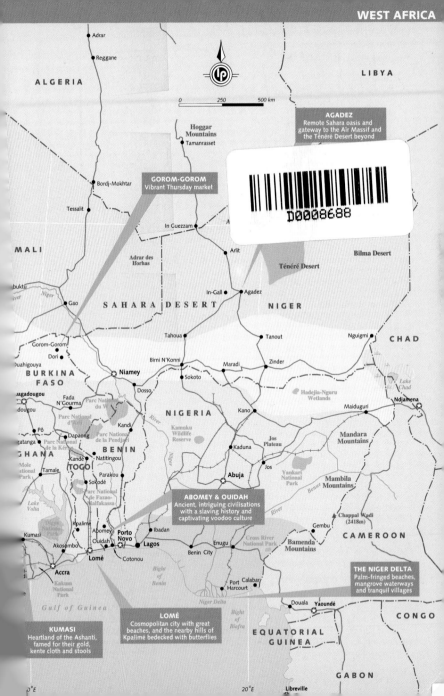

WEST AFRICA

AGADEZ
Remote Sahara oasis and gateway to the Aïr Massif and the Ténéré Desert beyond

GOROM-GOROM
Vibrant Thursday market

D0008688

ABOMEY & OUIDAH
Ancient, intriguing civilisations with a slaving history and captivating voodoo culture

THE NIGER DELTA
Palm-fringed beaches, mangrove waterways and tranquil villages

LOMÉ
Cosmopolitan city with great beaches, and the nearby hills of Kpalimé bedecked with butterflies

KUMASI
Heartland of the Ashanti, famed for their gold, kente cloth and stools

ALGERIA

LIBYA

Adrar

Reggane

Hoggar Mountains
Tamanrasset

Bordj-Mokhtar

Tessalit

MALI

In Guezzam

Arlit

Adrar des Iforhas

Ténéré Desert

Bilma Desert

buktu
Niger
River
Gao

SAHARA DESERT

In-Gall

Agadez

NIGER

Gorom-Gorom
Dori
Ouahigouya

Tahoua

Tanout

Nguigmi

CHAD

BURKINA FASO

Niamey

Birni N'Konni

Maradi

Zinder

Lake Chad

agadougou
Fada N'Gourma
Parc National du W

Dosso

Sokoto

Hadejia-Nguru Wetlands

Ndjamena

dougou

Pô
Dapaong

Parc National d'Arli

Katanga
Parc National de la Kéra

Kandi

NIGERIA

Kamuku Wildlife Reserve

Kano

Maiduguri

Maidugur

Mandara Mountains

GHANA

Kandé
Natitingou

BENIN

Kaduna

Jos Plateau

Mole National Park

Tamale

TOGO

Parakou

Sokodé

Jos

Yankari National Park

Mambila Mountains

Benue River

Chappal Wadi (2418m)

Lake Volta

Parc National de Fazao-Malfakassa

Abuja

Kpalimé

Abomey

Porto Novo

Ibadan

Gembu

Douga National Park

Kumasi

Akosombo

Ouidah

Lomé

Cotonou

Lagos

Enugu

Benin City

Cross River National Park

CAMEROON

Bamenda Mountains

Accra

Kakum National Park

Bight of Benin

Port Harcourt

Calabar

Niger Delta

Douala

Yaoundé

CONGO

Gulf of Guinea

Bight of Biafra

EQUATORIAL GUINEA

GABON

0°E

20°E

Libreville

0   250   500 km

West Africa
4th edition – April 1999
First published – September 1988

Published by
Lonely Planet Publications Pty Ltd ABN 36 005 607 983
90 Maribyrnong St, Footscray, Victoria 3011, Australia

Lonely Planet Offices
Australia Locked Bag 1, Footscray, Victoria 3011
USA 150 Linden St, Oakland, CA 94607
UK 10a Spring Place, London NW5 3BH
France 1 rue du Dahomey, 75011 Paris

Photographs
Glenn Beanland, Graeme Counsel, Corinne Else, David Else, Victor Englebert, Pamela Kleeman, Jason Lauré, Alex Newton, Christine Osborne, Ingrid Roddis, Miles Roddis, April Smith, Ray Tipper, Windrush Photos, Dennis Wisken

Many of the images in this guide are available for licensing from Lonely Planet Images.
email: lpi@lonelyplanet.com.au

Front cover photograph
Woman in movement/walking to market, Bani, Burkina Faso
(Mike Skelton for Plan International)

ISBN 0 86442 569 4

Contents – Text

2 Contents – Text

GHANA   382

GUINEA   463

GUINEA-BISSAU   502

LIBERIA   526

Contents – Maps

MAP LEGEND

The Authors

David Else
After hitchhiking through Europe for a couple of years, David kept heading south and first reached Africa in 1983. Since then, he has travelled all over the continent, from Cairo to Cape Town, and from Sudan to Senegal, via most of the bits in between. David has written several guidebooks for independent travellers including Lonely Planet's *Africa – the South*, *Trekking in East Africa*, *The Gambia & Senegal* and *Malawi, Mozambique & Zambia*. He has contributed to LP's *Africa on a shoestring* and *East Africa*, and has also written a guide to Zanzibar. When not in Africa, David lives in the north of England, where he's permanently chained to a word-processor, and travel means driving to London and back.

Alex Newton
Raised in Madison, Georgia, Alex joined the Peace Corps in the 1960s. Following almost three years' service in Guatemala as an agricultural adviser, he worked for four years on Wall St as a lawyer. He then studied development economics and French, and ended up in West Africa working on development assistance programs. He moved on to similar work in Ecuador, where he met his wife Betsy. Together they lived and worked in Bangladesh for five years. In addition to *West Africa*, Alex has also worked on LP's *Central Africa* and *Bangladesh* guides. Alex and his family are now living in Kazakstan, working for USAID, and bid travellers look them up.

Jeff Williams
Jeff was born in Greymouth, New Zealand, and currently lives with his wife Alison and son Callum in Brisbane in the Australian state of Queensland. He is variously author, co-author or contributor to Lonely Planet's *Western Australia*, *South Africa, Lesotho & Swaziland*, *Africa on a shoestring*, *New Zealand*, *Tramping in New Zealand*, *Australia*, *Outback Australia*, *Washington DC & the Capital Region* and *USA* (Plains States). He is currently working on a Middle Eastern overland guide, *Istanbul to Cairo*. He enjoys skiing and walking, and would like to show Callum the Sahel desert one day.

Mary Fitzpatrick
Mary grew up in Washington, DC, and has travelled extensively in Africa, Asia and Europe. For the past five years she has worked in Africa, first on development projects in Mozambique, more recently as a freelance writer in Liberia and Sierra Leone. Mary has also contributed to Lonely Planet's *Africa on a shoestring*.

Miles Roddis

Always an avid devourer and user of guidebooks, Miles came late to contributing to them. Over 25 years he lived, worked, walked and ran in eight countries, including Laos, Sudan, Spain and Egypt. He celebrated retirement by cycling 12,000 miles around the rim of the USA. Convinced that the bike is humankind's greatest invention, but for velcro, he enjoys agitating for cyclists' rights. Wild about wilderness, he's trekked, among other trails, the Zagros Mountains in Iran, Britain's Pennine Way and the Pyrenees from the Atlantic to the Mediterranean. He writes for outdoor and athletic magazines and has contributed to Lonely Planet's *Walking in Britain* and *Africa on a shoestring*, and was coordinating author of *Walking in Spain*.

FROM THE AUTHORS

David Else For help, advice, guidance and hospitality as I researched and wrote this 4th edition of *West Africa* I'd like to thank the following people.

Firstly, a big thank you to Corinne Else, my wife, who helped considerably with the research and writing of this book. Secondly to Angela Kalisch, tourism research assistant extraordinaire, who skilfully covered Casamance and parts of Gambia that other writers couldn't reach. In Britain help also came from Chris Scott, seasoned Saharan traveller, and Tricia Barnett (Tourism Concern), while Lonely Planet staff in France, Australia and USA also helped with background information – thanks to Leonie Mugavin, Caroline Guilleminot and Sacha Pearson. Dr Katie Abu helped with the language section.

In Gambia, thanks to: Ann Rivington and Fodeh Trawally for endless valuable introductions, contacts and pointers; Andrew Samuel, Red Tobin, Baba Ceesay and Allan O'Meachair of the National Council for Arts and Culture in Banjul, for historical and cultural information; Anne Barrett (National Environment Agency)and Val Smith (Gambia Tourism Concern) for useful advice on appropriate and sensitive tourism; Ann Slind and Kekoi Koma in Basse, for information on upcountry Gambia; Paul Murphy, Research and Development Officer at the Department of National Parks & Wildlife, and Louise Kempton, Ecotourism Development Officer, for willingly sharing time, beers and expertise.

In Guinea-Bissau, special thanks to Eric Feron of IUCN for details on national parks and an enlightening view on community-based conservation; and to US Peace Corps volunteers Kim Snody, Fernando da Costa, Emilio Torres, Veronica of Bigene and Amee of Bubaque.

In Mali, thanks to: Rod Grant, Rachel Hollis and Peter Bennett, for good company and help with gathering material; Scottish bikers Andy Bannerman and Caroline Lindsay for route information; Sarah Tyley, Nick Hudson, Ann Baker and the rest of the UNAIS crowd for background on Bamako nightlife and other aspects of the country; (Bamako and Kita); Boubacar Ouologuem of Bandiagara for an invaluable insight into Dogon culture; Heleen Warmerdam, Anja Koster and Belco Bah of Ashraf Tours, for detailed background information.

In Senegal, thanks to: Sam & Liesbeth Floré-Van Camp in Dakar, who kept me constantly up to date with info, from downtown bus routes to obscure desert border-crossings; Nicole Fonck-Deruisseau in St-Louis, for advice on the spot and frequent updates from northern Senegal; Jean-Pierre Pieters and the team at Toubakouta; Mamadou Gaye, Chief of the Commercial Division, Manufactures Sénégalaises des Arts Décoratifs in Thiès; Boubacar Diaw of Dakar, for leads on good restaurants and some background on West African music; Peace Corps Volunteers Andrew Chase, Lynnea Ladouceur, Kathy Buescher, Laura Klebman and Jennifer Beaston for information on Kolda, Tambacounda, Kedougou and Niokolo-Koba; Samba Faye of Ziguinchor, for insights into backcountry Casamance; and special thanks to the Chiche clan of Casamance – Veronique and Philip in Ziguinchor, Jean-Pierre and Marie at Cap Skiring – for providing unlimited time, never-ending advice, bikes, cars and boats, plus an email socket just when we needed it most.

Finally, greetings to the travellers we met on the road who shared with us their company and thoughts, especially Carsten Kölle (Germany) and Barry Gillmore (Ireland). Hope to bump into you again some day.

Dedication from David I'd like to dedicate this book to the African guy who came up to me in Tambacounda taxi park with a copy of the last edition of *West Africa* clutched in his hand. He'd recognised me from the photo in the book. Coming from Banjul where he'd just finished work, he was heading for Lagos to visit family. 'I've seen many tourists with this book, and know it has good information to help me. Thank you', he said. It made my day. Thank YOU.

Alex Newton Alex would like to thank his wife, Betsy Wagenhauser, for her continuing support of his Lonely Planet work.

Jeff Williams Thanks go to all the helpful people who answered my schoolboy French questions. And to: Randy Arsenault, you are a great mate and excellent travelling companion and musician – I hope you remember all those great impromptu gigs; in Nigeria, Anne and Jo the mighty VSOs, the staff of the International Institute of Tropical Agriculture in Ibadan, Jordy and Matthew from the Australian High Commission, Lagos, the beautiful people of Port Harcourt and Brass Island, the bosses of the Outside Inn, Victoria Island, and the Hare and runners of the Lagos Hash House Harriers; in Togo, Émile and Marie and the rest of the boules team at Le Galéon, Kodjoviakopé; the guys at Bar Belgica, Lomé, and the butterfly men in Kpalimé; in Benin, the folk at Hôtel La Bodega and Le Calao, Cotonou; and in Niger, Aristide at the Ali Baba Bar, Danielle the Canadian, and the guys at Hôtel Maourey, Niamey. Finally, in Queensland, thanks to Callum and Alison for putting up with late nights (and Dad away from home).

Miles Roddis In Burkina Faso, my thanks go to Peace Corps volunteers Glen Davis in Kaya, Paul Dowling and Alecia Modahl in Ouahigouya and to Felicity Williams in Bobo for some particularly astute comments. Also, to M Isidore Nabouloum, Directeur de la Promotion Touristique, Dr Nestor Da for his insights into local languages, Mario, the wise and sentimental hunter, Hassan Idar, Arryn Blumberg and Andrew McNeil, who fulfilled their promise to write, Colin Smith, Ann Cassiman – and the jovial geography teachers from Denmark who brightened a lampless night in Gorom.

For Ghana very special thanks go to John Mason for all his help, particularly on the environment, national parks and community-based tourism sections, to Nina Chachu in Kumasi and to Katie Abu for her insights into Ghana's rich variety of peoples and languages. Thanks also to Mr Oti Awere, Regional Director of Tourism in Kumasi, Katrina Browning for her stop-press feedback from the field, Shrikant Ashar, the ebullient survivor, for his streetwise tips on Accra, brothers Adam and Suleiman Abdulai in Tamale and, from the Peace Corps, Don Evans and Scott Arche, plus Amy Babchek, Chris Frederick, Stuart Levenbach and Kevin Thompson, with whom I shared a brainstorming breakfast over the frontier in Bobo. Readers Jane Allison, Phil and Philippa Grant and Gavin Nathan sent in some particularly useful and detailed updates – and Campbell Rule of Edinburgh is responsible for the toe-curling pun on the Rastas of Labadi Beach.

In Côte d'Ivoire, very special thanks to Annabel Kershaw and Marco Landra, who took me into their home after 12 dusty weeks on the road. Also, to David Dunn for his good humoured email responses, to fellow-writer, M René Babi, Directeur Régional du Tourisme, Korhogo, and to M Serge Dion, Directeur de La Bourse de Tourisme in Man. Ralph Kadel of GTZ gave me a crystal-clear briefing on ecotourism in Taï National Park and Martial Alferoff was helpful in updating Marahoué National Park. Abdul Karim Sako put himself out to help in Man and Maurice Beugre was a genial canoe companion in Sassandra. Peace Corps volunteers Tricia Hampton and Nafy Mahoney, together with Joseph Hellwig communicated their enthusiasm for Odienné and volunteers Michelle Ryba and Billy di Diego were invaluable for Abidjan eating, bussing and clubbing. My appreciation also to Anna Theuff and Laura Renfrew in Abidjan.

In all three countries, updates from readers Marcel Pointet, Dirk Hoftijzek and Annie van Gansewinkel were particularly informative – as were the detailed trip notes of Ito Kazuto, the intrepid Japanese cyclist, expressed in his charmingly idiosyncratic English.

Special thanks too to Jim and Pam Richards for checking out Stateside information, to Tristan and Damon for cheerfully responding to their Dad's always urgent and sometimes peremptory requests. And, saving the best till last, to Ingrid, my most critical and best reader, whether with me on the road or keeping the home fires burning.

Mary Fitzpatrick Special thanks to Margaret Ohaion for the research assistance; to Joseph Michels for help in gathering background materials; and to my father, Don Michels, who early on instilled in me a fascination with the world's beauty and diversity and more recently spent numerous hours helping me track down missing bits and pieces of information for my chapters.

In Guinea, many thanks to Patrick Murphy and Mouctar Diallo for their time and assistance; to Sédibinet Sidibé at the University of Faranah and Mamadou Ilias Diallo at the Direction Nationale des Forêts et de la Faune for information on Guinea's national parks; to Sarah Muscroft for all the help in Guéckédou; to Andreas Heil for the tour of Faranah; and, to all the Peace Corps volunteers who generously offered information and hospitality, in particular Bev Roberts and Herb Caudill in Mali, Amanda Galton and Amy Blasen (for the information on their climb of Mt Nimba), Suni Elgar, Daniel Cozart, Karen O'Brien, Susan Melville Church, Scott Sackett, Kerry Philp, Lynne McIntyre, Duane Duke, Jamie Folsom, Shanda Steimer, Jennifer Jurlando and Jen Villemure. Thanks also to Ted Peck, Julie Harrold, Wick Powers, Dieter Herzhauser, Scott Smith, Kevin Bohrer (for information on his Bossou excursion), Rick Evans, Charlotte Langeveld, Joyce, David, Clara and Bethany, and to Teresa Foday.

In Liberia, I extend particular gratitude to Kathleen List for her assistance and generosity in always being available to answer yet another question. Thank you also to Mr Theo Freeman of the FDA's Wildlife Conservation Division; Mr James Wolo of the Ministry of Information, Culture and Tourism; Mr Ben Tur Tur Donnie and Mr William Draper at SCNL; and, Thomas Banks of West African Safaris. For mapping assistance and help upcountry, thanks to Steve Fakan, Celeste Staley, Lance Salisbury, Shawn Messick, Shannon Fischer, John Hare, Mary Mertens and Paul Sutherland.

In Sierra Leone, many thanks to Tommy Garnett for the information on environmental issues, to Doug Henry for help with the Mende phrases (which unfortunately didn't make it in), to Joseph Opala for the assistance and background materials provided prior to the coup, and to Samuel Hamid Kadil in Bo for the proofreading and invaluable tips.

Finally, thanks most of all to my husband, Rick, for his endless support, encouragement and enthusiasm.

This Book

The first two editions of *West Africa* were written and researched by Alex Newton. For the 3rd edition, David Else joined Alex. For this, the 4th edition, David Else coordinated the project and updated the introductory chapters, The Gambia, Guinea-Bissau, Mali and Senegal. Alex Newton updated Cape Verde and Mauritania. Jeff Williams updated Benin, Niger, Nigeria and Togo. Mary Fitzpatrick updated Guinea, Liberia and Sierra Leone. Miles Roddis was responsible for updating Burkina Faso, Côte d'Ivoire and Ghana.

From the Publisher

First of all, a big thanks to all the authors, and especially to coordinating author David Else, for putting up with so much and sticking with it even when things seemed to be going backwards. Thank you!

Inhouse, many people helped guide *West Africa* through the maze of book production and out into the glare of the real world. Heading the editorial expedition was Isabelle Young, with much help from Sally Dillon, Emily Coles, Bethune Carmichael, Kirsten John, Janet Austin, Joyce Connolly and Alan Murphy. Anne Mulvaney stepped in to help with map checking. The cartographical expedition (motto: you can never have too many maps) was led initially by Glenn van der Knijff and later by new recruit Rodney Zandbergs. Rodney was ably supported in his efforts by Sarah Sloane, Derek Percival, Sonya Brooke, Piotr Czajkowski and Maree Styles. Anna 'Layout' Judd was responsible for laying the book out, and also assisted with mapping. Paul Piaia managed to find climate charts for all 16 countries. Matt King coordinated the illustrations, which were drawn by Sarah Jolly. The cover design was done by Margaret Jung. Quentin Frayne was responsible for putting together the Language chapter. Senior editors Sam Carew, Katrina Browning and Michelle Glynn and senior designer Verity Campbell provided endless assistance, guidance and moral support. Publishing manager Geoff Stringer kept a watchful eye on progress from his honeymoon.

Several other people contributed to this book: Katie Abu advised us on people and traditional religion, and wrote many of the colour features as well as some of the boxed text; John Graham helped with the arts sections and wrote the colour features on masks, figurative sculpture and bronze casting; Graeme Counsel helped with the music sections; David Andrew wrote the Birds section; and Ingrid Roddis wrote the colour feature on Asafo and Posubans. Thanks to Professor Ablade Glover of the Artists Alliance Gallery in Accra for permission to reproduce the Ashanti symbols and proverbs, and to Chris de Wilde for help with the Maison des Esclaves boxed text. Traute Tuckfeld of the German Tourist Board put us all straight on German postcodes.

The colour features were made possible with the help of Ann Porteus of the Sidewalk Gallery in Tasmania; most of the photographs in those sections were taken by Dennis Wisken.

THANKS

Many thanks to the travellers who used the last edition and wrote to us with helpful hints, advice and interesting anecdotes. Your names appear in the back of this book.

13

Foreword

ABOUT LONELY PLANET GUIDEBOOKS

The story begins with a classic travel adventure: Tony and Maureen Wheeler's 1972 journey across Europe and Asia to Australia. Useful information about the overland trail did not exist at that time, so Tony and Maureen published the first Lonely Planet guidebook to meet a growing need.

From a kitchen table, then from a tiny office in Melbourne (Australia), Lonely Planet has become the largest independent travel publisher in the world, an international company with offices in Melbourne, Oakland (USA), London (UK) and Paris (France).

Today Lonely Planet guidebooks cover the globe. There is an ever-growing list of books and there's information in a variety of forms and media. Some things haven't changed. The main aim is still to help make it possible for adventurous travellers to get out there – to explore and better understand the world.

At Lonely Planet we believe travellers can make a positive contribution to the countries they visit – if they respect their host communities and spend their money wisely. Since 1986 a percentage of the income from each book has been donated to aid projects and human rights campaigns.

Updates Lonely Planet thoroughly updates each guidebook as often as possible. This usually means there are around two years between editions, although for more unusual or more stable destinations the gap can be longer. Check the imprint page (following the colour map at the beginning of the book) for publication dates.

Between editions up-to-date information is available in two free newsletters – the paper *Planet Talk* and email *Comet* (to subscribe, contact any Lonely Planet office) – and on our Web site at www.lonelyplanet.com. The *Upgrades* section of the Web site covers a number of important and volatile destinations and is regularly updated by Lonely Planet authors. *Scoop* covers news and current affairs relevant to travellers. And, lastly, the *Thorn Tree* bulletin board, and *Postcards* section of the site carry unverified, but fascinating, reports from travellers.

Correspondence The process of creating new editions begins with the letters, postcards and emails received from travellers. This correspondence often includes suggestions, criticisms and comments about the current editions. Interesting excerpts are immediately passed on via newsletters and the Web site, and everything goes to our authors to be verified when they're researching on the road. We're keen to get more feedback from organisations or individuals who represent communities visited by travellers.

> Lonely Planet gathers information for everyone who's curious about the planet – and especially for those who explore it first-hand. Through guidebooks, phrasebooks, activity guides, maps, literature, newsletters, image library, TV series and web site we act as an information exchange for a worldwide community of travellers.

Research Authors aim to gather sufficient practical information to enable travellers to make informed choices and to make the mechanics of a journey run smoothly. They also research historical and cultural background to help enrich the travel experience and allow travellers to understand and respond appropriately to cultural and environmental issues.

Authors don't stay in every hotel because that would mean spending a couple of months in each medium-sized city and, no, they don't eat at every restaurant because that would mean stretching belts beyond capacity. They do visit hotels and restaurants to check standards and prices, but feedback based on readers' direct experiences can be very helpful.

Many of our authors work undercover, others aren't so secretive. None of them accept freebies in exchange for positive write-ups. And none of our guidebooks contain any advertising.

Production Authors submit their raw manuscripts and maps to offices in Australia, USA, UK or France. Editors and cartographers – all experienced travellers themselves – then begin the process of assembling the pieces. When the book finally hits the shops some things are already out of date, we start getting feedback from readers, and the process begins again ...

WARNING & REQUEST

Things change – prices go up, schedules change, good places go bad and bad places go bankrupt – nothing stays the same. So, if you find things better or worse, recently opened or long since closed, please tell us and help make the next edition even more accurate and useful. We genuinely value all the feedback we receive. Julie Young coordinates a well-travelled team that reads and acknowledges every letter, postcard and email and ensures that every morsel of information finds its way to the appropriate authors, editors and cartographers for verification.

Everyone who writes to us will find their name in the next edition of the appropriate guidebook. They will also receive the latest issue of *Planet Talk*, our quarterly printed newsletter, or *Comet*, our monthly email newsletter. Subscriptions to both newsletters are free. The very best contributions will be rewarded with a free guidebook.

Excerpts from your correspondence may appear in new editions of Lonely Planet guidebooks, the Lonely Planet Web site, *Planet Talk* or *Comet*, so please let us know if you *don't* want your letter published or your name acknowledged.

Send all correspondence to the Lonely Planet office closest to you:

Australia: Locked Bag 1, Footscray, Victoria 3011
UK: 10a Spring Place, London NW5 3BH
USA: 150 Linden St, Oakland CA 94607
France: 1 rue du Dahomey, Paris 75011

Or email us at: talk2us@lonelyplanet.com.au

For news, views and updates see our web site: www.lonelyplanet.com

HOW TO USE A LONELY PLANET GUIDEBOOK

The best way to use a Lonely Planet guidebook is any way you choose. At Lonely Planet we believe the most memorable travel experiences are often those that are unexpected, and the finest discoveries are those you make yourself. Guidebooks are not intended to be used as if they provide a detailed set of infallible instructions!

Contents All Lonely Planet guidebooks follow the same format. The Facts about the Country chapters or sections give background information ranging from history to weather. Facts for the Visitor gives practical information on issues like visas and health. Getting There & Away gives a brief starting point for researching travel to and from the destination. Getting Around gives an overview of the transport options when you arrive.

The peculiar demands of each destination determine how subsequent chapters are broken up, but some things remain constant. We always start with background, then proceed to sights, places to stay, places to eat, entertainment, getting there and away, and getting around information – in that order.

Heading Hierarchy Lonely Planet headings are used in a strict hierarchical structure that can be visualised as a set of Russian dolls. Each heading (and its following text) is encompassed by any preceding heading that is higher on the hierarchical ladder.

Maps Maps play a crucial role in Lonely Planet guidebooks and include a huge amount of information. A legend is printed on the back page. We seek to have complete consistency between maps and text, and to have every important place in the text captured on a map. Map key numbers usually start in the top left corner.

Although inclusion in a guidebook usually implies a recommendation we cannot list every good place. Exclusion does not necessarily imply criticism. In fact there are a number of reasons why we might exclude a place – sometimes it is simply inappropriate to encourage an influx of travellers.

Introduction

Call it mystique or adventure, whatever, West Africa has a power of attraction which, despite its sometimes primitive conditions, continues to entice western travellers. They certainly don't come because it's comfortable. The rural Sahel is a hot, dusty and frequently featureless landscape, distances are long and transport is frequently rough, while in tropical cities such as Freetown and Monrovia every time it rains the electricity goes off and the sewers overflow.

But beneath the sometimes tough exterior, this most diverse of regions contains a delicious vitality and a wonderfully contrasting range of experiences that are hard to find elsewhere. Travel here could find you camel trekking on the edge of the Sahara, hiking on forest trails, meandering along

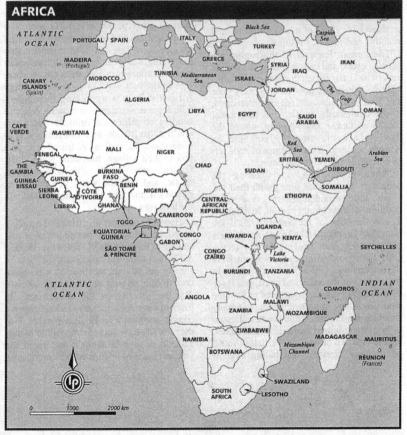

AFRICA

ATLANTIC OCEAN

PORTUGAL SPAIN
ITALY
Black Sea
Caspian Sea
TURKEY
MADEIRA (Portugal)
GREECE
SYRIA IRAQ
IRAN
CANARY ISLANDS (Spain)
MOROCCO
TUNISIA Mediterranean Sea
ISRAEL
JORDAN
The Gulf
OMAN
ALGERIA
LIBYA
EGYPT
SAUDI ARABIA
CAPE VERDE
MAURITANIA
Red Sea
Arabian Sea
MALI
NIGER
SENEGAL
CHAD
ERITREA YEMEN
DJIBOUTI
THE GAMBIA
BURKINA FASO
SUDAN
GUINEA-BISSAU
GUINEA
BENIN
SIERRA LEONE
CÔTE D'IVOIRE
NIGERIA
SOMALIA
LIBERIA
GHANA
CENTRAL AFRICAN REPUBLIC
ETHIOPIA
TOGO
CAMEROON
EQUATORIAL GUINEA
CONGO
UGANDA
SÃO TOMÉ & PRÍNCIPE
GABON
CONGO (ZAÏRE)
RWANDA
KENYA
SEYCHELLES
BURUNDI
Lake Victoria
TANZANIA
ATLANTIC OCEAN
ANGOLA
MALAWI
COMOROS
INDIAN OCEAN
ZAMBIA
MOZAMBIQUE
ZIMBABWE
NAMIBIA
Mozambique Channel
MADAGASCAR
MAURITIUS
BOTSWANA
RÉUNION (France)
SWAZILAND
SOUTH AFRICA
LESOTHO

0   1000   2000 km

idyllic palm-lined creeks, bartering for goods in a crowded market, learning to drum, lounging on the beach, dancing the night away in a sweaty nightclub, watching flocks of pelican and flamingo take flight, or marvelling at large and intricate mud-brick mosques. Accommodation could be in a traditional village hut or a five star hotel. Either way, Africa is just outside the door.

The natural features are as beautiful as they are rich and varied, from tranquil lagoons and coastal islands, mangrove deltas, dense rainforest, savanna plains, sand dunes and lush wooded hills to the great rivers such as the Niger and the Gambia, which defines in name and course a country's very existence. These natural environments harbour an impressive range of mammal species and stunning and prolific birdlife.

The human features of the region are equally varied and enticing: from the simple huts of mud and thatch in remote upcountry villages, where life goes on at an easy pace and local traditions are deeply entrenched, to the boulevards, traffic jams and tower blocks of Dakar and Abidjan, where the local inhabitants enviably combine an African soul with a Gallic sense of style left over from French colonial days.

Wherever you go, encountering the people of West Africa, along with their art, music, culture and traditions, is a major highlight of travel in the region. In Timbuktu and the edge of the Sahara, you'll see nomadic Tuareg perched on their camels and covered with flowing indigo robes. Only their penetrating eyes look out from the turbans wrapped around their heads. In the villages of the Sahel and coast, you'll see men in traditional dress gathered around the chief discussing important matters or simply shooting the breeze, while women dressed in brightly coloured material pound millet, tend to children or work in the fields. You'll go to large markets, fascinating even if you're not buying, which take all day to walk round and even longer to work out what half the goods are. At night in the villages, you'll probably hear drums and, in the Sahel, be offered the traditional three glasses of tea. You'll see village festivals where *griots* sing and play or the men dance with elaborate masks. And with good timing you can witness large ceremonies, some of which attract people from across the whole region, such as the Gerewol festival in Niger, or the Muslim durbars in northern Nigeria.

What is just as interesting, however, is simply meeting local people in everyday situations. In cities and towns you may find indifference, as in any part of the world, but in rural areas people invariably meet you with a warmth and directness, which at first may be unsettling but soon translates into hospitality and genuine friendliness which makes European reserve seem out of place. One of the best ways to appreciate modern African culture is by talking to people – fellow passengers, market traders, cigarette vendors or palm-wine drinkers. From this you'll make friends, and then really start to understand the region. A friend will take you to their village, introduce you to their family, show you the bars with the best music, and tell you when you're getting ripped off and how to accomplish tasks in the best way.

How do you meet this friend? Travelling by public transport in 2nd or 3rd class and staying in budget hotels is one way. Hanging out in bars and local cafes is another. Just be sure to get beyond the hustlers who make their living serving or disserving tourists. Try the schools or the universities. In Francophone Africa, many students enjoy a conversation with an English speaker. Plus they usually have lots of time – little money and lots of time. Make just one friend and you will see how open West Africans can be.

Facts about the Region

HISTORY

The national boundaries of West Africa are recent phenomena imposed on the region by European colonial powers just over a century ago; before this, West Africa had its own states and kingdoms. Because these modern political borders bear little relation to the territories of West Africa's myriad ethnic groups, an understanding of the history of the region is essential to an understanding of its people and culture.

This section provides an overview of history in the West African region, and mainly covers the period before European influence significantly penetrated the interior. For detailed accounts of the colonial and postcolonial histories of individual countries, see the country chapters.

Prehistory

Much archaeological evidence of the world's earliest human inhabitants has been found in Africa. Controversy exists among researchers, but most accept that the first hominids (upright-walking human-like creatures) evolved in Africa nearly four million years ago and by about two million years ago changing climatic and environmental conditions had resulted in the evolution of several hominid species, including *Homo habilis* (handy man) and *Homo erectus* (upright man). By about 1.5 to one million years ago, *Homo erectus* seems to have become dominant on the savannas of Africa, developing tool-making abilities and the use of fire. This species evolved into *Homo sapiens* (thinking man), essentially the same as modern humans.

Archaeological evidence suggests that 750,000 years ago these early people were hunting the ancestors of present-day elephants and cutting up the carcasses with large stone hand-axes. By 150,000 years ago people were using lighter stone points, spearheads, knives, saws and other finer tools for a variety of hunting and gathering activities.

Archaeologists classify this period of tool-making as the Stone Age.

The Advent of Agriculture

Around 10,000 years ago, the most recent Ice age came to an end. The world's climate got warmer and there was more rain. This allowed people to cease their hunter-gatherer lifestyle and to domesticate crops and animals. Evidence from 10,000 to 6000 years ago indicates that agricultural development occurred in the savanna regions now occupied by the Sahara Desert.

From around 5000 BC, as the global climate continued to alter, the savanna started to become drier, making farming more difficult and forcing the early farmers to move. The climatic changes also meant that the vegetation south of the savanna became less dense, so this area, today called the Sahel, was occupied instead.

Evidence discovered in the Sahel, dating from 4000 to 3000 BC, indicates that by this time people had domesticated cattle, and were also harvesting or cultivating indigenous plants, including millet (a cereal crop), yam (a root tuber) and African forms of rice. Remains of pottery, stone hoes and digging tools dating from around the same period provide further evidence of a sedentary, non-nomadic, lifestyle. Other tools, including hand-scythes used for cutting grasses, have also been found.

Early Societies

As in other parts of the world, agriculture led to the development of organised societies, as communities had to develop systems of co-operation or control. Additionally, farming could support larger numbers of people, so populations started to expand.

The earliest evidence of an organised society in West Africa dates from 1200 BC in Mauritania, where remains of stone villages and domestic animals have been found. Similar remains have been found in northern Nigeria. It is likely that settlements of this type were established across the Sahel, which was better watered and more vegetated than it is today.

Of the early societies who inhabited the Sahel during this period two dominant groups emerged: the first along the River Niger, and the second around Lake Chad, not surprisingly the two areas most suitable for agriculture. The people built large stone villages and even towns, and seem to have been in contact with other African peoples, particularly on the southern shores of the Mediterranean. Ancient rock paintings discovered in the Sahara Desert indicate that horse-drawn chariots were used to cover these great distances – the precursors of today's trans-desert overlanders.

The Iron Age

The earliest remaining evidence of ironworking in West Africa is found in central Nigeria and dates from around 450 BC. Knowledge of ironworking was introduced to the region either from Egypt via the Nile Valley and Lake Chad, or across the Sahara from North Africa. Some authorities hold that the use of iron was actually developed

in West Africa and that the knowledge went the other way, *to* Egypt.

Ironworking had massive ramifications across the region because iron tools were much more efficient than those made from stone or bronze. It was now possible for people to clear forest, which until then had hindered farming (especially cereal production) and expand or migrate into new territories. The process was usually gradual (see the boxed text 'African Migrations – An Explanation' on this page for more details) as weaker tribes were slowly absorbed by intermarriage with more powerful groups, but there were probably some quicker invasions too – iron was also good for making weapons.

Cities & Empires

Improved farming techniques meant that societies in West Africa continued to develop. The town of Jenné-Jeno (in present-day Mali), established between the 1st and 3rd centuries AD, has been called the first urban settlement in West Africa. It is likely that several similar settlements were established around this time. By 500 AD, towns and villages were dotted across the region.

African Migrations – An Explanation

When discussing the migrations of African peoples in the precolonial era, it's important not to imagine a sudden mass movement, with vast numbers marching great distances to conquer new lands (although this did occasionally happen). In this context, a migration is a gradual expansion over hundreds, maybe even thousands, of years, made up of many short moves – from valley to valley, or from one cultivation area to the next – with dominant peoples slowly absorbing and assimilating other groups in the process. The most successful migratory group in Africa were the Bantu people, originally from the area that is now Nigeria and Cameroon, who had been slowly expanding through the forests of Central Africa from as early as 2000 BC. The introduction of iron suddenly speeded up this process and the Bantu spread through the Congo basin to reach the East African plateau in around 100 BC. Over the next thousand years they moved down the continent as far as present-day Zimbabwe and South Africa. Today, the vast majority of indigenous peoples in Africa south of the equator are of Bantu origin. It is important to note, however, that there is no longer a single tribe or ethnic group called the Bantu. The term is now used to define the large language group to which most East and southern African ethnic groups belong.

As the 1st millennium progressed, trade increased significantly between the regions south and north of the Sahara. Goods transported across the desert included salt, gold, silver and ivory; there was also trade in slaves. Some of the early settlements on the edge of the desert were well placed to take advantage of the trade (and eventually control it) so they increased in size, wealth and power. Large villages became towns or city-states, and a few even developed into powerful confederations or empires.

The Birth of Islam

Islam was founded in Arabia by the Prophet Mohammed around the year 620 AD (for more details see the Religion section later in this chapter). This gave rise to a period of expansionism, as Arab peoples spread across North Africa, bringing the new religion with them. Many of North Africa's Berber people adopted the new religion. From around 900 AD, Muslim traders from present-day Morocco and Algeria brought Islam across the Sahara to the Sahel.

For many centuries after the introduction of Islam in West Africa it remained the religion of the rulers and the wealthy. Generally, ordinary people did not adopt the new religion and retained their traditional beliefs. However, rulers skilfully combined aspects of Islam and traditional religion in the administration of the state. This fusing of beliefs remains a feature of West African life today.

Early Empires

The Empire of Ghana (no geographic connection with the present-day country of Ghana) was the first major state of its kind to be established in West Africa. It was originally founded in the 5th century AD by the Soninké people and flourished from the 8th to 11th century. The capital was Kumbi Saleh in present-day Mauritania, about 200km north of modern Bamako (Mali). Power was based on the control of trans-Saharan trade, and at its height the empire covered much of present-day Mali and parts of eastern Senegal.

Islam was introduced by traders from the north, and adopted by local merchants and some members of the political elite, but the Empire of Ghana did not fully embrace the new religion. The empire was destroyed in the late 11th century by the better armed Muslim Berbers of the Almoravid Empire from Mauritania and Morocco.

At around the same time the Tuklur (or Tekrur) Empire was established by the Tuklur people in what is now northern Senegal. It also based its power on control of the trans-Saharan trade, and flourished during the 9th to 10th centuries.

Empire of Mali

In the middle of the 13th century Sundiata Keita, leader of the Malinké people, founded the Empire of Mali in the region between the present-day countries of Senegal and Niger. By the beginning of the 14th century the empire had expanded further, and controlled nearly all trans-Saharan trade, making the rulers of Mali incredibly wealthy. They embraced Islam with great enthusiasm. When Emperor Mansa Musa went on a pilgrimage to Mecca in the early 14th century, he took an entourage of 60,000 people. In Egypt, he presented so many people with lavish gifts of gold that the metal's value slumped for several years.

During this period the trans-Saharan trade reached its peak, and the wealth created meant Mali's main cities became major centres of finance and culture. Most notable was Timbuktu, where two Islamic universities were founded, and Arab architects were brought in to design new mosques, some of which can still be seen today.

Empire of Songhaï

While Mali was at the height of its powers, the people of Songhaï had established their own city-state to the east around Gao. This became powerful and well organised, and by the middle of the 15th century had eclipsed the Empire of Mali and incorporated Timbuktu and Djenné. A hallmark of the Songhaï Empire was the creation of a professional army and a civil service with provincial governors. The state even subsidised Muslim scholars, judges and doctors. By the 16th century Timbuktu was an important commercial city with about 100,000 inhabitants. This golden period ended with an invasion by Berber armies from Morocco in the late 16th century.

Later States & Empires

To the west of Mali, on the coast near the site of present-day Dakar in Senegal, the Wolof people established the Empire of Jolof (also spelt Yollof). Meanwhile, to the east of Mali and Songhaï the Hausa people created several powerful city-states, such as Katsina, Kano and Zinder (which are still important trading towns today), but they never amalgamated into a single empire. East of here, on the shores of Lake Chad, yet another empire, that of Kanem-Borno, was founded in the early 14th century and at its height covered a vast area including parts of present-day Niger, Nigeria, Chad and Cameroon. It remained a powerful force in the region until the 19th century.

To the south of the Sahel empires, mostly in the period between the 13th and 16th centuries, several smaller states were established in forested areas and where gold was produced. These states prospered from trade with their larger northern neighbours. They included the kingdoms of Benin (in present-day Nigeria), Dahomey (Benin), Mossi (Burkina Faso), and Akan-Ashanti (Ghana).

European Interest

Around this time in Europe, interest in West Africa was growing. The trans-Saharan trade carried gold from the coastal regions via the Mediterranean to the courts and treasuries of countries such as England, France, Spain and Portugal. As early as the 13th century, the financial stability of several major European powers depended largely on the supply of West African gold. There were frequent reports of the wealthy empires south of the Sahara (the use of Timbuktu as a metaphor for a faraway place possibly dates from this time) but no European had ever visited the region.

Prince Henry of Portugal (1394-1460; known as Henry the Navigator) encouraged explorers to sail down the coast of West Africa. His intention was to bypass the Arab and Muslim domination of the trans-Saharan gold trade and reach the source by sea. By the early 15th century, Portuguese ships had reached the Canary Islands and the coast of what is now Western Sahara. In 1443 ships reached the mouth of the River Senegal, and a year later another ship rounded a peninsula on the coast of Senegal, which was named Cabo Verde or Green Cape. (It is now called Cap Vert, the site of Dakar, and should not be confused with the Cape Verde Islands.)

In a series of later voyages the Portuguese pushed further south: Sierra Leone in 1462, Fernando Po (now Bioko in Equatorial Guinea) in 1472 and Cape Cross (Namibia) in 1485.

Early Portuguese Trade

On the West African coast (which had become known as Guinea) the Portuguese made contact with local chiefs and started to trade for gold and ivory. Thus, the great empires of the Sahel lost their monopoly and started to decline but the coastal states benefited from contact with the new arrivals, and continued to prosper.

In 1482 the Portuguese built a fortified trading post at Elmina, on the coast of today's Ghana, which was the earliest European structure in sub-Saharan Africa. But trade never fulfilled the hopes of the earlier pioneers. Elmina became a staging point for the increasing number of ships sailing between Portugal and the Far East, where commodities were proving far more profitable than those from Africa.

By 1500, Portuguese ships had also sailed some distance upstream along the Senegal and Gambia rivers, using these waterways as vital routes into the interior. (It has been suggested that the River Gambia's name derives from the Portuguese word *cambio*, meaning 'exchange' or, more likely in this context, 'trade'.) But West Africa had few other large rivers which allowed access to

The Slave Trade

Although slavery had existed in West Africa for many centuries, the Portuguese massively increased the trade, taking slaves to work on the large sugar plantations which had been established in Portuguese settlements on the other side of the Atlantic (including present-day Brazil) between 1575 and 1600.

Fort William, Anomabu, one of a string of old slave-trading forts along the Ghanaian coast.

By the 17th and 18th centuries, other European nations (particularly England, Spain, France and Holland) had established colonies in the Americas, and were growing sugar, tobacco, cotton and other crops. Huge profits could be made from these commodities, and the demand for slaves to work the plantations was insatiable.

In most cases, the European traders encouraged Africans on the coast to attack neighbouring tribes and take captives. These were brought to the coastal slaving stations and exchanged for European goods such as cloth and guns, enabling more neighbours to be invaded and more slaves to be captured. A triangular trans-Atlantic trade route developed – the slaves were loaded onto ships and transported to the Americas; the raw materials they produced were transported to Europe; and finished goods were transported from Europe to Africa once again to be exchanged for slaves and to keep the whole system moving. The demand for slaves was maintained because conditions in the plantations were so bad that life expectancy after arriving in the Americas was often no more than a few years.

Exact figures are impossible to come by, but from the end of the 15th century until around 1870 (when the slave trade was abolished) up to 20 million Africans were captured. Between a quarter and half of this number died, mostly during transportation. Accounts written at the time describe hundreds of slaves packed tightly between decks so low there was only room to lie down. Food or water was often not provided and the faeces or vomit from those above fell through the planking onto those lying below. It is not surprising that only around 10 million actually arrived in the Americas. These figures are hotly debated by historians, and sometimes obscure the main issue, which is that whatever the actual numbers, the slave trade was undeniably cruel and inhuman.

---

the interior and trade remained essentially a coastal operation.

The Rise of Islam

In the interior, events took a different course. The expansion of Islam, which had first moved south of the Sahara with traders at the end of the 1st millennium, and later with conquerors (such as the Moroccan invasion of Songhaï in 1590), continued to gather pace. A particular type of Islam called Sufism, which emphasises mystical and spiritual attributes, became popular. A central aspect of Sufism is the influence of religious teachers, many of whom are ascribed divine powers and the ability to communicate with Allah. (Orthodox Islam is essentially more egalitarian and does not allow for intermediaries of this nature.) Commentators have suggested that this master-follower relationship found favour in West Africa because it mirrored the hierarchical social structures already in place.

Various factors, including the decline of the old empires, the increased power of the coastal states, the rise in European influence, and the corresponding rise in trade and slavery, as well as the introduction of guns, had led to a period of instability across much of the West African region, particularly in the Sahel. Islam filled the vacuum and gathered momentum through the 17th and 18th centuries. The leaders became particularly powerful and their followers enthusiastically carried the faith across the region. The Fula people, a large group which spread across the northern part of West Africa, were particular adherents.

Islamic holy wars (called 'jihads') were declared on groups of nonbelievers. The leadership influenced followers in political and economic matters, as well as religion, and several Muslim states became established. These included Futa Toro (in northern Senegal), Futa Djalon (Guinea), Masina (Mali) and the Sokoto state of Hausaland (Niger and Nigeria). The long-term effect was that Islam became the dominant religion of the Sahel, which it remains today.

European Expansion

While Islam was becoming firmly established, European interest was moving away from the coast towards the interior. Explorers included Mungo Park, the Scottish doctor who travelled from the River Gambia to reach the River Niger in present-day Mali. Later British explorers included Clapperton, who reached Kano in northern Nigeria, and Landers, who finally established that the Niger flowed into the Atlantic. Meanwhile, other explorers were trying to reach the fabled city of Timbuktu – the

Frenchman René Caillié was finally successful in 1828.

As European influence grew through the first half of the 19th century, the jihads were fought less against 'infidel' Africans, and more against the Europeans – particularly against French forces, who were pushing ever deeper into this part of the region. The most notable leader of the time was Omar Tall (also spelt Umar Taal), who led a major campaign against the French from around 1850 until he was killed in 1864. After his death, the jihads continued as the Marabout Wars in Senegal until the 1880s.

Mungo Park

The first half of the 19th century (from 1795 to 1850) is usually regarded as the main period of 'modern' European exploration in the interior of West Africa.

Exploration focused on solving two main puzzles: the position of Timbuktu, the mysterious 'city of gold', and the route of the River Niger. Although the river's existence was well known, its source and mouth, and even its direction of flow, were a mystery to the geographers of Europe.

In 1795, the London-based Association for Promoting the Discovery of the Interior Parts of Africa sent a young Scotsman called Mungo Park to the River Gambia. Sailing upstream, he based himself near Georgetown, where he learnt several local languages, and then set off across the plains, with just two servants and three donkeys. He took a north-eastern direction, crossing the River Senegal, getting captured and escaping, and eventually reached the River Niger at Ségou, confirming that it flowed in a northerly direction.

In 1801 Park returned to the River Gambia and again set out for the Niger. By the time he reached the River Niger, many of his crew had died. Park and the rest of the party encountered the same fate at the Bussa Rapids in the east of present-day Nigeria.

Early Colonialism

In the second half of the 19th century, the trans-Atlantic slave trade came to an end (although it continued in some parts of Africa for many decades more). This was the result partly of a liberalisation of attitudes brought on by the European Age of Enlightenment, but also due to the Industrial Revolution which led to a demand for stable, compliant colonies supplying raw materials and providing a market for finished goods.

In West Africa, the main European powers had established pockets of territory on the coast. These included the French enclave of Dakar (which would become the capital of Senegal), and the British ports of Freetown (Sierra Leone) and Lagos (Nigeria). Portugal was no longer a major force, but had retained some territory – notably Bissau (capital of today's Guinea-Bissau). There had been several military expeditions to the interior, with the French active mostly in the Sahel regions and the British penetrating the region mostly from the south coast. Various minor treaties were made with local chiefs, but there was still little in the way of formally claimed territory.

By the 1870s, political events in Europe meant competition among nations (including France, Britain, Belgium and the recently formed state of Germany) was great, but to a large extent their battle for dominance was played out in Africa, in a sudden rush of land-grabbing that became known as the 'Scramble for Africa'.

The Scramble for Africa

This land-grabbing frenzy was triggered in 1879 by King Leopold of Belgium's claim to the Congo (which later became Zaïre, and more recently was renamed Congo). France responded by establishing territory in the neighbouring area, which became known as French Congo (now Congo-Brazzaville) and Gabon. Meanwhile, the British were increasing their influence and showing interest in territories in East Africa, as part of a plan to control the headwaters of the Nile, and in turn the strategic Suez Canal, the route to India. Germany's leader, Bismark, said he

also wanted 'a place in the sun' and claimed various bits of Africa, including Togo and Cameroon.

All the European powers wanted to strengthen their positions and occupy territories as soon as possible. In 1881 France invaded Tunis, and in 1882 Britain invaded Egypt. In the following year, Britain staked a claim to much of East Africa, and to territories in West Africa – such as Gambia, Sierra Leone, the Gold Coast (Ghana) and Nigeria.

At the same time France claimed much of the Sahel belt, eastwards from their territory in Senegal. France also claimed much of the Sahara itself, to link up with their possessions in North Africa, which had become French territory earlier in the century.

The various claims of the European powers were settled at the Berlin Conference of 1884-85, when most of the continent of Africa was split neatly into colonies. Britain got a few West African coastal territories plus most of East and southern Africa, Belgium got the Congo, Germany kept Togo and Cameroon (and added what were to become Tanzania and Namibia to its far-flung empire), while Portugal kept Guinea-Bissau, the islands of Cape Verde, Equatorial Guinea and the territories in the south which would become the modern states of Mozambique and Angola. France was awarded most of West and Central Africa – a vast area covering almost a third of the entire continent which became known as Afrique Occidentale Française (French West Africa) or the French

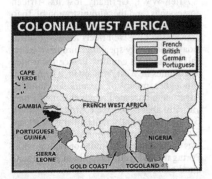

COLONIAL WEST AFRICA

French
British
German
Portuguese

CAPE VERDE

GAMBIA

FRENCH WEST AFRICA

PORTUGUESE GUINEA

NIGERIA

SIERRA LEONE

GOLD COAST

TOGOLAND

Soudan (to distinguish it from the Anglo-Egyptian Sudan, now the modern state of Sudan).

It seems that the European powers were mostly happy with the results of the Berlin Conference. The map of Africa had been neatly divided up and coloured in. What the Africans thought of the conference remains unrecorded – not surprisingly, they weren't invited to attend.

The 20th Century

Following the Berlin Conference, the European powers consolidated their presence in the new colonies. Although there was a great deal of anti-European feeling among African people, local resistance was generally sporadic. Where uprisings did occur they were usually easily put down by well-armed European soldiers.

Despite some lip service to the introduction of civilisation to the 'heathen natives', the main aim of the European governments was to exploit the colonies for raw materials. In some areas, gem and gold mining was developed but generally West Africa had little in the way of bulk minerals such as coal. Consequently, labour-intensive plantations were established, and cash crops such as coffee, cocoa, rubber, cotton and groundnuts (peanuts) soon came to dominate the economies of the fledgling colonies, and to be a major source of employment (not always voluntary) for local people.

After WWI, Germany lost its African possessions, and the administration of Togo and Cameroon was entrusted to Britain and France (the divisive effects are still evident today). Generally speaking, through the first half of the 20th century, France controlled its colonies in West Africa with a firm hand, although a policy of *assimilation* allowed Africans to become French citizens (if they virtually abandoned their African identity). Britain was slightly more liberal in its approach towards its colonies, although there was no equivalent assimilation policy, while Portugal ruled its tiny empire in Africa with a rod of iron.

Independence

After WWII, a rising tide of nationalism developed in the colonies, and there were increasingly loud calls for independence to be granted. Although these were at first fiercely resisted by France and (to a lesser extent) by Britain, the colonial rulers eventually capitulated. In 1957, Ghana became the first country in Africa to gain independence, followed by Guinea in 1958. The big year was 1960, when independence was granted to Benin, Côte d'Ivoire, Nigeria, Togo, Senegal and several other countries. Through the early 1960s most other countries in the region became independent. In 1965, Gambia was the last British colony in Africa to gain independence.

Once again, the former powers had different approaches to the new independent states: France encouraged its former colonies to remain closely tied in a trade-based 'community', and most did (Guinea was a notable exception). Britain reduced its power and influence in the region, while Portugal grimly hung on to its colonies for another decade or longer. France maintained batallions of its own army in several former colonies, while Britain's provision of military assistance was more behind the scenes.

During the rest of the 1960s and into the 1970s the early optimism started to fade. Colonialism had created fragile economies based on cash crops prone to huge price fluctuations and ethnic tensions were created by artificial boundaries or divide-and-rule policies. Border disputes, separatist uprisings and civil wars became common events, and this continued into the 1980s. Elected leaders were unable or unwilling to combat their nation's economic and social problems, and military takeovers and coups d'état became more frequent. Corruption, embezzlement and mismanagement by presidents and other politicians also became common problems in West Africa, and life for ordinary people became increasingly hard.

During the Cold War period, anticommunist dictators were propped up with finance and arms from the west (with the backing of transnational corporations who still stood to gain from the region's raw materials), while leaders who declared themselves Marxist were similarly supported by the Soviet bloc. Rebels, separatists and opposition figures often found it easy to get backing from whichever side was not behind that country's leader, and for many years, Africa (along with other parts of the developing world) became the superpowers' battleground and the site of many unpleasant 'dirty wars', all too easily forgotten today.

The 1990s and the end of the east-west split led to dramatic changes throughout West Africa, and these are discussed in more detail in the Government & Politics section later in this chapter and in the individual country chapters.

GEOGRAPHY

West Africa can be divided into three main geographical areas that form horizontal bands across the region: the northern band consists of desert; the southern band is woodland and forest; and in between is a semidesert zone called the Sahel – see the boxed text for more details. The characteristics of the different geographical areas are discussed in the Climate and Flora & Fauna sections following.

West Africa has few mountains, and much of the region is flat or gently undulating plateau, although a few highland areas break the monotony. These include the range along the border between Nigeria and Cameroon (the highest point, Chappal Wadi, is 2418m); the Jos Plateau and Shebsi Mountains in Nigeria; the hills around Mt Bintumani (1945m) in Sierra Leone; the rocky Aïr Massif in Niger; the hill country around Mt Nimba (1752m), covering the border area between Guinea, Côte d'Ivoire and Liberia; and the hills of the Fouta Djalon in western Guinea, which also spread into south-eastern Senegal. The peaks of the volcanic Cape Verde islands are also notable; Mt Fogo is the highest at 2839m. For the sake of completeness, Mt Cameroon (4100m), just over the Nigerian border in Cameroon, should be mentioned, as it rises far above any other West African contender.

The Sahel

The Sahel is the part of West Africa between the Sahara Desert in the north and the forested zone of the south – a vast horizontal band stretching from the Atlantic coast into the countries of Chad and Sudan.

Usually described simply as 'semidesert', within the Sahel there are many different subregions: in the north, near the true desert, the Sahel is dry and very sparsely vegetated; in the south, nearer the forests, the Sahel gets more rainfall and contains areas of light woodland. Additional factors such as mountains or rivers can also influence the vegetation pattern within the Sahel. Other definitions used for this area include semidesert savanna, Guinea savanna, Sudanese savanna, dry savanna or dry woodland savanna. To the nonscientist it's all rather confusing, which is why 'Sahel' is such a convenient catch-all term.

The countries covered by this book usually considered to be all or partly in the Sahel are (from west to east) Senegal, Gambia, Guinea, Mali, Burkina Faso, Niger and Nigeria. However, the boundaries are not fixed, and much of northern Mali and Niger is true desert, while southern Nigeria and south-eastern Guinea are in the forest zone. (It's also important to realise that the 'forest zone' term is used in areas where the *natural* vegetation is forest. In these areas much has been cleared for farmland.) In the same way, the northern parts of the coastal countries of Côte d'Ivoire, Ghana, Togo and Benin are relatively dry, and so are sometimes described as having a Sahel climate or vegetation.

The term 'Sahel' (or 'Sahelian') is also used to describe characteristic aspects of the region. For example, 'Sahel architecture' refers to the mud-brick and render style used to such stunning effect on the great mosques found in Mali and Niger. In the same way, you'll come across 'Sahel music' or 'Sahel food'.

Although West Africa's highland areas are limited, they create headwaters for several rivers. The largest river in the region is the Niger, which rises in the Fouta Djalon highlands of Guinea and flows in a great curve (Niger Bend or Boucle du Niger) through Mali north-east to Mopti, where it spreads out to form a maze of swamps and channels called the Niger Inland Delta. The top of the Bend touches the edge of the Sahara near Timbuktu, and the river then flows south-east through Niger and Nigeria to enter the Atlantic at the vast Niger Delta west of Port Harcourt.

Other major rivers of the region include: the Senegal, in the north of the country of the same name, and forming the border with Mauritania; the Gambia, again giving its name to the country it flows through; the Casamance in southern Senegal; the Volta in Ghana and Burkina Faso; and the Benue (a major tributary of the Niger) in Nigeria.

While some of West Africa's boundaries may be loosely defined, the region's irrefutable western and southern limit is the Atlantic Ocean. Many major cities – Dakar, Banjul, Bissau, Conakry, Freetown, Monrovia, Abidjan, Accra, Lomé, Cotonou, Porto Novo and Lagos – are strung along the coast like beads in a chain, in some areas forming an almost constant linear urban sprawl, cut only by national frontiers.

CLIMATE

This section gives an overview of West Africa's climate patterns. More specific details are given in individual country chapters.

In the northern parts of West Africa temperature patterns are essentially hot from April to September, and cool (or not so hot) in the winter from October to March, although places on the coast (eg Nouakchott in Mauritania) will be relatively cooler than those deep in the interior (eg Gao in Mali).

In the southern parts of West Africa temperatures are high from October to February, at their peak from March to May, then lower from May to September, although again much depends on distance from the ocean and sometimes the variations throughout the year are not great.

In the coastal countries minimum temperatures are fairly constant throughout the year, but in the northern parts of West Africa, minimums are much lower in January than they are in May or August. Deep in the desert, water bags have even been known to freeze briefly on winter nights.

The West African climate is dominated more by rainfall than by temperature, and the dry and wet seasons are important factors to consider when planning your trip. Generally, the dry season in the southern coastal countries is November to April, while in the Sahel countries it's October to May. The rainy season in the coastal countries is May to October, and the wettest areas are Guinea, Sierra Leone, Liberia and south-eastern Nigeria, where the monthly rainfall can top 400mm. In the Sahel countries, the rainy season is from June to September. In all areas, rainy periods get shorter, and rainfall levels decrease, as you go further north and further away from the ocean.

Weather patterns have become more unpredictable in recent years, so don't expect the wet and dry seasons to work like clockwork any more – be prepared for unexpected weather conditions, which can affect travel.

Humidity is another important climatic factor. Dry heat (eg in the Sahel) is always easier to handle than wet heat (eg on the coast).

The Harmattan

This is a dry wind that blows from the north, usually in December, January and February, when the skies of most West African countries are grey with dust from the Sahara. Even when the wind stops blowing, conditions remain hazy until the first May rains. On bad days in the harmattan season visibility can be reduced to around 1km, which results in plane delays, but generally, travel itself isn't too badly affected – although photographers can expect 'overcast' pictures.

ECOLOGY & ENVIRONMENT

Ecological and environmental issues such as deforestation, soil erosion, air and water degradation, urban encroachment, habitat and wildlife destruction, and the conservation of natural resources are increasingly pertinent in West Africa, just as they are in many other parts of the world. Some local issues are discussed in this book, but they should not be regarded in isolation. It is important to realise that most environmental and conservation matters are complex and interconnected to wider economic and political situations on a national or global scale.

For example, all over West Africa, an ever-increasing human population puts great demands on the land and natural resources. It is generally agreed that these resources need to be conserved, and one way of doing this is to lower the rate of population growth. But to suggest that the solution simply involves contraception, sterilisation or a change in cultural attitudes is narrow. Conservationists taking a broader perspective say that the rapid population growth is closely linked to poor living conditions, which in turn is linked to social issues such as lack of education and health care. They argue that it is not reasonable to expect people with no money or little food to worry about conservation in its widest sense; the root of the problem – poverty – needs to be addressed.

Poverty & Resources

Methods for the alleviation of poverty in West Africa, and other poor countries, vary considerably. International bodies such as the World Bank favour large-scale economic development, initiated by loans, on the assumption that this will eventually provide income for citizens. Opponents of this argument hold that such economic development can cause environmental damage: heavy industry creates air and water pollution, and inevitably requires the use of natural resources. Large-scale farming also causes pollution and soil erosion, and frequently leads to the displacement of people from their land, which results in increased poverty levels, a drift towards urban centres and

further environmental degradation in rural areas. (See Economy later in this chapter for a fuller discussion of these issues.)

Moreover, even if the grand economic plans were successful, so that Africa's population growth stabilised and higher living standards were achieved, this does not solve the overall problem. Currently, the developed world uses a far greater proportion of the earth's resources than the developing world (for example, an urban citizen of Britain, Australia or the USA consumes over 50 times more than a poor rural inhabitant of Niger or Guinea-Bissau), and these resources are being used at an unsustainable rate already. If the 'poor' countries 'caught up' with the rich countries, the earth's resources would be put under more pressure and wouldn't be able to support everyone anyway. Put simply, the ideal (some would say idealistic) solution is to raise living standards in Africa, but at the same time reduce western consumption, with everyone using resources at a sustainable rate.

When African environmental issues are discussed, there is often a tendency to emphasise local problems (wood-burning creates deforestation; over-grazing causes soil erosion), but the global imbalance in the use of natural resources shows that environmental issues are never clear-cut, and often need to be addressed on a global scale.

The Ivory Debate

Possibly the most striking example of how environmental issues are never clear-cut is the emotive debate about the conservation of elephants and the international trade in ivory. Although East and southern Africa are more noted for their elephant populations, the issue is also relevant in West Africa.

Throughout the 1970s and 1980s, large-scale poaching reduced Africa's elephant populations to less than 20% of their earlier levels. In 1990, the Convention on International Trade in Endangered Species (CITES) banned the worldwide ivory trade. At the same time there was an increase in funds for the protection of elephants, and across the continent herds began to recover.

However, in the southern nations of Zimbabwe, Botswana and Namibia, elephant populations were already healthy. Through the 1990s these countries put forward increasingly strong arguments for the trade to be legalised so that funds from sales of ivory could go to conservation projects that would benefit both animals and people. In June 1997 CITES allowed Zimbabwe, Botswana and Namibia to resume selling ivory from March 1999, in a strictly controlled way so that poached ivory could not be 'laundered' through the legal trade.

In West and Central Africa, the effects were noticed immediately. In December 1996 the British *Times* newspaper quoted an International Fund for Animal Welfare representative who discovered 280 poached elephant carcasses in the border area between Gabon and Congo-Brazzaville: 'where you have a legal trade, inevitably an illegal trade will follow'. Through 1997, several other conservation bodies, including Care for the Wild, stated that poachers were stockpiling illegal ivory to be ready for the new wave of trading. In Ghana's Mole National Park, two elephants were killed in June 1997 – the first since 1988.

Conservationists who favour a trade resumption say that legalising ivory sales in southern Africa cannot be directly linked to an increase in poaching in West Africa. They cite other factors such as poor national park management and lack of suitable habitat. They believe that poachers will disregard the international status of the elephant, and kill anyway, so that only a legal market value will encourage local people to protect 'their' animals against poachers. But conservationists in West Africa see the push for reintroduction of a legal trade as selfish. While southern African elephant populations may be secure, a resumption in the ivory trade may be enough of a boost for poaching to push the West African elephant herds into extinction.

Deforestation

Deforestation is another major environmental issue currently facing most parts of West Africa. Increased population growth, and a corresponding increase in the demand for farmland, means areas of natural forest and woodland are continually being cleared. Also, bush fires are started by local farmers to promote new growth for livestock, control pests such as tsetse flies and to flush out wild animals, which can then be hunted. On a larger scale, rainforests in some countries are being commercially logged, while in many countries wooded areas are cleared for plantations to produce cash crops – often for export, so that countries can earn the currency desperately needed to pay off interest on the loans provided by the World Bank and other institutions.

Whatever the reason, this clearing of natural woodland leads to soil erosion, and eventually the reduction of cultivable areas. More immediately, the loss of woodland also means reduced water catchment and a decease in the availability of traditional building materials, foodstuffs and medicines. On top of that, the destruction of wooded areas leads to the loss of vital habitats for many of the region's bird and animal species.

In some countries this issue is being addressed. For example, forestry projects in Gambia and Ghana aim to 'manage' remaining natural woodland. These areas are not simply fenced off; instead they are utilised in a sustainable way for the benefit of local people. Dead wood can be used for timber, fruits and edible leaves can be collected, or grasses can be harvested for thatch. These products can be used or sold, but all the activities take place without destroying the growing trees. In this way the local people see the forest as a source of produce, income or employment, and have a real incentive to protect it in the long term.

Community-Based Conservation

The forestry projects are just one example of how environmental schemes can never really be successful without the willing inclusion of local people. 'Community-based conservation' is a vital buzz word, as organisations recognise the importance of including local inhabitants in environmental planning, and that national parks and other protected areas are unlikely to succeed in the long term unless local people can obtain real benefits. The sometimes altruistic environmental sentiments often expressed in the west (that forests or other natural areas should be conserved simply because they look nice) is a luxury that the people of Africa can ill afford.

Established thinking among conservationists for many years regarded human populations as a negative factor, and in many instances local inhabitants were excluded from national parks or other protected wildlife areas because it was assumed that they damaged natural resources. But now, if there is a tangible benefit for local inhabitants, then natural environments have a much better chance of evading complete destruction. In many instances, one of the benefits available to local people is money earned from tourists who come to visit wildlife or wilderness areas. This is discussed further under Responsible Tourism in the Regional Facts for the Visitor chapter.

FLORA & FAUNA
Vegetation

The vegetation zones of West Africa are linear, and correspond to the three main bands outlined in the Geography section earlier in this chapter.

Forest & Woodland Much of the coastal area lies between 5° and 10° north of the equator, where rainfall is heavy. The natural vegetation created by this climate is dense rain-fed lowland forest (or just 'rainforest') where trees can reach heights of 45m. The upper branches form a continuous canopy, often blocking light from the forest floor which hinders growth of smaller plants, although vines and other epiphytes are a feature of this vegetation zone. In woodland areas the trees tend to be lower and more spread-out so that their upper branches do not form a continuous canopy, which allows other plants to grow in between.

It is important to emphasise that vast areas of this natural vegetation have been cleared for logging and agriculture, so that very little of the original West African forest remains, except in parts of Liberia, Sierra Leone and south-western Côte d'Ivoire. Areas of woodland exist in the southern parts of Benin, Ghana, Guinea, Nigeria and Togo.

Savanna & Semidesert In the northern parts of the coastal countries the climate becomes drier. The forest and woodland give way to a vegetation zone defined as 'savanna and semidesert', where the landscape consists primarily of well-dispersed trees, the most common being various species of acacia, and low scrub bush, although ribbons of dense gallery forest occur along river courses. (Gallery forest is similar to rainforest but is fed by ground water, rather than rain, so many of the vines characteristic of rainforest are absent.) This zone is usually called the Sahel, and covers most of Senegal, southern Mali and Niger, Burkina Faso and northern Nigeria.

Desert North of the Sahel lies the true desert, where rainfall and vegetation growth is minimal. Of the countries in this book, the desert covers northern Mali and Niger, plus most of Mauritania.

Mammals

You may hear it said that people visit East Africa to see the animals and West Africa to see the people. While these aspects are probably the main attractions for each region, it does not mean there are no animals to see in West Africa. The region's national parks and wildlife reserves contain most of the classic African mammal species – including elephant, lion and leopard – although these are rarely seen. Buffalo also exist here, but these are the forest type – smaller and redder than the East African version.

Animals more readily seen include several beautiful antelope species, such as bushbuck, reedbuck, waterbuck, kob, roan, eland, oribi, sitatunga and various gazelle and duiker. The Sahel-dwelling dama gazelle is the largest gazelle species in Africa, but this animal is now close to ex-

The Baobab Tree

Along with the flat-topped acacia, the baobab tree *(Adansonia digitata)* is an instantly recognisable symbol of Africa. Its thick, sturdy trunk and stunted root-like branches are featured on countless postcards and brochures. Baobabs grow in most parts of West Africa, and in many other areas of the continent, usually in savanna zones where rainfall is limited. Many cultures have their own version of a story that displeasing a deity who plucked it in anger and thrust it back into the ground upside down. Hence the root-like branches.

However, despite the misdemeanours of its ancestor, today's baobab is held in high regard by local people. Its wizened appearance, combined with an ability to survive great droughts and live for many hundreds of years, means the baobab is often revered and believed to have magical

powers. Very old trees develop cavities and these are sometimes used to inter a revered *griot* (praise singer). Smaller holes are used by birds and animals.

The baobab has many practical uses for local people too. The hollow trunk sometimes holds rainwater, making a useful reservoir in times of drought. The tree's large pods (sometimes called 'monkey bread') contain seeds encased in a sherbet-like substance which can be eaten or made into a drink. The pods themselves are used to make cups or bowls (often for drinking palm wine). Any not suitable for this purpose are used as fuel. They burn slowly and are especially good for smoking fish. The leaves of the baobab can be eaten when chopped, boiled and made into a sauce. They can also be dried and ground into a paste to use as a poultice for skin infections and joint complaints. Even the flowers are used for decoration at ceremonies.

tinction as its grazing lands have been taken over by cattle or reduced by desertification. Wild pig species include giant hog and bush pig (the West African species is browner than those in East Africa and often called the red river hog), which inhabit forest areas, and warthog, frequently seen in drier savanna areas.

Possibly the best known and most easily observed mammal species of West Africa are the monkeys. These include several types of colobus and green or vervet monkey. Other primates include mangabey, baboon, galago (bushbaby), as well as the chimpanzee troops for which some parks here are world famous.

In the rivers, including the upper reaches of the Niger and Gambia rivers, hippopotamus can sometimes be seen, but hunting and the restriction of natural grazing grounds mean their numbers are low. Some hippo have adapted to live in saltwater and exist in coastal areas, and a few forest areas of West Africa are home to very small populations of pygmy hippos, which are less aquatic than their larger cousins.

Other marine mammals which you may encounter include dolphin, especially where the region's main rivers meet the ocean, and manatee (sea-cow) – giant seal-like relatives of the elephant, which inhabit mangrove and delta areas along the coast.

Watching mammals is not always straightforward. Most are very shy, and poaching has reduced populations considerably in the last 20 years in West Africa.

Birds

The West African region is renowned for its birdlife – see the special section 'Birds of West Africa' later in this chapter.

Reptiles & Amphibians

West Africa's most notable reptile is the Nile crocodile, which was once abundant all over the region. These days its numbers have been much reduced by hunting and habitat destruction, and very few remain, although you may see them along the larger rivers such as the Gambia, Senegal and Niger. Two lesser-known species, the dwarf crocodile and slender-nosed crocodile, also occur. In several countries, including Mali and Côte d'Ivoire, crocodiles are regarded as sacred.

Along the coast of West Africa, and on some of the offshore islands, turtles can be seen. The females come to the beaches to lay eggs in the sand, sometimes several hundred in one laying, but the species is in decline as nesting areas are damaged or inhabited by humans. Additionally, adults are hunted or suffer from the effects of water pollution – specifically from floating plastic bags, which they mistake for food and try to eat.

Other reptiles to watch for – but which shouldn't inspire paranoia – are snakes. West Africa has a complement of both venomous and harmless snakes, but most fear humans and you'll be lucky to even see one. The largest snake is the python, which grows to over 5m in length. It's harmless to humans. Another snake worth mentioning is the puff adder, which reaches about 1m in length, and like all reptiles enjoys sunning itself. Although it isn't aggressive, it is very slow and is sometimes stepped on by unwary people before it's had time to wake up and move out of the way. And when stepped on it bites. Take care when hiking in bush areas, especially in the early morning when this snake is at its most lethargic.

Lizards are ubiquitous in West Africa from the desert to the rainforest, and from the bathroom ceiling to the kitchen sink. The largest of these is the monitor (often up to 2m in length), which spends a lot of time lying around rivers and water holes, perhaps dreaming of being a crocodile. You're more likely to see agama – lizards about 20cm long with purple bodies and orange heads, energetically doing press-ups on walls and boulders. And in any house or small hotel you'll inevitably see geckos, running around on the walls or hiding behind pictures, with their sucker-like feet and near-transparent skin. They can appear alarming, but you'll soon get used to these harmless creatures – they help to keep the flies down too.

Other insect-eaters include frogs, which inhabit riverside reeds and mangroves, and toads, which are happier out of water than their froggy relatives.

Insects

The forest areas of West Africa are particularly rich in insect life, and the list of species is mind-boggling (many more are yet to be recorded by science). Entomologists will have their own agendas but the casual traveller won't fail to notice huge centipedes and millipedes, colourful spiders and columns of viciously biting safari ants. You may not see termites, but you won't fail to see termite mounds – solid towers of soil and sand up to 3m high where each grain has been painstakingly glued together with the termites' adhesive saliva. The forests are also particularly rich in butterflies.

Insects to be wary of include scorpions, which often hide under stones or logs and can sting if disturbed or threatened. They can also crawl into shoes or under sleeping

National Parks in West Africa

For many travellers, the main problem in West Africa isn't the lack of animals – it's the lack of easy access to national parks where they can be seen. Many parks are in remote areas where access by public transport is not always possible, and walking in the park itself is usually forbidden. Walking safaris, as found in East and southern Africa, are virtually unknown.

Generally, the national parks do not receive many visitors, and tourist facilities are limited or nonexistent. For some people, this is an attraction – they find it more satisfying to stalk and observe the animals rather than jostle for space with other visitors.

Having said that, several parks can be visited on a locally organised tour, or simply by hiring a taxi. Details are given in the individual country chapters.

A selection of West Africa's major parks is listed here. These are the best known or easiest to reach; other parks and protected wildlife areas are covered in the individual country chapters. Some are open year-round, but others are open only in the dry season from November to the end of May. In December, some park tracks may still be waterlogged, and dense vegetation makes spotting animals difficult. Later in the year, animals are easier to see as the ground cover withers, but the parks get hot and dusty. Just before the rains break is an excellent time for viewing, but conditions can be very uncomfortable.

Benin	Parc National de la Pendjari
Burkina Faso	Parc National d'Arli
Côte d'Ivoire	Parc National de la Comoë, Parc National de Taï
Gambia	Abuko Nature Reserve, Kiang West National Park
Ghana	Mole National Park, Kakum National Park
Niger	Parc National du W
Nigeria	Yankari National Park
Senegal	Parc National aux Oiseaux du Djoudj, Parc National du Niokolo-Koba, Parc National du Delta du Saloum

Whenever you visit, binoculars are highly recommended, and some good compact models are available. Observing behaviour or picking out beautiful markings with binoculars is so much more rewarding than squinting at some vague brown beast in the distance.

bags during the night, so give everything a shake if you're sleeping in the bush.

Field Guides

At some national parks, locally produced booklets detail local birds and other animals. If you have a deeper interest, a good regional field guide is recommended. Some bird books are listed in the special section 'Birds of West Africa' and in the Flora & Fauna section of the chapter on Gambia, the major birding destination in the region.

For mammals, the classic volume for many years has been *Mammals of Africa* published by Collins, but it's now a little dated. The recently published *Kingdon Field Guide to African Mammals* by Jonathan Kingdon is highly regarded by naturalists. The author is a leading authority, and the book covers over a thousand species, discussing ecology, evolutionary relationships and conservation status as well as the more usual notes on identification and distribution, with colour pictures and maps throughout.

BIRDS OF WEST AFRICA

African spoonbill

West Africa is an area so vast, and encompasses so many different habitats, that only a brief summary is possible here. Over a thousand bird species have been recorded in the region, from the Sahara Desert through savanna woodlands to the rich tropical forests of Liberia and Ghana. Many species are endemic (ie found nowhere else); others are passage migrants that fly down the Atlantic coast to and from their wintering grounds; and still more are nomads that fly from one part of Africa to another, taking advantage of seasonal plenty before moving on. If this is your first visit to West Africa you will be delighted by the abundance and diversity of birdlife; if you are a seasoned African birdwatcher you will find a host of species here not found in the eastern and southern parts of the continent.

© MIKE McKAVETT – WINDRUSH PHOTOS

Painted snipe

BIRD HABITATS

Many birds are wide-ranging, but the vast majority have feeding, breeding or other biological requirements which restrict them to a habitat or group of habitats. Thus, ducks are adapted to feed in water and are rarely found far from it. A brief rundown of West African bird habitats follows. Of course, creatures as mobile as birds are not restricted to their preferred environment (in fact, the habitat of some birds, such as swallows and swifts, could perhaps best be described as 'air'), but travellers will probably notice the change in variety of birds as they move from area to area.

Visit as wide a range of habitats as possible to see the full diversity of birdlife in West Africa.

Cities, Towns & Villages

Since these will be the first stop for nearly all visitors, it is worth mentioning a few birds that will be seen around human settlement. Swifts, swallows and martins nest under the eaves of buildings; the grey-headed sparrow is a widespread representative of the cosmopolitan sparrows; and the red-billed firefinch frequents grain stores and village compounds.

Keep your eyes open – many travellers have their first introduction to African birds on and around their hotel.

Look out for the gorgeous little cordon-bleus and firefinches flitting among the vegetation around hotels and other dwellings; starlings and the brilliant yellow-crowned gonolek may be seen feeding on lawns; and weavers make their presence felt in noisy colonies. The piapiac is a long-tailed member of the crow family that is sometimes seen around towns and villages.

Ocean Shore & Estuaries

The narrow strip where land meets sea is a rich habitat that attracts humans and animals alike to feast on creatures such as crustaceans and shellfish. Birds adapted to feeding in these habitats include waders such as oystercatcher and plover, and the reef egret, which stalks fish and crabs.

Major rivers such as the Benue, Casamance, Gambia, Niger, Senegal and Volta have extensive mangrove-lined tidal estuaries. Mangrove trees form the first line of defence against the destructive power of the sea by breaking down wave action and stabilising mud with their strong root system. Historically they have been dismissed as 'swamps', but mangroves are now recognised as an important ecological resource. At low tide the mud floor is exposed and makes a rich feeding ground for migratory waders like sandpiper, stint, curlew, godwit and plover. Small birds such as sunbirds feed in the mangrove canopy and larger water birds, such as heron, ibis and spoonbill, may roost or nest among the larger stands.

> Freshwater habitats provide some of the best opportunities to view birds for beginner and expert alike.

Waterways

The major river systems of the region – and the associated fringing (or 'gallery') forests, grasslands and swamps – support an astonishing variety of birds. Different groups of birds use waterways in different ways: some hunt along the shoreline or probe the soft mud at the water's edge, others stride on long legs into deeper water to seek prey. Some kingfishers perch on overhanging vegetation and dive into the water, and warblers, finches and rails skulk in dense vegetation.

Low-lying areas may flood after rains to create extensive ephemeral swamps which are often superb for birdwatching. Egrets, herons and other wading birds stalk the shallows; the dainty jacana walks across floating vegetation on its ridiculously long splayed toes; and finches nest and feed in fringing reed beds.

Savanna & Woodland

Large swathes of West Africa are characterised by savanna dominated by a mixture of small trees – the typical African landscape. Much woodland has been cleared or modified by human activities, but good stands remain in national parks and other reserves. There can be rich bird pickings in this habitat, from the perplexing cisticolas to huge birds of prey, and from weavers and finches to starlings, rollers and bush shrikes.

© DAVID TIPLING – WINDRUSH PHOTOS

Black-headed plover

Rainforest

Rainforest occurs in areas of high rainfall from Guinea-Bissau to Nigeria, although this habitat is increasingly under threat from clearing for agriculture. Good stands of forest remain in protected areas and these are usually great for birdwatching. Although they are perhaps the most complex and diverse ecosystems on earth, rainforests are little understood and are disappearing faster than scientists can catalogue their contents, let alone study their inhabitants. In these forests a great number and variety of birds are found, including many which have a restricted range or are unique to West Africa, for example the bizarre bald crow.

Arid & Semi-arid Areas

The Sahara Desert covers large areas of northern Mauritania, Mali and Niger, giving way to semi-arid Sahel in the southern parts of these countries and in parts of Senegal and Burkina Faso. This sparsely vegetated landscape shaped by low rainfall comes to life briefly after rains but is usually low in species and diversity. It is a habitat seldom visited by birdwatchers, but supports a few interesting species including wheatears, desert finches and migrants stopping over to or from their northern breeding grounds.

THE BIRDS

The following is a group by group description of some of the birds travellers may see in West Africa. For more detailed information, you should refer to one of the guides mentioned under Books later in this section. Birds that are less likely to be spotted have been left out: for example, a peculiarly African group known as flufftails are so shy as to be virtually invisible. Instead, we have listed common, unusual or spectacular species.

Birds of Prey

Over 50 species, including hawks, eagles, vultures and falcons, are found in West Africa. They can be seen almost everywhere, and travellers will soon notice a few species, from soaring flocks of scavenging vultures to the stately bateleur eagle watching for prey. Many have specialised prey or habitat requirements; for example, the osprey and striking African fish eagle feed almost exclusively on fish.

Try to get an early start because most birds are active during the cooler hours of the day, especially in arid regions and during hot weather.

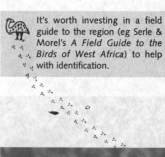

It's worth investing in a field guide to the region (eg Serle & Morel's *A Field Guide to the Birds of West Africa*) to help with identification.

Griffon vulture

© DAVID TIPLING – WINDRUSH PHOTOS

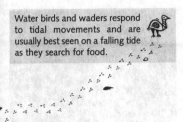

Water birds and waders respond to tidal movements and are usually best seen on a falling tide as they search for food.

Seabirds

Into this broad category can be lumped a number of bird families which hunt over the open sea. They include the various petrels and shearwaters, which usually live far out to sea and only return to land to breed; the beautiful gannets, which feed by plunging from a great height after fish; and the fish-eating cormorants and shags, which also make use of brackish and freshwater habitats. Fea's petrel is an extremely rare species that breeds only on the Cape Verde islands.

Waterfowl

This large group includes the familiar ducks and geese, although there are comparatively few species of ducks and geese in the region. As their collective name suggests, they are found almost exclusively around waterways. Waterfowl are strong fliers and can move vast distances in response to rainfall. They may be more easily seen after rains; in particular the large, black-and-white spur-winged goose can be abundant at such times. Several of the region's species are migrants from other parts of Africa or northern Europe. Residents include the whistling-duck and the diminutive African pygmy-goose.

Knob-billed duck

Long-Legged Wading Birds

Virtually any waterway will have its complement of herons, egrets, storks, spoonbills and ibis. All have long legs and necks, and bills adapted to specific feeding strategies: herons and egrets have dagger-like bills for spearing fish and frogs; spoonbills have peculiar, flattened bills which they swish from side to side to gather small water creatures; ibis have long, down-curved bills to probe in soft earth or seize insects; and storks have large powerful beaks to snap up small animals and fish. Members of this group range in size from the tiny, secretive bitterns to the enormous goliath heron, standing 1.4m tall, and the ugly marabou stork, which feeds on carrion. An unusual member of this group is the hamerkop, a small heron-like bird that makes an enormous nest of twigs and grass.

Hamerkop

Cranes

These graceful, long-legged birds superficially resemble the storks and herons, but are typically grassland-dwelling birds. The one species found in the region – the black crowned crane – is eccentrically adorned with a colourful crest.

© ERIC WOODS – WINDRUSH PHOTOS

© ROY GLEN – WINDRUSH PHOTOS

Migratory Waders

Every year migrating shore birds leave their breeding grounds in the northern hemisphere and fly to their wintering grounds south of the Sahara. Generally nondescript in their winter plumage, these migratory waders present an identification challenge to the keen birdwatcher. A number of species are also resident. With few exceptions these birds are found near fresh and saline waterways, feeding along the shores on small creatures or probing intertidal mud for worms. The migrants include the long-distance champions, the sandpipers and plovers, while residents include the boldly marked lapwings and the odd dikkops – a lanky, cryptic, nocturnal species with weird wailing cries.

Pigeons & Doves

Familiar to city and country dwellers alike, members of this worldwide family have adapted to virtually every habitat. For example, the various turtledoves and the tiny Namaqua dove feed on the ground while the African green pigeon leads a nomadic life following the fruiting of trees. Two species are common inhabitants of gardens and human settlements – the cosmopolitan rock dove and the laughing dove.

Wattled plover

Turacos

These often beautifully coloured, medium-sized forest birds can be difficult to see because of their habit of remaining hidden in the forest canopy. The violet turaco is a stunning bird, although you may only catch a tantalising view as one flies across a clearing, showing its vivid crimson wing patches. The grey plantain-eater is perhaps the drabbest – but also one of the commonest – of the seven species found in West Africa.

European travellers will recognise many common European migratory species, including swallows, swifts and waders, enjoying the hot African sun.

Barbets & Tinkerbirds

Barbets are closely related to woodpeckers but rather than drilling into bark after grubs, they have strong, broad bills adapted to eating fruit and a variety of insect prey. Barbets are often brightly coloured and perch conspicuously; the tinkerbirds are noisy but tiny and sometimes difficult to see.

Honeyguides

Honeyguides display some of the most remarkable behaviour of any bird. They seek out mammals such

Namaqua dove

RAY TIPPER

African fish eagle

© PETER CRAIG-COOPER – WINDRUSH PHOTOS

Bateleur eagle

© ROY GLEN – WINDRUSH PHOTOS

Yellow-billed stork

© MICHAEL GORE – WINDRUSH PHOTOS

African paradise flycatcher

African pygmy goose

Goliath heron

White-faced tree ducks

Red-throated bee-eater

Giant kingfisher

Red-billed hornbill

Blue-breasted kingfisher

Carmine bee-eater

African hoopoes

Yellow-billed oxpecker

Splendid sunbird

Pied kingfisher

Some West African birds are stunningly colourful – look out for bee-eaters, especially the carmine bee eater, rollers, kingfishers, brilliantly iridescent sunbirds and the violet turaco.

One of the pleasures of birdwatching in West Africa is that beautiful and spectacular species aren't always rare.

Abyssinian roller

as the ratel (honey badger), genet, mongoose or baboon, or even humans, then 'guide' them to a beehive. Once it has attracted the attention of a 'helper', a honeyguide flies a short way ahead then waits to see if it is being followed. In this way it leads them to the hive which the obliging creature breaks open and robs while the honeyguide feeds on the wax, larvae and eggs of the bees.

Kingfishers

Colourful and active, the 12 species of kingfisher found in West Africa can be divided into two groups: those which typically dive into water after fish and tadpoles (and as a result are found along waterways); and those that are less dependent on water because they generally prey on lizards and large insects. Of the former, the giant kingfisher reaches 46cm in size and the jewel-like malachite and pygmy kingfishers a mere 14cm. Of the not-so-colourful 'forest' kingfishers, the blue-breasted kingfisher is a boldly patterned example.

Bee-Eaters, Rollers & Hoopoe

The bee-eaters range in appearance from gorgeous to merely brilliant and are always watchable. Twelve members of this family are found in West Africa. Some species are commonly seen perched on fences and branches – sometimes in mixed flocks – from which they pursue flying insects especially, as their name suggests, bees and wasps. They may congregate in thousands and you won't easily forget seeing a flock of the stunning carmine bee-eater.

The rollers are closely related to bee-eaters and most of the six species are common. Rollers are not as gaudy as bee-eaters, usually being decked out in blues and mauves; the Abyssinian roller sports two long tail feathers. Mention should also be made of the hoopoe, a black and white bird with a salmon-pink head and neck and a bizarre crest.

Hornbills

Hornbills are medium-sized birds of forests and woodland that sport massive, down-curved bills. Two groups, the African grey and red-billed hornbills, are reasonably common; the extraordinary ground hornbill moves about in groups along the ground and stands nearly 1m tall.

Owls

These nocturnal birds of prey have soft feathers (making their flight inaudible), exceptional hearing and can turn their heads in a 180° arc to locate their prey. There are many species in the region, ranging from the diminutive scops owls to the massive eagle owls, which can be up to 65cm in length. The prey varies according to the species, from insects, mice and lizards among the smaller species to the roosting birds and small mammals favoured by others. Pel's fishing owl hunts along rivers and feeds exclusively on fish.

Owls have inspired fear and superstition in many cultures, but their elusiveness makes them eagerly sought by birdwatchers.

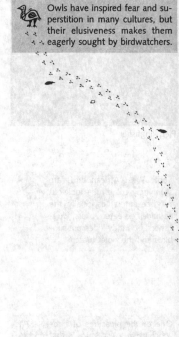

Nightjars

Another nocturnal group, these small birds are not related to owls, although their plumage is soft and their flight also silent. Nightjars roost on the ground by day, their subtle coloration making them perfectly camouflaged among the leaves and twigs. At dusk, they take to the wing and catch insects. Although they are not uncommon, you may be oblivious to their presence until one flies up near your feet. The identification of several species is difficult and often relies on call, but when disturbed during the day nightjars typically fly to a nearby branch or perch, allowing you to have a closer look. The incredible standard-winged nightjar is the region's most spectacular example.

Swifts & Swallows

Although unrelated, these two groups are superficially similar and can be seen chasing insects in the air just about anywhere. Both groups have long wings and streamlined bodies adapted to lives in the air; both fly with grace and agility after insects; and both are usually dark in coloration. However, swallows differ in one major aspect: they can perch on twigs, fences or even the ground whereas swifts have weak legs and rarely land except at the nest. In fact, swifts are so adapted to life in the air that some are even known to roost on the wing. There are many examples of the swallow family in the region; two that are often seen around human habitation are red-rumped and mosque swallows.

Cisticolas

These drab little warblers are common and widespread, but are sometimes difficult to see and even harder to identify. Many are so similar they are most easily separated by their calls, which are the basis of their common names such as singing, croaking, siffling and zitting cisticolas. Cisticolas are typically found in long grass and riverside vegetation.

Zitting cisticola

Senegal firefinch

Have patience – and don't give up. Most birds are shy creatures requiring much time and effort to spot.

Bald Crows

Two extraordinary birds in this group are found in the rainforests of West Africa. Known as bald crows, they superficially resemble the true crows (to which they are not related), but are white and grey with a bald, bright red, grey or yellow head. Little is know of these rare birds, although they appear to frequent caves in dense forest.

Weavers & Finches

This large group includes many small but colourful examples, readily seen in flocks along roads and wherever there is long grass. All are seed eaters and while some, such as the various sparrows, are not spectacular, others develop showy courtship plumage and tail plumes of extraordinary size.

Weavers are usually yellow birds with varying amounts of black in their plumage. They can become pests in cultivated areas, as they are voracious seed eaters, and often form big nesting colonies right in the centre of towns. Sparrows come typically in shades of brown and grey. Widows (also called why-dahs) are similar while not breeding, but during courtship males moult into black plumage with red or yellow highlights. Widows also develop striking tail plumes during courtship – the enormous tail of the exclamatory paradise widow can be more than twice the bird's body length.

Starlings

Africa is the stronghold of these gregarious and intelligent birds, and many species are found in West Africa. Several species of the so-called glossy starlings – including the purple, long-tailed and blue-eared glossy starlings – may be seen in fast-flying, noisy flocks. All are magnificent birds with iridescent blue and purple plumage, although they may prove an identification challenge when they occur in mixed flocks. The yellow-billed oxpecker is another member of this family and can be seen clinging to livestock or game, from which it prises parasitic ticks and insects.

Sunbirds

Sunbirds are small, delicate nectar feeders with sharp, down-curved bills. The males of most species are brilliantly iridescent while the females are drabber. Spectacular species include the pygmy sunbird, whose slender tail plumes almost double its 9cm length, the copper sunbird and the violet-backed sunbird.

Long-tailed glossy starling

WHERE TO LOOK FOR BIRDS IN WEST AFRICA

Birds will be encountered virtually everywhere in your travels, although weather and temperature can affect the number of birds you see. Most countries in the region have reserves set up to protect wildlife and wildlife habitats, and these are good places to concentrate your efforts. Some countries also have reserves specifically for birds.

In the tiny state of **Gambia**, bird diversity is astonishing – 540 species have been recorded and the country's unusual shape makes many good birdwatching sites easily accessible. Abuko Nature Reserve is closest to the capital Banjul, and hosts a surprising diversity within its 130 hectares. Many forest species are easier to see here than in other parts of the country and observation hides have been set up. Tanji Bird Reserve, on the Atlantic coast, protects a patchwork of habitat on the flyway for migrating birds. Although it covers only 600 hectares, almost 300 species have been recorded in Tanji. Kiang West National Park is one of the country's largest protected areas and a good spot to see a large variety of wildlife, including birds. The adjacent north shore of the river is known as the Baobolong Wetland Reserve in recognition of its international importance.

Senegal has six national parks, plus a number of areas set aside as reserves to protect wildlife. Among the protected areas near the mouth of the River Senegal in the north are the Langue de Barbarie and Djoudj national parks. Both are superb sites, famous for vast pelican and flamingo flocks, and Djoudj is a UNESCO World Heritage site where almost 400 bird species have been recorded. The magnificent Parc National du Niokolo-Koba, also a World Heritage site, protects more than 9000 sq km of savanna and associated habitats; it is the last stronghold of Senegal's large mammals and about 350 bird species have been recorded.

The rainforests of **Côte d'Ivoire's** Parc National d'Assagny are home to a large variety of birds and in Parc National de la Marahoué nearly 300 species have been recorded. Parc National de la Comoë also supports an abundance of birds.

Good birdwatching sites in **Mali** include Lac Faguibine 50km north of Goundam – one of the best places in the Sahel for seeing migratory birds. In **Benin**, Parc National de la Pendjari supports a variety of birdlife, and in Burkina Faso the lake at Le Barrage,

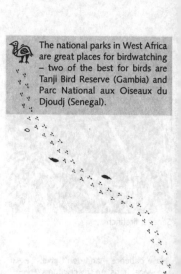

The national parks in West Africa are great places for birdwatching – two of the best for birds are Tanji Bird Reserve (Gambia) and Parc National aux Oiseaux du Djoudj (Senegal).

Pink-backed pelican

© DAVID TIPLING – WINDRUSH PHOTOS

African jacana

Ranch de Nazinga and Lac de Tengréla are all worth a look.

In **Ghana**, Kakum Nature Park, Owabi Wildlife Sanctuary, Bia National Park and Bui National Park are all good for birding, and over 300 species have been reported in Mole National Park.

Public access to **Mauritania's** remote Parc National du Banc d'Arguin may be restricted during the breeding season, but it is one of the best sanctuaries in West Africa. Its location makes it a crossroads for a host of birds migrating between Europe and southern Africa.

Sierra Leone's Tiwai Island Wildlife Sanctuary has more than 120 bird species including hornbills, kingfishers and the rare white-breasted guinea fowl. The smaller Mamunta-Mayoso Wildlife Sanctuary protects a wetland area about 30km south of Makeni and provides a vital refuge for many bird species. Around Mt Bintumani the endangered rufous fishing-owl has been sighted. Various habitats in Outamba-Kilimi National Park support many species, including kingfishers, hornbills, herons, hawks and the spectacular great blue turaco.

Nigeria offers some fine birding: Yankari National Park has a stunning array of some 600 species in its various habitats; Okomu Sanctuary, less than an hour from Benin City, hosts cranes and hornbills; try also Kamuku Wildlife Reserve, near Birnin Gwari, and the Hadejia-Nguru Wetlands, 200km north-east of Kano, an important resting place for migratory birds and endemic species. Gashaka Gumpti National Park near the Cameroon border is the largest national park in Nigeria and has a diverse ecology.

Small models of binoculars don't weigh much but can make a huge difference to your trip, even if you're not normally a keen birder.

SOME TIPS FOR WATCHING BIRDS

A pair of binoculars will reveal the subtleties of form and plumage not usually detected by the naked eye. Be warned – once you've seen the shimmering colours of a glossy ibis or the brash tones of a bee-eater through binoculars you may get hooked! Binoculars will also considerably aid identification and help you nut out the subtle – and vexing – differences between difficult groups such as cisticolas.

Basic models can be purchased quite cheaply from duty-free outlets. If you get serious about bird-watching you may want to invest in better quality optics. Some brands come in handy, pocket-sized models. You may also want to consider buying a spotting scope. With a magnification usually at least twice that of binoculars, they can give stunning views. The drawback is their size (they must be mounted on a tripod for best results); on the other hand, a camera can be attached to some models and a scope then doubles as a telephoto lens.

Other suggestions to help you get the most out of birdwatching in West Africa include:

Helmeted guinea fowl

- Approach birds slowly and avoid sudden movements or loud talk. Many species are quite approachable, allowing opportunities for observation and photography.
- Birds are not usually too concerned about people in a vehicle or boat and stunning views can often be obtained from the roadside. Cruises on the rivers and through mangroves are a popular and fun way to birdwatch in some parks and reserves, notably in Gambia and Senegal.
- Do not disturb birds unnecessarily and never handle eggs or young birds in a nest. Adults will readily desert a nest that has been visited, leaving their young to perish.
- Always ask permission before birding on private property, and avoid military areas.

BOOKS

Although West Africa encompasses a huge area, there are few books that specifically cover the region's birdlife. *A Field Guide to the Birds of West Africa,* by W Serle and GJ Morel, is a compact little guide that illustrates about 650 species and describes over 1000. For more detailed information, plus excellent illustrations, on all African birds, consult the six volume *Birds of Africa* by EK Urban, CH Fry and S Keith.

Country or area-specific field guides can be used in some places, but very few individual West African countries are covered in this way. A notable exception is Gambia, where worldwide fame as a top-quality birdwatching destination has inspired several guides, including the superb *A Field Guide to the Birds of The Gambia and Senegal,* by C Barlow, T Wacher and T Disley, which illustrates 570 species and describes all those so far recorded in the Senegambia. Although a bit heavier than the average paperback, this is an essential purchase for any serious birdwatcher. *A Birdwatchers' Guide to The Gambia* by Rod Ward is a finely researched book on birding sites and likely sightings.

Specific field guides to other West African countries include the excellent *Birds of Liberia* by W Gatter. More specialised treatments of the region's

Part of the fun of birdwatching is learning – take a notebook and pencil!

birdlife include: *Forest Birds in Côte d'Ivoire*, by ME Hartshore, PD Taylor and IS Francis; *The Birds of Ghana: An Annotated Checklist*, by LG Grimes; *The Birds of Nigeria: An Annotated Checklist*, by JH Elgood; and *The Birds of Togo: An Annotated Checklist*, by RA Cheke and JF Walsh. Most of these titles do not have colour illustrations, but will give you an idea of what to expect or look for.

David Andrew

Tips for Budding Photographers

That perfect picture proving elusive? Here are some hints from Lonely Planet's top photographer, Richard I'Anson.

- Get close and fill the frame as much as possible
- The bird must be recognisable
- Use 300mm or 400mm lenses
- Use fast film 200 ISO or 400 ISO
- Use fast shutter speeds, 1/500 or 1/1000
- Use autowinder/motor drive

© MIKE McKAVETT – WINDRUSH PHOTOS

Red-cheeked cordon-bleu

GOVERNMENT & POLITICS

The end of the Cold War had a profound impact on African political systems. Previously, dictators argued that democracy wasn't necessarily the best system for Africa. In truth, this was a façade for tyranny, but as long as a dictator remained loyal to either the west or the eastern bloc, they were supplied with arms and bilateral (country-to-country) 'aid' money to prevent any chance of a switch to the other side. That the dictators squandered the money, raped their countries and brutally oppressed their subjects was conveniently overlooked.

Towards the end of the 1980s and into the 1990s, as the peoples of Eastern Europe threw out their dictators, Africans began looking at their own leaders and wondered what right they had to stay in power for so long without periodic public approval. At the same time, support to Africa from the Soviet bloc dwindled, so the western nations had less need to prop up their own allies. Suddenly, the dictators' positions started to look decidedly shaky as pro-democracy and multiparty movements sprang up in many parts of Africa.

These moves towards democracy were supported by the USA, through the World Bank, and by the French government, both demanding further political reform in return for financial assistance. Although more laudable than the old-style support for dictators, critics hold that the sudden interest in African democracy is based firmly on economic motives – a stable country makes more money – rather than on a desire for basic freedoms or human rights.

One of West Africa's most autocratic governments was in Benin, but at a major political gathering in 1990, delegates demanded and received long-time president Mathieu Kérékou's resignation (although he retained control of the army) along with a new constitution and the promise of free, multiparty elections. A new government was elected in 1991, but became increasingly autocratic, and four years later Kérékou was voted back into power. Despite the return to power of this notorious dictator the move was seen as a strong endorsement of Benin's new democratic system.

Similar events occurred in Mali during 1991, when President Moussa Traoré (in power since 1968) was ousted. The new leadership is now supporting a multiparty system and open elections. In Côte d'Ivoire, everyone expected political chaos when their leader for some 35 years, Houphouët-Boigny, died, but his appointed successor, Henri Konan-Bédié took over in one of the smoothest transitions in recent history and, under pressure, submitted himself to elections, which he won resoundingly. In Ghana, Jerry Rawlings, who thrust his way to power by army coup, has twice had his legitimacy confirmed by elections, acknowledged as free and fair.

On the flip side, in Niger, the new democratic multiparty system produced a weak, unstable government, which was overthrown in a coup in 1996, although elections for a new president and national assembly were held the following year. Even in apparently stable countries coups are still a real possibility, as illustrated by Gambia's 1994 military takeover and the coup in Guinea-Bissau in 1998.

It is indicative of the region's political status that at a 1997 West African heads-of-state meeting, seven of the 12 leaders attending had come to power in a coup. Genuine multiparty democracy is still far from being guaranteed across the region.

ECONOMY
The Figures

The countries of West Africa are the poorest in the world, and their economic figures make grim reading. The most common yardstick is per capita gross national product (GNP), which is calculated by dividing what a country 'earns' annually by its total population – giving an indication of what each inhabitant produces per year. By this measure, Sierra Leone is the poorest of the West African countries, with a per capita GNP of US$160. Gambia, Guinea-Bissau, Liberia, Mali and Niger all have per capita GNPs of US$250 or less, putting them among the poorest 10 countries in the world. Even oil-rich Nigeria shows just US$280, while most other West African countries, including Benin, Burkina Faso, Gambia, Ghana and Mauritania, show between US$300 and US$500. The high rollers are Senegal and Côte d'Ivoire (both with US$600) and Cape Verde (US$930). In contrast, most western industrialised nations have per capita GNPs of around US$20,000. In crude terms, the average western citizen is up to 100 times richer than their West African counterpart.

The per capita GNP figure is admittedly a very blunt instrument, as it is concerned only with economic values. Because of this, the United Nations devised the Human Development Index (HDI), which measures the overall achievements of a country according to factors such as life expectancy and education standards, as well as income. The results didn't change much. Sierra Leone still came out as the poorest country in the world, with Niger ranking 173rd out of 175 countries, closely followed by Burkina Faso at 172 and Mali at 171. Most other countries in West Africa were ranked low, with Senegal at 160, Mauritania 150, Côte d'Ivoire 145, Nigeria 141 and Ghana 132. Cape Verde was the highest at 123.

The Facts

What does it mean? In human terms, this poverty gives a life expectancy of less than 50 years in most parts of West Africa and as low as 44 years in some countries. Literacy rates are also very low, especially among women. Between 100 and 200 children in every 1000 die before the age of five, but annual birth rates are around 3% – the highest in the world. Unemployment is also very high. People have no money to buy food and can only grow cereal crops, so nutritional intakes are very low, which makes a large proportion of the population – especially children – susceptible to disease, for which there are very few medical services. It's a depressing scenario, and likely to get worse – 'The gap between Africa and the rest of the world is widening' (the *Economist*, 1997).

But there is an an even darker picture behind the scenes. Along with most other developing countries, the economies of West Africa are dominated, some say suffocated, by debt.

International Debt

It all started in the 1970s. The rise in oil prices meant commercial banks in the west had spare cash they needed to farm out, lending billions of dollars to developing countries, in West Africa and around the world, with little concern for safeguards or collateral. At the same time, western governments and international bodies such as the World Bank and the International Monetary Fund (IMF) also encouraged developing countries to take on loans. Sometimes it went beyond encouragement – loans were foisted or even forced on developing countries as part of so-called development projects. Many loans were linked to the production of cash crops or minerals for export, or for sales of imported goods (such as armaments) from which the lending countries would benefit. Generally speaking, the money was wasted, spent by dictators on their military, presidential palaces and other impressive buildings, inefficient nationalised industries or grandiose schemes like dams and motorways. And billions of dollars were simply embezzled. In some countries, the loans may have led to improvements, but in West Africa there were very few benefits. Very little, if any, reached the ordinary people.

Meanwhile the prices for commodities (such as cotton grown in Mali or groundnuts in Senegal) dropped, and the countries of West Africa earnt less from their exports, and found it increasingly hard to meet their interest payments. At the same time, the cost of importing western manufactured goods went up, creating an imbalance of trade which still affects many West African countries today. For example, in Benin and Mali, the cost of their imports is 33% more than the value of their exports; Senegal's import costs are double its export values; and Guinea-Bissau's import costs are four times its export values.

The Debt Crisis in Africa

Things came to a crunch in the early 1980s, when the term 'debt crisis' was coined. It was a crisis for the West African nations and other developing countries who could no longer afford to pay interest, but even more of a crisis for the major banks who stood to lose their money.

To avert the crisis, several western governments bailed out the banks (with taxpayers' money) while the IMF and other lenders introduced 'structural adjustment' or restrictions on the spending allowed by the debtor countries. In West Africa, this may have helped to control corruption and inefficiency, but for ordinary people things got worse – their wages went down, the price of food went up and services such as schools or hospitals were cut.

Despite the economic warning signs, and despite the suffering of the poor in the developing world, the loans kept going out and the debts keep piling up. Even today, the IMF continues to provide loans: so that interest on other loans can be paid. The World Bank is owed five times more today than it was 10 years ago. And the crisis is as big as it ever was.

Opponents of the World Bank, the IMF and other large development organisations point out that, quite apart from human and environmental costs, loans fail on an economic front too. Despite the billions of dollars in development loans that have been pumped into Africa in the last 30 years, most countries are now far worse off economically than they were at independence.

Debt in West Africa Today

In sub-Saharan Africa today, around 15% of countries' export earnings go on 'servicing' debt (ie paying off the interest, not the loan itself). In West Africa the percentage is higher – up to 50% of total export earnings in some cases. This means less money gets spent on useful things like schools and hospitals. Niger, for example, pays three times more on debt servicing than it does on health care and education. In Guinea-Bissau and Côte d'Ivoire, the debt they owe is three times more than their total annual earnings. On a global scale, the developing world owes the developed countries over two trillion US dollars, and pays over US$700 million in interest every day. Maggie O'Kane, writing in the *Guardian*, puts it

African Aid Money – Friends Indeed!

It's quite usual for emergency aid money to go from western countries to Africa, but very rare to find it going in the other direction. So when the Canadian farming community of St Elizabeth, near Quebec, was badly hit by ice storms in early 1998, they were very surprised when citizens in the town of Sanankoroba, near Bamako, the capital of Mali, heard about the disaster and decided to help. A collection raised CFA40,000 (about US$80), which was sent to St Elizabeth with a message of sympathy. A report by Alex Duval Smith in the British *Guardian* newspaper quoted collection organiser Moussa Konate: 'We are aware that the money they have received from us is symbolic. But it shows that giving has to do with the heart, not the sum'. This was not the first time the people of St Elizabeth and Sanankoroba had been in touch – the two settlements have been twinned for over a decade – but until now, the Canadians (each almost 100 times richer than their Malian counterparts) were doing all the material giving – especially when Sanankoroba was damaged by floods in the mid-1990s.

Moussa Konate's sympathy message quoted a Malian proverb: 'If you cannot share the meagre resources you have today, you will not know how to share the smallest part of your wealth tomorrow'. He went on to say, 'After all we have received, this is the least we can do. It is completely normal to help friends in need'.

more starkly: 'Every baby born in the developing world owes US$482'.

It has become increasingly obvious, and bitterly ironic, that although loans from the World Bank and other institutions are supposed to help developing nations, in reality they are a way to siphon money from the poor countries to the richer countries. And while the western financial institutions benefit, the vast majority of people in Niger, Mali, Gambia and the rest of West Africa continue to suffer. This is not to say that government corruption and inefficiency are not major problems in the region, but the outstanding debts which absorb so much money are an undeniably significant factor.

The Solution?

There are increasing calls from various charitable, human rights, church and welfare organisations for the western banks and nations to write off the loans to developing countries. The argument goes that they're never going to get the original money back, and the annual interest repayments only go to stifle the poor nations' economies and harm the populations. The debtor countries claim that the interest they've paid over the years equates to many times more than the original debt anyway.

To put the figures in some kind of perspective, the US$16 billion that sub-Saharan Africa owes the west is the cost of a fleet of jet fighters. Put another way, the US$6 billion required to provide adequate education for children in all developing countries is just 1% of what the world spends every year on its militaries. Here's another one, from the United Nations: to provide universal access to basic social services, and to alleviate income poverty would cost roughly US$80 billion – less than the combined net worth of the world's seven richest men.

A few western nations have agreed to write off some loans, but others remain resolute that the money must be repaid. The IMF and World Bank also indicate that some loans might be written off, but this may not be for another decade. Simple rescheduling is more likely, but even then only if the poor

countries introduce economic reforms – on World Bank and IMF terms.

On a personal scale, what can travellers in West Africa do? Just be aware is the main thing. See the wider picture. Don't overlook the part that your own government or bank back home plays in the enforcement of debt repayments in the developing world. Consider banking or investing with institutions who have ethical policies. And don't be fooled by claims in your home country about loans from western governments, banks and financial institutions 'helping' the poor of West Africa. In many cases they're doing the exact opposite.

EDUCATION

Generally speaking, all the countries in West Africa have state education systems which follow patterns established by their colonial powers, ie a primary stage, a secondary stage and a tertiary stage. In Islamic countries, Quranic schools operate in parallel to the state education system.

In most countries primary education is theoretically available for all children, whereas only those who pass relevant examinations can go to secondary school and university. In reality, which children go to school and how far up the ladder they progress is determined by their family income rather than by academic performance; poor children may not be able to afford school fees or extra items like uniforms and books (especially when they want to go beyond primary school). Also, children from poor families may be kept away from school to work in the fields or to provide income from other employment.

Across the region, these problems are compounded by restrictions on the government revenue available for education. Although many West African countries spend a relatively high proportion of public cash (higher, in percentage terms, than some western countries) the actual amount per child is still very low.

The end result is simply not enough schools to cater for the number of children. Many schools have to operate two 'shifts'

Female Genital Mutilation in West Africa

Female genital mutilation (FGM), often euphemistically termed 'female circumcision' or 'genital alteration' is widespread throughout West Africa. The term covers a wide range of procedures, from a small, mainly symbolic, cut to the total removal of the external genitalia (known as infibulation). In West Africa, the procedure usually involves removal of the entire clitoris. The World Health Organization's estimates range from about 30 to 59% of women altered in Côte d'Ivoire to about 90% of women altered in Sierra Leone.

Although outsiders often believe that FGM is associated with Islam, in fact it predates the religion (there are historical records of infibulation dating back 6000 years). The procedure is usually performed by midwives on girls and young women. They sometimes use modern surgical instruments but usually it's with a razor blade or a piece of glass. If the procedure is done in a traditional setting the girl will not be anaesthetised, although nowadays many families take their daughters to clinics to have the procedure performed by a trained doctor. Complications, especially in the traditional setting, include infection of the wound leading to death or scarring which makes childbirth and urination difficult.

In West Africa, genital alteration is seen as important for maintaining traditional society. An unaltered woman would dishonour her family and lower its position in society, as well as ruining her own chances for marriage – an altered woman is thought to be a moral woman, and more likely a virgin. Many believe that if left, the clitoris can make a woman infertile or damage, even kill, her unborn children.

Although FGM is deeply ingrained in West African societies, there are moves to make it illegal. Five countries have banned the procedure, although there are doubts about how well this is working. Practitioners are afraid of being arrested, but find it hard to go against tradition. In other countries, women's groups are trying to raise awareness about the dangers.

Jane Rawson

with one lot of children coming in the morning, and another in the afternoon. Even so, classes may hold over 100 pupils, sitting three or four to a desk, and sharing books and pens. At the same time, teachers are grossly underpaid, and many become understandably demoralised so that standards slip further. Consequently, literacy rates across West Africa are low.

ARTS
Art & Craftwork

West Africa has a rich artistic heritage and tradition, including sculpture (in wood, bronze and other materials), masks, fabulous textiles, jewellery, basketwork and leatherwork. See the colour features on arts throughout this book for a guide to the diversity in style and technique that you will find in the region. More specific details are given in the Arts sections of the individual country chapters.

For a deeper insight into West African arts, the Books section in the Regional Facts for the Visitor chapter lists some recommendations for further reading and, when you are on the road, even a brief museum visit can help to make sense of what you see.

Literature

West Africa has a rich heritage of traditional storytelling, and modern-day writers are no less prolific. Listed here is a brief selection of classic works by African authors of international renown. All are pan-African, or universal, in their scope, and all are highly recommended, wherever you travel in the region. For more information, see also the Arts sections in the individual country chapters, and the Books section in the Regional Facts for the Visitor chapter.

For a good introduction to the literature of the region, by far the most useful anthology is the *Traveller's Literary Companion – Africa*, edited by Oona Strathern, which contains over 250 prose and poetry extracts from all over Africa, with an introduction to the literature of each country, plus a list of 'literary landmarks' – features that appear in novels written about the country. Poetry anthologies include *The Heinemann Book of African Poetry in English*, edited by Adewale Maja-Pearce, and *The Penguin Book of Modern African Poetry* edited by Moore & Beier.

West African literature is undeniably dominated by Nigerian writers. These include Wole Soyinka who won the Nobel Prize for Literature in 1986, only the fifth person from a developing country, and the first from Africa, to achieve this accolade. He is primarily a playwright – *A Dance of the Forest*, *The Man Died*, *Opera Wonyosi* and *A Play of Giants* are some of his more well known works – and has also written poetry (including *Idane & Other Poems*), novels (including *The Interpreters*), and the fantastical childhood memoir, *Ake*. He is a man with a social vision and strong beliefs who doesn't mind lambasting those in power, although he uses a writing style that is far from simple.

Amos Tutuola is another Nigerian whose *The Palm Wine Drinkard* was published in the early 1950s and is often regarded as the first great African novel, a link between traditional storytelling and the modern form. Dylan Thomas, poet and critic, described it as 'brief, thonged, grisly and bewitching'. It's still a classic; about an insatiable drunkard who seeks his palm-wine tapster in the world of the dead.

Better known, perhaps, is Chinua Achebe, also of Nigeria. His *Things Fall Apart* (1958) is a classic, which has sold over eight million copies in 30 languages – more than any other African work. Set in the mid-19th century, this novel studies the collision between precolonial Ibo society and European missionaries. Particularly interesting is Achebe's penetration beyond colonialism to a moral examination of Africa and Africans. A more recent work is *Anthills of the Savannah*, a satirical study of political disorder and corruption. It was a finalist for the 1987 Booker Prize in the UK.

The position of 'best-known African author' was taken by Ben Okri, yet another Nigerian, when his novel *The Famished Road* won the Booker Prize in 1991. When critics grumbled that to appreciate the book's style and symbolism the reader had to 'understand Africa', Okri recalled reading Victorian novelists such as Dickens while a schoolboy in Nigeria. His combination of modern style and traditional mythological themes continues in later novels *Songs of Enchantment* and *Astonishing the Gods*.

Buchi Emecheta, from Nigeria, is one of Africa's most successful women authors. Her novels include *Slave Girl*, *Rape of Shavi* and *Kehinde*, focusing with humour and irrepressible irony on the struggles of African women to overcome their second-class treatment by society.

Another well known West African writer is Ken Saro-Wiwa (for more details, see the boxed text 'Ken Saro-Wiwa' in the Facts about Nigeria section of that chapter), although outside Nigeria he is famous for his politics rather than his writings. He became a household name in the mid-1990s when he was executed by the Nigerian authorities for protesting against the activities of an international oil company which he claimed resulted in the genocide of the Ogoni people. His last novel was *Pita Dumbroks Prison*.

The African Child (also called *The Dark Child*) by Camara Laye of Guinea was first published in 1954, and is the second most widely printed novel by an African. Laye was born in Guinea in 1924, studied in France and returned to write this largely autobiographical work, in which he describes his childhood among the Malinké tribe, surrounded by ritual magic and superstition, and his emergence into manhood and independence.

Ghana's foremost writer is Ayi Kwei Armah – not a well known name outside the

West African Cinema

A small but significant West African film industry has existed in the region since the heady days of newly won independence in the 1960s. At that time, some countries in the region nurtured cultural links with the Soviet Union, and several directors trained in Moscow, returning home to make films – often with state support or funding – based on overtly Marxist themes.

Common themes explored by the first wave of postcolonial film makers included the exploitation of the masses by colonialists, neocolonialists and, later, corrupt and inefficient independent governments. Another theme was the clash between tradition and modernity. Films frequently portrayed African values – usually in a rural setting – suffering from western cultural influence in the shape of industrialisation or urban deprivation.

The 1970s was the zenith of African film making, and many films from this era still inspire the new generation of directors working today. However, through the 1980s and 1990s, directors have found it increasingly hard to arrange other essential aspects of film making, such as finance, production facilities and – most crucially – distribution. The lack of a good distribution network for African films makes it hard for travellers to see them, even though most of the continent's directors (outside South Africa) are from West Africa – particularly the Francophone countries. Every town has at least one cinema, but the films on show are invariably American action or Indian drama, rather than anything from, or relevant to, West Africa. A notable exception is the biennial FESPACO film festival held in Burkina Faso (for more details see the boxed text in the Ouagadougou section of the Burkina Faso chapter).

Following are a few major names and films to look out for. From Senegal, a leading figure is Ousmane Sembène, whose works include *Borom Sarret* (1963), the first commercial film to be made in postindependence Africa. Sembène's later films include *Xala* and *Camp Thiaroye*. Other Senegalese directors and films to look out for include: Ahmed Diallo (*Boxumaleen*), Mansour Wade (*Picc Mi*), Amadou Seck (*Saaraba*) and Djibril Diop (*Le Franc*).

Mali's leading director is Souleymane Cissé, whose 1970s films include *Baara* and *Cinq Jours d'Une Vie*. Later films include *Yeelen*, a prize-winner at the 1987 Cannes festival, and *Waati*, which was made in South Africa. Other Malian film makers include Alkady Kaba (*Wamba*), Sega Coulibaly, Adama Drabo, Abdoulaye Ascofare and Cheik Omar Sissoko (*Finzan* and *Gimba* – the latter the winner of the Etalon de Yennega, Africa's 'Oscar', at the 1995 FESPACO).

Film makers from Burkina Faso include Djim Mamadou Kola, whose career stretches from *Le Sang de Paris* (1971) to *Etrangers* (1993), Gaston Kaboré (*Wend Kuuni* and *Zan Boko*), and Idrissa Ouedraogo, the only West African film maker to find genuine commercial success in the west; his films include *Yaaba* and *Samba Traoré*, and most recently *Kini and Adams*.

country although *The Beautiful Ones Are Not Yet Born*, published in 1969, is a classic tale of corruption and disillusion in postindependence Africa.

Another classic is *God's Bits of Wood* by Sembéne Ousmane (Senegal), one of the few well known and readily available Francophone novels in English, and probably the most widely acclaimed book by any Senegalese author. It describes a railway workers' strike and the emergence of African political consciousness as the colonial era comes to an end. Another Senegalese writer is Mariama Bâ, whose brief but incisive novel *So Long a Letter* was first published in 1980 and won the Noma Award for publishing in Africa. The awkward transition between traditional and modern society is explored by a woman narrator whose much-loved husband suddenly takes a second, much younger, wife.

MUSIC OF
WEST AFRICA

usic is a major feature of West African culture, and some of the continent's most famous musicians come from this region. Music is everywhere – loud with a pounding beat from the market cassette stalls, pure and sweet straight from a singer's mouth, scratchy and distorted on a bush taxi radio, in the background at restaurants and in your face at bars and nightclubs. For many travellers, experiencing West African music, with its haunting rhythms and melodies, is the highlight of their trip.

African music can be divided into two categories – traditional music and pop music. Traditional music is predominant in rural areas, whereas pop music is largely an urban phenomenon. This division is not clear cut, however, because African pop draws inspiration from the styles and rhythms of traditional music.

TRADITIONAL MUSIC

For the majority of West Africans, traditional music is at the heart of their culture. Traditional music can be harder for foreigners to appreciate than the modern styles. To the uninitiated it may sound random, or simply monotonous. However, if you listen carefully you can begin to follow and pick out the structure of the piece. If you are listening to a drum ensemble, try and focus on the sound (or rhythm) produced by just one

Title page: Salif Keita plays concerts all over the world but returns regularly to Mali for inspiration.

Left: Music is at the heart of West African culture, serving an important social purpose.

of the drums – you'll begin to notice how it fits in with the others, and the whole pattern will become clearer. It's important to remember that typiically African music is polyphonic and polyrhythmic, which means that there are many rhythms occurring simultaneously, without one dominating the other. This allows the listener to pick out certain melodies or rhythms and concentrate on them, which is what the dancers do.

An essential feature of traditional music is that it serves a social purpose. Not only does each social occasion have its own type of music but, in addition, there are different kinds of music for women's groups, hunters, warriors etc.

Traditionally, the instruments used were made from whatever was at hand, such as these cowbells, which are played in many West African countries.

In much of West Africa (including Mali, Senegal, Guinea, Guinea-Bissau, Gambia, and parts of Côte d'Ivoire, Ghana, Burkina Faso, Niger and Mauritania) music was traditionally the province of one social group, the *griots*. The term 'griot' (pronounced *gree-oh*) is of French origin and means minstrel, musician or praise singer. 'Griot' is a useful general term, but each linguistic group has its own word – *jali* in Mandinka, *gewel* in Wolof and *gawlo* in Fula (Pulaar).

Many West African societies were, and still are, highly stratified with the nobility at the top and the descendants of slaves at the bottom. Artisans (blacksmiths, weavers, leatherworkers etc) are a rank above the lowest. Griots were traditionally part of the artisan class, and they fulfil many important social functions.

Historically, griots had a close relationship with the royal courts, where they acted as translators and diplomats, but it was their role as oral historians that made them so important. In West Africa, the younger generation traditionally learns about the history of their society through word of mouth. The role of griots in this is crucial because they are the retainers of their culture's history, which they reveal through narratives recited or expressed in songs. For example, all griots know the epic of Sundiata, which describes the exploits of the warrior who founded the Empire of Mali in the 13th century AD. This song is well known throughout West Africa, and is just one of a large repertoire of narratives, including anticolonial songs, praise songs to famous warriors and love songs.

Griots are also genealogists, and at weddings, naming ceremonies and other important events they are called upon to recount the names and deeds of the host's ancestors. Like other artisans, they are thought to possess spiritual powers, and this, coupled with their knowledge of the past, leads people to fear them.

TRADITIONAL INSTRUMENTS

A distinctive aspect of traditional music is the instruments used. Traditional musicians generally use instruments made from local materials, such as gourds, leather, cow horns and shells.

Drums

A quick visit to almost any museum in West Africa will give you a good idea of the variety of drums used by musicians. These include the kettle, cylindrical and frame (similar to a tambourine) drums, as well as goblet and hourglass-shaped ones. Drums are usually covered with cowhide or goatskin, although some use skin from a gazelle, or even a snake. The immense variety of shapes and sizes reflects the diversity of natural materials available in West Africa. Another reason is that drums not only serve as musical instruments but also as tools of communication. The drums used for long-distance messages are often made from the trunks of trees and can easily weigh several hundred kilograms. Drums are also used to announce the arrival of important people.

The variable pitch quality of the tama drum, produced by squeezing the drum under the musician's arm, is the reason for its common name: 'talking drum'.

The *tama* drum of the Wolof has become familiar in the west through its use in the music style known as *mbalax*, popularised by Youssou N'Dour (see the boxed text on the following page). The tama is a small, single-faced drum with strips of leather fixed to the skin and base, which, when squeezed under the musician's arm, change the tension of the surface of the skin and, therefore, its pitch. This variable pitch quality gives rise to the name 'talking drum', and good players can obtain a wide range of notes.

Another type of talking drum is used extensively in juju music (see the Juju Music section later for an explanation of this style). The player strikes the skin with a hooked stick, squeezing and releasing the tension of the skin to obtain the desired pitch.

The *djembe* is a popular drum used from Ghana to Senegal. The skin is usually of goat-hide (sometimes with the hair still attached), stretched over a barrel-shaped drum and fastened by leather cord.

Drums are not usually played alone, but are often part of an ensemble. The Ewé people of Ghana are well known for their skill in drumming, and their drum ensembles can include up to 10 musicians. Tubular iron bells, gourd or calabash rattles and a large variety of

Youssou N'Dour

Youssou N'Dour began his singing career at an early age, taking inspiration from his mother who was a gawlo (the Tukulor word for griot). He first performed at traditional ceremonies and it wasn't long before the extraordinary beauty of his voice caught the attention of a local nightclub owner who offered him a regular spot at his club, the Miami.

After singing with a few different bands (notably the Star Band), Youssou formed Etoile de Dakar in 1979. Their first cassette, *Xalis*, was a huge hit. The band's fusion of traditional Wolof rhythms using the tama drum with a funky Latin-based sound (a style known as mbalax) proved irresistible and launched Youssou into super-stardom. Etoile de Dakar and, later, Super Etoile, have released over a dozen CDs and cassettes which are easily available all over West Africa.

On the international stage he has collaborated with other singers, notably Neneh Cherry (on the superb *7 seconds*) and Peter Gabriel. His style continues to be the trendsetter in Senegal, where he remains the undisputed king of mbalax.

upright drums make up the group and the rhythms are irresistible. You can also hear drum ensembles in Senegal, Gambia, Nigeria, Guinea-Bissau and Burkina Faso.

Stringed Instruments

There is a huge variety of stringed instruments in West Africa, from a one-string plucked lute *(moolo)* or bowed fiddle *(riti-riti)* to the 21-string *kora*. The kora is historically the instrument of the griots, and is arguably one of the most sophisticated instruments in sub-Saharan Africa. It is a cross between a harp and a lute, with its strings divided into two rows, one of 11 strings, the other of 10. These are supported over a long neck (usually made of rosewood) by a wooden bridge, with a notch for each string, which is often ornately carved. Studs fasten the hide to the gourd and are often arranged in interesting patterns, which sometimes feature the player's name. The instrument is held upright in the lap of the seated player who plucks the two rows of strings with the thumb and index finger of each hand. Kora players are often very highly skilled musicians who start learning their craft in early childhood. They are found throughout the Sahel, especially in Gambia, Mali, Senegal and Guinea.

Kora players can be heard at naming day or wedding ceremonies, which take place in cities, towns and villages throughout the region. Urban performances are more difficult to come by, although in tourist areas such as Gambia's Atlantic Coast resorts, hotels and restaurants often put on kora performances – look out for the talented Bajaly Suso, who often

The kora, the instrument of the griots: even if you are tone deaf, you can still appreciate its exquisite form.

DAVID ELSE

plays here. You could also try asking around at the local markets in the region; people should be able to point you in the right direction.

There is quite a wide range of kora music available internationally, with a much greater range within West Africa. For an excellent example of kora music performed in the traditional style, look for the recordings by Jali Nyama Suso, a Gambian who wrote the country's national anthem. He appears on a two record set *A Search for the Roots of the Blues* as well as *Songs from The Gambia*. Other good kora players include Guinean Jali Musa Jawara (younger brother of pop star Mory Kanté) whose recording *Soubindoor* is worth finding, and Gambians Dembo Konté and Kausa Kouyate who collaborated on the excellent *Simbomba*. In a different style is the kora music of Lamine Konté, from the Casamance region of Senegal, whose best work appears on *The*

Mory Kanté

Mory Kanté is the musician responsible for bringing electrified kora music to the dance floors of North America and Europe. His smash hit Yeke Yeke was a chart buster in France and he has had considerable success with his CDs Ten Kola Nuts and Tatebola.

Born in Kissidougou (Guinea) into a family of blacksmiths, his first instrument was the balafon. He found early success with the Rail Band of Bamako in the early 1970s, where he was the second singer to Salif Keita. The band wasn't big enough for both singers and Salif left to join Les Ambassadeurs. It was during this time that Kanté began learning the kora.

Kanté's music blends the traditional Guinean styles with western big-beat pop. Drum machines, synthesizers, pulsating bass and great production are his hallmarks, into which he weaves complex and intricate kora lines. Yeke Yeke has become his signature tune. The song concerns blacksmiths and comes from his album Akwaba Beach, which is available on CD internationally and can be found easily on cassette in Guinea and Mali.

Kora of Senegal Vols 1 & 2. Delicately structured and with a Cuban feel, his music is well worth finding.

Another excellent kora player is the Malian Toumani Diabaté, whose classic recording *Djelika* features some of Mali's best musicians.

The *xalam* (pronounced *khalam*), as it's known in Wolof, is another important instrument of the griots. It's also known as *ngoni* in Bambara, *hoddu* in Fula and *konting* in Mandinka. It has three to five strings, which are plucked. The body of the xalam is carved out of a tree trunk to form a 'boat' shape, with goatskin (traditionally, the skin of a male gazelle) stretched over the opening and fastened to the sides by wooden pegs. A smooth piece of narrow wood serves as the neck, with the strings (originally thin strips of leather, but now fishing line is usually used) attached to it by leather collars. Interestingly, this instrument is regarded by musicologists as the ancestor of the banjo. Two of West Africa's most revered musicians (both now dead), Mali's Banzoumana Sissoko and Guinea's Kouyate Sory Kandia, were ngoni players.

Wind Instruments

The most common wind instrument is the flute. Fula shepherds are reputed to play the most beautiful flute music, using an instrument made from a length of reed. You'll also see flutes made from millet stalks, bamboo and gourds. Other wind instruments include animal tusk horns and trumpets made from gourds, metal, shells or wood. They are found all over West Africa and take a slightly different form in each area.

Xylophones

The *balafon* is a type of wooden xylophone with between 15 and 19 rectangular keys made out of a hardwood. These are usually suspended over a row of gourds, which amplify the sound. The player (sometimes two) is usually seated and strikes the keys with two wooden mallets. The balafon is the name given to the instrument played by griots, and other types of xylophones have different names depending on the particular language group in the region. Souleymane Traoré, a Malian balafon player, has two very good recordings: *Hommage à Lamissa Bangaly* and *Confirmation*.

The balafon is one type of xylophone played by griots in West Africa.

POP MUSIC

African pop music can be said to have begun at the end of the 19th century with the beginning of the colonial era. Africans were then exposed for the first time to western music (via phonographs and church choirs) and western instruments (through regimental orchestras), and also through the music and instruments brought by sailors to Africa's busy ports. African musicians incorporated this wide variety of new sounds and influences into their own compositions, and it wasn't long before the music evolved into unique and popular African styles. A brief description of the major forms follows.

Highlife

During colonial times, Ghana was the richest country in the region and, not surprisingly, was where the influence of European music was felt the most. What emerged was a westernised style called 'highlife'. The western influence was very noticeable in the dance bands that played to the African elites in the cities, less so in the bands which played in the hinterland. The new bands combined acoustic guitars with rattles, drums and other traditional instruments.

During WWII, Allied troops stationed in West Africa spread more new musical ideas, especially the then-popular 'swing' music. After the war, bands had a wide repertoire of sounds, including calypso. They began touring West Africa, igniting the highlife fire everywhere, and continuing to assimilate foreign musical styles. Black music from across the Atlantic had a big impact, especially jazz and soul.

Sahel Pop Music

Riding the crest of the world music wave is the sound of West Africa's Sahel countries – Mali, Senegal and Gambia – with Guinean music following closely behind. From these countries come many of today's leading singers and musicians. The roots of their music offers an interesting insight into the development of their styles.

In the 1960s and 70s Cuban music was a major influence on the musical styles of the region. At the same time, many West African nations embarked on 'Authenticité' campaigns which sought to encourage musicians to keep traditional African roots in their modern music. As a result, many musicians used the stories and melodies from the past in their new compositions. Ensembles and groups of musicians, called 'orchestras' were established whose aim was to reinvent and revitalise traditional songs. Their influence on the West African music scene was enormous, and is the origin of today's distinct Sahel pop style.

Oumou Sangaré

Oumou Sangaré, the 'Songbird of Wassoulou', is one of the great singers of Mali and easily the country's most famous female singer. Her first cassette, *Moussolou*, released in 1989, sold well over 200,000 copies in West Africa alone, and that figure doesn't include the bootleg recordings! Her distinctive style of music is known as *wassoulou*, after the region of south-western Mali where Oumou was born. What typifies wassoulou music is the use of the *kamelengoni*, or 'youth harp', which sounds a lot like a funky bass guitar.

Oumou's popularity, especially with the younger generation, is based on her lyrics. Her songs frequently address issues of direct concern to women in Mali and challenge their traditional roles. She sings, for example, of the difficulties of arranged marriages, the freedom to choose a lover, and the daily sacrifice and toil of a woman's life in Mali. Her songs are passionate, direct and beautifully crafted, and have caused quite a sensation among the more conservative elements of Mali society.

Be on the lookout for performances by her in Bamako. Oumou has made three CDs, including *Ko Sira*, all of which are superb.

ALEX NEWTON

BOTH PHOTOS BY DENNIS WISKEN/SIDEWALK GALLERY

Top: Learning their craft – musicians at the Academy of African Music & Arts in Kokrobite, Ghana, where you can arrange lessons in traditional African music, drumming and dance.

Middle: The anthropomorphic design of this wooden Dan slit drum (left) may be an expression of the identification of the musician with his instrument. The *sanza* or thumb piano (right) is widely used throughout West Africa.

Bottom: In West Africa music is everywhere, and is an important feature of most ceremonies and rituals, like these rooftop festivities in Kano, Nigeria.

JASON LAURÉ

Top: Bells, like this Baoulé one, can be made in a variety of forms and from many different materials, including wood, iron, bronze or ivory.

Middle: A balafon, a type of xylophone that is typically West African, has a series of gourds to amplify the sound.

Bottom: Kora players like Ablaye Diabaté are highly skilled musicians who start learning their craft in early childhood.

There were many superb recordings made during this era. While some original cassettes are available in the region, many are now available on CD internationally, and can be found in good record stores worldwide. From Senegal, look out for the legendary Orchestra Baobab, who have three CDs out, and also The Royal Band and Canari de Kaolack. A six volume set of CDs entitled *Dakar Sounds* showcases the major stars of the Senegalese scene.

From Mali, Salif Keita's original band – the Rail Band of Bamako – is excellent, as is his follow-up combination, Les Ambassadeurs. The Regional Orchestras of Mali series, through the Baerenreiter-Musicaphon label, are an absolute must for fans of this style.

Guinean music of the period was dominated by the government-controlled Syliphone label, which released recordings by Bembeya Jazz National, Keletigui et ses Tambourinis, Camayenne Sofa, and the all-female police group Les Amazones de Guinée, among a host of others.

Economic downturns in the 1980s led to the disbandment of most of these groups, but their music paved the way for the next wave of West African artists.

From Senegal, Youssou N'Dour's mbalax style is well known. It's a fusion of frenetic rhythms from the tama drum with funky bass and guitar lines creating an irresistible combination to dance to, and aficionados of his style should seek out his earlier recordings with Etoile de Dakar. As popular as N'Dour is Baaba Maal, whose music incorporates traditional instruments alongside electric guitars.

From Mali the hugely popular Oumou Sangaré has three CDs out, and her funky *wassoulou* sound is the latest thing in West African pop music. If you like the style look out for recordings by Sali Sidibé. Other

Ali Farka Touré

Ali Farka Touré is probably the most famous acoustic guitarist to come out of Africa. His style of music, similar to that of John Lee Hooker, clearly indicates the close relationship that the blues has with traditional West African music. His songs evoke a strong sense of place and he has adapted many traditional songs from a variety of Mali ethnic groups.

Born in the Timbuktu region of Mali, Ali Farka Touré began playing the *njurkel*, a traditional one-string horsehair lute, at the age of 10. He is not of the traditional griot caste, and because of this (and perhaps because of his outstanding musicianship!) local griots objected to his playing the instrument and he was made to stop. It was not until he was 18 that he began to play the guitar.

He performs at many blues concerts throughout the world, and to date he has released six CDs, including a collaboration with Ry Cooder.

good Malian women singers include Tata Bambo Kouyaté, Ami Koita, and Kagbe Sidibé.

Blues lovers should check out Ali Farka Touré who is now a major international star. His blues-derived guitar sound clearly indicates the close relationship between his style and that of Chicago blues.

Guinean artists include Mory Kanté, whose 'kora funk' style is very popular in Europe, and Sékou Diabaté, aka Diamond Fingers, the wonderful guitarist who played with Bembeya Jazz.

Afro-Beat

Afro-beat is a fusion of African melodies and rhythms with jazz and soul, popular particularly in Nigeria, and 'invented' in the 1960s by Fela Anikulapo Kuti (often known simply as Fela). Fela's songs dealt with corruption and police brutality, among other issues, and focused attention on the way in which Nigeria was being governed. As a result, Fela was imprisoned on several occasions on trumped-up charges.

Fela, who died in 1997 was probably Africa's best known and respected musician. Some of his best recordings are *Lady*, *Army Arrangement*, *Zombie*, and *Confusion*.

Similar in style is Sonny Okosun, who had a massive hit in 1978 with *Fire in Soweto*. His reggae-based music, while not as political as Fela's, retains many elements of highlife.

Juju Music

In the 1920s in Lagos, traditional Yoruba talking drums (see Traditional Instruments earlier) were incorporated with the popular 'palm-wine' guitar style to form a new music known as *juju*. Juju music is characterised by sophisticated guitar work and tight vocal harmonies, backed by traditional drums and percussion. It is one of the best loved styles in Nigeria.

The early exponents of juju found some commercial success through the release of their music on 78 rpm records, although it wasn't until the introduction of amplification after WWII that juju really began to take off. Juju took over from highlife in Lagos during and after Nigeria's civil war (1967-70). Many of the highlife musicians were Igbo, who left Lagos for their eastern homeland to escape discrimination.

The leading musicians are King Sunny Ade, Ebenezer Obey and Shina Peters. Sunny Ade was influenced by Afro-beat and is probably the most famous juju musician. Check out his album *Synchro System*, which is excellent. Shina Peters is the latest juju star, and is particularly popular with the younger crowd.

Congo Music

While fads in pop music come and go, there is one style that is universally popular – the music of Congo-Brazzaville and Congo (Zaïre). This is the only music that is truly pan-African, popular from Senegal to Zimbabwe. The reason for this is that the Congolese artists produce some of the best dance music in the world – a heady mix of swirling guitars, punchy brass sections, bubbling bass and tight vocals.

It all began just after WWII, when radio stations began popularising the early Cuban rumba stars. 'Congo-bars' began to appear, offering dance music as well as refreshments. This early music featured acoustic guitars and empty bottles for percussion, but it eventually evolved into electric ensembles featuring a lead guitarist with a brass section and backing vocalists. With the arrival of the electric guitar and amplification, large orchestras emerged, many elaborating on traditional rumba patterns or modernising traditional songs.

In 1953, in Congo (Zaïre), the popular band African Jazz featuring Dr Nico was established, followed three years later by the famous OK Jazz led by Franco, Africa's all-time most influential musician (and still one of its most popular despite his recent death). While musicians are constantly adding new ideas and arrangements to their songs, their music still retains the basic rumba framework. So if it sounds Latin, it's probably Congolese.

Another big star is Tabu Ley (aka Rochereau). Other leading musicians and groups include Kanda Bongo Man, Sam Mangwana, Papa Wemba, Langa Langa Stars, Bella Bella, Pierre Moutouri and Pamelo Mounka (both from Congo-Brazzaville) and Akédéngue (from Gabon). Leading female artists include M'Bilia Bel, Tshala Muana, M'Pongo Love and Abeti, all from Congo (Zaïre), and Nayanka Bell (from Côte d'Ivoire).

The Cuban Influence

The influence of Cuban music was pervasive in many other West African countries. In the 1960s and 1970s the pop music of Guinea, Mali, Cote d'Ivoire, and in particular, Senegal, was strongly influenced by Latin styles. The large orchestras of this period featured brass sections with brilliant soloists, and their music was based on Latin styles like the rumba. Some groups of the time sung in Spanish. The salsa style was very popular in Senegal, with Africando (look out for the excellent CDs *Trovador* and *Tierra Tradicional*) and Le Super Cayor being the main exponents. Unlike the Congolese form, salsa music moves away from a reliance on electric guitars, and utilises flutes, violins, and a big-band type brass section, and this style has enjoyed a revival in recent times.

Makossa Music

Cameroon's distinctive *makossa* music has become increasingly popular in recent years throughout much of West Africa. It's a fusion of Cameroon highlife and soul, and is strongly influenced by Congo music, with great use of the electric guitar.

The biggest star is still Manu Dibango, whose hit *Soul Makossa* in the mid-1970s put makossa music on the African musical map. His jazz-influenced music is more for listening to than for dancing. Francis Bebey and Isadore Tamwo are also extremely popular, while Sam Fan Thomas is Cameroon's king of *makassi*, a lighter sound than makossa but just as catchy. Other makossa stars include Sammy Njondji, Moni Bile, Toto Guillaume and Ekambi Brillant.

Cape Verdean Music

Although not as popular as other music styles in West Africa, Cape Verdean music is nevertheless worth mentioning because of its distinctive, fast-paced Latin style. The dominant role of the guitar and electric piano without traditional African instruments set it apart. The leading musicians can change quickly; those currently popular include Cesária Évora, Tam Tam 2000, Bana and Paulino Vieira.

THE MUSIC SCENE IN WEST AFRICA

The music industry in West Africa is huge and employs a significant section of the workforce. It's easy to find locally recorded cassettes (and imported CDs in large cities) of West and Central African music. Every town market has a small cassette shop, and in many places young men with boxes full of cassettes wander the streets. It's a good idea to go into a store and ask to hear something by the local recording stars. There is no better way to get to know the different styles and you may end up buying a cassette of next year's international hit.

Unfortunately, cassettes in West Africa are often of poor quality, as cheap tapes are used and the recordings themselves have often been pirated. It is possible (for a higher price) to obtain the original cassette, which will have a better sound than copies, but these are often in short supply and it can be difficult to tell an original release cassette from a pirated copy (one indication is that a cassette cover of a copy is usually poorly overprinted). If you buy at a shop, you can listen to the tape first. Original cassettes cost US$3 to US$4, while cheap copies are around US$2. Alternatively, rather than buying a poor quality cassette you can ask at a cassette shop (where the pirating is usually done anyway) for music from an original tape to be copied onto a tape of your own. Most stall owners will be happy to oblige (for a small extra charge) and you can choose your own selections.

To see a West African band you normally need to be in one of the capital cities, although in some countries venues are surprisingly limited. The best cities in West Africa for hearing live music performances are Lagos, Accra, Dakar, Abidjan, and Bamako. At weekends in Accra and elsewhere in Ghana, you can find live bands at many of the nightclubs. Other cities where you can find live bands include Conakry, Praia, Bissau and Niamey.

More details on local stars and names to look out for are given in the country chapters.

COMPILATIONS, BOOKS & MAGAZINES

A good introduction to African music is *Africa Never Stands Still*, a boxed set of three CDs with a 48 page booklet. For a fix of pure West

African sounds, highly recommended is *The Music in my Head*, a compilation CD with magical and influential tracks by Youssou N'Dour, Salif Keita, Franco and the cream of the region's singers and bands, from the 'golden age' of the 1970s to the sophisticated 1990s. There's also a five CD series focussing on music from Senegal and Gambia called *Sénégal Flash*, and a two volume CD anthology on Malian music called *Musiques du Mali*.

Recommended books include *The Da Capo Guide to Contemporary African Music* (published in the UK as *Stern's Guide to Contemporary African Music*) by Ronnie Graham, which has a musician-by-musician guide, short surveys of each country's music and an extensive discography, although this has been out of print since the early 1990s. *African Rock* (also titled *African All Stars: the Pop Music of a Continent*) by Chris Stapleton and Chris May is a good introduction to the pop music scene, as is *West African Pop Roots* by John Collins and *Africa Oh Yeah* by Graeme Ewens. The Rough Guide to *World Music* has a good section on West Africa.

The Roots of the Blues, by Samuel Charters, describes the author's journey to West Africa in search of traditional music. Other good books on traditional music include *African Music: A People's Art*, by Francis Bebey; and *The Music of Africa*, by JH Kwabena Nketia.

The UK magazine *Folk Roots* is a good source for the latest news and interviews. Scholarly journals include *African Music* and the *Journal of Modern African Studies*.

MUSIC SHOPS

Many large shops now have World Music or African Music sections where you can buy CDs, cassettes and even a few good old-fashioned vinyl LPs. Specialist world music shops in Britain include Stern's (☎ 0171-387 5550, fax 388 2756; after 22 April 2000 ☎ 020-7387 5550, fax 7388 2756) 74 Warren St, London W1P 5PA, which also runs a worldwide mail order service, and will send you their extensive catalogue on request. In the USA, Africassette Music (☎ 313-881 4108, fax 881 0260, email rsteiger@africassette.com), PO Box 24941, Detroit, MI 48224, also have a mail order service. Both places offer a wide selection of books on African music. In Australia, contact Blue Moon (☎ 03-9415 1157, fax 9415 1220), 30 Johnston St, Fitzroy, Vic 3065.

Graeme Counsel, Alex Newton, David Else

SOCIETY & CONDUCT

One of the highlights of travel in West Africa is meeting the people, and you'll get a lot more from your visit by knowing something about how West African society functions and what the social customs are.

As in any part of the world, the best way to learn about a society's conduct is by people-watching. The first thing to remember is not to worry: Africans are generally very easy-going towards foreigners, and any social errors that you might make are unlikely to cause offence (although they may cause confusion or merriment). Having said that, there are a few things that are frowned upon. These include: public nudity, open displays of anger, open displays of affection (among people of the same or opposite sex), and vocal criticism of the government or country.

Minding Your Manners

If you get invited to share a meal, there are a few customs to observe. You'll probably sit with your hosts on the floor, and it's sometimes polite to take off your shoes. It may be impolite, however, to show the soles of your feet, so make sure you observe local form.

The food is served in one or two large dishes, and normally eaten by hand. Beginners will just pick out manageable portions with their fingers, but experts dig deep, forming a ball of rice and sauce in the palm of the hand before swallowing. Everybody washes their hands before and after eating. As an honoured guest you might be passed choice morsels by your hosts, and it's usually polite to finish eating while there's still food in the bowl to show you have had enough.

If all this sounds too daunting, you probably won't offend anybody by asking for a spoon. But however you eat, remember it is absolutely essential to use only the right hand, because traditionally the left hand is used for personal toiletries.

Social Structures

Many West African peoples organise their society along hierarchical lines, with status determined by birth. At the top are traditional noble and warrior families, followed by farmers, traders and persons of low caste – for example blacksmiths, leather workers, woodcarvers, weavers and musicians. Slaves were once at the bottom of the social hierarchy. Although this status does not exist any longer officially, many descendants of former slaves still work as tenant farmers for the descendants of their former masters.

Modernity is eroding traditional hierarchies. Today, the government official who shows contempt for a rural chief may actually be a member of a lower caste who went away to the city and acquired an education and an office job.

Ceremonies are very important in traditional societies as they reinforce social structures. Much of Africa's cultural life revolves around events such as baptisms or naming ceremonies, circumcisions, weddings or funerals. At baptisms guests bring gifts for both the mother and father – a small amount of money is perfectly acceptable. There will be a ceremony followed by a meal, typically a slaughtered sheep or goat. At weddings there is likely to be an official ceremony followed by more festivities at the family's home. Most events involve traditional music and dancing, when men and women may dance separately. If there's modern music, younger people of both sexes may dance together. Either way, if you want to join in, observe the form.

Village festivals (*fêtes* in French) may be held to honour dead ancestors, local traditional deities or to celebrate the end of the harvest. Some festivals include singing and dancing, some favour parades, sports or wrestling matches. In other areas you may see puppets used to tell stories, or elaborate performances with masks, which play an important part in traditional life.

For more information on specific festivals, see the Public Holidays & Special Events section in the Regional Facts for the Visitor chapter.

Marriage

In many parts of West Africa, marriage is an expensive affair. Gifts from the groom to the bride's family can easily cost several hundred dollars – not exactly peanuts in a region where annual incomes of US$200 are typical. Many men cannot afford to get married before their late 20s or 30s.

Despite the financial constraints, in traditional society (among Muslims and some non-Muslim people), men who can afford more than one wife usually marry two, three or even four women (the Quran allows up to four). You will be told (by men) that women are not averse to the custom, and that the wives become like sisters, helping each other with domestic and child-rearing duties. In reality, however, most first wives definitely don't like their husbands marrying again. On the other hand, there's not much they can do, as leaving a marriage simply because a husband takes another wife would bring shame to the woman's own family. She might be cast out of the family home or even physically beaten as punishment by her own father or brothers. A particularly incisive account of the clash between modern and traditional views on polygamy is given in *So Long a Letter* by Miriama Bâ (for more details, see Books in the Facts for the Visitor section of the Senegal chapter).

Greetings

Great importance is placed on greetings in West Africa. Muslims will almost certainly start with the traditional Islamic greeting *salaam alaykum* (peace be upon you), to which the reply is *wa alaykum as-salaam* (and upon you be peace), and then go onto 'How are you doing?', 'How is the family?', 'How are the people of your village?', to which the reply is usually *al-humdu lillah* (thanks be to God). In cities, the traditional greetings may give way to shorter versions in French or English but they're never forgotten.

Although it's not necessary for foreigners to go through the whole routine, it's important to use greetings whenever possible. Even for something simple like exchanging money or asking directions, always start with 'Good day, how are you? Can you help me please?'. Launching straight into business is considered rude.

If you can learn greetings in the local language, you will be an incredible hit. Even a few words make a big difference – see the Language appendix for more details.

Deference

In traditional societies, older people (especially men) are treated with deference. Teachers, doctors, and other professionals (usually men) often receive similar treatment. Thus, when you meet people holding positions of authority, such as police officers, immigration officials or village chiefs (you've guessed it – usually men) it is very important to be polite. Officials are usually courteous but can make things awkward for you, and this is when manners, patience and

Shaking Hands

The emphasis on greetings makes shaking hands important. At social gatherings, men should go around the room, greeting and shaking hands with other men, and maybe with older women. Do the same when you leave. Always use a soft handshake. Macho knuckle-crackers are considered rude, and even more inane than they are in the west.

Western women will usually find that the same rules apply to them. However, some Muslim men prefer not to shake hands with women, and West African women usually don't shake hands with their male counterparts, so it might be considered odd if you do. However, most western women in traditional situations generally find they hold the privileged position of 'honorary man' and any extraneous handshaking will not cause offence.

cooperation on your side are essential to get you through. Undermining an official's authority or insulting an ego may only serve to waste time, tie you up in red tape and inspire closer scrutiny of future travellers.

At the other end of the spectrum, children rate very low on the social scale. They are expected to do as they're told without complaint and defer to adults in all situations. Unfortunately for half the region's population, the status of women is only slightly higher. In traditional rural areas, women are expected to dress and behave with appropriate modesty, especially in the presence of chiefs or other esteemed persons.

When visiting rural settlements, it is a good idea to request to see the chief to announce your presence and request permission before wandering through a village. You will rarely be refused.

Another consideration is eye contact, which is usually avoided, especially between men and women in the Sahel. So if a West African doesn't look you in the eye during a conversation, remember they're being polite, not cold.

Dress

West Africans place great importance on appearance and generally dress conservatively. So it's not surprising that clothes worn by travellers are often considered offensive (eg singlets, shorts or tight trousers). In Africa, the only people wearing shorts or tatty clothes are children, labourers or the poor, which is why bare-legged travellers often get treated with contempt.

For women, apart from the disrespect you are showing to local sensibilities, you also make things harder for yourself – don't be surprised if kids laugh, adults treat you disdainfully, and some young guns see you as easy prey. From a practical point of view, keeping reasonably covered with loose-fitting clothes helps prevent sunburn.

In many West African cultures women's breasts are not considered offensive or sexually attractive, whereas legs and buttocks are. Women travellers should keep this in mind when planning what clothes to wear.

Les Modes d'Afrique

Any West African who can afford to dress well does so with a regal quality. In the big cities, you'll see everything from the latest Parisian fashions to the most traditional outfits. For most people, the traditional outfit here is the *grand boubou*. For men, this is an elaborately embroidered robe-like garment reaching the ground, with deep vents down each side; baggy trousers and a shirt are worn underneath. This outfit is invariably worn on important occasions, and sometimes in everyday situations. The woman's boubou is similar, but may have even more embroidery, and is often worn with a matching headscarf. For more everyday wear, women wear a loose top and a length of colourful printed cotton cloth (*pagne*) around the waist for a skirt.

Begging

In Africa, there is no government welfare cheque for the unemployed, crippled, homeless, sick or old, so the only social security system is the extended family. People with no family are forced to beg, although the extended family support system is very effective, and there are remarkably few beggars considering that West Africa is the poorest area on earth.

Because helping the needy is part of traditional African culture, and one of the pillars of Islam by which Muslims reach paradise, you will see even relatively poor people giving to beggars. If you want to give, even a very small coin is appreciated. If you don't have any change, just say 'next time' or something similar. Of course, sometimes it's hard to differentiate between hustlers and genuine, deserving cases – those in dire need, with no family support, such as the blind, crippled and old, or unmarried women with babies. If in doubt, consider giving money to the beggars local people give to also – they are the best judges of who is deserving and who is not.

Gifts & Tips

'Do you have something for me?' or *'Donnez-moi un cadeau'* becomes a familiar refrain everywhere you go, usually from children, but also from youths and adults. Part of this expectation comes from a belief that anyone God has been good to (and all foreigners are thought to be rich – which, relatively, they are) should be willing to spread some wealth around. People may ask for your hat, shoes or camera, or simply for money, all within a couple of minutes of meeting you. But generally, this is just a 'worth a try' situation, and your polite refusal will rarely offend.

Even if your refusal to give a gift is accepted, you may be asked by your new-found friend for your address, so that you can become pen-friends or correspondents. Don't be surprised if the letters you get a few months later include copious greetings, reports on the health of family members – and a request for some money. Once again,

Wari

Wari is a board game (similar in principle to backgammon) which is played all over West Africa. It has various names (including *woro, aware, woaley, awélé, ayo* and *kboo*) and rules vary from region to region. The game is played in other parts of Africa, and in many other countries around the world.

Wari boards can be very simple or very elaborate, but in West Africa they are nearly always rectangular, about 50cm long, with two rows of six cups each. Where no real board is available, a makeshift one will be scratched on rock or scooped out of the sand. Although names and rules vary, the main principles of the game are always the same: two players move beads or counters across the board from cup to cup, 'capturing' the opponent's beads where possible. Some boards also have extra cups at one or both ends for storing captured beads. To play well involves being able to assess numbers without counting, a vital skill for nomadic pastoralists who may have introduced the game across Africa. The game's origins remain a mystery, although anthropologists agree it has been played in Africa for many thousands of years.

it's a 'worth a try' situation. You can send some money if you like (many travellers do) – but cash in an envelope nearly always gets 'lost' at the post office. Your best option is to politely refuse to give out your address in the first place.

When a gift is given in return for some service it becomes more like a tip, (although

Kola Nuts

These are yellow or purple nuts, about half the size of a golf ball, which are sold in the streets and markets everywhere in West Africa. They are known for their mildly hallucinogenic effects. They make a good portable gift if you want to carry something to give people in exchange for their kindness. They last longer if you keep them moist but they go mouldy in a day or two if kept sealed in a plastic bag. Despite their popularity among West Africans, most foreigners find them too bitter to chew and anyone looking for a high is usually disappointed.

in Francophone countries both words translate as *cadeau*). Simply being pointed in the right direction is not a significant service, whereas being helped for 10 minutes to find a hotel probably is. When deciding how much to give, enough for a drink (tea, coffee or soft drink) is usually sufficient. If you're not prepared to offer a tip, don't ask for significant favours. Do remember, however, that some people will help you out of genuine kindness and will not be expecting anything in return.

Things sometimes work the other way. West Africans are frequently very friendly towards foreigners and even after a few minutes of talking they may offer you food or a bed for the night. You may want to repay such kindness with a gift: tobacco, tea or perfume are all portable, and kola nuts are good, but money is usually the easiest thing to give, and is always appreciated. When deciding how much money to give, consider what you would have paid for a similar meal or hotel room. Experiencing local hospitality definitely enhances your travelling experience. Using it as a way merely to save money makes you a low-down grubby parasite.

Be aware, however, that in tourist areas you'll encounter local men who make a living by talking to foreigners, then providing 'friendly' services (from information and postcards to hard drugs and sex) for money. Avoid these hustlers unless you really need something and don't mind paying.

Bribery

A gift or tip becomes a completely different matter when you have to pay to get something done. In this case it's effectively a bribe (also called *cadeau* in Francophone countries or 'dash' in English-speaking countries such as Gambia and Ghana). For example, a border customs official may go through your belongings then ask: 'Don't you have something extra?' implying that if you don't give them a gift the search could go on for hours.

The best way to deal with this is to feign ignorance and simply bluff your way through. If this doesn't work, state clearly that you are not going to give anything. Occasionally requests may become threats, such as denying entrance to the country. This is usually just a bluff, although it can last several minutes. It is essential to remain polite. You might ask to see a senior officer, but never make threats back. Give the official plenty of room to back down and save face. In virtually all cases, you'll soon be allowed to continue.

If your documents are not all in order, you're more vulnerable. It helps to know the regulations, however, because sometimes officials trump up totally fictitious ones simply to create a bribe situation.

Sometimes you have to play the system. For example, if officials are slow in processing a visa request, offering a small dash or cadeau may be your only option. But tread very carefully here. Never simply offer to pay. Wait to see if the official hints for something extra, if any 'special fee' is required to speed up the process.

RELIGION

The religions of West Africa fall into three main categories: Islam, Christianity and traditional beliefs. Accurate figures are impossible to find because there's considerable overlap between religions, and many grey areas, but in general Christianity is more widespread in the southern coastal countries than in the northern Sahel countries. For more details, see the Religion sections in the individual country chapters.

Islam

Origins of Islam Between the years 610 and 620 AD in the city of Mecca, Saudi Arabia, the Prophet Mohammed called on the people to turn away from pagan worship and submit to Allah, the one true god. His teachings appealed to the poorer levels of society and angered the wealthy merchant class. In 622 AD Mohammed and his followers were forced to flee to Medina. This migration, the Hejira, marks the beginning of the Islamic calendar, year 1 AH. By 630 AD (8 AH) Mohammed had gained a larger following and returned to Mecca. He died in 632 AD but within two decades most of Arabia was converted to Islam. Over the following centuries, Islam spread through North and West Africa, down the coast of East Africa, into several parts of southern and eastern Europe and eastwards across Asia.

The Five Pillars of Islam The five pillars of Islam are the basic tenets that guide Muslims in their daily lives, and are as follows:

shahada – The profession of faith: 'There is no god but Allah, and Mohammed is his Prophet'.
salat (prayer) – Muslims must face Mecca and pray at dawn, midday, mid-afternoon, sunset and nightfall.
zakat (alms) – Muslims must give a portion of their income to the poor and needy.
sawm (fasting) – Ramadan commemorates Mohammed's first revelation, and is the month when all Muslims fast from dawn to dusk.
haj – Pilgrimage, usually written *hadj* in West Africa.

For more information on Islamic holidays, including a table of dates, see the Public Holidays & Special Events section in the Regional Facts for the Visitor chapter.

The Hadj It is the duty of every Muslim to make the pilgrimage to Mecca at least once, if they have good health and the money for the journey. This can involve a lifetime of saving money; it's not unusual for families to save up and send one member. Before the advent of air travel, the pilgrimage used to involve an overland journey of a year or more. In West Africa, those who complete the pilgrimage receive the honorific title of Hadj for men, and Hadjia for women. If you meet someone with this prefix, you may appreciate the honour this bestows on them in the community.

Tips for the Traveller in Islamic Countries

- When you visit a mosque, take off your shoes. Women should cover their head and shoulders with a scarf. In some mosques, women are not allowed to enter if prayers are in progress or if the imam (prayer leader) is present; in others, there may be separate entrances for men and women.
- If you have hired a guide or taxi driver for the day, remember he'll want to say his prayers at the right times – so look out for signs indicating that he wants a few moments off, particularly around midday, late afternoon and sunset. Travellers on buses and bush taxis should also be prepared for prayer stops at these times.
- Despite the Islamic proscription against alcohol, some Muslims may enjoy a quiet drink. Even so, it's impolite to drink alcohol in their presence unless they show approval.
- Some strict Muslim men prefer not to shake hands with women.
- During Islamic holidays, shops and offices may close. Even if the offices are officially open, during the Ramadan period of fasting, people become soporific (especially when Ramadan falls in the hot season) and very little gets done.

Islam in West Africa By the early years of the 2nd millennium Islamic influence had spread from North Africa across the Sahara. By the 14th century many African rulers, particularly in the Sahel, had adopted Islam. For example, the Empire of Mali was a Muslim state, and cities like Djenné and Timbuktu became major centres of Islamic teaching.

In its journey from Arabia to West Africa, Islam adapted to local conditions by evolving features which would not be recognised by purists in Cairo or Mecca. Most notable of these are the marabouts – holy men who act as a cross between priest, doctor and adviser for local people. In some countries, especially Senegal, they wield considerable political power.

Today, roughly half of all West Africans are Muslim, particularly those living in the desert and Sahel countries. There are not many adherents of Islam in the coastal areas except for the immigrants from the north.

Traditional Religions

Before the arrival of Muslim and Christian evangelists, every race, tribe or clan in West Africa practised their own traditional religion. While many people in the Sahel converted to Islam, and those in the south converted to Christianity, traditional religions remained strong in many parts of the region. Today, traditional beliefs frequently exist alongside established aspects of Islam or Christianity, and firm lines between one set of values and another are impossible to draw.

When discussing traditional beliefs, terms such as 'juju', 'voodoo' and 'witchcraft' are frequently employed. In certain contexts these may be correct, but they cannot be applied to all African religions.

There are hundreds of traditional religions in West Africa, although many overlap considerably, but no great temples or written scriptures. For outsiders, beliefs and traditions can be complex and difficult to understand as can the rituals and ceremonies surrounding them. However, several common factors can be outlined, although the description here provides an overview only, and is necessarily very simplified.

Almost all traditional religions are animist, meaning they are based on the attribution of life or consciousness to natural objects or phenomena. Thus a certain tree, mountain, river or stone may be sacred because it represents a spirit, is home to a spirit, or simply *is* a spirit. Instead of 'spirit', some authorities use the term 'deity' or 'god'. The number of deities each religion accepts can vary, as can the phenomena that represent them. The Ewé of Togo and Ghana, for example, have over 600 deities, including one representing smallpox.

Several traditional religions accept the existence of a Supreme Being or Creator, as well as the spirits and deities, although this figure is considered too exalted to be concerned with humans. Communication is possible only through the lesser deities or through the intercession of ancestors. Thus, in many African religions, ancestors play a particularly strong role. Their principal function is to protect the tribe or family, and may on occasion show their pleasure or displeasure. Many traditional religions hold that the ancestors are the real owners of the land, and while it can be enjoyed and used during the lifetime of their descendants, it cannot be sold. Displeasure may be shown in the form of bad weather or a bad harvest, or as a living member of the family becoming sick.

Communication with the ancestors or deities may take the form of prayer, offerings (possibly with the assistance of a holy man, or occasionally a holy woman) or sacrifice. Requests may include good health, bountiful harvests and numerous children. Many village celebrations are held to ask for help from (or in honour of) ancestors and deities. The Dogon people from the Bandiagara Escarpment in Mali, for instance, have celebrations before planting to ensure good crops, and after harvests to give thanks.

Totems, fetishes and charms are also important aspects of traditional religions. For more details, see the colour feature between pages 160 and 161.

PEOPLE & LANGUAGES

The number of 'tribes' or ethnic groups in West Africa is huge, and is one of the most fascinating aspects of travel in the region. Guinea-Bissau, a country of less than a million people, has at least 20 ethnic groups. Most other countries have a similar diversity. The colonial powers ignored this diversity, and created states which incorporated many groups, all with vastly different languages, religions and cultures. At the same time, they imposed artificial borders across the territories of some ethnic groups, so today the Hausa are found in Niger and Nigeria, and the Malinké (and the closely related Mandinka) are found in Guinea, Côte d'Ivoire, Mali, Senegal and Gambia.

In some countries, the population may be fairly evenly divided among ethnic groups, but in other countries a single group may predominate, either through sheer numbers, or through a disproportionate control of the political system. In Mali, for example, the largest ethnic group, the Bambara, represents only 23% of the total population, but controls most aspects of the government and economy.

For more information on the people of West Africa, refer to the colour features throughout this book, as well as the Population & People sections of the individual country chapters. For a list of useful phrases in the main West African languages, French and Portuguese, see the Language appendix.

Official Languages

Of the 16 countries in West Africa, French is the official language in eight (Benin,

---

You Say Mandingo, I Say Mandinka ...

As you travel through West Africa, you'll soon realise that many of the people groups have different names. For example, the Fula who are found in Senegal, Guinea, Mali and other countries are variously known as the Fulani, the Fulbe or the Peul. Their language is known as Fula or Pulaar. Name differences may also arise when groups are divided into subgroups, as sometimes the name of a relatively minor clan is given to the whole group. Similarly, spellings of names can vary, either according to the language of the country's original colonial power, or as linguistic studies become more phonetically precise. For example, Peul can be spelt Peulh, and Tamashek (the language of the Tuareg) is generally spelt Tamachek by French speakers. The Toucolour of northern Senegal are now often more accurately called the Tukulor, while the Igbo of Nigeria are now often termed the Igbo.

Confusion can also arise when the definitions of ethnic groups don't always correlate with those for language groups. Normally an ethnic group is defined as a people sharing the same language – a common tongue is the most fundamental aspect which links the people of the group together – but linguists and anthropologists can give language groups confusingly wide or narrow margins, sometimes incorporating several subgroups (or sub-subgroups) which are determined by languages that may be mutually unintelligible, even though they share a common root. Thus the Malinké people of Senegal and Guinea and the Mandinka people of Gambia are sometimes seen as the same ethnic group with different names determined only by geography, while linguists point out that their languages differ in some respects and therefore the two peoples should be categorised separately – even though their languages are both part of the wider Manding language group. And to add even further to the confusion, both the Malinké and the Mandinka are sometimes called the Mandingo.

The upshot of all this is not to expect a clear-cut picture. Expect people, groups, tribes and languages to have a variety of spellings, and you'll be far less confused as you travel.

Burkina Faso, Côte d'Ivoire, Guinea, Mali, Niger, Senegal and Togo), English in five (Gambia, Ghana, Liberia, Nigeria and Sierra Leone) and Portuguese in two (Cape Verde and Guinea-Bissau). Arabic is the official language of Mauritania. It might seem like an awful legacy of the colonial period that the official languages are non-African, but they have a useful role. Where relations between different ethnic groups are strained, the official language is regarded as 'neutral'. For a government to choose one local language for the official language would be politically disastrous, and only some of the people would be able to speak it anyway.

An interesting feature of the European languages' influence is that the same African word or sound is spelt differently, according to the nationality of the original colonial recorder. For example, the Jola people in Gambia (a former British colony) spread over the border into Senegal (a former French colony) where they are known as the Diola. Similarly, the city of Djenné in Mali might just have easily been spelt 'Jenay' had the country been a British colony rather than French. Interesting too is the fact that the Fula people who are spread across much of northern West Africa were identified by the French as 'Peul' and by the English as 'Fulani', the former being the singular and the latter the plural used by these people to identify themselves.

For travellers in West Africa, it is essential to be able to speak a few words (or more) of the official language in each country. Assuming most readers of this book have at least a basic grounding in English, communication in the English-speaking countries of Gambia, Sierra Leone, Liberia, Ghana and Nigeria will be straightforward. In Francophone countries, although some English is spoken in tourist areas, once you get off the beaten track even a handful of French words will make things much easier. The same applies in the Portuguese-speaking countries, although French is commonly spoken in tourist areas of Guinea-Bissau. In Mauritania, although Arabic is the official language, French is widely spoken.

Indigenous Languages

West African languages are classified by linguists and anthropologists in a complex (and constantly shifting) system of groups and subgroups. The following outline is necessarily very simplified.

The West Atlantic group of languages, as the name implies, is found along the western coastal regions of Senegal, Gambia, Guinea-Bissau and Sierra Leone. Principal or well known languages in this group include Wolof, Jola, Bijago, Temne and Fula (also called Fulani or Pulaar). Fula has also spread inland through northern Senegal, northwestern and northern Guinea and central Mali.

The Kwa group of languages is spread along the southern Atlantic coast from Liberia through the southern parts of Côte d'Ivoire, Ghana, Togo and Benin to Nigeria. Principal or well known languages in this group include Ashanti, Ewé, Fon, Yoruba, Ibo, Bassa and Krahn.

The Voltaic group of languages lies to the north of the Kwa group, covering the northern parts of Côte d'Ivoire, Ghana, Togo and Benin, and much of Burkina Faso. Principal or well known languages in this group include Mossi, Bassari and Dogon.

Across the north of the region, language groups include Arabic and Chadic (of which Hausa, spoken in Niger and Nigeria, is the most prominent). Languages also used in this region, but not part of the Arabic or Chadic groups, include Tamashek (also spelt Tamachek), spoken by the Tuareg people, and Songhaï, spoken in the Gao region. In central Nigeria, some languages belong to the Bantu group, related to the languages spoken throughout East and southern Africa.

Unrelated to any of the languages already listed is the distinct Mande group, found mostly in southern Mali and much of Guinea, with significant pockets in Senegal, Gambia, Burkina Faso, Sierra Leone, Liberia and Côte d'Ivoire. Principal or well known languages in this group include Malinké (and the closely related Mandinka), Bambara, Bozo, Mende, Dan, Kpelle and Susu.

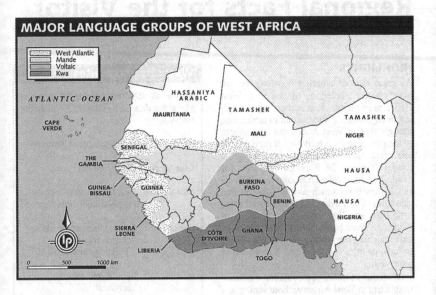

MAJOR LANGUAGE GROUPS OF WEST AFRICA

West Africans tend to be multilingual and this, combined with the use of common languages, means the many different languages used in the region are not a problem. However, many political issues can be more clearly understood when viewed in terms of ethnicity, and language is usually the chief identifying marker of each ethnic group. For example, the north of Sierra Leone is inhabited by Temne-speaking people (part of the West Atlantic group), while the south of the country is inhabited by Mende speakers (part of the completely unrelated Mande group). A major feature of Nigeria is the delicate tripartite balance between the Igbo, Yoruba and Hausa people, with their different histories, cultures and religions. Matters are further complicated when colonial boundaries split the territory of an ethnic group, as with the Ewé people who straddle the border between Ghana and Togo. One of the few benefits is that the Ewé traditionally supply teachers of French in English-speaking Ghana and of English in French- speaking Togo.

Creole Languages

A creole language is formed by the combination of African and European languages. Examples in West Africa include Crioulo (a mixture of Portuguese and various local languages) in Guinea-Bissau and Cape Verde, and Krio (a mixture of English and African languages from all over the region introduced by freed slaves) in Sierra Leone.

Regional Facts for the Visitor

HIGHLIGHTS

At great risk of creating controversy, we have chosen a selection of places in West Africa most visitors find interesting, rewarding or enjoyable. It's important to remember, though, that in West Africa the atmosphere of the places and the activities of their people are often more interesting than tangible tourist 'sights'. In Bamako in Mali, for example, you could rush around the city's official attractions (such as the mosque and museum) in half a day, but if you spend more time here, strolling through the markets or along the river bank, sitting in a pavement cafe watching the world go by, or just talking to local people, you'll get much more out of your visit.

With that in mind, you could have a memorable trip in West Africa without seeing any of the highlights mentioned here. In fact some travellers may want to avoid them because they are in this book! Still, some places are unique and particularly fascinating, and some have been recognised as sites of global significance by UNESCO.

In **Mauritania**, the remote Parc National du Banc d'Arguin, a vast bird sanctuary between the ocean and desert, is a major attraction, although it's impossible to reach without your own vehicle. **Cape Verde's** stunning scenery alone makes it well worth a visit, while a specific highlight might be the port town of Mindelo, which has a charming Mediterranean atmosphere and lively nightlife.

On the coast, **Gambia** is a natural gateway and introduction to the region. It's compact and easily reached from Europe, with long beaches, a beautiful river, lively markets and good birdwatching. **Senegal** has a host of attractions, including the lively markets of Dakar and the fascinating colonial centres of Gorée and St-Louis, but Casamance usually gets most votes – a lush region of forest, palms, lagoons and waterways, with a network of cheap *campements* (lodges) and

World Heritage Sites	
Sites in West Africa considered to be of global significance by UNESCO include the following:	
Benin	Royal palaces of Abomey
Cape Verde	Cidade Velha
Côte d'Ivoire	Parc National de Taï
	Parc National de la Comoë
Ghana	Coastal forts and castles
	Ashante traditional buildings in Kumasi
Mali	Djenné (old town)
	Timbuktu
	Falaise de Bandiagara (Dogon Country)
Niger	Réserve Naturelle Nationale de l'Aïr et du Ténéré
	Parc National du W
Senegal	Île de Gorée
	Parc National aux Oiseaux du Djoudj
	Parc National du Niokolo-Koba

ideal for exploring by bike. The Siné-Saloum Delta is similarly beautiful, and more readily experienced by boat or on foot.

Inland from Senegal, the countries of the Sahel stretch in a great band across the continent. In **Mali**, the area around Mopti is the jewel in the crown of West Africa; from here the cities of Djenné and Timbuktu, and the fascinating Dogon Country can be reached. This area boasts intriguing traditional architecture and culture, a rich history, the

FESTIVALS & CEREMONIES

A highlight of any trip to West Africa is witnessing one of the many ceremonies that are an important part of traditional West African culture. Events such as naming ceremonies, weddings and circumcisions take place everywhere, and you may be invited to take part. You'll also see village festivals, where people celebrate the end of a harvest, give thanks to a deity or honour their ancestors. All these ceremonies usually involve singing, dancing and other festivities, and are fascinating to watch – and great fun too! Some larger ceremonies attract people from across the whole region.

Box: Nomadic herder painted to enhance his beauty for the Gerewol festival in Niger. Photograph by Victor Englebert.

Middle: Music features in many traditional ceremonies such as this naming ceremony in Bakau, The Gambia.

Bottom: In Niger each September you can see the famous Gerewol, a week-long event during which the young Wodaabé herders paint their faces to make themselves beautiful and then line up in long rows for the single women to inspect. This is followed by camel races, ritualistic combat and long hours of dancing into the night.

CHRISTINE OSBORNE

VICTOR ENGLEBERT

VICTOR ENGELBERT

JASON LAURÉ

Top: Masks have a central role in the traditional culture of many West African peoples, and dances with masks, like this Dogon dance in Mali, are performed all over the region.

Bottom: In northern Nigeria during the major Muslim celebrations, you'll see long processions of elegantly dressed men galloping in mad fashion through town on their elaborately decorated horses.

MASKS

In West Africa there is a staggering range of shapes and styles of masks, from the tiny 'passport' mask of the Dan to the plank-like *sigui* mask of the Dogon, which can tower over 3m in height.

Usually created by a professional artisan, masks can be made of wood, brass, tin, leather, cloth, glass beads, natural fibres and even (in the case of the Ashanti) gold.

Masks are made in a number of forms, including face masks and helmet masks (which cover the whole head), headdresses which are secured to the top of the head and the massive *nimba* mask of the Baga tribe in Guinea, which is actually carried on the dancer's shoulders.

The mask is only part of a complex costume which often covers the dancer's entire body. Made of plant fibre or cloth, often with elaborate appliqué, the costume is usually completed with a mane of raffia surrounding the mask. Most masks are associated with dance, although some are used as prestige symbols and worn as amulets. The famous ivory masks from the Kingdom of Benin are worn around the waist and are referred to as hip masks.

It is when the mask is worn in a dance in combination with the costume, and accompanied by percussive music and song that it comes alive, conveying its meaning to the audience who are receptive to its symbolic place in their specific tribal identity.

An illustration of the staggering variety of masks seen in West Africa: Bobo sun mask (top), the huge nimba mask of the Baga (middle) and the miniature 'passport' masks of the Dan (bottom).

Masked dances fulfil a variety of functions, including the following:

Ritual – associated with secret societies and cults; ceremonies include initiation and coming of age formalities.

Fertility – associated with agriculture and the appeasement of ancestor and nature spirits to ensure a successful harvest.

Burial – dances and celebrations designed to assist the spirit of the dead to forsake the earth and reside with the ancestors.

Entertainment – community-based dances and theatrical plays created for social education and enjoyment.

JASON LAURÉ

Top: Wooden fish headdress from the Ebrié Lagoon, Côte d'Ivoire. Photograph by Dennis Wisken/Sidewalk Gallery

Bottom: To appreciate a mask fully, you need to see it in use with the rest of the costume, like this plank mask worn by a Dogon dancer.

Masked dances can also be associated with healing and divination and, in the past, social control.

West African masks are usually classified as anthropomorphic (human) and zoomorphic (animal). The anthropomorphic masks are often carefully carved and can be very realistic. Many tribal groups use masks representing a beautiful maiden whose features reflect the aesthetic ideal of the people. The zoomorphic masks mostly represent dangerous and powerful nature spirits, and can be an abstract and terrifying combination of gaping jaws, popping eyes and massive horns. Some masks combine human and animal features. These convey the links between humans and animals – the ability to gain and control the powers of animals and the spirits they represent.

Christianity, Islam and the 20th century have had a major impact on West African masked dance. Many dances are no longer performed

Top: Marionette headdresses like this one (left) are used by the Bambara in satires and comedies to represent various stereotyped characters; in Sierra Leone, Mende women wear helmet masks like this (middle) in their secret societies; horned headdress from Ghana (right).

Bottom: Plank masks – the checked pattern on the Bobo mask (left) represents the separation of good from evil; the rectangular mask of the Toussain (middle) represents the female, while a helmet mask represents the male; the *kanaga* mask of the Dogon (right) symbolises a bird.

and sometimes those that are have changed from being sacred rituals to forms of social entertainment.

Masking traditions were never static and many have incorporated new aspects. It is still possible to see masked dances in West Africa, although these may be specially arranged 'tourist' performances. Getting to see the real thing, however, is simply a matter of being in the right place at the right time.

John Graham, Alex Newton, David Else

Top: The Senoufo *kponiugo* mask (left) represents a mythical being who acts as a protector of the community. It combines features of various animals, including the tusks of a warthog, and looks appropriately terrifying. In complete stylistic contrast are the two Bobo antelope masks, one male, with the tall plank structure (middle), and one female, with a figure instead of the tall crest (right).

Bottom: The crest on this Bambara mask (left) represents the growth of millet, indicating the importance of agriculture. The function of the Dan bird's beak mask (middle) is to act as a protector of the village. Other Dan masks are smoothly polished and characteristically naturalistic; women's masks have slits for eye holes (right), while men's masks have large round eye holes.

beautiful River Niger, bustling market towns, and good hiking.

In **Burkina Faso** try to plan for a Wednesday afternoon arrival in Gorom-Gorom, in ample time for its swirling Thursday market – an ethnic kaleidoscope where Sahel meets savanna. If you have your own transport, the Parc National d'Arli is rich in birdlife and offers a good chance of spotting leopard, crocodile and antelopes.

Niger has a beautiful desert landscape, with a thin, green fertile band along the River Niger, where you'll find the top-quality Parc National du W – the only place in the Sahel where giraffe can be seen. To the north is the *banco* (mud brick) city of Agadez, with its distinctive mosque, the stark and dramatic Aïr Massif and the rolling dunes of the Ténéré Desert.

Back on the coast, **Guinea-Bissau** is often overlooked, but the islands of the Bijagos Archipelago are idyllic, with good beaches and fascinating local culture. Next door is **Guinea**, where the highlight is undoubtedly the Fouta Djalon, a wide area of beautiful rolling hills, with cool climate and endless hiking opportunities.

Both **Sierra Leone** and **Liberia** have suffered from the effects of war but when things eventually normalise, travellers can return to the highlights of the Freetown peninsula in Sierra Leone, which has excellent beaches and good hiking, or to Sapo National Park in Liberia, which encompasses one of West Africa's largest remaining rainforests. If this national park proves to be unreachable, the beautiful beaches along the coast between Robertsport, Monrovia and Buchanan are consolation enough.

Côte d'Ivoire has many highlights. In the west, you'll find a range of pristine beaches near Sassandra, a lagoonside fishing village well worth visiting in its own right. Further west, the Parc National de Taï offers controlled ecotourism in Côte d'Ivoire's largest rainforest. Man is a great base for getting to know the Dan (also known as Yacouba) people and their rich culture of dances and masks, while from Korhogo you can visit the artisan villages of the Senoufo.

Suggested Itineraries

A lot depends on the time and money you have available, but the main factor affecting the number of places you can reach is your form of transport. Although a significant number of people tour West Africa in their own vehicle, the great majority of travellers use buses, bush taxis and trains, and get to most places at fairly low cost, albeit sometimes quite slowly. A hired car or organised tour cuts delays, and can be the only way to visit some national parks, but it's much more expensive.

If time is limited, it's probably better to concentrate on visiting just one or two places rather than rushing to too many places and only skimming the surface.

You should count on a two week minimum to do the region any justice. With two weeks, you could fly to/from Dakar (Senegal) or Banjul (Gambia) and do a circular tour of Senegal and Gambia, or you could fly to/from Accra and do a tour of Ghana. With three weeks you could go further afield, perhaps visiting Senegal and Mali, or Ghana and Côte d'Ivoire.

Open jaw tickets (see the Getting There & Away chapter for more details) allow you to fly into one city and out of another, and an increasingly popular route is to fly into Dakar, travel through Senegal, Mali and Burkina Faso to Ghana and fly out of Accra. You could do this route in four weeks, but five or six weeks would be much better, and two months would allow time to visit other countries too. For example, from Senegal, you could go north into Mauritania, or loop down through Guinea-Bissau and Guinea before reaching Mali or Côte d'Ivoire.

In a grand tour of anything between three and six months, you could start in Dakar or Gambia, head south and east through Guinea-Bissau, Guinea, Côte d'Ivoire and Ghana, before heading east into Togo, Benin or Nigeria, or north into the Sahel regions of Burkina Faso or Niger and then following the River Niger through Mali, returning to the start via Mauritania.

Ghana is buoyant and has long since sloughed off its reputation as the poor relation of the region. Accra's nightlife can rival any neighbouring capital's, while Kumasi, deep in the homeland of the Ashanti people, has the area's largest market. The coast west of Accra is rich in fishing villages and beaches. On many of its promontories and headlands are the remains of old colonial trading and slaving forts. Cape Coast Castle and St George's Castle, Elmina, both have excellent museums.

Benin has a remarkably diverse host of attractions including frenetic Cotonou, the stilt villages near Ganvié, the voodoo and old slaving centre of Ouidah, and several national parks. Smaller **Togo** is known for its beaches, but cosmopolitan Lomé, and the nearby 'butterfly hills' of Kpalimé are also popular destinations.

Nigeria is the giant of West Africa and overpopulated, crime-ridden Lagos can be hellishly difficult. However, the historic cities of Kano, Kaduna and Zaria are a refreshing contrast, or you can escape the bustle by retreating to Yankari National Park, or exploring the tranquil waterways and islands of the Niger Delta, and the cool Jos Plateau.

PLANNING
When to Go

The best time to visit West Africa is the dry period from November to February (for more details see the Climate section in the Facts about the Region chapter). Any time up to April (in the southern coastal countries) or May (in the Sahel countries) is also dry; from here it gets progressively hotter. From May/June to September/October is the rainy season, which is usually considered bad for travelling, although in the Sahel rain only falls for a few hours per day, keeping temperatures down and the skies clear of dust.

The main problem during the rainy season is getting around. Most major roads in the region are tar or all-weather dirt, but minor roads can turn to mud or be virtually washed away. (Wildlife reserves are usually closed from June to November, as tracks are impassable.) With your own 4WD vehicle you'll probably be OK, but travellers on public transport will have little chance of reaching some of the more remote spots. If you plan to do a lot of upcountry travel during the rains, you'll need patience, a sense of humour and a good book to while away the delays.

Another factor to consider is the tourist season. Although West Africa is not a major tourist destination compared with other parts of the continent, there are some areas where tourists congregate at certain times of the year. For example, hotels along the coasts of Senegal and Gambia are packed with European sunbathers on package tours from December to March (and to a lesser extent, in November and April). The Casamance region of Senegal and the Dogon area of Mali are also crowded at this time, especially in December and January.

You might also want to consider timing your trip to coincide with the festivals that are a major highlight in many countries. If you're planning to visit the Sahel countries, you should be aware of the dates of the major Islamic holidays, especially Ramadan. For more details on festivals and holidays see the Public Holidays & Special Events section later in this chapter.

What Kind of Trip

In West Africa *any* kind of trip is possible. If time is limited, you can visit the region for just a few weeks and get a lot out of it. If time is of no consequence, there's enough to keep you going for three months at least.

If you prefer to go alone, solo travel is always one of the best ways to meet and get to know local people. Getting around by public transport is straightforward, and local people are always ready to help (although in cities and towns people tend to be more indifferent to foreigners). Women travelling alone are rare, but not at all unknown, and can enjoy the region, provided they keep certain considerations in mind – for more information, see the Women Travellers section later in this chapter.

Travelling as a couple, or with a friend or two, may cut you off a bit from local people (you'll talk to each other on the bus, rather than to the people sitting next to you) but does open up more possibilities. Costs tend to drop, as you can share hotel rooms, and in national parks or wilderness areas the cost of hiring guides or boats can be shared. With a small group, you can also consider hiring a car or maybe a boat (eg for a trip down the River Niger in Mali), for a few days so as to reach areas which are more problematic or time consuming by public transport.

A third travel option is to go by organised tour, either arranged locally and lasting a few days or something set up in your home country and covering anything from two weeks to several months. A tour takes care of time-consuming aspects such as sorting out food and accommodation, but is usually more expensive than doing things yourself. For those with limited time and a bit of cash it can be a good way of simply enjoying your trip. Some parts of West Africa can only be reached by organised tour, so solo travellers should team up with others, while small groups can arrange 'private tours', and have some room for price negotiation. For more details, see Organised Tours in the Getting There & Away chapter.

Maps

For regional coverage the Michelin map *Africa: North and West* (sheet No 953, formerly No 153) is one of the few maps in the world to achieve something like classic status. The detail is incredible, given the limitations of scale (1:4,000,000), and the map is regularly updated. (It's the kind of map that lingers in bookshops for ages, so check that you are buying the most recent version.) Even so, you should expect a few discrepancies between the map and reality, particularly with regard to roads, as old tracks get upgraded and once-smooth highways become potholed disasters. However, no overland driver would be without this map. It's even lent its name to The 153 Club whose members have driven across the Sahara and around West Africa.

Other maps include the Bartholemew *Africa West* (1:3,500,000) which does not have the route accuracy of the Michelin, but does have the advantage of contour shading, which gives a better idea of the region's topography. To put the region in the wider context (or possibly for wider travels) Bartholemew's *Africa: Continental Travel Map* shows all the main routes and towns, with contour shading, and makes a very nice souvenir to pin on the wall after your trip.

Maps of individual countries are described in more detail in the relevant chapters, but worth noting is the Institut Géographique National (IGN) *Pays et Villes du Monde* series, which includes Benin, Burkina Faso, Côte d'Ivoire, Guinea, Guinea-Bissau, Mali, Niger, Senegal and Togo. IGN also produces *Carte de l'Afrique* sheets but these were surveyed in the 1960s and don't seem to have been updated since. For the former British colonies, including Nigeria and Gambia, the *Traveller's Map* series produced by Macmillan is the best. International Travel Maps covers several African countries including Ghana, Sierra Leone, Gambia and Senegal.

What to Bring

When deciding what to bring, it's always best to keep your luggage to a minimum, as a light bag makes travel so much easier. Some travellers bring all they need in a backpack small enough to pass as hand luggage on the plane. With a small, light bag you're unencumbered in crowded situations, you can avoid having your belongings loaded onto bus roof racks (and possibly damaged and tampered with) and you're less likely to have hassles with luggage fees on bush taxis. Generally the duration of your journey makes little difference to the amount of kit you need.

Backpack For carrying your gear, a backpack is most practical. Many travellers favour travelpacks which turn neatly into a 'normal'-looking holdall. It's a good idea to pack your clothes and other gear in plastic bags inside your backpack to protect them from moisture and dust. A smaller day-pack can be useful for when your main bag is left at a hotel.

Clothes For day-to-day travel all you need is a few shirts or T-shirts, trousers and/or a skirt, shorts, underwear, socks, a strong pair of shoes and flip-flops (thongs) or sandals for showers and beaches. A hat is essential, and a light sweatshirt is useful from December to February in the Sahel. If you visit during the rains, a waterproof jacket should complete your outfit. Anything else you find yourself without can easily be bought along the way, either new, second-hand, or tailor-made.

West Africans like to dress well if they can, especially in the cities, so it might be worth taking a set of smart clothes for special occasions such as visa applications, crossing troublesome borders, or if you're invited to somebody's house.

Generally, military-style gear isn't recommended, as you may be taken for a soldier. See also Dress in the Society & Conduct section of the Facts about the Region chapter for more details on appropriate dress in West Africa.

Equipment Camp sites are limited, and cater mainly for travellers with their own vehicle, so it's not worth backpackers lugging around a tent and camping gear. A lightweight sleeping bag is useful in the cooler months, particularly if you're sleeping on roofs, as is often an option. A sheet sleeping bag is useful for cheap hotels where bedding is either not provided or less than appealing.

Absolute essentials include a basic medical kit (see the Health section later for more details), mosquito net, water bottle, water purifier and filter, torch and spare batteries.

Optional items include camera and film, binoculars, universal washbasin plug, travel alarm clock, Swiss Army-style knife, a length of cord for drying clothes or securing the mozzie net, sewing kit and small calculator (for working out exchange rates or bargaining in markets). A padlock can be useful to secure your pack from opportunistic thieves, and for when hotel locks are dodgy.

Don't forget boring things like a wash kit and towel (although some travellers class these as optional too).

RESPONSIBLE TOURISM

Tourism is one of the largest industries in the world, and the effects of tourists on destinations can be substantial. But they can be positive – for example, tourists may pay to visit areas which have interesting wildlife or natural features such as waterfalls and forests, and if some of this money goes to the local inhabitants then they benefit personally and have an incentive to protect the areas and the animals. For more details, see the Ecology & Environment section in the Facts about the Region chapter.

While schemes like this allow the local inhabitants to maintain their traditional lifestyles, there is also the option for income generated by the jobs that tourism creates, such as wildlife rangers, tour guides and various posts in hotels, lodges and camps. Further spin-offs include the sale of crafts and curios.

The link between tourism and conservation has been positively exploited in Ghana, for example, where village projects in some areas such as the Bobiri Forest Reserve and the Tafi-Atome Monkey Sanctuary offer tourists nature trails and trained guides, as well as simple food and accommodation. Part of the money the park earns from tourism is used to improve village resources, providing people with drinking water and veterinary care for their livestock. Thus, local people have a stake in park development. In Côte d'Ivoire, a village tourism project now exists in Parc National de Taï, one of West Africa's largest stands of rainforest, and clearing and poaching have decreased dramatically in recent years.

Even in protected areas which may not be of great interest to tourists, or may be difficult to reach, if local people can gain some benefit (for example, from employment or indirectly through wood harvesting or limited hunting) rather than being completely excluded, that essential incentive to protect the area is still present. This has happened in some protected areas in Gambia, including Kiang West National Park, where the continuation of certain activities, such as cattle grazing and (more controversially) rice cultivation, is permitted, and at Niumi National Park, where community groups have been established which give local people a formal voice in the park management structure – ideally so they can benefit from the sustainable use of natural resources. On the Gambian coast, areas of ecological importance are being earmarked as tourist attractions in their natural state. The local people stand to benefit from the income this will attract, which in turn will hopefully ensure the area's long-term survival.

Ecotourism

Although tourism can be a saviour in some instances, it can also have very negative effects, particularly when destinations cannot cope with the number of tourists they attract, leading to damage to natural ecologies and human environments. In an effort to counter these negative effects, some companies offer 'eco-friendly' holidays; but this, along with 'ecotourism' is one of the most overused and meaningless terms around. Don't be fooled by travel companies claiming to be 'eco-friendly' just because they do things outdoors. Activities such as desert driving, hiking, boating, wildlife viewing or sightseeing trips to remote and fragile areas can be more environmentally or culturally harmful than a conventional hotel holiday in a specially developed resort.

Environmentalists point out that although tourism relies on natural resources such as healthy wildlife populations or rich cultural traditions, it often does little to sustain them. If you want to support tour companies with a good environmental record, you have to look beyond vague 'eco-friendly' claims and ask what they are really doing to protect or support the environment and the people who live there.

Visitors to Africa are often asked by environmental organisations to consider the amount of money they pay during their holiday, and to ensure that as much as possible stays within the 'host' country to the benefit of local people. Overland truck passengers and independent backpackers can contribute just as much to local economies as high-rolling tourists who come to a country on a short all-inclusive trip paid for overseas.

But tourism's effect is not just financial. It is just as important for visitors to behave in a manner which limits their impact on the natural environment and the local inhabitants. To be a responsible tourist you have to question some of your own actions and those of your tour companies. You also have to look pretty closely at the actions of governments, both local and around the world. Being a responsible tourist doesn't mean you have to get depressed and spoil your holiday. In fact, by asking a few questions and getting a deeper insight, it can make your trip even more rewarding.

Guidelines for Responsible Tourism

A British organisation called Tourism Concern (☎ 0171-753 3330, fax 753 3331, email tourconcern@gn.apc.org; from 22 April 2000 ☎ 020 7753 3330, fax 7753 3331), Stapleton House, 277-281 Holloway Rd, London N7 8HN, UK, has come up with a set of guidelines for travellers interested in minimising the negative impact they have on the countries they visit. These include:

• Save precious natural resources. Try not to waste water. Switch off lights and air-conditioning when you go out. Avoid places which clearly consume limited resources such as water and electricity at the expense of local residents.
• Support local enterprise. Use locally owned hotels and restaurants and support trade and craft workers by buying locally made souvenirs. But help safeguard the environment by avoiding souvenirs made from local wildlife, particularly endangered species.
• Ask before taking close-up photographs of people. If you don't speak the language, a gesture will be understood and appreciated.
• Please don't give money, sweets, pens etc to children. It encourages begging. A donation to a recognised project – a health centre or school – is more constructive.

- Respect for local etiquette earns you respect. Politeness is a virtue in most parts of the world, but remember that people have different ideas about what's polite. In many places, revealing clothes are insensitive to local feelings. Similarly, public displays of affection are often culturally inappropriate.
- Learn something about the history and current affairs of the country. It helps you understand the idiosyncrasies of its people, and helps prevent misunderstandings and frustrations.
- Be patient, friendly and sensitive. Remember that you are a guest.

For more information, try their Web site at www.gn.apc.org/tourismconcern. In the USA, the Rethinking Tourism Project (PO Box 581938, Minneapolis, MN 55458-1938, email RTProject@aol.com) is a similar organisation.

TOURIST OFFICES

Apart from a few small pockets, West Africa isn't geared for tourism, and tourist offices are few and far between. Some countries run small tourist offices at their embassies, and a call here before you leave home may elicit some brochures or help with specific travel information.

When you're travelling, some countries may run a Ministry of Tourism information office, but apart from a few tatty brochures you're unlikely to get much here. Notable exceptions – where a town or city may have a genuinely useful tourist office – are listed in individual country chapters. Some tour companies or hotels where staff are happy to provide information for independent travellers are also listed where appropriate.

VISAS & DOCUMENTS
Passport

Before travelling in West Africa, make sure you have enough free pages in your passport. You will need around two pages per country – one for the visa and another for the border stamps, plus extra pages for countries where you may have to report to police along the way. Some officials prefer passports which

---

Visa Photos

Nearly every visa application requires between two and four passport photos. Two is the usual number, but regulations change from embassy to embassy, and from day to day, according to the whims of the issuing clerk. If you're planning to get several visas along the way, take a good supply of photos. Black and white or colour is acceptable. If you run short, you can usually get more taken at camera shops in large towns. In smaller places you'll usually be able to find the village photographer, complete with an ancient wooden pin-hole camera and tripod, who can do the job for you.

---

expire at least three months after your trip ends.

Visas

This section contains general information about visas – for the specific details on who needs what for where, see the Facts for the Visitor sections of the individual country chapters.

Visas are normally available from embassies, consulates or high commissions, and should be obtained before arrival in a country, as they are rarely issued at land borders. Visas are sometimes available at airports, but if you're flying from outside Africa, airlines usually won't let you on board without a visa anyway. If you are only visiting one or two countries it might be a good idea to get your visas before you leave. If you're on a longer trip, you can get them as you go along. This gives you more flexibility, but does require careful planning – see the table for guidelines on where you can get which visas.

A fee is usually payable, and can vary from a few dollars up to US$50 or more. Prices may also vary according to where you buy the visa. Check how long the visa is valid for, and from when, as this may help determine where you get your visa. Multiple-entry visas, which allow you to enter a

Getting Visas in West Africa

This table shows where you can get visas within West Africa for other West African countries. The row along the top lists the countries you may want visas for, while the first column lists the countries where you may want to get them. For visa applications, it's usually best to go to the embassy first thing in the morning. Visas are often ready within 24 hours. You will need at least two photos per application. Note that generally Nigerian embassies only issue visas to residents of the country you're in, or to those with a letter of introduction from their embassy.

VISAS FOR:

AVAILABLE IN:	Benin	Burkina Faso	Cape Verde	Côte d'Ivoire	Gambia	Ghana	Guinea	Guinea-Bissau	Liberia	Mali	Mauritania	Niger	Nigeria	Senegal	Sierra Leone	Togo
Benin		F	–	F	–	✓	–	–	–	–	✓	F	–	✓	–	F
Burkina Faso	–		–	✓	–	✓	–	–	–	✓	F	–	–	✓	–	F
Cape Verde	–	F		F	–	–	✓	✓	–	✓	–	✓	✓	✓	✓	–
Côte d'Ivoire	✓	✓	–		–	✓	✓	✓	–	–	✓	–	✓	✓	✓	–
Gambia	–	–	–	–		–	✓	–	✓	–	✓	–	–	✓	✓	✓
Ghana	✓	✓	–	✓	–		✓	–	✓	✓	–	✓	✓	✓	–	F
Guinea	✓	F	✓	✓	–	✓		–	✓	✓	✓	–	–	✓	–	F
Guinea-Bissau	–	F	–	F	✓	–	✓		–	–	✓	–	✓	✓	✓	–
Liberia	–	–	–	✓	–	✓	✓	–		–	–	–	✓	✓	–	F
Mali	–	✓	–	✓	–	–	✓	–	–		✓	✓	–	✓	–	F
Mauritania	–	F	–	F	–	–	–	–	–	✓		–	✓	✓	–	F
Niger	✓	F	–	F	–	–	–	–	–	✓	✓		✓	–	✓	✓
Nigeria	✓	✓	✓	–	✓	–	✓	✓	–	✓	✓	–		–	✓	F
Senegal	–	F	✓	✓	✓	–	✓	✓	–	✓	✓	–	–		✓	–
Sierra Leone	–	–	–	–	–	✓	✓	–	✓	–	–	–	–	–		–
Togo	✓	F	–	F	–	✓	–	–	–	–	–	–	–	–	–	

F = issued by French embassy

country more than once without the hassle of getting a new visa, can be useful for some countries, although they usually cost more than single-entry visas. When applying for a visa you may have to show proof that you intend to leave the country (eg an air ticket) or that you have enough funds to support yourself during your visit.

If you need visas to several countries before you leave home, or there's no relevant embassy in your home country, you could consider using a visa agency. Prices and quality vary, so it's worth taking the time to shop around.

Travel Insurance

A travel insurance policy to cover theft, loss and medical problems is a good idea. Some policies offer lower and higher medical-expense options; the higher ones are chiefly for countries such as the USA, which have extremely high medical costs. There is a wide variety of policies available, so check the small print.

Some policies specifically exclude 'dangerous activities', which can include scuba diving, motorcycling and even trekking. A locally acquired motorcycle licence is not valid under some policies.

Hospitals in Africa are not free, and the good ones are not cheap. You may prefer a policy which pays doctors or hospitals directly rather than you having to pay on the spot and claim later.

If you have to claim later make sure you keep all documentation. Some policies ask you to call collect (reverse charges) to a centre in your home country where an immediate assessment of your problem is made.

Check that the policy covers ambulances or an emergency flight home. Air ambulances and urgent international flights are frighteningly expensive.

Other Documents

Other documents you may need include: proof of your vaccinations, especially yellow fever (see the Health section later for more details); your driving licence and an International Driving Permit (if you intend to hire a car – see the boxed text for more details); a membership card for a national youth hostelling association (which may get you cheap accommodation in affiliated hostels – although there are very few in West

---

International Driving Permit

An International Driving Permit (IDP) is easily and cheaply issued in your home country – usually by a major motoring association (in Britain it's the AA) – and is very useful if you're driving in countries where your own licence may not be recognised (officially or unofficially). It has the added advantage of being written in several languages, with a photo and lots of stamps, so it looks much more impressive when presented to car rental clerks or policemen at road blocks.

Africa); and a student or youth card (occasionally good for various discounts).

Photocopies

Photocopies of all your important documents, plus tickets and credit cards, will help speed up replacement if the originals are lost or stolen. Keep these, and a list of your travellers cheque numbers, separate from other valuables, and leave copies with someone at home so they can be faxed to you if necessary.

EMBASSIES & CONSULATES

It's important to realise what your own embassy – the embassy of the country of which you are a citizen – can and can't do to help if you get into trouble.

Generally speaking, embassy staff won't be much help in emergencies if the trouble is remotely your own fault. Remember that you are bound by the laws of the country you are in. Your embassy will not be sympathetic if you end up in jail after committing a crime locally, even if such actions are legal in your own country.

In genuine emergencies you might get some assistance, but only if other channels have been exhausted. For example, if you need to get home urgently, a free ticket home is exceedingly unlikely – the embassy would expect you to have insurance. If you have all your money and documents stolen, it might assist with getting a new passport, but a loan for onward travel will be out of the question.

Some embassies used to keep letters for travellers or have a small reading room with home newspapers and magazines, but these days the mail holding service has usually been stopped and even the newspapers tend to be out of date.

See the Facts for the Visitor sections of the individual country chapters for addresses and contact details of embassies and consulates. Note that in some parts of Africa, countries are represented by an 'honorary consul' who is not a full-time diplomat but is usually an expatriate with limited duties.

MONEY

Specific details on currencies and places to exchange money are given in the Facts for the Visitor sections of individual country chapters. Throughout the regional chapters and in countries where inflation is high we have quoted prices in US$ as these rates are more likely to remain stable, whereas local currencies may go up and down.

CFA Franc

The principal currency of the region is the West African CFA franc (pronounced *see-eff-ahh* in French and commonly called 'seefa' by English-speaking travellers). CFA stands for Communauté Financière Africaine, and the West African CFA franc is

The CFA & the Euro

In early 1994, France devalued the CFA from 50:1 to 100:1, sending shock waves through West Africa. Most prices rose by 125 to 150% and imported goods by up to 190% – not enough to completely offset the devaluation, but enough to put many products outside the grasp of local buyers. Any West African saving money for a trip abroad, or to buy something imported, such as a washing machine, saw their savings effectively halved. The biggest winners were foreign travellers – dollars and pounds now buy more CFA, which makes the cost of a visit far more reasonable.

But beware. On 1 January 1999, the euro comes into existence as the currency of the European Union, of which France is a member. The CFA will then be attached to the euro, a situation that is full of uncertainty, as the other countries in the European Union may not be as well-disposed to the CFA as France historically has been.

So, at the very least, be prepared for another devaluation, or, as seems more likely, the CFA may be floated to find its own natural level against international currencies. If this happens, visitors will be even better off. Be prepared for confusion.

used in Benin, Burkina Faso, Côte d'Ivoire, Guinea-Bissau, Mali, Niger, Senegal and Togo. It can also be used (or easily exchanged for local currency) in some other West African countries, such as Gambia, Guinea and Ghana. On a practical note, it allows travellers to go from one West African CFA country to the next without changing money.

The CFA is fixed against (and supported by) the French franc at a rate of 100:1, effectively making it a 'hard' currency. For travellers, the practical result of this arrangement is that some banks will change FF cash into CFA without charging a fee or commission. Note, however, that some exchange bureaus do charge a fee and you always have to pay a commission when changing travellers cheques into CFA.

Even though the CFA is considered hard currency, exchanging it in countries outside the region is difficult. In East Africa, the banks act like it's funny money. In the USA and most parts of Europe, even major banks won't accept it. In short, the CFA is hard currency only in West Africa and France.

Note that another block of countries (including Cameroon and Gabon) uses the Central African CFA franc, which is also linked to the French franc at 100:1. The Central African CFA is interchangeable with the West African CFA.

Exchanging Money

In CFA countries, major international currencies such as UK£ and US$ (cash or travellers cheques) can be changed in capital cities and tourist areas, but elsewhere French francs are more readily dealt with. In the non-CFA countries, most banks will handle French francs, UK£ or US$.

You can change your money into local currency at banks or foreign exchange ('forex') bureaus. Because West Africa is dominated by the CFA you'll find your own finances much more straightforward if you carry at least some of your money in French francs. Indeed, in smaller towns (and some of the larger ones too) in the CFA countries, you'll have difficulty changing anything but

French francs. We get many letters from travellers who got stuck without money because they relied totally on US$ and had no French francs. In short – take some!

In addition, carrying French francs makes budgeting easier, as you always know the exchange rate. Large hotels, tour companies, some shops and small hotels, and even a few buses, will accept French francs cash instead of CFA, so you'll always have something to fall back on.

Cash & Travellers Cheques Cash is more convenient than travellers cheques but cannot be replaced. Travellers cheques are refundable if lost or stolen, so taking a mix of cash and travellers cheques is best. Well known brands of cheque are better to deal with as they're more likely to be recognised by bank staff.

Carry some cash with you, say 3000FF or US$500, as a contingency fund for emergencies. (Don't forget, it's a good idea to carry some of your money in French francs.)

It's worth taking a mixture of high and low denominations of cash and travellers cheques. Thus, if you're about to leave the region, you can change enough currency for just a few days without having loads of spare cash to get rid of.

Bank Charges & Commissions

When you're exchanging money, note that charges and commissions vary between banks. The bank charge may be a flat fee (around US$2) or a commission (usually between 1 and 2%), and sometimes you have to pay a charge *and* a commission. Exchange rates can differ between banks, so it's important to check these too. The bank with the higher commission may also offer a higher exchange rate – so you could still be better off. If you're dealing with CFA and French francs, of course, much of this is academic. The rate is fixed at 100:1 so all you have to compare between banks *is* the charge or commission.

Note also that the USA changed the design of the US$100 bill in the mid-1990s and old-style US$100 notes are not accepted at places that don't have a light machine for checking watermarks.

ATMs Automated teller machines (ATMs) exist in some capitals and other large cities in West Africa and, in theory, accept credit and debit cards from banks with reciprocal agreements. We've heard from travellers who have successfully drawn cash from ATMs, but also from others who have drawn a blank or even lost their card.

Credit, Charge & Debit Cards You can use a credit card or charge card to pay for some items, but these are limited to top end hotels and restaurants, car rental and occasionally air tickets. You can also use your card to withdraw cash in some banks in the region. Contact your card company to see which banks in which countries accept your card. American Express and Visa are the most widely accepted.

You'll also need to ask your bank or card company about charges, and arrange a way to pay your card bills if you're travelling for more than a month or so.

The advantage of debit cards is there's no bill to pay off (if you have the money in your account of course), so they are more suited for longer travels.

It's normally not wise to rely totally on plastic, as computer breakdowns can leave you stranded. Note also that in some countries drawing cash by card can take more than a day. Details are given in each country chapter.

International Transfers If you think your finances may need topping up while you're away, ask your bank about international transfers. This can be a complicated, time-consuming and expensive business, but if you're travelling for a long time it can save the worry (and sheer bulk) of carrying large wads of notes and cheques around. Western Union Money Transfer has representatives in many West African countries.

Currency Regulations Except in CFA countries and Liberia, the import and export of local currency is either prohibited or severely restricted – typically limited to the equivalent of about US$10 – although enforcement of this regulation is fairly lax. On leaving non-CFA countries, it's usually not possible to reconvert local currency into foreign currency (except in Gambia where it's quite straightforward). As part of their fiscal control, some countries use currency declaration forms. More details are given in individual country chapters.

Black Market In some countries, artificially low fixed exchange rates create a demand for unofficial hard currency, so you can get more local money by changing on the so-called 'black market'. In CFA countries, this is not an issue because buying and selling currency is easy and the rates are pegged to the French franc. In many other countries, banks and forex bureaus offer floating rates, so any black market has also disappeared. You may be offered 5% more than bank rates by shady characters on the street but it's likely to be a scam. If they offer 10% you *know* it's a scam!

In some countries, unofficial moneychangers are tolerated by the authorities. For example, if you're crossing from a CFA country to a non-CFA country, there's rarely a bank at the border, and moneychangers operate in border towns, or at the border itself, quite openly under the eyes of police and customs officials. It's important to be alert, though, as these guys pull all sorts of stunts with bad exchange rates or folded notes.

In some cities and towns, if the banks are closed, unofficial moneychangers also operate, usually around markets or outside banks and post offices. But changing money this way is not advised. Even if the moneychanger is straight, you don't know who's watching from the other side of the street.

Safer options involve changing money at top end hotels or tour companies, although rates can be lousy. Another is to ask discreetly at a shop selling imported items.

'The banks are closed, do you know anyone who can help me ...?' is better than 'Do you want to change money?'. In Liberia changing money in shops is tolerated because the banks don't offer exchange facilities.

In countries with a real black market, where you can get considerably more for your money, don't forget that this is morally questionable and against the law. What's more, dealers often work with corrupt policemen and can trap you in a set-up where you may be 'arrested', scared to death and eventually lose all your money.

Security

To keep your money, passport and air ticket safe from pickpockets, secure a pouch, either around your neck or waist, under your clothes. Keep a separate purse or wallet containing a small amount of money for day-to-day purchases so you don't have to fish around under your clothing all the time.

Costs

Compared with many other parts of the developing world, travel in West Africa is not cheap. Travellers who have been in East Africa, South America, India or even parts of Europe, get a nasty shock when they come here. Very generally speaking, prices of things in West Africa are around 50 to 75% of what they are in Europe, Australasia or North America. Obviously there are exceptions: locally produced items (including food and beer) may be much cheaper, while imported items may be twice what they cost in the west.

Accommodation costs start from about US$5 a night for a bed in very basic local resthouses, to US$10 to US$15 for something a bit more comfortable, US$25 to US$50 for mid-range hotels, and up to US$100 or US$200 for top end establishments.

Food can be very cheap if you eat from markets and street stalls. In local restaurants, plan on meals costing between US$2 and US$7. In capital cities or resort areas, meals at places catering mainly for foreigners can easily cost US$30 for two.

Transport options are equally varied: you can go by pick-up for a nominal fee or rent a car for US$100 a day or more. Most people go by bush taxi, bus or train, and throughout the region expect to pay about US$1 to US$2 per 100km. When estimating your costs, you should also include extra items such as visa fees, national park admission charges, plus the cost of organised tours or activities, such as hiking, where local guides have to be hired. Taking all these aspects into account, shoestring travellers could get by on US$10 to US$15 per day (or even less). For a bit more comfort, US$20 to US$25 per day is a reasonable budget. With US$30 to US$50 per day or more at your disposal, you could stay in decent hotels, eat well and travel quite comfortably (if good transport is available!).

Tipping & Bargaining

Tipping can be a problem in West Africa because there are few clear rules applicable to all people. The situation is further complicated because tipping is related to the concept of gift giving (see also the entry on Gifts & Tips in the Society & Conduct section of the Facts about the Region chapter). Throughout West Africa, only the wealthy are expected to tip. This means well-to-do locals and nearly all foreign visitors.

The Fine Art of Bargaining

In some West African countries, bargaining over prices, often for market goods, is a way of life. Visitors often have difficulty with this idea, as they are used to things having a fixed value, whereas in West Africa commodities are considered worth whatever their seller can get for them. It really is no different to the concept of an auction and should be treated as one more fascinating aspect of travel in the region.

Basics

In markets selling basic items like fruit and vegetables some traders will invariably put their asking price high when they see you, a wealthy foreigner. If you pay this – whether out of ignorance or guilt about how much you have compared with most local people – you may be considered foolish, but you'll also be doing fellow travellers a disservice by creating the impression that all foreigners are willing to pay any price named! You may also harm the local economy: by paying high prices you put some items out of the reach of local people's reach. And who can blame the traders – why sell something to a local when foreigners will pay twice as much? So in cases like this you may need to bargain over the price.

Having said that, many traders will quote you the same price that locals pay, particularly away from cities or tourist areas. It is very important not to go around expecting *everybody* to charge high. It helps, of course, to know the price of things. After the first few days in a country (when you'll inevitably pay over the odds a few times) you'll soon get to learn the standard prices for basic items. Remember, though, that prices can change depending on where you buy. For example, a soft drink in a city may be one-third the price you'll pay in a remote rural area, where transport costs have to be paid for. Conversely, fruit and vegetables are cheaper in the areas where they're actually grown.

Souvenirs

At craft and curio stalls, where items are specifically for tourists, it's a completely different story: bargaining is very much expected. The trader's aim is to identify the highest price you're willing to pay. Your aim is to find the price below which the vendor will not sell. People have all sorts

Anyone staying in a fancy hotel would be expected to tip porters and other staff, but there would not be the same expectation from a backpacker in a cheap hotel.

Everyone, locals and foreigners, is expected to tip around 10% at the better restaurants, but check the bill closely to see if service is included, as it frequently is. At the more basic restaurants and eating houses no tips are expected from anyone. There's a grey area between these two classes of restaurants, where tipping is rarely expected from locals, but may be expected of foreigners. Even wealthier West Africans will sometimes tip at the smaller restaurants, not so much because it's expected but because it's a show of status.

In privately hired taxis, tipping is not the rule among locals, but drivers expect well-heeled travellers to tip about 10%. In bigger cities that see lots of foreigners, such as Dakar (Senegal), Abidjan (Côte d'Ivoire) and Lagos (Nigeria), taxi drivers may still hope for a small tip, even from backpackers. In shared taxis around cities tipping is almost unheard of.

POST & COMMUNICATIONS

Post and telephone services are quite reliable in most of West Africa, but in all

---

The Fine Art of Bargaining

of formulae for working out what this should be, but there are no hard and fast rules. Some traders may initially ask a price four (or more) times higher than what they're prepared to accept, although it's usually lower than this. Decide what you want to pay or what others have told you they've paid; your first offer should be about half this. At this stage, the vendor may laugh or feign outrage, while you plead abject poverty. The trader's price then starts to drop from the original quote to a more realistic level. When it does, you begin making better offers until you arrive at a mutually agreeable price.

And that's the crux – *mutually agreeable*. You hear travellers all the time moaning about how they got 'overcharged' by souvenir traders. When things have no fixed price, nobody really gets overcharged. If you don't like the price, it's simple – don't pay it.

Some people prefer to conduct their bargaining in a stern manner, but the best results seem to come from a friendly and spirited exchange. There's no point in losing your temper when bargaining. If the effort seems a waste of time, politely take your leave. Sometimes traders will call you back if they think their stubbornness may be losing a sale. Very few will pass up the chance of making a sale, however thin the profit.

If traders won't come down to a price you feel is fair (or you can't afford the asking price), it either means they really aren't making a profit, or that if you don't pay their prices, they know somebody else will. Remember the traders are under no more obligation to sell to you than you are to buy from them. You can go elsewhere, or accept the price. This is the raw edge of capitalism!

countries the service to/from towns and cities tends to be better. In rural areas the service can range from slow to nonexistent. For more specific details on rates and prices see the Facts for the Visitor sections of the individual country chapters.

Post

Letters sent from a major capital take about a week to reach most parts of Europe, and about two weeks to reach North America or Australasia. Don't rely on this though, every now and again it can take a lot longer for a letter to arrive. If you're in a hurry, a courier service is an alternative; DHL, for example, has offices in almost every capital city in West Africa.

If you want to receive mail, you can use the poste restante service. This is where letters are held for your collection at a post office (which in French-speaking countries is called a PTT). Although smaller post offices may offer this service, it's usually more reliable to use the main post office (called the General Post Office or GPO in English-speaking countries) in a capital or large city.

Letters should be addressed clearly to you (with your family name in capitals) at Poste Restante, General Post Office (English-speaking countries) or PTT (Francophone countries), then the town and country where you want to collect the mail.

To collect your mail, go to the post office and show your passport. Letters sometimes take a few weeks to work through the system, so have them sent to a place where you're going to be for a while, or will be passing through more than once. Some poste restantes make a charge when you collect mail, and some only hold it for a limited time (around a month).

Some hotels and tour companies operate a mail-holding service, and American Express customers can have mail sent to Amex offices.

Telephone & Fax

Most cities and large towns have public telephone offices (either as part of the post office

or privately run) where you can make international calls and send faxes. Telephone and fax connections to places outside West Africa have improved greatly recently because international calls now go by satellite.

Calls between African countries, however, are sometimes relayed on land lines or through Europe, in which case the reception is usually bad – assuming you can get a call through in the first place. Another problem with calls within Africa is the waiting time between placing your call with the operator and actually getting through, which can be minutes or hours depending on the locality and time of day. Calling from the USA,

---

International Telephone Codes

To West Africa

To phone West Africa from abroad, you need to use the country code. This is preceded by an international access code (usually ☎ 00 or 010), often represented by a + sign. In many West African countries, city or area codes are not used, so go straight to the individual number you need.

Country codes for West African countries are given in the facts box at the start of each country chapter.

From West Africa

To phone Europe/USA/Australasia from West Africa, first dial the international access code (see above) then the code of the country you want to reach, then the city or area code (omitting the 0), then the individual number.

Australia	+61
Belgium	+32
Canada	+1
France	+33
Germany	+49
Netherlands	+31
New Zealand	+64
South Africa	+27
UK	+44
USA	+1

Europe or Australasia to West Africa is usually easier.

Costs for international calls and faxes to Europe, the USA or Australasia start at about US$3 per minute, although a few countries offer reduced rates at night. In some West African countries you can buy stored-value phonecards at post offices or telephone offices. Using these solves the problem of finding the correct coins for calls, and usually makes international calls slightly cheaper. At some airports and top end hotels in the major capitals, telephones may accept credit cards, but bear in mind that the rates can be extremely high.

If you would rather have somebody else pay for the call (or add the charges to your own home bill), it may be possible from some countries to dial directly to an operator in your home country. You can then reverse the charges, or charge the call to a phone company charge card. 'Home direct' numbers are usually toll free but if you are using a public phone booth you may need a coin or local phonecard to be connected with the relevant home operator. Access numbers vary from country to country, and are currently only available in a few West African countries. Check with your home phone company before you leave for the latest information. Note that home direct services can end up being more expensive than paying the local direct-dial tariff.

Another type of phonecard that may be available in some countries is a Country card that gives you a discount on calls to specified countries.

Telegram
This archaic method of communication is often overlooked, but if all you want to do is to send an 'All OK' message to loved ones at home, it can be cheaper than phone or fax. A 10 word minimum (including address) is sometimes imposed but the charge is rarely more than US$3. Ask at main post offices.

Email & Internet Access
In some countries, telephone offices also offer an email service, but this is still in its infancy and not always reliable. Internet centres (and even a few Internet cafes) can be found in most capital cities, where you can send email simply by paying to use a terminal for an hour or longer. Receiving email is less straightforward. Some Internet centres won't allow one-off messages to be sent to them for you to pick up, as they're geared to local companies and individuals setting up subscriptions.

Many hotels and tour companies have email facilities and will allow clients to send and receive messages, usually at a minimal cost.

INTERNET RESOURCES
The World Wide Web is a rich resource for travellers. You can research your trip, hunt down bargain air fares, book hotels, check on weather conditions or chat with locals and other travellers about the best places to visit (or avoid!). Some Web sites that may be of interest to travellers to West Africa are listed in the boxed text on the following page.

The Lonely Planet Web site (www.lonely planet.com) is a good place to start looking. Here you'll find succinct summaries on travelling to most places on earth, postcards from other travellers and the Thorn Tree bulletin board, where you can ask questions before you go or dispense advice when you get back. You can also find travel news and updates to many of our most popular guidebooks, and the subWWWay section links you to the most useful travel resources elsewhere on the Web.

BOOKS
This section lists publications covering the whole (or most) of West Africa. For more information see also Literature under Arts in the Facts about the Region chapter, and the Arts and Books sections of individual country chapters.

Some specialist publications are listed in the Flora & Fauna section of the Facts about the Region chapter, and in the special sections 'Birds of West Africa' and 'West African Music'. If you're planning to take

Internet Resources

If you have access to the Internet, you can get hold of all sorts of information about West Africa. Some Web sites that may be worth checking out include:

Index on Africa
http://www.africaindex.africainfo.no/index.html
Put together by the Norwegian Council for Africa, this site claims to be a comprehensive guide to the continent on the net – and is. Surf this site for a long reading list, links to other web resources, and country-by-country information on music, craft, facts and figures, culture, cooking (even recipes!), a language database, and media links.

African Birdclub
http://www.africanbirdclub.org/
This UK-based organisation's site provides interesting reading for those going to West Africa to birdwatch. The site includes excerpts from the association's newsletter, good photos, and links to other bird sites.

The Electronic African Bookworm
http://www.hanszell.co.uk/navtitle.htm
This directory of more than 400 links is designed for the book publishing industry, but travellers could make the most of the useful links to African media, Africa-studies resources, and the impressive set of African literature links.

Arts and Life in Africa Online
http://cas15.cas.uiowa.edu/
This site, set up by the University of Iowa, has a heap of information on countries and specific peoples, and lots of good links to museums, exhibits, miscellaneous African resources and the African Studies Centres of other American universities.

The Elephant – African Search Engine
http://www.alphablondy.com/websearch/index.html
Although not specifically West African, this search engine has lots of good links, especially for West African music.

In addition, Lonely Planet's homepage (www.lonelyplanet.com) has links to sites on selected West African countries, including Ghana and Côte d'Ivoire.

---

your own vehicle to or around West Africa, a selection of handbooks is listed in the Land section of the Getting There & Away chapter.

Note that bookshops and libraries search for publications by title or author, so publisher details have not been included unless particularly relevant. Also note that we have only listed titles available in English; there are many more publications in French.

Lonely Planet

If you're looking for more in-depth coverage of the countries covered by this book, Lonely Planet has a travel guide to *The Gambia & Senegal*. For onward travel, the guide to *East Africa* includes Tanzania, Uganda and Kenya, while *Africa – the South* includes Malawi, Zambia, Zimbabwe, Namibia, Botswana, South Africa and other countries.

Also look out for *Mali Blues: Travelling to an African Beat*, by Lieve Joris, published in Lonely Planet's travel literature series. It's a collection of four stories set in Mali, Mauritania and Senegal, in which the writer captures the rhythms of everyday life in the region, and tells the uplifting and tragic stories of its people.

For Francophone Africa, Lonely Planet's *French phrasebook* is, of course, highly recommended.

Exploration & Travel

This selection of books covers exploration and travel in the West African region, from precolonial times to the present day.

Travels in West Africa, by Mary Kingsley, was written in the late 19th century and, despite the title, is mostly confined to Cameroon and Gabon. It captures the spirit of the age, as the author describes encounters with wild places and wild people, all the while gathering fish specimens and facing every calamity with flamboyance, good humour and typically Victorian fortitude.

The Fearful Void, by Geoffrey Moorhouse, is a classic account of the author's 1970s attempt to cross the Sahara west to east, going via Chinguetti in Mauritania and Timbuktu in Mali, partly because nobody had done it before and partly to examine the basis of fear – 'an extremity of human existence'.

Impossible Journey: Two Against the Sahara, by Michael Asher, is an enthralling account of the first successful west-to-east camel crossing of the Sahara, starting in Mauritania and passing through Mali and Niger before ending at the Nile. Asher's wife, who joined him on the trip a short time after their meeting and marriage, took the stunning photos.

Desert Travels, by Chris Scott, is a lighthearted and readable account of various journeys by motorbike in the Sahara and West Africa, as the author graduates from empty-tanked apprentice to expert dune-cruiser and desert connoisseur.

Anatomy of Restlessness, by Bruce Chatwin, is a collection of writings by the same author, which includes discussion of his most recurring theme – the clash between nomads and settled civilisations – and a section on his 1970 visit to Timbuktu. This theme is also explored in his famous book *The Songlines*, which includes brief descriptions of Mauritania's nomadic Namadi people.

Chatwin's bewitching *Photographs & Notebooks* contains an intriguingly eclectic collection of pictures and observations from his travels, mainly in Mauritania, Mali and Benin.

For a more unusual kind of travel book, try *The Ends of the Earth*, by Robert Kaplan. The author visits areas frequently seen as cultural, political and ecological devastation zones, including West Africa, analysing what he sees (Liberian refugee camps, the breakdown of society in Sierra Leone, the massive growth of urban poverty along the coastal strip from Lomé to Abidjan) in terms of the present and the future – about which he cannot help but be darkly pessimistic.

Fiction

The Viceroy of Ouidah, by Bruce Chatwin, tells the story (partly based on fact) of a Brazilian trader stranded on the Slave Coast in the 17th century. But it's much more than this; with unique style and characteristic insight Chatwin also writes about history, imagination, human wanderlust and the spirit of Africa.

A Good Man in Africa, by William Boyd, is a humorous novel about a junior diplomat's struggles to maintain composure, all the time dealing with diplomats, presidents, girlfriends and the weather. *Brazzaville Beach*, set in West Africa, is far more mature, and discusses a range of themes, including the behavioural development of chimpanzees, human academic vanity, and depressing African civil wars.

The Music in My Head, by Mark Hudson, is an engaging and darkly amusing novel about the power, influence and day-to-day realities of modern African music, set in a mythical city, instantly recognisable as Dakar. The oppressive urban atmosphere is perfectly captured, and extra twists include an unreliable, Nabokovian narrator.

Reference

The nearest you'll get to a pocket library is *Africa*, by Phyllis Martin and Patrick O'Meara, with scholarly but accessible essays on a wide range of subjects including history, religion, colonialism, sociology, art, music, popular culture, law, literature, politics, economics and the development crisis.

The Resource Guide to Travel in Sub-Saharan Africa has an extensive, critical review of all guidebooks, maps, travelogues and specialist manuals to the region, plus information on travel magazines, bookshops, publishers, libraries, tourist organisations, special interest societies and conservation projects. Volume 1 covers East and West Africa.

History & Politics

A History of Africa, by JD Fage, and *A Short History of Africa*, by JD Fage and Roland Oliver, are both comprehensive and concise paperbacks, covering the whole continent.

Africa Since 1800, by Roland Oliver and Anthony Atmore, covers the precolonial period up to 1875, followed by partition and colonial rule, independence and the post-independence decades. Other books by the same authors include *Africa in the Iron Age* and *The African Middle Ages 1400-1800*.

African Civilization Revisited: From Antiquity to Modern Times and *A History of West Africa 1000-1800* are just two of the many books by Basil Davidson, a leading and influential writer on African history.

West Africa Since 1800, by JB Webster and AA Boahen, provides good in-depth treatment of the region in recent times.

The Africans, by David Lamb, is a portrait of early 1980s Africa, rich in political and social detail. The author visited 46 countries, revelling in midnight flights to witness little-known coups in obscure coun-

tries, but some critics suggest this rapid approach prevented in-depth understanding.

Africa: Dispatches From a Fragile Continent, by Blaine Harden, provides provocative and pessimistic reading on several topics, including the failure of African political leadership (the 'Big Man' syndrome).

In *Masters of Illusion – The World Bank and the Poverty of Nations* Catherine Caufield discusses the influence that the global development lending agency has had on poor countries around the world. The book's observations – that the social and environmental effects of projects are inadequately analysed – are shocking, while the conclusions – that despite loans totalling billions of US dollars the people of the developing world are worse off now than before – calls the whole institution into question.

Ecology & Environment

Africa in Crisis, by Lloyd Timberlake, emphasises that ecological issues cannot be regarded in isolation, and focuses on the political and environmental factors contributing to drought and famine in Africa, particularly the roles of international aid organisations and African leaders.

Squandering Eden, by Mort Rosenblum & Doug Williamson, is highly readable and proposes that broad-based stable development is dependent totally on workable relationships between African landholders and their environment.

African Silences, by Peter Matthiessen, is a deeply gripping, beautifully written book about the author's journeys through parts of West and Central Africa, and includes descriptions of research trips to estimate elephant populations in the region.

Arts

African Art, by Frank Willett, is a superb, well-illustrated and wide-ranging introductory paperback, while *African Art in Cultural Perspective*, by William Bascom, focuses on West and Central African sculpture. The large-format, full-colour and fantastically detailed *Africa Adorned*, by Angela Fisher, has an excellent section on West African jewellery and how it relates to cultural and social structures.

More specialist titles include: *A Short History of African Art*, by Gillon Werner; *African Traditional Architecture*, by Susan Denyer; *African Textiles*, by John Picton and John Mack, the best book on the subject (with numerous photographs); *Africa Through the Eyes of Women Artists*, by Betty La Duke; *African Hairstyles*, by Esi Sagay; and *Beads From the West African Trade*, by Picard African Imports. *Beads*, by Janet Coles and Robert Budwig, has a section on Africa, and is beautifully illustrated.

African Arts is a superb quarterly published by the African Studies Center (UCLA, Los Angeles, CA 90024), with good photography and well researched articles.

Dictionaries & Phrasebooks

Apart from Lonely Planet's indispensable *French phrasebook*, other phrasebooks include the *Portuguese Phrasefinder*, published by Collins Gem. For those words the phrasebook doesn't cover, the *French Dictionary* and *Portuguese Dictionary*, also published by Collins Gem, are much more comprehensive and only slightly larger than the phrasebooks.

NEWSPAPERS & MAGAZINES

There are no daily or weekly newspapers which cover the whole of West Africa, but several countries have national papers with good regional coverage. These are listed in the individual country chapters. Magazines covering the region, produced in English and available in most English-speaking countries (in Africa and elsewhere), include:

African Business Economic reports, finance and company news.
Africa Today Good political and economic news, plus business, sport and tourism.
Business in Africa A thick bi-monthly concentrating on business and tourism, with a bias towards West African and South African subjects.
Focus on Africa Published quarterly by the BBC, it has excellent news stories, accessible reports and a concise run-down of recent political events.

New African With a reputation for accurate and balanced reporting, it has a mix of politics, financial and economic analysis, features on social and cultural affairs, sport, art, health and recreation.
West Africa A long-standing and well respected weekly concentrating on political and economic news.

There are many more periodicals produced in French. The most widely available is *Jeune Afrique*, a popular weekly magazine covering regional and world events.

RADIO & TV

All countries in the region have state-run and commercial radio stations, although national TV is rarely received outside capitals and major towns. Details of local stations of interest to travellers are given in the country chapters.

International radio stations can be vital if you want to keep abreast of world events while travelling. These include Voice of America (for information on broadcast frequencies see their Web site on www.VOA .gov/) and the BBC World Service, which can be picked up on various short wave frequencies (listed in the BBC *Focus on Africa* magazine and on their Web site www.BBC .co.uk/worldservice/) and is also relayed on FM by several local radio stations.

Many top end and mid-range hotels have satellite dishes to receive international TV such as CNN and BBC World, as well as many French channels.

PHOTOGRAPHY & VIDEO

You'll find plenty of subjects in West Africa for photography (with a video or 'normal' camera), but if this is a primary reason for your visit it's important to avoid the harmattan season between December and mid-February (see the Climate section in the Facts about the Region chapter for more details).

Film & Equipment

Film in West Africa is expensive (from US$6 to US$14 for 24 or 36 exposures) because it has to be imported. Outside major capital cities only standard print film (not slide or large format) is available. Also, even if the expiry date is still good, the film may have been damaged by the intense African heat. It's best to bring all you need with you.

The sunlight in West Africa is frequently very intense, so most people find 100 ASA perfectly adequate, with possibly 200 ASA or 400 ASA for long-lens shots or visits to coastal areas in the rainy season.

Useful photographic accessories might include a small flash, a cable or remote shutter release, filters and a cleaning kit. Also, remember to take spare batteries.

Finally, a few airports have X-ray machines for checking baggage which may not be safe for film. Even so-called film-safe models can affect high-speed film (1000 ASA and higher), especially if the film goes through several checks during your trip, so you may want to use a protective lead bag – they're fairly inexpensive. Alternatively, carry your film in your pocket, and have it checked manually by customs officials.

For video cameras, you may find tapes in capitals and other large towns, but qualities and formats vary. While travelling, you can recharge batteries in hotels as you go along, so take the necessary charger, plugs and transformer for the country you are visiting.

TIME

Burkina Faso, Côte d'Ivoire, Gambia, Ghana, Guinea, Guinea-Bissau, Liberia,

---

Photography Hints

Timing
The best times to take photographs on sunny days are the first two hours after sunrise and the last two before sunset. This takes advantage of the colour-enhancing rays cast by a low sun. Filters (eg ultraviolet, polarising or 'skylight') can also help produce good results; ask for advice in a good camera shop.

Exposure
When photographing animals or people, take light readings on the subject and not the brilliant African background or your shots will turn out underexposed.

Camera Care
Factors that can spoil your camera or film include heat, humidity, very fine sand, saltwater and sunlight. Take appropriate precautions.

Wildlife Photography
For wildlife shots, a good lightweight 35mm SLR automatic camera with a lens between 210mm and 300mm should do the trick. Videos with zoom facility may be able to get closer. If your subject is nothing but a speck in the distance, try to resist wasting film but keep the camera ready.

Restrictions
Generally, you should avoid taking pictures of bridges, dams, airports, military equipment, government buildings and *anything* that could be considered strategic. You may be arrested or have your film and camera confiscated. Some countries – usually those with precarious military governments – are particularly hot on this. If in doubt, ask first.

Mali, Mauritania, Senegal, Sierra Leone and Togo are at GMT/UTC. Cape Verde is one hour behind. Benin, Niger and Nigeria are one hour ahead. None of the West African countries in this book observe daylight saving.

When it's noon in the following West African countries, not taking account of daylight saving, the time elsewhere is:

	Benin, Niger & Nigeria	Cape Verde	Other Countries
London	11 am	1 pm	noon
New York	6 am	8 am	7 am
Paris	noon	2 pm	1 pm
Sydney	9 pm	11 pm	10 pm

ELECTRICITY

The electricity supply throughout West Africa is 220V. Liberia also uses 110V. Plugs are usually the European two round pin variety. In former British colonies you may also find plugs with three square pins, as used in Britain.

WEIGHTS & MEASURES

The metric system is used in West Africa. To convert between metric and imperial units refer to the conversion chart at the back of this book.

LAUNDRY

Throughout West Africa, finding someone to wash your clothes is fairly simple. The top

---

Photography Hints

Photographing People

Like people everywhere, some Africans may enjoy being photographed, but others do not. They may be superstitious about your camera, suspicious of your motives, or simply interested in whatever economic advantage they can gain from your desire to photograph them. To some people in poor areas, a foreigner with a camera is seen, understandably, as simply a chance to make money. If you want a picture, you have to pay, although doing this is a controversial issue. Other locals maintain their pride and never want to be photographed, money or not. Some tourists go for discreet shots with long lenses, which smacks a bit of voyeurism. Others ask permission first. If you get 'no' for an answer, accept it. Just snapping away is rude and unbelievably arrogant.

Local people may agree to be photographed if you give them a picture for themselves. If you don't carry a Polaroid camera, take their address and make it clear that you'll post the photo. Your promise will be taken seriously. Never say you'll send a photo, and then don't. Alternatively, just be honest and say that so many people ask you for photos that it's impossible to send one to everyone.

Video photographers should follow the same rules, as most locals find them even more annoying and offensive than still cameras.

The bottom line is, always ask permission first, whether you have a still camera or a video camera.

Sacred Sites

Some local people are unhappy if you take pictures of their place of worship or a natural feature with traditional religious significance. In some instances, dress may be important. In mosques, for instance, wearing long trousers and removing your shoes may make it more likely that your hosts won't object.

end and mid-range hotels charge per item. At cheaper hotels, a staff member will do the job, or find you somebody else who can. The charge is also usually per item, but cheaper than at the big hotels, and often negotiable.

TOILETS

There are two main types of toilet in Africa: the western style, with a toilet bowl and seat; and the African style, which is a hole in the floor, over which you squat. Standards can vary tremendously, from pristine to unusable. Some travellers complain that African toilets are difficult to use, but it just takes a little practice to master a comfortable squatting technique.

In rural areas squat toilets are built over a deep hole in the ground. These are called 'long drops', and the waste matter just fades away naturally, as long as the hole isn't filled with too much other rubbish (such as paper or synthetic materials, including tampons – ideally these should be burnt separately).

Some western toilets are not plumbed in, but just balanced over a long drop, and sometimes seats are constructed to assist the people who can't do the business unsupported. The lack of running water usually makes such cross-cultural mechanisms a disaster. A noncontact hole in the ground is better than a filthy bowl to hover over any day.

HEALTH

Travel health depends on your predeparture preparations, your daily health care while travelling and how you handle any medical problems that may develop. While the potential dangers can seem quite frightening, in reality few travellers experience anything more than an upset stomach.

Predeparture Planning

Immunisations For some countries no immunisations are necessary, but the further off the beaten track you go the more necessary it is to take precautions. Be aware that there is often a greater risk of disease with children and in pregnancy. More details on

the diseases these immunisations protect against are given later in this section.

Plan ahead: some vaccinations require more than one injection, while some vaccinations should not be given together. Note that some vaccinations should not be given during pregnancy or in people with allergies – discuss with your doctor.

It is recommended you seek medical advice at least six weeks before travel. Record all vaccinations on an International Certificate of Vaccination, available from your doctor or government health department.

Discuss your requirements with your doctor, but vaccinations you should consider for West Africa include:

Diphtheria & Tetanus Vaccinations for these two diseases are usually combined and are recommended for everyone. After an initial course of three injections (usually given in childhood), boosters are necessary every 10 years.

Polio Everyone should keep up to date with this vaccination, which is normally given in childhood. A booster every 10 years maintains immunity.

Hepatitis A Hepatitis A vaccine (eg Avaxim, Havrix 1440 or VAQTA) provides long-term immunity (possibly more than 10 years) after an initial injection and a booster at six to 12 months.

Alternatively, an injection of gamma globulin can provide short-term protection against hepatitis A – two to six months, depending on the dose given. It is not a vaccine, but is ready-made antibody collected from blood donations. It is reasonably effective and, unlike the vaccine, it is protective immediately, but because it is a blood product, there are current concerns about its long-term safety.

Hepatitis A vaccine is also available in a combined form, Twinrix, with hepatitis B vaccine. Three injections over a six-month period are required, the first two providing substantial protection against hepatitis A.

Typhoid Vaccination against typhoid may be required if you are travelling for more than a couple of weeks in West Africa. It is now available either as an injection or as capsules to be taken orally.

Cholera The current injectable vaccine against cholera is poorly protective and has many side effects, so it is not generally recommended for travellers. However, in some situations it may be necessary to have a certificate as travellers are very occasionally asked by immigration officials to present one, even though all countries and the WHO have dropped cholera immunisation as a health requirement for entry.

Meningococcal Meningitis Vaccination is recommended for travellers to West Africa (as well as some other parts of the world). A single injection gives good protection against the major epidemic forms of the disease for three years. Protection may be less effective in children under two years.

Hepatitis B Travellers who should consider vaccination against hepatitis B include those on a long trip, as well as those visiting countries where there are high levels of hepatitis B infection, where blood transfusions may not be adequately screened or where sexual contact or needle sharing is a possibility. Vaccination involves three injections, with a booster at 12 months. More rapid courses are available if necessary.

Yellow Fever This disease is endemic in West Africa, and vaccination is recommended. You may have to go to a special yellow fever vaccination centre.

Rabies Vaccination should be considered by those who will spend a month or longer in a country where rabies is common, especially if they are cycling, handling animals, caving or travelling to remote areas, and for children (who may not report a bite). Pretravel rabies vaccination involves having three injections over 21 to 28 days. If someone who has been vaccinated is bitten or scratched by an animal, they will require two booster injections of vaccine; those not vaccinated require more.

Tuberculosis The risk of TB to travellers is usually very low, unless you will be living with or closely associated with local people in high risk areas such as West Africa and some other parts of the world. Vaccination against TB (BCG) is recommended for children and young adults living in these areas for three months or more.

Malaria Medication Antimalarial drugs do not prevent you from being infected but kill the malaria parasites during a stage in their development and significantly reduce the risk of becoming very ill or dying. Expert advice on medication should be sought, as there are many factors to consider including the area to be visited, the risk of exposure to malaria-carrying mosquitoes, the side effects of medication, your medical history and whether you are a child or adult or pregnant. Travellers to isolated areas in high risk countries may want to carry a

Medical Kit Check List

Following is a list of items you should consider including in your medical kit – consult your pharmacist for brands available in your country.

☐ **Aspirin** or **paracetamol** (acetaminophen in the USA) – for pain or fever.

☐ **Antihistamine** – for allergies, eg hay fever; to ease itch from insect bites or stings; and to prevent motion sickness.

☐ **Antibiotics** – consider including these if you're travelling well off the beaten track; see your doctor, as they must be prescribed, and carry the prescription with you.

☐ **Loperamide** or **diphenoxylate** – 'blockers' for diarrhoea, and **prochlorperazine** or **metaclopramide** for nausea and vomiting.

☐ **Rehydration mixture** – to prevent dehydration, eg due to severe diarrhoea; particularly important when travelling with children.

☐ **Insect repellent, sunscreen, lip balm** and **eye drops.**

☐ **Calamine lotion, sting relief spray or aloe vera** – to ease irritation from sunburn and insect bites or stings.

☐ **Antifungal cream or powder** – for fungal skin infections and thrush.

☐ **Antiseptic** (such as povidone-iodine) – for cuts and grazes.

☐ **Bandages, Band-Aids (plasters)** and other **wound dressings.**

☐ **Water purification tablets** or **iodine.**

☐ **Scissors, tweezers** and a **thermometer** – note that mercury thermometers are prohibited by airlines.

☐ **Syringes** and **needles** – for injections in a country with medical hygiene problems. Ask your doctor for a note explaining why you have them.

☐ **Cold and flu tablets, throat lozenges** and **nasal decongestant.**

☐ **Multivitamins** – consider for long trips, when dietary vitamin intake may be inadequate.

treatment dose of medication for use if symptoms occur.

Health Insurance Make sure that you have adequate health insurance. See Travel Insurance under Visas & Documents earlier in this chapter for details.

Travel Health Guides If you are planning to be away or travelling in remote areas for a long period of time, you may like to consider taking a more detailed health guide.

CDC's Complete Guide to Healthy Travel, Open Road Publishing, 1997. The US Centers for Disease Control & Prevention recommendations for international travel.
Staying Healthy in Asia, Africa & Latin America, Dirk Schroeder, Moon Publications, 1994. Probably the best all-round guide to carry; it's detailed and well organised.
Travellers' Health, Dr Richard Dawood, Oxford University Press, 1995. Comprehensive, easy to read and authoritative, although it's rather large to lug around.
Where There is No Doctor, David Werner, Macmillan, 1994. A very detailed guide aimed at someone, such as a Peace Corps worker, going to work in an underdeveloped country.
Travel with Children, Maureen Wheeler, Lonely Planet Publications, 1995. Includes advice on travel health for younger children.

There are also a number of excellent travel health sites on the Internet, which are worth checking out. From Lonely Planet's home page there are links at www.lonelyplanet .com/weblinks/wlprep.htm#heal to the World Health Organization and the US Centers for Disease Control & Prevention.

Other Preparations Make sure you're healthy before you start travelling. If you are going on a long trip make sure your teeth are OK. If you wear glasses take a spare pair and your prescription.

If you require a particular medication take an adequate supply, as it may not be available locally. Take part of the packaging showing the generic name, rather than the brand, which will make getting replacements easier. It's a good idea to have a legible prescription or letter from your doctor to show that you legally use the medication to avoid any problems.

Basic Rules

Food Even travellers with sensitive stomachs can usually eat traditional African food if they ease themselves in gently to the change of diet. In any kind of restaurant, you might get a bit of stomach trouble if plates or cutlery aren't clean, but that can happen anywhere, and it doesn't happen often.

However, it's wise to take a few basic precautions. Vegetables and fruit should be washed with purified water or peeled where possible. Beware of ice cream which is sold in the street or anywhere it might have been melted and refrozen; if there's any doubt (eg a power cut in the last day or two), steer well clear. Shellfish such as mussels, oysters and clams should be avoided as well as undercooked meat, particularly in the form of mince. Steaming does not make shellfish safe for eating.

In West Africa, local-style food is usually safer than western-style food because it's cooked much longer (sometimes all day) and the ingredients are invariably fresh. On the other hand, food in a smarter restaurant may have been lingering in a refrigerator – in a city which has power-cuts. Basically, if a place looks clean and well run and the vendor also looks clean and healthy, then the food is probably safe. In general, places that are packed with travellers or locals will be fine, while empty restaurants are questionable. The food in busy restaurants is cooked and eaten quickly with little standing around, and is probably not reheated.

Water The number-one rule is *be careful of the water* and especially ice. If you don't know for certain that the water in your glass or coming out of the tap is safe, assume the worst. Reputable brands of bottled water or soft drinks are generally fine, although in some places bottles may be refilled with tap water. Only use water from containers with a serrated seal, not tops or corks. Take care

Nutrition

If your food is poor, if you're travelling hard and fast and therefore missing meals or if you simply lose your appetite, you can soon start to lose weight and place your health at risk.

Make sure your diet is well balanced. Cooked eggs, beans and nuts are all safe ways to get protein. Fruit you can peel (eg bananas, oranges or mandarins) is usually safe and a good source of vitamins. Note, however, that melons can harbour bacteria in their flesh and are best avoided. Try to eat plenty of grains (including rice) and bread. Remember that although food is generally safer if it is cooked well, overcooked food loses much of its nutritional value. If your diet isn't well balanced or if your food intake is insufficient, it's a good idea to take vitamin supplements.

In hot climates make sure you drink enough – don't rely on feeling thirsty to indicate when you should drink. Not needing to urinate or small amounts of very dark yellow urine is a danger sign. Always carry a water bottle with you on long trips. Excessive sweating can lead to loss of salt and therefore muscle cramping. Salt tablets are not a good idea as a preventative, but in places where salt is not used much, adding salt to food can help.

with fruit juice, particularly if water may have been added. Milk should be treated with suspicion as it is often unpasteurised, although boiled milk is fine if it is kept hygienically. Tea or coffee should also be OK, since the water should have been boiled.

Water Purification The simplest way of purifying water is to boil it thoroughly. Alternatively, consider purchasing a water filter for a long trip.

There are two main kinds of filter. Total filters take out all parasites, bacteria and viruses, and make water safe to drink. They are often expensive, but they can be more cost-effective than buying bottled water. Simple filters (which can even be a nylon mesh bag) take out dirt and larger foreign bodies from the water so that chemical solutions work much more effectively; if water is dirty, chemical solutions may not work at all. It's very important when buying a filter to read the specifications, so that you know exactly what it removes from the water and what it doesn't.

Simple filtering will not remove all dangerous organisms, so if you can't boil water it should be treated chemically. Chlorine tablets will kill many pathogens, but not some parasites like giardia and amoebic cysts. Iodine is more effective in purifying water and is available in tablet form. Follow the directions carefully and remember that too much iodine can be harmful.

Medical Problems & Treatment

Correct diagnosis is vital. Self-diagnosis and treatment can be risky, so you should always seek medical help. In West Africa, most capitals and large towns have at least one hospital, as well as private clinics, surgeries and pharmacies. Where available, medical facilities are listed in the Information sections of large cities in individual country chapters. Alternatively, an embassy, consulate or good hotel can usually recommend a place to go for advice.

Although we do give drug dosages in this section, they are for emergency use only. Where relevant we have used the generic names of medicines – check with your pharmacist for brands available locally.

Antibiotics should ideally be administered only under medical supervision. Take only the recommended dose at the prescribed intervals and use the whole course, even if the illness seems to be cured earlier. Stop immediately if there are any serious reactions and don't use the antibiotic at all if you are unsure that you have the correct one. Some people are allergic to commonly prescribed antibiotics, such as penicillin; carry this information (eg on a bracelet) when travelling.

Everyday Health

Normal body temperature is 37°C (98.6°F); more than 2°C (4°F) higher indicates a high fever. The normal adult pulse rate is 60 to 100 beats per minute (children 80 to 100, babies 100 to 140). As a general rule the pulse increases about 20 beats per minute for each 1°C (2°F) rise in temperature above normal.

Respiration (breathing) rate is also an indicator of illness. Count the number of breaths per minute: between 12 and 20 is normal for adults and older children. For younger children, it's up to 30 breaths per minute, 40 for babies. People with a high fever or serious respiratory illness breathe more quickly than normal. More than 40 shallow breaths a minute may indicate pneumonia.

Environmental Hazards

Heat Exhaustion Dehydration and salt deficiency can cause heat exhaustion. Take time to acclimatise to high temperatures, drink sufficient liquids and do not do anything too physically demanding.

Salt deficiency is characterised by fatigue, lethargy, headaches, giddiness and muscle cramps; salt tablets may help, but adding extra salt to your food is better.

Anhidrotic heat exhaustion is a rare form of heat exhaustion that is caused by an inability to sweat. It tends to affect people who have been in a hot climate for some time, rather than newcomers. It can progress to heatstroke. Treatment involves removal to a cooler climate.

Heatstroke This serious, occasionally fatal, condition can occur if the body's heat-regulating mechanism breaks down and the body temperature rises to dangerous levels. Long, continuous periods of exposure to high temperatures and insufficient fluids can leave you vulnerable to heatstroke.

The symptoms are feeling unwell, not sweating very much (or at all) and a high body temperature (39 to 41°C or 102 to 106°F). Where sweating has ceased the skin becomes flushed and red. Severe, throbbing headaches and lack of coordination will also occur, plus confusion or aggression. Eventually the victim will become delirious or convulse. Hospitalisation is essential, but in the interim get victims out of the sun, remove their clothing, cover them with a wet sheet or towel and then fan continually. Give fluids if they are conscious.

Prickly Heat Prickly heat is an itchy rash caused by excessive perspiration trapped under the skin. It usually strikes people who have just arrived in a hot climate. Keeping cool, bathing often, drying the skin and using a mild talcum or prickly heat powder or resorting to air-conditioning may help.

Sunburn In West Africa you can get sunburnt surprisingly quickly, even through cloud. Use a sunscreen, hat, and barrier cream for your nose and lips. Calamine lotion or aloe vera are good for mild sunburn. Protect your eyes with good quality sunglasses, particularly if you will be near water or sand.

Jet Lag Jet lag is experienced when a person travels by air across more than three time zones (each time zone usually represents a one-hour time difference). It occurs because many of the functions of the human body (such as temperature, pulse rate and emptying of the bladder and bowels) are regulated by internal 24-hour cycles. When we travel long distances rapidly, our bodies take time to adjust to the 'new time' of our destination, and we may experience fatigue, disorientation, insomnia, anxiety, impaired concentration and loss of appetite. These effects will usually be gone within three days of arrival, but to minimise the impact of jet lag:

- Rest for a couple of days prior to departure.
- Try to select flight schedules that minimise sleep deprivation; arriving late in the day means you can go to sleep soon after you arrive. For very long flights, try to organise a stopover.

- Avoid excessive eating (which bloats the stomach) and alcohol (which causes dehydration) during the flight. Instead, drink plenty of noncarbonated, nonalcoholic drinks such as fruit juice or water.
- Avoid smoking.
- Make yourself comfortable by wearing loose-fitting clothes and perhaps bringing an eye mask and ear plugs to help you sleep.
- Try to sleep at the appropriate time for the time zone you are travelling to.

Motion Sickness Eating lightly before and during a trip will reduce the chances of motion sickness. If you are prone to motion sickness try to find a place that minimises movement – near the wing on aircraft, close to midships on boats, near the centre on buses. Fresh air usually helps; reading and cigarette smoke don't.

Most commercial motion-sickness preparations, which can cause drowsiness, need to be taken before you set off. Ginger (available in capsule form) and peppermint are natural preventatives.

Infectious Diseases

Diarrhoea Simple things like a change of water, food or climate can all cause a mild bout of diarrhoea, but a few rushed toilet trips with no other symptoms is not indicative of a major problem.

Dehydration is the main danger with any diarrhoea, particularly in children or the elderly as dehydration can occur quite quickly. Under all circumstances *fluid replacement* (at least equal to the volume being lost) is the most important thing to remember. Weak black tea with a little sugar, soda water, or soft drinks allowed to go flat and diluted 50% with clean water are all good.

With severe diarrhoea a rehydrating solution is preferable to replace minerals and salts lost. Commercially available oral rehydration salts (ORS) are very useful; add them to boiled or bottled water. In an emergency you can make up a solution of six teaspoons of sugar and a half teaspoon of salt to a litre of boiled or bottled water.

You need to drink at least the same volume of fluid that you are losing in bowel movements and vomiting. Urine is the best guide to the adequacy of replacement – if you have small amounts of concentrated urine, you need to drink more. Keep drinking small amounts often. Stick to a bland diet as you recover.

Gut-paralysing drugs such as loperamide or diphenoxylate can be used to bring relief from the symptoms, although they do not actually cure the problem. Only use these drugs if you do not have access to toilets, eg if you *must* travel. For children under 12 years loperamide and diphenoxylate preparations are not recommended. Do not use these drugs if the person has a high fever or is severely dehydrated.

Antibiotics may be required if you are experiencing the following: diarrhoea with blood or mucus (dysentery), any diarrhoea with fever, profuse watery diarrhoea, persistent diarrhoea not improving after 48 hours and severe diarrhoea. These suggest a more serious cause of diarrhoea and in these situations gut-paralysing drugs should be avoided.

In these situations, a stool test may be necessary to diagnose what bug is causing your diarrhoea, so you should seek medical help urgently. Where this is not possible the recommended drugs for bacterial diarrhoea (the most likely cause of severe diarrhoea in travellers) are norfloxacin 400mg twice daily for three days or ciprofloxacin 500mg twice daily for five days. These are not recommended for children or pregnant women. The drug of choice for children would be cotrimoxazole with dosage dependent on weight. A five day course is given. Ampicillin or amoxycillin may be given in pregnancy, but medical care is necessary.

Two other causes of persistent diarrhoea in travellers are giardiasis and amoebic dysentery.

Giardiasis is caused by a common parasite, *Giardia lamblia*. Symptoms include stomach cramps, nausea, a bloated stomach, watery, foul-smelling diarrhoea and frequent gas. Giardiasis can appear several weeks after you have been exposed to the parasite. The symptoms may disappear for a few days and then return; this can go on for several weeks.

Amoebic dysentery, caused by the protozoan *Entamoeba histolytica*, is characterised by a gradual onset of low-grade diarrhoea, often with blood and mucus. Cramping abdominal pain and vomiting are less likely than in other types of diarrhoea, and fever may not be present. It will persist until treated and can recur and cause other health problems.

You should seek medical advice if you think you have giardiasis or amoebic dysentery, but where this is not possible, tinidazole or metronidazole are the recommended drugs. Treatment is a 2g single dose of tinidazole or 250mg of metronidazole three times daily for five to 10 days.

Fungal Infections Fungal infections occur more commonly in hot weather and are usually found on the scalp, between the toes (athlete's foot) or fingers, in the groin and on the body (ringworm). You get ringworm (which is a fungal infection, not a worm) from infected animals or other people. Moisture encourages these infections.

To prevent fungal infections wear loose, comfortable clothes, avoid artificial fibres, wash frequently and dry yourself carefully. If you do get an infection, wash the infected area at least once daily with a disinfectant or medicated soap and water, and rinse and dry well. Apply an antifungal cream or powder like tolnaftate. Try to expose the infected area to air or sunlight as much as possible and wash all towels and underwear in hot water, change them often and let them dry in the sun.

Hepatitis Hepatitis is a general term for inflammation of the liver. It is a common disease worldwide. There are several different viruses that cause hepatitis, and they differ in the way that they are transmitted. The symptoms are similar in all forms of the illness, and include fever, chills, headache, fatigue, feelings of weakness and aches and pains, followed by loss of appetite, nausea, vomiting, abdominal pain, dark urine, light-coloured faeces, jaundiced (yellow) skin and yellowing of the whites of the eyes. People who have had hepatitis should avoid alcohol for some time after the illness, as the liver needs time to recover.

Hepatitis A is transmitted by contaminated food and drinking water. You should seek medical advice, but there is not much you can do apart from to rest, drink lots of fluids, eat lightly and avoid fatty foods. **Hepatitis E** is transmitted in the same way as hepatitis A; it can be particularly serious in pregnant women.

There are approximately 300 million chronic carriers of **hepatitis B** in the world. It is spread through contact with infected blood, blood products or body fluids, for example through sexual contact, unsterilised needles and blood transfusions, or contact with blood via small breaks in the skin. Other risk situations include having a shave, tattoo or body piercing with contaminated equipment. The symptoms of hepatitis B may be more severe than type A and the disease can lead to long term problems such as chronic liver damage, liver cancer or a long term carrier state. **Hepatitis C** and **D** are spread in the same way as hepatitis B and can lead to long term complications.

There are vaccines against hepatitis A and B, but there are currently no vaccines against the other types of hepatitis. Following the basic rules about food and water (for hepatitis A and E) and avoiding risk situations (hepatitis B, C and D) are important preventative measures everyone should take.

HIV & AIDS Infection with HIV, the human immunodeficiency virus, may lead to the acquired immune deficiency syndrome (AIDS), which is a fatal disease. HIV is a major problem in many parts of the world, including West Africa. Any exposure to blood, blood products or body fluids may put the individual at risk. The disease is often transmitted through sexual contact or dirty needles – vaccinations, acupuncture, tattooing and body piercing can be potentially as dangerous as intravenous drug use.

HIV/AIDS can also be spread through infected blood transfusions; some developing countries, including countries in West Africa, cannot afford to screen blood used for transfusions. If you do need an injection, ask to see the syringe unwrapped in front of you, or take a needle and syringe pack with you. However, fear of HIV infection should never preclude treatment for serious medical conditions.

Intestinal Worms These parasites are most common in rural, tropical areas. The different worms have different ways of infecting people. Some may be ingested on food such as undercooked meat (eg tapeworms) and some enter through your skin (eg hookworms). Infestations may not show up for some time, and although they are generally not serious, if left untreated some can cause severe health problems later. Consider having a stool test when you return home to check for these and determine the appropriate treatment.

Meningococcal Meningitis This very serious disease attacks the brain and can be fatal. There are recurring epidemics in various parts of the world, including much of sub-Saharan Africa.

First symptoms include fever, severe headache, sensitivity to light and neck stiffness which prevents forward bending of the head. There may also be purple patches on the skin.

Death can occur within a few hours, so urgent medical treatment is required. Treatment is large doses of penicillin given intravenously, or chloramphenicol injections.

Schistosomiasis Also known as bilharzia, this disease is transmitted by minute worms. They infect certain varieties of freshwater snails found in rivers, streams, lakes and particularly behind dams. The worms multiply and are eventually discharged into the water.

The worm enters through the skin and attaches itself to your intestines or bladder. The first symptom may be a general feeling

of being unwell, or a tingling and sometimes a light rash around the area where it entered. Weeks later a high fever may develop. Once the disease is established abdominal pain and blood in the urine are other signs. The infection often causes no symptoms until the disease is well established (several months to years after exposure) and damage to internal organs irreversible.

Avoiding swimming or bathing in fresh water where bilharzia is present is the main method of preventing the disease. Even deep water can be infected. If you do get wet, dry off quickly and dry your clothes as well.

A blood test is the most reliable way to diagnose the disease, but the test will not show positive until a number of weeks after exposure.

Sexually Transmitted Diseases Gonorrhoea, herpes and syphilis are among these diseases; sores, blisters or rashes around the genitals, discharges or pain when urinating are common symptoms. In some STDs, such as wart virus or chlamydia, symptoms may be less marked or not observed at all especially in women. Chlamydia can make men or women infertile before they've noticed symptoms. Syphilis symptoms eventually disappear completely but the disease continues and can cause severe problems in later years.

While abstinence from sexual contact is the only 100% effective prevention, using condoms is also effective. The treatment of gonorrhoea and syphilis is with antibiotics. The different sexually transmitted diseases each require specific antibiotics.

Typhoid Typhoid fever is a dangerous gut infection transmitted by contaminated water and food. Medical help must be sought.

In its early stages sufferers may feel they have a bad cold or flu on the way, as early symptoms are a headache, body aches and a fever which rises a little each day until it is around 40°C (104°F) or more. The victim's pulse is often slow relative to the degree of fever present – unlike a normal fever where the pulse increases. There may also be vomiting, abdominal pain, diarrhoea or constipation.

In the second week the high fever and slow pulse continue and a few pink spots may appear on the body; trembling, delirium, weakness, weight loss and dehydration may occur. Complications include pneumonia, perforated bowel or meningitis.

Insect-Borne Diseases

Filariasis, leishmaniasis, sleeping sickness, typhus and yellow fever are all insect-borne diseases, but they do not pose a great risk to travellers. For more information on these illnesses, see Less Common Diseases later in this section.

Malaria This serious and potentially fatal disease is spread by mosquito bites. If you are travelling in endemic areas it is extremely important to avoid mosquito bites and to take tablets to prevent this disease. Symptoms range from fever, chills and sweating, headache, diarrhoea and abdominal pains to a vague feeling of ill-health. Seek medical help immediately if malaria is suspected. Without treatment malaria can rapidly become more serious and can be fatal.

If medical care is not available, malaria tablets can be used for treatment. You need to use a malaria tablet which is different from the one you were taking when you contracted malaria.

The standard treatment dose of mefloquine is two 250mg tablets and a further two six hours later. For Fansidar, it's a single dose of three tablets. If you were previously taking mefloquine and cannot obtain Fansidar, then other alternatives are Malarone (atovaquone-proguanil; four tablets once daily for three days), halofantrine (three doses of two 250mg tablets every six hours) or quinine sulphate (600mg every six hours). There is a greater risk of side effects with these dosages than in normal use if used with mefloquine, so medical advice is preferable. Be aware also that halofantrine is no longer recommended by the WHO as emergency standby treatment, because of side effects, and should only be used if no other drugs are available.

Travellers are advised to prevent mosquito bites at all times. The main messages are:

- wear light-coloured clothing
- wear long trousers and long-sleeved shirts
- use mosquito repellents containing the compound DEET on exposed areas (prolonged overuse of DEET may be harmful, especially to children, but its use is considered preferable to being bitten by disease-transmitting mosquitoes)
- avoid perfumes or aftershave
- use a mosquito net impregnated with mosquito repellent (permethrin) – it may be worth taking your own
- impregnating clothes with permethrin effectively deters mosquitoes and other insects

Dengue Fever This viral disease is transmitted by mosquitoes and occurs mainly in tropical and subtropical areas of the world. Generally, there is only a small risk to travellers except during epidemics, which usually occur during and just after the rainy season.

The *Aedes aegypti* mosquito, which transmits the dengue virus, is most active during the day, unlike the malaria mosquito, and is found mainly in urban areas, in and around human dwellings.

Signs and symptoms of dengue fever include a sudden onset of high fever, headache, joint and muscle pains (hence its old name, 'breakbone fever') and nausea and vomiting. A rash of small red spots appears three to four days after the onset of fever. Dengue is commonly mistaken for other infectious diseases, including influenza.

You should seek medical attention if you think you may be infected. Infection can be diagnosed by a blood test. There is no specific treatment for dengue. Aspirin should be avoided, as it increases the risk of haemorrhaging. Recovery may be prolonged, with tiredness lasting for several weeks. Severe complications are rare in travellers but include dengue haemorrhagic fever (DHF), which can be fatal without prompt medical treatment. DHF is thought to be a result of a second infection with a different strain (there are four major strains) and usually affects residents of the country rather than travellers.

There is no vaccine against dengue fever. The best prevention is to avoid mosquito bites at all times – see the malaria section earlier for advice.

Cuts, Bites & Stings

Bedbugs & Lice Bedbugs live in various places, but particularly in dirty mattresses and bedding – look for spots of blood on bedclothes or on the wall. Bedbugs leave itchy bites in neat rows. Calamine lotion or a sting relief spray may help.

All lice cause itching and discomfort. They make themselves at home in your hair (head lice), your clothing (body lice) or in your pubic hair ('crabs'). You catch lice through direct contact with infected people or by sharing combs, clothing and the like. Powder or shampoo treatment will kill the lice and infected clothing should then be washed in very hot, soapy water and left in the sun to dry.

Insect Bites & Stings Bee and wasp stings are usually painful rather than dangerous. Calamine lotion or a sting relief spray will help relieve discomfort and ice packs will reduce the pain and swelling. However, in people who are allergic to them, severe breathing difficulties may occur and they may require urgent medical care.

Scorpions often shelter under stones, but can creep into shoes or clothing (if you're sleeping in the bush), and their stings are notoriously painful. Check before dressing.

Cuts & Scratches Wash well and treat any cut with an antiseptic such as povidone-iodine. Where possible avoid bandages and Band-Aids, which can keep wounds wet. Coral cuts are notoriously slow to heal and if they are not adequately cleaned, small pieces of coral can become embedded in the wound.

Ticks You should always check all over your body if you have been walking through a potentially tick-infested area (such as long grass where cattle are grazing) as ticks can cause skin infections and other more serious diseases. If a tick is found attached, press down around the tick's head with tweezers, grab the head and gently pull upwards. Avoid pulling the rear of the body as this may squeeze the tick's gut contents through the attached mouth parts into the skin, increasing the risk of infection and disease. Smearing chemicals on the tick will not make it let go and is not recommended.

Snakes Travellers in West Africa very rarely see a snake let alone get bitten by one. However, to minimise your chances of being bitten you should always wear boots, socks and long trousers when walking through undergrowth where snakes may be present. Don't put your hands into holes and crevices, and be careful when collecting firewood.

If you are unlucky enough to get bitten, remember that snake bites do not cause death immediately and in some areas antivenenes may be available. Immediately wrap the bitten limb tightly, as for a sprained ankle, and then attach a splint to immobilise it. Keep the victim still and seek medical help, if possible with the dead snake for identification. Don't attempt to catch the snake if there is a possibility of being bitten again. Tourniquets and sucking out the poison are now comprehensively discredited.

Less Common Diseases

The following pose a small risk to travellers, and so are only mentioned in passing. Seek medical advice if you think you may have any of these diseases.

Cholera This is the worst of the watery diarrhoeas and medical help should be sought. Outbreaks of cholera are generally widely reported, so you can avoid such problem areas. *Fluid replacement is the most vital treatment* – the risk of dehydration is severe as you may lose up to 20L a day. If there is a delay in getting to hospital then begin taking tetracycline. The adult dose is 250mg four times daily. It is not recommended for children under nine years or for pregnant women. Tetracycline may help shorten the illness, but adequate fluids are required to save lives.

Filariasis This is a mosquito-transmitted parasitic infection found in parts of Africa (and elsewhere). Possible symptoms include fever, pain and swelling of the lymph glands, swelling of a limb or the scrotum, skin rashes and blindness. Treatment is available to eliminate the parasites from the body, but some of the damage already caused may not be reversible. Medical advice should be obtained promptly.

Leishmaniasis This is a group of parasitic diseases transmitted by sandfly bites, found in many parts of Africa (and elsewhere). Cutaneous leishmaniasis affects the skin tissue causing ulceration and disfigurement, and visceral leishmaniasis affects the internal organs. Seek medical advice as laboratory testing is required for diagnosis and correct treatment. Bites are usually painless, but itchy. Avoiding sandfly bites is the best precaution – yet another reason to cover up and apply insect repellent.

Rabies Rabies is a fatal viral infection found in many countries. Many animals can be infected (such as dogs, cats, bats and monkeys) and it is their saliva which is infectious. Any bite, scratch or even lick from a mammal should be cleaned immediately and thoroughly. Scrub with soap and running water, and then apply alcohol or iodine solution. Medical help should be sought promptly to receive a course of injections to prevent the onset of symptoms and death.

Sleeping Sickness In parts of tropical Africa tsetse flies can carry trypanosomiasis or sleeping sickness. The tsetse fly is about twice the size of a housefly and recognisable by the scissorlike way it folds its wings when at rest. Only a small proportion of tsetse flies carry the disease but it can be fatal without treatment. The only prevention is to avoid getting bitten. The flies are attracted to large moving objects such as cars, to perfume and aftershave, and to colours

like dark blue. Swelling at the site of the bite, five or more days later, is the first sign of infection; this is followed within two to three weeks by fever.

Tetanus This disease is caused by a germ which lives in soil and in the faeces of horses and other animals. It enters the body via breaks in the skin. The first symptom may be discomfort in swallowing, or stiffening of the jaw and neck; this is followed by painful convulsions of the jaw and whole body. The disease can be fatal. It can be prevented by vaccination.

Tuberculosis TB is a bacterial infection usually transmitted from person to person by coughing but may be transmitted through consumption of unpasteurised milk. Milk that has been boiled is safe to drink, and the souring of milk to make yoghurt or cheese also kills the bacilli. Travellers are usually not at great risk as close household contact with the infected person is usually required before the disease is passed on.

Typhus Typhus is spread by ticks, mites or lice. It begins with fever, chills, headache and muscle pains followed a few days later by a body rash. There is often a large painful sore at the site of the bite and nearby lymph nodes are swollen and painful. Typhus can be treated under medical supervision.

Seek local advice on areas where ticks pose a danger and always check your skin (including hair) carefully for ticks after walking in a danger area such as a tropical forest. A strong insect repellent can help, and serious walkers in potentially infested areas should consider having their boots and trousers impregnated with benzyl benzoate and dibutylphthalate.

Yellow Fever This viral disease is endemic in many African countries and is transmitted by mosquitoes. The initial symptoms are fever, headache, abdominal pain and vomiting. Seek medical care urgently and drink lots of fluids.

Women's Health

Gynaecological Problems Antibiotic use, synthetic underwear, sweating and contraceptive pills can lead to vaginal fungal infections, especially when travelling in hot climates. Fungal infections are characterised by a rash, itch and discharge and can be treated with a vinegar or lemon-juice douche, or with yoghurt. Nystatin, miconazole or clotrimazole pessaries or vaginal cream are the usual treatment. Maintaining good personal hygiene and wearing loose-fitting clothes and cotton underwear may help prevent these infections.

Sexually transmitted diseases are a major cause of vaginal problems. Symptoms include a smelly discharge, painful intercourse and sometimes a burning sensation when urinating. Medical attention should be sought and male sexual partners must also be treated. Remember that in addition to these diseases HIV or hepatitis B may also be acquired during exposure. Besides abstinence, the best thing is to practise safe sex using condoms.

Pregnancy It is not advisable to travel to some places while pregnant as some vaccinations normally used to prevent serious diseases are not advisable in pregnancy eg yellow fever. In addition, some diseases are much more serious for the mother (and may increase the risk of a stillborn child) in pregnancy eg malaria.

Pregnant women should avoid all unnecessary medication, although vaccinations and malarial prophylactics should still be taken where needed. Additional care should be taken to prevent illness and particular attention should be paid to diet and nutrition.

WOMEN TRAVELLERS

In general, women travellers (alone or with other women) in West Africa will not encounter significantly more gender-related problems, including sexual harassment, than they might in other parts of the world. Many women travellers report that, compared with North Africa, South America and some western countries, the region is

Positive Vibes

So much advice for women travellers concentrates on negative aspects – the following reader's letter is a refreshing and very welcome antidote.

I am a 22-year-old white female, and spent three months completing a gigantic loop through Senegal, Mali, Niger, Benin, Ghana, Côte d'Ivoire and Guinea. I travelled mostly alone and on a small budget. My gender had a profound influence on my trip, but far more than instances of sexual harassment, although I received invitation after invitation from consul officials, border guards, taxi drivers and market vendors.

I always wore a skirt and covered my hair, but often found myself surrounded by men. But not all these situations centred around requests for sex or visa papers – it's just that men are more likely to be in a situation to interact with foreign travellers. I often found myself among a crowd of 15 youths at a bus station – just the sheer numbers can be daunting! – and I won't elaborate on the tedious and lengthy learning process involved in understanding how to recognise innuendos, separate nice boys from those with ulterior motives and generally how to raise the red flag at the appropriate time.

Eventually, though, I did learn, and felt very comfortable going solo. I went to Agadez, and hiked 100km through the villages of the Fouta Djalon. And people took excellent care of me. People got my passport back for me from awkward border guards. They brought me home, showed me around, and gave me unlimited supplies of manioc and bananas. Once, even the local chief of police brought me back to his house, so his wife could take care of me.

Once I'd learnt how to react, it seemed that locals knew I'd been travelling for a while, and I certainly found it increasingly easy and enjoyable to be in Africa.

Amy Marsh

safe and unthreatening, and that friendliness and generosity are met with far more often than hostility.

Having said that, sexual harassment is a possibility, and this is discussed later in this section. And, of course, there are some parts of West Africa where mugging is a risk and, as in any place worldwide, women (particularly lone women) are generally seen as easy targets, so it pays to keep away from these areas. Particular risk areas are listed in individual country chapters.

When it comes to evening entertainment, West Africa is a conservative, male-dominated society and women travellers may come up against a few glass walls and ceilings. Cultural conventions often dictate that women don't go to bars without a male companion, and trying to buck the system may lead to trouble.

Because of these prevailing attitudes, it can be hard to specifically meet and talk with local women in the countries you're travelling through. It may require being invited into a home, although because many women receive little or no education, language can sometimes be a problem. However, this is changing to some extent because a surprising number of girls go to school while boys are sent away to work. This means that many of the staff in tourist offices, government departments and so on are educated young to middle-aged women, and this can be as good a place as any to try to strike up a conversation. In rural areas, a good starting point might be women teachers at a local school, or staff at a health centre.

When you're actually travelling, the best advice on what can and can't be undertaken safely will come from local women. Unfortunately, many white expatriates are likely to be appalled at the idea of lone female travel and will do their best to discourage you with horrendous stories, often of dubious accuracy. Having said that, although some countries in this region are considerably safer than other parts of the world, hitching alone is not recommended. Use common sense and things should go well.

Sexual Harassment

Despite sexual harassment being less of a problem for women travellers in West Africa than it is in some other parts of the world it is something that women, particularly lone women, have to occasionally deal with when travelling here. Unwanted interest is always unpleasant, but it's worth remembering that although you may encounter a lewd border official, or an admirer who won't go away, real harm or rape is actually very unlikely.

Part of the reason for the interest shown in you arises from the fact that local women rarely travel long distances alone, and a single foreign female is a very unusual sight. Another reason is that, thanks to imported TV and Hollywood films, western women are frequently assumed to be promiscuous.

What you wear may greatly influence how you're treated. African women dress conservatively, in traditional or western clothes, so when a visitor wears something significantly different from the norm, she will draw attention. In the minds of some men this peculiar dressing will be seen as provocative. In general, look at what other women are wearing and follow suit. Keep most of your legs covered, at least below the knee, with trousers, skirt or culottes.

If you're in an uneasy situation, act prudish. Stick your nose in a book. Or invent an imaginary husband who will be arriving shortly either in the country or at that particular spot. If you are travelling with a male companion, one of the best ways to avoid unwanted interest is to introduce him as your husband.

Tampons & Sanitary Towels

Tampons and towels (usually imported from Europe) are available from pharmacies or large supermarkets in capitals and large towns in West Africa. In tourist areas they are also available from shops at hotels. See the glossary for French terms for these items.

GAY & LESBIAN TRAVELLERS

All the countries covered in this book are conservative in their attitudes towards gays and lesbians, and gay sexual relationships are culturally taboo and rare to the point of nonexistence (although some homosexual activity – especially among younger men – does occur in some areas). In most places, open displays of affection are generally frowned upon, whatever your orientation, and show insensitivity to local feelings.

A USA-based tour company offering specialist tours, including West Africa, for gay men and women is All Continents Travel (☎ 800-368 6822 or 310-645 7527, fax 310-645 1071), 5250 West Century Blvd, Suite 626, Los Angeles, CA 90045.

DISABLED TRAVELLERS

People who don't walk will not have an easy time in West Africa. Even though there are more disabled people per head of population here than in the west, wheelchair facilities are virtually nonexistent. In the capitals of some countries, a few official buildings are constructed with ramps and lifts – but not many, and probably not the ones you want to visit.

SENIOR TRAVELLERS

West Africa is generally not ideal for senior travellers (on the assumption that you want to rough it less than younger folk) as good hotels are limited, and travel by public transport can be hard work. Having said that, we've heard from several retired people who have journeyed in West Africa and had a wonderful time, coping with deprivations that may have 20-year-olds rushing for the first flight home. Much comes down to attitude and expectations, rather than number of years.

TRAVEL WITH CHILDREN

In countries with a mainstream tourism industry some package tour hotels cater for families with children, and in large cities top end hotels usually have rooms with three or four beds for only slightly more than a double. Alternatively, arranging an extra bed or mattress so that children can share a standard adult double is not generally a problem.

Baby Basics

We were delighted to hear from a Canadian family who travelled for six weeks in Senegal, Guinea and Guinea-Bissau with a one-year-old baby, and sent the following tips for tiny travellers:

'In West Africa, travelling with a baby was not too difficult, even though life is different. People constantly wanted to touch him, and even though this bothered us on occasion, it was not serious. Most of the time we enjoyed the contact. We learned to travel light, and went with one 50 litre backpack and a baby carrier which also carried another 10 litres of luggage. Clothes could be washed every day, and dried while wearing them.

- We used small chlorine pills to clean water that was not bottled – apparently iodine may be harmful to children.
- In every capital we found nappies at grocery stores selling imported items. Sometimes the quality was poor so we secured them with strong sticky tape.
- Baby cereal and powdered milk were available in most towns, even small villages, and prices were similar to those at home.

In Senegal our baby got a rash caused by the heat and humidity. This was not dangerous, and with soothing powder it was gone in two days.

After the hot and humid temperatures of West Africa, we went to Europe and spent another six weeks hiking in the Alps and Pyrenees before returning home.'

Gino Bergeron, Julie Morin
& 'little Thomas'

Other than that, there are very few child-oriented facilities in West Africa. In nontourist hotels there are no discounts for children – a bed's a bed, whoever sleeps in it. Likewise, on public transport if you want a seat it has to be paid for. Most local kids go for free on buses but spend the whole journey on their parent's lap.

Highlights of the region that appeal to adults (markets, mosques, mud-brick architecture, endless desert wilderness) don't have such a hold over children. Additionally, distances can be long, especially on public transport, so parents need to have a good supply of distractions. ('Let's count how many black goats we can see ...')

On the plus side, some people we've heard from who have travelled with children in West Africa found the experience more enriching. Because foreign children are an unusual sight, they're a great conversation starter.

Lonely Planet's book *Travel With Children* by Maureen Wheeler provides sound advice (and ideas for games on the bus).

DANGERS & ANNOYANCES
Personal Safety

It is very important not to make sweeping statements about personal safety in West Africa. While there may be considerable risk in some areas, other places are completely safe. The danger of robbery with violence is much more prevalent in cities and towns, rather than in rural or wilderness areas. Most cities have their dangerous streets and beaches, but towns can differ; there's more of a danger in those frequented by wealthy foreigners than in places off the usual tourist track.

The Sahel countries are some of the safer places in the world, although Dakar has got much worse in the last few years and many people have had bags snatched and pockets picked, sometimes violently (see Dangers & Annoyances in the Dakar section of the Senegal chapter). In cities such as Banjul (Gambia) and Bamako (Mali), attacks are not unknown, but generally the accompanying violence is limited. Travellers have on occasion been pushed to the ground and had day-packs or cameras stolen, but they haven't been knifed or otherwise injured. (In

Considerations

Lest we get too paranoid, remember this. Considering the wealth of most tourists, and the unimaginable levels of poverty suffered by most West Africans, the incidence of robbery or theft in most countries in the region is incredibly low. Even a shoe-string traveller's daily budget of US$10 a day is more than the average local labourer makes in a month.

When you sit in a bus station sipping a couple of soft drinks, which cost a dollar, and you see an old man selling fans made carefully from palm leaves for about a quarter of this price, or a teenage youth trying to earn the same amount by offering to clean your shoes, it reminds you with a jolt that the vast majority of local people are decent and hard-working, and want from you only respect and the chance to make an honest living.

these cities, it's rare to hear of thieves carrying guns.)

In some of the southern cities, the picture is not the same. The worst place by far is Lagos (Nigeria), followed by Abidjan (Côte d'Ivoire). In countries recovering from civil war (such as Sierra Leone and Liberia) another danger is that of harassment and violence by rebel groups or former combatants, especially in rural areas. More specific details are given in the individual country chapters.

Safety Tips

The warnings in the previous section are not designed to put you off travelling in West Africa, but they are designed to make you more aware of the dangers. Some simple precautions will hopefully ensure you have a trouble-free trip. Remember, many thousands of travellers enjoy trips to this region, and have no problems, because they are careful as required. The precautions listed

Scams – What to Look Out For

The main annoyance you'll come across in West Africa are the various hustlers, touts and con men that pray on tourists. Although these guys are not necessarily dangerous, some awareness and suitable precautions are advisable. A few examples of the dazzling array of scams and con tricks that the hustlers of West Africa have perfected follow. Some are imaginative and amusing; others are serious and a cause for concern.

Dud Cassettes

Street sellers walk around with boxes of cassettes by local musicians. You browse, you choose, you pay. And then when you get back to your hotel and open the box it's got a cheap blank tape inside. Or the tape itself is missing, or the music is by a completely different artist. Tapes sealed in cellophane are normally fine, and of reasonable quality, but look at or try to listen to tapes before buying them.

Phone Numbers

You give your address to a local kid who says he wants to write you letters. He asks for your phone number too, and you think 'no harm in that'. Until the folks back home start getting collect calls in the middle of the night.

Remember Me?

A popular trick in the tourist areas is for local lads to approach you in the street pretending to be a hotel employee or 'son of the owner'. There's been a mix-up at the shop. Can you lend him some money? You can take it off the hotel bill later. He'll know your name and room number, and even give you a receipt. But, surprise surprise, back at the hotel they've never heard of him, and the money is never seen again. The way to avoid the trap is to be polite but firm: you don't remember anyone, and you'd like to be alone.

Sock Sellers

A youth approaches you in the street with socks for sale. Even though you don't want them he follows you for a while. His buddy approaches from the other side and also tries to persuade you to buy the socks. He bends down to show you how well the socks would go with your outfit. You are irritated and distracted, and while you bend down to fend him off, whoosh, the other guy comes in from the blind side and goes straight for the pocket with your wallet in. The solution? Be firm, walk purposefully, stay cool, and never buy socks in the street.

A Nice Welcome

You may be invited to stay in someone's house, in exchange for a meal and drinks, but your new friend's appetite for food and beer may make this an expensive deal. More seriously, while you are dining, someone else will be back at the house of your 'friend' going through your bag. This scam is only likely to be tried in tourist areas (we heard about it in St-Louis in Senegal) but remember in remote and rural areas you'll quite often come across genuine hospitality.

Police & Thieves

If you're unwise enough to sample local narcotics, don't be surprised if dealers are in cahoots with the local police, who then come to your hotel or stop you in the street and find you 'in possession'. Large bribes will be required to avoid arrest or imprisonment. The solution is easy – don't buy drugs from strangers.

below are particularly relevant to cities, although some may apply to other places too.

- Carry as little as possible. Thieves will be less interested if you're not carrying a day-pack, camera and personal stereo. Consider leaving them in your room. Even passports, travellers cheques and credit cards can sometimes be left behind, if the hotel has a reliable safe or security box.
  If your hotel isn't too secure, then you will have to carry your valuables with you. You have to work out which is the safest option on a case by case basis. (Note that in many countries it's law to carry your passport at all times – although you're very unlikely to be stopped in the street by police and asked for it.)
- Be discreet. Don't wear jewellery or watches. Use a separate wallet for day-to-day purchases, and keep the bulk of your cash out of sight, hidden in a pouch under loose-fitting clothing. For more advice, see the entry on Security in the Money section earlier.
- Try not to look lost. Walk purposefully and confidently, and don't obviously refer to this guidebook. Tear out the pages you need, or photocopy them, or duck into a shop of cafe to have a look at the map and get your bearings.
- Avoid back streets and risky areas at night. Take a taxi. A dollar or two for the fare might save you a lot of pain and trouble.

A final suggestion is to hire somebody locally to accompany you when walking around a risky area. It's usually not too difficult to find someone who wouldn't mind earning a few dollars for warding off potential molesters – ask at your hotel.

PUBLIC HOLIDAYS & SPECIAL EVENTS

Public holidays vary from country to country, but some are observed in nearly all countries, including New Year's Day and Christmas Day. Official holidays for each country are listed under Public Holidays & Special Events in the Facts for the Visitor sections of the individual country chapters.

Islamic Holidays

Important Islamic holidays, when much of West Africa's commercial life comes to a stop, include the following:

Tabaski Price Hikes

Two weeks before Tabaski, sheep prices rise steeply, as every family is expected to provide one during the celebrations. Those who cannot afford a sheep are socially embarrassed, and most will do anything to scrape up the money. One-third of the slaughtered animal is supposed to be given to the poor, one-third to friends, and one-third is left for the family. If you can manage to get an invitation to a Tabaski meal (it usually takes place after prayers at the mosque), you'll be participating in Muslim West Africa's most important and festive day of the year.

Tabaski (also called **Eid al-Kebir**) commemorates Abraham's readiness to sacrifice his son on God's command, and the last-minute substitution of a ram. It also coincides with the end of the pilgrimage to Mecca, and is the most important Muslim event, marked in most countries by great feasts with roast sheep and a two day public holiday.

Eid al-Fitr is the second major Islamic holiday, and marks the end of Ramadan, the annual fasting month when Muslims do not eat or drink during daylight hours but break their fast after sundown. Throughout Ramadan, offices usually grind to a halt in the afternoon.

Eid al-Moulid celebrates the birthday of the Prophet Mohammed. It occurs about three months after Tabaski.

Since the Islamic calendar is based on 12 lunar months, with 354 or 355 days, these holidays are always about 11 days earlier than the previous year. The exact dates depend on the moon and are announced for certain only about a day in advance.

Festivals & Cultural Events

There are many fascinating festivals that take place throughout the year in various countries of the region. Following is a selection of some of the more important and spectacular ones. For more details, see the individual country chapters. Note that many

Islamic Holidays

Hejira year	Eid al-Moulid*	Ramadan begins	Eid al-Fitr	Tabaski
1419	06-07-98	19-12-98	18-01-99	28-03-99
1420	25-06-99	08-12-99	07-01-00	17-03-00
1421	14-06-00	27-11-00	27-12-00	06-03-01
1422	03-06-01	16-11-01	16-12-01	23-02-02
1423	23-05-02	05-11-02	05-12-02	12-02-03
1424	12-05-03	25-10-03	24-11-03	01-02-04

*Also called Prophet's Birthday

of the dates listed here are approximate – check locally before setting off.

January

Paris-Dakar Motor Rally (1–22)
Africa's biggest auto race; the route changes slightly every year, but usually finishes with a mad dash along the beach from St-Louis to Dakar in Senegal.

February

Fêtes des Masques (throughout February)
Spectacular festivals with masked dancing, held in the Man region of Côte d'Ivoire.

Argungu Fishing & Cultural Festival (15)
Three-day festival held on the banks of the River Sokoto in Nigeria; includes spectacular displays of fishing, duck hunting and swimming, as well as diving competitions and canoe racing.

Carnival
Latin-style street festival in Bissau (Guinea-Bissau), with masks, parties and parades. Usually held in the first two weeks of February, sometimes later.

FESPACO
Film festival, held in Ouagadougou (Burkina Faso) in the last week of February every odd year.

March

Mardi Gras
Major celebration in Cape Verde, with street parades every day leading up to Lent.

April

Senegalese National Day (4)
Senegal's biggest public celebration; coincides with the West African International Marathon in Dakar.

Fête du Dipri (8–9)
Held in Gomon (Côte d'Ivoire), where you'll see masked dancing, healing ceremonies and sacrifices.

May

Deer Hunt (Aboakyer)
Famous festival held in Winneba (Ghana) on the first weekend in May; the main event is a competitive antelope hunt between two groups of men.

July

Bakatue Festival
Colourful harvest thanksgiving feast, with music and dancing, held in Elmina (Ghana) on the first Tuesday of July.

August

Oshun Festival
Famous Yoruba festival in Oshogbo (Nigeria) on the last Friday in August, with music, dancing and ritual sacrifices.

September

Igname Festival
Fire dances are a highlight of this festival in Bassar (Togo), held at the beginning of September.

Fetu Afahye Festival
Colourful carnival, on the first Saturday in September in Cape Coast (Ghana).

Biennal (9–22)
National sport and cultural festival, held in Bamako (Mali) every two years, starting around the second week of September.

La Cure Salée
Annual celebration by the Fula herders in Niger, famous all over Africa. Usually held in the first half of September, near In-Gall.

November

Abissa Festival (2)

Festival of the Prophet Atcho, held at Grand Bassam, Côte d'Ivoire, and nearby at Gbregbo (near Bingerville).

December

Igue/Ewere Festival (7–15)

Colourful seven-day festival with traditional dances, a mock battle and a procession to the palace to reaffirm loyalty to the oba. Held in Benin City (Nigeria).

Cattle Crossing (10–12)

Vibrant annual festival of Fula cattle herders in Diafarabé (Mali); the date is not fixed until November.

ACTIVITIES

Cycling

In several parts of West Africa (notably tourist areas such as the Gambian coast and Senegal's Casamance region), bikes can be hired by the hour, day or week, and can be a good way to tour a town or area. Your choice may range from a new, imported mountain bike (*vélo tout terrain* or VTT in French) to ancient, single gear, sit-up-and-beg steel roadsters. Costs range from US$1 to US$10 per day, depending on the bike and the area.

Information on bringing your own bicycle for a more extensive tour of West Africa is given in the Bicycle section of the Getting Around the Region chapter.

Paris-Dakar Rally

The Paris-Dakar Motor Rally, also known simply as 'Le Dakar', is recognised as being one of the world's longest, hardest and most dangerous driving events. The Paris-Dakar Rally was thought up by French racing driver Thierry Sabine. It was first held in 1979, although adventurous motorists have been crossing the Sahara since the 1920s. The race is held annually in January, usually starting in Paris and finishing in Dakar (except the year it went all the way to Cape Town). The race always crosses the Sahara Desert, although the exact route changes every year. In 1998 the route went from Paris through France, Spain, Morocco, Western Sahara, Mauritania, Mali and Senegal. The route distance is around 10,000km and takes 20 days to complete, with speeds of well over 150km/h being achieved on open stretches of sand. (For details of routes, check out the Paris-Dakar Rally Web site on www.dakar.com/indexus.html.)

The pace, heat and terrain are so tough that of the 400 or so vehicles that start each year, less than half (and sometimes only around one-quarter) of this number cross the finishing line. Categories include motorbikes, cars and trucks, and among the big names are international auto manufacturers such as Citroën and Yamaha who spend millions of US dollars on drivers, machines and support teams to ensure top rankings. Of equal interest are the 'privateers' – individuals or amateur teams who compete on shoestring budgets and keep the spirit of the original adventurers alive.

Some commentators have questioned the morality of a million dollar orgy of western consumerism blasting its way through the poverty-stricken Sahel. The sponsorship money the rally generates, for example, equals 50% of Mauritania's total aid budget, and each rally stage burns 10% of Mali's total annual fuel consumption. In fact, so much petrol is needed by the competitors that 'host' countires run short, some aid and relief operations report being unable to move their trucks for weeks.

Competitors get killed most years, but when innocent villagers (who account for 75% of the overall numbers of deaths) get run over by speeding cars with a value many times the lifetimes' earnings of an entire town in, say, Mali or Senegal, the contrast is brought even more sharply into focus.

Fishing

For most travellers, deep-sea sports fishing is prohibitively expensive, costing well over US$100 a day per person. For those still interested, facilities are available in some countries, including Côte d'Ivoire, Gambia, Mauritania and Senegal.

Football (Soccer)

Soccer is Africa's most popular participation and spectator sport. If you want to play, the universities and municipal stadiums are by far the best places to find a good-quality game, but outside every town in Africa is a patch of ground where informal matches are played most evenings (in coastal areas, the beach is used). The ball may be just a round bundle of rags, and each goal a couple of sticks, not necessarily opposite each other. You may have to deal with puddles, ditches and the odd goat or donkey wandering across the pitch, but the game itself will be taken seriously. Play is fast and furious, with the ball played low. Foreigners are usually warmly welcomed and joining in a game is one of the best ways to meet people. If you bring along your own football (deflated for travelling) you'll be a big hit.

Hash House Harriers

Just about every city in the world has a branch of this international social running club. However, it's almost exclusively an expatriate scene, often male-dominated, with its own rules and traditions, and with a set of elaborate beer-drinking rituals afterwards that are as important as the run. If you've 'hashed' elsewhere you'll know the scene, and can usually locate local hash-runs by asking embassy staff, volunteers or expatriate workers. If you've never hashed before – steer clear.

Rock Climbing

West Africa has very little in the way of climbing. While expatriates living in, say, Guinea or Ghana may find some outcrops suitable for one-pitch routes or 'bouldering', as a visitor it's generally not worth lugging rock climbing equipment around West

Soccer in West Africa

All the countries in West Africa have football leagues and tournaments, in which teams from different towns and cities compete on a national or regional basis, but international competitions cause the greatest excitement among football fans. Africa's main international competitions include the African Champions League and the CAF Cup (CAF is Africa's football governing body), both held annually. In the 1998 CAF Cup, West African teams included Jasper United (Nigeria), Real Tamale (Ghana), Energie Sport (Benin) and Jeanne d'Arc (Senegal).

The most high-profile event, and the one which most captures the enthusiasm of Africans throughout the continent is the Africa Cup of Nations, held in January every two years. In the preliminary rounds, 34 national teams compete, and the 16 best teams are gathered together in one place for the final rounds.

The 1998 Africa Cup of Nations was held in Burkina Faso, and West African national sides included Ghana, Côte d'Ivoire, Guinea and Togo, as well as surprise qualifiers Burkina Faso. The competition was won by South Africa, who beat Egypt 2-0 in the final.

West African football is usually dominated by Nigeria, but they were disqualified from the 1998 tournament. Nearly all the players in the national side play for top European clubs. After Nigeria's victories at the 1994 Cup of Nations and the 1996 Atlanta Olympics, and their strong showing at the 1998 World Cup, one of the biggest unanswered questions of Burkina 98 was 'would Nigeria have won if they'd been there?'. We'll have to wait until the next Africa Cup of Nations – Zimbabwe 2000 – to find out. The Nigerian women's team is worth keeping an eye out for too.

For the latest results and more details on all the African international competitions, wired fans can check out the CAF Web site, www.cafonline.com.

Hiking

West Africa has many interesting possibilities for hiking, but the set-up in this region is very different from that in East or southern Africa. There are few high mountains or wilderness areas with good walking conditions, so much of the hiking is in populated areas, where paths pass through fields and villages. This is a great way to interact with the local inhabitants, and on foot you can meet on more equal terms rather than stare at each other through the windows of a bush taxi.

If you're interested in wildlife, you can also walk in some of West Africa's national parks and reserves. However, most trails (if they exist at all) are generally quite short, designed more as an introduction to the vegetation and its inhabitants than as a way of covering long distances. For something more demanding, there are opportunities for longer treks or hiking expeditions, but the region has little in the way of organised routes so you often need to use your imagination and be prepared to adapt your plans as you go.

In some places, because of the distances involved (or just to take a break from walking), it may also be necessary to use donkeys, hitching or public transport to get around. The range of transport, and the need for adaptability, is all part of the fun.

Country	Area	Features	Rating
Benin	Natitingou & Somba Country	Somba architecture and culture	E
Burkina Faso	Banfora	Lush green countryside, rock formations	V
Cape Verde	Brava Island	Mountainous island, numerous short hikes	V
	Mt Fogo (2839m)	Volcanic crater; last major eruption 1995	V
	Ribeira Grande valley	Spectacular views from the peak	V
Côte d'Ivoire	Man area	Hills, waterfalls, art and culture	V
	Parc National de Taï	Dense rainforest, chimpanzees; special permit required	E
The Gambia	Abuko Nature Reserve	Various habitats, birds	E
	Bijilo Forest Park	Coastal woodland, informative trails, birds	E
Ghana	Gambaga Escarpment (Nakpanduri)	Good views from the escarpment	E
	Ho	Forested hills, villages	V
	Hohoe	Mt Afadjato (885m), waterfalls, villages	V
	Kakum National Park	Unique walkway above the forest floor	E

Africa. The main exception is the area of Hombori, in Mali, where some spectacular rock formations stand high above the desert floor and attract a small but growing number of serious rock climbers from Europe (see the boxed text 'Rock Climbing' in the Mali chapter for more details). Another area with rock climbing potential is the Bandiagara Es-

	Hiking

Country	Area	Features	Rating
Ghana (cont)	Mole National Park	Guided walking safaris; animals and birds	E
Guinea	Fouta Djalon	Scenic, hilly region	V
Guinea-Bissau	Ilha de Bolama	Few visitors, good beaches and interesting local culture	V
	Ilha de Bubaque	Beaches, fields, villages	V
Mali	Bandiagara Escarpment	Spectacular landscape, Dogon art and culture	V
Nigeria	Cross River National Park	Guided walks to see gorillas	V
	Gashaka Gumpti National Park	Extended walks on rough terrain	V
	Gembu	Tea estates, cattle farms	V
	Jos Plateau area	Ganawuri Mountains	V
	Mandara Mountains	Rocky foothills, unusual butterflies and monkeys	V
Senegal	Casamance	Scenic lowland region, excellent accommodation	V
	Siné-Saloum Delta	Coastal woodland, monkeys, birds; travel by canoe	E
Sierra Leone	Freetown Peninsula and Sugar Loaf Mountain	Forested mountains, great views, Krio villages	E
	Kabala area	Wooded hills, waterfalls	E
	Mt Bintumani (1945m)	Remote region, mountain forest, high peak	H
	Outamba-Kilimi National Park	Rivers, forest, animals, birds	V
	Tiwai Island Wildlife Sanctuary	Pristine rainforest, high concentration of primates	E
Togo	Kpalimé area	Forested hills, butterflies	V
	La Fosse aux Lions	Savanna woodland, cliffs of the Tamberma people	V
	Parc National de Fazao-Malfakassa	Forested hills	E
	Vallée de Tamberma	Culture and architecture	V

E – easy and/or short hikes (less than one day or 10km)
H – harder and/or longer hikes (more than 10km, over several days or in tougher conditions)
V – various lengths and standards

carpment, also in Mali. The famous French climber Christine Destiville established some routes here (and featured prominently in a TV film about climbing in Dogon Country) several years ago, and groups from Europe occasionally follow her footsteps (and handholds). Nigeria, too, has some good routes, on granite outcrops in the north. For more details see the boxed text 'Rock Climbing' in the Nigeria chapter.

Swimming & Water Sports

All along the coast of West Africa, you have a huge choice of beaches where swimming is a major attraction. Some beaches are very touristy, whereas others may be inhabited by local fishing communities or completely deserted. Wherever you go, it is important to note that in many areas the beaches can slope steeply and the waves create a vicious undertow. Never plunge into the ocean without first taking reliable local advice.

A safer, if less adventurous, option may be to use a swimming pool. Most large cities have a public swimming pool (*piscine*), and major hotels often have pools that nonguests can use for a small fee.

For sailing, there are clubs in various cities along the coast, but they rarely have boats available for hire. Your other option is to hire a small sailing boat at a tourist area, such as Gambia's Atlantic Coast or Senegal's Petite Côte. Day trips on large crewed yachts are available in Dakar, Banjul, Freetown and occasionally Abidjan.

Sailboards are available for rent in Senegal (Dakar and the Casamance beach area), the Atlantic Coast resorts (Gambia), Freetown (Sierra Leone), Abidjan and Sassandra (Côte d'Ivoire), and Lomé and Lac Togo (Togo). Dakar is also a base for scuba diving and kayaking.

ACCOMMODATION

In all the countries covered in this book, you'll find a wide range of places to stay. If you plan to travel at the luxury end of the scale, however, West Africa has very few top-class hotels outside the capitals, and offers little in the way of exclusive wildlife lodges or tented camps as found in East or southern Africa. Independent travellers on tighter budgets are fairly well catered for, although there are hardly any backpacker lodges. However, in most towns accommodation (of variable quality) is available.

Throughout West Africa standards vary but quality generally reflects price. Hotels at the top end of the range have clean, air-conditioned rooms with private bathrooms. In the mid-range, rooms probably have fans instead of air-con, and usually have a bathroom, but there may not always be hot water. Near the lower end of the range, hotel rooms are not always clean (they are sometimes downright filthy), bathrooms are usually shared and often in an appalling state, and a smashed window may provide fresh air. Many hotels – of whatever quality – double as brothels; the standard of the room reflects the standard of the clients.

Most towns and villages in Francophone countries have a *campement*. This could be loosely translated as 'inn', 'lodge', 'hostel' or even 'motel', but it is not a camp site (ie a place for tents), although some campements also provide areas where you can pitch a tent. Traditionally, campements offered simple accommodation, less elaborate than hotels. However, while some campements remain cheap and simple, others are very good quality, with prices on a par with mid-range hotels. You'll find the occasional *auberge* (small hotel) too – again with a wide range of quality.

In many parts of West Africa, particularly in the Sahel during the hot season, people often sleep outside their hut or on the flat roof of their house, as it's much cooler. In some hotels this is also possible, and carrying a mattress onto the roof is usually allowed if you ask. The cool breeze can be a godsend, and the views of the stars an extra bonus. In trekking areas such as Mali's Dogon Country, it has become established practice for visitors to sleep on the roof of the campements in each village.

Maisons de passage ('houses for travellers') tend to be on the basic side. Often near markets or bus stations, they provide a bed for travellers and little else. They invariably double as brothels.

Some hotels charge for a bed only, with all meals extra. If breakfast is included it's usually on a par with the standard of accommodation: a full buffet in more expensive places, coffee and bread further down the scale. In many countries a government tourist tax is also charged.

There are not many dedicated camp sites in West Africa, and those which do exist cater mainly for overlanders in their own vehicle. However, some hotels and campements allow camping, or provide an area where tents can be pitched. Grassy sites are very rare – you often have to force pegs through hardpacked gravel.

FOOD

Eating West African food need not mean eating poorly – the region has some wonderfully tasty dishes. However, the quality of food varies considerably from country to country. In desert countries like Mauritania or Niger ingredients are limited. The countries with the best range of food are those along the coast, where rainfall is plentiful and the crops are varied.

Street Food

A feature of West African travel is the availability of 'street food' – ideal if you're on the move or prefer to eat little and often. Street food rarely involves plates or knives – it's served on a stick, wrapped in paper or in a plastic bag. It also tends to be very cheap.

On street corners and around bus stations, especially in the morning, you'll see small booths selling pieces of bread with fillings or toppings of butter, chocolate spread, mayonnaise or sardines. In the French-speaking countries, the bread is cut from fresh French-style loaves or baguettes, but in the English-speaking countries the bread is often a less delicious soft, white loaf. Price depends on the size of the piece of bread you want, and the type of filling. It's quite usual to ask for, say, a CFA75 chunk, with CFA75 of mayonnaise, giving you a sandwich for CFA150 (US$0.25).

One of the region's finest institutions (found mainly in the French-speaking countries) are the coffee stalls where clients sit on small benches around a table and drink glasses of Nescafé mixed with sweetened condensed milk, served with French-style bread, butter or mayonnaise for around

Vegetarian?

Vegetarianism is rarely understood in West Africa, although you can easily find food without meat – it's what most poor people eat – but how easy you find sticking to a vegetarian diet here depends to some extent on how strictly you adhere to your principles. Even the simplest vegetable sauce may sometimes have a small bit of meat or animal fat in it, and chicken is usually not regarded as 'real' meat.

Vegetarian restaurants in this part of the world are as rare as hen's teeth, although you can find vegetarian dishes at some Asian and Indian restaurants in the main cities. If you eat eggs and dairy products, pizzas and omelettes make a change from the ubiquitous bean and vegetable dishes. Street food is an excellent option – fill up on cassava, yam and plantain chips, bread with mayonnaise, egg or chocolate spread, and fried dough balls.

Alternatively, head for the markets and do your own catering – but steer well clear of the meat and fish sections unless you're hoping to convert a friend. There's always plenty of fresh fruit and vegetables (usually sold in piles of four or five pieces), as well as nuts, including dollops of ground peanuts (local-style peanut butter) arranged on banana leaves. Bread and tins of margarine are always available. Banana and ground peanut sandwiches made with fresh bread are a delicious and nutritious option.

If your taste buds are pining for cheese, you may be in for a disappointment – unless you like the ultra-processed triangular varieties, which are generally available from larger supermarkets.

US$0.50. Some also offer tea (made with a Lipton teabag), or even Milo, and a more enterprising 'caféman' might fry up eggs or serve sardines. Many coffee stalls are only open in the morning.

In the Sahel countries, usually around markets, you'll see women with large brown bowls covered with a wicker lid selling yoghurt, which is sometimes mixed with pounded millet and sugar. This sells for around US$0.15 a portion – you can eat it on the spot, or take it away in a plastic bag. A variation is where the millet is boiled before being mixed with the yoghurt to make more of a porridge.

In the evenings you can buy *brochettes* (small pieces of beef, sheep or goat meat skewered and grilled over a fire) or lumps of roast meat sold by guys who walk around pushing a tin oven on wheels. Around markets and bus stations, women serve deep-fried chips of cassava or some other root crop.

In Francophone countries, grilled and roast meat, usually mixed with onions and spices, is sold in shacks (basically an oven with a few walls around it). These are called *dibieteries*, and you can eat on the spot (a rough bench might be provided) or take away. To feed one or two, ask for, say, CFA1000 worth (about US$2).

Another popular stand-by in the larger cities are Lebanese-style *chawarmas,* thin slices of lamb grilled on a spit, served with salad (optional) in Lebanese-style bread (pitta) with a sauce made from chickpeas. These cost about US$1.

Meals

For something more substantial than street food, West African meals typically consist of a staple served with a sauce, and it's the great variety of ingredients that make the sauce interesting. Dishes can be simple or very complex according to the skill of the cook, the availability of ingredients and the budget of the customers.

Some travellers have been lucky enough to stay with local people, where a great way to repay their hospitality is to pay for a special meal for the whole family. This way you'll also be able to see how meals are put together. For the full picture, visit the market with the lady of the house (it's always the women who do the cooking in domestic situations) and see the various ingredients being bought.

Staples One of the most common staples, especially in the Sahel, is rice. Millet is also common, although this grain is usually pounded into flour before it is cooked. In most rural areas this is done by hand with a large wooden mortar and pestle, sometimes for several hours. The millet flour is steamed and then moistened with water until it thickens into a stiff 'porridge' that can be eaten with the fingers. Sorghum is a similar grain crop, and is prepared in much the same way, although it's not used as much as millet.

In the countries nearer the coast, staples may be root crops such as yam or cassava (also called manioc), which are pounded before being cooked. They're served as a near-solid glob, called *fufu* or *foufou* – picture mashed potatoes mixed with gelatine and very sticky. You grab a portion (with your right hand, please!) form a ball, dip it in the sauce and eat. In the coastal countries, plantain (green banana) is also common – either fried, cooked solid or pounded into a fufu.

Sauces Sauces are made from whatever is available. In some Sahel countries, ground-nuts (peanuts) are common, and a thick brown groundnut sauce is often served, either on its own or with meat or vegetables mixed in with the nuts. Sometimes deep orange palm oil is also added. Sauces are also made with vegetables or the leaves of staple food plants, such as cassava. Okra is popular, particularly in coastal countries – the result is a slimy green concoction. Other vegetables used in meals include potatoes (*pommes de terre* in French), sweet potatoes (*patates*), onions (*oignons*), green beans (*haricots verte*) and tomatoes (*tomates*). For flavouring, chillis may be used, and look out for *jaxatu* (pronounced *ja-ka-too*), like a green or yellow tomato but extremely bitter.

Stock cubes or sachets of flavouring are ubiquitous across the region (Maggi is the most common trade name) and are often thrown into the pot as well. Where it can be afforded, or on special occasions, meat or fish is added to the sauce; sometimes succu-lent slices, sometimes heads, tails and

Le Menu

In all French-influenced countries the *menu du jour* (often shortened to *le menu*) is the meal of the day, usually offered at a special price. If you want to see the menu, ie the list of meals available, ask for *le carte*. Here you may find the *plat du jour* (dish of the day) which, again, is usually offered at a special price.

bones. See the individual country chapters for more details on regional specialities.

Where to Eat

The best place to eat, if you're lucky enough to be invited, is at somebody's house. Most days, though, you'll be heading for a restaurant. The smallest, simplest eating houses usually have one or two meals available each day. It's usual to ask what they have, and base your choice – if any – on that. Meals will usually be straightforward – bowls of rice or another staple served with a simple sauce.

In slightly smarter places your choice may also include fried chicken or fish served with hot chips (*frites*). Cooked vegetables such as green beans may also be available. Up a grade from here, mainly in cities, you'll find mid-range restaurants catering to well-off locals and foreigners. They may serve only 'international' dishes, such as steaks or pizzas, and these meals are usually expensive, particularly if some of the ingredients have been flown in from Europe. Ironically, local specialities, such as fish and rice, may cost the same in this kind of place.

In many cities and tourist towns, 'fast food' is available. This refers less to the time it takes to serve, and more to the type of meal served – pizzas, burgers, hot dogs and Lebanese pitta bread sandwiches.

Fruit

Availability depends on the season, but your choice is always quite good and increases as you head south from the Sahel into the coastal countries. The choice includes oranges, mandarins and grapefruits (all often with green skin despite being ready to eat), bananas (many different colours and sizes), mangoes (also many varieties), pineapples and guavas.

DRINKS
Alcohol

You can often find imported beers from Europe and America, but about 45 brands of beer are brewed in West Africa, with Nigeria alone producing about 30. Some beers are European brands, brewed locally, others are specific to the region. Quality is often very good. Brands to look out for include: Club (Ghana, Nigeria and Liberia), Flag (Côte d'Ivoire and Senegal), Star (Sierra Leone, Ghana and Nigeria), Harp and Gulder (Nigeria and Ghana). Guinness is found in several countries too.

In the Sahel a rough, brown and gritty 'beer' made from millet is common, but West Africa's most popular home brew is palm wine. The tree is tapped and the sap comes out already mildly fermented. Sometimes yeast is added and the brew is allowed to ferment overnight, which makes it much stronger. In Nigeria, it is even bottled in factories.

Guinness Power

West African males firmly believe that Guinness, locally brewed, enhances nocturnal performance. It's drunk not only for its intrinsic delicious bitterness but also as a fortifier. 'Guinness: the Power' shout the slogans on hoardings and wayside bars or, lest there be any ambiguity, 'Guinness: the Power of Love'. Also, although we all know size doesn't count, you'll see 'Guinness: the Big One'. Who knows where the rumour started? If it was one of the Guinness reps, they deserve the Freedom of the City of Dublin.

Soft Drinks

International and local brands of soft drinks are sold virtually everywhere. A tiny shop in a remote village may sell little food, but the chances are they'll have a few dusty bottles of Coca-Cola or Pepsi for sale. (Coke is called 'Coca' in French-speaking countries.) Bottled mineral water is quite widely available in cities, towns and tourist areas.

Home-made soft drinks include ginger 'beer' and *bisap*, a purple mixture made from water and hibiscus leaves. These drinks are usually sold in plastic bags by children on the street. Although they are refreshing, the water may not be clean, so they're probably worth avoiding.

As with beers, prices for soft drinks vary from dirt cheap at the side of the road to extortionate at posh restaurants. As a guide, the price of a soft drink is nearly always about half the price of a beer at the same place. Beer prices at hotels and restaurants are quoted throughout this book, so you'll easily be able to tell how much a Coca-Cola or Pepsi costs at the same place.

Tea & Coffee

In the Sahel countries, tea comes in two sorts. There's the type made with a tea bag (its local name is 'Lipton tea' even if the brand is actually something else), and there's the tea drunk by the local population – made with green leaves (often imported from China) and served with loads of sugar in small glasses. Mint is sometimes added, or the tea may be made from mint leaves alone. Half the fun of drinking local-style tea is the ritual that goes with it, taking at least an hour. Traditionally, the tea is brewed three times and poured from a small pot high above the glass.

Coffee is almost exclusively instant coffee (Nescafé is the usual brand), although *where* you drink it will determine the flavour. At the coffee stalls mentioned under Street Food earlier, it's mixed with sweetened condensed milk, and in some areas the water may be infused with a local leaf called *kinkiliba* which gives it a woody tang – unusual but not unpleasant when you get

over the shock. If you drink coffee at a smarter restaurant it will come as a cup of warm water, with the coffee in a sachet in the saucer – you add milk (usually powdered) and sugar as required.

SHOPPING

A major feature of travel in West Africa is the vast range of artistic and craftwork items found across the region. These include masks, statues and other woodcarvings, hand-made textiles with a fantastic variety of colours and patterns, glass beads and jewellery made from gold and silver, as well as a fascinating assortment of pots, urns, stools, weapons, musical instruments and agricultural tools.

Whether you're a serious collector or just looking for a souvenir from your trip, you'll find plenty to choose from, and prices are always more reasonable than they are at home. Of course, many of the items you'll see in shops and markets are made expressly for the tourist trade, although these are often copies of traditional items. Even contemporary pieces of art are usually based on traditional designs.

Making items for sale is not new either: the oldest 'tourist' art in sub-Saharan Africa was produced by the Sapi people of Sierra Leone in the 15th century – they sold ivory salt pots and trumpets to the Portuguese traders.

See the colour features on sculpture, masks, textiles and jewellery later in this book for more details of the types of art and craftwork available. As well as these, other items commonly seen in West Africa are baskets and pottery with intricate designs, which are almost always produced by women. Leatherwork, with colourful incised patterns, mostly made from goat-hide, are created by men in the Sahel region.

Cassettes of local music are also good to buy – for more details see the special section 'West African Music', as well as the Shopping sections of individual place entries.

Antiques

Older wooden sculptures, particularly masks, headdresses and stools, from all

TEXTILES

West Africa is famous for the beauty, vitality, colour and range of its textiles. Wool, cotton, nylon, rayon and silk are woven on a variety of looms, usually by men. Most cloth is woven in narrow strips which are sewn together. As many West Africans now wear western clothes, the skills required to produce the finer textiles are disappearing. The colourful cloth, in two or three pieces, worn by women all over West Africa, is usually imported or locally produced 'Dutch wax', a factory-made material using stencils and the batik wax process.

Kente & Adinkra Cloth

Probably the best known West African fabric is the colourful *kente* cloth from Ghana, made by the Ashanti people for whom clothing is one of the most obvious and important marks of distinction in society. The basic garment for men is a long rectangular piece of cloth *(ntoma)* passed over the left shoulder and brought around the body like a toga. The most impressive of all materials used in such garments is silk, which is woven in narrow, brightly coloured strips with complex patterns and a wealth of hues. Kente cloth is worn only in the southern half of Ghana and is reserved mainly for prestigious events.

BOTH PHOTOS BY DENNIS WISKEN/SIDEWALK GALLERY

The Ewé also weave kente cloth, but the designs are somewhat different. The motifs used include geometric figures. Every design has a meaning, and some are reserved exclusively for royal families.

The earliest kente cloth was all cotton, but starting from the 18th century the Ashanti weavers began incorporating designs using unravelled imported Dutch silk. Today only the higher priced kente cloth contains silk (or imported rayon). The weaving is done exclusively by men, usually outdoors. Adinkra cloth, also from Ghana, is just as impressive, although perhaps less well known. It is a colourful cotton material with black geometric designs or stylised figures stamped on it. The word *adinkra* means farewell, and Ghanaians consider this fabric most appropriate for funerals.

Top: Shuttle and pulley

Right: The fabulous colours of kente cloth, which is woven in narrow strips and sewn together.

Originally the printing was done on cotton pieces lying on the ground. Today, the cotton fabric is cut in long pieces, spread on a raised padded board and held in place by nails. The symbolic designs are cut on calabash stamps, and the dye is made from the bark of a local tree called *badie*. The printer dips the calabash into the hot dye and presses it onto the fabric. Each colour has a special significance: vermilion (red) symbolises the earth, blue symbolises love, and yellow is for success and wealth.

JASON LAURÉ

Bogolan Cloth

Bogolan cloth (*bokolanfini* in Bambara and often simply called 'mud cloth') comes from the Sahel region of Mali, but can be found in markets all over the region. The cloth is woven in plain cotton strips, sewn together and dyed yellow using a solution made from the leaves of a local tree, and then covered in designs using various types of mud for colour. The mud comes from different sources: from sandstone outcrops for reds and oranges and from riverbeds for blacks and greys. The cloth is left to dry in the sun, and the mud designs are then removed, leaving their imprint – the effect is very striking.

Designs are traditionally geometric and abstract, but bogolan cloth made specifically for sale to tourists are more representational, showing animals, markets or village scenes. Some designs are very complex and involve many hours of work by the artists, who are all women. Bogolan cloth is usually used for wall hangings or bedcovers, but waistcoats, caps and bags are also made from it.

DENNIS WISKEN/SIDEWALK GALLERY

Top: Adinkra stamps. There are over 60 different adinkra symbols, each with a specific meaning. Photograph by Dennis Wisken/Sidewalk Gallery.

Middle: Preparing adinkra cloth for stamping.

Bottom: Heddle pulleys like this Baoulé one are often decorated with fine carvings, in keeping with the aesthetic sensibilities of the weaver.

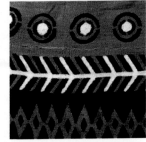

Indigo Cloth

Another classic West African fabric is the indigo-dyed cotton worn as robes and headdresses primarily by the Tuareg. Indigo comes from the *indigofera* plant and the indigo vine. The plant is crushed and fermented, and then mixed with an alkaline solution producing the dye. The dyed cloth is often beaten with a mallet to produce a sheen. West African tribes noted for the use of indigo include the Hausa, Baoulé, Yoruba and Soninké.

The Yoruba produce an indigo-dyed cloth, called *aderi*, with designs applied using the tie-dye technique or by painting motifs with a dye-resistant starch.

Top: Bogolan or mud cloth – the striking geometric designs on these three examples are produced using different types of mud.

Bottom: The deep blue of indigo cloth, like this one decorated with a tie-dyed pattern, is characteristically associated with the Tuareg people.

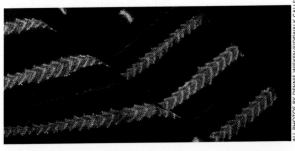

Other Textiles

The Fula have a caste of weavers called Maboube who produce blankets known as *khasa*, which are made from sheep's wool mixed with camel hair. These are used during the cold months. The Maboube also make rare and expensive wedding blankets. These large and elaborately detailed textiles are displayed around the marriage bed.

The Fon and the Fanti are known for their appliqué banners and flags. Shapes of people and animals are cut from colourful material and carefully sewn onto a cloth panel.

The Hausa are known for their embroidery, which was once hand-stitched onto their robes and caps. Although now machine-stitched, the designs remain unchanged. In keeping with Islamic culture the designs are nonfigurative.

John Graham, Alex Newton, David Else

Top: Tuareg blanket (left); all over West Africa, women like these Yoruba mothers use lengths of cloth to carry their babies on their backs (right).

Middle: Fula finery on display.

Bottom: Hausa cloth (left) and wax-resist cloth (right) with a cowrie shell design, widely used throughout West Africa.

JEWELLERY

Jewellery is important in Africa, to both men and women; in West Africa you'll find a large and fascinating variety. Because it's portable, jewellery is a great thing to collect during your travels.

For West Africans, beads are often more than simple adornment. They are used as objects representing spiritual values and can play major roles in community rituals such as birth, circumcision, marriage and death. Beads are often made of glass, which was quite rare in West Africa until the arrival of Europeans in the Middle Ages. Local jewellers copied the highly decorative glass millefiori trading beads from Venice, which featured flowers, stripes and mosaic designs. Discarded bottles and medicine jars were pulverised into a fine powder to remake into glass beads. Many glass beads are tiny and sold by weight, hence their name 'pound beads'. Today, the Krobo in Ghana still melt powdered glass in terracotta moulds, while the Nupe of Bida in central Nigeria wind molten glass on long iron rods to make beads and bracelets. Many of the beads still come from Europe. Referred to as *bakim-mutum* by bead traders throughout West Africa, they are commonly worn by village chiefs and elders as a sign of power and wealth.

In Mali you'll see large amber beads worn by Fula women. The Dogon also treasure amber and use it in their necklaces, bracelets and pendants. The Dogon also use beads made of stone or terracotta incised with geometrical patterns. A variety of other materials are used in Africa for making beads, including coral, shells, copal, amazonite, silver, gold and brass. Women sometimes have to make do with cheaper elements. Among the Bella, for instance, plastic and imitation amber beads are sometimes used, while coins may replace silver in jewellery.

Rings in West Africa can be stunning. In Burkina Faso, look out for Bobo bronze rings, which often have intricate designs, including a tick

Top: Glass trade beads

Middle: Amber beads (top two) and Mauritanian glass beads (lower two)

Bottom, from left to right: Ghanaian agate beads; glass millefiori trade beads; and Chevron Venetian glass trade beads.

bird, a warrior on horseback or a chameleon. In Mali, older Dogon men wear large bronze rings as a sign of status. All over the region you'll find beautiful dark green malachite jewellery, usually from Congo (Zaïre). Cowrie shells are often used to decorate pieces of jewellery; for a long time these shells were used as money all over Africa.

In most areas the preferred metal in jewellery is gold, but in and near the Sahara the Tuaregs and Moors prefer silver. In West Africa, both metals are nearly always sold by weight, and the artwork is included in the price. The Ashanti are famous for their goldwork in jewellery, ornaments and staffs. The Tuareg are renowned for their intricate silverwork, in jewellery and the decoration of the handles of their daggers. Tuareg men and women often wear silver crosses as pendants around their necks. These come in various designs, characterised by protective symbolism. Some incorporate circle and phallus designs, fertility symbols; those representing a camel's eye or jackal tracks are symbolic of power and cunning.

Top: Some examples of the superb rings found in West Africa – Tuareg silver rings and Lobi bronze rings.

Bottom, clockwise from top left: How to wear it – a Fula woman in her finery; Tuareg carnelian pendant; Ashanti bronze beads; Ashanti gold ornaments; and Tuareg silver crosses, each design representing a different protective symbol.

Markets

The markets in West Africa are large, vibrant, colourful and always fascinating. The best are those in Abidjan, Dakar, Bamako, Banjul, Kano, Lomé, Niamey and Ouagadougou, but the markets in smaller places are also well worth a visit.

There are two main sorts of market. There are the ones where local people come to buy and sell everyday things such as fruit, vegetables and other items like clothes and farm tools. In larger places, you'll also see stalls selling radios, cassette players and other electrical goods, imported shoes, hardware and car parts. The second type of market is aimed more at tourists, where you can buy art and craft items. In some places the main market and the tourist-oriented craft market are combined and these can be the most interesting to visit.

Bargaining

When it comes to buying souvenirs, bargaining is usually the name of the game. Many items do not have a fixed value, and prices have to be negotiated (see the boxed text 'The Fine Art of Bargaining' in the Money section earlier in this chapter) but this is not always true. With cloth sold by the metre, for example, you can expect little or no lowering of the price. The same is true of gold and silver; if the trader tells you the price and you come back with an offer one-third that amount, don't be surprised if they are genuinely insulted and refuse to talk further. In these cases, try to get a feel for prices beforehand. Ask knowledgeable locals or check out a fixed-price shop or hotel gift shop; prices in the market are typically half those in the stores. If you don't enjoy bargaining, stick to the fixed-price shops.

Hassles

Most travellers love to visit markets, but a few find them extremely intimidating or annoying experiences. It can be hard dealing with eager traders when they grab you by the arm and not-so-gently pull you over to their stall 'just to see' (*pour voir seulement*). Although traders in city or tourist markets are often very pushy, in local markets tourists are treated just like any other person there. If you want to sample a big traditional market, go early when the stalls are just opening and the vendors are still in low gear. It's usually cooler then as well.

As for persistent traders, if you really don't want anything they're offering, say 'No thanks' and move on. Once you move into another trader's pitch they'll usually back off. If they keep pulling you and you find it really offensive, let them know in no uncertain terms – if your actions are clear, they'll stop.

In a few markets, the hassle can verge on danger, as pickpockets work the crowds or gangs of youths posing as merchants can surround tourists and snatch bags and cameras. For tips on safety, see the Dangers & Annoyances section earlier in this chapter.

over West and Central Africa are often sold in tourist markets. Some of the dusty pieces are genuine, which raises questions about whether we should encourage the people of Africa to sell off the best parts of their cultural inheritance. Others are replicas made specifically for sale – although they usually still have a nice 'worn' look, which you may find more preferable to the gloss of many new items.

Note that items which are authentic and valuable cannot be exported under the laws of most West African countries. Since very little art purchased by nonexperts fits this description, it's more a matter of being hassled by customs than doing something illegal. Nevertheless, in some countries such as Mali, Nigeria and Ghana, for genuine antiques you must get an export permit – usually from the museum in the capital. If the piece looks old, it might be worth letting the museum check it before you purchase, to avoid difficulties later.

Bringing Items Home

When you buy a new woodcarving you may find it has cracked by the time you get home. New wood must be dried slowly. Wrapping the carvings in plastic bags with a small water tray enclosed is one technique. If you see tiny bore marks with white powder everywhere, it means the powder-post beetle (frequently confused with termites) is having a fiesta. There are three remedies – zap the beasts in a microwave oven, stick the piece in the freezer for a week, or drench it with lighter fluid. You could also try fumigating items. Be warned that if you have wooden objects with insect damage, the items may be seized by customs and you will have to pay to have them fumigated.

If you buy textiles, note that some dyes, including indigo, may not be colour-fast. Soaking cloth in vinegar or very salty water may stop the dye running, but this method should only be used on cloth of one colour. Adinkra cloth is not meant to be washed.

Getting There & Away

This chapter tells you how to reach West Africa from other parts of the world and how to leave the region after your travels. More specific details on transport options are given in the Getting There & Away sections of individual country chapters.

AIR
Airports & Airlines
You can fly to any major airport in West Africa from anywhere in the world, but some routes and destinations are more popular (and therefore usually cheaper) than others. The main international airports in West Africa of most use to tourists are Abidjan (Côte d'Ivoire), Accra (Ghana), Bamako (Mali), Dakar (Senegal) and Lagos

Stop Press – Air Afrique

As we went to press, Air Afrique suspended flights to the USA, France and South Africa. These may resume, however, and flights within West Africa were not affected.

(Nigeria). There are also regular charter flights from some European countries to Banjul (Gambia). Flights to other places in the region are less convenient, or considerably more expensive, or both.

Where you fly to in the region depends on where you want to visit, but don't automatically aim for the airport nearest your intended starting point. Even if you want to start your travels in, say, Mali you may still find it cheaper and easier to fly to Banjul first, from where you can travel overland or take a short regional flight.

Most major European airlines serve cities in West Africa. There are regular Air France flights from most parts of Europe to all the Francophone countries. Similarly, British Airways serves former British colonies, such as Ghana, while TAP Air Portugal is Guinea-Bissau's main link with Europe. Many other European airlines fly between Europe and West Africa, including Sabena, Lufthansa, Alitalia and Aeroflot. Other airlines serving specific countries are detailed in the Getting There & Away sections of the individual country chapters. Although there are a few flights between the USA and West Africa, most visitors from North America fly via Europe, as do visitors from Australasia.

Several African airlines also fly regularly between Europe and West Africa (a few also serve North America). Air Afrique has the most extensive network (although note the warning given at the beginning of this section), run jointly by all the former French colonies, but some other West African countries have a national airline with flights to/from Europe or other parts of Africa. These include Ghana Airways, Nigeria Airways and Air Mauritanie. Other African airlines that serve the West African region include EgyptAir, Royal Air Maroc and Ethiopian Airlines. Although the routes offered by these airlines can be longer than those of European carriers, their prices are often cheaper – ideal for travellers with plenty of time but less money to spare.

Whichever airline you decide to take, it may be worth checking out the possibility of an open jaw ticket (ie flying into one country and out of another). Sometimes, though, even if you want to do a linear trip (starting in Dakar and finishing in Niamey, Niger, for example), it might be easier and cheaper to get a long haul standard return (in and out of Dakar) and a one way regional flight (Niamey to Dakar) at the end of your trip.

Buying Tickets

To buy a ticket, it's usually not worth contacting airlines directly as their prices aren't the cheapest. Travel agents provide you with better deals and a wider choice. Buying a plane ticket can be an intimidating business, so it's always worth taking time to do it properly. Start as soon as you can: some cheap tickets must be bought months in advance, and some popular flights sell out early.

To find a suitable travel agent, look at the advertisements in weekend newspapers or travel magazines, or look on the Internet. Once you've got a list of five or six, start phoning around. Tell them where you want to fly to, and they will offer you a choice of airline, route and fare. The fare is normally determined by the quality of the airline, the popularity of the route, the duration of the journey, the time of year, the length of any stopovers, the departure and arrival times, and any restrictions on the ticket.

Not all scheduled flights are direct. For example, if you fly from London to Dakar on KLM-Royal Dutch Airlines, you have to change planes at their hub in Amsterdam. Likewise, if you go with TAP Air Portugal, you have to change at Lisbon. If you go on an African airline there's more chance of a

Travelling on the Internet

A few hours surfing the Web can help give you an idea of what you can expect in the way of good fares as well as be a useful source of information on routes and time-tables.

Many student travel organisations and budget travel agents have Web sites with air fare information. All the major airlines have Web sites, and although they can be useful, they are usually not good for discounts. Most online flight reservation services on the Web need credit card details and, as many are US-based, they will only deliver to North American addresses. Users from other areas can still browse available flights and fares.

Travel Agents
STA Travel
www.statravel.com.au or
www.statravel.co.uk
Council Travel
www.counciltravel.com
Campus Travel
www.campustravel.co.uk

Airlines
Air Ivoire
www.air-ivoire-info.com
Air France
www.airfrance.fr

Online Ticket Sellers
Travel.com.au
www.travel.com.au – handles bookings for travel out of and around Australia.
Flifo
www.flifo.com – has an easy log-in procedure, cheap flights and good flexibility.
Microsoft Expedia
expedia.msn.com/daily/home/default.hts
– definitely has the prettiest interface.
Easy Sabre
www.easysabre.com – good information, if you can get to it!
Travelocity
www.travelocity.com – good once you've got past the frustrating log-in procedure.

direct flight, for example London to Accra on Ghana Airways, or Paris to Abidjan on Air Afrique. Flights where you have to change planes are usually cheaper than those which go direct.

Charter flights are generally cheaper than scheduled flights, and are usually direct too, so they are well worth considering. Some charter flights come as part of a package that includes accommodation and other services, but most charter companies sell 'flight only' tickets, which are often very good deals.

Several airlines offer 'youth' or 'student' tickets, with sometimes significant discounts for people under 26 (sometimes 23) or in full-time education. Regulations vary, and not all agents will tell you about these offers. If you think you might be eligible, contact a specialist student travel agency – there's usually at least one in university towns and cities.

When comparing costs, you'll find that the cheapest flights are advertised by obscure 'bucket shops'. Many such firms are honest, but there are a few rogues who will take your money and disappear. If you feel suspicious, pay only a small deposit. And once you have the ticket, ring the airline to confirm that you are actually booked on the flight before paying the balance. If they insist on cash in advance, go somewhere else.

Some agents may tell you that the cheap flights in the ad are fully booked, 'but we have another one that costs a bit more ...'. Or the agent may claim to have the last two seats available for the whole month, which they will hold for two hours only. These are all old tricks. Don't panic – keep ringing around.

You may decide to opt for a more reliable service by paying more than the rock-bottom fare. You can go to a better known travel agent (such as STA Travel, who have offices worldwide, Campus Travel in the UK, Council Travel in the USA or Travel CUTS in Canada) or to a small independent agent, where your money is safe if they are 'bonded' ie members of a trade organisation

(eg ABTA in the UK, AFTA in Australia or AATA in the USA) that guarantees to protect your money in case of problems.

Once you have your ticket, keep a note of the number, flight numbers, dates, times and other details, and keep the information somewhere separate from money and valuables. The easiest thing to do is to take a few photocopies – carry one with you and leave another at home. If the ticket is lost or stolen, this will help you get a replacement.

It's sensible to buy travel insurance as early as possible. If you get it the week before you fly, you may find, for example, that you're not covered for delays to your flight caused by industrial action. For more details see Travel Insurance under Visas & Documents in the Regional Facts for the Visitor chapter.

Travellers with Special Needs

If you have special needs of any sort – you've broken a leg, you're vegetarian, travelling in a wheelchair, taking the baby, terrified of flying – you should let the airline know as soon as possible so that they can make arrangements. You should remind them when you reconfirm your booking (at least 72 hours before departure) and again when you check in at the airport. It may also be worth ringing round the airlines before you make your booking to find out how they can handle your particular needs.

Disabled travellers will find that airports and airlines can be surprisingly helpful, but they do need advance warning. Most international airports in Europe, North America and Australasia will provide escorts where needed, and there should be ramps, lifts, accessible toilets and reachable phones. Aircraft toilets are likely to present a problem; travellers should discuss this with the airline at an early stage and, if necessary, with their doctor.

Deaf travellers can ask for airport and inflight announcements to be written down for them. Airports in Africa probably won't have these facilities.

Guide dogs for the blind will often have to travel in a specially pressurised baggage

Air Travel Glossary

Baggage Allowance This will be written on your ticket and usually includes one 20kg item to go in the hold, plus one item of hand luggage.

Bucket Shops These are unbonded travel agencies specialising in discounted airline tickets.

Bumped Just because you have a confirmed seat doesn't mean you're going to get on the plane (see Overbooking).

Cancellation Penalties If you have to cancel or change a discounted ticket, there are often heavy penalties involved; insurance can sometimes be taken out against these penalties. Some airlines impose penalties on regular tickets as well, particularly against 'no-show' passengers.

Check-In Airlines ask you to check in a certain time ahead of the flight departure (usually one to two hours on international flights). If you fail to check in on time and the flight is overbooked, the airline can cancel your booking and give your seat to somebody else.

Confirmation Having a ticket written out with the flight and date you want doesn't mean you have a seat until the agent has checked with the airline that your status is 'OK' or confirmed. Meanwhile you could just be 'on request'.

Courier Fares Businesses often need to send urgent documents or freight securely and quickly. Courier companies hire people to accompany the package through customs and, in return, offer a discount ticket which is sometimes a phenomenal bargain. In effect, what the companies do is ship their freight as your luggage on regular commercial flights. This is a legitimate operation, but there are two shortcomings – the short turnaround time of the ticket (usually not longer than a month) and the limitation on your luggage allowance. You may have to surrender all your allowance and take only carry-on luggage.

Full Fares Airlines traditionally offer 1st class (coded F), business class (coded J) and economy class (coded Y) tickets. These days there are so many promotional and discounted fares available that few passengers pay full economy fare.

ITX An ITX, or 'independent inclusive tour excursion', is often available on tickets to popular holiday destinations. Officially it's a package deal combined with hotel accommodation, but many agents will sell you one of these for the flight only and give you phoney hotel vouchers in the unlikely event that you're challenged at the airport.

Lost Tickets If you lose your airline ticket an airline will usually treat it like a travellers cheque and, after inquiries, issue you with another one. Legally, however, an airline is entitled to treat it like cash and if you lose it then it's gone forever. Take good care of your tickets.

MCO An MCO, or 'miscellaneous charge order', is a voucher that looks like an airline ticket but carries no destination or date. It can be exchanged through any International Association of Travel Agents (IATA) airline for a ticket on a specific flight. It's a useful alternative to an onward ticket in those countries that demand one, and is more flexible than an ordinary ticket if you're unsure of your route.

No-Shows No-shows are passengers who fail to show up for their flight. Full-fare passengers who fail to turn up are sometimes entitled to travel on a later flight. The rest are penalised (see Cancellation Penalties).

On Request This is an unconfirmed booking for a flight.

Air Travel Glossary

Onward Tickets An entry requirement for many countries is that you have a ticket out of the country. If you're unsure of your next move, the easiest solution is to buy the cheapest onward ticket to a neighbouring country or a ticket from a reliable airline which can later be refunded if you do not use it.

Open Jaw Tickets These are return tickets where you fly out to one place but return from another. If available, this can save you backtracking to your arrival point.

Overbooking Airlines hate to fly empty seats and since every flight has some passengers who fail to show up, airlines often book more passengers than they have seats. Usually excess passengers make up for the no-shows, but occasionally somebody gets bumped. Guess who it is most likely to be? The passengers who check in late.

Point-to-Point Tickets These are discount tickets that can be bought on some routes in return for passengers waiving their rights to a stopover.

Promotional Fares These are officially discounted fares, available from travel agencies or direct from the airline.

Reconfirmation At least 72 hours prior to departure time of an onward or return flight, you must contact the airline and 'reconfirm' that you intend to be on the flight. If you don't do this the airline can delete your name from the passenger list and you could lose your seat.

Restrictions Discounted tickets often have various restrictions on them – such as needing to be paid for in advance and incurring a penalty to be altered. Others are restrictions on the minimum and maximum period you must be away, such as a minimum of 14 days or a maximum of one year.

Round-the-World Tickets RTW tickets give you a limited period (usually a year) in which to circumnavigate the globe. You can go anywhere the carrying airlines go, as long as you don't backtrack. The number of stopovers or total number of separate flights is decided before you set off and they usually cost a bit more than a basic return flight.

Stand-by This is a discounted ticket where you only fly if there is a seat free at the last moment. Stand-by fares are usually available only on domestic routes.

Transferred Tickets Airline tickets cannot be transferred from one person to another. Travellers sometimes try to sell the return half of their ticket, but officials can ask you to prove that you are the person named on the ticket. This is less likely to happen on domestic flights, but on an international flight tickets are compared with passports.

Travel Agencies Travel agencies vary widely and you should choose one that suits your needs. Some simply handle tours, while full-services agencies handle everything from tours and tickets to car rental and hotel bookings. If all you want is a ticket at the lowest possible price, then go to an agency specialising in discounted tickets.

Travel Periods Ticket prices vary with the time of year. There is a low (off-peak) season and a high (peak) season, and often a low-shoulder season and a high-shoulder season as well. Usually the fare depends on your outward flight – if you depart in the high season and return in the low season, you pay the high-season fare.

compartment with other animals, away from their owner; though smaller guide dogs may be admitted to the cabin. All guide dogs will be subject to the same quarantine laws (six months in isolation etc) as any other animal when entering or returning to countries currently free of rabies such as Britain or Australia.

Children under two travel for 10% of the standard fare (or free, on some airlines), as long as they don't occupy a seat. They don't get a baggage allowance either. 'Skycots' should be provided by the airline if requested in advance; these will take a child weighing up to about 10kg. Children between two and 12 can usually occupy a seat for half to two-thirds of the full fare, and do get a baggage allowance. Pushchairs can often be taken as hand luggage.

The UK

Numerous airlines fly between Britain and West Africa. Air France has a particularly good network, serving most cities in West Africa, with the added bonus of departures from regional airports, such as Manchester. Other airlines linking Britain and West Africa include Air Afrique, British Airways, Ghana Airways, KLM, Nigeria Airways, Sabena, Swissair, TAP Air Portugal and Royal Air Maroc.

For an idea of the prices you should expect to pay for scheduled flights between Britain and West Africa, return flights from London to Dakar start at about UK£400 to UK£500, while London to Accra costs from UK£350 to UK£400. Low season return fares between London and Abidjan or Bamako are around UK£500 or UK£550, respectively. During popular periods (such as the dry season for countries that are popular tourist destinations or at busy holiday times such as Christmas or the end of Ramadan), prices may rise by another UK£100.

Cheaper fares are available to Banjul on charter flights catering for package tourists. Flights go mostly from London, but there are also departures from regional airports. The leading charter flight and tour operator is The Gambia Experience (see Organised

Tours later in this chapter). Others include Kuoni and Thomsons. You can buy flight tickets direct from the operators or from many high street travel agents. Flight-only fares are around UK£300 return, but some agents offer special deals that include accommodation – often in reasonable hotels – for only a little extra. Even if you don't stay in the hotel all the time, it can still be worth taking this offer; the airport transfers and first or last night bed can be very useful. Last-minute flight-only stand-bys can drop to UK£200 or less – ideal if your dates are flexible. One-way flights may be cheaper, and some amazing deals are available if you're *very* flexible (see the boxed text).

There are many travel agents competing for your business. London is usually the best place to buy a ticket, although there are specialist travel agents outside the capital who are often just as cheap and can be easier to deal with. It's worth checking the ads in weekend newspapers or travel magazines, but the following main players are a good starting point. Note that from 22 April 2000, you will need to replace the 0171 in London telephone numbers with 0207.

Africa Travel Centre
  (☎ 0171-388 4163; email africatravel@easynet
  .co.uk) 21 Leigh St, London WC1H 9QX

Never Too Late

We heard from an Aussie traveller who flew into London's Gatwick airport from somewhere sunny in the USA, not looking forward to a few months of work in the British winter. Walking through the airport he saw a two week flight and luxury accommodation holiday in Gambia offered by a late-deal specialist for UK£99 (about US$150). The only catch was that the flight left that same morning. He grabbed his bag from the reclaim, bought the ticket and two hours later was flying back out of London, heading for West Africa and the sunshine once again.

African Travel Specialists
  (☎ 0171-630 5434) Glen House, Stag Place, Victoria, London SW1E 5AG
Bridge the World
  (☎ 0171-911 0900) 52 Chalk Farm Rd, Camden Town, London NW1 8AN
Campus Travel
  (☎ 0171-730 8111) 52 Grosvenor Gardens, London SW1W 0AG, also with offices in large YHA Adventure shops and universities/colleges around the country (for telephone bookings call ☎ 0171-730 2101, 0161-273 1721 or 0131-668 3303).
STA Travel
  (☎ 0171-361 6262) London branches include 117 Euston Rd NW1 (which has a dedicated Africa desk); 85 Shaftesbury Ave W1; and 40 Bernard St (near Russell Sq) WC1. There are also branches in Manchester, Bristol and most large university towns.

If you came into West Africa on a one way ticket or overland, you might need to get a one way flight home. Some suggested cities in West Africa to buy tickets are listed in the Continental Europe section, following. For cheap flights direct to Britain, there are regular charter flights from Banjul to London and other cities, from around UK£ 200 – probably the cheapest way to get from West Africa to Europe. The main holiday company operating these flights is The Gambia Experience. More details are given in the Getting There & Away section of the Gambia chapter.

Continental Europe

You can fly from any European capital to any city in West Africa, but some routes are more popular and frequent (and usually cheaper) than others. There's a particularly good choice of destinations that can be easily reached via Paris on Air France and Air Afrique.

Return fares on scheduled flights from France to several West African capitals start at around 3000FF (around US$500) and go up to around 4000FF (around US$650) during popular periods (such as holiday times), although you can find charters to Senegal for as little as 2000FF, especially in the less popular periods. There are also

some good options to Senegal from Belgium: Brussels to Dakar returns range from around Bf20,000 (around US$500) to Bf30,000 (US$750).

As a starting point, travel agents and tour operators you could try in **France** include:

Any Way
  (telephone sales only ☎ 01 803 008 008)
Council Travel
  (☎ 01 44 41 89 80) 1 place de l'Odéon, 75006 Paris
Nouvelles Frontières
  (☎ 01 41 41 58 58) 87 blvd de Grenelle, 75015 Paris, plus numerous other branches in France and French-speaking countries
Nouvelle Liberté
  (☎ 01 55 00 66 66) 2 rue du Dr Lombard, 92441 Issy-les-Moulineaux
Voyageurs en Afrique
  (☎ 01 42 86 16 60) 55 rue Sainte-Anne, 75002 Paris

In **Belgium**, you could try the following:

Acotra World
  (☎ 02-512 86 07) rue du Marché aux Herbes 110, 1000 Bruxelles
Connections
  (☎ 02-550 01 00) rue du Midi 19-21, 1000 Bruxelles
Eole
  (☎ 02-217 27 44) chaussée de Haecht 43, 1210 Bruxelles
Joker Toerisme
  (☎ 02-426 00 03, email luc callewaert@joker .be) Verdilaan 23, 1083 Ganshoren
Nouvelles Frontières
  (☎ 02-547 44 44) blvd Lemonnier 2, 1000 Bruxelles

If you didn't come on a return ticket, you can buy flights to any major European airport, from most capital cities in West Africa. However, when it comes to buying a ticket out, some cities are much better than others, with a wider choice of airlines, flights and prices. The best places to get flights to various European destinations are Dakar and Abidjan. Second for choice are Bamako and Accra. Cheap charter flights to France from Lomé (Togo) are also available. Lagos also has a good choice, but it's not worth going there just for a flight home.

North America

Although North Americans won't get the great deals that are available in London, there are a few discount agencies which keep a look out for the best air fare bargains. Look in major weekend newspapers or travel magazines for travel agents' advertisements. The magazine *Travel Unlimited* (PO Box 1058, Allston, MA 02134) publishes details of the cheapest air fares and courier possibilities for destinations all over the world from the USA. STA Travel (☎ 800-777 0112) and Council Travel (☎ 800-226 8624) have offices in major cities nationwide. Use Council Travel's toll-free number or check out their Web site (www.counciltravel.com).

STA Travel offices in the USA include the following:

- (☎ 800-781 4040 or 800-925 4777) International Group Services: 5900 Wilshire Blvd, Suite 2110, LA, CA 90036
- (☎ 310-824 1574) 920 Westwood Blvd, Los Angeles, CA 90024
- (☎ 415-391 8407) 51 Grant Ave, San Francisco, CA 94108
- (☎ 212-627 3111) 10 Downing St, New York, NY 10014

To comply with regulations, some agents are associated with specific travel clubs. The following is a list to get you started – some also arrange tours and make other on the ground arrangements. Some of the companies listed under Organised Tours later in this chapter also sell flights.

Falcon Wings Travel
(☎ 800-230 4947 or 310-417 3590) 9841 Airport Blvd, Suite 818, Los Angeles, CA 90045
Flytime Tours & Travel
(☎ 212-760 3737, fax 594 1082) 45 West 34th St, Suite 305, New York, NY 10001
Magical Holidays to Africa
(☎ 800-223 7452) 501 Madison Ave, Fl 14, New York, NY 10022
Pan Express Travel
(☎ 212-719 9292 or 719 2937) 25 West 39th St, Suite 705, New York, NY 10018
Uni Travel
(☎ 314-569 2501) PO Box 12485, St Louis, MO 63132

For an idea of prices, some agents sell Air Afrique direct flights from New York to Dakar and Abidjan with APEX (discounted tickets that must be paid for in advance) return fares from about US$1200 and US$1700, respectively. Excursion fares are more but allow a stopover (eg in Dakar en route to Abidjan).

Most airlines between the USA and West Africa go via Europe, in which case it may be cheaper to fly on an economy hop to London and then buy a discounted ticket onwards from there.

Canadians will probably also find the best deals travelling via Europe, especially London or Paris.

Australasia

There are not many route options from Australasia to West Africa. Most people fly via Europe, with flights starting at around A$2600. Going via East or South Africa is another option, although sometimes it's cheaper or more flexible to buy a round-the-world ticket, which sell for around A$2500. Another option is to fly on EgyptAir, via Cairo, to Accra, Abidjan or Lagos for around A$2300. Whichever way you go, discuss your options with several travel agents before buying. Few have had much experience with inexpensive routings to Africa.

In Australia and New Zealand, inexpensive deals are available mainly from STA Travel, which has branches in all capital cities and on most university campuses. In Australia phone ☎ 1300-360 960 for the latest fares, and ☎ 131 776 for details of your nearest STA office. In New Zealand phone STA on ☎ 0800-100 677. For more options check the ads in travel magazines and weekend newspapers.

Africa

Many travellers on long trans-Africa trips fly some sections, either because time is short or simply because land routes are virtually impassable. One section frequently hopped is the Western Sahara (because it can be tricky for travellers without vehicles) by flying between Dakar or Nouakchott (Mauritania) and Casablanca (Morocco). See the Getting There & Away sections in the Senegal and Mauritania chapters for more details.

For travellers going between West Africa and East or southern Africa, another section usually flown over is the great mass of Congo (Zaïre), along with Gabon, Congo-Brazzaville, Cameroon and usually Nigeria too. The best places to get flights in East or southern Africa are Nairobi (Kenya), Harare (Zimbabwe) or Johannesburg (South Africa), from where the easiest and cheapest flight options go mostly to Accra or Abidjan.

If you're going the other way – from West Africa to East or southern Africa – the same routes are also your best options. The most popular flights leave from Accra or Abidjan and go to Nairobi, Harare or Johannesburg. There are also regular flights between Lagos and Jo'burg. Note that some flights between West Africa and East/southern Africa are direct (eg Air Afrique flies between Abidjan and Jo'burg), while others are a little more meandering (eg Ethiopian Airlines covers the same destinations, but goes via Addis Ababa). Some sample fares are given in the relevant country chapters.

LAND
Border Crossings
If you're travelling independently overland to West Africa – whether hitching, cycling, driving your own car or going by public transport – you can approach the region from three main directions: from the north, across the Sahara; from the south-east, through Cameroon; or from the east, through Chad.

If you're coming from the north, the main border crossing points into West Africa are at Bordj-Moktar and Assamakka where the trans-Saharan routes through Algeria enter Mali and Niger. However, these routes are effectively closed to travellers due to political unrest in Algeria, so nearly all trans-Saharan tourist traffic goes from Morocco and Western Sahara into Mauritania, where the main border crossing point is just north of Nouâdhibou. This Western Sahara route is by far the most popular overland way to West Africa. Most travellers heading this

way have their own vehicles, and options for drivers and those on public transport are outlined briefly in the boxed text 'Crossing the Sahara' on the next page. It is very unusual for travellers to go south to north on this route, particularly as it is officially forbidden to cross overland from Mauritania in this direction. However, some alternative options do exist, and are outlined in the boxed text.

If you come into West Africa from the south-east, crossing from Cameroon into Nigeria, the most popular border crossing in the southern parts of these countries is Mfum-Ekok between Mamfé and Ikom. If you're travelling in the northern regions there are several more crossing points – Jimeli, between Mora and Maiduguri is one of the busiest.

Your final option is to come into West Africa from the east, travelling from Ndjamena (Chad), either straight to Maiduguri (Nigeria), crossing the border near Ngala, or going the 'long way round', crossing the border on the northern side of Lake Chad, on the route to Nguigmi (Niger). More details on these routes are given in the Getting There & Away sections of the Niger and Nigeria chapters.

Taking Your Own Vehicle
Driving your own car or motorbike to West Africa (and then around the region and possibly onwards to East or southern Africa) is a vast subject far beyond the scope of this book. Some recommended manuals which cover this subject are listed later in this section. These cover matters such as equipment, carnets, insurance, recommended routes (and their current conditions), driving techniques, maintenance, repairs, navigation and survival. Note, however, that these books are usually pretty thin on practical information about places to eat and sleep (mainly because most overlanders use their vehicle as a mobile hotel) and general background information about the country, such as history, economy etc. So we leave the practical vehicle information to the experts, and hope drivers find our guidebook invaluable for everything else!

Crossing the Sahara

There are three main routes across the Sahara leading to West Africa: the Route du Hoggar (through Algeria and Niger); the Route du Tanezrouft (through Algeria and Mali); and the Western Sahara Route (through Morocco and Mauritania). Since the early 1990s the Tanezrouft and Hoggar routes have been virtually unused by travellers, initially due to antigovernment Tuareg rebellions in Mali and Niger, and more recently due to civil unrest in Algeria, where foreigners have been targeted by antigovernment terrorists. Thus, all drivers and nearly all independent travellers (hitching or using public transport) now use the Western Sahara Route to reach West Africa.

Anybody planning to travel in the Sahara should check out the excellent Web site put together by desert specialist Chris Scott, www.users.globalnet.co.uk/~ckscott/.

Warning

It is unlikely that either the Route du Hoggar or the Route du Tanezrouft will become usable for tourists in the next few years, so only the briefest of information is included here. Do not travel on these routes without first checking the current security situation. Note that, although we hear rumours of the occasional intrepid traveller still crossing via Algeria, this is unequivocally dangerous and cannot be recommended.

Route du Hoggar

The Route du Hoggar through Algeria and Niger is tar except for the 600km section between Tamanrasset ('Tam') and Arlit, although the tar is in poor shape on many sections. The fabulous Hoggar Mountains and Aïr Massif are well worth extra diversions, and the route passes several magnificent outcrops of wind-eroded rocks, while Agadez, at the end of the route, is one of the most interesting desert towns in West Africa.

Route du Tanezrouft

The Route du Tanezrouft runs through Algeria and Mali, via Adrar and the border at Bordj-Moktar, to end in Gao. It is technically easier than the Route du Hoggar, even though the dirt section is over 1300km, and has a reputation for being monotonous, although some travellers find that the sheer size and remoteness of the desert is better appreciated here. This consideration is more than outweighed by the significantly increased risk factor. Help, should you need it, is likely to be a long time coming.

Western Sahara Route

Travel through Morocco is pretty straightforward (see Lonely Planet's *Morocco* guide). About 500km south of Agadir you enter the disputed territory of Western Sahara. This former Spanish colony was occupied in 1976 by Morocco, who flooded it with settlers. Since then an armed movement called the Polisario Front has been fighting for an independent state and proper recognition of the indigenous Sahrawi people – most of whom have been stuck in refugee camps in Algeria for over two decades. A shaky cease-fire was negotiated in the early 1990s, with Mauritania and Algeria acting as peace brokers. Elections allowing local people to choose between independence and Moroccan integration have been due for some years, but are continually bogged down as both sides haggle over who will be allowed to vote.

The main road continues through the Western Sahara, running along the coast, all the way to Dakhla. There are a couple of cheap hotels and a camp site (which also has some rooms)

Crossing the Sahara

where all the overlanders stay, and this is the best place to find other vehicles to team up with. If you're hitching, there's a thriving trade in second-hand cars being driven from Europe (especially France) to sell in West Africa, and these drivers are sometimes happy to give lifts to travellers, although sharing costs is expected. Hitchers are not allowed in Mauritanian vehicles, and there have been occasional scams where hitchers with local drivers have been abandoned in the desert unless they pay a large 'fee'.

South of Dakhla all traffic must join one of the twice-weekly convoys (currently departing on Tuesday and Friday) organised by the Moroccan military. Drivers must register with the sûreté, as well as the 'province' (to get permission to proceed towards Mauritania), then get customs clearance before going to the army headquarters to register their vehicle for the convoy itself.

The convoy drives for 300km towards Mauritania, but the army vehicles turn back about 8km before the actual border, leaving the tourist vehicles to carefully follow the route through the minefields to reach the Mauritanian border post. The mines are a real danger, and this section is pretty nerve-wracking. After border formalities it's another 100km and several checkpoints to the town of Nouâdhibou.

From Nouâdhibou, most vehicles go south down the coast to Nouakchott, through the Parc National du Banc d'Arguin, including a 160km stretch along the beach at low tide, with soft sand on one side and waves breaking over your windscreen on the other. Some cars, most bikes and hitchers go east on the train to Choûm, and then take the road via Atâr and Akjout to Nouakchott. For more details on these options, see the Getting Around section in the Mauritania chapter.

We had a very interesting readers letter from Barry Gilmore who had travelled widely overland in Africa, and was determined to get home without his feet leaving the ground:

After several months in West Africa, I travelled from Senegal to Nouakchott and then to Nouâdhibou via Choûm and the iron-ore train. It was a battle to get on the only passenger carriage on this 3km-long line of wagons, but well worth the fight, and the price of 600 ougiya. You can ride for free on the open wagons as some poor locals do, but this is only for the truly desperate and crazed adventurers. Even inside the crowded carriage the desert night was cold, but the atmosphere was good – there was even some singing and dancing.

In Nouâdhibou I had trouble continuing my journey north. It is not permitted officially to travel from Mauritania to Western Sahara by land. Unofficially, you can find guides who will show you where to jump off the train about 30km to the east of the main border and lead you through the minefields, but this costs 40,000 ougiya and is highly risky. I tried to go by sea to Las Palmas in the Canary Islands, but the twice-monthly cargo boats no longer take passengers. I found some fishing boats who were ready to take passengers but there was nothing going for up to a month. A traveller I met dubbed Nouâdhibou the Hotel California because it was so hard to leave.

In the end I went on the Air Mauritania flight (twice weekly) to Las Palmas, which was expensive at 45,000 ougiya one way, but I was glad to escape Nouâdhibou after 10 days of increasingly frustrating hanging around. I stayed a week in the Canaries, then got back to the African mainland by flying to Laayoune in the Western Sahara. This flight cost 22,000 pesetas (around US$150). From there I travelled by bus through Morocco to cross the Straits of Gibraltar and eventually reach Europe.

The *Sahara Handbook*, by Simon Glen, is the long-standing classic manual if you're coming to West Africa overland in your own vehicle. Although it concentrates on the Algerian trans-desert routes, which are currently closed to traffic, it also includes coverage of the northern Sahel, and much of the general information is relevant.

Sahara Overland (published by Trailblazer) is a brand new book to look out for. The author, Chris Scott, is a desert specialist, and this detailed and comprehensive book covers all aspects of the Sahara for travellers on two or four wheels, with information on established and new routes (including those in Mauritania, Mali, Niger and Libya), and over 100 maps.

Africa by Road, by Bob Swain and Paula Snyder, is recommended once you're across the desert. Half the book is no-nonsense advice on everything from paperwork and supplies to driving techniques, while the other half is a complete country-by-country rundown.

The *Adventure Motorcyclists Handbook*, by Chris Scott, covers all parts of the world where tar roads end. It contains stacks of good information on the Sahara and West Africa, all combined with humour and personal insights.

Shipping a Vehicle If you want to travel around West Africa using your own car or motorbike, but don't fancy the Sahara crossing, another option is to ship it. The usual way of doing this is to load the car onto a ship in Europe and take it off again at either Dakar or Banjul (although Abidjan and Tema, in Ghana, are other options).

Costs range from US$500 to US$1000 depending on the size of the vehicle and the final destination, but apart from cost your biggest problem is likely to be security – many drivers report theft of items from the inside and outside (such as lights and mirrors) of their car. Vehicles are usually left unlocked for the crossing and when in storage at the destination port, so chain or lock all equipment into fixed boxes inside the vehicle. Getting a vehicle out of port is frequently a nightmare, requiring visits to several different offices where stamps must be obtained and mysterious fees paid at every turn. You could consider using an official handling agent or an unofficial 'fixer' to take your vehicle through all this.

Two British bikers wrote to us with details of how they shipped their motorcycles between London and Banjul, and back again, with Allied Pickfords (☎ 0181-219 8000, fax 219 8001; from 22 April 2000 ☎ 020-8219 8000, fax 8219 8001). The process was 'very slick', and the return trip cost UK£1100 per bike.

SEA

For most people, reaching West Africa by sea is not a viable consideration. The days of working your passage on commercial boats have long gone, although a few lucky travellers do manage to hitch rides on private yachts sailing from Spain, Morocco or the Canary Islands, to Senegal, Gambia and beyond. Alternatively, several cargo shipping companies run from Europe to West Africa, with comfortable officer-style cabins available to the public. (There are very few options from the USA). A typical voyage from London takes about eight days to Dakar and 13 days to Abidjan. Costs vary according to the quality of the ship, but don't take this option if you want to save money – Europe to Dakar is around US$1500 to US$1800 per person in a double cabin.

For more information, see *Travel by Cargo Ship*, a handy book by Hugo Verlomme, or contact one of the following specialist agents:

Associated Oceanic Agencies Ltd
(☎ 0171-930 5683, fax 839 1961) 103 Jermyn St, London SW1Y 6EE, UK
Strand Voyages
(☎ 0171-836 6363, fax 497 0078) Charing Cross Shopping Concourse, Strand, London WC2N 4HZ, UK
Freighter Travel Club of America
3524 Harts Lake Loop, Roy, WA 98580, USA (publishers of *Freighter Travel News*)
Freighter World Cruises
(☎ 626-449 3106, fax 449 9573) 180 South Lake Ave, No 335-1, Pasadena, CA 91101, USA (publishers of *Freighter Space Advisory*)

ORGANISED TOURS

Two main sorts of tour are available. On an overland tour, you go all the way from

Europe to West Africa, visiting several countries, which usually takes two months (or possibly up to six). On an inclusive tour you fly to your destination and spend two to three weeks in a single country. Between these two types is the option of joining an overland tour for a short section (usually three to five weeks), flying out and back at either end.

Where relevant, details of tours organised by local companies are listed in the Getting Around sections of the individual country chapters.

Overland Tours

For these trips, you travel in an 'overland truck' with about 15 to 28 other people, a couple of drivers/leaders, plus tents and other equipment. Food is bought along the way and the group cooks and eats together. Most of the hassles (such as border crossings) are taken care of by the leader. Disadvantages include a fairly fixed itinerary and the possibility of spending a long time with other people. Having said that, overland truck tours are extremely popular.

Many overland truck companies are based in Britain, so most tours start in London and travel to West Africa via Europe and Morocco. Tours can be 'slow' or 'fast', depending on the number of places visited along the way. Some form part of a longer trans-Africa trip to/from Nairobi or Harare.

Many people don't have the time for long-distance trips between Europe and West Africa, so most overland companies also arrange shorter trips, for example London to Banjul or Dakar. Most overland companies can arrange your flights to join and leave the tour. Alternatively, some of the specialist travel agents listed in the Air section earlier can also arrange tours.

The overland tour market is dominated by British companies, although passengers come from many parts of the world. Following is a list of some UK-based overland tour companies offering trips in West Africa. Note that from 22 April 2000, you'll need to replace the 0171 and 0181 codes in London phone numbers with 0207 and 0208, respectively.

Acacia Expeditions
(☎ 0171-706 4700, fax 706 4686) 23A Craven Terrace, London W2 3QH
Africa Explored
(☎ 01633-880224, fax 882128) Rose Cottage, Summerleaze, Magor Newport NP6 3DE
African Trails
(☎ 0181-742 7724, fax 742 8621) 3 Flanders Rd, London W4 1NQ
Dragoman
(☎ 01728-861133, fax 861127, email brox@dragoman.co.uk) Camp Green, Kenton Rd, Debenham, Stowmarket IP14 6LA
Economic Expeditions
(☎ 0181-995 7707, fax 742 7707) 29 Cunnington St, London W4 5ER
Encounter Overland
(☎ 0171-370 6845, fax 244 9737) 267 Old Brompton Rd, London SW5 9JA
Exodus Overland
(☎ 0181-673 0859, fax 673 0779) 9 Weir Rd, London SW12 0LT
Guerba
(☎ 01373-858956, fax 838351) Wessex House, 40 Station Rd, Westbury BA13 3JN
Oasis Overland
(☎ 0181-759 5597, fax 897 2313) 33 Travellers Way, London TW4 7QB
TransAfrique
(☎ 01908-378028) 9 Rockspray Grove, Milton Keynes MK7 7AE
Truck Africa
(☎ 0171-731 6142, fax 371 7445, email truckafrica@zambezi1.demon.co.uk) 37 Ranelagh Gardens Mansions, London SW6 3UQ

Also well worth checking is a small British company called Saharan Expeditions (email saharanex@geocities.com or check out their Web site www.geocities.com/Baja/Dunes/3258), exporting all sorts of vehicles through Europe, Morocco and Mauritania to Gambia and Senegal, with spare seats sold to the public at very reasonable prices.

In North America and Australasia overland tour companies are represented by specialist travel agencies, and the best place to start hunting for details are the advertisements in travel magazines and weekend papers.

Inclusive Tours

This type of tour includes your international flight, transport around the country, food, accommodation, excursions, local guide and so on. They are usually around two to three weeks long, and ideal if you want to visit West Africa but lack the time or inclination for long-distance overland trucks.

The number of inclusive tour companies operating in West Africa is much smaller than in East or southern Africa, but there's still a fair selection. Some of the overland companies listed earlier also run shorter inclusive tours, and this can be one of the best ways to reach the more unusual destinations such as Niger or Côte d'Ivoire, which are not usually covered by the inclusive tour companies.

Wherever you live, when it comes to buying inclusive tours, as with flights and overland tours, the best place to begin looking is the advertisements in the weekend newspapers and travel magazines. The following list will provide some idea of the range of companies available. Give them a call, ask for a brochure, see what appeals, then take it from there.

Many inclusive tour companies operating in West Africa are based in **Britain**, although many of these take clients from all over the world. Some companies you could try include the following:

Afrikan Heritage
(☎ 0171-328 4376; from 22 April 2000 ☎ 020-7328 4376) 60B Rowley Way, London NW8 0SJ. Gambian-run tours based in Gambia.

Brekete West Africa Tours
(☎ 0181-933 7889; from 22 April 2000 ☎ 020-8933 7889) 48 Grange Farm Close, South Harrow HA2 0BQ. Small, personalised company running tours to Ghana, with links to the Academy of African Music and Arts.

Dragoman (listed under Overland Tours)

Drumdance
(☎/fax 01524-64616) 11 Bank Rd, Lancaster LA1 2DG. Cultural, musical and special interest tours for independently minded travellers.

Exodus (listed under Overland Tours)

Explore Worldwide
(☎ 01252-344161 or 319448, fax 343170, email info@explore.co.uk) 1 Frederick St, Aldershot GU11 1LQ. Well established company offering a huge range of adventurous and active tours and treks, including Mali.

Guerba (listed under Overland Tours)

Insight Travel
(☎ 01995-606095, fax 602124, email insight@provider.co.uk, Web site www.illustrations.co.uk/users/insight-travel) 6 Norton Rd, Preston, Lancashire PR3 1JY. This small agency, run by a former VSO field director in Ghana, offers trips based in Kumasi, with the opportunity of living with a Ghanaian family; activities offered include birdwatching, touring Ashanti craft villages, and lessons in dance, music or weaving.

Karamba Experience
(☎/fax 01603-872402, email karamba@gn.apc.org, Web site www.karamba.co.uk) Ollands Lodge, Heydon, Norwich NR11 6RB. Holidays in Senegal, concentrating on learning to play drums and other African instruments, as well as time for the beach and other excursions.

Limosa Holidays
(☎ 01263-578143, fax 579251) Suffield House, Northrepps, Norfolk NR7 0LZ. Specialist birding trips, including Gambia.

Naturetrek Chautara
(☎ 01962-733051, fax 736426, email sales@naturetrek.co.uk) Brighton Airesford, Hampshire SO24 9RB. Bird and wildlife specialists; offers a tour in Mali.

The Gambia Experience
(☎ 01703-730888, fax 731122, email gambia@serenity.co.uk) Kingfisher House, Rownhams Lane, North Baddesley, Hampshire SO52 9LP. Leading operator of package holidays to Gambia, with some options in Senegal, plus a selection of specialist birding, fishing and cultural tours; sells excellent-value charter flights.

Travelbag Adventures
(☎ 01420-541007, fax 541022, email mail@travelbag-adventures.co.uk, Web site www.travelbag-adventures.co.uk) 15 Turk St, Alton GU34 1AG. Small group, adventurous holidays all over the world, with an unusual trip to Cameroon and exploratory tours planned to other parts of West Africa.

Wildwings
(☎ 0117-984 8040, fax 961 0200) International House, Bank Rd, Bristol BS15 2LX. Birding and wildlife specialists; expeditions and tours worldwide, including Senegal and Gambia.

In **France**, companies to try include the following:

Explorator
(☎ 01 53 45 85 85) 16 rue de la Banque, 75002 Paris. Destinations include the Sahara region, Senegal, Gambia and Mali.

Nouvelles Frontières
(☎ 01 41 41 58 58) 87 blvd de Grenelle, 75015 Paris, plus numerous other branches in France and French-speaking countries. Wide range of mainstream holidays and adventurous tours all over West Africa and beyond.

Terres d'Aventure
(☎ 01 53 73 77 77) 6 rue Saint-Victor, 75005 Paris. Various adventurous trips in West Africa and the Sahara region, including Senegal and Mauritania.

Voyageurs en Afrique
(☎ 01 42 86 16 60) 55 rue Sainte-Anne, 75002 Paris. Tours in Senegal, plus hotel booking and car rentals for independent travellers.

In the **USA**, there are only a few companies which actually operate inclusive tours in West Africa. Most act as agents or representatives for other companies based in Europe or Africa, or can provide you with a trip tailor-made to your own requirements. Companies include:

Adventure Center
(☎ 510-654 1879 or 800-227 8747) 1311 63rd St, Emeryville, CA 91608

Born Free Safaris
(☎ 800-372 3274 or 818-981 7185, fax 818-753 1460) 12504 Riverside Dr, North Hollywood, CA 91607

Cross Cultural Adventurers
(☎ 703-237 0100, fax 237 2558) Box 3285, Arlington, VA 22203

Mountain Travel-Sobek
(☎ 800-227 2384, fax 510-525 7710) 6420 Fairmount Ave, El Cerrito CA 94530

Museum for African Art
(☎ 212-966 1313) 593 Broadway, New York, NY 10012. Offers cultural tours.

SafariCentre
(☎ 310-546 4411or 800-223 6046, fax 310-546 3188) 3201 N Sepulveda Blvd, Manhattan Beach, CA

Turtle Tours
(☎ 888-299 1439 or 602-488 3688, fax 602-488 3406) Box 1147, Carefree, AZ 85377

West African Safaris
95361 (☎ 209-847 7710, fax 847 8150) PO Box 365, Oakdale, CA

Wilderness Travel
(☎ 800-368 2794 or 510-558 2488, fax 510-558 2489) 1102 Ninth St, Berkeley, CA 94710

In **Canada**, the situation is very similar to that in the USA, with most companies acting as agents or representatives for other companies based in Europe or Africa. Possible starting points include the following:

Adventures Abroad
(fax 604 303 1076) Vancouver

Adventure Centre & Trek Holidays
(☎ 416-922 7584 or 800-276 3347) 25 Bellair St, Toronto, Ontario M5R 3L3

Connections Travel
(☎ 604-738 9499) Suite 210, 1847 West Broadway, Vancouver BC V6J 1Y6

In **Australasia**, many of the tour companies listed earlier are represented by specialist travel agents, including the following:

Peregrine Adventures
(☎ 03-9662 2700) 258 Lonsdale St, Melbourne, Vic, or (☎ 02-9290 2770) 38 York St, Sydney, NSW, Australia. Agents for Guerba.

Getting Around the Region

This chapter briefly outlines the various ways of travelling around West Africa. For more specific details see the Getting There & Away and Getting Around sections of the individual country chapters.

AIR

Distances are great in Africa, and if time is short a few flights around the region can considerably widen your options. Even within a country, flying can save vital days or hours for those on tight schedules (eg between Mopti and Timbuktu in Mali).

Some airlines and airports are very good, some are bad and some are definitely worth avoiding. Don't be surprised if you have to wait half a day at check-in (always bring a good book), or if during the flight the cabin crew try to keep the door from coming off. (Sometimes they *don't* try to stop the door coming off, as was our experience on one flight during research for this book!) Other horror stories involve airport clerks issuing more boarding passes than seats, and some unlucky passengers being dumped on the runway. Usually, however, there's not a lot of choice, with only two or three airlines operating between most major cities.

Flying within West Africa is not cheap because the distances are often great – for example, from Dakar (Senegal) to Abidjan (Côte d'Ivoire) is equivalent to flying halfway across the USA. Some sample one-way fares are: Dakar to Bamako in Mali (about 500km) US$150, and Banjul (Gambia) to Accra in Ghana (about 1000km) US$250. Return fares are usually double the one way fares. Some West African airlines offer youth or student fares and these are always worth asking about.

It's usually better to buy tickets in West Africa through a travel agency, rather than from the airline. They can explain the choice available, without you having to visit several airline offices, and the price is usually the same. They may also help you with refunds

if anything goes wrong. Usually, tickets issued by one airline are not acceptable ('endorsable') on another airline.

Once you've bought your ticket don't forget to reconfirm your reservation, even if the ticket says 'OK'. If you can't get a confirmation, you'll be put on the waiting list. Although far from ideal, this is not a completely disastrous situation. Your chances of getting on the plane are frequently quite good if you get to the airport early.

BUS & BUSH TAXI

The most common forms of public transport in West Africa are bus (*car* in Francophone countries) and bush taxi (*taxi brousse*). Buses may be run by state-owned or private companies. Bush taxis are always private, although the driver is rarely the owner of the vehicle. Vehicles are usually located at bus and bush taxi parks, called *gare routière* in Francophone countries, 'garage', 'lorry park' or 'motor park' in English-speaking countries and *paragem* in Portuguese-speaking countries. The gare routière is usually in the centre of town, near the market. Most large cities have several gares routières, one for each main direction or destination.

In some countries buses are common and bush taxis are hard to find; in other countries it's the reverse. Either way, travel generally costs between US$1 and US$2 per 100km, although fares depend on the quality of the vehicle and the route. On routes between countries (eg between Ouagadougou in Burkina Faso and Abidjan in Côte d'Ivoire) costs can be more because drivers have to pay additional fees (official and unofficial) to cross the border. You can save money by taking one vehicle to the border and then another on the other side, but this can prolong the trip considerably.

Touts at the Gare Routière

At most gares routières, bush taxis leave on a fill-up-and-go basis, but problems can arise when you get more than one vehicle covering the same route. This is when a tout (called a *coti-man* in some countries) can earn money by persuading you to take 'his' car, and they'll tell you anything to get you on board: 'this one is very fast', 'this minibus is going soon', 'this bus is a good cheap price' etc. Another trick involves putting your baggage on the roof rack as a 'deposit' against you taking another car.

One consolation is that you're not being targeted because you're a wealthy foreigner. The touts hassle everybody. Try and check which vehicle has the most passengers, as this is usually the one to go first. But essentially it's a gamble. And the touts do nothing to make decisions any easier!

Bus

Long distance buses (sometimes called a 'big bus', *grand car,* to distinguish it from a minibus) vary in size – usually between 35 and 70 seats – and services vary considerably between countries and areas. On the main routes buses are often good quality, with a reliable service and fixed departure times (arrival times may be more fluid).

On quiet roads in rural areas, buses may be incredibly ancient, and may have frequent breakdowns and regular stops to let passengers on or off. These buses have no timetable, and usually go when full or when the driver feels like it. Generally, bus fares are cheaper than bush taxi fares for a comparable route.

You may arrange a long ride by bus or bush taxi, and find yourself transferring to another vehicle somewhere along the way. There is no need to pay more – your driver pays your fare direct to the driver of the next vehicle – but unfortunately it can mean long waits while the arrangements are made.

On some main-route buses, you can reserve in advance, and this is often advisable. In many countries you book a place but not a specific seat. Just before the bus leaves, names get called out in the order that tickets were bought, and you get on and choose the seat you want. It's rather like answering the register at school. Indeed, some passengers reply 'present' when their name is called out.

Bush Taxi

A bush taxi is effectively a small bus. Almost without exception, bush taxis leave when full of passengers, not according to a timetable. As soon as one car leaves, the next one starts to fill. Depending on the popularity of the route, the car may take half an hour or several days to fill. Either way, drivers jealously guard their car's place in the queue.

Early customers can choose where to sit. Latecomers get no choice and are assigned to the least comfortable seats – usually at the back. The best time to catch bush taxis is usually early morning, although departures are sometimes determined by market days, and then the afternoon may be best.

Luggage Fees

In many countries transport fares are fixed by the government, so the only way the bush taxi drivers can earn a bit extra is to charge for luggage. Local people accept this, so travellers should too, unless of course the amount is unreasonable. The fee for a medium-sized rucksack is usually around 10% of the fare. Small bags will be less – a good reason for travelling light. Some travellers carry bags the size of a fridge and they're often the ones complaining the loudest. If you think you're being overcharged, ask other passengers – out of earshot of the driver. When you know the proper rate, stand your ground politely and the price will soon fall.

There are three main types of bush taxi in West Africa, as follows.

Peugeot 504 These cars, assembled in Nigeria or imported from Europe, are used all over West Africa and are also called *cinq-cent-quatre*, Peugeot-taxi, *sept-place* and *brake*. With three rows of seats, they are built to take the driver plus seven passengers. In some countries this limit is observed. In others it's flagrantly flouted. All 504s in Mali, for example, take the driver plus nine passengers. In Guinea you might be jammed in with at least a dozen adults, plus children and bags, with more luggage and a couple of extra passengers riding on the roof. That these cars do hundreds of thousands of kilometres on some of the worse roads in the world is a credit to the manufacturer and the ingenuity of local mechanics.

Quality varies. Some drivers are safe and considerate; others verge on insanity. Some cars are quite new (there are quite a few Peugeot 505s, the later model, around these days) and well maintained, with comfortable seats. Others are very old, reduced to nothing more than chassis, body and engine: there's more weld than original metal, tyres are bald, most upholstery is missing, and little extras

like windows, door handles and even exhaust pipes have long since disappeared.

If a bush taxi looks like it's going to get uncomfortably full you can buy two seats for yourself – it's simply double the price. Likewise, if you want to charter the whole car, take the price of one seat and multiply it by the number available, then add some more for the equivalent of seven people's luggage.

If a group of passengers has been waiting a long time, and there's only two or three seats to fill, they may club together and pay extra so as to get moving. If you do this, don't expect a discount because you're saving the driver the hassle of looking for other passengers – time is not money in Africa. If you pick up someone along the way, however, the fare they pay goes to the passengers who bought the seats, not to the driver.

Minibus Many routes are served by minibuses (*minicars*) – usually seating about 12 to 20 passengers. In some countries these are just large bush taxis, but in others they fill a category between bus and bush taxi. Typically about 25% cheaper than 504s, they can be more comfortable than old 504s, although slower (which usually means safer). Police

Love 'em or hate 'em, bush taxis are the ultimate West African experience.

checks at roadblocks take longer to negotiate because there are more passengers to search.

Pick-Up With wooden seats down the sides, covered pick-ups (*bâchés*) are definitely 2nd class, but are sometimes the only kind of bush taxi available. They officially take around 16 passengers but are invariably stuffed with people and baggage, plus a few chickens (live, of course), and your feet may be higher than your waist from resting on a sack of millet. Up on the roof go more bags, bunches of bananas, extra passengers and goats (also live). Bâché rides are often very slow, and police checks at roadblocks are interminable as drivers or passengers frequently lack vital papers. The ride is guaranteed to be unpleasant unless you adopt an African attitude, which means each time your head hits the roof as the vehicle descends into yet another big pothole, you roar with laughter. There's nothing like local humour to change an otherwise miserable trip into a tolerable, even enjoyable, experience.

TRUCK & HITCHING

In many countries, as you venture further into rural areas, the frequency of buses or bush taxis drops dramatically – sometimes to nothing. Then the only way around is to ride on local trucks, which is what the locals do. A 'fare' is payable to the driver, so in cases like this the line between hitching and

---

Warning

Bush taxi drivers often race along at hair-raising speeds and overtake blind to reach their destination before another car can get in front of them in the queue for the return journey. In addition, drivers can be sleepy from an 18 hour work day. If you feel unsafe, rather than complain about the dangerous driving, say you're feeling sick. Drivers seem to care more about keeping vomit off their seats than about dying under the wheels of an oncoming lorry.

---

public transport is blurred – but if it's the only way to get around you've got no choice anyway. Usually you'll be riding on top of the cargo – it may be cotton or rice in sacks, which are quite comfortable, but it might be logs or oil drums, which aren't.

If you want to hitch because there's no public transport going from the gare routière, you'll normally have to go well beyond the town limits, as bush taxi drivers may take umbrage at other vehicles 'stealing' their customers. Even so, you'll probably still have to pay for your lift – but at least you'll get moving more quickly.

Hitching in the western sense (ie because you don't want to get the bus, or more specifically because you don't want to pay) is also possible, but may take a very long time. The only people giving free lifts are likely to be foreign expatriates, volunteer aid-workers, or the occasional well-off local (very few West Africans own a car).

Most people with space in their car are likely to want payment – usually on a par with what a bus would have cost. The most common vehicles for lifts of this sort are driven by locals working for international agencies, government bodies or aid and relief organisations; all over West Africa you'll see smart white Land Cruisers with words and badges on the doors (eg UNESCO, Ministry of Energy or 'Save the Sahel'), never more than a few years old, always going too fast, and always full of people. But beggars can't be choosers, and if you've been waiting all day and one of these stops for you, in you'll get however distasteful it might be.

However, as in any other part of the world, hitching or accepting lifts is never entirely safe, and we therefore don't recommend it. Travellers who decide to hitch should understand that they are taking a small but potentially serious risk. If you're planning to travel this way, take advice from other hitchers (locals or travellers) first. Hitching in pairs is obviously safer, and hitching through less salubrious suburbs, especially at night, is asking for trouble.

TRAIN

There are railways in Mauritania, Senegal, Mali, Côte d'Ivoire, Ghana, Burkina Faso, Togo, Benin and Nigeria. Some services run only within a country, but there are also some international services, notably between Dakar and Bamako, and between Ouagadougou and Abidjan.

Some services are relatively comfortable, with 1st class coaches, which may be air-conditioned. Some also have sleeping compartments, with two or four bunks. Other services are 2nd or 3rd class only, and conditions can be uncomfortable, with no lights, no toilets and no glass in the windows (no fun on long night journeys). Some trains have a restaurant on board, but you can usually buy things to eat and drink at every station along the way.

CAR & MOTORCYCLE

Some general points about driving your own vehicle to and around West Africa (or shipping it) are covered in the Land section of the Getting There & Away chapter. Your other option is to rent a car or motorbike. Whether you rent or bring you own vehicle, especially the latter, there are a few things to be aware of, as follows.

The most important thing to remember is that throughout West Africa, traffic drives on the right – as in continental Europe and the USA – even in countries which have a British colonial heritage (such as Gambia). Your next major consideration is the location of the principal routes. Some dirt roads can be used year-round, while others are impassable in the rains, and you can't necessarily tell this from road maps. Some tar roads become so badly potholed that a dirt road would be much better. Conditions can change from year to year, so the best way to keep up to date is to talk to other drivers, although you should also try to use the most recent maps you can.

The quality, availability and price of fuel (petrol and diesel – called *essence* and *gasoil*, respectively, in the Francophone countries) varies between countries, and also between rural and urban areas. Where tax-ation, subsidies or currency rates make petrol particularly cheaper in one country than its neighbour you'll inevitably find traders who have carried large drums across the border and sell 'black market' fuel at the roadside.

To drive a car or motorbike in West Africa you will need a driving licence and, ideally, an International Driving Permit (see the boxed text in the Visas & Documents section of the Regional Facts for the Visitor chapter for more details). If you're hiring a car, the rental agency will provide all your insurance papers – make sure they are up to date.

If you're bringing your own vehicle you'll need to arrange a *carnet* – a document for the car to prevent you importing or exporting it illegally. This is covered in more detail in the specialist manuals listed in the Land section of the Getting There & Away chapter.

Rental

There are car rental agencies in most capital cities and tourist areas. Most international companies (Hertz, Avis, Budget etc) are represented, plus smaller independent operators, but renting is invariably expensive – you can easily spend in one day what you'd pay for a week's rental in Europe or the USA. If the small operators charge less, it's usually because the vehicles are older and sometimes not well maintained. But sometimes it's simply because their costs are lower and they can do a better deal, so if you've got the time, check around for bargains. You will need to put down a large deposit (credit cards are usually good for this).

It's very unlikely you'll be allowed to take a rental car across a border, but if you are (for example from Gambia into Senegal) make sure the paperwork is valid. If you're uncertain about driving, most companies can provide a chauffeur at very little extra cost – sometimes it's cheaper because you pay less for insurance.

In tourist areas, such as Gambia and Senegal, it is also possible to hire mopeds and motorbikes. In most other countries there is no formal rental available, but if you want to hire a motorbike (and know how to ride one) you can usually arrange something by asking around at an auto parts shop or repair yard, or by asking at the reception of your hotel. You can often be put in touch with someone who doesn't mind earning some extra cash by renting out their wheels for a day or two. Remember, though, that matters such as insurance will be easily overlooked, which is fine until you have an accident and find yourself liable for all bills.

Taxi Hire As an alternative to hiring a car, consider using a taxi by the day. It will probably cost you less (anywhere from about US$20 to US$50 per day), and if the car breaks down it'll be the driver's problem. You can either hire a city taxi or a bush taxi. Whichever, make sure it's mechanically sound before agreeing to anything. Even if you know nothing about cars, just looking at the bodywork or listening to the engine will give you an idea.

The price you pay will have to be worth the driver taking it out of public service for the day. If you want a deal including petrol, he'll reduce the speed to a slow trot and complain incessantly every time you take a

Car Hire – Beware!

If you have never driven in a developing country before, hiring a self-drive car is not something to be undertaken lightly. Road conditions outside the capital are often bad and, apart from the potholes, dangers include people and animals moving unexpectedly into your path. Smaller roads are not tarred, so you need to be able to drive comfortably on dirt. There are very few signposts, so you should take a map and be able to read it. You also need to be aware that outside capital cities, phones are few and far between, should you need to contact your rental company in case of breakdown. Having some basic mechanical knowledge, at the very least being able to change a wheel, is very useful.

detour. But a fixed daily rate for the car, while you pay extra for petrol, is much easier to arrange. Finding a car with a working petrol gauge may be tricky, but you can work on the assumption that the tank will be empty when you start, and if you allow for 10km/L on reasonable roads (more on bad roads) you should be OK.

BICYCLE

Cycling is a cheap, convenient, healthy, environmentally sound and, above all, fun way to travel. On top of this, you'll probably get more out of your visit as you often stay in small towns and villages, interact more with the local people, and eat West African food more frequently. In general, the remoter the areas you visit, the better the experience.

Traditional touring machines will cope with most tar roads (and some good dirt roads) without too much trouble, but generally, a fat-tyred mountain bike is more suitable. Motorists are more cause for alarm than any road surface. Cyclists are regarded as 2nd class citizens in West Africa even more than they are in western countries, so make sure you know what's coming up behind you and be prepared to take evasive action onto the verge, as local cyclists are often forced to do. A small rear view mirror, mounted on your helmet or the handlebars, is worth considering.

Other factors to consider are the intense heat, the long distances and places to stay. The best time to cycle is in the cool dry period from mid-October to February. Even so, you'll need to work out a way to carry at least 4L of water. If you get tired, or simply want to cut out the boring bits, bikes can easily be carried on bush taxis.

Consider starting off along the coast of Ghana or in Gambia and southern Senegal: the distances between major points of interest in these areas are manageable. If you're camping near settlements in rural areas, ask the village headman each night where you can stay. Even if you don't have a tent, he'll find you somewhere to stay.

You won't be able to buy crucial gismos for your bike when it breaks down somewhere in the back of beyond, so carry sufficient spares, and have a good idea about how to fit them. In particular, punctures will be frequent. Take at least four spare inner tubes, some tyre repair material and a spare tyre. Consider the number of tube patches you might need, square it, and pack those too. Anyone considering doing some serious cycling in West Africa should contact their national cycling association. Useful contacts include:

Cyclists' Touring Club
  (☎ 01483-417217, fax 426994, email cycling@ctc.org.uk). British organisation that provides members with details on cycling in many parts of the world.
International Bicycle Fund
  (☎/fax 206-628 9314, email ibike@ibike.org, Web site www.ibike.org/bikeafrica) US-based, low-budget, socially conscious organisation, arranges tours and provides information.

If you haven't got a bike of your own, but fancy a few days pedalling, there are a couple of places in tourist areas where bikes

Bringing a Bike to West Africa

You can ride all the way to West Africa, or you can bring your bike with you on the plane. If you choose the latter option, you can partially dismantle it and put the pieces in a large bag or box, or simply wheel your bike to the check-in desk, where it should be treated as a piece of baggage. Some airlines don't even include 'sports equipment' in the baggage allowance, while others may charge around US$50 extra because your bike is not standard size.

If you take the latter option you'll probably still have to remove the pedals, partly deflate the tyres and turn the handlebars sideways. This way the baggage handlers see a bike and are unlikely to pile suitcases on top of it. Some travellers say that if your bike doesn't stand up to airline baggage handlers it won't last long in Africa anyway, but that's a matter of opinion.

can be rented. Otherwise, local people in villages and towns are often willing to rent their bikes for the day to travellers; ask at your hotel or track down a bicycle repair man (every town market has one).

BOAT

At several points along the West African coast you can travel by boat, either on a large passenger vessel or by local canoe. Some of the local canoe trips are definitely of the informal variety, and many are extremely dangerous.

On most major rivers in the region, a passenger boat service serves towns and villages along the way, and can be an excellent way to see the country. Possibly the most popular boat trip for travellers is along the River Niger in Mali, but other riverboat options exist, for example along the Gambia and Senegal rivers.

LOCAL TRANSPORT
Bus & Minibus

Many capitals have well developed city bus networks, as well as minibuses, connecting the city centre and suburbs. In most other cities, it's minibuses only.

Shared Taxi

Many cities have shared taxis which will stop and pick up more passengers even if they've already got somebody inside. Some run on fixed routes, and are effectively a bus, only quicker and more comfortable. Others go wherever the first passenger wants to go, and other people will only be picked up if they're going in the same direction. They normally shout the name of the suburb they're heading for as the taxi goes past. Once you've got the hang of this system it's a good way to get around cities. It's quick, safe and quite cheap. It's always worth checking the fare before you get in the car though, as they are not always fixed, and meters don't usually apply to shared trips. If you're the first person in the taxi, make it clear that you're expecting the driver to pick up others and that you don't want a private hire (*déplacement*, 'charter' or 'town trip') all to yourself.

Private Taxi

Only in the bigger cities, such as Dakar, Abidjan and Ouagadougou, do taxis have meters (*compteurs*). Otherwise, bargaining is required or you'll be given the legally fixed rate, which is not negotiable. The fare at most airports into town is fixed, but some drivers (at Dakar for example) will try to charge at least double these. The price always includes luggage unless you have a particularly bulky item. Also, fares invariably go up at night.

ORGANISED TOURS

Compared with most areas of the world, West Africa has very few tour operators. Tour companies are usually based in the capital cities, and typically offer excursions for groups (rather than individuals) from one-day to one-week trips, or longer. On most tours, the larger the group, the lower the cost per person. More details are given in the individual country chapters.

Benin

Benin is again becoming a popular West African destination. The country has now emerged from its Marxist past and taken on a new vibrancy. It competes with neighbouring Togo as the pick of the small countries on the Gulf of Guinea coast of West Africa.

The fishing villages built on stilts are one of the most famous images of Benin and are a must-see even if they are a little touristy these days. In the rural areas, life goes on as it has for centuries, and voodoo, which originated in Benin and eastern Togo, is still practised. In Ouidah, the old slave-trading centre on the coast, and Abomey, the centre of the Kingdom of Dahomey, one of Africa's former great empires, you may even witness a ceremony.

The national parks in the north – Pendjari and W – are some of the best places to see animals in West Africa.

Part of Benin's charm is that it has almost no tourist infrastructure, apart from Cotonou's large hotels. The tantalising Beninese food is another reason for coming here. Memorable experiences include organising a sleeper on the night train to Parakou, or haggling with pirogue operators around the fringes of Lac Nokoué. Benin suits the truly independent traveller.

BENIN AT A GLANCE

Capital: Porto Novo
Population: 5.5 million
Area: 112,622 sq km
Head of state: President Mathieu Kérékou
Official language: French
Main local languages: Fon, Bariba, Dendi
Currency: West African CFA franc
Exchange rate: US$1 = CFA600
Time: GMT/UTC +1
Country telephone code: ☎ 229
Best time to go: January & February

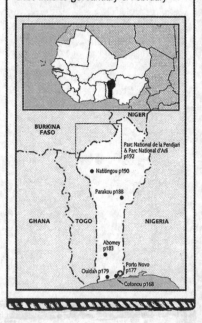

Facts about Benin

HISTORY

Over 350 years ago, the area now known as Benin was broken up into numerous small principalities. One of the chiefs quarrelled with his brother and, around 1625, settled in Abomey. He then conquered the neighbouring kingdom of the Dan, which became known as Dahomey, meaning 'in Dan's belly' in Fon. Each king pledged to leave to his successor more land than he inherited, a pledge they all kept by waging war with their neighbours, particularly the powerful Yoruba of Nigeria. At the same time, the Portuguese, and later other European powers, established trading posts along the coast, notably at Porto Novo and Ouidah.

The Kingdom of Dahomey soon became rich by selling slaves – usually prisoners of war – to these traders and received luxury items and guns in return, thus enabling them to wage war against neighbouring kingdoms. For well over a century, an average of 10,000 slaves per year were shipped to the Americas (primarily Brazil and the Caribbean, in particular Haiti), taking their practice of voodoo with them. As a result, southern Dahomey became known as the Slave Coast.

In the late 1800s, the French gained control of the coast and defeated the Kingdom of Dahomey, making it a colony and part of French West Africa. During the 70-year colonial period great progress was made in education. Dubbed the 'Latin Quarter of West Africa' by the French, Dahomey became famous for its educated elite. These citizens were employed by the French and the Senegalese as principal advisers to government officials throughout West Africa. This eventually backfired – the educated elite became extremely vocal and began campaigning against 'assimilation' and for equality; they even produced a newspaper attacking the French.

Independence

After WWII, the people of Dahomey formed trade unions and political parties. When Dahomey became independent in 1960, Hubert Maga became the country's first president. Almost immediately, the former French colonies started deporting the Dahomeyans who had been running the administration. Back in Dahomey without work, they were the root of a highly unstable political situation. Three years after independence, after seeing how easily some disgruntled army soldiers in Togo staged a coup, the military did the same in Dahomey.

During the next nine years, Dahomey had four more successful military coups, nine more changes of government and five changes of constitution: what the Dahomeyans called in jest *le folklore*.

The Revolution

In 1972, Lt Col Mathieu Kérékou seized control and formed a revolutionary government. Initially portraying themselves as a group of officers outraged by tribalism and political chaos, Kérékou's government soon attracted more radical elements.

Two years after his coup, Kérékou announced that from then on Marxism would be the country's ideology. To emphasise the break from the past, he renamed the country 'Benin'. As part of the revolution, the government required schools to teach Marxism, set up collective farms and ordered students to work part time on them. It assigned areas of cultivation and production goals to every district and village, formed state enterprises,

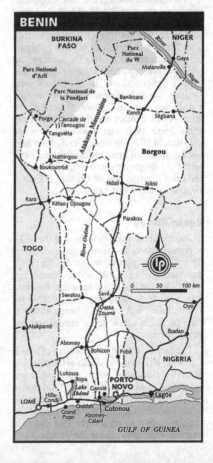

created a single central trade union and inculcated a more militant spirit in the army.

However, the revolution was always more rhetorical than real. The economy fell into a shambles: inflation and unemployment rose and salaries remained unpaid for months. People soon lost interest in the Marxist-Leninist ideology foisted on them by the regime. In one year alone, there were six attempted coups. In the late 1980s, workers and students went on strike.

In December 1989, the French recommended to Kérékou that the government hold a national conference and adopt constitutional changes. Kérékou followed their advice, renouncing Marxism-Leninism and calling for the drafting of a new constitution. Dissidents used the occasion to blame the government for leading the country into total bankruptcy, and for corruption and human rights abuses. To Kérékou's total surprise, the 488 delegates then engineered a coup, leaving him as merely head of the army. A new cabinet was formed with Nicéphore Soglo (a former dissident) as prime minister. In 1991 there were calls for a new constitution and free multiparty elections were held. Soglo defeated Kérékou in a free and open election and, in exchange, France stepped up aid significantly.

Benin Today

It all seemed too good to be true. In the wake of popular discontent over economic austerity measures (partly caused by the 1994 devaluation of the CFA) and increasing autocracy by the Soglo government, Kérékou was voted back into power in March 1996. The balloting was seen as a strong endorsement of Benin's new democratic system of government.

The jury is still out on the extent to which Kérékou has distanced himself from his previous dictatorial ways and slavish endorsement of Marxist ideology. Yet Benin is now being touted as a model of successful democratisation in Africa. The future of the country looks fairly bright and there is renewed optimism among the people.

GEOGRAPHY

Lying between Nigeria and Togo, Benin measures roughly 700km long and 120km across in the south, widening to about 300km in the north. It is a small country: about two-thirds the size of Portugal. Most of the coastal plain is a sand bar that obstructs the seaward flow of several rivers. As a result, there are lagoons a few kilometres inland all along the coast. The biggest lagoon is Lac Nokoué, which forms the northern city limits of Cotonou and the southern limits of Porto Novo, the country's nominal capital. Lac Nokoué's outlet to the sea passes through Cotonou, dividing the city almost in half. The famous fishing town of Ganvié is constructed on stilts in this lagoon. The country's major river, the Ouémé, flows into Lac Nokoué.

As you travel inland, the land remains flat but the coastal plains are replaced by a forested plateau with dense vegetation. In the far north-west, where Benin's two major wildlife parks (Pendjari and W) are, the Atakora Mountains reach 457m in height.

CLIMATE

In the south, there are two rainy seasons – April to mid-July and mid-September to the end of October. The north has one rainy season from June to early October. Areas in the Atakora region occasionally receive heavy rainfall. In the north temperatures can reach 46°C, while the coastal south is cooler, with temperatures ranging from 18 to 35°C. Harmattan winds blow from the north from December to March. The hottest time of the year is from March to June.

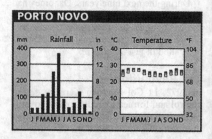

PORTO NOVO

ECOLOGY & ENVIRONMENT

Although much of southern Benin was originally covered by rainforest only small patches now remain. Deforestation and desertification are the major environmental problems. In the north, droughts have severely affected marginal agriculture, while poaching is threatening the small remaining wildlife populations.

FLORA & FAUNA

Significant vestiges of wildlife are found in Parc National de la Pendjari and Parc National du W, including herds of elephants. The southern part of Benin is heavily burnt out as the human population scrambles for remaining areas to cultivate.

GOVERNMENT & POLITICS

The Marxist-inspired constitution, the Loi Fondamentale, of 1977 was rescinded in 1988 and a new constitution was ratified two years later. The latter vested legislative authority in the hands of a 64 member national assembly and executive power in the president, who is elected by universal suffrage for five-year terms with a maximum of two terms, and in the Council of Ministers, including a prime minister who the president appoints.

The constitution also created a true multiparty system. The main political parties today are the Rassemblement Africain pour le Progrès (RAP), which is the ruling party, the Union National pour la Démocratie et le Progrès (UNDP) and the Rassemblement Démocratique Dahoméen (ROD).

ECONOMY

Benin is primarily a country of subsistence farming, with agriculture accounting for more than 35% of GNP. Yams, cassava and corn are the principal food crops, followed by sorghum, beans, millet and rice, while cotton and palm oil are the main export crops. Cotton, the production of which has grown spectacularly during recent years, now accounts for more than three-quarters of export earnings. Imports, however, exceed exports by about 60%.

The GNP per capita is around US$370, which has dropped about 25% in recent years.

POPULATION & PEOPLE

Over half of Benin's people belong to one of five ethnic groups – Fon, Yoruba, Bariba, Betamaribé and Fula (also called Fulani or Peul). For more information on the Yoruba, see the colour feature between pages 704 and 705.

The Fon (and the related Adja) comprise nearly 40% of the population in Benin. Migrating from south-western Nigeria in the 13th century to southern parts of Benin, they established a kingdom in what is known today as the village of Allada.

The Yoruba (called Nagot locally), who also migrated from Nigeria, occupy the southern and mid-eastern zones of Benin and are the second-largest ethnic group in the country, comprising 12% of the population.

The Bariba, who live primarily in the north and comprise about 8% of the population, are found mostly in the Borgou region. According to legend, they migrated from the Bussa and Ife areas of Nigeria. Their most famous kingdom in Benin was centred at Nikki, and they have remained relatively aloof towards southern Benin because of their distant location and the slave raids which occurred in the north prior to the arrival of the colonial powers.

The term Somba is a misnomer for the Betamaribé who live in the north-west, in the area of the Atakora Mountains. They have lived for hundreds of years in seclusion from industrial and western influence and have managed to keep much of their traditional culture intact (for more details see the boxed text 'The Somba' on p189).

The Fula live primarily in the north and comprise about 6% of the population.

ARTS
Art & Craftwork

The cultural history of Benin is rich, and traditional Beninese art has brought international attention to the legendary Kingdom of Dahomey.

Traditionally, art served a spiritual purpose, but under the Fon kings, artisans and sculptors were called upon to create works that evoked heroism and enhanced the image and prestige of the rulers. Until the 19th century, these Fon kings forbade artists and brass/silver casters to work outside the palace walls. They became the historians of the era, creating richly coloured appliqué banners that depicted the events of past and reigning kings. Originally hung on walls and paraded during ceremonies, these colourful banners are still made today. You won't have any problem finding modern-day examples; these are usually black material with figures cut out of imported coloured cloth and sewn on. They usually illustrate animals, hunting scenes and the panther-god Agassou, for example.

Don't miss the bas-reliefs at the Royal Palace Museum in Abomey. These are polychrome bas-reliefs in clay that were used to decorate the palace, temples and chiefs' houses. The palace has been restored by the Getty Conservation Institute and has been designated a UNESCO World Heritage site.

Sculpture produced for the voodoo cults is considerably less refined than that supplied to the king. Figures called bochio are carved from the trunk of a tree and placed at the entrance of the village to discourage malevolent spirits. Some voodoo wood figures are combined with a variety of materials, such as bottles, padlocks and bones, to embody them with power. Moulded figures of unfired clay represent Legba (a Fon god) and receive daily libations for the protection of the home.

Music

Angélique Kidjo is now a major international star, and is very popular. Other well known Beninese recording artists include Yonass Pedro, Nel Olivier and Yelouassi Adolphe and the bands Orchestre Poly-Rythmo and Disc Afrique.

Dance

There's a great variety of traditional dances and songs that you may encounter while

Angélique Kidjo

Angélique Kidjo was born in Ouidah, which is known for its strong links to voodoo and traditional beliefs. She believes music can't exist without spirituality and regards voodoo as bringing energy and spirituality to everyday life. She believes that most people outside Africa only project voodoo's negative side and misunderstand the role it has.

Her particular style of music is an eclectic mix of soul, jazz, and reggae. She has produced a number of hits that have been popular on dance floors around the world, and on her album *Fifa* (Freedom) she mixed recordings of traditional singers and musicians into her compositions.

Some critics have questioned the lack of 'African-ness' in her music, her response is that such a question would never be directed at a European artist, and asks why African musicians are expected to remain firmly within their traditions. Her songs address issues which are at the heart of many of Africa's social problems, such as in *Houngbati* (Push Them), a song about homelessness. Her debut album *Parakou* is recommended, as is her third, *Aye* (Life), which includes the international hit *Agolo*.

Graeme Counsel

travelling through the interior of Benin. Depending on the circumstances and events, these dances and ceremonies may be of a religious or cultural nature, or may concern the vital forces of the universe. They may also give praise or be a simple manifestation of joy, sorrow or communion with the spirits of the dead.

SOCIETY & CONDUCT

Within the narrow borders of Benin is an array of different ethnic groups (for more details see the Population & People section earlier), which adds to the diversity and charm of the country. Despite the underlying tensions between the southern and northern regions, the various groups live in relative harmony and have intermarried.

Most of the ethnic groups are patrilineal and many groups still practise polygamy. It appears, however, that this practice is becoming increasingly rare among urban and educated Beninese. Marriages were and are still arranged by the families and divorce is rare.

Most families support themselves through agriculture. Women control the local food distribution system, including the transport of produce to the market and the subsequent barter and sale.

RELIGION
While 20% of the population is Christian (Roman Catholics and fewer Protestants) and 15% are Muslims, most retain traditional beliefs. For more information on these beliefs, see the boxed text on this page.

LANGUAGE
French is the official language in Benin. Fon is the main language in the southern parts, while Bariba and Dendi are the principal languages in the north. Villages bordering Nigeria and Benin speak Yoruba, which is often referred to as Nagot. See the Language chapter for useful phrases in French, Fon and Yoruba.

Facts for the Visitor

SUGGESTED ITINERARIES
Cotonou is a fascinating example of urban Africa and worth a week's stay. Add several more days to explore nearby tranquil Porto Novo, the capital, and Ganvié, the lacustrine stilt village, but return to Cotonou in the evening. Those interested in voodoo will

Voodoo in Benin

The traditional religion of Benin conforms to the general pattern found in West Africa. There is a supreme being, and a host of lesser gods or spirits that are ethnically specific to their followers and part of the spiritual world also inhabited by a person's ancestors. Traditional priests, variously known as fetish priests and priestesses or juju men, are consulted for their power to communicate with particular spirits and seek intercession with them. This communication is achieved through spirit possession and through ritual, which often includes a gift or 'sacrifice' of palm wine, gin or food such as eggs, chickens and goats. The grace of the spirits is essential for protection and prosperity, and some can be harnessed to malicious and selfish ends.

Fon and Ewé slaves exported through the Dahomey Kingdom took these spirits or Loa and their religious practices with them, establishing in Haiti and Cuba the religion now known as vodou (as it is currently spelt). Originally 'vodun' meant 'the hidden' or 'mystery'. Like the Obeah and Macumba religions, vodou developed independently, acquiring new spirits and incorporating features of Roman Catholicism that echoed aspects of its own beliefs. This 'vodou' version of African-derived religion has been both demonised and distorted by Hollywood.

The label 'vodou' also stuck in modern Benin where the Marxist government of Kérékou outlawed it as being inimical to a rational and socialist work ethic. Since a democratic government was installed here in 1989, traditional religious practice has been permitted. Vodun was formally recognised as a religion by the government of Benin in Februrary 1996. Most of the country's 30% (and growing) Christians live in the south of the country while the 15% (and growing) who are Muslim are mainly in the north. Many, irrespective of the world religion to which they belong, also revere and seek protection and favours from the spirits to which they are tied by birth.

Katie Abu

BENIN

Highlights

Voodoo Culture

Abomey   *(The South)*
This World Heritage site was once the centre of the great Kingdom of Dahomey. It is also a voodoo centre with many temples and statues.

Ouidah   *(The South)*
Another important voodoo centre, but with a darker past – many slaves left from here, never to return, a fact commemorated by the poignant Point of No Return memorial. The Casa do Brazil museum is another must-see.

Architecture

Ganvié   *(Around Cotonou)*
The most visited of the extraordinary stilt villages on Lac Nokoué, this is a major tourist attraction.

National Parks

Parc National de la Pendjari *(The North)*
Elephant, hippo, buffalo, crocodile and lion are easily seen at this, the best of Benin's national parks with facilities for tourists.

Relaxation

Nightlife   *(Cotonou)*
Cotonou is a great place to have a drink or dance the night away at one of the myriad bars and nightclubs in Rue des Cheminots.

Beaches   *(The South, Cotonou)*
The long, palm-fringed white-sand beaches at Grand Popo make this an ideal place to idle away a few days, while in Cotonou, Jonquet Plage is the best of the city's beaches.

---

want to visit Ouidah and walk the Routes des Esclaves, a poignant reminder of a darker past. Grand Popo, further west, is for beach lovers. Lac Ahémé north of Grand Popo is surrounded by peaceful fishing villages. In Abomey you can see the royal palace of the Dahomey Kingdom and explore the area on bicycle, uncovering voodoo relics and disintegrating palace walls. Parakou, further north, is a good stopping point for a day, and handy for Natitingou and Parc National de la Pendjari. You could easily spend a week here, climbing and cycling, exploring the castle-like houses, looking for wildlife and cooling off in waterfalls.

PLANNING

Many roads in the south are impassable during the rainy season (April to mid-July and mid-September to the end of October). Parc National de la Pendjari may be inaccessible during the northern rainy season, May to October. The Michelin map *Africa: North & West* is sufficient for most travel.

VISAS & DOCUMENTS
Visas

Visas are required for all travellers except nationals of ECOWAS countries. The Benin embassy in Washington requires US$20 for single-entry visas, which are valid for stays of up to 90 days. Multiple-entry visas are not available. There is no embassy in London, so travellers from the UK must get one in Paris or elsewhere. If you're in a hurry and don't have time to get a visa, you could fly to Lomé (Togo) and take a taxi from there to Cotonou (three hours).

Benin visas are readily obtainable at the Togo border on the coastal road between Lomé and Cotonou. The border post at Hilla-Condji is open 24 hours, but you might have to bribe someone to get a visa at night. It costs CFA4000 (about US$8) but is good for only 48 hours; however, extensions are easy to obtain in Cotonou.

The only other border post that may issue visas is Malanville, at the Niger border – but don't count on it.

Visa Extensions Extensions for up to 30 days are issued without problems in three to four days by the immigration office of the Ministry of Interior (☎ 31 42 13) in Cotonou.

TOTEMS, FETISHES & CHARMS

An important feature of traditional religions are 'totems' – objects (usually animals) which serve as emblems for a particular tribe or clan, usually connected with the original ancestor of that group. It is taboo for a member of the clan whose totem is, for example, a snake to harm any snake – because that would be harming the ancestor. Other totems include lions, crocodiles or certain birds.

Fetishes are another important feature. These are sacred objects (sometimes called charms) and can take many forms. For example, bird skulls and other animal parts may be used as charms by a learned elder for helping people communicate with their ancestors. Another example are the decorated trees or mounds of earth guarding the entrance to villages. The elders (usually men) dealing in these sacred objects are sometimes called fetish-priests.

The most common charms found all over West Africa are small leather or metal amulets, often containing a sacred object, worn by people around the neck, arm or waist. These are called *grisgris* and are usually worn to ward off evil or bring good luck. Many West African Muslims also wear grisgris, called *t'awiz* in other Islamic countries, often with a small verse from the Quran inside.

Top: Small Lobi pendant fetish

Middle left: Dan woman's house fetish, usually presented to a woman on marriage, and kept as a protective spirit throughout her life.

Middle right: Monkey totem

Bottom, clockwise from left: Tuareg brass amulet; small monkey fetish; and Bobo chameleon fetish.

BRONZE CASTING

West Africa is famous for its traditions of casting brass and bronze using the lost wax technique, *cire perdue* in French. (Bronze and brass are different compounds but it is not usually possible without scientific analysis to distinguish between them, and the terms are used interchangeably here.) The process involves creating a sculpture out of wax. The sculpture is then dipped in a solution of silt and mud. When dry, clay is built around the form to create a strong mould. The mould is then heated and the wax melted out. Molten bronze is then poured into the empty mould and when cool the mould is broken away to reveal the bronze sculpture. Each cast is thus unique. This process is thought to have produced the 1000-year-old beautifully intricate bronzes of Ibo Ikwu, which can be seen in the Nigerian National Museum in Lagos. Today, latex is often used instead of wax, creating even finer detail.

West Africa's best known castings were created for the Kingdom of Benin in present-day Nigeria. Plaques, statues and masks were produced to ornament the palaces and compounds of the kings and chiefs. The Yoruba cast ritual staffs called Edan. These comprise male and female figures in bronze, surmounting an iron tip and joined together by a chain.

In Ghana, the Ashanti are famous for their gold ornaments and jewellery, worn by royal families. Figurative weights for weighing gold were also cast, and often symbolised the colourful proverbs for which the Ashanti are known. Crab claws, groundnuts, locusts and even chicken feet were cast using a similar technique.

John Graham

Top: Bronze scorpion (Côte d'Ivoire)

Middle, from left to right: Bronze plaque in the Benin-style (Nigeria); bull and owl (both from Burkina Faso).

Bottom, inset in text: The Ashanti make brass weights, like this one, for weighing gold, using the lost wax method.

Bottom, from left to right: Intricate detail on a Benin-style bronze head (Nigeria); pair of figures (Yoruba), called Edan, joined by a chain signifying the force of the earth; a bronze ceremonial container (Dogon).

A 30 day extension costs CFA12,000; applications are accepted only until 11 am.

Other Documents

For entry, you will need an International Vaccination Certificate or other proof of immunisation against yellow fever.

EMBASSIES & CONSULATES
Benin Embassies & Consulates

In West Africa, Benin has embassies in Côte d'Ivoire, Ghana, Nigeria and Niger but not in Togo or Burkina Faso. For more details see the Facts for the Visitor section of the relevant chapter.

Elsewhere, Benin embassies and consulates include the following:

Belgium
(☎ 02-354 94 71)
5 ave de l'Observatoire, Brussels 1180
France
(☎ 01 45 00 98 82)
87 ave Victor Hugo, Paris 75116
Germany
(☎ 0228-34 40 31 or 34 40 32)
Rüdigerstrasse 10 Postsech, 53178 Bonn
UK
(☎ 0181-954 8800, fax 954 8844; from 22 April 2000 ☎ 020-8954 8800, fax 8954 8844)
Dolphin House, 16 The Broadway, Stanmore, Middlesex HA7 4DW
USA
(☎ 202-232 6656, fax 265 1996)
2737 Cathedral Ave NW, Washington, DC 20008

Benin has embassies in Congo (Zaïre) and Canada. There's a consulate in Switzerland.

Embassies & Consulates in Benin

These include the following, all in Cotonou:

France
Embassy:
(☎ 30 02 25)
Route de l'Aéroport near the Presidential Palace.
Consulate:
(☎ 31 26 38, 31 26 80)
In the city centre, two blocks behind the post office on Ave de Général de Gaulle

Germany
(☎ 31 29 68)
In Patte d'Oie, on Blvd de France, one block from the US embassy
Ghana
(☎ 30 07 46)
Route de l'Aéroport
Niger
(☎ 31 40 30)
One block behind the post office
Nigeria
(☎ 30 11 42)
Blvd de la Marina, several hundred metres east of the Sheraton
USA
(☎ 30 06 50)
Rue Caporal Anani Bernard, in Patte d'Oie, near the French embassy

Visas for Onward Travel

In Benin you can get visas for the following neighbouring West African countries:

Burkina Faso, Côte d'Ivoire & Togo
Three-month visas for these countries are issued by the French consulate in 24 to 48 hours. You should expect to pay about CFA20,000. Transit visas (CFA6000) can also be obtained.

Ghana
Visas take two days to issue and cost CFA 12,000 (CFA30,000 for multiple entries), which is considerably more than at the Ghanaian embassy in Togo.

Niger
The embassy issues visas within 24 hours. It's open weekdays from 8 am to noon and 3 to 6.30 pm (CFA22,500). If you get there early and are polite you may receive your visa the same day.

Nigeria
Like most Nigerian embassies, they issue visas for residents only, although they may consider your case if you have a letter from your embassy. It's open weekdays from 10 am to 2 pm and issues visas in 24 hours.

BENIN

CUSTOMS

There is a restriction on the amount of CFA that you may export (CFA25,000). If you import a large amount you should declare it because you will be allowed to export only what you declare.

MONEY

The unit of currency in Benin is the CFA franc.

Euro €1	=	CFA660
1FF	=	CFA100
UK£1	=	CFA950
US$1	=	CFA600

POST & COMMUNICATIONS

Cotonou's main post office has a good poste restante service, a telecommunications office, where you can make and receive phone calls, and an Internet cafe. For more details, see Information in the Cotonou section later. There are no telephone area codes.

PHOTOGRAPHY & VIDEO

A photo permit is not required, but be careful when taking shots of museums, fetish temples and cultural and religious ceremonies. You could upset a lot of people and end up being cursed. These rules are not clear cut, so it's best to ask first. For more general information see the Photography & Video section in the Regional Facts for the Visitor chapter.

NEWSPAPERS & MAGAZINES

The three dailies in Cotonou don't really fulfil their role as 'newspapers', but you may be able to glean local football results and seesawing political accusations from them. Some of the weekly papers are more readable. Foreign newspapers and magazines can occasionally be found at newspaper stands. The cultural centres may have week-old copies of foreign dailies.

RADIO & TV

The state-run radio broadcasts in English, French and local languages. TV, usually poorly presented, comes on when least expected during the day. At night you may be lucky to see re-runs of Michael Jackson's *Thriller*.

HEALTH

A yellow fever vaccination certificate is required for all travellers and malaria is a risk year-round throughout the whole country, so you should take appropriate precautions. It's best to only drink water that has been treated. For more general health information, see the Health section in the Regional Facts for the Visitor chapter.

WOMEN TRAVELLERS

Benin presents no specific problems for women – see the boxed text in this section for one woman's perspective on this. In the bars of Cotonou a white woman may be in some ways considered 'fair game' by local men, especially along Rue des Cheminots; go as part of a group. For more general information and advice, see the Women Travellers section of the Regional Facts for the Visitor chapter.

DANGERS & ANNOYANCES

Benin is a relatively secure country with only limited incidents of crime that tourists can avoid by simply being cautious.

Never walk on the beach alone and, even when walking with someone, don't carry or wear any valuables. Even a cheap watch can attract thieves and there have been numerous muggings on the beach. Most city beaches are closed at night, so avoid being there after dusk.

BUSINESS HOURS

Business hours are weekdays from 8 am to 12.30 pm and 3 to 7 pm; Saturday from 8 am to 12.30 pm. Government offices are open weekdays from 7.30 am to 12.30 pm and 3.30 to 6.30 pm, closed Saturday and Sunday.

Banking hours are generally weekdays from 8 am to 12.30 pm and 3 to 6.30 pm (but can vary greatly).

Travelling in Benin – a Woman's Perspective

Liza Debevec, who spent some time travelling on her own through Benin and Burkina Faso, found both countries to be safe and friendly. She had the following advice for women travellers in Benin:

In Benin where I started my journey I met local women just by talking to them on market stands (not in Cotonou, because the market is too big and they are too money oriented, but in smaller towns like Abomey etc). The thing to do would be to start the conversation with the vendors, women who are selling things you have no interest in buying. On days when there are not many customers these women get bored and are happy to talk to strangers; I actually ended up staying with one of these women, she invited me to her home after seeing me at the market for three days in a row.

In terms of clothing, dress normally. Don't be half naked (hot pants or microskirts would be inadvisable), but you don't need to be wrapped up from head to toe. I suppose long pants are good for travelling in bush taxis, buses and trains since you get a lot of dust and you are squashed in these vehicles and if your bare leg is brushing against some guy's leg for a few hours he might make a move on you (BUT I'm not saying this will happen). I had some traditional African dresses made for me early on and I wore those most of the time. I made a big mistake in bringing a lot of white shirts with me (having read somewhere that mosquitoes don't like light colours) and I had to wash the dust off much too often.

The attitudes of people of Burkina Faso and Benin on women travelling alone are usually quite positive once they get over the fact that you are a woman travelling on your own – where is your husband and all that stuff. I guess you should react according to your own judgement – you could say that your husband is in the next village or he is back home but is coming to join you or whatever and then they are happy, some people don't even mind the fact that you are on your own and that there is nobody waiting for you back home. Nobody ever treated me badly just because I was travelling alone; the only thing is that you might get more marriage proposals and I even had a guy suggest to me that I should become a nun (being on my own and all that he said that it would give my life some purpose!).

I have only one suggestion for any traveller (male or female) who intends to spend more than a month in these parts of the world. Get involved in some project or have some sort of reason for your travels (especially if you are travelling on your own) because that way you have a goal and it makes you feel less of a tourist in a land of the poor.

Liza Debevec

PUBLIC HOLIDAYS & SPECIAL EVENTS

Benin celebrates the usual Christian and Muslim holidays. See Public Holidays & Special Events in the Regional Facts for the Visitor chapter for a table of dates of Islamic holidays. In addition to these, Benin has holidays on 1 January (New Year's Day), 16 January (Martyr's Day), 28 February (Liberation Day), 1 May (Labour Day), 1 August (Independence), 26 October (Armed Forces Day), 4 December (Republic Day) and 31 December (Harvest Day).

Apart from the colourful, annual Muslim celebrations in the northern towns (Parakou and Kandi for instance), the other main event is the on-again off-again International Festival of Voodoo which is periodically held in Abomey (ask at the tourist office in Cotonou).

Every four years or so there is the seasonal 'whipping ceremony' in Boukombé, which seems to go on until the young men are satisfied that they have literally beaten other men in neighbouring villages black and blue (and themselves are covered with bruises). There are also many voodoo celebrations in Ouidah and Abomey; visiting these is usually a matter of luck.

ACTIVITIES

The beaches around Cotonou, with the exception of Jonquet Plage, are fairly ordinary. For better swimming, head for the beaches at Grand Popo and the Bouches du Roy. Many of the large hotels have swimming pools that nonguests can use – and you don't have to worry so much about theft of your valuables.

If you get the chance, rent a bicycle (but don't expect 18-speed mountain bikes) and cycle around Porto Novo or Abomey. There are few organised hikes but there is nothing to prevent you walking from village to village on the fringes of Lac Nokoué, taking pirogue rides for some stretches.

ACCOMMODATION

It is fairly easy to find rooms (usually with fans) for less than CFA3000 all over the country, even in Cotonou. Several of these have restaurants attached. Most towns have very decent mid-range hotels from about CFA8000.

FOOD & DRINKS

The food in Benin is similar to that in Togo, and is unquestionably among the best in West Africa – see the entry on Food in the Togo chapter for more details.

The local beer, La Béninoise, is a passable drop. The adventurous could try palm wine, *tchapallo* (a millet-based local brew) or *sodabe* (a good alternative fuel for NASA's fleet of space vehicles).

Getting There & Away

AIR

The main airport is on the western fringe of Cotonou, in Cocotiers. Several West African airlines (Air Gabon, Nigeria Airways, Ghana Airways and Air Afrique) serve some of the main cities in neighbouring countries.

The departure tax is CFA3000. Compared with some other West African countries, departure from Cotonou is far less of a hassle.

Europe & the USA

There are direct flights between Paris and Cotonou on Air France and Air Afrique and Sabena has flights to/from Brussels. Standard economy fares from Europe on the major airlines (Sabena and Air France) are similar – about US$950 return. Air Afrique is cheaper, but less reliable. If the flight schedules to Cotonou are not convenient or if you're having problems getting a visa to Benin, consider flying to Lomé (Togo) and taking a taxi from there to Cotonou (three hours).

Between the USA and Cotonou, you can take Air Afrique a few times a week from New York to Abidjan in Côte d'Ivoire (US$800/1050 one way/return), transferring from there to Cotonou (US$130 one way) on the same airline.

Africa

One-way fares to West African destinations on Air Afrique include the following: Lagos (Nigeria) for CFA22,000, Niamey (Niger) for CFA100,650, and Ouagadougou (Burkina Faso) for CFA131,450. If you're heading to East Africa via Lagos, you may find it cheaper to fly from Cotonou to Lagos (CFA17,050) and transfer airlines there rather than going overland to Lagos. This way you'll avoid having to get a Nigerian visa and escape the hassles of Lagos. You'll also be safely tucked away in the transit lounge, therefore avoiding all the chaos of the airport itself.

Border Crossings

There are three main border crossings into Benin – Hilla-Condji (from Togo) in the south-west, Kraké (the Nigerian border) in the south-east, and Malanville (from Niger) in the north. The Hilla-Condji crossing from Togo is relatively trouble-free, unlike the other two. The northern border of Benin is open from 7 am to 7.30 pm, so if you're driving keep that in mind when leaving Cotonou. The borders at Togo and Nigeria on the coastal route are open 24 hours.

Another good crossing point from Togo into Benin is at Kétao, east of Kara. Note that this border closes at 6 pm.

LAND

Niger

Getting a taxi from Cotonou to Parakou is easy and takes from six to eight hours; to the Niger border at Malanville it's another six hours. The entire trip costs CFA9500. From the border post at Gaya there are minibuses to Niamey (CFA3500).

The Cotonou to Parakou road is tar, so you can travel the entire 1062km to/from Niamey quite smoothly.

Nigeria

The trip by bush taxi from Cotonou to Lagos costs CFA2750 and takes about three hours. Minibuses are cheaper (CFA2500) but the trip takes much longer.

In Cotonou, bush taxis leave for Lagos frequently throughout the day in Cotonou from the Gare du Dantokpa. Going to/from Lagos, you could save money by taking a taxi just to the border and changing there, because taxi fares on the Nigerian side are much lower than in Benin. If you do this, you will need to change money at the border or carry naira with you.

If you have your own vehicle, the driving time between Lagos and Cotonou is only three hours. Avoid arriving or leaving Lagos at rush hour (the 'go slow' – 6 to 10 am and 3 to 7 pm) – it's a mess.

Togo

Peugeot 504 bush taxis from Lomé make the trip along the coastal road to Cotonou in three hours. The fare is CFA2200 by minibus and CFA2750 by bush taxi. In Cotonou, bush taxis leave for Lomé at all hours of the day and into the early evening from the Gare de Jonquet, not far from the centre of town.

Getting Around

BUSH TAXI & MINIBUS

Benin has no large buses, so minibuses and Peugeot 504 bush taxis are the principal means of public transport between towns. In Cotonou, there are four main *gare routières* (bush taxi parks), each serving different areas and routes – see Cotonou Getting There & Away and Getting Around sections later for more details. A Peugeot 504 bush taxi costs CFA600 to Ouidah, CFA2000 to Abomey, CFA2750 to Lagos or Lomé and CFA8000 to Parakou, while minibuses generally cost about 25% less and take much longer.

TRAIN

The train between Cotonou and Parakou via Bohicon (the stop for Abomey, 9km to the west) takes from 10 to 12 hours. There's a daily morning train in either direction and every other day there's also an evening train with a sleeper coach. There is no dining car on the sleeper train, so be prepared. Bedding (a sheet) is provided, but you'll need to bring warm clothing.

Second-class seats on the train are significantly cheaper than taking a bush taxi but the carriage tends to be crowded with humanity and produce. First class, which costs CFA 1800 to Bohicon and CFA5000 to Parakou, is about as comfortable as you'll find on any train in West Africa. The train also has a *couchette* (sleeping car) on the night run; a bunk is CFA3000 to Bohicon and CFA7500 to Parakou. Food is available at stations along the way.

CAR & MOTORCYCLE

Petrol costs about CFA200 per litre, but in recent years the price has fluctuated a bit because of the political turmoil in Nigeria and Benin's critical dependency on Nigeria for its petrol. In Nigeria, petrol is much cheaper, so much of it is carried illegally across the border into Benin and sold on the black market at prices slightly below the official rate. Just look for the guys along the roads with 1L to 5L bottles.

Rental cars are readily available in Benin. See the Cotonou Getting Around section for details on rates.

LOCAL TRANSPORT

In all towns, you'll find motorcycle-taxis, commonly referred to as *zemi-johns* or *zemidjans*. While they are by far the fastest and most convenient way of getting around the cities, they are not as safe as regular taxis. They are virtually everywhere in Cotonou as well as the larger towns. You'll recognise them by the driver's yellow and green shirt (purple and green in Parakou). Hail them just as you would a taxi. Be sure to discuss the price beforehand or when you arrive at your destination the driver may demand an obscene fare. The typical fare is CFA100 to CFA250, depending on the length of the trip.

Cotonou

Although the official capital of Benin is Porto Novo, Cotonou (population around 800,000) with its Atlantic port is the capital in everything but name. Cotonou means 'mouth of the river of death' in Fon – a reference to the role the Dahomeyan kingdom played in the exportation of slaves. In 1868, Cotonou was ceded to the French, but this was challenged in 1892 by the Dahomeyan King Behanzin, leading to the Franco-Dahomeyan campaigns of 1892, and ending in the defeat of the king and the formation of the French protectorate of Dahomey.

Although not the most exciting of West African cities, Cotonou has its attractions. In addition to some fairly good beaches only a few kilometres from the centre of town,

there are several good nightclubs, international hotels, and craft centres. It is also one of the best places in West Africa for trying African food. However, if you are not overwhelmed by the daily screech of thousands of zemi-johns and the resultant pollution then you are the most hardened of travellers!

Orientation

The heart of town is the intersection of Ave Clozel and Ave Steinmetz. Going north-east along Ave Clozel, one of the city's two main thoroughfares, you pass over the old bridge into the Akpakpa sector; the road eventually turns into the highway to Porto Novo and Lagos. The new bridge is further to the north; the wide Blvd St Michel (which becomes Ave du Nouveau Pont), the other main road, passes over it into Akpakpa, eventually connecting up with Ave Clozel.

There is no readily available *good* map of the city.

Information

Tourist Information The Direction du Tourisme et de l'Hôtellerie (☎ 30 19 84 or 30 10 19), at the Carrefour des Trois Banques, has an 80 page booklet, *Passeport pour le Bénin*, in French or English for CFA1000. Air Afrique's free *Benin: Guide Touristique* has some additional information.

Money The best bank for changing money is Ecobank-Benin (☎ 31 40 23), near Marché Ganhi, which is the agent for Western Union Money Transfer. It's open weekdays and Saturday (from 9 to 11.30 am); all other banks except the one at the Sheraton are closed at the weekend. The Financial Bank gives advances on Visa cards quickly and easily (but applies exorbitant fees).

There's a thriving black market for the Nigerian naira and CFA around the Jonquet district. The rate for the CFA is essentially the same as the bank rate; the difference is you can get money any day and virtually at any hour.

Post The main post office is just off Ave Clozel in the heart of town. The poste restante here is excellent. To mail packages overseas, head for the Centre de Tori (☎ 30 10 48), opposite the airport. Packages up to 5kg cost about CFA12,500 or less.

Telephone & Fax For overseas telephone calls and faxes, go to the telecommunications office, in the heart of Cotonou on Ave Clozel; it's open from Monday to Saturday between 7.30 am and noon and Sunday from 9 am to 1 pm. The cost of a call to the USA, UK or Australia is about CFA2400/3600/4200 for one minute. You can also make an international call and have the person ring you back. You can receive faxes here (CFA 600 to receive up to four pages; the fax number is 31 38 37).

Email & Internet Access There is the Sogimex Internet cafe, in Jonquet near the corner of Ave van Vollenhoven and Rue de Soc Gbeto; the basic service is CFA1600 and transmission/computer time is added. It is open 8 am to 9 pm Monday to Saturday.

Travel Agencies & Tour Operators Two of the best agencies are Bénin-Tours (☎ 30 05 46) at the Sheraton and Top Tours & Safaris (☎ 31 10 87). Both offer a wide range of information and tours, including pirogue fishing and trips by boat from Cotonou to Ganvié. Two others include Sitrexci Voyages (☎ 31 47 80), on Rue Goa and good for discounted fares, and C&C Benin Voyages (☎ 31 49 24) on Ave Clozel several blocks east of the old bridge.

Bookshops Papeterie Soneac on Ave Clozel, across from the main post office, is the largest and most popular bookshop in town. It has a large selection of books and postcards. The Librairie Nôtre-Dame (☎ 31 40 94), next to the cathedral, has an excellent selection of cultural and historical books on Benin.

Cultural Centres The Centre Culturel Français (☎ 30 08 56) is next to the French embassy on Route de l'Aéroport; its library is open daily from 9 am (closed Sunday and Monday). Movies are often screened at the American Cultural Center (☎ 30 03 12), just off Blvd de la Marina.

Medical Services The Polyclinique les Cocotiers (☎ 30 14 31) is a private and efficient clinic at the Carrefour de Cadjehoun, across from the PTT Cadjehoun.

The best stocked pharmacy is Pharmacie Camp Ghezo (☎ 31 55 52), one block north of Olymp Coiffure, just around the corner from the US embassy. For a *pharmacie de garde* (all-night pharmacy), try Pharmacie Jonquet (☎ 31 20 80) on Rue des Cheminots in the Jonquet district. The pharmacy in the Grand Marché du Dantokpa is another good well-stocked place, with friendly, helpful staff.

Dangers & Annoyances The beachfront between the Sheraton and Hôtel de la Plage is the area that has seen the greatest increase in muggings. Also take care in the Jonquet and Ganhie business districts from late afternoon onwards.

Grand Marché du Dantokpa

A 'must see' in Cotonou is the huge, picturesque Grand Marché du Dantokpa which borders the lagoon and Blvd St Michel. This lively market has everything from food items (which occupy the entire first floor), blank cassettes, radios, wax cloth, baskets, religious paraphernalia and pottery to bat wings and monkey testicles. The wax cloth selection is the best in Cotonou and, like all items, it's all sold in one area.

One of the more amusing things you may find here is a love fetish, *le fetiche d'amour*. Rub it into your hands, whisper a girl's or boy's name to it seven times, touch the person and he or she is yours. The price is determined in a ceremony where a fetisher, to the sound of chanting and gongs, hurls into the air a piece of rope with bits of animals hanging off it.

Beaches

The closest good beach is the one to the east of the city centre, behind PLM Hôtel Aledjo

BENIN

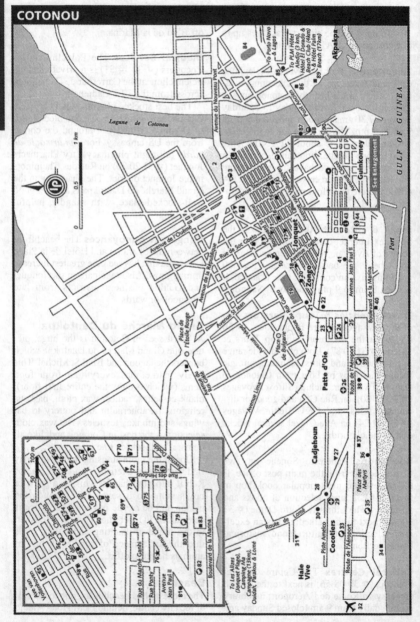

COTONOU

Lagune de Cotonou

Avenue du Nouveau Pont

GULF OF GUINEA

Akpakpa

To PLM – Hôtel
Aledjo (3 km),
Hôtel El Dorado &
Beach Club (4km)
& Hôtel Palm
Beach (17km)

84

85
86

87
88

90

Guinkomey

See Enlargment

Port

Avenue Steinmetz

Avenue de l'Ouémé

Avenue de la République

Rue de Soc Gbeto

Place de
l'étoile Rouge

Place du
Roi Glélé

Avenue St Jean

Avenue Kléber

Place O
de Bulgarie

Avenue Roi Guézo

Jonquet

Zongo

Avenue Jean Paul II

Boulevard de la Marina

41

40

19
20
21
22

23
24
25

Avenue Lima

Patte d'Oie

26

Route de l'Aéroport

38   39

Cadjehoun

27

28

30   29

Place des
Martyrs

37

36

35

Avenue Dodds

Route de
Lomé

31

Cocotiers

33

34

To Les Alizes
(Jonquet Plage),
Camping (4ha
Campagne (32km),
Ouidah, Parakou & Lomé

32

Piste Amélco

Hale
Vive

Route de l'Aéroport

Enlargement

Avenue Steinmetz

Avenue Proche

Rue Gor

Avenue Vauban

Rue Ponty

Avenue Jean Paul II

Rue du Marché Ganhi

Boulevard de la Marina

Avenue Clozel

Rue des Honcous

Avenue Dodds

70   71

72

73   78
    75

74

77
79

83

80

82

81

68
69
67
66
65
64
63

62
61
60
59
58
57
56
55
54
53
52
51
50

PLACES TO STAY
1 Hôtel l'Étoile
7 Hôtel de France
15 Hôtel de l'Amitié;
   Hôtel des Familles
16 Hôtel Babo
20 Hôtel de l'Union
34 Hôtel Bénin-Sheraton
37 Hôtel Croix du Sud
40 Hôtel du Port
49 Hôtel le Crillon;
   Hôtel Vickinfel
50 Hôtel Concorde; Ciné Vog
67 Hôtel Bodega
83 Hôtel de la Plage
86 Hôtel Pacifique;
   Le Vieux Nègre Nightclub
89 Hôtel du Lac

PLACES TO EAT
5 Maquis Akwaba
8 Restaurant la Serre
9 Mama Bénin
11 Dunya Restaurant
17 Restaurant l'Amitié
18 Maquis le Pili-Pili
25 Bangkok Terrasse
27 Restaurant la Harmattan
31 L'Oriental
46 Le Lagon Grill; Street Food
47 Le Calao
48 D'Union Glacier Bar Maquis
51 Royal Toffa
52 Chez Fatou
53 La Terrasse
58 China Town
61 Acropole
63 Café au Lait

64 Pâtisserie la Caravelle
69 La Gerbe d'Or
70 Mik-Mac
72 Prisunic Supermarket
80 Street Stall

OTHER
2 Grand Marché du Dantokpa
3 Gare du Dantokpa
4 Mosque
6 Église St Michel
10 Ciné le Bénin
12 Nigeria Airways
13 Coronné d'Or
14 Gare Abomey (Missébo)
19 Halle des Arts; Centre de
   Promotion de l'Artisanal;
   Discotheque New York, New
   York; Sorrento Restaurant
21 Place de la Revolution
22 Pharmacie Camp Ghezo
23 German Embassy
24 US Embassy
26 Hospital
28 Carrefour de Cadjehoun
29 Polyclinique les Cocotiers
30 Pharmacie Haie Vive
32 Airport
33 Ghanaian Embassy
35 Nigerian Embassy
36 American Cultural Center
38 La Présidence
39 French Embassy;
   Centre Culturel Français
41 Ministry of the Interior
   (Visa Extensions)
42 Carrefour des
   Trois Banques

43 Direction du Tourisme
   et de l'Hôtellerie
44 Bank of Africa
45 Sogimex Internet Cafe
54 Gare Guinkomé (North)
55 Gare Itajara
56 Autogare Jonquet (West)
57 Rue des Cheminots Clubs:
   Le Quartier Latin; Le 2001;
   Le Must; L'Ancien Pattaya;
   La Paix Joie; Le Soweto;
   Playboy
59 Pharmacie Jonquet
60 La Romancero
62 So What!
65 Sitrexci Voyages
66 Costa Rica
68 Train Station
71 Three Musketeers
73 Marché Ganhi;
   American 24
74 Telecommunications
   Building (OPT);
   Papeterie Soneac
75 Financial Bank
76 Police
77 Post Office
78 Ecobank-Benin
79 Niger Embassy
81 Air Afrique
82 French Consulate
84 Stadium
85 C&C Bénin Voyages
87 Institut Géographique
88 Gare de l'Ancien
   Pont (East)
90 Cathedral; Librairie
   Nôtre-Dame

and extending east to Hôtel El Dorado (4km east of the centre). It gets crowded at weekends. A little further out (11km west of the centre) is the superb beach fronting Les Alizes (see the Places to Stay – Budget section following). The best beaches, however, are further west of Cotonou – at Ouidah (41km) and Grand Popo (80km).

Places to Stay – Budget

Camping The only true camping ground near Cotonou is *Camping Ma Campagne* (☎ 36 01 63), 13km from the heart of Coto-

nou on the coastal road to Lomé. It's clearly marked and only 5km from the launching point for boats to Ganvié. The facilities are not the best, but camping costs only CFA 1200 per person and the bar's frosty beers are reasonably priced. Meals here cost around CFA1500. To get here from central Cotonou, stand by the main mosque on Blvd St Michel and look for a minibus headed north-west towards Ouidah; the fare is CFA250.

Les Alizes hotel also permits camping in a secure area (see listing in the following Hotels section).

Don't try camping at an unofficial camp site, even in a car: it's illegal and if the police find you, you could spend a night in jail. Thieves are notorious at the beaches.

Hotels The long-standing *Hôtel Babo* (☎ 31 46 07), on Rue Agbeto Amadoré, five blocks south of Église St Michel, has for many years been the most popular cheap hotel. Unattractive rooms with cockroaches cost from CFA2800 to CFA4250 (with fan and toilet). Request one on the top level as they are more spacious and airy.

Two blocks to the east is *Hôtel de l'Amitié* (formerly Hôtel Camer). It has spartan but large, clean and airy rooms for CFA 3500 (CFA4000 with bathroom, including a flush toilet); check the sturdiness of your bed. There's a lively open-air bar next door. Just around the corner is the pink *Hôtel des Familles* (☎ 31 51 25), which has adequate rooms with fan for CFA6000/7000.

At *Hôtel Pacifique* (☎ 33 01 45) you simply cannot beat the price for the quality of the rooms and bathrooms, and the relatively central location. Single or double rooms with fan cost CFA4500/8500, including breakfast. Ask for a room at the back, as those on the street side are a bit noisy. The hotel is just south-east of the old bridge, on the road to Porto Novo. If you walk across the bridge at night be alert, as robberies have occurred there.

Hôtel le Crillon (☎ 31 51 58), in the city centre around the corner from the Ciné Vog, is not a bad choice either. It has rooms with fans starting at CFA7000, which includes breakfast, amazingly clean bathrooms and friendly service. Check the mattress before taking your room, however, because some of them are in terrible condition. *Hôtel Vickinfel* (☎ 31 38 14, fax 31 18 02), a few doors to the east seems much more upmarket from external appearances (it has an impressive foyer). We weren't allowed into the rooms, but visitors report that they are OK. Just around the corner on Ave Steinmetz is *Hôtel Concorde* (☎ 31 13 45), with rooms starting at CFA7500. It has good management and very clean rooms with bathrooms. It is often

completely booked, however, so you might have to go early in the morning to get a room.

Many readers recommend *Les Alizes* (☎ 31 29 74), 11km west of Cotonou on Jonquet Plage at the end of Avenue de la Francophonie and beyond Carrefour Houenoussou. It is probably the best value accommodation in Benin. The bungalows have double beds with mosquito nets, oil lamps and bucket showers, and it's only CFA4000 to CFA4500 per bungalow. Slowly, electrical wonders such as fans and lights are being added, but the ambience is already superb. There are *paillotes* (thatched sun shelters) on the beach, deck chairs and showers so you can clean up after a swim. The bar is well situated and the restaurant has a great selection of dishes – *brochettes* (kebabs) for CFA2800, grilled *côte d'agneau* (lamb) for CFA3200, sandwiches (CFA1200) and grilled sole (CFA3000).

Places to Stay – Mid-Range

Hôtel Bodega (☎ 31 29 74, fax 31 32 62) has been revamped considerably and is undoubtedly the best accommodation for the price in central Cotonou. Clean single/double rooms with bathroom in this French-run place start at CFA11,000/13,000. There is an excellent restaurant below, a pool table and the very swish Marilyn Disco – see the Places to Eat and Entertainment sections, following.

North of Blvd St Michel on Ave du Roi Guezo is the 25-room *Hôtel de France* (☎ 32 19 49), which is a bit off the beaten path, but all the taxi drivers know it. It's well maintained and has spacious, clean rooms with fans and carpets for CFA8000 (CFA10,000 with air-con). A couple of kilometres to the north-west is the *Hôtel l'Étoile* (☎ 30 26 41), on Place de l'Etoile Rouge. Despite the remote location, it gets its fair share of business and has rooms with fans starting at CFA7500 (CFA13,500 with air-con). There is a restaurant and small bar and the meal of the day is CFA4000.

If you want to stay in a more central location, check out *Hôtel de l'Union* (☎ 31 27

49), on Blvd St Michel and opposite the Halle des Arts. Rooms cost CFA8000 (CFA 14,000 with air-con), but the service is woeful and the rooms are tiny and dark.

Hôtel du Port (☎ 31 44 44) is the best mid-range hotel in town because of its professional service and high-quality rooms. Prices range from CFA18,000 for a carpeted air-con room with bathroom to CFA26,000 for a spacious pool-front bungalow. The restaurant is quite expensive, but they have Sunday barbecue specials, which are delicious, and a popular disco.

If you're desperate, consider the antiquated *Hôtel de la Plage* (☎ 31 25 61) nearby. It has improved considerably since we last saw it but still has a decaying postcolonial air. Grubby single/double '2nd class' rooms start at CFA16,000/18,000. The CFA20,000/22,000 '1st class' units with air-con and bathrooms are slightly better but still very poor value (compared with Hôtel Bodega). It has a small pool out the back, accepts American Express and has a beach in front which smells, as it has long been used as a local toilet.

Heading east out of town, *Hôtel El Dorado* (☎ 33 09 23), 4km from the centre, has a nice breezy ambience and is a good value mid-range hotel. Standard rooms with fans cost CFA12,000 and have large bathrooms, comfortable beds and tiled floors. You can also get larger bungalows for CFA20,000. The facilities include tennis courts, an excellent long pool and a small one for children, a work-out room, table tennis and a clean private beach. The main drawback of the El Dorado is the location. Finding taxis out here is no problem (CFA250 for a zemi-john), but finding one at night to take you into town is nearly impossible. Also, at weekends the pool and beach here are often very crowded and thieves abound.

Much further east along the coastal highway, 17km from central Cotonou, is the new *Hôtel Palm Beach* (☎ 33 00 67), a nice hideaway right on the beach. It has one of the best restaurants in Cotonou for grilled and fresh seafood. Rooms are spacious and start at CFA16,000 with air-con and TV.

Places to Stay – Top End

For luxury accommodation, head for the huge *Bénin-Sheraton* (☎ 30 01 00, fax 30 11 55), on the beach on the outskirts of town near the airport. Rooms cost CFA 80,000 (CFA10,000 more for one with an ocean view). Nearby, the long-standing *Hôtel Croix du Sud* (☎ 30 09 54) is much better value. It has good amenities, including the United Nations Club which has a pool, tennis courts, volleyball and offers horse riding. Singles/doubles cost from CFA 25,000/28,000 to CFA28,000/31,000, including breakfast.

If you're looking for a beach hotel and won't be going to the city centre very often, you may prefer the four star *PLM Hôtel Aledjo* (☎ 33 05 61), 3km east of the centre. Large doubles cost from about CFA43,000, including 15% tax, and singles are also available. The restaurant at the Aledjo serves good but expensive food. Except in the peak of the winter season, the place is like a mortuary, and finding a 'hearse' for your last trip to town can be deadly.

The only top end hotel near the city centre is *Hôtel du Lac* (☎ 33 19 19). The rooms are sunny, spacious, exceptionally clean and have TVs and telephones. Singles/doubles cost CFA24,000/40,000, including 15% tax and breakfast. There is an excellent restaurant, with great lagoon and port views.

Places to Eat

Cheap Eats Superb *brochettes* can be found all over Cotonou in the late afternoon and at night – just look for the smoking grill spiled with meat on sticks. They sell for CFA400 to CFA500. The *stalls* in front of Le Lagon Grill on Ave Steinmetz, north of Hôtel Concorde, are perennially good. A plate of hot chips with tomato or onion sauce for CFA500 and delicious meat with Maggi soup and onions is CFA500.

There are also *omelette men* who set up shop around dusk and work until about 10 am the next day. They are everywhere, and you can usually spot their long tables with hot chocolate, coffee and tea containers spread across the top. You can get an entire breakfast here for CFA350. A favourite is the small stall *Café au Lait* just east of Ave Steinmetz, in a street north of Ave Clozel – the breakfasts here are consistently good (an omelette is CFA125 and coffee CFA 100). Another *stall* diagonally across from Hôtel de la Plage is also good.

The *sandwich ladies*, off Ave Clozel, about 100m north of La Gerbe d'Or patisserie, allow you to create your own sandwich with avocado, spaghetti, beef, eggs, pasta and loads more.

On the same street as Hôtel Babo, the Senegalese *Restaurant l'Amitié*, has excellent groundnut (peanut) sauce and rice dishes for less than CFA800. It's a great lunch time place – it ranks among the best. They serve from noon to 4 pm and from 8 pm until late.

Le Lagon Grill on Ave Steinmetz, near Hôtel Concorde, has grilled chicken and chips, and is open late. *Chez Fatou* has for years been a popular hang-out and has very good Nigerian food. The prices are reasonable and it's open at all hours of the night. It's on Ave Steinmetz, near Le Lagon Grill. The long-standing *Mama Bénin* has an overwhelming selection of West African dishes (CFA300 to CFA1000). It's behind the Ciné le Bénin, and is open for lunch and dinner.

African *Maquis le Pili-Pili* (☎ 31 50 48), a couple of blocks behind Hôtel de l'Union, is one of Cotonou's best. It's a slightly upmarket restaurant with a great ambience and excellent food; prices range from CFA2500 to CFA4000.

Maquis Akwaba is another great restaurant right off Blvd St Michel, near St Michel market. It is most impressive, with dishes from all over the region, including Senegal, Nigeria, Cameroon and Côte d'Ivoire. Ask about their Sunday specialities; you can also make special requests.

Royal Toffa (☎ 31 23 33) on Ave Steinmetz is where the Benin government ministers and diplomats go. Prices are high, but the food is said to be only average. The menu is African and European.

Perhaps the best culinary discovery this time was *Dunya*, one street south of Blvd St Michel and to the west of Rue de Soc Gbeto. The meal begins with a complimentary plate of *crudités* and the main meal includes a choice of rice, couscous or spaghetti. The superb *mafé* (mutton and peanut sauce) and *poulet yassa* (chicken with onions and tomatoes) with rice are both CFA2500.

Asian *China Town*, just off Rue des Cheminots in the heart of Jonquet, is a simple but nice place with low prices, good food and friendly service. Also try the attractive *Bangkok Terrasse* on Route de l'Aéroport. The interior is simply charming but the portions are small.

European For relatively moderate prices, it's hard to beat the very popular *Le Calao* (☎ 31 24 26), an attractive small restaurant in the heart of town, on Ave Steinmetz, near the Ciné Vog. The *menu du jour* is CFA4000, but lobster will set you back CFA8000.

La Bodega, in the hotel of the same name, is one of the consistently best French and Italian restaurants in town. It has great pizzas; the house special, the Bodega has everything, and is CFA4000. Other good choices include beef brochettes CFA3200, spaghetti carbonara CFA3100 and grilled chicken CFA3000. A few doors away to the north is *La Romancero*, a cosy bar which has a similar menu to La Bodega.

Restaurant la Serre, has French food for reasonable prices (CFA2500 to CFA5000). It's around the corner from the intersection of Blvd St Michel and Rue de Soc Gbeto.

Restaurant la Harmattan has been around for years and has a long-standing reputation among expatriates, though you'll rarely hear them raving over the food. It's not far from the statue at the Place des Martyrs and is under a large straw hut.

La Terrasse (☎ 31 52 08) in the city centre on Rue Guinkomey, a block northwest of Flash Video, is an upmarket restaurant with specialities such as Spanish rice dishes, couscous, *raclette* and fondue; most main courses are around CFA4000.

Sorrento (☎ *31 57 79)* is the only authentic Italian restaurant in Cotonou. It has decent pizza and other Italian and French dishes. It's within the Halle des Arts complex (at the back) on Blvd St Michel, about 2km from the centre, and is open for lunch and dinner. *Costa Rica*, diagonally across the road from Hôtel Bodega, is a good place for pizza, grilled steak and delectable shrimp dishes. It has great draught beer on tap too.

Lebanese *Mik-Mac* (☎ *31 39 79)*, directly across from Pâtisserie la Caravelle on Ave Clozel, has quick service and takeaway. One of the best restaurants in town is *L'Oriental* (☎ *30 18 27)*. With the exception of the Sheraton, it has the best and largest buffet in Cotonou; it's on Wednesday and Sunday nights and costs CFA 5000. It's open every evening and is in Quartier Haie Vive; going north take the first road on the right after Pharmacie la Haie Vive.

Cafes & Patisseries The most popular place for fresh bread, croissants and other pastries is *La Gerbe d'Or*, on Ave Clozel. It opens at 7 am; on the lower level they sell bread, pastries, yoghurt, milk and ice cream. On the second level is the restaurant/ice cream parlour (closed Monday), which has a full menu plus sandwiches, hamburgers and chips. Further along the street, on Ave Clozel at the intersection with Ave Steinmetz, is *Pâtisserie la Caravelle*, which has a quaint coffee shop and a terrace restaurant overlooking the city centre. It's open daily.

The best ice cream in town is served at *D'Union Glacier Bar Maquis* next to Hôtel le Crillon; pistachio ice creams are CFA 500. The pleasant restaurant here has a full menu if you wish to dine before tucking into your dessert.

Self-Catering In the heart of the city, around Marché Ganhi, are a number of good supermarkets, including *Prisunic*, the newest and largest. *American 24* is just across the street and has many expensive US products, while *La Pointe* has an impressive selection of wines and imported fruit.

Locally bottled mineral water is sold at all supermarkets; you'll find chilled bottles at patisseries such as La Gerbe d'Or and La Caravelle.

Entertainment

Bars There are *buvettes* (small bars) all over Cotonou, and both beer and mixed drinks are unquestionably cheaper than elsewhere. The liveliest bars in town are along the Jonquet strip after dusk. *Le Calao*, on Ave Steinmetz, has a popular bar with good beer on tap. It's very animated in the evenings. Other nearby stalwarts are *Costa Rica*, *La Romancero* and the outdoor *Le Lagon Grill*. *Three Musketeers*, near the cement works and just off Ave Clozel, has a quiet, more upmarket English-theme pub on the ground level with draught beer on tap. If you can't find a place to drink in Cotonou you have lost either your sense of smell or your sight.

Nightclubs There are a number of good nightclubs in Cotonou, regardless of the type of crowd and music you're in search of. The Jonquet strip is full of them, and they're wild and wicked. Just down from Le Quartier Latin (see the Music Venues section following) is the live, uncensored *Le 2001*; it's small, smoky and crowded, but it's good for dancing and has friendly owners. Other decadent places in the area are *Le Must*, *L'Ancien Pattaya*, *La Paix Joie*, *Le Soweto* and *Playboy*. They are equally animated and all have good, upbeat music. In the Halle des Arts is the plush *New York, New York*, which is a haven for prostitutes with fetishes for mirrors.

Le Téké at the Sheraton is a lot of fun on holidays and special occasions, when there's a crowd, otherwise it's usually pretty dead. *Le Vieux Nègre* is a fabulous Cameroonian nightclub that often has dancers from Cameroon performing traditional dances. It's across the old bridge, next door to Hôtel Pacifique.

Music Venues There are a number of places where you can go to hear a wide variety of live music. The *Marilyn* jazz bar in the Hôtel Bodega is a classy place featuring local musicians, but drinks are very expensive. *So What!*, off the southern end of Ave Steinmetz, is the most popular jazz club in town and has a variety of traditional Benin musical performers and contemporary jazz artists. It's a nice and casual open bar, above Librairie Buffalo; entry is CFA2000 and worth it. Recently *Le Quartier Latin* (formerly Afrikan Nights) in Rue des Cheminots has been pumping out the sounds with visiting bands from Lagos, some of them established reggae, jazz or Afro-beat stars; there's no entry fee, but a donation is greatly appreciated when the hat comes around.

Cinema Most cinemas in Cotonou have reopened in the last couple of years (they were closed during the Marxist period) and screen two movies per day. Good choices are Ciné le Bénin near the Halle des Arts, Ciné Vog on Ave Steinmetz, and Concorde in Akpakpa, near the new bridge. Tickets are usually about CFA5000 per movie. You can see good films at the American and French cultural centres; both offer monthly pamphlets with upcoming program details.

Shopping

If you're not looking for anything in particular and just want to browse, the Centre de Promotion de l'Artisanal, just west of the Halle des Arts on Blvd St Michel, is a good place to do this. The shops here offer a wide variety of woodcarvings, bronze sculptures, batiks, leather goods, jewellery and the famous Benin appliqué banners.

The Coronné d'Or (☎ 31 58 64) on Ave Steinmetz, a block south of Nigeria Airways, has an impressive selection of bronzework, wall hangings, wood sculptures and jewellery. It is open from 9 am to 1 pm and 3 to 8 pm Monday to Saturday. Hôtel du Port has a nice boutique, open every day from 10 am to noon and 3 to 7 pm. It sells beautiful bathrobes, handbags, jewellery and other art and craftwork from Togo, Côte d'Ivoire and Congo (Zaïre).

For recordings of Beninese music, the best place is along the road just behind Marché Ganhi. Angélique Kidjo's recordings *Fifa* and *Ayé* cost about CFA2000. Other cassettes cost from CFA1000 to CFA 1200.

Getting There & Away

Air Aeroflot (☎ 30 15 74) and Air France (☎ 30 18 15) are out on Route de l'Aéroport; Air Afrique (☎ 30 21 07) is on Ave Clozel; Ghana Airways (☎ 31 42 83), Air Gabon (☎ 31 20 67) and Cameroon Airlines (☎ 31 52 17) are all on Ave Steinmetz, halfway between Ave Clozel and Blvd St Michel; Sabena (☎ 30 03 55) is on the Place des Martyrs; and Nigeria Airways (☎ 31 52 31) is on Ave du Gouverneur Ballot.

Bush Taxi & Minibus Bush taxis for Lomé and Ouidah leave from Autogare Jonquet on Rue des Cheminots, a couple of blocks west of Ave Steinmetz. Those for Parakou leave from Gare Itajara a block away. Gare Abomey, which serves Abomey and is often called Missébo, is at the eastern end of Ave van Vollenhoven, one block east of Ave Steinmetz. Bush taxis for Lagos leave from Gare du Dantokpa at the new bridge, while those for Porto Novo leave from there and from Gare de l'Ancien Pont, on the corner of Ave Clozel and Rue des Libanais. A bush taxi costs about CFA300 to Porto Novo.

Train See the main Getting Around section earlier in this chapter for more details of train services. The train station is in the heart of town one block north of Ave Clozel and several blocks west of Ave Steinmetz.

Getting Around

To/From the Airport The official fare for a taxi from the city centre to the airport is CFA2000 (CFA750 for the 3km to the Sheraton). From the centre you can get this price, but at the airport most drivers will probably demand a higher price. You can cut costs, if you don't have much to carry, by walking from the airport down Route de l'Aéroport to the Place des Martyrs (20 minutes) and catching a shared cab from there to the centre, which will only cost CFA150 to CFA250.

Taxi Most motorcycle-taxi fares vary according to the distance, but CFA100 to CFA120 is typical. Fares of regular taxis are CFA150 for a shared taxi (double that for fairly long trips) and CFA600 for a taxi to yourself. By the hour, taxis cost about CFA2000; rates double at 9 pm.

To avoid the gare routières in Cotonou, stand along Blvd St Michel or near the university hospital where most taxis (for any destination within Benin) pass before departing Cotonou. However, for taxis to Lomé and Lagos, you will need to go to the gare routière because they don't leave from here until they're full.

Car Hertz (☎ 30 19 15) has a booth at the airport and Bénin Tours is at the Sheraton (☎ 30 01 00). Typical rates for a Citroën or the equivalent are about CFA17,500 per day, as well as CFA200 per kilometre, plus CFA6000 a day for insurance and 12% tax (ie about CFA70,000 plus petrol if you average 200km per day). A Peugeot 504 costs roughly 10% more.

AROUND COTONOU
Ganvié

The main attraction near Cotonou is Ganvié, where the 18,000 inhabitants live in bamboo huts on stilts several kilometres out on Lac Nokoué. It's a place that has been overrun by so many tourists that many children find it profitable to beg and will allow you to photograph them if you pay. You'll only be contributing to the problem if you agree.

However, for those travellers with a human eye Ganvié provokes a mixture of fascination, pathos and respect. While it is possible to hire a pirogue to explore other less-visited villages on the lagoon, visiting Ganvié is still worthwhile, especially if you have a knowledgeable guide.

In the 18th century the Tofinu fled here from the warring Fon kingdoms in the north, where the land could no longer support the growing population. The swampy area around Lac Nokoué was excellent protection against the Fon kingdoms because a religious custom banned their warriors from venturing into the water.

All the houses, restaurants, boutiques and the one hotel and post office in Ganvié are on wooden stilts about 2m above water level. The people live almost exclusively from fishing. As much breeders of fish as they are fishermen, the men plant branches on the muddy lagoon bottom. When the leaves begin to decompose, the fish congregate there to feed. After several days, the men return to catch the fish in a net. Most of the

Ganvié is the most accessible – and most visited – of the stilt villages on Lac Nokoué, originally built to escape the warring Fon whose religion forbade them from entering the water.

pirogues are operated by women, who do the selling of produce at market. Loaded with spices, fruits and fish, these pirogues are a colourful sight.

The best time to see Ganvié or other villages on the lagoon is early in the morning when it is still fairly cool. Unfortunately, the pirogue rental place doesn't open until 8 am. Alternatively, try the late afternoon when the sun has lost its force.

Taking close-up photographs is nearly impossible because the people, especially the women, object to having their pictures taken. Please respect their wishes.

Places to Stay & Eat It's possible to sleep in Ganvié; some of the locals don't mind renting rooms and there is also the *Aptam Inn* – a quaint little bungalow-hotel which has very nice huts and decent bathrooms with flush toilets. The quoted price is CFA12,000, which includes a three course dinner and breakfast. However, the price is negotiable. Regardless of where you stay in Ganvié, sleeping here can be expensive because you must pay twice for the pirogue (the second time to pick you up): about CFA3500 extra per person. However, you may be able to negotiate or hitch a pirogue ride with someone who is going to the morning market at the launching point in Abomey-Calavi.

Alternatively, there's the *Ganvié Bungalow Hôtel* (☎ 36 00 39) in Abomey-Calavi at the launching point. It has four very decent air-con rooms for about CFA9000. Next door is *La Pirogue*, a pleasant restaurant that offers a costly four course meal for CFA3750.

Getting There & Away To get to Ganvié you must go to Abomey-Calavi (not to be confused with Abomey) on the western side of the lagoon. A shared Peugeot 504 bush taxi from Cotonou costs CFA750 and takes 25 minutes. Most of them leave from the Gare du Dantokpa, or just hail one along Blvd St Michel. Most drivers will let you off right at the embarkation point but if yours won't, just walk down the hill (1km)

to the pirogue moorings. You'll need to return to the top of that hill to find a taxi back. A taxi (not shared) from Cotonou costs CFA4000.

From the embarkation point, you can get either a motorised boat or a pirogue across the lagoon to Ganvié. By motorised boat, the return trip takes about 1½ hours and costs CFA7500 for one person (CFA5500 each for two to four people and CFA4200 each for five to nine people). By pirogue, the cost is CFA5000 (CFA4500 each for two to four people) and the return trip takes 2½ hours. The pirogue is more serene, and you'll be able to talk to people passing by and hear the fishermen singing.

It's possible to get a cheaper pirogue ride to Ganvié or to some of the less-visited lagoon villages from other points around the lagoon, but finding a pirogue driver is no easy task. One such place is Akossato, a village 5km north of Abomey-Calavi. Be aware, however, that some of these unregulated pirogues are less seaworthy than the regulated ones and in recent years there have been cases of pirogues capsizing. To avoid scams, don't pay the full amount to the drivers/piroguers until the motorboat or pirogue is well and truly under way.

The South

PORTO NOVO

Even though the president lives in Cotonou and most commercial activities are centred there, Porto Novo, 32km to the east, remains the official capital.

Dating back to the 16th century, Porto Novo was named by the Portuguese after a town in Portugal to which they thought it bore a certain resemblance. The town has numerous buildings dating from early colonial times and has apparently seen better days. The Portuguese and wealthy Yoruba families once lived here and you can see a few of their homes, now dilapidated, in the old quarter to the east of the market.

Today, Porto Novo is a town of 130,000 people and is fairly active because of its proximity to Nigeria. It's possible to cover the town on foot but there are motorcycle-taxis everywhere, ready and willing to take you anywhere for a song.

Around 3km north of the city centre is Ouando, which has a fairly active market and some lively night spots. Porto Novo is also a good place to look for pirogues to take you to some of the less-visited villages on the Lac Nokoué.

Musée Éthnographique de Porto Novo

Opened in 1966, but revamped with funding from President Mitterrand (ex-president of France) after his visit in 1983, what was once a colonial-style structure housing orphans is now an interesting museum. Retracing the history of the kings of Porto Novo, it has a wonderful collection of old Yoruba masks, some dating back to the 17th century. Other items on display are fetishes, carved drums and costumes. It's a couple of blocks north-west of Place Jean Bayal, and is open every day from 9 am to noon and 3 to 6 pm. The entrance fee is CFA1000.

Palais Royal du Roi Toffa

Now officially called the Musée Honmé (☎ 21 35 66) but better known as the Palais Royal, this walled compound was the residence of King Toffa, who signed the first treaty with the French in 1883, conferring much territory to them. The kingdom of Porto Novo was one of the longest lasting in sub-Saharan Africa. It ended with the 25th king in 1976, when the five dynasties in Porto Novo had a disagreement and let the kingdom die.

Far from luxurious by western standards, but nevertheless fascinating, the Palais Royal gives you a good idea of how African royalty lived. Built in the late 17th century and remodelled numerous times, it has finely carved doors, interesting old photos and King Toffa's royal carriage. It is on Rue Toffa two blocks south of the central market. Admission is CFA1000 and it's open daily from 9 am to noon and 3.30 to 6 pm.

Mosque

Don't miss the unique mosque north of the market in the town centre. Originally a

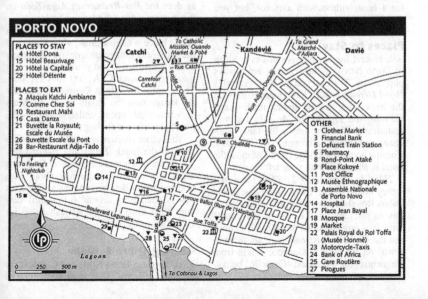

PORTO NOVO

PLACES TO STAY
4 Hôtel Dona
15 Hôtel Beaurivage
20 Hôtel la Capitale
29 Hôtel Détente

PLACES TO EAT
2 Maquis Katchi Ambiance
7 Comme Chez Soi
10 Restaurant Mahi
16 Casa Danza
21 Buvette la Royauté;
   Escale du Musée
26 Buvette Escale du Pont
28 Bar-Restaurant Adja-Tado

OTHER
1 Clothes Market
3 Financial Bank
5 Defunct Train Station
6 Pharmacy
8 Rond-Point Ataké
9 Place Kokoyé
11 Post Office
12 Musée Éthnographique
13 Assemblée Nationale
   de Porto Novo
14 Hospital
17 Place Jean Bayal
18 Mosque
19 Market
22 Palais Royal du Roi Toffa
   (Musée Honmé)
23 Motorcycle-Taxis
24 Bank of Africa
25 Gare Routière
27 Pirogues

To Catholic Mission, Ouando Market & Pobé
Catchi
Kandévié
To Grand Marché d'Adjara
Davié
Rue Catchi
Carrefour Catchi
Route d'Ouando
Rue Adjara-Tocadji
To Feeling's Nightclub
Rue Obalédé
Rue du Port
Avenue Ballot (Rue de l'Hôpital)
Rue Toffa
Boulevard Lagunaire
Lagoon
0 250 500 m
To Cotonou & Lagos

Brazilian-style church, built in the late 1800s, it has been converted into a mosque and painted in seemingly 20 different hues, making it perhaps the most colourful building in West Africa.

Markets

The Grand Marché d'Adjara, 10km east of Porto Novo on a back road to Nigeria, is held every fourth day, and is one of the most interesting in Benin. You'll find drums and other musical instruments, unique blue and white tie-dyed cloth, some of the best pottery in Benin, baskets and the usual fare. Pirogues are used to transport goods from nearby Nigeria. The daily clothes market (with numerous bargains) is on Rue Catchi.

Pirogue Rides

For a pirogue ride to some lagoon villages rarely visited by foreigners, the best place to inquire is next to the lagoon, about 50m east of the bridge. There's no fixed price because the pirogue men are rarely approached by foreigners. A trip in a non-motorised pirogue to the nearest villages takes about four hours. For this they ask around CFA20,000/30,000 for a boat without/with a motor, but you should be able to bargain.

Places to Stay

Ask around for inexpensive places to sleep in Porto Novo, as new places are always popping up. The best and the most central is *Hôtel Détente*, which has a large paillote in the back – perfect for drinks, reading and viewing the lagoon. Inside is a bar and restaurant. Clean rooms with fans, armchairs and shared bathrooms cost CFA3000. Coming across the bridge from Cotonou, the hotel is about 300m to your left (west).

Hôtel la Capitale (☎ 21 34 64) is a four storey hotel on Rue Toffa, 500m east of the Palais Royal and not far from the market. It has no restaurant and its overpriced rooms with fans cost about CFA6500. Also check out the *Catholic mission* (there are three in town) on the road to Ouando, 1.5km from the centre, but your best 'Catholic' behaviour is expected at all times.

The most expensive hotel in town is *Hôtel Dona* (☎ 21 30 52) on Rue Catchi, 1km north of the town centre. The 20 comfortable rooms cost CFA7000/9000 for singles/doubles with fans and CFA10,000/12,000 with air-con. They are rarely fully booked. *Hôtel Beaurivage*, with 19 rooms, has a more lively ambience and overlooks the lagoon on the western end of town, 1.5km from the centre. Air-con rooms with two beds cost about CFA9000.

Places to Eat

For cheap African food, it's hard to beat *Comme Chez Soi* on the western side of Rond-Point Ataké. The restaurant has a selection of dishes from CFA350 to CFA500. Another place that looks good is the *Maquis Katchi Ambiance* at the intersection of Rue Catchi and Route d'Ouando. Try the local speciality, *agouti*, which is grasscutter, a large rodent. Locals swear by *Restaurant Mahi*, just south of Place Kokoyé; hearty meals such as mutton, *njame* (yam) and sauce are from CFA300 to CFA400. *Buvette Escale du Pont*, adjacent to the gare routière, has cheap drinks and a good African menu, as does the *Bar-Restaurant Adja-Tado* on the western side of the lagoon bridge.

For more expensive western-style food, a good choice is *Casa Danza*, a block south of the Musée Éthnographique on the same street. It's attractive and you can get a decent meal for around CFA1500 to CFA3000. There's also *Buvette la Royauté* and *Escale du Musée* near the Palais Royal. Both are very reasonably priced, and have a full menu, plus lighter fare including sandwiches.

Your other alternatives may be the restaurants at the hotels *Dona* and *Beaurivage*, which are much more expensive. *Feeling's* nightclub, on Blvd Lagunaire about 1km north of Hôtel Beaurivage, has a restaurant that is open from around 6 pm until very late. It has European and African dishes for CFA1000 to CFA3000.

Getting There & Away

Taxis between Porto Novo and Cotonou are available all day. They cost CFA300 and leave in Porto Novo from the intersection in front of the bridge. To Abomey from Porto Novo is CFA1700.

In Cotonou, taxis to Porto Novo leave from Gare du Dantokpa and Gare de l'Ancien Pont, or alternatively just hitch along the road east of the Pont Ancien.

Getting Around

If you are up to it (and experiences in Cotonou may well have scared you) the best way to see Porto Novo is by zemi-john. A full town tour with the driver waiting should cost no more than CFA5000 for the day.

OUIDAH

About 42km west of Cotonou is Ouidah (population 30,000), the voodoo centre of Benin and the second most popular tourist site in the country. (For more information about voodoo, see the boxed text 'Voodoo in Benin' in Facts about Benin earlier in this chapter). Until the wharf was built at Cotonou in 1908, Ouidah had the only port in the country. Its heyday was from 1800 to 1900, when slaves from Benin and eastern Togo were shipped from Ouidah to the USA, Brazil and Haiti, where the practice of voodoo remains strong. Good preliminary reading is Bruce Chatwin's excellent *The Viceroy of Ouidah*, which tells part of the story of early Portuguese settlement – and creates a suitable mood for your visit.

A walk to the beach can be interesting and culturally enlightening; it's 4km south of town. You'll pass a big lagoon with people fishing and a small Ganvié-like village. There are voodoo ceremonies every weekend during the dry season – ask around (and be careful when taking pictures).

Many travellers pass Ouidah without ever seeing the town because of the bypass road around the northern side. The centre of town is about 2km from this road.

Musée d'Histoire d'Ouidah

Also called the Voodoo Museum, the Musée d'Histoire d'Ouidah is part of an old Portuguese fort (Fortaleza São João Batista) built in 1721. The exhibits focus on the slave

trade and the resulting links between Benin and Brazil and the Caribbean. There are also all sorts of artefacts of the voodoo culture and rooms presenting Benin's influences on its descendants in Haiti, Brazil and Cuba. You'll be shown skulls, ghost clothes, Portuguese gifts to the kings of Dahomey, old maps, engravings, photos showing the influence of Dahomeyan slaves on Brazilian culture, and traces of Brazilian architecture that the repatriated slaves brought back with them to Africa.

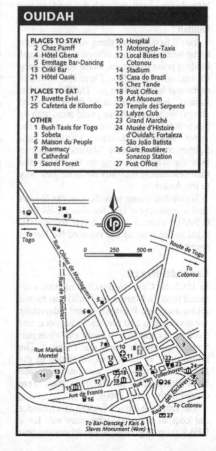

OUIDAH

PLACES TO STAY	
2	Chez Pamff
4	Hôtel Gbena
5	Ermitage Bar-Dancing
13	Oriki Bar
21	Hôtel Oasis

PLACES TO EAT	
17	Buvette Evivi
25	Cafeteria de Kilombo

OTHER	
1	Bush Taxis for Togo
3	Sobeta
6	Maison du Peuple
7	Pharmacy
8	Cathedral
9	Sacred Forest
10	Hospital
11	Motorcycle-Taxis
12	Local Buses to Cotonou
14	Stadium
15	Casa do Brazil
16	Chez Tande
18	Post Office
19	Art Museum
20	Temple des Serpents
22	Lafyze Club
23	Grand Marché
24	Musée d'Histoire d'Ouidah; Fortaleza São João Batista
26	Gare Routière; Sonacop Station
27	Post Office

The museum is open daily from 9 am to 6 pm (closed for lunch from 1 to 3 pm); the entrance fee is CFA1000, which includes a guide (a further tip is expected). It's two blocks east of the market.

Route des Esclaves

The 4km path, which is the main road to the beach, starts near the Musée d'Histoire d'Ouidah. There are lots of fetishes along the way as well as monumental statues of old African symbols. This is the route that the slaves took to the coast to board the ships. Numerous historical and supernatural legends are associated with this road, giving it significance even today to the residents of Ouidah.

You'll pass through three villages en route to the beach. The third village was the actual holding point for slaves, as the fort was only for taking head counts. There is a beautiful **memorial** here, known as 'The Point of No Return', here in honour of those departed slaves. Walk through this grand arch, with its bas-relief depicting slaves in chains, to the water. Imagine the slaves climbing into lighters to go out to the 'slavers', turning to hear the waves crashing on the beach and then descending into dark holds on their way to the Americas.

If you don't want to walk, you can always find a motorcycle-taxi for about CFA1000 (CFA500 extra if you visit the fishing villages to the west of the Point of No Return memorial).

Casa do Brazil

In 1992 the Casa do Brazil (sometimes referred to as La Maison de Brazil) was turned into a museum. It displays works depicting voodoo culture and the black diaspora, and has a good collection of black and white pictures of voodoo rituals – don't miss it. The house itself is the former residence of the Brazilian governor and was later occupied by a Portuguese family until they were ousted in the early 1960s.

The entrance fee is CFA500; this includes the cost of a guide, who may ask for a CFA500 tip to go upstairs to where the best photos are. Casa do Brazil is a 15 minute walk from the centre, near the civil prison. Plenty of zemi-johns pass by.

Temple des Serpents

Snakes are especially important in Ouidah because, traditionally, they were fetishes and the principal object of worship. This explains why there's a sacred python temple here. It's in the centre of town, half a block from the cathedral, but has become something of a tourist trap and appears less sacred because of this. A small tour costs a ridiculous CFA500 (extra for photos), for which you'll get an explanation of the temple and some of the voodoo traditions. Don't expect too much. Inside the temple they'll lead you into a very small room, lift up some boards, and *voilà* – harmless, sleeping snakes.

Sacred Forest

This park consists of a small array of African deities representing fascinating legends and myths. The deities are placed on the spiritual site where King Kpassé, the founder of Ouidah, turned into a tree to hide from his adversaries. The tree, a rare and huge *iroki* tree, is still alive today. Be sure to bow before Legba (the trickster in the voodoo pantheon and the 'guardian of the house') when you enter the park. The caretaker/guide will expect a tip for his informative tour.

Places to Stay & Eat

One of the best and cheapest places in town is **Ermitage Bar-Dancing** (☎ 34 13 89), a block east of the huge *maison du peuple*. It has a very African feel and a pleasant terrace bar. The three rooms here cost about CFA3000 each.

Another possibility is **Oriki Bar** on Rue Marius Moutel which is about a kilometre south of the crossroads on Route de Togo. The singles/doubles with fan and bathroom are very good value at CFA2500/3000.

Others prefer **Chez Pamff**, on the northern edge of town, behind the Sobeta office. From Hôtel Gbena on the bypass road, take the road north for one long block, then the first right for a couple of hundred metres.

The rooms at Chez Pamff have fans and are good value at CFA3500. The hotel also serves excellent African food, with dishes starting at CFA750. Across the road they have a new annexe, where excellent doubles with bathroom are CFA6500.

There are two upmarket hotels in Ouidah. The best value for money is the new *Hôtel Oasis* (☎ 34 10 91), which is in the heart of town not far from the fort and opposite the Sonacap petrol station. It has spacious, clean and airy rooms with air-con and bathrooms for CFA9000. The restaurant serves special African dishes upon request and these are both excellent and filling. The other top end place is *Hôtel Gbena* (☎ 34 12 15), on the bypass road 2km north of the town centre. Even though the spotless rooms have air-con and bathrooms, at CFA16,000 they're expensive. The restaurant serves western-style food; the *menu du jour* costs CFA3000.

For more good Beninese food, head for *Cafeteria de Kilombo*, an open-air restaurant across from the Musée d'Histoire d'Ouidah, or the open-air *Buvette Evivi*, across from the post office in the main square; meals cost from CFA400. Also worth trying is the new *La Tasse d'Or*, with meals from CFA600 to CFA1500.

Entertainment

The terrace bar at *Ermitage Bar-Dancing* is definitely the place to go for a drink at night. The bar-dancing *J Kais* on the beach road (Route des Esclaves) is a popular place for a drink and serves good meals (from CFA2500 to CFA4000). When the disco is operating entry is CFA1000. Another handy bar is *Chez Tande*, across from the Casa do Brazil. The best bar-dancing in the centre of town is *Lalyze Club*, which is open until late; entry is CFA500 and large beers are CFA375.

Getting There & Away

In Cotonou, bush taxis for Ouidah leave from Autogare Jonquet, while in Ouidah those for Cotonou leave from the Sonacop petrol station in the heart of town. At both stations, taxis are easiest to catch in the morning, although at the Sonacop station

you will almost always find Peugeot 504s headed for Cotonou. If not, one option is to go out to the Route de Togo and try hailing one from there – the fare to Cotonou is CFA400. This is also the place for hailing taxis for the Togo border.

There is also a bus to Cotonou (CFA300); it leaves from the main square.

GRAND POPO

About 80km west of Cotonou and 20km east of the Togo border, Grand Popo is renowned for its beaches and is the best getaway spot in Benin for travellers to spend a few idle days on the sand. Travelling here via the coastal highway from either Cotonou or Lomé, you may see white flags flying from poles in small villages along the way; they identify voodoo practitioners.

The only hotel is the popular and highly recommended *L'Auberge de Grand Popo*, which has a very casual atmosphere and is right on the beach. It has rooms in a restored colonial building. It costs CFA3000/5000 for singles/doubles with fans and from CFA6950/8000 to CFA11,000/12,000 for the newer, more spacious air-con rooms. The menu is quite impressive, but the meals are not cheap. Many visitors to Grand Popo just camp on the beach, although the owners of the auberge will try their best to tell you that it is not allowed. They no longer offer camping in their grounds.

Getting There & Away

From Cotonou, take a bush taxi from Autogare Jonquet and have it drop you off at the Grand Popo junction on the main coastal highway, 20km east of the Togo border; the fare is CFA750. Take a motorcycle-taxi from the junction to the auberge (CFA200). Leaving shouldn't be difficult, as there is usually someone there with a vehicle who will be willing to drop you off at the main road junction.

POSSOTOMÉ & BOPA

If you're looking for a place that's off the beaten path, head for the northern shores of Lac Ahémé, 40km south-east of Lokossa.

There are fishing villages all around the lake, the main ones being Possotomé and Bopa, and the setting is very pleasant, with coconut palms everywhere. Few travellers come this way. The villagers may help you to make arrangements for pirogue trips around the lagoon.

Possotomé, which is connected by road to Lokossa, is famous for its thermal springs, the country's primary source of mineral water. You can visit the factory here which has been set up near the source for bottling the water. From the village you can rent a pirogue for a trip to the nearby fishing villages, including Bopa and Oussa Tokpa, or simply to ride around the lagoon.

Bopa is on the western side of the lake and is a fascinating village. The practice of voodoo here may be the most avid of anywhere in Benin. Ask around to see if you can meet a local fetisher.

Lokossa, halfway between Grand Popo and Abomey, is a convenient spot to find taxis east to Possotomé and Bopa and north to Abomey. If you stop here, check out the lively market (it operates every five days).

Places to Stay & Eat
In Lokossa, *Hôtel Étoile Rouge* has a bar-restaurant and 20 rooms, four with air-con.

Near the thermal springs at Possotomé is a 20 room hotel, *Village Club Ahémé* (☎ 45 02 20). It's on the water's edge and has bungalows with fans for CFA6500 (CFA12,000 for a double with air-con) and a surprisingly good restaurant with excellent service. Breakfast costs CFA1500 and full meals cost around CFA5000.

Getting There & Away
From the coastal highway take the turn-off north to Lokossa. About 20km south of Lokossa you'll come to the Marché de Comé intersection. Take the dirt road heading east just after the Co-op store for 17km to the lake and Possotomé. The fork to the left heads towards the hotel and Bopa. The former is about 500m down that road, on your right. For a bush taxi to either village, look around the Marché de Comé intersection.

ABOMEY & BOHICON
If you have time to visit only one town outside Cotonou, Abomey would be a good choice. It's 144km north-west of Cotonou on a tar road. Abomey is in Fon country and was the capital of the great Kingdom of Dahomey. The main attraction is the restored Royal Palace and the excellent museum inside, which covers the history of the kingdom, and there is a wealth of other things to explore. The town itself, with picturesque *banco* (mud brick) houses, is pleasant to walk around.

Orientation & Information
Abomey is the real attraction, but Bohicon 9km to the east is close to the train line and the major north-south highway.

Once you get to Abomey there are few main roads – dirt streets radiate from the central market passing banco houses and historic palaces. Use the water tower as a point of reference. Only the museum has information on the town's history; the rest is easy to discover yourself. Aux Délices de France, on the western side of the market, is the place to change money.

Royal Palace Museum
The palace compound must once have been the most incredible structure in West Africa. The first palace was constructed in 1645 by the third king of Dahomey. Each successive Fon king built his own palace so that by the 19th century the palace compound was huge, with a 4km-long perimeter and a 10m-high wall enclosing an area of 40 hectares and housing a court of 10,000 people.

The palace museum you can visit today dates from 1818 and consists only of the palaces of the last two great kings to live there – Ghézo and Glélé. Fleeing from the French in 1892, Glélé's son, Béhanzin, the 10th king, ordered the palaces to be burned. As a result, only a small section of the palace compound is standing – the courtyards and ceremonial rooms, and the houses where the kings' wives lived.

Most of the palace compound was devoted to altars for dead kings, who were buried

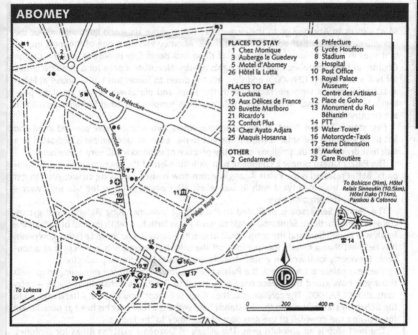

ABOMEY

PLACES TO STAY
1 Chez Monique
3 Auberge le Guedevy
5 Motel d'Abomey
26 Hôtel la Lutta

PLACES TO EAT
7 Luciana
19 Aux Délices de France
20 Buvette Marlboro
21 Ricardo's
22 Confort Plus
24 Chez Ayato Adjara
25 Maquis Hosanna

OTHER
2 Gendarmerie

4 Préfecture
6 Lycée Houffon
8 Stadium
9 Hospital
10 Post Office
11 Royal Palace
   Museum;
   Centre des Artisans
12 Place de Goho
13 Monument du Roi
   Béhanzin
14 PTT
15 Water Tower
16 Motorcycle-Taxis
17 5eme Dimension
18 Market
23 Gare Routière

To Bohicon (9km), Hôtel
Relais Sinnoutin (10.5km),
Hôtel Dako (11km),
Parakou & Cotonou

Route de la Préfecture

Route de l'Hôpital

Rue du Palais Royal

To Lokossa

0   200   400 m

there. The people thought it fitting that their deceased kings have entourages in the afterlife, so they held annual human sacrifices, mainly of convicts and prisoners of war.

On the exterior of the palace are **bas-reliefs** which depict the history of the Dahomey Kingdom. Although many of the reliefs were destroyed in the fire, some have been saved and restored. These reliefs were a major factor in UNESCO's decision to classify the palace as a significant World Historic site.

Inside the museum a guide will show you rooms containing the relics of the kings. In one room, the Room of Arms, are the **thrones** of 11 of the 12 Dahomey kings – the last king was a puppet of the French and his subjects threw away his throne. These 11 thrones are all made from elaborately carved wood and a few are decorated with silver and copper. Ghézo's throne is particu-

larly large and is mounted on four skulls (not real) of vanquished enemies.

Behind the 11 thrones are the magnificent **appliqué banners** of the royal family. These wall hangings, which have been restored, depict some of the country's bloody history, particularly the battles. One of them shows a scene of Glélé using a dismembered leg to pound his enemy's head. In the same rooms are carvings of the panther Agassou.

In other museum buildings, you'll see lots of voodoo artefacts, skulls, Portuguese items (ranging from pistols to sets of china) and the traditional housing of King Glélé's 800 wives. You are not allowed to take photos of any of this.

The palace museum is open daily from 9 am to 3.30 pm. The entrance fee is CFA 2000, which includes a guide (who expects a tip as well). The museum tour takes about an hour, at the end of which your guide

The Dahomey Trail

Most visitors to Abomey go to the museum and then move on – and learn little about the incredible civilisation that once flourished there. Abomey was once one of the most important sites in West Africa – as important as Kano and Benin City in Nigeria and the Dogon Country in Mali. There are many other sights nearby. Negotiate a price for a motorcycle-taxi for half a day (about CFA4000) and then ask the driver to follow this trail – inquire at Hôtel la Lutta for drivers who are familiar with the stops and places where you can take photographs. The trail leads to unrestored palaces, fetish temples and other Dahomeyan relics in the countryside.

First stop is **Temple Zéwa**, a voodoo temple where two women were covered in oil and left to be eaten by red ants. Zéwa was the last to die. Each voodoo temple is dedicated to a different divinity (death, smallpox etc) – the practice of voodoo is still very active here.

The **Palais Ghézo** is now a crumbling ruin with little left of the once impressive mud ramparts. Better restored is the **Palais Agonglo** which now houses a weaving centre; you can get access to the main courtyard with its bas-reliefs after paying a tip to the site supervisor – restoration is still ongoing here.

The **Temple Sémassou** is dedicated to the wife of Dahomey King Aglongo and gynaecological deformations. Sémassou is said to have given birth to a fetish instead of a child; the fetish was buried here and the temple built above it. Nearby is a large white fetish *sans* penis. It is believed that a female tourist broke off the oversized erect penis and kept it as a souvenir. Previously local women would straddle it to ensure their future productivity.

The next palace is the largest, the **Palais Glélé**. Little is left, but the remaining mud walls show you how grand this palace once was. Head to the **Palais Béhanzin** at Djimé – entry costs about CFA1000. The caretakers in the village will escort you around. Afterwards, go to the **Béhanzin statue**. It is said that he stands here without a roof over his head as punishment for allowing the downfall of the Kingdom of Dahomey to the French.

The next stop is an absolute gem. The village of **Dozoéme** exists as it has for centuries, with its *forgerons* (blacksmiths) fashioning implements in their crude forges as they once did exclusively for the Dahomey kings. They now produce farm implements and kitchenware. They are amusing to talk to and they laugh at a foreigner's interest in their trade. They expect payment for photos (CFA500).

Head to the **Palais Akaba**, once the most important of the palaces. Little is left of the ramparts, but the sheer size is overwhelming. The name Dahomey originated here – two brothers Dan and Akaba fought for the right to succession. Dan was killed and the name 'Dahomey' comes from combining Dan and *homey* (in his belly).

Before returning to the museum to tie all the threads together, stop off at Agbodo to see the remains of the **moat** which once surrounded Abomey. It has largely filled in with debris over time but was once 60m deep and 15m wide and stretched for many kilometres around the town.

---

takes you to the Centre des Artisans next door, where you'll see appliqué banners being made. The quality is better than that of most appliqué work found in Cotonou, but asking prices are high. At this centre you'll also see artisans working on all kinds of other crafts.

Places to Stay

The best cheap establishment in Abomey is *Hôtel la Lutta* (☎ 50 03 43), down a rambling dirt road south-west of the market. Mr 'La Lutta' (Adjolohoun Jean-Constant) is a never-ending source of information on Abomey and the Dahomey kingdoms – the 'trail' described in this section is his suggestion. Simple double rooms with fans and showers are CFA3500. The food here is delicious; salads are CFA1600 and a large *plat du jour* CFA2400.

The pleasant *Chez Monique* (☎ 50 01 68) is at the far north-western end of town down a dirt road. The garden has a delightful tropical ambience, exotic birds and straw huts. The rooms (from CFA8000) have insect screens and fans and the shared bathrooms are exceptionally clean. The meals are very good but not cheap, mostly CFA2500 a dish.

Auberge le Guedevy, about 2km north of the town centre, is a modern two-storey hotel that has a good restaurant with a European and African menu and a wide selection of cold drinks. Rooms cost CFA6500 for a double with fan and bathroom (CFA10,000 with air-con).

Motel d'Abomey (☎ 50 00 75) on the north-western side of town, 1km from the centre, is the largest and best hotel in Abomey. The rooms are pretty basic, with carpeting and air-con, and cost CFA10,000/15,000 for singles/doubles. It also has larger bungalows with TVs and large bathrooms from CFA18,000. The restaurant serves expensive European food; there's also a pleasant paillote bar outside where you can have a drink.

Some travellers prefer to stay in Bohicon, 9km to the east. *Hôtel Dako* (☎ 51 01 38) on the Cotonou to Parakou highway, 2km south of Bohicon, has nothing to offer other than a pool and, at weekends, a nightclub. The restaurant serves bland European meals and expensive drinks. Air-con rooms cost CFA12,000, including breakfast, and are cramped and expensive for the quality. For a large room with balcony you'll have to pay CFA18,000 to CFA25,000.

A much better choice is the pleasant *Hôtel Relais Sinnoutin* (☎ 51 00 75) on the same road and 500m closer to Bohicon. It's well managed and they serve western-style and African food (CFA1000 to CFA2000). A spotlessly clean room with fan and shared bathroom is CFA5000 (CFA6000 with bathroom), while air-con rooms are CFA8000.

Places to Eat

Just across the street from Hôtel Dako in Bohicon is the maquis *La Bonne Marmite* which serves wonderful African sauces with couscous, rice and pounded yam at lunch time (before 2.30 pm) and in the evening. You can expect to pay from CFA200 to CFA600 for a filling meal.

In Abomey, look around the market area for cheap street food. At the stall called *Chez Ayato Adjara* you can get a delicious meal for CFA400 to CFA600. A speciality here is *pâte de maïs* (made from mashed maize) with meat and cheese sauce or with *gombo* (okra) sauce; both are excellent. Other choices are *Hôtel la Lutta* (see Places to Stay earlier in this section); *Ricardo's*, on the Lokossa road, which is also one of the better bars; *Luciana* on the Route de l'Hôpital for African dishes; *Confort Plus*, another good drinking spot, across from the gare routière; *Maquis Hosanna* (formerly Maquis de Zou) opposite the market, on the southern side; and *Buvette Marlboro* on the Lokossa road for inexpensive lunches (CFA550).

If you're self-catering, *Aux Délices de France* stocks lots of French goodies.

Entertainment

In Abomey, try *The Prestige* at Motel d'Abomey – it's one of the fanciest places in town. A more animated crowd will be found at the air-conditioned *5eme Dimension*, not far to the east of the market; entry is CFA1500, which includes a drink, and from then on drinks are CFA1000.

During the day in Bohicon, you could try the pool at Hôtel Dako; it's open daily from 10 am to 6 pm and costs CFA1500.

There is the ever-popular buvette *Mochas*, at the crossroads on the Parakou to Cotonou road; and the buzzing *Buvette de le Musso: Nouvelle Dimension*, which has good street chop (CFA500) and cold beers – ask any taxi driver to take you here.

Getting There & Away

In Cotonou, bush taxis for Abomey leave throughout the day and early evening from

Gare Abomey, or more conveniently from anywhere on Blvd St Michel (CFA1500).

Shared taxis and motorcycle-taxis go between Abomey and Bohicon during the day and in the early evening; the fare is CFA150. Vehicles continuing to Parakou leave frequently from the gares routières in Abomey and stop off in Bohicon. In Bohicon, to hail a taxi headed north towards Parakou, just stand along the main road and wave.

Alternatively, you could take the train. From Cotonou, the train takes 2½ hours to get to Bohicon, from where you can catch a taxi to Abomey. The Cotonou to Parakou morning train, stopping at Bohicon, leaves in either direction at 8 am. The evening train from Cotonou leaves at 7 pm on Tuesday, Thursday and Saturday; from Parakou it leaves at 6 pm on Wednesday, Friday and Sunday. The fare from Cotonou to Bohicon is CFA1500 for 1st class, CFA850 for 2nd class and, on the night train only, CFA4500 for a sleeper.

Getting Around

It's possible to rent bicycles for about CFA 1500 a day – just ask around town.

DASSA ZOUMÉ

Dassa Zoumé, which is 200km north of Cotonou on the main north-south highway, lies roughly halfway between Cotonou and Parakou. It's one of the most picturesque places in Benin.

Dassa, the 'city of 41 hills', has a buzzing population of 30,000, and is the next major town you come to after Bohicon. It has some awesome rock formations that have houses built around them. Dassa is also renowned for its annual pilgrimage (La Grotte) for Catholics throughout West Africa, who come to pay homage to the Virgin Mary who is said to have appeared here once. It has evolved into more of a social than religious gathering these days.

For *cheap lodging*, ask around the gare routière. The most expensive place in town is the *Auberge de Dassa* (☎ 53 00 98), which is opposite the roundabout (*rond-*

point) on the major highway. It has rooms with fans for CFA8000 (CFA13,000 with air-con) and an excellent restaurant, which serves great pepper steaks and desserts.

For details of how to get to Dassa Zoumé, see the Savé Getting There & Away section following.

SAVÉ

Savé, 160km south of Parakou, is the home of many Yoruba people who migrated from Nigeria, and is a convenient place to cross over to Nigeria. If you enjoy rock climbing, stop here as there are accessible rock formations. Many of these rocks have a great deal of history behind them and are considered sacred, hence the name La Montagne Sacrée. Centuries ago, to counter attacks from their enemies from the south, the inhabitants would flee to the rocks and strategically placed boulders, then roll them down the hills as the enemy approached. There are also areas in these hills where village elders would go to pray to the deities.

The town's nicest hotel is *Les Trois Mammelles*, which is an overly ambitious hotel with large spacious rooms with comfortable beds, and balconies overlooking the hills and much of Savé. The CFA6500 price is entirely negotiable. There's a popular open-air bar where you can enjoy the view of Savé over a cold beer.

Getting There & Away

Getting to Dassa and Savé is relatively painless by bush taxi. You can catch direct bush taxis from Cotonou from under the new bridge next to the Grand Marché du Dantokpa. Taxis leave in the early afternoon once they fill up. The fare is CFA3000 to Dassa and CFA3500 to Savé. It's quicker to stand along Blvd St Michel and catch a taxi to Bohicon. In Bohicon, it's fairly easy to hail taxis on to Dassa and Savé as they pass through the centre of town.

You can also get to Dassa and Savé by train. The day train from Cotonou arrives at Bohicon usually between 10.30 am and noon and at Dassa and Savé roughly one and two hours later, respectively.

The North

PARAKOU

Parakou (population 92,000) is a bustling metropolis at the end of the train line. It was a major slave-market town in the 19th century. Today it is the administrative capital of the Borgou region. While there's not much to see, it is a convenient place to stop for the night if you're heading on to the wildlife parks or further north.

The centre of town is the area around the cinema at the intersection of Route de l'Aéroport, Rue des Cheminots and Route de Transa. There are three banks here and the Grand Marché is three blocks away to the south-east.

Places to Stay

The long-standing *Hôtel les Canaries* (☎ *61 11 69*), about 400m east of the train station, has two courtyards with rooms opening onto them. Single/double rooms with fans, shared baths and showers cost CFA2000/3200 (CFA 5000/6500 with bathroom and CFA6500/7800 with air-con). The restaurant closes fairly early.

A notch up is the *Auberge Mon Petit Père* (☎ *61 10 57*), on the northern side of town on the Malanville road (Route de Transa). It's a delightful six-room auberge with spotless singles/doubles with fans for CFA4500/5500, and excellent meals include couscous, pounded yam and other African specialities.

The long-standing but declining *Hôtel OCBN* (☎ *61 10 57*), in a quiet area just east of the train station and surrounded by trees and shrubs, has large clean single/double rooms for CFA4000/5000; breakfast is CFA900.

For years, the most popular top end hotel has been *Hôtel des Routiers* (☎ *64 04 01*). It's a French-run establishment on Route de Transa, 500m north of the heart of town. You can't help but relax in the garden setting with its clean pool. There's also an excellent tennis court and a good, but expensive, French restaurant (the *plat du jour* is CFA6000 and large beers are CFA1000).

Rooms with fan are CFA19,000/21,000 for singles/doubles and air-con rooms are CFA 22,000/25,000. Cheaper rooms with cold water only are CFA14,000/15,000.

Hôtel la Princess (☎ *61 01 32*), however, is now the liveliest hotel in town and has a wide range of rooms. For CFA7500 to CFA10,500, you can get a small room with a fan and bathroom. The deluxe rooms (CFA12,500 to CFA17,200) are spacious, carpeted bungalows with telephones and satellite TV.

Hôtel Central (☎ *61 01 24*) lacks ambience and is therefore difficult to recommend. The rooms, however, are quite cosy and cost from CFA11,500 to CFA16,000. The *restaurant* serves both European and African meals, and the *menu du jour* costs CFA 4500.

Places to Eat

For inexpensive African food, head for the unmarked *La Face Douane*, next to Hôtel OCBN. It is extremely popular at seemingly all hours of the day and serves *pâte* for CFA150 plus several sauces for around CFA300. An excellent place for street food is at the intersection about 200m north-east of the Hôtel les Canaries, along the road running in front of the hotel.

Many locals speak highly of *Les Palmiers* at the back of Hôtel les Canaries, but business seems to wax and wane. One of their more popular dishes is chicken and chips (CFA1500). *Les Marmites du Roi*, one street south of Route de l'Hôtel Canaries, also has great African selections – dishes cost from CFA2500 to CFA3500 and excellent salads are CFA1200. You dine outdoors under paillotes.

Chez Mamou is a small buvette that serves good cheap street food such as rice, couscous, salad and chicken. It's north of the town centre on Route de Transa opposite *Le Miel* bakery. The bakery is a good place for vegetarian sandwiches, ham and cheese sandwiches, ice cream and, in the mornings, croissants and coffee.

La Belle Epoque (☎ *61 10 25*), which is on the northern side of town near Hôtel la Princess, serves excellent French fare but

BENIN

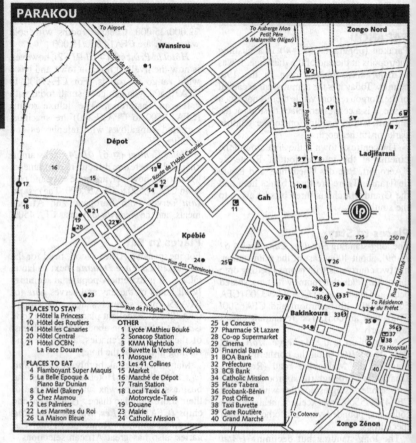

PARAKOU

To Airport

To Auberge Mon
Petit Père
& Malanville (Niger)

Zongo Nord

Wansirou

●1

Route de l'Aéroport

Route de Transa

3● 4▼

2■

5▼

6●

●7

Dépot

Route de l'Hôtel Canaries

13● 12
14● ●

9▼ ▼8

Ladjifarani

16

15

10■

●17

○18

●21

19●
●20

22●

C
11

Gah

●23

Kpébié

24● 25▼

▼26

Rue des Cheminots

28● 29 ●
30● ●31

27●

Rue de l'Hôpital

0   125   250 m

Rue du Marché

To Résidence
32★ du Préfet

Bakinkoura 33●

34●

35●

36●
37
39●

38

To Hospital

To Cotonou

Zongo Zénon

40●

PLACES TO STAY	OTHER	25 Le Concave
7 Hôtel la Princess	1 Lycée Mathieu Bouké	27 Pharmacie St Lazare
10 Hôtel des Routiers	2 Sonacop Station	28 Co-op Supermarket
14 Hôtel les Canaries	3 KMM Nightclub	29 Cinema
20 Hôtel Central	6 Buvette la Verdure Kajola	30 Financial Bank
21 Hôtel OCBN;	11 Mosque	31 BOA Bank
La Face Douane	13 Les 41 Collines	32 Préfecture
	15 Market	33 BCB Bank
PLACES TO EAT	16 Marché de Dépot	34 Catholic Mission
4 Flamboyant Super Maquis	17 Train Station	35 Place Tabera
5 La Belle Epoque &	18 Local Taxis &	36 Ecobank-Bénin
Piano Bar Dunian	Motorcycle-Taxis	37 Post Office
8 Le Miel (Bakery)	19 Douane	38 Taxi Buvette
9 Chez Mamou	23 Mairie	39 Gare Routière
12 Les Palmiers	24 Catholic Mission	40 Grand Marché
22 Les Marmites du Roi		
26 La Maison Bleue		

the pizza is only average and prices are on the high side. The salade niçoise is excellent value for CFA1500. The most outstanding restaurant in town is *La Maison Bleue*, near the Bank of Africa. The wide choice on the menu is refreshing. Main dishes range from CFA2500 to CFA 5000.

Entertainment

For a nightclub, try *KMM* (formerly Savane) on Route de Transa, two blocks north of Hôtel des Routiers. *Le Concave*, off Rue

des Cheminots, is also a lot of fun. It's more casual and much less expensive than KMM, but finding a motorcycle-taxi in the wee hours of the morning is more difficult.

Another place worth trying is *Piano Bar Dunian* in La Belle Epoque. It's more sophisticated and suits a sedate crowd.

If you're just after a drink, buvettes abound – two favourites are *Les 41 Collines* across from the Hôtel les Canaries; and the animated *Buvette la Verdure Kajola*, a local favourite in Ladjifarani.

Getting There & Away

Bush Taxi & Minibus The bustling gare routière is in the centre, near the Grand Marché. Peugeot 504s to Cotonou take six hours and cost CFA6000. Beware: if your taxi is not full upon departure or if people are not going the entire distance, the taxi will stop endlessly en route and you will probably be dumped into another taxi in Bohicon. This will lengthen your travel time considerably.

Bush taxis for the border town of Malanville (Niger) take five hours and cost CFA 3500 plus extra for luggage, while a bus or minibus costs CFA2500 and takes about seven hours. They all leave either from the gare routière in the centre or from the Sonacop petrol station on the northern side of town. Bush taxis east to the Togo border take at least three hours because the road is not tar. The Togo border closes at 6 pm and the Niger border closes at 7.30 pm.

Train You can save money by taking the train – a relaxing trip far removed from taxi or minibus hell. There are two trains a day, in each direction, one in the morning and one in the evening. The morning train from Cotonou leaves at 8 am. The evening train from Cotonou leaves at 7 pm on Tuesday, Thursday and Saturday; from Parakou it leaves at 6 pm on Wednesday, Friday and Sunday.

DJOUGOU

Djougou is a lively crossroads town 134km north-west of Parakou. Most people passing through are on their way east to Togo or north to Natitingou.

If you're looking for hiking opportunities, don't overlook the area around Djougou. The famous Somba people live mostly to the north, but the Tanéka villages near Djougou are also very picturesque.

Motel de Djougou (☎ *80 01 40)* is not very good for the price, but it does have a bar-restaurant. Singles/doubles with fans and showers cost CFA5500/6500. For cheap *food*, try the area around the gare routière and adjoining market.

The Somba

Commonly referred to as the Somba, the Betamaribé people are concentrated to the south-west of Natitingou in the plains of Boukoumbé on the Togo border, and to the south-east around Perma. They live in the middle of their cultivated fields, rather than together in villages, so their compounds are scattered over the countryside. This custom is a reflection of their individuality and helps maintain a good distance from their neighbours.

The Betamaribé, like their close relatives in Togo, the Tamberma, have avoided Islamic and Christian influences. Most are devout animists. Once famous for their nudity they now wear clothes, but they still hunt with bows and arrows.

What's most fascinating about the Betamaribé is their houses. Called *tata somba*, they consist of small, round, tiered huts that look like miniature fortified castles. The ground floor is reserved for the animals. The kitchen is on the intermediate level. From there, you ascend to the roof where there are rooms for sleeping and a terrace for daytime living.

If you're travelling to Kara, there are good connections to the border. It's also fairly easy to find vehicles heading north to Natitingou. The gare routière is next to the market. Any vehicle heading from Parakou to Natitingou should stop in Djougou.

NATITINGOU

About 200km north-west of Parakou and pleasantly located at an altitude of 440m in the Atakora Mountains, Natitingou is the starting point for excursions to Somba country to the east and south, as well as to Parc National de la Pendjari to the north.

The Musée d'Arts et de Traditions Populaires de Natitingou is behind the tourist agency, Atacora. It has an interesting history and some fascinating artefacts from the

BENIN

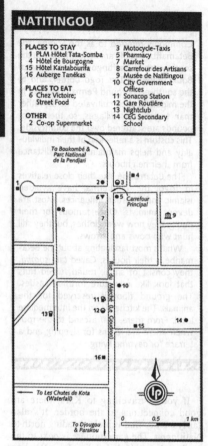

NATITINGOU

PLACES TO STAY
1 PLM Hôtel Tata-Somba
4 Hôtel de Bourgogne
15 Hôtel Kantabourifa
16 Auberge Tanékas

PLACES TO EAT
6 Chez Victoire;
   Street Food

OTHER
2 Co-op Supermarket

3 Motocycle-Taxis
5 Pharmacy
7 Market
8 Carrefour des Artisans
9 Musée de Natitingou
10 City Government
   Offices
11 Sonacop Station
12 Gare Routière
13 Nightclub
14 CEG Secondary
   School

To Boukombé &
Parc National
de la Pendjari

Carrefour
Principal

Rue du Marché de Coudon

To Les Chutes de Kota
(Waterfall)

To Djougou
& Parakou

0   0.5   1 km

Somba region. The exhibition includes
various musical instruments (bells, violin,
drums and flutes), jewellery, crowns and
other ceremonial artefacts. Most interesting
is the habitat room which has models of the
different types of *tata somba* (houses of the
Betamaribé – see the boxed text on the previous page for more details) with an
explanation of why certain models are used.
It is open from Tuesday to Saturday between
8.30 am and 1 pm and 3 to 7 pm.

You could also check out **Les Chutes de
Kota**, a waterfall 15km south-east of Nati-

tingou. It's off the main highway, on a well-
maintained dirt road. It's a nice place to have
a picnic and for at least half the year during
the rainy season, you can swim in the pool
of water at the bottom of the falls.

Places to Stay & Eat
Auberge Tanékas (☎ 82 15 52) is nice and
quiet and one of the cheapest places to stay
in Natitingou. It's on the southern outskirts
of town on the road to Djougou, on your left
as you enter Natitingou and about 2km from
the centre. Spacious singles/doubles with
fans and showers cost CFA5000/6000. The
hotel's restaurant is also quite popular and
offers chicken, steak, omelettes and African
specialities; the *menu du jour* costs around
CFA2500 and most main dishes are in the
CFA1500 to CFA2800 range. On the road to
the CEG secondary school is **Hôtel Kantabourifa** (☎ 82 17 66). It has quiet, clean
singles/doubles for CFA5000/6000 (CFA
8000/9000 with air-con), and a restaurant.

Hôtel de Bourgogne (☎ 82 12 40), on the
road running east from the Carrefour Principal, is a two storey hotel with a restaurant
and singles/doubles for CFA8000/10,000
with air-con, less with fan.

The best hotel by far is **PLM Hôtel Tata-
Somba** (☎ 82 11 24), which is at its liveliest
during the national park's open season. It
has air-con singles/doubles with bathrooms
for CFA22,000/26,000 (25% cheaper in the
period from 1 June to 30 September). The
facilities include a classy restaurant (CFA
2000 for breakfast and CFA6000 for other
meals), a pool and a reproduction of a tata
somba. You can also book rooms for the
lodges at Parc National de la Pendjari here.

There are plenty of opportunities for
drinking cheap beer and trying **street food**, or
just hanging out in Natitingou.

Getting There & Away
Usually at least one vehicle every morning
goes from Parakou to Natitingou (CFA
3500). It starts filling up early in the morning. If you miss it, don't worry; there are
many more vehicles to Djougou (134km)
and from there it's usually not difficult to

find a ride to Natitingou. For a vehicle from Natitingou to Parakou or Cotonou, go early in the morning to the gare routière. A bush taxi direct to Cotonou costs around CFA 8000. Buses are cheaper, but they are much slower and break down frequently. There are other taxis for Parakou and Cotonou that leave during the day when they fill up.

BOUKOUMBÉ

On the border with Togo, 43km south-west of Natitingou via a very scenic road, Boukoumbé is definitely a place worth visiting if you're in the Natitingou area. About 15km before town you'll pass near **Mt Kousso-Kovangou**, the highest mountain in Benin. About 3km further along this road you'll pass the Belvédère de Koussou-Kovangou, an observation point which offers fantastic views of the area.

The Boukoumbé market is the town's major attraction and not to be missed. The market here is as much a social event for people from near and far around the region to get together and drink *chouk* (sorghum beer) and party as it is for selling produce. Every four years or so, there is a whipping ceremony, in which the young men of the area beat each other black and blue. Boukoumbé is one of the few areas in Benin where you can buy traditional smoking pipes, which are truly rare souvenirs.

Places to Stay & Eat

Some way of the road which runs by the Catholic mission is a nice hotel with three decent rooms, the *Auberge Villageoise de Tourisme*; it has a restaurant.

Chez Pascaline in the Zongo area is the best place to eat in Boukoumbé. It is reportedly 'wickedly nice', with fantastic and inexpensive wild-game meat, salads, rice and beans. This is also a good place to inquire about lodging with locals and the possibility of visiting nearby tatas. *Street food* can be found in the market area.

Getting There & Away

There is at least one taxi every day from Natitingou to Boukoumbé; the fare is

CFA1000. The trip only takes two hours, but the waiting time can be longer as the taxi starts filling up around 9 am and may not leave before 3 pm.

PARC NATIONAL DE LA PENDJARI

This national park (275,000 hectares), 45km north of Natitingou, adjoins the Parc National d'Arli in Burkina Faso and is bordered on its western and eastern side by the River Pendjari. It's much more developed for tourism than the Benin side of Parc National du W, so it receives the most visitors. It's open only from 15 December to 15 May, the best viewing time being near the end of the dry season when the animals hover around the water holes.

Half the fun is looking for the animals. A recent census indicates that about 850 elephant, 2000 buffalo, 1250 hippo and 350 lion live in Pendjari. Readers have reported that wildlife is easily seen; one reader reported seeing lions three times in three days.

The park entrance fee is CFA5000 (valid for 30 days), plus you must pay a camera fee of CFA1000 and also CFA2000 for each night you stay in the park. You must have a guide (about CFA5000 per day), and he will expect to be provided with food and drink.

Places to Stay & Eat

Many visitors stay in Natitingou and make excursions from there, but you'll have a better chance of seeing animals if you stay at the park itself. That's because very early morning is the best time for spotting animals, when they tend to congregate at the water holes. Because of the presence of lions, there are only certain areas, including the Mare Yangouali and Pont d'Arli, where *camping* is permitted. The park wardens can show you where.

In Tanguiéta, at the southern tip of the park, there are two very rustic *campements* – one of these is beside the river and has low prices. There's also *Chez Basille*, which is a small hotel-restaurant in town.

PLM has a new *hotel* at the Cascade de Tanougou, well located for an early morning

BENIN

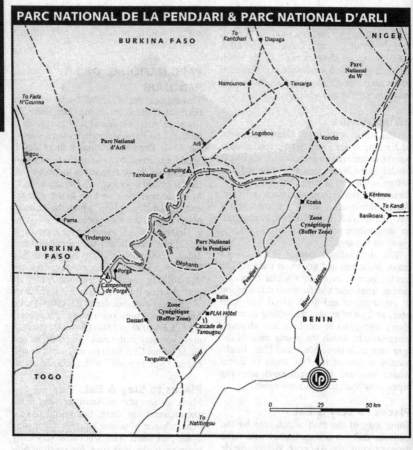

PARC NATIONAL DE LA PENDJARI & PARC NATIONAL D'ARLI

walk and swim at the falls. The circular bungalows have a bathroom behind a dividing wall. It is CFA6000/8000 for a single/double from December to May (CFA4000/6000 in the off season); meals are CFA3500 from December to May (otherwise CFA3000). Book with PLM in Cotonou (☎ 33 11 85) or in Natitingou (☎ 82 11 24). Most people keep going north to Porga. There, at the entrance to the park, is **Campement de Porga** (☎ 82 11 24). It's a larger place with a restaurant and basic singles/doubles with fans which are CFA13,500/15,000 (CFA19,000/

21,000 with air-con). Nile perch and meat in season are restaurant specialities.

Getting There & Away

The main entrances to Pendjari are roughly 100km north of Natitingou. To get to the park from Natitingou, take the dirt road heading north for 45km to the fork in the road at Tanguiéta, a village on the southern end of the park. From there most visitors head north-west for 59km to Porga near the Burkina Faso border. This village is the main entrance to the park and there's a campement near the gate. Alternatively, head about 40km north-east from Tanguiéta to Batia, the other park entrance. Many people prefer the latter because the route is shorter and in equally good condition. You can't walk into the park (hiking is not permitted), so go to one of the hotels in Natitingou and hitch a lift with travellers who have vehicles. Sharing the Hôtel Tata-Somba's Land Rover is another possibility. Travel agencies in Cotonou will organise trips, but they are expensive.

KANDI

This town, 213km north of Parakou on the way to Niger, is worth a stop for its market. The Bariba and Peul (Fula) people give the town a distinctive northern character, as do the voluptuous mango trees.

At the southern entrance to town is the *Auberge du Carrefour*, while at the other end is the *Baobab 2000* (aka the Campement); both provide bucket showers. The new *La Recontre Auberge* (☎ 63 01 76) has been recommended by travellers. It has rooms with fans/air-con for CFA5000/7000 and a small paillote restaurant which serves African and European food. *Gargoterie de Kandi* behind the market is the place to eat. Good buvettes include *La Nouvelle Cité Jerusalem* and *Aux Parc des Princes*.

Any bush taxi heading north to Malanville will pass through Kandi.

MALANVILLE

This town is in the far north at the Niger border, on the main highway between Cotonou and Niamey. The ride from Parakou is scenic. Look for women selling red-skinned

cheese on the way. Market day is Sunday, which is the best time to visit because of the rich mix of people you'll see.

The dirty *campement* at the entrance to town is one place to stay, but the newer *Rose des Sables* (☎ 67 01 25), with fans or air-con rooms, is reportedly good value for your CFA. For *food*, look around the outskirts of the gare routière.

A bush taxi to from Malanville to Parakou takes about five hours (CFA3000). A rare bus or minibus takes seven hours (CFA 2500).

From Malanville, a taxi to the Niger border costs about CFA200 and then a motorcycle taxi from there to Gaya in Niger (where you can get taxis to Niamey) is an exorbitant CFA500, but it is a long way to walk.

PARC NATIONAL DU W

The Benin section of Parc National du W (pronounced *dou-blay-vay*) is about twice as large as Pendjari – W is adjacent to the park of the same name in Niger. The one across the border is more accessible and has the best viewing trails (see the relevant section in the Niger chapter for more details). Pendjari, W and d'Arli form, in effect, one big park and are surrounded by buffer zones managed for hunting (*zones cynégétiques*). You may see elephant, buffalo, hippo and crocodile and several species of antelope.

To get to du W, go north-east from Batia for 100km to the intersection with the dirt road connecting Kondio (Burkina Faso) and Kérémou. Kérémou is the major entry point to the park on the Benin side. You will need your own 4WD transport.

Burkina Faso

Burkina Faso, previously known as Haute (Upper) Volta, is too often merely on a traveller's route to somewhere else. However, it is well worth visiting for its own sake; it's a place to slow down, step down a gear and unwind for a week or two. Despite the strutting, macho national slogan, 'la patrie ou la mort, nous vaincrons' (the fatherland or death, we shall overcome), Burkinabe, as they are called, are agreeably laid-back.

The capital, Ouagadougou (pronounced *waga-doo-goo*) – or simply Ouaga – has little to detain you for more than a few days. But the countryside, a gradation from desert and purest Sahel in the north through to the savanna of the central plateau and the rainforest lushness of the extreme south-west, is well worth exploring, and the people are as varied as the terrain.

Facts about Burkina Faso

HISTORY
The earliest known inhabitants of present-day Burkina Faso were the Bobo, Lobi and Gourounsi, who were in the area by the 13th century. By the 14th century, Mossi peoples had begun to move westward from settlements near the River Niger.

The first Mossi kingdom was founded more than 500 years ago in Ouagadougou. Three more Mossi states subsequently arose in other parts of what today is Burkina Faso, all paying homage to Ouagadougou, the strongest. The government of each of the states was highly organised, with ministers, courts and a cavalry known for its devastating attacks against the Muslim empires in Mali. They also fostered a rigid social hierarchy in which other ethnic groups within their domains were relegated to the lowest level. Only a few groups in the south-west, including the Bobo, Lobi and Senoufo, escaped subjugation.

BURKINA FASO AT A GLANCE

Capital: Ouagadougou
Population: 10.4 million
Area: 274,122 sq km
Head of state: Captain Blaise Compaoré
Official language: French
Main local languages: Moré, Dioula
Currency: West African CFA franc
Exchange rate: US$1 = CFA600
Time: GMT/UTC
Country telephone code: ☎ 226
Best time to go: November to February

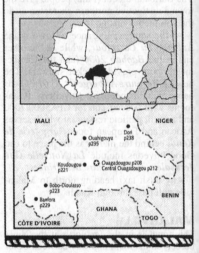

During the 'Scramble for Africa' in the second half of the 19th century, the French, expanding their territory in the continent's western bulge, broke up the traditional Mossi states rather than reaching an accommodation with the traditional rulers. Exploiting the latter's internal rivalries, they had established their sway over the entire region by the early 20th century.

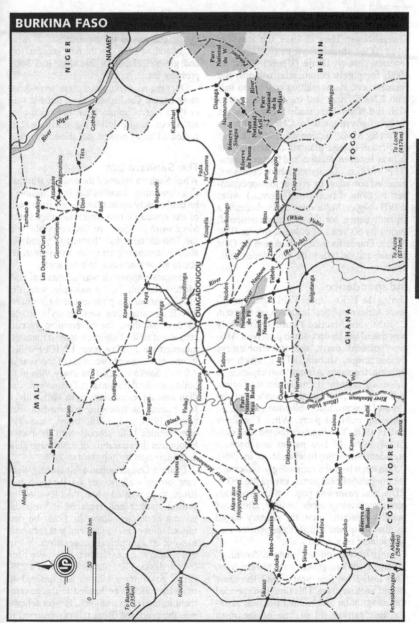

BURKINA FASO

At first, the former Mossi states were assimilated into the vast Colonie du Haut Sénégal-Niger. Then, in 1919, the area was hived off for administrative convenience as a separate colony: Haute (Upper) Volta. In 1932, for purely commercial reasons, the French sliced it up, grafting more than half onto Côte d'Ivoire and the remainder onto Mali and Niger. This made it easier for the colonial government in Côte d'Ivoire to recruit the Mossi, forcing them to work there on French-owned plantations and on the railway between Abidjan and Ouagadougou. (This tradition of emigrant labour continues, impelled nowadays by greater job opportunities in Côte d'Ivoire and Ghana.) After WWII, Upper Volta once again became a separate entity, but the disparity continued; during its 60 years of colonial rule in West Africa, France focused its attention on Côte d'Ivoire and did little to develop Upper Volta.

Independence

During the 1950s, Upper Volta's most prominent African political leaders were Ouezzin Coulibaly and Maurice Yaméogo. Coulibaly was one of the leaders of the pan-West African political party, the Rassemblement Démocratique Africain (RDA), which was fighting for more African participation in colonial government throughout the region. Yaméogo was one of the founders of the Union Démocratique Voltaïque (UDV), an opposing political party. When Coulibaly died in 1958, Yaméogo negotiated the amalgamation of the two parties and became president following independence in 1960.

Yaméogo became increasingly autocratic, banning all political parties except the UDV-RDA, and governing poorly with disastrous economic consequences. In 1966, after mass popular demonstrations, the military staged its first coup and jailed Yaméogo for embezzlement on a grand scale.

In 1970, the military stepped down, allowing a civilian government to take over. This lasted for four years, until the army staged another coup. This time it suspended the constitution and banned political activity. But getting rid of one of the most

powerful trade unions in Africa was not so easy. Following a nationwide strike in 1975, the unions forced the government to raise wages and, in 1978, got the new constitution and general elections that they had been pressing for.

Over the next five years there were three more coups. The last and most notable was in 1983 when Captain Thomas Sankara, an ambitious young left-wing military star, staged a bloody putsch and seized power.

The Sankara Era

When Sankara renamed the country Burkina Faso, meaning 'Land of the Incorruptible', he deliberately coined the phrase from each of the country's two major languages: the Moré word for 'pure' or 'incorruptible' and the Dioula term for 'homeland', and set about restructuring the economy to promote, above all, self-reliance in rural areas.

Sankara's approach was unconventional. Modest Renault 5s, for example, were the official cars of the president and his ministers. Blitz campaigns were his style. In one 15 day marathon, the government vaccinated about 60% of children against measles, meningitis and yellow fever. UNICEF called it 'one of the major successes of the year in Africa'. Sankara called on every village to build a medical dispensary. The government then sent representatives from each village for training as front-line paramedics. Between 1983 and 1986, more than 350 communities built schools with their own labour and the education of school-age children increased by one-third to 22%.

Finding Ouagadougou a bit shabby, Sankara ordered all houses on the principal streets to be painted white, then levelled the central market and replaced it with the present concrete horror. In 1985, he dismissed most of his cabinet and sent members to work on agricultural cooperatives. It was mainly show; a month later, they were back at their desks. Then Sankara imposed a 25% cut in government salaries and ordered all rents for 1985 to be handed to the government instead of to landlords. His pet scheme was the proposed Sahel railway, planned to be a 375km link between Ouagadougou and Tambao on the Mali border, the site of rich manganese and limestone deposits. Although economists calculated that it could never be profitable, Sankara went ahead. In early 1987, he inaugurated the first 33km leg to Dousin, all done with 'voluntary' village labour. Today, it reaches Kaya, 98km from Ouaga, and is unlikely ever to get any further.

Sankara was charismatic and the masses loved him for his blunt honesty. In 1986, he engaged the country in a five day war with Mali, which merely enhanced his popularity. But, while he had widespread popular support, Sankara antagonised powerful interests such as the trade unions, landlords and many western countries – particularly the USA and France, upon whom the country had long been economically dependent. He did not live to see the realisation of his socialist policies. In late 1987, a group of junior officers seized power. Sankara was taken outside Ouagadougou and shot.

But Thom Sank, as he's still known throughout the country, lives on in peoples' memories. Every 15 October, the anniversary of his overthrow, the regime mounts a stilted celebration, while the 'Sankarists' pay their own more spontaneous, genuine homage. His simple grave has become a place of discreet pilgrimage.

Burkina Faso Today

Under Sankara the economy improved and there was little government corruption. Financial books were kept in good order, debt financing was kept to a minimum and budgetary commitments were adhered to. Most importantly at that time, people developed a genuine pride in their country.

The new junta was headed by Captain Blaise Compaoré, Sankara's former friend and co-revolutionary, and son-in-law of the late Houphouët-Boigny, Côte d'Ivoire's long-standing leader. Compaoré attempted unsuccessfully to discredit Sankara with a 'rectification' campaign, designed to correct the 'deviations' of the previous government while still embracing the revolution. But the first act – dismantling the local cells of the revolutionary defence committees that had threatened and often replaced traditional power structures in rural areas – couldn't have been more counter-revolutionary.

In late 1991, Compaoré achieved a degree of legitimacy when, as sole candidate and on a low turnout, he was elected president. This legitimacy was compromised, however, when Clément Ouedraogo, the leading opposition figure, was assassinated a couple of weeks later. In 1992, the government party, the Organisation pour la Démocratie Populaire (ODP), won 78 of the 107 seats in the national assembly amid widespread accusations of fraud. In the subsequent legislative elections of 1997, the ODP, restyled the Congrès pour la Démocratie et le Progrès (CDP), received a suspect 95% of votes cast by those who bothered to turn out. Fresh presidential elections were scheduled for 1998, but were yet to materialise by late 1998.

GEOGRAPHY

Landlocked Burkina Faso has a variety of landscapes. The harsh desert and semidesert of the north resembles the terrain of its neighbours, Mali and Niger. But Burkina is only in part a country of the Sahel. Its dominant feature is the vast central laterite plateau, where hardy trees and bushes thrive, which gives way to woodland and savanna further south. In the south-west, around Banfora, the rainfall is heavier and there are forests as well as irrigated sugar-cane and rice fields.

The French named the country Upper Volta after its three major rivers – the Black, White and Red Voltas, known today as the Mouhoun, Nakambe and Nazinon rivers. All flow south into the world's largest artificial lake, Lake Volta, in Ghana.

CLIMATE

The main rains fall between June and October. From December to February the weather is marginally cooler, with midday maximums only occasionally exceeding 35°C.

BURKINA FASO

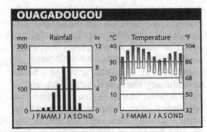

During this period, the dry heat is more bearable, although the dusty harmattan winds produce hazy skies. The hot season, when the mercury can rise well above 40°C in the capital, is from March to early June.

ECOLOGY & ENVIRONMENT
Burkina suffers acutely from two related forms of environmental damage: deforestation and soil erosion. Some sources attribute a GNP loss as high as 9% annually to such degradation.

Nowadays, Ouagadougou is surrounded by a 70km stretch of land virtually devoid of trees. That's because firewood accounts for 94% of the country's energy consumption. Carts bringing wood from afar are a common sight on the roads leading to the capital. This and commercial logging, together with slash-and-burn agriculture and animal grazing, has increased desertification, particularly in the north.

But all is not gloom. Small-scale projects supported by nongovernmental organisations have been the most successful at addressing these issues. For example, farmers have been encouraged to return to traditional methods of cultivation, in particular the building of *diguettes*, stone lines laid along field contours which slow water run-off, maximise water penetration and reduce erosion. These have had considerable impact, preventing soil levels from decreasing.

FLORA & FAUNA
The drier northern part of the country is the domain of trees such as acacia (including the gum arabic tree *Acacia senegal*, whose sticky resin is used in chewing gum) and the baobab. The word 'baobab' is a corruption of the Arabic *abu habeb*, (seed bearer), and the tree looks as though it's been tipped upside down, its profusion of spindly branches like networks of roots. (For more information about baobabs, see the boxed text 'The Baobab Tree' in the Flora & Fauna section of the Facts about the Region chapter.)

Further south, tamarind and mango trees predominate while, in pockets of the south and south-east, the vegetation, similar to that of neighbouring Benin becomes more lush. Here, in the Parc National d'Arli and Ranch de Nazinga lies the best chance of spotting large mammals.

GOVERNMENT & POLITICS
The head of government is the president. The country also has an elected national assembly. According to the constitution, both presidential and legislative elections follow a five year cycle. The last elections to the national assembly were held in 1997, and at the time of going to press, the presidential election was still awaited. Behind the scenes, the traditional leaders still exert considerable influence; the Moro-Naba, the leader of the Mossi, for example, will be consulted before any major political decision is taken.

ECONOMY
Burkina has scarcely any exploitable natural resources apart from its decimated forests, and remains one of the world's five poorest countries. Its agriculture, which still employs some 90% of the work force, is largely dependent upon capricious rainfall.

During Sankara's time, foreign debt was low and the GNP rose from an average of 3.1 to 4.6% per annum, making Burkina one of the very few countries in Africa to enjoy per capita GNP growth during the 1980s. On the negative side, external investment and western aid – now once again flowing – was reduced to a trickle.

A 5% growth rate was sustained in the early 1990s and in 1994 Burkina was one of only five African countries in a position to export food. Agriculture, despite the unpredictable rains, remains a buoyant sector, not least because of a highly successful World Health Organization river blindness (onchocerciasis) eradication program, which has led to the repopulation and recultivation of large fertile areas.

At the macro level, Burkina is successfully implementing reforms dictated by the 1993 IMF and World Bank Structural Adjustment Program. It has also adjusted less painfully to the 1994 devaluation of the CFA than some other West African countries. However, while this may have cheered the international bankers, the poorest have suffered and international debt is again soaring.

POPULATION & PEOPLE

With more than 10 million people, Burkina Faso, occupying an area about half the size of France, has some 60 ethnic groups. The largest of these is the Mossi, who make up about half the population and are primarily concentrated in the central plateau area, including Ouagadougou. The Bobo live in the west around Bobo-Dioulasso, while the far south-west around Gaoua is home to the Lobi. To their east, and transcending the border with Ghana, are the Gourounsi. In the Sahel areas of the north, you'll find Hausa, Fula (also known as Peul or Fulani), Bella and Tuareg peoples, many still seminomadic, while the Gourmantché predominate in the east around Fada N'Gourma.

ARTS

Art & Craftwork

Burkina is an excellent place to look for masks and woodcarvings. While each ethnic group in Burkina has its own artistic style, that of the Mossi, the Bobo and the Lobi is the most famous. In the museums of Ouaga and Bobo you'll see examples of all three. The tall antelope masks of the Mossi and the butterfly masks of the Bobo are perhaps the best known, while the Lobi are well known for their figurative sculptures. For more details, see the colour feature between pages 224 and 225.

Music

Established local stars include Black So Man, Nick Domby, Youssou Camporé, Georges Ouedraogo, Nakelse Emmanuel and Amity Méria, a female vocalist. The group Farafina, originally from Bobo, continues to make waves but nowadays spend most of their time in Europe. Among the up-and-comers are Jean-Claude Bamogo, Roger Waongo and, for traditional music, Zougn Nazaganda.

SOCIETY & CONDUCT

Ceremonies and *fêtes* (festivals) are mainly based on the rhythms of the seasons and rites of passage – a festival to celebrate a bounteous harvest or planting time, the moment of renewal and regeneration, weddings, funerals and an adolescent's formal transition to adulthood. For more information see the Society & Conduct section in the Regional Facts for the Visitor chapter.

RELIGION

Because the Mossi were so successful historically in resisting Muslim invaders, today only about 25% of the people, mostly those living in the north, follow Islam. Some 10% are Christian and the remainder continue to observe traditional beliefs, based mainly on ancestor and spirit worship.

LANGUAGE

The official language is French. Of some 60 local languages, the most significant is Moré, the language of the Mossi and others living on the central plateau, spoken by more than half the population. Dioula is the lingua franca, the language of the market, even though, within Burkina, it's nobody's mother tongue. It's very closely related to Bambara, the major language of neighbouring Mali. Other significant local languages include Fula, Gourmantché and Gourounsi, spoken by people of the same name.

See the Language chapter for a list of useful phrases in French, Moré, Dioula and Fula.

Facts for the Visitor

SUGGESTED ITINERARIES

If you have a week at your disposal, you should plan on visiting Ouagadougou, Bobo-Dioulasso (Bobo) and, schedule allowing, Gorom-Gorom. If you arrive by air, your stay will probably begin in Ouagadougou, a friendly, relaxed capital city with an active nightlife. Allow at least three days. Mark Wednesday in your diary – that's the day to take a bus north-east to

Highlights

Markets

Ouagadougou
Despite its stark concrete shell, Ouaga's market is a bustling Aladdin's cave inside.

Bobo-Dioulasso   *(The South-West)*
Another busy urban market; this one is smaller than Ouaga's, and more relaxing to wander through.

Gorom-Gorom   *(The North)*
Held only on Thursday, this market is an ethnic melting pot where nomads meet farmers and herders. Not to be missed.

Cultural Events

FESPACO   *(Ouagadougou)*
The film event of the African continent, held biennially in February – be sure to book your accommodation well in advance.

Cultural Festival   *(The South-West)*
If you can, try to catch Bobo's Semaine Nationale de la Culture, a festival of music, dance and theatre, held in April during even years (alternating with FESPACO).

Festival des Arts Africains *(Ouagadougou)*
With artwork on display from all over the continent, and held annually in October, this festival is a great time to be in Ouaga.

Traditional Music

Urban   *(The South-West)*
Bobo's nightclubs really come to life at the weekends, while traditional music is offered up by the bars of the popular quarter of Balomakoté.

Rural   *(The South-West)*
The Lobi have their own musical tradition, and a good place to hear traditional Lobi music is in the simple cafes of Gaoua.

Traditional Architecture

Rock houses   *(The South-West)*
The fascinating troglodyte dwellings, hewn into the hillside, at Koro (near Bobo) are well worth making a detour for.

Lobi compounds   *(The South-West)*
Gaoua is a good base for exploring Lobi country, where traditional Lobi mud-brick compounds can be seen.

Mosques   *(The North)*
The village of Bani has seven fine mud-brick mosques, their minarets forming an impressive skyline as you approach.

National Parks & Natural Features

Parc National d'Arli   *(The South & South-East)*
Burkina's major national park, where you have a good chance of spotting a variety of animals and birds.

Ranch de Nazinga   *(The South & South-East)*
Established originally to rear deer and antelope for hunters, a visit here is possible as a day trip from Ouagadougou, if you're mobile.

Les Pics de Sindou   *(The South-West)*
There are good opportunities for walking or more challenging trekking in this craggy chain, 50km from Banfora.

Gorom-Gorom, stopping en route to explore the Sahel-style mosques of Bani. Thursday is Gorom-Gorom's unmissable market day. Head back to Ouaga that same evening, since transport on other days of the week is much harder to find. Take the bus to Bobo, which merits a couple of days at least; the train is slower and notoriously unpunctual and an internal flight is expensive and no quicker.

With two weeks to spare, plan on spending more time in the south-west, journeying by bus or train from Bobo to Banfora in the country's 'green' belt, an area with opportunities for hiking and cycling (allow at least three days). Travel on to Gaoua, further to the east in the heart of Lobi country and accessible from both Banfora and Bobo.

Returning to either town, most travellers now head over the border by bus, bush taxi or train to Ferkessédougou in Côte d'Ivoire or beyond. An alternative for lovers of wildlife who are around between December and May is to join a tour or hire a vehicle in Ouaga – access by public transport is well-nigh impossible – and make a three to four day return trip to visit the Parc National d'Arli or its less abundant neighbour, the Ranch de Nazinga.

PLANNING

If possible, try to avoid the rainy season between June and October, when the humidity's high and roads may be temporarily blocked.

The Institut Géographique in Ouagadougou produces a good map of Burkina, the *Carte Touristique et Routière*, and less helpful town maps of Ouaga and Bobo.

VISAS & DOCUMENTS
Visas

Everyone except ECOWAS nationals needs a visa. You can buy a tourist visa at Ouagadougou airport in return for CFA10,000 and two photos.

Burkina Faso embassies usually issue multiple-entry visas valid for three months.

They require two photos and may ask for proof of yellow fever vaccination. In countries where Burkina is not represented, French embassies normally issue them on its behalf. Typical costs are US$25 in the USA, UK£20 in Britain and 195FF from French embassies.

Visa Extensions Visas can be extended at the *sûreté* (room 22) on Blvd de la Révolution in Ouagadougou (open weekdays from 7.30 am to 12.30 pm and 3 to 5.30 pm). A one month extension costs CFA10,000 plus two photos and is usually ready the same day if you go early.

Other Documents

Proof of vaccination against yellow fever is mandatory and is usually checked on arrival at airports and most land borders.

EMBASSIES & CONSULATES
Burkina Faso Embassies

In West Africa, there are embassies in Côte d'Ivoire, Ghana, Mali and Nigeria. For more details, see the Facts for the Visitor section of the relevant country chapter.

Burkina Faso embassies elsewhere include the following:

Belgium
 (☎ 02-345 66 09)
 16 place Guy-d'Arezzo, Brussels 1180
France
 (☎ 01 43 59 90 63)
 159 blvd Haussmann, 75008 Paris
Germany
 (☎ 0228-33 20 63)
 18 Wendelstadtallee, 53179 Bonn-Bad Godesberg
USA
 (☎ 202-332 5577)
 2340 Massachusetts Ave, NW, Washington, DC 20008

In the UK, there is an honorary consul (☎ 0171-738 1800, fax 7738 2820; from 22 April 2000 ☎ 020-7738 1800, fax 7738 2820) at 5 Cinnamon Row, Plantation Wharf, London SW11 3TW.

BURKINA FASO

Embassies & Consulates in Burkina Faso

Embassies or consulates in Ouagadougou include the following. All embassies or consulates listed in this section are open from Monday to Friday.

Côte d'Ivoire
(☎ 31 82 28)
Corner of Ave Raoul Follereau and Blvd du Faso

France
(☎ 30 67 74)
Blvd de la Révolution, 100m west of the Palais Présidentiel

Germany
(☎ 30 67 31)
Rue Joseph Badoua

Ghana
(☎ 30 76 35)
Ave d'Oubritenga, opposite the UNESCO office

Mali
(☎ 38 19 22)
2569 Ave Bassawarga, just south of Ave de la Résistance

Nigeria
(☎ 30 66 67)
Ave d'Oubritenga, 1km north-east of Place des Nations Unies

USA
(☎ 30 67 23)
Ave Raoul Follereau, south of the French embassy

If you're British and in trouble, contact the honorary consul (☎ 31 11 37, fax 31 05 03).

Visas for Onward Travel

Benin and Niger don't have embassies in Burkina Faso and the French consulate doesn't issue visas on their behalf, so if you intend to travel directly from Burkina Faso you'll need to plan ahead. If you just want to slip over the border to Benin to explore the Parc National de la Pendjari, you can get a 48 hour visa at the border post. Information about visas for other neighbouring countries is listed below.

Côte d'Ivoire

Visa costs vary substantially according to nationality. If you're French, a one month single-entry visa costs CFA20,000. Canadians pay CFA27,500, while UK and Irish nationals are stung for CFA35,000. If you're lucky to hold a US passport, it's free. The embassy's open from 7.30 am to midday and 3 to 5 pm. You need three photos and can collect your visa the next day.

Ghana

'All visitors entering the embassy for any negotiation are requested to be decently dressed', says the plaque at the entrance gate. Another eccentric feature is that the embassy insists upon a local address in Ghana. Just pluck a hotel from one of the Places to Stay sections in the Ghana chapter and they'll be happy. The embassy, open from 8 am to 2 pm, charges CFA12,000 for a one month visa, issued within 48 hours. Bring four identical photos.

Mali

The consulate is open from 7.30 am to 4 pm. One-month visas cost CFA12,000 and are issued the same day.

Togo

The French consulate issues visas for Togo. Single-entry visas cost CFA16,500 for a stay of up to one month and CFA19,500 for up to three months (CFA23,000 for multiple entry). The consulate is open from 8.30 to midday and visas are issued within 24 hours. Note that their Togolese visa is only valid for 48 hours after crossing the border, but it can be extended in Lomé.

The Canadian embassy (☎ 31 18 94) represents Australia in consular matters.

CUSTOMS

There's no restriction on the import or export of CFA or foreign currencies. If you want to take out an artefact that's manifestly old and valuable, play safe and get an export certificate from the Directeur du Patrimoine National in Ouaga. Inquire at the tourist office.

MONEY

The unit of currency in Burkina Faso is the CFA franc.

Euro €1	=	CFA660
1FF	=	CFA100
UK£1	=	CFA950
US$1	=	CFA600

The best – often the only – banks for changing money nationwide are the Banque Internationale du Burkina (BIB), which has a branch at Ouaga airport, and the Banque Internationale pour le Commerce, l'Industrie et l'Agriculture du Burkina (BICIAB). Both change US$, French franc and UK£ travellers cheques, for which the BICIAB charges a flat rate of CFA2360 per transaction. At the time of writing, the BICIAB was not accepting Thomas Cook, Visa, MasterCard or Citicorp cheques.

Other banks include the BICAO and the Banque Nationale de Paris. None give cash against a credit card.

POST & COMMUNICATIONS

The post offices in Ouagadougou and Bobo-Dioulasso offer a poste restante service – for more details see the Information sections in the relevant place entries.

Phonecards cost CFA2400 for 20 units and CFA5325 for 50, and are available from the post office in Ouaga and a few other retail outlets. Except in Bobo, they're of little use elsewhere. Similarly, off-the-street Internet access is, for the moment, confined to the capital.

There are no telephone area codes in Burkina.

PHOTOGRAPHY & VIDEO

You no longer need a photo or video permit. Your freedom, however, is far from absolute. The official off-limits list is formidable, and includes airports, bridges, reservoirs, banks, any military installations, police stations or government buildings, including the Palais Présidentiel and post offices, train stations and bus and bush taxi parks, TV/radio stations, petrol stations, grain warehouses, water towers, industrial installations and indigent people. For more general information and advice, see the Photography & Video section in the Regional Facts for the Visitor chapter.

HEALTH

You'll need a yellow fever vaccination certificate to enter the country. Malaria exists year-round throughout the whole country, and you should take appropriate precautions against it.

Meningitis outbreaks, although rarely widespread, occur in the Sahel areas, especially during the dry season. Several travellers have reported being asked for proof of inoculation against meningitis when arriving at land borders, especially between Mali and Burkina. This isn't a standard requirement, but it may be demanded if there's a local epidemic on either or both sides of the frontier.

Onchocerciasis, or river blindness, once a scourge, has been all but eradicated. Bilharzia (schistosomiasis) exists in many lakes and ponds, so you should avoid paddling or swimming in these. For more information on these and other health matters, see the Health section in the Regional Facts for the Visitor chapter.

WOMEN TRAVELLERS

Burkinabe are, in general, a laid-back, friendly and polite people, and women travellers are unlikely to meet any more hassle here than in other countries in the region.

For more information and advice, see the Women Travellers section in the Regional Facts for the Visitor chapter.

DANGERS & ANNOYANCES

Burkina remains one of the safer countries in West Africa, but crime isn't unknown, particularly around big markets and bus stations, where it's usually confined to petty theft and pickpocketing. It's usually only a problem to look out for in Ouagadougou and Bobo-Dioulasso; knives are rarely flashed.

BUSINESS HOURS

Business hours are from 7.30 am to midday and 3 to 5.30 pm, Monday to Friday, and from 9 am to 1 pm on Saturday. Government offices close Saturday and Sunday.

Banking hours are weekdays from 7 to 11.00 am and 3.30 to 5 pm.

PUBLIC HOLIDAYS & SPECIAL EVENTS

Public holidays include 1 January (New Year's Day), 3 January, 8 March (Women's Day), Easter Monday, 1 May (Labour Day), Ascension Day, 4 and 5 August, 15 August, 15 October (anniversary of Sankara's overthrow), 1 November (All Saints Day), 25 December (Christmas Day) and variable Islamic holidays. See the Public Holidays & Special Events section in the Facts for the Visitor chapter for a table of estimated dates of the Islamic holidays.

FESPACO is the biennial festival of African cinema, which takes place in Ouaga in odd-numbered years during February or March. In even-numbered years, Ouaga hosts the Salon International de l'Artisanat de Ouagadougou which attracts artisans and vendors from all over the continent. This event alternates with Bobo's Semaine Nationale de la Culture, a week of music, dance and theatre held every even year during March or April. Each October, Ouaga plays host to the annual Festival des Arts Africains and all over, all the time, there are traditional festivities or *fêtes*, especially in the Bobo area.

ACTIVITIES

There are opportunities for hiking and biking around Banfora. You can sign up for organised safaris to both the Parc National d'Arli and the Ranch de Nazinga.

ACCOMMODATION

It's fairly easy to find basic rooms with fan and shared facilities for between CFA3500 and CFA4500. In Ouaga and Bobo, you can be lodged comfortably with air-con for between CFA7000 and CFA10,000. There's a lodging tax of CFA300 per person per night in addition to 18% VAT, except at the cheapest hotels. Both are usually included in the rate you'll be quoted.

Within Ouaga and Bobo you have to pay a *taxe de séjour*, also known as a *taxe communale*. It's a once-off payment, irrespective of the number of nights you stay at a hotel, and is calculated at CFA500 per person per hotel star rating.

FOOD

Food lacks the variety of some other West African countries. As is usual in the region, sauces are the mainstay. There's *riz sauce* (boiled rice with a sauce to pour over), *riz gras* (gooey rice cooked in animal fat, usually tomato flavoured), *sauce de poisson* (a fish-based sauce), *boeuf sauce aubergine* (sauce with beef and eggplant), *mouton sauce tomate* (sauce with mutton and tomatoes), *ragoût d'igname* (a yam-based stew), *riz sauce arachide* (rice with peanut sauce) and *sauce gombo* (a sticky okra-based stew).

Sauces are always served with a starch, usually rice or the Burkina staple, *tô*, a millet or sorghum-based *pâte* (a pounded dough-like substance). Stewed *agouti*, (grasscutter, a large rodent) is a prized delicacy, as is *capitaine* (Nile perch). Lunch is the main meal; at night, grilled dishes are popular.

DRINKS

Bottled Lafi spring water (CFA400 for a 1.5L bottle) is safe, as are the plastic sachets of Yilembe. Bullvit, the local soda water, is a refreshing alternative to sticky *sucreries* (soft drinks).

Castel, Flag, Brakina and So.b.bra (just that; pronounced *so-bay-bra*) are popular and palatable lager-type beers.

Getting There & Away

AIR

Burkina Faso's international airport is in Ouagadougou. The national carrier is Air Burkina; other airlines servicing Burkina are Air Afrique and Air France.

There's an international departure tax of CFA7700, which is normally included in the price of your ticket. Check to be sure.

Europe & the USA

Both Air France and Air Afrique have four flights a week between Ouaga and Paris. Sabena connects Brussels and Ouaga three times a week. An undiscounted one way ticket costs around CFA625,000. For most of the year, Corsair runs a weekly flight to Paris for CFA180,000 one way. From Paris, a one way flight to Ouagadougou costs between 1800FF and 2300FF, more during the peak months of July and August. Other cut-price options are Air Algérie (weekly, CFA 240,000 to Paris) and Aeroflot (every two weeks, CFA260,000 to Paris or London).

For travel to/from the USA, you have to transfer in Paris, Brussels, Dakar (Senegal) or Abidjan.

Africa

There's a daily flight to Abidjan on either Air Afrique or, more cheaply, Air Burkina (CFA62,000). Air Ivoire (CFA71,500) has two flights a week. Air Burkina flies to Bamako (Mali) for CFA59,000 and Lomé (Togo) for CFA73,000, as does Air Afrique, which has direct flights from Ouaga to Niamey (Niger), Dakar and Cotonou (Benin). Air Ivoire used to offer a 35% student discount but this may have been discontinued.

For travel to/from East and southern Africa, you need to pick up a connection in Abidjan or Dakar. Refer to the Getting There & Away sections of the Côte d'Ivoire and Senegal chapters for details.

LAND
Benin

A SOTRAO bus (CFA4000) runs every Sunday from Ouaga to Tanguiéta in Benin. There's a twice daily STMB bus (225km, four hours, CFA2000) and daily minibuses (CFA3000) between Ouagadougou and Fada N'Gourma. Onward transport to the border (CFA3000) is scarce and fills up slowly. Except on market day (Monday), it's even scarcer from the border to Tanguiéta (65km, CFA2500), from where there's at least one taxi a day to Natitingou.

Côte d'Ivoire

Bus & Bush Taxi Large buses, mostly packed with migrant Burkinabe workers, leave Ouaga and Bobo daily for Bouaké (925km from Ouaga, CFA13,500), Yamoussoukro (CFA13,500) and Abidjan (CFA14,500). The full 1175km trip takes at least 24 hours – more if your bus overnights at the border. UTB runs a daily service. Sans Frontière has three departures a day and more at peak periods, either direct or with a change in Bobo.

From Bobo, Compagnie Transport and SOTRAKOF run to Niangoloko (CFA1400) near the border and also to Ouangolodougou

Border Crossings

The main land border crossings are at Niangoloko for Côte d'Ivoire; Tanguiéta for Benin; 15km south of Pô for Ghana; 40km south of Bitou for Togo; east of Kantchari for Niger; and west of Tiou for Mali. Borders tend to be closed by 5.30 pm or 6.30 pm at the latest, and note that there is a time change of one hour going from Burkina into Benin or Niger.

(CFA4000) in Côte d'Ivoire. Sans Frontière has at least one bus a day to Ferkessédougou, Bouaké (both CFA8000) and on to Abidjan (CFA12,000).

You can get a Peugeot 504 direct from Ouaga to Abidjan, but it's more pleasant and less exhausting to do the journey in stages. A trans-border bush taxi between Bobo and Ferkessédougou costs CFA6000.

Train The train between Ouaga and Abidjan, once an enjoyable experience in its own right, has declined considerably in recent years. Nowadays, there are no sleeping berths and only snacks and drinks are available, although you can buy food and drink from vendors at stops en route. Timings are decidedly speculative; a chalkboard at the station at Ouaga announces the '*arrivée probable*' of '*l'Express*' from Abidjan. It leaves Ouagadougou on Tuesday, Thursday and Saturday mornings and typically takes something over 24 hours.

The 1st/2nd class fare is CFA24,000/ 17,500 to Abidjan, CFA17,300/12,700 to Bouaké and CFA12,200/8100 to Ferkessé-dougou. It's well worth paying the extra for a comfortable 1st class seat as 2nd class can be very overcrowded.

Ghana

A Ghanaian STC bus makes the 24 hour journey from Ouaga via Tamale (363km, CFA8000) and Kumasi (720km, also CFA 8000 from Ouaga) to Accra (1000km, CFA 10,000), leaving from the gare routière on Monday and Friday, in principle at 8.30 am. You need to buy your ticket in advance from the STC office (☎ 30 87 50) in Ouaga.

SOTRAO has a daily bus from Ouaga to Pô (144km, CFA1250), 15km from the frontier, from where there's infrequent transport to the border (CFA1000) and on to Bolgatanga in Ghana (45km, CFA1000). A bush taxi from Ouaga to Pô costs CFA2500.

Mali

STMB (daily) and Sans Frontière (daily except Saturday) run from Bobo to Bamako (15 hours, CFA8000) via Koutiala and

Ségou. Some buses go all the way from Ouaga to Bamako (CFA12,500). Sans Frontière also has a daily service from Bobo to Mopti (12 hours, CFA7000) via San. For other options, refer to Getting There & Away in the Bobo section of this chapter.

If you're heading for Dogon Country, from Ouaga you can take an STMB bus to Ouahigouya and another to Koro in Mali (4½ hours, CFA2000), then on by bush taxi to Bankass (CFA2500) and then Mopti (CFA3000).

Niger

Bus & Bush Taxi Niamey (500km, 12 hours, CFA7500) is not well served from Ouagadougou. SOTRAO has a Thursday bus and SNTN runs on Wednesday. Buy your ticket in advance from the relevant bus company office. Sans Frontière has a daily service to Kantchari (CFA4500), from where there's intermittent transport to the frontier.

Minibuses to the Niger border (CFA5000) leave from Ouagadougou's main gare routière but they're not frequent. It's CFA2000 from the border to Niamey.

Car & Motorcycle The straight driving time from Ouagadougou to Niamey is about 10 hours. A more adventurous route is via Kaya and Dori, then on a very lightly trafficked road to Gothèye in Niger. From there, you follow the River Niger south to Farié, where for CFA700 you can take a ferry across and continue a further 62km to Niamey. This route is scenic, off the beaten path and in fairly good condition except from mid-July to September.

Togo

At the time of writing, there were no buses connecting Ouaga and Togo. STCB used to link Ouaga with Dapaong in northern Togo – it might be worth checking whether this service has resumed.

There are direct bush taxis from Ouaga to Lomé (965km, CFA15,000), but it's cheaper to travel in stages. Take a minibus first to Bitou (40km from the border, CFA4000), then on to Dapaong (CFA2000). Expect heavy searches at the border, which closes at 6.30 pm.

The nonstop driving time from Ouagadougou to Lomé is about 20 hours, and the roads are tar and in good condition except for some heavily potholed stretches in Togo.

Getting Around

AIR
Air Burkina has four flights a week between Ouagadougou and Abidjan or Bamako, via Bobo-Dioulasso (CFA22,290).

BUS
Buses are the most reliable and comfortable way to get around the country. They're no more expensive than minibuses, which are often overcrowded and take time to fill up. Major transport companies, such as STMB, SOTRAO, SOGEBAF and Sans Frontière, have large buses (cars) with schedules, guaranteed seating and fixed departure times; many leave from their own offices rather than the bush taxi parks.

BUSH TAXI & MINIBUS
Minibuses and bush taxis (taxis brousses), mostly ageing Peugeot 504s, cover all the major towns, as well as outlying communities that large buses don't serve. Most leave from the gares routières (bush taxi parks), and the morning is the best time (frequently the only time) to find them. Minibuses are usually one-third cheaper than Peugeot 504s.

TRAIN
There are two train routes in Burkina but both are infinitely slower than road transport. For the record, the Abidjan-bound Express (a manner of speaking only) leaves Ouaga on Tuesday, Thursday and Saturday morning and arrives in Bobo some seven hours later. In the opposite direction, the train is scheduled to depart Bobo at 12.55 am on these same days but rarely achieves this. The 1st/2nd class single fare is CFA7200/4800.

There's also a Saturday train between Ouagadougou and Kaya, leaving Ouaga at 8.20 am and returning from Kaya at 2.30 pm the same day (CFA2000/1500 for 1st/2nd class). Cancellations, even changes of day, are frequent. Unless you're a railway aficionado, take the bus.

CAR & MOTORCYCLE
Tar roads are driveable year-round. During the rainy season, you may find your progress impeded by rain barriers, which are lifted once temporary flooding further down the road has abated.

A litre of petrol costs CFA360, premium (super) is CFA400 and diesel (gasoil) is CFA300.

HITCHING
Locals don't hitch. If they take a ride from passing traffic, they expect – and are expected – to pay. You should do the same, a fair price being the equivalent of a seat in a bush taxi. See also the Trucks & Hitching section in the Getting Around the Region chapter for more general information on hitchhiking in the region.

ORGANISED TOURS
Because the wildlife parks and reserves are inaccessible by public transport, your only options are to hire a 4WD or take a tour. For details, see the relevant sections later in this chapter.

Ouagadougou

Ouagadougou became the capital of the Mossi empire in 1441 and, 250 years later, was chosen as the permanent residence of the Moro-Naba, the Mossi king. The town grew up around the imperial palace and was extended during colonisation. Its more recent expansion was largely fuelled by the country's rural exodus.

There's not a great deal to turn your head in Ouaga but it has a relaxed atmosphere and

BURKINA FASO

OUAGADOUGOU

PLACES TO STAY
1 Hôtel Silmandé
2 Hôtel Ricardo
7 Le Pavillon Vert
8 Auberge les Manguiers
13 Hôtel le Dapoore;
   Restaurant le Chalet Suisse
37 Hôtel Oubri
42 Ouaga Camping
43 Hôtel OK Inn; Vacances OK Raids

PLACES TO EAT
9 Restaurant-Bar la Farigoule
20 Le Jardin Bambous
29 Black & White Maquis
32 Restaurant Tam-Tam; Restaurant
   le Lotus d'Or; SOGEBAF Bus Station

34 La Chaumière
41 Cité l'An II

OTHER
3 Race Track
4 SOTRAO Bus Station
5 Neerwaya Cinema
6 Le Monde Nightclub
10 STMB Bus Station
11 Marché Sankariaré
12 Bush Taxis for Dori & Gorom-Gorom
14 Bar Matata Plus; Le Casino
15 Yalgado Hospital
16 Italian Embassy
17 Nigerian Embassy
18 Ghana Embassy
19 UNESCO

21 Gendarmerie
22 Palais Présidentiel; Ministries
23 French Embassy
24 Institut Géographique
25 National Assembly
26 Côte d'Ivoire Embassy
27 US Embassy
28 American Cultural Center
30 Lycée Marien Ngouabi
31 Stade du 4 Août
33 Sans Frontière Bus Station
35 Moro-Naba Palace
36 Wakati Nightclub
38 Senegal Consulate
39 Airport
40 Mali Embassy
44 Gare Routière

To Kaya (98km)

Reservoir

To Ouahigouya (182km)

Reservoir

To Fada N'Gourma (219km)

Avenue Yatenga

Boulevard Anateng

Avenue de la Liberté

Rue des Écoles

Rue Mon Gressioron

Avenue d'Oubritenga

Blvd Charles de Gaulle

Avenue du Conseil de l'Entente

Avenue N Mandela

Avenue du Capitaine

Avenue Kadiogo (Route de Bobo)

Rue Kouandia

Rue Joseph Badoua

Avenue Nkrumah

Ave Boumedienne

Canal

Sec Central Ouagadougou Map (Page 212)

Ave Coulibaly

Avenue de la Résistance du 17 Mai

Avenue Bassawarga

To Le Camping Poko-Club (12km) & Bobo-Dioulasso (356km)

Rond-Point de l'Avenue Bassawarga

To Fada N'Gourma (219km), Niger & Togo

Boulevard Circulaire

To Léo (165km)

To Pô (142km)

0   0.5   1 km

you'll find the people open and accessible. It's a relatively compact city which is easy to get around on foot. Some of the main boulevards have dedicated lanes for two-wheelers and there are traffic lights – which are observed – at all major intersections.

The central market, despite being housed in a forbidding concrete monolith, is well worth a browse and, after dark, the town's nightlife warms up; several places have live music almost every night of the week.

Ouagadougou is the capital of African film. If you enjoy cinema, the best time to be here is during the biennial FESPACO, Africa's premier film festival, when the whole city parties. The films, almost all African, are both fascinating in themselves and an excellent way to learn about the continent's culture and society.

Orientation

Ouaga's built on a fairly regular grid pattern and the streets are well signed. Take your

bearings from the unmistakable globe at the centre of the busy Place des Nations Unies, from which the city's five main boulevards lead. The human heart of town is the nearby Grand Marché, or central market, completed in 1989.

Along Ave Yennenga are a concentration of budget hotels and inexpensive places to eat. Ave de la Résistance and Ave Nkrumah, parallel but quite different in character, have several of Ouaga's swankier restaurants and upmarket clubs.

Around Marché Sankariaré and Ave de la Liberté are some of the city's best bargain hotels, cheap drinking places and earthy 'in' clubs.

Maps Librairie Diacfa, Hôtel Silmandé and Hôtel de l'Indépendance should have in stock a good 1:10,000 map of Ouaga (CFA 2000) and a 1:1,000,000 one of Burkina. Both are produced by the Institut Géograph-

BURKINA FASO

FESPACO

The nine day Pan-African Film Festival, FESPACO, is held every odd year in the second half of February in Ouagadougou (in even years it is held in October in Tunis). In recent years it has become such a major cultural event that it attracts celebrities from around the world.

This home-grown event started in 1969 when it was little more than a few African film makers getting together to show their 'shorts' to interested audiences. Since then it has helped stimulate film production throughout Africa. In 1997 more than 200 films from Africa and the diaspora in the Americas and the Caribbean were viewed. Some 20 are selected to compete for the Étalon de Yennenga, FESPACO's equivalent of the Oscar. For more general information on West African cinema, see the boxed text in the Arts section of the Facts about the Region chapter.

Three Burkinabe film makers who have won prizes here and developed international reputations are Idrissa Ouedraogo, who won the 1990 Grand Prix at Cannes for *Tilaï*; Souleymane Cissé, who won the Prix du Jury at the 1987 Cannes Festival for *Yeelen*; and Gaston Kaboré, whose film *Buud Yam* was the 1997 winner of the Étalon. Among the film makers from other West African countries, those from Mali and Senegal have also taken many prizes.

Ouaga is always at its best during FESPACO as the city is invariably spruced up for the occasion and everyone seems to be in a festive mood. All the city's cinemas are used, each screening different films starting in the late afternoon. Hotel rooms are hard to find, so advance booking is essential. For videos of award-winning African films, contact California Newsreel (☎ 415-621 6196), 149 9th St, Suite 420, San Francisco, CA 94103, USA.

ique, at whose headquarters on Blvd de la Révolution they and other maps are on sale.

Information

Tourist Information Look for the sign 'ONTB' (Office Nationale du Tourisme Burkinabé) stuck to the entrance door of the dusty tourist office (☎ 31 19 59) opposite the Hôtel Nazemsé. It has little but a pamphlet or two to offer and the counter staff, when they're present, are not particularly helpful.

Le Pilote is a free guide which appears intermittently and has useful information on Ouaga and Bobo. The more slender *Burkina à Faire* comes out monthly. Both publications can be picked up in major hotels and restaurants.

Money The BIB facing the central market gives efficient service and significantly better rates than its competitors. Its official policy is not to charge commission for changing travellers cheques, although some travellers report deductions being made. The 1st floor exchange office of the BICIAB on Ave Nkrumah is also efficient. You can change currency notes without hassle and around the clock at the Hôtel de l'Indépendance, although the rate is not so favourable.

Post & Communications There is a poste restante service at Ouagadougou's main post office (open weekdays from 7.30 am to 12.30 pm and 3 to 5 pm). Charges are CFA500 per collected letter and they will hold mail for one month.

You can make international phone calls at ONATEL offices in Ouagadougou from 7 am to 10 pm daily. A three minute call costs CFA4500 to France, CFA5000 to the UK and CFA8250 to the USA and Australia.

Ouaga's fax office, in the post office building, is open Monday to Saturday from 7.30 am to noon and 3 to 5.30 pm (CFA750 per received page, fax 33 81 30).

At the friendly Cyber Club Évasion (☎ 31 41 07, fax 31 22 94, email evasion@fasonet .bf) you can log on at CFA3000 for 20

minutes. It costs CFA1000 to send an email and CFA300 per incoming message.

Travel Agencies & Tour Operators

Several agencies offer individualised or programmed tours around Burkina. Those that stand out for reliability and the range of tours are Kenedia Travel (☎ 31 59 69, fax 31 59 70), Vacances OK Raids at the Hôtel OK Inn (☎ 38 27 49, fax 30 48 11, email okraid@ mail.cenatrin.bf), L'Agence Tourisme (☎ 30 70 83, fax 31 84 44; contactable via La Fontaine Bleue restaurant) and Safaris du Sourou (☎ 31 24 08, fax 31 24 10). Wundi Voyages (☎ 30 03 70, fax 30 03 70), based at Auberge les Manguiers (see Places to Stay – Budget), may also be worth trying.

Bookshops Librairie Diacfa is reasonably well stocked and carries a wide range of French and local magazines and newspapers. You'll find a few English-language newspapers and magazines at Hôtel Silmandé and Hôtel de l'Indépendance.

Radio For FM radio and news, tune to the following stations:

Radio Nationale	88.5
Radio France Internationale	94.0
Radio Pulsar	94.8
Canal Arc en Ciel	96.6
Radio Énergie	103.4
Horizon FM	104.4

Radio Pulsar carries programs of BBC Afrique, the BBC French-language service for Africa.

Medical Services Pharmacie Nouvelle on Ave Babangida is well stocked.

Dangers & Annoyances Most resident expatriates walk around Ouaga at night without qualms although it is, of course, prudent to watch your back, particularly on Ave Yennenga.

Should you have a problem in Ouaga, contact the police at the *commissariat central* (☎ 30 62 71).

Things to See

The **Musée National** was in crates at the time of writing and due to be temporarily housed in the Maison du Peuple, pending completion of custom-built premises on Ave Charles de Gaulle. Unless things change, it's open from 9 am to midday and 3 to 6 pm, Tuesday to Saturday, and admission costs CFA500. Highlights of the modest collection are its ancestral statues, especially those from Lobi country, and the masks and traditional costumes.

The **cathedral** is another heavy, stolid structure built to impress but not to charm. The **Maison du Peuple** (with its preplural-ism name, the Maison du Parti, still carved deep into its façade) claims to be inspired by Burkina's traditional architecture but it's a million miles from the grace and under-statement of traditional Burkinabe housing.

In an act of officially perpetrated vandal-ism, Thomas Sankara had the old **Grand Marché** razed and erected in its place the present ponderous concrete structure. But beneath the angular, unadorned roof, the traders have again made it their own. It's a maze of crowded alleys; keep your bearings or you'll spend ages trying to get out. There are some good craft stalls upstairs. In addi-tion to local handicrafts, you'll find cloth and ready-made garments from the cotton mill in Koudougou and blankets from Dori.

Steel yourself: the merchants here are – atypically for Burkina – at best importune and at times bordering on the aggressive.

Activities

Nonguests can go swimming in hotel pools at the Nazemsé (CFA1200), Ran, Indépen-dance, Palm Beach (all CFA1500), Relax (CFA2000) and Silmandé (CFA2500). The pool at Restaurant la Colombe costs CFA 700. There are also tennis courts at the Sil-mandé which outsiders can use and a billiard table at the Indépendance.

Places to Stay – Budget

Camping The small camping area at *Au-berge les Manguiers* (for more details see Hotels later in this section) is the best place

Moro-Naba Ceremony

Such is the influence of the Moro-Naba of Ouagadougou, the emperor of the Mossi and the most powerful traditional chief in Burkina Faso, that the government will always consult him before making any major decision. Most Moro-Nabas have had an imposing presence, possibly due in part to their ritual drinking of millet beer. The portly present Moro-Naba, the 37th, is no exception.

The Moro-Naba ceremony, *la cérémonie du Nabayius Gou*, takes place outside his palace around 7.15 am every Friday. It's a very formal ritual that lasts only about 15 minutes. Prominent Mossi arrive by car, taxi and mobylette, greet each other and sit on the ground according to rank: in the first row, the Moro-Naba's spokesman and his chief ministers and, behind them, other dignitaries in descending order of seniority. The Moro-Naba appears, dressed in red, the symbol for war, accompanied by his saddled and elaborately decorated horse. There's a cannon shot, his most senior sub-jects approach to give obeisance and His Majesty retires, while his horse is unsaddled and beats the bounds of the palace at a brisk trot.

The Moro-Naba reappears, dressed all in white, a sign of peace, and his servants invite his subjects to the palace for a drink; millet beer for the animists and a Kola nut concoction for the Muslims. It's much more than an excuse for an early morning tipple as, within the palace, the Moro-Naba gives audience and hands down his verdict on local disputes and petty crimes. The pre-ceding ritual serves to reinforce the Mossi social order.

The story behind the ceremony? As so often in Africa, there are several conflicting versions. The predominant one recounts how the Ouahigouya Mossi had stolen the Ouaga people's main fetish. As the king made ready for war, his ministers persuad-ed him to desist and undertook to recover the fetish.

BURKINA FASO

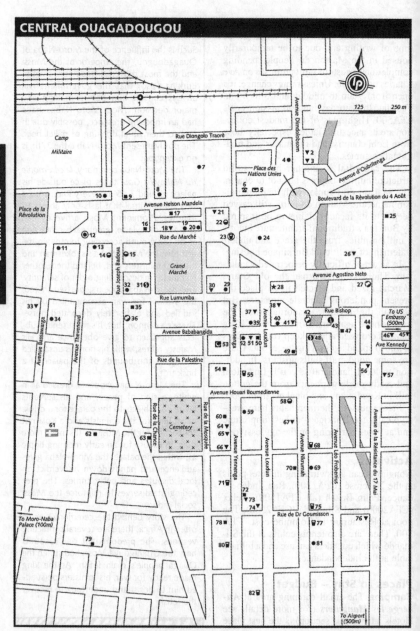

CENTRAL OUAGADOUGOU

Camp Militaire

Place de la Révolution

Rue Diangolo Traoré

Place des Nations Unies

Avenue Diindolobsom

Avenue d'Oubritenga

Boulevard de la Révolution du 4 Août

Avenue Nelson Mandela

Rue du Marché

Grand Marché

Rue Joseph Badoua

Rue Lumumba

Avenue Agostino Neto

Avenue Babangida

Avenue Yennenga

Avenue Loudun

Rue Bishop

To US Embassy (500m)

Ave Kennedy

Rue de la Palestine

Avenue Houari Boumedienne

Avenue Bassawarga

Avenue Thevenoud

Avenue Thevenoud

Cemetery

Rue de la Chance

Rue de la Mosquée

Avenue Yennenga

Avenue Loudun

Avenue Nkrumah

Avenue Léo Frobenius

Avenue de la Resistance du 17 Mai

Rue de Dr Goumisson

To Moro-Naba Palace (100m)

To Airport (500m)

0   125   250 m

CENTRAL OUAGADOUGOU

PLACES TO STAY
9 Ran Hôtel
16 Hôtel Central
17 Hôtel Relax; Safaris du Sourou
25 Hôtel de l'Indépendance
35 Hôtel Delwendé; Le Pub; Pâtisserie Moderne
47 Hôtel Nazemsé
49 Hôtel Belle Vue
50 Hôtel Continental; Café de la Paix
54 Hôtel Yennenga
60 Hôtel Idéal
62 Centre d'Accueil des Soeurs Lauriers
63 Fondation Charles Dufour
70 Hôtel Palm Beach
72 Pension Guigsème
78 Hôtel de la Paix
79 Hôtel la Rose des Sables

PLACES TO EAT
2 La Fontaine Bleue
3 Le Verdoyant
18 L'Eau Vive
21 Pâtisserie la Bonbonnière
26 La Colombe
30 La Gourmandise
33 La Forêt
37 Restaurant Sindabad
38 Le Vert Galant
41 Le Coq Bleu; Air Algérie; Aeroflot

45 Rive Droite
46 Le Belvédère
51 La Sorbetière
56 Pâtisserie de Koulouba
57 Le Tambarze
64 Chez Awa
65 Restaurant Riale
66 Café Salif
67 Restaurant Akwaba
73 Café Étalon
74 Nabonswende
76 Restaurant Allah Barka

OTHER
1 Train Station
4 Centre National d'Artisanat et l'Art
5 Post Office
6 ONATEL
7 Maison du Peuple
8 Air France; Sortilèges Artisan Shop
10 French Cultural Centre
11 Air Afrique
12 Place du Cinéaste Africain
13 Mairie
14 STWS Bus Station (buses for Koudougou)
15 STAF Bus Station (buses for Ouahigouya)
19 Gurnaam Supermarket
20 Librairie Diacfa
22 Bush Taxis for Togo & Benin; Total Station

23 Wassa Club
24 Palais de Justice
27 Canadian Embassy
28 Commissariat Central
29 Top Music
31 BIB Bank
32 Avis Car Rental; CICA building
34 Air Burkina
36 German Embassy
39 Ciné Burkina
40 Cyber Club Évasions; Pharmacie Nouvelle
42 Netherlands Embassy
43 Tourist Office
44 Sabena
48 BICIAB Bank
52 Marina Market; Café ONU
53 Grande Mosquée
55 Palladium Nightclub
58 STC Booking Office (buses for Ghana)
59 Super Sound Music Shop
61 Cathedral
68 New Jack Nightclub
69 Kenedia Travel
71 African Queen
75 Jimmy's Discotheque; Hôtel Yibi; Maquis Pili-Pili
77 Bar Taxi Brousse
80 Ludo Bar
81 Air Ivoire; Corsair
82 Sahel Nightclub

BURKINA FASO

to pitch your tent (CFA2000 per person or CFA3000 for two in a tent). *Ouaga Camping*, or Chez Bouda Abel, (CFA1500 per person), 1km behind the gare routière, has a barren, treeless ambience and travellers consistently report negatively on it.

If you have wheels, *Le Camping Poko-Club* (☎ 30 24 06), 12km out on the Bobo road and 4km beyond the police checkpoint, is another option. Prices are similar and even though there isn't much shade, the ambience is better and it has a reasonable restaurant.

Hotels The best place for price and ambience is *Fondation Charles Dufour* on Rue de la Chance. Profits from this basic hotel

and membership fees for the foundation (CFA10,000) go to support some 20 orphans whom Adama Yameogo feeds, lodges and educates. Even if you're not staying here, you might like to drop by and become a member; the cause couldn't be more deserving. There are two double rooms and one seven-bed dormitory. All beds, most of which have mosquito nets, cost CFA2000. If they're taken, you can sleep on a mattress on the floor for CFA1000. Shared facilities are rather grimy. Filling meals cost CFA1200 or you can cook for yourself.

The *Centre d'Accueil des Soeurs Lauriers* (☎ 30 64 90) within the cathedral compound is a safe and hassle-free place for women travelling alone. Accommodation in spotless rooms with mosquito net, shower and fan costs CFA4000 and copious meals are CFA1500.

Along Ave Yennenga are several cheap but seedy hotels which are not recommended for women travelling alone. Cheapest of the cheap is *Pension Guigsème* with singles/doubles at CFA3000/4000. The folk are friendly but the shower area recalls the black hole of Calcutta. *Hôtel de la Paix* (☎ 33 52 93) is good value. Clean rooms with fan and interior shower are CFA4000 (CFA5000 with bathroom), while self-contained air-con singles/doubles cost CFA6500/7000.

Hôtel Idéal (☎ 30 65 02) has overpriced singles/doubles with fan and shower for CFA6000/7500. The nearby *Hôtel Yennenga* (☎ 30 73 37), once a budget travellers favourite, has become increasingly grungy. At the time of writing, it was being extensively renovated.

Hôtel la Rose des Sables (☎ 31 30 14) directly south of the Catholic cathedral was also being refurbished when we visited. We can't give current prices but it's well worth considering for the friendliness of its staff and its pleasant garden.

Above the unprepossessing entrance of *Hôtel Delwendé* (☎ 30 87 57) on Rue Lumumba are decent singles/doubles with fan for CFA6500/8500 (CFA8500/9900 with air-con). All rooms have showers. The long 2nd-floor balcony is a great place for drinks and watching the street life below. Nearby, air-con singles/doubles with bathroom at *Hôtel Central* (☎ 33 34 17) are CFA8500/10500. It faces the market and has a good though overpriced restaurant.

On the northern side of town are two highly recommended French-run hotels. *Le Pavillon Vert* (☎ /fax 31 06 11) on Ave de la Liberté is a favourite haunt of both French expats and travellers. It's a friendly, tranquil haven with straw *paillotes* and a good open-air restaurant. Shed-like singles/doubles with fan and shared bathroom cost CFA4000/4500. Large rooms are CFA7000/7500 with bathroom and CFA13,000/13,500 with air-con. Nearby is the intimate *Auberge les Manguiers* (☎ 30 03 70, fax 30 03 75) which

also has a shady courtyard, where the cooking's just as good and the welcome (there's even a mini-library for guests) just as warm. Singles/doubles with fan or air-con range from CFA10,000 to CFA16,500.

South of Ave de la Liberté on Rue du Commerce, *Hôtel le Dapoore* (☎ 31 33 31) is good value. Rooms, all with bathroom, cost CFA5500/6500 for singles/doubles with fan and CFA8500/9500 with air-con. In its Chalet Suisse restaurant, only the tacky décor recalls the Alps and the service is snail-like and offhand.

Places to Stay – Mid-Range

Singles/doubles at *Hôtel Belle Vue* (☎ 30 84 98, fax 30 00 37) on Ave Nkrumah, all with TV, air-con and bathroom, are particularly good value at CFA13,500/14,500. After sunset, the terrace, although Spartan, is great for drinks and views of downtown. Spacious, carpeted rooms at the nearby *Hôtel Continental* (☎/fax 30 86 36) have the same facilities and prices. You can eat simply at the adjacent Café de la Paix, which is under the same ownership.

Despite its gloomy foyer, *Ran Hôtel* (☎ 30 61 06, fax 31 15 47) on Ave Nelson Mandela scores for its long pool, although the restaurant is mediocre. Air-con singles/doubles with TV cost CFA22,000/26,000 (CFA26,000/30,000 in a bungalow). *Hôtel Nazemsé* (☎ 33 53 28, fax 31 08 50) a block east of the BICIAB bank is a rather sterile concrete block, but the staff are friendly and willing. All rooms have air-con and TV. Singles cost from CFA23,000 and doubles from CFA25,500. The new *Hôtel Yibi* (☎ 30 73 70, fax 30 59 00) on the corner of Ave Nkrumah and Rue de Dr Goumisson has air-con singles/doubles with TV for CFA 25,000/28,000 and is already pulling in the tour groups.

The colonial *Hôtel Ricardo* (☎ 30 70 72, fax 33 60 48) is beginning to slip but the staff are welcoming and it remains a justified favourite of overland tour groups. Trophy heads stare down from the walls, there's a small aviary in the garden and you may find yourself sharing its pool with a pair of ducks from the reservoir over the wall. Singles/doubles with air-con and TV cost CFA25,800/28,800. It has a good restaurant, specialising in pizza, paella and grills. Although it's relatively remote, reception can have a metered taxi for you within five minutes.

Places to Stay – Top End
The French-owned *Hôtel OK Inn* (☎ 30 40 61, fax 30 48 11) is outstanding. Singles/doubles are CFA25,000/29,000 and bungalows are CFA36,000. It has a small menagerie, clean but short pool and a quality restaurant. Although on the southern outskirts, it offers a free shuttle into town five times a day.

Hôtel de l'Indépendance (☎ 30 60 60, fax 30 67 67), 1km east of the Grand Marché, has singles/doubles with air-con and satellite TV for CFA39,000/43,000. There's a 50m pool, access to Ouaga's major tennis club and a billiard table. At *Hôtel Palm Beach* (☎ 31 09 91, fax 36 68 39) on Ave Nkrumah all rooms have air-con and fridge. Singles start at CFA34,500 and doubles at CFA 39,500 and there's a good pool.

One block north of the Grand Marché is *Hôtel Relax* (☎ 31 32 33, fax 30 89 08) which has air-con singles/doubles for CFA41,000/46,000 with satellite TV and fridge. The hotel has a pool.

Ouaga's smartest is Sofitel's *Hôtel Silmandé* (☎ 30 01 76, fax 30 09 71), where rooms cost CFA68,000. It has a long pool, nightclub, a couple of restaurants, tennis courts and a great location, overlooking the reservoir.

Places to Eat
Cheap Eats There's a good choice of inexpensive street stalls and modest restaurants around Ave Yennenga and Ave Loudun. Perhaps the best value for money is *Chez Awa*, where the folk are friendly and the portions generous. Nearby is *Restaurant Riale*, also recommended, and the plain *Café Salif*, which is even cheaper. *Spaghetti sauce tomate* with meat and hunky vegetables, for example, will set you back no more than CFA300. *Café ONU* opposite the mosque is also cheap, though nothing special. *Café de la Paix* opposite Ciné Burkina is a notch above most of those along Ave Yennenga; it's also slightly more expensive. *Nabonswende* sells yoghurt and tasty spiced meat sandwiches.

Le Tambarze is a small rustic place on Ave de la Résistance with specialities such as couscous, ragout and *riz gras*. At the *Café Étalon* tables are brought outside at night. You can get an excellent steak and chips here for CFA2500 as well as cheaper African dishes.

Restaurant Sindabad is excellent value. You can munch through a hamburger (CFA 1250 to 2500 for a whopper among whoppers), eat more subtle international fare (under CFA2000) or choose from their range of Lebanese dishes (CFA1000 to 2750). If you're a group of five or six, go for their *mezze Libanais*, a table of 20 different dishes for CFA18,000. If you simply want a snack, they do a great range of pitta bread sandwiches, all for CFA750.

African *La Forêt* on Ave Bassawarga is an upmarket outdoor restaurant in a pleasant shady garden. It offers a few selections each day, all well prepared. Another good place in a relaxing outdoor setting is *La Colombe*. Among its African specialities are *poulet yassa* and *kedjenou* (both CFA2500) and *tieb bon djen* (strips of fried meat). Main dishes cost from around CFA3000 and you can use the swimming pool for CFA700.

For African food with international comfort, *Restaurant Akwaba* on Ave Nkrumah, with its mainly Ivoirian menu, is excellent. The service is good and the décor, with its vivid wall tapestries, is pleasant and marred only by the spectacularly kitsch ceiling fans. A main course with *foutou* or rice costs CFA3500 to CFA4000.

Ouaga has several Ivoirian-style maquis specialising in grilled dishes. They're better at night; some, in fact, only open in the evening. The popular *Cité l'An II* on Ave Bassawarga south of the centre is a spacious

BURKINA FASO

open-air place, very dimly lit at night. Another venue with a variety of grills is the vast *La Farigoule* near the STMB bus station. You can get cheaper fare at *Restaurant Allah Barka* on Ave de la Résistance, but the night-time atmosphere isn't so lively. However, the food, particularly the Senegalese *poulet yassa,* is good. The *Black & White Maquis* on Ave Boumedienne is laid-back and agreeable.

Asian Of the Chinese-Vietnamese restaurants, try *Le Jardin Bambous* (☎ 31 35 14) on Ave d'Oubritenga, or *Le Lotus d'Or (35 Ave Kadiogo),* 1.5km west of the central area.

Austrian *Restaurant Tam-Tam* (☎ 30 28 04) on Ave Kadiogo is open daily to midnight (closed Tuesday) and specialises in Austrian dishes.

French As you'd expect, Ouaga has some good and not necessarily expensive restaurants offering French cuisine. Don't miss *Restaurant l'Eau Vive,* a Ouaga institution which has an equally enjoyable branch in Bobo. It's run by an order of nuns and is closed on Sunday. At lunch time, it's an air-con oasis, clean and pleasantly decorated. On one side is the heaving central market and on the other a tranquil mature garden where you can dine in the evening. You also get Ave Marias, with optional participation, from the waitresses. The food is mainly French with a few African selections. There are set menus at CFA2000, CFA3000 and CFA4000 and an extensive and imaginative à la carte selection. It's exceptional value and you can be sure that every franc over costs goes to support the order's charitable works.

The French-owned *La Fontaine Bleue* (closed Tuesday) on Ave Dimdolobsom has an attractive outdoor setting and serves delectable if pricey French and African cuisine. Go steady on the drinks which are particularly expensive. The long-standing *La Chaumière* (☎ 31 18 25; closed Thursday), 1.5km south-west of the centre on Ave Coulibaly, is a local favourite and has Alsatian and Belgian specialities. At *Le Pub,* small, friendly and central near Hôtel Delwendé, a tasty entrée plus main dish costs under CFA5000 and the French owner has a great selection of jazz CDs. The *Rive Droite* (☎ 31 22 99) on Ave Raoul Follereau serves an imaginative range of dishes for under CFA5000.

The fanciest place for quality French cooking is the recommended *Le Coq Bleu* on the corner of Ave Nkrumah and Ave Bababangida. It may be more expensive than the competition but it offers excellent value for money. The blue décor's tasteful and soothing but the schmalzy background music will have you scraping off the wallpaper.

And let's not forget the best of the hotel restaurants. *Auberge les Manguiers* and *Le Pavillon Vert* in particular offer good food in pleasant surroundings. The cuisine at the *OK Inn,* a favourite haunt of French expatriates, is impressive although expensive and for a weekend blow-out, nothing beats their Sunday lunch buffet and barbecue.

Italian The *pizzeria* at Hôtel Central is friendly and good but overpriced. *Le Verdoyant,* also central, is more popular, more stylish and does excellent lasagne. On the outskirts, *Hôtel Ricardo* has excellent pizza as well as numerous Franco-Italian dishes. Until 8 pm, you can get there on a No 5 bus from Place des Nations Unies.

Le Belvédère (☎ 33 64 21) on Ave Raoul Follereau is open only in the evening and closed all day Tuesday. It doesn't try all that hard but it has an outdoor garden and an air-con dining room, serves good Italian and Lebanese food and bakes about the best pizza in town. It also does takeaway.

Le Vert Galant (closed Sunday lunch time and Monday) on Rue Lumumba has French fare and Italian dishes such as spaghetti carbonara, *osso bucco* and exquisite if pricey ice-cream desserts.

Patisseries Ouaga has some good patisseries, or pastry shops, most of which double as social meeting places. Hours are usually 6 am to noon and 3 to 7 pm. The longest running is *Pâtisserie la Bonbonnière* on Ave

Nelson Mandela, which has good pastries and a tantalising variety of ice cream. Try the idiosyncratic version of cappuccino with a thick blob of cream floating on top.

Also popular is *La Gourmandise* facing the market's south-eastern corner. It's on the 2nd floor and is great for watching the crowds. It stays open until midnight and serves beer and sandwiches. *Pâtisserie Moderne*, starker and without the view, is also well situated (near Hôtel Delwendé) for taking a break from market browsing.

La Sorbetière on Ave Bababangida facing Ciné Burkina is a popular breakfast spot for wealthier Burkinabe. But the really discriminating locals patronise the cool, spacious *Pâtisserie de Koulouba* on Ave de la Résistance, which has a range of sandwiches and the widest selection of pastries.

Entertainment

Bars *Wassa Club* (☎ 31 02 33) is a pleasant, open-air watering hole in the heart of town where you can also dine. Open during the daytime and until 1 am, it sometimes has live music and, less frequently, theatre. Popular and warmly recommended.

For late-night drinking, the liveliest area is along Ave Yennenga. The *Ludo Bar*, with its large drinking area at the back, and the nearby *African Queen*, are good, earthy and cheap.

Nightclubs There are two main fun areas: in the heart of town around Ave Loudun and Ave Nkrumah; and to the north, near Ave de la Liberté.

Downtown, for the city's hottest disco, head to *Jimmy's Discotheque*, a favourite with Ouaga's youth. Jimmy's has air-con and, with admission at CFA2500 and drinks the same price, is strictly for the well heeled. Nearby, *New Jack* is a similarly flash joint with much the same prices.

Another lively place is *Sahel's* which has drumming and live reggae music every night (no cover charge). *Maquis Pili-Pili* has live blues music on weekends and also serves food. Across the street, *Taxi-Brousse*

has outdoor tables where you can watch the scene on the street for free. Closer to the centre, *Palladium* (CFA500 cover) features live music and has a large dance floor as well as food, including good brochettes and other snacks.

North of the railway at *Bar Matata Plus* (no cover charge), dancing to a live band starts at around 9 pm. If you weary of the Matata, drift to its near-neighbour, *Le Casino*. According to club cognoscenti, *Le Monde* on Ave de la Liberté, the current 'in' spot, offers the best value entertainment in town.

Last but not least, don't overlook the *Wakatti* (CFA300 cover), worth the trip south along Ave Bassawarga.

Cinemas *Ciné Burkina*, built for FESPACO in the late 60s, has a wide screen and good seats. It regularly shows African-produced films plus recent international releases and a diet of kung fu and Bollywood potboilers. The *Neerwaya* is a pleasant alternative, one block west of Ave Kouanda.

Shopping

Supermarkets Marina Market facing the Grande Mosquée is the best stocked supermarket. Prices are similar at Gurnaam on the north side of the Grand Marché.

Art & Craftwork The Grand Marché merits a visit. For details, see the separate entry earlier in this section. Among the smaller boutiques, Sortilèges (☎ 31 60 80) next to Air France is outstanding and prices are fixed. Batimo-B near Hôtel Central is another quality shop and the tiny, less sophisticated Boutique d'Artisanat at the Wassa Club is also worth visiting.

The Centre National d'Artisanat et d'Art (☎ 30 68 35) on Ave Dimdolobsom is open Monday to Friday from 8 am to noon and 3 to 6 pm. Prices are fixed and the money goes directly to the artisan, but with an amount to cover the centre's overheads. The quality is mixed but take time to look over the bronze statues, wooden sculptures and

BURKINA FASO

colourful batiks. Apprentices and artisans here will gladly take you around their workshops and show you their craft. Follow your ears to the courtyard where blacksmiths hammer and shape inventive and witty items from scrap iron.

Embroidered tablecloths and napkins, and woven rugs are the speciality of the Centre de Formation Feminine Artisanale, a women's cooperative sponsored by the Austrian Catholic mission. It is in Gounghin, off the road to Bobo-Dioulasso on the western outskirts of town. Hours are from 7.30 am to noon and 3.30 to 5.30 pm weekdays and until noon on Saturday. Visit Le Centre du Tannage for leather goods. It's on the eastern outskirts of town on the road to Fada N'Gourma, opposite the prison. Bus No 1, which passes along Ave Nelson Mandela, serves both places.

Should you happen to visit Burkina Faso in late October, you will coincide with Ouaga's annual Festival des Arts Africains, which is held in front of the Maison du Peuple. Artisans and art dealers from all over the continent come here to sell their wares.

Music For cassettes of African music (about CFA1500), try Top Music, Super Sound or Musique Sans Frontières, all on Ave Yennenga.

Getting There & Away

Air For details of international flights to/from Ouagadougou, see the Getting There & Away section earlier in this chapter. Air Burkina flights between Ouaga and Abidjan or Bamako make a stop in Bobo four times a week.

For confirming flights or ticket sales, the following airlines have offices in Ouagadougou, most within a few blocks of the Grand Marché:

Aeroflot
   (☎ 30 71 29) Ave Nkrumah
Air Afrique
   (☎ 30 60 20 or 30 60 21) Ave Bassawarga
Air Algérie
   (☎ 31 23 01) Ave Nkrumah

Air Burkina
   (☎ 31 53 25) Ave Bassawarga
Air France
   (☎ 30 63 65, 30 63 66 or 30 63 67) Ave Nelson Mandela
Air Ivoire
   (☎ 30 62 07) Ave Nkrumah
Corsair
   (☎ 30 40 55) Ave Nkrumah
Sabena
   (☎ 30 58 80 or 30 58 51) Ave de la Résistance

Bus Most bus companies leave from their own depots rather than the gare routière. You'll find the major ones marked on the two maps of Ouaga. There are several departures daily for Bobo, Ouahigouya and Koudougou. Buses for most other destinations in Burkina leave only in the morning, usually between 7 and 9 am.

Major companies operating the Ouaga to Bobo route (355km, five hours, CFA3000 to 4000) are SOGEBAF, which has almost hourly departures, SOTRAO (previously called X9) with two buses a day and Sans Frontière with three. STMB has five departures a day, including its 2 pm air-con service with high-decibel video – CFA1000 more and worth every franc of it.

Of the larger companies serving Ouahigouya (180km, three hours, CFA2000), STMB has three departures a day and SOGEBAF has four. For SOTRAO buses south-west to Gaoua (433km, CFA4000), see the table on the opposite page. Both STMB and Sans Frontière have a twice daily service to Dori (4½ hours, CFA3000) via Kaya. STMB runs twice daily eastbound to Fada N'Gourma (3½ hours, CFA2000).

STMB, a relative newcomer on the scene is, for the moment at least, the most reliable operator. It covers the following destinations (fares are in CFA):

destination	frequency	fare
Bobo	daily x 5	4000
Dori	daily x 2	3000
Fada N'Gourma	daily x 2	2000
Gorom-Gorom	Mon, Wed, Sat	4000
Ouahigouya	daily x 3	2000

SOTRAO provides the most extensive service, with more than a dozen routes in all. Below are the main destinations and fares (in CFA) from Ouaga; returns are the same day, unless shown otherwise.

destination	frequency	fare
Bobo	daily	3000
Dédougou/Nouna	Mon, Wed, Sat (returns next day)	2850
Djibo	Wed, Sat	2250
Dori/Gorom-Gorom	Mon, Wed, Sat (returns next day)	3750
Fada N'Gourma	Mon, Wed, Sat	2000
Gaoua	Mon, Wed, Sat (returns next day)	4000
Kaya	Mon Wed, Sat	1250
Kongoussi/Djibo	Wed, Sat	1900
Namounou	Mon, Wed, Sat	4250
Pô	daily	1250
Tiébélé	Tues, Wed, Sat, Sun	1500
Tougan	Thur (returns Fri)	2250

Bush Taxi & Minibus Most bush taxis and minibuses leave in the early morning from the gare routière, 4km from the centre on the southern outskirts of town. To get there, a shared taxi costs CFA250 or you can take bus No 3.

Bush-taxi fares tend to be a quarter to a third more than that of a minibus – which is rarely any cheaper than a bus. Minibuses to the borders of Togo, Benin and Côte d'Ivoire also leave in the morning from the gare routière at the Total petrol station near the Wassa Club.

Train It really isn't worth your while. For the sorry details, see Train in the main Getting Around section earlier in this chapter.

Getting Around
To/From the Airport The 2km taxi journey to the centre is about CFA1000 (50% more to Hôtel Silmandé). It's also possible to walk; Ave Yennenga, with its hotels, is only 1km away. You could also catch bus No 5, which heads north on Ave Nkrumah

(two blocks west of the airport) toward the Place des Nations Unies.

Bus A network of SOTRAO buses covers the city. They start running at 6 am and stop at 8 pm. The names of the city neighbourhoods are posted on their front and bus stops are clearly indicated with the route number. Fares are CFA100 for a single journey and CFA150 for a connecting trip.

Most of the six bus lines pass along some part of Ave Nelson Mandela; the post office and the Place des Nations Unies are major bus stops.

No 1 goes east-west from the Zone du Bois along Ave d'Oubritenga, Ave Nelson Mandela and Ave Kadiogo (the road to Bobo).

No 2 also goes east-west. It starts on the Hôtel Silmandé Rd, passes along Ave d'Oubritenga and Ave Nelson Mandela, then heads northwest on Ave Yatenga (the Ouahigouya road).

No 3 passes the gare routière, then heads north on Ave Bassawarga to the centre of town and east on Ave Nelson Mandela and Ave d'Oubritenga to the Zone du Bois.

No 4 takes a more circuitous route, passing north along Ave Yennenga to Ave Nelson Mandela, then east along Ave Nelson Mandela and Blvd de la Révolution, north again to Ave de la Liberté, then west along Ave de la Liberté and past Marché Sankariaré towards the stadium.

No 5 goes south-north. It starts several hundred metres west of the gare routière and passes north along Ave Nkrumah (near the airport) towards the Place des Nations Unies, continuing along Ave Dimdolobson, across the reservoir and past Hôtel Ricardo.

No 6 goes east-west, starting beyond the university and heading west on Blvd Charles de Gaulle and Ave Boumedienne toward Place de la Révolution, north on Ave Kouanda through Ciné An III and eventually westward.

Taxi Green shared taxis, mostly beaten-up old Renaults, cost CFA150 for a ride within town. The basic rate for a private taxi (orange or green), which you commission just for yourself, is CFA500 and more for longer journeys. If you bargain hard, one by the hour will cost CFA2500, or about CFA15,000 plus petrol for a full day. Rates double after 10 pm.

Taxis are not too difficult to find during the day. At night, you'll find them, among other places, at the petrol station near the Wassa Club and outside the Ran and Indépendance hotels.

Car Since insurance costs escalate if you drive yourself, it's cheaper to hire a car with a driver, which usually costs an extra CFA 4000 to 5500 per day. There are agencies or prowling agents at most major hotels.

Vacances OK Raids (☎ 38 27 49, fax 30 48 11, okraid@mail.cenatrin.bf) is reliable and significantly cheaper than the competition. Typical costs including driver are CFA 20,000 per day for a small car (CFA 35,000 out of town) and CFA65,000 for a 4WD. Unusually, there's no charge per kilometre.

The long-established Burkina Auto Location (☎ 30 60 61, fax 30 67 67), based at the Hôtel de l'Indépendance, charges CFA 25,500 per day for a Peugeot 306 plus CFA140 per kilometre (CFA190 out of town) and CFA56,000 for a 4WD (CFA220 per kilometre out of town). Avis (☎ 30 61 59) one block west of the market offers its usual international standard of service – at international prices. In all cases, if you order in advance your vehicle can be waiting for you at the airport.

More cheaply than the above, but without the same guarantee of reliability, you could try Auto Location Service (☎ 33 56 69) on Ave Yennenga.

Bicycle & Mobylette The going rate for bicycles is CFA1500 to CFA2000 a day, and for mobylettes is between CFA4000 and CFA6000. Despite the swarms of mobylettes revving at every junction, there's no rental system. However, by asking at your hotel or around the market, you'll locate one. You can leave both bicycles and mobylettes safely for CFA50 at one of the myriad two-wheeler parks around town.

AROUND OUAGADOUGOU
Koudougou

Koudougou, with a population of 40,000, is a dusty little city, 97km to the west of Ouaga-

dougou. Burkina's third-largest settlement, it owes its commercial importance to the Faso Fani cotton mill, 3km out of town. With its wide, shaded avenues, Koudougou is a tranquil if unexciting place to stroll around after visiting the market, which has a vitality out of proportion to its size. It's a good base for exploring the nearby picturesque villages such as **Goundi** (8km) or **Sabou** and its crocodile lake (25km).

Places to Stay Cheapest is the *Auberge Boulkiemdé*, where singles/doubles with fan and shower are CFA3500/4000. There's a small restaurant and an external dancing *piste* – a mixed blessing if you're early to bed. *Hôtel Espérance (☎ 44 05 59)* is highly recommended and well worth the 1km walk from the centre. The folk are friendly and a clean room with fan and shower is CFA 4500.

Hôtel Photo Luxe (☎ 44 00 87) at the eastern entrance to town is relatively new but already running downhill; the pool's empty and the satellite dish doesn't work. But it has spotless rooms with fan and shower for CFA6500 (CFA8500 with air-con). Singles/doubles/triples with air-con are CFA10,000/11,000/15,000. It has a restaurant, a couple of bars and, at weekends, the town's best nightspot.

Two hotels with confusingly similar names but under separate ownership are *Hôtel Yelba Central* and *Hôtel Yelba Annexe*. Both have been recently renovated and are spick, span and good value. The Yelba Annexe *(☎ 44 09 89)* has clean singles/doubles with fan for CFA5000/6000 (CFA 6500/8000 with air-con). All rooms are with bathroom and there's a decent, reasonably priced restaurant. The Lebanese proprietor of the Yelba Central runs a tight ship. Singles/doubles with fan and shower cost CFA 6000/8000 (CFA9000/15,000 with air-con and bathroom). The quality justifies the difference in price from its near-namesake.

Hôtel Toulourou (☎ 44 01 70), three blocks east of the train station, was built by Maurice Yaméogo, local boy made good and Burkina's first president. With its attractive,

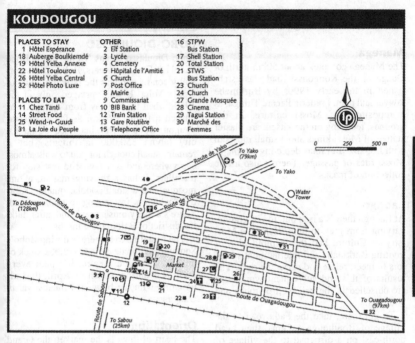

KOUDOUGOU

PLACES TO STAY	OTHER	16 STPW
1 Hôtel Espérance	2 Elf Station	Bus Station
18 Auberge Boulkiemdé	3 Lycée	17 Shell Station
19 Hôtel Yelba Annexe	4 Cemetery	20 Total Station
22 Hôtel Toulourou	5 Hôpital de l'Amitié	21 STWS
26 Hôtel Yelba Central	6 Church	23 Church
32 Hôtel Photo Luxe	7 Post Office	24 Church
	8 Mairie	27 Grande Mosquée
PLACES TO EAT	9 Commissariat	28 Cinema
11 Chez Tanti	10 BIB Bank	29 Tagui Station
14 Street Food	12 Train Station	30 Marché des
25 Wend-n-Guudi	13 Gare Routière	Femmes
31 La Joie du Peuple	15 Telephone Office	

BURKINA FASO

air-con restaurant and shaded garden, it's weathered the years well. All rooms have air-con. A single with bathroom costs CFA 9500. Doubles with communal facilities are CFA17,000 (CFA19,000 with bathroom). Guests can hire a hotel car to visit Sabou (CFA20,000 self-drive, CFA25,000 with driver).

Places to Eat The choice is limited. In addition to restaurants and bars at the major hotels, there are a few modest places.

For African food, try *Wend-n-Guudi*, one block south of the main mosque. The food is unexciting, though cheap. You can also get good brochettes and guinea fowl on the street opposite the station road or inexpensive food in pleasant, simple surroundings at *Chez Tanti* nearer the station.

Best for African food, day or night, is the restaurant-bar *La Joie du Peuple*. A spa-

cious open-air place with funky paintings on the walls and recorded music, it has three or four African sauces to choose from. At night, it's also the best place for drinks and dancing.

Getting There & Away Both STWS and STRW have seven buses a day from Monday to Saturday (there's no Sunday service) between Koudougou and Ouaga (two hours, CFA1000). Both leave from their offices south and west of the market respectively. There are also frequent Peugeots and minibuses departing from the gare routière.

Loumbila Goat Farm

This French-run farm, 15km from Ouaga on the Kaya road, is a popular weekend retreat for residents of the capital. You can stroll by the lake, have a relaxing drink, nibble the rich goat cheeses and, at weekends, enjoy a barbecue of – you've guessed it, goat – surrounded by free-roaming farm animals.

Manega

The Manega complex about 50km north of Ouaga on the Kongoussi road was established in the early 1990s by Burkinabe lawyer and poet, Frédéric Pacéré Titinga, as a repository of Mossi culture. In the grounds, teetering on the kitsch, are plaster statues of Mossi kings and a small museum with life-size dioramas depicting the major Mossi rites of passage. There's also a fine collection of masks.

Laongo

At Laongo there's a rich outcrop of granite, varying from grey to pink. Here, the Ministry of Culture had the inspired idea of inviting Burkinabe and international sculptors to meet, relate and carve the rock. The results of this and subsequent workshops are chiselled in the pell mell of rocks and boulders.

To get there, take the Fada road to the village of Boudtenga (32km), then head north-east on a dirt road to the village of Laongo.

Crocodile Lakes

If crocodiles give you a frisson, there are a couple of sacred lakes within reach of Ouaga. The ritual's the same at each; you arrive, you're assailed by kids from whom you buy a live chicken at a sacrificial price, it's fed to a croc which lumbers out of the water and photos are taken of you, them and, grinning the widest, the croc.

Sabou, 88km west on the Bobo road and 20km from Koudougou, is on the tour bus circuit and is the more hideous because of this fact. **Bazoulé** is less of a tourist trap but is catching up fast. Take the Bobo road to the village of Tanghin Dassouri (about 30km), then head north for 6km on a dirt road.

At Sabou, you can stay at the simple *Campement Hotelier* (CFA4000).

The South-West

BOBO-DIOULASSO

Bobo-Dioulasso means 'Home of the Bobo Dioulas'. For many years, Bobo, as it's normally contracted, was the principal town of Upper Volta. It was upstaged only in the 1950s when the railway from Abidjan was pushed a further 360km as far as Ouagadougou. Bobo is Burkina's second-largest city (about 350,000 inhabitants) but it remains small enough for you to walk almost everywhere and is a favourite rest stop for travellers. It has a thriving market, a fine mosque, and a small popular quarter, Kibidwe, which is fascinating to roam around. There's a lively music scene and, after dark, the district of Balomakoté throbs.

The best time to be here is during Bobo's Semaine Nationale de la Culture, a week of music, dance and theatre. It's held every even year during March or April, thus alternating with the biennial film festival in Ouaga.

Orientation

The heart of town is the market, the Grand Marché. From the train station, Ave de la Nation leads south-east to Place de la Nation, while Ave de la Liberté heads north-east to Place du Paysan. The town's commercial core is the triangular area defined by these two roundabouts and the train station. The area south and east of the market houses many of the hotels, restaurants and banks.

You may find a map of the town at Librairie Socifa, if they have any left in stock.

Information

There is a poste restante counter at the post office.

Money Both BICIAB and BIB banks change money, including French franc and US$ travellers cheques, for which you'll need proof of purchase. The rate is usually better at BIB and they don't charge commission. Banks in Mali and Côte d'Ivoire

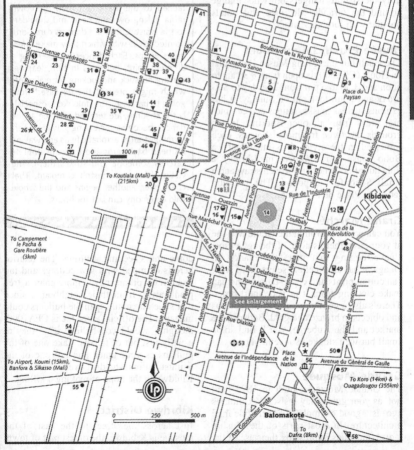

BOBO-DIOULASSO

PLACES TO STAY
1 Hôtel Méridien
8 Hôtel Hamdalaye
11 Hôtel Central
19 Ran Hôtel
21 Hôtel 421
23 Hôtel Soba
29 Hôtel Renaissance
32 L'Auberge
36 Hôtel Relax
38 Hôtel Teria
40 Hôtel l'Entente
45 Hôtel Watinoma
54 Casafrica

PLACES TO EAT
16 Restaurant la Casa
25 Nouvelle Boule Verte
30 Restaurant-Bar l'Entente
35 L'Eau Vive
39 Restaurant Togolaise;
   Boulangerie Pâtisserie
   la Bonne Miche
41 La Sorbetière
42 Café des Amis
44 Restaurant Delwinde

OTHER
2 SOGEBAF Bus Station
3 Gare de Dédougou
4 STMB Bus Station
5 Gare de Mopti
6 Marché du Soir
7 Stadium
9 Ciné Sanyon
10 Sans Frontière Bus Station
12 Grande Mosquée
13 Librairie Socifa
14 Grand Marché
15 Air Afrique;
   Mobylette Rentals
17 SOTRAKOF & Compagnie
   Transport Bus Station
18 Cathedral
20 Train Station
22 Artisan Shops
24 BICIAB Bank
26 Sûreté
27 Post Office
28 ONATEL
   Telephone Office
31 Booby Supermarket
33 Le Makoumba Nightclub
34 BIB Bank
37 Oxygène Nightclub;
   Chicken Vendor
43 Rakieta Bus Station
46 Air Burkina
47 Momba So Nightclub;
   Air Ivoire
48 Mairie
49 Soweto Bar
50 Centre Culturel Français
51 Gendarmerie
52 Café le Colsa
53 Hospital
55 Brakina Brewery
56 Musée Provincial
   du Houët
57 Haut Commissariat
58 Concorde
   Bar-Restaurant

BURKINA FASO

are much more of a challenge, so if you're headed to either, change your money here.

Radio For news and music, tune to FM stations Radio Arc-en-Ciel (89.8), Horizon FM (102.7), Radio Nationale (89.8) and RFI (Radio France Internationale; 99.4).

Dangers & Annoyances Bobo is generally a safe city. Avoid, however, the small river – more a trickle – where travellers report there's a risk of being mugged.

You'll need to be firm with some particularly persistent hangers-on who lounge around the Grande Mosquée and hotels popular with foreign visitors.

Musée Provincial du Houët

The small but interesting Musée Provincial du Houët (CFA500) is open from 8.30 am to noon and 3.30 to 6 pm from Tuesday to Saturday and 9 am to 1 pm on Sunday. It has exhibits such as masks, statues and ceremonial dress from all over Burkina. In the grounds are three traditional houses, each furnished in the style of its inhabitants: a Bobo house in red *banco* (mud-brick), a Fula hut of branches and woven straw and a small Senoufo compound. The museum faces the Place de la Nation.

Grand Marché

You can wander through the Grand Marché at your ease; there's none of the aggressive sleeve-tugging that mars the market in Ouaga. It has an excellent selection of African cotton prints and cheap tailors who can make clothing from it in very short order. There's also a good choice of masks, drums and objects in bronze and gold. Between the market and the Auberge, you'll find some small but well stocked souvenir shops.

Grande Mosquée

The Grande Mosquée, built in 1893 (and not, as your guide may insist, 3½ centuries ago) is a good example of Sahel-style mud architecture. In most parts of the Muslim world, mosques impress by their use of the

Fêtes des Masques

In the Bobo region, whenever there's a major funeral – such as that of a village chief, which takes place six months or so after his death – it's accompanied by a late-night *fête des masques* which features Bobo helmet masks, as well as other types of masks.

Masked men dance to an orchestra of flute-like instruments and narrow drums beaten with curved canes. Sometimes they're dressed in bulky black-and-brown raffia outfits, resembling scarecrows. Attached to the mask is a mop of brown raffia, falling over the head and shoulders to the waist. Often the dancers carry long pointed sticks with which they make enormous jumps. Each dancer, representing a different spirit, performs in turn, leaping, waving his stick and looking for evil spirits which might prevent the deceased from going to paradise. The onlookers, especially the children, are terrified and flee as the dancer becomes increasingly wilder, performing strange acrobatic feats and waving his head backwards and forwards until he catches someone and strikes them. The victim, however, mustn't complain. That chase over, another begins and the whole wild ceremony can last for hours.

dome and sweeping vaulting. The interior here is cramped with low ceilings and fat, unadorned pillars never more than a tree plank away from their neighbours, since that's the maximum span the builders could manage. The official entry fee is CFA1000, though – would you believe it? – they're usually just out of tickets. Take one of the mullahs as your guide and not one of the animist loafers who drift over the road from Kibidwe in the hope of making a killing.

Kibidwe District

Just across the street to the east of the mosque is Kibidwe, the oldest part of town.

MOSSI

Concentrated in the central plateau area in and around Ouagadougou, the Mossi are the largest and most powerful people group in Burkina Faso. Moving westward from the River Niger in the 14th century, they established powerful kingdoms in present-day Burkina. Known for their rigid social hierarchies and elaborate social rituals, they still exert considerable political influence today. Historically, they resisted invasion by the Muslim Empire of Mali, and as a result mostly follow traditional beliefs.

Artistically, the Mossi are best known for their tall wooden antelope masks, often over 2m high and painted red and white. The top section distinguishes a female antelope mask from a male one; the former features a human female figure, while the latter is a nonhuman plank-like structure. At the bottom of the mask is a small, oval face bisected by a serrated vertical strip, with triangular eyeholes on either side. They were originally principally worn at funerals.

BOBO

The Bobo, who escaped subjugation by the Mossi, live in the west of Burkina Faso around Bobo-Dioulasso, and are renowned for their masking traditions, involving many different types of masks, including the famous butterfly and helmet masks.

The large, horizontal butterfly masks are typically 1.5m wide and painted red, black and white. They are worn during funeral rites and when invoking the deity Do in ceremonies asking for rain and for fertility of the fields, especially at planting time.

Top: Mossi wooden antelope mask – these plank masks can be over 2m tall.

Middle: Small brass pendant, Bobo

Bottom: Bobo butterfly mask, used in fertility rites, as a symbol of renewal.

The form of a butterfly is used because butterflies appear in great swarms immediately after the first rains and are thus associated with the planting season. The dancer twists his head so rapidly that the mask almost appears to be spinning. Other animals used for these zoomorphic masks include the owl, buffalo, antelope, crocodile and scorpion. These masks are usually tall, with bold coloured patterns similar to the butterfly masks.

LOBI

The Lobi live in the south-west of Burkina Faso, and also in northern Côte d'Ivoire and Ghana. They follow traditional, ancestor-based beliefs and their traditions are some of the best preserved in Africa. They live in distinctive fortress-like mud-brick compounds.

The Lobi don't use masks. Most of their woodcarvings are of human figures, typically 35cm to 65cm high, representing deities and ancestors. They are used for ancestral shrines, and years ago were found in every home. The Lobi also carve staffs and three-legged stools with human or animal heads, and combs with human figures or geometric decorations. What distinguishes Lobi carvings is their rigid appearance, with arms straight down by the sides of the body, and the realistic, detailed rendering of certain body parts, particularly the navel, eyes and hair.

Top: The seat is the most important piece of furniture in West Africa. These Lobi chairs incoporate anthropomorphic features, probably representing ancestor worship.

Bottom, from left to right: The rich variety of Lobi sculpture, including an old wooden ancestor figure, an unusual two-headed sculpture and a fertility symbol in the shape of a pregnant woman.

You won't get around alone, so give in gracefully, make a contribution 'for the elders' and let yourself be guided; the best of the youths know their neighbourhood well, though their English is minimal. You'll see blacksmiths, potters, weavers and Sya, the house of the ancestors and traditionally the oldest building in Bobo.

Activities

Nonguests can use the hotel pools at L'Auberge (CFA1000), Ran and Relax (both CFA1500).

Places to Stay – Budget

Two places on the west side of town are highly recommended. The hyperfriendly *Casafrica* (☎ 98 01 57) in its green and peaceful compound charges CFA4000/5000 for singles/doubles with mosquito net and fan (CFA5000/6000 with bathroom). Travellers can also camp for CFA1500 a person. Large beers are CFA375 and it has good meals. The Franco-Swiss owned *Campement le Pacha* (☎ 98 09 84) is 3km west of the centre near the gare routière. All rooms have communal facilities. Singles/doubles with mosquito net and fan cost CFA5000/6000 (CFA9500/10,500 with air-con). There is a great garden restaurant but drinks are expensive. Camping costs CFA1500 per person. A shared taxi from the centre to either costs CFA200 (more after 8 pm).

Hôtel Méridien (☎ 98 03 42) is friendly, good value and handy for most bus depots. Rooms with fan begin at CFA4000 and air-con singles/doubles cost CFA7500/9300. The roof terrace is bleak but breezy and has a great view over the city.

In the centre, *Hôtel Hamdalaye* (☎ 98 22 87) three blocks north of the market is excellent value. Spruce singles/doubles with fan cost CFA3500/4500 (CFA4500/5500 with bathroom) and air-con rooms with bathroom are CFA8000. The nearby *Hôtel Central* (☎ 97 01 47) charges CFA3600/4600 for singles/doubles with fan and mosquito net (CFA4100/5100 with bathroom) and has a terrace restaurant. On the other

side of the market, *Hôtel Renaissance* has singles with fan for between CFA4000 and CFA7000 (doubles CFA5000 to CFA8000) and air-con rooms for CFA9000.

Hôtel l'Entente (☎ 97 12 05), a travellers favourite, has a pleasant bar-restaurant set in a garden, and large singles/doubles with fan and mosquito net starting at CFA4500/5500 (CFA10,000/10,500 for attached bathroom and air-con). Nearby, *Hôtel Teria* (☎ 97 19 72) charges CFA5500/6500 for singles/doubles with mosquito net, fan and shower, and CFA8500/9500 for large rooms with air-con. It has a reasonable restaurant.

Places to Stay – Mid-Range

At the *Hôtel Watinoma* (☎ 97 20 82), air-con singles/doubles with bathroom and TV cost CFA14,500/17,000. The *Hôtel 421* (☎ 97 20 11) has rooms with bathroom for a negotiable CFA11,500 with fan and CFA 17,000 with air-con and satellite TV. Its restaurant menu, inspired by the owner's stays in France and China, is varied and inventive. *Hôtel Relax* (☎ 97 22 27) has a pool and, with singles from CFA14,500 to CFA27,500 and doubles between CFA 16,500 and CFA29,500, is good value within its category. *Hôtel Soba* (☎ 97 10 12) has long been popular with travellers. It was closed for renovation when we passed by.

Places to Stay – Top End

L'Auberge (☎ 97 17 67) is a friendly and recommended place on Ave Ouédraogo with a pool, a couple of billiard tables, a good restaurant and a sidewalk terrace. Singles/doubles with TV and air-con are CFA 22,000/24,000. The rather soulless *Ran Hôtel* (☎ 97 09 00) near the train station also has a pool. Its singles range from CFA22,000 to CFA28,000 and doubles from CFA 26,000 to CFA32,000. At weekends the nightclub next door can be noisy.

Places to Eat

Cheap Eats You can eat cheaply and well at the friendly, unnamed *restaurant* at the east end of Ave Ouédraogo. *Street vendors* sell juicy whole grilled chickens for CFA1500, notably outside the Restaurant Togolais and on the corner near Oxygène Nightclub. The relaxing *Café des Amis*, two blocks east of the market, is good for light snacks.

African The *Restaurant Togolais* on Rue du Commerce is a good inexpensive place even if there's not much that's specifically Togolese on offer. *Restaurant Delwinde* on Ave Alwata Diawara is known to locals as Chez Tanti Abi and has an unusually extensive and equally reasonable menu. Many of the hotel restaurants also offer African dishes.

French Bobo's good for mid-range dining. The recommended *L'Eau Vive* (closed Sunday), where you can eat under the stars, is sister to the restaurant of the same name in Ouaga. Also run by nuns, the cooking's imaginative, the menu's varied and the sisters are pleasant. Main dishes cost between CFA 2500 and CFA4500 and all come with potatoes or vegetables. Save a corner for their tooth-sucking desserts. It's on the corner of Rue Delafosse and Ave Alwata Diawara.

Restaurant la Casa (don't confuse it with the run-down nightclub of the same name) is two blocks west of the market at the end of a shady arbour. It's a green and peaceful place where all dishes are served with rice, chips or vegetables and are in the CFA2000 to CFA3000 range.

In the same price range, the friendly *Nouvelle Boule Verte*, three blocks south of the market, is excellent value and offers mainly French plus a few African dishes. It's well managed and has what is possibly Bobo's cleanest toilet and washbasin with soap and towel; other attractions are dazzling white tablecloths, ice-cold beers in frosted glasses and, to round off the meal, real espresso coffee. You could also try *Restaurant l'Entente* nearby (not to be confused with the restaurant of the Hôtel l'Entente, nor with the upstart place of the same name on the north side of town!).

You can eat well at several hotel restaurants, in particular those of *L'Auberge*, *L'Entente*, the *421* and the *Teria*.

Cafes & Patisseries *La Sorbetière* near the Place de la Révolution is outstanding – spotlessly clean and with neatly turned-out staff. Its pastries are varied and delicious and it also has sandwiches and large portions of pizza. They make real espresso coffee and their own ice cream (CFA225 a scoop). Try the coconut and you'll melt. Slightly cheaper and less spick-and-span, *Boulangerie Pâtisserie la Bonne Miche* two blocks south-east of the market has excellent bread and a range of pastries.

Entertainment

Bobo only really comes to life at weekends; on weekdays, you're likely to be the only clients. One exception is the popular quarter of Balomakoté, rich in traditional music, from which the internationally acclaimed group, Farafina, emerged. (Don't be misled by the hustlers who offer to take you to hear them play; they're far away, living it up in Europe.) Here, you'll enjoy great music in small, unpretentious *buvettes* where you can drink *chopolo*, the local millet-based beer.

Bars *Café le Colsa* is a tranquil open-air bar two blocks north-west of the Place de la Nation, which, like all bars, is best at night. *Soweto Bar*, two blocks south of Place de la Révolution, is often crowded and slightly seedy. The garden of *Hôtel L'Entente* is laid-back, while the street-side terrace of the *Auberge* is great for a drink and watching life pass by.

Nightclubs *Momba So*, where you can also eat well, is popular. Other top places for dancing include *Oxygène* and *L'Entente* (separate from the adjacent restaurant, see Places to Eat, and not to be confused with other places of the same name!). The most 'in' place – but fashion changes fast – is *Le Makoumba* near the market.

Alternatively, head south from the centre to the friendly, outdoor bar-restaurant *Concorde*. A shared taxi costs CFA150 and, to return, the owner will dragoon his son, a taxi driver by profession.

Cinemas The modern *Ciné Sanyon* is an excellent air-con cinema which shows good films, including runs and reruns of Burkinabe productions which have won international acclaim.

Shopping
Booby supermarket carries the widest range of goods in town.

Getting There & Away
Air Air Burkina (☎ 97 13 48) has four flights a week to/from Ouaga (CFA22,300), three to Abidjan (CFA6,700) and one to Bamako (CFA39,000). Its office is on Rue Malherbe. Air Afrique (☎ 98 19 21) has a sales office at the south-west corner of the market.

Bus The bigger bus companies have their own depots, most of them near the centre of town. Others use the gare routière.

STMB runs between Bobo and Ouaga five times a day (five hours, CFA4000). It's well worth paying an extra CFA1000 to take the 2 pm air-con service. Sans Frontière has three buses every day to Ouaga (CFA4000) and at least one (more at peak periods) to Ferkessédougou (CFA8000) in Côte d'Ivoire and on to Bouaké (CFA8000) and Abidjan (CFA12,000). It also has one which leaves daily except Saturday for Bamako (CFA 8000) in Mali via Ségou. SOGEBAF runs almost hourly during the day to Ouaga and SOTRAO has two services to Ouaga a day.

Rakieta is a good local company which serves a variety of destinations in the south-west. In addition to its Ouaga service, it has, for example, buses departing punctually nine times a day for Banfora (CFA800). It also runs twice daily to Gaoua (CFA3000). Compagnie Transport and its neighbour, SOTRAKOF, run four services a day to Banfora at the slightly cheaper price of CFA700. Some buses from all three companies continue on to Niangoloko (CFA1400), 20km short of the frontier, then a further 25km to Ouangolodougou (CFA4000) in Côte d'Ivoire.

If you're headed to Mali, a daily bus leaves the Gare de Mopti on Ave Ponty at around 2 pm for Bamako (CFA8000) via Koutiala (CFA5000) and Ségou (CFA6500). There's also a daily run which departs at approximately 4 pm for San (CFA5500) and on to Mopti (12 hours, CFA7000). Peugeot bush taxis, at the same price, also leave from the Gare de Mopti for both destinations from about 7 am. For more information, see also Mali in the main Getting There & Away section earlier in this chapter.

If you're aiming for Dédougou (six hours, CFA2500), the Gare de Dédougou near the Marché du Soir has buses departing daily at 3 pm.

SOTRAO buses leave from its depot (☎ 97 03 58) on Ave Binger. Departures include the following (fares are in CFA):

destination	frequency	fare
Dédougou	Wed, Fri, Sun	3000
Diébougou	Mon, Tues, Wed, Sat	1800
Gaoua	Tues, Sat	3500
Hamélé	Mon, Wed, Sat	2700
Ouaga	daily x 2	4000
Tougan	Fri, Sun	3300

Bush Taxi & Minibus Nearly all leave from the gare routière about 3km west of the city centre. To get there, head west along Rue Malherbe. Fares are CFA4500 to Ouaga and CFA1000 to Banfora – slightly higher than the bus fare.

Train The train from Ouaga to Abidjan passes through Bobo on Tuesday, Thursday and Saturday afternoon. The return, heading for Ouaga, is scheduled to arrive about 3 am. It's invariably late and isn't worth considering. Fares (1st/2nd class) are CFA4900/ 3200 to Ferkessédougou, CFA10,000/6600 to Bouaké and CFA16,700/11,100 to Abidjan.

Getting Around
Taxi Taxis are plentiful and most trips within town cost between CFA150 and CFA250. Prices increase after 10 pm and luggage costs extra. A shared taxi from the market to the gare routière costs CFA200 and a private one is CFA500.

BURKINA FASO

Bicycle & Mobylette To rent a bicycle for the day, ask at your hotel or around the market. CFA1500 to CFA2000 is a reasonable price.

For a mobylette, expect to pay between CFA3500 and CFA4000 a day and CFA5000 for a motorbike. André Dabiré at the Hôtel Central rents a few and you'll find others for hire outside the Air Afrique office. During the rainy season, visiting the surrounding villages by bicycle or mobylette can be a sticky experience.

AROUND BOBO-DIOULASSO

The traditional houses in the villages around Bobo are characterised by their tall conical roofs and narrow storehouses linked by earth walls, which give the compounds the look of squat medieval castles.

During the dry season, all of the following sites except the hippo pool are an easy bike ride from Bobo.

La Guinguette & Koumi

La Guingette is a crystal-clear bathing area, 18km from Bobo in a lush forest, the Forêt de Kou. Although it's popular at weekends, you'll probably have the place to yourself during the week. There's an entry fee of CFA1000. Thieves have been a problem but don't let this deter you. Camping is possible but it's safer to ask the locals for a place to sleep in the village.

On the way, pause at the village of **Koumi** which has some fine ochre two-storey adobe houses, typical of the area.

From Bobo, take the Sikasso road to Koumi (15km). Just after the village, turn right and then take a left fork along a narrow, rough dirt track. After passing two villages, take a sharp right alongside the forest and follow the track to the river.

Koro

The village of Koro is 14km east of Bobo, just off the main Ouagadougou road. Perched on the hillside, its houses, hewn into the natural rock, are unique in the area. There's an entry fee of CFA500.

Mare aux Poissons Sacrés

This sacred fish pond is some 8km south-east of Bobo, in the village of Dafra. The surrounding hills and the pond, at the base of a cliff and a 20 to 30 minute walk from the nearest parking spot, are memorable; the fish less so. Chickens, which you can buy on the spot, are sacrificed and thrown to the over-gorged *poissons sacrés* (sacred fish). It's all rather gruesome with chicken feathers everywhere. Don't wear gold jewellery or anything red; both are prohibited at this sacred spot. A few louche characters prowl the place and there have been instances of mugging, so go in a group.

From Place de la Nation in Bobo, head south-east on Ave Louveau. After about 8km, ask for the turn-off to the right for Dafra. Everybody in the village knows the way to the pond. A taxi there and back from Bobo should cost about CFA5000.

Mare aux Hippopotames

Some 66km north-east of Bobo there's a lake with hippos. Access to the lake isn't easy and the hippo population doesn't compare with that of Lac de Tengréla (see Around Banfora). The local fishermen will take you in a pirogue to see them but they're tough bargainers. A fact to ponder as you glide across the lake: more people are killed in Africa every year by hippos than by any other animal. The lake has bilharzia, so don't dive in.

Getting here is very difficult without a vehicle since there's no public transport beyond Satiri, which leaves you with a 22km walk. If you have wheels, head for Satiri, 44km north-east of Bobo on the dirt road to Dédougou. From there, take a rough dirt road north-west which, after about 15km, forks to the left (south) towards the lake. From July to September this road is often impassable.

BANFORA

Banfora lies on the Ouagadougou-Abidjan train line and is a stopping point for buses between Bobo and Côte d'Ivoire. Apart from its market, there's little of interest in town. This said, it's an ideal base for visiting the lush, green surrounding countryside, one of the more beautiful areas in Burkina and ideal for a tour on two wheels. The major attractions are Lac de Tengréla (7km to the west), the Cascades de Karfiguéla (15km north-west), the nearby Dômes de Fabedougou and, much further to the west, the stunning rock formations around Sindou. Wherever you head, you'll be riding alongside and

through irrigated rice and sugar-cane fields, established on a collective farm scale with Chinese assistance in the 1980s.

For changing money, the BICIAB bank facing the market accepts only French francs – in cash.

Places to Stay

Hôtel le Comoé (☎ 88 01 51) with its pleasant courtyard and good restaurant is justifiably popular with travellers. It's a 15 minute walk or CFA150 taxi ride from the

BURKINA FASO

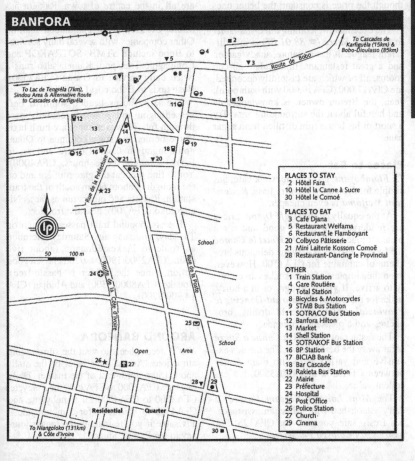

BANFORA

To Cascades de Karfiguéla (15km) & Bobo-Dioulasso (85km)

Route de Bobo

To Lac de Tengréla (7km), Sindou Area & Alternative Route to Cascades de Karfiguéla

Route de la Préfecture

Route de la Côte d'Ivoire

Rue de la Poste

School

School

Open Area

Residential Quarter

To Niangoloko (131km) & Côte d'Ivoire

0   50   100 m

PLACES TO STAY
2 Hôtel Fara
10 Hôtel la Canne à Sucre
30 Hôtel le Comoé

PLACES TO EAT
3 Café Djana
5 Restaurant Weifama
6 Restaurant le Flamboyant
20 Colbyco Pâtisserie
21 Mini Laiterie Kossom Comoë
28 Restaurant-Dancing le Provincial

OTHER
1 Train Station
4 Gare Routière
7 Total Station
8 Bicycles & Motorcycles
9 STMB Bus Station
11 SOTRACO Bus Station
12 Banfora Hilton
13 Market
14 Shell Station
15 SOTRAKOF Bus Station
16 BP Station
17 BICIAB Bank
18 Bar Cascade
19 Rakieta Bus Station
22 Mairie
23 Préfecture
24 Hospital
25 Post Office
26 Police Station
27 Church
29 Cinema

train or bus stations. Singles/doubles with fan, netted windows and shower cost CFA4500/5000 (CFA6500 with bathroom) and it has a few rooms with air-con (CFA10,000). It has a partially open-air bar-restaurant and there's sometimes dancing to recorded music on Saturday night.

Rooms at the more central *Hôtel Fara* (☎ 88 01 17) are around a large, rather lifeless compound. They're clean and all beds have mosquito nets. One with fan and shower costs CFA7000 (CFA7500 with twin beds). Air-con rooms with bathroom are CFA9500. There are two categories, even though the price is constant; the better ones are larger and have superior furniture.

The excellent, welcoming three-star *Hôtel la Canne à Sucre* (☎ 88 01 07) is in a different league. It has a mature, shady garden and a great restaurant. Immaculate air-con rooms, all of which are tastefully decorated, are CFA17,000 (CFA19,000 with bathroom). Jean, the Breton owner, is knowledgeable and helpful about the surrounding area. Try a snort of his house rum distilled from sugar cane.

Places to Eat

Le Flamboyant, a shady sidewalk cafe, has simple food. Nearby, the very basic *Restaurant Weifama* is even cheaper.

At the equally central *Café Djana*, prices are moderate, the food's good and it's a pleasant place to linger. At *Hôtel le Comoé* the food is also good – try the delicious brochette of capitaine for CFA1500. However, even the simplest of dishes takes an eternity to arrive. If you're hungry or in a hurry, make for the nearby *Restaurant-Dancing le Provincial* which has cold drinks, brochettes and a pleasant ambience.

The restaurant at *Hôtel la Canne à Sucre* is far away the best in town. The menu's extensive and varied and, with main dishes between CFA2500 and CFA3500, it's excellent value.

The *Mini Laiterie Kossom Comoë*, a dairy established with Canadian assistance, has fresh, safe yoghurts for CFA125. For pastries, try *Colbyco Pâtisserie*.

Entertainment

As well as the three hotels there are a number of small *buvettes* in Bobo, which are all good for a drink. The paillote of *Bar Cascade* is a relaxing place for a sundowner. And, if you want to impress the folks back home, drop by the *Banfora Hilton*. It's in fact a modest restaurant and dancing place, although you'll be lucky to find any dancing going on, except at weekends.

Getting There & Away

The gare routière and company bus stations are all in the centre of town. Rakieta has nine comfortable buses a day to Bobo (1½ hours, CFA800) with guaranteed seating. Other companies with several daily services to Bobo include STMB, SOTRAKOF and Compagnie Transport. Rakieta also runs a twice daily service to Gaoua (CFA2500). Bush taxis to Bobo cost CFA1000.

The large buses headed south to Ferkessédougou and Abidjan generally pass through full. However, there are bush taxis to the border and some continue to Ouangolodougou in Côte d'Ivoire and on to Ferkessédougou (five hours, CFA4000). You'll find them at the gare routière and on the main drag about 600m south of the train station. Rakieta and others run as far as Niangoloko (CFA700), near the frontier.

The southbound train passes through on Tuesday, Thursday and Saturday afternoon en route to Ferkessédougou (about five hours, CFA2900/1900, 1st/2nd class; a good option, since the border is hassle-free), Bouaké (CFA8000/5300) and Abidjan (CFA 14,700/9700).

AROUND BANFORA

You'll need wheels to visit the surrounding attractions. Ask at your hotel or the stalls about 150m north-east of the market. Daily rates are CFA2000 to CFA2500 for a bicycle, CFA3500 to CFA4000 for a mobylette and CFA4500 to CFA5000 for a motorcycle – advisable if you're making the longer journey to the Pics de Sindou.

Lac de Tengréla

Whatever your level of fitness, this lake, less than 10km west of Banfora on a good dirt road, makes a pleasant bicycle ride and is easy to find. You'll see fisherfolk, a variety of birdlife and, if you're lucky, hippos. There's a fee of CFA250 and a pirogue trip costs CFA1000 per person.

You can spend the night in one of the simples paillotes at *Farafina Buvette*, owned by Suleimane, exuberant, dreadlocked and drum-crazy. The buvette, which serves capitaine or carp fresh from the lake, also makes a pleasant drinks or lunch stop, and you'll probably be treated to a throbbing recital from his percussion school.

To get to the lake, take the dirt road which forks right at the Total petrol station in Banfora, then after about 6km turn left for the village of Tengréla. The lake is a further kilometre beyond the village.

Cascades de Karfiguéla

Some 15km north-west of Banfora, these waterfalls are at their best during and just after the rainy season – when, unfortunately, it can be difficult, impossible even, to negotiate the dirt tracks leading to them. But, whatever the season, it's worth the journey. From below, you approach them through a magnificent avenue of mature mango trees; the chaotic jumble of rocks over which the water splays is a sight in itself.

You can camp beside the pool at their base. In the dry season, bring your own water as the pool will be too muddy.

From the waterfalls, you can walk or ride to the **Dômes de Fabedougou** by following the main irrigation pipe eastwards. They're an escarpment-type formation and good for rock climbing.

Travelling from Bobo to Banfora, you could also stop off at the **Chutes de la Comoé**. Less impressive than the Karfiguéla falls but easier to get to, they're near Toussiana, about 25km north of Banfora and just west of the highway to Ouagadougou.

Getting There & Away It's not easy to get here alone. Of two alternative methods, the

simpler is to follow the road to Sindou and then turn right at a sign near the Karfiguéla falls turn-off. You risk going astray on the tracks leading through the sugar-cane plantations and, in this mega agri-business, there are few human beings to direct you. When you reach a T junction and the main irrigation canal, which leads from the head of the falls, your troubles are over; just follow it to the left (upstream).

Alternatively, save yourself the possible frustration and take a guide (CFA3000 to CFA3500 per day) and ride pillion on a hired mobylette.

Pics de Sindou

The Sindou rock formations (entry CFA 1000) are a narrow, craggy chain which extend north-east from the dirt road, which you follow from Banfora for about 50km.

The tortured cones of these structures, sculpted and blasted by the elements, were left behind when the surrounding softer rocks eroded away.

This area is ideal for a short, steep stroll, a day hike or even a couple of days' trekking, for which you'll need to bring all your own food, gear and water. There's plenty of flat ground at the base of the fingers and chimneys where you can stretch a sleeping bag.

You can also overnight for CFA1000 at the basic but very friendly *Auberge Soutarala* in the small village of Sindou, 2km beyond the Pics, where the drinks are cool and the food simple and filling. Turn left at the mini-roundabout as you enter the village, and then go down a lane beside the dispensary.

GAOUA

Gaoua is a good base for exploring Lobi country. There's a vital Sunday market and, if you like your music traditional and untainted, it has some great *boîtes*, or informal nightclubs, with live music. There's no lack of choice and the Cabaret Pastis has been particularly recommended. There's also a small museum (CFA1000) devoted to Lobi culture. For more details on Lobi art and

BURKINA FASO

Lobi Traditions

Lobi traditions are some of the best pre-served in Africa. The *dyoro* initiation rites, which take place every seven years, for example, are still widely observed. For three to six months, young boys undergo severe physical tests of their manhood and learn the clan's oral history and the dos and don'ts of their culture. Lobi art, in particular the wooden carvings (which play an essential role in protecting the family), is highly regarded by collectors.

What's most fascinating for travellers, however, is the architecture of rural Lobi homes. The compounds are rectangular and – rarely for constructions of mud – sometimes multistorey. Each, with its high mud-brick walls and scarcely a slit for windows, is like a miniature fortress. Unlike most Africans, who live in villages, the Lobi, like the Somba and Tamberma in northern Benin and Togo, live in their fields; a family compound may be several hundred metres from its nearest neighbour.

With such strong traditions, it's not surprising that in rural areas the Lobi don't warm easily to foreigners. Be particularly cautious about your behaviour. Don't take photos without express permission, for instance, or even offer sweets to children. In towns such as Gaoua, however, the Lobi can be very friendly, and if you're invited to have some *chapalo*, the local millet beer, by all means accept.

culture, see the colour feature between pages 224 and 225.

Places to Stay & Eat
For cheap accommodation try *L'Hôtel de Poni* (☎ 87 02 00), which faces the main square and charges CFA4000 for a room, or the *Hôtel 125*. The *Hôtel Hala* (☎ 87 01 21), just outside town, offers the best accommodation by far and serves excellent Lebanese fare. For cheap food, your best bet is *La Porte Ouverte*.

Getting There & Away
From Ouaga, SOTRAO buses (CFA4000) leave on Monday, Wednesday and Saturday. They also run from Bobo to Gaoua (CFA3500) on Tuesday and Saturday. Both services return from Gaoua the following day. Rakieta has a twice daily service to and from both Bobo (CFA3000) and Banfora (CFA2500).

Bush taxis run from Gaoua to Ouaga, Bobo and Banfora and, more frequently, to Diébougou, from where there's transport to/from Bobo.

The dirt road from Banfora to Gaoua (197km) is badly rutted in places. The one between Bobo and Gaoua (210km) via Diébougou is in good condition, as is the highway from Ouaga to Gaoua (385km) via Pâ and Diébougou. From Ouaga, you can drive to Gaoua in five or six hours.

AROUND GAOUA
Loropéni
Loropéni, 39km west of Gaoua on the road to Banfora, is the site of some ancient ruins whose origins remain unknown. The local Gan people call the complex the *maison de refus*. The structures themselves are far from overwhelming; their interest lies in their being among the very few stone remains in West Africa.

To get there, head west out of town on the Banfora road for 3.5km. At the top of a small hill, take a track to the right for about half a kilometre.

BOROMO
Boromo is halfway between Ouaga and Bobo. Although the main section of the Parc National des Deux Bales is quite far away, there are several areas within 10km of Boromo where elephant sightings are common.

The only place to stay is the *Relais Touristique* (☎ 44 06 84), which has clean singles/doubles with fan for CFA3500/4500 (CFA5500/7000 with air-con). It's also the only place for food apart from the stalls at the bus halt.

The South & South-East

FADA N'GOURMA

Fada, 219km east of Ouaga, is the major town between the capital and Niamey in Niger. It's also the turn-off point for Parc National de la Pendjari and Natitingou, both in Benin. It makes a convenient overnight stop if you're travelling to/from Niger or Benin. Its heart is the market and the tiny gare routière nearby, both on the main drag. There's a BIB bank, where you're unlikely to be able to cash travellers cheques.

Places to Stay & Eat

The cheapest place to stay is *Le Campement*, if it's still open, just across the main highway from the gare routière. Singles/doubles cost CFA2000/3000. The best hotel is the *Auberge* (don't confuse it with the singularly dirty Auberge Liberté, also in town). It charges CFA5000/5500 for singles/doubles with fan and bathroom (CFA6000/7000 with air-con). It has several paillotes with comfortable chairs and a popular outdoor bar-restaurant where meals start at CFA1500.

There are usually several vendors selling inexpensive local food around the gare routière. At the south-east corner of the market is a small *food stall* where you can get coffee, good yoghurt and minced-meat sandwiches. *Restaurant de la Paix* next to the Auberge has an attractive shaded eating area and offers standard fare for about CFA1500.

Getting There & Away

STMB has a twice daily service between Fada and Ouaga (225km) and SOTRAO runs every Monday, Wednesday and Saturday. Both cost CFA2000. Transport for Niger and, especially, Benin is scarce and fills up slowly. For the Parc National d'Arli, most travellers continue east to Kantchari before heading south.

KOUPÉLA

Koupéla, 137km east of Ouaga, is a lively intersection where major routes from Togo, Niger and Ouaga converge. There are several cheap and very basic hotels: the *Hôtel Bon Séjour* and the *Campement* beside the Bar Calypso both cost CFA2500 a room, and neither is far from the intersection.

PARC NATIONAL D'ARLI

In the south-east on the border with Benin, Parc National d'Arli is Burkina's major national park. (For a map of the park and the surrounding area, see p192.) Here, you have by far the best chance of spotting a variety of animals. The park lies on a flood-prone lowland plain, bordered to the south-east by the River Pendjari. It's part of the same ecosystem as Benin's Parc National de la Pendjari, just across the river.

Animal species common to both parks include hippopotamus, elephant, warthog, baboon, monkey, lion, leopard, crocodile and various kinds of antelope. Bird species are also very varied.

With your own vehicle, you can also see the Burkina side of **Parc National du W** to the east of Arli on the Niger border; the entrance is via Diapaga. Both parks are usually open from 15 December to 15 May. Entrance is CFA5000 per person, plus CFA1000 for the obligatory guide.

If you have wheels, it's also possible to cross the border to visit Parc National de la Pendjari and the Benin section of Parc National du W. At the frontier, you can buy a 48 hour visa for CFA8000.

Places to Stay & Eat

In Ouaga, you can reserve rooms at *Les Pavillons Safari d'Arli* through L'Agence Tourisme (☎ 31 84 43, fax 31 84 44), who manage the complex. There's an attractive lodge, thatched-roof bungalows and an air-con bar-restaurant overlooking a clean pool. Rooms with fan and bathroom cost CFA16,000 (CFA18,000 with air-con) and the fixed menu is CFA5000. At Les Pavillons, you can arrange to hire a 4WD and camping near the lodge is also possible.

BURKINA FASO

Getting There & Away

Without your own transport, Parc National d'Arli is extremely difficult to reach since public transport will only take you so far – and not far enough. You can hire a 4WD or you can take an organised tour (see the Ouagadougou Information section for more details). The latter's prices may seem expensive but they're highly professional, and once you tot up park charges, lodging and the hire of a compulsory guide and tracker plus car rental, it's scarcely cheaper to go it alone.

For the main (eastern) entrance, take the highway from Ouaga to Niamey as far as Kantchari (389 km), then head south on a dirt road to Diapaga (56km), Namounou (25km) and Arli (48km). The nonstop driving time is about seven hours.

The alternative route via the western entrance is more scenic. At Fada N'Gourma, head south to Pama (109km), where there's simple lodging, then Tindangou, 15km further. From there, it's an 85km trip northeast to Arli. This route will save you about 90km but it's tougher and takes about 1½ hours longer.

SOTRAO buses leave Ouaga for Namounou on Monday, Wednesday and Saturday. From Namounou, however, traffic is very scarce.

RANCH DE NAZINGA

South of Ouaga near Pô and the Ghanaian border, the Ranch de Nazinga (also called the Réserve de Nazinga) was established with Canadian assistance. The project sought to restock the area by raising species of deer and antelope – hence the name 'ranch' – and releasing them into the wild.

Many, alas, have been shot and most of the ranch's elephants have migrated westwards to the contiguous **Forêt de Sissili**, richer in animals, where accommodation is available in bungalows (CFA12,500). In the Nazinga reserve, there's a chance of seeing various kinds of antelope and monkey, warthog, crocodile and a variety of birds species. A guide is compulsory (CFA2000 per outing) and, unlike in many national

parks, you can walk, but with caution. Entrance is CFA1000 per vehicle and CFA8000 per person. There's also a camera tax of CFA500 (CFA1000 for video). If you reserve in advance (☎ 30 84 43), it's possible to hire a 4WD for CFA15,000 per half day.

Places to Stay & Eat

Three-room *chalets* with bucket showers cost CFA5000 a night and must be reserved in advance through the tourist office in Ouaga (☎ *31 19 59*). Basic *huts*, which cost CFA500 per person, are bare rooms without mattresses, screens or locking doors. Meals are expensive and poor quality so it's better to bring your own food. If you're caught in Pô, try *Bar la Montagne* or, near the radio mast, the *Auberge*, which also has a bar and simple restaurant.

Getting There & Away

Driving time from Ouaga is three hours and a 4WD is essential. Take the tar road south to Pô (176km), then a dirt road west towards Léo. After 15km you'll come to a sign pointing south to Nazinga, some 40km further. You can rent a 4WD vehicle inside the park. The cost is CFA15,000 per day or CFA7500 per half day.

Access without a vehicle is very difficult. There's a daily SOTRAO bus between Ouaga and Pô, but from there it's an expensive taxi journey.

TIÉBÉLÉ

Tiébélé, 40km due east of Pô via a dirt track, is in the heart of Gourounsi country and famous for its fortress-like, windowless traditional houses. They're decorated in geometrical patterns of red, black and white by women, working with guinea fowl feathers. From Tiébélé, you can go another 10km to the border village of **Boungou**, famous for its potters.

The North

Heading north-west from the capital, the road is tar as far as Ouahigouya and good quality as far as the border with Mali. Travelling north-east, you have tar to Kaya and good compact dirt as far as Dori; from there it's shake, rattle and roll on a rough track all the way to Gorom.

OUAHIGOUYA

Ouahigouya (pronounced *waee-goo-ya*), 182km north-west of Ouaga by tar road, is the country's fourth-largest city. It's a quiet place, except on Saturday night. Much of the activity during the day is around the

market and on the long main drag. At night, the lively areas are around Ouahigouya's two cinemas.

Finding a taxi is virtually impossible, so if you're without a vehicle, be prepared to walk unless you happen upon someone with a mobylette willing to take paying passengers.

The two banks in town, BICIAB and BIB, change French francs in cash but don't seem to have heard of dollars.

It's an easy walk to **Le Barrage** and its lake, some 300m beyond Hôtel de l'Amitié.

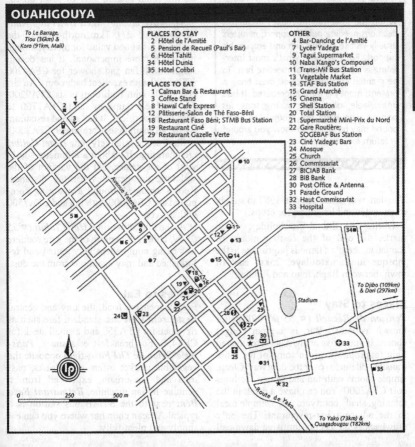

OUAHIGOUYA

To Le Barrage, Tiou (36km) & Koro (91km, Mali)

Avenue Yatenga

PLACES TO STAY
2 Hôtel de l'Amitié
5 Pension de Recueil (Paul's Bar)
6 Hôtel Tahiti
34 Hôtel Dunia
35 Hôtel Colibri

PLACES TO EAT
1 Caïman Bar & Restaurant
3 Coffee Stand
8 Hawaï Cafe Express
12 Pâtisserie-Salon de Thé Faso-Béni
18 Restaurant Faso Béni; STMB Bus Station
19 Restaurant Ciné
29 Restaurant Gazelle Verte

OTHER
4 Bar-Dancing de l'Amitié
7 Lycée Yadega
9 Tagui Supermarket
10 Naba Kango's Compound
11 Trans-Mif Bus Station
13 Vegetable Market
14 STAF Bus Station
15 Grand Marché
16 Cinema
17 Shell Station
20 Total Station
21 Supermarché Mini-Prix du Nord
22 Gare Routière;
    SOGEBAF Bus Station
23 Ciné Yadega; Bars
24 Mosque
25 Church
26 Commissariat
27 BICIAB Bank
28 BIB Bank
30 Post Office & Antenna
31 Parade Ground
32 Haut Commissariat
33 Hospital

Stadium

To Djibo (109km) & Dori (297km)

To Yako (73km) & Ouagadougou (182km)

Route de Yako

0 250 500 m

Maison du Naba Kango

A short walk north-east from Ouahigouya's market, the Maison du Naba Kango dates back to the days of the Yatengo Kingdom, a precolonial rival of the principal Mossi kingdom, centred in Ouaga. The compound, a traditional mud construction, contains houses for the naba's 30 or so wives, several granaries, a small, plain reception room for guests and a fetish house, forbidden even to the naba's children.

The modesty of the compound is deceptive. The naba, king of Yatengo province, whose inhabitants are mainly Mossi, is second only to his counterpart in Ouaga. When the government makes important decisions needing public support, ministers usually visit to consult him and engage his support. For travellers, what's most interesting is the possibility of meeting him. To be granted an audience, you must bring a present; money is most appreciated. If he's unavailable, one of his young sons, *les princes*, who hang out around the compound may be willing to show you around in return for a tip.

The dam was constructed in 1987 to supply town water and irrigation for crops.

During the Eid al-Fitr holiday, which marks the end of the fasting month of Ramadan, there's a famous pilgrimage to the mosque in **Ramatoulaye**, 25km east of town, between Baghélogo and Rambo.

Places to Stay

Pension de Recueil (☎ 55 00 09), better known as Paul's Bar, is a great budget choice. If you arrive at night, look for the red light (appropriate, given some of the more transient clientele) over the doorway. Clean, simple rooms with fan and shared facilities cost CFA3000. You can have a drink in the relaxing, shady courtyard and a simple meal in the adjacent bar-restaurant. The only drawback is the deeply intrusive dawn call

to prayer from the nearby mosque. Paul, who invested his retirement money in the hotel, is friendliness itself. If you ask him, he'll show you the nearby compound where his wife brews chapalo, the local millet beer.

Hôtel Dunia (☎ 55 05 95), run by a friendly Syrian couple since the early 1970s, charges CFA6000/9000 for rooms with fan/air-con and bathroom. It's like stepping into someone's home. There's a sitting room with satellite TV (often empty) and a shady area in front, pleasant for a meal or drink. Madame's cooking is homely, plentiful and quite the best in town. The Dunia is on the south-eastern side of town on the Route de Señanega.

The government-owned **Hôtel de l'Amitié** (☎ 55 05 21), 1km north-west of the centre, is also good value for money, though it's much more impersonal. It has decent singles with fan and shower for CFA4200 (CFA5600 with excellent bathroom). An air-con single with bathroom costs CFA9200. For double occupancy, add CFA1700 to each of these prices. It has a good restaurant where all main dishes are under CFA2000.

Staff at the relatively new **Hôtel Colibri** are charming. It's about a kilometre south-west of the centre, but the warmth of the welcome compensates for the distance. Rooms arranged around a maturing compound are CFA4000 with fan and CFA7500 with air-con.

At the time of writing, **Hôtel Tahiti** (☎ 55 03 09) about 300m north of the gare routière was being comprehensively gutted and refurbished and may again rise from the dust.

Places to Eat

For inexpensive food, the tiny and central **Restaurant Ciné** has standard fare such as riz sauce for CFA350 and a small steak for CFA450. For breakfast or a snack, **Pâtisserie-Salon de Thé Faso-Béni** opposite the vegetable market offers cold drinks, pastries and ice cream, expressed from a genuine Italian machine. **Restaurant Faso Béni** next to the STMB bus station is a typical African chop bar where you can eat simply and plentifully.

Slightly more upmarket, *Restaurant Gazelle Verte* near the stadium is relatively new and well worth a visit. Craving an espresso coffee? Head for *Hawaï Cafe Express* which, in addition to coffee, serves good snacks. In the evening you can get grilled chicken and brochettes at the *Caïman Bar*, just behind Hôtel de l'Amitié. On Saturday evening, it's a good place to hang out until the nearby *Bar-Dancing de l'Amitié* (entrance CFA400) livens up, typically around midnight.

For the best food in town, visit *Hôtel Dunia* (see Places to Stay), where you need to order in advance.

Getting There & Away

All transport leaves from the gare routière or the market area. The standard bus fare between Ouahigouya and Ouaga (180km, three hours) is CFA2000 (CFA1000 to Yako, en route) and CFA3000 by bush taxi. There's no lack of choice: SOGEBAF buses depart every two hours from 6 am to 8 pm and both STMB and STAF have three buses a day.

For Bobo, you can go via Tougan or Dédougou, but it's much easier to make the dog's leg via Ouaga. STMB runs two daily buses north-east to Djibo (CFA1500), where you can catch onward transport the next day to Dori (CFA3000 more). The road to Dori is dirt and well maintained.

The road to Mali is in good condition, but deteriorates once you cross the border. The most comfortable option is to take the bi-weekly STMB bus (Thursday and Saturday, leaving at 6 am) to Koro in Mali (CFA2000). Most days, there's a bush taxi or truck in each direction, but there's little traffic on the road; you may have to wait ages for a vehicle to fill up and then find yourself sleeping at the border. On Saturday, market day in Koro, you stand a better chance of finding transport deeper into Mali.

KAYA

Kaya, 98km north-east of Ouaga, is a potential stopover on the way to Dori and Gorom-Gorom. Market day is every three days and a rather low-key affair despite its wide selection of fabrics and leatherwork. You can visit the Swiss-funded Morija Rehabilitation Centre (also known as Tuum Tuumde), which sells handicrafts made by the centre's handicapped artisans. At the Marché du Bétail, 3km east on the road to Dori, you can see tanners and weavers at work. Lac Dem is 16km north-west of town via a rough dirt road (look for a sign near the market). If you haven't a vehicle, try renting a mobylette at the market.

Places to Stay & Eat

The cheapest place is the friendly *Mission Catholique* on the north-western outskirts of town towards Kongoussi. It has two rooms with shower but no fan for CFA2500. For about the same price, you can also stay at the *Relais Touristique*, known to locals simply as 'L'Auberge', on the road to Dori. The rooms without fan or mosquito nets are nothing special, but there's a good breeze from the nearby lake. Even if you don't stay here, it's a great place for a drink or meal as its terrace offers a scenic view of the lake. Decent cheap food includes brochettes (CFA200) and *frites* (CFA400).

There are two newish and more expensive hotels; *Hôtel Sanmatenga* on the city's southern edge near the police post and, more expensive, *Hôtel Zinoogo* (☎ 45 32 54), where singles/doubles with fan cost from CFA4000/4500 and air-con rooms are CFA11,000/15,000. It has satellite TV and one of the city's top restaurants.

Other good places to eat include *L'Escale* on the road south to Ouaga, *Mon Chou*, heading east, and *Resto les Amis* in the heart of town. Opposite L'Escale is *Paillote Plus*, which has food and dancing.

Getting There & Away

All buses between Ouaga and Dori stop on the outskirts of Kaya. The fare is CFA1000 and the journey takes about two hours. Additionally, SOTRAO (CFA1250) runs three times a week, specifically to Kaya. Several minibuses (CFA1500) cover the route from dawn to dusk. If you're headed north-west, you can bypass the capital by taking a daily minibus which goes almost directly to Ouahigouya (via Kongoussi).

There's a weekly train service on Saturday between Kaya and Ouaga, but it's notoriously unreliable and not worth considering.

DORI

Dori is 261km north-east of Ouaga and 98km beyond Kaya. Its small daily market isn't a patch on Gorom-Gorom's Thursday spectacular but it's worth a short browse. One speciality is the prized Dori blankets, woven from wool provided by the semi-nomadic pastoralists who camp around the town's large pool. At the small Liptako women's cooperative, you can see members weaving cloth for napkins, aprons and table-cloths. The cooperative's another outlet for Dori blankets.

Places to Stay

If you're after quiet, friendly accommodation, the *Hébergement de Dori* (also known as Hébergement Sahel) east of the centre has singles/doubles with fan and bucket shower for CFA2500/3000 and a modest, cheerful bar-restaurant. The *Auberge Populaire* on the northern side of town on the road to Gorom-Gorom, also known as Chez Tanti Véronique, has no-frills rooms with shared facilities for CFA3000. Its large adjacent bar is a lively place to spend the evening or an irritating sleep inhibitor, depending upon your mood and the hour.

Accion Sociale 2km south-east of town on the Sebba road rents out its conference facilities to travellers when they're not in use. Clean beds cost CFA1000 in a dormitory and

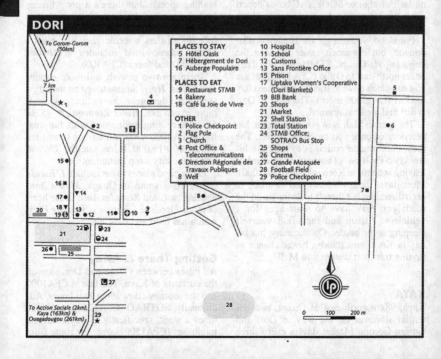

DORI

PLACES TO STAY
5 Hôtel Oasis
7 Hébergement de Dori
16 Auberge Populaire

PLACES TO EAT
9 Restaurant STMB
14 Bakery
18 Café la Joie de Vivre

OTHER
1 Police Checkpoint
2 Flag Pole
3 Church
4 Post Office & Telecommunications
6 Direction Régionale des Travaux Publiques
8 Well
10 Hospital
11 School
12 Customs
13 Sans Frontière Office
15 Prison
17 Liptako Women's Cooperative (Dori Blankets)
19 BIB Bank
20 Shops
21 Market
22 Shell Station
23 Total Station
24 STMB Office; SOTRAO Bus Stop
25 Shops
26 Cinema
27 Grande Mosquée
28 Football Field
29 Police Checkpoint

To Gorom-Gorom (50km)

7 km

To Accion Sociale (2km), Kaya (163km) & Ouagadougou (261km)

0   100   200 m

CFA1500 in a private room. *Hôtel Oasis* was built by the Italians to house road construction workers (they built the tar highway between Ouaga and Kaya) and was later converted into a hotel. It's beginning to slide but still represents good value. All cabins have air-con and bathroom. Single/double occupancy in the smaller ones (called, with some exaggeration, bungalows) costs CFA 7500/9500. Larger ones (styled in an even greater flight of fancy as mini-villas) are CFA15,000/17,000 and include a spacious sitting area.

Places to Eat

You can eat simply at *Restaurant STMB*, where riz sauce costs CFA350, and *Cafe la Joie de Vivre* with riz gras at CFA200 and spaghetti for CFA300. The *Hôtel Oasis* has a small restaurant serving cold drinks and meals, which are simple, nourishing and inexpensive but not the quality you'd expect from a hotel of this category.

Getting There & Away

Both STMB and Sans Frontière run a twice daily service between Dori and Ouaga (4½ hours, CFA3000). SOTRAO has three buses a week from Ouaga to Gorom-Gorom which make a stop in Dori. Bush taxis and minibuses to/from Ouaga cost CFA 4500/3000.

AROUND DORI
Bani

It's well worth stopping at Bani, about 35km south of Dori on the road to Ouaga. Its claim to fame is its seven fine mud-brick mosques. You'll know you've arrived at this small, predominantly Muslim village when you see their minarets, the only structures over one storey high, stabbing like fingers at the sky. Begin at the large mosque in the centre of the village and work your way up the hill to the outlying structures.

All transport between Ouaga and Dori stops here, but don't delay your departure until too late since there's nowhere to stay.

BURKINA FASO

If you're more used to the walled and domed mosques of the Middle East, you might not at first recognise that these striking whitewashed mud-brick structures perform the same function.

The Gold Mines of Assakane

All around the main extraction area, which is exploited intermittently and on an industrial scale by an American company, hundreds of labourers mine a meagre existence. The government has parcelled out the land into small concessions, many owned by traders in distant Ouaga. The workers, descending rickety shafts, some more than 30m deep, haul out the rocks of ore which they crack and pan. Some days are good, many are bad and, whatever the pickings, the owner takes a 2:1 split.

To get there, you'll need a 4WD. Just north of Dori, take the right fork as far as Falagountou, then head west for 15km.

GOROM-GOROM

Gorom's main attraction is its market, held on Thursday, which gets into full swing about 11 am.

Places to Stay

At the police station, you'll probably have to pay a CFA1000 per day *taxe de campement touristique* for the dubious privilege of staying at one of Gorom's two unimpressive hotels. On arrival, you'll be steered towards *Le Campement Hôtelier* (☎ 66 01 44), also known as the Relais Touristique, a complex of traditional huts constructed by a long-departed French tour company; today it's declining and overpriced. Single/double rooms with toilet and shower cost CFA 6000/6500. To take excursions, ask at the campement for a member of the local guides association.

If price counts, resist the pressure and ask for the basic *Auberge Populaire*. If it's still operating, rooms with bucket shower cost CFA4000 and you can also pitch a tent in the grounds.

Places to Eat

There are few alternatives to the overpriced food at the *Campement* (over CFA2000 for rice and a quarter of the scrawniest chicken ever to scratch the dust). The best of these is the friendly *Restaurant Inssa* beside the Shell petrol station. There are also a couple of undistinguished *Togolese chop houses* in the market, a small *cafe* beside the bus terminus and another by the Salle de Video.

Getting There & Away

The road between Dori and Gorom is in vile condition. Both STMB and SOTRAO buses

---

Gorom-Gorom Market

Gorom-Gorom's Thursday market is the most colourful in all Burkina, if not the entire Sahel. In addition to African cotton prints, Tuareg silver, beads and leatherwork, including sandals, scabbards and bags, you'll also find the food of the desert: dates; *lait caillé*, or curdled milk; sweet-tasting *tamaré*, a wild, red bean-like fruit sold in the form of a ball and used by the nomads as a thirst quencher; and *gib-gib*, a large rock-like sweet made from crushed seeds. The animal market, where camels, goats, sheep, donkeys and cattle are all traded, is just beyond the nearby town pond.

You'll see a variety of Sahel and Sahara ethnic groups: the Tuareg proudly on their camels and their former slaves, the Bella, who've taken over many of their erstwhile masters' skills in leatherwork, Fula herders and Songhaï farmers, each in their traditional dress.

The Tuareg men are easily identified by their oval features, long, flowing robes *(boubous)*, indigo turbans and elaborate silver swords. The Bella, both men and women, favour black or grey gowns with wide belts of richly decorated leather. Most elaborately dressed of all are the Fula women. You can recognise them by their vivid, multicoloured dresses and complex hairstyles, usually braided and decorated with silver threads, tiny chains and colourful beads. They carry their wealth with them in the form of beads, bracelets, heavy earrings or necklaces, many of solid silver with dangling Maria Theresa dollars.

(seven hours, CFA4000) leave Ouaga on Monday, Wednesday and Saturday, returning the next day. Every day, there's a few minibuses from Ouagadougou to Dori for (CFA1500).

AROUND GOROM-GOROM

You can hire a 4WD with driver from the hangers-on at Le Campement and visit some of the nearby Tuareg villages.

Further afield, Markoyé and Oursi can be visited as a day trip. **Markoyé**, 40km north-

east of Gorom-Gorom on a sandy track towards the Niger border, has a vibrant camel and cattle market every Monday. It's the only day when you can be guaranteed a ride. A minibus leaves Gorom at 7.30 am, returning at 6 pm.

Oursi, some 35km north of Gorom, has some spectacular sand dunes, **Les Dunes d'Oursi**. If you can tear yourself from your bed, set off at 4 am to catch the sunrise gilding their crests. If you haven't got your own transport, you'll need to hire a 4WD from Le Campement.

Cape Verde

The Cape Verde islands lie in the Atlantic Ocean, 445km off the coast of West Africa. Geographically they are more in line with the Azores and the Canary Islands than the African mainland, and trade-wise they have little to do with West Africa, but ethnically there are close connections.

When Charles Darwin visited here over a hundred years ago, he noted that such 'an utterly sterile land possesses a grandeur which more vegetation might spoil'. But there's more to Cape Verde than the environment. There are Mediterranean-style houses with verandas, *praças* (squares) with orchestra stands, cobbled streets, Portuguese wine (*vinhos verde*), with your Portuguese meals, distinctive fast-paced music with Latin rhythm as well as African inspiration, and a relatively well-educated people. Cape Verde may not be action-packed, but if the idea of islands with a Portuguese ambience, a barren and rocky landscape and guaranteed sun seems intriguing, you'll be delighted with a visit here.

Facts about Cape Verde

HISTORY

When Portuguese mariners first landed on the Cape Verde islands in 1456, the islands were barren of people but not of vegetation. Seeing the islands today, it's hard to imagine that they were sufficiently *verde* (green) in those years to entice the Portuguese to return six years later to the island of Santiago (also called São Tiago) to found Ribeira Grande (now Cidade Velha), the first European city in the tropics.

The Portuguese established vineyards, but working on the plantations was no easy task, so almost immediately slaves were brought from the West African coast to do the hard labour. The islands also became a convenient base for ships transporting slaves to Europe

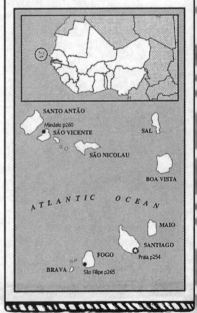

and the Americas. The wine exported to Portugal was of good quality and added to the islands' prosperity. However, it was this very prosperity that attracted pirates, who

242

occasionally attacked the towns. England's Sir Francis Drake sacked Ribeira Grande in 1585.

Droughts

Cape Verde continued to prosper, but in 1747 the islands were hit with the first (in recorded Cape Verdean history) of many droughts that have plagued them ever since. The situation was made worse by people chopping down trees and goats destroying the moisture-retaining ground vegetation.

Three major droughts in the late 18th and 19th centuries resulted in well over 100,000 people starving to death. The proportion of the population that died in each was huge: 44% in 1773-76, 42% in 1830-33 and 40% in 1863-66, but the Portuguese government sent almost no relief during any of the droughts. The decline of the lucrative slave trade in the mid-19th century was another blow. Cape Verde's heyday was over.

At the end of the 19th century, with the advent of the ocean liner, the position of the

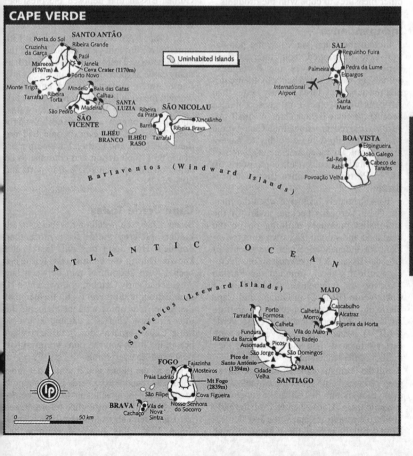

islands on the Atlantic shipping lanes made Cape Verde an ideal location for resupplying ships with fuel (imported coal), water and livestock. The deep, protected harbour at Mindelo on São Vicente became an important commercial centre.

However, the droughts continued. During the first half of the 20th century, the following percentages of the population were wiped out: 15% in 1900-03, 16% in 1920-22, 15% in 1940-43 and 15% in 1946-48. Starvation was becoming a way of life. The Portuguese still did nothing, neither helping to build water retention dams nor taking other measures to cope with the droughts.

Independence

Although the Cape Verdeans, the population who developed from intermarriage between African slaves and Portuguese colonisers, were treated badly by their colonial masters, they fared slightly better than Africans in the other Portuguese colonies because of their lighter skin. A small minority received an education; Cape Verde was the first Portuguese colony to have a high school. By independence, a quarter of the population could read, compared with 5% in Portuguese Guinea (now Guinea-Bissau).

This ultimately backfired when the literate Cape Verdeans became aware of the nationalist pressures building up on the mainland and started their own joint movement for independence with the people of Guinea-Bissau. A Cape Verdean intellectual, Amilcar Cabral, founded the Partido Africano da Independência da Guiné e Cabo Verde (PAIGC) in Guinea and Cape Verde in 1956, later renamed the Partido Africano da Indepêndencia de Cabo Verde (PAICV). Because the Cape Verdeans were better educated than the Guineans, they took over the leadership.

But the Portuguese dictator Salazar wasn't prepared to give up his colonies that easily, even though the British and French had given up theirs. Consequently, from the early 1960s, the people of Cape Verde and Guinea-Bissau fought one of the longest African

liberation wars. In fact, most of the fighting took place in Guinea-Bissau (see the History section in the Guinea-Bissau chapter for more details) because the liberation movement simply wasn't as strong in Cape Verde. Also, middle-class Cape Verdeans were not keen to dissociate themselves from Portugal, and the islands were more isolated. Finally, in 1975, following Salazar's death, Cape Verde gained independence from Portugal. For five years afterwards, Cape Verde and Guinea-Bissau (which had gained its own independence in 1974) talked about a union of the two countries, but a 1980 coup in Guinea-Bissau that deposed the president (who was of Cape Verdean origin) put an end to that.

In 1985, Cape Verde witnessed its 17th consecutive drought year and its 31st in the 20th century. There was only a third as many cattle as there had been in 1969. Only Santo Antão remained green enough to warrant the islands' original name. The following year Cape Verde had heavy rains, ending its longest and harshest drought ever. This time, however, people had not died. The USA and Portugal made up most of the 85% food deficit and continue to do so – food aid represents 50% of imports and 60% of GNP.

Cape Verde Today

Since 1986, the weather has been much kinder and crop yields have more than doubled. How long this will last is not known. During the century, the norm has been 100 to 200mm of rain between late August and early October, followed by a 10 month drought. Survival is still the name of the game, and coping with the elements the only strategy. There's a gamble in everything Cape Verdeans do. If farmers plant before the rains and the rains are minimal, they can lose everything.

One of the things you'll remember most about your trip to Cape Verde is the strength of the people's attachment to their homeland. Even if the droughts return, Cape Verdeans aren't about to desert these islands. Since 1991, this peaceful country has become a flourishing democracy and has opened its economy considerably, resulting in significantly increased private investments from abroad, a higher growth rate and many more tourists. By 1998, 20 state industries had been privatised, tourism had grown to 30,000 visitors annually, and a stock exchange was about to open.

GEOGRAPHY

There are 10 major islands (nine of them inhabited) and five islets, all of volcanic origin. The capital city is Praia on Santiago. The island's interior is mountainous and is more interesting than that of São Vicente, which has the country's major harbour and second-largest city, Mindelo. Two other important islands with stunning landscapes are Santo Antão and Fogo. On the top of the former are perhaps the most beautiful mountains in all of Cape Verde. Fogo, with the islands' highest peak, Mt Fogo (2839m), is a good place for hiking.

Sal, sandy and flat except for several large hills, has many kilometres of sunny white beaches. Brava, the smallest of the inhabited islands, is one of the most picturesque and has a good beach. Another very scenic island, with beautiful mountains and valleys, is São Nicolau.

CLIMATE

Rainfall is not evenly distributed. In most areas, however, rainfall is typically limited to several downpours between late August and early October. The rest of the year is marked frequently by gusty winds and, during the harmattan season, occasionally by low visibility. If you're hiking in the mountains between April and June, you may also encounter considerable fog.

Cape Verde has the lowest temperatures of any country in West Africa and the variance is minimal, from a minimum night-time average temperature of 19°C in February and March to a maximum daytime average temperature of around 30°C from May to November. From December to March, you'll need a sweater.

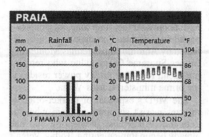

ECOLOGY & ENVIRONMENT

Soil erosion is a major environmental problem. The steep slopes, torrential rains, rapid water run-off and strong winds cause extensive erosion. People add to the problem by cultivating in steep and arid areas. The country has made heroic efforts to combat these problems. In the countryside you'll see the evidence – over 15,000 contour ditches to slow water run-off and 2500km of dams for controlling streams. Cape Verde also has a major reforestation program.

FLORA & FAUNA

There is very little natural vegetation on the islands – and certainly little to suggest now why the Portuguese called the islands *verde*. Only 20% of the land is arable. Cape Verde has less fauna than just about anywhere in Africa. There are no large mammals and even the birdlife is meagre, although birdwatchers should be on the look-out for the rare Rzao Island lark; otherwise, look to the seas. If you take a ferry, you may spot some dolphins and flying fish but you'd have to have extraordinary luck to spot a whale. Fish in the area include nurse shark, barracuda, angel shark, octopus, squid, manta ray and dogtooth tuna.

GOVERNMENT & POLITICS

In early 1991, Cape Verde held its first-ever direct presidential and multiparty parliamentary elections. A year before, Carlos Veiga, a Portuguese-trained lawyer, helped create a right-of-centre party, the Movimento Para a Democracia (MPD). It was swept into power with more than 70% of the vote on a platform of a more market-oriented economy. At the same time, the country's president, Aristides Pereira, was soundly defeated by António Mascarenhas Monteiro, a former Supreme Court judge who remains president. Real day-to-day power resides in the prime minister, Carlos Veiga.

The MPD's espousal of market-oriented reforms wasn't so different from what the defeated PAICV was advocating and had already begun implementing. Today, Veiga's government, re-elected in 1996, is encouraging foreign and joint ventures in fishing, light industry and tourism.

In many ways, Cape Verde is the best-run country in Africa. Politically, the country is a stable democracy and has an outstanding human rights record and no political prisoners. There is an absence of ethnic or religious conflict and no political violence, perhaps because of the homogeneous population and high literacy.

ECONOMY

Based on the UN's quality of life index, Cape Verde comes out on top in West Africa. Health standards are the highest in West Africa. From 1975 to 1995, life expectancy leapt from 46 years to 66 years, 50% higher than the sub-Saharan African average. Cape Verde is relatively well off, with by far the highest GNP per capita (US$930) in West Africa. This is because Cape Verdeans receive considerable money from relatives overseas, mainly in the USA, and from foreign aid. Since 1991, the government has moved rapidly towards a free-market capitalistic system and most government enterprises have been privatised. The country is now on a roll, with real growth averaging 5.5% a year, and foreign investment is pouring in. The country is also attracting more and more tourists by building hotels and tourist facilities on Sal.

POPULATION & PEOPLE

Cape Verde has a population of 400,000, one of the lowest population growth rates in Africa and the longest life expectancy. It is also the only country in West Africa with a population of primarily mixed European and African descent. The original inhabitants of Cape Verde were Portuguese colonisers. Black slaves started coming shortly afterwards, and by the 17th century there was a mixed Cape Verdean population as a result of intermarriage, although the rulers were still Portuguese. This intermixing of the Portuguese settlers and their African slaves forged a distinct Cape Verdean nationality with its own highly individual culture.

EDUCATION

The rate of literacy in Cape Verde is 68%, the highest in West Africa. This is due mostly to the emphasis that the government has given to education, even during colonial

CAPE VERDE

So What Do Cape Verdeans Do?

Cape Verde has an amazingly successful food-for-work program. Some 25% of working rural people, mainly farmers, are employed this way. Many others are employed in transport services, which account for over two-thirds of the country's foreign earnings. This stems from Cape Verde's strategic position as a refuelling and servicing point for international air and maritime traffic.

Despite the successful food-for-work program, the country's biggest problem is unemployment, which is thought to hover around 25%. Foreign investment has helped to reduce this, but only a bit. As a result, many men resort to drinking, especially the locally produced *grogue*. Although maize is the staple food, most irrigated land is used for growing sugar cane to produce the rum. Since 1993, the government has been attempting to encourage the use of such land for other crops but progress is slow.

times. Virtually all children of primary school age attend school. Attendance at secondary schools is considerably less.

ARTS
Craftwork

The islands' traditional crafts are weaving, ceramics, basket and mat making. The baskets come mostly from the rural areas of Santiago and the pottery is mostly from Boa Vista. Mats are made primarily on Brava, Fogo, Santiago and Santo Antão, and pottery comes mostly from Boa Vista, Maio, Santiago and Santo Antão.

Literature

While Cape Verde has the smallest population of any country in West Africa, its literary tradition is one of the richest, diverse and most developed in the region. Prior to independence, a major theme in Cape Verdean writing was the longing for liberation. As far back as 1936, a small clique of intellectuals founded a literary journal, *Claridade*, which lasted until 1960. Their aim was to express a growing Cape Verdean identity, including an attempt, by using Crioulo in some of their writings, to elevate this language to one of literary merit. Since independence, the journal has been replaced by *Raizes*, which has also helped revive both Portuguese and Crioulo writing.

The dominant themes of the local literature have been the sea and the oppression of the slave trade, although more recently racial discrimination has been a common theme. The poet, Jorge Barbosa, became well known with his publication of *Arquipélago*, which is laden with melancholy reflections on the sea and longings for liberation. Expressing the contradictory desires of many Cape Verdeans to leave a country with a declining economy and to establish a national identity, he wrote in *Poema do Mar*: 'The demand at every hour, to go is brought to us by the sea, the despairing hope for the long journey, and yet always be forced to stay'. (*Two Languages, Two Friends – A Memory* by Jorge Barbosa, 1986).

Music

Cape Verdean music falls into three categories. The two oldest musical styles are *mornas* and *coladeiras*. Mornas are basically mournful and express homesickness. They have an emphasis on the lyrics and are similar to the Portuguese *fado* style, from where they may have originated. The most

Cesária Évora

The undisputed star of *mornas* and *coladeiras* is Cesária Évora, who hails from Mindelo. She has made numerous international tours and, at the time of writing, is on top of the charts in France, where she records. Her crowning achievement was in 1997 when, in the second annual all-African music awards ceremony held in South Africa, she stole the show, running away with three of the top 13 awards including top female vocalist. In so doing, she vaulted Cape Verdean music out of the realms of the unknown. One of her top recordings, is *Mar Azul*. She is amazingly modest about her success, however, and continues living a fairly normal life in Paris.

famous writer of mornas was Eugénio Tavares, born in 1867.

Coladeiras, in contrast, are more romantic, typically sentimental love songs, and unlike mornas, tend to be upbeat and are frequently danceable. The top singers are Cesária Évora (see the boxed text on the previous page) and Bana, plus Tito Paris and Paulino Vieira. Others musicians to look out for include Marizia, Dina Medina, Chandinho Dédé, Lura, Ano Nobo, Kodé Di Dona, Chico Serra, Luis Morais and the group Tam-Tam 2000.

The newest less 'polite' style of music is called *funaná* and originated in the late 70s with the group Bulimundo. Very lively, it's a distinctive fast-paced music with a Latin rhythm and is great for dancing. It usually features players on the accordion and other musicians tapping two pieces of metal together. The top singer today is Ildo Lobo. Leading funaná bands are Exitos de Oro and Ferro Gaita.

SOCIETY & CONDUCT

The vestiges of Portuguese culture are much more evident than those of African culture. The food is basically Portuguese but other aspects of the culture are distinctly Cape Verdean, such as the colourful textiles and ceramics.

RELIGION

About 80% of the people are Roman Catholics. Even though many slaves coming here were from predominantly Muslim countries in West Africa, Islam never took hold and today there are few Muslims.

LANGUAGE

Portuguese is the official language. People also speak Crioulo, an Africanised creole Portuguese. It is slightly different from that spoken in Guinea-Bissau.

See the Language chapter for a list of useful expressions in Crioulo.

Facts for the Visitor

SUGGESTED ITINERARIES

Arriving at Sal airport, you could spend a few days on the beach at Santa Maria or alternatively you could head for Mindelo, the country's most interesting city. Two days here should be sufficient. You could then take the daily ferry over to Santo Antão, the best island for hiking. If you have only a week, after a few days here you could head for Praia town for a day, followed by a couple of days exploring the rest of the island.

If you have two weeks, you could spend longer hiking on Santo Antão or you could head for Fogo, where you could climb Mt Fogo and spend a day in São Filipe. You could then head over to Brava by ferry for a couple of days hiking, before heading back to Praia. With three weeks at your disposal, you could do all of the above and also explore some of the less visited islands such as São Nicolau.

VISAS & DOCUMENTS

Visas

Visas are required by everyone and are usually easy to obtain. In the USA simply mail your passport, one photo and US$13 to the Cape Verde embassy in Washington. Visas are issued routinely for stays of 30 days and more if you ask. Dakar, in Senegal, is one of only a very few countries in West Africa where you can get a visa for Cape Verde. If there's no Cape Verde embassy, try the nearest Portuguese embassy – it may have authority to process applications. You can always get a visa at the airport on arrival. You need from US$15 to US$20.

Visa Extensions For visa extensions, visit the police station on Rua Serra Pinto on the Platô in Praia.

Other Documents

Proof of yellow fever vaccination is not required unless you are coming from an infected area (see the Health section for more details).

Highlights

Natural Beauty & National Parks

Santiago island
Picturesque villages and impressive mountain views are found throughout the interior of Santiago, as well as several good beaches.

Mt Fogo   *(Fogo)*
A striking ash-covered volcano with an impressive huge crater surrounding it, which makes a pleasant and not too strenuous hike.

Santo Antão island
Beautiful mountainous interior with verdant valleys and forests – the best island for hiking.

Culture

Mardi Gras   *(Mindelo)*
This carnival is the country's most colourful and vibrant celebration; so popular that you'll need to book flights and lodgings several months in advance.

Praça Amilcar Cabral   *(Mindelo)*
Walking around the park is a popular activity in the evening, and at weekends a band livens things up even more – not to be missed!

Platô market   *(Praia)*
This vibrant food market in the centre of town is a good place to people-watch – or buy supplies.

Activities

Trekking
Cape Verde offers some of the best hiking in West Africa, especially on Santo Antão, Fogo, São Nicolau, Brava and Santiago. Hiking is relatively easy and trips tend to be short, rarely exceeding a day.

Windsurfing   *(Sal)*
Many European travellers come to the islands just to windsurf – the best season is November to mid-May when winds are strong but constant.

Diving   *(Sal, Santiago)*
Some of the best in West Africa. No need to bring your own equipment as you can generally rent it here.

Beaches   *(Sal)*
Miles of white sand and sunshine year-round; the best beach is at Santa Maria.

EMBASSIES & CONSULATES

Cape Verde Embassies & Consulates

In West Africa, there are Cape Verde embassies in Guinea and Senegal. For more details, see the Facts for the Visitor section of the relevant chapter. Elsewhere, Cape Verde embassies or consulates include:

France
(☎ 01 42 25 63 31)
92 blvd Malesherbes, 75017 Paris

Germany
(☎ 0228-265002)
Fritz-Schaeffer-Strasse 5, 53113 Bonn

Netherlands
(☎ 070-346 9623, fax 346 7702)
Koninginnegr 44, 2514 AD

Portugal
(☎ 01-301 5271, fax 301 5308)
33 Ave Restelo, 1400 Lisbon

USA
(☎ 202-965 6820)
3415 Massachusetts Ave, NW, Washington DC 20007

There are also Cape Verde embassies and consulates in the Canary Islands, Germany, Italy, the Netherlands and Portugal. Note that Cape Verde has no representative in the UK.

Embassies & Consulates in Cape Verde

There are several embassies in Praia (Santiago island), including:

CAPE VERDE

Visas for Onward Travel

If you're going on to Senegal, visas cost CVE440 and take up to 48 hours to process. For visas to Guinea-Bissau and Guinea, go to the Ministry of Foreign Affairs in Praia (Praça 10 de Maio).

France
(☎ 615589)
Rua da Prainha near Hotel Trópico, Prainha
Germany
(☎ 612076)
Same building as French embassy
Portugal
(☎ 615602 or 615603)
Rua da Assembleia Nacional, Achada de Santo António
Senegal
(☎ 615621)
Rua Abilio Macedo, opposite the US embassy
USA
(☎ 615616, fax 611353)
81 Rua Abilio Macedo, Platô

There are also embassies and consulates in Mindelo (São Vicente island), including France (at the French Cultural Centre), Portugal (Avenida 5 de Julho), the Netherlands (Rua Senador Vera-Cruz) and Switzerland (off Avenida Januario Leite). There are honorary consuls for Belgium and Britain.

CUSTOMS

There is no restriction on the import of local or foreign currencies unless you bring in large amounts. Importing alcohol is technically not allowed.

MONEY

The unit of currency is the Cape Verde escudo (CVE), divided into 100 centavos. It's not a hard currency, but it's stable.

CFA1000	=	CVE170
Euro €1	=	CVE120
1FF	=	CVE16
UK£1	=	CVE170
US$1	=	CVE100

Banks accept travellers cheques in most major currencies. Changing money on the parallel market may not be strictly legal, but the police do little to control it. The rate is virtually the same as at the banks. Banks for changing money are the Banco Comercial do Atlântico and the Caixa Económica do Cabo Verde. Their service is quick and their rates are good.

POST & COMMUNICATIONS

The postal service is reliable and reasonably quick to the USA and Europe. Letters for the poste restante should be marked 'Lista da Correios'. Post offices (correios) are open weekdays from 8 am to noon and from 2.30 to 5.30 pm, also mornings on weekends in some towns.

The country has no internal telephone area codes. A call to another island is a local call and cheap. Public telephone booths are easy to find but you'll need a phonecard, obtainable at any post office. Alternatively, call from a post office. Calling anywhere internationally is easy. The cost is about CVE520 per minute to the USA and most of Europe.

BOOKS

Publications in English on Cape Verde are extremely scarce and include Cape Verde: Politics, Economics and Society by Colm Foy (1988), Atlantic Islands by Anne Hammick and Nicholas Heath (1994), and The Fortunate Isles by Basil Davidson (1989).

The only bookshops are in Praia and Mindelo and the selections are meagre.

NEWSPAPERS & MAGAZINES

Among the newspaper selection is Novo Jornal Cabo Verde, a government publication which appears thrice weekly, and A Semana, a weekly newspaper supported by the opposition.

Literary magazines include Artiletra, which comes out bi-monthly and contains lots of poetry, and Fragmentos, which has interesting prose.

PHOTOGRAPHY & VIDEO

No permit is required. Nevertheless, avoid photographing military installations. In general, Cape Verdeans are much less likely to object to their photos being taken than people elsewhere in West Africa, but you should always ask permission first. Film is readily available, and there are one-hour developing shops in Praia and Mindelo. See the Photography & Video section in the Regional Facts for the Visitor chapter for more general information.

HEALTH

A yellow fever vaccination is theoretically required if you have been in an infected area within the previous six days. Malaria is not a problem on most of the islands, but there is a limited risk from September to November on Santiago. For more information on these and other health matters, see the Health section in Regional Facts for the Visitor chapter.

The water in most towns is treated and is generally safe, although you're probably better off with bottled water, which is readily available.

Hospitals in Cape Verde are fairly good by West African standards and pharmacies are fairly well stocked.

WOMEN TRAVELLERS

Cape Verde has got to be one of the safest countries in West Africa for solo women travellers – problems are rarely encountered. Still, it would be wise to take the usual precautions.

For more general information and advice, see the Women Travellers section in the Regional Facts for the Visitor chapter.

DANGERS & ANNOYANCES

Praia (Santiago island) is probably the safest capital city in West Africa. On the other islands, Mindelo and the other major towns are equally safe. Wallet snatchings, even in the country's most touristy town, Santa Maria (Sal island), are rare.

BUSINESS HOURS

Business hours are weekdays from 8 am to 12.30 pm and 3 to 6 pm, and Saturday from 8 am to noon. Government offices are open on weekdays from 8 am to noon. Banking hours are weekdays from 8 am to 2 pm; closed weekends.

PUBLIC HOLIDAYS & SPECIAL EVENTS

Annual holidays in Cape Verde are 1 January (New Year's Day), 20 January (National Heroes' Day), 1 May (Labour Day), 5 July (Independence Day), 15 August (Assumption Day), 1 November, 8 December (Immaculate Conception) and 25 December (Christmas Day).

Cape Verde's main festivals include the Mardi Gras which is held all over Cape Verde in February or March, the largest being in Mindelo (São Vicente island); Nhô São Filipe, the Fogo island fiesta held on 1 May; and the Festival de Música, held in Baia das Gatas, São Vicente island, in August.

ACTIVITIES

Windsurfing, scuba diving and deep sea fishing off Santa Maria (Sal island), plus trekking in the mountains, especially on Santo Antão, which has verdant valleys and great ocean views, are major attractions. Many people on package tours from Europe spend their entire vacation at Santa Maria enjoying these water sports. The best seasons are mid-November to mid-May for windsurfing (constant strong winds), May to December (especially June to October) for diving, and April to November (especially June to October) for fishing (rays, barracuda, marlin, wahoo, shark). Trekking and cycling are good year-round.

ACCOMMODATION

Just about everywhere there are budget hotels with rooms in the US$10 to US$16 (CVE1000 to CVE1500) range. All of the major towns have at least one place to stay, but small towns generally do not. In some

CAPE VERDE

towns all you may find is the *pousada municipal* (town resthouse) which typically has several rooms. There are no camp sites but camping on a remote beach is possible and generally safe. In addition to the many midrange hotels, there are now hotels of international standing in Praia, Mindelo and Santa Maria (Sal island).

FOOD & DRINKS

Cape Verdean food is basically Portuguese, but some dishes are unique to the islands. The national dish is *cachupa*, a tasty stew of several kinds of beans plus corn and various kinds of meat, often sausage or bacon. A particularly delicious dish is *pastel com diablo dentro* (pastry with the devil inside) – a mix of fresh tuna, onions and tomatoes, wrapped in a pastry made from boiled potatoes and corn flour, deep fried and served hot. Soups (*caldo*) are also popular. One of the most common is *caldo de peixe* (fish soup) which has a bit of everything. Vegetarians may find non-meat cachupa and soups, as well as yoghurt.

For drinks, there's *grogue* (grog), the local sugar cane spirit, and *ponch* (rum, lemonade and honey) and Ceris, a decent bottled local brew.

ENTERTAINMENT

Entertainment is limited primarily to bars and nightclubs. Promenading around the praças on an evening or weekend is always great fun, even in smaller towns. Cinemas are noisy affairs and good for laughs.

SHOPPING

Cape Verde has little in the way of things to buy. The traditional crafts (weaving, pottery, baskets and mats) are available here and there. Markets are a good place to look. The best place for souvenirs is the Centro Nacional Artesanato in Mindelo which has unique offerings including some colourful tapestries and toys, including large model ships.

Getting There & Away

AIR

All international flights, except those from West Africa, arrive at Sal island. There are frequent onward flights to Praia (Santiago island) and Mindelo (São Vicente) with TACV (Cabo Verde Airlines).

TACV has flights once a week from Boston, Lisbon, Paris, Amsterdam, Frankfurt and Bergamo (Italy). There are also flights from Lisbon several times a week on TAP Air Portugal and weekly flights from Moscow on Aeroflot. You can fly from New York and Johannesburg on South African Airways, and from Buenos Aires and Rio de Janeiro.

From West Africa, TACV provides connections to Praia from Dakar (Senegal), Bissau (Guinea-Bissa), Conakry (Guinea) and Banjul (Gambia). Air Senegal, which is definitely inferior, also has two weekly flights to/from Dakar but bookings on it from abroad are problematic and unreliable.

SEA

There is a boat that connects Dakar and Praia but not on a regular schedule. Freighters from Europe include the *Monte Verde* and the *TBN*, which originate from Rotterdam, and the *Atlántis* and the *Stadt Leer*, which sail from Leixões (Portugal). There's no passenger service on any of these vessels but talk with the captain – you might succeed in getting a berth.

Getting Around

AIR

TACV serves all the inhabited islands – see Getting There & Away in the individual island sections for contact details. Internal flights are slightly cheaper if you buy the ticket in Cape Verde. But if you'll be taking three or more internal flights, you may find it advantageous to purchase TACV's 22-day

Cabo Verde AirPass, which can be purchased abroad from travel agents or in Cape Verde directly from TACV. Flights are often full, so reserve as far in advance as possible. If flights are full, try stand-by at the airport. No-shows occur frequently.

MINIBUS, BUS & TAXI

On Santiago island, private minibuses (marked *aluguer* – for hire) provide regular connections to all major towns. There are also bus service on the major routes on São Vicente, Santo Antão and Sal. Elsewhere, your only choice may be taking taxis and hitchhiking. Hitching is easy and payment is sometimes expected. It's usually safe but see the Trucks & Hitching in the Getting Around the Region chapter for a general warning on the possible risks of hitching.

CAR

Four of the islands have car rental agencies. The largest company is Alucar. An ordinary driving licence is all that's required. The cost of renting a car, usually a 4WD, is typically CVE4000 to CVE5000 a day plus petrol. Taking a driver is not required. A credit card is not necessary.

BICYCLE

Cycling is a good way to get around the islands, but you may have to bring your own. See the boxed text 'Bringing a Bicycle to West Africa' in the Getting Around the Region chapter for more information.

BOAT

There are ferry connections to all nine inhabited islands. Four ferries have short routes (one to 12 hours) with fixed schedules; see the individual island sections for details. Some of them have no cabins, only benches. In addition, the larger *Sotavento* and the *Barlavento* have week-long schedules, stopping at all islands except Maio and Santo Antão. They stop at each port for only few hours, making island-hopping impossible (unless you want to stay for more than a few days or combine ferries and planes).

The *Sotavento* has a counterclockwise schedule, starting from Mindelo and stopping at Brava (alternate sailings only), Fogo, Praia (Santiago), Sal, São Nicolau and back to Mindelo. This takes six or seven days and the day of departure changes each time, making advance planning difficult. The *Barlavento* alternates between a clockwise schedule and a counterclockwise one. Departures are often on Mondays but not always.

Every few days, the Companhia Nacional de Navegação Arca Verde posts a new 10-day schedule in front of its various offices (see individual island sections). Here's a sample schedule for the *Sotavento*:

port	departs
Mindelo	Tuesday, 4 pm
Brava	Wednesday, noon
Fogo	Wednesday, 6 pm
Praia	Thursday, 8 pm
Sal	Friday, 10 pm
São Nicolau	Saturday, noon

It arrives back at Mindelo on Sunday at 6 am.

For a bit extra, you can reserve a bunk in one of the four-berth cabins on these two vessels. There are basins but no showers, and there are usually drinks but no food or water.

Santiago

This was the first island to be settled and is the major island of the Cape Verde archipelago, with 147,000 inhabitants, about 40% of the country total. Attractions include the relaxed capital city, Praia, the first settlement, Cidade Velha, superb beaches at Tarrafal and the mountainous interior.

PRAIA

Praia is Cape Verde's largest city (population 75,000). It has the country's most colourful food market (for other goods, there's Sucupira market) and some lovely beaches. The town centre, on a fortress-like plateau (*platô*) overlooking the ocean, is quite imposing. Despite these attractions, many travellers find a day or two here is enough.

CAPE VERDE

CAPE VERDE

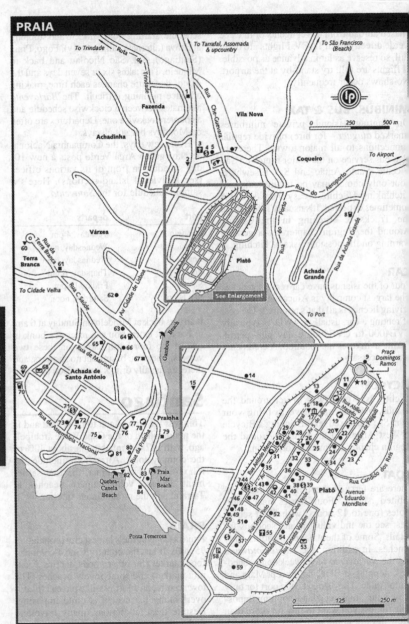

PRAIA

To Trindade — Ruta da Trindade
To Tarrafal, Assomada & upcountry
To São Francisco (Beach)

Rua Che-Guevara

Fazenda
Vila Nova

0   250   500 m

Achadinha

Coqueiro

To Airport

Rua do - Aeroporto

Rua do Porto

Várzea

Platô

Achada Grande

Rua da Achada Grande

Terra Branca
Rua da Terra Branca

To Cidade Velha

Rua C. Saúde
Av. Cidade de Lisboa

See Enlargement

To Port

Gamboa Beach

Rua de Marconi

Achada de Santo António

Prainha

Rua da Assembleia - Nacional

Rua da Prainha

Quebra-Canela Beach

Praia Mar Beach

Ponta Temerosa

Praça Domingos Ramos

Rua Abílio Macedo

Rua Martires de Pidjiguiti

Rua Cândido dos Reis

Rua António Maia

Rua Serpa Pinto

Rua Guiné-Cabo Verde

Platô

Avenue Eduardo Mondlane

Av Unidade

Rua Teixeira Valdadim

0   125   250 m

PRAIA

PLACES TO STAY
1	Pensão Eurolines
11	Residencial Paraíso
26	Residencial Anjos
40	Hotel Felicidade
46	Residencial Solmar
50	Residencial Sol Atlántico
61	Hotel Luar; Vehicles for Cidade Velha
65	Aparthotel Holanda
67	Hotel Marisol
74	Hotel Americano
79	Hotel Trópico
84	Pousada Praia Mar

PLACES TO EAT
2	Restaurante le Paris
6	Garden Grill
15	Restaurante Hong Kong
16	Casa de Pasto Amelia
20	O Celeiro
21	Doce Vita Snack Bar
25	Lanchonette Aquarium
27	Lanchonette Atryum
32	Restaurante Avis
34	Restaurante Flor de Lys
48	Snack-Bar Cachito
60	Restaurante Li
69	Churrasqueria
77	Restaurante O Poeta
82	Restaurante Panda

OTHER
3	Church
4	Caixa Económica do Cabo Verde
5	Classic Auto Rental
7	SEAGE
8	Zéro Horas
9	High School
10	Immigration Police
12	Senegalese Embassy
13	Air Senegal
14	Sucupira Market; Minibus Station
17	Museum
18	Arca Verde (Ferry Information)
19	US Embassy
22	Photo Quick
23	Hospital
24	Instituto Cabo Verdeano do Livro et do Disco
28	Praiatur
29	Orbitur
30	Air Portugal
31	Plateau Bus Stop
33	Praça 10 Maio
35	Livraria Diocesana
36	Tropictur
37	Cinema
38	Casa Felicidade
39	Money Exchange
41	Verdean Tours

42	Minibuses & Taxis
43	Market
44	Termfrio (Groceries)
45	Caixa Económica do Cabo Verde
47	TACV
49	Farmacia Modern
51	Praça Alexandre Albuquérque
52	Cabetur Travel Agency
53	Post Office
54	French Cultural Centre
55	Church
56	Banco Comercial do Atlântico
57	Municipal Council
58	Parking Lot
59	Palácio da República
62	Palácia do Governo
63	Alucar Car Rental
64	Shell Station
66	Mercado Pilorinho
68	Post Office
70	Discoteca A Ilha
71	Banco Comercial do Atlântico
72	Supermercados Felicidade
73	TACV
75	National Assembly
76	Portuguese Embassy
78	French & German Embassies
80	Peace Corps
81	Russian Embassy
83	Beach Parking; Bicycle Rental

CAPE VERDE

Information

Money The Banco Comercial do Atlântico (☎ 615529) and Caixa Económica do Cabo Verde (☎ 615561) change money. Money-changers around the Platô market give similar rates.

Post & Communications The post office, three blocks east of the main praça, is open Monday to Friday until 5 pm and on Saturday and Sunday mornings.

Travel Agencies & Tour Operators The oldest travel agency is Cabetur (☎ 615551, fax 615553). If you send them a fax of your itinerary they can make hotel and flight arrangements, and also help with car rental. Other agencies are Praiatur (☎ 615746, fax 614500), Tropictur (☎ 611240), Orbitur and Verdean Tours on Rua Serpa Pinto.

Bookshops The Instituto Cabo Verdeano do Livro et do Disco on the Platô is excellent for local publications, but has virtually no publications in English.

Museums

The museum on the Platô is in a restored old house. The display includes pottery, wooden kitchen utensils, baskets and a few nice indigo weavings. It's open Monday to Friday from 3 to 7.30 pm, and at the weekend from 10.30 am to 2 pm and 3 to 7 pm on Saturday, and from 10 am to 2 pm and 3.30 to 7 pm on Sunday.

Beaches

The most popular beach is a tiny one just east of Pousada Praia Mar. The beach west of the Praia Mar, Quebra-Canela, is better because it's not so packed and the body-surfing is good.

Places to Stay – Budget

Residencial Sol Atlántico (☎ 612872) on the Platô looks like a dump but inside it's pleasant enough and the rooms, with shared bathroom, are good for the price (CVE1100/1500 singles/doubles). For years the most popular budget hotel has been *Hotel Felicidade* (☎ 615585). Clean single/double rooms with shared bathroom (hot-water showers) cost CVE1500/2000. The more homely *Residencial Solmar* (☎ 613639) has much larger rooms at CVE1500/2500, with bathroom.

There are two other possibilities, both well maintained but devoid of charm. *Residencial Paraiso* (☎ 613539) charges CVE 2000/3000-3500 for singles/doubles, while *Residencial Anjos* (☎ 614178) costs CVE 2000/2700. Others, a kilometre or more from the Platô, are *Aparthotel Holanda* (☎ 612293), *Pensão Eurolines* (☎ 616655) and *Hotel Luar* (☎ 632121).

São Francisco Beach

The best beaches on the southern side of Santiago Island are at São Francisco, 12km north-east of Praia. There's no bus so you'll need to hitchhike, easiest on weekends, or take a taxi. Take the airport road and hang left just after crossing the bridge and follow that road to the end. Bring food and water as there are no drinks stalls or cafes. If you reserve in advance, you can stay at Kingfish (☎ 611661); about CVE3000 a room, plus food. This delightful hideaway on the beach caters mostly to Germans with advance bookings. There are three rustic bungalows and a main lodge.

Places to Stay – Mid-Range & Top End

Hotel Americano (☎ 621431, fax 621432) charges CVE3800/4500-5000. *Hotel Marisol* (☎ 613652, fax 611612), which also overlooks the sea, is much nicer and better located. Air-con singles/doubles with TV cost CVE3900/4650. The city's top new address is *Hotel Trópico* (☎ 614200, fax 615225). Singles/doubles with air-con and heating cost CVE7000/8000. The long-standing *Pousada Praia Mar* (☎ 613777) charges CVE5000/6000.

Places to Eat

City Centre For value you can't beat *Casa de Pasto Amelia* on the Platô. A big Cape Verdean meal costs about CVE500. It's open daily except Sunday. *Restaurante Flor de Lys* has similar food and slightly lower prices. The most popular place with travellers is *Restaurante Avis* (☎ 613079). Most dishes range from CVE400 to CVE700 but you can also get cheaper fare. Two other late-night places are *Lanchonette Aquarium* and *Doce Vita Snack Bar* (☎ 612590).

One place that has very good vibes is *Lanchonette Atryum*. It's mainly a place for drinks but you can also get light meals. Another is *Snack-Bar Cachito* facing the park. The Hotel Felicidade's attractive *Restaurante Panorama* is the most upmarket restaurant on the Platô.

Suburbs *Hotel Marisol* is still a favourite. A typical Portuguese meal costs CVE950. For great ice cream and sundaes, try *Ártica* next door. *Restaurante O Poeta* (☎ 613800) and *Churrasqueria* in Achada de Santo António are both worth trying; the former overlooks the ocean but the food is mediocre. *Restaurante Panda* (☎ 614397) offers Chinese fare and is better. *Restaurante Li* in Terra Branca also serves Chinese food.

Others that are worth a mention include *Restaurante le Paris* (☎ 613464) and *Hotel Eurolines*, both on Avenida Cidade de Lisboa. The inviting open-air *Garden Grill Restaurante* (☎ 612050) nearby occasionally has live entertainment.

Grand Mosque at Bobo-Dioulasso, Burkina Faso.

ALEX NEWTON

APRIL SMITH

VICTOR ENGLEBERT

The daily grind: Yoruba girls collecting water.

Market traders in Cotonou, Benin.

Street traders shelter in the shade of the mosque in the main street in Porto Novo, Benin.

APRIL SMITH

DAVID ELSE

Sampling the different snacks for sale along the way is just part of the fun of taking public transport.

ALEX NEWTON

ALEX NEWTON

The old and the new: traditional fetish carvings contrast with modern art in Côte d'Ivoire.

Self-Catering For groceries, try *Termfrio* and *Casa Felicidade* on the Platô and *Supermercados Felicidade* in Achada de Santo António. For bread and pastries, head for *O Celeiro* on the Platô.

Entertainment
Bars & Nightclubs In the centre, the best places for a drink are *Lanchonette Atryum*, *Restaurante Avis* around the corner, and *Doce Vita*. For a popular local hang-out, try the small *Flor de Lys*.

Most nightclubs have a cover charge of around CVE200 to CVE300 on weekdays and CVE500 on Fridays and Saturdays. The three best nightclubs are *Doce Vita* on the Platô, *Zéro Horas* on Rua da Achada Grande, and *Discoteca A Ilha* in Achada de Santo António.

Cinema The *Cine-Teatro* has shows at 6.30 and 9.30 pm. The best films, however, are shown at the French Cultural Centre and are free. See the schedules outside.

Getting There & Away
Air TACV (☎ 615813, airport 615821) has flights to Sal, Mindelo, Fogo, Maio, Brava and Santo Antão. See those sections for details.

Land There are private minibuses to most towns. They leave next to Sucupira market. Those for Tarrafal depart every day starting around 9.30 am and cost CVE250.

Sea Ferries leave from the port but tickets and schedules can be obtained at Arca Verde (☎ 615497, fax 615496) at 153 Avenida 5 de Julho. The *Furna* plies between Praia, Fogo and Brava (see the Fogo section for schedules); other ferries head for Maio and Boa Vista (see the sections on those islands later in this chapter).

Getting Around
To/From the Airport A taxi from the airport to the centre costs CVE140 in prin-

ciple but CVE200 in practice. There are no buses, but walking the 1.5km to the centre is a possibility.

Taxi Fares are about CVE140 for a short trip in town. By the hour, CVE500 to CVE600 is fair.

Bus Large Transcor buses connect the Platô with all sections of the city. Destinations are marked on the windshields. Private minibuses, marked *aluguer* (for hire), charge slightly more.

Car Your best bets are Classic Auto Rental (☎ 615555 or 615556) a block east of Avenida Cidade de Lisboa or Alucar.

CIDADE VELHA
Cidade Velha, once called Ribeira Grande, is 10km west of Praia. A UNESCO World Heritage site, it was the first town built by the Portuguese in Africa. It's quite run-down – the most notable structures are the ruins of the old **Cathedral**, constructed in 1693 during the city's heyday, and the **Pillory** in

Cidade Velha – Slaves & Pirates

In the late 16th century, Ribeira Grande, with its good harbour and reliable source of water, was the principal stopping point for slave ships sailing between West Africa and the Caribbean. Some ships dropped off slaves, to be sold and eventually shipped away, usually to the West Indies. Ribeira Grande became the most important Portuguese settlement outside Portugal. For England, Portugal was a great rival, and for English pirate, Sir Francis Drake, this prosperous Portuguese enclave was irresistible. In 1585, on one of his world-wide voyages, he came here. His 1000-plus men plundered the town and forts. When one was killed, Drake took revenge by setting it all aflame. The town was rebuilt, however, and continued to prosper through the following century.

CAPE VERDE

the park where enslaved captives were chained up and put on display. Check the harbour as there are often fishing vessels. Afterwards, walk up the hill to **Fort Real de São Filipe**. It's remarkably well preserved and commands an unforgettable view of the village.

Getting There & Away

Buses from Praia leave from Sucupira market. Finding a minibus back to Praia can take a while, so consider coming by taxi instead and having your driver wait. Alternatively, walk back.

SÃO DOMINGOS, SÃO JORGE DOS ORGÃOS & PICOS

São Domingos is 25km north of the capital on the inland road to Tarrafal. The gardens in the valley are lovely and the surrounding area will give you an idea of what the formidable mountainous interior is like. Facilities include *Bar-Restaurant Morena* (☎ 611252) and a hotel, *Pousada Bela Vista* (☎ 611475).

In São Jorge, 15km further, you'll have fantastic views of the island's highest peak, the **Pico de Santo António** (1394m). This is a good place for hiking. For a bed, call ahead to *Rancho Relax* (☎ 711183).

Further along is Picos, affording stunning views of an impressive basaltic outcrop nearby. The **botanical gardens** are lower down. *Pensão Sossego* (☎ 613637) has rooms.

To get to any of these villages, take any bus to Assomada and get off en route.

ASSOMADA

Assomada is the largest town in the interior. It has a lively market and older buildings. For a room (CVE1500) and a meal, try *Asa Branca* on the main drag.

Just north of town is a monstrously large **silk cotton tree**, which is thought to be some 500 years old. At over 50m around at the base, it must be one of the largest of its kind. To get there, head for Boa Entrada, a short walk north out of town, then to your right

and down into the valley. You can't miss the tree.

Getting There & Away

In Praia, minibuses for Assomada leave from Sucupira market starting around 9.30 am.

TARRAFAL

Tarrafal's white-sand, palm-lined beach is no match for Santa Maria's but it's the main one on the island's northern side. From the bay on the northern side you can walk northward via a path leading up the cliffs. There's a scuba-diving centre (CVE3010 per dive, including equipment and boat) next to Hotel Baia Verde.

Places to Stay

Hotel Sol Marina (☎ 661219), overlooking the bay, has breezy rooms (CVE1500) with bathrooms. The clean but sterile *Pensão Mille et Nuits* (☎ 661463) two blocks south of the park charges CVE1500/2000 for single/double rooms while *Pensão Tá-Tá* (☎ 661125) just across the street charges CVE1300/1800. The friendly *Hotel Mar Azul* (☎/fax 661289), further down the same street, is excellent value and charges CVE2000 a room. The tropical *Baia Verde* (☎ 661128, fax 661414), overlooking the bay, is the best hotel. Single/double bungalows cost CVE2600/3000. Cabetur's bland *Hotel Tarrafal* (☎ 661785) costs slightly more.

Places to Eat

Casa de Pasto Sopa de Pedra just south of the central park serves cheap food. *Bar-Restaurant Graciosa* (☎ 661128) is next door; most dishes cost CVE300. A block south is *Pensão Tá-Tá*. The food is good but not cheap. The best restaurant is at the *Baia Verde*.

If you come here by the coastal route, a good place to stop for a meal and room (CVE1800) is *Hotel Careca* (☎ 731090) in Calheta overlooking the ocean.

Getting There & Away

Minibuses for Praia (CVE250) depart from the western end of the central park.

São Vicente

São Vicente is where you'll find Cape Verde's prettiest city (Mindelo) and a small, stark mountainous interior that, although less interesting than that of nearby Santo Antão, is only minutes away by taxi.

If you travel inland, three places worth visiting are Monte Verde, the island's highest peak (750m), and the beaches at Calhau and at Baia das Gatas, 15km east of Mindelo. A good time to come here is August when the Festival de Música in Baia das Gatas takes place.

MINDELO

Mindelo (population 50,000) is Cape Verde's deepest port and its liveliest town. The heyday was in the late 19th century when the British operated a coaling station to fuel ships. Today it's still animated but the wildness has gone. **Praça Amilcar Cabral** is vibrant from 6 to 11 pm. At weekends a band plays from 7 to 8.30 pm. Much of what there is to see and do is on or off Rua de Lisboa. The town's Portuguese **colonial houses** are painted in pastel colours with white trim, and look very picturesque. The city, with the sea on one side and tall barren hills on the other, also features cobbled streets, lined with palms.

Information

Tourist Office The tourist information centre on Avenida 5 de Julho has postcards, hotel prices, maps of the various islands and schedules of ferries to Santo Antão.

Money Banco Comercial do Atlântico is on Rua de Lisboa. At Caixa Económica (☎ 615561), nearby on Rua Santo António, you can purchase or cash American Express travellers cheques, and possibly other travellers cheques too.

Post & Communications There's a post office (good for postcards) on Rua Camões, opposite Praça Amilcar Cabral. It's open until 5 pm Monday to Saturday; 9 to 11 am on Sunday.

Travel Agencies & Tour Operators

Cabetur (☎ 313847 or 313859, fax 313842), the oldest agency, is at Rua Senador Vera-Cruz 57, and FL Viagens & Turismo is at Hotel Porto Grande. Both agencies arrange island tours.

Things to See & Do

From the old **Palácio de Presidente**, now the office of the island's governing council, you could walk down Rua de Lisboa to the newly restored old **food market**. Further on is the **Centro Cultural do Mindelo** at the harbour. Open weekdays from 8.30 am to 12.30 pm and 2.30 to 7 pm, the centre has exhibits and is the best place to buy books (in Portuguese) on Cape Verde. Outside is a tall **monument** commemorating the first flight, in 1922, between Lisbon and Rio. The two pilots stopped here en route. Three blocks south along Avenida Marginal is the restored **Torre de Belem**, a 1920's replica of the much older tower of the same name outside Lisbon. Just beyond is the photogenic **fish market**. The main beach, **Praia Laginha**, is north of the port.

Mindelo's Mardi Gras

Mardi Gras (usually in February) is by far the best time to be in Cape Verde but it's also when the islands are most crowded. While celebrations and parades are held all over the islands, those at Mindelo are the best. Preparations begin several months in advance and on Sundays you can see the various groups practising, marching up and down the streets. The fanciful costumes, however, are worn only on the celebration days.

CAPE VERDE

MINDELO

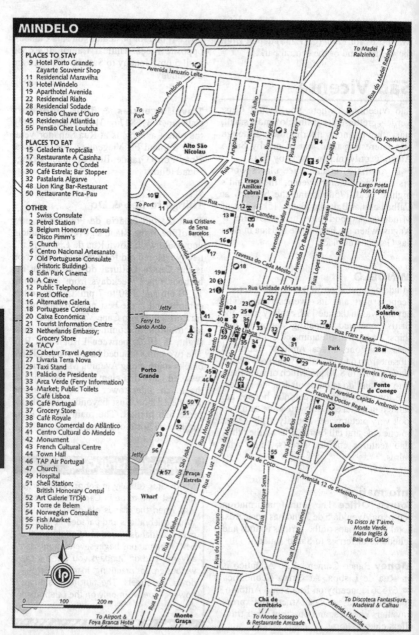

PLACES TO STAY
9 Hotel Porto Grande;
   Zayarte Souvenir Shop
11 Residencial Maravilha
13 Hotel Mindelo
19 Aparthotel Avenida
22 Residencial Rialto
28 Residencial Sodade
40 Pensão Chave d'Ouro
45 Residencial Atlantida
55 Pensão Chez Loutcha

PLACES TO EAT
15 Geladeria Tropicália
17 Restaurante A Casinha
26 Restaurante O Cordel
30 Café Estrela; Bar Stopper
32 Pastalaria Algarve
48 Lion King Bar-Restaurant
50 Restaurante Pica-Pau

OTHER
1 Swiss Consulate
2 Petrol Station
3 Belgium Honorary Consul
4 Disco Pimm's
5 Church
6 Centro Nacional Artesanato
7 Old Portuguese Consulate
   (Historic Building)
8 Edin Park Cinema
10 A Cave
12 Public Telephone
14 Post Office
16 Alternative Galeria
18 Portuguese Consulate
20 Caixa Económica
21 Tourist Information Centre
23 Netherlands Embassy;
   Grocery Store
24 TACV
25 Cabetur Travel Agency
27 Livraria Terra Nova
29 Taxi Stand
31 Palácio de Presidente
33 Arca Verde (Ferry Information)
34 Market; Public Toilets
35 Café Lisboa
36 Café Portugal
37 Grocery Store
38 Café Royale
39 Banco Comercial do Atlântico
41 Centro Cultural do Mindelo
42 Monument
43 French Cultural Centre
44 Town Hall
46 TAP Air Portugal
47 Church
49 Hospital
51 Shell Station;
   British Honorary Consul
52 Art Galerie Ti'Djô
53 Torre de Belem
56 Norwegian Consulate
57 Police

Places to Stay – Budget

Time has stopped at the *Pensão Chave d'Ouro* (☎ 311050). Still maintained fairly well, it charges CVE1000/1200 for singles/doubles with clean shared bathrooms. Rooms on the 3rd floor are about 30% cheaper. The 2nd floor rooms have lots of character – high ceilings and old-style furnishings. Nearby, the tiny *Residencial Rialto* on a side street off Rua Santo Antonio is similarly priced and usually full, and the old *Residencial Atlantida* (☎ 313918) just off Rua Senador Vera-Cruz charges CVE1000 for inferior rooms.

The modern *Residencial Sodade* hotel (☎ 313556) on Rua Franz Fanon offers a decent restaurant and spotlessly clean singles/doubles with fans and bathrooms for CVE1700/1950 including breakfast. *Pensão Chez Loutcha* (☎ 321634, fax 321635) on Rua de Coco has been given good reviews. It charges CVE1600/2500, including breakfast, for singles/doubles with bathrooms. Twice weekly, musicians perform at the restaurant.

Places to Stay – Top End

Residencial Maravilha (☎ 322216, fax 322217) in Alto São Nicolau is an attractive modern place. Singles/doubles cost around CVE4000 to CVE4500. The small well-run *Aparthotel Avenida* (☎ 324497, fax 322333) on Rua Santo António is more central. Single/double rooms cost CVE2970/3470. The old majestic *Porto Grande* (☎ 323190, fax 323193) facing Praça Amilcar Cabral has recently been renovated and charges CVE6000/7000 for singles/doubles. It features a swimming pool. Nearby, *Hotel Mindelo* on Avenida 5 de Julho is likely to cost the same when completed in 1999. For a beachfront hotel, check the windy new *Foya Branca* (☎ 316373, fax 316370) just beyond the airport. Singles/doubles cost CVE4500/8500.

Places to Eat

Pensão Chave d'Ouro has a nice old-world atmosphere and serves very good Cape Verdean food (a meal costs about CVE500). You can get sandwiches, light meals and ice cream at the popular *Geladeria Tropicália* near Hotel Mindelo. The rustic *Restaurante Pica-Pau* (☎ 315507) at Rua Santo António 42 is marvellous and open daily. The seafood and rice, *arroz de marisco* (CVE650), and lobster get rave reviews; there's also less expensive fare and alcohol. *Restaurante O Cordel* (☎ 322962) across from the Palácio offers top service. Most dishes are around CVE600.

Restaurante Amizade (☎ 323917) 1km south-east of the centre on Rua 1 in Monte Sossego specialises in seafood, as does the *Lion King Bar-Restaurant* (☎ 316410) on Prainha Doctor Regala; the latter sometimes has music. *Restaurante A Casinha* on Rua Cristiane de Sena Barcelos is worth a look, and highly recommended is *Pensão Casa Velha*, 5km east of the centre at Mato Inglês near the island's highest peak.

Entertainment

Bars Many bars are on or just off Rua de Lisboa. *Café Portugal* has been renovated and lost its charm, but *Café Royale* still draws crowds, including for breakfast. The tiny *Café Lisboa* is better for espresso.

Nightclubs Three of the hottest places are *A Cave* (☎ 311864) in Alto São Nicolau, *Je T'aime* (☎ 311591) in the eastern suburbs of Bela Vista, and the intimate *Disco Pimm's* (☎ 314597) downtown on Rua Senador Vera-Cruz. All open around 10.30 pm.

Cinema The *Cine Edin Park* next to the Porto Grande has foreign films, all dubbed in Portuguese. Shows are at 6 and 9 pm. The *French Cultural Centre* (on Rua de Lisboa) shows classic French films.

Shopping

Don't miss the Centro Nacional Artesanato opposite the park, which features unusually colourful tapestries, plus whimsical toys, dolls, ceramics and batiks. In the back you can see the tapestries being made. It's open

CAPE VERDE

weekdays from 8 am to noon and 2.30 to 7 pm; Saturdays 9 am to 1 pm. For art and ceramics, try Alternative Galeria on Avenida 5 de Julho and Art Galerie Ti'Djô on Avenida Marginal.

Getting There & Away

Air TACV (☎ 321524 or 321528, airport 323717 or 323718) on Avenida 5 de Julho has at least one flight a day to Sal (CVE 6149), one or two flights a day to Praia (CVE6149) and São Nicolau, flights on Thursday and Saturday to Santo Antão (CVE3800) and infrequent flights to other islands.

Sea The *Sotavento* and the *Barlavento* connect Mindelo with most islands (for example CVE750 to São Nicolau). For up-to-date prices and schedules, contact Arca Verde (☎ 313516, fax 312055); see also the Getting Around section at the start of this chapter. Ferries for Santo Antão depart across from the cultural centre; you can buy tickets there or at Arca Verde (see the Santo Antão section for details of ferries and times).

Getting Around

The taxi stand is on Avenida Fernando Ferreira Fortes. Taxis charge CVE600 to the airport.

If you want to rent a vehicle, Alucar (☎ 311150, fax 315169) is in Monte Dji Sal. Turicar (☎ 312847) is on Rua do Douro south of town.

AROUND SÃO VICENTE

For views of Mindelo and the bay (provided it's a clear day), take a taxi to **Monte Verde** (6km), the island's highest peak (750m). Cars can go nearly to the top; alternatively, it's an hour's hike.

The most popular beach is at **Baia das Gatas**, 15km east of Mindelo. There's no bus service but on Sundays you may be able to hitch a ride (follow Avenida 12 de Setembro to the outskirts). To hire a taxi costs CVE1000 to CVE2000, depending how long you stay. In August, Baia really livens up when the international music festival takes place here.

There's another beach at **Calhau**, 20km south-east of Mindelo. On Sundays, Chez Loutcha here is open for meals.

Santo Antão

When you see the long southern cliff, you may think Santo Antão is barren and treeless. But this is Cape Verde's greenest island, with awesome scenery, pine and cedar trees and a European-like climate. Verdant valleys lead down towards the ocean, providing magnificent views and making this the best island for hiking and mountain biking.

RIBEIRA GRANDE & PORTO NOVO

Ribeira Grande, the administrative centre, is nothing special but the location – hemmed in by steep cliffs and the Atlantic Ocean – is at least a bit unusual. Porto Novo, the major port some 20km away on the eastern coast, is somewhat less interesting. Both have a church, central praça and bank.

Places to Stay & Eat

In Ribeira Grande, *Residencial Aliança* (☎ 211246) has clean singles/doubles for CVE1500/1700 including breakfast (CVE 2000/2500 with bathroom). *Residencial 5 de Julho* (☎ 211345) charges CVE1400 (CVE 2000 with bathroom). Both are average but often full; the friendly owners will help find taxis. They serve standard meals as do *Esplanada Nova Aurora* and *Restaurante Progreso*. Meals cost around CVE500.

In Porto Novo, *Pensão Lizette* (☎ 211586) charges CVE1400/1800 for singles/doubles with bathrooms. Also worth trying is *Pousada Municipal*. For food, try *Lizette* or *Restaurante Bitty Nelly*.

In Paúl, *Residencial Vale do Paúl* (☎ 231319) charges CVE1000 for a room with shared bathroom; breakfast and other meals are extra. There are only five rooms, so call to reserve.

Hiking on Santo Antão

One of the most popular routes is up Ribeira Grande valley, which starts a few kilometres south-west of Ribeira Grande town. You can walk from Ribeira Grande (taking the road towards Cruzinha da Garça) or, to save an hour or so, take the occasional minibus which goes up the valley for several kilometres. A guide (around CVE1000) can be helpful but isn't essential. After several kilometres of flat road, take a left and start going up. Initially, the slope is gentle and crops are everywhere. You'll soon pass through a small village where you can get drinks and water. Houses, mostly stone, are spread out along the route. Further on, the gradient gets steeper. After an hour or so, you'll reach the cooler summit, with spectacular views if you aren't clouded in. Continue along the path and you'll eventually come to a dirt road. Take a left on it and continue walking (north-eastward) along the plateau; within an hour or so you'll come to the trans-island road, where you can hitchhike to Ribeira Grande or Porto Novo. The hike takes at least half a day, usually longer. Some travellers arrange for taxis to pick them up at the top (about CVE2500).

A second popular hike is along the coastal road from Ribeira Grande east to Paúl and Janela (16 km). Or hitchhike to Paúl (10km) and begin the hike there.

A third hike begins at Paúl and goes inland up the Vale do Paúl, an exceptionally verdant and lovely valley. The road passes by fields of sugar cane to Passagem (4km) and on up to Cova Crater (1170m) and the trans-island road. There's a small swimming pool (CVE100) in Passagem and a cafe open on weekends. That pretty village is where much of Cape Verde's grogue is distilled. You can also do this hike in the opposite direction.

A fourth hike is along the Ribeira das Fontainhas, departing westward from Ribeira Grande to Cruzinha da Garça via Fontainhas. You can stop en route at Ponta do Sol, a particularly picturesque village.

A fifth hike is up the trans-island road from Porto Novo to Cova Crater.

Getting There & Away

Air TACV (☎ 211184) has flights to Ponta do Sol airport, the island's main airport, on Wednesday direct from Praia (CVE6448) and on Thursday and Saturday from Praia via Mindelo (CVE3800 from Mindelo).

Sea The ferries from Mindelo (CVE440) take an hour and the seas are often quite rough. The *Ribeira Paúl* leaves from Mindelo Monday to Saturday at 8 am (8.30 am Saturday) and Porto Novo at 11 am. The more comfortable ferry, the *Mar Azul*, departs Mindelo Tuesday to Thursday at 8.30 am (Porto Novo at 11 am), Friday at 3 pm (Porto Novo at 5 pm), Saturday at 8 am (Porto Novo at 11 am) and Sunday at 9 am (Porto Novo at 5 pm).

Fogo

The major attraction of this island is **Mt Fogo volcano** (2839m). It last erupted in 1995. Another attraction is the pretty town of São Filipe. The scenic cobbled road encircling the island connects São Filipe and Mosteiros, the coffee capital at the northern tip of the island, and is punctuated by hamlets with lava block houses.

On the eastern slopes of the volcano is where much of Fogo's coffee is grown, while on the northern slopes is the forest of Monte Velha, with pine and eucalyptus trees. Inside the crater and around Achada Grande you'll see vineyards. Fogo coffee and red wine, although low in quality, are both hallmarks of Fogo and are well worth trying.

CAPE VERDE

Mt Fogo

The conical Pico do Fogo volcano sits on the floor of a huge depression, with a diameter of some 8km, called Chã das Caldeiras ('plain of craters'). A crater with a precipitous cliff bounds all sides of this plain, where people farm and grow grapes, except on the eastern side where the *pico* (volcano) is located. If you hike up the crater, you'll see the black volcano in the distance. The depression was produced within the last 100,000 years when some 300 cubic km of the island collapsed and slid into the sea to the east. Later, the eastern side was filled by the volcano.

The main cone has been inactive for over 200 years. Subsequent eruptions have taken place on the sides of the volcano. The latest eruption, in 1995, occurred to the south-west of the cone, producing a long fissure to the south of the villages in Chã das Caldeiras. The north-eastern end of that fissure still gives off gases, so be warned – don't get too close. The lava stopped short of the villages but covered some vineyards. Today, people are again growing crops here.

Despite the latest eruption, the volcano's cone remains intact and can still be climbed on the northern side. But the climb is now more difficult because the slopes are covered in slippery cinders, which can easily cause you to fall. Hiking boots are essential. The taxing ascent (a climb of 1000m up a 30 to 40° slope) takes three to four hours, but the view from top is magnificent. Afterwards, you can run down in 45 minutes!

Make sure you get here early – you'll need to climb the volcano first thing in the morning to avoid the heat. This means departing São Filipe at around 5 am. Alternatively, come the previous afternoon and camp. When you arrive you could visit part of the fissure which is still giving off gas (the 1995 vent) and arrange for a guide for the following day. The easiest route to the 1995 vent from the road is from the south-east (upwind of the fumarole), along the eastern edge of the recent lava flows.

A guide for the volcano (about CVE2000) is essential because the routes change monthly due to constantly falling ash. You'll find them in Chã das Caldeiras. Avoid climbing during or after rain because water can trigger rock falls. Instead, climb the huge crater around the volcano, starting from Fernan Gomes (for the northern rim) or from Curral Grande (for the western rim).

You can reach the southern rim from almost anywhere along the road between Achada Furna and Coxo. The climb, roughly 1500m, takes three or four hours (one down) and is a bit easier than climbing the volcano.

Simon Day

SÃO FILIPE

Perched on a cliff with a black-sand beach below, São Filipe features numerous praças and colourful houses. The town is divided into two sections, with an old stone wall between them. The lower section includes the market, town hall, church and old customs house. For centuries, the people on either side have made this a social division, like two clans vying for power. Walking around, you'll see old *sobrados*, homes of the town's elite. Their ancestors are buried in an interesting cemetery down the hill from the church.

A good time to visit São Filipe is 1 May, when the town's fiesta, Nhô São Filipe, takes places. You'll probably have to get here by ferry as planes are fully booked for many weeks in advance. Plus, finding a place to stay can be extremely difficult. The

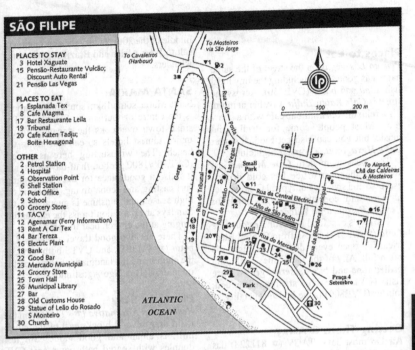

SÃO FILIPE

PLACES TO STAY
3 Hotel Xaguate
15 Pensão-Restaurante Vulcão; Discount Auto Rental
21 Pensão Las Vegas

PLACES TO EAT
1 Esplanada Tex
8 Cafe Magma
17 Bar Restaurante Leila
19 Tribunal
20 Cafe Katen Tadju; Boite Hexagonal

OTHER
2 Petrol Station
4 Hospital
5 Observation Point
6 Shell Station
7 Post Office
9 School
10 Grocery Store
11 TACV
12 Agenamar (Ferry Information)
13 Rent A Car Tex
14 Bar Tereza
16 Electric Plant
18 Bank
22 Good Bar
23 Mercado Municipal
24 Grocery Store
25 Town Hall
26 Municipal Library
27 Bar
28 Old Customs House
29 Statue of Leão do Rosado S Monteiro
30 Church

To Mosteiros via São Jorge
To Cavaleiros (Harbour)
To Airport, Chã das Caldeiras & Mosteiros
Small Park
Rua da Central Eléctrica
Alto de São Pedro
Rua do Mercado
Praça 4 Setembro
Park
Wall

ATLANTIC OCEAN

0   100   200 m

town's celebration of Mardi Gras is a festive time – see the boxed text 'Mindelo's Mardi Gras' in the Mindelo section earlier for more information on these celebrations in the islands.

The beach far below the town is clean but the undertow is strong. **Praia da Salina** outside São Jorge, 17km to the north on the western route to Mosteiros, is better.

If you're headed for Mosteiros, go to the market; there's at least one minibus every morning (around CVE600). For Mt Fogo, consider hiring a taxi, which is usually cheaper than renting a car for the day. For a car, try Discount Auto Rental (☎ 811480) or Rent a Car Tex (☎ 811818, fax 811819), both on Rua de Central Eléctrica. Car rental costs CVE3500 to CVE4000 a day. If you don't mind camping overnight in the crater, look for a minibus for Chã das Caldeiras – difficult to find.

Places to Stay

The unmarked *Pensão-Restaurante Vulcão* (☎ 811896) on Rua da Central Eléctrica has singles/doubles with shared bathrooms for CVE1000/1100.

Pensão Las Vegas (☎ /fax 811281), 150m west of the market, has spotless rooms for CVE1800/2500, including breakfast. There are hot-water showers, fans, balconies and refrigerators well stocked with beer and soft drinks in each room.

Hotel Xaguate (☎ 811222, fax 811203), on a bluff overlooking the sea, is the town's 'top' hotel, but it's dreary. Singles/doubles with bathrooms (no hot water) cost CVE 2000/2600. Nonguests can use the pool for CVE250.

In **Mosteiros**, you can stay at the pleasant *Pensão Restaurante Christina* (☎ 831045). A single/double is CVE1000/1600 with shared bathroom, CVE1800/2500 with own bathroom; prices include breakfast. Meals cost around CVE500.

Places to Eat

Pensão Las Vegas on the street of the same name has good food, including the tiny local fish, *lapa* and *buzio* (CVE230). Across the street is *Cafe Katen Tadju*. Livelier at night, it's a relaxing open-air bar-cafe with a straw roof. Most people come for drinks and music, but you can also get food. It's over *Boite Hexagonal*, a popular nightclub.

The pleasant modern *Cafe Magma* just south of the post office has cold drinks, espresso and snacks. For typical Cape Verdean fare and copious servings, head for *Pensão-Restaurante Vulcão*.

The city's best food is at *Bar Restaurante Leila* (☎ 811214) across from Central Eléctrica. It's open every day, and at night it's often full. Any of the fish dishes, including grilled tuna and *bife de serre* (grilled serre fish) (CVE400 each), are recommended; lobster (CVE800) is the house speciality.

Getting There & Away

Air On most days, TACV (☎ 811228) has two flights from Praia to São Filipe (CVE3317). There's also one weekly flight from Praia to Mosteiros. You'll need to reconfirm your return flight before 3 pm (when the office closes). A taxi into town (2km) costs CVE250; by truck it's CVE100.

Sea The *Furna* departs Praia Mondays at 10 pm for Fogo (CVE1300), Fogo Tuesday at noon for Brava, Brava Tuesday at 6 pm for Praia, Praia Wednesday at 10 pm for Brava, Brava Thursday at noon for Fogo, and Fogo Thursday at 6 pm for Praia. The *Sotavento* and the *Barlavento* also stop here. For details, visit Agenamar (☎ 811012) across from TACV.

Sal

Sal has several large hills. Worth visiting is the salty crater, **Pedro da Lume**, east of Es-

pargos (the largest town and 2km from the airport in the centre of the island). Until the middle of the 20th century the exportation of salt to West Africa and Brazil supported the islanders.

SANTA MARIA

Santa Maria, some 18km south of the airport, is the centre of tourism on Sal island. The small town overlooks the ocean, with the major tourist hotels spread out along the beach. The windsurfing here is superb (CVE700/1800 per hour/half-day rental) and it's also a good place for deep-sea fishing, surf casting and scuba diving. Winter is the high season and sunshine is guaranteed. On Sundays at 11 am, don't miss the enchanting singing at the church near the praça.

There are two good travel agencies: Cabetur (☎ 421305), and CVTS both between the church and the landmark windmill on the main drag (Rua Ngo Agostinho).

Places to Stay

Residencial Alternativa (☎ 411616), on the main drag several blocks east of the windmill, is clean and good value. Singles/doubles with shared bathrooms cost CVE 1500/2250 (CVE2000/2600 with own bathroom). The upmarket *Restaurante Nhã Terra* (☎ 421109) just east of the windmill has some excellent value singles/doubles (CVE2000/2500). The modern *Pousada da Luz* (☎ 421138) is clean but sterile and in a remote location. Singles/doubles are CVE 2500/3500.

On the beach, two of the best large tourist hotels are *Morabeza* (☎ 421111, fax 421005), with singles/double rooms for CVE4945/8050, and *Hotel Belorizonte* (☎ 421080, fax 421210) next door (CVE 4700/5700).

Places to Eat

For sandwiches, snacks and good yoghurt, you can't beat *Pastela'ria Relax* on the main drag. The unpretentious open-air *Restaurante Bar Esplanada Soleil* next to the park is often packed. Most dishes range from CVE450 to CVE600; sandwiches are less. At night, the Mateus band often performs here. Also popular is *Restaurante Nhã Terra* (☎ 421109); most fish dishes are CVE500. *Restaurante Grill Por Do Sol* near the park and overlooking the ocean is good for beers and grilled fish. The open-air 2nd floor *Restaurante Americos's* facing the church is also good for drinks and views. For an upmarket place with good fish, try *Restaurante O Piscador* around the corner from the park.

Getting There & Away
Taxis to Santa Maria cost CVE600 from the airport (CVE700 from Espargos). Minibuses ply between the two towns (CVE70). Hail them on the main drag facing the windmill.

ESPARGOS
Espargos is a small quiet town but in the evenings things liven up, especially around the central Praça 19 de Setembro. It's alongside the main north-south drag, Rua 5 de Julho. That road heads north from the large intersection at the southern entrance to town where you catch all minibuses. For good views, climb the large hill just outside of town (30 minutes from the centre of town to the top).

Places to Stay
Casa da Angela (☎ 411327) on Rua Abel Djassi on the northern side of town is highly recommended; CVE1500/2000 for spotlessly clean singles/doubles with hot-water bathrooms. *Residencial Central* (☎ 411113, fax 411366) facing the main square has pleasant single/double rooms for CVE1500/2000. You can get meals here. The modern upmarket *Hotel Atlántico* (☎ 411210, fax 411522) at the southern intersection is lifeless except when flights are delayed, and waiting passengers are lodged here. Rooms are good value though, at CVE2400/2950.

Places to Eat
Restaurant Salinas (☎ 411799), on the main drag two blocks south of the park, is recom-
mended; grilled fish costs CVE460. A block further south is *Restaurant Arcada*, which offers indoor and outdoor dining. The restaurant with the nicest ambience is the small *Bar Violão* near Angela's. For drinks and music afterwards, try the lively *Bar Esplanada Recanto* across the street. The more plebeian *Restaurant Max* around the corner from Angela's advertises itself as a 'family place'. In the area around the central park you'll find *Restaurante Sivy*, which is good for snacks and yoghurt, and the lively *Snack Bar Tanha Fina*, which is better for drinks. For groceries, try *Super Mercado Central* facing the park.

Getting There & Away
Air TACV (☎ 411268) has up to three flights a day to Praia (CVE6149), one or two flights a day to Mindelo (CVE6149), and five flights a week to São Nicolau and Boa Vista. At the airport there's a bank, tourist booth with maps, Cabetur travel agency (☎ 411545, fax 411098), airline offices, and Transcor (☎ 411439) and Alucar (☎ 411089) car rental agencies. Taxis from the airport to town (2km) charge CVE150. Or hail a minibus on the highway in front of the airport.

Sea The *Sotavento* and the *Barlavento* stop at Palmeira, the port near Espargos. See Boat in the Getting Around section earlier in this chapter for details of times and fares.

Other Islands

BRAVA
Brava is the smallest of the inhabited islands and densely populated. It was settled in the late 17th century by refugees from Fogo fleeing an eruption of the island's volcano and gained fame in the 19th century as a source of whalers for American ships. Many of them eventually settled around Boston.

The mountainous landscape of the island offers numerous short hikes. From the port of Furna on the eastern side to Fajã d'Agua on the verdant western side near the airport, the distance is only 10km. The best of two good beaches is at the latter. Vila de Nova Sintra is the tiny capital in the centre (500m altitude). From there, you could hike 3km eastward down to Vinagre via Santa Barbara or, somewhat longer, westward to Cova Joana and then on to Nosso Senhora do Monte or Lima Doce, both nearby. To Fajã d'Agua, hike or take a minibus, although there aren't many.

Places to Stay & Eat

In Vila de Nova Sintra, try *Pensão Restaurante Paul Sena* (☎ 851312); a clean room with bathroom is CVE1000, and breakfast and other meals are available. The *Pousada Municipal* (☎ 811220) has only three rooms (CVE1500 with bathroom). For meals, try the *Esplanada* or the *Pousada Bar Restaurant Português* (☎ 851446 or 851376); you may also be able to get a room at the latter. The best place to stay and eat, however, is in Fajã d'Agua at *Manuel Burgo Ocean Front Motel* (☎ 851321); singles/doubles with bathroom cost CVE1000/1500.

Getting There & Away

TACV (☎ 851192) has flights to/from Praia on Monday, Tuesday, Thursday and Friday (CVE4426). The airport is near Fajã d'Agua. (See the Fogo section for ferry schedules and the main Getting Around section earlier in this chapter for details about the *Sotavento* and *Barlavento*.)

SÃO NICOLAU

With seven peaks over 500m, São Nicolau is a great place for hiking. The highest peak, **Monte Gordo** (1312m), is only 8km west, as the crow flies, from **Ribeira Brava**, the island's capital. The island's most fertile area is the beautiful verdant **Fajã valley** just north of that peak. In many other areas, the landscape is rugged and dry.

Minibuses from Tarrafal, the port, for Ribeira Brava (26km) travel along a spectacular winding road that goes all the way to the northern coast, skirting Monte Gordo and then back inland to Ribeira Brava. (You could get off halfway and hike in the Fajã valley or down a path eastward to Ribeira Brava.)

The best time to visit Ribeira Brava is in February or March during Mardi Gras as the celebrations are second only to Mindelo's.

Places to Stay & Eat

In Ribeira Brava, *Residencial Sila* (☎ 351188) offers singles/doubles for CVE 500/1000, and there's a restaurant. *Pensão Jumbo* (☎ 351315) charges CVE1000 for a room (CVE1200 with bathroom), and *Pensão Jardim* (☎ 351117) charges CVE 1200/1500, with bathroom. The best is *Pensão da Cruz* (☎ 351282) where singles/doubles are CVE1000/1800 with shared bathroom; slightly more if you want your own bathroom. Meals are available if you order in advance. Good restaurants include *Casa de Pasto Lino Évora* and *Restaurant Bela Sombra Dilila*.

In Tarrafal, single/double rooms cost CVE1000/1200 at *Residencial Lidio Gomes Martins* (☎ 361187). For food, try *Bar Patché*, *Esplanada Tarrafal* or *Casa de Pasto Lino Évora*.

Getting There & Away

TACV (☎ 351161) has flights to/from Mindelo once or twice daily and to/from Sal five times weekly. The airport is 5km south-east of Ribeira Brava. About once a week you can get here from Mindelo or Sal on the *Sotavento* or *Barlavento*. See the Getting Around section earlier in this chapter for more details about these boats.

BOA VISTA

Not many travellers come to Boa (population 4000), but the few who do are usually very warmly received. Sal-Rei, the island's capital and port, offers no 'must-see'. What's interesting is to travel around the island. There are only a few minibuses to Rabil (7km), so count on hiring a vehicle. Your hotel manager may know where to find one. Better, bring a bike (you'll need to bring your own as there is nowhere to rent bikes on the islands) – with the exception of the island's three mountains to the east, the island is fairly flat. One of the best beaches is Santa Mónica on the south-western side.

Places to Stay & Eat

Residencial Bom Sossego (☎ *511155*) charges CVE1500/2000 for singles/doubles with bathroom; CVE1000/1500 without. *Residencial Boa Esperança* (☎ *511170*) has rooms for CVE1200/1400, including breakfast. Both serve meals as does *Bar-Restaurant Rosalita*. The upmarket *Hotel Dunas* (☎ *511225, fax 511384*) charges CVE2350/2700 for singles/doubles with bathroom, balconies facing the ocean and breakfast. Another good place is *Marine Club Boa Vista* (☎ *511285*) on Rua 5 de Julho (CVE5500 with full board).

Getting There & Away

TACV (☎ *511186*) has flights to/from Praia (CVE4428) every day except Friday and to/from Sal five times a week. The *Porto Novo* plies between Praia and Sal-Rei, departing Praia every Thursday at 8 pm and Sal-Rei every Friday at 6 pm. The *Barlavento* stops here, too.

MAIO

Maio (population 5000) is flat and desertlike. You may be the only traveller here and are likely to be well received. It was once an important salt-collecting centre controlled by the British, hence the main city and port, Vila do Maio, is commonly called Porto Inglés. There's a good beach, Bitche Rotche, just outside town. There are no buses but Garage Tote sometimes rents cars (typically CVE3000 a day).

Places to Stay & Eat

Hotel Bom Sossego (☎ *551365, fax 551327*) costs CVE1400/2000 for singles/doubles with hot-water bathrooms. The friendly *Hotel Marilú* (☎ *551347*) has clean singles/doubles with bathrooms for CVE2000/2800. Both offer food (order in advance), or try *Restaurant Mascarenhas*. *Club des Tortues* on a beach 5km from town has attractive stone bungalows; CVE5000 for doubles, and meals are available.

Getting There & Away

TACV (☎ *551256*) has flights to/from Praia (CVE2711) every day except Sunday. The *Porto Novo* ferry departs Praia Tuesdays at 5 am and Vila do Maio Wednesdays at 6 pm.

CAPE VERDE

Côte d'Ivoire

Many developing countries bear little relation to their capitals and Côte d'Ivoire, more developed than most in West Africa, is an extreme example.

In the regions, the people are welcoming and friendly. Culturally diverse, they produce some of the area's finest art such as the haunting masks of the Dan (also known as Yacouba), Baoulé and Senoufo, and the latter's famous Korhogo cloth. It's a land rich in festivals and popular traditions, such as the stilt dances and child juggling of the Man region.

Parc National de la Comoë, in the northern savanna lands, is the largest in West Africa, while Parc National de Taï preserves the country's last significant belt of rainforest. The hills around Man offer some good opportunities for walking. There are fine beaches and fascinating fishing villages on the Atlantic coast, where Grand Bassam, the original colonial capital, maintains a faded charm.

Today, Côte d'Ivoire boasts two capitals. Yamoussoukro, the titular capital, is the birthplace of former president Houphouët-Boigny, and its portentous Basilica, a near replica of St Peter's in Rome, is his final resting place. In a beautiful lagoon setting, Abidjan, known as the 'Paris of West Africa', is the economic capital, and claims all the embassies and ministries and most of the commerce. The skyscrapers, restaurants and boutiques of Le Plateau, the Hôtel Ivoire (West Africa's most famous hotel) and the splendid modern cathedral are in marked contrast to the vibrant popular quarters of Treichville and Adjamé, where migrants from all over Côte d'Ivoire and further afield have made their homes. On the downside, Abidjan comes second to Lagos as the region's most dangerous city (see the boxed text 'Safety Considerations' in the Abidjan section later for more details).

If the twin capitals' cosmopolitan charms leave you cold, simply bypass them. Comfortable long-distance buses run along the excellent network of tar roads, and even the smallest town can offer clean, inexpensive accommodation.

CÔTE D'IVOIRE AT A GLANCE

Capital: Yamoussoukro
Population: 14.7 million
Area: 322,465 sq km
Head of state: President Henri Konan Bédié
Official language: French
Main local languages: Mande, Malinké, Dan, Senoufo, Baoulé, Agni, Dioula
Currency: West African CFA franc
Exchange rate: US$1 = CFA600
Time: GMT/UTC
Country telephone code: ☎ 225
Best time to go: Year-round

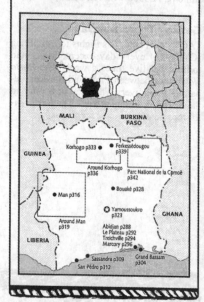

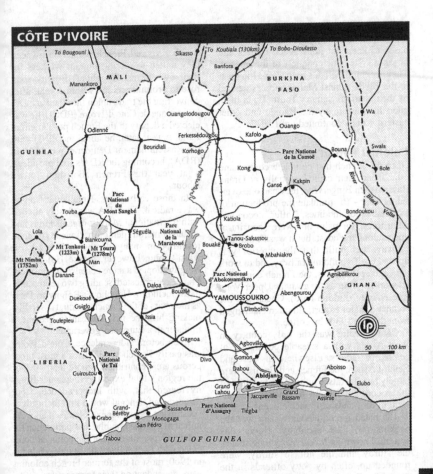

CÔTE D'IVOIRE

Facts about Côte d'Ivoire

HISTORY

The major ethnic groups in Côte d'Ivoire all came relatively recently from neighbouring areas. The Krou (or Kru) people migrated eastward from Liberia around 400 years ago; the Senoufo and Lobi moved southward from Burkina and Mali. It wasn't until the 18th and 19th centuries that the Akan people, including the Baoulé, migrated from Ghana into the eastern area and the Malinké (also called Mandingo) from Guinea moved into the north-west.

The Portuguese were the first Europeans to arrive. Compared with neighbouring Ghana, Côte d'Ivoire suffered little from the slave trade. European slaving and merchant ships preferred other areas along the coast with better harbours. France took no interest until the 1840s when the French, under their king, Louis-Philippe, enticed local chiefs to grant

French commercial traders a monopoly along the coast. Thereafter, the French built naval bases to keep out non-French traders and began a systematic conquest of the interior. They accomplished this only after a long war in the 1890s against Malinké forces headed by the illustrious Samory Touré. Even then, guerrilla warfare by the Baoulé and other eastern groups continued until 1917.

Colonial Period

Once the French had complete control and established their capital, initially at Grand Bassam then Bingerville, they had one over-riding goal – to stimulate the production of exportable commodities. Coffee, cocoa and palm trees (for palm oil) were soon introduced along the coast, but it wasn't until the railway was built that the interior was opened up. To build the railway and to work the cocoa plantations, the French conscripted workers from as far away as Upper Volta (present-day Burkina Faso). Cocoa was the country's major export, although challenged from the late 1930s by coffee.

Côte d'Ivoire was the only country in West Africa with a sizeable population of *colons*, or settlers. Elsewhere in West and Central Africa, the French and English were largely bureaucrats. But here, a good third of the cocoa, coffee and banana plantations were in the hands of French citizens.

The hated forced-labour system was the backbone of the economy. Under this system, known as *la corvée*, young males, the sturdy and the not so sturdy, were rounded up, often by petty officials in the pay of the French and drawn from a neighbouring, antagonistic tribe, and compelled to work on private estates or public sector projects, such as the railway.

Houphouët-Boigny

Born in 1905, the son of a wealthy Baoulé chief, Félix Houphouët-Boigny became Côte d'Ivoire's father of independence. After studying medicine in Dakar, he became a medical assistant, prosperous cocoa farmer and local chief. In 1944, he turned to politics and formed the country's first agricultural

trade union – not of labourers but of African planters. Opposing the colonial policy which favoured French plantation owners, they united to recruit migrant workers for their own farms. Houphouët-Boigny soon rose to prominence and within a year, after converting the trade union into the Parti Démocratique de Côte d'Ivoire (PDCI), he was elected a deputy to the French parliament in Paris. A year later, he allied the PDCI with the Rassemblement Démocratique Africain (RDA), becoming the RDA's first president. That year the French abolished forced labour.

In those early years, Houphouët-Boigny was a radical. The RDA was closely aligned with international Marxist organisations and staged numerous demonstrations in Abidjan, resulting in many deaths and arrests. It wasn't long, however, before Houphouët-Boigny adopted a more conciliatory position. France reciprocated, sending two representatives, including Houphouët-Boigny to Paris as members of the French national assembly, making him the first African to become a minister in a European government.

Even before independence, Côte d'Ivoire was easily French West Africa's most prosperous area, contributing more than 40% of the region's total exports. Houphouët-Boigny feared that, with independence, Côte d'Ivoire and Senegal would find themselves subsidising the poorer ex-colonies if all were united in a single republic. His preference for independence for each of the colonies coincided with French interests; at independence in 1960, most of the former French colonies were dependent on their former ruler.

Independence

Houphouët-Boigny naturally became the country's first president. Leaders throughout Africa offered varying strategies for development. Houphouët-Boigny was at one extreme, favouring continued reliance on the former colonial power.

He was also one of the few leaders who promoted agriculture and gave industrial development a low priority – at least initially. While almost every other African country short-changed the farmer with low produce prices to subsidise industrial development, Houphouët-Boigny's government gave farmers good prices and stimulated production. Coffee production increased significantly, catapulting Côte d'Ivoire into third place behind Brazil and Colombia in total production. By 1979, Côte d'Ivoire had become the world's leading cocoa producer, as well as Africa's leading exporter of pineapples and palm oil. The Ivoirian 'miracle' was foremost an agricultural miracle. In most other African countries, agriculture failed to deliver the goods.

French technicians assisted in the program. In the rest of Africa, Europeans were largely driven out following independence. In Côte d'Ivoire, they poured in. The French community grew from 10,000 to 50,000, mostly teachers and advisers. In 1975, two out of three top managerial personnel were foreigners, mostly French. Critics argued that Houphouët-Boigny had sold out to foreign interests. However, the president was clearly calling all the major shots and, with a strong economy, few Ivoirians complained. For 20 years, the economy maintained an annual growth rate of nearly 10%.

The fruits of growth were widely enjoyed since the focus of development was on farming – the livelihood of some 85% of the people. Another reason was the absence of huge estates; most of the cocoa and coffee production was in the hands of hundreds of thousands of small producers. Literacy rose from 28 to 60% – twice the African average. Electricity reached virtually every town and the road system became the best in Africa, outside South Africa and Nigeria. Still, the numerous Mercedes and the posh African residences in Abidjan's Cocody quarter were testimony to the growing inequality of incomes and the beginnings of a class society.

Politically, Houphouët-Boigny ruled with an iron hand. The press was far from free. Tolerating only one political party, he eliminated opposition by largess – giving his opponents jobs instead of jail sentences. Several half-hearted coup attempts in the early 60s were easily suppressed. All those arrested were eventually released.

Not all investments were wise: Houphouët-Boigny was Africa's No 1 producer of 'show' projects. So much money was poured into his birthplace, Yamoussoukro, that it became the subject of jokes. Many of the state enterprises were terribly managed and corruption was rampant. But since the economy was booming, the government could afford to err.

The Big Slump

The world recession of the early 80s sent shock waves through the Ivoirian economy. The drought of 1983-84 was a second body blow. For four years from 1981 real GNP stagnated or declined. In 1984, the rest of Africa was gleeful as the glittering giant, Abidjan, was brought to its knees for the first time with constant power blackouts. Overlogging finally had an impact and timber revenue slumped. Sugar had been the hope of the north, but world prices collapsed, ruining the huge new sugar-refining complexes there. The country's external debt increased threefold and Côte d'Ivoire had to ask the IMF for debt rescheduling. Rising crime in Abidjan made the news in Europe. The miracle was over.

Houphouët-Boigny slashed government spending and the bureaucracy, revamped some of the poorly managed state enterprises, sent home a third of the expensive French advisers and teachers and, most difficult of all, finally slashed cocoa prices to farmers in 1989 by 50%.

Early 1990s

In 1990, hundreds of civil servants went on strike, joined by students who took to the streets protesting violently, blaming the economic crisis on corruption and the lavish lifestyles of government officials. The unrest was unprecedented in scale and intensity, shattering Houphouët-Boigny's carefully cultivated personality cult and forcing the government to accede to multi-party democracy. The 1990 presidential elections were opened to other parties for the first time; however, Houphouët-Boigny still received 85% of the vote.

Houphouët was becoming increasingly feeble, intensifying the guessing game of who he would appoint as his successor. A master politician, he kept everyone speculating. Finally, in late 1993, after 33 years in power as Côte d'Ivoire's first and only president, 'le Vieux' died at the estimated age of 88. His funeral, which took place at the Basilica in Yamoussoukro, was large and impressive, with many African heads of state in attendance, but only one non-African head of state: France's President Mitterrand, accompanied by a delegation of 80, including virtually the entire cabinet!

Houphouët's silently hand-picked successor was Henri Konan-Bédié, a Baoulé and speaker of the national assembly. (The recently amended constitution conveniently designated the speaker as first in succession.) He was far from universally popular among PDCI party barons. Nevertheless, after some brief political infighting in the days following the funeral with Prime Minister Alassane Ouattara, his main rival, Bédié emerged in complete control and Ouattara resigned.

Côte d'Ivoire Today

Economically, the 'African Elephant', as Ivoirians are fond of referring to their country, is getting back on its feet. Although still dangerously vulnerable to the vicissitudes of world coffee and cocoa prices, the country is seeking to diversify – notably into tourism. The 1994 devaluation of the CFA franc was, on balance, of benefit to Côte d'Ivoire as the leading exporting country in the CFA zone. Inflation is being reined in and growth rates, although much less spectacular than in the boom years, are steady.

On the political front, Bédié achieved further legitimacy in open presidential elections in 1995, receiving 95% of the vote, while his party, the PDCI, won an overwhelming victory in legislative elections over a bickering and fragmented opposition. On the downside, true democracy is stifled

by the application of the 'parenthood clause', which stipulates that both a candidate's parents must be Ivoirian. Bédié plays this marked card to deflect potential opponents. On occasion he has also used more strong-arm tactics, locking up critics, including journalists, who are too vocal.

GEOGRAPHY

Côte d'Ivoire is about the size of Germany or New Mexico. The central area, where most of the coffee and cocoa grows, is a fairly uniform flat or gently undulating plain. The western area around Man is rolling hill country with several peaks over 1000m. In the drier north, the land becomes savanna and sparse woodland, as in the vegetation of Parc National de la Comoë.

Little remains of the dense rainforest which once covered most of the southern half of the country. The residue is mostly confined to the south-west, inland from the coast and towards the border with Liberia, including the spectacular Parc National de Taï.

A unique coastal lagoon with its own ecosytem stretches from the Ghanaian border westward for nearly 300km.

CLIMATE

In the south, the rains fall heaviest from May to October, with a dry interlude in August and early September. In the drier northern half, the rainy season extends from late May to early October, with no August dry spell. The south is humid, but temperatures rarely rise above 32°C. In the north, from early December to February, when

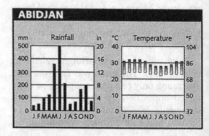

midday maximums are regularly above 35°C, the harmattan blows in from the Sahara and greatly reduces visibility.

FLORA & FAUNA

The northern part of the country is typical savanna grassland interspersed with acacia and other bushes and trees. Further south, the predominant indigenous tree, large and fronded, its fruit dangling like hand grenades, is the mango. The most evident varieties across a wide band in the south, coffee and cocoa, have both been introduced. In the south-east and south-west are massive groves of native palm, tapped for its oil, of which Côte d'Ivoire is the world's second-biggest producer after Malaysia. The last remaining primary forest is in the south-west.

In the Parc National de Taï, where poaching has been successfully controlled, species of rainforest animals, absent for decades, are returning. The Parc National de la Comoë is the best place to observe the birds and animals of the savanna.

ECOLOGY & ENVIRONMENT

The major threat to Côte d'Ivoire's diverse flora and fauna is the expansion of agricultural lands: from 3.1 million hectares in 1965 to nearly eight million in 1995. The rainforests are being cut down at a tragic rate; between 1977 and 1987 Côte d'Ivoire lost 42% of its forest and woodland – the highest loss in the world. The corresponding figures for neighbouring Ghana and Liberia, for example, were 8% and 0%, respectively; for Brazil it was 4%. Since the late 1980s, the volume of timber exports has declined by about one-third, but hardwood exports are still on a level with those of Brazil, a country over 20 times larger. The timber industry is one of the culprits; hundreds of logs float in the lagoon around Abidjan and ships are loaded wood, including mahogany, samba, sipo, bété and iroko, for export.

GOVERNMENT & POLITICS

The head of state and commander in chief of the military is the president, who is elected by universal suffrage every five years. The president in turn appoints a council of ministers, including the prime minister. The legislature consists of a national assembly whose 175 members are also popularly elected to five-year terms. The speaker of the assembly is authorised to assume the presidency in case of the president's death. The ruling party, the PDCI, has operated for many decades, but multipartyism has existed only since 1990. There are now some 40 officially recognised opposition parties, the main ones being the Front Populaire d'Ivoire (FPI), the Parti Ivoirien des Travailleurs (PIT) and the Rassemblement des Républicains (RDR).

Conservation & Ecotourism: the Taï Example

The Parc National de Taï team have had remarkable success in preserving West Africa's largest rainforest from further destruction. The key has been to give those who previously made a living from forest resources a stake in its development. An element of the revenue from tourism is used to improve the quality of life of villagers by, for example, setting up a primary health-care centre, improving drinking water and providing veterinary support for livestock. In Guiroutou, the villagers are being encouraged to share in the controlled development of tourism as owners of cafes and planned rural accommodation.

As a result, logging and encroachment by small landholders has ceased and poaching, controlled also by much stricter surveillance, has diminished significantly. Hunters turned gamekeepers, the locals actively help in repelling the main threat: poachers who slip over the border from neighbouring Liberia.

CÔTE D'IVOIRE

ECONOMY

In the agricultural sector, Côte d'Ivoire rates many superlatives – largest producer of cocoa in the world, largest producer of coffee in Africa (and third largest in the world) and largest producer of cotton in Francophone Africa. However, despite serious efforts at diversification (palm oil, rubber, bananas and pineapples in the south, and sugar cane and cotton in the north), coffee and cocoa still represent more than half of export earnings – about the same as in 1960. As a result of the collapse of these commodities on world markets in the early 1980s, Côte d'Ivoire has become the world's largest debtor on a per capita basis.

The rude shock of the CFA devaluation did little for the debt problem but gave a spurt to the economy, resulting in a positive growth rate in 1994, the first in years. This rose to 7% in 1996, thanks to good coffee and cocoa harvests and stable world prices.

The infrastructure, the fruit of investment when times were good, is there and functioning. There are nearly 4000km of well maintained tar road, linking all major towns, the inter-urban transport system is good and electricity reaches significantly more of the rural community than anywhere else in West Africa.

One bright prospect is the rise of oil and gas production. Two new offshore oil and gas fields are expected to make the country self-sufficient in both. The fuel has begun to flow but it's unlikely that it will ever be a bonanza. For the foreseeable future, Côte d'Ivoire, although diversifying, will remain vulnerable to world prices for its two primary products, cocoa and coffee.

POPULATION & PEOPLE

There are more than 60 ethnic groups among the country's 14.7 million people. They divide into four principal groupings. The Akan (Baoulé and Agni primarily) live in the eastern and central areas and constitute about 35% of the population. The largest single group of Akan is the Baoulé (around 20% of the population), who separated from the Ashanti in Ghana around 1750 and mi-

grated west into the central area. The Krou ethnic group originated from present-day Liberia and Ghana. The Bété are its most numerous subgroup and, at about 18% of the population, the second-largest ethnic group in the country. The Voltaic group includes the Senoufo, animists and renowned artisans who live in the north around Korhogo, and the Lobi, who transcend the borders with Burkina Faso and Ghana.

Finally, the Mande, who live in the north and west, include the Malinké, numerous around Odienné, and the Dan, renowned for their impressive masks and dancers on stilts, who inhabit the mountainous region around Man.

See also the colour feature between pages 304 and 305 for more information on the main people groups of Côte d'Ivoire.

There are also some 30,000 French, more than 100,000 Lebanese, and immigrants, from all over West Africa, including an estimated two million from Burkina Faso.

ARTS
Art & Craftwork

The art of Côte d'Ivoire is among the most outstanding in West Africa. Three groups stand out – the Baoulé, the Dan and the Senoufo. Among the traditional arts that are especially prized are Korhogo cloth (for more details, see the boxed text 'Korhogo Cloth' in the Korhogo section later in this chapter), from the north, Dan masks of wood or copper from the Man region, traditional musical instruments in wood, bronze pots for unguents and creams and Senoufo statues. Although nowadays almost entirely factory produced, *pagnes*, the dazzling, brightly coloured lengths of cloth which the women wear, reflect popular colour combinations and designs, even though healthy experimentation is also rife.

Literature

The doyen of Côte d'Ivoire's literature is Bernard Dadié, who is credited with writing the country's first play, first poetry anthology and first collection of short stories in French. He has a warm, simple style, even

Art of Côte d'Ivoire

If you're looking for masks or woodcarvings, Côte d'Ivoire is a good place to come.

Dan masks, which demonstrate a high regard for symmetry and balance, are a good example of expressiveness achieved primarily through form. Traditionally, they were often carved spontaneously, inspired perhaps by a beautiful face. The most common mask is that of a human face, slightly abstract but with realistic features, a smooth surface, protruding lips, slit or large circular eyeholes and calm expression. These masks often have specific uses; a mask representing a woman, for example, is used to prevent women from seeing uncircumcised boys during their initiation into adulthood.

Other common Dan carvings include large spoons for serving rice; such spoons typically rest upon two legs of human form.

Baoulé masks typically represent an animal or a human face. The facial masks, traditionally used in commemorative ceremonies, are very realistic. They are often intended to portray particular individuals who can be recognised by their facial marks and hairstyles. Other Baoulé masks, however, are far from realistic. The *kplekple* horned mask, for example, represents a forest demon and is very stylised. The same is true of the painted antelope and buffalo masks, called *goli*, which have large open mouths and are intended to represent bush spirits.

The Baoulé also carve figures of individuals and spirits. These often incorporate fine details and a shiny black patina. Baoulé carvings called *colon* representing a person wearing European-style clothing are sold all over West Africa. Current opinion is that, far from portraying a colonial official, such figures represent a person's other world mate – *blolo bian* for men and *blolo bla* for women. Of course these days most are carved for the tourist trade and not necessarily by a Baoulé carver.

Senoufo masks are highly stylised, like the animal masks of the Baoulé. The most famous perhaps is the 'fire-spitter' helmet mask, which is a combination of antelope, warthog and hyena. Powerful and scary, it is said to represent the chaotic state of things in primeval times. The human face masks, on the other hand, can often have a very serene expression. One that you'll see everywhere in the tourist markets is the *kpelie* mask which features a highly stylised hairdo, thin eyes, small round mouth, various facial markings and two horns. The Senoufo also carve a great variety of statues, mostly female, which are used in divination and other sacred rituals.

when expressing his dissatisfactions. One of his first novels, published in 1970, is *Climbié*, an autobiographical account of his childhood. Other works translated into English include *The Black Cloth* (1987) and *The City Where No One Dies* (1986).

Aké Loba is best known for *Kocoumbo* (abstracted in *African Writing Today*, 1967), an autobiographical novel of an impecunious, uprooted African in Paris being drawn towards militant communism. Ahmadou Kourouma's first hit novel was *The Suns of Independence* (1981), the wry, humorous story of a disgruntled village chief, deposed following independence. His second novel, *Monné, Outrages et Défi*, written in 1990 after 22 years of silence and yet to be translated into English, took that year's Grand Prix Littéraire d'Afrique Noire – Francophone Africa's premier literary prize.

Among younger writers, Bandama Maurice won the same honour in 1993 for his novel *Le Fils de la Femme Mâle*. Two novelists and poets who are also widely read throughout Francophone Africa are Véronique Tadjo and Tanella Boni.

CÔTE D'IVOIRE

Music

Côte d'Ivoire's best known musical export is Alpha Blondy, whose reggae style has achieved considerable international success. An early great, and probably his best recording, is *Apartheid is Nazism*. Other reggae stars are Serge Kassy, Ismael Isaac and Tiken Jah Fahkoly. Top female vocalists include Aïcha Koné, Monique Seka and Nayanka Bell. Gadji Celi plays more traditional Ivoirian music. Les Salopards and Les Poussins Chic, with their right-on, in-your-face lyrics, surged from the popular quarters of Abidjan.

Other Ivoirian stars include the late Ernesto Djedje, whose cassette *Zigblithy* is superb. Good jazz combos include Les Woody and Groupe Awana. Last but not least, listen for Meiway, guaranteed to set the hips swaying.

RELIGION

Although the country has two of the largest Catholic cathedrals in the world, only about 12% of the people are Christian, including Protestant and some peculiarly African sects. One particularly interesting 'born-again' amalgam of Christianity and tradition is the faith of the Harristes, a sect founded by William Wade Harris, who was born in Liberia in 1915. Some 23%, mostly the Malinké and Dioula, are Muslims, living primarily in the north. The remaining 65% of the people practise traditional religions based upon ancestral worship.

LANGUAGE

French is the official language. Principal African languages include Mande and Malinké in the north-west, Dan (in the area around Man), Senoufo (in and around Korhogo), Baoulé and Agni in the centre and south – and Dioula, the market language everywhere. See the Language chapter for a list of useful phrases in French, Dioula, Senoufo and Dan (Yacouba).

Facts for the Visitor

SUGGESTED ITINERARIES

If you arrive direct from the developed world, consider saving Abidjan until last. That way, you'll appreciate its uniqueness in an African context.

If you're visiting Côte d'Ivoire for only a week – the minimum to get anything from it – plan on a couple of days in Abidjan, followed by two in one of the west coast resorts, such as Sassandra, before heading north to Yamoussoukro (one night), with its amazing Basilica, then back to Abidjan.

With three weeks or more at your disposal, we suggest a pentagon-shaped tour, embracing the beaches and fishing villages of the Atlantic coast, culturally rich Man and Korhogo, Yamoussoukro, then back to Abidjan. If your time's more limited, you can easily select from this menu.

Before leaving Abidjan, spend a day or, better, stay overnight in the old colonial capital of Grand Bassam. Then head along the coast westwards. If you have transport and an ample budget, consider cosseting yourself for a day or two at the luxury hotels in Monogaga or Grand-Béréby. If you're travelling independently, aim for Sassandra or one of the basic, Robinson Crusoe beach camps to its west (three days). Nature lovers should build in a visit to Parc National de Taï, for which you need to make arrangements in San Pédro – allow three days. From San Pédro, swing north to Man, the base for visiting some of the nearby villages of the Dan people, and the surrounding hills, ideal for a spot of hiking (three to four days). Then on to Korhogo which merits another three to four days as you explore the nearby villages of the Senoufo people.

Korhogo is also the base for visiting, in December to May, Parc National de la Comoë (three days or more, including travelling time). From Korhogo, head south to Yamoussoukro, the titular capital (one or two nights), then back to Abidjan to soak up the remaining days at your disposal.

If you're worried by Abidjan's justified reputation for crime, simply bypass it –

HIGHLIGHTS

Beaches & Fishing Villages

Sassandra *(West Coast)*
An interesting Fanti fishing village in its own right and a good base for exploring the magnificent beaches to its west.

West Coast
Superb beaches at Monogaga and Grand-Béréby, great surfing at Grand Lahou and a fascinating fishing village on stilts at Tiégba.

Assinie *(East Coast)*
Perhaps the best beaches on the Ivoirian coast. A favourite with European package tours.

Natural Features & National Parks

Parc National de Taï *(West Coast)*
A fine example of controlled ecotourism within Côte d'Ivoire's largest remaining rainforest.

Parc National de la Comoë *(The North)*
Encompassing savanna and forest; Comoë is particularly rich in birdlife.

La Dent de Man & Mt Tonkoui
(West Coast)
A pair of challenging hills; spectacular views from the summit reward a strenuous ascent of La Dent, and the panorama from Mt Tonkoui is even better.

People & Culture

Senoufo *(The North)*
Around Korhogo, you can see traditional potters, blacksmiths, basket weavers and painters of Korhogo cloth; also masked dances.

Dan/Yacouba *(The West)*
Man is a good base for exploring the fascinating Dan villages and seeing masked dances.

Museums

Musée National *(Abidjan)*
With more than 20,000 items of varying quality, the quantity can be overwhelming – be selective.

Adja Swa Museum *(The Centre)*
In Yamoussoukro, this small, excellently documented private museum has pieces from around the country.

Péléfero Gbon Coulibaly Museum
(The North)
This small museum of Senoufo art and artefacts in Korhogo is well worth visiting.

Markets & Craftwork

Marché de Cocody *(Abidjan)*
With handicrafts from all over West Africa, and particularly good for beads and textiles.

Centre Artisanal, Korhogo *(The North)*
A wide range of Senoufo artefacts – it's a co-operative so you know your money is going in the right direction.

Architecture

Basilica, Yamoussoukro *(The Centre)*
Love it or hate it, you won't fail to react to this near clone of St Peter's in Rome; don't miss the breathtaking stained glass windows.

Cathédrale St Paul *(Abidjan)*
Daring and innovative, its tower is a stylised St Paul and the nave his trailing robes.

Le Plateau *(Abidjan)*
Architectural highlights include La Pyramide and the chunky, copper-coloured towers of the Cité Administrative.

Grand Bassam *(East Coast)*
A walk around the Vieux Quartier will give you a feel of what the original colonial settlement was like.

Food

Maquis
Côte d'Ivoire's contribution to eating out in West Africa. Try the chicken kedjenou, almost a national dish, with attiéké, grated cassava.

CÔTE D'IVOIRE

you'll still have a stimulating stay in Franco-phone Africa's culturally richest country.

PLANNING

Since the intercity roads are all tar, the rains shouldn't impede your travels too much. However, it's probably best to avoid the heaviest downpours during May, June and July.

The Michelin 1:800,000 map (No 957) gives the best coverage of Côte d'Ivoire. There's no decent map of Abidjan. Don't bother to buy the only available one of Abidjan (*Plan d'Abidjan* by Éditions A Benois) since it's impossible to read or to navigate by. Indeed, many local expats cheekily photocopy the one in this book!

VISAS & DOCUMENTS
Visas

Everyone except nationals of ECOWAS countries needs a visa, although US nationals don't need one for stays of less than 90 days. Visas are usually valid for three months and are good for visits of up to one month. The cost varies quite substantially depending on your nationality and where you are applying for it.

Visa Extensions Visas can be extended at the police headquarters near the main post office in Abidjan. An extension, valid for up to three months, costs CFA14,000 (plus two photos) and is ready the same day if you apply early. The visa section is open from 8 am to noon and 3 to 5 pm on weekdays.

Other Documents

A yellow fever vaccination certificate is mandatory.

EMBASSIES & CONSULATES
Côte d'Ivoire Embassies & Consulates

In West Africa, Côte d'Ivoire has embassies or consulates in Burkina Faso, Ghana, Nigeria and Senegal. For more details, see the Facts for the Visitor section of the relevant country chapter.

Elsewhere, embassies include the following:

Belgium
  (☎ 02-672 23 57)
  234 ave Franklin-Roosevelt, Brussels 1050
France
  (☎ 01 53 64 62 62)
  102 ave R-Poincaré, 75116 Paris
Germany
  (☎ 0228-21 20 98)
  Königstrasse 93, 53115 Bonn
UK
  (☎ 0171-235 6991; from 22 April 2000 ☎ 020-7235 6991)
  2 Upper Belgrave St, London SW1X 8BJ
USA
  (☎ 202-797 0330)
  2424 Massachusetts Ave, NW, Washington, DC 20008

Embassies & Consulates in Côte d'Ivoire

Embassies and consulates in Abidjan, mostly in Le Plateau district unless otherwise indicated, include the following:

Benin
  (☎ 41 44 13)
  Rue des Jardins, Les Deux Plateaux
Burkina Faso
  (☎ 21 13 13)
  2 Ave Terrasson de Fougères
France
  (☎ 20 05 05)
  Rue Lecoeur
Germany
  (☎ 21 47 27)
  Immeuble le Mans, Rue Botreau-Roussel
Ghana
  (☎ 33 11 24)
  Résidence la Corniche, Blvd du Général de Gaulle
Guinea
  (☎ 22 25 20)
  Immeuble Crosson Duplessis, Ave Crosson Duplessis
Liberia
  (☎ 33 12 28)
  Immeuble Taleb, Ave Delafosse
Mali
  (☎ 32 31 47)
  Maison du Mali, Rue du Commerce

Visas for Onward Travel

In Côte d'Ivoire, you can get visas for the following neighbouring countries. Note that the UK embassy issues visas to Sierra Leone and Kenya, and the French embassy issues visas to Togo.

Burkina Faso

Three-month visas cost CFA13,000 and are issued within 24 hours. The consulate is open from 8 am to 2.30 pm. The small consulate in Bouaké (☎ 63 44 31) also issues visas.

Ghana

Visa applications only accepted from 8.30 am to 1 pm on Monday, Wednesday and Friday. It requires four photos, CFA12,000 and 48 hours to issue visas.

Guinea

The consulate is open from 9 am to 3 pm. One-month visas cost CFA20,000 for all except US nationals, who pay CFA32,500. You need three photos and visas are issued within 48 hours.

Liberia

Three-month visas, issued the same day, cost CFA20,000 for most nationalities and CFA25,000/30,000 for US/UK citizens. The embassy's open from 9 am to 12.30 pm and 1.30 to 4 pm.

Mali

One-month visas cost CFA10,000 (issued within 24 hours). The embassy is open from 8 am to 12.30 pm and 2.30 to 4 pm.

Niger
(☎ 26 28 14)
Blvd Achalme, Marcory

Nigeria
(☎ 21 19 82)
Blvd de la République

Senegal
(☎ 33 28 76)
Immeuble Nabil, off Rue du Commerce

UK
(☎ 22 68 50)
Immeuble les Harmonies, Blvd Carde
USA
(☎ 21 09 79)
5 Rue Jesse Owens

Canada, Germany, Japan and the Netherlands also have embassies in Abidjan.

MONEY

The unit of currency is the CFA franc.

Euro €1	=	CFA660
1FF	=	CFA100
UK£1	=	CFA950
US$1	=	CFA600

Banks for changing money include, in Abidjan, Citibank and COBACI (previously Barclays; it's particularly swift and operates extended banking hours from 8 am to 3 pm) and, nationwide, BICICI (Banque Internationale pour le Commerce et l'Industrie en Côte d'Ivoire), BIAO (Banque Internationale pour l'Afrique Occidentale), SGBCI (Société Génerale de Banques en Côte d'Ivoire) and SIB (Société Ivoirienne de Banque). In Abidjan, only banks in Le Plateau will change money. In the provinces, most banks will only accept French francs and, sometimes, US$. The commission charged, like the rate of exchange, varies significantly from bank to bank; SGBCI, for example, imposes a fee of CFA2500 on notes and CFA3750 on travellers cheques, whatever quantity you change.

Banks are equally cavalier about which travellers cheques they'll accept. BIAO, SGBCI and COBACI honour Thomas Cook travellers cheques, while Citibank, BICICI and SGBCI accept American Express. COBACI will give a cash advance against both Visa and MasterCard and SGBCI against Visa.

POST & COMMUNICATIONS

Post offices in Côte d'Ivoire are easy to recognise; they're all painted blue and white and are called SIPE (Société Ivoirienne de la

CÔTE D'IVOIRE

Poste et de l'Épargne). An air mail letter costs CFA280 to Europe, CFA400 to the USA and CFA750 to Australia.

International telephone calls and faxes can be made from CI Telecom offices in major towns. A three minute call costs CFA3500 to the UK, CFA4000 to the USA and CFA5000 to Australia (there's a cheaper off-peak rate for the US and UK). Phonecards are handy for local and international calls. Cards with 20/50/150 units cost CFA 1500/3500/11,000.

The local dial-in number for the American AT&T chargecard is ☎ 00 111 11 and for the British BT chargecard, ☎ 00 111 14.

NEWSPAPERS

The main government newspaper is *Fraternité Matin*, while *La Voie* is very much the mouthpiece of the opposition FPI party. *Le Jour* steers an independent course between the two.

HEALTH

You will need to have a yellow fever vaccination certificate to enter the country. Malaria risk exists throughout the country, year-round, so you should take appropriate precautions. For more information on these and other health matters, see the Health section in the Regional Facts for the Visitor chapter.

There are a couple of good clinics in Abidjan – see Information in the Abidjan section later for more details. The hospital in Ferkessédougou, run by Baptist missionaries, is excellent.

WOMEN TRAVELLERS

With the possible exception of the few coastal resorts which are becoming package tour favourites, women travellers are unlikely to meet hassle, provided that they dress with the decorum that the locals observe. For more general information and advice, see the Women Travellers section in the Regional Facts for the Visitor chapter.

DANGERS & ANNOYANCES

For the capital's special security risks, see the boxed text 'Safety Considerations' in the Abidjan section. Abidjan apart, the rest of Côte d'Ivoire, including its provincial cities, is as safe as anywhere else in West Africa.

The Atlantic has fierce currents and a ripping undertow and every year there are several drownings, often of strong, overly confident swimmers.

BUSINESS HOURS

Business hours are from 8 am to noon and 2.30 to 6 pm weekdays, and mornings only on Saturday. Government offices are open from 7.30 am to noon and 2.30 to 5.30 pm weekdays. Banking hours are from 8 to 11.15 am and 2.45 to 4.30 pm weekdays.

PUBLIC HOLIDAYS & SPECIAL EVENTS

Public holidays are held on 1 January (New Year's Day), 1 May (Labour Day), 28 May (Mothers' Day), 7 August (Independence Day), 15 August (Assumption), 1 November (All Saints), 15 November (Fête de la Paix), 7 December (National Day), 25 December (Christmas Day), Easter Monday, Ascension Day and Whit Monday. Various Islamic holidays are also celebrated – for a table of estimated dates for these holidays, see the Public Holidays & Special Events section in the Regional Facts for the Visitor chapter.

Côte d'Ivoire is rich in festivals. Some particularly exuberant ones are the masked

Table Football

If you want an instant icebreaker in Côte d'Ivoire, hone your skills at table football – known here, as throughout the Francophone world, as *babyfoot*. At even the most modest wayside halt, you'll find a battered, much abused table, the colours of the rival teams all but effaced, surrounded by a buzz of players, spectators and self-appointed advisers.

dances, *fêtes des masques*, in the villages around Man during February. Others include the Fête de l'Abissa in Grand Bassam (late October or early November), the Fête des Harristes in Bregbo near Bingerville 15km east of Abidjan (1 November), the carnival in Bouaké (March), the Fête de Papa Nouveau at Toukouzou near Jacqueville (12 September) and the Fête du Dipri, held each March or April in Gomon, 100km north-west of Abidjan.

ACTIVITIES

The area around Man is good for hiking. For swimming, there are unlimited possibilities all along the coast (see the sections on the East Coast and West Coast later in this chapter for details of the best beaches). Grand Lahou has great potential for surfing.

Côte d'Ivoire isn't particularly rich for birdwatchers, although it's worth polishing your binoculars before visiting Taï and Comoë national parks or the last remaining coastal rainforest around San Pédro.

ACCOMMODATION

In Abidjan, you can find a clean, basic room with fan from CFA4000 and one with air-con and bathroom from CFA6000. There's a good selection of mid-range hotels for between CFA8000 and CFA15,000.

Outside Abidjan, rates are slightly lower, although the choice, of course, is much more restricted.

FOOD

There are three staples in Ivoirian cooking: rice, *foutou* and *attiéké*. Foutou is a dough of boiled yam, cassava or plantain, pounded into a sticky paste similar to mashed potato and so glutinous that it sticks to your palate. Attiéké is grated cassava with a subtle taste and texture very like couscous.

They're invariably served with a sauce, such as *sauce arachide* made with ground-nuts (peanuts), a hot *sauce graine* made with palm oil nuts, *sauce aubergine* (eggplant), or *sauce gombo* and *sauce djoumgbré*, both with a base of okra (ladies' fingers). *Aloco*, which is a dish of ripe bananas fried with

Maquis

The *maquis* is Côte d'Ivoire's great contribution to eating in West Africa. Much copied by the country's Francophone neighbours, a typical maquis is a reasonably priced open-air restaurant where you eat under a thatched *paillote*. At lunch time, those that open (many open only in the evening) usually offer a few sauces with globs of meat or fish accompanied by some form of carbohydrate, usually rice, bread or attiéké. In the evenings, the grills sizzle with meat, fish or poultry, normally served smothered in an onion and tomato salad.

chilli in palm oil, is a popular street food. *Kedjenou* – chicken simmered with vegetables in a mild sauce and usually served in an attractive earthenware pot – is almost a national dish. Many restaurants will serve you a whole chicken unless you specify that you only want half.

DRINKS

Fizzy drinks are widely available. Youki Soda, a slightly sweeter version of tonic water, is a good thirst quencher. *Bandji* is the local palm wine, which is especially palatable when it's freshly tapped. Distilled, it makes a skull-shattering spirit known as *koutoukou*.

The standard beer is Bock Solibra, which locals order by asking for 'une soixante-six', a 660mL bottle. If you've a real thirst, go for *une grosse bière*, a hefty 1L bottle. For a premium beer, call for a locally brewed Tuborg, or try a Flag or its smaller brother, Flagette.

Getting There & Away

AIR

The main international airport is in Abidjan, at Port Bouët on the south side of town. The main airlines serving the country are Air Afrique and Air France.

There's a departure tax of CFA3000 on international flights. When you buy your ticket or reconfirm your flight, check whether this is included in the ticket price.

Europe & the USA

The standard one way fare to Europe is about CFA350,000. Both Air Afrique and Air France have daily flights to Paris. Sabena flies to Brussels and KLM-Royal Dutch Airlines to Amsterdam, both twice weekly, while Swissair has three flights a week to Zürich. British Airways has a twice weekly flight to London.

A cheaper and, as a result, often fully booked alternative is TAP Air Portugal which has one weekly flight to Lisbon. The cheapest option is by Corsair which has a weekly flight to/from Lyon and Paris for CFA186,000. From Paris, its flights to Abidjan cost between 1700FF and 2050FF, except during the peak months of July and August.

Between New York and Abidjan, Air Afrique has a few flights a week. The cheapest way to/from Australia is by EgyptAir, with a change of planes in Cairo.

Africa

Air Afrique serves most capitals in West and Central Africa. Air Ivoire has two flights a week to Bamako (Mali), Conakry (Guinea), Monrovia (Liberia) and Ouagadougou (Burkina Faso). It's about 20% cheaper than the giants, as are other small national airlines, such as Air Burkina and Air Mali.

There are daily flights between Abidjan and Accra (Ghana), Bamako, Conakry, Dakar (Senegal), Lagos (Nigeria), Lomé (Togo) and Ouagadougou,. There are also at least four flights a week between Abidjan and Banjul (Gambia), Cotonou (Benin), Freetown (Sierra Leone), Monrovia and Niamey (Niger).

Ethiopian Airlines has four flights a week to Addis Ababa, all via Nairobi. EgyptAir flies twice weekly to Cairo, and Middle

East Airlines (MEA) once a week to Beirut (Lebanon).

Abidjan and Johannesburg (South Africa) are linked four times a week by South African Airways, twice by Air Afrique and once by Air Gabon.

LAND
Burkina Faso

Bus & Bush Taxi From Abidjan to Ouagadougou, the routes are tar all the way. The border with Burkina Faso closes around 6.30 pm and reopens at 8 am.

Large *cars* (buses) depart daily from Abidjan, Yamoussoukro and Bouaké for Bobo-Dioulasso and Ouagadougou. Bus companies include Sans Frontière with three departures a day, and UTB with one.

The trip from Abidjan to Ouagadougou (1175km, CFA14,500) takes at least 24 hours – much more if the bus overnights at the border, which closes at 6.30 pm and where lodging is available. The fare from Yamoussoukro (925km) to Ouagadougou is CFA13,500 and CFA12,000 from Ferkessédougou (585km).

From Ferkessédougou, it's better to take a bush taxi to Bobo-Dioulasso (230km, five hours, CFA6000) or on to Ouagadougou (CFA8000) as the bush taxi passes through border controls more swiftly than a bus. A Peugeot 504 direct to Ouagadougou from Abidjan is CFA15,000 and CFA14,000 from Bouaké or Yamoussoukro.

Train The optimistically named express leaves the Treichville train station in Abidjan on Tuesday, Thursday and Saturday morning and arrives in Ouagadougou about 25 hours later. The 1st/2nd class fare is CFA16,700/12,500 to Bobo-Dioulasso

Border Crossings

The main land border crossings are north of Ouangolodougou for Mali and Burkina Faso, Elubo for Ghana and west of Danané for Guinea and Liberia.

(18 hours) and CFA24,000/17,500 to Ouagadougou. Only snacks and drinks are available, although you can buy food and drink from vendors at stops en route.

This once-stylish train continues to deteriorate. All the same, don't discount undertaking an element of the trip by rail – for instance the trans-frontier leg, between Bouaké or Ferkessédougou and Banfora or Bobo-Dioulasso. The scenery is attractive and, on those occasions when the train's in motion, it fairly hurtles along.

Ghana

The coastal road connecting Abidjan and Accra is all tar and in good condition.

The best bus service is STIF's Ecowas Express, recently introduced, which will probably settle down to three runs a week between Abidjan and Accra (550km). It's far superior to the Ghanaian STC bus which runs daily, except Sunday, from its bus station south of Treichville. Leaving in principle – but rarely in practice – at 8 am, it arrives 12 to 14 hours later depending on the delay at the border, which is always long and tedious. The fare is CFA8500 plus CFA500 for luggage and a whip-round at the border to cover bribes to border officials, for which the going rate is about CFA1000. Tickets must be purchased the day before departure.

It's cheaper and faster to take a bush taxi from the Gare de Bassam in Abidjan to Takoradi in Ghana (about CFA4000), from where there are frequent connections to Accra.

You can also travel from Abidjan to Kumasi (555km) in Ghana via Agnibilékrou. There are no direct buses, but you can do the journey in stages from Abidjan to Abengourou, then on to the border. Don't forget to collect an exit stamp from the police/immigration at Agnibilékrou. From the Ghanaian border there are taxis heading to Kumasi.

On the northernmost route from Ferkessédougou to Bole (370km), taxis go from Ferkessédougou to Bouna (eight to 12 hours, CFA7500) and from there to the border with Ghana (CFA1000). From the border, there's a canoe that will take you across the Black Volta River for a standard fee. On the far bank are moneychangers (change enough to get yourself to Tamale) and minibuses for Bole (39km). In Bole, there's a cheap grubby motel without electricity or running water. A daily bus leaves there for Tamale at 6 am.

Guinea

A taxi or minibus from Danané will drop you at the border (50km, 1½ hours, CFA 2500), which is open 24 hours, from where you can catch transport to Lola (35km) and on to N'zérékoré (45km). Be sure to get your passport stamped at the police commissariat in Danané.

An alternative route goes via Odienné and Kankan, but this is in poor condition and infrequently travelled. You will probably have to hitch a ride with a truck. Allow two days.

Liberia

Since the situation in Liberia is unstable, check first in Abidjan and again with the police *commissariat* in Danané to find out if the border is open and whether it's safe to travel.

The main route into Liberia is from Danané to Sanniquellie (90km) via Kahnple. You should be able to get a minibus from Danané to the border (1½ hours, CFA1000) and a taxi on the other side.

The unpaved section between Man and Ganta (Liberia) is in good condition and driveable year-round. You can also go along the Ivoirian coast to Tabou and proceed to Harper, just over the frontier. From Harper, cut inland to Zwedru, Tapeta and Ganta. This route takes three to four days and only expert drivers with 4WD vehicles should attempt it from May to November, when the Liberian section becomes very muddy.

Mali

From Abidjan to Bamako, the routes are tar all the way. The border with Mali closes around 6.30 pm and reopens at 8 am.

There are several buses a week from Abidjan to Bamako, going via Sikasso and Bougouni, but few travellers do this long,

Bus Routes & Fares

from	to	distance	duration	fare (CFA)	bus company & station
Abidjan					
	Aboisso	120km	2 hours	1000	STA from Gare Routiére d'Adjamé or Gare de Bassam
	Bouaké	355km	5 hours	3000	STIF or UTB from Gare Routiére d'Adjamé
	Ferkessédougou	590km	9 hours	4000	CTM, TBO or UTRAFER from Gare Routiére d'Adjamé
	Grand-Bassam	45km	45 mins	500	UTAB from Gare Routiére d'Adjamé via Gare de Bassam from where minibuses and bush taxis also leave
	Korhogo	640km	10 hours	4000	CK, CTK or DB from Gare Routiére d'Adjamé
	Man	580km	9 hours	4000	Fandaso, BAN, Tramoci or CTM from Gare Routiére d'Adjamé
	Sassandra	260km	5 hours	2500	ETS or SKT from Adjamé
	Yamoussoukro	200km	3 hours	2000	UTB or YT buses from Gare Routiére d'Adjamé
Korhogo					
	Bouaké	285km	5 hours	2500	DB or CK opposite the Grand Marché
	Ferkessédougou	55km	1 hour	1000	TBO or minibus from Agip station
	Odienné	235km	5 hours	3500	postal van from post office daily (except Sunday) at 8 am
Odienné					
	Man	275km	5 hours	3000	one minibus/bush taxi daily or the 7 am daily (except Sunday) postal van from behind the post office
Yamoussoukro					
	Man	330km	6 hours	3500	CTM or STIF, from the depot on Ave Houphouët-Boigny

tedious two day journey in one hit. The fare to Bamako is CFA15,000.

Minibuses make the journey from Ferkessédougou to Bamako (CFA8000). There is a more frequent service as far as the frontier, beyond which you can pick up another vehicle for Sikasso (CFA4000). There's only one bus a week between Odienné and Bamako (CFA5000) and traffic is very light

on the trans-border road between Odienné and Bougouni.

Getting Around

AIR

Prices of internal flights are reasonable. From Abidjan, Air Ivoire flies three times a week to Korhogo (CFA22,000), Man

(CFA24,000) and Bouaké (CFA20,000). As we went to press, a new airline, Air Continental, had started to operate within Côte d'Ivoire, with return flights from Abidjan to Korhogo for CFA86,000, to Bouaké for CFA70,000 and to San Pédro for CFA86,000.

There's a departure tax of CFA800 on domestic flights.

BUS

The country's large, modern buses *(cars)* are slightly cheaper and significantly more comfortable than bush taxis. Most have fixed departure times and don't charge extra for luggage. The table shows journey times, typical fares and bus companies for routes between selected towns.

BUSH TAXI & MINIBUS

Bush taxis (ageing Peugeot 504s or covered pick-ups, known as *bâchés*) and minibuses cover major towns and outlying communities not served by the large buses. Their main advantage is that they leave at all hours of the day and not at a fixed departure time. In general, their fares are slightly higher than those of buses.

TRAIN

The northbound express for Ouagadougou leaves Abidjan's Treichville station on Tuesday, Thursday and Saturday morning. It's slower than bus or bush taxi and it bypasses Yamoussoukro. The 1st/2nd class fare to Bouaké (6½ hours) is CFA6700/4800 and, to Ferkessédougou, CFA11,800/8600. You're better off in every sense on the bus.

CAR

Petrol costs CFA385 per litre (CFA410 for super, or premium) and diesel *(gasoil)* is CFA265. The road system is among the best in West Africa and highways between major towns are all tar. One exception is the road from Korhogo to Odienné, which is paved only as far as Boundiali and in lamentable condition from there to Odienné.

LOCAL TRANSPORT

For details on taxi transport in Abidjan, see Getting Around in the Abidjan section following.

In most other towns, the fare for a ride in a shared taxi is CFA125. If your destination is far off the regular route, the driver may want you to hire the whole taxi, which will usually be expressed as *quatre places* – in other words, you are being asked to pay for four fares which, at CFA125 each, adds up to CFA500. In the same way, the driver may respond *deux places* or *trois places* when you state your destination.

ORGANISED TOURS

Pistes Africaines (see Information in the Abidjan section later for contact details) have an office in Abidjan and local reps in Korhogo and Man, and can lay on an English-speaking guide. They offer tours in both regions and also a 10 day 'adventure circuit', which includes trekking in Parc National de Taï and canoeing on the River Bandama. Other companies offering tours include Haury Tours and Ivoire Voyages Tourisme, also based in Abidjan.

Abidjan

Abidjan was an unimportant town until it became a major port in 1951, when the French finished the Vridi Canal connecting the Ébrié Lagoon with the ocean. Since then, its population has skyrocketed from 60,000 to 3.5 million people.

If you've just flown in from the USA or Europe, you won't fully savour the uniqueness of Le Plateau, the business district. But if you arrive after a few weeks of bussing and bush taxi-ing around West Africa, you'll gasp.

Your first glimpse will probably be from across the lagoon. Water in the middle ground, offset by daring high rises puncturing the sky – it could be Boston or Seattle in the USA. If you can ignore the dispossessed, the beggars and street hawkers who've slipped in from another world, the impression's sustained; smart hotels and

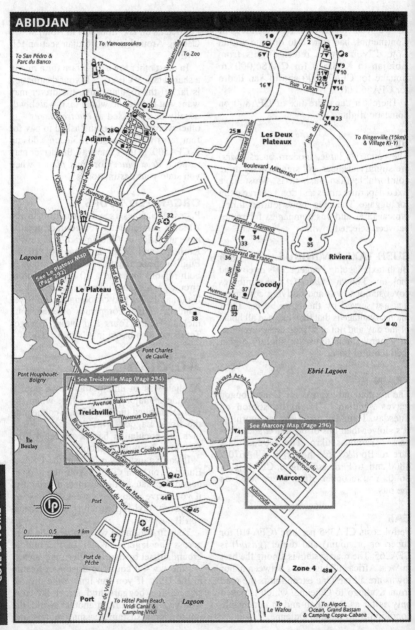

ABIDJAN

To San Pédro &
Parc du Banco

To Yamoussoukro

To Zoo

Lagoon

Adjamé

Les Deux
Plateaux

To Bingerville (15km)
& Village Ki-Yi

Le Plateau

See Le Plateau Map
(Page 292)

Riviera

Cocody

Pont Charles
de Gaulle

Pont Houphouët-
Boigny

Ebrié Lagoon

See Treichville Map (Page 294)

Treichville

Avenue Blaka

Avenue Dadié

Avenue Coulibaly

See Marcory Map (Page 296)

Île
Boulay

Marcory

Zone 4

Port

0   0.5   1 km

Port de
Pêche

Port

To Hôtel Palm Beach,
Vridi Canal &
Camping Vridi

Lagoon

To
Le Wafou

To Airport,
Ocean, Grand Bassam
& Camping Coppa-Cabana

ABIDJAN

PLACES TO STAY	14	Restaurant Georges V; Nem	4	Pistes Africaines; Cyber Espace
18	Hôtel Patient		Bassac; Pâtisserie Choc	5	Shared Taxis for Adjamé
23	Le Provençal		Gourmand	8	Benin Embassy
25	Le Palm Club	15	Hamburger House; Festival	12	Cash Center Supermarket
26	Hôtel du Nord		des Glaces (Le Vallon Shop-	17	Gare Nord (SOTRA)
27	Hôtel de la Gare;		ping Centre)	19	Adjamé Train Station
	Restaurant l'Escale	16	Pizzeria St Remi;	20	Shared Taxis for Grand Bassam
29	Hôtel Banfora		La Reine de Saba	21	STIF Bus Station
38	Hôtel Ivoire	22	Le Phenecien; Hayat	28	Gare Routière d'Adjamé
40	Hôtel Golf		Supermarket	30	Marché d'Adjamé
48	Hôtel Ibis Marcory	24	Taj Mahal	31	Musée National
		33	Allocodrome	32	Polyclinique Internationale
PLACES TO EAT	34	Le Pékin		St Anne-Marie
3	Le Datcha	36	La Dolce Vita; Le Mechoui;	35	Université de Cocody
6	Evening Grilled Chicken		Hollywood Café; Marché de	37	Institut Géographique
	Vendors		Cocody	39	Musée Municipal d'Art
7	Nuit de Saigon	41	Restaurant de la Paix		Contemporain de Cocody
9	Farafina	47	Restaurant des Pêcheurs	42	Shared Taxis for Adjamé
10	Nuit de Bangkok;			43	Gare de Bassam
	Restaurant Asia	OTHER	44	Cristal Jazz Club
11	Restaurant Baie d'Along	1	Hypermarché SOCOCE	45	STC Bus Station
13	L'Automatic; Nem Saigon	2	Commissariat de Deux Plateaux	46	Hospital

boutiques, chic Ivoirian ladies clacking along on high heels, on their way to restaurants of four star Parisian quality – and prices to match – with their smooth escorts, chattering away in impeccable, accent-less French. You'll sense the same atmosphere in the leafy residential areas of Cocody and Les Deux Plateaux.

But Abidjan has two faces. Adjamé, on the north side of town, plus Marcory and Treichville to the south of Le Plateau, linked by two major bridges, are areas in which rural immigrants have settled – they remain pure Africa in all its vitality and urban poverty.

Orientation

Abidjan spreads around the inlets and along the promontories of the large Ebrié Lagoon. Le Plateau, with its boulevards and skyscrapers, is the hub of the business and government districts.

Across a finger of the lagoon, east of Le Plateau, is the exclusive residential district of Cocody. North of Cocody lies the equally chic residential and restaurant district of Les Deux Plateaux.

To the north of Le Plateau is the popular quarter of Adjamé and the main *gare routière*, Gare Routière d'Adjamé. South of Le Plateau, across two busy bridges are Treichville, another popular area, full of vitality especially at night, and Marcory, of little interest in itself but safe at night and offering a selection of budget and mid-range hotels plus superb street food and maquis.

The international airport and main marine port are at Port Bouët, further south, on the Atlantic Ocean.

Information

Tourist Information The Office Ivoirien du Tourisme et de l'Hôtellerie (OITH) (☎ 20 65 00) is opposite the main post office on Place de la République in Le Plateau. However, there's little point in passing by until they complete their proposed visitors' reception centre.

The weekly free French-language guide *Abidjan Sept Jours*, although mainly packed with TV schedules and small ads, is useful for checking what's on around town. *Visions*

CÔTE D'IVOIRE

Safety Considerations

Abidjan can easily induce paranoia. The uniformed security guards on major buildings and vanloads of security guards setting out at nightfall to guard the villas of Les Deux Plateaux and Cocody recall scenes from *Robo Cop*. But it's not as bad as it was – or as the more lurid travellers tales would have you believe – and tough, even brutal, enforcement measures have decreased crime rates in recent years.

It can be dangerous and the incidence of mugging and theft is still high. However, with reasonable precautions you can reduce the risk significantly. Treichville nowadays is fairly safe by day, but don't walk around after dark when even the commercial district of Le Plateau can be dicey. The precincts of Treichville's nightclubs are a favourite haunt of no-gooders. The Gare Routière d'Adjamé is notorious for theft, sometimes with violence. And walking over either bridge between Treichville and Le Plateau is a particular risk, even in broad daylight.

If you're attacked or lose anything, especially if you intend to claim insurance reimbursement, contact the Commissariat du Premier Arrondissement in Abidjan (☎ 32 00 22). Each certificate of theft costs around CFA7000.

de Côte d'Ivoire (CFA2000) is published every three months in French and English.

Money The only places that will change money are the main branches of the banks in Le Plateau. If you're stuck with Central African CFA francs and the banks turn their noses up at them, as they're likely to, try Air Gabon on Ave Delafossa.

American Express is represented by SDV Voyages (☎ 24 23 52, fax 20 21 99) on Ave Christiani in Treichville, west of the *gare lagunaire* (ferry terminal). It's open weekdays from 8 am to 12.30 pm and 2 to 6 pm and until 12.30 pm on Saturday.

At the airport, you'll find a forex bureau beside the Air Ivoire check-in counter and there's also a branch of the SIB bank.

Post & Communications Poste restante in Abidjan's Le Plateau post office is open from 7 am to noon and 2.30 to 5.30 pm weekdays. Letters cost CFA600 each to collect and are held for one month.

International telephone calls and faxes can be made easily between 7 am and 6.30 pm, Monday to Saturday, and from 8 am to noon, Sunday, on the 1st floor of the CI Telecom office in the giant EECI building on Place de la République.

CyberEspace (☎ 42 68 16) on Rue des Jardins in Les Deux Plateaux is an Internet cafe. It's open every day from 9.30 am to 12.30 pm and from 3 to 10 pm. Online costs are CFA5000 an hour. To send an email costs CFA500 per transmission, and you can prepare your messages offline for CFA50 per minute.

Travel Agencies & Tour Operators Pistes Africaines (☎ 41 17 18, fax 41 66 75) is in Rue des Jardins in Les Deux Plateaux. They offer tours and also hire out camping equipment.

Haury Tours (☎ 22 16 54, fax 22 17 68, email haury@africaonline.co.ci), on the 2nd floor of the Chardy building in Le Plateau, is an affiliate of the French leisure giant, Nouvelles Frontières, and has several off-the-peg one-day tours from Abidjan, plus trips deeper into the provinces. Ivoire Voyages Tourisme (☎ 43 01 74, fax 43 50 45, email IVT@africaonline.co.ci), based at the Hôtel Golf, offers similar services. All three tour companies are highly professional and can provide personalised tours and car hire with a driver.

Saga Voyages (☎ 329870), opposite Air Afrique in Le Plateau, can assist with finding discounted fares.

Bookshops Librairie de France is very good. Its main shop is on Ave Chardy. It carries a smaller selection of titles at other branches around the city.

Medical Services Two recommended hospitals in Abidjan are the Polyclinique Internationale Sainte Anne-Marie (☎ 44 32 29) just off Blvd de la Corniche near Cocody and Clinique Avicennes, Boulevard Achalma, in Marcory. The free weekly, *Abidjan Sept Jours*, lists 24-hour pharmacies and doctors on emergency call.

Musée National

The Musée National (☎ 22 20 56) is just over a kilometre north of Le Plateau market and is open from 9 am to noon and 3 to 6 pm, Tuesday to Saturday. Recently renovated, it has a collection of over 20,000 objects, including wooden statues and masks, pottery, ivory and bronze. Many of the buses heading for Adjamé pass nearby.

Cathédrale St-Paul

This cathedral is bold and innovative. Designed by the Italian Aldo Spirito, it's open from 8 am to 7 pm daily. The tower is a huge stylised figure of St Paul (bearing, it must be said, a remarkable resemblance to one of the Simpson family from certain angles) with the nave sweeping boldly behind him like trailing robes. Inside, the stained glass tableaus are as warm and rich as those of the Basilica in Yamoussoukro. Note in particular the one behind the altar depicting God blinding St Paul on the road to Damascus, the storm on Lake Galilee with Jesus pointing the way ahead as the disciples jettison the cargo and, opposite, the tableau of the first missionaries stepping ashore to a scene of African plenty – elephants, gazelles, luxuriant palms and smiling villagers. Although closed at the time of writing, the tower lift (CFA500) may again be functioning.

Le Plateau

Step back and look up at some of the buildings of Le Plateau; they're as breathtaking close up as from a distance. La Pyramide on the corner of Ave Franchet d'Esperey and Rue Botreau-Roussel, designed by the Italian architect Olivieri, was the first daring structure, although, now more than 25 years old, it's beginning to show its age. Nearby is

the striking head office of the BCEAO bank. Looming over the cathedral are the towers of the Cité Administrative on Blvd Angoulvant, giant copper-coloured slabs with fretted windows. The shimmering Ministry of Posts & Telecommunications building on the corner of Ave Marchand and Rue Lecoeur, all rounded angles and curves soaring skywards, contrasts with its cuboid, right-angled neighbours.

And poke your head into the spacious and airy Centre Culturel Français. Its architecture owes everything to France. By contrast, the exciting wood and scrap-metal sculptures in the patio with its open-air cafe are a happy meeting of two cultures.

Parc du Banco

The Parc du Banco, only 3km from town to the north-west, is a lush rainforest reserve

The Outdoor Laundrette

Every day, some 375 *fanicos* (washermen), mostly Burkinabe and none Ivoirian, jam together in the middle of a small stream near the Parc du Banco, frantically rubbing clothes on huge stones held in place by old car tyres. Afterwards, they spread the clothes over rocks and grass for at least half a kilometre (never getting them mixed up) and then iron them. Any washer not respecting the strict rules imposed by the washers' trade union, which allocates positions, is immediately excluded.

The soap is black and sold by women who make it from palm oil in small wooden sheds on the hills surrounding the stream. It all starts at dawn when the fanicos head off on their rounds to collect the laundry; they begin arriving in single file at the stream around 6.30 am. The best time to be here is between 10.30 am and noon when the action is at its peak. You'll get some superb photos, although payment is expected. In the afternoon, all you'll see is drying clothes.

LE PLATEAU

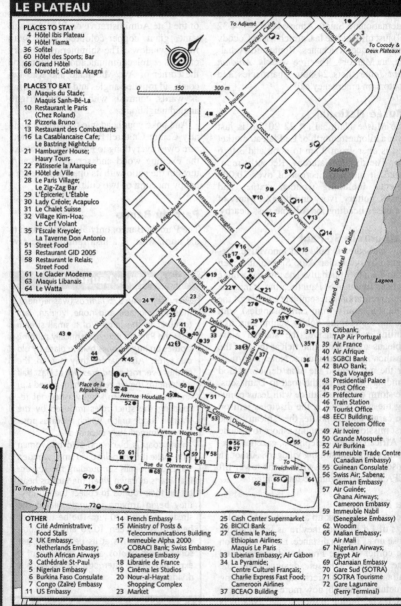

PLACES TO STAY
- 4 Hôtel Ibis Plateau
- 9 Hôtel Tiama
- 36 Sofitel
- 60 Hôtel des Sports; Bar
- 66 Grand Hôtel
- 68 Novotel; Galeria Akagni

PLACES TO EAT
- 8 Maquis du Stade;
   Maquis Sanh-Bé-La
- 10 Restaurant le Paris
   (Chez Roland)
- 12 Pizzeria Bruno
- 13 Restaurant des Combattants
- 16 La Casablancaise Cafe;
   Le Bastring Nightclub
- 21 Hamburger House;
   Haury Tours
- 22 Pâtisserie la Marquise
- 24 Hôtel de Ville
- 28 Le Paris Village;
   Le Zig-Zag Bar
- 29 L'Épicerie; L'Étable
- 30 Lady Créole; Acapulco
- 31 Le Chalet Suisse
- 32 Village Kim-Hoa;
   Le Cerf Volant
- 35 l'Escale Kreyole;
   La Taverne Don Antonio
- 51 Street Food
- 53 Restaurant GID 2005
- 58 Restaurant le Relais;
   Street Food
- 61 Le Glacier Moderne
- 63 Maquis Libanais
- 64 Le Watta

To Adjamé
To Cocody & Deux Plateaux
Stadium
Lagoon
Place de la République
To Treichville
To Treichville
To Treichville

- 38 Citibank;
   TAP Air Portugal
- 39 Air France
- 40 Air Afrique
- 41 SGBCI Bank
- 42 BIAO Bank;
   Saga Voyages
- 43 Presidential Palace
- 44 Post Office
- 45 Préfecture
- 46 Train Station
- 47 Tourist Office
- 48 EECI Building;
   CI Telecom Office
- 49 Air Ivoire
- 50 Grande Mosquée
- 52 Air Burkina
- 54 Immeuble Trade Centre
   (Canadian Embassy)
- 55 Guinean Consulate
- 56 Swiss Air; Sabena;
   German Embassy
- 57 Air Guinée;
   Ghana Airways;
   Cameroon Embassy
- 59 Immeuble Nabil
   (Senegalese Embassy)
- 62 Woodin
- 65 Malian Embassy;
   Air Mali
- 67 Nigerian Airways;
   Egypt Air
- 69 Ghanaian Embassy
- 70 Gare Sud (SOTRA)
- 71 SOTRA Tourisme
- 72 Gare Lagunaire
   (Ferry Terminal)

OTHER
- 1 Cité Administrative;
   Food Stalls
- 2 UK Embassy;
   Netherlands Embassy;
   South African Airways
- 3 Cathédrale St-Paul
- 5 Nigerian Embassy
- 6 Burkina Faso Consulate
- 7 Congo (Zaïre) Embassy
- 11 US Embassy
- 14 French Embassy
- 15 Ministry of Posts &
   Telecommunications Building
- 17 Immeuble Alpha 2000
   COBACI Bank; Swiss Embassy;
   Japanese Embassy
- 18 Librairie de France
- 19 Cinéma les Studios
- 20 Nour-al-Hayat
   Shopping Complex
- 23 Market
- 25 Cash Center Supermarket
- 26 BICICI Bank
- 27 Cinéma le Paris;
   Ethiopian Airlines;
   Maquis Le Paris
- 33 Liberian Embassy; Air Gabon
- 34 La Pyramide;
   Centre Culturel Français;
   Charlie Express Fast Food;
   Cameroon Airlines
- 37 BCEAO Building

with pleasant walking trails. The entrance fee is CFA300. Near the park entrance is Africa's largest outdoor laundrette, where hundreds of washermen scrub clothes in the River Banco and thrash them against the rocks. Take bus No 20, 34 or 36 from the Gare Nord in Adjamé on the road north to Yamoussoukro or bus No 20 from the Gare Sud in Le Plateau, south of Place de la République.

Hôtel Ivoire

In Cocody, the Hôtel Ivoire, West Africa's premier hotel, is a small city in itself. It has everything from an ice-skating rink, bowling alley, seven tennis courts, cinema and casino to a grocery store and a major art shop. Take bus No 86 from Gare Sud, No 84 from Gare Nord or No 74 from Gare de Marcory.

Musée Municipal d'Art Contemporain de Cocody

This small museum (☎ 44 83 54), an easy stroll east from Hôtel Ivoire in Cocody, has a stimulating permanent collection of works by contemporary Ivoirian and other African artists and regularly mounts temporary exhibitions. Entry is free. It's open 9 am to 1 pm and 3 to 6.30 pm. It's scheduled to move to custom-built premises on Ave Latrille by the new millennium.

Activities

You can play tennis at the Hôtel Ivoire and for CFA1500, nonresidents can use the pool. You can swim and play tennis or hire sailboards at Hôtel Golf. The Ivoire Golf Club has the best 18-hole golf course in West and Central Africa.

Places to Stay – Budget

Camping There are two camping possibilities, both small and on the beachfront and each charging CFA1500 per person. The better is the very friendly *Coppa-Cabana*, 17km east of Abidjan along the ocean road to Grand Bassam. It has showers, a paillote

bar-restaurant and basic singles/doubles with fan for CFA3000/4000. It's on a frequent shared taxi (CFA500) route from the Gare de Bassam.

Camping Vridi is in the Vridi Canal area between Hôtel Palm Beach and Coco Beach. It also has basic rooms for CFA1500 per person. It's often deserted since the water supply's unreliable and there's no electricity. From Le Plateau, take bus No 18 or 53 (or bus No 24 from Treichville) to the Coco Beach sign, then walk back 500m.

Hotels – Treichville Although the crime level has fallen, Treichville can still be dangerous after dark, when it's prudent to take a taxi back to your hotel.

Hôtel Fraternité near Cinéma l'Entente is a friendly place where the manager takes the security of his guests seriously. It costs CFA2500 for a small, basic room and CFA 3000/5000 for a larger one with fan/air-con. The pink five-storey *Hôtel le Succès* (☎ 25 36 16, fax 25 81 53) near the corner of Rue 25 and Rue 14 is another possibility if you don't mind the gloomy brown paintwork inside. All rooms have showers. Those on the ground floor are CFA3500 (CFA4000 with fan) and are used mainly by guests hiring rooms by the hour. The upper rooms with air-con (CFA5000) are much better value. Ask for one with a balcony.

Hôtel le Prince (☎ 24 17 38) on Ave 20 has recently undergone a radical facelift. Rooms with shower and fan for CFA6000 (CFA8000 with air-con) are excellent value. A patio restaurant and bar are planned as the next stage of the overhaul. *Hôtel Atlanta* (☎ 24 25 08, fax 25 32 04) is a further step up. Rooms, all with bathroom, cost CFA5000 with fan and CFA7000 to CFA10,000 with air-con.

Hôtel l'Ariegeois (☎ 24 99 68) 500m north of the Treichville train station on Blvd de Marseille has simple rooms with air-con and bathroom for CFA7000. Next door but one, *Hôtel de France* has a pleasant courtyard and rooms with similar facilities. Singles/doubles cost CFA9000/10,000 but they're amenable to bargaining. (Don't be

CÔTE D'IVOIRE

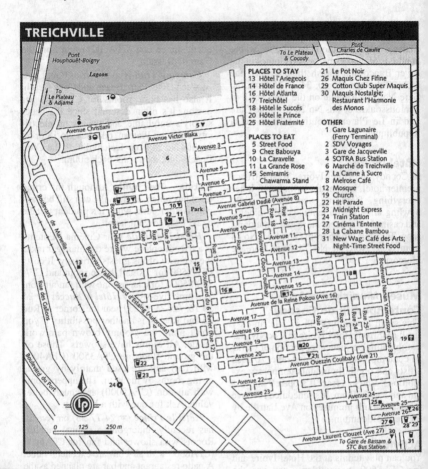

TREICHVILLE

PLACES TO STAY
13 Hôtel l'Ariegeois
14 Hôtel de France
16 Hôtel Atlanta
17 Treichôtel
18 Hôtel le Succés
20 Hôtel le Prince
25 Hôtel Fraternité

PLACES TO EAT
5 Street Food
9 Chez Babouya
10 La Caravelle
11 La Grande Rose
15 Semiramis
   Chawarma Stand

21 Le Pot Noir
26 Maquis Chez Fifine
29 Cotton Club Super Maquis
30 Maquis Nostalgie;
   Restaurant l'Harmonie
   des Monos

OTHER
1 Gare Lagunaire
   (Ferry Terminal)
2 SDV Voyages
3 Gare de Jacqueville
4 SOTRA Bus Station
6 Marché de Treichville
7 La Canne à Sucre
8 Melrose Café
12 Mosque
19 Church
22 Hit Parade
23 Midnight Express
24 Train Station
27 Cinéma l'Entente
28 La Cabane Bambou
31 New Wag; Café des Arts;
   Night-Time Street Food

CÔTE D'IVOIRE

tempted by the overpriced and unwelcoming Hôtel Terminus, opposite the station.)

Hotels – Adjamé At night, Adjamé is scarcely safer than Treichville, so a hotel with its own restaurant where you can dine after dark is an advantage.

Hôtel Patient (☎ 37 22 41) to the east of the Gare Nord has clean singles/doubles with air-con and shower for CFA6500/7500 (CFA8500 with bathroom). It has its own bar and restaurant. *Hôtel de la Gare* (☎ 37 18

56) across the road from the Gare Routière d'Adjamé is often full by mid-morning. Basic rooms with shower begin at CFA3500 (from CFA4500 with fan and CFA5000 with air-con). There's a good, inexpensive restaurant next door.

Hotels – Marcory Marcory is considerably safer than either Treichville or Adjamé.

The friendly *Hôtel Pousada* is a cheery and particularly active whorehouse. Rooms with shower cost CFA4000 and CFA6000 with air-con. It has been warmly recommended – as a hotel, let's make it quite clear! – by several readers. It's superior to the nearby *Hôtel Copacabana*, of the same genre, whose only virtue is its cheapness, with basic rooms for CFA4000.

At the more conventional *Hôtel le Souvenir* (☎ 26 12 56) a couple of blocks west of the Gare de Marcory all rooms have bathroom. Those with fan cost CFA4000, while larger ones with air-con and TV are a bargain at CFA7000.

Places to Stay – Mid-Range

Treichville The long-established *Treichôtel* (☎ 24 05 59, fax 25 45 35) on Ave 16 is beginning to show its age. Rooms, all with air-con and bathroom, cost between CFA 11,000 and CFA14,000.

Adjamé *Hôtel Banfora* (☎ 37 02 52), near the Gare Routière d'Adjamé is the best choice in this part of town. It has air-con rooms with bathroom for CFA8000 to CFA10,000 and a pleasant terrace restaurant. The long-standing *Hôtel du Nord* (☎ 37 04 63, fax 37 56 48) has two small ground floor rooms with air-con for CFA7000 and less cramped air-con rooms upstairs for CFA 8000 (CFA10,000 with bathroom). Order in advance if you want to eat at their small restaurant.

Marcory Buses from Le Plateau and Treichville stop right outside the multi-storey *Hôtel Konankro* (☎ 26 16 28) on the main drag, Ave de la TSF. All rooms have bathrooms and cost CFA7500 with fan and between CFA8500 and CFA10,000 with air-con. At the friendly *Hôtel le Repos* (☎ 26 32 57) rooms are ranged around a small interior courtyard. Those with fan cost CFA7000 while ones with air-con and TV are from CFA8000 to CFA10,000. It has a pleasant, active bar. Marcory's would-be finest is the significantly overpriced *Hôtel Hamanieh* (☎ 26 91 55, fax 26 78 94) on Blvd de Lorraine, a dour modern establishment with air-con singles/doubles for CFA21,000/31,000, including obligatory

full board, where the restaurant portions are so small as to be insulting.

Le Plateau The cheapest lodging in Le Plateau is *Hôtel des Sports* (☎ 33 19 58) on Rue du Commerce. Its sparsely furnished air-con rooms with bathroom cost CFA7000 with fan and between CFA11,000 and CFA15,000 with air-con. There's a lively bar-restaurant downstairs.

Les Deux Plateaux The *Palm Club* (☎ 44 49 95), the one-time Palme Industrie guesthouse, has rooms with air-con and bathroom for CFA12,000. *Le Provençal* has comfortable air-con rooms from CFA11,000.

Places to Stay – Top End

As you'd imagine, Abidjan isn't short on luxury hotels. At the less expensive end, the shoreside *Palm Beach* (☎ 27 42 16, fax 27 30 16), 20 minutes drive south of the centre in Vridi, is excellent value. Singles/doubles cost CFA27,000/32,000 and it has a good saltwater pool.

In Le Plateau, the *Grand Hôtel* (☎ 32 12 00, fax 32 98 60) off Rue du Commerce has a Gallic feel and a maturity that its flash, up-market competitors lack. It has a tranquil patio and dining area. Rooms are CFA 21,000/28,000. *Ibis Plateau* on Blvd Roume (☎ 21 01 57, fax 21 78 75) and its clone, *Ibis Marcory* (☎ 24 92 55, fax 35 89 10) both have a small pool and rooms for CFA33,000/ 36,000.

Rooms at the somewhat run-down *Novotel* (☎ 21 23 23, fax 33 26 36) cost CFA 50,000/58,000. It too has a pool. In the Riviera area bordering the lagoon and a 15 minute taxi ride from the centre, the relaxing *Hôtel Golf* (☎ 43 10 44, fax 43 05 44) has a pool and offers tennis and windsurfing. Rooms are CFA69,000/80,000. *Hôtel Tiama* (☎ 21 08 22, fax 21 64 60) on Blvd de la République is conveniently central and has rooms for between CFA80,000 and CFA90,000. At *Sofitel* (☎ 22 11 22, fax 21 20 28) rooms facing the lagoon cost CFA100,000 while those facing inward are scarcely a snip at CFA94,000.

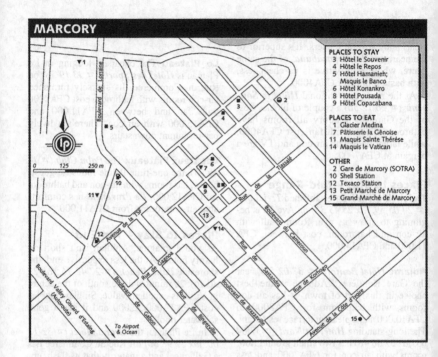

MARCORY

PLACES TO STAY
3 Hôtel le Souvenir
4 Hôtel le Repos
5 Hôtel Hamanieh;
   Maquis le Banco
6 Hôtel Konankro
8 Hôtel Pousada
9 Hôtel Copacabana

PLACES TO EAT
1 Glacier Medina
7 Pâtisserie la Gênoise
11 Maquis Sainte Thérèse
14 Maquis le Vatican

OTHER
2 Gare de Marcory (SOTRA)
10 Shell Station
12 Texaco Station
13 Petit Marché de Marcory
15 Grand Marché de Marcory

Last, but hardly least, the 750-room *Hôtel Ivoire* (☎ 44 10 45, fax 44 00 50) remains the city's finest and West Africa's most famous. Single/double rooms will cost you CFA98,000/112,000 (CFA123,000/141,000 in the tower).

Places to Eat

Cheap Eats In Adjamé, *L'Escale* at the Hôtel de la Gare has a good selection of inexpensive dishes. Slightly more expensive, the restaurant at *Hôtel Banfora* is equally pleasant.

If you're staying in Treichville, there's tasty *street food* on Ave Victor Blaka, just east of the market.

Le Plateau, strangely enough, is superb for inexpensive food, mainly at lunch time. Vendors on the short street between Ave Nogues and Rue du Commerce are so popular that you'll have to wait in line. *Res-taurant le Relais* is a spruce, friendly place with main dishes for under CFA1000. They also do demon fruit juices. Across the street, the bustling *Maquis Libanais* serves chawarma and other Levantine dishes.

On the open ground east of the Grande Mosquée, hungry lunch timers mill around the women with their simmering pots. There's also a cluster of small, highly recommended lunch time *stalls* at the base of the towers of the Cité Administrative on Blvd Angoulvant. *La Casablancaise* on Blvd de la République is a pleasant cafe, with a variety of selections for under CFA 2500.

In Les Deux Plateaux at evening time, you can get half a juicy grilled chicken and a plate of *attiéké*, yam chips or *aloco* for CFA1000 from the *roadside vendors* about 500m south of the *Club SOCOCE* hypermarket, within which are several good value places to eat. *Nem Bassac* and *Nem Saigon* on Rue des Jardins serve inexpensive Vietnamese food.

The seething area around Marcory's *Petit Marché* is great for grilled fish and meat. The *Allocodrome* on Rue Washington in Cocody is active from 4 pm until late. Some 30 vendors grill fish, chicken and beef, and the competition is such that you can eat satisfyingly for under CFA1000.

For burgers, you can't beat *Hamburger House*, which has an outlet in Le Plateau on Ave Chardy east of the Nour-al-Hayat shopping complex and another in Les Deux Plateaux at the Vallon shopping centre. A burger, chips and soft drink cost about CFA2000.

African In Le Plateau, the garden paillote of the long-standing *Restaurant des Combattants* is relaxing and inexpensive. The small *Restaurant GID 2005* has a good, mainly African menu. *Maquis du Stade*, where a meal costs about CFA2000, has a more extensive menu and is open until 6 pm. Its neighbour, the *Maquis Sanh-Bé-La*, is quieter and less expensive.

If you fancy African food in air-con comfort with impeccable service, visit *Farafina* (☎ 41 60 74) on Ave Crosson Duplessis in Les Deux Plateaux which has a wide range of dishes. The quality doesn't come cheaply. *Espace 351* in Cocody is a popular venue. At lunch time, there are sauce dishes for around CFA1500 and, in the evening, grills at under CFA4000. There's live music every Tuesday and Wednesday and cabaret on Thursday.

In Treichville, *Chez Fifine* serves African dishes during the day and delicious grills at night. At *La Grande Rose* you can get a filling three-course meal for under CFA3000. *Chez Babouya* must rank as Abidjan's most unusual restaurant. It simulates a Mauritanian tent with cushions on the floor, low tables and an amazing collection of photographs of old Hollywood movie stars. The food's plentiful but not great – a fixed menu with wine is CFA5000. The friendly *Pot Noir* has a variety of sauces and other specialities for under CFA2000. One of the best areas for maquis food, particularly late at night, is around the Cabane Bamboo nightclub. Within easy walking distance, you'll find open-air grills facing the club, the *Maquis Nostalgie* and the similar *Restaurant l'Harmonie des Monos*, also known as Chez Jacqui, plus the rather more expensive *Cotton Club Super Maquis*.

In Marcory, *Maquis le Vatican*, with its 1st floor terrace, is perhaps the most pleasant of the maquis, although, strangely, it's often nearly empty. Try, in particular, their delicious whole chicken *kedjenou* for CFA3000. The quiet, partially open-air *Maquis Sainte Thérèse* about 100m north of the Texaco petrol station, equally underpatronised and almost as good, is slightly cheaper.

Asian & Indian There's no shortage of restaurants serving Chinese or Vietnamese cuisine. In Le Plateau, there are several, all good and similarly priced, in the cluster of eating places where Blvd du Général de Gaulle meets Ave Chardy. They come, go and change names but *Le Cerf Volant* and *Village Kim-Hoa* seem here to stay.

Another concentration is on Rue des Jardins in Les Deux Plateaux. Among the best, *Nuit de Saigon* (☎ 41 40 44) is air-con and attractive. It has a large menu and is open daily for lunch and dinner. Most dishes are in the CFA3000 to CFA6000 range. Perhaps the best Chinese/Vietnamese restaurant of all, and at a price which reflects its quality, is *Le Pékin* in Cocody.

Also in Les Deux Plateaux, the *Taj Mahal* has a long menu of relatively inexpensive but not very inspiring dishes between CFA 2000 and CFA3000.

French In Le Plateau, *Le Watta* offers both French and local cuisine. Open at lunch time and until 11 pm, the food is good and reasonably priced. The fine prospect over the lagoon is marred only by the constant drone of traffic from the motorway below. (As an aperitif, you may care to try their 'Blondy

Mary', item 78 on the menu). *Restaurant le Paris*, also known as Chez Roland, has a pleasant atmosphere and does great, uncomplicated French fare at quite moderate prices.

There's a golden triangle of fine restaurants, mostly French, where Ave Chardy, Rue Botreau-Roussel and Blvd du Général de Gaulle meet. Not all are outrageously priced but check the menu before you sit down; the business menu at the excellent *Le Paris Village* (☎ 22 26 17), for example, starts at CFA15,000. Two intimate, highly recommended alternatives are *L'Étable* (☎ 22 23 93), renowned for its steaks and meat dishes, and *L'Épicerie* (☎ 22 66 54). *Le Chalet Suisse* (☎ 21 66 43) serves Swiss and French specialities and is a little more moderately priced.

Italian Most Italian restaurants offer both Italian and French cuisine. In Le Plateau, the popular *Pizzeria Bruno* (closed Sunday) does big, tasty pizzas for between CFA4000 and CFA5000. *La Taverne Don Antonio* (☎ 21 89 51) is somewhat fancier and more expensive. In Les Deux Plateaux, *Au Pastel* (☎ 41 35 80) draws praise from both locals and expats.

Reasonably priced and with pleasant service, *La Dolce Vita* (☎ 44 57 79) in the Marché de Cocody is justifiably one of the most popular restaurants in town, where it's essential to reserve.

Lebanese You'll find Lebanese restaurants and chawarma outlets all over town. In Le Plateau, *Charlie Express* is a friendly, human-scale kiosk at the base of La Pyramide.

Les Deux Plateaux has three excellent Lebanese places within an easy walk of each other on Rue des Jardins. *L'Automatic* does great chicken chawarmas for CFA600 and most main dishes are within the CFA1500 to CFA2000 range. The friendly *Le Phenecien* is more intimate while *Restaurant Georges V*, is scarcely more expensive and just as good. The air-con *Le Mechoui* in Marché de Cocody has more style and is a pleasant place to linger for an evening.

In Treichville, the *Semiramis* is great for chawarmas and takeaways, while *La Caravelle* does copious, all-inclusive menus for CFA2500. *Restaurant de la Paix* (☎ 26 09 80) on Rue de la Paix in Marcory has excellent Levantine food that is well worth going out of your way for.

Seafood There are two excellent lagoonside restaurants. Known to most taxi drivers, they're at the beginning of the road to Vridi, a 15 minute ride south from Le Plateau. *Le Petit Bateau* (☎ 25 29 67) does a superb three-course menu, including lobster, for CFA7000. Next door, the long-standing *Chez Cakpot* (☎ 27 40 86) is very similar. Both offer succulent grilled *gambas* (prawns), *langoustines* (crayfish) and *langoustes* (lobster). They're open from noon to 10 pm daily.

Another good seafood restaurant is the significantly more expensive *Restaurant des Pêcheurs* (☎ 25 52 89) at the Port de Pêche in the port area. It's open for both lunch and dinner every day except Sunday.

Other Cuisines If you fancy Caribbean cuisine at a price, you have a choice between *Lady Créole* (☎ 21 66 67) and *L'Escale Kreyole* (☎ 22 40 46), both in Le Plateau. *La Reine de Saba* in Les Deux Plateaux offers good Ethiopian cuisine.

Patisseries In Le Plateau, *Pâtisserie la Marquise* is a small, elegant pastry shop, open until 6.30 pm, which also does lunchtime sandwiches and pizzas for CFA1500 to CFA3000. In Marcory, *Pâtisserie la Gênoise* is friendly and does an imaginative dish of the day for around CFA1500. The *Pâtisserie Choko Gourmand* in Les Deux Plateaux does everything superbly: cakes, pastries, buttery croissants and – surprisingly difficult to find in one of the world's major coffee-growing countries – excellent, fresh, real coffee. Strongly recommended.

Entertainment

Bars & Nightclubs In Le Plateau, the bar of the *Hôtel des Sports* on the Rue du Commerce is a favourite watering hole for French expats and Francophile Ivoirians. Pricey, with its bustle and energy it could have been transplanted from Marseille. Open at night, *Acapulco* on Ave Chardy is an expensive cosy bar. The lounge bar of the *Sofitel* has a stunning view over the lagoon to *Hôtel Ivoire* where, from around 5 to 10 pm, the lobby resonates with the sounds of a lively band. *Melrose Café* on Blvd Delafosse in Treichville is a popular spot for a drink and a snack. *Hollywood Café* in the Marché de Cocody, with an American flavour, is also popular, while the terrace of *Restaurant Georges V* on the Rue des Jardins is a pleasant place to sip a beer and watch life.

If you go clubbing in Treichville, as many expat residents do, play safe and take a taxi to the door. *La Canne à Sucre* on Blvd Delafosse has energy but is something of a low dive, popular with the French military. Clustered together between Ave 26 and 27 and east of Rue 38 are several nightclubs: *La Cabane Bambou* has a live band and no cover charge, the recently opened *New Wag* is developing a following and, beside it, the *Café des Arts* is an outdoor bar with live music at weekends.

More upmarket, *Hit Parade* (cover CFA5000) on Blvd Delafosse attracts a young, predominantly expat crowd and has a good restaurant upstairs. Nearby, *Midnight Express* (cover charge CFA4000, which is sometimes waived if you arrive early) has full-length mirrors for the most narcissistic movers and shakers. At the *Cristal Jazz Club* on Blvd Valéry Giscard D'Estaing opposite the Gare de Bassam make sure that you get the right door. From one, you'll hear great jazz blasting; the other leads to a disco. Drinks at both cost CFA5000.

If you like your jazz cool and Coltrane, visit *Le Zigzag* in Le Plateau. There's no cover charge and beers cost CFA2500. A short walk away on the corner of Ave Terrasson de Fougères and Blvd de la République, *Le Bastring* is also popular.

Traditional Music & Dance The restaurant at *Le Wafou* (☎ *25 62 01*), a waterside complex of handicraft shops, does dinner with a folky cabaret. Popular with the package tours and saturation advertised, it smacks more of a theme park than a genuine cultural experience. Much more authentic is *Le Village Ki-Yi* (☎ *43 20 05*) on Blvd Mitterrand which offers a show with dinner, Wednesday to Saturday. The resident troupe, Le Groupe Ki-Yi M'bock enjoys national fame as singers, dancers and musicians.

Cinemas All English-language movies are dubbed into French. The three best cinemas, all excellent, are: *Cinéma Ivoire* at Hôtel Ivoire and, in Le Plateau, *Cinéma Le Paris* between Rue Botreau-Roussel and Rue Lecoeur and *Cinéma Les Studios* on Blvd de la République, one block north of the market.

Shopping

Supermarkets Abidjan has two established supermarket chains: Hayat and the cheaper, gaudier Cash Center. A recent arrival is the French franchise, Tati. The vast Hypermarché SOCOCE (pronounced *soc-o-say*) in Les Deux Plateaux is worth a visit for its own sake; you need to pinch yourself to confirm that you really are still in Africa.

Markets The Marché de Treichville, once a treasure trove, has burnt down and is nothing but twisted metal and sagging concrete. The Marché d'Adjamé on Blvd Abrogoua is the cheapest in Abidjan but it is spread out and caters primarily to locals, although it does have a good selection of fabrics.

The Marché de Cocody on the corner of Rue Washington and Blvd de France is much more compact and manageable. Its top floor is geared more for the tourist market. It's good for beads, bronze and malachite and occasionally has a fine woodcarving. It has an excellent range of batiks and other textiles from Côte d'Ivoire (Korhogo and Bouaké cloth) and further afield, such as Mali mud cloth, *kente* cloth from Ghana, Benin appliqué and Tuareg wedding blankets.

Art & Craftwork Apart from the markets, the best place for quality artisan goods is the magnificent La Rose d'Ivoire at Hôtel Ivoire.

Passing the quick-carve, off-the-peg items in the cabinet by the entrance, you descend into an Aladdin's cave of fine pieces. It's worth going just to browse but don't expect any bargains. It's open from 9 am to noon and 3 to 8 pm daily. Galeria Akagni next to the Novotel on Blvd de la Paix also has some excellent pieces but prices are equivalent and the selection is much more limited. Both, despite their air of gentility, are amenable to bargaining.

Textiles African print material is generally sold in a length of three *pagnes*, the quantity required to make a blouse, skirt and the wide strip which swathes a baby, bobbing on its mother's back. The cheapest is Fancy, from Ghana, which costs CFA8000 to CFA12,000 per pagne. Côte d'Ivoire wax prints are around CFA18,000, while Dutch prints cost between CFA25,000 and CFA30,000. The fabric shops along Rue du Commerce in Le Plateau have fixed prices. Outstanding among them is Woodin, one block east of the Novotel, which will sell by the single pagne or metre. It's a kaleidoscope of colour and swirling shapes and worth a visit for the sensual pleasure alone.

Gold & Silver The finest silver and 18-carat gold work is at the Hôtel Ivoire. The Marché de Cocody has a good selection, as do the small jewellery shops in Treichville. There are several along Blvd Delafosse facing the Bracodi brewery. Gold is sold by the gram according to the current rate and the price includes workmanship. For silver, it's essential to bargain.

Music Abidjan, where many artists record, is about the best place in West Africa to buy African music. In Le Plateau, try Studio 33 next to the Librairie de France on Ave Chardy. The manager of the well stocked JAT Music outlet, on the ground floor of the Nour-al-Hayat shopping complex, is friendly and ready with advice. It's also worth trawling the music shops on Ave 16 in Treichville. Boomers has been particularly recommended.

Music cassettes sold on the street are a third of the price but of poor quality.

Getting There & Away

Air The airport is at Port Bouët on the south side of town. For details of international and domestic flights to/from Abidjan, see the Getting There & Away and Getting Around sections earlier in this chapter. For reconfirmation of flights and ticket sales, the following airlines have offices in Abidjan:

Air Afrique	☎ 20 30 00
Air Burkina	☎ 32 89 19
Air Continental	☎ 27 62 10
Air France	☎ 21 90 93
Air Gabon	☎ 21 55 06
Air Ivoire	☎ 21 36 36
Air Mali	☎ 32 19 62
British Airways	☎ 32 00 55
Corsair	☎ 22 16 94
EgyptAir	☎ 32 57 19
Ethiopian Airlines	☎ 21 93 32
Ghana Airways	☎ 32 27 83
KLM-Royal Dutch Airlines	☎ 32 00 55
Middle Eastern Airways	☎ 22 62 82
Sabena	☎ 21 29 36
South African Airways	☎ 21 82 50
Swissair	☎ 21 55 72
TAP Air Portugal	☎ 21 17 55

Bus & Bush Taxi The main bus station is the shambolic Gare Routière d'Adjamé, some 4km north of Le Plateau. All buses and most bush taxis leave from here. There's frequent transport to all major provincial towns. Peugeot 504 bush taxis tend to cost about 30% more than the large buses. You'll have less hassle if you decide in advance which bus company you want to travel with and head straight for its depot. For more information on fares, routes and bus companies, see the table in this chapter's Getting Around section.

To avoid the chaos of Adjamé on arrival in Abidjan, disembark at Yopougon station on the outskirts of the city, one stop before Adjamé; almost all buses stop at Yopougon. A taxi to the city centre costs slightly more, but it's well worth the extra. This doesn't work as well on departure, as buses are often full when they leave Adjamé, with no seats left by the time they get to Yopougon. Whatever you do, avoid using Adjamé at night as robberies and muggings are common.

There are two small stations in Treichville. Bush taxis and minibuses for destinations east along the coast such as Grand Bassam, Aboisso and Elubo at the Ghanaian border, leave primarily from the Gare de Bassam at the corner of Rue 38 and Blvd Valéry Giscard d'Estaing south of Treichville (see the Abidjan map). A bush taxi costs CFA400 to Grand Bassam (35 minutes) and CFA1200 to Aboisso (1½ hours). Transport for Bassam and Aboisso also departs from Gare Routière d'Adjamé and costs CFA100 more. Buses for Jacqueville leave from the tiny, unmarked Gare de Jacqueville in Treichville, 200m east of Houphouët-Boigny bridge. The only company serving this route is 3A Express which has frequent departures between 6 am and 7 pm (CFA800).

Train There are three train stations in Abidjan – Le Plateau, Adjamé and Treichville – from which the express to Ouagadougou departs three times a week. For more details on train times and fares, see the Getting Around section earlier in this chapter.

Getting Around

To/From the Airport Abidjan airport is no longer the threatening experience that travellers tales would have you believe. Walk out, turn sharp left and continue for about 20m to an overhead sign, 'Tête de Stationnement', at the head of a long line of waiting orange taxis. When your turn comes, ensure that the driver switches on his meter. If he refuses, establish a price, which shouldn't exceed CFA3000. If he sticks, make a show of getting out; you'll quickly reach an accommodation and, if not, there are plenty more behind him.

A metered taxi will cost about CFA1500 to Marcory, CFA2000 to Treichville, CFA 2250 to Le Plateau and CFA3000 to Cocody (Hôtel Ivoire area). If you're travelling between midnight and 6 am, rates double. Bus No 6 connects the airport with the central area; the cost is CFA160. If you reserve ahead, Hertz, Avis and Europcar will meet you with your car. There's a free shuttle service to major hotels.

Bus The city's SOTRA buses tend to be crowded, but they're in good condition and cheap – CFA160 for most destinations and CFA200 for outlying areas. They display their route number, which also features on bus-stop signs, but only rarely their destination. Even so, armed with the information below, it's not difficult to navigate around town.

The major bus station in Le Plateau is the Gare Sud south of Place de la République. Other stations are the Gare Nord in Adjamé 500m north of the train station and Gare de Marcory at the northern end of Ave de la TSF in Marcory. The buses on most lines operate from about 6 am to between 9 and 10 pm. Routes include:

No 0/9 Gare Nord, Le Plateau (Cité Administrative, Blvd Clozel, Ave Delafosse, La Pyramide building, Rue Botreau-Roussel), Gare de Marcory

No 2 Gare Nord, Marché d'Adjamé, Le Plateau (National Museum, Blvd Clozel, Blvd de la République, post office), Treichville (market and train station), Gare de Marcory

No 3 Gare Nord, Le Plateau (Musée National, Blvd Clozel, Ave Delafosse, La Pyramide building, Rue Botreau-Roussel, Rue du Commerce, Ave du Général de Gaulle), Marché de Treichville, Gare de Bassam, Gare de Marcory

No 6 Airport, Blvd de Marseille, Treichville hospital, Marché de Treichville, Gare Sud

No 12 Gare Nord, 220 Logements roundabout, Le Plateau (Cité Administrative, Blvd Clozel, Blvd de la République, Gare Sud), Marché de Treichville, Gare de Bassam, Port Bouët

No 14 Williamsville, Adjamé, Marcory

No 18 Gare Sud, Marché de Treichville, Gare de Bassam, autoroute, airport turn-off, Hôtel Palm Beach, Vridi Canal

No 21 Cocody, Le Plateau, Treichville

No 22 Gare Nord, Le Plateau (Cité Administrative, Blvd Clozel, Blvd de la République, post office), Treichville (market, Cinéma l'Entente)

No 24 Marché de Treichville, fishing port area, Vridi Canal, Hôtel Palm Beach, autoroute, Koumasi

CÔTE D'IVOIRE

No 25 Gare Sud, Ave Christiani, Marché de Treichville, Gare Koumasi

No 26 Gare Koumasi, Le Plateau (Rue Botreau-Roussel, La Pyramide building, Ave Delafosse, Blvd Clozel, Cité Administrative), Gare Nord

No 28 Le Plateau (Gare Sud, Blvd de la République, Blvd Clozel, Cité Administrative), Marché de Cocody, Université de Cocody, Riviera, Hôtel du Golf

No 31 Marché de Treichville, Gare de Marcory

No 35 Gare Nord, Ave Reboul, Terminus Gobélé, Les Deux Plateaux

No 74 Gare de Marcory, Le Plateau (Rue Botreau-Roussel, La Pyramide building, Blvd Clozel, Cathédral de St Paul), Marché de Cocody, Hôtel Ivoire

No 81 Gare Nord, Ave Reboul, Université de Cocody, Route de Bingerville

No 82 Le Plateau (Gare Sud, Blvd de la République, Blvd Carde, Cité Administrative, Musée National), Ave Reboul, Les Deux Plateaux

No 84 Gare Nord, Ave Reboul, Marché de Cocody, Hôtel Ivoire

No 86 Le Plateau (Gare Sud, Rue Roussel, La Pyramide building, Blvd Clozel, Cité Administrative), Marché d'Adjamé, Gare Routière d'Adjamé, 220 Logements roundabout, Marché de Cocody, Université de Cocody

For travel between Marcory and Le Plateau, buses No 14 and 74 take the autoroute and are much quicker than the other options, which wind their way through Treichville.

Taxi Taxis in Abidjan are reasonably priced. The fare from the Gare Routière d'Adjamé to Le Plateau, for example, is about CFA700. Drivers generally switch on the meter without prompting. Do check, however, that it's set to tariff No 1. The more expensive No 2 rate only applies between midnight and 6 am. Taxis by the hour cost about CFA3000 if you bargain. Racing at death-defying speeds is quite normal; don't be diffident about asking your driver to slow down. Seat belts are compulsory, although not always worn.

Shared taxis, called *woro woro*, cost between CFA125 and CFA200, depending on the length of journey. They vary in colour according to their allocated area. Taxis in Treichville, for example, are red. One red route is between the Gare de Bassam in Treichville and Blvd du Général de Gaulle at the intersection just north of the Gare Routière d'Adjamé. The fare is CFA150 in a shared taxi and CFA100 in a minibus. Grey-and-white taxis run from the Gare Routière d'Adjamé to Les Deux Plateaux, yellow taxis run between there and Cocody and there are green ones in Marcory and blue in Yopougon.

Car Hiring a car is expensive. The big multinationals are all represented: Europcar (☎ 25 12 27, fax 25 11 43), Hertz (☎ 25 77 47, fax 25 42 14), Avis (☎ 32 80 27, fax 32 66 75) and Budget (☎ 25 60 11, fax 25 45 09). Their prices are almost identical. Typically, a small car costs CFA23,000 per day, including compulsory insurance, in Abidjan and CFA26,000 outside. An extra fee for petrol of CFA200 per kilometre is also charged. A 4WD is CFA51,000 per day plus CFA435 per kilometre. To hire a driver costs CFA10,000 per day in the Abidjan and CFA20,500 outside. A 20% tax is added to the total cost.

Prices are somewhat lower at smaller agencies such as Ivoirienne Location de Voiture (ILV) (☎/fax 25 27 67), Axe Location (☎ 26 65 86, fax 26 65 87) or VACI Car Hire (☎ 26 91 55, fax 26 78 94). This last, for example, based at the Hôtel Hamanieh in Marcory, hires a Peugeot 405 or 505 with driver and unlimited mileage for CFA35,000 per day all-inclusive in town and CFA45,000 per day for travel outside.

Boat Abidjan has a good ferry service on the lagoon. It goes from Treichville to Abobo-Doumé (across the lagoon, west of Le Plateau) to Le Plateau to Treichville again (in that sequence; it's a long ride from Treichville to Le Plateau). Taking a *bateau-bus* (ferry) is a great way to the see the city from a different perspective. It's also a way of avoiding the dangerous walk across one of the bridges linking Le Plateau and Treichville. The gare lagunaire in Le Plateau is 100m east of Pont Houphouët-Boigny. The fare from there across the lagoon to the Treichville ferry terminal, also east of Pont

Houphouët-Boigny, is CFA140 and CFA240 to Abobo-Doumé. There are several departures every hour from about 6 am to 8.30 pm.

AROUND ABIDJAN

Île Boulay

SOTRA Tourisme (☎ 32 17 37) offers a 1½-hour round trip (CFA2000) across the lagoon to Île Boulay, south-west of Le Plateau. The boat leaves from the gare lagunaire in Le Plateau at 9.30 am on Saturday and Sunday. If 10 or more passengers turn up, there's also a boat at 3 pm on these days, plus Wednesday and Thursday afternoon. You get a unique perspective of Abidjan's high-rises and also a sense of how immediate traditional Côte d'Ivoire, with its fishing villages, coffee, banana and cassava groves, is to the urban Gargantua. The boat chugs alongside the port and pokes its nose into the 2.7km-long Vridi canal, whose completion in 1951 led to the city's phenomenal expansion. It makes a short stop on the island at Eden Roc, a decaying resort established by a black American, Benoit Brown, long since returned to the USA.

Bingerville

Bingerville, 15km to the east via Blvd Mitterrand, was built on the highest point of land within easy reach of the lagoon. It became the colonial capital in 1901 when the French abandoned Grand Bassam after an outbreak of yellow fever, and was succeeded in its turn by Abidjan in 1934.

For such a long period of occupancy, very little remains. The fine Governor's palace, now an orphanage, is the only building of any consequence. The botanical gardens make for a pleasant stroll. Established by the French as a repository for trees with medicinal and, being French, culinary properties, they're well maintained. But a great educational opportunity has been lost; there's no explanatory leaflet and the only signs are on the commemorative trees planted by dignitaries such as the prime minister of the time and his cabinet members (the one planted by the wife of the current president is ravaged by caterpillars – could this be a portent?).

East Coast

GRAND BASSAM

Grand Bassam, some 45km to the east of Abidjan, can be visited in a day, but its sadly crumbling colonial buildings deserve more of your time. The narrow strip of land between ocean and lagoon, known as Ancien Bassam, is where the French first established their capital, distancing themselves from the locals, whose own settlement across the lagoon expanded as servants' quarters.

Grand Bassam was declared capital of the French colony in 1893, but a mere six years later, a major yellow fever epidemic broke out, prompting the French to move their capital to Bingerville. Bassam, it seemed, was headed for oblivion. Construction of a wharf two years later, however, brought new life and substantial new construction. In 1931, when the French built another wharf in Abidjan, three golden decades came to an end. The *coup de grâce* was the opening of the Vridi Canal.

Today, Grand Bassam is a schizophrenic sort of place. During the week, you'll almost have the place to yourself. At weekends, especially during the dry season, it seems as though half of Abidjan has fled the capital and fetched up here. In addition to the pull of its beaches and restaurants, visitors are also drawn by its boutiques, artisans and craft shops. Beware of the surf and the dangerous tides; every year someone drowns offshore.

The ideal way to visit Grand Bassam is on foot. Alternatively, you can hire bicycles opposite the Centre Céramique. Call by or ring ☎ 30 15 67 and ask for Marie-Jo.

The best time to visit is in late October or early November during the colourful week-long Fête de l'Abissa festival, when the N'Zima people honour their dead.

Colonial Buildings

Confident structures with spacious balconies, verandas and shuttered windows were the style of the day. Of the colonial-era

CÔTE D'IVOIRE

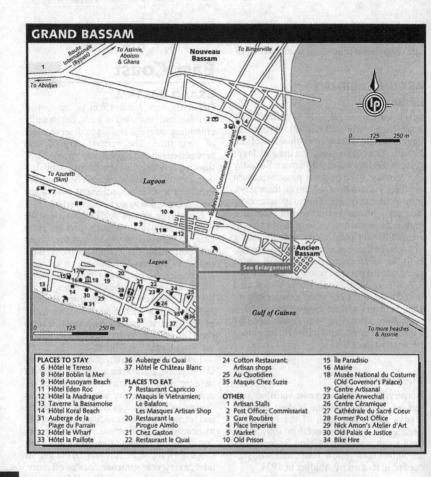

GRAND BASSAM

To Assinie, Aboisso & Ghana

To Bingerville

Nouveau Bassam

Route Internationale (Bypass)

To Abidjan

To Azuretti (5km)

Lagoon

Boulevard Gouverneur Angoulvant

0   125   250 m

Lagoon

See Enlargement

'Ancien Bassam'

Gulf of Guinea

To more beaches & Assinie

0   125   250 m

PLACES TO STAY	36 Auberge du Quai	24 Cotton Restaurant;	15 Île Paradisio
6 Hôtel le Tereso	37 Hôtel le Château Blanc	Artisan shops	16 Mairie
8 Hôtel Boblin la Mer		25 Au Quotidien	18 Musée National du Costume
9 Hôtel Assoyam Beach	PLACES TO EAT	35 Maquis Chez Suzie	(Old Governor's Palace)
11 Hôtel Eden Roc	7 Restaurant Capriccio		19 Centre Artisanal
12 Hôtel la Madrague	17 Maquis le Vietnamien;	OTHER	23 Galerie Arwechall
13 Taverne la Bassamoise	Le Balafon;	1 Artisan Stalls	26 Centre Céramique
14 Hôtel Koral Beach	Les Masques Artisan Shop	2 Post Office; Commissariat	27 Cathédrale du Sacré Coeur
31 Auberge de la	20 Restaurant la	3 Gare Routière	28 Former Post Office
Plage du Parrain	Pirogue Almilo	4 Place Imperiale	29 Nick Amon's Atelier d'Art
32 Hôtel le Wharf	21 Chez Gaston	5 Market	30 Old Palais de Justice
33 Hôtel la Paillote	22 Restaurant le Quai	10 Old Prison	34 Bike Hire

CÔTE D'IVOIRE

buildings, mostly constructed between 1894 and 1920, the Governor's palace (now the costume museum), with its imposing outer staircase, and the *mairie* (town hall) have been restored. Most of the remainder, including the old *palais de justice* (law courts), the elegant former post office, tax office, customs houses, prison and hospital, are vacant now and in various stages of decay, although commendable efforts are at last being made to rescue what's still capable of being saved. The costume museum sells an

excellent leaflet (CFA300) containing a map, suggested walking tour and description of each building.

Musée National du Costume

The Musée National du Costume, formerly the governor's palace, across the road from the old palais de justice, is well worth a visit. It has a small but interesting collection of traditional clothing of the Baoulé, Senoufo, Malinké and Dan peoples. There are also examples of old Korhogo cloth,

SENOUFO

The Senoufo live in Côte d'Ivoire, Burkina Faso and Mali, and are renowned as skilled farmers. The Senoufo hold animals in high regard. They believe that when someone dies they're transformed into the clan's animal totem. Many of their dances, therefore, are associated with animals. In Natiokabadara, near Korhogo, they perform the dance of the leopard men. Such a dance also takes place throughout the Senoufo area when the boys return from one of the Poro (part of the secret Lô association) initiation-training sessions. In all dances, masks, often of animal heads, are instrumental in making contact with the gods and driving away bad spirits.

Blacksmiths hold a special position in Senoufo society. Their relationship with iron, from the earth, and with fire invests them with special power, and their caste presides over funerals. When someone dies, the corpse is carried through the village in procession, while men in grotesque masks chase away the soul. Immune to evil spirits, the blacksmiths dig the grave and carefully position the corpse inside, after which they present a last meal to the deceased, then feast and celebrate.

Top: Senoufo cloth, usually woven by the Dioula (traditionally weavers and traders) and decorated by the Senoufo.

Middle, clockwise from top left: Senoufo furniture: articulated chair; a zoomorophic stool; and a bed with a built-in headrest.

BAOULÉ

The Baoulé originally separated from the Ashanti in Ghana. They live in the eastern and central areas of Côte d'Ivoire. They believe in another, parallel world to our own, the *blolo*, meaning 'elsewhere' or 'the beyond'.

Invisible to ordinary mortals, it's inhabited by people just like themselves. A man may even have a *blolo bla*, a wife from beyond, and a woman her *blolo bian*, her other husband. As in real relationships, the other man or woman can influence the partner's wellbeing, marital stability or sex life, usually negatively.

When this happens, the clan's soothsayer will recommend that the other-world partner be 'called in' or 'brought down' to prevent further havoc. This can be done in two ways: either by moulding a cone of fine kaolin clay mixed with secret herbs or by fashioning a clay or wooden statue of the 'other'. In this way, the parallel-world partner can be controlled and their damage limited.

DAN (YACOUBA)

The Dan (also known as the Yacouba) inhabit the mountainous area around Man in Côte d'Ivoire. Masks are an important part of Dan culture. Each village has several great masks which represent its collective memory and which are glorified during times of happiness and abundance. Masks are not made simply to disguise the face during celebrations; nor are they seen as works of art. The mask is a divinity, a repository of knowledge. It dictates the community values which give the clan cohesiveness and help to preserve its customs. Nobody ever undertakes any important action without first addressing the mask to ask for its assistance. Whether the crops will be good or bad, for example, depends upon the mask; likewise, whether you will have a son or daughter.

Top, from left to right: Fine art typical of the Baoulé – ceremonial container, wooden slingshot, stool and mouse oracle. Mouse oracles are used by Baoulé soothsayers. A mouse is shut in the vessel, and the oracle bones and a handful of rice are scattered on a plate, which is placed inside the container. As the mouse runs across the plate gathering rice, it moves the bones, and the pattern of the bones tells the soothsayer the answer to the problem.

Bottom: Dan mask – the wide open eye holes indicate that it is a male mask.

models of Ivoirian architecture, some truly fascinating old photographs of Côte d'Ivoire during the colonial period and a small but quality selection of masks. In the grounds, there's an artisans' workshop. It's open from 9 am to noon and 3 to 5.45 pm daily, except Monday and Tuesday morning. Admission is free, although a tip is appreciated.

Centre Artisanal & Centre Céramique

The handicraft centre is a cooperative with a fairly wide selection of artisan goods of souvenir quality at reasonable prices. It's open from 8 am to 5 pm daily, as is the ceramic centre, where you can see potters at work.

Places to Stay

At weekends, it's essential to ring in advance and reserve. The top end hotels tend to vary their prices between the brief high season and the rest of the year; we quote the latter.

Places to Stay – Budget

The pleasant, friendly *Auberge du Quai* (☎ 30 10 75) has only four rooms, which are CFA6500/9500 with fan/air-con. The *Auberge de la Plage du Parrain* (☎ 30 15 41), right on the beach, has had a face-lift. Rooms, all with bathroom and mosquito net, cost between CFA6000 and CFA7000 with fan and CFA12,000 with air-con. It has an attractive paillote bar, where they'll prepare meals to order (CFA2500 to CFA3500).

Places to Stay – Mid-Range

Is it the sea air? Both hotels in this category are exceptionally friendly places. *Hôtel Boblin la Mer* (☎/fax 30 14 18), west of town, has rather cramped rooms overlooking the ocean for CFA8000/15,000 with fan/air-con. There's a decent restaurant and you can even have a massage from the qualified Italian co-owner. The new *Le Château Blanc* (☎ 30 18 11) is run by a jovial Frenchman who took early retirement from the oil industry in order to enjoy a less stressful

life, and is more private club than hotel; they'll take you if they like you. Rooms with air-con are CFA15,000 and there's great live jazz on Saturday evening and an extended Sunday lunch time. The food (CFA8500 for the set menu) is French and great.

Places to Stay – Top End

There's a strip of first-rate hotels facing the Gulf of Guinea to the south; all have swimming pools and rooms with air-con and bathroom. Working from east to west, the small *Hôtel la Paillote* (☎ 30 10 76), yet another friendly place, has good food. Its singles/doubles cost CFA15,000/18,000. *Hôtel le Wharf* (☎ 30 15 33, fax 30 10 68), also French-owned, offers bed and breakfast for CFA19,000/25,000. It has its own beach and a good restaurant. *Koral Beach* (☎ 30 16 26, fax 30 12 63) is a laid-back place. It's the most African of the options and has a good restaurant overlooking the ocean. Spacious rooms are between CFA 17,500 and CFA25,000.

Heading west of town, *Taverne la Bassamoise* (☎ 30 10 62, fax 30 12 96) is Grand Bassam's most expensive hotel. It has a tennis court and its own beach. Rooms are CFA31,500/44,000. Bungalows at the *Hôtel la Madrague* (☎ 30 15 64, fax 30 14 59), which has a great shoreside restaurant, are CFA18,000/20,000. The new *Hôtel Eden Roc* (☎ 30 17 75), where rooms cost CFA 20,000, has both air-con and terrace restaurants, specialising in seafood and Provençal cuisine, and live music on Saturday nights.

Hôtel Assoyam Beach (☎ 30 15 57, fax 30 14 74), with restaurant and attractive beach, has cosy singles/doubles for CFA11,000/ 22,500. If you fancy something more strenuous than a sprawl on the beach, Grand Bassam's newest hotel, *Le Tereso* (☎ 30 17 57, fax 30 19 97), owned by the French travel giant, Nouvelles Frontières, offers a range of sporty, keep-fit, Club Med-like activities. Rooms cost CFA 25,000/26,000.

Places to Eat

There are two basic places in the heart of town: *Maquis Chez Suzie* east of the Centre

Céramique and *Au Quotidien* facing the lagoon, a welcoming bar and restaurant where you can get sauces for CFA500 and half a grilled chicken for CFA1300. At *Maquis le Vietnamien* (closed Thursday) north-west of the Musée National du Costume, you can eat well from the extensive menu, with dishes priced from CFA2500 (closed Thursday). Its neighbour, *Le Balafon*, has main dishes ranging from CFA3500 to their lobster at CFA5000.

Restaurant le Quai, also known as Chez Pierrot, serves both African and French dishes in a relaxing lagoonside setting. To work up an appetite, you can usually arrange with the owner to hire out the restaurant's pirogue for a nominal fee. On the same street are *Restaurant la Pirogue Almilo*, thatch-roofed and also overlooking the lagoon, and, much in the same genre, *Chez Gaston*.

East of Chez Gaston, the new *Cotton Restaurant*, also called Chez Roger, with its primarily French menu, is very pleasant, whether for a meal or a drink. For Italian food, *Restaurant Capriccio* has a fine up-market menu, while you can get pizza at the new *Île Paradisio*, which also functions as a nightclub.

Shopping

Ancien Bassam Masques Club, beside the Balafon Restaurant, belongs to Joseph Njie from Gambia. He's knowledgeable and informative about his display and speaks excellent English.

There are several more artisan shops on and around the old Place Commerciale. Facing Restaurant le Quai, for example, is the Galerie Arwechall, which is not at all pushy and has good quality work. For modern African oil paintings, visit Nick Amon's Atelier d'Art (☎ 30 17 09) and savour his brilliantly coloured paintings.

Nouveau Bassam At the entrance to town, coming from Abidjan, the highway is lined with 50 or more artisan stalls selling caneware, cloth, carvings, masks and other crafts. Bargain hard and beware of imitation 'antiques'.

Getting There & Away

Minibuses (CFA300) and bush taxis (35 minutes, CFA400) leave Abidjan from the Gare de Bassam and also from the Gare Routière d'Adjamé (CFA100 more). UTAB has a bus service from Abidjan (Gare Routière d'Adjamé via Gare de Bassam) for CFA500. In Grand Bassam, the gare routière is beside the Place Impériale roundabout, north of the lagoon. From there, minibuses and bush taxis leave for Assinie and also Aboisso (both CFA1000), on the way to Ghana.

ASSINIE

Some 85km east of Grand Bassam, Assinie, near the tip of a long sandspit where the Canal d'Assinie meets the mouth of the Abi Lagoon, has magnificent beaches. The preserve of rich weekenders from Abidjan and package tours from Europe, it has little to do with Africa.

Accommodation, exclusively at the top end, includes the vast *Club Med* (☎ 30 07 17); the similar *Les Palétuviers* (☎ 30 08 48), also called Valtour, in nearby Assouindé; and the *African Queen Lodge* (☎ 35 47 10, fax 35 92 70) 3km from Assinie, with 12 bungalows. For the first two hotels, you must reserve in advance.

The more reasonably priced *Assouindé-Village* (☎ 35 36 85), set well back from the ocean, has 45 bungalows for about CFA 25,000/45,000 (half board). Reservations are required.

From Abidjan, head first for Grand Bassam, from where there are irregular bush taxis to Assinie. By car, take the right fork 28km east of Grand Bassam.

West Coast

JACQUEVILLE

Jacqueville, 50km west of Abidjan, is a small coastal community with a fine beach.

Today, it retains few vestiges of either its time as an entrepôt for the slave trade or its French heritage, except for several dilapidated colonial houses along the coast.

Places to Stay & Eat

If price is your only concern, head for **Hôtel Relax**, 600m from the bus station. The **Campement de Jacqueville** (☎ 31 51 21), only a short walk from the bush taxi stand, fronts onto a pleasant stretch of beach. Attractive thatched-roof bungalows cost around CFA8000, camping is about CFA 3000 and there's an agreeable open-air restaurant. Readers have also recommended **Chez Laura** (☎ 57 71 21), about 2km east of Jacqueville and run by a retired English-woman, where half board costs CFA12,000.

The top establishment is the modern **Hôtel M'Koa**, which faces the lagoon and features a pool and nearby private beach. There's a restaurant and all rooms have air-con.

Getting There & Away

Buses of the 3A Express company run several times a day. In Abidjan they leave from the tiny Gare de Jacqueville, just east of Houphouët-Boigny bridge; the fare is CFA800. If you're driving, be prepared for the 20 minute ferry crossing of the Ebrié Lagoon en route.

DABOU

Dabou, 49km west of Abidjan, is a potential rest stop for those en route to Tiégba or Grand Lahou. If you get stuck here, the principal hotel is **Le Fromager**, which has rooms for around CFA4500 (CFA8500 with air-con) and meals for about CFA2500. There's transport to Dabou from the Gare Routière d'Adjamé in Abidjan.

TIÉGBA

West of Dabou, old Tiégba is a fascinating lagoon village of houses on stilts. The villagers, however, did not seem overly welcoming and you may need to bargain hard for a pirogue for the trip. Having said this, hiring a pirogue for a trip around Ébrié

Lagoon is well worth the haggle. There's a CFA500 village tax.

The only hotel is **Aux Pilotis de l'Ébieyé** (☎ 37 09 99) near the boat dock on the mainland, where most people now live. It has four clean rooms and its terrace bar facing the lagoon is a good place for a drink. It's closed during most of the wet season and reopens in August. You can also stay in a local home. Aim for a price around CFA1500.

Getting There & Away

There's only one overcrowded minibus a day (CFA850) from Dabou to Tiégba, leaving about 5 pm and returning the next morning at 6 am. Expect to pay around CFA5000 for a private taxi – easily arranged in Dabou but infrequently available in Tiégba. The Tiégba turn-off is about 30km west of Dabou on the road to Grand Lahou. From there, it's about the same distance on a rough dirt road through rubber plantations.

GRAND LAHOU

At the mouth of the River Bandama, Grand Lahou was occupied successively by the English, Germans and Dutch. In 1890, it was transformed into an important trading post by the French. After a brief period of prosperity, it virtually died. Today, it's a tranquil seaside village, similar to Grand Bassam except that the old colonial buildings are even more decaying and there are fewer palm trees. The modern section, Grand Lahou II, is on the mainland, while the old quarter is on a thin sand bar facing the ocean.

Grand Lahou is one of the best spots along the coast for surfing. Because of the larger waves and undertow, however, swimming here is especially dangerous. It's also a great place for nature lovers; a few kilometres upstream is **Parc National d'Assagny** (admission CFA1500), a dense rainforest which is home to a large variety of birds and some of the country's few remaining forest elephants. It has observation decks for viewing and guards to accompany you on a walk through the park. Trips here by pirogue can be arranged at Bandama Lodge.

Places to Stay & Eat

At the eastern end of the sand bar, beside the mouth of the River Bandama, is *Bandama Lodge* (☎ 52 10 22), an old hunting lodge in a shaded area between beach and lagoon. It has a bar-restaurant and bungalows with mosquito net and shower for about CFA 8000. For cheaper accommodation, try *Chez Tantie Agathe* in the middle of the old quarter. *Paillotes* without electricity or water cost about CFA1500.

Getting There & Away

There are direct buses to Grand Lahou from the Gare Routière d'Adjamé in Abidjan. You've also a reasonable chance of picking one up in Dabou.

To get to the old quarter facing the ocean, take a ferry across Tagba Lagoon; it operates daily from 7 am to 6.30 pm. If you're adventurous and are headed back to Abidjan, ask around for a *pinasse*. These large, motorised canoes usually travel at night and the trip takes about 10 hours.

SASSANDRA

Sassandra, 71km east of San Pédro, is a great base for visiting the spectacular beaches to its west – if you have your own transport. It's also an interesting Fanti fishing village on a scenic river estuary. (The Fanti, renowned as fishing people, are recent arrivals from present-day Ghana.) It was originally established by the Portuguese in 1472, who named it São Andrea. Settled successively by the British and the French, who developed it mainly as an outlet for timber from Mali, it went into swift decline once the port at San Pédro was constructed in the late 1960s. Today, you can still see several old colonial buildings, such as the governor's house, and the town is small enough to explore on foot.

You can hire a pirogue (aim for around CFA5000 for three hours) and be poled and paddled across the estuary to a soggy island of mangroves, then on to the tiny village of **Glodié**, on the sand bar. Or you can make a six-hour round trip upstream to see the hippos. It's slow progress, though, and your backside will recall the journey for days to come. The alternative is to take a motorboat (inquire at Le Campement or La Terrasse hotels) for around CFA40,000.

You can walk for free and enjoy some spectacular views. Optional routes include a 10 minute ascent up to Hôtel la Terrasse, an attractive circular route up the hill from Safari Plaza Maquis to the hospital, returning via Maquis la Croisière; or an easy stroll to the sadly ruined governor's house at the end of the peninsula.

Places to Stay

The cheapest place to stay, if you can stand the stench of fish, is *La Cachette du Wharf*, sandwiched between the covered fish market and the port. Rooms with a bare light bulb, bed and fan cost CFA2500. It may be short on life's luxuries but the fine view of the bay compensates. *Chez Tantie Youyou* (☎ 72 01 20) is, you might say, a different kettle of fish. Strongly recommended, it sits beneath coconut palms and a giant flame tree, right on the river estuary. Great setting, great food and friendly folk. Rooms, in cabins or small bungalows, cost from CFA 5000 to CFA6000 with bathroom, fan and mosquito net and between CFA8500 and CFA10,000 with air-con.

The small *Hôtel Grau* (☎ 72 05 20) is French-run. Its most basic rooms with fan cost CFA5000. All other rooms have a clean, tiled bathroom and cost CFA6000 with fan and CFA10,000 to CFA12,000 with air-con. The bar is a popular watering hole with expats.

Le Campement (☎ 72 0515) is the only hotel right on the beach and the only one with a freshwater pool (CFA2500 a day, including a drink, for nonguests). Once splendid, it's now showing its wrinkles, but it still has charm, the staff are pleasant and the beach is safe for bathing. All rooms have bathroom and air-con. Singles/doubles/

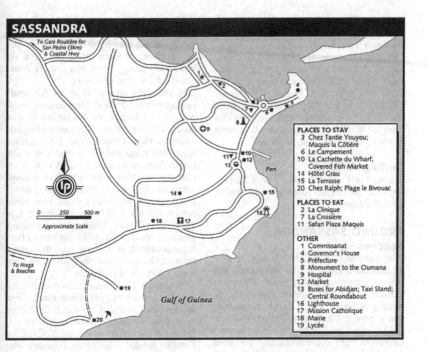

SASSANDRA

To Gare Routière for
San Pédro (3km)
& Coastal Hwy

To Niega
& Beaches

0   250   500 m
Approximate Scale

Gulf of Guinea

Port

PLACES TO STAY
3   Chez Tantie Youyou;
    Maquis la Côtière
6   Le Campement
10 La Cachette du Wharf;
    Covered Fish Market
14 Hôtel Grau
15 La Terrasse
20 Chez Ralph; Plage le Bivouac

PLACES TO EAT
2   La Clinique
7   La Croisière
11 Safari Plaza Maquis

OTHER
1   Commissariat
4   Governor's House
5   Préfecture
8   Monument to the Oumana
9   Hospital
12 Market
13 Buses for Abidjan; Taxi Stand;
    Central Roundabout
16 Lighthouse
17 Mission Catholique
18 Mairie
19 Lycée

triples cost CFA12,000/14,000/18,000 and they also have larger, rather musty studios, which can accommodate up to six, for CFA25,000.

La Terrasse (☎ 72 02 00) is at once hotel, restaurant and bar – and excels at all three. The 500m walk up the steepish hill is a must, if only to sip a drink and enjoy the stupendous view of the port, sand bar, estuary and inland forest. Bungalows and cabins, all with bathroom and air-con, cost CFA15,000 during the week and CFA20,000 at the weekend.

Places to Eat

There's plenty of *street food*, including delicious fresh fish, around the market and central roundabout. You'll recognise *Safari Plaza Maquis*, north of the central roundabout, by the strings of dried coconuts hanging like shrunken heads from its breezy terrace. The speciality is grilled fish (CFA 2200 to CFA3000). What's on offer, which may include barracuda or swordfish, depends on that day's catch. They do a demon stuffed crab. Help the survival of an endangered species by abstaining from the turtle steak.

Two other simple maquis, more drinking dens than restaurants, are *La Croisière*, north of the monument to the Oumana, and *La Clinique*.

Hotel food is particularly good. At the top end, *La Terrasse* has a small, carefully chosen à la carte selection and a menu of the day for CFA6000. *Le Campement* has a more extensive menu but you can't rely on all dishes being available. *Le Grau* in the Hôtel Grau offers good, reliable French cuisine and Chez Tantie Youyou's restaurant, *La Côtière*, has equally delicious fare in a pleasant waterside setting.

CÔTE D'IVOIRE

Getting There & Away

The ETS and SKT transport companies both run two buses a day (five hours, CFA2500) between Abidjan and Sassandra, leaving Sassandra from the central roundabout. Peugeot 504s and minibuses connect Sassandra and San Pédro (1½ hours, CFA1500). In San Pédro, they leave from the main gare routière and in Sassandra from the small bus station some 3km north of town. They take time to fill up.

Getting Around

Shared taxis around town cost CFA125, even for the longish journey to the station for San Pédro.

AROUND SASSANDRA
Beaches

With one exception, all the beaches are west of Sassandra along a well maintained dirt road. Accommodation is mostly Robinson Crusoe – simple without electricity or running water. To reach all but the nearest, you'll have to take a taxi. The trip to Plage Niega, the furthest beach, costs around CFA4500. For the return journey, you need to make firm arrangements in advance with a taxi driver.

The nearest, **Plage le Bivouac**, is a 45 minute walk to the *lycée* (school), then about 10 minutes down a narrow footpath. Alternatively, you can take a shared taxi as far as the school (CFA125) or hire one all the way for CFA1500. There, *Chez Ralph*, the only dwelling, has a magnificent setting right on the sandy beach, beneath the palm trees and beside a small lake, where crocodiles lurk beneath the waterlilies. Small cabins cost CFA3000 and larger ones are CFA6000. All have simple straw mattresses and mosquito nets. It's CFA1000 per person to pitch your own tent. You can get cold Cokes (CFA500) and small Flag beers (CFA500), since Ralph does a daily run into town to collect ice. Meals are CFA2000 to CFA2500 and, if you order in advance, he will lay on a four course special for CFA4500. Even if you don't overnight, it's well worth a visit for lunch or a laze on the beach.

The next beach westward is the stunning **Plage Niezeko**. There's no accommodation but, if you ask the village chief, you can put up your tent or sleep under the stars. At **Vodiéko**, a luxury hotel was nearing completion at the time of writing.

If you have wheels, drop by the small fishing port of **Drewen** (pronounced *dray-van*). Some 8km from Sassandra, it was founded by one Charles Drewen, an English trader. At **Plage Latéko**, about 10km further west, Raymond and his brothers rent out *simple huts* on the sand for CFA3000. It's a friendly, relaxing place and they'll cook meals on request. At **Plage Godé**, Michel Godé, son of the village chief, runs some simple shelters. Full board, it's reported, is about CFA10,000. While you're walking along the beach, look out for the rusting Portuguese cannon. A warning, though: women travellers have reported physical hassle from some members of staff here.

There are three beachside possibilities near the village of **Poly**. *Chez Basil, Chez Marcel* and, at Poli-Crique a little further west, *Chez Ousman*, signed, unless the villagers have torn it down yet again, 'Camping Farafina Beach'. The young Ivoirians who run it are friendly and their fish meals are delicious. The beachside bamboo huts with mosquito net cost CFA2500, each with a basic but clean toilet.

The final and brightest jewel in this necklace of beach paradises is **Niega**, about 4km further west, where the road ends. With its curling breakers, it's a popular surfing venue. Its other great attraction is the dense equatorial forest stretching inland. For a modest fee, the village boys will guide you along the narrow trails. There's a simple campement, *Niega Plage*, about 1.5km before the village, whose setting is idyllic.

At the time of writing, a luxury holiday village, *The Best of Africa* (☎ 72 07 74) at **Dagbego** 35km east of Sassandra, was nearing completion.

Parc Naturel de Gaoulou

On a small island up the River Sassandra and 12km from town by road, a French couple have established this mini-paradise, ideal for wildlife spotting. A simple hut costs CFA 4000 and meals are CFA5000. There's also a one-off entry fee of CFA1000 and a daily tourist tax of CFA500. It's essential to reserve in advance through Marco at Hôtel la Terrasse (☎ 72 02 00) in Sassandra; the owners intend to limit human impact and keep the place small and beautiful.

From the camp, you can take a short nature walk or pirogue trip, with an excellent chance of seeing hippos.

SAN PÉDRO

San Pédro, 330km west of Abidjan, is the country's second major port, built from nothing in the late 1960s. Much of the country's timber, palm oil, rubber, coffee and cocoa is exported from here.

You may find yourself spending a night in town en route to Sassandra, some 70km to the east, Grand-Béréby, about 60km to the west, or northwards to Man and Dan territory. It won't be wasted. The Cité area in the heart of San Pédro throbs, particularly after dark. Although set back from the sea, it has a dockside vitality. There's such a profusion of maquis that you could eat out for a month without repeating yourself and enough bars-dancing to see you through to the dawn after next. You'll find most hotels and restaurants in the commercial centre.

The main public **beach** is 1km west of the port, just beyond Maquis l'Horizon. The commercial port has no interest; you can't even peer through its concrete boundary wall. The small, reeking area where the fishing boats moor, however, is well worth a browse.

Places to Stay – Budget

Camping The Vietnamese proprietress of *Maquis l'Horizon* will let you camp (CFA1000 per person) in the grounds, right beside the ocean, if she likes the look of you.

Hotels At the popular *Hôtel Bahia* (☎ 71 27 33) in the centre of town, Felix, the Ghanaian manager, speaks good English. Well furnished singles/doubles, with clean, tiled bathroom and fan cost CFA4500/5000 and larger air-con rooms are CFA8000/9000. The relatively new, scrupulously clean *Hôtel San Pédro* is highly recommended. All rooms cost CFA4000/4500 with fan and bathroom and CFA6000/7000 with air-con. At *Hôtel le Relais* nearby all rooms have bathrooms. There's one room with fan (CFA4000) and the rest have air-con (from CFA5500). *Hôtel Poro* (☎ 71 22 60) charges CFA5000 for a clean room with shower and fan and between CFA7000 and CFA8000 for air-con. The three storey *EnHôtel* (☎ 71 20 93, fax 71 22 83), near the post office and St Paul's church, is rather soulless. It has clean rooms with fan/air-con and shower for CFA5000/11,000 (CFA6000/15,000 with bathroom).

Places to Stay – Mid-Range

Hôtel Arso (☎ 71 24 74, fax 71 20 26) is a tour-group favourite. The pool is empty these days and the restaurant menu is limited to a couple of dishes, but its air-con rooms are good value at CFA8000 to CFA10,000. The monolithic five-storey *Hôtel Atlantic* (☎ 71 18 14, fax 71 15 48) on Rue du Commerce is a rather forbidding place with a gloomy lobby and reception. It has average-sized rooms with fan for CFA6000 and ones with air-con for CFA12,000 to CFA13,000.

Places to Stay – Top End

The city's top establishment is *Hôtel Balmer* (☎ 71 22 75, fax 71 27 83), 4km west of the port and a CFA1000 taxi ride from town. It's ideally located in large, well tended grounds on a rocky site overlooking the ocean and a safe, sandy beach. Prices of luxury bungalows vary according to season: basic single/double rooms are between CFA25,000/35,000 and CFA30,000/44,000.

The adjacent and almost as pleasant *Village Hôtel les Hauts de Digboué* (☎ 71 11 40) is an easy walk from the public beach. Comfortable bungalows cost CFA18,000/22,000 and they have a pool (CFA2500 for nonguests) and nine-hole golf course. A reader reports favourably on the new *Hôtel*

SAN PÉDRO

PLACES TO STAY
1 Hôtel Bahia
2 Hôtel le Relais
3 Hôtel San Pédro
7 Hôtel Poro
17 EnHôtel;
   Maquis le Noble
22 Hôtel Atlantic;
   Restaurant Hoang Oanh;
   Le Médiator Nightclub
26 Hôtel Arso

PLACES TO EAT
5 Maquis Marine
8 Maquis des Amis
9 Restaurant le Cavally
14 Restaurant la Terrasse
23 Nem Stand
24 Bar-Restaurant le Rock 'N
25 Cheap Maquis
32 Restaurant la Langouste
33 Maquis la Cannelle
34 Maquis l'Horizon

OTHER
4 Ex-Cinema
6 Le Triangle
   (Bars Dancing)
10 BICICI Bank
11 Rond-Point de La Cité
12 Hospital
13 SGBCI Bank
15 St Paul's Church
16 Post Office
18 Commissariat

19 Market
20 La Baraka;
   Raffiné Supermarket
21 ADK Building;
   Parc National
   de Täi Office
27 Fishing Boats
28 Direction du Port
29 Palm Industrie
30 Sipo Nightclub
31 Banque Centrale

Sophia (☎ 71 34 34), right on the beach and with quality – and prices – to match.

Places to Eat

San Pédro is great for eating out. There are plenty of inexpensive places around the gare routière and the Cité has a stomach-challenging variety of good restaurants and maquis.

There's a superb, animated strip of cheap *maquis* and drinking places, wedged one beside another, in the same block as the

market. It's invidious to pick any out since the fare (grilled fish and attiéké for CFA 1000 to CFA1500 or an entire grilled chicken with attiéké for CFA3000) is much the same. *Maquis des Amis*, however, a short walk north, stands out. As friendly as its name implies, it's no frills and basic. The food is plentiful, simply delicious and popular with Ivoirians and expats alike. *Maquis le Noble* (☎ 71 20 93), within the EnHôtel and more upmarket, is also good. If you'd rather be inside with air-con, try *Maquis*

Marine or *Restaurant le Cavally*, which is similarly priced and also has a few Togolese selections.

If you're hankering after an evening away from Africa, *Bar-Restaurant le Rock 'N* – just that – *(☎ 71 20 02)* run by a sparky young Frenchman, is *the* place. Main dishes cost between CFA4000 and CFA5000 and they make their own pasta and do pizzas. With its crisp tablecloths, hip music, blow-ups of James Dean, Mickey Rourke and Elvis Presley, it's also great for a drink or snack. There's even a pinball machine.

Restaurant la Terrasse on Rue du Commerce has Lebanese food. You can get good but pricey Vietnamese cuisine at the *Restaurant Hoang Oanh* in the same block as the Hôtel Atlantic and inexpensive fare from the *nem stand* (selling Vietnamese rissoles) just opposite.

Maquis l'Horizon, 1km west of the port and beside the beach, has both standard maquis food and Vietnamese specialities, mostly around CFA3500. It's open daily from 10 am to 10 pm. *Restaurant la Langouste (☎ 71 19 00)* closer to the port on Route de l'Hôtel Balmer has an attractive terrace, great for a drink, overlooking the waves. Upmarket and French-run, it specialises in fish dishes (from CFA4200) and seafood, especially lobster (from CFA8200). Also on the coast, you're guaranteed a great meal at either of Hôtel Balmer's restaurants, and especially at *Maquis la Cannelle*, which was awarded the title of Côte d'Ivoire's best new restaurant in 1996.

Entertainment

Head for what locals call Le Triangle where you'll find half-a-dozen *bars-dancing* belting out the rhythms. For something more structured – and expensive – try *La Baraka* or *Le Médiator*, both near the Hôtel Atlantic, or *La Grotte*, out near the gare routière, or *Sipo Nightclub*, opposite the port.

Getting There & Away

Air Continental (☎ 71 34 34, at the new Hôtel Sophia) has flights between San Pédro and Abidjan for CFA86,000 return.

Buses and bush taxis leave from the main gare routière, some 4km north of the Cité. It's at the northern limit of Rue du Commerce, beside the Rond-Point d'Abidjan. Buses to Abidjan (six hours, CFA3500) either go via Gagnoa or follow La Côtière, the highway which parallels the coast, some distance inland. ATP has nine departures daily and STP, TKP and TCF each have several.

UTB has a twice daily service to Bouaké (CFA6000) via Gagnoa (CFA3000) and Yamoussoukro (CFA5000). CTM runs two buses a day between San Pédro and Man (6½ hours, CFA4000). If you're aiming for Danané, near the border with Liberia, BST runs a daily minibus via Man. For travel west to Tabou (or Grand-Béréby en route) and east to Sassandra, you'll have to take a bush taxi; they charge CFA1500 to either town and the trip takes about 1½ hours.

Getting Around

Shared taxis around town, including to the port or gare routière, cost CFA125.

AROUND SAN PÉDRO

It's worth a day's excursion from San Pédro to enjoy the superb beaches at **Monogaga**. Here you can stay at the upmarket *Langouste d'Or (☎ 24 84 80, fax 24 81 97)* and, at the time of writing, more accommodation was under construction. Minibuses run from San Pédro's gare routière. To get here under your own steam, take the coastal highway eastwards towards Sassandra. After 27km, turn right at a clearly signed junction and continue for a further 11km.

GRAND-BÉRÉBY

Grand-Béréby, a fishing village some 50km west of San Pédro, has magnificent beaches. On one side is a protected bay with calm waters, while on the other the surf is pretty good. Unlike its rivals, it's also reasonable for snorkelling. Bush taxis between San Pédro and Tabou stop here.

The luxury *Hôtel la Baie des Sirènes (☎ 71 15 20, fax 71 10 32)* has 75 attractive bungalows beside the ocean and backing

CÔTE D'IVOIRE

onto a 40 hectare park. Room costs vary substantially according to season; on average, a double costs about CFA50,000 (CFA 60,000 with half board). Play safe and reserve at weekends.

The only alternative, if it's still open, is *Hôtel Mani* in the village. It has an affable Ivoirian owner, a restaurant and 10 bungalows which cost about CFA3000.

PARC NATIONAL DE TAÏ

Parc National de Taï, with its 454,000 hectares, is one of the largest remaining areas of virgin rainforest in West Africa. You'll see trees over 45m high, with massive trunks and huge supporting roots. They block out the sun, preventing dense undergrowth from developing, thus making walking through the forest quite easy. It's a unique experience. The towering trees, hanging lianas, swift streams and varied wildlife create an enchanting environment.

For more information about the park's special conservation scheme, see the boxed text 'Conservation & Ecotourism: the Taï Example' in the Ecology & Environment section of Facts about Côte d'Ivoire.

The park is in a very rainy, humid area, so the best time to visit is from December to February, when there's a marked dry season. In these months, you can get there by car; at other times, a 4WD is strongly recommended.

Because it's so special and so fragile, access to the park and the number of visitors are strictly controlled. To reserve in advance – which is essential – phone or fax the park's office in San Pédro (☎/fax 71 17 79 or 71 23 53). It's in the ADK building on Rue du Commerce. Normally, you need to call by to collect your *permis touristique* (tourist permit), although you can pick it up by arrangement in Guiroutou.

The all-in price of CFA20,000 per person per day includes simple accommodation, full board and guided excursions (at present you can't explore the park without a guide). These, for the moment, are three: a walk through the forest; a chimpanzee-viewing visit; and a two day expedition, including overnight camp, to Mont Niénokoué (396m), the highest point in the park.

Getting There & Away

If you have your own vehicle, from San Pédro, head west to Tabou, from where a 145km dirt road via Grabo (68km) takes you to the park office at Guiroutou. Under your own steam, you'll need to take three bush taxis: San Pédro to Tabou, another on to Grabo and a third as far as Guiroutou, from where it's a 7km walk to the campement.

If you're coming from the north with your own transport, head for Duekoué. From there, it's a tar road as far as Guiglo, then dirt to Taï and Guiroutou. Since this

---

Chimpanzees of Parc National de Taï

A Swiss husband and wife team, Hedwige and Christophe Boesch, did some fascinating research in Taï with chimpanzees. The chimps live in large communities of 60 to 80 individuals but forage in small groups. What is particularly interesting is how they have learned to select and use stones for cracking nuts. If you're in the park during kola nut season (November to February), listen for the cracking sounds, which can be heard up to a kilometre away.

Equally fascinating is how the chimps hunt for monkeys. It's a group activity which involves a high degree of teamwork to catch the more agile prey. If they discover a monkey high up in a tree, one group of chimps will silently encircle it while another group climbs up and forces the monkey to jump to an adjacent tree. When he jumps, one of the chimps, already in place, may pull the branch aside, causing the monkey to fall into the hands of the chimps below. These tactics are quite different from those recorded by researchers elsewhere.

route is sparsely travelled and serviced, it's probably easier for independent travellers to take a bus from Man to San Pédro, then head north again by bush taxi. If you want to try your luck from Man, take a CTN bus to Guiglo then do the Guiglo to Taï leg by STIF bus or the daily postal van (*courrier postal*). From Taï to Guiroutou there are infrequent pick-ups.

BOUBÉLÉ

Boubélé is a tiny Fanti fishing village with an out-of-the-way beach. It's 4km (which you'll probably have to walk) from the highway between San Pédro and Tabou, 56km west of Grand-Béréby. On the way, you'll pass through groves of palm trees.

The *Village Hôtel de Boubélé* (reservations from Abidjan ☎ 43 01 74) is a top class hotel in a superb location along the River Houou, next to the ocean. Closed temporarily, it should again be functioning. It costs about CFA25,000 for an air-con bungalow with mosquito net and full board. The owner will make arrangements for trips with the Fanti fishing people.

A good hour's walk down the beach will bring you to **Tolou** where, for around CFA1500 a person, you can hire one of the six palm-leaf huts on the beach. It's a fantastic spot and the people are very friendly. Fresh water is available.

TABOU

Tabou, near the Liberian border, is on the main road 16km west of the Boubélé turnoff. Bush taxis from San Pédro charge CFA1500 and take about 1½ hours. If you're headed for Liberia, you must get your passport stamped here. The border is the River Cavally, 27km further west and reachable by bush taxi.

The *Hôtel Campement*, beside the beach at the eastern limit of town, has doubles from CFA3000 to CFA6000. It's a friendly place with a garden and large veranda. *Hôtel Kleh* (☎ 72 40 98), just behind the palais de justice, has air-con rooms and a restaurant.

The West

MAN

Man, known as the 'city of 18 mountains' (*la cité des 18 montagnes*), nestles at the base of lush green hills and has the most beautiful location of any inland Ivoirian town. It's a good base for walking or for exploring the fascinating Dan villages nearby.

Man's main attraction, the covered market, burnt down in 1997. The market used to be a treasure-trove of fabrics, fetishes and woodcarvings, particularly masks. Until it is reconstructed, the merchants are dispersed around town.

There are three craft shops worth exploring: one facing Hôtel CAA, one beyond Hôtel les Cascades and another opposite Hôtel Leveneur. For more information on Dan masks and woodcarvings, see the boxed text 'Art of Côte d'Ivoire' in the Facts about Côte d'Ivoire section.

The best time to be in the Man region is when there are Dan festivals with masked dancing (February is particularly good). To find out where and when a festival is on, contact the Bourse de Tourisme.

Information

The Bourse de Tourisme (☎ 79 20 76) is open, in principle, from 8 am to 6 pm weekdays and until 12.30 pm on Saturday. They have few, if any, maps or brochures but they can arrange an official guide (about CFA 8000 per day) and car hire, with driver but not fuel. They'll also suggest and arrange tailor-made excursions to the surrounding villages.

Places to Stay – Budget

Camping You can camp in the grounds of the *Hôtel Beau-Séjour*, a favourite overnight spot for budget overland tours, at CFA1500 per person.

Hotels *Hôtel Fraternité* (☎ 79 06 89), just south of the gare routière, has simple rooms with shower for CFA2500 (CFA3500 with bathroom and fan). The place is a bit on the

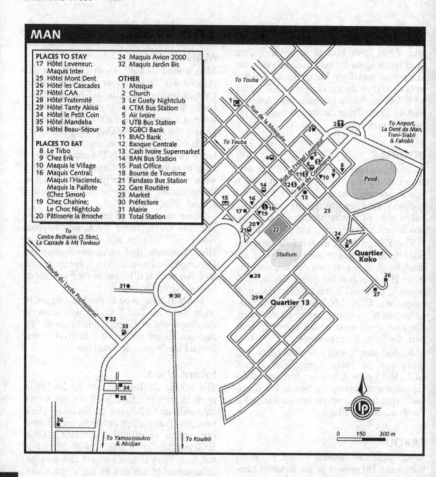

MAN

PLACES TO STAY
17 Hôtel Leveneur;
     Maquis Inter
25 Hôtel Mont Dent
26 Hôtel les Cascades
27 Hôtel CAA
28 Hôtel Fraternité
29 Hôtel Tanty Akissi
34 Hôtel le Petit Coin
35 Hôtel Mandeba
36 Hôtel Beau-Séjour

PLACES TO EAT
8 Le Tirbo
9 Chez Erik
10 Maquis le Village
16 Maquis Central;
     Maquis l'Hacienda;
     Maquis la Paillote
     (Chez Simon)
19 Chez Chahine;
     Le Choc Nightclub
20 Pâtisserie la Brioche

24 Maquis Avion 2000
32 Maquis Jardin Bis

OTHER
1 Mosque
2 Church
3 Le Guety Nightclub
4 CTM Bus Station
5 Air Ivoire
6 UTB Bus Station
7 SGBCI Bank
11 BIAO Bank
12 Banque Centrale
13 Cash Ivoire Supermarket
14 BAN Bus Station
15 Post Office
18 Bourse de Tourisme
21 Fandaso Bus Station
22 Gare Routière
23 Market
30 Préfecture
31 Mairie
33 Total Station

To Touba

To Touba

To Airport,
La Dent de Man,
Tieni-Siabli
& Fakobli

Rue de la Mosquée

Rue de l'Hôtel Leveneur

Rue du Commerce

Pond

To
Centre Bethanie (2.5km),
La Cascade & Mt Tonkoui

Route du Lycée Professionnel

Quartier
Koko

Stadium

Quartier 13

To Yamoussoukro
& Abidjan

To Kouibli

0   150   300 m

---

run-down side but it's friendly, the bath-rooms are clean and there's a small, pleasant bar. Prices are identical at *Hôtel Tanty Akissi* (☎ *79 01 08*) on the next street, although rooms are rather cramped. Tanty, who pre-pares good Ivoirian food, also has much larger rooms with air-con for CFA5000. Here too, there's a small bar.

In the centre, *Hôtel Mont Dent* (☎ *79 03 94*) has basic rooms with clean beds and showers for CFA2500 (CFA3000/3500 with fan and bathroom). Just up the hill, *Hôtel*

CAA (☎ *79 11 22*) is distinctly superior. Im-maculately clean doubles with bathroom cost CFA4000 with fan and CFA6000 with air-con. The cosiness of its rooms belies the hotel's unfinished air – the result of an over-ambitious extension plan that ran out of cash. From it, you get a fine view of Man and the surrounding hills.

The *Centre Bethanie* (also called, incor-rectly, the Mission Catholique) sits in tranquil grounds on the western side of town, some 2.5km (about CFA250 by taxi) from the centre. Turn right off Route du Lycée Professionel opposite the Collège Catholique de Second Cycle, from where it's clearly signed. All rooms come with mosquito net but no fan. Singles/doubles with shared bathroom are CFA2500/3000 (CFA4000/4500 with bathroom) and they have a few air-con rooms at CFA6000.

Hôtel Mendeba (☎ 79 03 41) on the southern outskirts of town is great value, despite its more remote location. Rooms are clean and have bathrooms. They cost CFA4000 with fan and CFA5000 with air-con. *Hôtel le Petit Coin* (☎ 79 03 91) one block north is also spruce and has rooms with fan and shower for a bargain CFA2500 (CFA3500 with bathroom) plus a few with air-con at CFA5000.

Places to Stay – Mid-Range

Hôtel Leveneur (☎ 79 14 81) north-east of the gare routière is friendly and conveniently central. A vast, if stark, air-con room with shower costs CFA6000 (CFA8000 with bathroom). It has a pleasant although uninspiring restaurant and the terrace is a good place to have a drink and watch people.

If you're mobile, *Hôtel Beau-Séjour* (☎ 79 08 55) on the south-western outskirts of town with its thatched-roof bungalows, attractively decorated with paintings, is a good choice. Rooms with air-con cost between CFA5000 and CFA12,000 and they have a few with fan for CFA3500. It has a pleasant paillote restaurant, where dishes on the mainly French menu cost about CFA3000.

Hôtel les Cascades (☎ 79 02 52, fax 79 07 73) in the Quartier Koko, once the best in town, seems, after a change of ownership, to be sliding rapidly down the hill on which it stands. When we visited, the only signs of near-life were the receptionist and a couple of bored good-time girls. Rooms cost CFA8500/10,000 with fan and CFA10,000/12,000 with air-con, plus a difficult-to-justify CFA3000 if you want TV. But its clean pool (CFA1500 for nonguests) is the only one within easy reach of the town centre, and they can't spoil the great view of Man with its corona of mountains.

Places to Eat

Cheap Eats The best place for cheap *street food*, night and day, is around the main gare routière. Man has many simple, inexpensive open-air maquis serving much the same grilled fare, some of which are open only in the evening. *Maquis Avion 2000* near the market, for example, has tasty grilled fish for about CFA1000. Others worth sampling are *Chez Erik*, *Maquis Central*, its near-neighbour *Maquis Inter* and – especially recommended – *Le Tirbo*.

For fast food, you can get great Lebanese chawarma sandwiches (CFA750), hunky hamburgers (CFA1000 to CFA1300) and pizzas (between CFA2000 and CFA3000) from *Chez Chahine*, just across the street from L'Hacienda.

African For a more sophisticated venue, try *Maquis le Village* on Rue du Commerce, where they serve good grilled chicken for about CFA2500 a plate. In the same category, the newish *Maquis Jardin Bis* on the Route du Lycée Professionel has quickly built up a faithful local following.

French *Hôtel Leveneur* has decent but unspectacular French food. Most dishes are in the CFA2500 to CFA3500 range and they do a menu of the day for CFA2500. You'll eat much better in more agreeable surroundings at the French-run *La Paillote* (or Chez Simon) nearby. It has a huge paillote in the heart of a quiet garden. The menu is mostly French with a few African selections, including chicken *kedjenou*. Here too, most dishes are between CFA2500 and CFA3500. There's a Dan singer who serenades diners, if you like that sort of thing, while his small son trails in his wake, looking deeply and understandably embarrassed. Nearby is *L'Hacienda* which serves simpler, less expensive but quite pleasant meals.

Patisseries The French-managed *Pâtisserie la Brioche* is a great place for a terrace breakfast or morning coffee. It does good cakes and pastries and buttery croissants that melt in the mouth.

Entertainment

Man has two nightclubs, with two very different characters. *Le Choc* is more disco, catering to rich Ivoirians and expats, such as personnel from the diamond mines some 45km away, who hit town at weekends to whoop it up. It's closed on Sunday. *Le Guety* (closed Monday), is much more vibrant and African. Both have a first-drink charge of CFA2500.

Getting There & Away

Air Air Ivoire has three flights a week between Man and Abidjan (CFA24,000).

Bus There are three major companies in town, CTM, BAN and Fandaso, and each has five services daily between Man and Abidjan (nine hours, CFA4000), most of them travelling via Yamoussoukro (CFA3500). CTM also has a twice daily service to/from San Pédro (6½ hours, CFA4000), to which there are also a few minibus departures a day. For Bouaké (CFA4000), UTB has three departures a day and CTM one. Avoid Les 18 Montagnes buses; their accident rate is appalling, even by local standards.

Bush Taxi The main gare routière for minibuses and bush taxis is on Rue du Commerce. Peugeot 504 taxis to Abidjan cost about CFA5000. Minibuses headed north to Biankouma (CFA500), Touba (CFA1000) and Odienné (CFA3000) leave from the gare routière on the Touba road, 2km north of the centre, while those bound for Danané (CFA1500) leave from the central market.

Waiting for a minibus to Odienné to fill up can take hours. Much more punctual and reliable is the *courrier postal* (postal van) that leaves every day except Sunday from the post office at 8 am, arriving in Odienné some five hours later. It costs CFA3000, plus CFA500 for heavy luggage, and fairly flies, pausing briefly at major towns and villages to pick up and drop off mail.

Getting Around

The Bourse de Tourisme opposite the gare routière can arrange a car hire for about CFA15,000, including driver but not fuel. Another place for car hire is the Total station opposite the gare routière.

AROUND MAN

La Cascade

La Cascade is a waterfall within a bamboo forest some 5km west of town on the road to Mt Tonkoui. The entry fee is CFA200. A shared taxi seat costs CFA125 although, since it's off the regular routes, you may have to take all four places (CFA500).

August and September are the months of fullest spate, when you can swim at the base of the waterfall. As the dry season progresses, from late December onwards, however, the water slows to scarcely a trickle. The site's very run-down, despite the optimistic sign proclaiming future renovations – including, bizarrely, a zoo. The purported bridge of vines *(pont de lianes)* is in fact made of rope and the one-time restaurant is abandoned and crumbling.

Mt Tonkoui

Mt Tonkoui (1223m), topped by a giant communications tower, is the second highest peak in Côte d'Ivoire and a further 16km of steep, winding road beyond La Cascade. Just before a T-junction where you turn left, about 3km before the summit, you'll see, on the right, a quinine plantation, established by an enterprising Ivoirian who returned from pharmaceutical training in France.

The views from the summit are breathtaking and extend as far as Liberia and Guinea, although not during the harmattan season (December to March). If they're not too busy, the telecommunications engineers may let you go up the 325 steps to the observation balcony at the top of the tower.

La Dent de Man

For hikers, a major attraction is La Dent de Man, Tooth of Man, a steep molar-shaped mountain (881m) north-east of town. The walking track is much more interesting and challenging than the route up by road to Mt Tonkoui and the view from the crest is

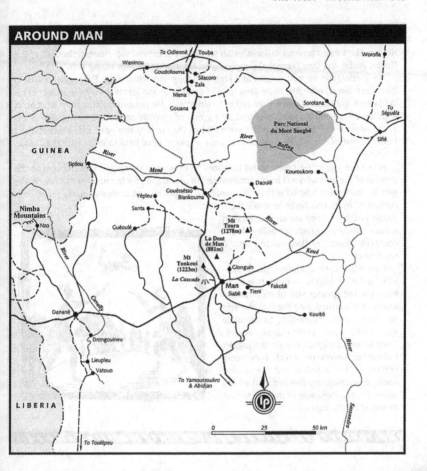

AROUND MAN

superb. Take a shared taxi (CFA250 per person) to the village of Zobale, 4km from town. There, the inhabitants ask for a CFA 500 village tax.

From the village, strike due east to take the path which follows the contour line and southern flank of the hill which lies between you and La Dent. After 10 minutes of steepish ascent, the track levels out as you stroll beside plantations of coffee, cocoa and bananas plus, at ground level, cassava, mountain rice and gombo (okra). In the distance you can see the coffee and rice-processing

plant, the only building of significance to the south-east. After about 1¼ hours, take a minor track to the left. Here, the steep stuff begins – about 45 minutes of fairly gruelling ascent beneath shady trees. Allow 4 to 4½ hours for the round trip, including a breather at the summit. Carry lots of water and keep looking down at your feet and the stunning clouds of butterflies which they disturb.

For a bigger challenge, try Mt Nimba (1752m) at the tripartite border with Liberia and Guinea, which you approach via Danané.

The Child Jugglers

No, we don't mean precocious Indian-club swingers but men of superhuman strength of the Guéré, Wobé and Dan (Yacouba) peoples, who literally juggle with young girls.

The preparation for both juggler and juggled is long and demanding. The juggler retires to the sacred forest, where he undergoes tests of endurance and learns the arcane secrets of his skill, which are handed down from father to eldest son. He remains isolated from all contact with the village and his food, prepared by a group of specially nominated young girls, is left at the edge of the forest. The girls, selected when they're only five years old, are kept apart from the rest of the village children and wear a special headdress to emphasise their separateness.

When the juggler returns from his isolation, he offers two sheep and four chickens to the families of the girls who will be his accomplices. In preparation for the ritual performance, the girls are washed in a liquid with secret medicinal properties and drink an equally secret concoction of roots and herbs to make them supple and light. Their lips are coated with a black substance which, it's believed, encourages silence, for they mustn't utter a word or cry.

Four adolescent drummers and a sidekick, a junior juggler whose role is to highlight the greater skill of his superior, warm up the crowd. And then, as the girls roll their heads, trance-like, to stimulate the spirits, the performance begins. They're tossed high in the air, the juggler brandishes knives on which they seem certain to be impaled and the crowd becomes increasingly frenzied. But all the while, the countenances of the girls remain as still as death masks ...

Villages

The villages around Man, most of which charge an officially agreed fee of CFA500, are all accessible by car. They're well used to tourists. To diminish the hassle, ask for the village chief, who will usually impose a degree of order. If you need a place to stay, he can normally find you somewhere and someone to cook you a meal. At most villages you'll be presented with a sliding scale of charges; this much to see a couple of masks, that for the full 'troupe' and, like taxi-dancers, so much per dance or duration.

For travellers with wheels, an interesting circular route of around 250 to 300km, preferably with an overnight stop built into it, is north from Man to Biankouma and Gouéssésso, then west to Sipilou on the Liberian border, south to Danané, and back (east) to Man.

Tieni-Siabli Thirteen kilometres east of Man on the tar road to Fakobli is Tieni-Siabli. Easily reached by bush taxi, Tieni is an old village on a cliff overlooking two

BASILIQUE DE NOTRE DAME DE LA PAIX

For miles around Yamoussoukro in Côte d'Ivoire you'll see the famous Basilica, set squat against the skyline like a giant, pearl-grey boiled egg. Some of the facts about this lacquered aluminium building are startling. Completed in 1989, it was built in just three years by a labour force of 1500, working day and night. This compares with the more than a century it took to build St Peter's in Rome, to which it bears a striking and deliberate resemblance. The price tag was roughly US$300 million, a sum matching half the national budget deficit, and annual maintenance costs run at about US$1.5 million.

Although the cupola is slightly lower than St Peter's dome (by papal request), it's topped by a huge cross of gold, making it the tallest church in all Christendom. Inside, each of its 7000 seats is individually air-conditioned, a system used only on the two occasions when the Basilica has been full: at its consecration by a reluctant Pope John Paul II and at the funeral of the man whose faith in God, and not a little in himself, was responsible for its creation. The Basilica can accommodate a further 11,000 standing worshippers and as many as 300,000 pilgrims in the 3-hectare plaza – an area slightly larger than St Peter's. (There are only about one million Catholics in the entire country.)

Except for its architect, Pierre Fakhoury, an Ivoirian of Lebanese descent, and its toiling construction workers, it owes nothing to Africa. Stop in front of the second bay to the left of the entrance. There, frozen in stained glass, are the architect, the French lady who chose the furnishings, the French foreman and the French stained glass

Top: The famous pearly dome of the Basilica.

Bottom: Although the architect is an Ivoirian, the design of the Basilica owes little to Africa.

master craftsman. And, at Christ's feet, the conceiver, who bankrolled it all, one Felix Houphouët-Boigny.

Acres of marble from Spain, Italy and Portugal and the exquisite stained glass panels fashioned in Bordeaux were all shipped in. There's even a replica of Michelangelo's Pieta, sculpted by a local artist – in Italian marble from Carrera.

There's another dimension to arguments against such visible signs of material excess. As proponents of the Basilica will rhetorically ask, were there no poor in France when Chartres Cathedral was lovingly built? And was England affluent when the spires of Canterbury Cathedral first stabbed the sky?

What's certain is that you'll catch your breath as you cross the threshold and see the 36 immense stained-glass windows, all 7400 square metres of them, with their 5000 different shades of warm, vibrant colour. It's like standing at the heart of a kaleidoscope.

The visitors' entrance is on the south side. Take your passport, which the uniformed guard holds until you leave. The Basilica's open from 8 am to 5 pm daily except on Sunday, when it opens at about 11.30 am, after mass. Entrance to the Basilica is free but you'll need to engage a guide (fee discretional) if you want to take the lift to the top of the cupola (CFA1000).

Left: The breathtaking stained glass windows of the Basilica.

fertile valleys; below is the newer, larger and less interesting village of Siabli.

Fakobli About 9km further east on the banks of a River Sassandra tributary is Fakobli, where you can hire a pirogue for a river trip to view hippos and crocodiles. The village is renowned for the Tematé dance, performed by young Wobé girls at the end of the rice harvest.

Biankouma Some 44km north of Man on the paved road to Touba, Biankouma is famous for its acrobatic Goua dances, which usually take place on Sunday. The new part of town on the main highway is of no interest. In the old section, several kilometres away on a hillside, the traditional houses are noted for their decorative paintings in kaolin clay. The old part is also rich in fetishes. It is forbidden to photograph many of the fetish houses, so you should ask before taking pictures.

For a bed, check the *chambres de passage* near the pharmacy at the market (about CFA1500 for a room) or the more expensive *Hôtel du Mont Sangbé*, which has rooms with fan and bathroom plus a restaurant. The kids who trail you everywhere can lead you to either.

Gouéssésso This Dan settlement, 12km west of Biankouma, is famous for its unusual tourist hotel, *Motel les Lianes* (☎ 63 33 95 or 32 75 03), which is unique in Côte d'Ivoire and constructed to look exactly like the adjoining village. Rooms cost CFA 18,000, less in July and August. The area's good for hiking and you can cool off in the hotel's pool. About 4km away, there's a short bridge made of vines. You'll need a guide to find it – if it's still there; at the time of writing, it was down, although the villagers assured us that it would rise again.

Further north on the road to Touba is **Gouana**, famous locally for its enormous, 200-year-old tree and its giant termite mound. **Niena**, up the road, is renowned for its masked dancers.

Stilt Dancers

A frequent photo in tourist brochures of Côte d'Ivoire is of masked dancers performing incredible feats on their three-metre stilts. This is a speciality of a very select group of young Dan men in the mountainous area around Touba. During the three to five years of training, the dancers must tell no one, not even their wives, what they're doing. Once initiated, they become empowered to communicate with the spirits who, during the dancing, direct their elaborate, acrobatic stunts, all to the sound of chanting and drums – to the crowds' delight.

TOUBA

This mainly Malinké town, 115km north of Man, has a colourful Saturday market. The main attraction of Touba, however, is the stilt dancers living in villages to the south – well publicised in tourist brochures and posters. Three villages are especially famous: **Goudofouma**, 10km or so south along the main highway, **Booni** and **Zala**, which is 7km south of Touba, then 15km east along a dirt road. Perched on a 500m-high rock, Zala has

322 The West – Danané

magnificent views of Touba and its environs. It's also a centre for hang-gliding – something of a minority sport hereabouts. In early January, when the strong harmattan wind is blowing off the savannas, there's a hang-gliding festival for aficionados from all over Africa.

Places to Stay & Eat

Hôtel l'Escale du Port (☎ 70 70 63) is the best in town and a favourite with tour groups. It has 10 air-con rooms and an excellent restaurant. Nearby is the more modest yet clean and quite acceptable *Hôtel la Savane*. For both, the landmark is the multifingered signpost near the Petit Marché.

Getting There & Away

There are minibuses to/from Man (CFA 1000). You can also get here from both Man and Odienné on the daily postal van, the *courrier postal*. Buses of the BAN company run between Touba and Abidjan, via Man.

DANANÉ

Travelling from Guinea or Liberia, Danané (about 80km west of Man) is the first major town you hit. Its two gares routières – east *(est)* for Man and west *(ouest)* for the Liberian and Guinean borders – are about 2km apart at the eastern and western ends of town respectively, so you may want to take a taxi (CFA125) from one to the other. When arriving or leaving, be sure to get your passport stamped by the police in the centre; otherwise you'll be sent back.

Not far from Danané are some of Côte d'Ivoire's last remaining **ponts de lianes** (vine or creeper bridges), which cross the River Cavally. The major ones are near three villages south of town: Drongouineu (14km), Lieupleu (22km) and Vatouo (30km). The one at Lieupleu (negotiable fee, CFA1000) is the easiest to get to; it's 2km east of the road to Toulépeu and signed. The cheapest way to get there is to catch a minibus (CFA600) for Toulépeu and ask the driver to drop you off at the sign. Otherwise, a taxi costs about CFA4500 return.

Places to Stay & Eat

A recommended budget place is *Hôtel Tia Étienne* (☎ 70 03 88), 500m west of the eastern gare routière. Basic rooms are CFA3000 (CFA3500 with fan and bathroom, CFA6000 with air-con) and they do decent meals for between CFA2000 and CFA2500. There's even wine – at a price. Other budget choices are *Hôtel de la Frontière* (☎ 70 02 10), which has a restaurant (meals from CFA2500), small, gloomy rooms from CFA3000 and an abundance of mosquitoes; *Hôtel le Marquis*, with rooms for around CFA2000; and *Hôtel le Refuge*, with tiny doubles for about CFA3000.

Simon, of La Paillote fame in Man, owns *Hôtel des Lianes*, opposite the eastern gare routière. Air-con doubles with bathroom are CFA7000 and the restaurant's quite good.

Getting There & Away

Minibuses and bush taxis (CFA1500) to Man go from the eastern gare routière. STIF has three buses a day from Yamoussoukro via Man. For more details about onward transport to Liberia and Guinea, refer to the main Getting There & Away section earlier in this chapter.

The Centre

YAMOUSSOUKRO

Yamoussoukro is the capital of Côte d'Ivoire – officially designated so in 1983 – but one without embassies, ministries or significant commercial life. Originally a village called Ngokro with no more than 500 inhabitants, it has swollen to more than 100,000 people because of the whim of one man, Félix Houphouët-Boigny, who happened to be born hereabouts and who wanted to glorify himself, his family and his ancestors. With its lightly trafficked six-lane highways bordered by more than 10,000 streetlights and leading nowhere in particular, and its

YAMOUSSOUKRO

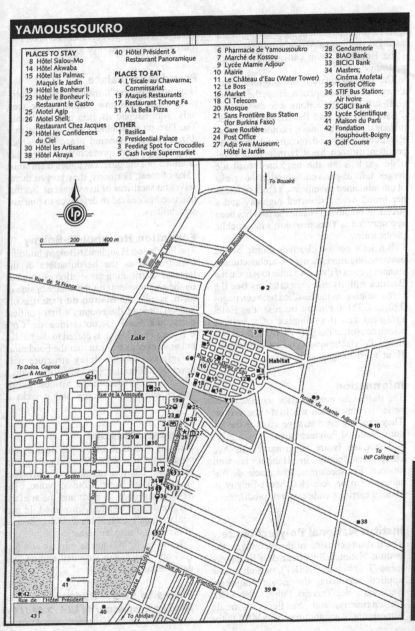

PLACES TO STAY
8 Hôtel Sialou-Mo
14 Hôtel Akwaba
15 Hôtel las Palmas;
    Maquis le Jardin
19 Hôtel le Bonheur II
23 Hôtel le Bonheur I;
    Restaurant le Gastro
25 Motel Agip
26 Motel Shell;
    Restaurant Chez Jacques
29 Hôtel les Confidences
    du Ciel
30 Hôtel les Artisans
38 Hôtel Akraya

40 Hôtel Président &
    Restaurant Panoramique

PLACES TO EAT
4 L'Escale au Chawarma;
   Commissariat
13 Maquis Restaurants
17 Restaurant Tchong Fa
31 A la Bella Pizza

OTHER
1 Basilica
2 Presidential Palace
3 Feeding Spot for Crocodiles
5 Cash Ivoire Supermarket

6 Pharmacie de Yamoussoukro
7 Marché de Kossou
9 Lycée Mamie Adjour
10 Mairie
11 Le Château d'Eau (Water Tower)
12 Le Boss
16 Market
18 CI Telecom
20 Mosque
21 Sans Frontière Bus Station
    (for Burkina Faso)
22 Gare Routière
24 Post Office
27 Adja Swa Museum;
    Hôtel le Jardin

28 Gendarmerie
32 BIAO Bank
33 BICICI Bank
34 Masters;
    Cinéma Mofetai
35 Tourist Office
36 STIF Bus Station;
    Air Ivoire
37 SGBCI Bank
39 Lycée Scientifique
41 Maison du Parti
42 Fondation
    Houphouët-Boigny
43 Golf Course

CÔTE D'IVOIRE

grandiose monuments set just far enough apart to be inconvenient for walking, it's a lasting testament to Africa's greatest curse – the Big Boss, who can get away with anything.

The Habitat quarter, the original town, always resisted occupation. Here, the market bustles, the nightlife along Rue du Château d'Eau beats out and the tranquil lakeside maquis do good business. People are gradually humanising and reclaiming what the president usurped. Small farmers plant vegetable gardens on the neglected roadside verges, tufts of grass push through the cracks of unmaintained pavements, a chicken fusses her brood over a deserted highway and a stretch of boulevard beside the lake has been appropriated as Yamoussoukro's most public public toilet.

But let's not be churlish. Some of the overweening monuments are architecturally stunning, even if they owe little to Africa: the Basilica with its many superlatives (see the colour feature on the Basilica between pages 320 and 321 for more details), the Hôtel Président and the complex of structures which constitute the INPHB, the Institut National Polytechnique (you've guessed it) Houphouët-Boigny.

Information

The staff at the tourist office seem scarcely better informed than the first-time visitor. They can, however, arrange visits to the Institut National Polytechnique.

The Cash Ivoire supermarket on Ave Houphouët-Boigny in Habitat is well stocked. For medicines, Pharmacie de Yamoussoukro on Ave Houphouët-Boigny in Habitat carries a wide range of products.

Institut National Polytechnique

The institute consists of three colleges: the Institut National Supérieur de l'Enseignement Technique (INSET), which trains applied scientists, the École Nationale Supérieure des Travaux Publics (ENSTP), for engineers, and the École Normale Supérieure Agronomique (ENMSA), for agricultural specialists. Each building is a jewel of contemporary architecture. The tourist office can arrange guided visits.

Presidential Palace

Houphouët-Boigny's massive palace complex, where he is now buried, can be seen only from beyond its 5km perimeter wall. The lake on its southern side is home to a dozen or more languid crocodiles which supposedly lend protection. Every day around 5 pm the guardian tosses them some 15kg of meat. Formerly, they gorged themselves on sacrifices of live chickens, but that practice has ceased in deference to tourists' sensibilities.

Fondation Houphouët-Boigny

The Fondation Houphouët-Boigny building (constructed as the headquarters of the largesse-distributing association established by the ex-president) on the southern side of town, is near the **Maison du Parti**, the old headquarters of the country's first political party, the Parti Démocratique de Côte d'Ivoire. The Maison is closed to the public, but at weekends you can tour the Fondation, an impressive four-storey structure with several auditoriums (including one with a capacity of 4500), huge air-con public spaces and marble floors. All it lacks is people.

Adja Swa Museum

Meaning 'heritage house' in Baoulé, this private museum (CFA1500) brings together more than 200 fine examples of craftsmanship from all over Côte d'Ivoire. The lighting, for once, is great and the artefacts are simply and tastefully displayed. In particular, there's a small but superb collection of masks and wooden statues.

It's open from 9 am to midday and 5 to 7.45 pm, Tuesday to Saturday, and on Sunday afternoon.

Places to Stay – Budget

Hôtel les Confidences du Ciel (☎ 64 11 04) a few blocks south of the mosque is a bargain and the young staff are very friendly. '*Dormir moins cher, manger sainement*' (sleep cheaper, eat healthy), goes its slogan. Cramped rooms with fan and shower cost CFA2500 while somewhat larger ones with air-con are CFA3500. The restaurant, however, isn't always open. Nearby, in the same area, *Hôtel les Artisans* (☎ 64 02 27) has more spacious, spotless rooms with bathroom and fan/air-con for CFA4000/6000. It's beside a garage with 'Peugeot' written large on its roof, which is clearly visible from the main drag.

In the lively Habitat quarter, attractive paillotes with fan and bathroom cost CFA 5000 at the new *Hôtel Sialou-Mo* (which means 'thanks, mother' in Baoulé). They're the same price as the undistinguished, shower-only rooms in the main block. The small *Hôtel Las Palmas* (☎ 64 02 73) a couple of blocks to the south of Rue du Château d'Eau has rooms with fan and shower for CFA3000 to CFA5000. They also have a couple of air-con rooms at CFA6000. At *Hôtel Akwaba* (☎ 64 25 84) gloomy rooms with bathroom and fan cost CFA5000. Their air-con rooms at CFA7000 are larger and altogether more pleasant.

Places to Stay – Mid-Range

Rooms at all the mid-range hotels have bathroom and air-con. Several are clustered near the gare routière. Two of the best are at petrol stations, although separately owned and managed. *Motel Agip* (☎ 64 30 43) near the lake has decent air-con rooms for CFA7000, as well as a pleasant bar and small restaurant. *Motel Shell* (☎ 64 11 27), run by two brothers from Lyon, has a bar, popular with French expats, an excellent, if rather pricey restaurant and, in the garden, a veritable mini-zoo where three giant tortoises lumber amid the geese, hens, a crested crane, a gazelle and an antelope. The mongooses, chimps, baby hippos and a pair of lions are more confined, for their sake and yours. Attractive rooms cost CFA12,000.

Opposite, *Hôtel le Bonheur I* (☎ 64 00 61) and *Hôtel le Bonheur II* (☎ 64 00 31, fax 64 09 42) are of near-identical quality,

and have carpeted rooms, with telephones and bathrooms, for CFA10,000 and bigger rooms with satellite TV for CFA13,000 to CFA15,000. Both have good French-style restaurants. Le Bonheur I is the more flexible, offering, in addition to its à la carte choices, *menus* at CFA3500, CFA4500 and CFA5500, plus a '*menu maquis*'.

Recently completed, *Hôtel le Jardin* (☎ 64 38 51, fax 64 34 39), beside the Adja Swa Museum, has large rooms with bathrooms, new furniture and satellite TV from CFA10,000 to CFA12,000, and is especially good value. Further east, the modern *Hôtel Akraya* (☎ 64 11 31) has singles/doubles with TV and radio for CFA14,000/16,000.

Places to Stay – Top End

The town's finest is *Hôtel Président* (☎ 64 15 82, fax 64 05 77) to the east of the golf course, now a member of the InterContinental hotel chain. Whether you consider staying here could depend on your address. Moderate differential pricing for nationals and non-nationals is acceptable enough; but the discrepancy here is huge. If you're a resident, you pay CFA27,000 for a room in the tower and CFA21,000 for one in the annexe. The rest of the world forks out CFA60,000 and CFA40,000, respectively. All rates are between 10% and 30% cheaper at weekends.

Places to Eat

Cheap Eats During the day, several *shacks* around the Marché de Kossou on the Rue du Château d'Eau in Habitat sell dishes such as *sauce graine* and *riz sauce* for CFA350 a plate. There's also an abundance of *stalls* near the gare routière, serving mostly snack food and brochettes.

African Yamoussoukro has some excellent maquis. *Maquis le Jardin* (☎ 64 14 22) opposite Hôtel Las Palmas is upmarket and popular with well-heeled Ivoirians (as you travel the country, you may come across the offspring it's spawned in Ferké and Man). More expensive than most, with dishes in the CFA2500 to CFA4000 range, the quality justifies the price. On the downside, their Julio Iglesias and similar international pap music can be an irritant.

Down by the lake's edge on the south side of Habitat, maquis cluster one beside another and several have pleasant terraces overlooking the water. There's no great difference between menus and prices. Ones which we and other travellers have enjoyed include, from west to east, *Maquis le Jardin's* own lakeside terrace (offering the same menu but without the muzak), *Super Maquis le Palmier*, the restaurant of *Hôtel Akwaba*, *Les Alizés* and *La Paillote*.

Other Cuisines The unpretentious *Restaurant Tchong Fa* (☎ 64 27 43) south of the Habitat market has a wide selection of Chinese dishes at very reasonable prices. They also do takeaways, which you can order by phone. For simple Middle Eastern cuisine, visit *L'Escale au Chawarma* on Ave Houphouët-Boigny. The French-owned *A la Bella Pizza* on the corner of Ave Houphouët-Boigny and Rue de Sopim (closed Monday) serves great pizzas for CFA1800 to CFA3000.

You can eat very well at Motel Shell's *Chez Jacques* and *Restaurant le Gastro* at Hôtel le Bonheur I. At Hôtel Président, the *Restaurant Panoramique*, with its magnificent wrap-around views, is great for a drink or meal. The menu of the day is worth every franc of its CFA8000 price tag – there are fresh flowers and slender bronze gazelles on every table and the service is impeccable. À la carte entrées cost between CFA 2000 and CFA3000 and main dishes are CFA3000 to CFA5000.

Entertainment

Bars & Nightclubs At night, the liveliest area of town is around Rue du Château d'Eau in Habitat, where several modest bars blare out funky music. *Le Boss* is good for dancing. More upmarket places include *Masters*, a fancy disco, and *Sugus*, appended to Hôtel le Bonheur II. The latter is open Wednesday to Saturday and both have a cover charge of CFA2000 to CFA2500, depending on the night.

The classiest joint in town is *Kotou* at Hôtel Président, hopping at weekends but often moribund during the week.

Cinema The cinema at Hôtel Président (CFA1000) shows recent releases. It has screenings at 6.30 and 9 pm every evening.

Getting There & Away

Onward travel in all directions is, in principle, easy from Yamoussoukro, which is a transport hub. However, many buses roll through full. Nevertheless, with a little patience you'll be on your way. Day or night, buses leave for Abidjan (three hours, CFA2000), Bouaké (1½ hours, CFA1500), Korhogo and Man (each CFA4000) and San Pédro (six hours, CFA5000). Bush taxis are more expensive. Typical prices are CFA3500 to Abidjan and CFA4000 to Man.

Most transport leaves from the main gare routière, except Sans Frontière buses, which run to Abidjan and Burkina Faso and have their own station beside the Route de Daloa, and buses of the STIF company, whose station is south of the centre on Ave Houphouët-Boigny.

STIF, which is highly recommended, has at least 10 buses a day to both Abidjan and Bouaké and three to Danané via Man. STIF is set apart from the gare routière both physically and in terms of its services. Departures are announced by loudspeaker, they issue baggage tickets and have two efficient windows which, unlike some of their competitors, don't issue tickets for buses they know to be full. There's even a mosque if you want to take out a little heavenly insurance before departure.

Getting Around

A seat in a shared taxi is CFA125, even as far as the INP, although you'll have to pay more to get to the Basilica in its splendid isolation. They're difficult to find after 9.30 pm. By the hour, taxis cost about CFA3000.

PARC NATIONAL DE LA MARAHOUÉ

This national park is 80km west of Yamoussoukro. A quarter of its 1010 sq km is savanna woodland and the rest is dense forest. There are several trails and four viewing towers. At the River Marahoué (also known as the Bandama Rouge), about 20km from the Hôtel Campement at the main entrance, you can hire a canoe or kayak and the chances of seeing hippopotamus are good.

Baboons too are fairly plentiful and you may see some of the shy, smaller forest elephants, of which there are about 25. Other animals include monkeys, chimpanzee, buffalo, waterbuck, hartebeest and various kinds of antelopes. Nearly 300 species of birds have been recorded here as well as more than 150 different plants and trees.

The park's open year-round, although access is often cut during the rainy season, and you can walk around freely.

Places to Stay

The *Hôtel Campement* is at the main entrance. It has bungalows with air-con for CFA15,000 and cheaper doubles with fan. There are also plans to open dormitory accommodation. For the latest information, ask at Motel Shell in Yamoussoukro, who manage the hotel and run the simple restaurant. There's a park fee (CFA2500 a day) and a compulsory guide fee (CFA3000).

Getting There & Away

If you have transport, head west from Yamoussoukro on the road to Daloa. At Gobazra, about 25km west of Bouaflé, take the well signed dirt road leading north, which brings you to the park entrance and Hôtel Campement after 7km. Alternatively, take any bus or bush taxi going towards Daloa and ask to be dropped off in Gobazra.

You can arrange car hire in Yamoussoukro through Motel Shell or, once you arrive, you can hire the campement Range Rover for CFA40,000 per day, inclusive of driver.

BOUAKÉ

In the heart of Baoulé country, Bouaké, some 100km north of Yamoussoukro, is the country's second-largest city with a population of around half a million. Its numbers increased dramatically in the early 1970s when villagers, dispossessed of their lands by the waters from the giant Kossou dam, headed for the big city. Since then, the continuing stream of economic migrants from all over Côte d'Ivoire and from neighbouring Burkina Faso has been tolerated and even encouraged by the government, which seeks to divert the human flood from further inundating Abidjan.

There's little to see apart from the extensive market, so many travellers give the city a cursory look and pass on. Bouaké sprawls, but the centre and the Koko district, where the Baoulé are concentrated, can be covered on foot. For more information about the Baoulé, see the colour feature between pages 304 and 305.

The main north-south highway is Ave Houphouët-Boigny, in the centre of which is the Rond-Point du Grand Marché. Southwest of the roundabout is the Quartier du Commerce, the commercial district, while the much livelier Koko quarter is to the west. Wherever you are, you can use the tall telecommunications tower in the post office grounds as a landmark.

Bouaké has a particularly good bookshop, the Nouvelle Librairie de Côte d'Ivoire in Quartier du Commerce, which has postcards, a wide selection of books, including titles on African art and culture, and French periodicals and newspapers.

You can make international phone calls from the CI Telcom centre, near the station. Centre Voyages (☎ 63 13 52) is the city's top travel agency.

Grand Marché

Bouaké's market must be one of the most ethnically varied in the country, reflecting the diversity of its people and their eating and purchasing patterns. In it, you'll find Baoulé leatherwork and intricately woven *pagnes*, the lengths of fabric worn by

CÔTE D'IVOIRE

BOUAKÉ

PLACES TO STAY
9 Hôtel le Monde
14 Hôtel de la Gare
15 Ran Hôtel
23 Hôtel Bakary
27 Hôtel Provençal
36 Hôtel Phenecia
41 Hôtel du Centre
50 Hôtel le Lion d'Or
51 Hôtel l'Éléphant

PLACES TO EAT
1 Restaurant
4 Maquis 501
7 Food Stalls
8 Super Maquis l'Opéra
11 Maquis le Pigeon Club;
   Maquis le Phénix
29 Pâtisserie les Palmiers;
   Centre Voyages
33 Restaurant Deauville;
   Pâtisserie du Commerce
34 Chez Donald
38 Maquis le Beaumanière
39 Maquis Walé
45 Maquis le Sahel
46 Restaurant
   Black & White
53 Maquis Mandela
54 Tantie Alpha

OTHER
2 Marché Koko
3 Total Station
5 Agip Station
6 Rond-Point de Koko
10 School
12 Total Station
13 Grande Gare
   (STIF Bus Station)
16 Cathédrale St-Michel
17 Gare Routière
18 Rond-Point
   du Grand Marché
19 Préfecture
20 Grand Marché
21 Petite Gare
   (STIF Bus Station)
22 UTB Bus Station
24 Train Station
25 CI Telecom
26 SOCOCE Supermarket
28 Post Office;
   Telecommunications Tower
30 Nouvelle Librairie
   de Côte d'Ivoire
31 Pharmacie du Carrefour
32 Air Afrique
35 BIAO Bank
37 BICICI Bank
40 Savannah Nightclub
42 Air Ivoire
43 Gendarmerie
44 Club Sportif Amical
47 Cinéma Centrivoire
48 Cinéma le Capitole
49 French Cultural Centre
52 Place de la Paix

To Hôtel Entente (1km),
Hôtel Iroko,
Sans Frontière (3km),
& CK (5km) Bus Station
& Ferkessédougou

To Hôtel le Baron,
Hôtel de l'Air (5km)
& Airport (10km)

To Brobo

Quartier
Air France II

Rue de la Boulangerie Koko

Rue de l'Aéroport

Rue du Camp Militaire

Route de Bouini

Route de l'Avenir

Koko

Quartier du
Commerce

Ave Houphouët-Boigny

Ave Gabriel Dadié

La Route de Carnaval

La Route du Batik

Rue Jacque Aka

TSF Nord

Nimbo

To Maquis Chez Mado,
Hôtel Jean Mermoz,
Hôtel le Lac Vert (5km),
Chez l'Artiste du Batik (3km)
& Abidjan

To Chez
Mado

500 m
0   250   500 m

women, Senoufo cloth, Dan masks and arte-facts from all over the country. The fruit and vegetable section is equally varied, al-though you may find yourself gagging if you pass by the butchers towards the end of a hot day.

Cathédrale St-Michel

This modern cathedral is worth a short visit. When empty, it's like a vast hangar. What brightens the warehouse gloom are the ab-stract stained glass windows which contrast with the representational style of those in the Basilica at Yamoussoukro. Notice also the black Madonna in bronze to the left of the altar.

Places to Stay – Budget

For rock bottom prices with commensurate facilities, there's the dreary *Hôtel Bakary* with basic, grubby rooms for CFA2000 (CFA3000 with fan). The *Hôtel de la Gare*, up a dirt road in an unmarked building west of Hôtel Bakary, yet identifiable by the bar's loud music, also has rooms for CFA2000 (CFA2500 with fan). Hookers outnumber guests and it's probably best avoided by solo women travellers. *Hôtel Entente* (☎ 63 37 52), 1km north of the central roundabout, has tiny rooms with shower and fan for CFA3000 and one with air-con for a bargain CFA4000. Some 200m further north, just off but clearly visible from the road, is the gaunt, four-storey *Hôtel Iroko* (☎ 63 37 09), which is superior. Large rooms with fan/air-con and bathroom are CFA3000/5000. Even better is the small *Hôtel le Lion d'Or* (☎ 63 62 22) in TSF Nord, where all rooms have bathrooms and are CFA3500/5000 with fan/air-con.

Moving up a notch, *Hôtel le Monde* (☎ 63 15 38) in Koko is another small place which charges CFA4000 for carpeted rooms with large, comfortable beds and clean bathrooms (CFA5000 with air-con). *Hôtel le Baron* (☎ 63 58 44), although off the beaten track, is a good choice. It's clearly signed, on the airport road, 200m before Hôtel de l'Air. From the turn-off, it's 800m down a dirt road. Rooms cost CFA4000/5000 with fan/air-con. They're spick and span with tiled

floors and bathroom and there's an attractive thatched-roof maquis next door. South of the town centre, *Hôtel Jean Mermoz* (☎ 63 80 27) has good-value rooms with bathroom and fan/air-con for CFA4000/6000.

Places to Stay – Mid-Range

All hotels in this category have rooms with air-con and bathroom. The two best are both on the outskirts of town, a CFA500 taxi ride from the centre. *Hôtel de l'Air* (☎ 63 35 37, fax 63 28 15) is highly recommended. A comfortable room with a large bed costs CFA8500 (CFA10,000 with twin beds). It has an excellent restaurant with French and African dishes, mostly in the CFA1800 to CFA3500 range. The only drawback is its lo-cation, 5km north-west from the heart of town on the airport highway. At the opposite extremity, some 5km south on the Abidjan road, the new *Hôtel le Lac Vert* has spotless, attractively decorated rooms with tiled bath-rooms for CFA6000/8000 with fan/air-con. There's an attractive roof-top bar which catches the breeze. Set back some 300m on the left of the highway, its name is written large on the front wall.

In the Quartier du Commerce, *Hôtel du Centre* (☎ 63 32 78) is a cut above the com-petition. It has a pleasant adjoining restaurant and charges CFA9000/10,000 for decent singles/doubles with satellite TV. Two other options are *Hôtel Phenecia* (☎ 63 48 34) which has good small/large rooms for CFA7500/8500 and *Hôtel Provençal* (☎ 63 34 91) opposite the post office. Don't be de-terred by the latter's dowdy exterior and tunnel-like corridors. The rooms, all with tiled bathroom and a bleak balcony over-looking the street, are surprisingly pleasant. Rooms cost CFA8500/9500 (CFA10,500/ 12,500 with bathtub). *Hôtel l'Éléphant* (☎ 63 25 28) is reasonably priced at CFA8000/10,000 for singles/doubles with TV and has a good restaurant.

Places to Stay – Top End

The large, rather characterless *Ran Hôtel* (☎ 63 20 16, fax 63 40 32) beside the train station has rooms with satellite TV for between CFA23,000 and CFA25,000, and a large pool.

Places to Eat

Cheap Eats The area around the gare routière and market abounds in cheap, simple *stalls* selling cheap, simple food. There are several more shacks in Koko, near the Agip station.

Chez Donald a couple of blocks south of the post office is great for chawarma sandwiches (CFA500) and other inexpensive Lebanese fare.

African *The* place for African food is *Chez Mado*. It's unsigned and doesn't need to be since everyone in town knows where to find Mado's. Head for the Total petrol station some 2km south of the centre and take the first dirt road on your left (east) for about 150m. Sounds complicated? It's well worth the quest for some of Mado's holy gruel. For a sit-down place offering good African food, *Restaurant des Carrefours* on Rue de l'Aéroport is recommended.

In the Quartier du Commerce, the popular *Maquis le Sahel* is a cut above the rest. Open for lunch and dinner, it charges CFA2500 for a whole grilled chicken with *attiéké* and around CFA1000 for its other selections. *Maquis Walé* on Ave Houphouët-Boigny is a friendly, value-for-money place with a pleasant streetside terrace. Nearby, *Maquis le Beaumanière* is popular not only with diners but also with those who enjoy a little flutter; when the horses are running, the tables are packed with punters checking off their sweepstake cards.

Out in Quartier Air France II, *Maquis Chez Tantie Alpha* is one of the largest and most popular in town.

In the Koko district, maquis tend to be as popular for drinking as for eating. The shady, open-air *Maquis 501* south of Marché Koko, open only in the evening, is worth a visit, as is the rowdier, more animated *Super Maquis l'Opéra*. *Maquis le Phénix* and *Maquis le Pigeon Club* are side by side. The welcoming Pigeon Club may look dishevelled and dusty in comparison

with its sprucer neighbour but the food's just as tasty. It's unsigned, although Thérèse, the jolly owner known to all as Tantie Pigeon, promised us that she'd re-erect the sign. Let us know if it's there!

Asian For Chinese-Vietnamese food, *Restaurant Deauville* in Quartier du Commerce is reasonably priced, despite its relatively luxurious ambience, with most dishes for around CFA1700 – although they hit you hard on the drinks. Sit with your back to the window; their flashing neon sign is a veritable Chinese torture.

French Two places, quite different in character, stand out. *Maquis Mandela* (☎ 63 59 59) in Quartier Air France II, more conventional restaurant than maquis despite its paillotes, is hugely popular with locals. Its African items cost between CFA2300 and CFA3000, while its mainly French dishes are mostly CFA3000 to CFA4000. They also have a gourmet menu (*carte gastronomique*) with main dishes for CFA3000 to CFA6000 – although when you see the menu you'll probably be tempted to eat your way through all its offerings from the first entrée to the last dessert.

Restaurant Black & White near Maquis le Sahel has both an air-con dining room and a small, intimate outdoor thatched area. The French menu is varied and ambitious. With pizzas between CFA2700 and CFA3500 and main dishes between CFA3500 and CFA 5000 and a small beer at CFA900, its prices, for Bouaké, are as original as the menu. It's worth splashing out, all the same.

Patisseries A pleasant spot for breakfast or morning coffee is *Pâtisserie du Commerce* on Ave Houphouët-Boigny which also has inexpensive sandwiches and Lebanese fare. Even better for pastries is *Pâtisserie les Palmiers* with its wide selection of gooey cakes. To refresh yourself, there's nothing better than half an hour savouring the air-con while licking your way through one of their delicious ice creams.

Entertainment

The streetside terraces of *Hôtel Provençal* and *Hôtel Phenecia* are pleasant for a drink. For earthier African bars, head for Koko, which has several. *Savannah Nightclub* on Ave Houphouët-Boigny has three dancing *pistes* (floors) and a cover charge of about CFA2000, depending on the day.

Shopping

Chez l'Artiste du Batik is an exceptionally good place for buying quality batik – works of art rather than the usual quick-dip tourist fare. It's a small, well marked concrete cube, open daily, about 5km from the centre on the road to Abidjan. Mamadou Diarra, the gentle Malian artist who has used it as his studio since 1982, has four photo albums full of his designs, which he'll make to order. He'll also print your own pattern if you're specific enough.

Prices vary according to the complexity and originality of the design and the number of colours applied. Simple pieces start at around CFA1500. Batiks 1m long begin at about CFA5000 but can sell for as much as CFA16,000. A batik tablecloth for 12 typically costs CFA22,000.

Getting There & Away

Air Air Ivoire (☎ 63 34 37) has two flights a week to/from Abidjan (CFA22,000) and one a week to/from Korhogo (CFA12,550) and Ouagadougou (CFA54,100). Air Continental (☎ 63 74 64) also operates flights between Bouaké and Abidjan (CFA70,000 return). A taxi to the airport, about 10km from town, costs CFA1000.

Bus & Bush Taxi Most buses and bush taxis leave from the Gare Routière du Grand Marché. UTB runs more than 10 buses a day to/from Abidjan from its own station south of the market. It also has three services a day for San Pédro and Man. Once the market leader, UTB these days faces STIF competition (okay, okay, so it's pronounced *steef*…). On the routes where they coincide, STIF is markedly superior. They too run buses to Abidjan via Yamoussoukro, which

you can pick up at either their grande or petite gare at the Grand Marché. They also have a daily bus to Danané via Man and three to Daloa via Yamoussoukro.

CK has four buses a day to Ferkessé-dougou and Korhogo, leaving from their station about 5km north of the Rond-Point du Grand Marché. Sans Frontière has a minimum of one departure a day for Burkina Faso. Their station is also on Ave Houphouët-Boigny, about 3km north of the roundabout.

Standard fares are Abidjan (five hours, CFA3000), Yamoussoukro (1½ hours, CFA 1500) and Korhogo (four hours, CFA2500). A ticket costs CFA2500 to Ferké, CFA4000 to Man and CFA5000 to San Pédro.

Peugeot 504 bush taxis serve all of the same routes and charge about 50% more.

Train The train for Burkina Faso and Ouagadougou (1st/2nd class fare, CFA17,300/ 11,400) is scheduled to leave Bouaké early on Tuesday, Thursday and Saturday afternoon. For Abidjan, the bus is cheaper and more reliable.

TANOU-SAKASSOU

Some 12km east of Bouaké on the road to Bobo, Tanou-Sakassou is one of several villages in the Bouaké area where the women specialise in pottery-making.

The village is on the left and marked by a small artisans' cooperative sign. The pottery sculptures made here, in the form of animals or female heads, are very fine. You can buy a good example for around CFA 2500.

KATIOLA

About 55km north of Bouaké on the highway to Ferké, Katiola is the take-off point for the southern entrance to Parc National de la Comoë some 170km to the east. It has a huge pottery cooperative on the eastern outskirts. The pottery, heavily glazed and of tourist quality, is less interesting than seeing the women at work (for a fee) as they fashion perfectly symmetrical jugs without the aid of a pottery wheel.

Hôtel Makarwa and *Hôtel de l'Amitié* (☎ 65 43 63) are both inexpensive. *La Paillote*, 2km from the centre, has clean huts with showers and mosquito nets. The top place is the modern *Hôtel Hambol* (☎ 65 47 25) on the north side of town. It has air-con rooms for about CFA9500, a bar, restaurant, pool and nightclub.

The North

KORHOGO
A nine hour bus ride (640km) north from Abidjan, Korhogo, dating from the 13th century, is the capital of the Senoufo, who are best known for their woodcarvings and cloth – coarse raw cotton, like burlap, with painted or woven designs (for more details, see the boxed text 'Korhogo Cloth' later in this section). They're also renowned for their skilled blacksmiths *(forgerons)* and

---

The Lô Association

The secret Lô association of the Senoufo, which is divided into the Poro cult for boys and the Sakrobundu cult for girls, is essentially a way of preparing children for adulthood. The goal is to preserve the group's folklore, teach children about their tribal customs so that they can take over the various social duties of the community, and, through various rigorous tests, enable them to gain self-control. Their education is divided into three seven-year periods ending with an initiation ceremony involving circumcision, isolation, instruction and the use of masks. Each community has a 'sacred forest' where the training takes place. Many of the rituals involve masked dances; the uninitiated are never allowed to see them or the tests which the young people must undergo. However, some ritual ceremonies, such as the dance of the leopard men, occur in the village itself when the boys return from one of their training sessions, and these are open to all.

---

potters *(potiers)*. (For more details on Senoufo art and culture, see the boxed text 'Art of Côte d'Ivoire' in the Facts about Côte d'Ivoire section earlier and the colour feature between pages 304 and 305). Korhogo is therefore a popular destination for travellers; not so much for the town itself but as a base for visiting the nearby artisans' villages for which you'll need your own or hired transport.

The heart of town is the bustling market, near which are the major bus company offices and the BIAO bank, which will cash travellers cheques if you have your purchase receipt. The city's longest established hotel is named after Mt Korhogo, which is on the south-western outskirts of town and can be hiked in half an hour or so. Most government offices, including the police station and the small tourist office, the Délégation Régionale de Tourisme (☎ 86 05 84), are around Place de la Paix.

The tourist office can make arrangements for you to see some of the dancing for which the Senoufo are famous. There are many other guides around town, some of whom are quite competent. If someone offers their services, ask to see their *carte professionelle de guide*, proof that they're recognised by the Délégation and have followed its training course.

Things to See & Do
The small **Musée Régional Péléforo Gbon Coulibaly** was the home of the famous Senoufo chief, Péléforo Gbon Coulibaly, until his death in 1962. Abandoned until 1987, it reopened as a repository for traditional Senoufo crafts in 1992. It has some interesting old photographs, chiefs' chairs, Korhogo cloth and fine wooden statues and masks. It's open from 8.30 am to noon and from 3 to 6 pm, Tuesday to Saturday. Donations are accepted – 'thanks for your gift', the box cheerily announces in English.

Most of the city's woodcarvers live and work in a small district, the **Quartier des Sculpteurs**. At its heart is the **Maison des Feticheurs**, a small building dating from 1901. For a price, the old man who guards

KORHOGO

To Hôtel le Tisserin (500m),
Sinématiali &
Ferkessédougou

To Koni &
M'Bengue

0   200   400 m

To Boundiali &
Odienné

Route de Koni

Route de Boundiali

To Boundiali

To Kapélé, Foro &
Mt Korhogo

Petit Paris

Koko Nord

Servil
Kaha

Quartier des
Sculpteurs

Koro Sud

Dem

Residential

Route de Sirasso

To Waraniéné
& Sirasso

To Airport,
Dikodougou, Katia,
Napié, Farkaha
& Badikaha

Place
de la
Paix

Sinistre

Route de Dikodougou

Route de l'Adropont

To Airport,
Karakoro & Badikaha

Route de Ferkessédougou

Ave Coulibaly

PLACES TO STAY
1 Hôtel Kadjona
2 Hôtel les Avocats
4 Hôtel le Vert Paradis
6 Motel Agip;
   Vehicles to Ferké
7 Hôtel le Palmier
8 Hôtel Pèlerin;
   CK buses for Bouaké
20 Hôtel Gon
21 Hôtel du Centre Ville
22 Hôtel Mont Korhogo;
   Air Ivoire
28 Mission Catholique
39 Hôtel la Rose Blanche

PLACES TO EAT
5 Maquis l'Escale
18 Maquis le Katana
25 Maquis Alpha 2000
33 Chez Mousso
34 Maquis Jéricho
35 La Bonne Cuisine
36 Chez Donald

OTHER
3 Maison du Coulibaly
   Kassoum
9 Market
10 Maison des Feticheurs
11 Mosque
12 Cinema
13 BIAO Bank
14 SGBCI Bank
15 DB Bus Station
16 CK Bus Station
17 Pharmacie du Nord
19 Musée Régional Péléforo
   Gbon Coulibaly;
   Maquis les Lianes
23 BICICI Bank
24 CTK Bus Station
26 Post Office;
   Postal Van to Odienné
27 CI Telecom
30 Commissariat
31 Centre Artisanal
32 Préfecture
33 Mairie
37 Municipal Pool
38 Tourist Office

this place may agree to let you see the fetishes inside. In the vicinity, you'll find woodcarvers at work, all keen to show you around their storerooms.

Places to Stay – Budget

The two cheapest options are the stark, two storey *Hôtel Gon* (☎ 86 06 70) near the museum, which has bare rooms with shared bathroom for CFA2000 (CFA2500 with fan) and *Hôtel le Pèlerin* next to the market. Its rooms are poky but have fans, mosquito nets

and showers. Singles/doubles cost CFA2000/2500. The downside is the noisy disco next door.

A better place in the centre is *Hôtel le Palmier* on Route de Ferkessédougou south of the Agip petrol station. Rooms are CFA4000 with bathroom and fan and CFA5000 with chugging air-con. Don't be tempted to take their cheapest rooms which are unbelievably grubby and used intensively by the girls who hang around under the hotel's (literally) red light. Accommodation at the friendly *Mission Catholique* east of the post office has recently had a facelift and is excellent value. Trim rooms with mosquito net and shower cost CFA4000 (CFA5000 with air-con).

Hôtel du Centre Ville (☎ 86 13 34) across the road from the CTK bus station is more promising than its run-down exterior would suggest. Rooms are a bit stuffy but they're clean and cost CFA3500 with bathroom and fan and CFA5000 with air-con. *Hôtel le Tisserin* (☎ 86 05 92), heading north along Route de Ferkessédougou, is a good deal. Medium-sized singles/doubles with air-con, small tiled bathroom and comfortable bed cost CFA4000/4500). Although it has no restaurant there's a good maquis over the road. It's relatively remote but on a regular shared taxi route.

Places to Stay – Mid-Range

All rooms in these mid-range hotels have bathroom and air-con. The privately owned, French-run *Motel Agip* (☎ 86 01 13), although in the middle price bracket, offers top end quality. Almost always full, its immaculate rooms are a bargain CFA7500. The bar is homely and attractive and the garden restaurant has the best French cuisine in town. Also central, the new and friendly *Le Vert Paradis* has rooms from CFA7500.

At the relaxing *Hôtel la Rose Blanche* (☎ 86 06 13) all rooms have TV and carpets. Smallish rooms cost CFA7500/9000 and larger ones are CFA9000/12,000. They also have a decent restaurant. *Hôtel les Avocats* (☎ 86 27 30) makes up in comfort and reasonableness for its relative remoteness. Standard rooms cost CFA5000. For CFA 2000 more, you can have a 'semi-suite' with armchairs and table and, at CFA10,000, a suite with bedroom and separate lounge. There's a restaurant and shaded courtyard. The hotel can rustle up a taxi (CFA500) to take you to the centre.

Hôtel Kadjona (☎ 86 20 87) has well maintained rooms with TV for CFA8500/11,000. There's a pool, a restaurant and maquis, and in the grounds you can see a couple of Dioula weavers from the village of Waraniéné at their looms.

Most tours groups stay at *Hôtel Mont Korhogo* (☎ 86 02 93, fax 86 04 07), the city's top hotel. Rooms cost CFA11,000/13,500. Within its extensive, well maintained grounds, there's a pool (CFA800 for non-guests) and a good, if soulless restaurant. The hotel's *Le Poro Nightclub* (first drink, CFA2500) is active at weekends.

Places to Eat

La Bonne Cuisine east of Place de la Paix in the Sinistre district has dishes such as *sauce aubergine*, *sauce graine*, and *sauce gombo*, each for CFA500. At night, it becomes a maquis with grilled chicken for CFA2500 and grilled fish for CFA1500 to CFA2000, according to size.

Other congenial places, all serving much the same fare, include *Maquis le Katana* and *Maquis les Lianes* on either side of the museum, and, in the same area, *Maquis Alpha 2000*. *Chez Mousso* is an easy stroll east if you're staying at the Mission Catholique, while *Maquis l'Escale* is conveniently near the various bus stations, if you arrive starving or parched.

For a more upmarket maquis, try the one at *Hôtel Kadjona*. Also in the Sinistra district, *Maquis Jéricho* has a good reputation locally while, nearby, *Chez Donald* has chawarma sandwiches (CFA500), steak and chips (CFA2000), baby pizzas (CFA300) and good, safe ice cream.

By far the best French restaurant, for both food and ambience, is at *Motel Agip*; it offers a great three course meal for CFA4000 plus à la carte dining. The restaurant at *Hôtel Mont Korhogo* does a three course tourist menu for CFA4200 in addition to its ambitious range of French dishes. Although the food's decent enough, the place is short on atmosphere and you may find yourself the only eater in its spacious dining room.

Shopping

The Maison de l'Union des GVC d'Artisans du Nord, more commonly and less tongue-twistingly known as the Centre Artisanal, west of Place de la Paix on the road to Boundiali stocks good quality Korhogo cloth plus Senoufo carvings, pottery and bronze castings of less merit. Prices are reasonable and fixed. It's an excellent place to start your shopping or simply to browse and get a feel for what to look for in the market and in the nearby artisans' villages. It's open from 8 am to noon and from 2.30 to 6 pm daily.

Getting There & Away
Air Air Ivoire, whose office is in Hôtel Mont Korhogo, flies between Abidjan and Korhogo (CFA36,000 return) three times a week, with a stop en route at Bouaké or Man. Air Continental (☎ 86 01 65) also has flights to/from Bouaké for CFA 86,000 return.

Bus & Minibus Buses depart from each company's office; all are within easy reach of the market area. CTK and DB each run two services a day between Korhogo and Abidjan (eight to 10 hours, CFA4000) while CK has three. All offer a morning and evening departure. To save a day of your life and a night's accommodation, take the evening bus. If you arrive before dawn, you can continue sleeping on board. All buses make a stop in Yamoussoukro, to which you'll also pay CFA4000. DB and CK have at least two buses a day to/from Bouaké (four to five hours, CFA2500).

To Odienné (five hours, CFA3500), the best way to go is with the battered, windowless postal van, which leaves from the post office around 8 am every day except Sunday.

Minibuses, by contrast, take an eternity to fill up. A minibus costs CFA1000 to Ferkessédougou and CFA2000 to Boundiali, plus CFA200 or so for baggage.

Getting Around
A seat in a shared taxi costs CFA125. You'll have trouble finding one after 10 pm and, if you do, you'll have to pay more. By the hour, you should be able to get one for around CFA3000.

The tourist office (☎ 86 05 84) can arrange car hire (CFA20,000 plus fuel, including

Korhogo Cloth

You'll find Korhogo cloth in all of Côte d'Ivoire's major hotels as bedspreads, wall hangings, napkins and tablecloths. It's easy to recognise the coarse, cream-coloured cotton with either woven geometrical designs or fantastical painted animals and figurative shapes.

Its production illustrates the symbiotic relationship between two neighbouring but very different peoples. The Senoufo, animist and agriculturalist, grow the cotton, which they sell in its raw form to the Dioula, who are traditionally weavers and traders.

The Dioula women spin the cotton, which their menfolk weave into long strips. Being Muslim, they eschew anything figurative or representational. So they either weave in a variety of geometrical shapes or produce plain, unadorned cloth – which they sell back to the Senoufo.

Traditionally, the Senoufo painted this cloth with fantastical animals and bold allegorical motifs for their hunters and dancers and for young people undergoing initiation. Nowadays, it's very much for the tourist trade but the technique remains the same and the dyes – brown, black and burnt red – are still made from natural, local products.

Brown is the base colour, brewed from the fermented leaves of the *nangenmé* tree. For black, maize (corn) or millet cobs are left to ferment. When the transparent liquid which trickles off is daubed over the brown base, it becomes black. The juice for the burnt red colour comes from fermented sorghum stalks and is applied directly to the cream cloth.

To complete the cycle, the Senoufo sell the finished, dyed cloth back to the Dioula, the merchants.

Although some artisans have now moved to town, all weaving is traditionally done in the village of Waraniéné, 4km from Korhogo, while the dyes are applied in Farkaha, 35km to the south-east.

driver) and provide an English-speaking guide (CFA8000 per day).

AROUND KORHOGO

The villages around Korhogo, where you can see artisans at work, are well accustomed to tourists and prices are generally no lower than in town. Main villages of interest are Waraniéné for weavers (*tisserands*), Farkaha for painted Korhogo cloth, Sinématiali and Kanioraba for potters, Koni and Kasoumbarga for blacksmiths (for more information about Senoufo blacksmiths, see the colour feature between pages 304 and 305), Niofouin for traditional Senoufo architecture and Torgokaha for basket makers (*vanniers*).

Without a vehicle, it's difficult to see all but the nearest villages. Negotiate a price that's exclusive of petrol; otherwise, the driver will baulk at every small detour. It's well worth investing in a guide, even if you have your own vehicle, for their knowledge, to avoid getting lost and to parry the sometimes over-insistent villagers.

Waraniéné

The most touristy village is Waraniéné, in part because it's so accessible, only 4km south-west of Korhogo on the route to Sirasso. As in all Dioula communities, men weave while the women spin and spool the threads. Finished products include tablecloths, bedspreads, smocks and bedspreads. The weavers' cooperative there has set prices, which are considerably less than those in Abidjan.

Farkaha

The sleepy town of Farkaha, 35km southeast of Korhogo, makes most of the top-quality Korhogo cloth. As in Waraniéné, there's a cooperative, where bargaining is possible. To get here, take the old airport road to Napié (19km) and fork left for Farkaha, 16km further. At Katia, about halfway between Korhogo and Napié, several shops specialise in Korhogo cloth.

Sinématiali & Kanioraba

For pottery, head east for Sinématiali (30km on the tar road to Ferkessédougou) or, better

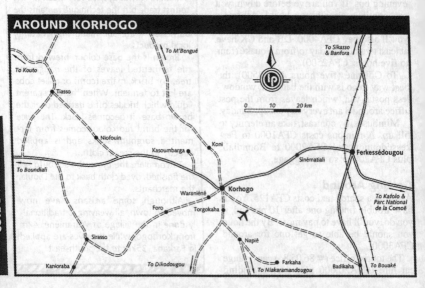

AROUND KORHOGO

still, south-west to Kanioraba (50km) via Sirasso. Although more difficult to reach, Kanioraba is a village of traditional round houses, while Sinématiali, once similar, now has ugly modern structures with metallic roofs.

Koni

At Koni, 17km north-west of Korhogo on the dirt road to M'Bengué, Senoufo blacksmiths make agricultural implements. If you're very lucky, you might see parts of the entire process in one visit: from mining the ore, by lowering men down shafts up to 20m deep, to smelting the iron and forging tools. Note that Senoufo smiths don't work on Friday.

Kasoumbarga

Kasoumbarga, 23km west of Korhogo, is another blacksmith centre. It also has a ruined 17th-century mosque, unusual in that it's round with a thatched roof. Take the tar Boundiali road for 14km then turn right (north). Kasoumbarga is 9km further.

Niofouin

Niofouin is interesting for its traditional Senoufo housing. Many of the mud-walled buildings with thick, straw roofs are in good condition. While some of the older structures may not be in perfect shape, they are less altered by incongruous modern features such as metal roofs than those of some other villages. Take the Boundiali road west out of Korhogo for 45km then go left (north-west) on a dirt road for another 12km.

Torgokaha

Torgokaha is 7km south of Korhogo on the road to Dikodougou and is noted for its basket and mat weavers.

BOUNDIALI

Some 98km west of Korhogo, this Senoufo town in the heart of the country's cotton belt has a good market, and is a good point of departure for visiting traditional Senoufo villages to see artisans at work. Around 30km north of Boundiali is **Kouto**, which has a beautiful 17th-century mosque with mud walls (and, ecumenically, a Catholic mission to stay at). On the way here, you'll pass **Kolia**, known as a pottery crafts centre. Both towns are also noted centres for blacksmiths, and you can watch them hauling the iron-rich earth from deep vertical shafts and washing it in the river before smelting.

Places to Stay & Eat

Hôtel Record, near the market, has clean rooms with bathroom for about CFA2500. *Hôtel Ledala* has also been recommended. You can eat at *Maquis de l'Indenie* (Chez Tanty Viane), on Ave Jean-Baptiste-Mockey, *Restaurant le Paysan* or *Restaurant le Carrefour de la Paix*.

Getting There & Away

Bush taxis leave from the gare routière for Korhogo (CFA2000) and, much less often, Odienné. You may find space on the postal vans, which pass through town in the late morning, one headed for Korhogo and the other for Odienné.

ODIENNÉ

Odienné (population 35,000) is in Malinké country and is predominantly Muslim. Historically, it's important for its strong support for Samory Touré, famous for his tenacious resistance to the French (see the History section at the beginning of the chapter for more details). Near the large mosque is the grave of Vakaba Tourié, the Malinké warrior who founded the city.

Today, most of the town's traditional houses have been replaced by unattractive modern buildings. However, the setting in a valley, 12km east of the 800m-high **Massif du Dinguélé**, is attractive. You could hire a taxi to the foot of the mountain and do a half-day (round trip) hike to the summit, from where the view's spectacular.

Take your bearings from the central roundabout and the four roads sprouting from it. The road north goes to Hôtel Kaoka,

Hôtel Romani and Lac Savané. The post office is on the short southern spur which ends at the *préfecture* (police station). Off this are Maquis le Yancadi and the Campement. Along Bamoko Rd, heading west, you'll find Air Ivoire, Restaurant les Étoiles, Hôtel des Frontières and Touristel. Eastwards, the road heads towards Boundiali and Korhogo.

At Hôtel les Frontières, they can give you information about, and just possibly arrange a tour of, the nearby Zievasso and Diougoro **gold mines**. At **Samatiguila**, 38km north, there's a well preserved 17th-century mosque. The adjoining museum has a small display of weapons from the time of Samory Touré. According to local legend, he called by the mosque to pray before sacking the town. However, rising to his feet, he was incapable of finding his way out. Eventually, the imam of the mosque led him to the exit, against Samory Touré's solemn promise that he'd spare the town.

Places to Stay

The *Campement*, opposite Maquis le Yancadi, has gloomy, spartan rooms with shower for CFA3000. Ones with bathroom and fan are CFA4000 (CFA5000 with aircon). The only other budget accommodation is *Hôtel Kaoka*, about 500m north of the roundabout, which is distinctly superior.

Hôtel des Frontières (☎ 80 02 03) is 1km west of town. Once the star of Odienné, it's beginning to slip, with lackadaisical staff and neglected maintenance. It has a pool (CFA 1000 for nonguests). Bungalow singles/doubles with air-con and bathroom cost CFA9000/10,000. A little beyond the hotel, take a dirt road to the right and you'll come to the new *Touristel* which, readers report, offers superior service and facilities at much the same price.

Hôtel Romani (☎ 80 05 06), beside the artificial Lac Savané, is an odd experience. It's about 4km beyond the roundabout and is well signed. Rooms with air-con and bathroom are between CFA9000 and CFA 11,000. What makes it so bizarre is that you may be the only presence at this massive investment in tourism – apart, that is, from the geese, horses, strutting peacocks and a lonely, tethered chimp who waves pathetically to all who pass.

Places to Eat

There are several *stalls* selling street food on the north side of the roundabout and on either side of the road leading westward from it. On the south-west corner is the unsigned *Chez Barry*, run by three friendly brothers and good for omelettes and simple snacks. Of the few maquis in town, *Le Yancadi*, 300m south-west of the post office, and *Les Etoiles*, about 1km west on the Bamoko road, are popular with locals.

Hôtel des Frontières has the best restaurant in town, offering mainly French cuisine. The menu of the day is CFA3500 and main dishes are between CFA1900 and CFA2500.

Getting There & Away

Buses and bush taxis all leave from the roundabout. Both EDT and FECTI have a daily run to Abidjan (15 hours, CFA5000), via Man (CFA3000), Daloa (CFA4000) and Yamoussoukro (CFA5000). The most reliable way of travelling to both Korhogo (235km) and Man (275km) is with the postal van, which leaves the post office around 8 am every day except Sunday for each town. Either way, the trip takes five to six hours and costs CFA3500.

FERKESSÉDOUGOU

Ferké, 231km north of Bouaké, is a crossroads town where the route north from Abidjan to both Mali and Burkina Faso intersects with the east to west route between Korhogo and Parc National de la Comoë. Should you overnight in transit, there's a good cluster of maquis and bars-dancing (active at weekends) near the Hôtel Senoufo and a large Thursday market. Ferké has one of the best hospitals in the country, run by Baptist missionaries and attracting patients from as far away as Ouagadougou and Bamako.

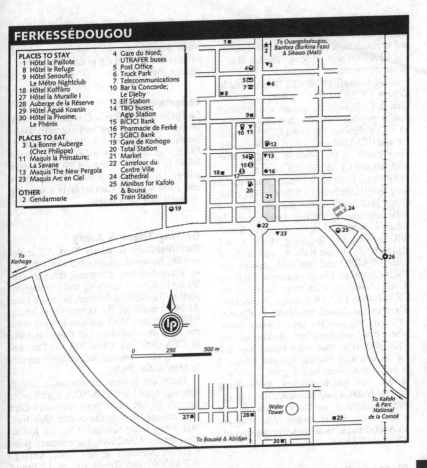

FERKESSÉDOUGOU

PLACES TO STAY
1 Hôtel la Paillote
8 Hôtel le Refuge
9 Hôtel Senoufo;
Le Métro Nightclub
18 Hôtel Koffikro
27 Hôtel la Muraille I
28 Auberge de la Réserve
29 Hôtel Aguié Koanin
30 Hôtel la Pivoine;
Le Phénix

PLACES TO EAT
3 La Bonne Auberge
(Chez Philippe)
11 Maquis la Primature;
La Savane
13 Maquis The New Pergola
23 Maquis Arc en Ciel

OTHER
2 Gendarmerie

4 Gare du Nord;
UTRAFER buses
5 Post Office
6 Truck Park
7 Telecommunications
10 Bar la Concorde;
Le Djeby
12 Elf Station
14 TBO buses;
Agip Station
15 BICICI Bank
16 Pharmacie de Ferké
19 SGBCI Bank
20 Total Station
21 Market
22 Carrefour du
Centre Ville
24 Cathedral
25 Minibus for Kafolo
& Bouna
26 Train Station

To Ouangolodougou,
Banfora (Burkina Faso)
& Sikasso (Mali)

To
Korhogo

0   250   500 m

To Kafolo
& Parc
National
de la Comoé

Water
Tower

To Bouaké & Abidjan

The town is essentially one long stem with sideshoots. The busiest area is the market and the roads bordering it to the west and south.

Places to Stay

Among the budget options, *Hôtel Koffikro* (☎ 88 01 97) two blocks west of the market, with its mosquito-netted windows and quiet compound, stands out. Rooms with shower cost CFA2000 (CFA2500 with fan) and the air-con rooms with bathroom at CFA4000 are even better value.

Hôtel la Paillote (☎ 88 05 86) styles itself as a blend *de la tradition et du moderne* (of the old and the new), but the 'moderne' is disintegrating and its paillotes, built of brick and mortar, not traditional materials, have deep fissures. The folk are friendly, however, and the price, at CFA2000 for a paillote with shower and CFA3000 with bathroom, is reasonable. Off the Bouaké road, south of the centre, *Hôtel la Muraille*

CÔTE D'IVOIRE

I (☎ *88 01 62)* is more remote but much better value. Spotless rooms with bathroom and armchair or sofa cost CFA2500 with fan and CFA4000 with air-con. There's also a small restaurant.

Hôtel Senoufo (☎ *88 03 23)* and *Hôtel le Refuge* (☎ *88 02 85)* are both relatively central. Le Refuge is superior, with friendly staff, a popular restaurant and clean rooms, all with bathroom. They cost CFA3500 with fan and CFA4500 with air-con. Rooms with shower only at the Senoufo are CFA4000 with fan and CFA5000 with air-con.

There are three more comfortable but still very reasonable hotels off the Bouaké road, about 2km south of the market. The best was once the sprawling *Auberge de la Réserve* (☎ *88 00 50)*, but it's going downhill fast and any lingering charm is not shared by its morose staff. A room with fan costs CFA4000 and one with air-con and TV is CFA6000. The restaurant is still fairly decent, however, with most dishes in the CFA1700 to CFA2500 range. Nowadays, it's way outclassed by *Hôtel la Pivoine* (☎ *88 03 90)* near the town's water tower, where trim, well furnished, tiled rooms cost CFA7000. (For that extra something, ask for the one with circular bed and mirrors!) It has a restaurant and a great first-floor terrace bar which catches the evening breeze. *Hôtel Aguiè Koanin*, also with bar and restaurant, is two blocks further east on a dirt road. Clean rooms with fan are CFA4000 and similar ones with air-con and TV cost CFA6500.

Places to Eat

In the cluster of places around Hôtel Senoufo, you can eat, drink and, at weekends, dance and be merry. *Maquis la Primature* and its neighbour, *La Savane*, have standard maquis fare in a pleasant ambience. At the former, you can get a litre of ice-cold beer for CFA475. *Maquis The New Pergola*, a block away, has a single large paillote and is earthier. The selections include braised fish/chicken for CFA1200/2500 and a whole chicken kedjenou for CFA1900.

La Bonne Auberge (Chez Philippe) opposite the Gare du Nord does a decent pizza while *Maquis Arc en Ciel* is an oasis of calm and a great place to unwind after exploring the market.

Entertainment

Le Djeby behind Bar la Concorde is lively at weekends. The new and currently fashionable *Le Métro* is a short stroll east. Ferké's smartest place is *Le Phénix*, beside Hôtel la Pivoine. It has a CFA1000 cover charge on Thursday (CFA2000 on Friday and Saturday). *La Concorde* is a relaxing open-air spot for a drink.

Getting There & Away

Bus Minibus & Bush Taxi All buses running between Abidjan and Korhogo call by Ferké but they often roll through full. UTRAFER has a morning and evening departure for Abidjan leaving from the Gare du Nord north of the centre (nine hours, CFA4000) and TBO has one leaving from the Agip petrol station. The fare to Bouaké is CFA2500 and CFA4000 to Yamoussoukro, where you can pick up a connection to Man or San Pédro.

There are several minibuses a day to Korhogo (one hour, CFA1000), which leave irregularly, once full, from the small Gare de Korhogo west of the centre. One bush taxi a day leaves around 9 am for Kafolo (five hours, CFA2500), the entrance point for Parc National de la Comoë, Ouango (CFA3000) and Bouna (up to 12 hours, CFA7500).

Vehicles for Burkina Faso and Mali leave from the Gare du Nord. To Burkina Faso, the bush taxi fare is CFA4000 for Banfora, CFA6000 to Bobo-Dioulasso and CFA8000 to Ouagadougou. To Sikasso in Mali, for which you may have to change vehicles at the border, the cost is CFA4500. If you push on to Bamako, it's CFA8000.

Train Trains from either Ouagadougou and Abidjan are scheduled to arrive at about

8.30 pm on Tuesday, Thursday and Saturday but they're frequently about two hours late. Heading south, the 1st/2nd class fare is CFA5000/3300 to Bouaké and CFA11,800/7800 to Abidjan. Northbound, fares are CFA4900/3200 to Bobo-Dioulasso and CFA 12,200/8100 to Ouagadougou.

BOUNA

Bouna is a good base for visiting the nearby villages of the Lobi people, which are noted for their unique adobe architecture. Compounds, called *soukala*, are castle-like structures with inner courtyards. The most attractive soukala can be found at Pouon, a small village 18km north-east of Bouna, reachable only during the dry season.

In Bouna, you can stay at *Hôtel Eléphant* (about CFA3500 a room) or the small *bar* (around CFA2500) across the street. If you're heading for Ghana, you need to stop at customs in town. A taxi to the border with Ghana at the Black Volta River (35km) takes 1½ hours and costs CFA750. There's a standard fee for crossing the river. For more details see the Ghana entry in this chapter's Getting There & Away section.

KONG

Kong is an old Dioula village dating from the 12th century. Its Sahel architecture and flat-roofed buildings are reminiscent of Mali. Much of the town was razed in the late 19th century by Samory Touré during a battle with the French. The most impressive building standing today is the banco Friday mosque with protruding wooden beams, built originally in the 17th century but much restored after Samory's rampage. You'll also find an old Quranic school and traditional mud houses with roof terraces.

Kong is west of Parc National de la Comoë, 34km south of the road between Ferké and Kafolo. Its only hotel is the *Campement*, with rooms for about CFA3000.

PARC NATIONAL DE LA COMOË

In the north-east corner of the country, Comoë (11,500 sq km), is the largest wildlife reserve in West Africa. Open from December to May, it has several entry points. The most widely used are Kafolo (also called Petit Ferké) in the north-west, and Gansé and Kakpin in the south. There's a daily park entry fee of CFA2000, which was reportedly about to increase significantly.

Sadly, it's no place for the budget traveller. While there's the occasional public transport to Kafolo, the southern entrances are not well served. Accommodation is expensive and, because walking in the park is prohibited out of respect for the lions, without private transport you're dependent on someone taking you on board.

A ride through the park takes you through savanna, forest and grassland. One of the most popular tracks broadly follows the River Comoë, which runs from Kafolo to Gansé. The whole trip, with frequent stops along the way, takes a full day. In the dry season, most of the wildlife is in this middle to western section of the park, where there's more water.

Lions, however, tend to be more abundant in the southern section, particularly in the *triangle de Kakpin* area, the top of which, bounded by the river, is roughly 30km north of Kakpin.

There's a good chance of seeing elephants, of which there are an estimated 100 in the park Other animals include species of pig, green monkey, hippopotamus, Anubis baboon, black and white colobus monkey, waterbuck, kob, roan and other kinds of antelope. Leopard also exist, but are rarely seen. Birds, on the other hand, are abundant: more than 400 species have been recorded here and one reader reported spotting 130 different types in three days.

At all three hotels bordering the park, you'll find guides. They're not obligatory, despite what they may say. However, with one, your chances of seeing animals will be greatly enhanced and, since tracks change and signs are very few, you won't go astray. The cost is negotiable; you should be able to get one for about CFA7000 a day.

The two tourist hotels, Comoë Sogetel and Comoë Safari Lodge, have vehicles which

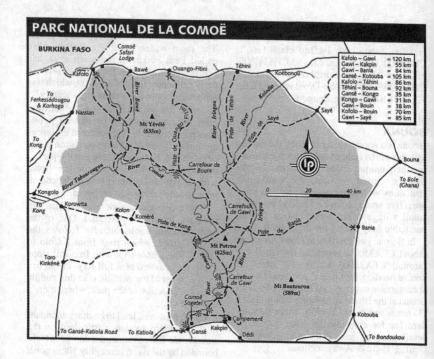

PARC NATIONAL DE LA COMOË

Kafolo – Gawi	= 120 km
Gawi – Kakpin	= 55 km
Gawi – Bania	= 84 km
Gansé – Kotouba	= 105 km
Kafolo – Téhini	= 86 km
Téhini – Bouna	= 92 km
Gansé – Kongo	= 35 km
Kongo – Gawi	= 31 km
Gawi – Bouin	= 38 km
Kofolo – Bouin	= 70 km
Gawi – Sayé	= 85 km

head out in the early morning and mid-afternoon, if there are enough clients. The cost per person for a half-day safari is CFA15,000.

Try to leave time for a pirogue trip on the River Comoë, interesting for both the scenery and the hippos. Both tourist hotels offer this service for about CFA5000 although, with the villagers, it's very much less.

Places to Stay & Eat

At the southern end, the *Campement* in Kakpin, 15km east of Gansé, has 17 traditional huts with bathroom but no air-con for about CFA7000, and a thatched-roof bar-restaurant with very basic food such as spaghetti and tinned tomato sauce. A reader recommends *Chez Ton Ton Guy* (about CFA10,000 per person), which is about 10km from Kakpin. It has a good restaurant and bar and the friendly French owner will

organise tours in the park or help you engage a good guide.

The park has two good top-end hotels of equal quality, both with pools and air-con. *Comoë Sogetel* (☎ 63 31 95 or 35 45 10) is at the southern entrance in Gansé near the River Comoë and has 25 Sudanic-inspired cabins. The 40-room *Comoë Safari Lodge* (☎ 32 70 73) is at the northern entrance near Kafolo. Rooms at either place are about CFA20,000 (CFA49,000 with full board for two).

Getting There & Away

Air Flying from Abidjan to Korhogo costs CFA36,300 return by Air Ivoire. You can hire a car there for about CFA20,000 a day plus petrol and including the driver. The cost per person for a two day all-inclusive package deal from an Abidjan tour operator is more than CFA100,000, including the airfare from Abidjan. You can also arrange one to three-day tours from Korhogo at Hôtel Mont Korhogo and Hôtel Kadjona.

Bus & Bush Taxi By bus or bush taxi, it's much easier to get to the northern entrance of Kafolo than the southern ones of Gansé and Kakpin, especially if you're departing from Ferké. Every morning there is at least one minibus headed from Ferké to Kafolo (three to five hours, CFA2500). The Katiola to Gansé route is not as well travelled and

finding a vehicle in Katiola is much more difficult.

Car Driving from Abidjan takes about 10 and 12 hours to the southern and northern entrances, respectively. The turn-off points are Katiola (407km from Abidjan) for Gansé (160km) and the southern entrance, and Ferkessédougou (584km from Abidjan) for Kafolo (121km) and the northern entrance. From either turn-off, it's jarring washboard roads the rest of the way.

The Gambia

Note

The Gambia's official name always includes 'The', but this is often omitted in everyday usage. In this book we have usually omitted 'The' for simplicity and readability.

THE GAMBIA AT A GLANCE

Capital: Banjul
Population: 1.1 million
Area: 10,690 sq km
Head of state: President Yahya Jammeh
Official language: English
Main local languages: Mandinka, Wolof, Fula
Currency: Dalasi
Exchange rate: US$1 = D10
Time: GMT/UTC
Country telephone code: ☎ 220
Best time to go: December to February (best climate), May to September (fewer tourists)

Warm temperatures and long golden beaches make Gambia ideal for rest and relaxation, and with a little more effort you can escape European-flavoured resorts and explore the country in greater depth. You can visit wildlife reserves, see African-style wrestling matches or take a cruise on the River Gambia. Birdwatchers are in for a real treat too – a wide range of habitats in a very compact area makes the country a world-class birding destination. The ease of getting around and minimal hassle makes Gambia an excellent introduction to the region, and cheap flights from Europe make it the perfect gateway to West Africa.

Facts about Gambia

HISTORY

Ancient stone circles and burial mounds along the River Gambia indicate that this part of West Africa has been inhabited by organised societies for at least 1500 years (for more details, see the History section of the Facts about the Region chapter). By the 13th century, the area was part of the Empire of Mali, which stretched between the present-day states of Senegal and Niger. During this period Mandinka traders migrated into the area, and introduced Islam, which remains the principal religion of Gambia.

The first Europeans to reach Gambia were Portuguese explorers who arrived in 1455 and traded with local inhabitants. By 1650 they were eclipsed by the British who estab-

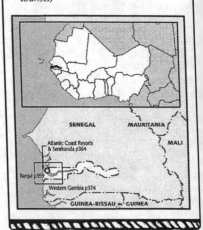

lished Fort James on an island 25km upstream from the mouth of the River Gambia. Twenty years later, the French built a rival fort at nearby Albreda, and during the 17th and 18th centuries the French and British vied for control of the region's trade. With tobacco and gunpowder the European traders purchased ivory, gold and slaves from local chiefs. In 1783 Britain gained all rights to trade on the River Gambia, and Fort James became one of West Africa's most infamous slave trans-shipment points.

The Colonial Period

When the British abolished slavery in 1807, Royal Navy ships began capturing slave ships of other nations, and Fort James was converted from a dungeon to a haven. As part of this crusade, in 1816, the British built a fort on Banjul Island, and established a settlement which was named Bathurst.

The River Gambia protectorate was administered from Sierra Leone until 1888, when Gambia became a full colony, but for the next 75 years Gambia was almost forgotten, and administration was limited to a few British district commissioners and the local chiefs they appointed.

In the 1950s Gambia's groundnut (peanut) plantations were improved, as a way to increase export earnings, and a few other agricultural schemes were set up. But there was little else in the way of services; by the early 1960s Gambia had less than 50 primary schools, and only a handful of doctors.

Independence

In 1960, when the rest of West Africa was gaining independence, Dawda Jawara founded the People's Progressive Party (PPP), but there was little else in the way of a local political infrastructure and Britain doubted that independence was feasible. Nevertheless, in 1965 Gambia became independent, and Jawara became prime minister. Without any official explanation, Gambia was renamed The Gambia. More understandably, Bathurst was renamed Banjul.

A viable future still seemed unlikely, but during the next 10 years, the world price for groundnuts increased, and the number of tourists grew even more dramatically – from 300 in 1966 to 25,000 a decade later – which enabled the tiny nation to survive and even prosper.

Economic growth translated into political confidence. In 1970 Gambia became a fully independent republic, with Jawara as president. Opposition parties were tolerated, but the tradition of political lethargy lingered on. The PPP government was deeply conservative and was accused by opponents of neglect and mismanagement.

The first major sign of discontent at the PPP's grip on the country came in 1980 when some disaffected soldiers staged a coup. In accordance with a mutual defence pact, the Senegalese army helped oust the rebels and, acknowledging this debt, Jawara announced that the armies of Gambia and Senegal would be integrated. In 1982 the Senegambian Confederation came into effect. Although political unity seemed a good idea, relations between the people and governments of Gambia and Senegal were never completely relaxed, and by 1989 the Confederation was dissolved. Tensions ran high for a while, but a new treaty of cooperation was signed in 1991.

Meanwhile, tourism became an increasingly vital source of foreign currency, as groundnut prices fell. There was increasing dissatisfaction in the rural areas as IMF restructuring cut agricultural subsidies. Malnutrition became common, but Jawara still enjoyed a large popular following, even though instances of government incompetence and corruption became increasingly evident.

The 1990s

Despite their many obvious failures, in April 1992 President Jawara and the PPP were re-elected for a sixth term. To the outside world, Jawara seemed to remain popular, so it came as some surprise when he was overthrown on 22 July 1994 in a reportedly bloodless coup led by young military officers. The coup leader, Lieutenant Yahya Jammeh, announced a new government headed by the Armed Forces Provisional Ruling Council (AFPRC). Ex-president Jawara was granted asylum in Senegal and Jammeh promised that the AFPRC would soon return to the barracks. When this never materialised, aid donors such as the USA and World Bank threatened to cut their support, and Gambia's tourist trade was badly affected.

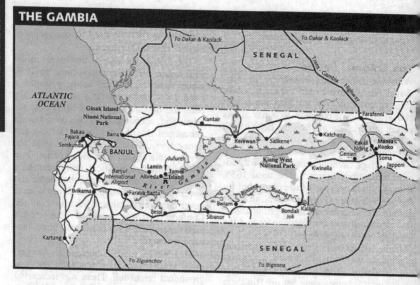

THE GAMBIA

In early 1995 Jammeh pragmatically announced that multiparty elections would be held the following year, and the British Foreign Office advised visitors that Gambia was safe once again. The 1996 elections were won by the AFPRC (now neatly renamed the Alliance for Patriotic Reorientation and Construction), and Jammeh was made president, completing his smooth transition from minor army officer to head of state in just over two years.

Elections for the national assembly in 1997 were dominated by the AFPRC, further consolidating Jammeh's position, although opponents' complaints of vote-rigging and the imprisonment of opposition leaders were supported by Amnesty International. Claims that multimillion US$ development loans had been diverted into overseas accounts of the president and other senior figures also surfaced, but were strongly denied.

Despite these machinations, life for most Gambians continued as normal, and many people regard Jammeh as a fresh force sweeping away the lethargy and corruption of the old days. Expectations are high, and

just how easy the future will be for the new government, and the country itself, remains to be seen.

GEOGRAPHY

The Gambia's shape and position epitomise the absurdity of the colonial carve-up of Africa, with its territory and very existence determined by the River Gambia. About 300km long, but averaging only 35km wide, Gambia is entirely surrounded by Senegal, except for about 80km of coastline, and has an area of around 11,000 sq km.

The Gambia has no hills or mountains, and the country is so flat that the River Gambia drops less than 10m in around 450km between the far eastern border and Banjul, the capital, at the river's mouth.

West of Banjul are the Atlantic Coast resorts of Bakau, Fajara, Kotu and Kololi, the centre of Gambia's tourist industry.

CLIMATE

The rainy season is from June to October, and the dry season is November to May.

THE GAMBIA

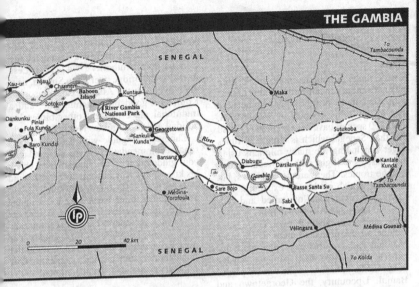

THE GAMBIA

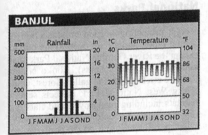

From December to mid-February average daytime temperatures are around 24°C. In October and November, and from mid-February to April, this rises to 26°C, up to around 30°C from July to September. Temperatures in the coastal areas are generally lower than these averages, while upcountry they are higher.

ECOLOGY & ENVIRONMENT

Some issues relating to Gambia are discussed under Ecology & Environment in the Facts about the Region chapter. A local organisation called Gambia Tourism Concern

(☎ 462057, fax 466180) is based at the Bakadaji Hotel in the Atlantic Coast resort of Kololi and welcomes visitors. They are involved in several schemes promoting sustainable and sensitive tourism in the country, and also produce *Concern* magazine – available around the resorts near Banjul.

FLORA & FAUNA

Vegetation is determined largely by the land's proximity to the coast or the River Gambia, which is lined with mangroves in the saline areas and with dense gallery forest further upstream. (For more details on mangroves see the boxed text in the Siné-Saloum Delta section of the Senegal chapter.) Away from the river, Gambia's position in the southern Sahel means natural vegetation consists mostly of dry grassland or open savanna woodland.

Gambia has few large mammals, although warthog and various antelope species can be seen in the national parks. Most notable are Gambia's primate populations – especially several species of monkey. The best place to observe monkeys is Abuko Nature Reserve (see the boxed text 'The Monkeys of Abuko' at the end of the Atlantic Coast Resorts & Serekunda section).

Birds

A wide range of habitats in a compact area makes Gambia a major birdwatching destination, and more ornithologists come here than to any other country in West Africa. Over 560 species have been recorded (just 80 less than Senegal which is almost 20 times larger), including the many migrants using the coast as a flight path between Europe and the tropics. There are no endemics, but 'specials' which get birders excited include Egyptian plover, swallow-tailed and red-throated bee-eater, Abyssinian roller, painted snipe and Pel's fishing owl. Good sites include all the protected areas listed under National Parks on this page, plus more unexpected areas like hotel gardens, sewage ponds or the mud flats in the scruffy part of Banjul. Upcountry, the Georgetown and Basse areas are also very rewarding.

Bird Books *A Field Guide to Birds of The Gambia & Senegal* by leading ornithologists Clive Barlow and Tim Wacher, with illustrations by award-winning artist Tony Disley, is undeniably the best, listing over 660 species, with colour plates, detailed descriptions and in-depth background information. But this 400 page hardback is no featherweight, and costs UK£26 (about US$40) in Britain. It is also available in Gambia. More portable and affordable is *Bird Watchers' Guide to The Gambia* by Rod Ward, a finely researched book which concentrates on birding sites and likely sightings, rather than detailed species descriptions.

Bird Guides Many birdwatchers hire local guides to show them good areas or identify 'difficult' species. You can arrange professional guides as part of an inclusive tour (see the list of operators under Inclusive Tours in the Organised Tours section of the Getting There & Away chapter), or contact one of the local tour companies listed in this chapter.

Some local guides have formed a loose organisation called Habitat Africa, headed by Solomon Jallow, contactable through Amadou Njie at Gambia International Airlines (☎ 472208) or Musa Jefang at the Gambia Ports Authority (☎ 472127). Less formally, the bridge over Kotu Stream, near the Novotel in the Atlantic Coast resort of Kotu, is a good birdwatching site, and a traditional place to meet other birders on holiday and local guides looking for work.

Choose your guide with care – get personal recommendations if you can, and take your guide out for a few hours first to check his knowledge and attitude. A fee of around D30 per hour, or D100 for a morning, is fair. Some guides offer week-long tours of the country for between D500 and D1250 per day, which includes a car and accommodation – but be warned that guides can overcharge wildly, or forget to mention that 'incidentals' (such as meals) are extra. Outright scams are also not uncommon.

National Parks

The Gambia has six national parks and reserves, protecting a good cross section of habitat types, and all are open to the public, except the River Gambia National Park (also known as Baboon Islands). Abuko Nature Reserve is a large tract of gallery forest, while Kiang West National Park protects several habitats including mangrove, mud flats and dry woodland. Baobolong Wetland Reserve (also spelt Baobolon) is on the north bank of the River Gambia. Niumi National Park and Tanji Bird Reserve are coastal, with dunes, lagoons, dry woodland and coastal scrub.

There are also several forest parks, established to provide renewable timber stocks, except Bijilo Forest Park which is primarily a nature reserve.

GOVERNMENT & POLITICS

The government is based on the British parliamentary system, and elections for president and members of the national assembly in 1996/97 returned the country to civilian rule, following the coup of 1994.

The dominant party is the Alliance for Patriotic Reorientation and Construction

(AFPRC), which holds 33 of the 45 elected seats in the national assembly. Other permitted parties with seats include the United Democratic Party and the Party of National Reconciliation. Four more members of the assembly, including the speaker, are appointed by the president. The next elections are due in 2002.

ECONOMY

The Gambia's economy is dominated by exports of groundnuts (peanuts) which account for 80% of gross national product (GNP), but as world prices of groundnuts have fallen, Gambia's balance of trade has been negative since 1975. Today, foreign debt stands at around US$500 million. Interest on loans owed to the World Bank and other institutions absorbs export earnings considerably.

The Gambia's other main economic activity is tourism, but despite its high profile this accounts for only 10 to 15% of GNP, mainly because package tours are paid for in visitors' home countries. The government spends vast sums on tourist-related projects, such as the new airport, thus diverting funds from agriculture and other sectors directly benefiting Gambians.

POPULATION & PEOPLE

Estimates in 1997 put Gambia's population at nearly 1.1 million. With an area of around 11,000 sq km, this gives a population density of around 100 people per sq km – the fourth highest in Africa.

The main ethnic groups are the Mandinka (comprising about 40%), Fula (about 20%) and Wolof (about 15%). Minor groups include the Sere and Jola. Among ethnic groups intermarriage is not uncommon. In Senegal, where all these groups are also found, most also have French names or French spellings of their names: Fula/Peul, Wolof/Oulof, Sere/Sérèr and Jola/Diola.

ARTS

Unlike other countries in the region, Gambia is not noted for the use of wooden masks and statues; however, costumes made of plant fibre are used in initiation ceremonies.

The traditional music of Gambia is outlined in the Society & Conduct section following. Gambian pop music is heavily influenced by the Sahel sounds of Senegal, Mali and Guinea, and most local artists who make it big soon disappear to the bright lights of Dakar.

Popular Gambian singers include Jaliba Kuyateh, Bubacar Jammeh and Abdel Kabirr. Older names to look out for include Guelwar and Ifang Bondi.

SOCIETY & CONDUCT

The Mandinka have strong musical traditions. Islamic feast days, such as the end of Ramadan, and family celebrations, such as a wedding or circumcision, or even the arrival of a special guest, are seen as good reasons for some music and dancing. Traditional instruments include the *kora* and *balafon* (see the special section 'West African Music' earlier in this book). Mandinka dances are based on common activities of everyday life, such as crop cultivation and fishing.

At Christmas-time in Banjul, crowds of people carry around large lanterns called *fanals*, while onlookers donate a few coins as a sign of their appreciation. This tradition originated during French colonial times in St-Louis in Senegal – for more details, see the St-Louis section in that chapter later in this book.

RELIGION

Over 90% of Gambians are Muslim. See the Religion section of the Facts about the Region chapter for more details on Islam.

LANGUAGE

English is the official language. A number of African languages are spoken, the principal ones being Mandinka, Wolof and Fula. See the Language chapter for a list of useful phrases in these languages.

Facts for the Visitor

SUGGESTED ITINERARIES

Cheap charter flights and quick flying times mean that a trip to Gambia of just one week is a very popular option for visitors from Europe. Overland travellers with more time to spare can easily spend a week in Gambia as part of wider travels around West Africa. You might want to spend a few days lazing on the Atlantic Coast beaches, combined with a few days to visit Banjul, Gambia's small and dusty capital, and to explore places nearby, such as the Bijilo and Abuko wildlife reserves, lively Serekunda market or Jufureh (the *Roots* village). If you cut out the beach, you could go further south down the coast to Tanji Bird Reserve or the fishing villages of Gunjur and Kartung, or even spend a few days touring upcountry Gambia, following the great river upstream to the old colonial outpost of Georgetown and the busy trading centre of Basse.

With two weeks you'd have time to laze on the beach and tour the country, visiting most of the places listed in the previous paragraph, but in a more relaxed manner. From Banjul you could also spend a day or two in the beautiful coastal area of Niumi National Park. If you go upcountry your first stop may be the mangroves and creeks of Bintang Bolong, or Farafenni which has a big weekly market. Wildlife fans should stop at Tendaba – the base for visiting Kiang West National Park and Baobolong Wetland Reserve. Further upcountry is peaceful Georgetown, from where you can reach Wassu Stone Circles or River Gambia National Park, and the lively trading centre of Basse, from where you can visit several surrounding villages – all with fascinating weekly markets.

With three or four weeks in Gambia, you could visit all the places listed earlier and also cross the border into Senegal, perhaps to Casamance or the Siné-Saloum Delta. For more ideas see the Suggested Itineraries section in the Senegal chapter.

PLANNING

When to Go

The climate pattern makes the high season from December to mid-February when conditions are dry and relatively cool. This is also the local trading season, when the harvest is completed and Gambians are more relaxed, perhaps with a bit of extra money to spend, so markets are noticeably busier at this time. October, November, March and April are not as busy.

The low tourist season is from May to September, which includes the June to October rainy season. Some travellers say this is the best time to visit because there are no crowds, the hotels are cheap, and rain only falls for a few hours each day – making the vegetation lush and the air crystal clear.

Maps

Macmillan's *The Gambia Traveller's Map* is the best, although not apparently available locally. It's easy to read, with most roads marked, plus a street map of Banjul, and the Atlantic Coast resorts. The locally produced *Map of Gambia* (D40) is quite simplified, but good enough to get you around. You can usually find copies in Atlantic Coast supermarkets and souvenir shops.

TOURIST OFFICES

The Gambia is represented in Britain by The Gambia National Tourist Office (☎ 0171-376 0093; from 22 April 2000 ☎ 020-7376 0093; email info@thegambia-touristoff.co.uk, Web site www.thegambia-touristoff.co.uk) based at The Gambian High Commission, Kensington Court, London W8 5DG. The friendly people here respond promptly to calls, faxes and email from Britain and abroad and will send a useful colour brochure called *Welcome to The Gambia* anywhere in the world.

VISAS & DOCUMENTS

Visas

Visas are not needed by most nationals of Commonwealth countries, Belgium, Germany, Italy, Luxembourg, the Netherlands, Scandinavia and Spain. Visas are normally

Highlights

Natural Features & National Parks

The River Gambia *(Upcountry Gambia)*
The river defines the country, and becomes increasingly beautiful as you go upstream. Several protected areas, including Kiang West and Boabolong, border the river.

Abuko Nature Reserve *(Around the Atlantic Coast Resorts)*
Gambia's flagship protected area, with beautiful forest trails – excellent place for seeing birds and monkeys, and within easy reach of the beach resorts.

Ginak Island & Niumi National Park
(Western Gambia)
Beautiful undeveloped beach, small traditional fishing villages and mangrove creeks make this an ideal spot for watching seabirds, with a chance of seeing turtles and dolphins.

People

Lumos *(Upcountry Gambia)*
These weekly markets are great fun, and a marvellous spectacle, even if you don't want to buy anything. The lumo at Farafenni is large and lively, and there are several more good lumos in the area around Basse.

Traditional Wrestling
(The Atlantic Coast Resorts & Serekunda)
Join the locals in watching one of their favourite traditional sports. Matches are most easy to find, and great fun, in Serekunda.

Albert Market *(Banjul)*
The large and lively heart of Banjul, with fruit and veg for the locals, cloth and crafts for the tourists.

Activities

Birdwatching
Gambia is a mecca for keen ornithologists, with endless possibilities for spotting both endemic and migrant species, and plenty for those with only a passing interest.

Music & Dance *(The Atlantic Coast Resorts, Western Gambia)*
Several hotels offer courses for learning to play drums and other traditional instruments. Or study local dance. Or just have a good time.

Cycling *(Banjul, The Atlantic Coast Resorts)*
The Gambia is ideal for touring by bike; distances are relatively short and traffic on the upcountry roads is light.

Beaches *(The Atlantic Coast Resorts)*
Gambia's coast is virtually one long strip of golden sand. Take your pick – there's a huge choice, from large lively resorts to secluded hideaways.

Fishing *(The Atlantic Coast Resorts)*
Numerous opportunities for relaxed days with rod and line on the rivers and mangrove creeks, or for serious deep-sea sport fishing out in the Atlantic.

---

valid for one month, and are issued in two to three days for the equivalent of around US$30, plus two photos. Visas may be issued at Banjul airport, if you look like a tourist and have a good excuse.

Visa Extensions Visa extensions are handled by the Immigration Office (☎ 228611) on Dobson St in Banjul, although there are

plans to move this office to the corner of Hill St and OAU Blvd.

EMBASSIES & CONSULATES
Gambian Embassies & Consulates

The few West African countries with Gambian embassies include Guinea-Bissau and Senegal. See the Facts for the Visitor section of the relevant country chapter for more details. Elsewhere, Gambian embassies and consulates include the following:

Belgium
(☎ 02-640 1049) 126 ave Franklin-Roosevelt, Brussels 1050
France
(☎ 01 42 94 09 30) 117, rue Saint-Lazare, 75008 Paris
Germany
(☎ 030-892 31 21, fax 891 14 01) Kurfurstendamm 103, Berlin
UK
(☎ 0171-937 6316; from 22 April 2000 ☎ 020-7937 6316) 57 Kensington Court, London W8 5DH
USA
(☎ 202-785 1399) 1155 15th St NW, Washington, DC 20005

The Gambia also has embassies in Canada, Japan, Portugal, Sweden and Switzerland.

Embassies & Consulates in Gambia

Embassies and consulates in Banjul and the neighbouring coastal resorts include:

Guinea
Liberation St, Banjul, next to Dabia Airways, above a shop called Marché Juboo Bah (the entrance is round the back)
Guinea-Bissau
(☎ 228134)
Liberation St, Banjul, upstairs next to the African Heritage Restaurant
Mali
VM Company Ltd, Cotton St, Banjul
Mauritania
(☎ 496518)
Just off Kairaba Ave, Fajara, near Weezo's Restaurant
Senegal
(☎ 373752)
Kairaba Ave, near the US embassy
Sierra Leone
(☎ 228206)
Hagan St, Banjul
UK
(☎ 495133/4, fax 496134)
48 Atlantic Rd, Fajara
USA
(☎ 392856/8, 391971, fax 392475)
Kairaba Ave, Fajara

Visas for Onward Travel

In Gambia, you can get visas for the following neighbouring countries. For visa applications it's always best to go to the embassy or consulate early in the morning, as lunch hours can be very flexible. You usually need to provide two photos.

Ghana
If you're flying into Ghana, Ghana Airways in Banjul can get you a visa; this costs US$20 and takes a week.

Guinea
Visas cost D400, and are issued the same day if you come in the morning.

Guinea-Bissau
The embassy is open in the morning only. Visas cost D100 and are issued the same day. It's just as easy to get visas in Ziguinchor (Senegal) where the consulate issues them on the spot for CFA5000.

Mali
The consul for Mali cannot issue tourist visas, but if you're flying you can get one at Bamako airport.

Mauritania
Visas are issued the same day for D150.

Senegal
Multiple entry visas cost D95 and take two days to issue.

Sierra Leone
Citizens of most non-African countries pay D500 for a single-entry one month visa.

For details of embassies not listed here, check in the phone book (most telecentres have one).

CUSTOMS

There are no restrictions on the import of local or foreign currencies, or on the export of foreign currency, but you cannot export more than D100.

MONEY
Currency
The Gambia's unit of currency is the dalasi (abbreviated to 'D'). Notes are D5, D10, D25 and D50. There is also a D1 coin. The dalasi is divided into 100 bututs. Many items can be paid for in CFA.

Exchange Rates
The dalasi exchange rate has been stable during the past few years, although they might have changed by the time you read this book.

CFA1000	=	D20
Euro €1	=	D13
1FF	=	D2
UK£1	=	D16
US$1	=	D10

Exchanging Money
Banks where you can change money include Trust Bank, Standard Chartered and BICIS, with branches in Banjul, Serekunda and the Atlantic Coast resorts. These towns also have several money changing bureaus. Up-country, the only place with a bank is Basse. There's also a bank at the airport. If it's closed, the police will help you find an unofficial but tolerated moneychanger (but they don't deal in travellers cheques).

In and around Banjul, changing cash or travellers cheques is fairly quick and straightforward. Generally the money changing bureaus give a slightly better rate for cash, and a slightly worse rate for travellers cheques, but as rates and commissions can vary, it might be worth shopping around.

Visa and MasterCard can be used to draw cash at all Standard Chartered Bank branches, for a flat charge of D100.

Black Market Dealers on the black market offer about 5% more than the banks, or the

same rate without commission, but generally it's hardly worth it, and there's always a risk of being short-changed or robbed if you deal on the street. However, if banks are closed, you'll find moneychangers around the post office in Banjul and at the souvenir stalls in Bakau (see Information in those sections for more details), and at the towns on the Trans-Gambia Highway.

POST & COMMUNICATIONS
The postal service out of the country is reliable; most cards and letters arrive at their destinations. Letters from Gambia to Britain cost D2; to USA and Australasia is D3. The best place for poste restante is the main post office in Banjul.

Most public telephone and fax offices run by Gamtel (the state telephone company) are open in the evening and at weekends. They run a good service. In and around Banjul you'll also find privately owned 'telecentres'.

Calls within Gambia cost around D8 for three minutes, and for international calls outside Africa about D35 per minute at peak time (7 am to 6 pm). Calls are cheaper by about 20% between 6 pm and 11 pm, and by about 33% between 11 pm and 7 am. Rates are also cheaper at weekends, when a call to Europe comes down to D20 per minute. You can also buy phonecards at Gamtel offices, which make international calls even cheaper.

BOOKS
Useful locally produced books include *An Overview of Protected Areas in The Gambia* by the Department of Parks & Wildlife, and *Sites & Monuments of The Gambia* by the National Council for Arts & Culture and available at the National Museum. Some field guides are listed in the Flora & Fauna section.

NEWSPAPERS & MAGAZINES
The Gambia Daily is nominally independent, but seen as the voice of the new government. The most outspoken is *The*

Daily Observer, although criticism was muffled after the paper's offices were temporarily closed in a government crackdown. The most interesting magazine for tourists is *Concern*, locally produced by The Gambia Tourism Concern organisation, available in some hotels and also sold by 'beach boys' as part of a scheme helping them to earn money without hassling visitors.

RADIO & TV

The Gambia's main radio stations include Radio Gambia, government-run and rather traditional, and Radio Syd, catering for tourists and locals, with broadcasts in Swedish and German as well as English. BBC World Service programs can be heard on Citizen FM (105.7 FM) although this was closed in 1998 for being 'anti-government'. The Gambia's main TV station is the government-run GTV.

PHOTOGRAPHY & VIDEO

No permit is required, but the usual restrictions apply – see the Photography & Video section in the Regional Facts for the Visitor chapter for more general information.

HEALTH

You'll need a yellow fever vaccination certificate if you're coming from an infected area. Malaria risk exists year-round in the whole country, so take appropriate precautions. For more details on these and other health matters, see the Health section in the Regional Facts for the Visitor chapter.

If you are sick or injured while in Gambia, the country's main government-run hospital is in Banjul, but there is a better selection of private clinics and doctors practising in the area around the Atlantic Coast resorts (see that section for more details). If you're up-country, the hospital at Bansang is the only one outside the capital.

DANGERS & ANNOYANCES

A combination of tourism and urban deprivation around Banjul and the tourist resorts means some drugs are cheap and readily available (a handful of grass can go for as little as D5), but despite what you may hear, no drug is legal in Gambia. If you're a smoker, be careful: some dealers are in cahoots with the police. Several tourists have been arrested (either by real policemen or impostors – it doesn't really matter) and forced to pay large bribes to avoid arrest and jail.

Other matters are discussed under Dangers & Annoyances in the Banjul and Atlantic Coast Resorts sections.

BUSINESS HOURS

Shops and businesses usually open Monday to Thursday from 8.30 am to noon and 2.30 to 5.30 pm and Friday and Saturday from 8 am to noon. Most banks in Banjul city centre are open mornings only, and close at around 11 am on Friday. Banks in the Atlantic Coast resorts and Serekunda open weekday afternoons and on Saturdays.

PUBLIC HOLIDAYS & SPECIAL EVENTS

Public holidays include 1 January (New Year's Day), 18 February (Independence Day), Good Friday, Easter Monday, 1 May (Worker's Day), 22 July (Anniversary of the Second Republic), 15 September (St Mary's Day) and 25 December (Christmas).

The Muslim holidays of Eid al-Fitr (end of Ramadan), Tabaski, Muslim New Year and Eid al-Moulid are also celebrated. For a table of dates of Islamic holidays, see the Public Holidays & Special Events section in the Regional Facts for the Visitor chapter.

ACTIVITIES

Most major hotels have swimming pools that nonguests can use for a fee. Otherwise, you have several beaches to choose from, although large waves, steep shelves and a heavy undertow can make some of them dangerous. In tourist areas you can hire sailboards, or arrange other water sports. Fishing – either in the creeks or out on the ocean – is also available (see Organised Tours in the

Roots Homecoming Festival

The third Roots Homecoming Festival was held in Gambia for one week in June 1998, and the Ministry of Tourism and Culture hopes it will develop into an annual event. Aimed primarily at Americans and Europeans of African descent, but open to all visitors, the festival includes displays of music, dance, art and craft, plus excursions to cultural sites (including, of course, the *Roots* village of Jufureh), and more serious seminars and educational workshops.

Venues for events and exhibitions include the National Museum and Arch 22 in Banjul, the museum at Jufureh, and the Alliance Française-Gambienne on Kairaba Ave near Serekunda. Official airlines and supporters of the event include Air Afrique in the USA, Sabena in continental Europe and The Gambia Experience in Britain, who all offer discounted fares to groups of festival participants and can provide more information.

Getting Around section). Cycling is a great way to explore the Gambian countryside – bikes can be hired in the Atlantic Coast resorts.

ACCOMMODATION

In Banjul and the nearby Atlantic Coast resorts there's a very wide range of places to stay, from simple guesthouses to international-standard hotels. Upcountry there are a few smart tourist lodges, but your choice is usually limited to basic establishments.

FOOD

Shoestringers should head for the cheap chop houses where plates of rice and sauce go for about D5. Or visit an *afra* where grilled meat is sold to take away at very reasonable prices. Even if you're not strapped for cash, it's well worth trying some local cooking during your visit, especially as the resort areas are dominated by burgers or chicken and chips. Traditional Gambian food is similar to Senegalese food (see the entry on Food in the Senegal chapter for more details), with the same ingredients and cultural background, although names and spellings may differ. Thick brown groundnut sauce called *mafay* is found everywhere. *Domodah* is another version, usually with meat or vegetables mixed in. Other meals include *benechin* (fish and rice), chicken *yasser* (marinated in onion and lemon sauce) and *yollof* rice – vegetables or meat cooked in a sauce of oil and tomatoes.

DRINKS

The local beer is JulBrew, usually served in 330mL bottles, but also as a draught beer in smarter bars and hotels. Prices for a bottle start at about D7 in the simplest watering hole, up to around D20 in posh restaurants. A traditional 'beer' made from millet looks brown and gritty and is common, but the most popular home-brew is palm wine.

SHOPPING

Keen shoppers can spend many happy hours browsing in Gambia's shops, stalls and markets. Woodcarvings vary in quality, but if you look hard enough you may well find something good that catches your eye. Tie-dyed or printed fabrics are also eye-catching, with vibrant designs and colours – but take care when you wash them. Very popular for tourists and locals are brightly coloured baggy trousers and 'Gambi-shirts'. Batiks are churned out in their hundreds but you may have to search to find something of quality – there are some good stalls in Serekunda and the coastal resorts. Even more portable, and found everywhere, are cloth paintings.

Getting There & Away

AIR

The Gambia's main airport is Banjul international airport, about 20km from the city centre, and about 15km from the Atlantic Coast resorts.

Airlines serving Gambia from Europe include Swissair, Sabena and Austrian Airlines, but most visitors come on charter flights as these are cheaper and usually direct.

The departure tax from Gambia is usually included in your ticket price. Check with your travel agent when buying the ticket, and again when reconfirming. If it is not included, the tax is levied at the airport (US$15/ UK£10, payable in any hard currency).

Europe & the USA

Swissair, Sabena and Austrian Airlines between them have five services a week. High season returns from London to Banjul are around UK£500 (US$750). From the USA, Delta Airlines tie in with the Swissair and Sabena flights, but it's cheaper to fly with Air Afrique to Dakar (see the Senegal chapter) and take a regional flight or travel overland from there to Gambia.

One of the cheapest ways of getting from Europe to Gambia is on a charter flight, available from holiday operators or travel agents. Although these cater mainly for package tourists, independent travellers can get 'flight-only' deals. The leading British operator is The Gambia Experience (☎ 01703-730888, fax 731122, email gam bia@serenity.co.uk) with one or two week flight-only deals from UK£275 return, monthly returns from UK£360, and three month returns from UK£430.

Sometimes, tour operators offer special deals which include accommodation with the flight for only a little extra. Even if you don't stay in the hotel all the time, the airport transfers and first or last night bed can be very useful. Last-minute stand-by fares can drop amazingly low – ideal if your dates are flexible.

From Gambia back to Europe, the cheapest scheduled flights cost UK£500 or US$750. The Gambia Experience (office at the Senegambia Hotel in Kololi) has charter tickets from UK£275 – and sometimes less – making this one of the cheapest places in West Africa to fly home from.

Africa

There are daily flights between Banjul and Dakar on Air Dabia and Air Senegal (D550 one way). Air Dabia also flies twice weekly to/from Conakry (Guinea) for D900 (one way) and Bamako (Mali) for D1350. Air Mauritania flies weekly to Bissau (Guinea-Bissau) for D550. Ghana Airways flies twice weekly to Conakry for D950, Abidjan (Côte d'Ivoire) for D2250 and Accra (Ghana) for D2450. Cabo Verde Airlines goes twice weekly between Banjul and Praia in Cape Verde for D3100 return. Air Guinée flies between Banjul and Conakry (one way D900, return D1200), once weekly via Dakar, and twice weekly via Labé in northern Guinea – perfect for reaching the Fouta Djalon.

If you're heading for North Africa, it's better to go overland to Dakar, from where there's a good choice of flights (see the Getting There & Away section of the Senegal chapter for more details.)

LAND

To reach Dakar from Banjul take the ferry across the River Gambia to Barra. There's a GPTC bus to Dakar at 9 am but you have to be quick off the ferry to get a seat. The next one goes between 10 am and noon, and the fare is D70 or CFA3500. Alternatively, you can get to Dakar by Peugeot 504 bush taxi for CFA3700 (D75), minibus for CFA3000 (D60) or bus for CFA2500 (D50). A 504 to Kaolack is CFA2000 (D40).

If you're coming from Dakar and think you might miss the last ferry across to Banjul (it leaves at 7 pm), accommodation in Barra is limited to a couple of sleazy hotels. You'd be better off staying in Kaolack or Missirah (see the Senegal chapter) and getting the ferry from Barra to Banjul next morning

Bush taxis for Ziguinchor leave from Serekunda (D50 or CFA2500). Some also go from Brikama. If you're heading for Kafountine, it's usually quicker to get a Ziguinchor taxi to Diouloulou (although the fare won't be any cheaper) and change there.

If you're heading east, from Basse bush taxis go to the Gambian border post at Sabi and then continue into the no-man's-land,

Border Crossings

The Gambia is completely surrounded by Senegal, and most vehicles running between the two countries are Senegalese, so drivers prefer to charge in CFA.

There are three main border points of interest for travellers: at Karang, north of Barra on the main road to/from Kaolack and Dakar; Seleti, south of Brikama, on the main road to Ziguinchor in southern Senegal; and Sabi, east of Basse on the road to Vélingara. There are also major border crossing points just south of Soma, and just north of Farafenni where the Trans-Gambia Highway between north and south Senegal cuts through Gambia. Along the border are several more minor crossing points, but these tend to be used mainly by local people.

At any border crossing there is usually a few kilometres of 'no-man's-land' between the Gambia and Senegal border posts. Most public transport goes across the border, simply stopping at both, but occasionally you may have to change transport on either the Gambia or Senegal side, and continue your journey in another vehicle.

where some of the most decrepit vehicles in the whole of West Africa wait to carry you to the Senegal border post and on to Vélingara. The fare for the first leg is D7 to D10. The second leg costs CFA400. From Basse, bush taxis only go when full, which can mean several hours of waiting, but one taxi usually leaves at 7 am (full or not). Beware of border guards trying to 'fine' you for not registering with immigration in Banjul (whether or not you have a visa): this is not required. In Vélingara a horse-drawn *caleshe* costs CFA250 per person across town to the bush taxi station for Tambacounda (CFA 1400 by 504, CFA1000 by minibus).

SEA

Some travellers take sea-going pirogues (open wooden boats) that are used by local people, although these don't run to a set timetable and are notoriously unsafe. Options include Banjul to Ziguinchor, or Banjul to Djifer in the Siné-Saloum Delta. For more details see the Getting There & Away section of the Senegal chapter.

Getting Around

BUS & BUSH TAXI

There are two main routes though Gambia: the dirt road along the north bank of the river, and the tar road along the southern bank. Both are well served by bush taxis and Gambia Public Transport Corporation (GPTC) buses. Fares are cheap – across the country by ordinary GPTC bus costs D60, or D70 on the express. Bush taxi fares are about the same as the ordinary bus.

CAR & MOTORCYCLE

It's possible to hire a car in Gambia's resort areas, but you might also consider using a tourist taxi – see Tours by Taxi later. Despite the British heritage, traffic in Gambia drives on the right, in line with most other countries in West Africa. Petrol costs D8.50 per litre, and diesel (called *gasoil*) D6.50 per litre.

BOAT

A company called River Gambia Excursions (☎ 495526 or 996903), operates a boat between Lamin Lodge (near Banjul) and Georgetown. At the time of writing this only runs to order for groups, but the owner plans to start up a regular public service, so phone or look out for details.

BICYCLE

Some general information about cycling in West Africa is given in the main Getting Around chapter. If you've never cycled in Africa before, Gambia is an ideal place to start. We've heard from many travellers, particularly British, who take bikes on the cheap charter flights to Banjul and enjoy a couple of weeks cycling in the sun. The landscape is flat and the distances between major points of interest are not so great. Alternatively, hiring a bike for a few days or a week is a great way to get around the country. See Getting Around in the Atlantic Coast Resorts section for more details.

LOCAL TRANSPORT

Local public transport, such as city minibuses and shared taxis, is pretty much limited to Banjul, Serekunda and the surrounding area (see those sections for details). In the Atlantic Coast resorts and at the airport you will also find green 'tourist taxis' – catering specifically for tourists – for more details, see Private Taxis in the Atlantic Coast Resorts Getting Around section. From some other towns around the country, local transport runs to outlying villages, but on no fixed schedule, and usually tying in with market days. Details, where appropriate, are given throughout this chapter.

ORGANISED TOURS
Tour Companies

Taking an organised tour can be a good way to get around if time is short or money not a prime concern. All tour companies are based in the Atlantic Coast resort area. Large hotels offer excursions but smaller independent companies usually have lower prices. This is a very small selection, but gives you an idea of prices and options.

Creek & River Fishing
  (☎ 466573 or 496798) Angling specialists based at Il Mondo Restaurant, Kotu. Rates start at D400 per person per day, including tackle, tuition, lunch and a no-catch-no-pay guarantee. More serious sport fishing trips start at around D550 per person per day.
Gambia Adventure Safaris
  (☎ 460239) Office in Kololi, near the Sene-gambia Hotel; has tours to Georgetown or Tendaba for D900, and offer a 'Roots' tour by land for D350.
Magic Tours
  (☎ 374874, 460737 or 993599) All the standards, plus horse riding for D550 to D700 per day, and dolphin-spotting for D350 to D400 per day. A two day horse riding trip in the Tanji area is D1000, and a three day boat and camping trip via Jufureh and Georgetown is D1200.

Pleasuresports
  (☎ 462125 or 992125) Boat tour specialists aimed at groups, but independent travellers are welcome to book direct, which is cheaper too. A 'Roots' tour costs D200 if you make your own way to the port.
Tropical Tours
  (☎ 460536, fax 460546) Shop near the Sene-gambia Hotel in Kololi. Tours include: the 'Roots' village of Jufureh by boat for D375 and south coast beach safari for D350. Special trips (such as birding, brewing, bee keeping and traditional medicine) are also available.

Tours by Taxi

Drivers of green tourist taxis offer tours at fixed prices but you should check carefully about extras you are expected to pay. Also check the 'itinerary': most drivers are reliable and considerate, but some like to go as quickly as possible before leaving you stranded at a line of tacky souvenir stands. Some sample prices (per car) for a four seater taxi from Bakau, Fajara, Kotu or Kololi are: to Lamin and Abuko D350, Tendaba D1000 and Georgetown D2500.

We've heard from several travellers who have enjoyed tours by taxi; the driver's local insights have added considerably to the experience, and visits to far-flung family in country compounds can turn out to be the best part of all.

Banjul

Banjul is one of the smallest capitals in Africa, with all of 50,000 inhabitants, and feels more like a large village than a national metropolis. It lies on an island, unable to expand, with a sleepy down-at-heel ambience, although the area around Albert Market and the main streets are lively and colourful during the day.

Because Banjul has nowhere to grow, the adjacent boom town of Serekunda has become the unofficial capital. Nearby is the Atlantic Ocean coast where several villages have grown over the last 20 years to become thriving holiday resorts. These areas are

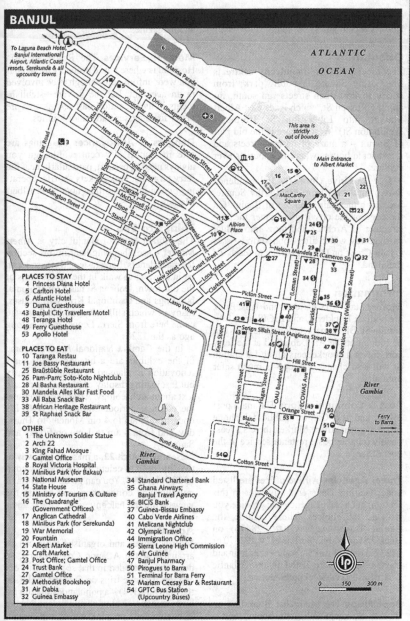

BANJUL

To Laguna Beach Hotel,
Banjul International
Airport, Atlantic Coast
resorts, Serekunda & all
upcountry towns

ATLANTIC
OCEAN

This area is
strictly
out of bounds

Main Entrance
to Albert Market

MacCarthy
Square

River
Gambia

Ferry
to Barra

River
Gambia

PLACES TO STAY
4 Princess Diana Hotel
5 Carlton Hotel
6 Atlantic Hotel
9 Duma Guesthouse
43 Banjul City Travellers Motel
48 Teranga Hotel
49 Ferry Guesthouse
53 Apollo Hotel

PLACES TO EAT
10 Taranga Restau
11 Joe Bassy Restaurant
25 Braüstüble Restaurant
26 Pam-Pam; Soto-Koto Nightclub
28 Al Basha Restaurant
30 Mandela Alles Klar Fast Food
33 Ali Baba Snack Bar
38 African Heritage Restaurant
39 St Raphael Snack Bar

OTHER
1 The Unknown Soldier Statue
2 Arch 22
3 King Fahad Mosque
7 Gamtel Office
8 Royal Victoria Hospital
12 Minibus Park (for Bakau)
13 National Museum
14 State House
15 Ministry of Tourism & Culture
16 The Quadrangle
   (Government Offices)
17 Anglican Cathedral
18 Minibus Park (for Serekunda)
19 War Memorial
20 Fountain
21 Albert Market
22 Craft Market
23 Post Office; Gamtel Office
24 Trust Bank
27 Gamtel Office
29 Methodist Bookshop
31 Air Dabia
32 Guinea Embassy

34 Standard Chartered Bank
35 Ghana Airways;
   Banjul Travel Agency
36 BICIS Bank
37 Guinea-Bissau Embassy
40 Cabo Verde Airlines
41 Melicana Nightclub
42 Olympic Travel
44 Immigration Office
45 Sierra Leone High Commission
46 Air Guinée
47 Banjul Pharmacy
50 Pirogues to Barra
51 Terminal for Barra Ferry
52 Mariam Ceesay Bar & Restaurant
54 GPTC Bus Station
   (Upcountry Buses)

0   150   300 m

covered separately in the Atlantic Coast Resorts & Serekunda section.

Orientation

The focal point of Banjul city centre is MacCarthy Square, a public park, from where several main streets run south, including Russell St, which leads past Albert Market into Liberation St (formerly Wellington St). West of here is the old part of Banjul – a maze of narrow streets and ramshackle houses where few tourists ever venture.

July 22 Drive (formerly Independence Drive) runs west from MacCarthy Square, becoming the main road out of Banjul. On the edge of the city it goes under the vast structure of Arch 22 and turns into a dual carriageway which after about 4km crosses Oyster Creek on Denton Bridge to reach the mainland.

Information

Money Standard Chartered and Trust Bank are both on Buckle St, and BICIS is on Liberation St. Black market moneychangers can be found outside Air Dabia and at the ferry port. Several shopkeepers along Liberation St will also change money – a much safer option.

Post & Communications The main post office and the Gamtel public telephone office are near Albert Market; there's a reasonably reliable poste restante service at the post office.

Travel Agencies Airline offices are listed under Getting There & Away later in this section, but a travel agency can provide you with all the choices. These include: the Banjul Travel Agency (☎ 228473) on Buckle St and Olympic Travel (☎ 222370 or 222371) on Dobson St. Some other tour and travel agencies are listed in the Atlantic Coast Resorts & Serekunda section.

Bookshops The Methodist Bookshop on Buckle St keeps religious books, and a pretty good stock of general books, papers and magazines.

Medical Services The Royal Victoria Hospital is where you'd probably be taken if you were unfortunate enough to be involved in an accident, but the private establishments in the Atlantic Coast resorts area are better for illnesses and minor injuries.

Dangers & Annoyances Muggings are rare in Banjul city centre although you always need to be alert, particularly near the ferry terminal. Pickpockets are rife, operating on the ferry and most notably in Albert Market.

Things to See

The vibrant heart of Banjul city is **Albert Market** – see Shopping later in this section for more details. For a taste of the past, it can be interesting to walk in the quiet streets of the **old town**: Dobson St has a few colonial buildings and traditional Krio-style houses, many of which still belong to families who came here from Sierra Leone, some as long ago as the 1820s.

In the **Gambia National Museum** some of the exhibits are a bit dog-eared, but a renovation is planned. Upstairs is a dusty but fascinating display of photos, maps and text about archaeology, African peoples and the colonial period. Entrance is D10. It's open from 8 am to 4 pm Monday to Thursday, and from 8 am to 1 pm on Friday and Saturday.

Nearby is **Arch 22**, a massive gateway to the city, built to celebrate the military coup of 22 July 1994. You can go up to the small museum and coffee shop, and admire the views from the balcony.

Activities

Most activities and organised tours can be arranged at the Atlantic Coast resorts, so details are included in that section. One exception is canoe trips on Oyster Creek (see the map on p374) – a popular destination for birdwatching, fishing or just messing about in boats. Many people come on trips organised by hotels, but you can arrange things informally a day in advance at the 'port' (a patch of mud with a few boats tied up) by Denton Bridge.

Places to Stay

Not many tourists stay in Banjul city, preferring instead the coastal resorts, but if you come to experience Africa, rather than a slice of Europe laid down on the tropical coast, you might prefer it here.

The cheapest place in town, complete with red light out front, is the *Banjul City Travellers Motel*, on Dobson St, charging D75 a room (single or double), but it's dirty and the toilets are disgusting. A less unpleasant cheapie is the *Teranga Hotel* on Hill St, with rooms at D80.

A much better deal is the welcoming *Ferry Guesthouse* on Liberation St, where big, airy singles/doubles cost D85/115 (or CFA5000/6500). Breakfast is not available, but it's easy to find something at the food stalls at the ferry terminal opposite. Another friendly place is the *Duma Guesthouse* (☎ 228381) on Louvell Square in the heart of old Banjul, where clean rooms with fans cost D80/100. Also in the old part of town is the *Abbey Guesthouse* (38 Grant St) off Albion Place. This charming building used to be the German consulate and has a great balcony. Rooms are basic but spacious, and cost from D80 to D100 for one to three people. The shared bathrooms are fine, the food is good and cheap, and the manager is very friendly.

The *Apollo Hotel* (☎ 228184) on Orange St is large and soulless, with reasonably clean rooms at D160/260 with bathroom and fan. Couples can share a single. By far the best value is the *Princess Diana Hotel* (☎ 228715) on July 22 Drive. Formerly the Kantora Hotel, it was renamed by the friendly Egyptian owner. Clean air-con rooms cost D165/200 including breakfast. An evening drink at the sidewalk tables is a great way to meet a mixed bag of guests from all over West Africa and other parts of the world.

The only top end place in central Banjul is the *Atlantic Hotel* (☎ 228601, fax 227861).

The official rates for air-con singles/doubles are D850/1100, but these are often discounted. There's a swimming pool and facilities for tennis and water sports.

Places to Eat

Chop shops with plates of rice and sauce for D3 to D5 include the *Taranga Restau* near the minibus park on Albion Place, and the nearby *Joe Bassy Restaurant*. There are a few more cheapies along Sam Jack Terrace. Also worth trying are the *food stalls* in Albert Market; some cater mainly for locals while others are more for tourists (both with prices to match).

The *Pam-Pam* on Clarkson St serves good chawarmas and other snacks for D15. Similar places in the same area are the *Ali Baba Snack Bar*, the *Mandela Alles Klar Fast Food*, and the *St Raphael Snack Bar* on Picton St.

The restaurant at the *Princess Diana Hotel* does good meals for about D35. For a better selection, the *African Heritage Restaurant* on Liberation St serves snacks for around D25, and main meals, such as spaghetti bolognaise, for D40 to D60. A small glass of beer is D12 and soft drinks D8.

A few blocks away, the Austrian-style *Braüstüble Restaurant* has an attractive 'biergarten', cold draught beer (D13 for a small glass) and sandwiches. Meals in the dining room include chicken at around D40 and steaks from D75, plus some Teutonic selections.

For Lebanese food, the smart *Al Basha Restaurant* (☎ 229799, 10 Nelson Mandela St) is open for lunch only, with main courses for D50.

Entertainment

The *Soto-Koto* on Clarkson St near the Pam-Pam restaurant is lively on weekends (after midnight) or when there's a band playing. You can have a good time here, but some foreigners have been hassled and it might be worth going with a Gambian friend to avoid this. Entrance is D10. The *Melicana* on Picton St is more upmarket.

Shopping

If you go in the main entrance of Albert Market you'll pass stalls selling clothes, shoes, household and electrical wares, and just about everything else. Go further back and you reach the area where the fruit and vegetables are sold – a colourful area worth a look even if you're not buying bananas or yams. Beyond here you reach the stalls catering mainly for tourists (the Craft Market), where you can browse through a wide range of carvings, fabrics, batiks, paintings, drums and other traditional musical instruments.

For cassettes of African music, the best place seems to be Kerewan Sound on Russell St, near the main entrance to Albert Market. Upstairs is the Camara Jua recording shop, which also has a good selection.

Getting There & Away

Air For details of international flights, see the main Getting There & Away section earlier in this chapter. For reservations, offices of the main airlines are listed below. Except Sabena, all are in Banjul centre.

Air Dabia
 (☎ 227463) Liberation St
Air Guinée
 (☎ 227585 or 225035) Leman St
Cabo Verde Airlines
 (☎ 222029) Hagan St
Ghana Airways
 (☎ 228245) Buckle St
Sabena
 (☎ 496301, 496302 or 496303) 97 Kairaba Ave, Fajara

Bus GPTC buses run several times a day between Banjul and Basse Santa Su. The GPTC bus station is on Cotton St. Ordinary buses leave at 6.45, 7.30, 9 and 10 am and at 1 pm. The fare is D30 to Soma, D50 to Georgetown, and D60 to Basse, and the journey to Basse takes around eight hours.

The express bus leaves at 8 am, and costs D10 more to reach each destination. The special express bus (Serekunda, Brikama, Soma and Bansang only) leaves at 11 am, and costs D22 more than the ordinary bus. Reservations are not possible, so to be sure of

a seat (particularly on the express and special express) get the bus from the Jimpex Rd depot, in Kanifeng near Serekunda – this is easier anyway if you're staying on this side. The buses leave from here half an hour before their timetabled departure time from the Cotton St station, and you pay an extra D2.

Bush Taxi Minibuses to Brikama, upcountry towns and southern Senegal all go from Serekunda garage (bush taxi park). For more details see Getting There & Away in the Atlantic Coast Resorts & Serekunda section.

Boat Ferries run between Banjul and Barra officially every one to two hours, from 7 am until 7 pm, but there are frequent delays and often one ferry is out of action. Get a ticket (D3) from the booth before going aboard.

If the ferry isn't running, pirogues run across although the ride can be scary (or downright dangerous) in choppy conditions. The fare is D3 to D5 per person – always check before boarding. Pirogues also run at night, although the fare (and the risk) rises considerably. We heard from two travellers who missed the last ferry and were charged US$50 for a private 'charter'.

Getting Around

To/From the Airport A green tourist taxi from Banjul international airport to Banjul city centre is D150. The official fixed rates are painted on a board at the taxi rank, so bargaining is usually not required.

There is no airport bus but minibuses run along the main road between Brikama and Serekunda, passing the turn-off 3km from the airport.

Minibus & Shared Taxi Local minibuses run between Banjul, Serekunda and the other nearby towns, while yellow shared taxis run between Serekunda and Bakau/Fajara. The route between Serekunda and Kotu/Kololi is served by shared taxis and minibuses. Between Banjul and Fajara you have to change at Bakau or Serekunda. From Banjul to Bakau or Serekunda is D3, from Bakau or Serekunda to Fajara is D2.

Private Taxi For a yellow taxi to yourself (known as a 'town trip'), a short ride across Banjul city centre costs D10 to D20, but negotiation is required. From Banjul it's about D40 to Bakau, D50 to Serekunda and D60 to Fajara. Check the price with the driver before getting in. Green tourist taxis also do town trips, but charge more.

Car, Motorcycle & Bicycle Cars and bikes can be hired from various places in the Atlantic Coast resort area. See Getting Around in that section for details.

The Atlantic Coast Resorts & Serekunda

The Atlantic Coast resorts of Bakau, Fajara, Kotu and Kololi are the heart of the tourist industry, with about 20 hotels along this 10km strip of beach, and several others planned or under construction. Back from the beach are more hotels, with restaurants, bars, nightclubs, souvenir stalls and all the other paraphernalia of tourism.

In complete contrast, Serekunda is 100% Gambian – a major centre of activity, and the hub of the country's transport network. A stroll around the town or the thriving market (in reality the town *is* one big market) is highly recommended for a taste of unrelenting in-your-face urban West Africa.

Information
For embassies and consulates in the Atlantic Coast resorts see Embassies & Consulates in the Facts for the Visitor section earlier.

Money The main cluster of banks (BICIS, Trust Bank and Standard Bank) is in Bakau. Standard Bank is also in Kololi and on Kairaba Ave in Serekunda. In Bakau and Kololi, banks open in the morning (usually from 8 or 8.30 am to noon or 2 pm), as well as in the afternoon from 4 to 6 pm, and for a few hours on either Saturday morning or afternoon. The Standard Chartered Bank in

Serekunda is open Monday to Thursday 10 am to 4 pm; Friday and Saturday 9 am to noon.

There is an exchange bureau at St Mary's Food & Wine supermarket in Bakau, and another outside the Bungalow Beach Hotel in Kotu. The best place to change money in Serekunda (and handy if you're in Fajara) is the Castle Exchange Bureau, behind the petrol station at the end of Kairaba Ave.

If all the banks and exchange bureaus are closed, you can usually change money at a large hotel or at some supermarkets (although rates are rarely good). Alternatively, some of the souvenir stall owners in Bakau will change – but they only deal in cash.

Post & Communications The main post office is just off Kairaba Ave, about half way between Fajara and Serekunda. There are Gamtel offices in Bakau (near the banks) and Serekunda plus private telephone offices (telecentres) on Kairaba Ave near the junction with New Town Rd and another near the footbridge and water tower.

Travel Agencies See Information in the Banjul section earlier for a list of agents in Banjul city centre. Most other agents are on Kairaba Ave between Fajara and Bakau. These include Gambia International Airlines (☎ 374100 or 374101) in the Midway centre, which is the main ground handling and reservation agent for most airlines flying into Gambia, with plans to operate its own flights in the future, and Discount Travel (☎ 375677 or 375613, fax 375598).

Medical Services If you have a potentially serious illness such as malaria, head for the British-run clinic at the Medical Research Council on Atlantic Rd in Fajara. Other places include the Spanish-run International Clinic, near Weezo's restaurant just off the northern end of Kairaba Ave, and Westfield Clinic (☎ 292213) at Westfield Junction in Serekunda.

Dangers & Annoyances Petty thefts and more serious muggings have increased in

THE GAMBIA

ATLANTIC COAST RESORTS & SEREKUNDA

PLACES TO STAY
1 Sunwing Hotel
2 Cape Point Hotel
15 Bakau Guesthouse
20 Friendship Lodge
23 Angie's Inn
26 Ngala Lodge
28 Leybato Guesthouse, Restaurant & Bar
29 Fajara Hotel
31 Kombo Beach Novotel; Bungalow Beach Hotel
32 Bakotu Hotel
33 Fajara Guesthouse
34 Francisco's Hotel & Restaurant
39 Safari Garden Hotel
48 Malawi Guesthouse
55 Kanifeng YMCA Hostel
74 Green Line Motel; Horus Restaurant
75 Jalakunda Hotel
79 Badala Park Hotel
82 Palma Rima Hotel
84 Bunkoyo Hotel
85 Bakadaji Hotel & Restaurant
87 The Holiday Suites
88 Kololi Inn & Tavern; The Auberge
89 Keneba Hotel
90 Balmoral Apartments
93 Kairaba Hotel; Senegambia Hotel; Tafbel Hotel

PLACES TO EAT
3 Calypso Restaurant; Baoba Sunshine Bar
6 Sambou's Restaurant
7 Seven Towers Restaurant
8 The Clay Oven
10 Fountaineer Restaurant; Klas Veranda
12 Tee Dee's Relax Spot
16 Kumba Bar; Bakau Market
25 Royal China; Bakery
31 Il Mondo Restaurant & Bar; Paradise Beach Bar
35 Mama's
36 Wheels; Weezo's Restaurant & Bar
38 Michael's Grill
44 Antonico's; Le Lotus

45 Rum Runners Caribean Café, Restaurant & Cocktail Bar
49 La Parisienne
58 Madeleine's Inn
59 UK Fast Food
64 Sen Fast Food; Billal Pastry & Ice-Cream Shop
71 Santa Yalla Restaurant
72 Amadou Barry Restaurant
80 Oriental Pearl; The Panda
83 Luigi's Italian Restaurant
86 Janneh's Seafood & Vegetarian Restaurant
94 Dolphin Bar & Restaurant
95 Tao Asian Restaurant; Scala Restaurant; La Valbonne Italian Restaurant; Kololi Casino
97 Badala Beach Bar

OTHER
4 St Mary's Food & Wine Supermarket
5 Botanical Gardens
9 Kachikaly Crocodile Pool
11 Marie's Pub; Sali's Bar
13 Minibuses to Banjul & Serekunda
14 Catholic Church
17 Maroun's Supermarket; Bank
18 MacDomorro's
19 Sweden & Norway Consuls
21 Independence Stadium
22 Gena Bes Batik Factory
24 Banks; Gamtel Office; Souvenir Market; Taxis
27 British High Commission

37 Mauritania Consul General
40 Sabena
41 Telephone
42 Fajara Golf Club
43 Palm Wine Sellers
46 Petrol Station
47 US Embassy
50 Senegal High Commission
51 Afri-Swiss Travels
52 Mosque
53 Telephone
54 Water Tower
56 GPTC Bus Depot
57 Post Office
60 Alliance Française-Gambienne
61 Discount Travel
62 Castle Exchange Bureau
63 Eddy's Nightclub
65 Gamtel Office
66 Minibuses to Banjul
67 Joker's Bar
68 Mandela Cinéma
69 Garage (Bus & Taxi Station)
70 Market; Gamtel Office
73 Petrol Station
76 Police Station
77 Isamari Cinéma
78 Arena Babou Fatty (Wrestling Area)
81 Solomon's Beach Bar
91 Lamtoro Clinic
92 Tropicana Nightclub
96 Kololi Beach Club
98 Bijilo Forest Park HQ

this area over the last few years. Although incidents are minimal considering the large numbers of tourists, the following places should be treated with special care: in Bakau, the beach south and west of Cape Point, beyond the hotels and restaurants; the woods and cliff top in Fajara, between Leybato Guesthouse and the Fajara Hotel; and the path around Fajara golf course between Fajara and Kotu.

Many visitors complain about local 'bumsters' or 'beach boys' who loiter in the resort areas. High unemployment and no welfare system in Gambia means that for many young men hustling tourists is the only way to make money. Apart from acting as guides or selling souvenirs and other services, bumsters can earn commissions from tour companies and restaurants.

Some visitors hire bumsters as guides, either to show them around or just to keep other hustlers away, while others hire guides from their hotel to keep the bumsters off! Either way it's not at all essential. Be polite but firm in your decline of offers, or you may find it more rewarding to ignore them completely, although this may result in a short burst of harmless verbal abuse. If you get hassled in the market, complain to a stall holder that it's preventing you buying. The bumster will soon be chased off!

Things to See

In Bakau, the **Botanical Garden** is looking a little dilapidated, although it's still a peaceful shady place and good for spotting birds. Not far away, a road leads down to a jetty and small **port** where traditional fishing boats come and go. Morning is usually the busiest time.

Also in Bakau is **Kachikaly Crocodile Pool**, a sacred site for the local people who traditionally come here to pray – the crocodiles represent the power of fertility. Success rates are apparently high as many children in this area are named Kachikaly. The pool is a popular tourist spot, but this is probably the nearest you'll get to a crocodile anywhere in Africa without having your leg

Bijilo Forest Park

This small wildlife reserve on the coast at Kololi is easy to reach. It's a beautiful place to visit, and should be supported as it helps prevent more hotel development down the coast. A well maintained series of trails of different lengths leads through the lush and shady vegetation, and you'll easily see monkeys and numerous birds. There are several good viewpoints for looking at the scenery.

The monkeys are habituated to humans, mainly because many visitors feed them. Birds are more easily spotted on the coast side. The dunes near the beach are covered in grass and low bush, with tall stands of palm just behind. Further back, away from the dunes, the trees are large and dense and covered in creepers. Many trees are labelled, and you can buy a small booklet which tells you a little about their natural history, traditional uses and so on.

Admission is D20 per day. On weekdays a guide is sometimes available.

chewed off. The largest croc is called Charley and seems completely resigned to people touching his scales or popping flashguns in his eyes. Entrance is D10.

Activities

For swimming, all the major hotels have pools and most rent equipment for water sports; the typical charge for sailboards is about D35 an hour. The beaches are relatively safe, but undertow drownings still occur every year, so inexperienced swimmers should check conditions locally before plunging in.

Fajara Golf Club has the country's main golf course, where an 18 hole round with clubs and caddy is D250. Smooth grass is hard to grow here, so the holes are surrounded by well maintained 'browns', not greens! The club also has courts for tennis, squash and badminton.

Places to Stay

In the Atlantic Coast area, new hotels continue to pop up, while old ones close or change name. The list here is not complete, but gives a good cross-section of options, especially for independent travellers. There are bound to be a few more changes by the time you arrive.

Places to Stay – Budget

Bakau One of the cheapest places to stay is *Crocs Guesthouse*, a British-Gambian enterprise deep in the old part of Bakau near Kachikaly Crocodile Pool, with friendly management and clean, no-frills rooms at D75/150. You can cook your own food in the kitchen, or order meals (some hours in advance).

Bakau Guesthouse has large, clean, airy singles/doubles with bathroom, fan and fridge for D180/270. There's a kitchen for self-catering, and if you stay a week you get one free night.

Friendship Lodge (☎ 495830), next to (and part of) the Independence Stadium, has spotless rooms with air-con, mosquito nets and bathroom – a steal at D165/195. Doubles with fans are D165.

Fajara The *Malawi Guesthouse* (☎ 393012, fax 392227), off Kairaba Ave, has been popular for years and has doubles/triples with shared bathroom for D100/200 to D150/250. Rooms with bathroom are about D50 extra. The atmosphere is relaxed, and the management are a good source of local information. Services include laundry, bike hire, a 'travellers tips' book on the bar, a notice board advertising various local services, safe parking, and a mail-holding service for guests (your name, c/o Malawi Guesthouse, PMB 495, Serekunda, Gambia).

At the Fajara end of Garba Jahumpa Rd (south side), *Holland House* is primarily a Dutch-run coffee shop and second-hand goods emporium – look for the converted shipping container in the garden – but they have a few rooms for D100 per person, including breakfast.

East of Fajara, a good budget option is *Kanifeng YMCA Hostel* (☎ 392647), where simple but clean rooms with shared bathrooms cost D70/105, plus D10 for breakfast. It's also a training centre and often full, so phone first to see if there are vacancies.

Kololi The *Kololi Inn & Tavern* (☎ 463410) has a very African feel with brightly decorated rooms in thatched bungalows for D150/200 including breakfast. There is a small bar-restaurant, and a kitchen for guests. We've heard varying reports, but when we visited it was clean and friendly.

In the same area, the friendly *Keneba Hotel* (☎ 470093) gets good reviews from shoestring travellers. Small double bungalows with bathroom cost D175 including breakfast. You can get here on a minibus from Serekunda heading for Kololi; get off at the junction by the Tropicana Nightclub.

Serekunda The dreary *Jalakunda Hotel* has rooms at D125, but much better is the *Green Line Motel* (☎ 394015), where clean rooms with air-con and bathroom are D150/225, and meals around D30.

Sukuta South-west of Serekunda, *Sukuta Camping* (☎ 994149) has single and double rooms at D80/120 and camping for D45, plus D10 per car. This place is clean and safe, with shared fully functioning showers and toilets, a restaurant-bar and kitchen for self-catering. The friendly German owner has spent a long time on the road and knows about routes, spares, and where to buy and sell vehicles. He also has a couple of cars for self-drive hire (see Getting Around later in this section). From Serekunda, take any minibus towards Brufut or Gunjur, and get off near the junction where the roads to Gunjur and Brufut divide.

Places to Stay – Mid-Range

As well as being medium priced, several of the hotels in this range are small, owner-managed, and more used to dealing with individual travellers than the larger top end establishments (although many also cater for organised groups). All rooms have their own private bathroom, most hotels accept credit cards and several drop prices in the low season.

Bakau The *Cape Point Hotel* (☎ 495005, fax 495375) has attractive gardens with a small pool, singles/doubles for D300/375 (D400 with air-con) and apartments with two double rooms and kitchen for D600.

Fajara The *Leybato Guesthouse, Restaurant & Bar* (☎ 390275, 497186, fax 497562) overlooks the beach, with self-catering double bungalows from D300 to D400, or without kitchen for D150 to D200. No single rates are available, but the friendly manager says all prices are negotiable, especially for stays of more than one night. The Leybato is reached along a small dirt track off Atlantic Rd. It's a great place to stay, but you do need to be careful walking here at night.

The small and quiet *Fajara Guesthouse* (☎ 496122), has airy rooms at D290/360 and breakfast for D35. Up a grade is the popular *Safari Garden Hotel* (☎ 495887, fax 496042, email geri@commit.gm) a small British-Gambian enterprise with a friendly efficient atmosphere. Well decorated rooms with private terrace are spaced around a lush garden and swimming pool. Singles/doubles/triples cost D300/400/550 including a buffet breakfast.

On Atlantic Rd, *Francisco's Hotel & Restaurant* (☎ 495332) has comfortable air-con rooms at D650 including a full English breakfast.

Kotu & Kololi The *Bakadaji Hotel & Restaurant* (☎ 462307) has self-catering bungalows (with two double rooms, lounge and kitchen) for D500 per night, and doubles/triples at D300 with breakfast. It has extensive grounds, complete with access to the beach, and a flock of sheep to keep the grass short!

The nearby *Bunkoyo Hotel* (☎ 463199) is more upmarket, but small and homely, with comfortable singles/doubles at D350/450, and breakfast for D50. Also nearby is

Luigi's (☎ 460280, fax 460282), a family-run Italian restaurant where double rooms with a kitchen and bathroom cost D275 to D375 per night.

Places to Stay – Top End

Most top end hotels cater for groups of package tourists rather than independent travellers, so information here is cut to the bone. If you fancy some luxury after a long time on the road, prices for independent travellers may be reduced to half the advertised rate if you phone in advance, especially in the low season (when rates drop anyway). All rooms have air-con and private bathroom, and most include breakfast. Nearly all hotels are on the beach and have a pool. Most accept credit cards.

Bakau The *Sunwing Hotel* (☎ 495428, fax 496102) on Cape Point has singles/doubles for D560/800. Water sports are available.

Fajara The large and soulless *Fajara Hotel* (☎ 495605, fax 495339) has singles/doubles for D500/650. In contrast, *Ngala Lodge* (☎ 497672, 997429, fax 497429) on Atlantic Rd is small, stylish and exclusive, and has double suites for US$140.

Kotu The small *Bakotu Hotel* (☎ 495555, fax 495959) has a pleasant garden. Singles/doubles are D480/640. The *Bungalow Beach Hotel* (☎ 495288) is a two storey complex with many facilities, and singles/doubles for D660/860. The *Kombo Beach Novotel* (☎ 465466) is a large, high standard hotel with most facilities. It has singles/doubles for D1050/1250.

Kololi The *Palma Rima Hotel* (☎ 463380, fax 493382) on Badala Park Way has singles/doubles for D650/850. The *Kairaba Hotel* (☎ 462940, fax 492947), the finest of the large hotels, has singles/doubles for D700/850 to D1100/1250. The *Senegambia Hotel* (☎ 462718/9, fax 461839) has singles/doubles for D700/900 and is a good second to the Kairaba.

Places to Eat

Cheap Eats In the resort areas, most places to eat are aimed at tourists, so finding really cheap local-style meals can be difficult. The best options are in Bakau and Fajara. Otherwise you have to go to Serekunda.

Bakau to Kololi At the taxi ranks there's usually a couple of women cooking up *rice and sauce* for the drivers, which goes for about D5 a plate, and near Bakau market a Senegalese-style *caféman* sells coffee and bread with simple plates of food in the morning. *Tee Dee's Relax Spot*, near the junction of Atlantic Rd and Old Cape Rd, sells drinks, omelettes and bread, and plates of chop for D10 (which may need ordering in advance). Otherwise, the cheapest you'll find are the snack bars catering mainly to tourists. These include the lively *Kumba Bar* near the market on Atlantic Rd, where meals such as burgers or fish and chips cost from around D35.

Well worth checking out is the friendly *Baoba Sunshine Bar*, about 50m south along the beach from the smarter Calypso Restaurant. This local-style place is open to 8 pm and does great value meals such as fish and chips for D35, shrimp sandwiches for D20, and Gambian dishes for D25.

In Fajara, a very good place is *Michael's Grill* in a back street off Kairaba Ave, near the Safari Garden Hotel, with European dishes from around D35 and local meals from D25. Guests at the nearby top end hotels have been known to sneak down here for a taste of genuine Gambian cooking. *Afra Kairaba*, on the corner of Kairaba Ave and Badala Park Way, serves takeaway grilled meat in the evenings.

The restaurant at the *Malawi Guesthouse* (see Places to Stay – Budget) has good-value food, with a definite English flavour, and there's an extensive menu. Sandwiches are D15 to D25, cheap meals such as veggie or meat burgers cost from D20, Gambian specialities are D30, pie and chips is D45, and grills and curries cost from D40 to D75. 'Sunday lunch' (roast beef and Yorkshire pudding) is served any time any day for D50,

and the Friday evening all-you-can-eat buffet for D50 has people queuing at the gate.

At the far end of Kololi is the *Badala Beach Bar*, a rustic and surprisingly cheap place (considering its proximity to the major hotels) with beers for D10. This place is primarily a bar but they do good baked fish for around D35, although you need to order in advance. It's worth tying in a meal here with a visit to Bijilo Forest Park: place your order, then walk round the reserve for a few hours, by which time your food will be ready.

Serekunda There are several *cheap eating houses* around the market and taxi station entrance. Near the Green Line Motel are some more cheapies: *Restaurant de Guinea* and *Jollof Rice Restaurant*, plus the smarter *Horus Restaurant*, with friendly management, and European, Gambian and Egyptian food from D25 to D40.

On Kairaba Ave, *Sen Fast Food* is clean and popular. Next door is *Billal Pastry Shop*, where you can muse on quotes from the Quran painted on the wall while you eat. South of here's more cheap places, including *Santa Yalla Restaurant* and *Amadou Barry Restaurant*.

African & European There are many options to suit all tastes, both in the resort areas and Serekunda.

Bakau *Calypso Restaurant* has ocean views, a good relaxed atmosphere, seafood meals from D75 and Gambian dishes for around D50. *Sambou's Restaurant* has light meals from D35 up to large pepper steaks for D100. Down Saitmatty Rd *MacDomorro's* has a nice outside terrace and grills and seafood in the D30 to D70 range.

Fajara & Serekunda On the corner of Kairaba Ave and Atlantic Rd, *Mama's* is ever popular, with a vast menu of good-value European and Gambian meals, ranging from D35 to D50. Another great favourite is *Leybato Guesthouse, Restaurant & Bar*, with a quiet shady garden and most meals around D60. Nearby is the more stylish

Francisco's with grills from D60 to D85, and the *Safari Garden Hotel* where Gambian and imaginative vegetarian meals go for around D30 and seafood and grills from D40 to D80. Dining at the latter allows you use of the pool. Top of the top end restaurants is *Ngala Lodge*, where the Belgian chef specialises in wonderful fish dishes – a three course meal with drinks will set you back D300 to D500 per person.

Kairaba Ave offers many more choices. The best thing to do is stroll down during the day and check out your options, but here's a few names to get you started. *Wheels* offers grilled meat from D30 to D75, a garden setting and a boisterous bar. *The Butcher's Shop* is a delicatessen and cafe. *Antonico's* is an 'international restaurant' that receives good reviews from expats, and has a *kora* musician. *La Parisienne* is a French-style cafe. *Rose du Vents* is a French restaurant with main courses around D55 to D80. *Le Palais du Chocolat*, a cafe-patisserie with delicious cakes and ice creams, answers any calorie craving. *Madeleine's Inn* is a Swiss restaurant with an interesting menu of fish, pork and chicken dishes from D65 and steaks with various sauces from D75.

Kotu Right on the beach, *Il Mondo Restaurant* does good food from D50 to D100, and *Paradise Beach Bar*, nearby, offers sandwiches for D20, grills from D40 to D50 and Gambian dishes for D55.

Kololi Luigi's Italian Restaurant has pasta dishes from D75 and pizzas at D65 to D130. Nearby, *Bakadaji Hotel & Restaurant* does very good African and European food, with main courses for around D80. Even better value are the Thursday and Saturday night buffets which cost D110 and include traditional entertainment.

If you're looking for high standards, the *Scala Restaurant* in Kololi gets good reports, with specialities for D100. Nearby, with similar prices and an excellent reputation, is *La Valbonne Italian Restaurant*. Near the Kololi Inn is the highly recommended *Janneh's Seafood & Vegetarian*

Restaurant (☎ 461164) where tempting dishes include king prawns in garlic (D60), butterfish ragout and mushroom sauce (D50) and aubergine in batter (D40).

Asian & Indian In Bakau, the *Royal China Restaurant (☎ 497168)* offers main dishes for around D55, while on Kairaba Ave *Le Lotus (☎ 496026)* has good-value Vietnamese food at around D30 to D45. In Kotu, the highly rated *Oriental Pearl (☎ 460428)* serves main dishes from D45, or a set menu for D90 per person. Also in Bakau, for Indian food, *The Clay Oven (☎ 496600)* has main courses between D50 and D100, and side dishes another D30 to D50.

Other Cuisines *Weezo's (☎ 496918)* on Kairaba Ave is a smart Mexican restaurant where main courses are around D100. For Lebanese cuisine, the *Neptune Restaurant (☎ 460434)* in Kololi has main courses from D60 to D90. Consistently popular is *Rum Runners Caribbean Café, Restaurant & Cocktail Bar (☎ 497506)* on Kairaba Ave in Fajara, with meals like ladyfish creole (D65) and pineapple and seafood salad (D30).

Hotel Restaurants All the upmarket hotels have their own restaurants where nonguests are welcome. Most serve evening buffets – usually D100 to D150 for all you can eat.

Entertainment

Bars In Bakau, *Marie's Pub* is a shanty-like bar with cheap beer, Gambian clientele and reggae music, while along Atlantic Rd, just past the Botanical Gardens, on the other side of the road, is the breezy *One For The Road Bar*, with just two tables and a fridge. The more tourist-orientated *Tropic Smile Bar* bills itself as a 'fun pub' and has good music. The nearby *Kumba Bar* also serves food, and is popular with tourists and locals.

In Fajara, an excellent place for drinks at sunset is *Leybato Restaurant & Bar*. A stroll down Kairaba Ave or along the beach in Kotu and Kololi will reveal a wide range of smarter watering holes. Less smart, but

Palm Wine

For a cheap drink, local style, you could head for the palm wine sellers who work in a large stand of palm trees between Kotu Creek and Fajara golf course. Their selling area is in the bush off Badala Park Way, about half a kilometre down from the Shell station on the corner. There's no sign, and it can be hard to find, so the best way might be to ask a local for guidance, or take a taxi. However you get there, remember that this stuff can pack a punch – and the odd dud batch can knock you out cold!

Palm wine is collected by punching a hole in the tree just under the sprouting palm fronds.

always popular, is **Badala Beach Bar** (see Cheap Eats earlier).

Serekunda offers bars with a more local feel. Try **Bar Afra** near the Green Line Motel, the simple **Star Bar** near the mosque,

or **Joker's**, a smarter place at the southern end of Kairaba Ave, with a garden, restaurant and, sometimes, live music.

Nightclubs The **Metro Nightclub** near the Cape Point Hotel in Bakau is frequented by locals and tourists, and costs D25 to get in. At the smarter **Tam Tam 2000**, next to the Badala Park Hotel in Kotu, entrance is D75 or D100 per couple. In Kololi there are a few more choices, including **Jembey Fever** and the **Tropicana Club** with live bands, discos featuring reggae and international pop, and a lively mix of tourists and locals. In Serekunda, **Eddy's Nightclub** has live music every weekend, although this is very much a locals' place which rarely sees tourists.

Spectator Sports

The Gambia's main stadium is in Bakau, and this is the site for major football matches and other sporting events, which are advertised locally on posters around town.

Traditional wrestling occasionally takes place at the Bakau stadium but it's more interesting, and much more fun, to see matches at one of the several smaller 'arenas' (open patches of ground) in Serekunda. These include the Arena Babou Fatty, off Sukuta Rd, south-west of the Green Line Motel, and at the Arena Tuti Fall Jammeh, also on the west side of town, a couple of hundred metres south of Sukuta Rd. Matches take place in the late afternoon, usually on Sunday evening (less frequently in the dry season, and not during Ramadan). The entrance fee is D15 for tourists.

To get there, you can arrange a tour through a large hotel; the cost is about D150. Taxis do this trip for the same price, including waiting time. Alternatively, you can get to Serekunda by shared taxi for about D5, and follow the crowds to the arena.

Shopping

Maroun's Supermarket in Bakau is open 9 am to 7.30 pm daily except Sunday. Nearby is the Atlantic Supermarket, also open Sunday mornings. There are also supermarkets on Kairaba Ave and in the resorts near

Traditional Wrestling

Watching a traditional wrestling match is a fascinating experience and great fun. The preliminaries can be as entertaining as the actual fights. Wrestlers enter the arena in full costume, a loincloth of bright, patterned material arranged with a tail falling behind and their bodies and arms smothered in leather *grisgris* (charms). They then slowly strut around the ring, sometimes preceded by *griots* beating drums.

There are usually many matches, as they last only a few minutes until one contestant forces the other to the ground (technically one knee touching the ground ends the match). As many as four matches may be going on at once. And during the fight anything goes: biting, kicking, punching. No fancy hand-locks, technical throws, or points. Just get him down!

foreign). Also worth checking out is Tropical Souvenirs near the Senegambia Hotel in Kololi, which stocks a good selection of books, plus maps, postcards, clothing, film and batteries as well as carvings and other craft items.

Bakau Market has several stalls selling carvings, traditional cloth and other souvenirs. There is a string of similar stalls nearby along Atlantic Rd. Opposite the Gamtel office is a particularly hassle-free shop selling batiks and brightly coloured clothing of good quality, at reasonable prices. The Gena Bes batik factory on Garba Jahumpa Rd has a good selection of batiks and tie-dye cloth which sells for around D60 per metre. Several readers have recommended the tie-dye and batik factory in Serekunda owned by Mrs Musu Kebba Drammeh – all the taxi drivers know her place.

Getting There & Away

To/From the Airport A green tourist taxi from Banjul international airport to Serekunda is D100, and to any Atlantic Coast resort is D150. There isn't any public transport to the airport, but minibuses between Brikama and Serekunda can drop you at the turn-off 3km from the airport.

Bush Taxi & Minibus Bush taxis and minibuses go from the garage in Serekunda to upcountry towns on the south of the river (to Brikama is D4, Soma D30; Farafenni D35), and to places on the South Coast (Brufut D3, Tanji D5 and Sanyang D7). For more details on transport options to places in southern Senegal see this chapter's Getting There & Away section.

Getting Around

Some details on transport between the Atlantic Coast resorts and Banjul city centre are given in Getting Around in the Banjul section earlier.

Minibus & Shared Taxi From Bakau you can get minibuses and shared taxis to Banjul city centre or Serekunda. From Serekunda, outside the Gamtel office at the southern end

Kotu and Kololi. All stock local and imported food, books, toiletries, suncream, swim gear and newspapers (local and of Kairaba Ave, you can get shared taxis to Bakau.

Private Taxi Green 'tourist taxis' wait at ranks outside most large hotels. They do not have meters and prices are fixed. Some sample 'town trip' fares from Bakau: Kololi D120; airport D150; Banjul city centre D100 one way, D150 return.

Car & Motorcycle At the Kairaba Beach Hotel, AB Rent-a-Car (☎ 460926, fax 460023) has self-drive vehicles from D350 per day and D300 per day for six days. To this add D100 to D150 for insurance, and another 10% tax. All this has to be paid in cash, although the deposit of D10,000 can be paid by credit card. A cheaper and more flexible option is offered by Sukuta Camping (see Places to Stay), where self-drive car hire is an absolute bargain at D225 per day.

Bicycle Mountain bikes and traditional roadsters (of varying quality) can be hired from several hotels, or from private outfits nearby. Prices seem to be standardised: D20 per hour or D100 for a full day, but are all negotiable.

AROUND THE ATLANTIC COAST RESORTS & SEREKUNDA

South-east of Serekunda, near the airport, are two popular attractions: Abuko Nature Reserve and Lamin Lodge (see the map on p374). Both are easily reached from Banjul or the Atlantic Coast resorts.

Abuko Nature Reserve

Abuko has amazingly diverse vegetation for a park of only 105 hectares, partly because a stream runs through the centre, allowing gallery forest and savanna species to flourish. The diverse vegetation attracts a wide variety of birds – water and forest species – many of which are difficult to see elsewhere. Over 270 species have been recorded here, making this compact reserve one of the best places in West Africa for birdwatching.

Abuko also has a small animal orphanage and education centre, housing hyena, lion

and bushbuck, and in the forest you can see three types of monkey, as well as duiker, porcupine, bushbaby and ground squirrel. Pools are home to Abuko's population of crocodile – there are at least 50 individuals lurking here!

The reserve is open every day from 8 am to 7 pm. Early morning or late afternoon is best for birdwatching, although most of the hides face into the sun in the evening. Mid-morning is most popular for groups, and around midday is the quietest time. Although it's quite hot, there's plenty of shade, and this is a very good time to enjoy being in the forest. The main trail through the reserve takes about two hours, but there are a couple of shorter options indicated on the map at the main entrance gate.

The entry fee is D30. Leaflets describing the trees and animals can be bought at the ticket office.

Getting There & Away A private taxi to Abuko from one of the beach hotels costs about D300, including two hours waiting time. Alternatively, take a minibus from Serekunda towards Brikama (D2). The reserve entrance is on the right (west) of the main road (you pass the exit about 200m before reaching the entrance).

Lamin

This village is unremarkable in itself, but *Lamin Lodge* (☎ 495526) about 3km east of Lamin village, is a unique restaurant built on stilts and overlooking a mangrove creek. The lodge is where tour groups come for their 'Birds and Breakfast' trip (some people more for the breakfast than for the birds!) as the surrounding swamps and rice fields are great for birdwatching or strolling around. Meals cost about D50, and you can hire small motor boats (D150 per hour) or go out in a canoe with a paddler for D50. A ride to Banjul costs D250, and to Denton Bridge D350.

Lunch times are often busy in the tourist season, so you might consider coming here in the late afternoon for a gentle boat ride through the mangroves followed by a beer at sunset at the lodge.

The Monkeys of Abuko

Abuko is an excellent place to observe monkeys, especially in the morning or evening when they are most active. There are three types commonly found here: the green (or vervet) monkey, the red colobus monkey and the patas monkey (sometimes called the red patas). Within the reserve there are six troops of green monkey and six main troops of colobus monkey; each species has a total of about 140 individuals.

The green monkey has grey underparts and a light green-brown back with a black face surrounded by white fur. Instantly recognisable is the male's bright blue scrotum. The troops are adaptable and feed either in the savanna or the forest areas, and their diet consists of leaves, roots, fruit, insects and bird eggs. Even small birds get gobbled up.

The red colobus is, not surprisingly, red in colour, usually tending to black or dark brown on the back and a lighter russet on the underparts, and is larger than the green monkey. They prefer the higher parts of the gallery forest, rarely straying far from their territory, and can often be seen jumping from branch to branch. Unusually for monkeys, their diet consists largely of leaves.

The patas monkey is about the same size as the red colobus, although more slender, with longer legs and tail, and light brownish-red on the back and top of the head, with very light grey underparts and face. A prominent feature is the dark bushy eyebrows. They prefer the savanna parts of the reserve, and generally feed on the ground, only using trees for sleeping. They are far-ranging and often go beyond the reserve to raid crops and fruit trees near surrounding villages.

The three monkey species of Abuko live in relative harmony. Territories frequently overlap, and they do not compete for food. You may even notice different species cooperating. Young colobus and green monkeys can be seen playing together, while their adult counterparts help each other groom. The green monkeys are also the most alert and their warning cries are recognised by the other species. It is not unusual for the usually 'resident' colobus nearing maturity to leave their own troop and team up with a group of green monkeys to explore a wider area, before rejoining a new colobus troop to mate.

Lamin Lodge can be reached from the Atlantic Coast resorts by private taxi (D150 one way). Alternatively, from Serekunda you can take any minibus towards Brikama, get off in Lamin village, then follow the dirt road to the lodge.

Western Gambia

The Gambia's western border is the coast, only 50km long as the pelican flies, but over 80km if all the bays and promontories are included. The coast is divided into northern and southern sections by the mouth of the River Gambia. Beyond the Atlantic Coast resorts, the South Coast proper begins.

THE SOUTH COAST

This area is surprisingly seldom visited by independent travellers, although tourists from the big hotels often come this way on 'bush and beach' day trips. In the last few years, a couple of places to stay have opened, which means a visit here can be much less rushed, and you can see traditional fishing villages or enjoy the huge beaches long after the day-trippers have gone back to their hotels. The places in this section are listed north to south.

Tanji & Around

The main attraction is **Tanji Bird Reserve**, an area of dunes, lagoons, palms, dry woodland and coastal scrub, also incorporating Bijol

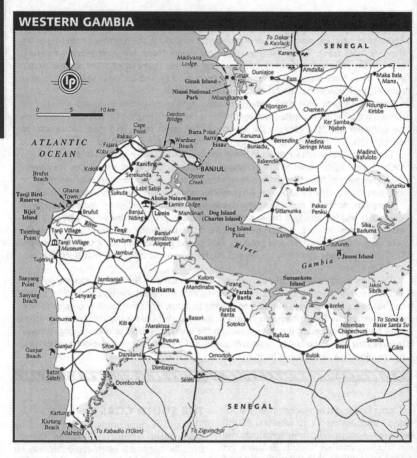

WESTERN GAMBIA

Island and its surrounding islets. The wide range of habitats supports a good variety of birds; almost 300 species have been recorded here. Although waders and water birds are the most obvious, this figure includes 34 species of raptor. Animals include vervet, patas and red colobus monkeys, hyena, porcupine and bushbuck. The reserve is also an important turtle breeding area.

From Serekunda, take a bush taxi to **Brufut Beach**, then it's easy to walk 2km to the Tanji Bird Reserve office, where you pay your D30 entry fee. Some bush taxis go all the way to Tanji village, past the office.

The village of **Tanji** is about 3km south of the reserve office. Here the *Paradise Inn* has double bungalows set in a tropical garden for about D200. About 2km further south is the fascinating **Tanji Village Museum** (open daily, D25) with huts of various ethnic designs, displays of traditional artefacts and furniture, a nature trail, and an artisan area with woodcarvers, blacksmiths and other artisans in action.

There's a small *bar-restaurant* and a simple hostel is planned.

Another possibility for food and drinks is the small, quiet and friendly *Suu Berry Beach Bar*, at **Tujereng Point**, about 3km south of Tanji village, and much nicer than the crowded bars at Sanyang Beach, a popular destination for day-trippers from the resorts.

Gunjur

Gunjur town is a D5 bush taxi ride from Brikama, along a dusty road through green farmland, sandy palm groves and grassy dunes, with creeks and lagoons where monkeys are often seen.

From Gunjur it's a 3km walk or D1.50 bush taxi ride to Gunjur Beach. Along the way you'll pass *Falconhurst Guesthouse* where owner Wilf Smedly offers singles/doubles for D50/75, and camping for D15. Use of the kitchen costs D15. Several travellers have written to us to recommend this place as a good base for a few days.

At **Gunjur Beach** there's a lot of activity: boats going in and out, nets being mended and fish being gutted. This is a place to sit down quietly, keep your camera out of sight, and just watch what's going on. If you want to sunbathe it's best to go along the beach to get a bit of seclusion and avoid upsetting the locals.

The European-style *Gunjur Beach Motel (fax 486026)* has bungalows for around D150 per person, and camping for D20 per person. About 2km further south is the hard to find *Rasta Kunda Camp*, a very laid-back local enterprise, with dilapidated huts for a highly negotiable D100.

Kartung

Kartung has a sandy main street, and the village centre is a market under the shade of a giant tree. *Morgan's Grocery* is a ramshackle shop, bar and restaurant, with simple meals like fish and rice for D20, where the friendly manager can set you up with birdwatching trips. *Follonko Resthouse* is a small low-key place charging D50 per person, where you can ask about the new

BoBoi Beach Bar and Camp Site, on the coast about 3km to the north. In the same area as the BoBoi, the *Halaheen Bar & Restaurant* is a lunch time stopover for tour groups, but in the evening it's quiet, and the beautiful beach is within easy walking distance.

On the southern edge of Kartung, opposite the school, a track leads west for 300m to a sacred crocodile pool, with several deceptively soporific inhabitants, believed by locals to hold powers of fertility.

If you continue southwards, past the police post, you get to a fork in the road (2km from the village); keep right and pass through grassy dunes to reach the beach where fishing boats land. Go left at the fork, to reach Kartung Fishing Centre and the River Allahein (also spelt Halahan), marking the border with Senegal.

If you're heading for Senegal get your passport stamped at the police post, then cross the river by dugout canoe (D1). On the other side you have to walk about 10km to reach Kabadio, between Kafountine and Dioubloulou.

THE NORTH COAST & NORTH BANK

The North Coast stretches all of 10km from the mouth of the River Gambia to the border with Senegal. In **Barra**, those with an interest in history may want to have a look at Fort Bullen, built by the British in the 1820s to help control slave shipping (for more information on slavery in West Africa, see the boxed text 'The Slave Trade' in the Facts about the Region chapter).

Ginak Island

The coastal island of Ginak (also spelt Jinak) is part of **Niumi National Park**, where the range of habitats (beach, mud flats, salt marsh, dunes, mangrove swamps, lagoons, grassland and dry woodland) makes for excellent birdwatching. Dolphins are often seen from the shore and turtles nest on the beach.

The park also protects small populations of manatee, crocodile and clawless otter, plus monkeys and various small antelopes.

There are even reports of the occasional leopard.

The only place to stay or eat is *Madiyana Lodge* (☎ 991994), in one of the most beautiful settings on the whole coast. A day's tour costs D450 per person, including a boat ride from Banjul and lunch. To also stay the night costs D300 for dinner, bed and breakfast. Independent travellers can phone the lodge direct or its owners, North Bank Tours (☎ 495950 or 995950, fax 495950), to see about joining a group. Alternatively, a private taxi from Barra to the mainland opposite Ginak costs D50, from where you go by dugout canoe (D2), across to the village of Ginak Niji and walk directly west across the island (20 minutes) to the lodge.

Jufureh & Albreda

Jufureh (formerly Juffure) became world famous in the 1970s following the publication of *Roots*, in which African-American writer Alex Haley describes how his ancestor Kunta Kinte was captured here and taken as a slave to America some 200 years ago. Today, Jufureh itself is nothing out of the ordinary – like many other villages along the River Gambia – but when the daily groups of tourists arrive things leap into action. Woman pound millet at strategic points, babies are produced to be patted and filmed, artisans in the craft market crank into gear, and an old lady called Binde Kinte (descendant of Alex Haley's own forebear) makes a guest appearance at her compound.

Albreda, half a kilometre from Jufureh, is a slightly more peaceful place, with huts and houses between baobabs and cotton trees. The main things to see here are the ruined 17th century 'factory' (fortified trading station) and museum (entrance D20, closed Sunday and Friday afternoon) with a simple but striking exhibition describing the history of slavery. Nearby is a small shop selling batiks and dyed cloth – with some of the best examples we saw in the whole country – where money from sales goes to the local primary school.

You can do this trip in a day, but if you're making the effort to come all this way, you

The Roots Debate

Alex Haley based his research on recollections of elder relatives, who knew that their African forebear's name was Kinte and he'd been captured by slavers while chopping wood for a drum outside his village. This later tied in with a story Haley was told by a *griot* at Jufureh. Critics have pointed out (quite reasonably) that the *Roots* story is flawed in many areas. Kinte is a common Mandinka/ Malinké clan name throughout West Africa, and the griot's story of Kunta Kinte's capture would hardly have been unique. Also, as the slave stations of Albreda and James Island had been very close to Jufureh for some decades, it's unlikely a villager from here would have been taken by surprise in this way.

The story of Alex Haley's ancestor is almost certainly true, but it's exceedingly unlikely that he actually came from here. Despite the inconsistencies, Haley seemed happy to believe he was descended from the Kintes of Jufureh, and the myth remains largely intact.

Detractors may delight in exposing fabrication, but there is a danger that the debate on the accuracy of Haley's story may obscure a much more serious, and undeniable, fact: the slave trade was immoral and inhuman, and had a devastating effect on Africa. Millions of men and women were captured by European traders, or by other Africans paid by Europeans, and taken to plantations in the Americas. Many historians also hold that their labour, and the slave trade itself, was fundamental to the economic development of Europe and the USA in the 18th and 19th centuries. For a more general discussion about the slave trade, see the boxed text 'The Slave Trade' in the Facts about the Region chapter.

should consider staying overnight; both Jufureh and Albreda are at their best in the evening, when the light is soft and most of the tourist groups have left.

Places to Stay & Eat In Albreda, the *Home at Last Hotel* has simple but very clean rooms at D80/100 for singles/doubles. At the *Jufureh Resthouse* facilities are similar and the price a lot higher, with rooms at D150/300, although this includes breakfast and may be negotiable.

Getting There & Away The usual (and easiest) way to visit Jufureh is by boat (see Organised Tours in the main Getting There & Away section earlier). Alternatively, take the ferry across to Barra, dodge the touts who try to get you into a private taxi, and find a shared taxi to Jufureh, which costs D10. If you want to do the trip in a day, you'll have to catch the first ferry.

James Island

James Island is in the middle of the River Gambia, about 2km south of Jufureh and Albreda, and most boat tours stop here. On the island are the remains of Fort James, originally built in the 1650s and the site of numerous skirmishes in the following centuries. (See History in the Facts about Gambia section for more details.) Today, the ruins are quite extensive, although the only intact room is a food store, which is often called the 'slave dungeon' because it sounds more interesting. The island itself is rapidly being eroded, and only the sturdy baobab trees seem to be holding it together. An interesting leaflet on the fort is available at the National Museum in Banjul.

Upcountry Gambia

Upcountry Gambia is what locals call everywhere away from the coast. As you travel inland from Banjul or Serekunda, the main road bypasses **Brikama**, so you may miss Gambia's third-largest town without even noticing, but the much-hyped wood-carvers' market is disappointing, full of hassle, and not worth the bother.

At **Mandinaba** most traffic turns south for Ziguinchor, and the main road becomes surprisingly quiet as it winds through fields, rice paddies, palm groves and patches of natural forest. Every 10km or so there's a village or sleepy junction where a dirt track leads north towards the River Gambia, never far away, but always frustratingly out of view.

Places in this section are described west to east.

BINTANG BOLONG

Bintang Bolong is a large meandering tributary of the River Gambia, which joins the main river about 50km upstream from Banjul. Its banks are lined with beautiful mangroves which are most easily explored from the village of Bintang, where *Bintang Bolong Lodge (fax 488058)* overlooks the river. Popular with tour groups, it's busy during the day but quiet in the evenings. Simple 'backpacker huts' cost D75 per person, and cottages built on stilts over the river cost D120/300, plus breakfast for D35. Boat rides are available, and the lodge is also a good base for walks in the surrounding fields and villages. To get there, most bush taxis stop at Killy from where a dirt road leads 3km to reach Bintang village and the lodge.

TENDABA

Tendaba is a small village on the southern bank of the River Gambia, 165km upstream from Banjul, dominated by the large *Tendaba Camp*, a popular destination for tour groups. Although the crowds can be disturbing in the high season, Tendaba is undeniably an excellent base for visiting Kiang West National Park and Baobolong Wetland Reserve. Accommodation costs D135 per person in small bungalows with shared bathrooms or D165 with bathroom. In the restaurant, breakfast is about D20, main meals D55 and the large evening buffet is D90.

An excursion by 4WD vehicle to Kiang West costs D90 per person (with a minimum of six people). Boat rides around the creeks of the Baobolong Wetland Reserve are the same price (with a minimum of four). There are lots of options for walking in this area; a good destination for the day is Toubab Kollon Point (see the Kiang West National

Park section following for more details) about 7km from the camp.

Getting There & Away

Tours to Tendaba Camp arranged at the Atlantic Coast resorts cost D900 to D1200 per person including transport, room, food and excursions. Green tourist taxis (carrying up to four people) charge about D800 to D1000 for the return trip. By bus, drop at Kwinella from where the camp (signposted) is 5km along the dirt road. You'll probably have to walk, but you may get a lift or meet the enterprising local who rents out his donkey and cart.

KIANG WEST NATIONAL PARK

Kiang West contains mangroves, creeks, mud flats and large areas of dry woodland and grassland. A major feature is the escarpment which runs parallel to the river: we're not talking Rift Valley here, but even 20m is significant in Gambia, and from this high point you can look over the narrow plain, where animals are often seen – especially at the three water holes. You might see baboon, colobus monkey, warthog, marsh mongoose, bushbuck, roan antelope and sitatunga (the bushbuck's aquatic cousin, adept at swimming or crossing water vegetation on its wide hooves). Other species in the park, although very rarely seen, include hyena, leopard, manatee, dolphin and crocodile. Birdwatching is also rewarding, with over 250 species recorded, including 21 raptors (the most impressive are the martial eagle and the bateleur), and some rarer birds such as the brown-necked parrot.

A popular place for viewing is **Toubab Kollon Point**, a promontory in the northeastern part of the park. Behind the point, the escarpment runs close to the river bank, and 2km west is a viewing hide overlooking a water hole which attracts a good range of animals, especially in the dry season.

BAOBOLONG WETLAND RESERVE

A tributary called Bao Bolong enters the River Gambia upstream from Tendaba. The Baobolong (also spelt Baobolon) Wetland Reserve contains several other bolongs (creeks), mangroves and salt marsh, and is a Ramsar site. The mangroves are some of the largest in the region, growing to over 20m to become a virtual 'forest'. Birds are a major attraction (including the rare Pel's fishing owl), but the reserve also protects various aquatic mammal species, such as manatee, clawless otter and sitatunga. The best way to experience this wonderful maze of islands and waterways is by boat, most easily arranged at Tendaba Camp (see the Tendaba section earlier).

SOMA & MANSA KONKO

Soma is a dusty fly-blown junction town where the main road between Banjul and Basse crosses the Trans-Gambia Highway. Nearby is Mansa Konko, originally an important chief's capital (the name means 'King's Hill'), then an administrative centre during the colonial era. Today, it's a sleepy ghost town, with a few reminders of earlier days still visible, such as the district commissioner's residence and the faded sign for Mansa Konko Lawn Tennis Club.

Places to Stay & Eat

If you get stuck in Soma, a dingy *resthouse* attached to the offices of the AFPRC near the petrol station has rooms for D50. Better is *Lamin Brothers' Resthouse* 3km north of Soma in Pakali Nding (where the road to Mansa Konko turns off east), charging D100 a double. For food, Soma has some basic *chop stalls*.

Getting There & Away

Buses between Banjul and Basse stop at the GPTC compound in Soma, where you can stretch your legs, buy a snack, or marvel at the large flock of scabby vultures that survive off the detritus discarded by passengers.

Other transport from Serekunda terminates here, and vehicles on to Georgetown and Basse leave from the bush taxi park in the town centre. If you're heading north from Soma, go to the River Gambia ferry by local bush taxi (D3), cross as a foot passenger (D2), then take another bush taxi to Farafenni (D2), where you'll find transport to Dakar.

FARAFENNI

Farafenni is on the Trans-Gambia Highway north of the River Gambia. It's a busy little town, much more pleasant than Soma. The main *lumo* (market) is on Sunday, when people come from surrounding villages, and merchants come from as far as Mauritania and Guinea to sell their wares. The border with Senegal is only 2km to the north, and the Gambian customs post is on the north side of town.

Places to Stay & Eat

Eddie's Hotel & Bar has been a popular travellers' meeting point for many years. Double rooms with bathroom cost D100 to D155, and you can eat chicken and chips or benechin for D25 in the shady garden courtyard. There's also safe parking, cold beer, and a disco at weekends. At the *Fankanta Hotel*, opposite the barracks, basic rooms with a shower cost D50. There are several *chop houses* on the main street.

Getting There & Away

Direct minibuses from Farafenni go to Serekunda most mornings for D35. For most other places you have to get to Soma and change. If you're heading for Dakar there are bush taxis for CFA5000.

RIVER GAMBIA NATIONAL PARK

Upstream of Farafenni is the River Gambia's transition zone where it changes from salt to freshwater. The mangroves thin out, thick forest grows down to the water's edge, and there are more islands. South of Kuntaur are five such islands, protected as the River Gambia National Park (also known as Baboon Islands National Park), the site of a privately funded project that takes chimpanzees captured from illegal traders, and rehabilitates them to live in the wild.

Boat rides can be arranged in Georgetown (D800 to D1000 per day) or Kuntaur (D200), but visitors are not allowed to land

or get close to the islands, partly because it interferes with the rehabilitation process, but mainly because the chimps can be very quick to attack humans, and males may vent their spleen on females and youngsters of their own troupe. Because of the dense cloak of gallery forest, it is not usually possible to see chimps anyway. And to get a proper view, you're close enough to be boarded by a bristling alpha male. This has happened – forcing people to rapidly abandon ship!

Boats are only permitted in the main channel between the islands and the east bank of the mainland, and are not allowed to approach the islands nearer than midstream. Guard posts are located on the west bank to enforce this rule. Boatmen often try to please their passengers by getting closer, but this should be positively discouraged.

If you visit the area, it's best to go with the attitude of having a good day out on this beautiful stretch of river. You'll quite likely see baboon and monkeys, and possibly hippo and crocodile too, plus an excellent selection of birds. And if you do see any chimps – while keeping a responsible distance – it will be an extra bonus.

GEORGETOWN (JANGJANG-BUREH)

Georgetown is on the northern edge of MacCarthy Island in the River Gambia, about 300km by road from Banjul. The local name for the town and island is Jangjang-bureh, and this has officially been reintroduced, but the old colonial name is still in use. The island is 10km long and 2.5km wide, covered with fields of rice and groundnuts, with ferry links to both river banks.

Although it was an important administrative centre during the colonial period, it is now a very tranquil town, but it is becoming more popular with tourists as the new lodges try hard to attract customers.

Things to See

On the waterfront are some old warehouses, crumbling away and being reclaimed by vegetation. Locals call the place the **slave** house but, although slaves were transported through Georgetown, these particular buildings were built in the second half of the 19th century, whereas slavery in British colonies was abolished in 1807.

A few local youths in Georgetown offer their services as guides, but this is not necessary and the hassle is very low-key. A few young men also tout for business at the ferry which crosses to MacCarthy Island from the main road on the southern river bank, and part of their story is that they'll 'protect' you from the guides in town, but again this is completely unnecessary.

Other places to visit include the **stone circle** of Lamin Koto, 1km away from the north bank ferry ramp and worth a look especially if you don't make it to the larger circles at Wassu. The passenger ferry runs on a fill-up-and-go basis, and the fare is D1.

Historians of exploration may want to head for **Karantaba Tenda** village, about 20km by road or river from Georgetown, where an obelisk marks the spot where Mungo Park started on his journey to trace the course of the River Niger (for more details on this journey, see the boxed text 'Mungo Park' in the History section of the Facts about the Region chapter).

Places to Stay

The *Government Resthouse* charges D60 per person: rooms are a bit run-down and musty, but clean and usually quiet. Another cheap option is *Alakabung Lodge*, where dark and dusty thatched huts costs D50 per person. Worth the extra cost is *Baobolong Camp*, set in lush gardens near the river, run by local birdwatchers Laurence and Jammeh. Rooms with bathroom cost D80 per person, breakfast is D35 and meals D30 to D50.

About 1km outside town, *Bird Safari Camp* (☎ 676108, fax 674004, email bsc@ commit.gm) has good quality rooms for D350 per person full board. This place is aimed at birdwatchers, and boasts a resident ornithologist, private hides and guided walks.

On the north side of the river, *Jangjang-bureh Camp* (☎ Banjul 495526) is an eclectic collection of rustic bungalows set in a maze-like garden. Lighting is by oil lamps, and a drink at the bar overlooking the river is a fine way to spend the evening. Rooms with bathroom cost D110 per person. A large buffet breakfast is D45, and other meals around D30 to D60. Motor boat trips (up to six people) cost D150 per hour, and kayaks can be hired for D250 per day.

To reach Jangjang-bureh Camp, go to *Dreambird Camp* on MacCarthy Island from where a transfer boat shuttles between the two – free for guests. Dreambird also has accommodation, with rooms at D75 per person.

Places to Eat

There are a few cheap *eating houses* around the market, and near the ferry is *BB Food & Drink* where friendly BB serves soft drinks, coffee, bread and eggs and can make a more substantial meal with advance notice. Beer is available at *Tida's Bar*, in a traditional compound reached through an unmarked green gate on the south-west side of the town.

Getting There & Away

Most buses and bush taxis turn off the main road between Soma and Basse to drop off passengers at the southern ferry ramp. Otherwise, you have to drop at Bansang, and take a bush taxi (D5) back. The ferry costs D0.50 for passengers. On the far side pick-ups run across the island to Georgetown for D1.50.

WASSU STONE CIRCLES

Wassu is on the north side of the River Gambia, 2km north of Kuntaur, about 25km north-west of Georgetown. The circles each consist of about 10 to 24 massive, reddish-brown stones, between 1m and 2.5m high and weighing several tonnes. This is one of the best examples of the enigmatic megaliths which are a feature of the area, but it has to be said they're not a major attraction for everyone. Go if you want to see evidence of ancient African cultures, but not if you're expecting Stonehenge.

From Georgetown, a bush taxi to Kuntaur waits most mornings at the north bank ferry ramp, but this only goes when full (which can take several hours), and even if you reached Wassu in reasonable time there may be nothing coming back. The fare is D7, so you could consider buying several seats which might persuade the driver to get moving. Your other option is a hired bike – but this would be an all-day expedition of 20km each way on a dirt road.

BASSE SANTA SU

Commonly called Basse, this is Gambia's easternmost town, a traditional trading centre, and by far the liveliest of the up-country settlements. The main market day is Thursday, but the streets are lined with shops and stalls, and the whole place is always quite busy – especially in the evening when local drinks stalls open and grilled meat shacks get fired up.

Down by the waterfront, an old colonial warehouse has been converted into a museum, cultural centre and restaurant called Traditions. With high quality pottery, leatherwork and cloth on show, it is a refreshing change from the tat sold on the coast. Particularly interesting are the items made from unbleached natural cotton in rich shades of yellow, gold and light brown.

Between June and February, this is also a good place to see the Egyptian plover, a rare species, known locally as the crocodile bird. Boat rides to see the birds (with a faint chance of seeing hippo and crocodile too) can be arranged here or with local boatmen.

Places to Stay & Eat

The *Plaza Hotel* overlooking the main square has grimy rooms at D50. Slightly better and D10 more is the nearby *Basse Guesthouse*. Infinitely better is the *Jem Hotel* where spacious airy rooms are D150/300. A final option might be the shabby *Government Resthouse*, about 2km from the centre, officially for government employees only, but we've heard from travellers who stayed for D60.

Around the garage are some tea shacks, and stalls and chop shops selling cheap

bowls of rice and sauce; *Fatu's* is highly recommended. In town, cheap restaurants include *No 1 Fast Food* and *No Flie Restaurant* with meals around D20. A better bet might be *F & B's Restaurant* on the main road south of the town, near the military camp, where chicken, fish or omelette and chips costs D15 to D30, and cold beer is a bargain D7.50. The delightful *Traditions* has tables on a balcony overlooking the river, and serves sandwiches or soups for D15 to D20, or burger and chips for D25.

Getting There & Away

GPTC buses between Banjul and Basse leave throughout the day (see the Banjul Getting There & Away section). From Basse, they go from the main road, not from the bush taxi park. Bush taxis and minibuses go to Soma for D30, the ferry ramp for Georgetown for D15, and Fatoto for D10.

For details on transport to Senegal, see the main Getting There & Away section earlier in this chapter. If you're heading even further afield a Peugeot 504 bush taxi goes more or less daily (passengers depending) to Labé in northern Guinea. The fare is CFA 14,000 and the trip takes around 24 hours (roadblocks depending).

Lumos around Basse

Several of Basse's surrounding villages have a weekly market (called a *lumo*) – all on a different day of the week. For example, at Lamwe, near Fatoto, the lumo is on Saturday; at Sabi, on the road towards Vélingara, it's Sunday; and at Sarengai on the north bank, it's Monday. Traders and shoppers come from other parts of Gambia, across the border from Senegal, and from as far as Mali, Guinea and Guinea-Bissau. Bush taxis from Basse run to wherever the lumo is that day, and visiting the market is always a lively and interesting day out.

Ghana

If an award were given for the country with the friendliest people in West Africa, Ghana would definitely be among the finalists. Accra isn't the most beautiful city in West Africa, but it's a Ghanaian city – not one catering to tourists or western expatriates. Ghanaians like to have fun. Accra and Kumasi on Saturday night are jumping – there's usually a choice of at least four or five live bands. Ghana is, after all, the place where highlife music got its start. It also has some of the most beautiful fabrics in West Africa; the most well known is the expensive and colourful *kente* cloth made by the Ashanti.

Ghana is the old 'Gold Coast', where Europeans came 500 years ago searching for Ashanti gold – and found it. Along the coast are a string of forts and castles that the Europeans left behind. Inside, your spirits will sink when you see how slaves were crammed into dank dungeons before being shipped to the New World.

Facts about Ghana

HISTORY

Present-day Ghana has been inhabited since at least 4000 BC, although little evidence remains of its early societies. Successive waves of migration from the north and east resulted in Ghana's present ethnographic composition. By the 13th century a number of kingdoms had arisen that were strongly influenced by the Sahel trading empires such as that of ancient Ghana (which incorporated western Mali and Senegal).

By the 18th century, the powerful Ashanti kingdom of the Akan people had conquered most of the other states and taken control of trade routes to the coast. Its capital, Kumasi, was highly organised, with facilities and services the equal of those in most European cities of the time.

The Portuguese arrived in the late 15th century to trade and to search for the fabled

GHANA AT A GLANCE

Area: 238,537 sq km
Population: 17.7 million
Capital: Accra
Head of state: Flight Lt Jerry Rawlings
Official language: English
Main local languages: Ga, Ewé, Twi
Currency: Cedi
Exchange rate: US$1 = C2350
Time: GMT/UTC
Country telephone code: ☎ 233
Best time to go: February & March, July & August

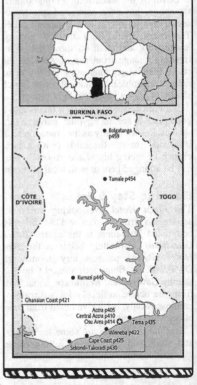

BURKINA FASO

• Bolgatanga p459

• Tamale p454

CÔTE D'IVOIRE

TOGO

• Kumasi p445

Ghanaian Coast p421

Accra p405
Central Accra p410
Osu Area p414 • Tema p435
Winneba p422
Cape Coast p425
Sekondi-Takoradi p430

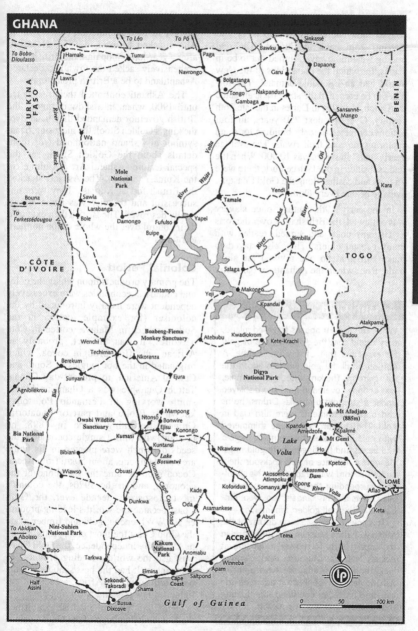

GHANA

GHANA

gold. In 1482, they built the first of several coastal forts and began to ship ivory and Ashanti gold back to Europe. The real trading wealth, however, turned out to be in slaves, for which the plantations of the New World had an insatiable demand. The fortunes to be earned in the slave trade attracted the Dutch, British and Danes in the late 16th century. Over the next 250 years, all four nations competed fiercely, building forts and capturing those of their rivals. The average yearly 'take' in slaves was 10,000. When the trade subsided in the 19th century, there were 76 forts and castles along the Gold Coast, an average of one every 6km.

In the early 19th century, once slavery was outlawed, the British took over the forts as customs posts and signed treaties with many coastal chiefs. They also stayed to make sure that no one revived the slave trade, from which the Ashanti, in particular

Ashanti Gold

When the first Europeans travelled inland, they found that the Ashanti's use of gold far exceeded that of any other tribe. A portion of all the gold went to adorn the ruling group. The king's stool, for example, was entirely covered in gold and displayed under a splendid umbrella. Drums, horns and other adornments were also clad in gold. The king or Asantehene shimmered with gold: his bracelets were made of gold and beads and his fingers bore gold rings. He wore a necklace of gold cockspur shells and a silk cord was draped over his shoulders, suspending three gilded ornaments. His anklets and his sandals, too, were embossed with small golden ornaments.

This splendid regalia is on display at the Manhiya Palace Museum in Kumasi and in the superb 'Arts for Power' exhibition at Accra's National Museum. And if you're lucky enough to coincide with a major Ashanti festival you'll see it adorning the king and his senior courtiers, accentuating their authority, power and wealth.

had profited handsomely. The Ashanti fiercely resisted domination by the British, who attacked Kumasi in 1873. However, after a year-long campaign, the British comprehensively sacked the town and declared Ashantiland to be a British protectorate.

The Ashanti continued their resistance until 1900, when, in a show of power, the British governor demanded they hand over the king's Golden Stool, the most significant symbol of Ashanti nationhood (for more details about the Golden Stool, see the special feature 'Ashanti Art & Culture' in the Kumasi section). The Ashanti attacked the British fort at Kumasi. They were unsuccessful and the city was again almost totally destroyed. The British then extended their control over the whole of the northern territories.

Colonial Period

The primary products upon which the colonial countries' economies were excessively dependent were usually introduced by the coloniser (for example, cotton in the Sudan, rubber in Malaya, coffee in Côte d'Ivoire). It was, in fact, probably an African who first brought cocoa, which originated in the hot jungles of South and Central America, to present-day Ghana. Tetteh Quarshie was a Ghanaian blacksmith working in Fernando Po, today known as Bioko and part of Equatorial Guinea. Returning home in 1898, he brought with him a single cocoa pod, the seeds of which were planted in his home area of Mampong, about 50km from Accra. Cocoa soon became the backbone of the economy, and in the 1920s, the colony's most prosperous decade ever, the Gold Coast became the world's leading producer. By WWI, cocoa, gold and timber made the Gold Coast the most prosperous colony in Africa. By independence, the Gold Coast was also the world's leading producer of manganese. It had the best schools and the best civil service in Africa, a cadre of enlightened lawyers and a thriving press.

Until 1948, when the British established the University College of the Gold Coast at

ASHANTI

Inhabiting the heart of the now thinning forest of southern Ghana are the Ashanti whose kingdom was famed for its gold, its royalty and traditional state organisation. One of the famous war leaders against the British was Yaa Asantewaa queen mother of Ejisu who in 1900 shamed the Ashanti army into entering battle by leading them herself.

As the political role of the state declined under colonial rule, a new source of wealth emerged. Cocoa underpinned the prosperity of town and village life and traditional crafts like stool carving, *kente* cloth weaving and goldsmithing continued to embellish the ritual and ceremony of

ALL FOUR PHOTOS BY DENNIS WISKEN/SIDEWALK GALLERY

Top: Ashanti wooden comb (left); stools, like this one (middle), are an important part of Ashanti culture and are said to be the receptacle of a person's soul; akuaba dolls like this one (right) are fertility figures carried by Ashanti women to induce pregnancy and ensure the successful birth of an infant.

Middle: Although spoons are not traditionally used in everyday meals, intricately carved spoons like this Ashanti one are used in ceremonies and are an indicator of status.

Bottom: Pomp and ceremony – drummers and a linguist carrying a golden staff precede an Ashanti chief.

VICTOR ENGLEBERT

traditional life. It is the aesthetic of traditional life and the chiefly ceremony that give Ashanti its magnetic appeal to the traveller in West Africa. In Europe and America too, some of the best known and appreciated African artefacts and symbols are Ashanti kente, stools and Adinkra symbols.

EWÉ

The Ewé people of Ghana and Togo are known for hard work, tidy villages and a love of education and church-going. Paradoxically they are also famous for the power of their traditional shrines and priests. There has been recent condemnation of the traditional institution of Trokosi, whereby young girls are given as virtual slave wives to priests in order to appease the spirits. The supreme deities of the Ewé are Mawu-Lisa, the female-male moon-sun twins.

Ewé kente cloth is subtly rather than brilliantly coloured and there is always a fine display of it at the Sometutuza festival in Agbozume. The Ewé *vu gbe* are their talking drums. The tonality of spoken language and the rhythm of particular phrases and proverbs are combined in drumming to produce messages that range from commonplace ones that everyone understands to a specialised repertoire known only to the master drummers. Drum language is used for communication, especially in times of crisis as well being part of religious song and dance. The drum cycle led by the Blekete drum dedicated to the deity of that name carries the message 'A feeble effort will not fulfil the self'. Ewé dances are widely appreciated for their fast and intricate movements, especially of the shoulders and feet. Atsia is a very ancient dance performed purely for the sake of style, while Agbodzo is executed to drum passages associated with the Agbo war shrine.

Katie Abu

Top: Family group, Ashanti

Bottom: All lined up and nowhere to go! These Ewé figures show the characteristic form used in many West African sculptures – short legs in relation to the trunk, arms by the side and eyes staring straight ahead.

Legon (now the University of Ghana), West Africans had to go abroad for advanced study. One such student was Kwame Nkrumah, who spent from 1935 to 1945 in the USA studying and teaching at Lincoln University in Pennsylvania. There he read and was influenced by African literature and Marxist writings, which were to inform much of his political behaviour.

In 1947, for example, Nkrumah, then Secretary General of the country's leading political party, the United Gold Coast Convention, impatient for immediate radical change, broke away and formed the populist Convention People's Party (CPP), with the slogan 'Self Government Now'. Two years later he called a general strike. The British responded by putting him in prison. While he was there, the CPP won the general elections of 1951. The British, impressed by how efficiently the CPP had gained votes despite Nkrumah's absence, released him and asked him to form a government.

Independence

Nkrumah agreed to abandon the party's slogan and work with the colonial administrators. In 1957, when Britain granted independence, Nkrumah cast aside the name Gold Coast in favour of that of the first great empire in West Africa – Ghana – even though the country had only a tenuous connection with the medieval empire. For Africa, it was a momentous occasion: Ghana was the first sub-Saharan African country to gain independence. For Ghana, it was the beginning of an economic nightmare and 25 years of almost continuous decline.

Nkrumah borrowed heavily to finance grandiose schemes. Many of his projects were wasteful – US$16 million was spent on a conference centre to host a single meeting of the Organisation of African Unity (OAU). At independence, Ghana had almost half a billion US dollars in foreign-exchange reserves; by 1966, the country was a billion dollars in debt. To compound things, world prices for cocoa tumbled from UK£247 a tonne at independence to below UK£100 a tonne by 1966.

Nkrumah's most grandiose project was Akosombo Dam, which was to be financed by the World Bank, other international banks and Valco, a US aluminium company. Although about 10,000 sq km of land was to be drowned under Lake Volta, Nkrumah calculated that the revenue generated would outweigh the loss of land, as it would allow projects like electrifying rural areas and irrigating the Accra plains. Valco, with its own agenda, wanted the dam to fuel its plants for smelting bauxite. However, Nkrumah, abandoned by other backers, was obliged to short-change his country by accepting Valco's offer of the dam in return for the right to all the electricity it needed, virtually at cost. With a steadily deteriorating economy, the projected private sector demand never materialised, and the electrification and irrigation programs were shelved for more than a decade.

To a continent of new nations desperate for political unity, Nkrumah, handsome, charismatic and articulate, was a hero. When he talked, people and nations listened. At home, however, he became increasingly ruthless. Within a year of independence, Ghana had become virtually a one party state. In 1958, he had approved a law providing for up to five years detention without trial or appeal. Four years later, an estimated 2000 to 3000 people were held in jail without trial. In 1962, a coup attempt led to a wide-scale purge.

Nkrumah alienated the business community by turning over much of the economy to state-run enterprises, very few of which became profitable. He alienated the west by his constant denunciation of imperialism and neocolonialism, the heavy accumulation of debts, and Ghana's commercial ties with the Soviet bloc. Perhaps worst of all, he alienated Ghana's army by setting up a private force answerable to him alone. The public, which appreciated the significant improvements in infrastructure and social services, became disillusioned by conspicuous corruption among the party's leaders. In 1964, Ghana had food shortages for the first time ever.

GHANA

GHANA

It was all too much. In 1966, while the president was on a mission to Hanoi, the army staged a coup. There was rejoicing in Ghana. Exiled to Guinea, Nkrumah died of cancer six years later.

The Great Decline

Between 1966 and 1981, Ghana suffered six governments, all corrupt or incompetent – except for one, led by Flight Lieutenant Jerry Rawlings, which lasted three months.

Probably no ruler was worse than Colonel Acheampong, who 'redeemed' the country in 1972, and then dissolved parliament. He considered a previous devaluation of the cedi an affront to the country's honour, and did the unheard of – he revalued the currency upward by 44%, even though it was already grossly overvalued.

Acheampong had a simple solution to all of Ghana's problems – print money. In 1976 alone, he increased the cedis in circulation by 80%. Inflation reached 12% a month. When he left office, the market value of the cedi was over 20 times the official exchange rate.

As the cedi became increasingly worthless, more and more cocoa – up to 50,000 tonnes a year – was smuggled across the borders to Togo and Côte d'Ivoire. Meanwhile, production fell from 430,000 tonnes in 1965 to 265,000 tonnes in 1978. Staple goods became scarce and people caught buses to Lomé in neighbouring Togo to buy essentials like washing powder, oil and milk. At the airport in Accra, customs officials inspecting the suitcases of passengers coming from London often found them filled with washing powder.

In 1979, two weeks before long-promised elections, a group of military officers led by Jerry Rawlings staged a coup. But the voting proceeded as planned and a new president was elected. Before handing over to a civil government, the coup leaders, relenting to pressure from the lower ranks, publicly executed three former heads of state, among them Acheampong, who was accused of massive embezzlement. Hundreds of other officers and business people were tried and convicted by impromptu 'people's' courts.

Then, after only three months in power, to everyone's amazement, Rawlings bowed out – just as he had promised.

Despite adopting very conservative economic policies and austerity measures, the new president, Hilla Limann, was unable to arrest the economy's downward spiral. Rawlings on the other hand, with his warnings of the need for vigilance against corruption, had enormous grass-roots support. At the end of 1981, Rawlings staged another coup and this time he stayed.

The Rawlings Era

Rawlings did the seemingly impossible. Since his takeover in 1983, the economy has grown on average by over 5% a year in real terms, the highest growth rate in Africa, while inflation, although still disturbingly high, dropped from 122% in 1983 to 29% in 1997. Export earnings regularly show 10% annual increases and manufacturing has risen from 3.6% of GDP to more than 10%.

What did Rawlings do? He bent to IMF and World Bank pressure. Between late 1983 and mid-1986, he devalued the currency 33-fold, and now the exchange rate floats. He also raised payments to cocoa farmers fourfold, laid off 28,000 civil servants in one year alone, removed price controls on all but 23 essential commodities, and sloughed off some unprofitable state enterprises. The government also renegotiated the one-sided agreement with Valco. In return, the World Bank and the IMF have rewarded Ghana amply with loans and funding. By 1988, the government budget was in surplus.

Major new hotels and other buildings have been constructed, roads have been improved, telecommunications and electricity has been extended to cover most of the country, and ports have been rebuilt. Farmers have replanted cocoa trees and reclaimed abandoned farms. Most noticeably, consumer goods are everywhere.

However, not everything has been a success. Many companies in the industrial area in Accra, for example, have had to curtail or stop production because they couldn't compete with the avalanche of foreign goods descending on Ghana. And it's increasingly difficult for the poor to access education and health services which were previously free.

During his time in office Rawlings has proved himself not only a man with guts but a maverick. When elected, instead of fostering the cult of personality, he ordered all pictures of himself removed from public places. And he tends to ride around in a jeep, not a limousine. In other ways, however, he's proved to be not so different from previous leaders. Those caught for corruption risk the firing squad. And, once, when football star Sarfo Gyambi refused to shake Rawlings' hand he was fined 25,000 cedis for 'breach of protocol'.

Ghana Today

Following a referendum approving a new constitution in early 1992, political parties were given complete freedom to form. In the subsequent presidential elections, the hastily formed, ill-organised parties feuded publicly among themselves. Parties included the People's National Convention (PNC), National Independence Party (NIP) and the National Convention Party (NCP). The main challenger, the New Patriotic Party (NPP), was led by Professor Albert Boahen. He failed to form an opposition coalition and lost the election to Rawlings, candidate of the National Democratic Congress (NDC), by a wide margin: 39 to 59% on a national turnout of 48% of the electorate.

Although the election was deemed fair by international observers, Boahen refused to accept the results and the NPP boycotted parliamentary elections the following month. Consequently only 29% of the electorate bothered to vote and the NDC collected all but 11 of the 200 seats. The elections left Rawlings' government in a stronger position than before, with a reasonable semblance of being democratic.

But despite Rawlings' successes, all was not well in Ghana. Ethnic clashes in the north-east in 1994 between Konkombas, their numbers swollen by an influx from neighbouring Togo, and Nanumbas, support-

ed by the powerful Dagomba, left more than 1000 people dead and many more displaced. In 1995, the army ruthlessly suppressed a renewed outbreak of ethnic killing.

In late 1996, Rawlings received 57% of the vote in presidential elections acknowledged as free and fair, leaving the combined opposition candidate, Dr John Kufour, trailing on 39%. In the 1997 parliamentary elections, which registered a 76% turnout, Rawlings' NDC took 133 of the 200 seats, with 65 falling to the opposition Great Alliance. With a clear mandate, the government of President Jerry Rawlings began its second term of office in January 1997. At much the same time, the appointment of Ghanaian Kofi Annan as UN Secretary General boosted national morale.

In 1998, in an effort to improve tax collection and spread the burden more equitably, the government again attempted to launch a value-added tax (VAT). This time, to prevent a re-occurrence of the riots instigated by 1995's hurriedly planned and subsequently aborted launch – the last occasion of major civil unrest in Ghana – the introduction was preceded by a carefully orchestrated campaign to inform Ghanaians.

Elections are next due in 2000. The constitution bars anyone from standing for a third four-year term of office. President Jerry Rawlings has already walked peacefully off the stage once before and the indications are that he will do so again. He has publicly endorsed his vice-president, Professor John E Atta-Mills, a former law professor, as his successor, thus scotching rumours that the First Lady, Nana Konadu Agyeman-Rawlings, might run on the NDC ticket and seek to keep the job in the family.

GEOGRAPHY

Ghana, stretching northward from the Gulf of Guinea, is about the size of Britain. It is generally flat or gently undulating. Only the low Akwapim mountain range in the east, sandwiched between Lake Volta and the border with Togo, breaks up the landscape.

The relatively dry coastal region is punctuated by saline lagoons and backed by a

GHANA

plain of low-lying scrubland. Around 25km inland, at the head of a mild escarpment, green forests roll northward. Although there are healthy areas of secondary growth, little virgin rainforest has survived the decimation of logging and the encroachment of small farms and coffee plantations. It's here, in the central and southern area, home of the Ashanti, that most of the cocoa is grown.

The northern third of the country, sitting on a plateau about 500m high, is hotter, drier and predominantly savanna or open woodland – an ideal climate for growing cotton.

Dominating the eastern flank of the country is Lake Volta – the world's largest artificial lake, about twice the size of Luxembourg. It's fed from Burkina Faso by the Black Volta and White Volta rivers.

CLIMATE

Ghana has three climatic zones. Along the coast, including Accra, rains fall from April to June and in September and October. Throughout the year, maximum temperatures are around 30°C, dropping three or four degrees during the brief respite between rainy seasons. The humidity is constantly

high, at about 80%. In the central forest region, the rains are heavier and last longer.

The north has one rainy season lasting from April to October. Midday temperatures rarely fall below 30°C, rising to 35°C and above in December to March when the rasping harmattan wind blows in from the Sahara. At this time, dust particles hang heavy in the air, making it constantly hazy.

ECOLOGY & ENVIRONMENT

Overgrazing by livestock (farmers have increased animal populations as water has become more available), coupled with the expansion of land under cultivation, is decreasing natural vegetation all over the country. This process is causing progressively larger areas of the northern savanna to resemble the arid lands of the Sahel. In the south, savanna is encroaching on areas which were previously forested. Cocoa is a forest-zone crop and growing it in cleared forests has contributed to this process in the centre. The timber and mining industries have also helped devastate the forests, in part as a result of their cutting and clearing practices. There are no longer any productive forests outside the government reserves.

On the brighter side, farmers and fishing people in the north who left the banks of Ghana's Sissili and Kulpawn rivers are now returning because the World Health Organization has controlled the fly that causes river blindness. The amazingly successful US$ 340 million project has essentially eliminated new cases of river blindness not only in Ghana but also in neighbouring countries.

Between November and February, giant turtles lumber ashore to their breeding grounds off the beaches at places such as Ada Foah and Winneba. At their most vulnerable, large numbers are killed. You can play your small part in aiding the survival of the species by abstaining from turtle steak if it features on a menu.

FLORA & FAUNA

The northern part of the country is typical savanna grassland where the thorny acacia is the dominant tree. Mole National Park is

Community-Based Nature Tourism

If you like your tourism simple, friendly and low-cost, visit some of the ecotourism projects being established by traditional councils and district assemblies. It's a new village-based venture, supported by the Ghana Tourist Board and the Peace Corps in collaboration with Ghana's Nature Conservation Research Centre.

A typical village will offer nature trails, trained guides, an information leaflet, simple food and, often, bicycle hire and basic accommodation in a guesthouse or with families. Projects that are up and running include the Estuary Beach Camp in Ada and the Tafi-Atome Monkey Sanctuary in the East, Larabanga at the gates of Mole National Park in the North, and Bobiri Forest Reserve and the Boabeng-Fiema Monkey Sanctuary in the Centre.

More villages, each with something special to offer, are joining the scheme. For the latest information, contact the main Ghana Tourist Board information centre (☎ 231817) off Barnes Rd in Accra, or regional offices.

Come soon, before the rush; in 1996, Ghana had about 250,000 visitors, but this figure is projected to rise to one million by 2010. Rural tourism is one of the main strands of Ghana's tourism development plan.

For more details of these and other ecotourism sites, hit the Ghana Ecotourism Web site, hosted by the Nature Conservation Research Centre, on www.ncrc.org.gh.

GHANA

the best place to observe the birds and animals of such an environment.

Much of the south is semideciduous forest and little of the primary forest remains. Cocoa, introduced in the early colonial period, is grown across a wide band in the south of the country. One protected area is Kakum National Park, home to nearly 600 different species of butterfly and where over 250 kinds of bird have been recorded. You won't see too many of these as you bounce along its unique canopy walkway, 30m above the ground at tree-top level but it's a unique experience, giving you – literally – a bird's eye view of the forest.

GOVERNMENT & POLITICS

Ghana's 1992 constitution allows political parties freedom to organise. Under it, the government is headed by an elected president and a 200-member parliament, which is also elected. Parliament is currently dominated by Rawlings' party, the NDC, which holds 133 seats. The next presidential and parliamentary elections are scheduled for 2000.

ECONOMY

Ghana is the world's second-largest cocoa producer after Côte d'Ivoire. However, in the early 1990s gold replaced cocoa as the country's leading export. The performance of both commodities was excellent in 1995 and 1996, although a fall in world prices subsequently hit hard. Tourism has recently overtaken timber as the third-biggest generator of hard currency and is predicted to become the lead earner within a decade. Timber revenue comes at a heavy price; little primary forest remains and secondary growth is being reduced at an alarming rate. Fishery resources are also in swift decline.

Since 1983, Ghana has had an average growth of 5% per annum – impressively high by sub-Saharan standards. Inflation, however, has been the plague of the last 25 years. Reaching a high of 70% in 1995, it was clawed back to 29% in mid-1997 and was expected to drop to single figures by the end of 1998, provided that the second attempt to introduce VAT is successful. The government is determined to sell off state enterprises and has disposed of more than half, including profitable plums such as Ashanti Goldfields.

Stability comes at a price; subsidies on health and education have been removed, although the government has promised a return to free basic education.

POPULATION & PEOPLE

Ghana's population of 17 million makes it one of the more densely settled countries in West Africa. Of this, 44% are Akan, a grouping which includes the Ashanti (also called Asante), whose heartland is around Kumasi, and the Fanti, who fish the central coast and farm its near hinterland. The Nzema, linguistically close to the Akan, fish and farm in the south-west.

Also fishers and farmers, the Ga are the indigenous people of Accra and Tema and distant migrants from present-day Nigeria. East of Tema are Dangme-speaking peoples, the largest being the Krobo, whose centre is Somanya. Further east, in the southern Volta region, are a large group, the Ewé.

The Dagomba inhabit much of the central north, including Tamale. Prominent neighbours are the Gonja to the south, Konkomba and Nanumba to the east and the Mamprussi and Kusasi to the north. In the north-east are the Frafra and, around Navrongo, the Kasena. The Dagarti, Lobi and Birfor live in the far north-west.

ARTS
Art & Craftwork

The principal art-producing tribes of Ghana are the Ashanti, the Ewé and the Lobi.

The Ashanti are famous for their kente cloth (metre for metre, probably the most expensive material in Africa), their distinctive block-printed *adinkra* cloth, their stools, which are among the finest in Africa, and their fertility dolls, as well as their goldwork and linguist staffs.

When the king makes a public appearance, he wears finest kente cloth, gold ornaments and jewellery. His attendants carry state swords of forged iron and carry linguist staffs which are topped with figura-

See Also ...

For more information about Ghana's rich artistic and cultural heritage, you may want to refer to the following:

Ashanti & Ewé
'Ashanti Art & Culture' pp440-43
Colour feature *between* p384 *and* p385

Dagomba
'Dagomba' p457

Ga
'Outdooring & Other Ga Rituals' p398

Lobi
Colour feature *between* p304 *and* p305

Art Colour Features
'Lost Wax Method of Bronze Casting'
between p160 *and* p161
'Textiles' *between* p128 *and* p129
'Figurative Sculpture' *between* p688 *and* p689

tive elements relating to Ashanti proverbs. The Ashanti don't use masks but carve figures for household shrines eg the *akuaba* doll which is used for fertility. The Ashanti are also famous for their miniature bronze sculptures which were once used for weighing gold.

Pop Music

Ghanaian highlife music was the most popular music in the region in the 1970s (for more details see the special section 'Music of West Africa' earlier in this book), and you can still pick up recordings by E.T. Mensah, Nana Ampadu, and The Sweet Talks. Highlife is still very big and there's a wide selection of artists to choose from. Popular Ghanaian stars include Ko Nimo, City Boys, Nana Acheampong, Kojo Antwi, Papa Yankson, Daddy Lumba, Nana Tuffuor, Blay Ambolley and George Darko.

Ko Nimo & Palm Wine Music

Ko Nimo is Ghana's foremost exponent of acoustic guitar highlife. He was taught classical guitar in his late 20s, and his delicate finger-picking style has absorbed a diverse range of influences ranging from jazz to classical. The traditional 'palm wine' style, however, still forms the basis of many of his compositions. This type of music was popular in West Africa in the 50s and 60s. Relaxed and informal, perhaps with someone tapping an empty bottle as an accompaniment, palm wine music was meant to entertain the customers at local bars, or wherever palm wine was being served. The guitarist would usually play for drinks and tips, and their songs dealt with the events of daily life, often with a comic touch.

In recognition of his services to music he was awarded a gold medal in 1997 by the Ghanaian president.

Ko Nimo is now in his early 60s, though he still performs regularly with his band, the Adadam Agofomma Group, at many venues throughout Ghana.

Graeme Counsel

SOCIETY & CONDUCT

Ghanaians are among the most laid-back people on a laid-back slice of the continent. But they aren't loud. You'll rarely hear shouting, and public displays of anger are uncommon. In an irritating situation, if you lose your cool, you'll probably lose your case. In common with many neighbouring peoples, Ghanaians are snappy dressers, particularly the women. A grubby T-shirt and sawn off jeans will arouse scorn, not sympathy.

RELIGION

Christians outnumber Muslims about two to one, with the Christians concentrated mostly in the south and the Muslims in the north. There are also substantial Muslim minorities in southern cities such as Accra and Kumasi. They usually live in a district called the Zongo, a Hausa word meaning 'ghetto' but without the pejorative overtones. The rest of the people (about 35%) practise traditional ancestral religions.

LANGUAGE

English is the official language. There are at least 75 local languages and dialects. Among the prominent ones are Ga in the Accra-Tema area, Ewé in the south-east and Mole-Dagbani languages in the north. The most widely spoken language is Twi which belongs to the Akan language group and is spoken in different versions throughout most of the central and southern parts of the country. Fanti-Twi is spoken along much of the coast west of Accra. The Ashanti version of Twi is not only spoken throughout the Ashanti homeland and in Kumasi but also serves as a lingua franca throughout much of the country and especially in Accra.

See the Language chapter for useful phrases in Ga and Twi.

Facts for the Visitor

SUGGESTED ITINERARIES

If you've only got two weeks to spare, you could try doing a triangle bounded by Accra, Takoradi, and, at the apex, Kumasi. Start in Accra (three to four days), then go to Cape Coast (three nights) and Elmina and on to Takoradi, taking in some of the coastal forts, villages and beaches (at least two nights) on the way. Take the night train from Takoradi to Kumasi, where you'll probably want to stay at least three nights, then back to Accra.

With four weeks to spare, you can do all of the above, adding in more days to explore the coast. When in Kumasi, radiate northwards to Tamale (one night) and on to Mole National Park (three nights), back to Tamale (one night) and return to Accra via Kumasi. Then you could graft on a visit to the east: Ada Foah (two nights), Akosombo (one night), on to Ho and Hohoe (three nights) and back to Accra.

GHANA

Highlights

Museums

National Museum   *(Accra)*
A repository of artefacts from around the nation; don't miss the well-documented Arts of Power exhibition.

Ashanti museums   *(The Centre)*
In Kumasi, the Prempeh II Jubilee Museum of Ashanti culture is not to be missed, while the Manhyia Palace Museum has an excellent guided tour and shows you how the Ashanti royals lived.

Volta Regional Museum   *(The East)*
This small but fascinating museum in Ho showcases exhibits from the time when the area was part of German Togoland.

Forts

Cape Coast Castle   *(The Coast)*
This UNESCO World Heritage site has a superbly informative museum.

St George's Castle & Fort St Jago, Elmina
                                      (The Coast)
Both these UNESCO World Heritage sites have excellent museums and guided tours.

Fort Good Hope, Senya Baraku *(The Coast)*
A small, well restored Dutch fort, where it's possible to overnight, although the accommodation is very basic.

Fort Kormantin, Abanze   *(The Coast)*
The most recently restored of the coastal forts; Louis Armstrong, the famous jazz trumpeter, claimed his ancestors were shipped from here.

Beaches

Ada   *(The East)*
An idyllic beach camp where the River Volta meets the Atlantic; in season, you can see giant turtles struggling ashore to lay their eggs.

Kokrobite   *(The Coast)*
Laze on the superb sandy beach here or take lessons in drumming and dancing at the Academy of African Music & Arts.

Busua   *(The Coast)*
Both a luxury hotel and a popular budget travellers hangout, this is the Ghanaian coast's most laid-back resort.

National Parks

Kakum National Park   *(The Coast)*
At tree-top level above the rainforest, you sway along a canopy walkway, unique in Africa.

Mole National Park   *(The North)*
A protected area of savanna – you'll need initiative to get here, but the rich bird and animal life make the journey worthwhile.

Walking

Ho   *(The East)*
Here you can walk around the mountain village of Amedzofe, which is excellent for birdwatching, and visit the Tafi-Atome Monkey Sanctuary.

Hohoe   *(The East)*
The easy ascent of Mt Afadjato is a pleasant walk and there are also walks to Tagbo and Wli waterfalls.

Boat Trips

Lake Volta   *(The East & Centre)*
Don't expect luxury, but the trip on the weekly Lake Volta ferry linking Akosombo and Yeji is a great alternative way to travel to the north of Ghana.

River Volta   *(The East)*
It's a full day's ferry trip between Akosombo and Ada, at the mouth of the estuary – definitely beats taking the bus.

Facts for the Visitor 393

PLANNING
When to Go
In the south the dry months, November to March plus July and August, are easier for travelling. In the north, avoid December and January, the hottest months. This is also when the harmattan wind blows in from the Sahara.

Maps
The *Tourist Map of Ghana* (1995), produced by the National Atlas Development Centre, details in a dizzying yet understandable array of symbols every feature you could want to know about – from shrines to cloth weaving villages to gold mines. It's excellent as a source of reference, but you'll need to supplement it if you're driving, as it doesn't distinguish between major and minor or tar and dirt roads.

Shell in collaboration with KLM have reproduced a map (US$3) with Accra on one side and, on the other, a road map of Ghana (reprinted in 1994 from an earlier Survey of Ghana map the date of which, perhaps wisely, they don't reveal). Both sides are useful but rather out of date.

The best map of Ghana is a 1:750,000 version produced by International Travel Maps of Vancouver, Canada.

VISAS & DOCUMENTS
Visas
Everyone except nationals of ECOWAS countries needs a visa. It's usually valid for three months from the date of issue and allows a one month stay.

In the UK, the Ghanaian consulate in London (open 9.30 am to 1.30 pm) requires UK£15 and four photos. Visas can take up to four days to process.

In the USA, both the Ghanaian embassy in Washington and the consulate in New York issue visas. They require four photos, a photocopy of your round-trip ticket and US$20 (US$50 for a multiple entry visa). Visas take three days to process and are good for visits of up to 30 days.

Note that visas are not issued at Ghana's borders.

Visa Extensions The best advice is – don't. It's much easier and less time consuming to hop over the border to Lomé in Togo and enter afresh with a new visa. If you go to Immigration Headquarters in Accra (☎ 221667 extension 215), you're in for a long and frustrating morning and a probable issuing delay of two weeks or more, during which they hold your passport. The penalty for staying on after your visa's expired can be severe.

Other Documents
Yellow fever vaccination certificates are routinely checked at Accra airport and most land borders. It's prudent to carry your passport or at least a photocopy of it at all times as police occasionally ask travellers for their papers.

Nowadays, the currency declaration form is almost redundant. However, officials will probably still go through the ritual of issuing and asking for one on your arrival and departure. But the attitude's relaxed and no one seems too concerned if you can't produce it. Keep your exchange receipts handy when leaving the country, just in case you run up against someone of the old school.

Export permits for wooden artefacts such as masks and sculptures which are antique – often defined by customs officers as anything not obviously new – are, in principle, no longer required. If you want to play it safe, you can get one without any hassle from the National Museum in Accra for a nominal fee.

EMBASSIES & CONSULATES
Ghanaian Embassies & Consulates
In West Africa, Ghana has embassies in Benin, Burkina Faso, Côte d'Ivoire, Guinea, Nigeria, Sierra Leone and Togo. For more details, see the Facts for the Visitor section of the relevant country chapter. If conditions stabilise in Liberia Ghana may reopen an embassy there. Elsewhere, embassies and consulates include the following:

Belgium
(☎ 02-0705 82 20)
7 General Wahisin Laan, B-1030 Brussels

GHANA

Canada
(☎ 613-236 0871)
1 Clemow Ave, The Glebe, Ottawa, Ont KLS 2A
France
(☎ 01 45 00 09 50)
8 Villa Said, 75116 Paris
Germany
(☎ 0228-36 79 60)
Rheinalle 58, 53173 Bonn
Japan
(☎ 03-409 3861)
Azabu, PO Box 16, Tokyo
Netherlands
(☎ 235 632 929)
Robijnlaan 13, Hoofdorp
UK
(☎ 0181-342 8686; from 22 April 2000 ☎ 020-8342 8686)
104 Highgate Hill, London N6 5HE
USA
Embassy:
(☎ 202-686 4520)
3512 International Drive, NW, Washington, DC 20008
Consulate:
(☎ 212-832 1300)
19 East 47th St, New York City, NY 10017

Ghana also has an embassy in Egypt.

Embassies & Consulates in Ghana

All embassies and consulates listed are in Accra (telephone area code ☎ 021).

Belgium
(☎ 776561, fax 773927)
Mile 4, Independence Ave
Benin
(☎ 774860)
19 Volta St, 2nd Close, Airport Residential Area
Burkina Faso
(☎ 221988)
Asylum Down, west of Mango Tree Ave
Canada
(☎ 228555, fax 773792)
46 Independence Ave, at Sankara Circle; represents Australia in consular matters
Côte d'Ivoire
(☎ 774611)
9 18th Lane, south of Danquah Circle
Ethiopia
(☎ 775928, fax 776802)
2 Milne Close

Visas for Onward Travel

In Ghana, you can get visas for the following countries.

For visa applications, embassies in Accra are open Monday to Friday and require two photos, except where indicated. Francophone countries insist upon payment for visas in US$, CFA or French francs, except Côte d'Ivoire which only accepts cedis.

Visas for Gambia, Kenya, Sierra Leone and other Commonwealth countries without high commissions in Accra are issued by the Ghana Immigration Service at Immigration Headquarters there. The process takes at least a week and the only sensible advice is to get them elsewhere.

Benin
The embassy is open from 8 am to 3 pm. Visas are issued for a maximum stay of two weeks but can easily be extended at Immigration in Cotonou. They cost US$20 and are issued within 48 hours, often faster.

Burkina Faso
The embassy is open from 8 am to 2 pm and gives same-day or 24 hour service. You'll need three photos and US$40 for a three month visa.

Côte d'Ivoire
Open from 8 am to 1.30 pm, the embassy issues visas in 48 hours. A one month visa, payable in cedis only, costs, for nationals of most countries, US$12.50 (but US$33 if you're British) and is normally valid for entry within 15 days of the date of issue.

Togo
Open from 7.30 am to 2 pm and 3 to 4.30 pm, the embassy requires three photos and US$20. A one month visa is issued within 24 hours. Alternatively, you can get one for the same price, valid for seven days, at the Aflao/Lomé border. For a longer stay, go to the sûreté in Lomé, where a one or three months extension costs about CFA10,000.

France
  (☎ 228571, fax 778321)
  12th Rd, off Liberation Ave
Guinea
  (☎ 777921)
  4 Norla St, Labone
Germany
  (☎ 221311, fax 221347)
  Valdemosa Lodge, 7th Ave Extension, North
  Ridge
Japan
  (☎ 775616, fax 775951)
  8 Tito Ave, off Jawaharlal Nehru Rd
Liberia
  (☎ 775160)
  Odiokwao St, Airport Residential Area
Mali
  (☎ 775160)
  8 Agostino Neto Rd, Airport Residential Area
Netherlands
  (☎ 773644, fax 773655)
  89 Liberation Ave, Sankara Circle
Niger
  (☎ 224962)
  House No E104/3 Independence Ave, 600m
  south of Sankara Circle
Nigeria
  (☎ 776158, fax 774395)
  Tito Ave, 1km north of Ring Rd
Togo
  (☎ 777950)
  Togo House, Cantonments Rd, 1km north of
  Danquah Circle
UK
  (☎ 221665, fax 664652)
  Gamal Abdul Nasser Ave
USA
  (☎ 775347, fax 776008)
  Ring Rd East, 300m east of Danquah Circle

Denmark, Egypt, Italy, and Spain also have embassies in Accra.

MONEY
Currency

The unit of currency is the cedi. For travellers cheques and small notes, exchange rates are less favourable than for cash in large denominations. The best currencies to bring are US$, UK£, French francs or German marks.

Because of Ghana's high inflation and the unstable exchange rate of the cedi, all prices in this chapter are expressed in US$.

Exchange Rates

CFA1000	=	C4000
Euro €1	=	C2800
1FF	=	C420
UK£1	=	C3900
US$1	=	C2350

Ghana, once one of the most expensive countries in Africa, now has a floating exchange rate and prices are generally very reasonable. Top end hotels may cover their backs by quoting prices in US$, but almost all will accept payment in cedis at the current exchange rate.

Exchanging Money

Privately operated foreign exchange bureaus (forexes) are found all over Accra and in major towns. They usually offer a better rate than the banks and are infinitely more convenient; you can be in and out in two minutes flat, your pockets stuffed with cedis. And stuffed they will be, since C5000 (about US$2) is the highest denomination note.

Don't even give the time of day to the occasional freelance moneychanger who may accost you; the rate won't be superior and it may be a sting.

Few banks outside Accra or Kumasi will accept travellers cheques. Not all forexes will take them and those that do tend to give much worse rates than the banks. Barclays bank in central Accra, for example, offers a rate which is only slightly below that for cash, whereas a forex's rate can be as much as 10% less.

The only place you can get cash advances (in cedis) on Visa and MasterCard is at Barclays in Accra. They charge 2% commission plus a US$3 fee for the approval telex and you can be in for a long wait. If you have a card issued in the USA, you'll get hit with commission on two exchange transactions: dollars to UK£ and UK£ to cedis.

American Express cardholders can get cash through the company's Ghanaian affiliate, Scantravel, in central Accra, on High St (☎ 664456, fax 663134), which charges a 2% commission.

Visa and MasterCard are increasingly widely accepted by major hotels and travel agencies. American Express and Diners, by contrast, tend to elicit nothing more than blank stares. Other banks that change money include: Ghana Commercial Bank (GCB), Standard Chartered, Social Security Bank (SSB) and Ecobank.

Spend up to your last cedi before leaving Ghana. You're not supposed to export more than a handful, and you wouldn't want to since once you're over the frontier no bank will look at them. Should you be stuck with a supply, you may be able to slough them off at a border town lorry park.

POST & COMMUNICATIONS
In Accra and most major towns, there is a 'communication centre' on every second street corner. These come complete with phone, fax and some of the planet's last remaining telex machines.

You need to establish in advance the cost of services, which is rather more than post office prices. Normally, the saving to you in time and nervous energy will more than compensate for the extra outlay.

Post
The main post offices in Accra and Kumasi have poste restante services. An air mail letter to the European Union costs US$0.35 and one to Australia or the USA, US$0.50.

Telephone
Area dialling codes within Ghana are listed in the table. The US AT&T phone company's access number within Ghana is ☎ 0191 and for the British BT charge card, call ☎ 0194. Outside Accra and Kumasi, make sure the operator understands how a charge card works, otherwise you'll be hit twice when they insist that you pay locally for your call.

You can make international phone calls from Ghana Telecom offices. Three minutes (the minimum for an operator-placed call) cost US$5 to the USA or the European Union and US$5.50 to Australia.

Area Dialling Codes	
Accra	☎ 021
Ada	☎ 0968
Akosombo	☎ 0251
Bolgatanga	☎ 072
Cape Coast	☎ 042
Elmina	☎ 024
Ho	☎ 091
Kokrobite	☎ 027
Kumasi	☎ 051
Mampong	☎ 0561
Navrongo	☎ 072
Sekondi-Takoradi	☎ 031
Sunyani	☎ 061
Tamale	☎ 071
Tema	☎ 022
Winneba	☎ 041

Fax
You can send and receive faxes at Telecom offices between 8 am and 6 pm on weekdays and until 2 pm on Saturdays. Incoming faxes, which are recorded, cost US$0.40 per received page and are held indefinitely.

When faxing at communication centres, be sure that you're only going to be billed for messages successfully transmitted and not for time spent trying to get through.

Email & Internet Access
Places offering Web access are mushrooming around Accra. See Information in the Accra section for details.

BOOKS
Ghana – A Travellers' Guide by Jojo Cobbinah contains some interesting cultural titbits. *Ghana Today* by Mylène Rémy, translated from the original French, captures the atmosphere well, although its prose tends towards the purple end of the spectrum. It's less comprehensive and less accurate as a guide for getting around. Albert van Dantzig's *Forts and Castles of Ghana*, although first published in 1980, remains the definitive work on the early European coastal

presence and is slim enough to slip into your back pocket.

For a taste of local cooking you could seek out *Ghanaian Favourite Dishes* by ADAEX Educational Publications.

RADIO

Ghanaian radio is a joy to listen to. The lively chat shows, in particular, give fascinating insights into local culture. Leading FM stations in and around Accra include the following:

GAR FM (95.7) – national radio with world news on the hour, every hour

Joy FM (99.7) – hourly news, including BBC World Service at 7 am and 3 pm

Radio Vibe (91.9) – news on the hour and wild music in between

Radio Gold (90.5) – cheap and cheerful

Groove Radio (106.3) – news every half-hour, great chat, eclectic music

PHOTOGRAPHY & VIDEO

You don't need a photo permit but, since many Ghanaians are suspicious of people taking photographs, ask permission first. In communities used to tourists, you may be asked to pay. And why not? You're intruding into their lives and they're performing a kind of service for you.

The usual restrictions on photographing apply – see the Photography & Video section in the Regional Facts for the Visitor chapter for more general information. Locals get agitated, for instance, if you try to snap the picturesque coastal fort at Anomabu, which nowadays serves as a prison.

HEALTH

A yellow fever vaccination is obligatory, and malaria is endemic year-round throughout Ghana, so you should take appropriate precautions. Schistosomiasis (bilharzia) is prevalent in Ghana, so avoid bathing or paddling in freshwater rivers or lakes. See the Health section in the Regional Facts for the Visitor chapter for more general information on these and other health matters.

WOMEN TRAVELLERS

The beaches within easy reach of Accra have their share of gigolos and predators. Otherwise, women can reduce the unlikely chance of other than a bit of verbal hassle by following the local example and wearing a longish skirt or sarong. The north of the country is Muslim, but their Islam is worn fairly lightly. There's no need to wear a headscarf, although a blouse or shirt that covers the shoulders would be appropriate. For more general information and advice, see the Women Travellers section in the Regional Facts for the Visitor chapter.

DANGERS & ANNOYANCES

As anywhere, large festivals tend to attract opportunist, out-of-town thieves and hustlers. Take care on the beaches all along the coast; they're notorious for petty theft and, in the vicinity of the capital, the occasional after-dark mugging.

Light-Outs

Power cuts, locally and charmingly called 'light-outs', are a feature of life in contemporary Ghana. There's nothing you can do but benignly accept them – and if they irritate you, think what it must be like to live with them, year-round, day in, day out. The problem is simple to define but much more difficult to solve. Water levels at the Akosombo Dam, which produces almost all of Ghana's electricity, plus a fair amount of Togo and Benin's consumption, have fallen to critical levels because of low rainfall. An astounding 40% of the turbines' output is gobbled up by the American-owned Volta Aluminium Corporation (Valco), a classic example of economic neocolonialism, to whom President Nkrumah mortgaged the nation on a 50-year renewable lease. Add to this politicians who failed to raise electricity prices in four years, during which time inflation more than doubled, so that production costs now way exceed revenue. No wonder it's dark at night.

GHANA

There's another sting to Ghana's tropical paradise beaches. Offshore, the Atlantic has fierce currents and a ripping undertow. Several bathers a year drown and often it's the strong, overly confident swimmer who's tugged under. Ask the locals, respect what they tell you and stay well within your depth. You'll also sometimes feel a squelch beneath your feet; too many of the beaches double as public toilets, so pick your way with care.

BUSINESS HOURS

Business hours are from 8 am to 12.30 pm and from 1.30 to 5.30 pm, Monday to Friday, and from 8.30 am to 1 pm Saturday. Government offices observe the same times but close Saturday.

Banking hours are from 8.30 am to 2 pm Monday to Thursday, 3 pm on Friday. A few bank branches are also open on Saturday from 8.30 am to 1 pm, as are most forexes.

PUBLIC HOLIDAYS & SPECIAL EVENTS

Public holidays fall on 1 January (New Year's Day), 6 March (Independence Day),

1 May (Labour Day), 1 July (Republic Day), the first Friday in December (Farmers' Day) and 25 and 26 December (Christmas).

Ghana also observes Good Friday, Easter Monday, and the Muslim festivals of Eid al-Fitr, at the end of Ramadan, and Eid al-Adha, both of which are determined by the lunar calendar. See the Public Holidays & Special Events section in the Regional Facts for the Visitor chapter for a table of Islamic holiday dates.

Ghana has many colourful festivals and events throughout the year, including Cape Coast's Fetu Afahye Festival (on the first Saturday of September), Elmina's Bakatue Festival (on the first Tuesday in July), Tamale's Damba Festival of the Dagomba people (dates vary according to the Muslim calendar) and various year-round Akan celebrations in Kumasi. In Winneba, Ghana's most famous festival – the Aboakyer (Deer Hunt) – is celebrated on the first weekend in May.

The Ashanti calendar is divided into nine cycles of 42 days called Adae, each of which is a special day of worship and rest. The last, or ninth Adae of the calendar is

'Outdooring' & Other Ga Rituals

The old Ga fishing villages towns are now all part of the Greater Accra-Tema urban complex. The Ga state symbol is an antelope standing on top of an elephant, meaning that the top is reached by wisdom, not size. Ga cultural identity is anchored in a series of life-cycle rituals that begin with the naming ceremony at eight days, and continue through puberty, marriage and death. Ga naming ceremonies, called 'outdooring' in Ghanaian English, are particularly elaborate and impressive. The religious rituals are performed early in the morning by the elders of the baby's father's family and relatives and guests come to congratulate the family and celebrate.

Homowo is the Ga harvest festival and takes place in August. For a month beforehand there is a traditional ban on drumming in the Accra-Tema area, which all ethnic groups must observe. On the day of Homowo the chiefs , the Mantses, of the Ga towns thank their gods for a good harvest and a special ceremonial dish made with corn and palm oil, *kpekple*, is distributed in the streets. In Ga houses throughout the city there is general merrymaking, and kpekple is eaten together with other party foods.

Katie Abu

marked all over the state by the week-long Odwira Festival (for more details see the special section 'Ashanti Art & Culture' in the Kumasi section later).

ACTIVITIES
The area around Ho and Hohoe, in the east, is great for hiking. Accra has an active Hash House Harriers running-and-drinking group. For details of the weekly run, inquire at Champs Sports Bar (☎ 021-228937). There are also opportunities for learning drumming and dancing. The Academy of African Music & Arts in Kokrobite, for example, offers residential courses.

ACCOMMODATION
You'll rarely have a problem finding a hotel in Ghana, even in the smallest provincial town. Budget accommodation in both the capital and provinces averages around US$5/7 a night for singles/doubles. For that you can get a decent room with fan and shared bathroom. Sleeping rough anywhere along the beaches is definitely not advisable; the chances of being robbed are high.

Every major town has reasonable midrange hotels. They usually have rooms with bathroom and a choice of either fan or aircon, and a bar-restaurant, although it may not be the best in town. Top end hotels are only found in Accra and Kumasi and at beach resorts such as Biriwa, Busua and Ada.

Outside Accra, there can be acute problems of water supply and pressure.

FOOD
Soups, which are really sauces, are the mainstay of the Ghanaian diet. They're usually fairly thick broths eaten with a starch staple such as *fufu*, *kenkey* or *banku*. Four of the most popular soups are *nkatenkwan, abenkwan, shito* and *nkita*. See the boxed text opposite for an explanation of some of the more common Ghanaian dishes and food terms you are likely to come across.

Stews or sauces are also popular, and include groundnut, eggplant (aubergine), fish, bean leaf, *forowe* and grasscutter, which

---

Ghanaian Grub

Starches
abolo – steamed corn dough
akla – pounded beans with palm oil
ametse – cassava and corn dough
ampesi – yam, plantain, cassava, sweet potato or cocoyam
apapransa – dried cornmeal
fufu – cooked cassava, plantain or yam, mashed and shaped into a ball
gari – coarse cassava flour
kenkey and *banku* – both are a sour, fermented corn mash which is wrapped in plantain leaves and boiled
kokonte – paste made of boiled cassava
kyekyirebetu – mashed plantains with palm oil

Soups & Sauces
abenkwan – soup made from pounded palm fruit and fish
agushie – pumpkin seed sauce, typically served with cooked yams
forowe – fish stew with tomatoes
nkatenkwan – groundnut (peanut) soup prepared with peanut butter, onions, tomatoes and fish or meat
nkita (also called light soup) – egg and tomato soup with fish or meat
palaver sauce – meat with spinach, efan and bitter leaves
shito – a fiery pepper sauce

Other Dishes
akapinkyi – green plantains with smoked fish and palm oil
emo dokon – beef with rice flour
gari foto – eggs, onions, dried shrimp and tomatoes accompanied by gari
gari jollof – gari with tomatoes and onions
jollof rice – rice with meat
kyemgbuma – crab with cassava, meat and tomatoes
mboteleba – fish or meat with crabs, tomatoes and abolo
oto – yams with eggs and palm oil
red red – blackeyed peas with gari and meat or fish, served with fried plantain

GHANA

is a large rodent. Egg curry, made with rice, tomatoes and groundnuts, is served in many cheap eating houses. *Omo tuo* are mashed rice balls with a fish or meat soup. This is a special dish, normally served only on Sunday, the day for family eating out. At the weekend, look for it advertised on chalkboards outside restaurants and chop houses. When in the north, try the delicious fried bean cakes called *kose*, which are also widely available in Accra and Kumasi during Muslim fasting month of Ramadan.

The least expensive restaurants are called 'chop bars'. Most open early in the morning and are closed by 6 pm. It's better anyway to have lunch rather than dinner at these since you can be sure that the food (chop) hasn't been sitting around for hours in the heat.

The cheapest food of all is sold on the streets by women. They'll typically have a mound of rice on a wooden table along with several sauces to choose from. One of the most popular street foods is *kelewele*, a delicious spicy dessert of fried plantains in long chips seasoned with ground chilli pepper and ginger. Another is *ntomo krakro* (fried sweet potato cakes). If you like the food, tell the cook it's 'sweet', meaning delicious.

DRINKS

A popular nonalcoholic beverage sold on the streets is *askenkee*, a linguistic corruption of *iced kenkey*. It's a milky-white drink made from fermented maize or corn. Fresh coconut milk is refreshing, safe to drink and considerably cheaper than bottled mineral water. Among home-brew alcoholic drinks, *pito* (millet beer) is the drink of choice in the north. Palm wine, which is altogether more subtle, is the preferred tipple in the south. Catch it when it's young. 'Tap before seven, drink before eleven', goes the local saying. The liquor contains so much natural sugar that it starts to ferment as soon as it meets the yeasts of the air. As the day grows older the wine becomes less refreshing, more sour – and more seriously alcoholic. Local beers and lagers vary in quality. Among the better ones, Star is a palatable

daytime drink, not too high in alcohol. Gulder is sweeter and heavier. Draught Bubra lager and stout are worth making a detour for. And, of course, as everywhere in West Africa, there's the reputedly performance-enhancing Guinness.

Bars in Ghana are often called 'Spot'. So you'll come across, for example, Lucky Spot, Lovers Spot or West End Spot.

SHOPPING

You'll find all the famous Ashanti art and craftwork, including kente and adinkra cloth, stools and fertility dolls, readily on sale in Accra as well as in Kumasi in the Ashanti heartland. The Thursday morning bead market at Koforidua, near Somanya, is about the best in West Africa for glass beads. The finest leatherwork comes from the north, where Bolgatanga woven baskets are also prized.

Getting There & Away

AIR

International flights arrive at Accra's Kotoka airport, about 8km from the centre of town. Major airlines include the national carrier, Ghana Airways, and British Airways.

The airport departure tax for international flights is US$20 (to be paid in cash, in US$). This is usually included in your ticket price, but check when you're buying your ticket or reconfirming your flight.

Europe & the USA

British Airways, Alitalia, KLM-Royal Dutch Airlines, Lufthansa, Swissair and Ghana Airways all have direct flights between Accra and Western Europe. The standard single fare is around US$1200.

The cheapest way to get to Ghana from Europe is with a discount ticket bought in London or Amsterdam.

From West Africa to Europe, many airlines – and certainly all the discount ones – will only accept US$ in cash. Balkan Airlines and Aeroflot vie for the lowest rates (around US$670) to major European destinations. Balkan has one flight a week via Sofia on Sunday, and Aeroflot flies via Moscow on alternate Thursdays.

To/from the USA, you can take Ghana Airways, which has twice weekly flights to New York, or Air Afrique, which has a transfer in Dakar (Senegal) or Abidjan (Côte d'Ivoire). Tickets for Ghana Airways long haul flights are cheaper than for their competitors' flights. They offer a 25% student discount on international flights only if you can produce a student ID and a letter of introduction from your college.

Africa

Within West Africa, Ghana Airways is one of the better airlines, although not without its delays and cancellations. It has three flights a day to Lagos (Nigeria)and either one or two a week to Banjul (Gambia), Conakry (Guinea), Cotonou (Benin), Dakar (Senegal), Lomé (Togo) and Monrovia (Liberia). You can also fly to most neighbouring countries with Air Afrique or Nigeria Airways. Ghana Airways and Air Afrique each have four flights a week to Abidjan while Air Ivoire has three.

Four airlines offer a direct link with East or southern Africa: Ethiopian Airlines has four flights a week (US$670) to/from Addis Ababa (two via Nairobi, Kenya; US$670), and Ghana Airways flies twice weekly to/from Harare (Zimbabwe) via Johannesburg (South Africa), which is also covered by South African Airways.

For travellers heading north, EgyptAir flies to/from Cairo (US$610) on Monday and Thursday.

LAND

The departure times that we give here for Ghana's government-run State Transport Corporation (STC) buses are very much statements of intent – buses rarely depart before every last seat is taken.

Burkina Faso

Between Accra and Ouagadougou, the usual route is via Kumasi, Tamale, Bolgatanga,

Border Crossings

The main border crossings are Paga, 16km north of Navrongo, for Burkina Faso, Elubo for Côte d'Ivoire and Aflao for Togo. Note that Ghana's borders all close promptly at 6 pm.

Navrongo and Pô. A direct STC bus runs to Ouagadougou from Accra (1000km, 24 hours, US$27) every Saturday at 8 am and from Kumasi (720km, 20 hours, US$21) on Wednesdays at 10 am. Going the entire distance in one sitting can be excruciating and you'll miss so much en route. It's better, and cheaper, to do the trip in stages. From Bolgatanga one or two bush taxis a day go to the border (45km, one hour, US$2) and on to Pô (US$2), 15km beyond the frontier. From there, SOTRAO runs a daily bus to Ouagadougou (three hours, US$2.50).

You can also enter Burkina Faso between Wa and Bobo-Dioulasso, going via Hamale (320km) or Léo. However, traffic is scarce and there's no direct transport on this route.

Côte d'Ivoire

The most popular route follows the coastal road via Elubo and Aboisso to Abidjan. STC buses run daily except Sunday between Accra and Abidjan (550km, 12 hours, US$17), leaving at 8 am. The trip normally takes 12 to 14 hours, depending upon the delay at the border, which is routinely two to three hours. Don't be surprised if the conductor passes the hat around for contributions to backhanders for police and frontier officials. The going rate is about US$2. The Trans-Ecowas Express, run by STIF, a company from Côte d'Ivoire, is much more reliable and comfortable. Introduced in late 1997, its service will probably settle down to three runs a week. In Accra, their station is in Achimota by the Neoplan building on Nsawam Rd. Call ☎ 233369 for the latest information. It's generally quicker and cheaper to take a bus or bush taxi from Accra to Takoradi, from where you can make Abidjan (US$7.50) in one hit.

GHANA

Another crossing is from Kumasi via Agnibilékrou; there are no direct buses on this route.

On the northernmost route, from Bole to Ferkessédougou (370km), you can get transport from Bole to the Black Volta River (the border), which you cross by canoe. A taxi from there to Bouna is US$2. Onward transport from Bouna to Ferkessédougou costs US$15 and takes eight to 12 hours.

Togo

STC buses leave twice daily for Aflao and Lomé from the company's second Accra station on the north side of Makola Market. STIF's Trans-Eccwas Express (see Côte d'Ivoire earlier in this section), with two runs a week (US$6), is a superior alternative.

For greater flexibility and speed, take one of the frequent taxis or minibuses which ply the coastal road between Accra and Aflao/ Lomé (200km, three hours, US$9). Once beyond customs and immigration, you're virtually in Lomé.

From Kpandu to Kpalimé (40km) there are direct shared taxis, but it's faster to take one to the border and then walk 1.5km on a well trodden footpath to the Togo border; it's the first track on the right after leaving Ghanaian customs. Some 120km north of Kpandu on the Hohoe to Yendi road is an obscure although easy crossing to Badou.

In the north, you can cross from Tamale via Yendi to Sansanné-Mango (220km) or Kara (260km) and from Bawku via Sinkassé to Dapaong (70km); transport is scarce on these routes.

SEA

Ships connect Tema with ports in numerous countries, including Nigeria, Côte d'Ivoire, Cameroon and South Africa. Inquire at the harbour authority in Tema for details; the Black Star Line's office in Tema (☎ 202088) also has information.

ORGANISED TOURS

One recommended tour operator is Insight Travel (☎ 01995-606095, fax 602124, email insight@provider.co.uk, or check out their Web site www.illustrations.co.uk/users/in sight-travel) based at 6 Norton Rd, Preston, Lancashire PR3 1JY. This small agency, run by a former VSO field director in Ghana, offers trips based in Kumasi, with the opportunity of living with a Ghanaian family. Activities include birdwatching, touring Ashanti craft villages, and lessons in dance, music or weaving.

Getting Around

AIR

Fan Airways is a new airline which flies a couple of Beechcraft planes. It operates daily flights between Accra and Kumasi (US$31) and, except Saturday, between the capital and Tamale (US$51). It also has two flights a week to Sunyani and Bolgatanga and one to Takoradi. Flights to all three destinations cost US$40 (one way).

Airlink, run by the Ghana Air Force, flies three times a week between Accra and Kumasi (US$27) and Tamale (US$42). Only Ghana Airways and M & J Travel Tours in Accra (☎ 773153) sell Airlink tickets. You can't reserve a flight so you have to arrive at the airport uncomfortably early if you're to be sure of a seat.

Golden Airways operated an ancient and, by all accounts, none too safe Antonov between Accra and Kumasi. At the time of writing, it was grounded at Kumasi airport. However, we were assured that they'd soon be in business again. Ring them in Accra (☎ 777978) to find out whether – and, above all, what – they're flying.

The newest fledgling in the skies is Muk Airways (who chose that particular name? And are they still on the payroll?), which began operations in late 1997. They operate Jetstream turboprop planes and fly daily except Saturday between Accra and both Kumasi (US$36) and Tamale (US$56). Their agents are Johnson Travel (Accra ☎ 777898, Kumasi ☎ 22905).

The departure tax for internal flights is US$0.25.

BUS

STC buses connect most major towns. Scheduled departure times are rarely observed, since buses don't usually leave until every last seat is filled. Conversely, and even more frustratingly, you may find a bus cancelled without warning if there aren't enough passengers. Service has deteriorated in recent years and it's frequently quicker to travel with one of the numerous private companies whose buses vary from nearly new to clapped out. Reliable operators are GPRTU and City Express. The latter's Bluebird service is particularly speedy although short on comfort. OSA is trustworthy but rickety and its network is more restricted.

Tickets are mostly sold only on the day of departure and, for popular routes, you need to get to the station early, since queues can be long. Avoid the flip-down aisle seats which can be real backbreakers on a long journey. The table in this section lists selected STC and City Express schedules and fares.

BUSH TAXI, TRO-TRO & MINIBUS

Bush taxis, also known as 'fast cars', are usually seven-seater Peugeot 504s – although they invariably squeeze in more than seven people. They fill up more quickly, make fewer stops and travel faster than buses. Consequently, their fares are rather more expensive. The other downside is that greater speed means even greater risk. Those plying the route between Accra and Kumasi have an alarmingly high crash rate.

Tro-tro is a catch-all category which these days embraces minibuses, pick-ups and the wooden framed boneshakers which were the first to be dubbed 'tro-tro'. They cover major and many minor routes, where buses and fast cars are loath to go. They're also cheaper than either. Many have been imported second-hand from Europe and still bear the name and logo of their original Dutch or German owner.

Many will demand a 'baggage fee'. Often this is legitimate, but look around to see if your Ghanaian fellow passengers are coughing up – and how much they're paying.

If you've arrived from a Francophone country, 'lorry park' and 'motor park' (the terms are used interchangeably) are the equivalent of the *gare routière* – the place

Bus Routes & Fares

from	to	distance (km)	duration (hours)	fares (US$)	frequency
Accra	Cape Coast	165	3	3	two STC buses daily
Accra	Kpandu	250	5	2	STC bus daily except Sunday
Accra	Kumasi	255	5	3	eight STC buses daily
Accra	Paga	830	18	13	STC three times weekly
Accra	Takoradi	240	4	4	hourly STC buses
Accra	Tamale	640	12 to 14	7	daily STC bus
Accra	Wa	710	15 to 18	13	weekly (Saturday) STC bus
Bolgatanga	Tamale	160	4	1.50	City Express three times daily
Cape Coast	Kumasi	200	4	3	daily City Express
Kete-Krachi	Tamale	285	11	9	daily City Express bus
Kumasi	Tamale	380	6 to 8	4	twice daily STC and City Express buses
Tamale	Wa	300	7	3	daily City Express bus

GHANA

where trucks and tro-tros and, in smaller towns often buses too, congregate.

TRAIN

Ghana's rail system is a triangular one, the points being Accra, Kumasi and Takoradi. The rolling stock is good and, like so many tro-tros and buses, was imported second-hand from Germany (look for some of the original signage on carriages and engines). But the trains creep along and are much slower and no cheaper than motorised transport. Unless you're a train enthusiast, the only line likely to interest you is the one between Kumasi and Takoradi – for more details, see the Sekondi-Takoradi Getting There & Away section later in this chapter).

CAR & MOTORCYCLE

Major roads in Ghana are generally in good condition apart from a badly potholed stretch between Kumasi and Techiman on the highway linking Kumasi and Tamale. Avoid it by taking a dogleg via Sunyani. Nearly all secondary roads are laterite or dirt.

Petrol costs US$0.35 per litre and diesel US$0.15.

BOAT

The *Yapei Queen* makes scheduled passenger runs up Lake Volta from Akosombo to Yeji, stopping at the small town of Kete-Krachi and villages along the way. It departs Akosombo on Monday at 4 pm, and arrives in Yeji 24 hours later. The southbound service leaves Yeji on Wednesday around 4 am and arrives in Akosombo on Thursday at 9 am. In principle, you can buy tickets in advance, but you may find yourself having to queue: get there early. A berth in a 1st class double cabin with bathroom and air-con costs US$20. Reserve in advance, as there are only two of them. A 2nd/3rd class ticket is US$9/8. The journey winds past beautiful coastal hills and is a great alternative to road travel.

The *Yapei Queen* also makes occasional unscheduled cargo runs to Buipe (US$24 in 1st class, US$13 2nd class and US$9 3rd

class). In addition, the *Buipe Queen* makes unscheduled cargo runs (3rd class only) to Yeji and/or Buipe. You sleep on deck directly above the engines, so pack earplugs. You'll also need to bring all food, because there's none on board. And don't forget the mosquito repellent!

From Yeji, two ferries run daily to Makongo (US$4), from where you can get onward transport to Tamale. A tro-tro between Buipe and Tamale costs US$2.

Bookings for all boats can be made at the dock, or through the Volta Lake Transport Co at Akosombo port (☎ 686) or in Accra (☎ 665300).

ORGANISED TOURS

Several travel agencies in Accra provide all-inclusive tours within Ghana. For more details, see under Information in the Accra section later in this chapter. Popular destinations are Kumasi and the surrounding area, the Akosombo Dam and Lake Volta, Mole National Park, Kakum National Park and the coastal forts.

Accra

Accra is a friendly, lively city, more interesting for its people than its places. It has several animated markets, an Arts Centre for those interested in local handicrafts, some attractive modern prestige buildings and an active nightlife. It's also safer than many African capitals.

With 1.7 million people, Accra is big and sprawling. Business and government offices are spread all over town – perhaps a legacy of the days when it was a scattering of villages controlled by seven branches of the Ga tribe, each with its own chief.

Orientation

The action area of Accra is bounded by the semicircular Ring Rd, whose four major junctions, or circles (from west to east, Lamptey, Kwame Nkrumah, usually known simply as Nkrumah or just 'Circle', Sankara

GHANA

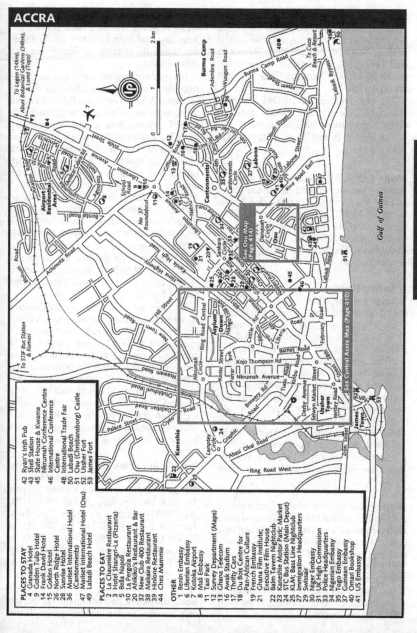

ACCRA

Gulf of Guinea

PLACES TO STAY
4 Granada Hotel
9 Golden Tulip Hotel
14 Frank David Hotel
15 State House & Kwame
26 North Ridge Hotel
28 Golden Hotel
36 Sunrise Hotel
Mariset International Hotel
(Cantonments)
47 Mariset International Hotel (Osu)
49 Labadi Beach Hotel

PLACES TO EAT
2 La Chaumière Restaurant
3 Hotel Shangri-La (Pizzeria)
5 Bella Napoli
10 La Pergola Restaurant
20 Afrikiko's Restaurant & Bar
32 New Club 400 Restaurant
38 Makaira Restaurant
39 Hinlone Restaurant
44 Chez Mammie

OTHER
1 Benin Embassy
6 Liberian Embassy
7 Kotoka Airport
8 Mali Embassy
11 Taxi Park
12 Survey Department (Maps)
13 Ghana Telecom
16 Awak Stadium
17 Thrifty Cars
18 Du Bois Centre for
Pan-African Culture
21 French Embassy
22 Ghana Film Institute;
Executive Film House
23 Balm Tavern Nightclub
24 Kaneshie Motor Park; Market
25 STC Bus Station (Main Depot)
27 KLM; Bass Line Nightclub
29 Immigration Headquarters
31 Swissair
30 Niger Embassy
31 UK High Commission
33 Police Headquarters
34 Nigerian Embassy
35 Togo Embassy
37 Guinean Embassy
40 Omari Bookshop
41 US Embassy

42 Ryan's Irish Pub
43 Shell Station
45 State House & Kwame
Nkrumah Conference Centre
46 International Conference
Centre
48 International Trade Fair
50 Labadi Beach
51 Osu (Christiansborg) Castle
52 Usher Fort
53 James Fort

and Danquah), are major landmarks and points of reference when people are giving directions. Much of the commercial district is along Nkrumah Ave and Kojo Thompson Rd, two parallel north-south highways which connect the Nkrumah Circle area and the city centre.

The fashionable area of Osu, south of Danquah Circle, is rich in restaurants, night-clubs, supermarkets and chic shops.

The airport is north-east of town, 8km from the centre.

Maps You've got a choice of two maps for finding your way around Accra: the Mobil and the Shell maps. The better one is pro-duced by Mobil. It's the same as the Shell version (see Planning in the Facts for the Visitor section earlier) but with a more up-to-date key. You'll find it at major Mobil service stations.

Information

Tourist Information The Ghana Tourist Board office (☎ 231817), open from 8 am to 5 pm Monday to Friday, is on the ground floor of a large grey building, 50m down Education Close, off Barnes Rd. The staff are friendly and willing but not too clued up. Among the items on sale are a tourist map of Ghana and Accra, a comprehensive cata-logue of hotels throughout the country and an informative booklet on popular festivals.

No Worries! The Indispensable Insiders' Guide to Accra, compiled and published by the North American Women's Association and targeted primarily at long-term visitors, is a mine of practical information about Accra.

Money Barclays (☎ 664901), on High St sells and cashes travellers cheques and gives cash advances on Visa and MasterCard. Scantravel (☎ 664456) on High St is the offi-cial representative of American Express. You'll find forexes all over town and espe-cially around the main post office and along Kojo Thompson Rd. For more details on changing money, refer to Money in the Facts for the Visitor section.

Post & Communications The main post office in Accra is open from 8 am to 5 pm weekdays and from 9 am to 2 pm on Satur-day. Its poste restante service is free and quite reliable.

International phone calls can be made from the Ghana Telecom offices on High St in central Accra or on Nehru Rd (still known to locals by its old name of Switchback Rd) in the Cantonments area. They're open daily from 7 am to 8 pm. If you're in Accra, you can also direct dial 24 hours a day with phonecards purchased at Ghana Telecom offices or at several other outlets around the city. They cost US$2.50 for 25 units, US$5 for 50 and US$9 for 100. An increasing number of public phones around town accept them. You'll need a minimum value of US$8 on a phonecard to make an international call.

You can send and receive faxes from the post office in High St; their fax number is ☎ 665960 or ☎ 662680. You can also phone and fax at the many communications centres around town.

The Internet Cafe, opposite the Niagara Hotel on Kojo Thompson Rd, charges US$5 per hour online and prints out incoming messages at US$0.15 a page. Or, you could combine browsing with bratwurst and a stein of beer at Aquarius, a German theme pub that also offers Internet and email ser-vices. Open from 11 am to midnight, they charge US$5 per online hour and incoming messages are free. The slick business centres at the Labadi Beach and other major hotels are markedly more expensive.

Travel Agencies & Tour Operators Travel companies with a proven track record for arranging local tours include Expert Travel & Tours on Ring Rd East (☎ 775498, fax 773937) near the US embassy, Speedway Travel & Tours (☎ 227744, fax 226188) on Tackie Tawiah Ave, Black Beauty Tours on Kwame Nkrumah Ave south of Farrar Ave (☎ 227078, fax 220062) and M & J Travel & Tours (☎ 773153, fax 774338), on 11th Lane.

Bookshops The best bookshop – in fact the only one that's more than adequate – is the one at the University of Legon, 14km north-east of the town centre. Omari bookshop, south-east of Danquah Circle, on Ring Rd East carries a few books on Ghana plus an unimpressive range of British and American publications. For foreign magazines and newspapers, go to the bookshops at major hotels or try the supermarkets in Osu.

Medical Services The best hospitals in Accra are private. The North Ridge Hospital (☎ 227328) has staff on 24 hour call. The SSNIT Hospital on Cantonments Rd in Osu also has a good reputation.

Three well-stocked pharmacies in Accra are Kingsway Chemist on Knutsford Ave near TCU Motors, Ghana Drug House on Asafoatsee Nettey Rd (opposite the ice company) and Circle Pharmacy on Fourth Circular Rd.

Dangers & Annoyances For such a large city, Accra has relatively few pickpockets. All the same, be on your guard around Independence Square, the old James Town area, Nkrumah Circle and the beaches; where muggings have occurred after dark.

Be particularly cautious of taking photos near Osu Castle, the President's office, which bristles with nervy soldiers who may view you as a spy or, worse, a journalist.

National Museum

The National Museum (☎ 221633), on Barnes Rd, is open from 9 am to 5.30 pm daily. Entry is US$1 plus an optional US$0.50 photography fee. A superbly documented exhibition, 'The Arts of Power', displays ceremonial chieftaincy regalia, such as royal stools, umbrellas, kente cloth, gilded sandals, swords and linguist's staffs. All these accessories reinforce the chief's authority and accentuate his physical presence.

Also on the main floor is some fine brass-work, including the famous Ashanti weights for measuring gold, and cabinets explaining local iron smelting techniques, the lost wax method for casting metal sculptures and how glass beads are made. Smaller displays feature masks, drums and wooden statues and the artefacts of other African cultures.

Outside is an armless statue of Kwame Nkrumah, resembling an African Venus de Milo. Torn from its pedestal outside Parliament House by rioters during the 1966 coup, it was re-erected in the museum garden many years later. It stands as a symbol of his partial rehabilitation, in the company of other relics and symbols of the past.

In the grounds is a pleasant restaurant (closed Sunday) which serves tasty Ghanaian dishes at lunch time (see Places to Eat for more details).

Independence Square

Independence Square, sometimes called Blackstar Square, is a huge parade ground (it can hold 30,000 people) backed by the sea. It marks the spot where, in colonial times, three ex-servicemen were shot while attempting to present grievances to the governor in a peaceful demonstration.

It is to Accra what Red Square is to Moscow. Its focal point is Independence Arch, a monolithic replica of the Arc de Triomphe (the parallel goes further – there's even an Eternal Flame of African Liberation flickering). The square, the huge stadium 200m to the north and the State House and Kwame Nkrumah Conference Centre (built in 1965 for the OAU conference), half a kilometre to the north-west of the stadium, are examples of Nkrumah's flamboyant style and vision. But the Big Man doesn't have a monopoly on prestigious buildings. Just behind the stadium and on Castle Rd across from the State House is the fine International Conference Centre, built as the venue for the 1991 Nonaligned Nations Conference.

From the square, towards the ocean, you can see Osu Castle. Built by the Danes around 1659 and originally called Christiansborg Castle, it's now the seat of government and is off limits to the public.

Du Bois Centre for Pan-African Culture

Dr Du Bois, an African American academic, champion of civil rights and African unity and adviser to Nkrumah, spent the last two years of his life in this villa, after having assumed Ghanaian nationality. His tomb and that of his wife are in the grounds. The Centre (☎ 773127), on Link Rd in Cantonments, is open from 8.30 am to 4.30 pm on weekdays, from 11 am to 4.30 pm, Saturday, and from 2 to 4 pm on Sunday.

It contains his library, as well as numerous memorabilia of his world travels and a photographic display of leading black personalities and political leaders. (Check whether the now deeply discredited Winnie Mandela is still there, smiling down.) The Centre organises occasional public lectures on Africa, jazz concerts and other musical performances which are advertised in the local press.

Kwame Nkrumah Memorial Park

Between the highway and the shore, diagonally opposite Parliament House, is Kwame Nkrumah Memorial Park, laid out in the early 1990s as a gesture of rehabilitation. Kwame Nkrumah's effigy, carved big, with arm outstretched and pointing the way forward, stands beneath a huge marble pile. With the playing fountains, the swathe of grass and the twin ranks of musicians at his feet, it's all on the monumental scale that he favoured and would have appreciated. The gardens are open, in principle, from 10 am to 6 pm. Admission, including an informative guided tour, is US$1 plus an optional US$1 for a camera and US$2 for a video.

National Theatre

The impressive Chinese-built National Theatre, on Liberia Rd, looms against the sky like the keel of a huge schooner. The inside's equally impressive. Check the billboards for forthcoming activities. One regular weekly event is the Sunday afternoon Concert Party (admission a bargain US$1), a Ghanaian music hall, or vaudeville, with sketches, songs and stand-up comedians. Even though most of it's in Twi, it's a fun afternoon out, where the audience reaction is as interesting as what's happening on stage.

Markets

At the city's major market, **Makola Market**, you'll find just about anything you might conceivably want. The market's particularly good for beads and fabrics (see also Shopping later in this section), for which the shops around the market and along Kojo Thompson Rd, Selwyn Market St and Derby Ave are also promising.

Accra's second major market, **Kaneshie Market**, on the western side of the city, on Graphic Rd, is rather more orderly than Makola but equally vital. The 1st level is for foodstuffs while the upper level is where you find textiles.

The **Obruni Wa Wu Market** specialises in second-hand goods, especially clothing. In Akan, *obruni wa wu* means 'the white man has died' and refers to the bale upon bale of used clothing, cast off and donated by conscience-salving westerners and sold here for a snip. The narrow lanes around Tema station are probably the largest used-goods store you've ever seen. You can buy a rumpled T-shirt for less than it would cost you to clean a dirty one. Saturday and Wednesday morning, when the new shipments of clothes arrive, is the best, but most crowded, time to shop here.

Even more interesting is **Timber Market** on Hansen Rd in the industrial area of Ussher Town. The fetish section, with its animal skulls, live and dead reptiles, strange powders, charms, bells, shakers, leopard skins, teeth, porcupine quills and juju figurines, is fascinating. People here are very friendly, but they'll also be curious about why you've come. Finding it is difficult without help from locals.

Arts Centre

The Arts Centre, also called the Centre for National Culture, is Accra's largest craft market. You'll find kente cloth, Ashanti sandals, beads, masks, woodcarvings, drums, brass and leatherwork.

You can see kente cloth weavers and woodcarvers at work. There's also an art gallery (closed Saturday) which displays and sells paintings by local artists. On Thursday to Sunday afternoons there's usually entertainment, including music, drumming, traditional dance and theatre. For what's on, check the chalkboard at the main entrance.

Other Things to See

Heading west from the Arts Centre, you pass, on your right, the original **Parliament House** and the **Supreme Court**. On the left is the **Anglican Holy Trinity Cathedral** (drop in for a look at its magnificent wooden barrel-vaulted roof). Continuing westward, you reach the vibrant yet dilapidated quarter of **James Town** and **James Fort**, which is now a prison and off limits. Next to it is an old lighthouse, 31m high and still in use.

Beaches

There are some beautiful sandy beaches near Accra, but remember that the tides and undertow are killers and countless tourists and Ghanaians, often competent swimmers, have drowned offshore. Labadi Beach resigns itself to a fatality or two every year.

Labadi Beach stretches eastward for several kilometres from the Labadi Beach Hotel. Just west of the hotel is a section open to the public. A bit further east is the main public beach. It's protected with a well guarded entrance, but crime is still a problem; never leave your belongings unattended. Because the place is so popular, it tends to be a haunt of tourist leeches and dope peddlars, so take care. You need to be wary of some of the Rastas, even though others are friendly and interesting to talk to – a case of pot luck, so to speak. There are several shaded places for eating and drinking plus showers and a lifeguard. The entrance fee is US$0.75.

Many local expats prefer **Coco Beach** in Nungua, 7km further east on the road to Tema and easily accessible by minibus or shared taxi. It's rarely crowded on weekdays and you can get food, drink and lodging at the Coco Beach Resort, which overlooks the shore. Watch your belongings; theft is a problem here as well. Both beaches are hideously overcrowded at weekends. If you have wheels and want somewhere more se-

cluded, head west of Accra to the unmarked beaches at Mile 13, Mile 14 and Mile 16 near Kokrobite.

Activities

Most of the top end hotels have pools which you can use for a daily fee, usually around US$3.

Places to Stay – Budget

Camping The best place for camping (US$4 per person) is the *Coco Beach Resort*, 7km east of Labadi Beach, on the eastern outskirts of town.

Hostels & Student Accommodation
The *YMCA* (☎ 224700) and the nearby *YWCA* (☎ 220567), on opposite sides of Castle Rd, are your cheapest options if you don't mind bunking with strangers.

The YMCA accepts only men and charges US$2 for a bed in a dormitory. Beds are usually available unless there's a large course going on.

Facilities at the YWCA, which normally only has rooms during school vacations and only accepts women, aren't as good. A bed costs US$2 per person in a four bed dormitory or US$3 in a double. It also has one double apartment with bathroom and small kitchen for US$8 per person. On the plus side, the YWCA has an excellent, moderately priced restaurant, open to all.

Two other vacation-time possibilities are the *University of Ghana* (☎ 275381) in Legon on the northern fringes of Accra, 14km from the centre, and *Accra Polytechnic* on Barnes Rd in the centre of town.

At both, student dormitory rooms become available from mid-July to the end of September, provided that the academic year hasn't been prolonged because of student disruption. The cost is about US$5 a person. Inquire at the office of student affairs at the university or polytechnic.

Hotels & Guesthouses – City Centre & Asylum Down Area If you want a rock-bottom priced hotel in the city centre, shack up at the dilapidated *Take Care Lodge*

GHANA

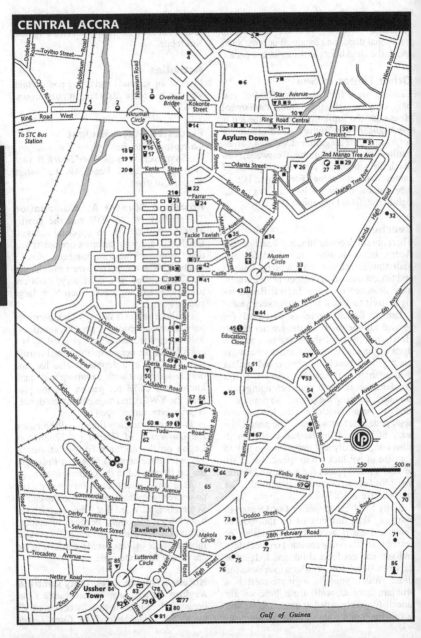

CENTRAL ACCRA

CENTRAL ACCRA

PLACES TO STAY
4   King David Hotel
5   C'est Si Bon Hotel
7   Kokomlele Hotel
9   New Haven Hotel
12 Kob Lodge
13 Marymart Hotel
22 Niagara Hotel
25 Asylum Down Hotel
28 Lemon Lodge
29 Korkdam Hotel
31 Gye Nyame Hotel
33 YMCA
34 Beverley Hills Hotel
37 St George's Hotel
38 Crown Prince Hotel
39 Hotel de California
40 Date Hotel
41 YWCA
44 Calvary Methodist
    Church Guesthouse
47 Nkrumah Memorial Hotel
56 Bellview Hotel
60 Gasotel
67 Novotel
84 Take Care Lodge

PLACES TO EAT
8   Tasha Food
10 Paloma Shopping Mall;
    Paloma Hotel
11 Bus Stop Restaurant
16 Terra Nova
    Restaurant & Bar
19 Wok Inn

26 Spicy Chicken
50 Elbi's Snack Bar
52 Best Cuisine
53 Antie Mary's Chop Bar
57 Cosmos Restaurant
58 Variety Chop Bar
82 Wato Bar & Restaurant
85 Smartstyle Kitchen

OTHER
1   Neoplan Motor Park
2   Tro-Tro Park
3   Taxi Park (for Labadi, Airport
    & Osu)
6   Accra Technical Training
    Centre (ATTC)
14 Air Afrique
15 Barclays Bank
17 Piccadilly Spot;
    Kilimanjaro
18 Container Spot
20 The Loom
21 Internet Cafe
23 White Bell; Glen's Bar
24 Miracle Mirage Nightclub
27 Burkina Faso Embassy
30 Alitalia; South African
    Airways
32 Lufthansa
35 Speedway Travel & Tours;
    & Avis Car Hire
36 Catholic Cathedral
42 Trust Cars Ltd
43 National Museum;
    Edvy Restaurant

45 Tourist Office
46 Nigeria Airways
48 Vicma Travel & Tours
49 British Airways; Balkan
    Airlines; Aeroflot
51 Standard Chartered Bank
54 British Council
55 Accra Polytechnic
59 Standard Chartered Bank
61 Cocoa House; Ghana
    Airways; Air Afrique;
    Air Ivoire; Ethiopian Airlines
62 Police Station
63 Train Station
64 Tudu Station
65 Makola Market
66 STC Buses (East)
68 National Theatre
69 Tema Station
70 Stadium
71 Independence Square
72 Arts Centre (Centre for
    National Culture)
73 Rex Cinema
74 Parliament House
75 Kwame Nkrumah
    Memorial Park
76 Labadi Lorry Park
77 Ghana Telecom
78 Standard Chartered Bank
79 Barclays Bank
80 Anglican Cathedral
81 Scantravel
83 Central Post Office
86 Independence Arch

(☎ 667064) on Lutterodt Circle near the post office. Singles/doubles with bathroom cost US$3/4. Even if you're on your own, go the extra dollar for a double, which are much bigger than the poky singles.

The sober, spotlessly clean **Calvary Methodist Church Guesthouse** (☎ 234507) has a notice in every room reminding that 'guests are expected to conform to a standard of conduct synonymous with decorum'. On the top floor of Reverend Gadiel Acquaah House on the eastern side of Barnes Rd, it's a great bargain and often full. Singles/doubles with fan and bathroom cost US$5/9 or US$8/11 with air-con. Breakfast is US$1 and a filling lunch or dinner is US$2.

The jury's out on the **Hotel de California** (☎ 226199), on the corner of Kojo Thompson and Castle Rds, a long-time travellers favourite. For some, it's friendly, lively and full of character. For others, it comes over as run-down and none too clean. What's certain is that it remains a great place to make contact with other travellers. For the same reason, it's an equally popular haunt of touts and professional clingers-on. Rooms with fans and shared bathroom cost US$6. Across the road, the **Crown Prince Hotel** (☎ 225381) has similar, somewhat smaller singles/doubles for US$6/7. They also have three rooms with air-con and bathroom which are a particular bargain at US$10.

Nearby, at the tranquil *Date Hotel* (☎ 228200) there's a pleasant interior patio where you can relax and switch off from the town. Singles/doubles with fan are US$5/6 or US$7 with bathroom.

The *Gasotel*, on Tudu Rd, is clean, comfortable and recommended. It charges US$7 for large, well furnished rooms with fan and bathroom, some with bathtub.

Asylum Down is a quieter area for budget hotels and is easily accessible by shared taxi. You also tend to get better value for your money out here. A long-standing travellers favourite is the clean, friendly *Lemon Lodge* (☎ 227857), on 2nd Mango Tree Ave, where rooms with fan and shared bathroom cost US$7. At the nearby *Asylum Down Hotel* (☎ 233104), on Odanta St, rooms are large and have overhead fans, comfortable armchairs, desks and clean shared bathrooms. The thatched-roof bar out the back is pleasant for a drink.

The *Marymart Hotel* (☎ 221011, email marymart@ghana.com) on Ring Rd Central is an endearingly disorganised, exceptionally friendly place where large rooms with fan, table and a couple of easy chairs cost US$9 or US$11 with bathroom.

Just north of Ring Rd Central, the *New Haven Hotel* (☎ 222053), on a dirt road which runs parallel to and between Star Ave and Ring Rd Central, has singles/doubles with bathroom for US$5/7. It also has a few air-con rooms for US$13. With rooms set around a quiet, green courtyard, it's a pleasant place to beach up. Nearby, the friendly *Kokomlele Hotel* is a favourite of upcountry VSOs. Singles/ doubles are US$3/4 or US$5 with bathroom. It has a simple restaurant which serves breakfast and lunch (US$2) and a colour TV blares on the patio, where you can get cold drinks.

Hotels – Elsewhere A clean room with fan and bathroom costs US$10 at the *Frank David Hotel*, near No 37 Roundabout on Liberation Ave. It's the place to head if you want to make contact with the Peace Corps, many of whose volunteers use it as a base when passing through the capital.

Places to Stay – Mid-Range
City Centre & Asylum Down Area At the *Bellview* (☎ 667730), on Tudu Crescent Rd, singles with fan and shared bathroom cost US$6.50, although the reception staff, if you can galvanise them into speech, will probably assure you that they're all taken. Doubles with bathroom cost US$11 with fan and US$14 with air-con. Avoid the hotel's dimly lit restaurant unless you've an evening to waste. You'll be better off materially, if not financially, at *St George's Hotel* (☎ 224699), one block north of Castle Rd, on Amusudai Rd. It has a restaurant and carpeted singles/doubles, all with large beds, air-con, refrigerator, comfortable chairs and decent bathroom for US$20.50/23.50.

The new *Beverley Hills Hotel* (☎ 224042), on Samora Machel Rd, is especially good value – at least for the moment while it's building up custom. Large air-con doubles with TV and fridge cost US$18 while even larger ones, which will take three or four people, are US$22. Will it last? Write and let us know – and avoid their absurdly exploitative breakfasts at US$3.50.

The equally new, well managed *Niagara Hotel* (☎ 230118, fax 230119, email niagara @ighmail.com), on Kojo Thompson Rd, is more upmarket but represents good value for money in its bracket. Singles/doubles with air-con, TV and fridge cost US$45/65 and doubles also have a kitchenette.

In Asylum Down, all rooms at the *Korkdam Hotel* (☎ 223221), next door to Lemon Lodge on 2nd Mango Tree Ave, have bathrooms. Singles cost US$13 with fan and US$14 with air-con. Doubles with air-con cost between US$20 and US$23. It has a shady terrace where you can get drinks and excellent kebabs, plus a decent restaurant inside.

It's in better shape than the run-down *Kob Lodge* (☎ 227647, fax 233066) on Ring Rd Central. But the place is clean, the staff are friendly and it's popular and often full. Singles/doubles cost US$11/16 or US$16/20 with air-con.

The *Gye Nyame Hotel* (☎ 223321, fax 226486), on 5th Crescent, is warmly recommended. Its singles/doubles are great value for money at US$40/47. Each has air-con, satellite TV, fridge and tiled bathroom with bathtub. The price includes breakfast and the staff are particularly pleasant.

On the northern side of Ring Rd Central, the *Paloma Hotel* (*☎/fax 231815*), above the Paloma Shopping Mall, has relatively small singles for US$45 and large singles/doubles for US$55/60, all furnished with TV and fridge.

Further north, 300m from the Ring Rd overpass, the *King David Hotel* (*☎ 229832, fax 233697*) has singles/doubles, all with air-con, fridge and TV, for US$45/55. It also has a decent restaurant and a small, rather soulless bar.

North of Ring Rd and Asylum Down, *C'est Si Bon Hotel*, north of the Accra Technical Training Centre (known to all as the ATTC) in Kokomlemle, is very good value although (perhaps because) it's a little away from the action. All rooms have a bathroom. Singles/doubles with fan cost US$9/11 and ones with air-con and TV cost US$16/20.

Osu In Osu, the small *Taj Guest House* (*☎ 778760, fax 779675, email harryinu@ africaonline.gh.com*), on 11th Lane, is a hyper-friendly place. Affiliated to the Tandoor restaurant, rooms with breakfast cost, in principle, US$60. This said, Harry, the owner, will usually cheerfully concede a considerable discount. Rooms have fridge and satellite TV, and the laundry service and Internet access is also free for guests.

Coco Beach The *Coco Beach Resort* (*☎ 766524*) is 7km east of Labadi Beach Hotel and is usually full at weekends. Singles/doubles cost US$22/24 or US$34/39 with air-con. The resort has a squash court, beach and restaurant.

Places to Stay – Top End
Most hotels in this category accept American Express, Diners and Visa cards, although MasterCard is less widespread.

Accra's only five-star accommodation is at the *Labadi Beach Hotel* (*☎ 772501, fax

772520*) on the eastern outskirts of town overlooking the ocean. Singles/doubles cost US$230/260. One star down is the *Golden Tulip Hotel* (*☎ 775360, fax 775361*), on Liberation Ave, near the airport. Singles cost between US$200 and US$220 while doubles range from US$225 to US$245. The other four star place is the French-managed *Novotel* (*☎ 667546, fax 667533*), near the town centre on Barnes Rd, with singles/doubles at US$148/172.

There are also several good *Mariset International* hotels: those in the Cantonments area (*☎ 777998, fax 773154*), on Wuogon Rd, and Osu (*☎ 774434, fax 772085*), two blocks west of the intersection of Labadi Rd and Ring Rd East, charge US$82/88 for singles/doubles, including breakfast. At around one-third of the price of the city's two smartest hotels, the Mariset establishments are all modern, comfortable and give excellent service.

The *Granada Hotel* (*☎ 775344, fax 774880*), where singles/doubles are US$50/80, is out near the airport, on the corner of Liberation Ave and Wide St. It's small and well managed and has a good restaurant and squash court.

The *North Ridge Hotel* (*☎ 225809, fax 221417*) is another well managed place with big rooms, a pleasant ambience and a good restaurant. Singles/doubles cost US$56/60. Rooms at the *Sunrise Hotel* (*☎ 224575, fax 227656*) are superior and range between US$59 and US$83. Both are on 8th Ave Extension in a quiet residential area.

Places to Eat
Cheap Eats All day and all over Accra, you'll find roadside stands serving coffee, hot chocolate, omelettes and bread. There are chop houses and modest cafes throughout town, many open only from lunch time to late afternoon.

City Centre & Asylum Down Area For *street food*, particularly in the evenings, it's hard to beat the vendors around Nkrumah Circle. During the day, there's a good selection in the area around the Arts Centre.

GHANA

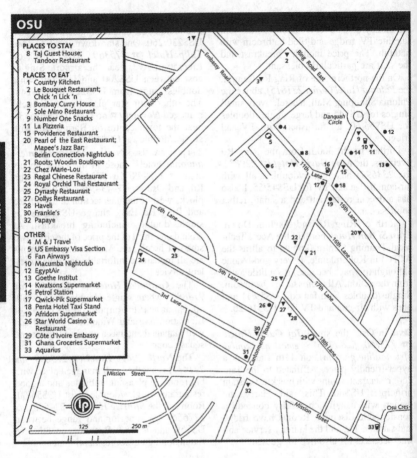

OSU

PLACES TO STAY
8 Taj Guest House;
   Tandoor Restaurant

PLACES TO EAT
1 Country Kitchen
2 Le Bouquet Restaurant;
   Chick 'n Lick 'n
3 Bombay Curry House
7 Sole Mino Restaurant
9 Number One Snacks
11 La Pizzeria
15 Providence Restaurant
20 Pearl of the East Restaurant;
   Mapee's Jazz Bar;
   Berlin Connection Nightclub
21 Roots; Woodin Boutique
22 Chez Marie-Lou
23 Regal Chinese Restaurant
24 Royal Orchid Thai Restaurant
25 Dynasty Restaurant
27 Dollys Restaurant
28 Haveli
30 Frankie's
32 Papaye

OTHER
4 M & J Travel
5 US Embassy Visa Section
6 Fan Airways
10 Macumba Nightclub
12 EgyptAir
13 Goethe Institut
14 Kwatsons Supermarket
16 Petrol Station
17 Qwick-Pik Supermarket
18 Penta Hotel Taxi Stand
19 Afridom Supermarket
26 Star World Casino &
   Restaurant
29 Côte d'Ivoire Embassy
31 Ghana Groceries Supermarket
33 Aquarius

Danquah Circle

0   125   250 m

Just north of Lutterodt Circle is **Smart-style Kitchen**. It has hamburgers and a variety of African dishes for about US$1.50, plus more expensive selections, including spaghetti and beef kebabs. South of the circle is the friendly, engagingly down-at-heel **Wato Bar & Restaurant**, on the 2nd floor of a triangular building. At lunch time, you can get a decent meal on the balcony and watch the crowds below. In the evening, you can sit out and enjoy a drink. It's closed at weekends. At night, you'd be

wise to take a taxi home since the area's not the safest after dark.

In the Kojo Thompson Rd area, **Elbi's Snack Bar**, on Liberia Rd Sth, does good rice and sauce dishes in a brisk and clean setting. The **YWCA** has an excellent, modestly priced restaurant, operating from 7.30 am to 5 pm, and open to all. The **White Bell** is a great, unpretentious roof-top place and is warmly recommended. Shaded and one floor up, it catches the breeze. It's schizophrenic; a quiet spot for midday lunch and, if you pick the right night, a throbbing dinner and dancing venue. Nearby, and just off Nkrumah Circle, the cheap and cheerful *Terra Nova* is equally good for a meal or a drink.

On Ring Rd Central, the long-standing *Bus Stop Restaurant* is clean, cheerful and efficient and attracts a friendly young crowd. It's open every day from 9 am to 10 pm. Nearby, *Spicy Chicken* serves chicken and snacks for under US$2.50. At the *Paloma Shopping Mall* on Ring Rd Central you can wander in traffic-free calm and choose from a variety of cuisines, including Ghanaian, Italian and Chinese and even Mexican, which is on offer at *Champs Sports Bar*. Also here is *Life Westward of Eden*, one of the very few places in town serving strictly vegetarian fare. Just a little north-west of the shopping mall, the jolly women who run *Tasha Food* dispense delicious food and warmhearted chat.

Osu There's plenty of choice in the Osu area; on Cantonments Rd you'll find lots of places. *Number One Snacks* on Danquah Circle is popular for drinks, including draught beer, and snacks. *Roots* is a slick American-style burger and salads joint which also does fish and chips, chawarma and simple grills. It's a place for night owls and early birds and is open weekdays from 7 am (when they serve mega breakfasts) to after midnight and around the clock on Friday and Saturday. Try their special Sunday morning Lebanese breakfast. *Frankie's* is something of an 'in place' and great for pastries and ice cream. *Papaye* provides a takeaway service and features what many claim to be the best charcoal-grilled chicken in Accra. The other contender for the town's champion chicken joint is *Chick 'n Lick 'n* (honest!), away from Cantonments Rd, on Ring Rd East, which specialises in roast takeaways.

African Many venues, such as Afrikiko or Country Kitchen, while open for dinner, serve African dishes only at lunch time.

City Centre & Asylum Down Area You can combine a visit to the National Museum with lunch at the excellent *Edvy Restaurant* in its grounds. Its special Wednesday buffet is an enjoyable way to sample a range of Ghanaian dishes.

Osu For the best Ghanaian restaurant in Accra, head for the *Country Kitchen* (☎ 229107) on Roberto Rd, a lunch time favourite during the week, open from noon to 10 pm, and well known to every taxi driver. The atmosphere's pleasant, the service is good, the food is fresh and it's excellent value. Ghanaian dishes cost between US$2.50 and US$4.50 and seafood dishes, including lobster thermidor, range from US$5.50 to US$9.

Another good place for reasonably priced Ghanaian food is *Providence Restaurant*, on Cantonments Rd, which has a small but tasty menu of African specialities and more expensive European dishes. It's open until 6 pm daily except Sunday.

Elsewhere *Afrikiko's* on Liberation Ave, open from 10 am to midnight, is a popular expat haunt. At once restaurant, bar and night time disco, it serves Ghanaian dishes for around US$3 and continental food for US$5 or so.

The precinct of a fuel station doesn't immediately sound like a promising location for a restaurant. But the African food at *La Pergola Restaurant*, beside the Elf station just north of No 37 Roundabout, is surprisingly good. It serves Ghanaian food (in the evenings as well) plus French and a few Ivoirian and Togolese dishes.

Asian & Indian Accra has some of the best Chinese restaurants in West Africa, and all are open every day.

Asylum Down Area If price is your major concern, the small *Wok Inn* on Nkrumah Ave is the cheapest and also does takeaways.

Osu The *Pearl of the East Restaurant* (☎ 774907) in Osu is also reasonable. Its outdoor area has music and a more casual ambience than the interior.

Two rivals for the title of best Chinese restaurant in town are the vast *Dynasty Restaurant* (☎ 775496), which features Peking cuisine, on Cantonments Rd, and, just around the corner, on 5th Lane, the *Regal* (☎ 773386). Its decor may not be as sumptuous as the Dynasty's (in fact it's positively tacky) but the food's just as succulent. It usually has a healthy number of Chinese customers – always a good sign.

The attractive *Royal Orchid Thai Restaurant* (☎ 662993), on 4th Lane in Osu, is in an old converted house. With dishes in the US$5 to US$10 range it doesn't come cheap, but the quality's well worth the price.

There's a trio of excellent Indian restaurants within walking distance of each other in Osu. *Haveli* (☎ 774714), on 18th Lane, is the favourite of favourites among those in the know. Main dishes cost between US$ 3.50 and US$7. You can also eat very well and rather more cheaply at the *Tandoor*, on 11th Lane. If you fancy a blowout, the *Bombay Curry House* does an all-you-can-eat buffet for US$5.50.

Elsewhere The attractive *Hinlone Restaurant* on Sithole Rd in the Labone area is many diners' favourite. It's wise to reserve in the evenings, since it's usually packed after 9 pm. *Chez Lien* (☎ 775356), in the Airport Residential Area, has magnificent Vietnamese fare, even if the portions are small. It also serves good French food.

European The acknowledged finest Italian restaurant in town is the *Bella Napoli* (☎ 778077), in the Airport Residential Area, on Volta St. It's expensive, but the cuisine is wonderful and includes a range of vegetarian dishes.

In Osu, try the recently opened *La Pizzeria*, on Ring Rd East. Nearby is the *Sole Mino* restaurant, on 11th Lane, which is equally new and establishing a reputation for itself.

If you have a hankering for German food, check the *Aquarius* on Osu Crescent. It has an extensive menu and good food, especially the potato salad and sausages.

Draught and German bottled beer are available, and the pub has a pool table, pinball, darts and table football. It also offers connection to the Internet.

You can enjoy fine French cuisine in Accra, albeit at a price. In the Airport Residential Area, opposite the Hotel Shangri-La, *La Chaumière* (☎ 772408), is a gourmet's delight, as is the French-owned *Makaira Restaurant* (☎ 778266) in Labone.

In Osu, on Cantonments Rd, you'll find *Chez Mammie* (☎ 775670), a small cosy place where reservations are essential at weekends, and the Swiss-run *Chez Marie-Lou* (☎ 227975), which has similar fare and prices but is less intimate. Try, in particular, their steaks or lobster.

Le Bouquet in Osu and *Chez Lien* in Airport Residential Area also offer a range of well prepared French dishes.

Lebanese Lebanese food is the longest standing of Accra's ethnic cuisines. The Syrian and Lebanese are as active in the restaurant business as they are in most other fields of commerce in town. You usually find a selection of tasty Middle Eastern dishes on a more wide-ranging 'continental' menu.

One of the best places in town for Levantine food is *New Club 400 Restaurant* (☎ 223723), which is in a fine old house on Independence Ave, just off Ring Rd East. You could easily make a meal out of the mezze alone. It's open daily except Sunday lunch time.

Both *Le Bouquet* (Osu) and the restaurant at the *Granada Hotel* (Airport Residential Area) have a range of Lebanese dishes on their menus, as does *Paloma Snack* in the Paloma Shopping Mall on Ring Rd Central.

Entertainment

Bars Most of the places we list here also feature in the Places to Eat section.

For atmosphere, day or night, head for the cheap and charmingly faded *Wato Bar & Restaurant* near the main post office. You can sit on the balcony and watch life pass by below. Take care here after dark. *Afrikiko* on Liberation Ave, about 300m

ASAFO AND POSUBAN

In the Fanti villages clustered around the coastal forts in Ghana, you may stumble across strange groupings of painted, sculpted figures representing animals, European ships, policemen, soldiers and even Adam and Eve. Before reaching for your camera, make sure you ask permission from the elders (you may well be asked to contribute to a

Top: Figures on a posuban at Elmina, perhaps representing Adam and Eve. Photograph by Miles Roddis.

Bottom: A striking posuban at Anomabu in the shape of a European ship.

libation, for which read a bottle of the local hooch). For these are posubans, which serve as religious shrines and gathering places for Asafo company meetings and rituals, while the often fantastical figures identify and advertise each company.

In the past, Asafo companies were primarily military groups devoted to the defence of the state. These days, they're primarily social groupings, which also exert political clout through, for example, their participation in the selection and enstoolment of the area chief. Larger towns may have several companies, open to both men and women. Each one is numbered and named and has its own individual emblems and regalia.

Ingrid Roddis

INGRID RODDIS

Dying for a drink? Just one of the many fantastic coffins made in Teshi, Ghana.

Picture perfect: children in Shama, Ghana, pose for the camera.

The old port at Bissau (Guinea-Bissau), from where boats go to the Bijagos Archipelago islands.

north of Sankara Circle, has an outdoor beer garden which is popular with expats. It's open from 10 am to midnight. You can get draught beer, snacks or a full meal and there's dancing, especially at weekends. The small, cheerful *Bus Stop Restaurant* on Ring Rd Central has good music in the evenings, when the mainly young crowd overflows onto the footpath. Large beers cost US$1.50 and you can buy a range of snacks and more substantial food. At night, a great place for drinking and viewing the more frenetic activity around Nkrumah Circle is *Terra Nova*, just south of the circle – but see the mild warning under Nightclubs in the next section.

In Osu, *Number One Snack Bar* is a good, inexpensive place for draught beer and light meals. Nearby is *Mapee's Jazz Bar*, which has good music.

Accra has three 'theme pubs', each with a predominantly expatriate clientele. In Osu, *Aquarius*, a bierkeller which also offers German food, is within staggering distance of *Ryan's Irish Pub* – the only place in Ghana with draught Guinness. *Champs Sports Bar* in the Paloma Shopping Mall on Ring Rd Central, run by an entrepreneurial Canadian ex-VSO and his Ghanaian partner, shows midday to midnight sport on its giant TV screen. On big match days and most weekends the place is packed.

Nightclubs Accra is one of the best places in West Africa for dancing, especially on Saturday night. The wildest joints are around Nkrumah Circle, where there's a slight risk of trouble as the night wears on, so you need to stay alert. On Nkrumah Ave, just south of the circle, *Piccadilly Spot*, colloquially known as 'Pick-a-Lady', is open-air, fun and vibrant, usually with a nightly reggae band and no cover charge. *Kilimanjaro* next door has a modest cover charge and is a darkly lit modern disco with more prostitutes. If you're wearing sandals you'll be refused entry, but you can often rent shoes from the cheery hookers outside. Just across the street is the popular *Container Spot*. All three are open from 8 pm daily and liven up from

about 10 pm. At any one of them you may be offered cocaine, gold smuggling, marriage, sex and several other deals best refused.

On Farrar Ave, *White Bell*, where you can eat well, is simple, friendly, altogether less disreputable, and a great dancing spot. *Glen's Bar* on Farrar Ave, one block west of White Bell, is a small New York-style bar with music and dancing. In the same area, 100m further west, *Miracle Mirage*, open Wednesday to Sunday, has outdoor tables and a disco with a good DJ.

For smarter, if less colourful, dancing places, head to Osu. Most have cover charges, typically around US$2.50. And if you fancy a flutter, call by *Star World*, which has a casino above its ground floor restaurant.

Of the Osu clubs, the loud *Berlin Connection*, on 15th Lane, is cool, comfortable and attractively furnished. Accra's newest club, *Macumba*, is on Ring Rd East and caters very much for the European disco set. Entry is US$4.50 and it opens Wednesday to Saturday. *Fusion* is another popular venue. More unusual is *La Cave du Roi* (cover charge Saturday only). With stalactites hanging from the ceiling and furniture resembling giant fungus, it's dimly lit and so tiny that if you don't arrive by 11 pm, you'll have to stand. *Mapee's Jazz Bar* has a live band at weekends.

Also good for jazz are *Bass Line* near KLM (closed on Tuesday), on Ring Rd Central, and the expensive nightclub at the *Golden Tulip Hotel*, which has a live combo on Saturday nights. The *Balm Tavern* in Kaneshie is good for both African music and jazz. It's closed on Monday and Tuesday and can be a bit soulless on weekdays. It's vigorous enough at weekends, especially on Friday, when it has a live band.

Cinema Ghana has an active and, of necessity, low-budget film industry, producing popular films for the local market. It's well worth making the effort to see one for its insights into local culture and everyday problems. The *Ghana Film Institute*, off Liberation Ave, across from the French embassy, shows the latest Ghanaian films

GHANA

and foreign releases and is often packed (US$2). Next door, the **Executive Film House** shows mostly recent US films. Both places have air-con and two nightly showings plus an extra Saturday session. Another large, central cinema is the **Rex** on Barnes Rd near Dodoo Street.

Shopping

Supermarkets There's no shortage of supermarkets. The Four Flowers, north-east of Sankara Circle off Nima Rd, carries a wide range of imported goods. Most of the other major ones, such as Ghana Groceries, Kwatsons, Qwick-Pik and Afridom, are in Osu, along Cantonments Rd. Locals are also increasingly turning to the minimarkets attached to larger petrol stations.

Art & Craftwork At the Arts Centre, which is open every day, you'll see a wide assortment of woodcarvings, masks, brass, baskets, blankets, leatherwork, paintings (not all of them Ghanaian) plus a variety of fabrics, including the famous kente cloth.

Makola Market is good for glass beads, although they're not particularly cheap. It has just about anything you could want to buy and is particularly rich in fabrics, including batiks and tie-dyes. Expensive Dutch wax cloth is everywhere, but you can find almost identical cloth made by Akosombo Textile Co that is almost as good and much cheaper. Zongo Lane, not far from the post office, has rows of small shops offering colourful prints.

The Loom, 200m south of Nkrumah Circle, is a tasteful, upmarket gallery specialising in fabrics and clothes as well as woodcarvings and statues. Even if you don't buy anything, pass by Woodin Boutique, next to Roots in Osu, a recently opened branch of the chic Abidjan store, and enjoy its dazzling display of fabrics.

One of Ghana's top artists, Glover, owns a gallery, which is worth a visit. It's on the road to Tema, a few kilometres past the Labadi Beach Hotel.

Music For cassettes of Ghanaian music, try the music shop by the Arts Centre. Open daily until 6.30 pm, it has an extensive collection and the staff can be helpful in selecting recordings. There are also lots of music stores on Nkrumah Ave just south of Nkrumah Circle. Street vendors selling tapes are another source. Prices are under US$3.

Getting There & Away

Air For details of international and domestic flights to/from Accra airport (☎ 776171), see the main Getting There & Away and Getting Around sections earlier in this chapter. International airlines with offices in Accra include:

Aeroflot
  (☎ 225289) Liberia Rd North
Air Afrique
  (☎ 230014 or 664122) Cocoa House, Nkrumah Ave
Air Ivoire
  (☎ 667522) Cocoa House, Nkrumah Ave
Alitalia
  (☎ 227873) Ring Rd Central, Asylum Down
Balkan Airlines
  (☎ 220491) Liberia Rd North
British Airways
  (☎ 667800) Liberia Rd North
EgyptAir
  (☎ 773537) Ring Rd East, 50m south-east of Danquah Circle
Ethiopian Airlines
  (☎ 664856) Cocoa House, Nkrumah Ave
Ghana Airways
  (☎ 221150) Cocoa House, Nkrumah Ave
KLM-Royal Dutch Airlines
  (☎ 224020) Ring Rd Central
Lufthansa
  (☎ 224030)
South African Airways
  (☎ 230722) Ring Rd Central, Asylum Down
Swissair
  (☎ 228150) Independence Ave

Bus For a breakdown of major routes from Accra and their fares and frequency, see the table in this chapter's Getting Around section. There are two STC bus stations in Accra. The main one (☎ 221912 for information) is just east of Lamptey Circle and serves destinations to the west and north Buses leave hourly for both Kumasi and Takoradi between 5 am and 5.30 pm and once a day for Tamale. In addition, two air-con buses a day run between Accra and Kumasi (US$4.50); these clip more than an hour from the standard journey time. It's well worth paying the extra for the coolness alone. The second, smaller STC terminal is next to Tudu station, at the northern end of Makola Market. From there, buses head east, serving towns such as Ho (US$1.50), Kpandu (US$1.75), Hohoe (US$2) and Aflao, which borders Lomé in Togo (US$1.75), to each of which there's one departure daily.

Private buses leave from three bus stations. Neoplan motor park, 250m west of Nkrumah Circle, serves points north such as Kumasi and Tamale. Buses for Tema, Ada, Ho, Aburi and the east leave from Tema station on Kinbu Rd in central Accra. Those for Cape Coast, Takoradi and other destinations to the west leave from Kaneshie motor park, half a kilometre west of Lamptey Circle.

Minibus, Tro-Tro & Bush Taxi Minibuses, tro-tros and bush taxis share with private buses the same three stations above and observe the same geographical distribution. In addition, those for Aflao/Lomé and Akosombo leave from Tudu station at the north-east corner of Makola Market.

Train There's little to induce you to take a train, unless you want to save a day's travelling by sleeping away the journey. There's one evening train a day to Takoradi and another to Kumasi, each arriving 10 to 12 hours later. There's no bar, no restaurant and no 1st class sleepers on the train. A 2nd class sleeper berth to Takoradi costs US$4 and, if you fancy sitting up all night, 1st/2nd class costs US$4/2.50. This is strictly for trainspotters.

Getting Around

To/From the Airport You'll be assailed as soon as you step outside Accra's Kotoka international airport. Don't be phased. Walk over the road, down the steps to the taxi rank and bargain. A private taxi (called a dropping taxi') to the city centre shouldn't cost more than US$5 – and half that for a journey to the airport.

For public transport into town (US$0.30), walk to the main highway (Liberation Ave) about 250m west of the airport and catch a tro-tro or shared taxi. Alternatively, a shared taxi from the airport to, for example, Nkrumah Circle costs US$0.80.

Taxi Finding a taxi is usually fairly easy except during rush hour (7 to 8.30 am and 5 to 7 pm). Late at night, you can find them in Osu on Cantonments Rd and outside the Novotel in central Accra.

Accra has three types of taxis: line taxis, dropping taxis and charter taxis. Line taxis are shared and travel on fixed runs from major landmarks or between circles. Most connect to one of the main circles, most commonly Danquah Circle, No 37 Roundabout and Nkrumah Circle. To get to an outlying neighbourhood from the centre, you'll probably have to take two taxis; one to a circle and another from there. At the major taxi parks like Neoplan motor park, Tema station and the one at No 37 Roundabout, waiting taxis have placards indicating their destination.

To hail a line taxi on the street, just hold out your hand and shout your destination. For Nkrumah Circle (usually called simply 'Circle') there's a special convention: point the index finger of your right hand towards the ground (never finger up and never your left hand or you'll unwittingly be signalling a fairly gross insult) and make a circular motion. If you enter an empty taxi, the driver will assume that you want a 'drop', a private run all to yourself, so make your intention clear if that's not the case. The standard rate is about US$0.20 between circles or major intersections. At night, fares (which are fixed) go up but not significantly.

Major routes include: Circle to Osu via Ring Rd; Circle to the central post office via Nkrumah Ave; Tudu station to Kokomlele; No 37 Roundabout to Osu; No 37 Roundabout to Labone; Makola Market to Osu; and Circle to the airport.

A dropping taxi is one you have to yourself. Rates, like just about everything in

Ghana, are negotiable. A journey within town costs around US$1.50. Charter taxis are similar and are hired for multiple destinations or a fixed length of time (US$4 an hour). On the street, you hail them in the same manner. Establish from the outset that fuel costs are the driver's responsibility.

Tro-Tro Tro-tros (US$10) ply the same town routes as line taxis and more. The main tro-tro parks in the centre are Tudu station and Tema station. Destinations they serve include Legon, Nungua, Tema, Asylum Down, New Town, Medina and Aburi. Neoplan at the north-west corner on Nkrumah Circle serves virtually every area of the city. The taxi park just west of the overpass near Nkrumah Circle serves Labadi Beach, the airport and Osu. The one further east at Sankara Circle (northern side) serves points north along Liberation Ave, including the airport and Legon. Tro-tros to Labadi and Osu leave from the Labadi lorry park on High St near Thorpe Rd.

Car Major car rental agencies in Accra include Hertz, Avis, Budget (☎ 668800) and Europcar. Vanef Tours (☎ 778265, fax 772423), 37 Achimota Rd, is the representative of Europcar. Both Hertz (☎ 223389) and Europcar have offices at the Golden Tulip Hotel. Speedway Travel & Tours (☎ 227744, fax 226188), 5 Tackie Tawiah Ave, has the Avis franchise, with a representative at the Labadi Beach Hotel (☎ 772501, fax 772520).

Local companies are usually cheaper, but their cars can be dubious. Three reliable agencies are Vicma Travel & Tours (☎ 232294, fax 234843) on Liberia Rd North, Trust Cars Ltd (☎ 228118, fax 222851) opposite the YWCA and Thrifty Cars (☎ 763654) at 10 Burma Camp Rd. Typical prices are US$50 per day and US$0.15 per kilometre for a family saloon car, or US$80 for a Mercedes 200 and US$90 for a 4WD, plus, for each, US$0.20 per kilometre.

AROUND ACCRA
University of Ghana
The university, founded in 1948, is in Legon, on the northern fringes of Accra and 14km

from the city centre. It has one of the prettiest and best maintained campuses in Africa. Its Balme Library, open from 8 am to 4.30 pm daily except Sunday, has a rich collection dating from the colonial era. The university also has the best bookshop in the country. Its botanical gardens are sadly run-down and can't compare with Aburi Gardens. All the same, they're a pleasant place for a stroll.

Getting There & Away Tro-tros leave from Tudu station in Accra. You can also pick one up from the tro-tro stop on the north side of Sankara Circle. If someone yells 'Old Road' or 'New Road', hop on; they're neighbourhoods just beyond Legon.

Aburi Botanical Gardens
Aburi, originally built by the British as a health and hill station, is on a ridge 20km beyond Legon and 34km north of Accra. It offers fine northward views of the forest and on a clear day you can make out Accra in the plains below. The botanical gardens (admission US$0.50), just beyond Aburi, are a popular weekend retreat. Established in 1890 with seedlings from all over the British Empire, they're home to an impressive variety of tropical and subtropical plants and trees. Look for the two tall 'monkey pot' trees from Brazil, which supposedly trap monkeys. The oldest tree, more than 150 years old, is a huge kapok tree facing the headquarters building. It's the only indigenous one the British didn't cut down.

A few kilometres before Aburi you'll pass **Peduase Lodge**, a weekend retreat for the president since Nkrumah's time.

Places to Stay & Eat Coming from Accra about 200m before the entrance to Aburi, you'll pass the well marked *Restaurant May & Lodge*. It's a relaxing place with a good view and decent meals at reasonable prices. It has only four guest rooms which are usually full at weekends. They cost US$8 and have bathrooms but no fans.

About 100m up the hill from the turn-off for the gardens is *Oleander Guest House* where prices are much the same. It's pleasantly decorated and homely and does wonderful family-style meals. Rooms are attractive and have fans, carpets and clean shared bathrooms. It also has larger rooms with private bathrooms.

Within the gardens, you can also stay at the old colonial-style *resthouse* (☎ 0876-22022) which charges US$9 for large, clean but basic rooms with shared bathroom. For a beautiful view of the gardens, ask for one on the front. The resthouse also has modern bungalows with fan and bathroom for US$11. Its restaurant, *Rose Plot*, serves basic fare from US$2 but has difficulty competing with the food and the view at the *Royal Restaurant*, about 200m away.

Getting There & Away Take a minibus (US$0.80) from Tema station in Accra.

The Coast

You'll enjoy the coastal area west of Accra, particularly Kokrobite, Biriwa, Cape Coast, Elmina and Busua. What makes it so special are the old slave-trading forts (see the colour feature between pages 432 and 433), the fishing villages, the beaches – and a unique National Park. Where else can you see 15 forts and castles along a 250km stretch of almost continuous beach, and feast on cheap seafood?

KOKROBITE

People come to Kokrobite, 32km west of Accra, for one or both of two reasons: to swim and laze on one of Ghana's cleaner beaches or to drum and strum at AAMA, the Academy of African Music & Arts.

AAMA (☎ 665987) is a beachside resort where you can take courses (from two hours to three months) in traditional African music, drumming and dance, or simply sunbathe and swim at the sandy palm-fringed beach. Founded by Mustafa Tettey Addy, a master drummer, it's now run by his two sons, Inusa and Kpani. One-on-one instruction in drumming or dancing costs US$4 an hour and

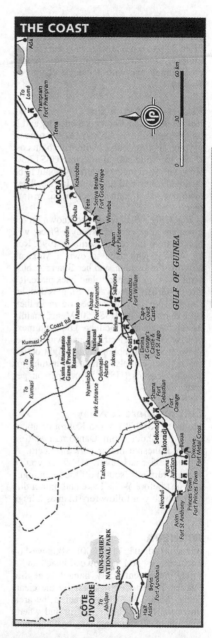

THE COAST

GHANA

US$6 for two hours. For groups, the price per person works out considerably less. From 2.30 to 6 pm at weekends the resident troupes, Akrowa and Obonu, drum – for free on Saturday and with a modest charge on Sunday.

Places to Stay & Eat

Kokrobite Beach Resort is owned by and is on the same site as AAMA. At the time of writing, singles/doubles with bathroom cost US$7/10, while bungalows were US$17.50. However, with mains electricity about to be installed, rates will undoubtedly rise. They have a good, if rather overpriced, restaurant.

Big Milly's Backyard, also known on the travellers grapevine as Wendy's Place, was hacked from the coastal scrub in 1995. Run by Wendy, who used to own a Mexican restaurant in London, and her Ghanaian husband, Seto, it's a friendly, laid-back place. It's also extremely good value. Singles/doubles cost US$5/6, or you can bed down in their large dormitory for US$2.50. Meals, mainly fish and vegetarian food, are good and inexpensive. Without electricity and with bucket showers, it's a simple paradise, right on the beach. They can also arrange drumming or dancing lessons (US$2.50 per person per hour).

Getting There & Away

Tro-tros (US$0.70) run to Kokrobite about every half-hour from Dansoman station within Kaneshie motor park in Accra. A private taxi costs about US$9. If you're driving, turn left (south) off the main highway just before Weija Lake and onto a dirt road, which you follow for 10km as it hugs the coast.

WINNEBA

Winneba (population 55,000), 64km west of Accra, has a good, uncrowded beach and a hotel, the eccentrically named huge Sir Charles Tourist Centre, right by the clean sandy shore. West of the hotel is the area where the fishing boats pull in and where upwards of 50 chanting, singing fishermen

haul in the dragnets. Nearby is a breeding ground for giant turtles. Little is being done to conserve them and between November and February large numbers are caught for food. You can play your small part in ensuring the survival of the survivors by refusing turtle steak if it features on your menu.

To the east, beyond the main public beach and the estuary lies a long stretch of peaceful coastline. If you've a penchant for faded colonial relics, visit the sad, weed-infested European cemetery near the beach, with its

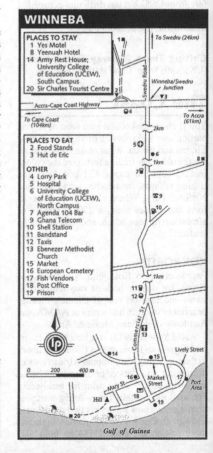

WINNEBA

PLACES TO STAY
1 Yes Motel
8 Yeenuah Hotel
14 Army Rest House; University College of Education (UCEW), South Campus
20 Sir Charles Tourist Centre

PLACES TO EAT
2 Food Stands
3 Hut de Eric

OTHER
4 Lorry Park
5 Hospital
6 University College of Education (UCEW), North Campus
7 Agenda 104 Bar
9 Ghana Telecom
10 Shell Station
11 Bandstand
12 Taxis
13 Ebenezer Methodist Church
15 Market
16 European Cemetery
17 Fish Vendors
18 Post Office
19 Prison

To Swedru (24km)

Swedru Road

Winneba/Swedru Junction

Accra-Cape Coast Highway

To Cape Coast (104km)

To Accra (61km)

2km

1km

1km

Commercial St

Lively Street

0 200 400 m

Mary St

Market Street

Hill

Port Area

Gulf of Guinea

Deer Hunt Festival

Winneba is home to Ghana's most famous festival – the Aboakyer (the Deer Hunt) – celebrated for more than 300 years and held on the first weekend in May. According to legend, Penkye Otu, a tribal god, demanded an annual sacrifice from his people. The main event, therefore, is a competitive hunt in which two Asafo (companies, or guilds of men), the Tuafo (No 1 company) and the Dentsifo (No 2 company), hunt an antelope to sacrifice. The first Asafo company to capture one alive with their bare hands and bring it back to the Omanhene (village chief) wins.

Each company has its own colours, emblems and flags, so it's easy to tell them apart. The Tuafo, in blue and white, are led by their captain who carries a cutlass and rides a wooden horse; the Dentsifo dress in red and gold and their captain, borne in a chair, wears an iron helmet and carries a sword and cutlass. Early on the Saturday morning the young men don their traditional battle dress and go to the beach to purify themselves and, after being 'blessed' with herbs, go on to the Omanhene's palace to greet the royal family and, finally, to the adjacent hunting grounds. Each group, singing war songs and wielding sticks and cudgels, is equipped with gongs, rattles, bells, bugles and whistles to flush out the antelope. The first to catch one alive rushes with his company to the Omanhene's dais, singing and dancing along the way and hurling taunts at their opponents. The Omanhene is then borne in a palanquin and paraded through the streets amid much drumming and shouting and the celebrations continue all night.

Next day, at 2 pm, the companies assemble before the Penkye Otu deity to question the oracle. The chief priest draws four parallel lines on the ground, one in white clay, one in red, another in charcoal and a fourth in salt. A stone is rolled down from the fetish. If it falls upon the white clay line, there will be a great drought. If it stops at the charcoal lines, this portends heavy rains. Landing on the salt line indicates that there will be plenty of food and fish, while settling upon the red line augurs war and strife. The hapless antelope is then sacrificed and cooked, the chief priest taking some of the hot soup with his bare hands and placing it on the Penkye Otu fetish. This offering is the *raison d'être* of the hunt and the festival concludes.

GHANA

graves of long forgotten Swiss missionaries and British civil servants.

Places to Stay & Eat

There's nowhere in Winneba that we can recommend unreservedly. If you're looking for inexpensive accommodation, the *Yes Motel* (☎ 22216), is clean and well maintained. Rooms with fan, bucket shower and shared toilet cost US$3. Others, with bathroom and a small sitting room, are a bargain at US$6.50. But it's 5km north of Winneba, on the main Accra to Cape Coast highway.

The *Army Resthouse* (☎ 22208) is, despite its name, open to the general public. It's on the south campus of the University

College of Education, Winneba (UCEW), towards the port. Rather run-down doubles with fan, bucket bath and flush toilet are US$6.

The *Yeenuah Hotel* (☎ 22161) is on a hill 4km from the centre of town. Take the dirt road leading east from the small Agenda 104 cafe and aim for the sole white two storey structure up the hill. Rooms with fan and shared bathroom cost US$4.50 or US$11 with bathroom. They also have larger apartments for US$15.50.

The *Sir Charles Tourist Centre* (☎ 22189) is in a huge, rather bleak compound overlooking the beach. Its most basic rooms with fan and shared bathroom are US$5.50. Bungalow prices vary according to whether they have a landward or seaward view. Singles cost from US$6.50, and doubles from US$11. It has a bar and an echoing restaurant, where you'll probably be the only diner. All in all, it's a rather sad, drab monument to a tourist bonanza that hasn't yet happened. But it's cheap, the staff couldn't be more friendly and the extensive beach alone is worth the overnight fee.

You can find *street food* at the stalls beside the lorry park. *Hut de Eric*, a short walk away, is nothing fancy but it offers the best food in town in clean surroundings.

Getting There & Away

Tro-tros, private buses and bush taxis for Winneba (US$0.75) and points further west leave Accra from Kaneshie motor park. Get off at the Winneba-Swedru Junction (61km), from where a shared taxi into town (5km) costs US$0.15 or US$0.75 if chartered. From Accra, you can also take a less frequent and more unpredictable STC bus.

AROUND WINNEBA
Senya Beraku

About 20km east of Winneba, Senya Beraku itself has little of interest, although the people are friendly and the beaches isolated. **Fort Good Hope** was the last fort to be built by the Dutch, in 1702, for the gold trade. It was expanded in 1715 when it was converted into a slave prison. Overlooking the sea, it has superb views. There's no admission charge and nowadays it's a basic guesthouse with one garret for US$3 and other less claustrophobic rooms for US$ 6.50. Bathrooms are communal and the fort is the only place in town with guaranteed water, drawn from the original Dutch underground reservoir. If you order in advance, they'll prepare dinner (US$2.50).

About 5km east of Senya Beraku by dirt road is **Fete**, one of the two best surfing spots, together with Dixcove, along the Ghanaian coast.

Several tro-tros a day go to Senya Beraku from Kaneshie motor park in Accra. Tro-tros and shared taxis are usually waiting at the junction on the main Accra to Takoradi highway, 8km from Senya Beraku.

Apam

Some 20km west of Winneba, Apam is a small fishing village whose main attraction is its fort. **Fort Patience** (or Fort Leydsaemheyt) was originally nothing more than a small two storey house flanked by two bastions. Nevertheless, it took the Dutch five years to build starting in 1697: hence the name. Later, they added other rooms, lost the fort to the British in 1782, regained it three years later and lost it again in 1868.

Admission is free. Serving as a *guesthouse*, it has a double distinction: at US$0.25 a room, it's the cheapest accommodation we found in Ghana – and the price had actually dropped since our previous visit. It can't be commensurate with a reduction in quality since nothing – a bare bed in a grubby room – could be more basic. Bring a torch (flashlight). More comfortable is the *King Pobee Hotel*, just off the main road, which offers doubles with fan for US$7.

Near the picturesque harbour is a great three storey *posuban*, an ensemble of statues which, in Fanti culture, represents a proverb or notable event in the community's history (see the colour feature between page 416 and 417). This one has mounted horsemen overlooked by a white-robed Jesus.

To get to Apam from Winneba, take a taxi or tro-tro west on the coastal road for 13km to the large, well marked Apam Junction, then another for Apam, which is 9km to the south.

CAPE COAST

Cape Coast (population 110,000) is called Oguaa in the local Fanti language. It was the British colonial capital until the administration moved to Accra in 1876.

Cape Coast Castle (see the colour feature between pages 432 and 433), is in the heart of town overlooking the sea. The castle and its superb museum, designed with support from the Smithsonian in Washington, are open from 9 am to 4 pm daily. Entry is US$4.50 or US$2.50 for students. Your

CAPE COAST

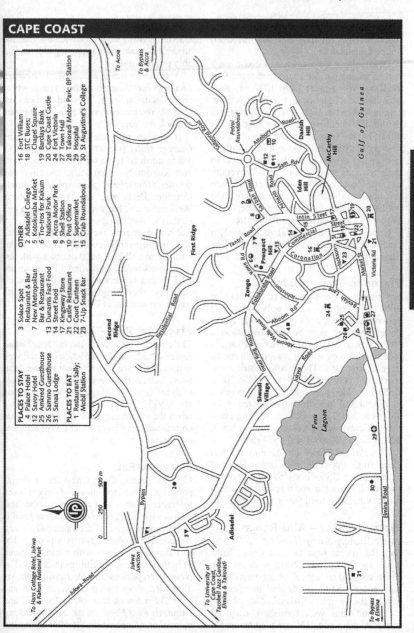

PLACES TO STAY
4 Palace Hotel
12 Savoy Hotel
25 Amkred Guesthouse
26 Sammo Guesthouse
31 Sanaa Lodge

PLACES TO EAT
1 Restaurant Sally;
    Mobil Station
3 Solace Spot
    Restaurant & Bar
7 New Metropolitan
    Bar & Restaurant
13 Dunamis Fast Food
14 Street Food
17 Kingsway Store
21 Castle Restaurant
22 Court Canteen
23 7-Up Snack Bar

OTHER
2 Adisadel College
5 Kotokuraba Market
6 Tro-tros for Kakum
    National Park
8 Accra Motor Park
9 Shell Station
10 Post Office
11 Supermarket
15 Crab Roundabout
16 Fort William
18 STC Buses;
    Chapel Square
19 Barclays Bank
20 Cape Coast Castle
24 Fort Victoria
27 Town Hall
28 Takoradi Motor Park; BP Station
29 Hospital
30 St Augustine's College

GHANA

ticket entitles you to join one of the hourly tours, led by articulate and well informed young Ghanaians.

Overlooking both town and coast are a pair of what are more keeps than forts: **Fort William**, which dates from 1820 and now functions as a lighthouse, and **Fort Victoria**, originally built in 1702 and heavily restored in the 19th century. You can't go inside either, but the panorama of the town and the sweep of bay as far as St George's Castle at Elmina to the west make the short ascent to their terraces worthwhile. The University of Cape Coast is at the western end of town just north of the bypass. You can buy good batiks and other crafts at the Cape Coast Women's Cooperative near the centre.

Cape Coast's Fetu Afahye Festival, a raucous carnival, takes place on the first Saturday of September.

Places to Stay – Budget

For a town of Cape Coast's size, the choice of hotels is poor. You have only two budget options in the centre of town. Fortunately, the better one, the new *Sammo Guesthouse* (☎ 33242), on Jukwa Rd, is great and warmly recommended by several readers. All rooms have ceiling fans. Those with shared bathroom cost between US$5 and US$6.50 or US$10 to US$11 with bathroom. There's a moribund roof-top bar from which the views are great, but don't go there seeking company. Meals, which you have to order in advance, are delicious and good value.

The *Palace Hotel* on Aboom Rd has clean singles/doubles with fan and shared bathroom for US$6/7 or US$9 with private shower. It has a bar and a restaurant which serves Ghanaian food for around US$2.50.

Places to Stay – Mid-Range

At the friendly *Savoy Hotel* (☎ 32805), on Sam Rd, rooms with fan and shared bathroom are US$13 or US$15 with air-con. There's a good restaurant, where main dishes cost under US$4. Just behind the Sammo hotel, the small *Amkred Guesthouse* (☎ 32868) has well furnished, carpeted rooms with air-con, TV and tiled bathroom

with bathtub for a bargain US$15.50 or US$13.50 with fan. With advance notice, the amiable caretaker will prepare good, reasonably priced meals.

A reader warmly recommends *Fairhill Luxury Guesthouse*, on the bypass, where rooms with air-con, TV and fridge cost US$29. You can either eat at their restaurant or cook for yourself.

If you've got wheels, consider *Hans Cottage Botel* (sic) (☎ 33621, fax 33623), 10km north of town on the road to Jukwa and Kakum National Park. 'A cosy and serene atmosphere that spells ultimate Comfort, Peace and Joy', says the blurb. Well, not quite, but with its crocodile pond, sunbirds, squabbling weaverbirds, monkeys and bar-restaurant overlooking an artificial lake, it's enjoyably eccentric. Simple rooms with fan are US$9.50 and doubles with air-con, satellite TV and tiled bathroom are US$35 and represent good value in their category; their single/double rooms with bathroom and fan at US$15/20 less so.

Places to Stay – Top End

The town's best hotel is the modern *Sanaa Lodge* (☎ 32570, fax 32898), a tranquil well maintained place on a hill near the westernmost entrance to town. Singles/doubles with air-con, TV, fridge, carpet and phone are US$50/60; prices will probably rise when the swimming pool and new wing are completed; they were under construction at the time of writing.

Places to Eat

Like its hotels, Cape Coast has a disappointingly restricted choice of decent, even tolerable, places to eat. One of the best areas in the heart of town for *street food* is at the intersection of Commercial St and Ashanti Rd. *Solace Spot*, is a popular bar and simple restaurant with a limited menu of both Ghanaian and European dishes. The *New Metropolitan Bar & Restaurant*, on Tantri Rd, does cheap Ghanaian food and beer. *7-Up Snack Bar*, on Jackson St, and *Dunamis Fast Food*, on the corner of Commercial and Coronation Sts offer filling but unexciting fare. The small cafe attached to **Kingsway Store** on Intin St serves excellent, inexpensive Ghanaian food. **Court Canteen**, one block south of Chapel Square, handy for the castle, does good local food at lunch time.

Restaurant Sally at the Mobil station on the bypass across from Jukwa Junction is worth the short journey from the centre. It's open from 9 am to 9 pm. If it's atmosphere you're after, particularly at weekends, head east of town to the **Tacobell Jazz Garden**, near the university's east gate. The food's good, even if the resemblance to the Texmex multinational is distant.

The only place that stands out, for both food and atmosphere, is the new **Castle Restaurant**, which juts out over the beach, right beside the castle. It does Ghanaian food at lunch time and international cuisine, any time. It's also an agreeable place to just have a drink, watch the waves and let the sea breeze play. It has live music at weekends.

Getting There & Away

In Accra, the principal station serving Cape Coast is Kaneshie motor park. There's a morning and afternoon STC bus service (three hours, US$3), departing from the company's main Accra station.

In Cape Coast, the STC bus terminal is in Chapel Square, 100m north of the castle. All other vehicles for Accra and Kumasi leave from Accra motor park on the corner of Sarbah and Tantri Rds. City Express has a daily run to Kumasi (four hours, US$3). Takoradi motor park is on the western side of town at the intersection of Elmina and Jukwa Rds, and primarily serves eastbound destinations. Tro-tros for Kakum National Park leave from Rowe Rd.

AROUND CAPE COAST
Biriwa

The nondescript fishing village of Biriwa, 13km east of Cape Coast, is nothing special. But just to its west is a fine 3km sandy beach, a popular spot at weekends, and the modern German-owned **Biriwa Beach Hotel** (☎ 042-

33333, fax 33555, email bbh@ncs.com.gh), on a bluff overlooking the sea. Singles/ doubles are US$63/69. The expensive restaurant, the best in the area, specialises in seafood and German dishes. The hotel's on the western edge of the village, just off the main coastal highway. Small – it only has nine rooms – and popular, advance reservation is essential, especially at weekends. There's public access to the magnificent sweep of beach below, where you can **camp**. Ask at reception for details.

Anomabu

Anomabu, about 5km east of Biriwa, is the site of **Fort William**, built by the Dutch in 1640, then captured and blown up by the British in 1664. A mere decade later, the British constructed a replacement, which they named Fort Charles, only to abandon and demolish it in the 1730s. The present, and third, fort, also built by the British, dates from 1756. One of the most handsome and best built forts on the coast, it now functions as a prison, so you can't visit it. Locals get nervy if they think you're trying to sneak a photo.

Anomabu has seven asafo shrines or posubans (for more details, see the colour feature between page 416 and 417), including a spectacular one in the form of a large painted ship: one for each of the seven companies or guilds represented in town.

Abanze

The restored **Fort Kormantin** looms above the small village of Abanze, 32km east of Cape Coast. Established in 1598 by the Dutch as a trading post, it was rebuilt by the English in 1645 as their first settlement along the coast of the Gulf of Guinea and named Fort York. When the Dutch recaptured it in 1665, they restyled it as Fort Amsterdam as a stylish thumbing of the nose at the English who, the previous year on the other side of the Atlantic, had taken possession of New Amsterdam and re-christened it New York.

This isn't the slave fort's only transatlantic connection. Louis Armstrong, the

GHANA

legendary 'Satchmo' himself, reckoned that his ancestors had been despatched as slaves from Kormantin. Ask the stentorian-voiced guide to show you the guest book. In it, you'll see the names of several visitors from Surinam, the one-time Dutch colony in Central America, who came here, seeking their roots. One of them is called Lafanti, recalling the Fanti, the dominant people along this part of the coast. Some are from Koromanti province in Surinam where, to this day, words of Fanti survive in the local patois, as do the Fanti traditions of flag waving and the title of paramount chief.

KAKUM NATIONAL PARK

Kakum National Park and the adjoining Assin Attandanso Game Production Reserve are 33km north of Cape Coast. It's a mixture of true rainforest and semideciduous forest that has been developed for ecotourism. The park protects 357 sq km but only about 14 sq km of virgin rainforest remain after years of selective logging before the area was declared protected.

The highlight of the park is its 350m cable and rope canopy walkway, with viewing stations linked by eight narrow suspension bridges along which you bounce, 30m above the forest floor. It's unique in Africa and one of only four in the world. It gives you a special bird's-eye view of the forest, up where 80% of its inhabitants – animal, bird and insect – live. However, since the park's not open at dawn or dusk, when mammals and birds are at their most active, go for the unique experience and perspective and don't expect any great wildlife viewing. Often the only sound is the chattering of insects and the creak of the ropes as you sway along.

The diverse and dense vegetation supports forest elephant, bongo, diana monkey, olive colobus monkey, red river hog, yellow-backed duiker and antelopes. In all, 40 species of larger mammals (including nine primate species), about 300 species of birds and a staggering 600 varieties of butterfly have been identified here. However, since the park receives more than 30,000 visitors a year, it's a fair bet that quite a pro-portion have already run scared. The *Field Guide to the Kakum Nature Park*, available at the park information centre, is well worth picking up. Before you set out, visit the park's superb, ecologically sensitive display, a masterpiece of gentle didacticism.

There's also a 2km nature trail (US$3), where you can learn a lot about medicinal plants.

The cost, an element of which goes towards upkeep of the park, is US$10, or US$5 with a student card or proof that you're a volunteer working in Ghana. You may find that the guides, although clearly well informed, are not overly informative. You really have to draw them out if they're to be more than simply accompanying guards.

Getting There & Away

In Cape Coast, go to Jukwa Junction on the bypass and head north-west from there past Jukwa to Abrafo (30km) and then 1.5km further to the park entrance. For tro-tros which pass by the entrance, go to the small station in Cape Coast on Rowe Rd.

ELMINA

Elmina ('The Mine' in Portuguese), is a town of some 20,000 people who live from fishing, fish processing, salt production and, increasingly, tourism. Protected on the south by the Atlantic, with a natural lagoon to the south-west and, to the east, a calm beach where large ships can land, it's a natural haven. It's famous for **St George's Castle** (open daily from 9 am to 4 pm, admission US$5, half price for students) and the much smaller **Fort St Jago** (see the colour feature between pages 432 and 433). Both are UNESCO World Heritage sites. Local names, such as Platte, Vroom, Vandyke and Plange, recall the offspring of Dutch soldiers and slaves. The main drag, Liverpool St, recalls the British period and the destination of most cargo which left the port.

The crowded Mpoben port on the lagoon side is an animated sight, particularly when the day's fishing catch is being unloaded in the afternoon. The town also has several interesting posubans.

Elmina's colourful Bakatue Festival takes place on the first Tuesday in July. A joyous harvest thanksgiving feast, one of its highlights is watching the priest in the harbour waters casting a net to lift a ban on fishing in the lagoon.

Places to Stay – Budget

Elmina courts upmarket tourism and the only decent budget option is the *Nyansapow Hotel (☎ 33955)*, previously called the Hollywood. It's on the northern edge of town, about six blocks north of the fort. Look for the hotel's sign on the main road into town. Clean singles/doubles cost US$5.50/9. All have fans and bathroom and open onto a pleasant courtyard.

Places to Stay – Top End

Near the town are four decidedly upmarket hotels, each overlooking the ocean. One kilometre east of town, you can really pamper yourself at the most luxurious, the *Elmina Beach Resort (☎ 33742, fax 33714)*. Opened in 1997, it has tennis courts, a swimming pool and an excellent restaurant. During the week, singles/doubles begin at US$98/144 and, on weekends, at US$81/115. At the *Oyster Bay Hotel (☎ 33605, fax 33643)*, singles/doubles cost US$50/60 and large 'executive' rooms are US$70/80. Prices and facilities at the adjacent *Harmony Beach Hotel (☎ 33678)* are much the same. The *Coconut Grove Beach Resort, (☎ 33646)*, 4km west of Elmina, is more remote and offers some fine shoreline walks.

Places to Eat

Choices, apart from the luxury hotels, are limited. The only relatively cheap place to eat is the open-air *Gramsdel J*, on the beach at the eastern edge of town. The *Castle Bridge Bar* overlooking the harbour is a pleasant spot for a drink.

Getting There & Away

Take a tro-tro (US$0.15) or a shared taxi (US$0.25) to Elmina from the Takoradi motor park in Cape Coast, near Kotokuraba Market or from anywhere along Elmina Rd.

Or you can hire a private taxi for about US$2. If you're coming from Takoradi, get dropped off at the Elmina turn-off, about 11km west of Cape Coast, from where you can walk or catch one of the buses coming from Cape Coast.

SHAMA

The small **Fort Sebastian**, built by the Portuguese about 1550, has been well restored. It was near ruins when the Dutch captured and renovated it in 1640, only to have it seized from them in 1664 by the British. A few months later, the Dutch regained control, re-rebuilt it and then held on for more than two centuries until it was ceded to Britain in 1872. The entrance fee is US$1 plus US$0.25 for a camera.

Where the Pra River joins the ocean, there's a colourful fish market from around 9 am until 6 pm, except on Tuesdays. (On Tuesday, no Fanti will put to sea for fear of enraging the sea monster.) Nearby, on the long peninsula, there's a beautiful sandy **beach**. Boatmen on the town side will ferry you across for a small fee or take you on longer excursions up the river.

The monolithic *Shama Hotel (☎ 23941)* – yet another coastal white elephant, echoing and empty – is great value. Rooms with fan, bathroom and hot water cost US$6.50 or US$9 with bathtub (but check first that the water's on). The hotel has a pleasant roof-top bar, where you can eat if you order in advance. The genial owner, a local boy made good, worked in England for 18 years and returned to invest in his home community.

Getting There & Away

Shama Junction is about 18km east of Takoradi, off the Accra to Takoradi highway. The town is 4km south via a tar road. A tro-tro from Sekondi to Shama costs US$0.25.

SEKONDI-TAKORADI

The twin city of Sekondi-Takoradi (population 270,000) has little of interest for travellers. You may find yourself spending a

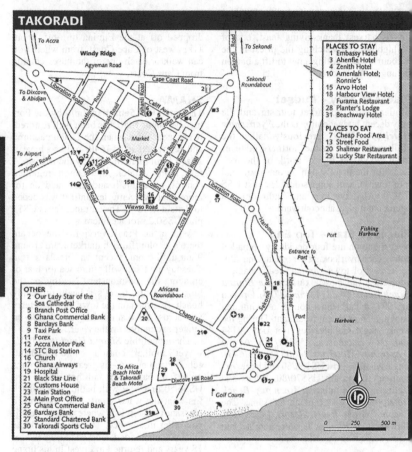

TAKORADI

To Accra

Windy Ridge

Agyeman Road

To Dixcove & Abidjan

Liberation Road

Hatford Road

Mozali Road

Ashanti Road

Califf Ave

John Sarpah Road

Cape Coast Road

Sekondi Road

To Sekondi

Sekondi Roundabout

To Airport

To Airport Road

Market

Market Circle

John Sarpah Road

Mamwewe Road

Kumasi Road

Obasi Road

Liberation Road

Axim Road

Collins Avenue

Wiawso Road

Accra Road

Africana Roundabout

Sekondi Road

Harbour Road

Niima Road

Chapel Hill

To Africa Beach Hotel & Takoradi Beach Motel

Dixcove Hill Road

Golf Course

Port

Fishing Harbour

Entrance to Port

Port

Harbour

Train Station

PLACES TO STAY
1 Embassy Hotel
3 Ahenfie Hotel
4 Zenith Hotel
10 Amenlah Hotel; Ronnie's
15 Arvo Hotel
18 Harbour View Hotel; Furama Restaurant
28 Planter's Lodge
31 Beachway Hotel

PLACES TO EAT
7 Cheap Food Area
13 Street Food
20 Shalimar Restaurant
29 Lucky Star Restaurant

OTHER
2 Our Lady Star of the Sea Cathedral
5 Branch Post Office
6 Ghana Commercial Bank
8 Barclays Bank
9 Taxi Park
11 Forex
12 Accra Motor Park
14 STC Bus Station
16 Church
17 Ghana Airways
19 Hospital
21 Black Star Line
22 Customs House
23 Train Station
24 Main Post Office
25 Ghana Commercial Bank
26 Barclays Bank
27 Standard Chartered Bank
30 Takoradi Sports Club

0   250   500 m

GHANA

night here, however, en route to or from Côte d'Ivoire, Ghana's coastal towns or Kumasi.

Sekondi, the older of the two cities, is a dull place. Only a few colonial buildings and **Fort Orange** might draw you there. Built by the Dutch in 1640, it was seized by the Ahantas in 1694 and abandoned in 1840 before being taken over in 1872 by the British, who turned it into one of their main trading posts. Today, it's a lighthouse. The British also built a fort here, Fort Sekondi, but few traces of it remain.

Takoradi was just a fishing village until it was chosen as Ghana's first deep-water seaport; since then it has prospered. The heart of town is Market Circle, 10km west of the centre of Sekondi. The motor parks and most of the cheap hotels and restaurants are near here.

The commercial port is about 2km southeast of Market Circle. It's closed to the general public. Near it are the main post office, the train station and several banks and shops. The better hotels and restaurants are on this side of town. The city's main beach is 2km south of Market Circle.

Places to Stay – Budget

The three storey *Embassy Hotel* (☎ 21088), at the junction of Cape Coast Rd and Liberation Rd has singles/doubles with large beds and shared bathroom for US$4.50/6. Noise can be a problem, from both the active bar-restaurant on the ground floor and the busy roads on either side. The friendly *Amenlah Hotel* (☎ 22543), on John Sarbah Rd, southwest of the market, has equally good rooms. Singles/doubles with fan and shared bathroom cost US$4/4.50 or US$6.50 with bathroom and they have one air-con room at a bargain US$10.50. It has a bar and a chop house.

The *Zenith Hotel* (☎ 22359), on John Sarbah Rd, north-east of the market, is built around a central courtyard, where a live band plays loudly and nightly. Singles/doubles with fans cost US$3.50/4.50 or US$6.50 with bathroom. It also has a restaurant, open on weekdays. On a Sunday morning, prepare to be inspired by the gospel singing from the church service upstairs. The *Arvo Hotel* has rooms with fan and clean sheets for US$4.50 or US$6.50 with bathroom. Rooms vary from cramped to large, so ask to see them first and insist upon the latter.

The *Beachway Hotel* (☎ 24734), On the balconied upper floors, where the views are best, the town water rarely rises. But it's a friendly, laid-back place where large rooms with fan and shared bathroom cost US$4, single, and between US$5.50 and US$7.50, double. If you order in advance, you can eat on their pleasant terrace. It's excellent value.

Places to Stay – Mid-Range

The *Harbour View Hotel* (☎ 23576), on Sekondi Rd, is something of a misnomer, since all it overlooks is the drab commercial port. But its singles/doubles with air-con for US$15.50/25.50 or US$10 with fan are reasonable value and it's right beside, and under the same ownership as, the Furama

Restaurant. The *Ahenfie Hotel* (☎ 22966), on Kumasi Rd, has clean singles/doubles with fan and bathroom for US$12.50/17.50 or US$26 to US$29.50 for a double with air-con, fridge and satellite TV. It has a disco (Saturday only) and an attractive air-con restaurant.

Places to Stay – Top End

Planter's Lodge (☎ 22233, fax 22230), has comfortable chalets with air-con and satellite TV (US$82), set in attractive flowering gardens. It also has a pleasant open-air restaurant, although it, like the rooms, is overpriced.

There are two relatively new hotels on the shore at the western end of town. The *Africa Beach* (☎ 23466, fax 21666) has bungalows for US$58, including continental breakfast. With its pool, bar and restaurant, it's a popular expat haunt at weekends, when it's advisable to reserve if you want a room. It's something of a ghetto – don't go there expecting to meet Ghanaians. Next door, just to the west, is the even newer *Takoradi Beach Motel* (☎ 21021, fax 21031), where singles/doubles cost US$70/80.

Places to Eat

There's inexpensive *street food* beside Accra motor park and look, too, around Market Circle, particularly on the east side. All along Mampong Rd are modest chop houses and street food. Of the budget hotel restaurants, the one at the *Zenith*, only open weekdays, has a great atmosphere and is inexpensive. The Amenlah Hotel has *Ronnie's*, a chop house serving simple food until 8 pm. For a more upmarket place with air-con, try the *Ahenfie Hotel*, which has a few Ghanaian dishes and a wide selection of other foods.

For Chinese cuisine, the *Lucky Star Restaurant*, on Dixcove Hill Rd, is superb and reasonably priced. The *Furama Restaurant* at the Harbour View Hotel has moderately priced Ghanaian dishes. Their patio's a pleasant place for a drink at sunset – but don't be tempted to photograph the port below. The long-standing *Shalimar*

GHANA

Restaurant, on the southern side of the Africana Roundabout specialises in Indian food, and is excellent value.

At the top end, the restaurant at *Planter's Lodge* has a good reputation locally.

Getting There & Away

Air Fan Airways has one flight a week (US$40) between Accra and Takoradi.

Bus, Tro-Tro & Bush Taxi STC has hourly buses to Accra, leaving from its station on Axim Rd. The trip takes around four hours and costs US$4. There are also daily STC buses to Kumasi. Their bus from Accra to Abidjan (daily except Sunday) passes through Takoradi and often has a few seats available. Accra motor park is the city's main vehicle departure point. Tro-tros and Peugeot 504s depart at all hours of the day and night for Accra. Those for Cape Coast, and Kumasi (via Cape Coast), also leave from here.

Taxis to Sekondi leave from the small taxi park on the south-west side of Market Circle. The fare is US$0.15 by shared taxi and US$1 by private taxi.

Train If you take the night train to Kumasi, you'll save yourself a night's accommodation, but you'll miss some attractive scenery en route. Two trains travel daily in each direction, departing at 6 am (except Sunday) and 8 pm. The morning one takes about eight hours, while the night train usually arrives about 9 am the following day. The cost is US$3/2 for 1st/2nd class. On the night train you can take a sleeper for US$4/3 in 1st/2nd class. There's also a daily run to Accra, departing Takoradi at 7.15 pm, but it's infinitely slower than road transport, taking 12 hours or more (US$4/2.50 in 1st/2nd class). Sleeping berths (US$4) are available only in 2nd class and there's no bar or restaurant.

DIXCOVE & BUSUA

Dixcove and Busua, each around 30km west of Takoradi, were for years a Mecca for beach lovers and budget travellers in the know. Now that they're an easy drive from

Accra, they've lost their off-the-beaten-track exclusiveness but are still well worth visiting.

Busua's **beach** is about the best on the coast, although its hotel doesn't enjoy the same distinction. Since a blight killed off the coconut palms which used to line the shore, the prospect is as bleak and bare as the Red Sea coast on the other side of the continent. Nevertheless, the long, white sand beach is still a great spot for just lazing in the sun and you can hire a boat to take you to the offshore island. Use of the beach is free; you only pay if you use the hotel's umbrellas or loungers. Don't let anyone tell you otherwise.

Dixcove is an undemanding 20 to 30 minute walk away, over the headland to the west, or a long 12km by road. But note that there are regular muggings on the headland track. Don't take it after dark and, in daytime, don't walk it alone.

On the shore of a rocky cove, Dixcove is a colourful fishing village. Its natural harbour is deep enough for small ships to enter – one of the reasons why it became the site of **Fort Metal Cross**, which overlooks the port. If you're visiting the fort, a word of

Fort Metal Cross

Fort Metal Cross was constructed by a certain Captain Dixon in 1691. Over the years, Dixon's Cove became shortened to Dixcove. Dixon made a cross of gold at the fort where he used to pray; hence its name. Built originally for trading purposes, the fort was converted to a slave entrepôt in 1775. At least two of the slaves, including a 15-year-old girl, were buried alive as sacrifices to appease the African gods. Both are buried in the courtyard.

The Dutch held the fort briefly from 1868 to 1872. It was among the first to be restored in the mid-1950s. The building is elegant, with arched doorways flanked by columns and a large open courtyard.

COASTAL FORTS IN GHANA

Most of the forts and castles (the terms tend to be used interchangeably) on the Ghanaian coast were built during the 17th century when Danes, British, Portuguese, Germans, French, Swedes and Dutch were vying for commercial dominance of the Gold Coast and the Gulf of Guinea. The castles and forts changed hands like a game of musical chairs – some as many as three times in five years. By the end of the 18th century, before the abolition of slavery in Europe, there were 37 such fortifications along Ghana's coastline.

Top: The ironically named Fort Good Hope, Senya Beraku, which, like many of Ghana's coastal forts, served as a slave trading centre in the 18th century.

Bottom: Fort Metal Cross, Dixcove, where you can savour the atmosphere by staying overnight.

Initially established as trading posts, principally for gold and ivory from the interior, many forts were later used as places to literally brand and store slaves ready for shipping. Up to 2000 people at a time were packed into dark, airless dungeons. By the 18th century the Dutch had exported over 65,000 slaves to European and US markets.

BOTH PHOTOS BY INGRID RODDIS

The major forts and castles east to west from Accra are listed below:

Osu Castle (also called Christiansborg Castle), Accra; now the seat of government and off limits to the public
Fort Good Hope, Senya Beraku, 50km south-west of Accra; offers simple accommodation
Fort Patience, Apam, 22km by road west of Winneba; offers very basic accommodation
Fort Kormantin, Abanze, 4km west of Saltpond; recently restored
Fort William, Anomabu, 18km east of Cape Coast
Cape Coast Castle, Cape Coast, 145km from Accra; superb museum
St George's Castle & Fort St Jago, Elmina, 13km west of Cape Coast
Fort Sebastian, Shama, 25km east of Sekondi-Takoradi
Fort Orange, Sekondi-Takoradi, 230km from Accra
Fort Metal Cross, Dixcove, 32km south-west of Sekondi-Takoradi; offers very basic accommodation
Fort Princes Town, Princes Town, 50km west of Sekondi-Takoradi; offers very simple accommodation
Fort St Anthony, Axim, 69km west of Takoradi
Fort Apollonia, Beyin, 65km west of Axim and 20km east of Half Assini

Nearly all forts are open to the public. Hours vary from the strictly enforced to any time you turn up, and entrance fees from nothing to US$5. At Cape Coast Castle and St George's, Elmina, an informed guided tour is included. At most others, custodians will impart their varying degrees of knowledge in variable English in return for a dash.

If your time is limited, make sure that you visit at least the big three: Cape Coast Castle, St George's Castle and Fort St Jago. All of them are deservedly UNESCO World Heritage sites.

Left: St George's Castle, Elmina, offers fantastic views over the coast and the town.

Cape Coast Castle

Built with slave labour by the Swedes starting in 1652, Cape Coast Castle changed hands five times over the 13 tumultuous years that followed, starting with the Danish and ending with the British. During the 211 years of British occupation, the castle was the headquarters of Britain's operations in West Africa, until, in 1876, they moved the capital of the Gold Coast to Accra.

The castle was not originally well built. Despite being strengthened and greatly enlarged from 1673 to 1694, walls collapsed and roofs leaked until an overhaul in the mid-1700s. The buildings, constructed around a trapezoidal courtyard facing the sea, are impressive, but the dungeons below are shocking. Several metres underground at the bottom of a ramp are the four dark, stale-smelling rooms on whose stone walls you can see the scratchings made by desperate inmates. From here no escape was possible for the 1500 slaves the castle held when full.

Below: Cape Coast Castle, its present whitewashed beauty belying its dark history as evidenced by the slave dungeons with their scratched walls.

St George's Castle & Fort St Jago

At the end of its rocky peninsula, St George's Castle in Elmina is clearly visible from a distance. Built in 1482 by the Portuguese, who came in search of the area's gold, it's the oldest European structure

INGRID RODDIS

in sub-Saharan Africa and predates the 'discovery' of the Americas. The Dutch captured the castle in 1637, then between 1652 and 1662 constructed Fort St Jago, on a hillock which dominates the castle. From then until 1872, when the Dutch ceded it to the British, the castle served as the African headquarters of the Dutch West Indies Company. Both the castle and the fort were expanded when slaves replaced gold as the major object of commerce, and the storerooms were converted into dungeons.

You'll leave with a deep impression of just how badly the captives were treated – it's amazing any of them survived. During the excellent one hour tour you'll see the slave quarters, the cells of the condemned people, the slave auctioning rooms and the governor's quarters. To quote the plaque you'll find here and at Cape Coast Castle:

In everlasting memory
Of the anguish of our ancestors.
May those who died rest in peace.
May those who return find their roots.
May humanity never again perpetrate
Such injustice against humanity.
We, the living, vow to uphold this.

Below: Fort St Jago, Elmina. Originally built by the Dutch, it provides an excellent vantage point over St George's Castle and the surrounding area.

INGRID RODDIS

warning: more than one woman traveller has reported that the staff at the fort have a tendency to grope women visitors.

Dixcove is renowned for its lobsters. You pay about US$6 a kilo and the staff of the Quiet Storm Hotel will cook them for you with jollof rice for US$1.50 per person.

Places to Stay

In Dixcove, your only option is the *Quiet Storm Hotel* where spacious, carpeted rooms with fan, shared bathroom and bucket shower cost between US$7 and US$9.

Over the headland, the upmarket *Busua Beach Resort*, beside the shore, seems to be in a state of permanent renovation. It has 26 chalets, all with air-con and bathroom, where singles/doubles cost US$31/43.

In Busua village itself, and in a different league, the new *Dadson's Lodge*, a converted private house, has singles with shared facilities for US$4.50 and large doubles with bathroom for US$11. Ask for a room overlooking the ocean.

Several villagers rent out simple rooms in the family compound. Neighbours can direct you to, for example, *Sabina's*, *Mary's* or *Elizabeth's*. Sabina, just before Busua Beach Resort, has three clean rooms with netting on the windows (US$4.50) and runs a neat, friendly chop house. Elizabeth has clean doubles with mosquito nets for much the same price, while Mary's place, down a narrow alley, has three rooms looking inward (US$3.50) and two overlooking the ocean (US$4.50). All, given enough notice, will prepare you a meal for under US$2.

Several readers have written in to recommend what is called, variously, the *Alaska Beach Bar*, Club or Resort, which is opposite Sabina's. Owned, implausible as it may seem, by a couple of Alaskans, day-to-day running is in the hands of 'the exceptionally friendly Mary', says one reader, and her husband Frank. It has simple huts with fans for US$7 and serves good, inexpensive food.

Places to Eat

In Busua, there's no shortage of locals who'll offer to cook some of the day's catch

for you – just ask around. All require at least an hour's notice. You can also eat well at the restaurant of the *Busua Beach Resort*, where main dishes cost between US$4 and US$10.

In Dixcove, even if you're not staying at the *Quiet Storm Hotel*, they'll cook you a meal if you order in advance. Otherwise, look around the harbour, where you can buy smoked fish and other *street food*.

Getting There & Away

From Takoradi, take the main coastal highway west for 20km to Agona Junction, then head south for 6km to where the road splits. The left fork leads to Busua and the right one to Dixcove, both 6km further.

From Takoradi, tro-tros serve both Agona Junction and Dixcove. You can usually catch a tro-tro (US$0.25) from Agona Junction to Dixcove or Busua fairly easily. Should a vehicle to Busua be a problem, take one to Dixcove and walk over the headland – but not alone and not after dark.

WEST OF DIXCOVE
Princes Town

Princes Town has a fort and a fine beach, but neither rival those at Dixcove and Busua. **Fort Princes Town**, which is open to visitors, was originally called Gross Friedrichsburg by the Prussians who built it in 1683. It was luxurious by the standards of the day, with a monumental gateway and an impressive bell tower. The Prussians soon abandoned it to a crafty African gold trader, John Conny. The Dutch seized it from him in 1725 and renamed it Fort Hollandia, after which it became a minor trading station until it was ceded to Britain in 1872. The caretaker lets people sleep here, and will cook for you by prior arrangement.

Getting There & Away It isn't easy. Princes Town Junction on the coastal road is about 15km west of Agona Junction. From there it's about 10km or so south along a sandy road the condition of which rivals quicksand after rain.

GHANA

Axim

Of main interest in Axim, 69km west of Takoradi, is **Fort St Anthony**. Built by the Portuguese in 1515, it's the second-oldest fort on the Ghanaian coast. Taken by the Dutch in 1642, it repeatedly changed hands between Britain and Holland. It's in good condition and today houses government offices. Admission is US$0.75 plus US$0.25 for a camera.

Nearby is the village of **Nkroful**, birthplace of Nkrumah, whose remains lie in a modest mausoleum.

Perhaps the best near-to-nature-yet-comfortable place on the whole Ghanaian coast is *Ankobra Beach* (☎ 0342 21349), 5km and a US$2 taxi ride by road from Axim or a shorter, pleasant shoreline walk. Large, tastefully decorated African-style huts in studiously wild grounds cost between US$22 and US$31 and a family bungalow with air-con, sleeping four, is US$49. Meals aren't cheap, and it's a long way to the next restaurant, but their five different lobster dishes at US$8 or their fish and meat platters for between US$4.50 and US$7 are exceptionally good value.

Beyin & Half Assini

About 65km further west from Axim are Beyin and **Fort Apollonia**. Built by the British between 1750 and 1770, it's the newest and sturdiest of the coastal forts.

Half Assini is nearby. It has a bank and the *Captain Williams Hotel*. From here you can catch a boat to Côte d'Ivoire, but it's a hassle as this route is not well travelled.

The East

TEMA

Tema, 25km east of Accra, is Ghana's fourth-largest city and the country's major port. It's a fairly sterile place with little of interest unless you happen to be leaving Ghana by ship.

It has grown faster than any other city in Ghana (from 35,000 inhabitants in 1961 to about 250,000 now), thanks to the construction of the Akosombo Dam, as a result of which Tema became the site of a huge aluminium smelter. Many other industries, such as oil refining, cocoa processing and cement making, are based here too.

Orientation & Information

The core of the city stretches from the port northward to the big roundabout at the beginning of the Accra to Tema toll road (US$0.20), constructed in Nkrumah's time to link Ghana's capital with its major port. The city's commercial centre is Community 1. There, you'll find the market, the post office and various shipping companies. Community 8 is livelier and most hotels are here.

Ghana's major shipping company is the Black Star Line (☎ 202088), whose office is just north of the port, on Port Link Rd. For other shipping agencies, inquire at the Ghana Port-Harbour Authority (GPHA), on Harbour Rd, near the port entrance.

Places to Stay

Near the port, the friendly *Sakumo Royal Hotel* (☎ 204911) has small single/double rooms with fan and external bathroom for US$5/8 and rooms with air-con, bathroom and fridge from US$12.50. In the same area, on Accra Coastal Rd, the *Harbour Terrace Hotel* (☎ 206575), has spacious rooms with bathroom and fan/air-con for US$6.50/9.

In Community 8, a simple place, which you can't beat for friendliness, is *Franco's Fast Food* (☎ 306835). Primarily what it proclaims itself to be, it also runs a few clean singles/doubles, all with bathroom, at US$6.50/7.50 with fan and US$9/10 with air-con. Just down the road, is *Hotel Lucia* (☎ 306134), where rooms cost US$9 with bathroom and fan. Others, well worth paying the extra for, are US$13.50 with air-con, fridge and TV. In the same district, *Page Hotel* (☎ 306068) has air-con rooms with TV for US$15. *Hotel du Planet* (☎ 302613) has rooms with bathroom and fan for US$9.50 and one room with air-con at

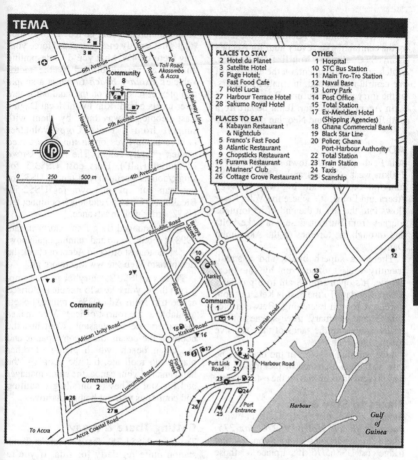

TEMA

PLACES TO STAY
2 Hotel du Planet
3 Satellite Hotel
6 Page Hotel;
   Fast Food Cafe
7 Hotel Lucia
27 Harbour Terrace Hotel
28 Sakumo Royal Hotel

PLACES TO EAT
4 Kabayan Restaurant
   & Nightclub
5 Franco's Fast Food
8 Atlantic Restaurant
9 Chopsticks Restaurant
16 Furama Restaurant
21 Mariners' Club
26 Cottage Grove Restaurant

OTHER
1 Hospital
10 STC Bus Station
11 Main Tro-Tro Station
12 Naval Base
13 Lorry Park
14 Post Office
15 Total Station
17 Ex-Meridien Hotel
   (Shipping Agencies)
18 Ghana Commercial Bank
19 Black Star Line
20 Police; Ghana
   Port-Harbour Authority
22 Total Station
23 Train Station
24 Taxis
25 Scanship

GHANA

US$12.50. Just across the street is the *Satellite Hotel* (☎ 302402), where superior rooms with fan/air-con cost US$10.50/13.

Places to Eat

In the port area, *Cottage Grove Restaurant* has inexpensive local dishes at lunch time. The *Mariners' Club*, a sailors' haven just north of the port, on Port Link Rd, is open to all.

Tema has several Chinese restaurants. In the centre you might try the *Furama Restau-rant*, on Krakue Rd. The long-standing *Chopsticks Restaurant*, on Hospital Rd, is popular, while the *Atlantic Restaurant* is on a par with Accra's finest.

You can eat at several of the hotels in Community 8. Alternatively, grab a bite at *Franco's Fast Food* or the Page Hotel's *Fast Food Cafe*, a hangout for Tema's youth, open from 7 am to 10 pm. The *Kabayan Restaurant & Nightclub* in Community 8, is open for dinner and has a live band on Friday nights.

Getting There & Away

Buses leave Tema's STC station, just north of the central market, every hour for Accra's main STC station. You'll find tro-tros, which are more frequent, on the east side of the central market and, in smaller numbers, at the lorry park on Turman Rd.

In Accra, tro-tros for Tema depart from both Tema station and Neoplan motor park.

ADA

Ada Foah, to give the town its full name, is 110km west of Accra and 20km from the junction on the main highway between Accra and Lomé. It's where the Volta River flows into the sea at the end of its tortuous journey from Burkina Faso, via Lake Volta and through the turbines of the Akosombo Dam.

There's a superb **beach** and a small, friendly tourist office run by the local people. It's open from 8 am to 6 pm daily except Sunday. To the east is **Keta Lagoon**, excellent for birdwatching. Between November and February, three species of sea turtle clamber up the sands of the extensive beach to lay their eggs.

One warning – swim in the ocean to be safe as there's a chance of picking up bilharzia (schistosomiasis) on the estuary side.

Places to Stay & Eat

At the top end, there's the German-owned **Paradise Beach Hotel** (☎ 276, fax 275) where singles/doubles with air-con, TV and fridge cost US$65/75. It's a place for those who enjoy water sports. Hotel guest or not, you can go waterskiing (US$8 a trip) or rent by the hour a windsurfer (US$11), catamaran (US$18) or, if you're really intent on destroying other people's pleasure, a jet ski (US$18).

At the dowdy, mildewed **Ada Hotel** (☎ 213), singles/doubles with ceiling fan and bathroom, complete with bathtub, are US$10/12. It's 500m from the extensive public beach, but that's about the only thing in its favour. Opposite is the wondrously named **Hushie-Hushie Bar**, where you can drink pleasurably and eat simply.

Ada's finest beach and least expensive accommodation can only be reached by canoe (that's not strictly true; you *could* force your way there by 4WD but you'd be despoiling an area as yet unpolluted by the motor vehicle). **Estuary Beach Camp** is a simple complex of reed huts on the sand bar where river meets ocean. Run by the local Dagma East people, it was built by them with support from a Peace Corps volunteer (whose name lives on in the largest reed shelter, grandly called 'The Amber Grove Memorial Hall'). Huts cost US$3/5 for single/double occupancy, a tent is US$2 or you can put up your own for US$2.50. Breakfast is US$1.50 and lunch or dinner are US$2; order well in advance.

Badly damaged by a freak storm in late 1998, it should be up and running again now. Ask at the tourist office in Accra or check the Ecotourism Web site www.ncrc.org.gh.

There's a US$0.25 entry fee to the camp. To get there, you take a 15 minute motorised canoe trip from Ada (US$3 return, tickets available at the tourist office). What makes the experience so pleasant is not just the boom of the ocean, the coconut palms and the clean beach, which plenty of other places can replicate, but the people – the helmsman of your canoe, the camp manager and his staff. They're unfailingly smiling and courteous without being smarmy.

Getting There & Away

Tro-tros (US$1.25) leave Accra's Tema station quite regularly for Ada. If you're travelling to Akosombo and beyond, there's no need to trek back to Accra. A ferry (US$1) runs three times a week up the Volta River as far as Asutsaure, near Kpong, from where you can easily get onward transport to Akosombo. It leaves Ada around 7.30 am and the journey takes up to 10 hours.

AKOSOMBO

The world's largest artificial lake, the 402km Lake Volta, backs up from Akosombo Dam, 104km north-east of Accra. The port is the terminus for a passenger boat service to Yeji

Akosombo Dam

Back in 1915, a far-sighted engineer, Albert Kison, realised that the Kwahu plateau was a rich bauxite deposit, that damming the Volta River at Akosombo could generate more than enough electricity for a huge foundry and that Tema could be converted into a deep-water port to export the aluminium. His conclusions, regarded as prohibitively expensive, gathered dust for 40 years until Nkrumah, keen to industrialise his country, picked up the idea. To finance the project, he was obliged to accede to the exceedingly harsh terms of Valco, the US company most interested in the project. Those terms were that, in return for constructing the dam, it would receive over two-thirds of the electricity generated for its aluminium smelter at Tema, that the price it paid for the electricity would be at cost, and that these generous terms would extend far into the future.

The project proved so expensive that the plans for extracting bauxite from the Kwahu plateau had to be shelved; the necessary raw material would be imported instead. Costs immediately escalated. Some 84,000 displaced people had to be relocated and at Tema a completely new port and town had to be constructed. Meanwhile, as work progressed, the world price for cocoa slumped sharply on several occasions. The drain on the economy was simply too much and, barely a month after Nkrumah inaugurated the dam in 1966, the army ousted him.

For years, the economy spiralled downward and Valco's savage terms allowed little potential for earning money from power generation, for realising the dam's potential for electrifying the country or for irrigating nearby farmland. Only now is the country truly beginning to benefit from its earlier sacrifices, but the dam's full potential is still far from realised.

The statistics regarding the dam and lake are impressive. The dam is 124m high and 368m wide and can generate 912,000 kilowatts of power. Except after severe droughts, there's potentially enough electricity to power all of Ghana and even a good portion of neighbouring Togo and Benin – but see the boxed text 'Ligh-Outs' in the Facts for the Visitor section. Because of the earthquake risk, the dam's not built of solid concrete but has a central nucleus of clay covered by a layer of crushed rock and outer walls covered with huge boulders.

Lake Volta, the world's largest artificial lake, stretches north from Akosombo for 402km. However, it has flooded 850,000 hectares of land (7% of Ghana's land surface) and much more remains to be done to compensate for this loss.

---

and for cargo ships heading north, which will also take a limited number of passengers.

The town of Akosombo, 2km before the dam and 6km before the port, was originally built to house the dam construction workers. There's a clean public pool (US$ 0.50) near the Volta hotel. Five kilometres south is **Atimpoku**, on the main road from Accra. Here you'll find the main lorry park and several cheap hotels and chop bars.

To visit the dam, you need a permit from the Volta River Authority (VRA) building, just down the hill from the Volta Hotel, or from the office of the VRA's Director of Power Operations in Accra. On Sundays, you can take a cruise (US$5) to nearby **Dodi Island** on the infelicitously named *Dodi Princess*. Leaving at 10 am, the trip takes six hours, with two hours on the island.

Ask permission before taking photos of the dam – something which, in principle, is forbidden even though thousands of shots from all angles must exist in family albums around the world.

Places to Stay & Eat

The stylish *Volta Hotel* (☎ 021-662639, fax 663791) is perched on a hill with sweeping views of the lake, dam and surrounding Akwamu highlands. It has a swimming pool and a terrace restaurant. Rooms, which start at US$80, have air-con, fridge and TV. A drink at the restaurant to savour the view is a must.

In Atimpoku, *Zito Guest House* (☎ 474), north-west of the Mobil station between Akosombo and Atimpoku, has four clean rooms with fan, bathroom and enormous bed for US$11. *Benkum Hotel* is also clean and has singles/doubles at US$5/6. The *Lakeside Motel* (☎ 310), south of Atimpoku towards Kpong, has a pleasant setting and rooms with fan for US$12 (US$15 with air-con). Readers have also recommended the *Sound Rest Motel*, about 6km from Akosombo on the Ho road. Its inexpensive rooms with shared bathroom are set around a central courtyard. You can camp (US$1.50) at *Aylos Bay Enterprise*, 5km from Akosombo near Adomi Bridge. This place has a delightful bar and restaurant and the owners intend to build a number of chalets.

You'll find excellent and exotic *street food* in the lakeside area. Specialities are fried shrimp sold in plastic bags, 'one man thousand' (minute fried fish), and abolo. The *Maritime Club*, 300m beyond the port, is lively at weekends. Closed on Wednesday, it has views of the lake and offers meals for about US$3.

Getting There & Away

Bus, Tro-Tro & Bush Taxi Buses, tro-tros and bush taxis for Akosombo (US$1) leave from Tudu station in Accra. Transport for Ho, Hohoe and Kpandu, which leaves from Tema station, also stops in Akosombo. STC doesn't serve Akosombo, but its daily services to these three towns pass nearby. If you have trouble finding transport directly to Akosombo, head for Atimpoku and take a taxi from the lorry park.

Boat Two leisurely, scenically attractive ways to travel onwards from Akosombo are by water. A weekly passenger service runs along Lake Volta between Akosombo and

Yeji, and more erratic, less comfortable cargo boats run as far as Buipe and, less frequently, on to Yapei. They make a great alternative to travelling northward by road. For details, refer to the Boat entry in the main Getting Around section earlier in this chapter. There's also a thrice-weekly river ferry between nearby Kpong and the small coastal resort of Ada at the mouth of the Volta River (for more details see the Ada section).

HO

Ho (population 65,000), in Ewé country, is the capital of Volta Region. About 80km beyond Akosombo and 184km north-east of Accra, it's a transit town for those on their way to Kpalimé in Togo. More importantly and in its own right, it's a good base for walking and for visiting some of the fascinating nearby villages.

The small **Volta Regional Museum** (admission US$1, closed Monday), behind the hospital on the western side of town is worth a visit. In addition to items of local and British colonial culture, you'll find relics of the period of German colonisation up to WWI, when the area was part of German Togoland. There's a small, helpful tourist office (☎ 560) in the State Insurance Corporation (SIC) building.

Places to Stay & Eat

The *E P Church Social Centre* has doubles with bathroom for US$7.50 and dormitory beds for US$2.50. It's at the church's headquarters, 1km from the centre, near the Basel Missionary monuments. The *Hotel de Tarso*, near the TV tower, has decent rooms for US$6. *Alinda Guest House* near the museum is in the same price range.

A little more upmarket is the *Peace Palace Hotel* (☎ 567) on the south-western side of town, off the road to Accra. It has eight air-con rooms and will prepare food on request. The best places in town are the attractive *Woezor Hotel* (☎ 8339) in its large compound and the *Freedom Hotel* (☎ 8158) a fair walk from the lorry park along the Kpalimé road. It has clean, comfortable rooms with fan and shared bathroom for US$6 (from US$9 with bathroom). Both hotels have restaurants.

For cheap food, try the lorry park or, better, *Dolly's Take Away Spot* beside the STC station. The *SSNIT cafeteria* serves plentiful, no-frills meals.

Getting There & Away

STC runs one bus a day (US$1.50) between Ho and Accra. It uses the smaller STC station in Accra, beside Makola Market. Private buses and tro-tros for Ho depart from nearby Tema station.

AROUND HO

Amedzofe

This mountain village, peeking above a forest reserve which is excellent for bird-watching, offers a waterfall within an easy stroll and stunning vistas from nearby **Mt Gemi**. You can stay at the *village resthouse* (☎ 091-301352), which you need to reserve through the Regional Administration Office or tourist office in Ho, or ask at the tro-tro stop for *Daria* or *Matilda*, who put up travellers (US$2.50 for a double).

Kpetoe

Kpetoe, a 15 minute tro-tro ride to the south-east of Ho, near the Togo border, is one of the country's major centres for kente cloth making. The attractive Ewé cloth sells for much less than the Ashanti version.

Tafi-Atome

Tafi-Atome, 25km north of Ho, is a superb example of ecotourism, developed by the villagers in cooperation with a Peace Corps volunteer. Local guides will take you to the **monkey sanctuary** (US$1.50), home to more than 200 sacred Mona monkeys, and on a tour of the village (US$0.75). You can stay with local families (singles/doubles, US$2.50/3.50) or take a half-board package (US$6.50) which includes evening entertainment such as drumming, dancing and story telling. You can also can rent a bicycle. A visit is strongly recommended.

Hohoe

Hohoe is another good base for walking and visiting nearby attractions. These include **Mt Afadjato** – 885m and Ghana's highest. The summit offers stupendous views of Lake Volta and the countryside below.

There are also a couple of more gentle walks, ending at the cool of a cascading waterfall. **Tagbo Falls** is a 45 minute hike from the village of Liate-Wote through indigenous forest and cocoa farms. The cliffs around the more spectacular **Wli Falls** (fee US$1), 45 minutes on foot from Wli village, are home during peak months to an estimated half a million fruit bats. When the season's right, you can also make a more strenuous two-hour trek to the upper falls. Hohoe is internationally famous as a centre for traditional herbal medicine.

There are several places to stay, including the *Grand Hotel* on the main street and, more upmarket, *Matvin Hotel* (☎ 0935-2134) and *Taste Lodge* (☎ 0935-8072), which also has a restaurant. Buses to Hohoe leave Accra's Tudu station once daily.

KETE-KRACHI

The original town of Kete-Krachi, once an important stop on slave trading routes, was flooded when Lake Volta was created. The new town is one of the lake's main ports, although the ferry dock is a 15 minute ride from town – and will become longer if the lake continues to recede. Kete-Krachi is also roughly the halfway point on the eastern overland route from Accra to Tamale.

The only accommodation in town is the spartan *Simon Hotel*, about 2km from the lake, where rooms with fan cost US$5.

There's a daily City Express bus between Tamale and Kete-Krachi (11 hours; US$9). Alternatively, there's a morning ferry between Kete-Krachi and Kwadiokrom on the west bank, from where you can take a bus to Kumasi (256km) via Atebubu and Mampong. The *Yapei Queen* stops here on the way to Yeji.

GHANA

ASHANTI ART & CULTURE

Ashanti have a matrilineally based social system, tracing descent through the female line so that a man's 'family' constitutes his sisters and their children, his mother and her relatives, while his wives and children belong to their own matrilineages. Marriage need not mean husband and wife setting up home together, but the wife will often send cooked food and visit later in the evening. Ashanti women are known for their independence, business acumen and influence in traditional politics.

When an Ashanti makes money they build a fine house in their home town or village, however remote that may be. Many small Ashanti towns boast a few houses whose magnificence is almost incongruous in simple villages, ill-served with basic facilities.

Funerals rather than marriages or naming ceremonies are the occasions that bring together family, townspeople and distant relatives – not surprising since traditional religion is ancestor-focused. At this time the streets of Ashanti towns teem with mourners and sympathisers wearing the distinctive funeral colours: black, red and shades of reddish-brown. Expenditure is lavish and there is a lot of socialising and drinking; new partners may be found, even business deals struck. At large funerals in towns some of the 'sympathisers' who join in the event have little to do with the family and never knew the deceased.

Adinkra cloth, together with kente cloth, is strongly associated with the Ashanti, who use it mainly for solemn occasions, when it is worn in toga-fashion. Designs are printed on cotton material using stamps cut on calabashes. The designs are symbolic, and each signifies a particular tradition or proverb.

Stools & Staffs

Stools feature prominently in Ashanti culture. There's an Ashanti saying: 'There are no secrets between a man and his stool', and when a chief dies his people say 'The stool has fallen'. Ashanti stools are among the most elaborate in Africa. Historically, certain designs, such as the seat supported upon the image of a leopard or elephant, were restricted to particular ranks within Ashanti society. The higher a person's status, the larger and more elaborate the stool.

Akoko nan tia ba, na ennkum ba
The hen treads upon its chicken but it does not kill them.

Mmarima Gwa
The man's stool: this is the first gift of a father to his son.

Mmaa Gwa
The woman's stool: it's usually the first gift presented by a man to his future bride.

Owo Foforo Adobe Gwa
This represents a snake climbing the palm-tree: 'attempting the impossible'.

Ntesie mate masie
Symbol of wisdom and knowledge: 'have heard and kept it'.

Kotoko
rennko a
we n'ami-
ade.
'his linguist
staff design

s a porcupine, the animal
symbol of the Ashanti:
ou can tell from the quills
whether the porcupine is
ready to fight or not. You
can easily tell when the
porcupine is serious'.

Legend of the Golden Stool

Komfo Anokye (the priest) drew the golden stool down from
the heavens, through dark clouds of thunder and dust, to rest
upon the knees of Osei Tutu, chief of Kumasi. Anokye collected nail and hair clippings from all the chiefs and queen
mothers, mixing them into a concoction that he smeared over
the stool. The soul of the Ashanti people now resided in that
stool, and Osei Tutu became their first Asantehene (king) although not even he was allowed to sit on the stool. The old
oppressor, the king of Denkyira, was defeated and his ornamental gold chains were hung on the golden stool. When a
neighbouring chief had a golden stool of his own made, the
then Asantehene Osei Bonsu invaded his state. The gold from
the offending stool was cast into two masks in effigy of its chief
and hung on the Ashanti golden stool.

If the stool was destroyed, so would be the Ashanti nation,
and that is why the Ashanti were ready to hand over their chief
to the British to be exiled, but not their stool, and fought a
bloody war to defend it. The war was lost and the stool was
hidden, tragically to be discovered years later by a bunch of
thieving road-builders who melted down its ornaments. The
restored stool is now kept at the palace in Kumasi where it is
brought out for sacred rituals. You can see a statue in Kumasi,
portraying Komfo Anokye reaching out and bringing down the
golden stool from heaven.

Dwannimmen
Ram's horn
symbol: 'it is
the heart and

not the horns that leads
a ram to bully'.

In social affairs stools act as symbols of authority, but the conse-
crated ones are homes to ancestral spirits and are 'fed' and 'given
drinks' during the Ashanti's Odwira Festival and at the Ga's Homowo
festival in the south. The first gift of a father to his son, and the first
gift bestowed by a man on his future bride, is a stool. Everyone has
their favourite; it would be heresy to sell or give it away. After death,
the deceased is ritually washed upon a stool, which is then placed in
the room for ancestral worship.

Chiefs consider stools to be their supreme insignia. There are
as many stool designs as there are chiefs, and the symbols
are infinite. Women's stools are different from men's.

There are also many linguist staff designs, all with
specific symbolism. Linguists, holding their staff, traditionally stand by the chief and speak on the chief's
behalf. When a request is made of the chief, usually elaborate and formally worded, the chief makes a monosyllabic
and, to the general public at least, probably inaudible
answer. The linguist then answers on the chief's
behalf, with a long speech well-laced with proverbs.
The post of linguist is hereditary, open to the talented

ASHANTI ART & CULTURE

Atuduro Kwadom Gwa
The keg of gunpowder stool – to be sat on with care ...

Pantu Gwa
The big spirit bottle (usually gin) stool, showing a European influence.

Sankofa
'It is no taboo to return and fetch it when you forget.' You can always undo your mistakes.

within the matrilineage of the linguist. The name Acheampong means great linguist, although the former head of state, General Acheampong, was notably bad at public speaking.

Festivals

The Ashanti calendar is divided into nine cycles of 42 days, called Adae. There are two special days of worship within each Adae when a celebration is held and no work is done, This is usually every sixth Sunday and then 17 days later on a Wednesday. The most important annual festival is the Odwira festival, which marks the last or ninth Adae.

Adinkrahene
Chief of all the adinkra designs, this forms the basis of adinkra printing.

Adae

On the day before, horn-blowers and drummers assemble at the chief's house and play until late at night. Early next morning, the chief's head musician goes to the stool house and drums loudly. The stool house, is a single dark room where the sacred stools are kept. These stools are thought to harbour the souls of the departed chiefs. The chiefs go there to ask their deceased forefathers for guidance and to offer them food and drink.

Eventually the chief arrives. The only people allowed inside are those who perform the rites and a few of the chief's relatives. Ritual food of mashed yam (fufu), eggs and chicken is then brought into the room; the chief places portions on each of the sacred stools inside. An attendant brings in a sheep on his shoulders. Its throat is cut, and the blood is smeared on the seats of all the stools. All then go outside to the courtyard, where the sheep is roasted and pieces of meat placed on each stool. The queen mother simultaneously prepares fufu and places some on the stools; the spirits do not eat salt, so none is used. Then a bell is sounded, indicating that the spirits are eating. Gin or schnapps is poured over the stools and the rest is passed around to all present. The ritual over, the chief retires to the courtyard and the merrymaking begins; drums beat and horns blast. The chief dons his traditional dress with regalia and sits in court, receiving the homage of his subjects. On some occasions, he is then borne in public in a palanquin shaded by a huge canopy, and accompanied by lesser chiefs.

Nkonsonkonson
Link or chain symbol of human relations. 'We are linked in both life and death. Those who share common, blood relations never break apart'.

Duafe
This wooden comb is one of the few purely representational adinkra patterns.

Odwira Festival

On Monday, the path to the royal mausoleum is cleared. On Tuesday, the day the ban on eating the new yam is lifted, tubers are paraded through the streets while the chief sexton proceeds to the royal mausoleum with sheep and rum to invoke the Odwira spirit. He then returns to the chief and is blessed; drumming follows well into the night. Wednesday is a day of mourning and fasting. People wear sepia-coloured attire and red turbans and there's lots of drinking and drumming all day long. Thursday is for feasting. Ritual food, including yam fufu, is borne in a long procession from the royal house to a shrine where it's presented to the ancestors. That night, when the gong strikes, everyone must go indoors; no one but the privileged few may see the procession of the dead, when the sacred stools are borne to the stream for their yearly ceremonial cleansing.

The climax is Friday, when the chief holds a great durbar, a grand meeting, at which all the subchiefs and his subjects come to pay their respects. The highlight is a great procession of elegantly dressed chiefs, the principal ones being borne on palanquins and covered by multi-coloured umbrellas.

Aya
This fern design is a symbol of defiance, meaning 'I am not afraid of you'.

Authors: Katie Abu, Alex Newton & Miles Roddis
With thanks to Professor Ablade Glover for permission to reproduce the adinkra and stools symbols and proverbs.

The Asantehene, the Ashanti king, is adorned with gold, dazzling onlookers and accentuating his authority and wealth.

The Centre

KUMASI

Kumasi, surrounded by rolling green hills, is a sprawling city of nearly a million people. Almost nothing remains of the original town, which was razed by the British in 1874 during the Fourth Ashanti War. It's the heart of Ashanti country, capital of the ancient kingdom and home to the Asantehene, the king, whose palace is open to visitors. It has an old fort (now a military museum), the Kwame Nkrumah University of Science and Technology, the palace museum of the Ashanti kings and the vast Kejetia Market, reputedly the largest in West Africa.

Ashanti culture is Ghana's richest and most self confident. In Kumasi, there are numerous colourful festivals in the summer and Akan religious ceremonies in honour of the ancestors are held at 42 day intervals throughout the year. In the area are Ashanti villages specialising in crafts such as goldsmithing, kente cloth weaving, adinkra cloth printing and the carving of Ashanti stools.

Orientation

The city's layout can be confusing because of its hilly environment. The action part is ringed by Bypass Rd, whose major junctions include Airport Roundabout (for the airport and Bonwire), Suame Roundabout (for Mampong and Tamale) on the northern side, and Ahodwo Roundabout, also known as Georgia Roundabout, on the southern side.

The heart of town is the market. The train station is just to its south. On the north-western side of the market are Kejetia Circle, a traffic-clogged roundabout with an endearingly kitsch representation of the revered Ashanti Golden Stool, and Kejetia motor park, the main transport park. The modern commercial district is in Adum, whose major landmark is Prempeh II Roundabout.

Information

Tourist Office The helpful Ghana Tourist Board office (☎ 26243) is within the National Cultural Centre complex. It's open from 9 am to 5 pm Monday to Friday and until noon on Saturday. The friendly staff can arrange guided tours of the city and surrounding craft villages.

Money At Barclays, on Prempeh II Roundabout, you can get money with a Visa card and they don't charge commission on travellers cheques. However, the service is outstandingly slow, even by local banking standards. Standard Chartered across the street is faster and will change both foreign notes and – against a fat commission – travellers cheques. The forexes, dotted all over town, are altogether more convenient for changing cash although many refuse travellers cheques.

Post & Communications The main post office on Stewart Ave is open from 8 am to 5 pm weekdays. It has an efficient 24 hour telecommunications office and a poste restante window (open weekdays from 8 am to 4.30 pm). Poste restante here is reliable and free.

Beside it is Ghana Telecom, where you can make international calls 24 hours a day. You can access the Web and send emails at CPC Ltd (☎ 24377), just off Asafo Roundabout. Open from 7 am to 8 pm, they charge US$1 per outgoing page and US$0.50 per page printout of incoming messages.

Travel Agencies & Tour Operators Kumasi Travel Agency (☎ 22217) and Johnson's Travel & Tours (☎ 22604), near-neighbours on 24 February Rd, are well established. Kay-Sika Travel & Tourism (☎ 24079), is also reliable. Kessben Travel Agency (☎ 27597, fax 24216), on Western Bypass Rd and M&J Tours (☎ 29337, fax 24216), just south of Prempeh II Roundabout will arrange tours of Kumasi and nearby attractions.

Medical Services The Benny Vee Pharmacy on Bantama High St carries a wider range of drugs than most and is open around the clock.

KUMASI

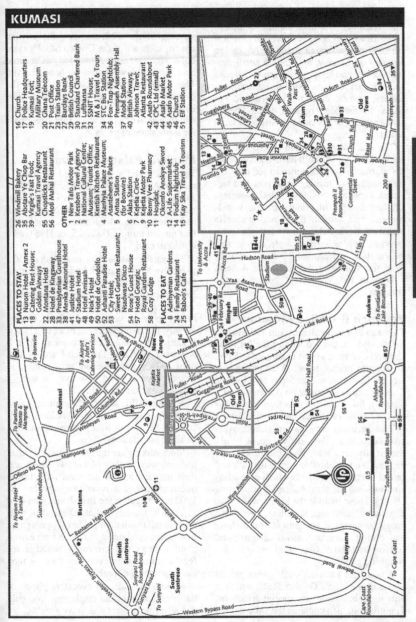

PLACES TO STAY
13 Nurom Hotel - Annex 2
18 Catering Rest House; Golden Airways
22 Montana Hotel
28 Presbyterian Guesthouse
33 Menka Memorial Hotel
41 Justice Hotel
47 Stadium Hotel
48 Hotel Amissah
49 Hok's Hotel
50 Hotel de Godolfo
53 Ashanti Paradise Hotel; City Hotel; Sweet Gardens Restaurant; Nsadwase Disco
57 Rose's Guest House

PLACES TO EAT
24 Adehyeman Gardens
25 Family Restaurant
25 Baboo's Cafe
26 Windmill Bakery
35 Abotare Ye Chop Bar
39 Virgie's Fast Food; Kumasi Travel Agency
55 Chopsticks Restaurant
56 Moti Mahal Restaurant

OTHER
1 New Tafo Motor Park
2 Kesben Travel Agency
3 National Cultural Centre; Museum; Tourist Office; Kentish Kitchen Restaurant; Asantehene's Palace
4 Manhyia Palace Museum; Asantehene's Palace
5 Antoa Station (for Bonwire)
6 Alaba Station
7 Kejetia Circle
9 Kejetia Motor Park
10 Benny Vee Pharmacy
11 Hospital; Okomfo Anokye Sword
12 A-Life Supermarket
14 Podium Nightclub
15 Kay Sika Travel & Tourism
16 Church
17 Police Headquarters
19 Kumasi Fort; Military Museum
20 Ghana Telecom
21 Post Office
23 Train Station
27 Barclays Bank
29 British Council
30 Standard Chartered Bank
32 Lufthansa; SSNIT House;
34 STC Bus Station
36 M & J Travel & Tours; Fox-Trap Nightclub; Prempeh Assembly Hall
37 Mobil Station
40 British Airways; Johnson Travel; Atlanta Restaurant
42 Asafo Roundabout
43 CPC Ltd (email)
45 Asafo Motor Park
46 Church
51 Elf Station

GHANA

Royal Georgia;
Royal Garden Restaurant;
Cozy Lodge

See Enlargement

To Nurom Hotel & Tamale
To Airport & Jofel's
To Bonwire
To Pankrono, Mampong
To University & Accra
To Kuntansi & Lake Bosumtwi
To Cape Coast
To Sunyani
To Cape Coast

Odumasi
Bantama
North Suntreso
South Suntreso
Danyame
Asukwa
New Zongo
Bimpeh Hill
Old Town

Kejetia Market
Stadium
Suame Roundabout
Sunyani Roundabout
Ahodwo Roundabout
Cape Coast Roundabout
Prempeh II Roundabout

Fuller Road
Guggisberg Road
Prempeh II St
Harper Road
Government Road
Raintree Rd
Cadbury Hall Road
Lake Road
Hudson Road
Maxwell Road
Asantewaa Road
Yaa Road
24 February Rd
Bantama Road
Bantama High Street
Wesleyan Road
Mampong Road
Kotoko Road
Odumah Rd
Zongo Road
Anloga Road
Nhyaeso Road
Ofinso Rd
Western Bypass Road
Southern Bypass Road
Cedar Avenue
Pine Avenue
Bekwai Road
8th St
11th St

National Cultural Centre

The National Cultural Centre complex, rather run-down now, is open daily from 8 am to 5 pm, although many activities are dormant on Sunday. It houses a small museum of Ashanti history, a library with books and magazines on Ashanti culture and history, several craft workshops and the Ghana Tourist Board regional office. There's also a restaurant (for more details see Places to Eat).

The craft workshops are spread out and not well signed, so you'll have to ask around. It's worth a little persistence to see the 'lost wax' method of making brass pots and figurines, kente and broadloom cloth weaving, adinkra dye-printing and potters, woodcarvers, and sandal, drum and umbrella makers at work. All items are for sale.

When you're satiated, refresh yourself with a flask of fresh palm wine (US$0.15) from the vendor at the miniature Ashanti village in the south-west corner of the complex.

Prempeh II Jubilee Museum

This rather cramped museum (admission US$0.50) is in the grounds of the National Cultural Centre. It's open from 9 am to 5 pm, Tuesday to Friday, from 10 am to 4 pm at weekends and from 2 to 5 pm on Monday. Constructed to resemble an Ashanti chief's house, it has a courtyard in front and walls adorned with traditional carved symbols.

The museum may be small and overcrowded and the surly guide only marginally less inert than the objects on display, but you shouldn't miss the rich and rare collection of artefacts which give a fascinating insight into Ashanti culture and history. These include the king's war attire, ceremonial clothing, jewellery, protective amulets, personal equipment for bathing and dining, furniture, royal insignia and some particularly fine brass weights for weighing gold.

Among the museum's intriguing photos is one of the king's **Golden Stool**, which is only brought out on very special occasions. The museum also contains the fake golden stool handed over to the British in 1900. After the occupation of Kumasi at the beginning of the 20th century, the British governor, aware of the Golden Stool's symbolic significance, demanded, as a final humiliating blow, that it be handed over. The Ashanti elders decided to dupe the British by making a replica stool. The British fell for the trick and the real stool, which was secreted away, didn't reappear for more than 20 years.

Manhyia Palace Museum

To get a feel for the life and times of a modern Ashanti ruler, visit Manhyia Palace and its museum. It's open from 9 am to noon and from 1 to 5 pm daily. Admission, which includes a video introduction and an excellent guided tour, is US$2.25, or US$1 with a student card.

The palace was built by the British in 1925 to receive King Prempeh I when he returned from a quarter of a century of exile in the Seychelles to resume residence in Kumasi (it was the least they could do since they'd blown up the previous royal palace). Consequently, the architecture has more of a Home Counties than an African flavour about it. It was used by Kings Prempeh I and II and, until 1974, by the present ruler, Otumfuo Opoku Ware II, who now lives in today's palace, just over the wall.

The pre-WWII and 1950s furniture – with the just possible exception of Ashantiland's first TV set – is of little interest apart from its regal associations.

More striking are the unnervingly lifelike, life-size wax models of the two kings and their mothers and of the most redoubtable queen mother, Yaa Asantewa, who led the 1900 revolt against the British and who died in exile in the Seychelles. Dressed in their royal regalia with their golden slippers (for a ruler's feet must never touch the bare earth), chunky rings and crowns – whether for feasts, funerals or everyday wear – they exude power and wealth.

Around the walls are evocative photos of the time and cabinets displaying fine gold and silver ornaments and brass weights.

Inquire here or at the Ghana Tourist Board if you're interested in having an appointment to meet the Asantehene. As his health isn't very good these days, his previously regular appearances have become more sporadic. However, you can occasionally arrange to meet the queen mother by advance appointment at the Secretariat on the eastern side of the palace grounds. If you're lucky enough to get an audience, etiquette demands presentation of a bottle or two of schnapps when meeting the royals.

Okomfo Anokye Sword

Set back from the roundabout, west of the National Cultural Centre, in the grounds of the Okomfo Anokye Teaching Hospital behind Block C (you still with us?) is the Okomfo Anokye Sword. The sword, partially visible, much rusted and enclosed in broken wood planks, has been in the ground for three centuries and has never been pulled out. According to Ashanti legend, it marks the spot where the Golden Stool descended from the sky to indicate where the Ashanti people should settle. If anyone ever pulls the sword out, the legend continues, their kingdom will collapse.

Kejetia Market

The centre of Kumasi is the huge, 10 hectare market with its 10,000 or so traders. Seen from above, its rusting tin roofs give the appearance of a vast shanty town. But below, despite two fires that swept through its narrow alleyways in 1995, it's throbbing, vital – and infinitely confusing.

It sells everything from foodstuffs to kente cloth, northern Muslim smocks, beads, Ashanti sandals, batik and bracelets. Other curiosities include smoked bush meat, such as monkey or bat, and fetish items, like vulture heads, parrot wings and dried chameleons.

Kente cloth, made locally, is a particularly good deal here. It's usually sold only in long pieces and price varies according to the composition of the material (cloth containing a mixture of cotton, silk and rayon is more expensive than all-cotton, for example) and weave (double weave is naturally more expensive than single).

Military Museum

Old Kumasi Fort and its museum merit a visit. They're open from 10 am to 5 pm Tuesday to Saturday ('Sunday and Monday: Off Duty', says the sign with a metaphorical click of the heels).

The fort was originally constructed by the Ashanti in 1820. In 1873, during the Fourth Ashanti War, it was razed by the British, who built the present structure in 1896. The most interesting section relates to the British-Ashanti war of 1900, when the Ashanti, led by their queen mother, Yaa Asantewa, temporarily besieged the fort, starving the British residents. The museum's major part is an extraordinary and diverse collection of booty amassed by the West Africa Frontier Force, forerunner of today's Ghanaian army, with items looted from the Germans in Togo in WWI and, in WWII, from the Italians in Eritrea and Ethiopia and from the Japanese in Burma.

There are some fascinating old maps and photographs from colonial and post-independence times. You'll also see the detention cells where serious criminals were kept and where many of them went blind from lack of light. A very professional guided tour, perhaps overly thorough for all but military buffs, takes about an hour and is well worth the US$1 fee.

Kumasi Hat Museum

For a quirky experience, call by the Nurom Hotel (see the Places to Stay – Budget section following). There, the owner, Chief Nana Kofi Gyemfi II, has assembled an amazing personal collection of hats from all over the world – more than 2000 of them. Beginning with his first headgear, back in 1928 when he was a young boy, he has assembled a collection of fedoras, sombreros, boaters, bowlers and much more that would be remarkable anywhere and which are truly astounding in fringe Kumasi.

Places to Stay – Budget

Camping You can camp in the spacious grounds of the *Presbyterian Guesthouse* for US$1.50 per tent. Alternatively, check with the friendly owner of *Rose's Guest House*, listed under top end hotels, as she has been known to allow camping there.

Hotels In Adum, the heart of town, there are three choices. The best is the two storey colonial-style *Presbyterian Guesthouse* (☎ 23879), all deep wooden balconies and high ceilings, on Mission Rd. Known locally as Presby's, it's popular with overland expeditions and a great place to meet other travellers. Large, basic rooms with twin beds are a bargain at US$2.50 per person. It's often full, so you'd be wise to call ahead and reserve a room. You can use the kitchen for free and there are several reasonable places to eat nearby.

The central *Montana Hotel* charges US$3/3.50 for sombre singles/doubles with fan and shared bathroom. To get there, go down a small alley on Odum Rd, just before the junction with Prempeh II St. The smaller *Nurom Hotel Annex II* is a notch better. It charges US$4/5 for spacious, clean singles/doubles with overhead fan and shared bathroom.

There are several good hotels on Accra Rd, which becomes 24 February Rd closer to the centre. The old-style *Menka Memorial Hotel* (☎ 26432) has large, reasonably clean rooms (the 2nd floor ones are better) with wide beds, fan, and decent shared bathroom for US$6.50. Two men – or for that matter two women – aren't allowed to share the same room, but such a restriction's fairly common in Ghana. At the *Justice Hotel* (☎ 22525), clean singles/doubles with fan and shared bathroom cost US$6/7, or US$8/10 with bathroom and US$15 with air-con. The best deal of all in this area, is the *Hotel de Gondolfo* (☎ 22866), where singles with shared showers cost between US$3 and US$5 and doubles between US$4.50 and US$7.

The *Nurom Hotel*, in Suame district on the northern outskirts of town, has pleasant doubles with bathroom for US$9, a bar, a restaurant – and a small but fantastic hat museum on the top floor.

During university vacations, you can also stay for around US$1 in *student residences* of the University of Science and Technology.

Places to Stay – Mid-Range

The *Ashanti Paradise Hotel* (☎ 24222) down a small lane off Harper Rd just north of Cadbury Hall Rd, where all rooms have a bathroom with hot water, is excellent value for money. Small but quite adequate rooms with fan cost US$9 and larger ones with tiled bathroom are US$13. Their air-con rooms with fridge, TV and carpet, cost US$22, or US$27 with bathtub and small living room. Although a little far from the centre, it's just off a regular shared taxi route. Readers sing the praises of their home cooking, which you need to order in advance.

The *Hotel de Kingsway* (☎ 26228), in a side street 100m north-east of Prempeh I Roundabout, is at the heart of things. Rooms with shared bathrooms cost US$12 while comfortable ones with air-con and bathroom range from US$17 to US$26. On the ground floor, there's a huge, desolate area for drinking and dancing which only comes to life on Saturday, when it's Old Timers Night. There's a rather gloomy restaurant with a limited range; choices are wider and better at places within easy walking distance of the Kingsway.

Several of the better mid-range hotels are near the stadium in the quiet residential area of Asukwa. At the *Stadium Hotel* (☎ 23647) rooms with fan and bathroom are US$15, or US$28 with air-con. It's a popular place in its category and is often full. The quiet *Hotel Amissah* (☎ 25601), two blocks away, in a side street off 8th St, has singles/doubles with air-con, large beds, plush carpet, refrigerator and satellite TV for US$25/29.

The old and endearing *Catering Rest House* (☎ 26506), on Government Rd, continues to try its best against slicker private sector competition. All rooms have a bathroom and, at US$16 with fan and US$20.50 for air-con, TV and fridge, including breakfast, they're excellent value if you don't mind general dowdiness. The *City Hotel* (☎ 23293), on Raintree Rd, which is state-wned, may once have been grand, but owadays it's decidedly threadbare. Air-con ooms with balcony and satellite TV cost etween US$24 and US$27 and the annexe as rooms with bathroom and fan for 'S$13.50. If you like the idea of shopping nd enjoying yourself under one roof, the omplex has a casino, numerous shops, eauty parlour, small grocery store, maga-ine stand and gift shop. The Nsadwase isco here, open on Friday and Saturday nly, is quite popular. The hotel's saving race is the excellent, independently man-ged Sweet Gardens Chinese Restaurant.

'laces to Stay – Top End

ir-con rooms with TV at *Nok's Hotel* (☎ 24438, fax 24162) on Hudson Rd cost etween US$41 and US$51 and represent ood value. The new *Cozy Lodge* (☎ 27030, x 27031) is in a quiet location. Carpeted ngles/doubles with air-con, fridge and TV ost US$47/51.

Hotel Georgia (☎ 24154, fax 24299), just ast of the Ahodwo Roundabout, is well run nd hospitable. It has good service, a small ttractive beer garden and comfortable ooms with air-con and colour TV. Like the ity Hotel, it has a great Chinese restaurant, e Royal Garden. Singles/doubles cost S$77/88. Rooms at *Rose's Guest House* (☎ 23500, fax 23500), on Harper Rd, cost S$33. It's a small, friendly hotel with a arden setting, air-con rooms with satellite V. The service is tops, the cook's a miracle orker and there's a good bar and restaurant ith an international menu. Even if you ither stay nor eat here, the garden's a good ace for a drink.

laces to Eat

heap Eats For good *street food*, sample e roadside cooking of the women who quat outside the Hotel de Kingsway and orthward along Prempeh II St. There are so lots of street food stalls next to the ilway line, just south of Kejetia Circle, and ongside the eastern wall of the stadium.

Two good places near Prempeh II Round-about are *Baboo's Cafe* and the *Windmill Bakery*. Both are open from breakfast time to around 7 pm. Warmly recommended by both locals and travellers, Baboo's is one of the few joints in town where you can get vege-tarian food. Cheerful and spotlessly clean, it specialises in Indian cuisine (try their blow-out curry lunch for US$4). They also serve good beef burgers (US$2), pizzas (US$2.50) and chunky sandwiches (US$1.50). The Windmill, on the eastern side of the round-about, is both restaurant and bakery. The service is fast and friendly and they do good Ghanaian meals (about US$2), including several vegetarian choices. They also offer a few European dishes – and a great breakfast selection.

If you're pushed for time, avoid the 1st floor *Family Restaurant*, opposite Baboo's, run by a wizened Lebanese in a pillbox hat. The food's fine, when it comes, although the portions tend towards the stingy side. Only the bill arrives with any degree of alacrity and the mosquitos are man-eaters.

In the heart of town, the *Podium Night-club* on Nsenie Rd does fast food takeaways during the day. There are several fairly in-expensive places to eat near the Menka Hotel on 24 February Rd. These include *Virgile's Fast Food*, 100m to the east, which stays open until midnight. The selections include hamburgers and chicken with fried rice or chips. Much cheaper beef skewers are grilled at night. A few metres further is the *Atlanta Restaurant*, next to Johnson Travel on 24 February Rd, which has a lively bar and serves both African and Chinese dishes. Not far away, in the stadium area, you'll find several small restaurants under the stands, including a Chinese one which serves huge portions.

There's good, no-frills Ghanaian food at the basic and popular *Abotare Ye Chop Bar* south-east of the STC station on Odum Rd.

African Within the National Cultural Centre, the thatched-roof *Kentish Kitchen Restaurant* is open for breakfast and until 10 pm. It serves a variety of Ghanaian dishes, including a few vegetarian options, at around US$1.50 a plate. It's also a pleasant spot to just sit and sip a drink between bouts of exploring the centre.

In greater comfort, **Jofel's Catering Services**, out on the airport roundabout, does excellent local meals for about US$3.50. The vast **Adehyeman Gardens**, just north of Kejetia motor park has good Ghanaian cuisine for around US$3 plus a variety of international dishes.

Asian & Indian Kumasi has particularly fine oriental cuisine. **Chopsticks Restaurant** (☎ 23221) is one of the city's top restaurants. Open only in the evenings and closed Monday, it serves succulent Chinese food, with most main dishes in the US$3 to US$5 range. It's deservedly popular and you'd be prudent to reserve.

Sweet Gardens, the Chinese restaurant at the City Hotel, and the **Royal Garden** at Hotel Georgia are also excellent.

The **Moti Mahal Restaurant** offers good Indian cuisine.

Entertainment

Bars There's no shortage of simple, cheerful spots in Kumasi. For somewhere a bit more flash, one of the best places for a drink, day or night, is **Adehyeman Gardens**. **Virgile's Fast Food** is simple and cheap and the relaxing garden at **Rose's Guest House** has calm and comfort. If you're dying for draught beer, head for the **Kentish Kitchen** restaurant at the National Cultural Centre, which is open until 10 pm.

Nightclubs If you're in Kumasi on a Saturday night, visit the **Old-Timers Club** at the Hotel de Kingsway in the heart of town. It attracts crowds, many in traditional dress. The dancing starts early, around 6 pm, lasting until 2 am. Since the 1950s, this legendary nightclub has been the home of Kumasi's major highlife bands, but those days are sadly gone and there's rarely live entertainment there or anywhere in town. One exception is **Adehyeman Gardens**. A local band performs there every Saturday evening.

Entrance is free and drinks and food are available.

The flashiest places in town include the **Podium Nightclub**, which serves ice cream and fast food during the day and mutates into a nightclub on Wednesday to Saturday evenings; the **Fox-Trap Nightclub** next to Prempeh Assembly Hall, **Masarati** (formerly Star Nite Club) near the stadium, and the **Nsadwase Disco** at the City Hotel. Most are open only from Thursday to Sunday.

Shopping

The best supermarket is the **A-Life** chain which has three stores in town. Their branch on Prempeh II St has the largest variety of stock.

Getting There & Away

Air Airlink has flights from Kumasi to Accra (US$27) at 6.30 am on Monday and Wednesday and at 6 pm on Friday. It flies from Accra to Kumasi, departing at 5 pm on Tuesday, Friday and Sunday. There are northbound flights to Tamale (US$42) on Monday, Wednesday and Friday. For information and reservations, go to M&J Travel & Tours (☎ 29337) in SSNIT House, just off Harper Rd.

Fan Airways (☎ 20087) has at least one flight daily to Accra (US$31) and flies to Tamale (US$36) Wednesday and Friday. Muk Airways flies daily except Saturday to both Accra and Tamale. The latter's agents in Kumasi are Johnson Travel (☎ 22905). Golden Airways, grounded at the time of writing, may be up and flying again.

Bus The STC bus terminal (☎ 24285, 21940 for information) is much more orderly than the seething Kejetia motor park. 'No Smoking, Selling, Standing or Preaching Allowed in the Bus', says the sign. Don't say we didn't tell you! It's on a clearly marked side road off Odum Rd. Eight buses a day go to and from Accra (255km, five hours, US$3). Those leaving at 8 am and 1 pm have air-con and are worth every cedi of the US$4.50 fare. STC runs buses twice a day to Tamale (380km, six to eight hours, US$

and also to Cape Coast (200km, four hours, US$3) and on to Takoradi. There's a Tuesday, Thursday and Saturday service to Bolgatanga and two buses a week, on Monday and Saturday, for Wa.

On major routes, OSA, GPRTU and City Express are equally reliable. City Express, for example, has a daily run to Tamale and a daily evening bus to Bolgatanga. Most services leave from Kejetia motor park.

Bush Taxi, Tro-Tro & Minibus Kejetia motor park, just west of the market, is by far the largest lorry park. In addition, vehicles for Sunyani, Cape Coast and Takoradi, plus some minibuses heading for Accra, leave from Asafo motor park on Fuller Rd. Trotros for many local destinations, including Kuntansi and Lake Bosumtwi, also depart from here. Vehicles for Tamale leave from New Tafo (Krofrom) motor park on the northern side of town. Those for Bolgatanga, Bawku, Tamale and Ouagadougou (Burkina Faso) use New Tafo motor park while minibuses to Tamale (again) and destinations in the Upper West depart from Alaba station off Zongo Rd, on the north-western side of the market.

Train Two trains a day go to Takoradi, departing at 6 am (except Sunday) and 8 pm. The morning one takes about eight hours while the night train usually arrives about 9 am the following day. If you take the latter, you'll save yourself a night's accommodation, but you'll miss some attractive scenery en route. The cost is US$3/2 for 1st/2nd class. The Accra train isn't even worth considering; it takes twice as long as road transport, has no bar or restaurant, and sleeping berths are available only in 2nd class.

Getting Around

Taxi There's no inner-city bus service, so shared taxis take their place. The standard fare is US$0.15. Most taxi lines start at Kejetia motor park and across the street at the intersection of Prempeh II and Guggisberg Rds. Two more lines head south along Harper Rd, starting from Ntomin Rd, behind the post office, and serve the areas of town beyond Ahodwo Roundabout. A private, or 'dropping', taxi normally costs under US$1 (US$1.50 for a longer run within town) and you can hire one by the hour for about US$3.

Car You can hire a car from the City Hotel and Hotel Georgia. A cooperative called Kumasi Airport Car Hiring Group has vehicles for rent in the large open space in front of the Asantehene's Palace. Both GPRTU and Protour have vehicles driven by trained driver-guides. Look for their distinctive blue uniforms.

AROUND KUMASI
Pankrono, Ahwiaa & Ntonso

These three craft villages lie north-east of Kumasi on the road to Mampong. They're very much on the tourist trail, so don't expect any special bargains or unique experiences. The first two are on the outskirts of Kumasi, beyond Suame Roundabout. **Pankrono** is a major pottery centre. One kilometre further is **Ahwiaa**, famous for its woodcarving. Two types of wood are used; the lighter one is sesée, the darker one, mahogany. Much wood purported to be mahogany is, however, dyed with shoe polish. You can have a stool made to order if you wish; a large one takes about three days. (If termites later become a problem, soak the stool with lighter fluid – or put it in the freezer.) **Ntonso**, 15km further on the same tar road, is the centre of adinkra cloth printing.

You can hire a private taxi to get to these towns or take a tro-tro from Kejetia motor park.

Bonwire

Bonwire, 18km north-east of Kumasi, is the most famous of the nearby craft villages and specialises in weaving kente cloth. The village receives lots of tourists and prices are no better than you'll find in Kumasi. It also has some fine traditional Ashanti housing compounds with enclosed inner courts.

Buses leave from Antoa station in Kumasi. They depart throughout the day and the cost is US$0.25.

Owabi Wildlife Sanctuary

At Owabi, a small sanctuary 16km north-west of Kumasi, just off the Sunyani road, you can stroll through the quiet forest. The Owabi River, which flows past Kumasi, has been dammed here, making it an important wetland area for birds and a few aquatic animals.

Lake Bosumtwi

Bosumtwi is a crater lake 38km south-east of Kumasi. It's a popular weekend venue for people from Kumasi, who come here to swim, canoe, fish, or just rest and enjoy the lush surrounding hills, which rise to more than 400m.

You can take an 8km motorboat trip across the lake for US$6. Or stroll the banks and visit some of the 30 or so small villages around the perimeter. You can cycle around its 30km circumference and swimming is safe.

Not only is Bosumtwi the country's largest and deepest natural lake (86m deep in the centre), but it's also sacred. The Ashanti believe that their souls come here after death to bid farewell to their god Twi. One interesting taboo is any form of dugout canoe, which is believed to alienate the lake spirit. So the fishermen head out on specially carved wooden planks, which they paddle either with their palms or with calabashes cupped in their hands.

Places to Stay & Eat At the lakeside, the very run-down *Sabon du Lac Hotel* has a pleasant covered patio overlooking the water. It has large basic rooms (US$9) with electricity and fan, but the shared bathrooms are filthy – not surprisingly since there's no running water and even drinking water can be hard to find. A better, but much more expensive, choice is the *resthouse*, high on a hill about 30 minutes walk from the lake. Owned and run by the district assembly, its chalets with two double beds costs US$25.

Bring your own food. To reserve, contact the district assembly (☎ 20146) or the Tourist Board office in Kumasi (☎ 26243).

It's possible to camp beside the lake or outside one of the nearby villages if you ask permission from the local chief.

Getting There & Away Minibuses run to the lake from Asafo motor park in Kumasi.

Bobiri Forest Reserve

Bobiri Reserve is a parcel of virgin, unlogged forest about 35km from Kumasi. It contains the **Bobiri Butterfly Sanctuary**, home to over 300 species of butterfly, and an arboretum with a detailed accompanying information sheet. It costs about US$20 per person to stay in the pleasant *guesthouse*.

To get there, take any vehicle going from Kumasi to Konongo or further south, and ask to be dropped off at Kubease, from where Bobiri is a 3km walk.

BOABENG-FIEMA MONKEY SANCTUARY

The twin villages of Fiema and Boabeng are 165km north of Kumasi via Nkoranza. The villagers have traditionally venerated and protected the black and white colobus and mona monkeys – more than 900 of them – which live in the surrounding forest. The animals, accustomed to humans, are so tame that they roam the streets and you're guaranteed close contact.

You can stay at the simple *guesthouse* (about US$ 4.50) which has a cook/caretaker and the villagers are developing a number of forest trails. The entrance fee to the sanctuary is US$2.50.

YEJI

Yeji, 216km north-east of Kumasi on the old Tamale road, is one of the main port towns on Lake Volta.

Rooms with shared bathroom at the *Alliance Hotel* have no running water, but they do have electricity from 6.30 to 10.30 pm. The *Volta Lake Hotel*, just down the street, is similarly priced but reportedly inferior. Doubles at the *Atlantic Hotel* cost US$3.50.

The 45 minute ferry to Makongo on the east bank runs twice a day: at 8 am, connecting with an OSA bus to Tamale (US$ 1.50), and at 3 pm. When you get off the ferry in Makongo, sprint for the bus or you'll have to stand for the five hour journey. The morning ferry connection with the bus isn't always reliable, so you may have to take a tro-tro.

For details of the lake steamer service to Akosombo, see the Boat entry in the main Getting Around section earlier in this chapter.

OBUASI

Obuasi (population 70,000) is 70km south of Kumasi on the Kumasi to Takoradi train line, in a steep valley surrounded by hills. Sitting upon some of the world's richest seams, it's the gold-mining centre of Ghana, owned by the recently privatised Ashanti Goldfields Corporation. The company conducts tours of the surface areas, although

Pollution from Gold Mining

A new law passed in 1989 encouraging small-scale mining saw a surge of unregulated quarrying and crude, manual extraction of the gold content. As a result, the already lifeless waters of the local rivers have been poisoned by mercury and other dangerous chemicals used in mining, the air is polluted by smoke containing arsenic and sulphur dioxide and it's impossible to grow crops around Obuasi and Tarkwa.

But people are no longer prepared to accept passively such contamination. In 1996, they staged a demonstration that was unique in Ghanaian history; as a protest against the environmental damage and government inaction, the traditional chiefs of the Tarkwa area marched through town wearing funeral cloth and red armbands, symbolising death.

you're unlikely to get underground. Tour days seem to vary. To reserve, phone the public relations officer (☎ 0582-494 or Accra 772190). It is, as you'd expect, a good place to buy gold items such as bracelets and earrings.

Places to Stay & Eat

There's no lack of hotels in a town which has so many contract workers. For a cheap room, try the modest *Black Star Hotel* or the *Sennet Hotel*. *Ceci's Lodge* and the *Silence Hotel* both have restaurants and rooms with fans. *Super Mambo* on the main street has self contained air-con rooms with fridge and TV for a bargain US$12. For more comfort at more cedis, check in at *Confidence Guest House* (☎ 0582-378) or *Anyinam Lodge* (☎ 0582-434). You can eat Chinese at *Goldfinger*, while the *Miners' Diner* offers the only Mexican food outside Accra.

Getting There & Away

The train between Kumasi and Takoradi passes through town twice a day in each direction. You can also take a bus or taxi from Kumasi; the trip takes from one to 1½ hours.

The North

TAMALE

Tamale (population 258,000), 640km north of Accra, is the capital and transport hub of the northern region. It's not exactly a swinging town. In fact, it's dead dull, except on Saturday nights. The heart of town is around the tall radio antenna (not to be confused with the smaller Ghana Telecom aerial). That's where you'll find the market, STC station and main motor park.

If you need to change money, the procedure at Barclays is simpler than at Standard Chartered, both near the town centre. The return on travellers cheques is also markedly better there.

The **market** is good for inexpensive leather goods (look out, in particular, for some stylish day-packs) and Ghana's north-

GHANA

ern cloths, especially those woven by the Gonja and Dagomba, which usually comes ready-tailored into women's dresses and men's smocks. A large man's smock should cost between US$18 and US$22 – a lot less than you'll pay in Accra.

The **National Cultural Centre** has an echoing auditorium with a solitary weaver and a few craft shops around the back. Nearby is a small compound where a Gonja and Mamprusi chief's compound are replicated; note the broken-pot decoration on the door jambs.

Colourful local celebrations include the Damba Festival and the fire festival of the Dagomba people. Dates of the Damba festival vary according to the Muslim calendar.

Places to Stay – Budget

Water is a chronic problem in Tamale. Whatever the array of showerheads, bath taps and bidets in your room, be prepared to sluice yourself with a bucket shower.

The *Alhassan Hotel* (☎ 23638), conveniently located near the motor park, has clean singles/doubles with fan and shared bathroom for US$4/5 (US$8 with bathroom). A room with fan at the friendly *Macos Hotel*, to the north of the town centre and clearly signed from the main drag, is US$4. The communal bathrooms are clean and – a rarity in Tamale – water spurts from the shower. There's no restaurant, but Emilia, the sociable landlady, will cook to order.

At the opposite end of town, off Salaga Rd, the neat, well maintained *Atta Essibi Hotel* (☎ 22569) is recommended for both atmosphere and friendliness. Clean singles/doubles with fan cost US$5/10, while those with bathroom are a rather overpriced US$16. The *Mirihca Hotel* (☎ 22935), nearby and on the other side of Salaga Rd, has

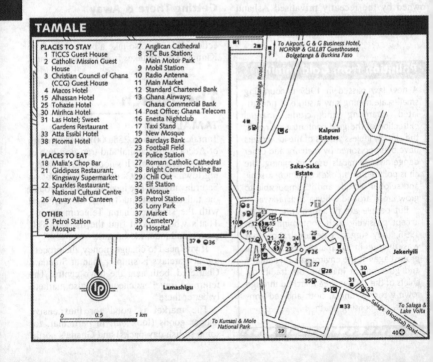

TAMALE

PLACES TO STAY
1 TICCS Guest House
2 Catholic Mission Guest House
3 Christian Council of Ghana (CCG) Guest House
4 Macos Hotel
15 Alhassan Hotel
25 Tohazie Hotel
30 Mirihca Hotel
31 Las Hotel; Sweet Gardens Restaurant
33 Atta Essibi Hotel
38 Picorna Hotel

PLACES TO EAT
18 Malia's Chop Bar
21 Giddipass Restaurant; Kingsway Supermarket
22 Sparkles Restaurant; National Cultural Centre
26 Aquay Allah Canteen

OTHER
5 Petrol Station
6 Mosque
7 Anglican Cathedral
8 STC Bus Station; Main Motor Park
9 Mobil Station
10 Radio Antenna
11 Main Market
12 Standard Chartered Bank
13 Ghana Airways; Ghana Commercial Bank
14 Post Office; Ghana Telecom
16 Enesta Nightclub
17 Taxi Stand
19 New Mosque
20 Barclays Bank
23 Football Field
24 Police Station
27 Roman Catholic Cathedral
28 Bright Corner Drinking Bar
29 Chill Out
32 Elf Station
34 Mosque
35 Petrol Station
36 Lorry Park
37 Market
39 Cemetery
40 Hospital

To Airport, G & G Business Hotel, NORRIP & GILLBT Guesthouses, Bolgatanga & Burkina Faso

Bolgatanga Road

Kalpuni Estates

Saka-Saka Estate

Jekeriyili

Lamashigu

To Kumasi & Mole National Park

To Salaga & Lake Volta

Salaga (Hospital) Road

0   0.5   1 km

rooms of similar quality. Singles with fan and shared bathroom cost US$7.50 and doubles with bathroom are US$12.50. Air-con rooms are in the US$16 to US$18 range.

The *Christian Council of Ghana (CCG) Guest House* on the Bolgatanga Rd, 2.5km north of the centre, has rooms with fan and shared bathroom for US$5, or US$6.50 with bathroom. They don't do meals, but guests can use the kitchen. Down a lane, just opposite, is the popular *Catholic Mission Guest House* (☎ 22265) in its leafy, mature compound. Singles/doubles with twin beds, fans and showers cost US$5.50/7 You can get lunch and dinner if you order in advance.

Places to Stay – Mid-Range
Several other local organisations, both church and lay, welcome visitors to their guesthouses, which are as good as any equivalent hotel and invariably more friendly. Like the mid-range hotels, they're often fully booked, so take the precaution of ringing to reserve.

The *Tamale Institute of Cross-Cultural Studies* (TICCS) (☎ 22914, fax 22836, email TICCS@africaonline.com.gh), another Catholic institution, is outstanding in its category. Go one block north from the Catholic Mission Guest House along the Bolgatanga Rd and turn left; it's about 500m along the road. Singles/doubles with fan and shared facilities cost US$12/17.50, or US$6 extra for air-con. The menu is international at lunch time (US$4) and Ghanaian for dinner (US$3). It's essential to reserve since, when courses are being held, there's little spare capacity.

About 4km further north on the Bolgatanga highway is the guesthouse of *NORRIP*, the Northern Region Rural Integrated Programme (☎ 23901 – and ask for the matron – no kidding!). Air-con rooms cost US$11 in chalets and US$13 in large caravans. For US$1, you can dunk yourself in the swimming pool of the adjacent Volta River Authority clubhouse.

One kilometre north of NORRIP and 1.5km to the right down a dirt road, is *GILLBT* (Tamale's hot on acronyms): the

Ghana Institute of Linguistics, Literacy and Bible Translation (☎ 22341). Their singles/doubles with fan and bathroom are US$9/12.50. They do lunches and dinners (sign up in advance) for US$2.50 or you can do your own cooking. It's a strictly no alcohol place.

Among the conventional hotels, the recently privatised *Tohazie Hotel* (☎ 23610), previously the Catering Rest House, charges US$10 for a bungalow with fan and bathroom and US$15 to US$17.50 for a large air-con room. It has a good restaurant.

The *Las Hotel* (☎ 22158), on Salaga Rd, has singles/doubles with fan for US$15/18 and doubles with air-con from US$20.50. All rooms are fairly spacious with tiled floors, clean sheets and work tables. It also boasts the city's best restaurant, the Sweet Gardens (see Places to Eat following).

The *Picorna Hotel* (☎ 22672), has for years been Tamale's best. Rooms, which cost between US$25 and US$27, have air-con, TV, refrigerator, comfortable chairs and modern bathroom. Cheaper singles at US$17 are similar but without TV or refrigerator. There's also a good restaurant, a bar, dancing on Saturday nights and an open-air cinema, active on Friday to Monday evenings.

The brand new *G&G Business Hotel* on the Bolgatanga Rd, with rooms at US$35, may now be open.

Places to Eat
For cheap Ghanaian food, check out the *street food* around the main market or visit the unmarked *Malia's Chop Bar*, opposite the central taxi stand and a particular favourite with locals. Just look for the crowd at lunch time. *Aquay Allah Canteen*, diagonally opposite the main police station, is open from 8 am to 6 pm and does a range of tasty, inexpensive local dishes.

Sparkles Restaurant, near the National Cultural Centre, despite its languid, offhand service, has decent enough food. It closes on Sunday. *Giddipass Restaurant* (can you resist such a name?) is popular with travellers; the staff smile and the service, although slow, is friendly. You can dine inside or out on their breezy, covered

GHANA

terrace. The menu's fairly extensive with most dishes costing around US$2.50.

Among the hotel restaurants, *Sweet Gardens Restaurant* at the *Las Hotel* has excellent Chinese cuisine. You can also eat well at the restaurant of the *Tohazie Hotel*, which has European fare for around US$3 to US$4, and at the *Picorna Hotel*.

Entertainment

The most popular drinking place for travellers is the terrace of *Giddipass*, although the overamplified music can kill conversation. Still in the centre, *Bright Corner Drinking Bar*, on Salaga Rd, is a small outdoor spot. While in the north, you ought to sample *pito*, the local millet brew, which is worth persevering with. You'll find it on sale at various places around the market.

Nightclubs, popular at weekends, include *Enesta Nightclub*, opposite the market, and *Chill-Out*, also known as Harry's Spot, a short walk from the *Tohazie Hotel*, whose own Saturday Old Timers' night also jumps. More upmarket, the *Picorna Hotel* shares in the Saturday night fever.

Getting There & Away

Air The airport is some distance north of town. Fan Airways (☎ 23645) has a daily flight, except Saturday, between Tamale and Accra (US$51) and Wednesday and Friday flights between Tamale and Kumasi (US$36). Muk Airways also flies daily except Saturday between Accra and Tamale (US$56). Airlink (☎ 2428), which uses the Ghana Airways office in Tamale, has flights on Monday, Wednesday and Friday to/from Accra (US$42 one way).

Tro-Tro, Bush Taxi & Bus Tro-tros, bush taxis and private buses all leave from the main motor park. The STC station is just behind it. There are twice-daily STC buses to both Kumasi (380km, six to eight hours, US$4) and Accra (640km, 12 to 14 hours, US$7).

OSA has a daily bus at 6 am for Makongo (US$1.50), from where you catch the ferry to Yeji and link with the Lake Volta steamer to Akosombo. They also operate the only bus service to Mole National Park (US$1.50), which leaves daily, in principle at 2.30 pm but usually later, once crammed to bursting point. They have a daily early morning run to Wa (US$3). City Express has a daily Bluebird express to Accra (US$6.50) and one to Kumasi (US$3). The buses are no more comfortable than any other, but they have pretensions: 'Bags of corn, groundnuts, yams and beans are not allowed on Bluebird buses', says the sign.

Bus travel to Bolgatanga (US$1.50) can be a problem since, although many head that way, most are already full when they roll through Tamale. City Express is your best choice. Your chances of finding space on a tro-tro or Peugeot are much better.

Getting Around

A taxi to the airport, which is quite a long way north of town, costs around US$3.

The best way to see Tamale and the surrounding areas is by bicycle. Near the main market and taxi stand, you can hire new Chinese-made bikes, strong and heavy as cast iron, by the hour (US$0.20) or day (US$1.50). One of the more scenic spins is north-west from the market, along Education Ridge Rd to the villages beyond; a satisfying 15km return trip.

To get to the accommodation options on the north side of town, you'll have little difficulty finding a shared taxi until about 9 pm.

AROUND TAMALE
Yendi

Yendi, 97km east of Tamale, is notable for its palace, an interesting fusion of Moorish and Sahelian styles. It's the home of the paramount Dagomba chief, the Ya-Na, who has 22 wives, distinguished by their shaven heads. Once a week there's a ceremony where his elders come with talking drums and praise-singers. It's not primarily a public spectacle, however, and you need to be invited. Yendi, like Tamale, is a good place to see the Damba and fire festivals of the Dagomba. The area was part of German Togoland until WWI. Many of the German

Dagomba

The traditional capital of Dagomba state is Yendi, the seat of their highest chief, the Ya-Na, who sits on a lion skin. Their chieftancy is a source of both pride and conflict for the Dagomba and the intrigue and tension between competing factions for succession at different levels is acute. The military nature of the Dagomba state is still evident from the use of muskets and horses in ceremony as well as swords in dances. They also have some of the most complex talking drum rhythms.

When the Dagomba arrived in the area as conquering horsemen the local people were culturally absorbed but the earth priests (Tendons) were retained because of their spiritual connection to the land. It was believed that Tendon, the god of the earth, would answer women's prayers faster than men's. So one day in a drought Dagomba men dressed as women and danced to their drums, asking for rain. Their prayers were answered and the dance, Bamaya, is still performed by men dressed as women.

The Dagomba fire festival takes place in July. According to legend a chief lost his son and was overjoyed when he found him asleep under a tree, but was angry that the tree had hidden his son. He punished the tree by having it burnt, and now on the night of the fire festival young men rush about with blazing torches.

Katie Abu

soldiers who died in conflict with the Dagomba are buried in the cemetery.

There are no hotels in Yendi, but there's a small **NORRIP compound**, where rooms have air-con and TV. It's prudent to reserve through the Tamale NORRIP Guest House (☎ 071-23901). Travellers also report that you can stay at the *police residence*, where a room with fan and mosquito net and clean, shared bathroom costs US$4.

The latter part of the road from Tamale to Yendi is in a vile state and no bus will attempt it. However, daily tro-tros and lorries make the two hour journey. It's possible to continue south by tro-tro to Kpandai and on to Kete-Krachi, where you can link in with a ferry to Akosombo.

Kpandai

Heading for Kete-Krachi from Tamale, you can make it here by tro-tro in one long day if you leave early from Tamale and find a tro-tro in Yendi going this far south. The road is in pitiful condition, especially the section between Kpandai and Kete-Krachi. Kpandai may look forsaken, but you'll find both food and cheap lodging here.

MOLE NATIONAL PARK

Mole National Park, Ghana's largest at 5198 sq km, has accommodation and tracks for 4WD access. It's open year-round; your optimum viewing time depends upon your reasons for going there. At the height of the harmattan from January to March, you'll see more animals and the nights are comfortably cool. For savouring the scenery, go when the rains are most intense, from July to September, when everything is a vibrant green and the skies are clear for most of the time. For watching birds, choose the transition time from rains into the dry season, between September and December, when the birds are courting and wearing their finest feathers – and when migratory birds from Europe are arriving. At the time of writing, the once-off entrance fee was US$1.75, but plans are afoot to raise this, probably to US$10 per day.

Animals you might see include roan antelope, elephant, baboon, buffalo, waterbuck, hartebeest, warthog, kob, oribi, hyena, jackal, various species of monkeys, and crocodile. More than 300 species of birds have also been recorded.

If you have your own transport, you'll see and experience much more by hiring one of the park wardens as a guide. If not, vehicle hire is relatively inexpensive – if it's functioning; the park's 4WD is frequently under repair. Many people find the walking safaris more stimulating. Treks leave twice a day, at

6.30 am and 3.30 pm, and last 2½ hours. A guide is mandatory and groups don't exceed six people. The fee is US$2 per person and a tip is expected.

Places to Stay & Eat

Since the one bus a day from Tamale arrives about 8 pm and leaves the next morning at 5.30 am, you need to budget for a minimum of two nights accommodation.

Within the park, you can stay at the *Mole Hotel* (☎ 0717-22041). If you want to make a reservation and can't get through, ring the Game and Wildlife Department in Accra (☎ 0217-65810), who will radio through your request. And do reserve; it's a long and hard journey to make to find yourself without a bed for the night. Weekends, local holidays and the months of July and August – peak holiday season in Europe – are particularly popular.

Perched on a hillock overlooking an artificial water hole where the animals gather, with baboons socialising in the trees outside your window, it's a superb setting. But remember that you're off the beaten track. There's rarely piped water and power comes from a generator, which functions from 7 to 10 pm. After a recent severe price hike without any corresponding enhancement of quality or service, the rooms now start at US$16 and are poor value for money. You can *camp* in the hotel grounds for US$2 per person.

There's a restaurant where, since provisioning is a problem, you need to order well in advance. A simple meal costs between US$2 and US$4.50 and the service is excruciatingly slow. You'd be wise to pack some provisions.

Fortunately for the traveller, the hotel no longer has a monopoly on accommodation with easy access to the park – you can also stay in Larabanga.

Getting There & Away

The reserve is 626km north of Accra and 135km west of Tamale. The turn-off for the park is on the Kumasi to Tamale highway at Fufulso, 298km north of Kumasi and 60km south-west of Tamale. From Fufulso, head west on a dirt road for another 60km to Damongo. The main entrance is 15km beyond Damongo at Larabanga.

A daily OSA bus runs from Tamale (US$1.50), leaving some time after 2.30 pm, once it's packed to the gunwales, and arriving at the park hotel about 8 pm. The same bus returns to Tamale the next day, leaving the park at 5.30 am.

Otherwise, from Tamale take a bus heading to Bole or Wa (you'll have to pay the full price to its final destination) and get off at Larabanga, 15km after Damongo. From there it's a 7km walk; hitching is virtually impossible.

LARABANGA

Larabanga, virtually at the gates of Mole National Park, is worth a visit – and perhaps a stay – in its own right. Its traditional claim to fame is its picturesque whitewashed mosque in the Sahel style. Of mud and pole construction, it's Ghana's oldest and reputedly dates back to the 13th century, when the trans-Saharan trade was at its most active.

The village also has a 'mystic stone', the subject of local legend, and a copy of the Quran that's almost as old as the mosque.

Larabanga's also an ideal, and economical, base for exploring Mole National Park. The small tourist office, built in the style of the mosque, is staffed by the local people. They offer tours of the village and mosque for US$2.00 per person.

You can rent bicycles for the 7km ride to the park, plus binoculars (both US$2.50) and 'bird identification kits'. And you can stay in the village's small *guesthouse* or with families for around US$2.50 per person.

Buses between Tamale and Wa or Bole pass through town.

BOLGATANGA

'Bolga', as it's known to locals, is the fast-growing capital of the Upper East Region and the major town between Tamale and the Burkina Faso border. It's also the craft centre of the north, with a fascinating central market which takes place on a three day cycle. (At the time of writing, it was in temporary premises on the Bawku Rd as extensive renovations were under way). Leatherwork and baskets are the speciality. In leather, for example, you can get sandals, handbags, wallets, briefcases, and day-packs – mainly reddish-brown and black with traditional designs. The multicoloured baskets, prized throughout Ghana, are tightly woven from raffia and range from minute to enormous. You'll also find place-mats and the famous Bolga straw hats. Visit, too, the shop next to the STC bus station, where goods have fixed prices.

There's a helpful tourist office (☎ 3416) near the Catholic Mission and a small museum in the same area whose two rooms focus upon the ethnology and culture of the north-east.

Things to Do

Take a tro-tro to **Tongo** (16km) if you want to hike or bike into the surrounding hills. You should have no problem renting a bike or hiring a guide there, but check first with the village chief as these scenic hills are sacred. To get there, go south for 8km to Winkogo on the Tamale road, then 8km east to Tongo.

Places to Stay

The friendly *Catholic Mission*, charges US$4/5 for clean, basic singles/doubles with shared facilities and has dormitory beds for US$2. A reader recommends *Hotel St Joseph's*, behind the National Investment Bank, where singles/doubles with bathroom cost US$3/3.50. It has a bar, a roof-top patio and serves good African food.

Two places on the south side of town are the *Royal Hotel Bolga*, on Tamale Rd, and

GHANA

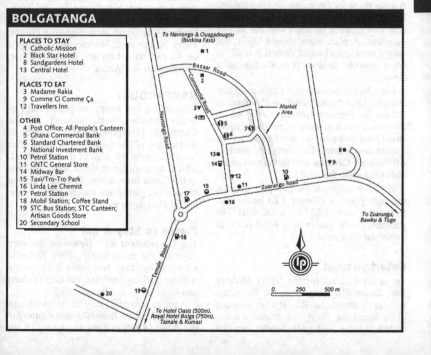

BOLGATANGA

PLACES TO STAY
1 Catholic Mission
2 Black Star Hotel
8 Sandgardens Hotel
13 Central Hotel

PLACES TO EAT
3 Madame Rakia
9 Comme Ci Comme Ça
12 Travellers Inn

OTHER
4 Post Office; All People's Canteen
5 Ghana Commercial Bank
6 Standard Chartered Bank
7 National Investment Bank
10 Petrol Station
11 GNTC General Store
14 Midway Bar
15 Taxi/Tro-Tro Park
16 Linda Lee Chemist
17 Petrol Station
18 Mobil Station; Coffee Stand
19 STC Bus Station; STC Canteen; Artisan Goods Store
20 Secondary School

To Navrongo & Ouagadougou (Burkina Faso)

Bazaar Road

Commercial Road

Navrongo Road

Market Area

Zuarungu Road

Tamale Road

To Zuarungu, Bawku & Togo

To Hotel Oasis (500m), Royal Hotel Bolga (750m), Tamale & Kumasi

0   250   500 m

the *Hotel Oasis*, 150m west of Tamale Rd down a dirt road. The former has doubles with fan and private bathroom for US$4.50. Singles/doubles at the Oasis, which has the same facilities, cost US$4/4.50.

The *Central Hotel* is somewhat run-down, but it's a welcoming place where rooms have air-con and bathroom, although water rarely reaches the taps. The *Sandgardens Hotel* (☎ 3464), off a side road 100m off Zuarungu Rd, has singles/doubles with fans and shared bathroom for US$4/5 or US$7.50 with bathroom. It may be possible to camp in the grounds.

The city's top hotel is the old, two storey *Black Star Hotel* (☎ 2346) on Bazaar Rd. It's popular with tour groups and has clean, reasonably attractive rooms with tiled floors and fans for US$4 with shared facilities and US$10 with bathroom.

Places to Eat

A great place for Ghanaian food is *Madame Rakia*, on Commercial Rd. She prepares only two or three dishes a day, but they're excellent. A plate costs around US$1, but only a prizefighter could demolish it all, so bring someone to share it or ask for half a bowl.

For a hearty breakfast or a light meal late at night, head further south on Commercial Rd for the friendly *Travellers Inn*, which also has a small grocery store. For cheaper *street food* and pito, the local brew, try the market area nearby. The clean and friendly *All People's Canteen* next to the post office has cheap chop from US$1.

If you're desperate for European cuisine, the only place is *Comme Ci Comme Ça*. Reckon on about US$5 for a full meal. The tranquil, shady garden is a good place to come just for a drink.

Entertainment

For a drink, head for the lively *Midway Bar*, diagonally across from the Travellers Inn on Commercial Rd. It's an outdoor place facing the street with music at a tolerable volume and grilled-meat vendors

nearby. You can also get a drink at the STC station's *canteen*.

Getting There & Away

Fan Airways operates a twice weekly flight (US$40) between Bolga and Accra.

The STC station is on the southern outskirts of town, on Tamale Rd. It runs three buses a week from Bolgatanga to Kumasi. In addition, if they're still running (STC has cut back savagely on its routes), there should be two early morning buses for Kumasi, one coming from Bawku and the other from Sandema via Navrongo. City Express runs three buses a day to Tamale (US$1.50), and an overnight service from Kumasi. Upgrading of the road between Bolga and Tamale, previously in horrendous condition, was nearing completion at the time of writing.

The tro-tro park in Bolga is just east of the roundabout. If you're headed to Ouagadougou, take a tro-tro from here to the Burkina Faso border at Paga. Bolgatanga is also a good point for crossing into Togo. From Bawku, you can catch vehicles to the border (30km) and on to Dapaong (Togo), 15km further east. Vehicles leave Bolga's tro-tro park daily for Paga, Bawku, Tamale, Wa, Kumasi and Accra.

NAKPANDURI

Nakpanduri is a sleepy, unspoilt village of neatly thatched huts, perched on the **Gambaga Escarpment**, 65km south of Bawku and 128km south-east of Bolga. You can walk along the edge of the escarpment, which has magnificent views, and drop down to the forest floor below. In the dry season the animals gather at a watering hole by the bridge 3km down the hill.

Places to Stay & Eat

The *Government Rest House* on the very edge of the escarpment offers fantastic views. It has only two fairly basic rooms with no cooking facilities, but they're clean and large and cost a bargain US$2.

Another possibility may be the guesthouse at the *Agriculture Rehabilitation Centre for the Blind (ARB)* in **Garu**, on the road from

Nakpanduri to Bawku. It has clean rooms with showers and, for a bit extra, the caretaker will let you use the centre's cooking facilities.

Getting There & Away

Nakpanduri is difficult to get to from Bawku unless you have wheels. Public transport is scarce, except on market day in Bawku, which occurs every three days, on the same day as Bolga's.

NAVRONGO

Navrongo (population 11,000) is 16km south of the Burkina Faso border. In the centre you'll see several crumbling, half-built structures. These were begun in the mid-70s by President Acheampong as a gift to this small town. Construction stopped when he was deposed and today the complex is just an eyesore. Much more harmonious is the Catholic cathedral which dates from around 1920. It's unusual in that it was constructed of *banco* in the traditional Sahel style and claims to be the world's largest cathedral built of mud – although how intense, you wonder, is the competition? The colourful interior decorations reflect the traditional designs of the Upper East Region.

For a side trip, visit the large dam and lake 8km away in **Tono**. The lake is 6km long and provides irrigation for the entire valley, whose fertility contrasts with the surrounding aridity.

The *Catholic Mission* on the south-east side of town rents out clean, cheap rooms for US$3. Another possibility is the *ICOUR Guest House* near the lake, which has a pool and rooms with air-con, although it's often full.

For cheap food and pito try the market area and *Tiko's* near the STC bus stop. *Crossroads* is a congenial bar, as is *Prison View* – despite the name.

Getting There & Away

Buses go every day to Kumasi, via Bolgatanga and Tamale, departing around 4.30 am. If you're headed only to Bolgatanga, it's better to take a tro-tro from the market as they depart more frequently.

PAGA

The attractive black and white geometrical patterns painted on the houses of Paga are peculiar to this area. This border town has a crocodile pond, a considerable income generator for the hustlers who hang around it. You'll be asked an absurd sum to have the crocodile summoned on land, more to be photographed with it; and yet more for a chicken to be fed, live and squawking, to the reptile. Unless you particularly want a photo for the folks back home of yourself sitting on the croc's back just before the sacrifice, it's cheaper and more humane to give the place a miss.

Travellers stuck here for the night can get a basic room at the *Paga Motel* for US$4. STC has three buses a week between Accra and Paga (US$13).

WA

Wa, capital of Upper West Region, and the small town of **Lawra** some 60km north on the Burkina Faso border, receive few visitors. The best time to come is the first week in October when both towns have festivals. During Wa's **Durbar festival**, the chief, elaborately dressed, sits in state to receive the homage of his subjects, on whom he showers hospitality and gifts. What makes the ritual here unique is that he must jump over a cow or, says tradition, he will be slain. Lawra's **Kobinah festival** features about 30 dancing groups which come from all over northern Ghana and Burkina Faso to participate.

Wa's imposing main mosque is a superb example of Sahel architecture, found more commonly in Burkina Faso and Mali. The dazzling white, traditional-style 19th century palace is the residence of the Wa-Na (the local chief). The area is renowned for its pito, the local brew, traditional smocks and xylophone players – all reputedly the best in Ghana.

GHANA

Places to Stay & Eat

The cheapest place to stay is the **Residency**, which has acceptable rooms with double beds, fans and shared bathrooms. The **Kunateh Lodge** (☎ 102) on Zongo St is good value. The manager is helpful and it has clean singles/doubles with fans and showers. For more comfort, the **Upland Hotel** (☎ 180), a 15 minute drive out of town, is the region's most popular and has good-value rooms with either fan or air-con.

Getting There & Away

OSA has a daily service to and from Tamale (US$3) via Damongo (near Mole National Park). It takes seven hours. The weekly STC bus from Accra leaves from the main STC station near Lamptey Circle. It runs on Saturday, costs US$13 and takes more than 15 hours, via Kumasi.

For travel to and from Kumasi, a tro-tro is a better option – it's faster, more frequent and only slightly more expensive.

Guinea

Guinea (sometimes called Guinea-Conakry to distinguish it from neighbouring Guinea-Bissau) used to suffer under one of the most oppressive regimes in Africa. But, following the death of President Sekou Touré in 1984, things began to change and today the country exudes a marked peppiness and economic vitality.

One of Guinea's major attractions is the vibrancy of its culture. Across the country, there's a strong tradition of live music, and any evening in Conakry you can find a musical celebration in the streets. Added to this is Guinea's spectacular landscape. The Fouta Djalon plateau, in the west of the country, has some of the most striking scenery in West Africa and is an excellent area for hiking.

Despite these attractions, Guinea is not prepared for tourism. Outside Conakry, most accommodation is quite basic (although this is beginning to change) and journeys by road can be long and hard. If you insist on creature comforts you may not enjoy Guinea. But if you're prepared to rough it, a visit here can be very rewarding.

Facts about Guinea

HISTORY
Rock paintings found in the Fouta Djalon indicate that Guinea was inhabited as early as 30,000 years ago. By 2000 years ago, the Coniagui, Baga and other smaller tribes had established isolated farming and fishing settlements along the coast and in the north-west. These were gradually pushed aside by influxes of Susu and Malinké following the fall of the Empire of Ghana. From the 13th century, the Malinké established dominance over much of Upper Guinea and by the 14th century all of Guinea had been incorporated into the powerful Empire of Mali. (For more information about this and other early empires, refer to the History section in the

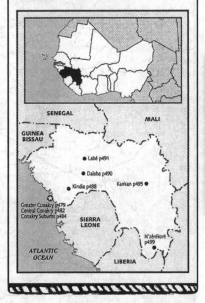

GUINEA AT A GLANCE

Area: 245,855 sq km
Population: 7.2 million
Capital: Conakry
Head of state: President General Lansana Conté
Official language: French
Main local languages: Malinké, Fula (Pulaar), Susu
Currency: Guinean franc
Exchange rate: US$1 = GF1320
Time: GMT/UTC
Country telephone code: ☎ 224
Best time to go: Mid-November

Facts about the Region chapter.) Around the 15th century – about the same time that Portuguese navigators first reached the Guinean coast – Peul (also called Fula) herders started migrating into the area and settled in the mountainous Fouta Djalon region where they established an influential theocracy.

In the 19th century, the Guinean hero, Samory Touré, led the fight against French colonialists. He was captured in 1898 and resistance gradually withered. Once the train line from Conakry to Kankan was completed, France began serious exploitation of the area, which by then had become part of French West Africa.

The most famous Guinean of all was Sekou Touré, born into a poor Malinké family and a descendant of Samory Touré. After becoming the foremost trade unionist in French West Africa he led the fight for independence; in 1956, while still holding communist views, he led a breakaway movement from the French parent union to form a federation of African trade unions.

Independence

In 1958, Charles de Gaulle offered the French colonies a choice between autonomy as separate countries in a Franco-African

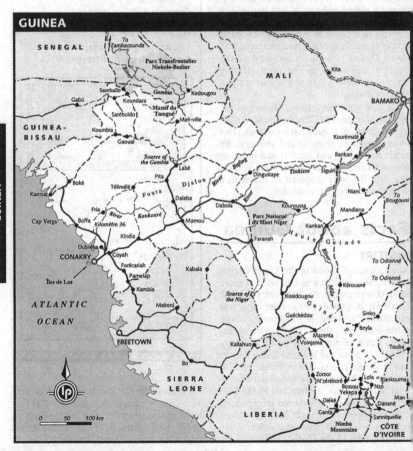

GUINEA

community or immediate independence. Sekou Touré declared that Guinea preferred 'freedom in poverty to prosperity in chains' and was the only leader to reject de Gaulle's proposal. Thus, Guinea became the first French colony to gain independence. Sekou Touré became an African legend in his own time and, as leader of Guinea's only viable political party, the country's first president.

De Gaulle, infuriated, immediately withdrew the French colonial administration. French private citizens fled with massive amounts of capital, thus assuring Guinea's economic collapse.

Wanting nothing more to do with the CFA franc, which was linked to the French franc, Touré introduced a new currency, the syli. But with French economic assistance gone, the new country badly needed foreign aid. Touré turned to the Russians, but the link with the USSR was short-lived.

The government continued on a socialist road, however, and in 1967 commenced a campaign of cultural revolution on the Chinese model, with state-run farms and weekly meetings of revolutionary units. It was an unmitigated disaster. As many as one million Guineans fled into neighbouring countries, while remaining farmers were able to work only one-quarter of the country's cultivable area.

The Reign of Terror

Sekou Touré appointed Malinké to all major government positions and treated his political opponents with cruelty. Following an unsuccessful Portuguese-led invasion of the country in 1970, he became paranoid, staying in Guinea for the following five years, and often speaking of a 'permanent plot' against his regime. Waves of arrests followed. Prisoners were sentenced to death, and torture became commonplace. In 1976, Touré charged the entire Peul population with collusion in an attempt to overthrow the government. The alleged leader of the plot was starved to death in prison while thousands of Peul went into exile.

A historic revolt by market women in late August 1977 turned the tide. As part of its program to discourage private trade, the government had decreed that all agricultural produce was to be delivered to state-run cooperatives. For the market women, many of whom had been among Touré's most ardent supporters, this was too much. Riots started in Conakry, then spread to Guinea's towns; the governors of Kindia, Faranah and Boké were killed. On hearing the women's complaints directly, Touré again legalised petty trade.

Sekou Touré died of heart failure in 1984, just before a scheduled conference of the Organisation of African Unity (OAU) that he was to chair in Conakry. Within days of his funeral a military coup was staged by a group of army colonels, including Lansana Conté, who became president of the country, and Diarra Traoré, who became prime minister. They denounced Touré and released around a thousand political prisoners, promising an open society and restoration of free enterprise.

The change of government opened up Guinea and returned it to the western fold, but tensions among the leaders led to more problems. Following a failed coup attempt in 1985 by Traoré, Conté was forced to face the urgent matter of reforming the economy. He introduced austerity measures to secure funding from the IMF, and a new currency, the Guinean franc, replaced the syli.

Guinea Today

Since the mid-1980s, incomes of many Guineans have risen, many exiles have returned and free enterprise is encouraged. Main roads and telecommunications have been improved, and rural tracks around the country are being rebuilt so that farmers can get their produce to market. People can talk freely and, while the press is still censored, reporters can usually express themselves without fear of reprisal.

For many Guineans, however, life remains hard. Life expectancy (46 years) and the rate of adult literacy (36%) are among the lowest in the world; under the UN's quality of life index, Guinea has ranked at or near the bottom every year since 1990.

GUINEA

In October 1991, after considerable pressure from within his government and from western donor nations, Conté agreed to proposals for a multiparty political system. In April 1992, the system was formally introduced and 17 parties were legalised; by July this number had doubled. In late 1993 it was announced that presidential elections would be held in December the same year; eight candidates stood for the post, including Conté. After a tense pre-election period marked by incidents of violence and temporary closing of the country's land borders, Conté won with just over 50% of the total ballot against a divided opposition and in the face of accusations of fraud and vote-rigging. Legislative elections followed in June 1995 amid continued tension and violence. While Conté's Parti de l'Unité et du Progrès (PUP) dominated, opposition parties managed to win a sizeable portion of the 114-member national assembly.

In February 1996, an army mutiny, instigated by lower-ranking soldiers protesting about poor salaries and benefits, threatened to become a full-blown coup as mid-level officers rapidly attached themselves to the movement. With considerable political savvy, Conté quelled the uprising by agreeing to redress the soldiers' grievances and took over the Defence Minister's portfolio in the process. However, in the intervening 48 hours, several dozen civilians were killed and widespread looting took place in Conakry.

Since then, things have remained relatively quiet although continued dissatisfaction among the military, ongoing instability in neighbouring Sierra Leone and Liberia, and the resulting pressures of up to half a million refugees pose constant threats to Guinea's stability.

As this book went to press, the next presidential elections were scheduled for late 1998.

GEOGRAPHY
Guinea has four zones: a narrow coastal plain; the Fouta Djalon plateau; north-eastern dry lowlands; and the forests of the south-east. The Fouta Djalon plateau, rising to over 1500m, is the source of the Gambia and Senegal rivers and of much of the Niger (although *the* source of the Niger lies south, near the Sierra Leone border). South-eastern Guinea is hilly and heavily vegetated; due to fires and cultivation little virgin rainforest remains.

CLIMATE
Guinea is one of the wettest countries in West Africa. Rainfall along the coast averages 4300mm a year, half of which falls in July and August, while the central mountainous region receives about 2000mm, more evenly distributed between May and October. Temperatures average 30°C along the coast, are somewhat cooler inland, and can fall to 10°C and below at night in Mali-ville and other high areas.

ECOLOGY & ENVIRONMENT
One of the major environmental concerns in Guinea is deforestation, although environmental exploitation has been mostly small-scale due to limited mechanisation. However, this is rapidly changing as the improved road system enables wood to be shipped out more easily, and as population pressures from some 500,000 refugees take their toll.

FLORA & FAUNA
Guinea has many designated protected areas (*forêts classée*), although in practice there is no enforcement of environmental regulations. The country also has two national parks: Parc Transfrontalier Niokolo-Badiar

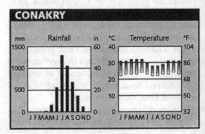

Guinea's National Parks

Since 1990, two national parks have been created in Guinea. **Parc National du Badiar** is in the far north-east of the country, near Koundara. Together with Senegal's Parc National du Niokolo-Koba, it encompasses a 950,000 hectare protected area (about 50,000 hectares of which are in Guinea), designated the Parc Transfrontalier Niokolo-Badiar.

While development on the Guinean side lags well behind that in Senegal, the park represents an important step for protecting the unique ecosystems of the region. There are no lodging facilities yet, but construction of a campement in Badiar is underway. The best access to the park is through the village of Kaparabima, past Sambaïlo, from where you can hike up to several good lookouts. To get there, take a bush taxi from Koundara to Sambaïlo (GF500); from there you'll have to charter a taxi to the village. Once in Kaparabima it's easy to find guides to the lookout points.

Park headquarters are scheduled to be moved from Koundara to Sambaïlo by mid-1998. In Conakry, information on the park is available from the Direction Nationale des Forêts et de la Faune on the Donka Route. The park is officially closed during the rainy season, from June to November.

In central Guinea, between Faranah and Kouroussa, is the 647,000 hectare (including inhabited buffer zones) **Parc National du Haut Niger** which protects one of the last remaining dry forest ecosystems in West Africa. Park headquarters are in Sidakoro, 45km from Faranah. There are a few rooms and prices range from GF3000 for students to GF8000 for foreign tourists; meals can be arranged. Reservations must be made in advance at the Sidakoro headquarters or through the Department des Eaux et Forêts at the University of Faranah.

Near the centre of the park, about 30km from Sidakoro, is the village of Somoria and a chimpanzee research station. There's a small campement at Somoria which can be reserved in Sidakoro.

To visit the park, you'll need your own transport though sometimes it's possible to get a lift with park staff at the University of Faranah. The park is open year-round.

near Koundara, and Parc National du Haut Niger, north-east of Faranah (see the boxed text for more details).

GOVERNMENT & POLITICS

The ruling PUP party dominates all three branches of government, although with 62% of the national assembly, it is one seat short of the majority required to make constitutional amendments. In addition to support from the Susus (President Conté is a Susu), the PUP is supported by the Guerzé, Toma, Kissi and other smaller groups in the Forest Region. The main opposition group is the Rassemblement du Peuple de Guinée (RPG), headed by Professor Alpha Conde. The RPG's main support comes from the Malinké, Guinea's second-largest ethnic group. The other major opposition group is the Union pour la Nouvelle République (UNR), headed by Mamadou Bah and supported primarily by Guinea's Peuls, who make up one-third of the population and are the largest single ethnic group.

While the opposition has been strong enough to influence some parliamentary votes – and despite the halting steps taken by the government towards true multiparty democracy – Guinea remains in many ways a one-man state, with authority in the hands of the president. During his term in office, Conté has consolidated control of several key areas and issued decrees enabling him to bypass his ministers. Following the February

1996 army mutiny Conté appointed a new cabinet and Guinea's first prime minister. Later, however, Conté stripped him of his primary portfolio, curtailing whatever authority he had.

ECONOMY

Although Guinea remains one of the world's poorest nations, the economic situation has improved markedly since President Conté took over. Since 1992, average annual growth rates have been above 4%, while inflation has dropped to about 5%. Clouding the picture are high rates of unemployment and underemployment. Rampant corruption – considered by many to be among the worst in Africa – discourages much-needed foreign investment.

Guinea has abundant natural resources, including large mineral deposits. Agriculture, much of it at subsistence level, and mining – particularly bauxite, used in the manufacture of aluminium – are the mainstays of the economy. Guinea has the third-largest known reserves of bauxite in the world, with an estimated 30% of the total, and mining revenues are the largest single source of government earnings. Guinea also has impressive reserves of diamonds, gold, iron, copper, manganese and uranium, although revenue potentials have not been realised in these resources. Lack of infrastructure and – in the case of diamonds and gold – illegal export have been major obstacles. Most of Guinea's iron ore deposits are around Mt Nimba, until recently inaccessible by paved road.

While many state-run enterprises, including the telecommunications industry, are slowly being privatised, progress is hampered by corruption and an opaque judicial system.

POPULATION & PEOPLE

Guinea's population is approximately 7.2 million, including up to 500,000 refugees from Sierra Leone and Liberia. Major ethnic groups are the Peul, who comprise one-third of the population, the Malinké , comprising just under one-third, and the Susu (about 20%). Fifteen other ethnic groups constitute the rest. Susu predominantly inhabit the coastal region, Peul the Fouta Djalon and Malinké the north and centre. Guinea' refugee population is concentrated in the south-east.

ARTS

Traditional music and dance have flourished in Guinea, due in part to government subsidisation during the Sekou Touré era. Guinea has a thriving local music industry (for more details, see the special section 'Music of West Africa' earlier in this book). It also has several widely renowned dance troupes. This cultural heritage is most accessible to visitors in Conakry, where musical concerts on the street are an almost daily occurrence, and where there are frequent dance performances at the Palais du Peuple.

The country's most famous cultural figure, however, is Camara Laye, author of L'Enfant Noir (see the Kouroussa section later in this chapter). Laye's book, which is considered one of the pre-eminent pieces of African literature, is full of fascinating insights into the traditions and daily life of Guinea's Malinké people.

SOCIETY & CONDUCT

One of the best times to experience traditional Guinean society is on Eid al-Fitr which marks the end of Ramadan and is one of Guinea's most important holidays. Families start preparing well in advance. On the day itself, everyone from grandparents to children dresses in their colourful best and heads for the mosques. You'll often see groups of young girls walking down the street, all wearing matching, elaborate *bou bous*, complete with headscarves to match or multigenerational gatherings of boys with their fathers and grandfathers, all in new outfits. Prayer mat and jewellery vendors are out in full force, hoping to capitalise on the event. Afterwards there are family celebrations, complete with neighbourhood street bands and traditional meals, which last until well into the night.

As Guinea is a traditional Muslim country, travellers should respect local sensibilities by not wearing sleeveless tops or short shorts; skirts (for women) or long trousers are preferable. For men, going without a shirt is not acceptable. Overall, the better dressed you are, the more respect you will enjoy and the easier time you will have in encounters with local authorities. During the Ramadan fasting period, you can show respect for locals by not eating or drinking in public.

RELIGION

About 80% of the population are Muslims, 7% Christians, and the remainder are adherents of traditional religions.

LANGUAGE

French is the official language, although it's often not spoken in remote areas. Major African languages are Malinké in the north, Pulaar (also called Fula) in the Fouta Djalon, and Susu along the coast. Learning some phrases in these local languages is essential if you'll be spending much time off main routes. See the Language chapter for a list of useful phrases in French, Malinké, Fula (Pulaar) and Susu.

Facts for the Visitor

SUGGESTED ITINERARIES

If you have a week or less in Guinea, a good option would be to spend two days in the capital getting orientated, then head to Kindia and spend a couple of days there exploring the town and visiting nearby attractions. Alternatively, you could fly from Conakry to Labé, then travel by road through the Fouta Djalon back to Conakry, with stops at Dalaba and Kindia en route. If you don't have time to leave Conakry, at least try to take a half-day excursion to Coyah or Dubréka. Upcountry Guinea is quite a contrast from the capital, and even going a short distance outside its boundaries would give you a glimpse of the rest of the country.

If you have two weeks, head from Kindia east to Mamou and then north to the Fouta Djalon, where you could easily spend five to six days or longer walking in the villages, or doing day excursions based in Dalaba.

For those fortunate enough to have a month or more, add north-eastern and south-eastern Guinea to the itinerary: from the Fouta Djalon region, head east towards Dabola, Kouroussa and Kankan. It's well worth pausing in Kankan for a few days before heading south towards Kissidougou. From Kissidougou, head east towards Macenta and N'zérékoré. The region around N'zérékoré can keep you busy for up to a week, including excursions to nearby Lola and Mt Nimba. From N'zérékoré you could fly back to Conakry or continue by road into Côte d'Ivoire. To make this grand loop with the minimum of backtracking, fly from Conakry to N'zérékoré. From N'zérékoré head towards Kankan via Macenta and Kissidougou. Then, continue from Kankan via Kouroussa towards Dabola and Mamou. Alternatively, from Dabola, you could go south to Faranah and then on to Mamou. From Mamou, go north through the Fouta Djalon to Labé. From Labé you could continue to Mali-ville or Koundara and on into Senegal or Guinea-Bissau, or alternatively fly or return by road to Conakry.

PLANNING

The best time to visit is mid-November, after the rains and before the dusty harmattan winds spoil the views.

The only map of Guinea readily available is the IGN one, although much of the road information is now outdated. It's on sale at Hôtel Camayenne (GF20,000) and at several stationery stores in Conakry.

The IGN in Conakry sells black and white or colour copies of topographical maps (scales 1:50,000 to 1:500,000) covering individual regions of the country for GF 10,000/20,000.

TOURIST OFFICES

Guinea has no tourist offices. *Dyeli*, a listings magazine available free at some hotels

GUINEA

Highlights

Historical Sites & Holy Places

Kankan area   *(The East)*
Samory Touré's stronghold and a spiritual centre for Malinké; nearby is Niani, once the capital of the powerful Empire of Mali.

Mosques *(Conakry, Fouta Djalon, The East)*
Conakry's Grande Mosquée is one of West Africa's largest, while those at Dinguiraye, Timbo and Fougoumba are also significant.

Kouroussa   *(The East)*
Birthplace of one of West Africa's most renowned authors, Camara Laye.

Fouta Djalon Region
Seat of the 18th-century Peul theocracy.

National Parks & Outdoor Activities

National Parks *(The East, Fouta Djalon)*
The big animals are almost gone, but Guinea still hosts some fascinating ecosystems.

Hiking & Biking *(Fouta Djalon, The Forest Region)*
The Fouta Djalon plateau offers some of the best hiking in West Africa, as well as biking opportunities; the lush Forest Region is also good for hiking and biking.

Canoeing   *(The East, The West)*
A good way to explore the River Niger and coastal Guinea's ecologically diverse mangrove swamps.

Beaches

Îles de Los   *(Around Conakry)*
For beach lovers – a relaxing getaway from the capital.

Cap Verga   *(The West)*
Palm-fringed beaches and fishing villages.

Culture

Music & Festivities   *(Conakry)*
Conakry is a good place to see impromptu musical performances and other neighbourhood festivities.

Markets
Bargaining is a must at Guinea's colourful markets; look for indigo cloth in Kindia and Labé and mud cloth around N'zérékoré and Lola.

Ethnic Diversity *(Fouta Djalon, The Forest Region)*
Experience Guinea's rich cultural mix, especially in the Fouta Djalon and Forest Region.

---

and travel agencies in Conakry, has details of local events.

VISAS & DOCUMENTS
Visas
All visitors, except nationals of ECOWAS countries, need a visa and an International Certificate of Vaccination or other proof of relevant vaccinations. Visas are not available at airports or land borders. Visas issued by embassies in Africa are usually valid for a maximum of one month (up to three months for visas issued outside Africa). Pre-

viously, tourist visas were frequently denied. This is generally not the case now, although a letter of invitation is often requested.

Visa Extensions Visas can be extended for up to three months at the Bureau of Immigration in Conakry for GF43,000 plus one photo; go to the third door on the right, marked Division Contrôle Séjour des Étrangers. Extensions are supposed to be processed within 72 hours, but it can take a week or more. For longer stays, you'll need a residency permit (valid for up to one year).

which requires four photos, GF353,000 and a good reason.

EMBASSIES & CONSULATES
Guinea Embassies & Consulates

Within West Africa, Guinea has embassies in Côte d'Ivoire, Gambia, Ghana, Guinea-Bissau, Liberia, Mali, Nigeria, Senegal and Sierra Leone. For more details see the Facts for the Visitor section of the relevant country chapter. Elsewhere, Guinea has embassies in the following countries:

Belgium
(☎ 02-771 01 26)
75 ave Vandendriessche, Brussels 1150
France
(☎ 01 47 04 81 48)
51 rue de la Faisanderie, 75016 Paris
Germany
(☎ 0228-23 10 98)
Rochusweg 50, 53129 Bonn

Visas for Onward Travel

In Guinea, you can get visas for the following neighbouring West African countries:

Burkina Faso & Togo
The French embassy (open Monday to Friday from 9.30 am to noon) issues one-month single-entry visas for either country for GF33,000 plus one photo.

Côte d'Ivoire
Open Monday to Friday from 8.30 am to 3 pm (Friday until 2 pm). One month single-entry visas cost GF25,000 to GF66,000, depending on nationality, plus three photos and are issued in three days.

Guinea-Bissau
Open Monday to Friday from 8 am to 2.30 pm (Friday until 1 pm). Prior to the recent difficulties in Bissau, one-month single-entry visas cost GF20,000 (GF45,000 for three-month multiple entry visas). You need two photos and visas are issued within two days. Same day service costs an additional GF5000.

Liberia
Open Monday to Friday from 8 am to 4 pm. Three-month single-entry visas cost GF40,000 (GF50,000 for multiple entry) plus one photo and are ready within 24 hours. Note that the Liberian consulate in N'zérékoré issues single-entry visas (GF40,000 plus two photos) in 24 hours.

Mali
Open Monday to Friday from 8 am to 4.30 pm. One-month single-entry visas cost GF7700 plus one photo, and are ready the same day if you go early.

Senegal
Open Monday to Friday from 8.30 am to 3 pm (Friday until 1 pm). One-month single-entry visas cost GF6000 plus four photos and are ready within 24 hours.

Sierra Leone
Open Monday to Friday from 9 am to 3 pm (Friday until 1 pm). One month single-entry visas cost between GF21,500 and GF66,000, depending on nationality, and are usually ready within 24 hours.

GUINEA

UK
(☎ 0171-333 0044; from 22 April 2000 ☎ 020-7333 0044)
20 Upper Grosvenor St, London W1X 9PB
USA
(☎ 202-483 9420)
2112 Leroy Place, NW Washington, DC 20008

Guinea also has embassies in Canada, Italy and Japan. In addition, there are consulates in Duisburg, Hamburg and Munich in Germany.

Embassies & Consulates in Guinea

Foreign embassies and consulates in Conakry include:

Belgium
(☎/fax 41 35 10) Cité des Nations, Villa 38, Kaloum
Benin
(☎ 46 17 47)
Madina, Matam, near the small mosque
Cape Verde
(☎ 42 11 37)
Minière, near the police station
Côte d'Ivoire
(☎ 45 10 82)
Blvd du Commerce
France
(☎ 41 16 05) Blvd du Commerce
Ghana
(☎ 46 15 12)
Super V Complex, Route du Niger
Guinea-Bissau
(☎ 42 21 36)
Donka Route, 500m north-east of Carrefour Bellevue
Liberia
(☎ 46 20 59)
Corniche-Nord, Dixin
Mali
(☎ 46 14 18)
Matam, next to the Office National des Hydrocarbures
Nigeria
(☎ 46 13 41)
Corniche-Sud, Coléah
Senegal
(☎ 46 28 34)
Corniche-Sud, Coléah
Sierra Leone
(☎ 46 40 84)
Carrefour Bellevue, next to A-Z Supermarket

UK
(☎ 46 16 80)
Corniche-Nord, Donka, opposite CNPG
USA
(☎ 41 15 23)
2nd Blvd and Ave 9, Kaloum

Other countries with embassies in Conakry include: Canada, Germany and Japan.

CUSTOMS

You are not allowed to export more than GF5000 in local currency; additional amounts will be confiscated on departure. There are no limits on the import or export of foreign currency. Currency declarations are only occasionally given out at the airport and are rarely checked.

To export art objects (generally interpreted to include anything made of wood), you'll need a permit from the Musée National in Conakry. Cost varies, but averages 10% of the value for items worth less than GF50,000 and up to 20% of the value for more expensive pieces. It's best to do this a day before departure and to bring purchase receipts.

MONEY

The unit of currency is the Guinean franc (GF).

CFA1000	=	GF2400
Euro €1	=	GF1575
1FF	=	GF240
UK£1	=	GF2230
US$1	=	GF1320

Most banks upcountry exchange only cash; if you're arriving overland carry some US$, French francs or CFA as they're easily changed almost everywhere. Black market dealers are widely used throughout Guinea (cash only); their rates are usually about 8% better than the bank rate.

The exchange counter at the airport is rarely open and has low rates. Neither this bank nor any other will change Guinean francs back into hard currency when you leave, even with exchange receipts. However, moneychangers can help you out. It all seems fairly open, but it's worth being as discreet as possible.

473 Facts for the Visitor

POST & COMMUNICATIONS

International mail is usually dependable, however Guinea's separate express mail service is not reliable.

All major towns have a PTT where you can make domestic and international calls, though line quality is frequently poor. Area codes are not used in telephone numbers within Guinea.

Guinea gained full Internet access in late 1997 and online services are rapidly increasing in the major towns.

PHOTOGRAPHY & VIDEO

Photo permits are not required, although police officers will often insist that they are and hassles are frequent. Don't snap government buildings, airports, bridges and military installations, and it's best not to use a camera at all in cities and towns unless you're sure the police aren't watching and locals don't object. Handy copies of a government decree expressly permitting tourist photos are available at the Ministry of Tourism and at some *préfectures* and hotels. The same restrictions apply to video.

Konica and Tudorcolor film are available in Conakry. For developing, the best is Labo Photo on Ave de la République in Conakry, although quality is erratic. For more general information, see the Photography & Video section in the Regional Facts for the Visitor chapter.

HEALTH

A yellow fever vaccination certificate is required from all travellers. Malaria risk exists year-round throughout the whole country, so you should take appropriate precautions. For more general information on these and other health matters, see the Health section in the Regional Facts for the Visitor chapter.

WOMEN TRAVELLERS

Women travellers are not likely to experience any special problems in Guinea. For more general information and advice, see the Women Travellers section in the Regional Facts for the Visitor chapter.

DANGERS & ANNOYANCES

Hassling and demands for bribes by poorly paid soldiers and customs officials, particularly at road checkpoints and the airport, are the major annoyances faced by travellers in Guinea. As long as your documents are in order, there is no need to pay these guys anything. Maintaining a respectful but relaxed attitude generally helps. The same is true if you're approached in more remote areas by someone with an immigration badge asking to see your documents.

Overall, travel in Guinea is relatively safe. However, bush taxis often drive at breakneck speeds and there are many road accidents. If you can get your driver to slow down, you'll probably be adding several years onto your life and his.

'C'est madame? ou bien mademoiselle?'

Women travelling on their own through Guinea will undoubtedly hear these words ad nauseam (roughly translated it means 'are you married or not?'). Sometimes, for example when you're filling out forms or registering at a hotel, it's not ill-intentioned. But all too often, it's a leering soldier who's a little too eager for company. Although there's not much you can do to prevent the question, having at least a fictitious husband can help in avoiding further advances.

Creative approaches can also work well in dealing with the constant demands for bribes. Greeting a *gendarme* as an old friend, inquiring about his family, exchanging a few words in the local language, or simply explaining – when he asks what you have for him – that you can offer a handshake but unfortunately nothing more, will usually diffuse the situation.

BUSINESS HOURS

Government offices are open Monday to Friday from 8 am to 4.30 pm (Friday until 1 pm). Some businesses (particularly airline offices) work government hours. Others are open Monday to Saturday from 8 am to 6 pm, except Friday, when they close at 1 pm. Many businesses also close between 12.30 pm and 2 pm or on Saturday afternoon. Banking hours are Monday to Thursday from 8.30 am to 12.30 pm and 2.30 to 4.30 pm, and Friday from 8.30 am to 12.30 pm and 2.45 to 4.30 pm.

PUBLIC HOLIDAYS & SPECIAL EVENTS

Public holidays include 1 January (New Year's Day), Easter Monday, 3 April (Declaration of the 2nd Republic), 1 May (Labour Day), 27 August (Market Womens' Revolt), 15 August (Assumption Day), 2 October (Independence Day), 1 November (Armed Forces Day) and 25 December (Christmas). Islamic holidays are also observed, and Ramadan is one of the biggest holidays; see the Religion section of the Regional Facts for the Visitor chapter for a table of dates.

ACTIVITIES

There is great walking and biking in the Fouta Djalon region; the Forest Region in the south-east is also good for biking. Fishing fans should come with a rod; there are streams and rivers all over the country, and it is a good way to pass the time. Deep-sea fishing is good off the coast by Conakry.

ACCOMMODATION

In Conakry, budget lodging is limited. Up-country, most towns have at least one place to stay, often with basic but cheap facilities, while larger towns generally have a range of hotels. Many places upcountry have no electricity from about February to May. Expect to pay up to GF7000 for budget lodging, and from GF15,000 for a room with amenities (usually bathroom and fan).

The government has recently implemented a tourism tax of GF2000 per person, applicable to top end hotels, such as the Novotel and the Hôtel Camayenne in Conakry, as well as some mid-range ones.

FOOD

Street food throughout Guinea is generally good, and there's at least one rice bar serving simple local dishes, usually rice with a sauce in every town. Shoestring travellers can keep their food budget under GF3500 per day. For those willing to spend more, there are some decent restaurants in most larger towns where you can eat well for GF6000 to GF15,000.

Getting There & Away

AIR

Guinea's only international airport is in Conakry (G'bessia), 13km from the centre of town. Regional flights leave from the Aerogare Nationale, next to the international airport. Be prepared for frequent cancellations and delays when travelling with the national carrier, Air Guinée.

Departure tax for international flights is usually included in the ticket; otherwise it's GF30,000. For regional flights, departure tax is GF20,000.

Europe & the USA

The only European airlines serving Conakry are Sabena (via Brussels), Air France (via Paris) and Aeroflot (via Moscow). Ghana Airways (via Accra) and Air Afrique (via Dakar or Abidjan) have flights to/from Europe, and Air Afrique has a direct flight between New York and Dakar. Royal Air Maroc flies from Conakry to Casablanca with onward connections to Europe and the USA; return fares to New York can be as low as US$900, although it's difficult to get seats.

Africa

The table in this section lists flights between Conakry and West African destinations.

Flights from Conakry (within West Africa)

destination	flights per week	airline	one way/ return fare (GF)
Abidjan (Côte d'Ivoire)	six	Air Afrique, Air Ivoire, Ghana Airways	210,000/295,000
Accra (Ghana)	two	Ghana Airways	435,000/620,000
Bamako (Mali)	two	Air Afrique, Air Guinée	151,000/302,000
Banjul (Gambia)	two	Air Dabia, Ghana Airways	115,000/230,000
Bissau (Guinea-Bissau)	two	TACV, Air Afrique	131,000/185,000
Dakar (Senegal)	five	Air Afrique, Air Guinée, Ghana Airways, Royal Air Maroc, TACV	150,000/300,000
Freetown (Sierra Leone)	six	Air Guinée, InterTropic, West Coast Airways	88,000/176,000
Monrovia (Liberia)	two	Air Guinée	110,000/189,000
Praia (Cape Verde)	one	TACV	204,000/407,000

You can also connect to Lomé (Togo), Niamey (Niger) and Cotonou (Benin) on Air Afrique via Abidjan, and to Bamako on Air France.

For southern and East Africa, you can connect to Johannesburg (South Africa) via Abidjan or Accra, and to Addis Ababa (Ethiopia) or Nairobi (Kenya) via Abidjan.

LAND

Côte d'Ivoire

The most frequently travelled route is between Lola and Man (about GF11,000) either via Nzo and Danané or via Tounkarata, Sipilou and Biankouma. During the rainy season, the stretches between Lola and the border are often impassable for 2WD.

Alternatively, you can go from Kankan to Odienné via Mandiana. Bush taxis run from Kankan to Mandiana and Noumoudjila, where you can find transport to Mininian and from there, onward to Odienné.

There's also a route between Beyla and Odienné (via Sinko). To/from Beyla you can get transport to N'zérékoré or to Kankan. It's better to cover as much distance as possible on the Côte d'Ivoire side, as many secondary roads in Guinea's Forest Region are in bad shape.

Guinea-Bissau

Due to political instability in Guinea-Bissau, some or all of these border crossings may be closed. Travellers should make inquiries locally before setting out.

The most popular route between Conakry and Bissau is via Labé, Koundara and Gabú, although the 100km stretch of road between Koundara and Gabú is in bad condition. From Koundara, there are direct bush taxis to Gabú, though it's often faster to travel in stages, first to Saréboïdo, then change to border transport.

On the Guinea-Bissau side, there's usually at least one pick-up a day between Gabú and the border. Your best chance for good connections is to coordinate your travels with Saréboïdo's Sunday market: vehicles from Gabú and Koundara go there on Saturday, returning on Sunday or Monday.

An alternative route from Conakry to Bissau goes via Boké and Koumbia to Gabú, though you often have to change vehicles at the border. The Boké to Koumbia road is in bad condition.

Boké bush taxis occasionally take the small track to Bissau via Kandiafara, but it's in bad condition, even during the dry season.

GUINEA

Border Crossings

Between Guinea and Guinea-Bissau the main border crossing is south-west of Koundara by Sáréboïdo. Between Guinea and Senegal, the main border crossing is just north of Koundara. There is also a border crossing north of Mali-ville near Kedougou, but the road is often impassable for vehicles. Border crossings between Guinea and Sierra Leone are at Pamelap, south of Coyah; at Gberia-Fotombu, south-west of Faranah; and by Medina Oula, south-east of Kindia. There are border crossings for Liberia at Diéké, south of N'zérékoré, at Thuo, south of Bossou, and at Daro, south-west of Macenta.

For both Guinea-Bissau and Sierra Leone, individual borders may be closed due to political instability in these countries; make inquiries locally before setting out.

Liberia

The route with the best road conditions is from N'zérékoré to Ganta via Diéké. Bush taxis go frequently from N'zérékoré to the border (GF5000), where you can change cars or walk the remaining 2km to Ganta. This border was temporarily closed in late 1997, so inquire before starting out.

Another route goes from Lola via Bossou to the border (GF1500); from here you'll have to walk a few kilometres to Yekepa. There's sporadic transport between Yekepa and Sanniquellie.

From Macenta, bush taxis go via Daro to the border (GF2000) and occasionally on to Voinjama, although the Voinjama road is often impassable. It's better to go from Macenta to Koyama, where you can find transport to Zorzor and on to Monrovia, although the Zorzor road is also in bad condition; allow two days to Monrovia. Both routes are only feasible in the dry season.

Mali

There's frequent transport to the border at Kourémalé from both Kankan (GF13,000)

and Siguiri (GF5000). A few times a week another direct service goes from both town direct to Bamako (about an extra GF6000 There's also a direct taxi once a week from Conakry to Bamako (GF45,000). Tax from Siguiri to Bamako sometimes take lesser-travelled route (better for cycling) pa alleling the River Niger via Bankan. You ca also go from Kankan via Mandiana Bougouni, although you'll have to travel i stages.

Senegal

The main route between Guinea and Seneg goes from Labé via Koundara to Tamb counda and Dakar (25 to 35 hours, G 45,000). During the rainy season the stretc between Labé and Koundara is slow or im passable for 2WD, although trucks ply th route frequently. From Koundara, there a several cars a week to the border, from whe there is frequent transport to Tambacound

There is a road between Mali (the tow Mali-ville) and Kedougou, but the road often impassable, even for 4WD. Mo people end up walking. See the Mali-vil section later in this chapter for more detail

Sierra Leone

As of late 1998, the Conakry to Freetow route via Pamelap was unsafe for travelle due to rebel fighting. Seek local advic before taking this journey.

Bush taxis run from Conakry to Freetow (330km, 10 hours, GF17,000). The road tar except for a 70km stretch near the borde Alternatively, you can take a bush taxi to th border at Pamelap (GF5000), then conne with vehicles on the other side. There a numerous checkpoints on this route; those Guinea are particularly onerous.

You can also enter Sierra Leone fro Faranah via a sparsely travelled road t Gberia-Fotombu on the border; from the you may find a truck heading for Kabal The crossing at Nongoa, west of Guéck dou, sees a lot of local traffic but is n feasible for onward travel in Sierra Leor due to insecurity near Kailahun. It's poss ble to reach Makeni in Sierra Leone fro

Kindia via Medina Oula (written Medina Oula on some maps) and Kamakwie. Bush taxis run from Kindia to the border; sometimes there's transport all the way to Kamakwie. In Sierra Leone, vehicles run between the border and Kamakwie, from where there's a daily bush taxi to Makeni. This route was unsafe for travellers as of late 1998 – seek local advice before setting off.

SEA & RIVER

Guinea-Bissau

Fishing boats go from Kamsar (south-west of Boké) to the Îles Tristao (five hours), from where you can get another boat to Guinea-Bissau. Be prepared to spend a few nights on the islands as the boats follow no set schedules.

Liberia

A boat runs once monthly between Conakry and Monrovia (36 hours, GF55,000/77,000 for deck/cabin). For schedules and reservations, go to Société Navale Guinéenne (☎ 41 27 51) on Blvd du Port, Conakry.

Sierra Leone

The ferry service is scheduled to resume between Conakry and Freetown. Inquire at travel agencies in Conakry for details.

Mali

Depending on river level, a barge runs once a week between Siguiri and Bamako (GF5000). See Getting There & Away in the Mali chapter for more details.

Getting Around

AIR

Domestic flights to/from Conakry use the Aerogare Nationale, next to the international airport. Coming from town you first reach the turn-off for the Aerogare Nationale; the international airport is a few hundred metres further on. For details on flight fares and schedules within Guinea see the Conakry Getting There & Away section. Departure tax for domestic flights is GF5000.

BUS

The government's TransGuinée buses run between Conakry and Kindia, Mamou, Labé, Kankan and Boké; most routes are serviced between one and three times weekly. Although the buses are fairly comfortable and less expensive than bush taxis, they're slow, break down often, and are rarely used by travellers. There are also several private bus companies covering these and additional routes, though they're more unreliable and run even less frequently.

For information on bus schedules, go to the Gare Voiture de Madina in Conakry. In Guinea, the term *gare voiture* is used for the bus and taxi park.

BUSH TAXI & MINIBUS

Bush taxis are the major form of transport in Guinea. They're usually Peugeot 504s, with six or nine passengers; fares in nine-seaters are slightly cheaper. If you want to charter *(déplacer)* a bush taxi for yourself , the cost should be the fare for one seat multiplied by the number of seats in the car . In general, transport is cheaper, faster and more frequent on or around market days.

Ferry crossings and road checkpoints, (the bane of travellers lives in Guinea) can add several hours on to journeys.

The cheaper, but more crowded and dangerous minibuses cover the same routes as bush taxis and are best avoided unless there's no alternative.

Sample bush taxi fares and journey times are listed in the table on the following page.

TRAIN

Note that passenger trains no longer run in Guinea.

CAR & MOTORCYCLE

If you are driving your own or a rented vehicle in Guinea, be sure the insurance and registration papers are in order as they will be frequently checked. Petrol averages GF850 per litre.

The main road east from Conakry to N'zérékoré via Mamou and Kissidougou is

GUINEA

Bush Taxi Fares & Journey Times

from	to	duration	fare
Conakry	Boké	5 hours*	GF10,000
	Kankan	13 hours*	GF22,000
	Kissidougou	11 hours	GF18,000
	Labé	9 hours	GF12,000
	Mamou	5 hours	GF7500
	N'zérékoré	20 hours	GF30,000
	Siguiri	15 hours*	GF30,000
Mamou	Labé	2½ hours	GF6000
Kissidougou	Kankan	5 hours	GF8000

*Timings are dependent on ferry crossings

tar and in reasonable condition. There's a ferry over the Mafou between Faranah and Kissidougou.

The coastal road from Conakry is tar and in excellent condition as far as Boké, dirt thereafter. There's a ferry over the River Pongo at Boffa.

From Mamou north, the road is tar as far as Labé; it's in bad condition thereafter.

In Upper Guinea, the Mamou-Dabola-Kankan road is tar and in excellent condition with the exception of a bad 80km stretch between Kouroussa and Kankan; there's a ferry over the Niger by Kouroussa. From Kankan to Siguiri (two ferry crossings), the road is dirt but OK; the road south from Kankan to Beyla is rough.

Secondary roads can get bad during the rainy season, especially in the south-east, although bush taxis usually find a way through. Conditions vary depending on how recently a road has been graded. At the time of research, the dirt roads from Dabola to Faranah and from Konsankoro to Macenta were in good shape, while those in most directions from Beyla were in bad condition.

BICYCLE

Although Conakry is too congested for cycling, many areas upcountry are excellent for mountain biking. Villages are spaced frequently enough that lodging and food are seldom a problem on longer trips. You'll need to be fully equipped with spare parts, as you won't find fittings for western-made cycles anywhere. Most towns have at least one shop that can mend flat tyres and take care of other basics.

Conakry

After being run down by Sekou Touré for a quarter of a century, Conakry is definitely on the upswing. It's now open and vibrant, with glitzy new shops, restaurants and nightclubs constantly appearing.

The city has a lot of African flavour too. If you walk around side streets on a Sunday, chances are you'll see a street celebration or two, and dozens of neighbourhood football (soccer) matches. Offshore are the Îles de Los with palm-fringed beaches.

Historically, Conakry was one of colonial France's major ports and in its heyday was apparently so attractive that it was described as the 'Paris of Africa'. Until the end of the 19th century, what is now Conakry's business district was an island, separated from the peninsula and mainland by a marshy channel (later bridged at the site of the Palais du Peuple).

Conakry's many good restaurants, picturesque tiny fishing harbours along the peninsula, friendly people and vibrant

GUINEA

GREATER CONAKRY

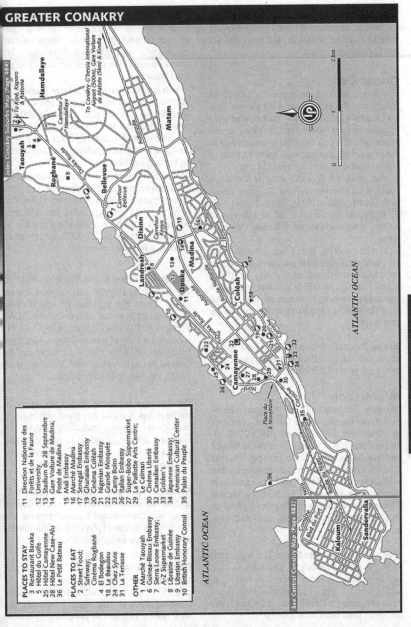

Joins Conakry Suburbs Map (Page 484)

To Conakry-G'bessia International
Airport (500m); Gare Voiture
de Matoto (5km) & Kindia

To Conakry, G'bessia International

Hamdallaye

Taouyah

Rogbané

Donka Route

Carrefour
Hamdallaye

Bellevue

Carrefour
Bellevue

Matam

Autoroute

Dixinn

Carrefour
Kegna

Landreah

Donka

Madina

Coléah

Route Niger

Corniche Sud

ATLANTIC OCEAN

Camayenne

Place du
8 Novembre

Corniche Nord

GUINEA

See Central Conakry Map (Page 482)

NORD
Route du Niger

Rte du port

Corniche

Kaloum

Sandervalia

ATLANTIC OCEAN

0 / 1 / 2 km

PLACES TO STAY
3 Restaurant Baraka
5 Hôtel du Golfe
25 Hôtel Camayenne
28 Hôtel New Case-Alu
36 Le Petit Bateau

PLACES TO EAT
2 Street Food;
 Safeway;
 Cinéma Rogbané
4 El Bodegon
18 Le Beaulieu
24 Chez Sylvie
31 La Terrasse

OTHER
1 Marché Taouyah
6 Guinea-Bissau Embassy
7 Sierra Leone Embassy;
 A-Z Supermarket
8 Librairie de Guinée
9 Liberian Embassy
10 British Honorary Consul

11 Direction Nationale des
 Forêts et de la Faune
12 University
13 Stadium du 28 Septembre
14 Gare Voiture de Madina;
 Poste de Madina
15 Marché Madina
16 Marché Madina
17 Senegal Embassy
19 Ghanaian Embassy
20 Cinéma Coléah
21 Nigerian Embassy
22 Grande Mosquée
23 Camp Boiro
26 Italian Embassy
27 Super-Bobo Supermarket
29 La Paillotte Arts Centre;
 Le Caïman
30 Cinéma Liberté
32 Canadian Embassy
33 Golden's
34 Japanese Embassy;
 American Cultural Center
35 Palais du Peuple

neighbourhood life will keep visitors busy for several days, and it's well worth making time to visit the capital before you head off for upcountry Guinea.

Orientation

Conakry's location on a narrow peninsula means that the city – now with almost 20% of Guinea's population – has nowhere to expand except northward, making it increasingly difficult to travel from one end to the other. This trip can take up to an hour in heavy traffic (every day until 11 pm).

The main north-south drag is the autoroute, which becomes Route du Niger closer to the centre and, in the business district, Ave de la République. Banks, airline offices and several restaurants are on or around this main street.

Ten kilometres north are the colourful Rogbané and Taouyah *quartiers* (suburbs), which are livelier than the city centre at night. Further out still is Ratoma with some upmarket hotels and restaurants, and beyond here the rapidly expanding quartiers of Kipé and Kaporo.

Maps Papeterie Hotimex (☎ 41 47 91) in town sells an excellent but expensive map of Conakry for GF37,000.

Information

Money The best bank for changing money is Banque Internationale pour le Commerce et l'Industrie de la Guinée (BICIGUI), although service is slow. Their main branch on Ave de la République accepts Thomas Cook, Visa and American Express travellers cheques, and will give cash advances against a Visa card. The SGBG (Société Général des Banques en Guinée) on Ave de la République also changes cash and travellers cheques.

Post & Communications The main post office is open Monday to Thursday from 8 am to 4.30 pm, Friday until 1 pm and Saturday until 2 pm. The unorganised poste restante charges GF500 per collected letter and will hold mail indefinitely.

Sotelgui (Guinea telecom) is open daily from 8 am to 10 pm. International calls average GF4800 per minute. There are card telephones, and phonecard vendors are found opposite the post office and throughout Conakry.

Sotelgui's fax window is open Monday to Saturday from 8 am to 8 pm. They charge GF1000 to receive one page (GF500 per page thereafter) and GF8000 to GF12,000 per page to send. Incoming faxes (fax 224 41 20 12) are held indefinitely, although there's no sorting system.

There are numerous private telecommunications centres around town, most slightly more expensive than Sotelgui. Hôtel Camayenne has an expensive but efficient business centre where you can even log on to the Internet for GF22,000/hour (reserved primarily for hotel guests).

Travel Agencies Karou Voyages (☎ 45 20 42, Ave de la République) is good for regional flights. For flights to Europe, it's best to go directly to an airline office. SDV-Voyages on Blvd du Commerce (☎ 41 14 91) is helpful for travel within Guinea. Flights to Freetown on West Coast Airways can be booked through Ambassador Voyages (☎ 45 38 03) on Ave de la République.

Bookshops Librairie de Guinée near the stadium has a small but good selection of books in French including works by Guinean authors. English-language magazines are on sale at Hôtel Camayenne, the Novotel and Super-Bobo Supermarket.

Medical Services Clinique Pasteur (☎ 41 25 55), two blocks south of Ave de la République, is recommended for emergencies and can provide names of physicians. Pharmacies in Conakry are fairly well stocked.

Dangers & Annoyances After 11 pm checkpoints are set up in many areas of the city. It is common practice for the soldiers manning them to stop passing vehicles and seek bribes. In order to pass, be prepared to

The Reign of Terror

Although almost 15 years have passed since Sekou Touré's death, his legacy continues to exert influence on many aspects of Guinean life. Some knowledge of his era is important for those wishing to understand modern-day Guinea.

A good place to start is Camp Boiro, in the centre of Conakry on the Donka Route, tactfully called Garde Républicaine on some maps. Originally constructed as a military camp, Boiro rapidly became synonymous with the worst atrocities carried out during Touré's 'reign of terror'. From 1960 until Touré's death in 1984, thousands of prisoners were tortured or killed at Camp Boiro, including many prominent figures. Every sector of society was affected, and almost all Guineans you meet can tell of a family member or friend who was there. Many prisoners were held for years in isolation; others were kept in a horrifying cement holding-pen open to the elements until they died.

Boiro was not the only camp of this kind in Guinea: there was another notorious one in Kindia, and smaller camps throughout the country. The bodies of many of those who died at Boiro have been lost. Others are buried in unmarked graves at the overgrown Nongo cemetery on the outskirts of town beyond Kaporo.

The present government is not eager to discuss this part of Guinea's history, and Camp Boiro is not open to the public. However, there are several private groups – primarily associations of family members of victims – working to restore the camp and make it into a memorial to serve as a foundation stone for democracy in Guinea and to remind others about the past so it will not be repeated.

For further reading on this era, check out the following Web site: www.guinee.net/

pay up to GF5000, depending on what type of vehicle you're in.

Despite its reputation, street crime in Conakry is no worse than in most other cities in the region. The places you're most likely to have trouble are taxi stands and markets, especially in Madina. Conakry's frequent traffic jams make it easy for bag snatchers to reach in vehicle windows, so keep hold of your belongings.

Things to See

The **Musée National** has a modest permanent collection of masks, statues and musical instruments, and more interesting temporary displays. It's just off Corniche-Sud in Sandervalia, and is open Tuesday to Saturday from 9 am to 6 pm, Sunday and holidays from 10 am to 5 pm. Entrance is free. There's a struggling restaurant on the grounds with drinks and inexpensive meals.

The **Palais des Nations** was to be the venue for the OAU conference in 1984, which was cancelled when Sekou Touré died. It served as the president's office until being partly destroyed in the February 1996 army rebellion; new quarters are under construction nearby. Near the palace are 50 Moorish-style villas, built to house African presidents during the conference meeting and now used as residences and offices.

The **Palais du Peuple** is a huge Chinese-built auditorium which serves as a forum for dance groups and other local performances.

The **Grande Mosquée**, financed primarily by Saudi Arabia and inaugurated in 1984, is impressive. It has an inner hall capable of accommodating 10,000 worshippers. Although visitors are not usually permitted inside, you can inquire at the Islamic Centre next door to arrange a tour. Sekou Touré's grave is in a small gazebo on the grounds.

It's worth stopping at the **university** to see its two large and interesting mosaics.

Conakry's biggest **market** is the hectic Marché Madina, but the best is Marché Taouyah in the suburbs.

GUINEA

Places to Stay – Budget

Inexpensive lodging is scarce in Conakry. The best by far is **Résidence Kaporo** (☎ *40 44 95 or 44 64 20*), 13km from the centre on the Donka Route extension, signposted on the right. It's GF10,000 for a tiny room with single bed, fan and shared bathroom, GF25,000/35,000 for a full-sized room with fan/air-con, and GF45,000 with bathroom. The whole place is spotless and safe. Breakfast is included in all prices.

Hôtel Mixte, signposted off the Donka Route extension in Kipé, has dingy rooms

with fan/air-con for GF20,000/25,000; most clientele rent by the hour.

Also in the suburbs, **Guesthouse Deborah** (☎ *43 17 61*), just off the Donka Route extension 300m after the turn-off to the Mariador hotels in Ratoma, has decent single/double rooms for GF35,000/40,000, although these can usually be negotiated down by at least GF5000, especially for longer stays. There's a restaurant and small roof-top terrace with sea views.

For the following three places, refer to the Greater Conakry map on p479. *Restau-*

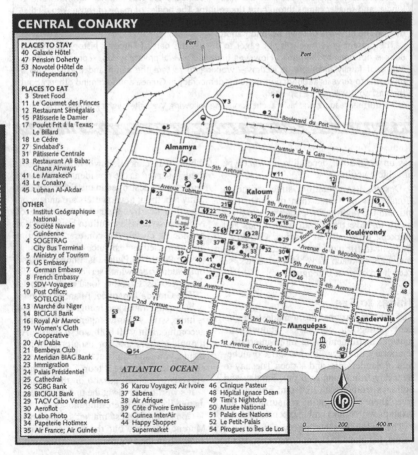

CENTRAL CONAKRY

PLACES TO STAY
40 Galaxie Hôtel
47 Pension Doherty
53 Novotel (Hôtel de l'Independance)

PLACES TO EAT
3 Street Food
11 Le Gourmet des Princes
12 Restaurant Sénégalais
15 Pâtisserie le Damier
17 Poulet Frit á la Texas; Le Billard
18 Le Cédre
27 Sindabad's
31 Pâtisserie Centrale
33 Restaurant Ali Baba; Ghana Airways
41 Le Marrakech
43 Le Conakry
45 Lubnan Al-Akdar

OTHER
1 Institut Géographique National
2 Société Navale Guinéenne
4 SOGETRAG City Bus Terminal
5 Ministry of Tourism
6 US Embassy
7 German Embassy
8 French Embassy
9 SDV-Voyages
10 Post Office; SOTELGUI
13 Marché du Niger
14 BICIGUI Bank
16 Royal Air Maroc
19 Women's Cloth Cooperative
20 Air Dabia
21 Bembeya Club
22 Meridien BIAG Bank
23 Immigration
24 Palais Présidentiel
25 Cathedral
26 SGBG Bank
28 BICIGUI Bank
29 TACV Cabo Verde Airlines
30 Aeroflot
32 Labo Photo
34 Papeterie Hotimex
35 Air France; Air Guinée
36 Karou Voyages; Air Ivoire
37 Sabena
38 Air Afrique
39 Côte d'Ivoire Embassy
42 Guinea InterAir
44 Happy Shopper Supermarket
46 Clinique Pasteur
48 Hôpital Ignace Dean
49 Timi's Nightclub
50 Musée National
51 Palais des Nations
52 Le Petit-Palais
54 Pirogues to Îles de Los

rant Baraka (☎ *42 13 03*), behind the CBG compound in Minière (part of Taouyah quartier), has a couple of air-con rooms from GF 30,000, although the owner may be willing to negotiate. As the rooms are near the restaurant, they can be noisy. *Hôtel du Golfe* (☎ *41 13 94*), off the Donka Route extension in Minière, has OK but overpriced singles/doubles from GF42,000/49,000.

The unmarked *Hôtel New Case-Alu* (☎ *46 37 07*), with restaurant and nice garden, is a decent place on Corniche-Nord, north of Place du 8 Novembre in Camayenne. Aircon rooms with bathroom are GF30,000/35,000 in the annexe/main building. The rooms in the annexe are a bit run-down, but those for GF35,000 are good value.

In town, *Pension Doherty* (☎ *44 38 75*), off Ave de la République, has tolerable aircon rooms with bathroom from GF27,500; most don't have outside windows.

Places to Stay – Mid-Range

Auberge Irena (☎ *42 10 63*), on the Donka Route extension in Ratoma, is a nice place with single/double rooms with bathroom, TV and telephone for GF50,000/65,000 including breakfast.

Hôtel-Restaurant César (☎ *44 72 60*), 500m from the Mariador Park hotel in Taouyah, has comfortable air-con rooms with bathroom for GF45,000/60,0000 in the main building/annexe.

Hôtel Mariador Résidence (☎ *41 27 52*), well signposted 800m off the Donka Route extension in Taouyah, has a seaside terrace, a pool and comfortable rooms from GF 65,000. The nearby *Hôtel Mariador Park* is a step down, but not bad, with rooms from GF58,200.

Le Petit Bateau (☎ *41 28 85*), 300m out in the water on a tiny stretch of land near the port (see the Greater Conakry map p479), has a nice pool and clean single/double rooms for GF55,000/75,000. The setting is pleasant with breezes from the sea, but isolated if you don't have wheels.

Galaxie Hôtel (☎ *45 10 03*), off Ave de la République, has fully equipped single/double air-con rooms for GF60,000/90,000, although the price will probably rise once renovations are completed; there's no restaurant as yet.

Places to Stay – Top End

Conakry's best is *Hôtel Camayenne* (☎ *41 40 89, email htlcam@leland-gn.org*) on Corniche-Nord; comfortable rooms with all the amenities start at GF175,000 including a good buffet breakfast. There's also a business centre with Internet facilities.

The *Novotel* (☎ *41 50 21*), at the tip of the Kaloum peninsula, has fully equipped rooms from GF99,000; the breakfast buffet is GF12,000 extra. Both these hotels have swimming pools.

Places to Eat

Places with good *street food* for under GF1000 include Marché du Niger and the stalls at the intersection of Corniche-Nord and Blvd du Commerce in town, and, out of town at Route Donka just south of Cinéma Rogbané.

For inexpensive African food in a restaurant, try *Restaurant Sénégalais*, on the corner of 9th Ave and 7th Blvd, which has filling meals for under GF2000. A step up is *Le Gourmet des Princes* (closed Sundays) on 5th Blvd, with a selection of dishes from GF2500. *Le Caïman* at La Paillotte Arts Centre in Camayenne (see the Greater Conakry map p479) is popular, although it's more expensive. In Kipé, *L'Africana* is a small streetside place on the Donka Route extension with inexpensive rice dishes. Opposite Hôtel Camayenne is the very popular *Chez Sylvie* (evenings only) with *attiéké* (cassava) and other dishes for about GF5000.

In the centre, on or near Ave de la République, are several inexpensive Lebanese and fast food restaurants. *Sindabad's* is clean, with good chawarmas for GF1500. *Restaurant Ali Baba* has chawarmas and pizza, while *Lubnan Al-Akdar* is good for felafel sandwiches. *Pâtisserie Centrale* (☎ *41 18 42*) has hamburgers, sandwiches and ice cream.

Also in the centre, for American-style

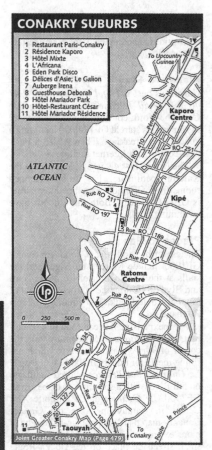

CONAKRY SUBURBS

1 Restaurant Paris-Conakry
2 Résidence Kaporo
3 Hôtel Mixte
4 L'Africana
5 Eden Park Disco
6 Délices d'Asie; Le Galion
7 Auberge Irena
8 Guesthouse Deborah
9 Hôtel Mariador Park
10 Hôtel-Restaurant César
11 Hôtel Mariador Résidence

ATLANTIC
OCEAN

To Upcountry
Guinea

Kaporo
Centre

Kipé

Ratoma
Centre

0   250   500 m

Taouyah

To
Conakry

Joins Greater Conakry Map (Page 479)

There's a selection of reasonably priced main dishes from GF6000; it's closed Sunday lunch. *Pâtisserie le Damier* (☎ *44 17 86*), opposite Marché du Niger, is open for breakfast and lunch Monday to Saturday. It has excellent French food from GF10,000 and breads and pastries to take away.

For places listed in this paragraph, refer to the Greater Conakry map on p479. *Le Petit Bateau* has OK meals for about GF10,000. It's worth a visit to enjoy the restaurant's relaxing setting on a pier jutting into the sea. Further out of town is the pleasant *La Terrasse* (☎ *46 50 04*), closed Sunday, with brochettes and grilled dishes for GF6000. *Le Beaulieu* (☎ *44 74 25*), just off Corniche-Sud, has a large selection of European food and a few African dishes from about GF5000. *El Bodegon* (☎ *42 14 60*), on the Donka Route extension in Hamdallaye, is a friendly place with good piña coladas, music on weekends, and meals for about GF6500. Cuban specialities are available on request. It's closed Sunday lunch.

Hôtel-Restaurant César's (☎ *44 72 60*) in Taouyah has pizzas and pasta dishes from GF5000. *Délices d'Asie* (☎ *42 21 22*), on the Donka Route extension, (closed Monday and Tuesday lunch) has good but expensive Vietnamese food and a terrace overlooking the sea. *Le Galion* (☎ *40 32 82*) next door has a seaside setting and main dishes from GF10,000. *Restaurant Paris-Conakry*, set on a cove 500m beyond Résidence Kaporo off the Donka Route extension, has excellent seafood stew and other dishes from GF 10,000.

Entertainment

Bars & Nightclubs Conakry has many good night spots, although most are in the suburbs. None get lively before 11 pm. Cover charges start around GF3000, more on weekends. Thursday and Saturday are the biggest nights.

Eden Park Disco, signposted off the Donka Route extension in Kipé, (GF8000 cover) has a good variety of music and plenty of dancing space. The nightclub at *La Paillotte Arts Centre* has good music and is

chicken, try *Poulet Frit á la Texas* on Route du Niger. *Le Billard* (☎ *41 49 76*) next door has meals from GF2000 and cheap *pressions* (beers).

Still in the centre, *Le Conakry* (☎ *41 26 82*), closed Sunday, has a quaint atmosphere and good service; the menu of the day costs GF10,000. *Le Marrakech* (☎ *45 21 53*) nearby has a selection of Moroccan and European dishes from GF7000. For the best Lebanese food in town, try *Le Cèdre* (☎ *41 44 73*), two blocks off Route du Niger.

always crowded. *Golden's*, one block off Corniche-Sud, is another popular place.

In town, the lively *Timi's Nightclub* in Sandervalia is open daily and popular with locals and expatriates. A seedy place with plenty of action is *Bembeya Club*, near the post office; it's best to go in a group as the area is not safe at night. For a change of pace, *Restaurant Petit-Palais* (☎ 45 40 10), opposite the Novotel has a karaoke bar upstairs open until 3 am (closed Sunday).

Music Venues To hear live Guinean music, check out *La Paillotte*, a local arts centre for Guinea's rising young stars. There are no set schedules: just turn up and see what's happening. It's on Corniche-Nord just north of Place du 8 Novembre.

Palais du Peuple often has good performances by local artists. Look out for advertisements at the Palais or in the free listings magazine, *Dyeli*.

Cinema *Cinéma Rogbané*, 10km from the centre, has shows most evenings; admission is GF1000. *Cinéma Liberté* on the autoroute is another place to try.

Shopping

Supermarkets Well stocked (but expensive) supermarkets include A-Z Supermarket at Carrefour Bellevue, Safeway in Hamdallaye, and Happy Shopper downtown.

Art & Craftwork The vendors opposite Hôtel Camayenne sell crafts of average quality, though occasionally they have interesting pieces. In general, it's better to buy baskets, textiles and other crafts upcountry as quality is higher and prices are lower.

For African print material, the Marché du Niger is best. A good place for tie-dyed cloth is the women's cooperative, Centre d'Appui à l'Autopromotion Feminine, with an outlet off Ave de la République.

Music The stalls in Marché du Niger stock tapes of current stars. Enima inside the Palais du Peuple is also a good place to look, especially for older recordings.

Getting There & Away

Air All domestic flights use the Aerogare Nationale near the international airport, 13km from town. Air Guinée, Guinea Inter-Air and Guinea Air Service fly from Conakry to Labé (GF44,000), Siguiri (GF 71,000), N'zérékoré (GF85,000) and occasionally Kissidougou (GF55,000) and Kankan (GF70,000). Flights are usually once or twice weekly, although schedules change constantly and prices vary slightly among the airlines. The planes are not the most luxurious and cancellations and delays are frequent.

For details on regional and intercontinental flights to/from Conakry see the main Getting There & Away section in this chapter.

In Conakry, most airline offices are on or near Ave de la République, including the following:

Aeroflot	☎ 41 41 43
Air Afrique	☎ 41 49 96
Air Dabia	☎ 45 39 05
Air France	☎ 41 36 61
Air Guinée	☎ 45 43 62
Air Ivoire	☎ 41 30 69
Cathay Pacific	☎ 41 47 38
Ghana Airways	☎ 45 48 13
Guinea Air Service (through Karou Voyages)	☎ 45 20 42
Guinea InterAir	☎ 41 37 08
Royal Air Maroc	☎ 41 38 96
Sabena	☎ 41 34 40
TACV Cabo Verde Airlines	☎ 45 23 30

Bus Long-distance buses leave from Gare Voiture de Madina, 6km from the centre (GF200 by shared taxi, or take an 'A' city bus). Buses usually leave around 8 am. Buses to Kindia and Mamou go almost every other day and to Labé and Kankan a few times a week. The luggage fee for large bags is GF3000, regardless of your destination. It's impossible to make reservations for most buses; you must go to the office at the gare voiture early (around 6 am) on the day of departure; take a taxi directly there (for safety, pay GF200 extra to go into the gare voiture) as it will still be dark. The Kankan

GUINEA

bus is the only one you can buy tickets for in advance at Gare Voiture de Matoto, 5km beyond the airport.

Bush Taxi & Minibus Bush taxis and minibuses for all upcountry destinations leave from Gare Voiture de Madina. Bush taxis for Siguiri also leave from the Magasin de Siguiri off Corniche-Sud. Bush taxis for Sierra Leone leave from Gare Voiture de Matoto, and from the Madina gare for the border at Pamelap. There's a postal van from the Poste de Madina to Kankan (Tuesday and Thursday, GF17,000), Labé (Tuesday and Friday, GF9000), Guéckédou (Tuesday and Thursday, GF17,000) and Kamsar (Monday/Thursday, GF8000); go the day before to confirm departure times.

Note Bush taxis going into Conakry don't enter the city at night, but stop at the infamous Kilomètre 36 and wait until dawn before finishing their journey.

Getting Around

To/From the Airport Taxis from town to the airport cost between GF2000 and GF5000, depending on your bargaining powers. From the airport into town (13km) should not cost more than GF5000.

Alternatively, catch a shared taxi from just outside the airport (GF200) or take the 'A' bus (marked 'Port' or 'Ville') into the centre (GF100).

Bus SOGETRAG has two main bus lines in the city: the 'C' line (marked 'Kaporo') from the centre to Kaporo, and the 'A' line (marked 'Matoto') from the centre to Matoto beyond the airport. Fares range from GF100 to GF250 according to distance. In the centre, both lines start at the roundabout opposite the port and pass along Ave de la République and Route du Niger until they reach Place du 8 Novembre, where the 'C' bus takes Route Donka and the 'A' bus continues on the autoroute.

Taxi A seat in a shared taxi around town costs GF200 per zone; most rides in the city

do not exceed this. A charter taxi costs a minimum of GF600, although most rides will cost GF1000; hotel taxis charge about double this. A taxi by the hour should cost about GF2500 if you bargain well.

Car & Motorcycle Europcar at the Novotel (☎ 41 50 21) and Avis at the Novotel and the Camayenne (☎ 41 40 89) have base rates of about GF50,000 per day plus mileage and chauffeur charges. For cheaper rates, try Guinée Cars (☎ 44 35 75) in the city centre or EGLPS (☎ 46 37 92) opposite Super-Bobo, which offers a range of related services for long-term visitors.

AROUND CONAKRY
Îles de Los

The Îles de Los are a group of small islands about 10km south-west of Conakry, used as a waystation for the slave trade and later by the British (who controlled the islands during much of the 19th century) to resettle freed slaves. They're now popular for weekend excursions; only three are inhabited.

Tiny **Roume** has a tranquil beach, good for swimming, and a hotel, *Le Sogue*, which has comfortable singles/doubles from GF 59,000/69,000, or GF99,000/170,000 (more at weekends) including transport and meals. Make reservations at Karou Voyages. Note that Le Sogue closes from mid-June to mid-October. There are also some basic *beach huts* for GF5000 per night.

Kassa is closer to Conakry and large enough for walks. Near the attractive main beach, Soro (GF1000 admission), are some dilapidated *bungalows* for GF25,000 (☎ 41 51 30). Meals are available with advance notice.

Tamara, used by the French and later by Sekou Touré as a penal colony, is less frequented by tourists as its beaches aren't particularly good, although it has some interesting hikes. Fotoba, with its small Anglican church, is the main village; there's no restaurant.

Getting There & Away A motorised pirogue leaves for Roume from Hôtel Camayenne from Friday to Sunday at 9.30 am (GF10,000 per person return). You can also hire your own pirogue for any of the islands from the beach near the Novotel, though it's unlikely you'll pay less than GF10,000. It's not unheard of for captains to inform you en route that they've run out of fuel, but for a small 'additional fee' they can get some from a friend.

Alternatively, regular pirogues leave the Novotel beach for Soro (GF500) and Fotoba (GF1000). Transport to the islands is sporadic during the rainy season when the seas get rough.

Coyah

Coyah, about 50km from Conakry and home of Guinea's bottled mineral water, is a possible place to stay if you want to avoid arriving late in the capital from upcountry.

Hôtel la Mariane, signposted off the Conakry road, has dumpy but bearable rooms with fan/air-con for GF10,000/ 15,000. *Chez Claude* (closed Friday) is a very decent French restaurant with a selection of delicacies from GF8000. It's a nice day excursion from Conakry for those with wheels. Claude has a couple of comfortable rooms which he is sometimes willing to rent out for GF45,000. The restaurant is signposted to the left as you arrive from Conakry. *Restaurant Kinsy*, 500m off the Conakry road, has meals for GF5000.

From Coyah, it's GF3000 in a bush taxi to Pamelap, GF2500 to Kindia and GF500 to Conakry.

Dubréka

Dubréka, 5km from Dubréka junction on the Boffa highway, is President Lansana Conté's home town and the starting point for excursions to several natural attractions. Near the town are some interesting mangrove swamps with a rich variety of bird and animal life. You can hire a pirogue locally, but be sure it's in good condition as it takes several hours to really get into the swamps.

Les Cascades de la Soumba make a good outing (except from February to May, when they dry up to a trickle). The cascades were

traditionally considered sacred by locals and were a site for sacrifices. Beneath the falls is a refreshing pool where you can swim. There is a nice *restaurant* here with meals for GF10,000, and nearby, six fully equipped single/double *bungalows* (☎ 45 32 45) for GF50,000/65,000, including breakfast. The owner can organise hikes into the surrounding area if you wish. The signposted turn-off is 11km after Dubréka junction on the Boffa highway; the cascades are 5km further down a dirt road. If you don't have transport, you'll have to charter a taxi for the day from Dubréka junction (about GF9000).

About 10km east of Dubréka are some good day hikes on **Mt Kakoulima** (1011m), and there are rock formations nearby, including **Le Chien Qui Fume**.

Kindia

Bustling Kindia is a good introduction to upcountry Guinea. The best day to visit is Sunday, when the market is in full swing. Kindia is also a good place to buy indigo cloth. You can see how it is made at the Cooperative des Teinturieres (open daily). About 5km north of town is the interesting Institut Pasteur (open Monday to Saturday), where research into snake venom is done; adjoining is a sad little zoo.

Bridal Veil Falls, 12km out of town, are overrated but worth a stop during the rainy season when they're at their fullest. There's a GF1000 entry fee and run-down *bungalows* for GF25,000 per night. Bring your own food as the restaurant is closed. You may be able to get a taxi heading for Mamou to drop you at the junction; otherwise, it's about GF3000 to charter your own.

Places to Stay & Eat In Kindia the proprietor of *Restaurant Mont Gangan* rents a room in his family quarters with mosquito net and bathroom for GF7500. The restaurant is pleasant, though you'll have to order ahead for most items on the menu.

Behind the train station, the declining *Hôtel Buffet de la Gare* (☎ 61 08 71) has dingy rooms for GF10,000 (no fan), GF 20,000 (fan) and GF35,000 (air-con).

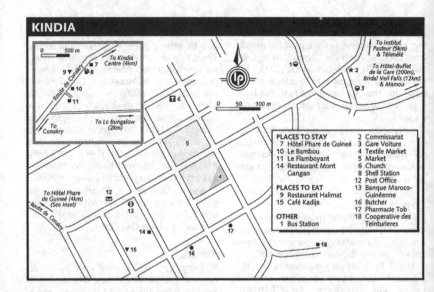

KINDIA

0   500 m

To Kindia
Centre (4km)

Route de Conakry

9 ▼   7
8

10

11

To
Conakry

To Le Bungalow
(2km)

To Institut
Pasteur (5km)
& Télimélé

To Hôtel-Buffet
de la Gare (300m),
Bridal Veil Falls (12km)
& Mamou

1 ●

★ 2

● 3

0   50   100 m

6

5

4

To Hôtel Phare
de Guinée (4km)
(See Inset)

Route de Conakry

12

9
13

14

15

16

17

● 18

PLACES TO STAY
7   Hôtel Phare de Guineé
10 Le Bambou
11 Le Flamboyant
14 Restaurant Mont
    Gangan

PLACES TO EAT
9   Restaurant Halimat
15 Café Kadija

OTHER
1   Bus Station

2   Commissariat
3   Gare Voiture
4   Textile Market
5   Market
6   Church
8   Shell Station
12 Post Office
13 Banque Maroco-
    Guinéenne
16 Butcher
17 Pharmacie Tob
18 Cooperative des
    Teinturieres

GUINEA

Much better, although inconveniently located 4km from town, is *Hôtel Phare de Guinée* (☎ *61 05 31*) with good, clean rooms from GF10,000 (GF20,000 with bathroom).

Le Bambou (☎ *61 08 39*), also out of town, has three clean, good value rooms with fan and mosquito net for GF15,000 (GF20,000 with bathroom). There's a satellite TV in the bar and meals from GF2500. The upmarket *Le Flamboyant* (☎ *61 02 12*) has comfortable rooms with fan/air-con and bathroom for GF40,000/50,000, including breakfast. They also have a pricey restaurant and a small pool.

Le Bungalow (☎ *61 01 43*) is also comfortable and slightly less expensive, with rooms with fan for GF30,000 or GF35,000 with air-con, including breakfast. It's 2km off the bypass road, opposite the President's farm; you'll need your own transport to get here.

The friendly *Café Kadija* in town has basic meals for under GF3000.

Restaurant Halimat (☎ *61 08 83*) has good French and African cuisine from about GF5000. It's best to call in advance.

Getting There & Away Daily taxis leave the gare voiture for Télimélé (GF5000), the Sierra Leone border (GF2500), Mamou (GF3500), Coyah (GF2500) and Conakry (GF3000). Buses from the bus station go several times weekly to Mamou and Conakry (both GF2500). There's a bypass road around town, avoiding Kindia centre.

Fouta Djalon

The Fouta Djalon plateau – an area of green rolling hills, 1000m peaks, orchards and farmland – is one of the most scenic areas of Guinea and the heartland of the country's Peul population. It's also one of the better hiking places in West Africa, especially from November to January when temperatures are cooler and the sky is not too dusty.

The towns listed below are in order of distance from Conakry.

MAMOU

Mamou, sometimes called the gateway to the Fouta Djalon, is a lively town with an inter-

Hiking in the Fouta Djalon

The Fouta Djalon is excellent for hiking (and mountain biking), as – unlike many other places in West Africa – you can essentially go at will. It's suitable either for an extended series of day trips based in one of the towns, or for village to village walking.

The villages are closely spaced, as in Nepal, except there are no teahouses. Lodging is basic (with villagers) and cheap, and limited food is available en route, although you should carry your own supplies as well as water-purifying tablets. Bring a jacket, as it gets chilly at night, especially near Mali-ville. It's advisable to use topographical maps from the IGN in Conakry (see Planning in the Facts for the Visitor section of this chapter for details).

The terrain is hilly, but not overly strenuous (except near Mali-ville, where there are some steep sections if you're climbing up the escarpment from Senegal). The scenery is pastoral, with wide views over rolling hills and small mountains. The language spoken in the region is Pulaar (Fula).

Outside the major towns (all of which, except Mali-ville, have a range of hotels and restaurants), there is no infrastructure and the area is not heavily visited, although tourism is increasing. Even so, you'll probably be the only tourist on the back paths.

esting mosque. There are several vine bridges nearby, including one at Soumay-ereya south of Marela. Also nearby is **Timbo**, former capital of the Fouta Djalon and, together with Fougoumba near Dalaba, an important religious centre for Guinea's Peuls.

Places to Stay

The cheapest place is *Hôtel Luna* (☎ 68 07 69), on the Dalaba road just to the east of the centre. Poorly ventilated rooms with mosquito net are GF5000, while better rooms

start at GF10,000. Rooms with two double beds and bathroom cost GF20,000. The unatmospheric *Hôtel Rama* (☎ 68 04 30), just off the main road, has acceptable rooms from GF15,000. *Clos Sainte-Catherine* (☎ 68 07 05), 3km from the centre on the Conakry road, has decent bungalows with bathroom for GF30,000; it's hard to find taxis back into town.

For business travellers or those affiliated with organisations, the *École Forestière* (☎ 68 06 34) sometimes rents out nice rooms from GF8000 and fully equipped cabins from GF18,000; this place does not accept independent tourists. It's about 3km from town on the Conakry road, opposite and just after Clos Sainte-Catherine.

About 40km from Mamou on the Kindia road is the *Mariador Hôtel Linsan*, which offers all the amenities in the middle of nowhere. Fully equipped rooms are GF 35,000 to GF47,000, and there's small pool and a restaurant which really does have almost everything on its menu.

Places to Eat

Mamou's best restaurant is *Chaoul & Fils* in Quartier Petel, 3km from the centre on the Dalaba road (GF250 in a shared taxi), with Lebanese dishes from GF2500.

Restaurant Hidalgo in town, on the Dalaba road, has omelettes and other basics for GF1000.

The more upmarket *Restaurant Luna* at Hôtel Luna has filling meals from GF2000.

Getting There & Away

Mamou is a major transport junction. Frequent bush taxis to Conakry (GF7500), Dalaba (GF2500), Labé (GF6000), Faranah (GF7000) and Dabola (GF7000) depart from the gare voiture.

DALABA

Dalaba, with its pretty pine groves and interesting nearby villages, makes a superb base for hiking or biking in this region. Before independence, the town was a therapeutic centre for colonial administrators and many buildings from the era remain.

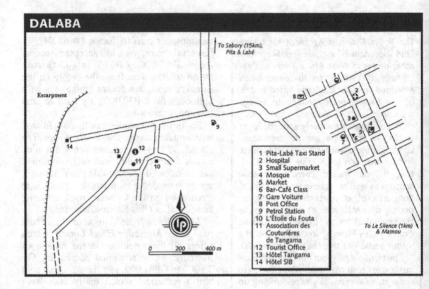

DALABA

To Sebory (15km),
Pita & Labé

Escarpment

To Le Silence (1km)
& Mamou

1 Pita-Labé Taxi Stand
2 Hospital
3 Small Supermarket
4 Mosque
5 Market
6 Bar-Café Class
7 Gare Voiture
8 Post Office
9 Petrol Station
10 L'Étoile du Fouta
11 Association des
   Couturiéres
   de Tangama
12 Tourist Office
13 Hôtel Tangama
14 Hôtel SIB

0   200   400 m

There's an excellent tourist office in the Chargeur Quartier with informative booklets in English and French detailing places of interest in and around Dalaba. They can help plan routes and arrange a guide if you want one, though it's not necessary. It can be difficult to change money in Dalaba, especially on Monday when many shops are closed. Market day is Sunday.

The Dalaba region is good for crafts. Places worth visiting include the Association des Couturières de Tangama for batiks and tie-dyed cloths, and the Group Artisanal Feminin Vanerie in Sebory (15km northwest of town) for baskets.

Places to Stay & Eat

The nicest place is *Hôtel Tangama*, a pleasant *pension* reminiscent of France. Simple, clean rooms with shared bathroom cost GF10,000 (GF15,000 with hot water), while comfortable one/two bed rooms with bathroom are GF25,000/35,000. The restaurant is good, with set menus for GF4000 (breakfast) and GF9000 (main meal). *L'Étoile du Fouta*, with dirty rooms and filthy common

bathrooms, is the cheapest place in town at GF5000 per night. Its *disco* is popular on weekends. *Hôtel SIB* (☎ 68 06 26) is Dalaba's luxury accommodation, with fully equipped but characterless rooms, which cost from GF35,000 to GF50,000, and an expensive restaurant. Views of the valley from the SIB's terrace are not to be missed, especially at sunset.

A kilometre out of town, *Le Silence* has good meals for GF 1700 to GF3000. Near the gare voiture are several rice bars. Madame Conté's *Bar-Café Class* is the best, with good attiéké from GF600.

Getting There & Away

Bush taxis for Pita (GF3000) and Labé (GF4000) leave from the Pita-Labé taxi stand on the main road. Bush taxis for Mamou (GF2500) and Conakry (GF10,000) leave from the gare voiture near the market. Most departures are in the morning.

PITA

Pita's major attraction are the **Chutes du Kinkon**. To get there, take the main road north out of town for 1km, then head left 10km down a dirt road to the falls. It's a good walk or an easy cycle. The setting is not ideal as the falls are below a hydroelectric plant, but they're still worth a visit. Camping is prohibited. Before visiting, you'll need a permit from the police station in Pita; it's free and usually not a hassle.

The three-tiered **Chutes de Kambadaga** are further away (about 35km) and rougher to reach; you'll need transport. To get there, follow the dirt road to Kinkon, then branch right (Kinkon is signposted to the left). It's a steep hike down to the bottom. There's a small bungalow where you can overnight for about GF5000; bring your own food and water-purifying tablets.

Places to Stay & Eat

The *Centre d'Accueil* behind the *préfecture* has run-down rondavels (huts) for GF5000 and better rooms with running water in the main building for GF10,000.

Hôtel Kinkon, in a tranquil setting north of town behind the public gardens, has basic, dirty rooms for GF5000.

For food, the best place is Oury's *Cool & Cozy Café* with meals for GF2000 or less. Oury speaks English and is a wealth of information on Pita and the surrounding area; it's well worth stopping by before setting off on any excursions. He can arrange guides for hikes to the falls and can help you find inexpensive accommodation with locals. The Cool & Cozy is behind Café-109 and opposite Video Club Le Sapin.

L'Amitié, signposted off the main road, has good hamburgers for GF3000 and TV on weekends. *Café-Restaurant Montreal* has good rice and sauce for GF600.

Getting There & Away

The postal van from Labé usually saves a few seats for passengers embarking in Pita. Bush taxis leave from the Rex Cinéma to Labé (GF1500) and Dalaba (GF3000) throughout the day, and twice a week to Télimélé (GF10,000).

LABÉ

Labé is the largest town in the Fouta and the region's administrative capital. There are hikes and excursions in the area, and in town, several indigo cloth cooperatives; one to try is Teinture-Promotion Labé. Although Labé has a bank, they're often reluctant to change money; shopowners may be able to help you out.

About 20km out of town on the Mali road is the signposted turn-off for the source of the River Gambia.

Places to Stay

The cheapest central lodging is the annexe of *Hôtel de l'Indépendance* (☎ 51 10 00) near the main gare voiture; basic rooms with shared bathroom are GF5000. The main part of the hotel across the street is much better, with good single/double rooms with bathroom for GF15,000/20,000.

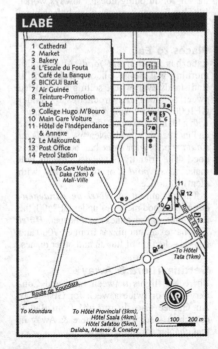

LABÉ

1 Cathedral
2 Market
3 Bakery
4 L'Escale du Fouta
5 Café de la Banque
6 BICIGUI Bank
7 Air Guinée
8 Teinture-Promotion Labé
9 College Hugo M'Bouro
10 Main Gare Voiture
11 Hôtel de l'Indépendance & Annexe
12 Le Makoumba
13 Post Office
14 Petrol Station

To Gare Voiture Daka (2km) & Mali-Ville
To Hôtel Tata (1km)
Route de Koundara
To Koundara
To Hôtel Provincial (3km), Hôtel Saala (4km), Hôtel Safatou (5km), Dalaba, Mamou & Conakry
0   100   200 m

GUINEA

Hôtel Saala (☎ *51 07 31*) is good value, with basic but clean rooms for GF5000 (from GF10,000 with bathroom). The only drawback is that it is 4km from the centre.

Also out of town is *Hôtel Provincial* with clean rooms for GF7000 (GF20,000 with bathroom, mosquito net and fan). Mouctar Paraya, a well known Guinean musician, often performs here at the weekend.

The nicest place in Labé is *Hôtel Tata* (☎ *51 05 40*), with comfortable, good value regular/large rooms with attractive tilework for GF20,000/25,000. The large rooms are a particularly good deal as they can sleep up to four people. Madame Raby, the owner, has lots of information on tourism in the area and can help organise excursions or arrange transport (including bicycle rental).

The glitzy *Hôtel Safatou* (☎ *51 11 09*), at the entrance to Labé, has fully equipped but characterless single/double rooms for GF35,000/40,000, including breakfast (but the air-conditioning doesn't always work). It's 5km from the centre and only feasible if you have your own vehicle.

Places to Eat

Labé has good *street food*. At the mid-morning and noon school breaks, you'll find stands everywhere selling beans, fried sweet potatoes and brochettes for under GF1000. The relaxing *Café de la Banque*, with a lounge and small library, serves coffee and inexpensive meals. Nearby, *L'Escale du Fouta* is pricey for a rice bar, but the food is good. The friendly Senegalese owner will make *yassa poulet* or other dishes with plenty of notice.

The restaurant at *Hôtel de l'Indépendance* has good meals for under GF2500; the restaurant in the annexe is cheaper. *Hôtel Tata* has excellent pizzas from GF7000 and a good selection of Italian and other dishes.

Getting There & Away

There are flights between Labé and Conakry once or twice a week for GF44,000. Air Guinée also fly to Labé from Banjul (Gambia) – see Getting There & Away in that chapter for more details.

Labé is an important transport junction, and the end of the tar road for onward transport to Senegal and Guinea-Bissau. Taxis for Mali (the town), Koundara and Senegal leave from Gare Voiture Daka north of town. Bush taxis for Conakry (GF12,000) and other destinations leave from the main gare voiture in the centre.

The postal van to Conakry (GF9000) departs Thursday and Sunday mornings from the main gare voiture; arrive by 7 am to get a seat.

MALI

Mali (sometimes called Mali-ville, to distinguish it from the country of the same name) is perched on the edge of the spectacular **Massif du Tamgué** just before its precipitous drop towards Senegal and the plains below. At over 1300m it's the highest town in the Fouta; the climate is cool and the scenery superb. If you don't mind roughing it a bit, it's an excellent base for hiking and mountain biking excursions into the surrounding area. In town, there's no electricity or running water, and only basic provisions.

On Sunday, Mali has a good **market**. Look for the honey vendors in the corner; they gather their wares from the baskets you see in the trees lining the road to Labé. Opposite the market is the Centre de Femme, a cloth-weaving cooperative with a small boutique.

Mali's most well-known attraction is **Mt Loura** and the **Dame de Mali** rock formation on its side. The top (look for the radio antenna) is 7km from town by bike (shorter if you hike), and offers unparalleled views. On a clear day you'll be able to see the River Gambia and Senegal. No permits are necessary to climb Mt Loura, despite what hotel staff or police at the town checkpoint may tell you.

Mt Lansa is another good excursion. It's a three hour hike to the top, from where there are excellent views over the surrounding countryside. You'll need a guide on the upper section of the mountain; ask him to point out the stone platform used for drumming messages to the villages below.

Places to Stay & Eat

The best is *La Dame du Mali* (also called the Mt Loura) which has basic rooms for GF3000 and GF5000 and meals on request. The dilapidated *Hôtel Tontou*, in the *préfet's* former house, has rooms for GF3000.

Café Montreal near the taxi stand has good omelettes and sandwiches.

Getting There & Away

There's at least one vehicle daily between Mali and Labé (120km, five hours, GF 7000). There's generally one vehicle per week to Kedougou (Senegal) in the dry season (GF12,000). Coming from Kedougou, you can usually get a lift on a motorcycle towards the border. After that, be prepared to walk the rest of the way – up to 12 hours – to Mali. Boys will be around to help carry your luggage.

The Mali to Koundara road is very bad; transport is only feasible on Saturdays, market day in Madina Woura where you'll have to change vehicle. Otherwise, you'll have to go via Labé.

KOUNDARA

Koundara is the starting point for visits to Parc Transfrontalier Niokolo-Badiar – see the boxed text 'Guinea's National Parks' in the Facts About Guinea section earlier for more details. The main language in this area is Pulaar (Fula). There are many ethnic groups in this area, including the Badiaranké, Bassari, Peul and Coniagui, and the colourful mixture makes this an interesting area to visit.

About 45km from Koundara on the Bissau border is **Saréboïdo**, with a good Sunday market attracting traders from Bissau, Senegal and Guinea.

Places to Stay & Eat

Hôtel Gangan has rooms for GF5000 and an undependable restaurant. Alternatively, try *Hôtel Mamadou Boiro*, which has rooms with mosquito nets for GF8000.

There are several *rice bars* and *salad stalls* near the gare voiture. In the mornings,

look for *gosseytiga*, a rice porridge with ground peanuts and sugar which is a speciality of the region.

Niokolo-Badiar Café near the Saréboïdo taxi stand has good coffee.

Thanks to its proximity to Bissau, you can usually find cold Superbock beer in Koundara.

Getting There & Away

The airport in nearby Sambaïlo has been upgraded in anticipation of development of Parc Transfrontalier Niokolo-Badiar, but there are no flights yet.

Bush taxis run frequently to Sambaïlo, Saréboïdo and Gaoual. There are daily bush taxis between Koundara and Labé (eight to 12 hours, GF13,000), and a direct taxi once a week between Koundara and Conakry (20 hours, GF25,000). For those driving their own vehicle, there is a ferry over the River Koumba between Kounsitél and Dinguétéri (GF2500).

The best transport to Boké is via Saréboïdo after its Sunday market; you'll need to change vehicle in Saréboïdo.

Several bush taxis a week head over the Senegal border, from where there's daily transport on to Tambacounda.

The East

In Haute Guinée (Upper Guinea), the hills and greenery of the Fouta Djalon give way to the reds and browns of the country's grassy, low-lying savanna lands. Although few tourists make it to this region, there's much of interest and it's an area well worth exploring.

DABOLA

Dabola's main attraction, apart from its peaceful setting amid some hills, is the Barrage du Tinkisso which supplies electricity for Dabola, Faranah and Dinguiraye. It's 8km from town, signposted on the Conakry road.

The best hotel is the *Tinkisso*, just out of town on the Conakry road, with spotless rooms with bathroom from GF30,000, and some basic bungalows in an isolated area 2km behind the main building for GF10,000 each.

The friendly *Hôtel le Mont Sincery*, signposted off the Conakry road, has rooms with fan and bathroom from GF15,000 and meals from GF3500.

The menu at *Chez Marie* is limited, but the food is good and the price is right (under GF2000). It's opposite the Tinkisso hotel.

Bush taxis leave daily in the morning to Faranah (1½ hours, GF5000), Mamou (GF 7000), Kouroussa (GF8000), Kankan (GF 12,000) and Conakry (GF13,000).

DINGUIRAYE

Dinguiraye is a small town whose main claim to fame used to be its mosque – until recently one of the largest thatched structures in Africa. Although renovations have replaced the thatching with more modern materials, it's still significant for students of Islam as the seat of an important regional sect founded in the mid-19th century by El Hadj Omar Tall.

For a place to stay, try *Madame Sow* who rents out basic rooms for GF5000.

Dinguiraye is about two hours off the main road. It's easier to get here by bush taxi from Dabola (GF5000, mornings only) than from Bissikrima.

FARANAH

President Sekou Touré hailed from this region, and Faranah still bears his marks. There's a dilapidated conference centre (now a hotel), an airstrip built to accommodate Concorde, and a large villa, which used to be a hotel but which is now closed.

Faranah is the starting point for visits to **Parc National du Haut Niger** (see the boxed text 'Guinea's National Parks' in the Facts for the Visitor section earlier in this chapter). It's also the highest point on the River Niger which is easily accessible, and only 150km from its source.

Behind Hôtel Cité de Niger is the house of renowned Guinean drummer Fadoumah Oularé; serious students can arrange lessons for a fee.

Places to Stay & Eat

Hôtel Kamal-Dhine is the best budget lodging. Simple but decent rooms with shower are GF5000, though this may increase when renovations are completed. It's unmarked, 2km from the centre off the Dabola road – turn right after the small bridge onto the dirt path paralleling the north side of the lake.

Le Bas-Fond, 1.5km from the centre on the Conakry road, is also cheap with a few basic rooms and meals from GF5000 each.

Hôtel Bati, 2.5km from the centre near the airport, has decent, rooms with fan and shared/private bathroom for GF12,000/ 15,000. The only problem is that it's isolated on the far side of the checkpoint; women travelling alone may not feel comfortable here. The Bati's restaurant has chicken or meat for GF5000; if you want something different, order well in advance.

Hôtel Cité de Niger, 1km from town off the Kissidougou road, has dirty, dilapidated double/triple rooms for GF15,000/18,000, and a noisy disco on Saturday evenings. There's no restaurant.

Getting There & Away

The bush taxi stand is on the main street next to the petrol station. Vehicles go daily to Kissidougou (GF5000), Mamou (GF 6000), Dabola (GF5000) and Conakry (GF12,000).

FOROKONIA

Between Faranah and Kissidougou and about 10km south of Banian (birthplace of Sekou Touré), a dirt road branches south towards the village of Forokonia (72km from the main road). Seven kilometres further is the muddy and unassuming **source of the River Niger**.

Public transport to Forokonia is limited; your best chance is a truck from Faranah market. Before setting out you'll need a permit, usually available from the préfecture

GUINEA

The East – Kankan 495

in Faranah or Banian (GF2000, negotiable). This is a border region and potentially sensitive; it's also a sacred area for the local people. Once in Forokonia, local youths will show you to *les sources* for about GF2000. You can find *lodging* in the village; expect to pay GF5000 for a bed in a hut and a simple meal.

KANKAN

Kankan, Guinea's second city and a university town, is a pleasant place with a Sahel feel, set on the banks of the River Milo (a large tributary of the River Niger). The capital of the ancient Empire of Mali was at **Niani**, 130km north-east of here, and today it's still an unofficial 'capital' for Guinea's Malinké people. Nearly every Malinké you meet, even as far away as Senegal and Gambia, regards Kankan as a spiritual home. Just over the river is the hill from which Samory Touré's famed nine month and nine day siege of Kankan and later stand-off against the French colonialists took place.

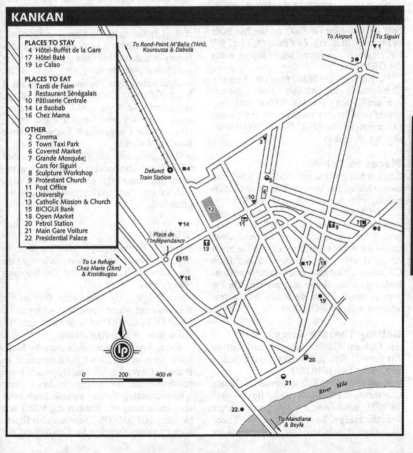

KANKAN

PLACES TO STAY
4 Hôtel-Buffet de la Gare
17 Hôtel Baté
19 Le Calao

PLACES TO EAT
1 Tanti de Faim
3 Restaurant Sénégalais
10 Pâtisserie Centrale
14 Le Baobab
16 Chez Mama

OTHER
2 Cinema
5 Town Taxi Park
6 Covered Market
7 Grande Mosquée;
   Cars for Siguiri
8 Sculpture Workshop
9 Protestant Church
11 Post Office
12 University
13 Catholic Mission & Church
15 BICIGUI Bank
18 Open Market
20 Petrol Station
21 Main Gare Voiture
22 Presidential Palace

To Rond-Point M'Balia (1km),
Kouroussa & Dabola

To Airport
To Siguiri

Defunct
Train Station

Place de
l'Indépendance

To Le Refuge
Chez Marie (2km)
& Kissidougou

To Mandiana
& Beyla

River Milo

0   200   400 m

GUINEA

The main sights are the colourful markets and the Grande Mosquée. The caretaker at the mosque will be glad to show you around for a small fee. Also worth a visit is the old presidential palace overlooking the river. It's closed now, although you can still walk around the grounds (no photos!).

Places to Stay

The best budget lodging is *Le Refuge Chez Marie* (☎ *71 05 41*), 3km from town on the Kissidougou road. Simple rooms with mosquito net are GF10,000; meals start at GF2000.

In town, the dilapidated *Hôtel-Buffet de la Gare* has dirty rooms from GF6000; the best are those for GF8000, on the 2nd floor of the main building. *Le Calao* (☎ *71 27 97*) has clean air-con rooms with running water for GF25,000.

For luxury, go to *Hôtel Baté* (☎ *71 26 86*). Comfortable single/double rooms with air-con and TV are GF37,000/47,000, including breakfast. Cheaper rooms with fan/air-con in the annexe cost GF22,000/27,000 (breakfast not included).

Places to Eat

Kankan has good street food and many rice bars. One of the best is *Restaurant Sénégalais*, with rice and sauce for GF300.

Chez Mama has good, inexpensive meals averaging GF1000. *Le Baobab* in the field behind the university – look for the baobab tree – is a popular place to relax in the afternoon; it offers inexpensive dishes from GF200. Another nice spot is *Pâtisserie Centrale*, good for coffee and pastries. On the Siguiri road, *Tanti de Faim* has a few western dishes for GF3500.

Getting There & Away

Air Guinée, Guinea InterAir and Guinea Air Service fly occasionally from Conakry to Kankan for GF70,000.

Bush taxis for all destinations, including Conakry (GF22,000) and Beyla (GF13,000), leave from the main gare voiture near the bridge. To N'zérékoré you'll need to change vehicle in Beyla; be prepared for

a long wait. There are also smaller taxi stands near Rond-Point M'Balia for Kouroussa (one vehicle daily in the afternoon) and near the Grande Mosquée for Siguiri.

Bush taxis to Côte d'Ivoire go via Mandiana to Noumoudjila, where you can find transport to Mininian and from there onwards to Odienné.

KOUROUSSA

Quiet Kouroussa is the birthplace of famed Guinean author Camara Laye, known in particular for his autobiographical *L'Enfant Noir* (often called *The African Child* or *The Dark Child* in English versions) about coming of age among the Malinké. You can still visit the family's simple compound, now occupied by Laye's brother and his family. It's about 1km from the centre on the road to the préfecture.

Your only lodging option is the unnamed *hotel* (GF10,000), about 1km north of the taxi stand near Restaurant Cobé. There are many *rice bars* near the taxi stand; otherwise, try *Le Cobe*, which has one or two standard dishes.

Bush taxis cost GF5000 to Kankan and GF8000 to Dabola and generally leave in the mornings. The postal van between Conakry and Kankan stops in Kouroussa, though it's often full.

SIGUIRI

Siguiri is the last major town en route to Mali. There are some good walks outside the centre with views of the Tinkisso and Niger rivers.

For lodging, try *Hôtel Tam Tam* on the Kankan road which has rooms with fan for about GF10,000. *Hôtel de la Paix*, near the radio mast, is slightly cheaper.

From Siguiri, two roads lead to Mali. Bush taxis generally go via Kourémalé to Bamako (seven hours). The secondary route paralleling the River Niger makes a great bike trip during the dry season. Bush taxis also leave daily for Kankan (GF8000) and Conakry (GF30,000). There are also flights once or twice a week from Conakry on Air

Guinée, Guinea InterAir and Guinea Air Service for GF71,000.

The Forest Region

Guinea's south-eastern corner is a beautiful region of hills, lush forests and streams, although deforestation is taking its toll. Liberia and Sierra Leone are nearby, and there's lots of smuggling going on. The area also has large refugee populations from these countries.

GUÉCKÉDOU

Bustling Guéckédou is known mainly for its large refugee population, and for its huge Wednesday market which attracts traders from all over Guinea and neighbouring countries.

The *Terminus*, 3km from the centre on the Kissidougou road, has clean rooms with shared bathroom for GF12,500 and a decent restaurant. The nightclub can get noisy on weekends.

Nearby is the similar *Bas-Fond*, slightly cheaper at GF10,000 per room but dirty and not worth the savings. Its restaurant is better, with hamburgers and meals from GF4000.

For good meals under GF2000, try *Chez Diallo*, directly opposite the Bas-Fond. *Le Mikado* nearby is expensive (GF10,000 for a full meal including beverage and starter), but portions are huge.

Bush taxis cost GF4000 to Macenta, GF3500 to Kissidougou and GF20,000 to Conakry.

KISSIDOUGOU

Kissidougou is a friendly town and the surrounding area, with gently rolling hills and many villages, is good for exploring on bicycle.

For food and lodging, *Hôtel Nelson Mandela*, signposted on the Kankan road, has decent rooms from GF15,000 and a nice restaurant with good, cheap food. *Hôtel de la Paix* is not as nice, but is cheaper at GF7000 per room; there's no restaurant. *Hôtel Bèlèfè* (☎ 98 12 34), signposted 500m from the market, has clean, well-equipped rooms for GF20,000 though most have only interior windows.

There are occasional flights between Conakry and Kissidougou on Air Guinée, Guinea InterAir and Guinea Air Service for GF55,000.

Bush taxis go daily to Faranah (GF5000), Conakry (GF18,000), Guéckédou (GF3500) and Kankan (five hours, GF8000). The scenic Kankan road is potholed between Kissidougou and Tokounou. For cyclists, Tokounou (where Friday is market day) makes a good stop; you can get basic supplies and arrange lodging with locals.

LOLA

Lola, near the borders of Liberia and Côte d'Ivoire, is the starting point for hiking up Mt Nimba (see the boxed text on the next page). There are several mud cloth cooperatives in town, including Cooperative Laanah des Teintures, 2km from the centre on the N'zérékoré road. In the past, Lola was known as a centre for traditional medicine. If you wish to learn more about local plants, staff at Hôtel Heinoukoloa can introduce you to the practitioners.

Hôtel Heinoukoloa has basic but acceptable rooms with toilets (no running water) and mosquito nets for GF4000/5000. It's about 1km off the main road behind the préfecture.

About 18km from Lola is **Bossou**, the site of a chimpanzee research centre. You need a guide to visit the chimps; this can be arranged at the checkpoint on the outskirts of Bossou. It's GF35,000 per guide (regardless of how many are in your group) if you see chimps, and GF10,000 if you don't. Mornings and evenings are the best times for viewings. There's one *hotel* in Bossou, at the base of the big hill, with simple but surprisingly decent rooms for GF3000.

From Lola, it's GF2500 by bush taxi to N'zérékoré, GF1000 to Bossou and GF2000 to Nzo. To the Côte d'Ivoire border, you can go via Nzo to Danané or via Tounkarata to Sipilou and Man. Both routes are in bad condition during the rainy season. There are

Hiking on Mt Nimba

Mt Nimba, Guinea's highest peak at 1752m, is part of the mountain range straddling Guinea, Côte d'Ivoire and Liberia. The summit offers excellent views of surrounding peaks in all three countries. The hike follows an old logging road, and you can ascend and descend in a day if you start out early enough.

Before setting off, you must get a permit at the préfecture in Lola, or after hours from the préfet at his house near the market. The fee is negotiable, usually around GF3000. From Lola, take a bush taxi towards Nzo and disembark after about 15km at the village of Gbakoré. The hike begins behind the health centre. It's a steep, winding four hour trek to the top.

If you want to overnight on the mountain, you can stay in abandoned forest ranger cabins (La Cité) about one-third of the way up; you'll need to first get the key (GF5000) from the guard in Gbakoré. Bring your own food and water-purifying tablets; there's running water at La Cité and a stream about halfway between there and the top.

The Nimba mountains host a rich variety of unique plant and animal life, including a rare type of frog. The range is under special UNESCO protection – to the dismay of some sectors of the Guinean government more interested in realising earnings from its iron ore reserves.

bush taxis to the Liberian border (GF1500), from where you'll have to walk a few kilometres into Yekepa.

MACENTA

Macenta is set in a scenic area of hills and streams. In the centre of the market is a theatre with occasional performances by local dance groups.

Hôtel Bamala, 3km from the centre off the N'zérékoré road, has clean rooms with bathroom from GF10,000 (GF20,000 with air-con), and one basic room for GF5000, although they may be reluctant to let you have it. Meals at the restaurant are about GF7000. If you want to sleep, be sure the disco is not operating.

Hôtel Watanga is an inconvenient 3km from the centre on the 'HCR' road, but the owner is friendly and is trying hard to get tourism going in the area. A room with running water is GF15,000. Plans are under way for a disco, but otherwise the hotel is in a quiet location backing onto woods with some walking trails. Meals are available upon request from GF5000.

For cheaper accommodation, your best bet is *Hôtel Palm* near the market, with dirty rooms from GF5000 and meals on request from GF1000.

Bush taxis go via Daro to the Liberian border and on to Voinjama. However, if you're heading to Monrovia, it's often faster to go from Macenta to Koyama and from there over the border to Zorzor as the Voinjama road is in terrible condition.

N'ZÉRÉKORÉ

N'zérékoré, the major city in Guinea's Forest Region, is a pleasant place and a good base for exploring the surrounding area.

There's a good mud cloth cooperative near the stadium where you can watch women making the cloth and dyeing it with kola nuts. It's better to buy from them directly, rather than from the neighbouring boutique as prices are cheaper and the women will receive more of the profits.

Further out of town is an artisanal village with a variety of woodcarvings, baskets and other crafts for sale.

During the dry season, the area around N'zérékoré offers endless possibilities for bicycle exploration. Many villages have vine bridges, particularly those along the River Oulé. There's a more accessible (and more touristy) vine bridge over the River Diani 3km off the main road at Silisu, 45km north-west of N'zérékoré. Further on, near Sérédou, is the Forêt Classée de Ziama, one of Guinea's few remaining rainforests. If

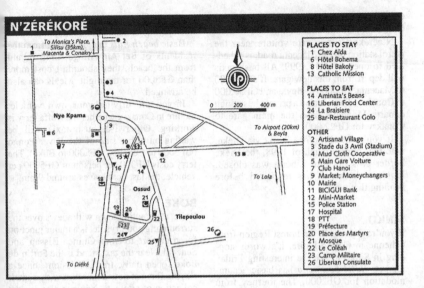

N'ZÉRÉKORÉ

To Monica's Place,
Silisu (35km),
Macenta & Conakry

Nye Kpama

To Airport (20km)
& Beyla

To Lola

Ossud

Tilepoulou

0   200   400 m

To Diéké

PLACES TO STAY
1 Chez Aïda
6 Hôtel Bohema
8 Hôtel Bakoly
13 Catholic Mission

PLACES TO EAT
14 Aminata's Beans
16 Liberian Food Center
24 La Braisiere
25 Bar-Restaurant Golo

OTHER
2 Artisanal Village
3 Stade du 3 Avril (Stadium)
4 Mud Cloth Cooperative
5 Main Gare Voiture
7 Club Hanoi
9 Market; Moneychangers
10 Mairie
11 BICIGUI Bank
12 Mini-Market
15 Police Station
17 Hospital
18 PTT
19 Préfecture
20 Place des Martyrs
21 Mosque
22 Le Coléah
23 Camp Militaire
26 Liberian Consulate

you want to stay in Sérédou, *Hôtel de l'Unité* has cheap rooms.

For those travelling onwards, the Liberian consulate in N'zérékoré's Tilepoulou quartier issues single-entry visas (GF40,000 plus two photos) in 24 hours. Follow signs for the Tilepoulou Refugee School, and then look for the house with a Liberian flag.

Places to Stay & Eat

The cheapest place is *Hôtel Bakoly* near the market, with basic rooms for GF2500 to GF6000 and meals on request. The much nicer *Hôtel Bohema*, in Nye Kpama quartier, is good value with clean rooms with bathroom from GF10,000.

At the other end of town, the *Catholic Mission*, (☎ 91 07 93), has simple but clean rooms with mosquito net and shower (shared toilet) for GF15,000. *Chez Aïda* (☎ 91 07 47) has three clean rooms for GF20,000/25,000, shared/private bathroom, and an excellent restaurant serving Senegalese and other dishes for GF4000 to GF6500.

N'zérékoré has excellent *street food* – some places to try are *Aminata's Beans*

south from the BICIGUI, and the ladies near the gare voiture selling rice and peanut sauce. The friendly *Liberian Food Center* has palm butter and other Liberian dishes from GF500.

Bar-Restaurant Golo is pricey but has a good selection of dishes for about GF6000. *La Braisiere* (☎ 91 04 28) is a nice place with meals from GF7000.

Monica's Place is well out of town and open only on weekends, but has good food and a great ambience. Meals are about GF6000.

Entertainment

For an afternoon drink, the best place is Jefferson's *Le Coléah*, opposite the mosque in Ossud quartier.

Club Hanoi, behind the market, is the best dance spot. It's open every Friday and Saturday evening; the GF2000 cover is usually waived.

Getting There & Away

There are flights once or twice a week between Conakry and N'zérérékoré on

GUINEA

Guinea Air Service, Guinea InterAir and Air Guinée for GF85,000.

N'zérékoré's new gare voiture, near the petrol station on the Macenta road, is scheduled to open in early 1999. All bush taxis will depart from this new gare. It's GF9000 to Macenta, GF6000 to Beyla and GF30,000 to Conakry. There's also a private bus which departs Mondays from the main gare to Conakry for GF22,000.

If you're heading for Liberia via Diéké, note that during much of 1998, the Diéké border crossing into Liberia was closed; inquire whether it has reopened before heading that way.

SINKO

If you're arriving in the Forest Region from Odienné in Côte d'Ivoire, it's worth stopping in Sinko to see the interesting Friday market. *Hôtel Soumano* has basic accommodation for GF2000. The journey from Sinko to Beyla can take up to five hours. From Beyla to N'zérékoré takes another five.

The West

While much of Guinea's coast is rocky or marshy and inaccessible, there are some beautiful spots worth discovering. Inland, the western part of Guinea has some interesting caves and other geological formations.

BOFFA

Boffa is a small coastal town en route to Guinea-Bissau and Senegal. If you get stuck at the ferry here, the dingy *Hôtel V Emmanuel* has rooms for GF8000. *Grand Hôtel Fatala* next door charges GF10,000 for similarly depressing accommodation. *Chez le Retraite* behind Hôtel Emmanuel will prepare simple meals for GF4000.

About 40km north of Boffa is the signposted turn-off leading 25km down to **Plage de Bel Air**, **Cap Verga**, the fishing village of **Kokoudé** and a beautiful coastline. Without your own transport, you'll need to charter a taxi in Boffa or be prepared for a long wait

at the junction for the occasional pick-up truck plying the route (GF1000).

Basic *beach huts* can be rented from the residents of **Bel Air** village, 2km inland from the beach; they shouldn't cost more than GF5000 for the night. Meals can also be arranged.

If you are driving your own vehicle, inquire in Conakry whether the Boffa ferry is working. Otherwise, bush taxis will be waiting on either side of the River Pongo (GF3500 to Conakry, GF5000 to Boké). The ferry costs GF300 per person or GF5000 per vehicle; the last boat leaves around 9 pm.

BOKÉ

Boké, a sprawling town with views over the surrounding countryside, is a major junction for transport to/from Guinea-Bissau and Senegal. Near the taxi stand is the **Fortin de Boké** (open daily, free admission), once a slaving fort but now a museum with a small collection of artefacts. You can also see the horrifying holding cells where slaves were kept before they were taken downriver to the coast.

Le Chalet (☎ 31 02 05), 2km from the centre on the Koundara road, has basic rooms with fan/air-con for GF10,000/15,000 and a noisy disco. Meals are available from GF2000 with advance notice. *Le Benda*, 3km from the centre on the Boffa road, has dirty, uncomfortable rooms for GF7000.

Direct bush taxis to Conakry cost GF 10,000; to Gabú in Guinea-Bissau it's GF16,000. Roads north of Boké are in bad condition.

FRIA

Fria is a bustling town in an attractive area, marred only by the enormous bauxite compound that dominates views on approach. The main reason to come here is to explore the geologically fascinating surrounding countryside. About 15km from Fria, beyond Wawaya village, are the **Grottes de Bogoro**. Hôtel Yaskadi in Fria can help arrange a guide. The **Grottes de Konkouré** can be reached by continuing out of town on the airport road and then down about 4km on a very rough road (best on bike or foot) to the River Konkouré. From there, it's an additional 10km or so to the 'Troisième Plage' where you can arrange a pirogue and a local guide to visit the grottoes. The trip is best done in the dry season when the river is calmer.

There are also interesting caves in **Tormélin**, between Fria and the main highway; they're about a 6km walk from the Tormélin mosque.

Places to Stay & Eat

The pleasant *Hôtel Mariam* (☎ *24 09 55*) on Route Unite-III is the best, with rooms with fan/air-con and bathroom for GF15,000/ 25,000. *Hôtel Yaskadi* (☎ *24 09 84*), 1km off Route Unite-III, has decent rooms with fan/air-con for GF15,000/20,000. *Hôtel Konkouré*, 2km from the centre on the airport road, is cheaper but not recommended. Dirty rooms are officially GF15,000, but negotiable down to GF10,000. *La Teranga* at the end of the airport road has good Senegalese and Guinean dishes for about GF2000.

Getting There & Away

Bush taxis go daily to Conakry (GF3000) and to Télimélé (GF8000), from where you can continue on to Gaoual and Koundara. Transport from Fria to the Boffa highway junction costs GF1500.

Guinea-Bissau

GUINEA-BISSAU AT A GLANCE

Capital: Bissau
Population: 1.1 million
Area: 36,125 sq km
Head of state: President João Vieira
Official language: Portuguese
Main local language: Crioulo
Currency: West African CFA franc
Exchange rate: US$1 = CFA600
Time: GMT/UTC
Country telephone code: ☎ 245
Best time to go: December to February

For travellers, Guinea-Bissau is a joy. It is home to some of the friendliest people on the continent, and has small towns with wide streets and flowering trees, and rarely a tourist in sight.

Bissau, the capital, has enjoyed an economic renaissance in the past few years and has a lively city centre, with crowded markets and busy street-stalls alongside pastel-coloured Mediterranean-style buildings.

For a change of pace, the Bijagos Archipelago, off the coast, offers tropical islands, azure waters, fine empty beaches and a fascinating culture.

Facts about Guinea-Bissau

HISTORY

The great Sahel Empire of Mali, which flourished between the 13th and 15th centuries AD, included part of present-day Guinea-Bissau. For more information on the precolonial history of this part of West Africa, refer to the Facts about the Region chapter.

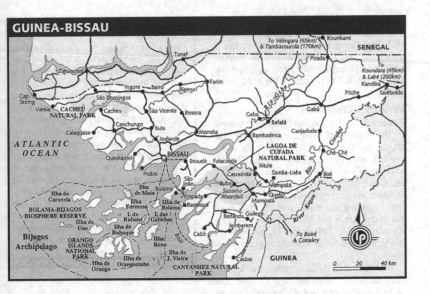

European Arrival

The first Europeans to arrive in Guinea-Bissau were Portuguese navigators, who had been exploring the coast of West Africa since the early 15th century. By around 1450, their ships reached Guinea-Bissau and other areas along the coast, where the Portuguese traded with the inhabitants for slaves, gold, ivory and pepper.

The Portuguese built many forts and trading stations along the coast, but their trade monopoly ended in the late 17th century when British, French and Dutch merchant adventurers entered the slave trade with particular enthusiasm. Over the following centuries, the surrounding territories became British or French possessions, but Portugal kept hold of what became known as Portuguese Guinea.

Portugal was content to trade on the coast and didn't lay claim to the interior until the 1880s, when the European powers carved up the continent. Even so, Portugal was unable to gain full control of the area until 1915, after a long series of wars with the local people. In the process, Portuguese Guinea ended up with the most repressive and exploitative of all the colonial powers.

Colonial Period

While Britain and France developed their West African colonies for the exportation of crops, the Portuguese administration here was weak and lethargic. Companies from other European countries were allowed to lease land for plantations, mainly to produce groundnuts (peanuts) and palm oil, but this changed in 1926 when the dictator Salazar came to power in Portugal and imposed restrictive customs duties on foreign companies. Direct Portuguese rule resumed, and it was simple: if you were a peasant, you planted groundnuts, like it or not. The oppressive regime was most notably characterised by the Pidjiguiti massacre of 1959, a pivotal event in Guinea-Bissau's recent history, when 50 striking dockworkers were shot by police at the Pidjiguiti pier in Bissau.

By the early 1960s, many countries in Africa were gaining independence from their European colonial rulers. Britain and France

GUINEA-BISSAU

changed smoothly from being colonials to neocolonials and still profited from trade with their former colonies. But Portugal's own weakness meant neocolonialism could not be imposed on liberated colonies, so Salazar refused to relinquish his hold.

War of Liberation

The result was the longest liberation struggle in the history of Africa: a guerrilla war waged by the Partido Africano da Independência da Guiné e Cabo Verde (PAIGC) with significant help from the Soviet Union and Cuba. Many PAIGC leaders were chosen from among the better-educated Cape Verdeans, including the leader and co-founder of the party, Amilcar Cabral. But it was from the mainland of Portuguese Guinea that the movement drew its strongest grass-roots support.

In 1961, the PAIGC entered Portuguese Guinea from neighbouring Guinea and started arming and mobilising the peasants. As the PAIGC's numbers grew to about 10,000 the Portuguese responded by increasing their troops to 25,000 plus 10,000 conscripted Africans. Yet within five years, half the country was in PAIGC hands. Internationally, Portugal became isolated. Foreign politicians and journalists visited the liberated area, and the struggle became front-page news during the early 70s.

The Portuguese continued to hold out in refugee-swollen Bissau, a few smaller towns, and pockets in the north-east where some of the Muslim Fula (one of the country's main ethnic groups) collaborated with the Portuguese in an attempt to preserve their social privileges. Their agents in Conakry (Guinea), where Amilcar Cabral the PAIGC leader was based, assassinated him in early 1973.

But the movement was too strong. The PAIGC organised nationwide elections in the liberated areas and proclaimed independence, with Amilcar Cabral's half-brother, Luiz (also a Cape Verdean), as president. Eighty countries quickly recognised the new government, but it still took Salazar's overthrow the following year for Portugal to do the same.

The PAIGC

The Partido Africano da Independência da Guiné e Cabo Verde (PAIGC) is viewed as a model for revolutionary armies in many parts of the world. The movement was successful largely because of its political strategy during the war of liberation. As each part of the country was liberated, the PAIGC helped villagers build schools, provided medical services and specifically encouraged widespread political participation. Amilcar Cabral insisted on a war of revolution, not of revolt, and he realised that society had to be completely reorganised if the people were ever to be genuinely free. Thus, from the very start of the war, the people of Guinea-Bissau believed in what they were fighting for.

Independence

Once in power, the new PAIGC government had more than a handful of problems. The Portuguese had seen Guinea-Bissau as little more than a cheap source of groundnuts, and had done almost nothing to develop the country. They left behind a few small factories, a brewery built for the Portuguese troops, 14 university graduates, and no doctors. Only one in 20 people could read, life expectancy was 35 years and 45% of children died before the age of five. During the war, rice production had fallen by 71% and rice had to be imported for the first time ever.

Politically, the PAIGC wanted a unified Guinea-Bissau and Cape Verde. However, this idea was abruptly dropped in 1980 when President Cabral was overthrown in a coup while he was visiting Cape Verde to negotiate the union. João ('Nino') Vieira took over and became president.

Despite the change of leader, Guinea-Bissau continued to follow a socialist path. The state controlled most major enterprises, Marxist literature was everywhere and political dissent was banned, although behind the dogma Vieira encouraged pragmatism and political neutrality. The Soviet Union provided arms and advisers while the west provided non-military aid.

But life remained hard for most people. Bissau's shops were almost empty and in rural areas foreign products were even more scarce. Vieira realised that Guinea-Bissau was making no progress under Marxism, and in 1986, after a serious coup attempt the previous year, the government completely reversed its policies, devalued the currency and began selling off almost all the state enterprises.

The 1990s

Vieira proved to be a shrewd politician, surviving three coup attempts while keeping the PAIGC in power. Government corruption and mismanagement were rife, but Vieira himself remained generally popular. He won the 1994 presidential elections, although 52% of the vote was hardly a landslide victory, especially with the power of the state and a well organised campaign behind him. However, opposition leader Kumba Yalla accepted the result and appealed for national unity, stating 'we don't want to become a second Rwanda'.

Away from political machinations, things also improved on the domestic front for most people in Guinea-Bissau. Unusually for an African nation, rural inhabitants have enjoyed a slight improvement in living conditions since the 1970s. Output from farmers increased (although not without problems – see the Ecology & Environment section later), while local produce and foreign goods were more readily available in shops and markets.

Despite the apparent political harmony, Guinea-Bissau's social situation remained poor, ranking 163rd out of 175 countries in the UN Human Development Index, and economically it is one of the 10 poorest countries in the world. Cracks began to show in early 1997, when teachers, health workers and other state employees went on strike, while students demonstrated in the streets of Bissau. One of their major complaints was about development money from

overseas nations which had gone 'missing' in the hands of the government.

Things suddenly came to a head on 7 June 1998, when an attempted coup took place. It was led by General Ansumane Mane, former head of the army, who'd been sacked by President Vieira in January, allegedly for supplying arms to rebels fighting for an independent Casamance in neighbouring Senegal. The coup was supported by soldiers at the main barracks and at the airport. These were surrounded by loyal government troops, with support from regiments sent in by Senegal and Guinea. As the two sides shelled and bombed each other, the surrounding residential districts were caught in the crossfire, and many people were killed.

Fighting continued through the rest of June and into July, and spread to other parts of Guinea-Bissau. Up to 90% of the army (totalling only 3500) backed General Mane, while President Vieira relied increasingly on the Senegalese and Guinean armies. The capital and most parts of the country were in a state of chaos, and the situation was very unsafe for local people and foreigners. The airport and the border with Senegal were effectively closed.

The rebels were reported to have support from the people of Guinea-Bissau, tired and disillusioned after many years of ineffective government. But this apparently made civilians legitimate targets in the eyes of the government troops and their Senegalese allies: news reports from mid-July told of several towns and villages being attacked, many people killed and atrocities committed. Food production and harvesting were interrupted, and by late July a total of 250,000 people had been displaced. Bissau became a ghost town, as residents fled to country areas or tried to reach Senegal, although border guards refused to let most refugees cross, and only a handful made it to Ziguinchor. Others tried to cross the border illegally, but came across land mines planted as part of the Casamance conflict (see Facts about Senegal in that chapter for more details). So as the soldiers slugged it out, once again it was innocent civilians who suffered most.

GUINEA-BISSAU

In August 1998, a tentative cease-fire was agreed, and peace negotiations were brokered by Portugal, other nations of the Portuguese-speaking community and several ECOWAS states including Burkina Faso, Gambia, Ghana, Nigeria and Senegal. Despite some cautious optimism, continued outbreaks of fighting in various parts of Guinea-Bissau continued for a few more weeks.

By October 1998, the rebels and the government had reached an agreement, allowing for the troops to return to their barracks and Guinea-Bissau's rulers to become more accountable. Elections are planned for early 1999, and in the meantime it is hoped that the thousands of civilian refugees can return to their homes and begin rebuilding the country. Although most observers are cautiously optimistic, the prospect of renewed fighting, or disturbances brought on by nationwide disruption, cannot be ruled out. The future for Guinea-Bissau is still far from certain.

GEOGRAPHY

Guinea-Bissau has an area of just over 36,000 sq km (about the size of Switzerland), making it one of West Africa's smaller countries. The coastal areas are flat, with estuaries, mangrove swamps and patches of forest. Inlets indent the coast and high tides periodically submerge the lowest areas, sometimes covering up to a third of the land surface. Inland, the landscape remains flat, with the highest ground (near the Guinea border) just topping 300m above sea level. Off the coast is the Bijagos Archipelago, consisting of 18 main islands, a few of which are beginning to develop tourist facilities, although some of the more remote areas rarely see visitors.

CLIMATE

The rainy season is from June to October, but the rainfall is almost twice as heavy along the coast than it is inland. Conditions are humid most of the time, especially in the months before the rains (March to May), when average maximum daytime temperatures rise to 34°C. Although daily maximums rarely fall below 30°C, this is quite bearable in the

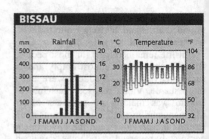

months after the rain, especially on islands which catch the sea breeze.

ECOLOGY & ENVIRONMENT

A major environmental issue is the rapid destruction of mangroves on the coast – some of the most important in Africa – due to the expansion of rice production in seasonally flooded areas. The increase in groundnut production also creates problems – the plants rapidly exhaust soil nutrients and farming methods lead to erosion.

Offshore, Guinea-Bissau has rich fishing waters, but the overfishing that has become a serious problem in neighbouring Senegal and Gambia may become an issue here if controls are not introduced.

FLORA & FAUNA

The natural vegetation of the inland areas is lightly wooded savanna, but much of it is under cultivation. You'll see rice fields and plantations of groundnuts, maize and other crops. The coastal zone is very low-lying and indented by many large creeks and estuaries, where mangroves are the dominant vegetation. Off the coast, the islands of the Bijagos Archipelago are also low-lying, and the vegetation is a combination of light woodland and mangrove.

Guinea-Bissau has several protected areas, including the flagship Bolama-Bijagos Biosphere Reserve, which contains the Orango Islands National Park (also called the Orango National Park) and the proposed Poilao Marine Park. On the mainland, the Cacheu Natural Park, near the border with

Senegal, protects a vast area of mangroves. In the south of the country, near Buba, the Lagoa de Cafada Natural Park protects a freshwater wetland area, which has also been gazetted as a Ramsar site. South of here the Cantanhez Natural Park is planned to protect estuarine mangroves and several 'sacred forests' which have cultural significance. Despite this impressive collection, it's important to note that tourist facilities in most parks are very limited, and in some cases nonexistent.

GOVERNMENT & POLITICS

Guinea-Bissau was ruled by the PAIGC, the sole political party, until 1991 when multiparty democracy was approved by the government. Members are elected to a 100 seat national assembly, and there is a separate election for the post of president. Opposition parties complain that the system is still stacked against them, but free speech is allowed and local human rights groups report that the country has no political prisoners. Since the coup of June 1998, the political situation is uncertain.

ECONOMY

On paper, Guinea-Bissau is one of the world's 10 poorest countries but, unlike many other West African nations, the heavy economic dependency on agriculture means people in rural areas normally survive relatively well. The main crops exported are cashew nuts, groundnuts (peanuts) and palm kernels, while the country is virtually self-sufficient in rice. Fishing is another growing industry, with fish exports accounting for more than 30% of export earnings. However, in all other sectors of the economy, Guinea-Bissau is highly dependent on overseas aid.

In mid-1997, the peso was abandoned as the national currency and Guinea-Bissau joined the West African CFA franc zone. Although prices rose, the change was generally welcomed, as inflation (which ran at 85% in 1996) has been brought under control.

POPULATION & PEOPLE

Current estimates put the population at more than one million, made up of 23 ethnic groups. The main groups are Balante (30%) in the coastal and southern regions, and Fula (20%) in the north. Other groups are the Manjaco (or Manjak) and Fulup (closely related to the Diola of Senegal) in the northwest, and the Mandinka/Malinké in the interior. The offshore islands are inhabited by the Bijago people. There's also a significant minority of people of mixed European and African descent.

For more information on culture of the Fula people, see the colour feature between pages 768 and page 769.

ARTS

While mainland Guinea-Bissau is not noted for the use of sculpted figures and masks, the Bijago people, due to their isolation, continue to maintain these traditions. Statues representing Iran, the great spirit, are used in connection with agricultural and initiation rituals. These are carved as a seated figure, sometimes wearing a top hat. Initiation masks are also carved, the best known being the Dugn'be, a ferocious bull with real horns. Other masks represent sharks, sawfish and hippos. The hippo masks are so massive that the dancer supports the mask with a pair of sticks carved as legs. One of the best times to see masks is in Bissau at carnival time (usually February or March).

On the mainland, traditional dance and music are influenced by the Mandinka/Malinké and Diola people of neighbouring Gambia and Senegal. The harp-like *kora* and the xylophone-like *balafon* are played, while women take turns to dance frantically in front of a circle of onlookers.

Modern music shares the same roots, and the Portuguese colonial legacy has given some sounds a Latin edge, especially among the larger orchestras. On the street and in bush taxis you'll hear little Sahel music and more salsa and Latin sounds. One of Guinea-Bissau's most popular groups is Super Mama Djombo, along with Dulce Maria Neves, N'Kassa Cobra, Patcheco,

GUINEA-BISSAU

Justino Delgado and Ramiro Naka, whose CD *Salvador* is available in Europe. These singers perform occasionally in some of Bissau's nightclubs.

SOCIETY & CONDUCT

The mainland people share many cultural aspects with similar groups in neighbouring Senegal and Guinea. In the Bijagos Archipelago, the people's customs are particularly interesting. On several islands, beliefs about death mean that bodies are placed in a canoe and taken to another island for burial so that their spirits do not haunt the living. On Ilha Roxa and some of the other islands, as soon as a young girl reaches puberty the young men venture forth with as much rice and other goods as they can afford in the hope of buying their way into her favour. She chooses a suitor, but if she's not pregnant within a year, or if a well stocked successor makes a better bid, she can get rid of her man and choose another. The man usually stays around only until she gives birth, and then he returns to his home and becomes eligible again for other liaisons. Children take the mother's name and are rarely able to identify their father.

RELIGION

About 40% of the people (mainly Fula and Mandinka/Malinké) are Muslims; they are concentrated more upcountry than along the coast. Except for a few Christians in the towns, the rest follow traditional beliefs.

LANGUAGE

Portuguese is the official language, but no more than a third of the people can speak it. Each group has its own language, but the common tongue is Crioulo – a mix of medieval Portuguese and local words. As Guinea-Bissau gets increasingly drawn into the Afro-Francophone world, quite a few people understand French – especially in tourist areas. See the Language chapter for a list of useful phrases in Portuguese, French and Crioulo.

Facts for the Visitor

SUGGESTED ITINERARIES

Most travellers with only a week to spare spend a day or two in Bissau, the capital. There's little in the way of 'sights', but the city has a nice relaxing feel. This could be combined with a few days visiting the country's major attraction, the Bijagos Archipelago, a group of islands to the south-west of Bissau. The island of Bubaque is the easiest to reach and most

Highlights

Natural Features

Bijagos Archipelago *(The Islands)*
Peaceful and idyllic islands off the coast, with beaches, palms, mangroves and traditional villages, easily reached from Bissau.

Cantanhez Natural Park *(The South)*
Tropical forest of sacred cultural significance, with good birds and monkeys and the chance of chimpanzee sightings.

Beaches *(The Islands)*
Beautiful golden beaches on several of the Bijagos islands.

People

Bissau Festival *(Bissau)*
Guinea Bissau's biggest carnival, with music, masks, parades, dancing and general good times; held in February.

Bijagos Dancers *(The Islands)*
Famous for their 'jungle-look' grass costumes and wonderful masks of cow and hippo heads.

Activities

Cycling *(The Islands, The North)*
An excellent way to explore the islands and remoter parts of the mainland; bikes can be hired in a few places or bringing your own would be ideal.

popular, with good beaches and a range of places to stay.

If you had two or three weeks to spare, you could simply spend more time on Bubaque, or visit some of the smaller islands – Galinhas is one of the easiest to reach. Alternatively, you could combine Bissau and the islands with time in the country's interior, heading north-west to the region around Canchungo, or south to the fascinating forested areas around Xitole and Catió, where travel is slow and patience a virtue. Another option is Gabú, a lively market town from where you can find onward transport to Guinea.

PLANNING
When to Go
The rainy season is from June to October, and the best time to visit is from late November to February, when conditions are dry and relatively cool. February is also carnival time in Bissau, although smaller festivals to celebrate the end of harvest in November and December take place in many towns.

Maps
By far the best map of Guinea-Bissau is produced by the Institut Géographique National (IGN), but it's not available in the country. The detail around the country is good, and there's a Bissau city map insert, but beware, some main streets have disappeared!

VISAS & DOCUMENTS
Visas
All visitors need visas. These are normally valid for one month and issued for around US$20 at embassies. They are not issued at land borders, but may be issued at the airport if you come from an African country where visas are not available.

Visa Extensions Extensions are easy to obtain at the central police station in Bissau. The process is straightforward, but costs seem to vary between CFA5000 and CFA20,000.

EMBASSIES & CONSULATES
Guinea-Bissau Embassies & Consulates
In West Africa, you can get visas for Guinea-Bissau in Senegal, Gambia and Guinea. For more details see the Facts for the Visitor section of the relevant chapter. Outside Africa, Guinea-Bissau has very few embassies or consulates. These are more or less limited to:

Belgium
(☎ 02-647 13 51)
70 ave Franklin-Roosevelt, Brussels 1050
France
(☎ 01 45 26 18 51)
94 rue Saint Lazare, 75009 Paris
USA
(☎ 202-483 9420)
2112 Leroy Place NW, Washington, DC 20008

Embassies & Consulates in Guinea-Bissau
All embassies and consulates are in Bissau, some in the centre, others along the road towards the airport.

Visas for Onward Travel

In Guinea-Bissau you can get visas for the following neighbouring West African countries. For visa applications, most embassies open from 8 am to noon or 2 pm; it's always best to go in the morning. You usually need two photos.

Gambia
One-month visas cost CFA15,000 and are issued on the same day if you come early.

Guinea
Two-month visas cost US$40 and take one or two days to issue; shorter, cheaper options may also be available.

Senegal
One to three-month visas cost CFA3000 and are issued in two to three days.

France
  (☎ 251031)
  Avenida de 14 Novembro, near the Hotel Hotti
  Bissau
The Gambia
  Avenida de 14 Novembro, 1km from Mercado
  de Bandim
Guinea
  (☎ 212681)
  Rua 12
Mauritania
  Avenida de 14 Novembro, opposite the
  Gambian embassy
Netherlands
  (☎ 201943)
  Rua Justino Lopes
Nigeria
  (☎ 212782)
  Avenida de 14 Novembro, opposite Mercado
  de Bandim
Senegal
  (☎ 212636)
  Just off Praça dos Heróis Nacionais
USA
  (☎ 252273, fax 252282)
  Avenida de 14 Novembro, near the Hotel Hotti
  Bissau

The consul for the UK is Mr van Maanen
(☎ 201224 or 211529, fax 201265), at the
Mavegro supermarket in Rua Mondlane
north of the Fortaleza d'Amura. The Belgian
consulate (☎ 201227) is in Rua Djassi.

MONEY
The unit of currency is the CFA franc.

Euro €1	=	CFA660
1FF	=	CFA100
UK£1	=	CFA950
US$1	=	CFA600

Banks include the Banco International de
Guinea-Bissau (BIGB) and Banco de Totto.
In Bissau banks change cash and travellers
cheques but the process is very slow. Outside
Bissau, there are few banks, so most travellers
change money in Bissau.

POST & COMMUNICATIONS
The postal service out of the country is
good, although slow – you're probably

New Money Confusion

In mid-1997 the peso was abandoned as
the national currency and Guinea-Bissau
adopted the West African CFA franc. This
caused some initial confusion as the rate
was pegged at 65 pesos to CFA1 and for a
meal which once cost 30,000 pesos, customers were asked to pay CFA461, even
though single CFA1 coins were rare and
change always impossible. Gradually things
have been rounded up or down to more
manageable amounts. Another confusing
aspect of the new currency is that many
local people call CFA50 'dez' (10), CFA100
'vinte' (20) and so on. You have to multiply the price asked for by five. Perhaps it's
because many people can't read the nu-
merals on the coins and notes, and the
traders use CFA5 as a base unit.

better off posting mail home from a neighbouring country such as Senegal or Gambia.
Travellers report that the poste restante in
Bissau is unhelpful and unreliable; one
wrote to say he couldn't collect his mail
because the clerk had been arrested, supposedly for stealing letters! The best place
for international phone calls or email is
Bissau – for more details see Information in
that section.

RADIO & TV
The national radio and TV stations broadcast
in Portuguese. Most interesting for travellers
is Radio Mavegro FM (100.0MHz) which
combines music with hourly news bulletins
in English from the BBC.

PHOTOGRAPHY & VIDEO
Photo permits are not required, but the
usual restrictions apply – for more information see the Photography & Video section in
the Regional Facts for the Visitor chapter.

HEALTH
A yellow fever vaccination certificate is required if you're coming from an infected

area. You should take precautions against malaria, as it exists throughout the year in the whole country. For more information on these and other health matters, see the Health section in the Regional Facts for the Visitor chapter.

Bissau and Bafatá both have hospitals and pharmacies, although the best hospital in the country is in Canchungo – for more details see the relevant sections later in this chapter.

WOMEN TRAVELLERS

The combined legacy of Portuguese assimilation and the role of women fighters in the liberation war, plus limited Islamic influence, means local women enjoy a certain degree of freedom. If you've travelled through Senegal or Mali, the sight of young women in jeans, couples holding hands in public, or men and women simply socialising comfortably together, makes a refreshing change. Although the atmosphere is relaxed, in rural areas women visitors may be more comfortable behaving and dressing conservatively. For more general information and advice, see the Women Travellers section in the Regional Facts for the Visitor chapter.

DANGERS & ANNOYANCES

See the Warning box at the start of this chapter. The conflict in Casamance (see the Senegal chapter for more details) occasionally spills over the border into northern Guinea-Bissau. Travellers heading for Varela should check the latest security situation.

Walking around at night is safer in Bissau than in just about any other African capital city. Nevertheless, crime is slowly increasing, so take the usual precautions. Avoid side streets and the port area at night.

BUSINESS HOURS

Shops and offices are open from 8 am to noon and 3 to 6 pm, or 8 am to 2 pm Monday to Friday. Shops also open on Saturday morning. Banks and post offices are open weekday mornings only.

PUBLIC HOLIDAYS & SPECIAL EVENTS

Official holidays include 1 January (New Year's Day), 20 January (death of Amilcar Cabral), 8 March (Women's Day), Good Friday, 1 May, 3 August (Pidjiguiti Day), 24 September (Independence Day), 14 November and 25 December (Christmas Day). Islamic feasts such as Eid al-Fitr (at the end of Ramadan) and Tabaski are also celebrated. See Public Holidays & Special Events in the Regional Facts for the Visitor chapter for a table of dates of Islamic holidays.

Guinea-Bissau's main event is the carnival which takes place in Bissau every February. Music, masks, dancing, parades and all-round good times are the order of the day. Small festivals are held in other towns around the country, at about the same time of year, although dates are not fixed so you need to ask locally for details.

ACTIVITIES

On the islands of the Bijagos Archipelago the sandy beaches mean swimming is a popular activity, while several of the smarter hotels in this area offer deep-sea fishing and other water sports. On the islands, and in some of the remoter parts of Guinea-Bissau, cycling is an excellent way to get around. Roads are quiet and distances between towns are not too long. There are no formal hire outlets, but you can usually arrange something just by asking around. For more serious exploration, you could consider bringing your own bike (for more information on this, see the Getting Around the Region chapter).

ACCOMMODATION

In Bissau, upmarket hotels are on the increase, but the choice in the budget range has shrunk in recent years. For this reason, many travellers head inland or to the islands, where accommodation is more reasonably priced and usually good value. Several specialist hunting and fishing camps for upmarket visitors flying in from France and Portugal exist. You may see signs along the roads, but as

GUINEA-BISSAU

these don't usually cater for independent visitors, details are not listed in this chapter.

FOOD & DRINKS

In Bissau, street food is surprisingly hard to find. Even coffee and bread stalls take some determined tracking down. However, in the last few years, Bissau's choice of patisseries has grown considerably, and there are several smarter restaurants serving good seafood. In rural areas, meat dishes may be monkey (*macaco*), so ask before ordering if beef, goat or vegetables are more to your taste.

Canned soft drinks and beers imported from Portugal are easy to find. Local brews include palm wine, as in many other West African countries. For a stronger home-brew, you may be offered *caña* (rum) which is 60% proof. You may also come across *caña de cajeu* (cashew rum), equally strong, and made not from the nuts, but from the fruit that surrounds them.

Getting There & Away

AIR

Guinea-Bissau's only airport is on the outskirts of Bissau. The main airlines flying to/from Guinea-Bissau are TAP Air Portugal and Air Bissau. The country is also served by several regional airlines, including TACV (the Cape Verde airline) and Air Mauritanie.

At the time of writing, departure tax for international flights was US$20, but this was included in some tickets. If you're flying out of Bissau, check the situation when you buy your ticket.

Europe & the USA

The only European airline serving Guinea-Bissau is TAP Air Portugal, with return flights from Lisbon (Portugal) for around US$750. A one way flight from Bissau to London is US$960. Air Afrique has a weekly flight to Bissau from Paris and Lisbon via Dakar (Senegal). Alternatively, get any flight from Europe to Dakar and change to a re-

gional airline. From the USA you can take Air Afrique from New York to Dakar, otherwise you'll have to go via Europe.

Africa

Air Senegal and Air Bissau between them have four flights a week between Bissau and Dakar (CFA87,000 one way). Air Bissau also has weekly flights to Conakry (Guinea) for CFA131,000 and, in partnership with TACV, flies weekly to Praia (Cape Verde) for CFA164,000 one way. Air Afrique links Bissau to Dakar, Abidjan (Côte d'Ivoire) and Conakry, with one or two flights each way per week, and Air Mauritanie has weekly flights to Casablanca via Banjul (Gambia) and Nouakchott (Mauritania). The most useful of these sectors is that between Banjul and Bissau (around CFA35,000 one way).

LAND

Guinea

Most travellers go via Gabú and Koundara. Bush taxis usually go daily for CFA2500 or GF5000, but it can take all day to cover this 100km stretch, although the winding road through the Fouta Djalon foothills is beautiful. You might have to change transport at

---

Border Crossings

Guinea-Bissau shares borders with Senegal and Guinea. For travellers going to/from Senegal, the busiest and most popular crossing point is at São Domingos, on the main route between Ingore and Ziguinchor, although there are also crossing points between Tanaf and Farim, and near Pirada, north of Gabú on the route to/from Vélingara and Tambacounda.

If you're heading to/from Guinea, most traffic goes via Kandika and Saréboïdo on the road between Gabú and Koundara, but there are also quiet tracks, open only in the dry season, which link south-eastern Guinea-Bissau and western Guinea, via Quebo and Boké.

Saréboïdo; tying in with the weekly Sunday market improves your options.

Another route for the intrepid involves taking the old truck (GF16,000) which leaves Gabú every few days for Boké, from where transport goes on to Conakry. You can also get to Boké from Quebo, but this route is slow, unless you tie in with Boké's market (Wednesday).

Senegal

Bush taxis go all the way between Ziguinchor and Bissau, via the border at São Domingos, Ingore and Bula, for CFA2500. The road is tar, but ferry crossings at São Vicente and Joalande mean the trip can take between four and eight hours. Passengers have to pay CFA100 for the ferry. The ferries may be replaced by bridges, and another new road is planned between Ingore and Bissora via Barro. (São Domingos used to be linked to Cacheu by ferry, and the main road to/from Bissau used to go through Canchungo, but this ferry no longer runs and all traffic between São Domingos and Bissau now goes through Ingore and Bula.)

You can also cross between Guinea-Bissau and Senegal by going from Farim (which has a small *pensão* if you need to stay overnight) from where bush taxis run to Tanaf in Senegal. Another option is to go via Gabú, from where a daily bush taxi goes to Tambacounda (via Vélingara) in Senegal for CFA5000.

Getting Around

AIR

There are no internal flights on the mainland. For details on flights to the islands see Getting There & Away in the Ilha de Bubaque section and the section on the Ilha de Orango later.

MINIBUS & BUSH TAXI

The main roads between Bissau and the towns of Gabú, Cacheu and Farim, and to the border at São Domingos, are all good tar.

Other roads are not so good and can be impassable in the rains. There are no bridges in Guinea-Bissau, so many road journeys require ferry crossings.

Public transport around the country consists mainly of minibuses and Peugeot 504 bush taxis on the main roads, and trucks or pick-ups called *kandongas* on rural routes. Mornings are always the best time to get transport. For an idea of fares, across the country from Bissau to Gabú (around 200km) is CFA2500 by 504, CFA2000 by bus and CFA1500 by kandonga.

BOAT

From Bissau, public passenger boats go to the islands of Rubane, Bubaque, Galinhas and Bolama, and to Catió and Enxudé on the mainland. Smaller boats and motor-canoes *(canoas)* also shuttle between Bissau and the islands.

For something more exclusive, you might consider a tour around the Bijagos Archipelago on the *African Queen*. An all-inclusive four day trip is CFA165,000 and you can get details from travel agencies in Bissau.

Bissau

Until the mid-1980s, Bissau was like a sleepy provincial town, with clean streets, few vehicles and a low noise level. On the down side, the commercial area was lifeless, food was scarce and there was a blackout nearly every night. But recently Bissau has become more like other African cities or, as some say, more 'Senegalised'. Now the centre is a hive of activity, with cars and taxis on the streets, stores full of foreign goods and thriving bars and nightclubs, although the small-town feel remains and the city is still calm compared with Dakar or Abidjan.

Orientation

Bissau's main drag is the wide Avenida Amilcar Cabral, running between the port and the Praça dos Heróis Nacionais. A block west on Avenida Domingos Ramos is the main market, the Mercado Central, and Praça

GUINEA-BISSAU

BISSAU

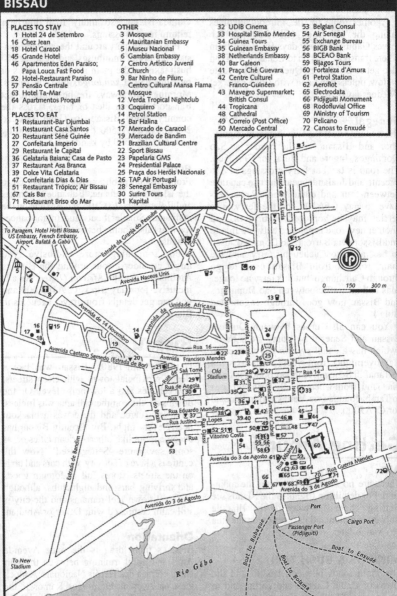

PLACES TO STAY
1 Hotel 24 de Setembro
16 Chez Jean
18 Hotel Caracol
45 Grande Hotel
46 Apartmentos Eden Paraiso;
   Papa Louca Fast Food
52 Hotel-Restaurant Paraiso
57 Pensão Centrale
63 Hotel Ta-Mar
64 Apartmentos Proquil

PLACES TO EAT
2 Restaurant-Bar Djumbai
11 Restaurant Casa Santos
20 Restaurant Séné Guinée
27 Confeitaria Imperio
29 Restaurant le Capital
36 Gelataria Baiana; Casa de Pasto
37 Restaurant Asa Branca
39 Dolce Vita Gelataria
47 Confeitaria Dias & Dias
51 Restaurant Trópico; Air Bissau
67 Cais Bar
71 Restaurant Briso do Mar

OTHER
3 Mosque
4 Mauritanian Embassy
5 Museu Nacional
6 Gambian Embassy
7 Centro Artístico Juvenil
8 Church
9 Bar Ninho de Pilun;
   Centro Cultural Mansa Flama
10 Mosque
12 Verda Tropical Nightclub
13 Coquiero
14 Petrol Station
15 Bar Halina
17 Mercado de Caracol
19 Mercado de Bandim
21 Brazilian Cultural Centre
22 Sport Bissau
23 Papelaria GMS
24 Presidential Palace
25 Praça dos Heróis Nacionais
26 TAP Air Portugal
28 Senegal Embassy
30 Surire Tours
31 Kapital

32 UDIB Cinema
33 Hospital Simão Mendes
34 Guinea Tours
35 Guinean Embassy
38 Netherlands Embassy
40 Bar Galeon
41 Praça Ché Guevara
42 Centre Culturel
   Franco-Guinéen
43 Mavegro Supermarket;
   British Consul
44 Tropicana
48 Cathedral
49 Correio (Post Office)
50 Mercado Central

53 Belgian Consul
54 Air Senegal
55 Exchange Bureau
56 BIGB Bank
58 BCEAO Bank
59 Bijagos Tours
60 Fortaleza d'Amura
61 Petrol Station
62 Aeroflot
65 Electrodata
66 Pidjiguiti Monument
68 Rodofluvial Office
69 Ministry of Tourism
70 Pelicano
72 Canoas to Enxudé

Ché Guevara, which has several popular bars and restaurants. On the north-western edge of the centre is Mercado de Bandim. From here Avenida de 14 Novembro leads west to the main *paragem* (bus and taxi park), the airport and most inland destinations.

Information

Tourist Information There's a small information office at the Ministry of Tourism on Rua Guerra Mendes, but its not much use to independent travellers. For hotels, camps and private transport, you're much better off at a travel agency or tour operator.

Money The BIGB on Avenida Amilcar Cabral is lethargic, but Banco de Totto in the narrow streets near the port changes French francs (travellers cheques and cash) at no commission. The change bureaus near the Mercado Central offer similar rates and quicker service. Outside business hours, you could deal with the moneychangers who loiter nearby, but this should be as a last resort as you might be set up for a con or robbery. The quickest and safest place to change money is at the Mavegro supermarket, about 300m east of Avenida Amilcar Cabral, where all currencies, cash or travellers cheques, are exchanged at bank rates with no commission.

Post & Communications The main post office (*correios*) is on Avenida Amilcar Cabral. To phone Europe, the post office and the nearby public telephone office charge CFA2000 per minute. Alternatively, buy phonecards from the post office and use them in the public booths outside. A card with 100 units costs CFA5000 and gives you three minutes to Europe.

Guinea Telecom's Internet centre on Rua Costa is open weekdays from 8.30 am to 1 pm and 4 to 7 pm, and charges CFA1000 per hour. Dunia Cybercafé on the eastern end of Avenida Naceos Unis is a bit more expensive but open on Sunday.

Travel Agencies & Tour Operators For international or domestic flights, and for information about hotels around the country,

agencies include: Guinea Tours (☎ 212409) on Rua 12 (English speaking); Bijagos Tours (☎ 212812) on Avenida Pansau Na Isna; Surire Tours (☎ 212024) on Rua de Angola; and Nimba Tours (☎ 251251) at the Hotel Hotti Bissau on Avenida de 14 Novembro.

Bookshops The bookstall on Praça Ché Guevara occasionally has foreign newspapers; otherwise try Papelaria GMS on Avenida Ramos, which has a small selection of English and French books and magazines.

Cultural Centres The Centre Culturel Franco-Guinéen (formerly the French Cultural Centre) on Praça Ché Guevara has a good selection of magazines (mostly French) in the downstairs coffee bar, and the notice board carries adverts for local cultural events. The US Information Service at the US embassy has a small library.

Medical Services Bissau's main hospital is the Simão Mendes (☎ 212816), east of the centre, but facilities are limited. There are pharmacies near the Hotel Ta-Mar and the Mercado Central.

Things to See

The **Presidential Palace** dominates Praça dos Heróis Nacionais at the northern end of Avenida Amilcar Cabral, but no photos are allowed, and it is forbidden to walk up the streets on either side. Next to the southern end of Avenida Amilcar Cabral are the narrow streets of the **old Portuguese quarter**, with some grand Mediterranean-style houses. South of here is the port and the nearby **Pidjiguiti Monument** (which commemorates the 1959 massacre of striking dockworkers), and to the east is the fort, **Fortaleza d'Amura**, surrounded by imposing walls and closed to visitors (although there are plans for the military to move out and for the fort to become a historic monument and museum). Amilcar Cabral's mausoleum is also here.

The **Museu Nacional** on Avenida de 14 Novembro is small, hard to find, and seems permanently closed. The exhibits might get

GUINEA-BISSAU

moved to the new museum proposed for the fort if that plan comes to fruition.

Places to Stay – Budget

Bissau's electricity is erratic, so be prepared for blackouts. All budget places have bucket showers rather than running water. Compared with many other West African capitals, there's a distinct lack of options.

Cheapest is the *Grande Hotel* on Avenida Pansau Na Isna, with no water, no electricity, no food and no beer. But what do you expect for CFA5000 a double? This place will surely be either closed or renovated by the time you arrive. So your first choice may be the *Hotel Caracol* on Avenida Caetano Semedo (also called Estrada de Bor), where doubles are CFA8000. The rooms have a bathroom just big enough to fit the large bucket of water. Nearby among the shacks is *Chez Jean*, with clean but cell-like singles/doubles rented by the hour; all night will cost you CFA5000/7500.

The *Pensão Centrale* on Avenida Amilcar Cabral is a long-time favourite to escape the dives, but only slightly better, although some rooms have had a lick of paint and there are new parasols on the balcony. Simple rooms with shared bathroom cost CFA8000 per person, with breakfast.

Much better value is *Apartmentos Proquil*, a couple of rooms above an export business of the same name in the narrow streets near the port. The friendly owner speaks French but is only available during office hours. Clean doubles with fan and bathroom cost CFA12,500.

Places to Stay – Mid-Range & Top End

All the hotels in this range have rooms with bathroom, air-con and running water.

The *Hotel-Restaurant Paraiso* on Rua Costa has fairly clean but pricey rooms for CFA25,000 (single or double), although the pleasant outdoor restaurant does good meals for around CFA4000. Same price but much better value is the *Apartmentos Eden Paraiso* (formerly the Jordani) on Avenida Pansau Na Isna. Also good is the refurbished *Hotel Ta-Mar* in the quiet, narrow streets near the port, where singles/doubles cost CFA26,500/32,500.

The *Hotel 24 de* Setembro (☎ 221026, fax 221033), north of the centre, charges CFA 37,500/44,000 with breakfast, but feels like a morgue with an empty lobby and empty pool (although the gardens are very nice).

The *Hotel Hotti Bissau* (☎ 251251, fax 251152), formerly the Sheraton, on Avenida de 14 Novembro, is Bissau's best, and takes credit cards. Rooms cost CFA63,000/75,000 and facilities include a large swimming pool (for guests only). The restaurant appears uninspiring but has an interesting though expensive menu, with meals from CFA4000 to CFA9000.

Places to Eat

The best place for *street food* and low-budget eateries is around Mercado de Bandim. A good cheap place is *Restaurant Séné-Guinée*.

For fresh bread and pastries to take away, try *Confeitaria Dias & Dias* behind the Grande Hotel. Alternatively, *Confeitaria Imperio* on Praça dos Heróis Nacionais is in a good position for watching the world go by, but not especially cheap with cakes for CFA500, and coffee with milk for CFA300. Smarter and better value is *Dolce Vita Gelataria* on Rua Vieira, with a mouthwatering selection of cakes, coffees and ice creams, all around CFA500.

The *Gelataria Baiana* on Praça Ché Guevara is OK for a drink with a view, but not worth visiting for food. Much better is the nearby *Casa de Pasto* with soft drinks for CFA400, beers for CFA500, snacks from CFA500 and meals up to CFA2000.

Next to the Apartmentos Eden Paraiso, *Papa Louca Fast Food* has chawarmas for CFA700, small pizzas for CFA1500 and pavement tables. *Cais Bar* down by the port on Avenida do 3 de Agosto has sandwiches from CFA300 and meals like beef and chips for CFA1000. East of here is the open-air *Briso do Mar*, a cheap and popular place with good atmosphere and music, beers for around CFA500 and meals from CFA1500. *Restaurant-Bar Djumbai* north of the centre has also been recommended.

The *Pensão Centrale* restaurant offers a filling three-course Portuguese meal (soup, main dish and fruit) for CFA3000, which is one of the best deals in town. For better surroundings, the *Restaurant Trópico* on Rua Vieira has a bar serving sandwiches from CFA500, and a very pleasant garden with meals in the evening from CFA3000.

Restaurante le Capitol on Rua Djassi has been recommended, with meals such as chicken or seafood for CFA2000 to CFA 3000, and Lebanese specials such as humous for CFA500 to CFA1000. *Casa Santos*, an old-style Portuguese restaurant on Estrada de Santa Luzia, serves good-value main courses from CFA2500 to CFA3500. With similar prices but better fare and ambience is *Asa Branca* on Rua Justino Lopes, which is particularly noted for its seafood.

Entertainment

Several of the restaurants listed above are also bars, but one of the best is *Briso do Mar*. More upmarket is *Bar Galeon* on Praça Ché Guevara, which is also a restaurant and casino.

Things get more lively if you go outside the city centre; the area around the Hotel Caracol has several good, cheap bars. Or cruise along Avenida Naceos Unis to *Bar Ninho de Pilun*, which has outdoor and indoor seating. Just behind is *Centro Cultural Mansa Flama* which is a good place for a drink in the early evening – later it has live music or a disco. Small beers cost CFA400. Down the road is the lively *Verda Tropical Nightclub*, and nearby is the sedate *Coquiero* with a garden terrace for drinks, plus a snack bar and restaurant. Nightclubs in the centre include *Tropicana* near the Grande Hotel, *Pelicano* near the port and *Kapital* on Rua Vieira. Other places to check for live music are the Centre Culturel Franco-Guinéen on Praça Ché Guevara and the Brazilian Cultural Centre near Avenida Francisco Mendes.

Shopping

The Mavegro supermarket, east of the centre, sells all kinds of imported items, from car tyres to stationery and shampoo, plus many kinds of food. Nearby, a mall called the Mavegro Shopping Centre is planned, with more than 30 shops inside.

For a more colourful experience, you can buy fruit at the Mercado Central, and the surrounding stalls sell Senegalese-style clothing and other souvenirs such as carvings. For music cassettes, try Discoteca Bamba. At Mercado de Bandim, there's more fresh produce, but very little in the way of arts and crafts. Your best place for this is the Centro Artistico Juvenil (closed Sunday), a training centre for young artists on Avenida de 14 Novembro. The fixed prices are reasonable, some pieces are very good, and there's no pressure to buy. Woodcarvings are also sold at stalls on the footpath outside the Pensão Centrale and on Avenida Mendes, by the old cinema (now a club renamed Sport Bissau).

Getting There & Away

Air Airlines represented in Bissau include: Air Bissau (☎ 212801) on Rua Vieira; Air Afrique (☎ 215000) under the Pensão Central; Air Senegal on Rua Vitorino Costa; and TAP Air Portugal (☎ 213993) on Praça dos Heróis Nacionais.

Bush Taxi & Minibus All bush taxis and minibuses leave from the paragem on Avenida de 14 Novembro. This used to be on the north side of the road, then was moved further out of town (beyond the Hotel Hotti Bissau) and about 500m south of the road. There are rumours that it might be moved again. It's always best to get transport in the morning. Minibuses to Bafatá cost CFA1500, and to Gabú CFA2000.

Boat Guinea-Bissau's ferries and boats are operated by Rodofluvial (☎ 212350). Sailing days and times are posted at their office near the port on Avenida do 3 de Agosto. For more details on the boats to Bubaque, Enxudé, Bolama and Catió, see the Getting

GUINEA-BISSAU

There & Away sections of the relevant towns and islands in this chapter.

Getting Around

To/From the Airport The airport is 8km from the centre. Taxis meet most flights, and charge anything from CFA2000 to CFA 20,000 to take you into town. To get a shared taxi or minibus, walk 200m to the roundabout at the start of Avenida de 14 Novembro, the road into the city.

Minibus Small minibuses painted blue and yellow called *toca-toca* run around the city, with most rides costing CFA100. The most useful route for visitors goes from Mercado de Bandim along Avenida de 14 Novembro towards the paragem and airport.

Taxi Taxis are painted blue and white, and a private hire costs about CFA500 for a short ride across town or CFA1000 from the centre to the paragem, but check the price with the driver before getting in.

Taxis will also pick up other passengers unless you specifically want a private hire, but this makes your ride cheaper. For example, a shared taxi from Mercado de Bandim to the paragem is CFA250 per person.

Car Tupi Rent-A-Car (☎ 211070, fax 215413) at the Hotel Hotti Bissau offers small cars for US$75 per day all-inclusive. A driver is US$20 per day.

The North

BAFATÁ

Bafatá, about 150km east (inland) by road from Bissau, is set on a hill overlooking the Rio Géba. It's one of Guinea-Bissau's largest towns, with about 10,000 inhabitants, but it's a quiet place. It's also where Amilcar Cabral was born. We heard from one traveller who hired a bike in Bafatá and cycled through 'fields, villages and beautiful jungle' to reach a ruined Portuguese outpost at Geba.

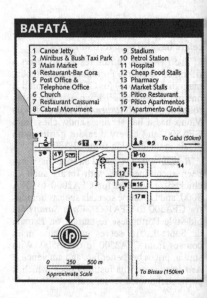

BAFATÁ

1 Canoe Jetty	9 Stadium
2 Minibus & Bush Taxi Park	10 Petrol Station
3 Main Market	11 Hospital
4 Restaurant-Bar Cora	12 Cheap Food Stalls
5 Post Office &	13 Pharmacy
Telephone Office	14 Market Stalls
6 Church	15 Pitico Restaurant
7 Restaurant Cassumai	16 Pitico Apartmentos
8 Cabral Monument	17 Apartmento Gloria

To Gabú (50km)

0   250   500 m
Approximate Scale

To Bissau (150km)

Apartmento Gloria, near a bar and disco of the same name, has very basic rooms for CFA1500/3000. Better is the nearby *Pitico Restaurant* which has a few *apartmentos* (rooms) opposite for CFA2500/5000. This is also a good place for food and beer, as is *Restaurant Cassumai* next to the church. There are also several *cheap eating houses* just south of the petrol station. For something more lively try the *Restaurant-Bar Cora* which becomes a nightclub some evenings.

Minibuses to Bissau (CFA1500) or Gabú (CFA500) depart from the market at the bottom of the hill.

GABÚ

Gabú is in the east of the country, a four hour (200km) minibus ride from Bissau. It's a lively town – especially in the evening when the large market and street food stalls come alive – and a major transport hub for eastern Guinea-Bissau and neighbouring parts of Guinea and Senegal. It's a good place to stay for a day or two and get a feel for upcountry life. If you crave activity, about 40km south of Gabú on the road to Boé is **Canjadude**, where you can hike up several rocky hillocks rising from the plain which give good views of the surrounding area. Farther south at **Ché-Ché** is a group of standing stones.

Places to Stay & Eat

One of the cheapest places to stay is the unmarked *Pensão Miriama Sago*, near the market, where fairly basic rooms cost CFA3500. Meals can be ordered, but nearby are several good cheap eating houses, including the clean and friendly *Restaurant Senegalese N'Dey* with big bowls of rice and meat sauce for CFA500. In the same part of town, the *Hotel Oasis* is basic and not worth the CFA5000 per person asked – although this may be negotiable. Much better value is the *Jovam*, north of the centre, a bar-restaurant-disco and hardware emporium, where spotless rooms with fan and bathroom cost from CFA6000 to CFA7500.

You can get *street food* and roast meat in the evening in the area around the market. Otherwise, the *Restaurant Oasis* does fish or chicken with chips on the terrace for CFA2000, but you have to order in advance.

They also serve beers, but our favourite was the outdoor *Bar Tudo na Iskina,* with low lights, cheap drinks, cheerful management and good music.

Getting There & Away

Minibuses to Bissau (CFA2000) go regularly through the morning, and there are usually one or two afternoon departures. If you're aiming for Guinea or Senegal see the Getting There & Away section earlier for details. You can easily change CFA into Guinean francs in the bush taxi and minibus park.

CANCHUNGO

This small sleepy town, north-west of Bissau, is a good stepping-off point for exploring the north-west of the country. The focus is the *praça* (square), ringed by shops, market stalls and a couple of small *restaurants* (one of them has cheap rooms).

To reach Canchungo, minibuses run direct from Bissau (CFA800), or you can change at Bula, which has a cheap restaurant-pensão on the main street. Note that the Canchungo road is 1km outside Bula: otherwise you'll miss half the traffic going your way.

CALAQUISSE

This peaceful and beautiful place is about 25km west of Canchungo on the coast, and a long way off the beaten track. However, there's a daily bush taxi from Canchungo, and Calaquisse has a small and friendly *hotel*, which has cheap rates and a disco on Saturday night. From here you can take walks through the surrounding woodland or reach a small port on the estuary about 2km away and stroll on the edge of the mangroves and salt marsh.

CACHEU

The small riverside town of Cacheu (pronounced *cash-ay-ou*), north of Canchungo, was once a major Portuguese slave-trading centre from which the infamous English pirate Sir Francis Drake was repulsed in 1567. You can visit the fort and see the cannons and some large bronze statues

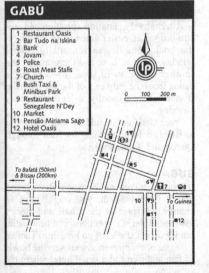

GABÚ

1 Restaurant Oasis
2 Bar Tudo na Iskina
3 Bank
4 Jovam
5 Police
6 Roast Meat Stalls
7 Church
8 Bush Taxi & Minibus Park
9 Restaurant Senegalese N'Dey
10 Market
11 Pensão Miriama Sago
12 Hotel Oasis

0   100   200 m

To Bafatá (50km) & Bissau (200km)

To Guinea

GUINEA-BISSAU

stacked in a corner and seemingly forgotten. The town's hotel has closed and is being renovated by an eccentric Frenchman who walks around with a parrot on his shoulder. Until this place reopens, ask at the small *restaurant* near the jetty about a local lady who rents very basic *rooms* for CFA1500. There are bush taxis from Canchungo.

CACHEU NATURAL PARK

Near Cacheu, this park is still in the early stages of being established, primarily to protect some large areas of mangrove (for more information on mangroves, see the boxed text 'Mangroves' in the Siné-Saloum Delta section of the Senegal chapter). The park office is a few kilometres before town, where simple *huts* for tourists are planned.

Things are still very much at an early stage here, but with help from the park staff you can arrange to hire a boat to go deep into the mangrove area. After your visit to the park, instead of returning to Cacheu town, you could get the boat to go off the main river and up the creek to drop you at São Domingos.

SÃO DOMINGOS

This border town, about 200km north-west of Bissau, is on the main route to/from Ziguinchor (Senegal). Most travellers pass through without stopping overnight, but if you get stuck the *Hotel Zulu* has been recommended by several travellers, with good cheap rooms and food. Or you can try the *Restaurant-Bar Paris* (one more example of increasing Francophone influence in Guinea-Bissau!) on the road towards Bissau, or any of the *food shacks* near the immigration office.

Most traffic between Bissau and Ziguinchor runs through São Domingos, stopping only for paperwork and passport checks at the border post. If you do need to change transport here, for example if you're heading for Varela, all bush taxis go from outside the border post.

VARELA

Varela is a village on the coast, about 50km west of São Domingos. The beaches here are

just as good as at Cap Skiring in Senegal, only a few kilometres away, but with far fewer people. Some travellers camp on the beach, others splurge CFA25,000 on a room at the mid-range *Aparthotel Jordani* on a low cliff overlooking the sea. But the best place is *Chez Helene* just over a kilometre from the beach, with rooms for one or two people at CFA10,000 (including breakfast), or large tents for hire for CFA5000. Camping in your own tent is also allowed. There's a bush taxi (CFA600) once or twice a day, running along the dirt road between São Domingos and Varela.

The South

Moving into southern Guinea-Bissau you leave the Sahel firmly behind and enter a beautiful region of forests and waterways. The bird and monkey populations are impressive, and this is the home of Africa's most westerly chimpanzee populations. Travel can be slow here but very rewarding.

A loop through the region might start with the weekly boat which goes every Tuesday from Bissau via Bolama to Catió (actually a point on the coast near Catió). It returns on Friday, and the one way fare is CFA2500.

Alternatively, **Enxudé** (pronounced *en-shu-day*) is an easier gateway to the south: the boat from Bissau runs daily except Sunday, stays an hour and then returns. As another option to Enxudé, you can get a canoa from the jetty east of the main port in Bissau– there's usually at least one every morning.

From Catió or Enxudé the loop takes you to Buba, before returning by road through Quebo and Xitole to Bissau.

BUBA

If you're travelling between Bissau and places further south, you might have to change transport at the small and sleepy town of Buba. Connections can be erratic, but if you get stuck it's no hardship. There's a couple of cheap *restaurants* serving bowls of fish and rice and a small *hotel* where the friendly French-speaking manager can set you up with a canoe ride on the nearby creek or advise on travel in the surrounding area. A minibus between Bissau and Buba costs CFA2700 – there's usually one each way every morning.

JEMBEREM

Jemberem is a small village 22km east of Catió, and the centre of a community-based conservation scheme connected with the proposed **Cantanhez Natural Park** – a good place to see birds, monkeys and possibly chimpanzees. The local women's association has set up the small *Raça Banana* guesthouse charging CFA1000 per night and the same for meals. Through them or the local chief you can arrange a guide (essential) to show you through the nearby sacred forest. A colourful booklet called *Cantanhez Forêts Sacrées* (in French) produced by an organisation called Tiniguena (☎ 251907) is available in Bissau and gives more information.

You can reach Catió on the weekly boat from Bissau. Alternatively, there's normally one vehicle a day from Bissau to Catió (CFA3000). You may have to go from Bissau to Buba by minibus (CFA2700) and change to a kandonga for the section to Catió. From Catió to Jemberem there's usually a kandonga every morning, which takes you across on the ferry. If you have wheels you can approach from Quebo on the bad dirt roads via Guilege. By public transport this journey takes a good deal of time and patience.

XITOLE & AROUND

Xitole is a village on the main road between Bissau and Buba, about 35km south of Bambadinca. Near Xitole, west of the main road on the north bank of the river, is a *campement* called *Casselinta*, which was still being finished in 1998. You can get details from travel agencies and tour operators in Bissau (see Information in the Bissau section).

About 20km further south and 4km east of the main road (look for the signs) is another

campement called *Samba-Loba* in an excellent setting on the Rio Corubal – an ideal base for exploration of the surrounding area. Bungalows cost CFA10,000 (one or two people) or CFA15,000 (three or four). Breakfast is CFA3000 and other meals are CFA7000. At Samba-Loba you can also arrange boat trips or guides to show you birds and monkeys and other wildlife (including maybe chimpanzees) in the surrounding forest.

About 25km south-east from Xitole, just east of the village of Mampatá (not to be confused with another village of the same name further west), the main road crosses the Rio Corubal near the **Saltinho waterfall** *(cascata)*, which is particularly impressive in the rainy season. Another new campement, called *Surire*, is planned nearby; you can get details from Surire Tours (☎ 212024) on Rua de Angola in Bissau.

The Islands

The Bijagos Archipelago is the island group off the coast of Guinea-Bissau. Several are uninhabited, while others are home to small fishing communities. The whole archipelago has been declared a Biosphere Reserve, and the southern Orango group of islands is a national park. The IUCN (World Conservation Union) and several other bodies are working to develop schemes which protect the natural environment and improve conditions for the islands' population.

The easiest islands to reach are: Bubaque, which has some wonderful beaches and some tourist infrastructure; Galinhas, where facilities are more limited; and Bolama, where they're nonexistent. Before you go to any beach, check the tides. When it's low the sea is miles away and you'll have to wade through thigh-deep mud to get a swim.

Getting There & Away

To get from Bissau to the islands, there's a fleet of decrepit and unreliable passenger boats (you can check departure times at the Rodofluvial office near the port) plus some smaller boats and canoes (no more reliable).

GUINEA-BISSAU

There are also good speedboats run by the top end hotels and fishing camps. When checking details, or looking for lifts, always ask about a canoa, as people will assume you only want to travel by *barco* (large boat). And ask specifically about the *Amor* (a boat owned by the Hotel Ambancana, the only hotel on Galinhas island) which doesn't seem to count as either barco or canoa.

ILHA DE BOLAMA

This island is about 40km south of Bissau. The island's main town, Bolama, was the country's capital during early colonial days, but it has been slowly crumbling away since 1941 when everything was transferred to Bissau. Architecture buffs will find the **old buildings** interesting, and readers have reported that the island is a great place to bring a bicycle. The closest **beach** is about 4km south of Bolama town, but the best beaches are along the far south-western end of the island, about 20km from Bolama town.

Getting There & Away

The ferry for Bolama town leaves Bissau every Tuesday and returns on Friday. There's another service on Saturday which returns on Sunday. The fare is CFA1500 each way. Another boat called the *Bambaya* sometimes

---

Bolama Bats

This is what one reader, MD Tinker, had to say about Bolama:

The island of Bolama is recommended for its pleasant scenery and interesting, decaying colonial atmosphere. It is now possible to find places to stay on the island. One of the most memorable aspects of the island is the truly amazing number of bats that swarm around at dusk in a massive black cloud darkening the sky and filling the air with noise. These bats, combined with the majestic decaying colonial architecture and a classic full moon, create a wonderful image.

---

goes to Bolama, on its way to the mid-range Bambaya Hotel on the mainland coast opposite the island. The transfer is CFA15,000 return. For more information on the hotel or boat contact a travel agent in Bissau. As a cheaper alternative, go to Enxudé from where you can catch a bush taxi to São João and then a canoa over to Bolama.

ILHA DE BUBAQUE

At the centre of the Bijagos Archipelago, this is one of the easiest islands to reach from Bissau. It's also the hub of the islands' transport system (such as it is) and the best place to find a boat to other islands. Bubaque has a good choice of places to stay and is an ideal place to slow down for a few days or weeks. The island's main (and only) town is also called Bubaque, which has a market, a bakery, some shops and a post office. All places to stay and eat are also in and around the town. There's also an **art exhibition** west of the church, with masks and carvings. IUCN runs a small **information centre** called Casa do Ambiente e da Cultura which has displays on local people and the islands' wildlife.

You can walk through the forest, palm groves and fields around the town, but most visitors come for the beaches: there's a little one near the Hotel Bijagos, but much better is **Praia Bruce** (pronounced *broo-see*) at the southern end of the island, about 18km from Bubaque town. Some hotels arrange transport to the beach or you can hire a bike. The road is rideable with a hard surface of shells and cement. There's the remains of a half-finished hotel, but nowhere official to stay. We've heard from travellers who hired bikes, brought supplies (and water) and slept on the beach.

Places to Stay – Budget

Nearest the port is *Pensão Cruz Pontez* with rooms (one to three people) for CFA5400. Breakfast is CFA650 and meals around CFA1500. Rates are negotiable for long stays. The owner Paulino is a happy, outgoing person and can advise on boats back to the mainland or other islands. Roughly 200m

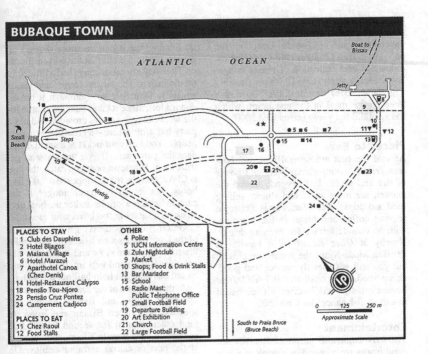

BUBAQUE TOWN

ATLANTIC OCEAN

Boat to
Bissau

Jetty

Small
Beach

Steps

Airstrip

South to Praia Bruce
(Bruce Beach)

0   125   250 m
Approximate Scale

PLACES TO STAY	OTHER
1 Club des Dauphins	4 Police
2 Hotel Bijagos	5 IUCN Information Centre
3 Maiana Village	8 Zulu Nightclub
6 Hotel Marazul	9 Market
Aparthotel Canoa	10 Shops; Food & Drink Stalls
(Chez Denis)	13 Bar Mariador
14 Hotel-Restaurant Calypso	15 School
18 Pensão Tou-Njoro	16 Radio Mast;
23 Pensão Cruz Pontez	Public Telephone Office
24 Campement Cadjoco	17 Small Football Field
	19 Departure Building
PLACES TO EAT	20 Art Exhibition
11 Chez Raoul	21 Church
12 Food Stalls	22 Large Football Field

to the south-west is *Pensão Cadjoco*, run by the Franco-Senegalese team of Johnny and Awa, where clean rooms cost CFA6500. Breakfast is CFA1000 and other meals are available. This place is set in a lush garden with its own well. On the east side of town is *Pensão Tou-Njoro*, another cheapie. Several travellers have also recommended *Campement le Balafon*, also known as Chez Titi, near the fields and palm groves on the eastern edge of town. Titi himself meets most boats at the port and will show you the way.

Places to Stay – Mid-Range & Top End

Good value is *Aparthotel Canoa*, east of the information centre, known to all as Chez Denis. Single/double rooms with bathroom and breakfast cost CFA8000/10,000. The bar-restaurant serves beers and soft drinks at CFA600, and genuine Portuguese or African

meals from CFA3000. Almost opposite is the *Hotel-Restaurant Calypso* (☎ 821116), a French, family-run place with a nice garden and cool bungalows around the swimming pool for CFA15,000/20,000. Drinks in the bar are CFA700 and meals are up to CFA3000. They have bikes for hire, and can arrange lifts to Praia Bruce for CFA5000.

To the west of the town's centre, *Maiana Village* (☎ 254118 or 821125) has a large swimming pool and private beach. Rooms are CFA16,500/22,000, and breakfast is CFA2500. French-style meals are CFA7000, or you can go for full board at CFA35,000/58,000. Boats and angling gear can be hired. The owners run a tight ship, catering primarily for European fishing groups, but they have a lot to learn when it comes to customer relations.

In the same price range as Maiana is *Club des Dauphins*, closer to the western end of

GUINEA-BISSAU

town, with a macho fishing atmosphere, and *Hotel Marazul*, a small, quiet place nearer the centre. South of Club des Dauphins, the once grand *Hotel Bijagos* (☎ 821144) is now a down-at-heel collection of musty bungalows, each costing CFA10,000 – possibly negotiable. Breakfast is CFA1500 and a three course meal in the restaurant (which has splendid sea views) costs CFA5000.

Places to Eat

Around the port are several workers' *bar-restaurants* serving cheap beers and bowls of rice and sauce. Just beyond, around the market, are more stalls and shacks selling food and drinks. *Bar Mariador* is a cheapie serving coffee and bread in the morning, with an outside terrace for evening drinks. Nearby at *Chez Raoul* (also known as Pension Meda-Njun) the rooms are closed, but you still get friendly service and good, cheap food, with omelettes (CFA1000) or Senegalese-style *thiéboudjenne* (rice baked in a thick fish sauce) for CFA1500.

Entertainment

The *bar-restaurants* mentioned earlier are good places for a beer. For a drink in lively surroundings, try *Zulu Nightclub*, down by the port.

Getting There & Away

Air A company called Astravia flies most days between Bissau and Bubaque, with extra services at weekends according to demand, but services are liable to cancellation or alteration with little notice and even less apology. You can get details at Guinea Tours in Bissau. The fare is CFA30,000 each way.

Several tour operators in Bissau offer special weekend deals including a flight, full accommodation for three nights at the Maiana Village hotel and boat trips for CFA125,000. For more details on travel agencies and tour operators in Bissau, see under Information in the Bissau section.

Boat It can be a daunting task finding out about ferries to Bubaque. Although two or

three large boats, all of dubious quality, leave Bissau every Friday for Bubaque and return on Sunday, the departure times depend on the tide. Asking around at the port in Bissau on Thursday afternoon may shed a little light on the matter. The largest ferry, *Sambuia*, is generally your best bet (although it breaks down a lot). Since it takes islanders home for the weekend, it is always crowded and has a party-like atmosphere – a great place to meet people. You buy your ticket at a small office near the port gates. If you want a seat, get there early. Whatever boat you catch, the fare is CFA2500. The trip is supposed to take five hours, but it can be much longer if the captain has a few drinks and/or the boat gets stuck on a sand bar (both frequent events).

On other days you may get a ride in one of the large canoes which occasionally make the trip. These are slow and the fare is negotiable. If the wind gets up, they give you an old can and you help bail out the water.

At the other end of the scale, several of the upmarket hotels and fishing camps run speedboats between Bissau and Bubaque (and other islands) for around CFA20,000 per person each way. In Bissau, look around at the port or ask at a travel agency. On Bubaque, ask about the *Estrellita* at the Hotel Marazul.

ILHA DAS GALINHAS

The island of Galinhas is between Bolama and Rubane, about 60km south of Bissau. There are a few small villages, and people grow crops on plots among the trees. The island is also the site of the old Portuguese prison and governor's house; you can walk across the island to see the crumbling building now gradually being consumed by the lush vegetation.

Places to Stay

The only place to stay is the friendly, low-key *Hotel Ambancana* right on the beach, facing west and with wonderful sunsets. A simple double costs CFA7500, or CFA9000 with bathroom. This price includes breakfast, and other meals are CFA5000. You can buy beers and other drinks, but as there are no shops or markets on the island, the hotel occasionally runs out of things. But it's a marvellous place; we've heard from people who planned to go for a few days and stayed for a week. Some money from the hotel supports the local village school.

Getting There & Away

The hotel's boat *Amor* goes from Bissau to Galinhas on Thursday or Friday and returns Sunday (and sometimes other days). The return fare is CFA7000. The boat is small and you'll get wet from the spray in choppy conditions. If you're heading to/from Bubaque, the *Amor* sometimes goes there, or will meet the *Sambuia* and you have to transfer from one to the other – quite an effort in a swell. Alternatively you can charter a canoa to reach Bubaque or other islands for around CFA30,000. (This is for a two way trip, but does not include waiting time of more than a couple of hours.)

More details on the *Amor* and the Hotel Ambancana are available in Bissau from the friendly and helpful owner – a businessman called Mr Sulai, who speaks French and a bit of English, and can usually be found at the Electrodata photocopy shop near the petrol station, 100m from the port.

ILHA DE ORANGO

West of Bubaque is Ilha de Orango which, along with several other islands, forms part of the **Orango Islands National Park** (also called Orango National Park). The vegetation is mainly palm groves and light woodland, with significant areas of mangrove and mud flats exposed at low tide. The park's inhabitants include rare saltwater species of hippo and crocodile, and the area is particularly good for birds. This is also one of the largest green and Ridley turtle nesting sites on the whole West African coast.

The obvious base for visiting the park and exploring this part of the archipelago is the *Orango Parque Hotel* (email orangotel@ sol.gtelecom.gw) near the village of Eticoga on the west coast of Orango, built with support from the park authorities and the local people. Local-style, good quality rooms cost from CFA20,000 per person including breakfast. There are also some *cheap huts* for rent at the national park headquarters in Eticoga village. Birdwatching and fishing can be arranged.

Access is by boat from Bubaque or Bissau, or direct to the island's airstrip by small plane run by Aerolitoral Bijagos (ask at a travel agent in Bissau for details).

OTHER ISLANDS

Some of the other islands in the Bijagos Archipelago have hotels or tourist facilities, but many remain almost completely untouched by modern civilisation. Where you get to depends on the time and money available, but wherever you go tread lightly: the Bijagos culture is precarious and such remote places are too often 'spoilt' by the behaviour of the people who visit them.

Ilha de Rubane is easily reached by canoa or small boat from Bubaque town and is an ideal spot for a day trip. On the island is the upmarket *Acaja Club*, totally devoted to fishing and mainly catering for fly-in guests. Independent visitors can stay for around CFA50,000 all inclusive. The nearby *Tubaron Club* is similar, and also has a fishing camp called *Les Carangues* on **Ilha de João Vieira**. Another upmarket place is planned for **Ilha de Maio** in the northern part of the archipelago, and there are two more fishing camps on **Ilha Roxa** (also called Ilha de Canhabaque).

Most of these places cater for upmarket visitors who pre-arrange their flight, accommodation and boat transfers as a package in Europe. If you fancy a spot of luxurious living and deep sea fishing in a predominantly French atmosphere, some of the travel agents listed under Information in the Bissau section earlier will be able to set you up.

GUINEA-BISSAU

Liberia

Warning

> ! With the withdrawal of West African peacekeeping forces, Liberia's already delicate security situation has become even more precarious. While travel is possible, visitors should allow sufficient time (and possibly also financial resources) to check out recent developments and to ensure some means of protection for themselves when in remote upcountry areas. At a minimum, this means registering with your embassy or leaving an itinerary with someone in Monrovia. In some cases, it may mean that independent-style travel is not feasible and that journeys must be made in a business or other official context. Visitors should be aware of extremes of poverty and destruction, both within Monrovia and upcountry.

For much of the past decade, Liberia was engulfed by brutal civil war. Since 1996, a tenuous calm has prevailed in the country. However, many areas remain factionalised and remote, and it is not yet a place for independent travellers. If peace consolidates and travel opens up, Liberia offers much to discover, including friendly people, lush landscapes and some of the last remaining rainforests in West Africa.

Facts about Liberia

HISTORY

The earliest inhabitants of Liberia are believed to have migrated south-east from the Sahel empires in the late Middle Ages. However, settlement of the area remained sparse because of the dense and inhospitable forests covering most of the country, and no great cities developed.

European contact with Liberia began in the 1460s with the arrival of Portuguese nav-

LIBERIA AT A GLANCE

Capital: Monrovia
Population: 2.8 million
Area: 111,370 sq km
Head of state: President Charles Ghankay Taylor
Official language: English
Main local languages: Kpelle, Bassa, Kru, Grebo
Currency: Liberian dollar
Exchange rate: US$1 = L$37
Time: GMT/UTC
Country telephone code: ☎ 231
Best time to go: November to April

igators who named several coastal features, including Cape Mesurado (Monrovia) and Cape Palmas (Harper). Because of the trading prominence of a pepper grain, the area soon became known as the 'Grain Coast'.

In the early 19th century the Grain Coast rose to the forefront of discussions within the abolitionist movement in the USA as a suitable place to resettle freed American slaves. After several failed attempts at gaining the agreement of local chiefs for such a venture, officials of the American Colonization Society (ACS) forced a treaty upon a local king at Cape Mesurado. Despite resistance by the indigenous people, settlement went ahead, and in April 1822, an expedition with the first group of black American settlers arrived at Providence Island in present-day Monrovia. Within a short time, under the leadership of the American Jehudi Ashmun who followed this initial expedition, the foundations for a country were established. Additional settlements were founded along the coast, notably at Greenville and Harper.

In 1839, Thomas Buchanan was appointed first governor of the new territory. He was succeeded in 1841 by Joseph Jenkins Roberts who expanded its boundaries and solidified cooperation among the various

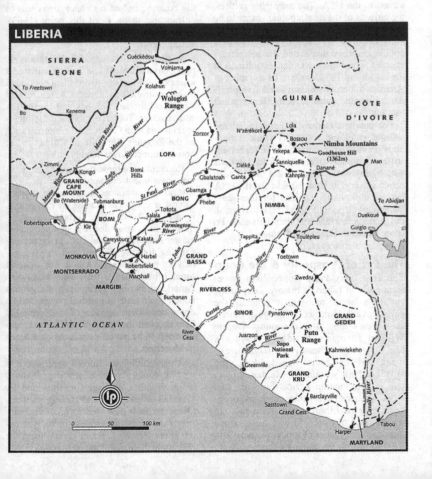

settlements. In 1846, the settlement at Cape Mesurado merged with others along the coast. A declaration of independence and a constitution, modelled on those of the USA, were drafted and in 1847 Liberia declared itself an independent republic (although citizenship excluded indigenous peoples). Roberts was elected the first president. Every successive president until 1980 was of American freed slave ancestry.

By the mid-19th century, about half of the 5000 black Americans who had originally migrated to Liberia had either died or had returned to the USA. The remaining settlers, the citizens of the new republic, came to be known as Americo-Liberians. Although constituting only a tiny fraction of Liberia's total population, they dominated the indigenous peoples. The Masonic Order, established in the country in 1851, came to be a symbol of Americo-Liberian solidarity and five presidents, starting with Roberts, were grand masters.

For nearly a century, Liberia foundered economically and politically while indigenous populations continued to be repressed, suffering under a form of forced labour which anywhere else would have been called slavery. In 1930, Britain and the USA cut off diplomatic relations for five years because of the sale of such labour to Spanish colonialists in what was then Fernando Po (now Bioko in Equatorial Guinea).

The Era of Prosperity & the Coup

The True Whig Party monopolised power from early in Liberia's history. Despite the country's labour recruitment policies, the party was able to project an image of Liberia as Africa's most stable country. During William Tubman's presidency (1944-71), this image led to massive foreign investment, and for several decades following WWII, Liberia sustained the highest growth rate in sub-Saharan Africa. Firestone and other American companies made major investments in Liberia, and Tubman – to whom much of the credit was due – earned praise as the 'maker of modern Liberia'. In the 1960s, iron ore mining operations were established near Yekepa by Lamco (Liberian-American Swedish Minerals Company), which soon became the largest private enterprise in sub-Saharan Africa.

The huge influx of foreign money, however, soon began to distort the economy, resulting in an exacerbation of social inequalities and increased hostility between Americo-Liberians and the local population. Viewing this development with alarm, Tubman was forced to concede that the indigenous people would have to be granted some political and economic involvement in the country; one of his concessions was to enfranchise them. Until this point (1963), 97% of the population had been denied voting rights.

William Tolbert succeeded Tubman as president in 1971. While Tolbert initiated a series of reforms, the government continued to be controlled by about a dozen related Americo-Liberian families and corruption was rampant. Tolbert established diplomatic relations with Communist countries such as the People's Republic of China, and at home clamped down harshly on opposition.

Resentment of these policies and of growing government corruption grew. In 1979, several demonstrators were shot in protests against a proposed increase in rice prices. Finally, in April 1980, Tolbert was overthrown in a coup led by an uneducated master sergeant, Samuel Doe. In the accompanying fighting, Tolbert and many high-ranking ministers were killed. For the first time, Liberia had a ruler who wasn't an Americo-Liberian, giving the indigenous population a taste of political power, and an opportunity for vengeance. The 28-year-old Doe shocked the world by ordering 13 ex-ministers to be publicly executed on a beach in Monrovia.

Although the coup turned over power to the indigenous population, it was condemned by most other African countries and by Liberia's other allies and trading partners. Over the next few years, relations with neighbouring African states gradually thawed. However, the flight of capital from the country in the wake of the coup coupled with ongoing corruption caused Liberia's economy to rapidly decline. During the 1980s, Liberia recorded the worst economic performance in Africa; real incomes fell by half, unemployment in Monrovia rose to 50%, and electricity blackouts became common.

Doe struggled to maintain his grip on power by any means available, including a sham 'election' held in 1985, largely to appease his major creditor, the USA. By the late 1980s, however, it was clear that opposition forces had had enough and were determined to topple him. Following a foiled post-election coup attempt, members of Doe's Krahn tribe began killing and torturing rival tribespeople, particularly the Gio and Mano in Nimba County.

Civil War

On Christmas Eve 1989, several hundred rebels led by Charles Taylor (former head of the Doe government's procurement agency) invaded Nimba County from Côte d'Ivoire. Doe's troops arrived shortly thereafter and indiscriminately killed hundreds of unarmed civilians, raped women and burned villages. Thousands of civilians fled into Côte d'Ivoire and Guinea.

Shortly after the invasion, Prince Johnson of the Gio tribe broke away from Taylor and formed his own rebel forces. By mid-1990, Taylor's forces controlled most of the country while Johnson's guerrillas had seized most of Monrovia; Doe was holed up with some loyal troops in his mansion. Refugees were streaming into neighbouring countries and Liberia lay in ruins. US warships were anchored off the coast and an ECOWAS peacekeeping force (known as ECOWAS Monitoring Group or ECOMOG) was despatched in an attempt to keep the warring factions apart.

It was all to no avail. Refusing to surrender or even step down as president, Doe and many of his supporters were finally wiped out by Johnson's forces. With both Johnson and Taylor claiming the presidency, ECOMOG forces installed their own candidate, political science professor Amos Sawyer, as head of the Interim Government

of National Unity (IGNU). Meanwhile, Taylor's National Patriotic Front of Liberia (NPFL) forces continued to occupy about 90% of the country, while remnants of Doe's former army and Johnson's followers were encamped within Monrovia itself.

After a brutal assault by Taylor on Monrovia in October 1992, ECOMOG increased its forces and in August 1993, the protagonists finally hammered out a peace accord at a UN-sponsored meeting in Geneva. The accord, known as the Cotonou Agreement, called for installation of a six month transitional government representing IGNU, NPFL and the third major player, ULIMO (United Liberation Movement for Democracy, Doe's former soldiers). When its mandate expired in September 1994 a new agreement, the Akosombo Amendment, was signed. It called for the formation of a new five-member Council of State to replace the IGNU. The amendment was rejected by the IGNU, however, which extended its own lifespan until mid-1995.

In August 1995, yet another peace agreement (the Abuja Accord) was signed by leaders of the main warring factions. This one lasted until 6 April 1996, when fighting erupted in Monrovia between NPFL and ULIMO. During April and May there was widespread looting, major sections of Monrovia were severely damaged, and nearly all resident foreigners and United Nations staff were evacuated.

August 1996 saw the negotiation of an amended Abuja Accord which provided for a cease-fire, disarmament and demobilisation by early 1997, followed by elections. At the same time, Ruth Perry, a former senator, was appointed to head the Council of State. Despite serious cease-fire violations and an incomplete disarmament process, elections took place on 19 July, with Charles Taylor and his National Patriotic Party polling an overwhelming majority (75%) in voting declared by international observers to have been largely free and transparent.

Since the elections, things have picked up markedly in Liberia. The change is particularly notable in Monrovia, where shops are well stocked and street life has recovered its vibrancy. Upcountry, some of the thousands of Liberian refugees have begun to return and daily life is slowly regaining its normal rhythms. Despite these improvements, the outlook for Liberia is clouded. In late 1997, there were several politically motivated attacks; many worry that the security situation will further deteriorate now that ECOMOG has withdrawn. It remains to be seen whether the present peace will provide a durable respite for Liberians or whether it will simply be yet another lull in the brutalities of the past decade.

GEOGRAPHY

With barely three million people within its 111,000 sq km, Liberia is sparsely populated in comparison with its neighbours, and large tracts of the country are uninhabited. The main population centres are around Monrovia on the coast, in the centre near Gbarnga and Ganta, in the north-west near the Sierra Leone border, and in the south-east near Harper.

The country's low-lying coastal plain is intersected by marshes, tidal lagoons and at least nine major rivers, the largest of which is the St Paul. Inland is a densely forested plateau rising to low mountains in the northeast.

CLIMATE

Monrovia is one of the two wettest capital cities in Africa (Freetown, in Sierra Leone, is the other), with rainfall averaging more than 4500mm per year along much of the Liber-

ian coast. Inland it's less – in some areas only about 2000mm annually. Temperatures range from 23 to 32°C in Monrovia, and are slightly higher inland, although humidity levels of more than 85% in the dry season (November to April) and more than 90% in the rainy season (May to October) often make it feel much warmer. There is little seasonal temperature variation.

ECOLOGY & ENVIRONMENT

Liberia is one of the last West African countries with significant rainforests. Originally found throughout the country, they now cover about 40% of total land area, primarily in the north-west near the Sierra Leone border and in the south-east by Sapo National Park.

Before the war, a variety of projects were under way targeted at preserving Liberia's unique ecosystems. Although these were forced to a halt during the war, a dedicated network of private individuals is working to increase interest in and support for conservation issues in the country. For information, the best contact is the Society for the Conservation of Nature of Liberia (SCNL) based at the Monrovia Zoo in Larkpase (PO Box 2628; ☎/fax 227 058).

One of SCNL's main projects in Monrovia is getting the zoo back on its feet. Extensive renovations are necessary, but it is hoped that by the end of 1998, they will open an education awareness centre on environmental conservation, as well as a reasonably priced guesthouse in the grounds. SCNL is also sponsoring a tree project in which acacia seedlings will be planted at up to 50 sites around the capital. Their informative newsletter, *The Pepper Bird*, is available at SCNL's offices.

In Monrovia you can get good sources of information on Liberian environmental issues from two other places. The Forestry Development Authority is on the 4th floor of the Ministry of Finance building on the corner of Broad and Mechlin Sts, and the Pan-African Wildlife Conservation Network can be contacted through Mr James Wolo at

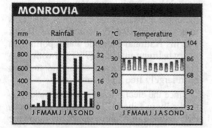

MONROVIA

Sapo National Park

While Liberia has at least half a dozen designated park areas, Sapo is the only official national park. Within its 1308 sq km, it contains some of West Africa's last remaining primary rainforest, as well as a variety of wildlife species, including forest elephant, pygmy hippo, chimpanzee and antelope. Nobody is really sure at this point about their numbers. It's generally agreed that wildlife is flourishing more now than before the war, although this could quickly change if logging interests – always a lurking threat – begin to encroach.

Surrounding the park is a 1.6km-wide buffer zone, which before the war was the site of a variety of agro-forestry projects aimed at sustainably balancing community needs with protection of the park's ecosystems. Some of these are now being revived on a very limited scale.

All park infrastructure was destroyed during the war, and at present Sapo is not accessible to independent travellers. However, given a few years of peace, this could quickly change. There's a strong network of private support, primarily in Liberia and the USA, to get Sapo going again.

Visitors seeking further information on the park should contact SCNL or the Forestry Development Authority (contacts for both are listed in the Ecology & Environment section on the facing page). The well-heeled can contact West African Safaris in the USA at PO Box 365 Oakdale, CA 95361 (☎ 209-847 5393), which plans deluxe package tours to Sapo beginning in late 1998.

the Ministry of Information, Culture and Tourism on Gurley St.

GOVERNMENT & POLITICS

Liberia's government is modelled after that in the USA, with popularly elected executive and legislative branches and a court system, although the present legislature was elected under a special proportional representation formula mandated by the peace accord provisions. With one notable exception (the appointment of former ULIMO-J leader Roosevelt Johnson as Minister of Rural Development), most ministerial positions are now filled by stalwarts of the governing National Patriotic Party.

ECONOMY

Liberia has an abundance of natural resources, including timber, gold, diamonds and iron ore, although potential revenues have never been realised. The economy, already weak before the war, is now in a shambles and World Bank data rank the country as one of Africa's poorest.

Agriculture has been the traditional mainstay of the economy; major crops before the war included coffee, cocoa, rubber, palm trees, fruit, rice and cassava. However, the number of Liberians involved in this sector dropped significantly during the past decade because of massive wartime displacement of rural communities; only slowly is this trend beginning to reverse.

Apart from resettling displaced populations, restarting an educational system, and reintegrating thousands of former fighters, Liberia is also faced with the task of rebuilding almost all infrastructure. A small but steady stream of outside investors has been visiting the country, but serious investment has been hampered by fears of further instability. Under any scenario, Liberia will remain heavily dependent on international aid for the foreseeable future.

POPULATION & PEOPLE

Liberia's population of 2.8 million (including 500,000 refugees still outside the country) consists overwhelmingly of people of indigenous origin. There are more than a dozen major ethnic groups, including the Kpelle in the centre, the Bassa around Buchanan, the Krahn in the south-east, the Mandingo (also called Mandinka) in the north and the Kru along the coast. The

Kpelle and the Bassa are the most numerous, making up about 20% and about 15% of the population, respectively. Americo-Liberians account for less than 3% of the total population. There's a sizeable Lebanese community in Monrovia who wield a disproportionate share of economic power. Large parts of Liberia are uninhabited or have very scattered populations, especially in the south-east. Almost one in every two Liberians were displaced from their home villages during the war.

ARTS

The arts of Liberia are well described in *Rock of the Ancestors* by William Siegmann with Cynthia Schmidt. These authors note that masks have traditionally been one of Liberia's most important art forms. They are viewed as having religious and moral significance and are used both to teach lessons and to entertain. The Gio in Nimba County to the north-east have some particularly rich traditions, including the *gunyege* mask, which is believed to shelter a power-giving spirit, and the *kagle* mask which is supposed to resemble chimpanzees. The Bassa are known for their *gela* masks, which often have elaborately carved coiffures, always with an odd number of plaits. *Rock of the Ancestors* contains many more details about Liberia's rich art tradition, so much of which was unfortunately destroyed during the war.

One of the most well known musical instruments – although by no means uniquely Liberian – is the 'talking drum', an hourglass shaped instrument whose upper and lower ends are connected by tension strings. When these are compressed by the drummer while holding it under one arm next to his body, the pitch increases producing a variable tone which gives the drum its name. The drum is beaten with a stick and not with the hands. (For more details, see the special section 'West African Music' earlier in this book.)

RELIGION

Almost half the population is Christian, close to 20% is Muslim and the remainder follows traditional religions.

Secret Societies

One of the most distinctive features of Liberian culture is the secret societies, called Poro for men and Sande for women. They're found throughout the country except in the south-east, and they're strongest in the north-west. Each has rites and ceremonies whose purpose is to educate young people in the customs of the tribe, preserve the group's folklore, skills and crafts, and instil discipline. Their contribution in preserving traditional ways has been significant.

Initiations, which used to involve as many as four years of training, now usually less, take place when children approach puberty. Initiates are easily recognised by their white painted faces and bodies and their shaved heads.

Hierarchies prevail; the most extreme example are the Poro among the Vai, which traditionally had 99 levels. Lower ranking members cannot acquire the esoteric knowledge of higher ranking members or attend their secret meetings. Ascending in the ranks depends on birth (leadership is frequently restricted to certain families), seniority, and the ability to learn the societies' beliefs and rituals.

The role of these societies has traditionally gone beyond religion and the education of the young, with zoes (Poro society leaders) wielding important political influence. The societies also control activities of indigenous medical practitioners, and they often judge disputes between members of high-ranking families or punish people for things such as theft and murder. A village chief who doesn't have the support of the Poro on important decisions can expect trouble enforcing them.

LANGUAGE

More than 20 African languages are spoken in Liberia, including Kpelle in the north-central region, Bassa and Kru along the coast, and Grebo in the south-east. English is the official language, although travellers often have difficulty understanding the local version. The following will help you get started:

dash	bribe
coal tar	tar road
waste	discard (waste the milk) or splash (waste water)
I beg you	please (with emphasis)
carry	give a ride to
wait small	just a moment please
kala kala	crooked, corrupt

Facts for the Visitor

PLANNING
The best time to visit Liberia is during the dry season, between November and April.

In Monrovia, the Cartographic Section on the ground floor of the Ministry of Planning and Economic Affairs building on Randall St has detailed maps of the capital and most other towns which they will copy for you for a negotiable fee.

Lion Stationery on Benson St sells second-hand maps of Liberia from about US$15. There are no commercially printed up-to-date maps of Monrovia or Liberia on the market.

TOURIST OFFICES
The Ministry of Culture, Information and Tourism in Monrovia can provide answers to specific queries – for more details see Information in the Monrovia section later. *Tourism in Liberia* is a free newspaper published in the USA with a variety of practical information on the country. It's updated annually and is available from the USA by writing to PO Box 365, Oakdale, CA 95361 or by calling ☎ 209-847 5393.

VISAS & DOCUMENTS
Visas
Visas are required by all except ECOWAS country nationals; travellers without proper documentation have been turned back at the airport. Regardless of visa duration, your length of stay will be determined on arrival: visitors are usually given 48 hours, with two weeks the maximum. This initial period can be easily extended at the Bureau of Immigration in Monrovia, on Broad St (open 9 am to 5 pm weekdays and until 3 pm on Saturday); it's US$14 for each additional 30 day period.

Exit Permits
An exit permit is required to leave the country. They're available from the Bureau of Immigration, cost US$5 and are valid for one week from date of issue. A typed letter of request is required for the application; there are typists near the entrance of Immigration.

For those leaving overland, exit permits are available at most border crossings, although you'll undoubtedly have to pay extra to convince officials to issue one; it's much better to get the permit in Monrovia.

Other Documents
Proof of vaccination against yellow fever and cholera is obligatory and will be scrutinised on arrival.

EMBASSIES & CONSULATES
Liberian Embassies & Consulates
In West Africa, Liberia has embassies or consulates in Côte d'Ivoire, Gambia, Ghana, Guinea, Nigeria and Sierra Leone (temporarily closed). See the Facts for the Visitor section of the relevant country chapter for more details. Elsewhere, embassies and consulates include the following:

France
  (☎ 01 47 63 58 55)
  8 rue Jacques Bingen, 75017 Paris
Germany
  (☎ 0228-352394)
  Hohenzollernstrasse 72, 53175 Bonn
UK
  (☎ 0171-221 1036; from 22 April 2000 ☎ 020-7221 1036)
  2 Pembridge Place, London W2 4XB
USA
  (☎ 202-723 0437)
  5201 16th St, NW, Washington, DC 20011

There are also embassies or consulates in Cameroon, Egypt, Ethiopia, Israel, Italy, Japan and Lebanon.

Embassies & Consulates in Liberia

Embassies and consulates in Monrovia include the following:

Belgium (honorary consul)
   (☎ 226 209)
   Bushrod Island Rd, Mezbau Building
Côte d'Ivoire
   (☎ 227 436)
   Ashmun St, at Air Ivoire (visa services only)
Guinea
   24th St and Tubman Blvd, Sinkor
Mali
   (☎ 223 061)
   Randall St, near Water St, Waterside
Mauritania (honorary consul)
   (☎ 225 416)
   Randall St, above Kailondo Travel
Nigeria
   (☎ 227 354)
   Nigeria House, Tubman Blvd, Congo Town
Senegal (honorary consul)
   (☎ 225 416)
   Randall St, same office as Mauritania
Sierra Leone
   Hotel Africa, Villa 18
UK (honorary consul)
   (☎ 226 056)
USA
   (☎ 226 370)
   United Nations Drive, Mamba Point

Egypt, India, Mauritania, Nigeria, Spain and Taiwan also have embassies in Monrovia.

If conditions stabilise, it's likely that several other countries will open diplomatic representations, including Ghana and Libya.

CUSTOMS

There's no restriction on the import or export of local or foreign currency, and there are no currency declaration forms.

For exporting artwork, permits are only required for quantities deemed in excess of normal tourist purchases or for items of exceptional value. They're available from Customs & Excise on the 3rd floor of the Ministry of Finance on the corner of

---

Visas for Onward Travel

In Liberia, you can get the following visas for neighbouring West African countries. For visa applications, most embassies are open weekdays from 9 am to 5 pm. You'll need to bring two photos, unless otherwise indicated.

Côte d'Ivoire

Open until noon on Saturday. Visas valid for up to three months cost US$50 plus one photo. They're usually ready the same day if you go early.

Guinea

Open until 2 pm weekdays. For one month single-entry visas you need US$40 (free for Americans) and they're usually ready within 24 hours.

Mali

Seven-day (maximum) single-entry visas are issued while you wait for US$25. Applications are accepted between 10 am and 2 pm.

Senegal

Single-entry visas are issued for US$20, and applications are processed within 24 hours. Be careful as there have been instances of fraudulent visas being issued which were later rejected in Senegal.

Sierra Leone

Visa services have been temporarily suspended. Previously, a three month single entry visa cost US$50 (US$100 for multiple entry) plus two photos and was processed immediately.

Mechlin and Broad Sts in Monrovia. Cost depends on quantity and value; base cost is US$5 plus a US$25 export fee.

MONEY

The unit of currency is the Liberian dollar (L$, sometimes called the 'liberty').

CFA1000	=	L$65
Euro €1	=	L$1
UK£1	=	L$50
US$1	=	L$37

The US dollar is also legal tender and widely used. Officially the two are on a par, but for all practical purposes, exchange is at a fluctuating rate of L$30 to L$40 for US$1. Given Liberia's unstable exchange rate, all prices in this chapter are expressed in US$. From Gbarnga northward, you'll need 'JJs' – notes issued by Charles Taylor during the war and distinctive because of the picture of former president Roberts on their face. JJs exchange at roughly twice the value of liberties against the US dollar. There's talk of replacing this three currency system with a single currency, but as yet no action.

Except for very large sums, banks in Monrovia will not do currency exchange. Most people change with one of the many Lebanese shop owners or on the street. Count your wads of L$ carefully when changing on the street. Moneychangers in Monrovia change CFA and UK£ but at unfavourable rates. In Monrovia, you can change liberties for JJs at Red Light motor park and with moneychangers in the city centre. Upcountry, you'll find moneychangers in all major towns.

Travellers cheques are virtually useless. If you get stuck, try the Liberia United Bank (LUBI) on Broad St, where you can sometimes change them for a 3% commission. Use the Randall St entrance and go upstairs. Some shop owners will accept payment for purchases in travellers cheques and give you the change in local currency.

POST & COMMUNICATIONS
Air mail letters cost US$0.80 (US$1.35 for express); the express service is usually reliable for letters, although 'express' is an exaggeration. Sending parcels through the Liberian post is not reliable. There's no poste restante.

There are no telephones upcountry, and in Monrovia international calls can only be made from the Liberia Telecom building on Lynch St. This service is available daily between 8 am and 10 pm. Rates are US$3 per minute to the USA and US$4 to Australia and Europe; there's a three minute minimum charge and a deposit is required. The only place to make collect calls is at the Nelson St Liberia Telecom office.

You can also send and receive faxes at the Nelson St Liberia Telecom office (fax 227 838, US$5 per page to send, US$1 to receive). It's open 8 am to 8 pm weekdays and 8 am to 5 pm on weekends. Incoming faxes are registered and held indefinitely (the collection window closes at 4 pm).

Liberia is not yet connected to the Internet.

INTERNET RESOURCES
The University of Pennsylvania and MIT both have excellent Web sites on Liberia: (www.sas.upenn.edu/african_studies/country_specific/liberia.html) and (groove.mit.edu/liberiapages); another one is that of the US-based Friends of Liberia (www.fol.org).

BOOKS
There's a wealth of English-language material on Liberia, much focused on post-1989 history, and most not available within Liberia. For interesting reading on Liberian art and culture, look for *Rock of the Ancestors* by William Siegmann with Cynthia Schmidt. It's actually a catalogue based on museum exhibits, but has some fascinating information on traditional Liberian artwork.

J Gus Liebenow's series of writings on Liberia (*Liberia, 1969 through 1987*) provides a fascinating look at the country's early history.

One of the best articles on more recent times is *The Final Days of Dr Doe* by Lynda Schuster (published in *Granta* 48, 1994).

PHOTOGRAPHY & VIDEO
Photo permits are issued within half a day by the Ministry of Information, Culture and Tourism (☎ 226 269) on Center St, Monrovia, for US$50 plus two photos. Government policy on photo permits is not clear, although police officers on the street will insist that you

First Traffic Light in Post-War Liberia

On Liberian Independence Day 1998, technicians of the Liberia Electricity Corporation turned on the first traffic light in Monrovia since July 1990 to commemorate the nation's 151st anniversary of independence.

It is the only traffic regulator functioning in a city dotted with personal power generators due to lack of a central electricity supply system since July 1990, when essential utilities broke down as the civil war entered the capital city. Many tax drivers who were seeing a traffic light for the first time made several trips across the intersection of Broad and Lynch streets, where the facility is located, out of sheer excitement.

need one. In any case, use a high degree of caution. Don't snap government buildings, airports, bridges and military installations, and it's best not to use a camera at all in cities and towns unless you're sure the police aren't watching and locals have no objection. See the Photography & Video section in the Regional Facts for the Visitor chapter for more general information.

Kodak film is available in Monrovia at some supermarkets, and at Sharp Showroom on Randall St. Sun Color on the same street does developing, but the quality is poor.

ELECTRICITY

Unlike the rest of West Africa, voltage in Liberia is 110V. However, many buildings are also wired with 220V. Sometimes outlets are marked, sometimes they're not, so ask before connecting appliances. Most plugs are US-style (two flat pins).

A few areas of Monrovia now have city power for part of the day, but blackouts and power surges are common. There's no power outside the capital.

HEALTH

You need a yellow fever vaccination certificate and proof of cholera vaccination as these are scrutinised on entry. Malaria risk exists year-round throughout the country, so you should take appropriate precautions. For more information on this and other health matters, refer to the Health section in the Regional Facts for the Visitor chapter earlier in this book.

St Joseph's Catholic Hospital (☎ 226 207) is the best for emergencies. Swed Relief has a clinic near the Freeport, open weekdays until 2 pm. Upcountry, your best option is Phebe Hospital near Gbarnga. Monrovia has several well stocked pharmacies, and most major towns upcountry have at least one pharmacy with basic medications (but check the expiry dates).

WOMEN TRAVELLERS

Liberia presents no specific problems for women travellers. For more general information and advice, refer to the Women Travellers section in the Regional Facts for the Visitor chapter.

DANGERS & ANNOYANCES

Although Liberia has stayed calm for well over a year, the peace is extremely fragile and demobilisation of the warring factions is not complete. In remote areas, it's not uncommon to encounter armed and traumatised ex-combatants. With the final withdrawal of ECOMOG troops in early 1998, it's likely that security conditions will deteriorate; targeted armed robberies are already increasing in Monrovia. If you're going to set off outside the capital, get a complete briefing first from people who know the situation; embassies and resident expatriates are the best sources. Overall, land mines are not a problem, though some have been found in areas of Firestone Plantation, and along the beach south of Buchanan.

Apart from security issues, the major hassles you'll face are constant requests for money and bush taxis driving at breakneck speed.

BUSINESS HOURS

Government offices are open 8.30 am to 4 pm Monday to Friday. Most businesses operate from 9 am to 5 pm Monday to Friday and from 9 am until 1 pm on Saturday. Banking hours are 9.30 am to noon Monday to Thursday and until 12.30 pm on Friday.

PUBLIC HOLIDAYS & SPECIAL EVENTS

Public holidays in Liberia include 1 January (New Year's Day), 11 February (Armed Forces Day), Decoration Day (2nd Wednesday in March), 15 March (JJ Roberts' Birthday), 11 April (Fast and Prayer Day), 14 May (National Unification Day), 26 July (Independence Day), 24 August (Flag Day), Thanksgiving Day (1st Thursday in November), 29 November (Tubman Day) and 25 December (Christmas). The biggest holiday is Independence Day.

ACCOMMODATION

Hotels are operating in Monrovia, although anywhere with a generator and water will be expensive. There are few hotels upcountry and those which do operate are generally very basic. Often the only accommodation is with missions or aid organisations, although these frequently do not have sufficient facilities to accommodate independent travellers. If you seek lodging in villages, most locals will be very welcoming and provide a space for you to set down a mat. Remember, though, that almost half of the Liberian people were displaced from their original homes during the war.

FOOD

Monrovia is the only city offering a variety of dining options; elsewhere, you'll have to rely on chop bars or simple meals. Traditional Liberian food consists of rice or a cassava-based staple (*fufu*, *dumboy* or GB) eaten with a soup or sauce, generally with greens and palm oil, and often with meat or fish. Popular dishes include *togborgee* (a Lofa County speciality made with *bitterbuoy* or *kittaly* vegetables and country soda), *palava* sauce (made with *plato* leaf, dried fish or meat and palm oil) and palm butter (a sauce traditionally from Maryland and Grand Kru counties and made from palm nuts). Upcountry, you should be prepared to be self-sufficient with food.

SHOPPING

Liberia was traditionally a good place to buy masks, baskets and textiles, and very slowly, craftmaking is reviving. In general, you'll find better items upcountry, but the selection is scanty everywhere.

Getting There & Away

AIR

There are no flights from Europe or the USA direct to Liberia; you must connect through Conakry (Guinea) or Abidjan (Côte d'Ivoire).

Within West Africa the only direct flights to Monrovia are from Conakry (twice weekly, Air Guinée, US$110/190 one way/return); from Abidjan (six to seven times weekly, Air Ivoire or Weasua, US$220/413); and from N'zérékoré in Guinea (weekly, Air Guinée, GF70,000). Air Guinée's service between Conakry and Monrovia is notoriously unreliable.

These flights now arrive and depart from Roberts international airport ('Robertsfield'), 60km south-east of Monrovia. Departure tax is US$30.

LAND
Côte d'Ivoire

Kingdom Transport Services and Yazu Ltd run a direct bus several times weekly from Monrovia to Abidjan and on to Accra via Sanniquellie. It's US$40 to Abidjan (US$60 to Accra), plus approximately US$20 for

LIBERIA

Border Crossings

Between Liberia and Sierra Leone, the main border crossing is at Bo (Waterside), although it's currently closed due to political instability in Sierra Leone. There is also a border post north of Bo (Waterside) at Kongo, although this may also be closed. Inquire locally for updated information.

Between Liberia and Guinea, there are border posts just north of Ganta, north of Voinjama, and at Yekepa. Border crossings with Cote d'Ivoire are just beyond Sanniquellie, and east of Harper near Tabou.

border fees etc. Schedules are irregular; inquire at the bus companies' office (☎ 226 588) in the BELCO building 50m beyond Bong Mines Bridge.

There are also daily bush taxis from Monrovia to Ganta and Sanniquellie near the border from where you can get transport to Danané and Man. Monrovia to Man takes 12 to 15 hours.

In the south, a road connects Harper with Tabou; you'll have to cross the Cavally River in a ferry (or canoe, if the ferry isn't operating). Service is erratic during the rainy season. Once over the river, you'll find taxis to Tabou, from where you can get transport to San Pédro and Abidjan.

Guinea

Taxis run daily from Monrovia to Ganta (US$13), where you can find transport to N'zérékoré. This border was temporarily closed in late 1998, so check before going.

In the dry season, you can go via Voinjama or Zorzor to Macenta (changing taxis at the border), although the roads on the Liberian side are in bad condition; allow two full days. From Yekepa it's a few kilometres walk to the border, where you'll find Guinean vehicles to Lola. From the border to Lola costs GF1500 (US$1).

Sierra Leone

The main crossing is at Bo (Waterside), al-

though this border is now closed because of the troubles in Sierra Leone. If it reopens, bush taxis should again ply the route between Monrovia and Freetown (650km, 15 hours, US$28). The road is tar the whole way except for a bad section between the border and Kenema.

Apart from numerous unofficial canoe crossings over the Mano River, there's another border post north of Bo (Waterside) at Kongo, although it's rarely travelled by taxis. The road on the Liberian side is in poor condition; allow a full day from Tubmanburg.

SEA

A boat runs monthly between Conakry and Monrovia (36 hours, US$50/70 deck/cabin). The schedule is set in Conakry, but staff at the Freeport 2km north-east of central Monrovia can give you an idea of the next arrival. Fishing boats run sporadically from San Pédro in Côte d'Ivoire to Harper.

Getting Around

AIR

There are no regularly scheduled domestic flights within Liberia. Weasua is available for charters.

All domestic flights use Spriggs-Payne airfield, 7km south-east of central Monrovia. There's no departure tax for domestic flights.

CAR, BUSH TAXI & MINIBUS

Road travel by public transport or otherwise is now possible throughout the country, although until the security situation stabilises further it is unwise to head off without first thoroughly checking things out in Monrovia. Most roads are dirt and many become nearly impassable during the rainy season. Major exceptions are the tar routes connecting the capital with Bo (Waterside), Tubmanburg and Buchanan, although there are some badly deteriorated stretches on the Buchanan road. The main road from Monrovia north-east is tar as far as Ganta.

Bush taxis go daily from Monrovia to Buchanan, Gbarnga, Ganta, Sanniquellie and

Bush Taxi Fares from Monrovia

to	distance (km)	duration	fares (US$)
Bo (Waterside)	140	2½ hours	4
Buchanan	150	3 hours	4
Harper	745	3 days	80
Sanniquellie	305	6 hours	16
Tubmanburg	70	1½ hours	3
Voinjama	395	11 hours	30

the Sierra Leone border, as well as to numerous other destinations. Several taxis weekly link the capital with almost everywhere else, although many routes (especially those connecting Zwedru with Greenville and Harper) are restricted during the rainy season. Minivans ('buses') ply most major routes, although they're more crowded and dangerous than bush taxis, and best avoided.

Sample journey times and fares for bush taxis are listed in the table. On most journeys the luggage surcharge should not exceed US$1 for a standard backpack. To charter a bush taxi, the price should be equivalent to the price for a single fare times the number of seats (five for small cars, nine for station wagons).

BOAT
Given the state of Liberia's road network, it's often faster to travel between coastal cities by boat. For those with time and a sense of adventure, fishing boats link most coastal cities. There are also frequent charter boats from Monrovia along the coast which sometimes have room for passengers. For more information on connections from Monrovia, see the Monrovia Getting There & Away section.

Monrovia

Monrovia suffered badly during the fighting of the past decade. Infrastructure was largely destroyed and most buildings gutted; many residents live in the most oppressive condi-

tions. However, despite its initially depressing appearance, the city has pep. It's also one of the friendliest capitals you are likely to visit in Africa. Pick a day when it's not raining, find some Liberian friends, and soon you'll forget you're walking around in what was only recently a war zone.

Information
For more details on changing money, and on post and communications services in Monrovia, see the relevant sections in Facts for the Visitor earlier in this chapter.

Tourist Office The Ministry of Culture, Information and Tourism on the corner of UN Drive and Gurley St can be helpful with specific questions if you're lucky enough to find the right people. However, they have no general tourist information.

Post & Communications The main post office, on the corner of Randall and Ashmun Sts, is open 8 am to 4 pm weekdays and 10 am to noon on Saturday.

Travel Agencies Karou Voyages (☎ 226 508) on Broad St is the best for regional and domestic flights. For booking Weasua flights and for intercontinental connections, try Gritaco Travel Agency (☎ 226 854). KLM-Royal Dutch Airlines has an office on Broad St, and Karou Voyages is the agent for Sabena/Swissair.

Bookshops Monrovia is not a good place to stock up on reading material; most books

LIBERIA

MONROVIA

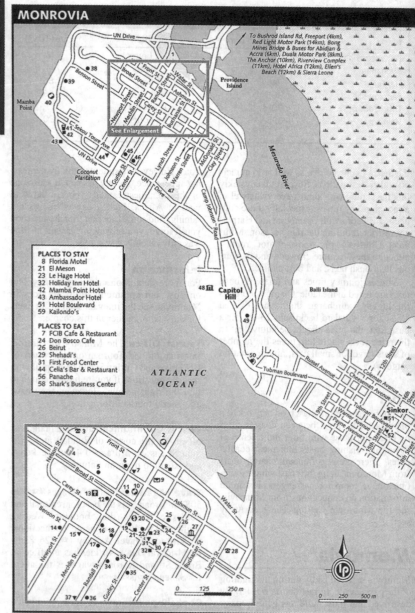

To Bushrod Island Rd, Freeport (4km),
Red Light Motor Park (14km), Bong
Mines Bridge & Buses for Abidjan &
Accra (6km), Duala Motor Park (8km),
The Anchor (10km), Riverview Complex
(11km), Hotel Africa (12km), Ellen's
Beach (12km) & Sierra Leone

PLACES TO STAY
8 Florida Motel
21 El Meson
23 Le Hage Hotel
32 Holiday Inn Hotel
42 Mamba Point Hotel
43 Ambassador Hotel
51 Hotel Boulevard
59 Kailondo's

PLACES TO EAT
7 FCIB Cafe & Restaurant
24 Don Bosco Cafe
26 Beirut
29 Shehadi's
31 First Food Center
44 Celia's Bar & Restaurant
56 Panache
58 Shark's Business Center

ATLANTIC
OCEAN

0   125   250 m

0   250   500 m

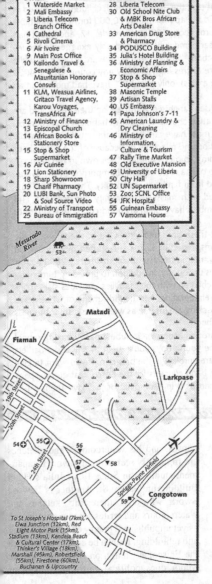

OTHER		
1	Waterside Market	
2	Mali Embassy	
3	Liberia Telecom	
	Branch Office	
4	Cathedral	
5	Rivoli Cinema	
6	Air Ivoire	
9	Main Post Office	
10	Kailondo Travel &	
	Senegalese &	
	Mauritanian Honorary	
	Consuls	
11	KLM, Weasua Airlines,	
	Gritaco Travel Agency,	
	Karou Voyages,	
	TransAfrica Air	
12	Ministry of Finance	
13	Episcopal Church	
14	African Books &	
	Stationery Store	
15	Stop & Shop	
	Supermarket	
16	Air Guinée	
17	Lion Stationery	
18	Sharp Showroom	
19	Charif Pharmacy	
20	LUBI Bank, Sun Photo	
	& Soul Source Video	
22	Ministry of Transport	
25	Bureau of Immigration	

27	National Museum	
28	Liberia Telecom	
30	Old School Nite Club	
	& MBK Bros African	
	Arts Dealer	
33	American Drug Store	
	& Pharmacy	
34	PODUSCO Building	
35	Julia's Hotel Building	
36	Ministry of Planning &	
	Economic Affairs	
37	Stop & Shop	
	Supermarket	
38	Masonic Temple	
39	Artisan Stalls	
40	US Embassy	
41	Papa Johnson's 7-11	
45	American Laundry &	
	Dry Cleaning	
46	Ministry of	
	Information,	
	Culture & Tourism	
47	Rally Time Market	
48	Old Executive Mansion	
49	University of Liberia	
50	City Hall	
52	UN Supermarket	
53	Zoo; SCNL Office	
54	JFK Hospital	
55	Guinean Embassy	
57	Vamoma House	

were lost during the war and those remaining are expensive. Occasionally, however, you'll find some decent second-hand books. A good place to look is the African Books & Stationery Store, which has Liberian history texts and some books by Liberians on Liberia.

Cultural Centres The US Information Service library is opposite the US embassy. Dated copies of the *International Herald Tribune* are available in the reading room.

Medical Services Pharmacies with a good selection of European and US items include American Drug Store & Pharmacy on Benson St (☎ 221 005, 8 am to 8 pm Monday to Saturday) and Charif Pharmacy on Randall St (8 am to 7.30 pm Monday to Saturday).

Dangers & Annoyances In Monrovia, there's a 10 pm to dawn curfew. Power is erratic or nonexistent in much of the city, so have a torch (flashlight) handy.

Things to See
The **National Museum** on Broad St is only a shadow of its former self. Much of the collection was destroyed or looted and all that remains is a handful of masks, drums and paintings accompanied by some interesting descriptions. However, it's still worth a visit; upstairs are a few dedicated and knowledgeable employees who will be happy to show you around. It's open from 8 am to 5 pm Monday to Saturday; admission is free.

Providence Island is where the first expedition of freed American slaves landed in 1822. There's not much to see now, although hopes are that the cultural centre will one day reopen.

Now in ruins, the **Masonic Temple** on Benson St was once Monrovia's major landmark. Since most Masons were Americo-Liberian descendants of the original settlers, the Temple was a prominent symbol of previous regimes. It was vandalised after the 1980 coup when the Masonic Order was

Liberia's Child Soldiers & Street Children

It's no secret that many of the guns shot during Liberia's civil war were wielded by young people. However, it is only since disarmament that the extent to which children were used in the factional fighting has become apparent. Of the approximately 20,000 former combatants disarmed under the August 1996 peace accord, about 4000 were under 17, and about half of these aged 15 or under. Although the disarmament figures probably exaggerate the involvement of children in the war (many factions pushed youths forward to disarm while withholding stronger forces), the numbers are distressingly high by any count. Of the 4000 young combatants (about 97% of whom are males), only about 8% have had more than an elementary level of schooling.

Now that the war is over, many of these disenfranchised youth are on the streets, and are often disillusioned and lacking sufficient education or skills to move to happier circumstances. While some were orphaned during the war, most have families but are unwilling or unable to return either for fear of community retaliation and rejection, or because of the difficulty of fitting into an established routine after spending so much time on their own in the bush.

These former combatants actually make up only a relatively small proportion of the overall number of young Liberians who are estranged from family or community. The near total suspension of schooling during the war, coupled with massive community displacement, and wartime deaths or separations from family members have led many hundreds more youth onto the streets, particularly in Monrovia.

There are several groups working to assist these boys and girls. One of the largest is the Catholic Salesian Fathers' Don Bosco Programs, based in Sinkor and staffed by a dedicated group of Liberians. At any one time, the program is in touch with approximately 2000 youths in Monrovia alone, and more at several centres upcountry. In addition to providing temporary night shelters, the program strives to reunify children with their families, provides skills training and works with communities to facilitate reintegration. For the girls, many of whom have turned to prostitution, health advice and counselling are offered as well as basic small business training to help them find an alternative livelihood.

Some skills training projects you may see around Monrovia include a pastry baking school and woodwork and craft centres. Many of the young boys you'll meet by the supermarkets and on the street in downtown Monrovia are enrolled in the program. If you want to give them some support, find out about upcoming band concerts for the Bosco Beat group, speak to staff at the Sinkor headquarters off Tubman Blvd in Monrovia, or just give them a few minutes of your time and attention.

---

banned. A grand master's throne from the temple, once used by William Tubman, now sits in dusty display at the National Museum.

Waterside Market is back in action and fun to walk around. You'll find everything here, although you must search for the good buys.

Art Exhibitions

Monrovia has a small circle of dedicated artists. Leslie Lumeh is one of the most well known, and his watercolours and sketches are frequently seen around town. His apartment-studio is in Suite 17 of Julia's Hotel Building on Gurley St. Another is Lawson Sworh, who does interesting sketches and watercolours and writes some good (though as yet unpublished) poetry on themes of war and rebuilding. He can be contacted through the Episcopal Church on Broad St. Wantue Major does political cartoons as well as paintings; some of his works are on display at the Mamba Point Hotel.

In addition to ongoing displays at Mamba Point Hotel, Celia's Bar occasionally has showings of local artists' work.

Activities

There are pools at Hotel Africa (US$5 per day for nonguests), Riverview Complex (US$5 per day for nonmembers) and Coconut Plantation (US$25 per month). Hotel Africa has a tennis court and there's a small squash court in Sinkor.

Places to Stay – Budget & Mid-Range

Good budget lodging is almost nonexistent in Monrovia. The best option is *Florida Hotel* on Front St with basic but acceptable rooms for US$16. It's reasonably clean, has a generator at night and fans in most rooms.

If they're full, try *Le Hage Hotel* on Gurley St. It's slightly cheaper at US$14, but has no other redeeming qualities. Women alone would probably not feel comfortable at either of these places.

The long-standing *El Meson* (☎ 227 871) on Carey St has decent rooms for US$40/60 single/double. There's running water for a few hours each morning and evening and generator power until 3 am.

The *Ambassador Hotel* is set on the beach off UN Drive and has acceptable but overpriced rooms for US$40; these benefits are marred by almost exclusive use for hourly rentals and the place isn't recommended.

If you don't mind noise and a sleazy atmosphere, *Kailondo's* (☎ 226 775) behind Spriggs-Payne airfield has a few new and comfortable rooms (next to its disco) with running water and generator for US$50; suites complete with centrally located toilet (right in the middle of the room) are US$100.

Places to Stay – Top End

Monrovia's best is *Mamba Point Hotel* (☎ 226 693, fax 226 050) along UN Drive on Mamba Point. For US$120/150 a single/ double and US$165 for a suite (plus 10% tax) you get a buffet breakfast and comfortable rooms with all the amenities.

Hotel Boulevard (☎ 227 348, fax 226 389) on the corner of 15th St and Tubman Blvd in Sinkor has comfortable rooms for US$100 a single, YS$125 a double and US$150 a suite, plus 10% tax. A 50% deposit is required at check-in. There are some good value rooms in an annexe for US$50/ 65 a single/double. They are primarily for long-term guests, but may be let out shortterm if not already booked.

Hotel Africa (☎ 226 039, ext 5610), 12km from the centre on the other side of the St Paul River, served as headquarters for UN operations in Liberia and has comfortable single/double rooms for US$115/175, plus 10% tax, although it remains to be seen whether conditions will be maintained once the UN departs.

Holiday Inn (☎ 224 332, fax 226 886), Carey St, has dark but moderately comfortable singles/doubles for US$75/100, plus 10% tax.

Places to Eat

The two best places for Liberian dishes are Carrington's *FCIB Cafe & Restaurant* and *Celia's Bar & Restaurant*.

Carrington's spotless, air-con restaurant is located in the walled compound directly behind the FCIB bank on the corner of Mechlin and Ashmun Sts, and features a different Liberian speciality each day from US$2. It's open daily except Sunday from about 11.30 am to 4 pm, and in the evenings until about 7 pm for drinks.

Celia's is a lively place with live music many evenings. It has an assortment of snacks and one or two main dishes from US$2; Celia will prepare to order with a few hours notice.

For good, inexpensive Lebanese food, the best is *Shehadi's*, Center St, with excellent felafels and other light dishes from US$3. It's open daily from 8 am to 8 pm (Sundays until 1 pm). Another place to try is *First Food Center*, Gurley St, with sandwiches and fast food from US$4.

Shark's Business Center, open Sundays and holidays only, is popular for ice cream and hamburgers. It's near Spriggs-Payne airfield.

For coffee and inexpensive snacks, try the friendly *Don Bosco Cafe* in the centre of Broad St opposite the Bureau of Immigration. Proceeds benefit a program for girls in distress.

The Anchor, on Bushrod Island (follow the signs to Island Hospital), is open in the evening only (closed Monday). It serves burgers, fish and chips and similar fare in large portions from about US$6. Occasionally there's live music.

Panache (☎ 226 629) in Sinkor is popular with groups, although the ambience is fairly mundane. Liberian specialities average US$13; seafood and other meals start at US$15. From the city centre, branch off Tubman Blvd on the airport shortcut road; it's a few hundred metres down on the left.

Further out of town, *Hotel Africa* has dishes from US$6. The indoor dining room is stale, but the outdoor tables are nice. *Beirut* (☎ 227 299), Center St, serves good but pricey Lebanese dishes for US$15.

The *Riverview Complex* restaurant (☎ 226 472) has a nice setting overlooking the St Paul River; it serves decent meals from US$10.

The meals at the *Mamba Point Hotel* are somewhat disappointing, but the restaurant has pleasant atmosphere and terrace overlooking the sea compensate. Main dishes start from about US$12. Their annexe, *Bitz & Pizzaz*, serves good pizzas from US$8.

Entertainment
Bars *Papa Johnson's 7-11* on Mamba Point has good views of the sea and is a popular watering hole for locals and expatriates alike. The terrace bar at *Mamba Point Hotel* is also popular for evening drinks. *Celia's* is full most afternoons and evenings, and sometimes has live music.

Nightclubs *Old School Nite Club* is co-owned by Liberian soccer star George Weah

and is popular. It's open Wednesday through Sunday evenings (US$10 cover charge on Friday and Saturday only).

Kailondo's has live music on Wednesday, Friday, Saturday and Sunday; it's most popular on Sunday afternoons.

The disco at the *Holiday Inn* draws a steady crowd of regulars (open Wednesday through Sunday; cover charge US$3 for men, US$1.50 for women). *Bacardi's Disco* at Hotel Africa (weekends only) is also popular; there's a US$4 cover charge.

Cinema *Rivoli Cinema*, on Broad St, may be operating again. For video rental, try Soul Source on Broad St.

Spectator Sports Soccer is popular in Monrovia; the local team, the Lone Stars, plays at the stadium near Elwa Junction, 12km south-east of town.

Shopping
Supermarkets There are several supermarkets in Monrovia selling a wide selection of products from the USA. A good one is Stop & Shop, with outlets on Benson and Randall Sts. The UN Supermarket on Tubman Blvd is also good, but doesn't have as wide a selection.

Art & Craftwork Craftmaking is slowly reviving. Try the artisan stalls diagonally opposite the US embassy on UN Drive – many items are imported or of average quality, but sometimes they have good pieces. Another place worth checking out is MBK Bros African Arts Dealer, Carey St, which sells (mostly imported) woodcarvings, musical instruments and stone statues; sometimes you'll come across a real find.

Textiles are sold by the *lapa* (2m) – the best place to look is Waterside Market near Gurley St.

Getting There & Away
Air For details on flights to and from Monrovia see the Getting There & Away section earlier in this chapter.

Bush Taxi & Minibus Bush taxis for Tubmanburg and the Sierra Leone border leave from Duala motor park, 9km north-east of the town centre. Transport for most other upcountry destinations, including the borders of Guinea and Côte d'Ivoire, leaves from Red Light, Monrovia's main motor park 15km north-east of the centre. Buses for Accra and Abidjan depart from the bus office near Bong Mines Bridge.

Boat Sam Kazouh (☎ 227 303) on the 1st floor of the Association of Evangelicals of Liberia building opposite PODUSCO on Randall St runs a weekly boat to Greenville (12 to 15 hours, US$30, deck seating only); days of departure vary. The boat leaves in the evening and then stays a day or two in Greenville before returning. If there are sufficient passengers, the boat continues to Harper (10 hours, US$50 from Monrovia).

A speedboat also goes sporadically between Monrovia and Harper (36 hours, US$60). Inquire at the 'fishing pier' at the port.

Getting Around

To/From the Airport Weasua is trying to organise a helicopter shuttle service between Robertsfield and Spriggs-Payne (US$25 one way), but for now your only option is US$2 for a shared taxi or US$12 in a private taxi. Shared taxis/private taxis from the city centre to Spriggs-Payne cost US$0.20/1.50.

Taxi Shared taxis are the primary means of public transport in Monrovia and can be a lot of fun. They operate on a zone system with prices ranging from US$0.10 to US$0.50. It's US$0.20 from the centre to Duala motor park and US$0.50 to Red Light motor park. Chartering a taxi within central Monrovia costs about US$1.35. Good places to catch a taxi include Waterside Market, Duala motor park and Broad St.

Car Mamba Point Hotel and Holiday Inn can both arrange car hire; otherwise, shopkeepers often have connections who can help. Petrol costs US$1.60 per gallon (US$1.50 for diesel).

AROUND MONROVIA

Currents on Liberia's beaches can be dangerous. Swimmers are frequently pulled in from Kendeja Beach, and there have been several drownings, so be warned.

In addition to the beaches listed below, countless beautiful spots line the coastline outside Monrovia, most accessible by unmarked dirt paths from the main road.

Shared taxis can drop you along the main road, from where you'll have to walk, usually between 1 and 2km.

Ellen's Beach

Ellen's Beach, just beyond Hotel Africa, is popular at weekends. It has large rocks offshore, moderate currents, and many people swim there. It has a kiosk where drinks are sold.

Kendeja

The beach at Kendeja, 15km south-east of the town centre on the Buchanan road, is prettier than Ellen's Beach and better for walking. The water is refreshing, although currents are strong. There's a US$0.50 admission fee and plenty of drink sellers.

Behind the beach is Kendeja Cultural Center, which is gradually being rehabilitated. It holds frequent dance performances complete with traditional costumes. The Ministry of Information, Tourism and Culture in Monrovia has scheduling information; admission averages US$0.75 per person. At weekends, you'll see the costumed dancers for free on the beach.

Thinker's Village

Thinker's Village (☎ 227 412), 1km beyond Kendeja, is the only beach offering food and lodging. Air-con rooms with bathroom are scheduled to open in early 1998 and will cost US$50; meals average around US$12. Admission to the compound costs US$0.75 at weekends.

Marshall

Marshall, about an hour's drive south-east from Monrovia, at the confluence of the Junk, Farmington and Little Bassa rivers with the sea, has a lagoon and a pretty stretch of beach which is usually deserted.

Firestone Plantation

Firestone – the world's largest rubber plantation – began in 1926 when the Firestone tyre company secured one million acres of land in Liberia at an annual rent of only US$0.06 per acre. In its heyday, the company employed 20,000 workers: more than 10% of Liberia's labour force, and Liberia was once known as the Firestone Republic.

After lying dormant during the war, Firestone is again operating, although at greatly reduced capacity; exports resumed in 1997. There are no regular tours, but you will probably to find employees on the grounds who can show you around and explain the tapping process. Stick to the beaten path, as Firestone is one of several areas in Liberia where land mines have been found.

The plantation is in Harbel, near Robertsfield airport. You'll need private transport to get here.

The Coast

ROBERTSPORT

Robertsport, once a relaxing beach town, was completely destroyed during the war. No infrastructure remains, although the beaches are still beautiful. They are said to offer some of the best surfing along the West African coast. During World War II, Robertsport was used as an Allied submarine base; you can still see relics of this era.

Lake Piso, separating Robertsport from the mainland, often flows onto the road during the rainy season; inquire first in Monrovia about conditions before heading there.

There is no lodging at Robertsport. There's a small fishing village in town with basic provisions only.

BUCHANAN

Buchanan is Liberia's second port and the capital of Grand Bassa County. During the war, the town was inundated by refugees fleeing fighting in the surrounding countryside, although infrastructure within its borders remained relatively intact.

Stick to the beaten path on the outskirts of Buchanan and in the vegetated strip bordering the beaches as some areas were mined during the war.

Things to See & Do

South-east of the port are some beautiful beaches, but beware of the strong currents. Follow the port road to the old Lamco Compound, then ask locals the way.

There's a large Fanti community in Buchanan. North-west of the town centre is their lively fishing village (Fanti Town) set on a colourful cove; you'll feel as if you've just walked into Ghana.

Places to Stay

Lodging is still at a premium in Buchanan. Apart from private guesthouses, your best bet is the NGOs Center, 2km north of the centre, which, despite its name, is also open to independent travellers. Fairly basic rooms in an office building cost US$10 per person with shared bathroom. Staff will cook meals for a reasonable fee if you supply the food. It's signposted and is 1.5km from the main road.

If you're desperate, try the Konah Motel near the main taxi stand with basic, dirty rooms for US$4; at least the owner is friendly. You can sometimes arrange with locals to rent a room for a few dollars at the old Lamco Compound, 3km south of the centre.

Places to Eat

For an inexpensive meal, try Franmah's Bar & Restaurant on Tubman St; it offers a variety of Liberian dishes from US$1.35 a plate.

Gbehzon near the port has a pleasant setting on the water, and prices are very reasonable. You can get drinks any time, and grilled fish or other simple meals with lots of advance notice.

Capital Hill is a decent chop house with dishes from US$1.35. For coffee or a snack,

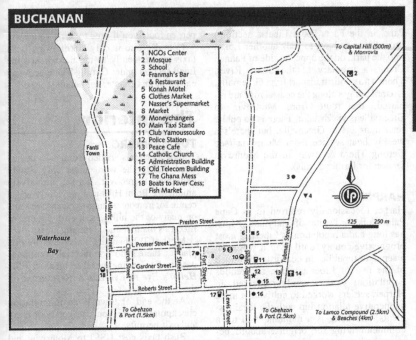

BUCHANAN

1 NGOs Center
2 Mosque
3 School
4 Franmah's Bar & Restaurant
5 Konah Motel
6 Clothes Market
7 Nasser's Supermarket
8 Market
9 Moneychangers
10 Main Taxi Stand
11 Club Yamoussoukro
12 Police Station
13 Peace Cafe
14 Catholic Church
15 Administration Building
16 Old Telecom Building
17 The Ghana Mess
18 Boats to River Cess; Fish Market

To Capital Hill (500m) & Monrovia

Fanti Town

Waterhouse Bay

Atlantic Street
Church Street
Prosser Street
Gardner Street
Roberts Street
Fuller Street
Fort Street
Preston Street
Kilby Street
Tumban Street
Lewis Street

0   125   250 m

To Gbehzon & Port (1.5km)
To Gbehzon & Port (2.5km)
To Lamco Compound (2.5km) & Beaches (4km)

---

try the *Peace Cafe* on Tubman St; proceeds assist children in distress.

Entertainment

The two hot spots for evening entertainment are *Club Yamoussoukro* on Kilby St and *The Ghana Mess* on Roberts St. Both are open every evening. Yamoussoukro's has dancing occasionally and The Ghana Mess sometimes has live music.

Getting There & Away

Bush taxis run daily to Monrovia (three hours, US$4). From Monrovia, it's better to get a taxi at Elwa Junction than at the hectic Red Light motor park. During the dry season several cars (4WD) a week travel to Cess River (US$10), an all-day journey on a bad road. It's often faster to take a fishing boat, although safety can be a serious concern. There are no set fees or schedules; boats

leave from Fanti Town and from the beach west of the centre.

Bush taxis for all destinations depart from the main taxi stand near the market; some taxis also leave from the junction on the Monrovia road several kilometres from town.

GREENVILLE

Greenville (sometimes called Sinoe) is the capital of Sinoe County. It was completely destroyed during the war, but is likely to quickly revive, thanks to its port and to significant logging interests in the area. It has a beach, but to reach the open sea you must cross a shallow lagoon. There is no commercial accommodation in town.

Greenville is the starting point for excursions to **Sapo National Park**, reached by driving (4WD only) 60km north to Juarzon and then heading south-east 5km to Jalay's

Town in the park's buffer zone. (For more details see the boxed text 'Sapo National Park' in the Facts about Liberia section.) From here you have to walk another 1.5km into the park, on the opposite side of Pahneh Creek, a tributary of the Sinoe River. There's no public transport from Greenville.

Until bridges along the coastal road are repaired, the route from Monrovia to Greenville is via Zwedru. There is no public road transport to Greenville, but there's a weekly boat service from Monrovia (see Getting There & Away in the Monrovia section for further details).

HARPER

Harper (occasionally referred to as Cape Palmas) is the capital of Maryland, which has long had a reputation as Liberia's most progressive county; until 1857 it was even a separate republic. In contrast with much of the rest of Liberia where indigenous populations were severely repressed, in Harper, settlers worked to cultivate a more cooperative relationship with the local residents, and there is a monument in town commemorating the original accord between settlers and locals.

Harper was also the seat of Liberia's first university (Cuttington, since transferred to Gbarnga), and the traditional centre of education in the country.

Now Harper is just a shell of its former self, and only ruins remain of the many fine old houses which once graced its streets, including President William Tubman's residence. The surrounding area, however, is very attractive.

A boat runs sporadically between Harper and Monrovia. See the Monrovia Getting There & Away section for further details.

Road access from Monrovia is via Tappita and Zwedru, then south to the coast. You'll need your own transport. Under good conditions, it's a three day journey in a 4WD; during the rainy season the road from Zwedru becomes impassable. There's no accommodation en route, other than what locals may offer (US$1/2 would be an appropriate amount). In Harper itself, the only

accommodation is with mission guesthouses. Food and other basics are available in Harper; en route you'll need to bring your own.

Côte d'Ivoire is only 20km away; bush taxis go frequently to the border. See the Land section under Getting There & Away earlier in this chapter for details.

The Interior

TUBMANBURG

Tubmanburg (also called Bomi) was devastated during the war and is only slowly beginning to recover. It's set attractively among the **Bomi Hills** and previously was a centre for iron ore mining – you can see scars on many of the hillsides. It also was one of Liberia's main diamond mining areas.

Most of Tubmanburg's residents are displaced; there's no commercial accommodation. For an inexpensive meal, try *Sis Helen's Eye to Eye Bar & Restaurant* on the main road.

At the end of town is an immigration checkpoint where you can get both entry and exit permits.

Bush taxis cost US$3 to Monrovia, and US$25 to either the Guinean or Sierra Leone borders, although direct transport to either country is infrequent. Most bush taxis for Sierra Leone go via Bo (Waterside).

GBARNGA

Gbarnga was Charles Taylor's centre of operations during the war and became virtually the second capital of Liberia. About 10km from Gbarnga on the Monrovia road is **Phebe**, site of Cuttington College. On campus are ruins of the old Africana Museum, which once had a very good collection of 3000 pieces. Now – thanks to looting and the war – only fragments remain. Efforts are under way to restore the museum, with pieces from the original collection being found in places like Brooklyn, New York. Unfortunately it's unlikely that many will ever be recovered.

About 30km north-west of Cuttington are the pretty **Kpatawe Falls**; take the dirt road opposite Phebe Hospital. You'll need either a bike or a 4WD; taxis don't ply the road. There's a village before the falls, but there's no accommodation or restaurants here.

About 40km north of Gbarnga on the Voinjama road, near Gbalatoah and just before the bridge over the St Paul River, is the site of former President Tolbert's house, **Tolbert Farms**, with beautiful views over the surrounding area.

Places to Stay & Eat
In Phebe, *Jalk Enterprises Restaurant & Store* (Josephine's) has adequate rooms with fan and shared bathroom for US$20 and a nice restaurant (closed Sunday lunch) offering one or two daily dishes.

If they're full, try *Villa de Via Classique*, a few kilometres further down the Monrovia road, which is said to have tennis courts and rooms for US$25.

In addition to the restaurant at Josephine's, Gbarnga has several chop bars.

About 60km from Gbarnga between Totota and Salala is the *Coo Coo Nest* (also known as Tubman Farms), formerly President Tubman's private residence and now a hotel with relatively comfortable rooms with bathroom for US$35 (US$50 when the generator is working). The name is said to come from Tubman's term of endearment for his daughter. When the generator works, there's also a disco and a restaurant. Across the road is a small coffee shop and a base for Charles Taylor's radio station.

Getting There & Away
Bush taxis go frequently from Gbarnga to Monrovia (six hours, US$10). Taxis from Gbarnga to Phebe Junction (US$0.60) leave from the taxi union parking lot at the top of the hill just off the highway. You need your own transport if you want to get to Coo Coo Nest.

GANTA
Ganta is a pleasant, bustling town 2km from the Guinean border. Its official name (and the one you'll still see on some maps) is Gompa City.

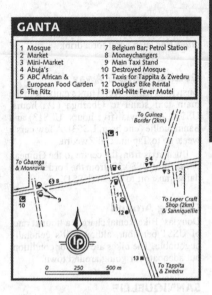

GANTA

1 Mosque	7 Belgium Bar; Petrol Station
2 Market	8 Moneychangers
3 Mini-Market	9 Main Taxi Stand
4 Abuja's	10 Destroyed Mosque
5 ABC African &	11 Taxis for Tappita & Zwedru
European Food Garden	12 Douglas' Bike Rental
6 The Ritz	13 Mid-Nite Fever Motel

On a street running north off the main road there's an interesting **mosque**, the design of which is said to be unique in Liberia. Just out of town on the Sanniquellie road is a good **craft shop** at the leper institution with excellent basketry and woodcarvings. It's open daily, except Sunday, from 8 am to 6 pm.

You can change money with the moneychangers around the taxi stands, or with shop owners.

Places to Stay & Eat
The only commercial lodging is *Mid-Nite Fever Motel* on the Tappita road; it has basic singles/doubles with surprisingly clean sheets (and with fan, if the generator is working) for US$7/9. Bring your own mosquito net.

Anthony Buster Clinton's *ABC African & European Food Garden*, has chicken and other meals from US$2.50. *Abuja's* next door is a more basic chop bar with rice dishes (around US$1) and drinks.

The *Mini-Market* opposite the market is the best stocked supermarket, selling a variety of basic provisions.

For cold drinks and dancing try *The Ritz* opposite the Tappita road. Opposite is *Belgium Bar*, also good for a drink.

Getting There & Away

Bush taxis leave several times daily from the main taxi stand to Gbarnga (1½ hours, US$3), Monrovia (five hours, US$13) and Sanniquellie (one hour, US$3). A few cars a week go to Tappita and Zwedru.

Bush taxis from the centre to the Guinean border cost US$0.30; from the border there's daily transport to Diéké (US$1).

Getting Around

Douglas' Bike Rental charges a 'tourist rate' of US$1 per hour, although it's generally negotiable. The bikes are in poor condition, but adequate for going around town.

SANNIQUELLIE

Sanniquellie is important historically as the birthplace of the Organisation of African Unity. On the main road into town is the building where William Tubman, Sekou Touré and Kwame Nkrumah met in 1957 to discuss a union of African states – a concept which was formalised in 1958 with the drafting of a preliminary charter. The compound is now used to house official visitors. Market day is Saturday.

Places to Stay & Eat

The only place to stay is the *Traveller's Inn Motel*, 500m off the main road; look for an inconspicuous white sign on the road from Monrovia. Basic rooms with shared bathroom are US$4 a single, US$7 a double and US$8 for a large room. There are a few *chop houses* along the main road, none worthy of distinction, and a few reasonably well stocked shops.

Getting There & Away

Bush taxis for the Côte d'Ivoire border (US$4) and Yekepa (US$3) congregate north of the market, while those for Ganta (US$3) and Monrovia (US$16) leave from the other end.

YEKEPA

Yekepa, in the north near the Guinean border and about 350m above sea level, has a pleasant climate and good views of the lush surrounding mountains, although the town itself has been completely destroyed. Former residents are only gradually beginning to make their way back. Given increased stability and infrastructure, the area holds potential for some good hiking, although you'll need a machete to hack through the underbrush. Nearby is **Guesthouse Hill** in the Nimba range, Liberia's highest peak at 1362m.

Before the war, Yekepa was the company town of Lamco and site of some of the world's richest iron ore deposits.

Places to Stay & Eat

There's no commercial accommodation in Yekepa. A few of the Lamco houses are in decent condition and their owners are sometimes willing to rent out rooms. *Ma Edith's* on the central market square is friendly and your best bet for a meal. Otherwise, try *Zay Duan Lay Food Center* near the market.

Getting There & Away

The Guinean border is just a few kilometres away; you'll have to walk as there's no transport. Transport from the border to Lola costs US$1.50. For Côte d'Ivoire, you'll have to go to Sanniquellie and then via Kahnple towards Danané.

There's no regular transport in or to Yekepa. Saturday, market day, is the only day when you can count on a lift to Sanniquellie.

Mali

MALI AT A GLANCE

Capital: Bamako
Population: 12 million
Area: 1,240,140 sq km
Head of state: Alpha Oumar Konaré
Official language: French
Main local languages: Bambara, Fula, Tamashek, Dogon, Bozo, Songhaï
Currency: West African CFA franc
Exchange rate: US$1 = CFA600
Time: GMT/UTC
Country telephone code: ☎ 223
Best time to go: October to February

Timbuktu is that place you always heard about, but could never find on the map. But now you know: it's in Mali, where you can also see the edge of the Sahara, the great River Niger, nomads on camels crossing the desert, and beautiful mud-brick mosques dating from medieval times. Other highlights include: Mopti, a busy river port and the centre of Mali's fledgling tourist industry; Djenné, an ancient city with one of the best markets in the region; and Bamako, the lively capital, large enough to have amenities and small enough to cover on foot.

Away from the towns, adventure seekers can travel down the River Niger by boat, head into the desert, or go trekking along the spectacular escarpment in Dogon Country, the Falaise de Bandiagara. All these are just some of the attractions that make Mali the jewel in the crown of West Africa.

Facts about Mali

HISTORY

In the 1st millennium AD, organised societies flourished in the Sahel, and included the Empire of Ghana (unrelated to the modern country of the same name) which covered much of today's Mali and parts of Senegal. This was followed by the great Empire of Mali, which in the 14th century stretched from the Atlantic Ocean to present-day Nigeria and controlled most of the extremely lucrative trans-Saharan trade. Timbuktu became a centre of commerce and Islamic culture during this period. The Empire of Mali was later eclipsed by the

Empire of Songhaï, which was finally destroyed by Berber armies from Morocco in the late 16th century. At the same time, the European maritime nations began circumventing the Saharan trade routes by sending ships along the coast of West Africa. They broke the monopoly and power of the Sahel empires, sending Timbuktu and the region's other cities into oblivion. For more details about the precolonial history of this region, see the Facts about the Region chapter earlier in this book.

The Colonial Period

By the end of the 19th century, Mali was part of French West Africa. Remnants of this colonial period visible today include the largest irrigation works (the Office du Niger, near Ségou) and the longest railway span (1200km between Dakar and Bamako) in West Africa. However, Mali always remained the poor relative of territories such as Senegal and Côte d'Ivoire. France's chief interest was in 'developing' Mali as a source of cheap cash crops (rice and cotton) for export.

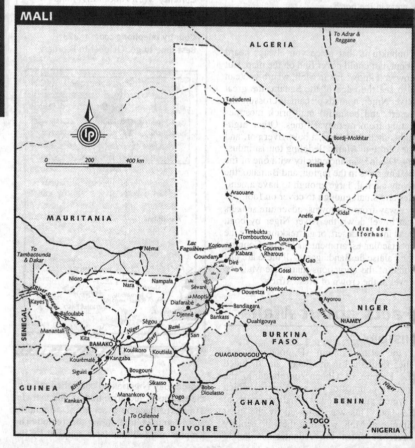

Independence

Mali became independent in 1960 (for a few months it was federated with Senegal) and its first president, Modibo Keita, embarked on an unsuccessful period of socialism, employing Soviet advisers, although political ties were also maintained with France. Newly formed state corporations took control of the economy, down to the level of supermarkets, but all began losing money except the cotton enterprise, which benefited from a fairly reliable world market. Ambitious planning schemes went awry, resulting in unpopular austerity measures. Eventually, in 1968, Keita was overthrown when a group of army officers, led by Moussa Traoré, staged a bloodless coup.

The Traoré Years

To the outside world, embroiled in the Cold War, things in Mali seemed relatively calm during the next two decades. Still, there were four coup attempts and a student strike which, according to Amnesty International, resulted in 13 young people being shot or tortured to death. Another cause for concern were the continual food shortages, which were conveniently blamed on the droughts but were largely due to government mismanagement.

In 1979, Mali was officially returned to civilian rule, although the single party permitted to exist remained tied to the military, and Moussa Traoré remained head of state. During the 1980s Soviet influence waned, and a free enterprise system was reinstalled. Several state-owned companies were sold, and the government withdrew from the grain business, long a recommendation of the west. By 1987, Mali had an estimated grain surplus of 150,000 tonnes – more than the deficit during the great 1983-84 drought. Adequate rainfall was the main reason, but policy change may have helped.

During the droughts of the 1980s the Tuareg people of northern Mali suffered considerably, leading to calls for an independent Tuareg state. In 1990 a group of Tuareg separatists attacked some isolated army posts in the Gao region, and the sol-

diers' heavy-handed retaliation led to further fighting. Militias made up mainly of Songhaï people, traditional enemies of the Tuareg, were drawn into the conflict: hundreds of people were killed on both sides and the north was in a state of virtual civil war through much of the early 1990s.

Meanwhile, there was disquiet in other parts of the country. Talk of multiparty democracy had begun in 1989 and became increasingly open, mainly through *Les Échos*, an opposition newspaper. In late 1990, a peaceful pro-democracy demonstration drew some 30,000 people onto the streets of Bamako, and in January 1991 a general strike for higher salaries paralysed the capital for two days.

Massive strikes and protests demanding multiparty democracy and freedom of the press continued through early 1991, reaching a head on 17 March when security forces met students and other demonstrators with machine-gun fire. Three days of rioting followed, during which 150 people were killed.

That three day slaughter finally provoked the army, led by Amadou Toumani Touré, to once again take control. Moussa Traoré was arrested, and around 60 senior government figures were executed. The Minister of Education and the president's brother-in-law were reportedly burned alive.

Touré established an interim transitional government, and gained considerable respect from the people of Mali, and the outside world, when he resigned a year later and kept his promise to hold multiparty elections.

The 1990s

Of the several political parties formed, the largest by far was the Alliance for Democracy in Mali (ADEMA), headed by Alpha Oumar Konaré, a scientist and former publisher of *Les Échos*. Konaré was elected president in June 1992 and ADEMA won a large majority of seats in the national assembly, but less than a year later serious anti-government rioting again broke out in Bamako. Konaré's immediate response was to put army patrols on the streets, but later he included several opposition figures in a reshuffled coalition government. However, in December 1993, five army officers were arrested, accused of plotting to overthrow the government, and in February 1994 there was more unrest in Bamako, this time with students protesting about the devaluation of the CFA franc.

Meanwhile, sporadic fighting between Tuareg rebels and government forces continued in the north. Konaré allowed more Tuareg representation in the army, civil service and government, but negotiations in mid-1994 struggled to find common ground, as some groups continued to demand an independent Tuareg homeland. The situation was complicated in the north by bandits exploiting the anti-government unrest. In 1995, vehicles on the roads around Gao were travelling in armed convoys.

In 1996 another truce was arranged, and Tuareg refugees began returning from Mauritania and Algeria (where they had gone to escape the unrest) to northern Mali – particularly the area around Timbuktu – where they now exist on hand-outs from aid organisations. This partly compensates for herds lost in the droughts and fighting, but it can never replace the traditional nomadic lifestyle, pivotal to the Tuareg's cultural identity, which so many have been forced to abandon.

Mali Today

Presidential and national assembly elections were held in 1997, with Konaré's ADEMA and the opposition Party for Unity Development and Progress the only runners. The process was marred by irregularities and took about four months to complete, but in the end Konaré was resoundingly re-elected with 96% of the vote (although only about one in five people voted). Nevertheless, Konaré's belief in negotiation and compromise seems to have won him the support of the people. Mali is a country on the up, with optimism in the air, as the government genuinely attempts to work towards a democratic multiparty system. The economy is improving and there has been increased spending on schools and health centres in rural areas.

The Tuareg issue lingers in the background, although by 1998 peace had returned to the north, and both Timbuktu and Gao could be reached by visitors. Despite genuine steps towards reconciliation, a few government hard-liners believe the Tuareg are a spent force. The only cloud on the horizon comes from cynics who say the Tuareg have been pacified with aid funds; if this money dries up, the Tuareg will be a people with nothing to lose and may pick up their guns again.

GEOGRAPHY

Mali is the largest country in West Africa measuring over 1.2 million sq km, and is divided into three main areas. In the north the Sahara Desert covers over half the country. The south is relatively well watered allowing cultivation without irrigation, and this area is the most densely populated. In between these two areas is the semidesert Sahel zone where rainfall can fluctuate which often causes great havoc for farmers.

Mali's major geographical feature is the River Niger, which flows in a great curve (the 'Niger Bend' or Boucle du Niger) through the country. The river rises in the Fouta Djalon highlands of Guinea, and flows north-east, past Bamako, to Mopti where it spreads out to form a maze of channels swamps and lakes called the Niger Inland Delta. The top of the Bend touches the edge of the Sahara near Timbuktu, and the river then flows south-east through Niger and Nigeria to the Atlantic.

CLIMATE

The rainy season is from June to September however, rainfall is rare in the north, heaviest in the south, and from 200 to 800mm per year in the Sahel. The hot season is from March to May, when temperatures frequently exceed 40°C. The harmattan blows from December to February.

ECOLOGY & ENVIRONMENT

Mali's most urgent environmental issue is desertification – a threat to virtually all parts of the country which are not desert already

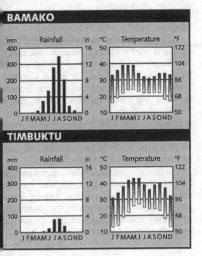

The Mopti and Gao areas are particularly affected, but even in the well watered south, forests have been cleared. The multiple causes of desertification stem, ultimately, from excessive population pressures, poverty and a high demand on wood for fuel and building. Overgrazing is another contributing factor, despite the droughts in the 1970s and 80s which severely cut Mali's livestock herds.

For a discussion of the impact of tourists on Mali's environment, see the Responsible Tourism section in Facts for the Visitor later.

FLORA & FAUNA

Mali is one of the Sahel countries of West Africa – for more information about the vegetation of the Sahel, see the boxed text 'The Sahel' in the Geography section of the Facts about the Region chapter.

Birds in Mali are mainly savanna species, but there's a good range for a country with no coast, and over 650 species have been recorded. Among the best places for birdwatching is the Niger Inland Delta downstream from Mopti, a vital oasis on the edge of the desert for native and migrant species. Other places along the river such as Ségou and San, or

outside Bamako on the roads to Koulikoro or Kangaba, can also be very rewarding. Bee-eaters and rollers are among the colourful birds commonly spotted, and Egyptian plover can also be seen. The country's only endemic is the Mali firefinch. For more general information on birds, see the special section 'Birds of West Africa' at the beginning of this book.

Mali is not a major wildlife destination, although a few large mammals can be found here.

National Parks

The Parc National de la Boucle du Baoule was once known for its large herds of elephant and buffalo, several species of gazelle and buck, and carnivores such as lion, but it is seldom visited today. The park lies in the west of the country between two large bends on the River Baoule, a tributary of the River Senegal. Its vegetation is predominantly wooded savanna. Access is restricted to tour groups or visitors in their own vehicle. However, no tour companies run trips here, as facilities are very limited and the wildlife has been ravaged by poaching. Most mammals are now restricted to remote parts of the park, although birdwatching is reported to be good. If you're particularly keen on visiting, more information might be available from Mr Togola, director of the Musée National in Bamako.

Mali's other protected areas are even more remote and inaccessible: the Parc National du Bafing, an area of hills near the Guinea border, and bordering the lake formed by the Manantali Dam, south-west of Kita; and the Réserve d'Ansongo-Menaka on the Niger border, south-east of Gao.

Of most interest to visitors, although still quite difficult to reach, is the Réserve de Douentza, a vast area of semidesert north of the main road between Mopti and Gao, which is home to Mali's remarkably hardy herds of desert elephant. For more details see the boxed text 'Elephants of Timbuktu' in the Around Timbuktu section later in this chapter.

MALI

GOVERNMENT & POLITICS

In August 1991 the country's constitution was changed to allow a multiparty political system. The national assembly has around 80 members elected by universal suffrage every three years. Head of state is the president, currently Alpha Oumar Konaré, described by *The Economist* as 'one of the truly democratic African leaders to have emerged in the last decade'. His party, the Alliance for Democracy in Mali (ADEMA), dominates the government but enjoys genuine popular support, although the last election was boycotted by opposition parties who remain divided. American advisers brought in to assist with the legislative progress have reported that there is a genuine desire within the Konaré government to democratise the political process. A constitutional court remains safely independent of the government, and a presidential council includes representatives from opposition parties, allowing them a platform denied by the ADEMA-dominated national assembly. There are few press restrictions, and government corruption is being seriously tackled.

ECONOMY

Mali's economy is dominated by agriculture; millet and rice are grown for domestic consumption, while export crops include cotton and groundnuts. After some decades in the doldrums, cotton production has increased, and Mali is now the second largest producer in Africa (after Egypt). Gold is being commercially mined, and economic reports indicate that Mali will soon become a major producer in Africa. Overall, however, the country still suffers from a negative balance of trade and the effects of international debt repayments. Per capita GNP is US$250, and according to the UN Human Development Index, Mali remains one of the poorest countries in the world.

POPULATION & PEOPLE

Mali's population is estimated at about 12 million people, with a population growth rate of 2.9%. This would be higher if Mali didn't have the world's second highest infant mortality rate (164 per 1000 live births).

Mali's most prominent ethnic groups are the Bambara (who call themselves Bamana), the Tuareg and the Dogon. (For more details on these people see the Society & Conduct section following and the colour feature between pages 608 and 609.) Other groups include the Fula (also called Peul), semi-nomadic herders widely spread across West Africa; the Bozo, traditionally fishers, found all along the River Niger; and the Songhaï, concentrated in the area around Gao.

There is considerable intermarriage between people of different ethnic groups, the common tie being Islam. Among some groups who do not intermarry, the *cousinage*, or 'joking cousins', relationship exists (eg between Dogon and Bozo).

ARTS
Art & Craftwork

Mali's famous sculptural traditions date back to the 12th century, when figures in terracotta, bronze and gold were created by the inhabitants of Djenné and surrounding towns. These sculptures usually depict a kneeling person with stylised eyes.

Woodcarvings made by the Bambara people are noted for their angular forms. Figures called *flanitokele* are carved in a rigid frontal posture with an elongated torso, arms held stiffly to the side, often with palms out, and conical breasts. Fine details are incised on the darkened surface using a hot knife. The Bambara also produce a wide range of masks and headdresses. Masks are usually bold and solid, with human and animal features incorporated into the design, and often used in secret society ceremonies. Perhaps no piece of African art is better known than the *chiwara*, a headpiece carved in the form of an antelope, and used in ritualistic dances. Air Afrique even uses the chiwara as its company logo.

The Bozo, who fish along the River Niger, sculpt a mask representing a sacred ram called *saga*.

The Bambara also produce striking bogolan or mud cloth – see the colour feature on textiles between page 128 and 129 for more details.

The art of the Dogon people is discussed in detail in the illustrated section 'The Dogon' later in this chapter.

Music

Mali's cultural diversity affords a wealth of great music, not only from the Bambara who dominate the scene, but also from the Tuareg, Songhaï, Fula, Dogon and Bozo people. Best known are the *griots* (also called *jalis*), a hereditary caste of musicians who fulfil many important functions in Malian society. You can easily tell whether a musician or singer comes from a griot family by their family name: Diabaté, Kouyaté and Sissoko are the most common. Many of Mali's modern singers are members of the griot caste, and you'll see and hear many musicians with these family names. The female griottes of Mali are famed throughout West Africa for the beauty and power of their voice, some of the most famous singers including Ami Koita, Fanta Damba, Tata Bambo Kouyaté and Mariam Kouyaté.

In Mali's early days of independence, the government encouraged African traditions in art and culture. Several state-sponsored 'orchestras' playing popular music were founded, whose members were technically employees of nationalised industries. Some of the greatest pop music to come out of Africa was produced by these orchestras, but much of it is very hard to obtain nowadays. Musicians with the legendary Rail Band de Bamako were actually employed by the Mali Railway Corporation. One of its most famous ex-members is Salif Keita, whose albums Soro and Ko-Yan were landmarks in the World Music explosion that swept across Europe in the 1980s and 90s.

Mali's wealth of talented female singers makes it difficult to pick out the best; however, as far as popularity in Mali goes, Oumou Sangaré would easily win. Her songs deal with contemporary social issues in Mali, and she addresses topics like polygamy and arranged marriages. Her style of music is influenced by the musical traditions of the Wassoulou region of south-western Mali, and features the kamelen-ngoni, a large six-stringed harp-lute. She has three CDs available internationally. If you like her music, also look out for recordings by Sali Sidibé and Kagbe Sidibé.

The enigmatic Ali Farka Touré is perhaps Africa's best known modern musician, although he's far more popular abroad than at home. His blues-influenced sound (he was a big fan of John Lee Hooker in the 60s) highlights similarities between the music of Africa and the Mississippi delta; some of his recommended releases are *The River* and *Radio Mali*.

Some of Mali's other popular artists include Les Amdassadeurs, Super Biton de

Salif Keita

Salif Keita is perhaps the most famous singer in West Africa. A direct descendant of Sundiata Keita, the founder of the Empire of Mali in the 13th century, Salif chose his career in music against the wishes of his family who considered such an occupation to be beneath their noble standing. In 1970 he joined the Rail Band of Bamako and later he left to form Les Ambassadeurs. In 1978 Salif left Mali for Côte d'Ivoire and created a new band, Les Ambassadeurs Internationaux, whose first release *Mandjou* was a great success. Playing the role of a *griot* in *Mandjou,* Salif sang the praises of the Touré family. The former president of Guinea, Sekou Touré, was so moved by it that he made Salif an Officer of the National Order. Salif's solo career began with the album *Soro*, a masterpiece that launched him onto the international stage, and which was one of the most influential recordings of African music in the 1980s.

An outspoken opponent of racism, a man 'with white skin and black blood' (he is albino), Salif now plays concerts in all corners of the world, returning to Mali regularly for inspiration.

Graeme Counsel

Ségou, Zani Diabaté, Toumani Diabaté and
Lobi. Rising Malian stars include Djenaba
Seck, Nahawa Doumbia, Teningnini Demba,
Fantani Touré, Souleymane Traoré and Kon
Kan Kon Sata.

SOCIETY & CONDUCT

The largest ethnic group in Mali are the
Bambara, concentrated in the south and west,
and comprising about one quarter of the
country's population. Many senior positions
in the government are occupied by Bambara
people. The Bambara are also renowned for
their art – especially woodcarvings.

The Tuareg inhabit the fringes of the
Sahara, and are found in Niger and other
countries, but most visitors encounter them
in Mali – especially in Timbuktu. The men
are famous for their flowing indigo robes
and turbans to protect them from sun and
sand. The cloth is traditionally dyed without
using water (a limited resource in the
desert) and over time the indigo becomes
impregnated in the skin, like a tattoo –
hence the romantic 'blue men of the desert'
title. The Tuareg people are fiercely proud
of their Caucasian descent and feel themselves to be superior to black Malians –
especially the Bambara, with whom they
have a history of conflict. The Tuareg were
famous for their fighting abilities and
artwork which, not surprisingly, adorns
swords and other metal objects.

The Dogon are incredibly industrious
farmers, and are famous for their complex
mythology and elaborate artistic abilities.
Their homeland is the Falaise de Bandiagara
(Bandiagara Escarpment), some 100km east
of Mopti, designated a World Heritage site
for its cultural and natural significance. (For
more details, see the illustrated section 'The
Dogon' later in this chapter.)

RELIGION

Approximately 75% of the population is
Muslim. The remainder of the people hold
traditional beliefs and a few are Christian,
although there is considerable overlap.
Islam in Mali is conservative but influential;
that less than 20% of women work outside
the home (the lowest rate in West Africa),
compared with around 50% in mainly non-
Muslim Burkina Faso, may be a reflection
of its cultural impact.

LANGUAGE

While French is the official language, the
most widely spoken African language is
Bambara, similar to the Mandinka/Malinké
spoken in Senegal and Gambia, and the
Dioula spoken in several countries to the
south. In contrast, the Dogon language is
spoken in a relatively compact area, but even
so it is divided into some 48 dialects, Sangha
being a major one. Other languages include
Bozo along the River Niger, and Songhaï
around Gao and Timbuktu. See the Language chapter for useful phrases in French,
Bambara and Dioula.

Facts for the Visitor

SUGGESTED ITINERARIES

If you've only got one week in Mali, you'll
almost certainly want to head for Mopti, the
centre of Mali's rapidly growing tourist
scene. This is also the base for visiting the
ancient mosque and market at Djenné and
for arranging a trip into Dogon Country.
Two weeks would make this journey less of
a rush, and you could also fit in Timbuktu
(although it would probably mean flying
there and back).

With three weeks you could really start to
do all of these places justice, spending a day
or two at Djenné (ideally tying in with the
great Monday market), a couple of days in
Timbuktu (plus another three or four getting
there by boat along the River Niger) and
putting aside anything from three to 10 days
for some top-quality hiking or trekking in
Dogon Country.

With four weeks or maybe some trimming
off the three-week trip outlined earlier, you
could spend a day or two in Bamako wandering around the lively streets and markets,
or stop off at the fascinating and non-touristy
town of Ségou. If you're travelling east, you
can reach Gao, from where transport contin-

Highlights

People

Dogon *(Dogon Country)*
Hard-working people with a culturally intact way of life and a complex belief system; welcoming, but proud.

Tuareg *(The River Niger Route)*
Fiercely proud nomadic desert-dwellers, famous for their hardy camels, swords and silver jewellery, and indigo robes which dye their skin blue.

Djenné *(The River Niger Route)*
Has a classic African market, one of the largest in the region, with the mosque providing a dramatic backdrop.

Architecture

Mosques *(The River Niger Route)*
In the Sahel, distinctive and elaborate mosques built from mud bricks represent the highest form of this traditional method. Djenné's mosque is the largest mud building in the world, while Timbuktu has some of the oldest mud buildings.

Dogon houses *(Dogon Country)*
Built at the foot of the escarpment and dotting the cliff itself, the Dogon's intricate styles make their homeland a deserved World Heritage site.

Natural Features

River Niger *(The River Niger Route)*
One of Africa's great rivers, scenically beautiful and a vital link between the main towns of Mali; the boat journey downriver through the Sahara Desert is the classic way to reach Timbuktu.

Falaise de Bandiagara *(Dogon Country)*
Dramatic line of red sandstone cliffs rising out of the plains and stretching for over 150km; home of the Dogon people and a superb area for trekking.

Activities

Trekking *(Dogon Country)*
The intricate cliffs of the Falaise de Bandiagara provide some of the best trekking in West Africa.

Camel treks *(The River Niger Route)*
Take an hour's ride out to the sand dunes, or a seven day trek deep into the Sahara; treks are best arranged in Timbuktu.

Birdwatching

Wide range of habitats, from desert to woodland, means a wide, although widely dispersed, range of species; the Niger Inland Delta is particularly good for herons and birds of prey.

ues to Niger. If you're heading south you can reach Sikasso, and there find transport into Côte d'Ivoire or Burkina Faso, or if Senegal is your next stop, you can go direct by express train, or break the journey at the rarely visited towns of Kita and Kayes.

PLANNING
When to Go

The rainy season is from June to September, and the hottest season from March to May, so a good time to visit is October to February. The harmattan blows from December, making November the best time to visit, but it's also the peak of Mali's tourist season. Many travellers come at other times of the year with no problems. For more suggestions see the Dogon Country section later.

Maps

The French IGN produces the excellent *Mali* (1:2,000,000) map in its Pays et Villes de

Monde series, but unfortunately it's not available in Mali itself. Your only alternative is the locally produced *Carte Touristique du Mali* available from the tourist office in Bamako; it's quite simplified, but shows the main routes and towns clearly enough.

RESPONSIBLE TOURISM

Mali is an increasingly popular tourist destination, and some places show signs of strain from the influx of outsiders. This is most notable in Dogon Country, where villages cannot cope with the extra rubbish tourism generates. It's quite common to see a dump of empty tins, mineral water bottles, toilet paper and other detritus only a short distance away from tourist accommodation. This is not stuff used by locals. It can't be buried and isn't burnt, so it just gets spread around by goats, birds and the wind.

More worrying than unsightly rubbish are the ineffectual toilets built for tourists at campements. Traditionally, most local people relieve themselves in the fields, away from the houses, but tourists need walls and holes in the ground. Unfortunately, these are often not deep enough and all the sewage just flows out over the rocks or sand, creating a health hazard for locals and visitors.

What can visitors to Dogon Country do to minimise their impact? If you're carrying your own food, carry out all your rubbish, at least until Bandiagara or another town (although anything you chuck away here will simply end up being tipped on the outskirts or into a dry river bed). If you're on an organised tour, speak to local guides, tour companies and *campement* owners and tell them that you find the rubbish unsightly and that it may be a hazard for local children. Consider staying only at the campements that make an effort to clean up and provide toilets with deep holes. For more on the impact of tourism, see the boxed text 'Dogon Souvenirs' in the Dogon Country section.

VISAS & DOCUMENTS
Visas
Everybody except French nationals needs a visa. One month visas are issued in two to three days, and usually cost US$15 (plus two photos). If there's no Mali embassy in your own country, you can apply by post to one in another country. Several travellers from Europe have reported that the staff at the Brussels embassy are much more on the ball than those in Paris.

Visas are issued at Bamako airport if you fly in from an African country where a visa was unobtainable. They cost CFA5000 and are valid for a week, but can be extended in Bamako. They are not usually obtainable at land borders, although some travellers have been issued temporary visas at Diboli for CFA5000, also extended in Bamako.

Visa Extensions Visa extensions beyond a month cost CFA5000 and are easy to get at Immigration in the *sûreté* building in Bamako, or at provincial police stations in places like Mopti or Timbuktu.

Registration
Foreigners used to have to register with the police in Mopti, Gao and Timbuktu. This involved filling in a form, while the police put a stamp and some illegible scrawl in your passport, for which you paid a CFA1000 'fee'. But times have changed: the tourist office in Bamako specifically informs visitors that registration is not required – and even where it might be, no fee is payable. However, some police officers don't seem to have caught on yet and still try to enforce this old rule. We've heard from several travellers who've happily crossed Mali without registering anywhere, while others have been persuaded to cough up in Mopti or Timbuktu.

If you come into Mali from Senegal on the train, you're supposed to register with the police at Kayes; no fee is payable and the process seems arbitrary, so most travellers don't bother. Likewise, you're supposed to register in Gao, but it's not clear if this requirement is still in force. It might be more important if you're leaving Mali via Gao, as the border guards on the road to Niamey might insist on seeing a police stamp.

EMBASSIES & CONSULATES
Mali Embassies & Consulates

In West Africa, Mali has embassies in Burkina Faso, Côte d'Ivoire, Ghana, Guinea, Senegal and Niger. For details, see the Facts for the Visitor section in the relevant country chapter. Outside Africa, Mali embassies or consulates include:

Belgium
  (☎ 02-345 74 32)
  487 ave Molière, Brussels 1060
France
  (☎ 01 48 07 85 85)
  43 rue de Chemin Vert, 75011 Paris
Germany
  (☎ 0228-357048)
  Basteistrasse 86, 53173 Bonn
USA
  (☎ 202-332 2249)
  2130 R St, NW, Washington, DC 20008

Embassies & Consulates in Mali

All embassies are in Bamako: some in the centre, others along Route de Koulikoro and others in Badalabougou, south of the River Niger.

Belgium
  (☎ 22 51 44)
  On Place du Souvenir, in the centre
Burkina Faso
  (☎ 22 31 71)
  North-east of the centre, just beyond the Hippodrome, 400m off Route de Koulikoro
Côte d'Ivoire
  (☎ 22 03 89)
  Above TAM travel agency on Square Lumumba
France
  (☎ 22 29 51)
  Square Lumumba
Guinea (☎ 22 29 75)
  South of the centre on Rue 313
Mauritania
  (☎ 22 48 15)
  In Hippodrome area, off Route de Koulikoro
Senegal
  (☎ 22 82 74)
  South of the centre, off Ave de l'Yser
USA
  (☎ 22 38 33)
  In the centre of town, corner of Rue de Rochester and Rue Mohammed V

Visas for Onward Travel

In Mali, you can get visas for the following neighbouring West African countries. For visa applications, most embassies open from 8 am to noon or 2 pm – it's always best to get there around 9 am. You usually need to provide two photos.

Burkina Faso
Visas cost CFA13,000 and are ready the same day if you come between 8 and 9 am.

Côte d'Ivoire
Visas cost CFA30,000 and are issued the same day.

Guinea
Visas cost CFA20,000 with a same day service.

Mauritania
Visas cost CFA7500 and are issued the same day.

Niger
Note that visas for Niger cannot be obtained in Bamako.

Senegal
Visas cost CFA5000 to CFA10,000, and are issued in 24 hours or less.

Togo
The French embassy issues visas for Togo.

The British honorary consul (☎ 22 47 38 or 22 25 30) is at the American International School in the suburb of Badalabougou. There are also honorary consuls for Italy, the Netherlands and Switzerland in Bamako.

CUSTOMS

Theoretically there is a limit on the amount of CFA that you can take out of the country, but whatever the rule it's rarely enforced. If you want to take a genuinely old artefact out of the country, you'll need an export permit, issued by the Musée National in Bamako for 10% of the value of the piece.

MONEY

The unit of currency is the CFA franc.

Euro €1	=	CFA660
1FF	=	CFA100
UK£1	=	CFA950
US$1	=	CFA600

Banks that change money include Banque de Développement du Mali (BDM), Banque Internationale du Mali (BIM) and Banque Malienne de Crédit et Depôt (BMCD), with branches in Bamako and other large towns. Commissions are invariably high, usually 2% with a minimum charge of CFA5000, then extra fees (sometimes up to CFA8000) for travellers cheques. Changing cash often takes a long time, and travellers cheques even longer. Staff prefer French francs, and outside Bamako often refuse to deal in anything else. You may also need to show travellers cheque purchase receipts.

If you've got French francs in cash you can always change them at larger hotels, tour companies or traders in main towns – usually with no commission. Some hotels and tour companies may also change travellers cheques.

You can get cash with a Visa card at BMCD in Bamako. BIM is the Western Union Money Transfer agent.

POST & COMMUNICATIONS
Post

Letter and parcel post out of Bamako or Mopti is reasonably reliable. Letters to Europe and the USA are CFA320. For sending large parcels home, the Colis Postal Office, off Blvd du Peuple in Bamako, offers a 'surface' service that's much cheaper than air mail – but it can take up to a year for things to arrive! The main poste restante is in Bamako.

Telephone

All large towns have a Sotelma public telephone office. Local calls cost CFA100 and between towns about CFA300 to CFA500 per minute. There are no area codes. Mobile phones begin with ☎ 77 and are more expensive to call.

International calls to Europe cost around CFA2000 per minute, but phonecards make them cheaper (they also have nice pictures on them). Most large towns have privately owned *télécentres* where the service is prompt and rates are only slightly higher. Reverse-charge (collect) calls cannot be made from anywhere in Mali, but to save money you could try a telegram; to Europe costs CFA2850 for 10 words (minimum).

Email & Internet Access

Sotelma, the state telephone company, is reported to be installing facilities in public telephone offices so that email can be sent and received.

BOOKS

Ségu by Maryse Condé is an epic novel following the generations of a family living in the River Niger trading town of Ségou. It has inspired many Dutch and French travellers to visit Mali.

Lieve Joris captures the essence of the country in *Mali Blues*, published in Lonely Planet's travel literature series, Journeys. Lieve travels to Bamako, Kayes and Dogon Country accompanied by famed Malian musician Boubacar 'Kar Kar' Traoré.

NEWSPAPERS & MAGAZINES

A couple of daily papers (all in French) are available in Bamako and other large towns, including *Le Republican*. International English-language publications, such as *Time* and *Newsweek* are usually available from bookshops in top-end hotels in Bamako, but are rarely seen elsewhere.

PHOTOGRAPHY & VIDEO

Photo permits are no longer required but the usual restrictions on photography apply –

see the Photography & Video section in the Regional Facts for the Visitor chapter for more general information. As in all parts of West Africa, whenever you want to photograph someone, ask permission first; this is particularly true in the Dogon area.

HEALTH

A yellow fever vaccination certificate is required to enter the country. Malaria risk exists throughout the country, year-round, and you should take appropriate preventative measures. See the Health section in the Regional Facts for the Visitor chapter for more general information on these and other health matters.

Most large towns have a hospital and pharmacy, although standards are low and supplies sometimes limited. The best services are in Bamako.

WOMEN TRAVELLERS

Mali is generally a safe place for women travellers, although the usual advice about travelling in a Muslim country should be followed. For more information and advice, see the Women Travellers section in the Regional Facts for the Visitor chapter.

DANGERS & ANNOYANCES

Crime rates in Bamako are low compared with some other cities in the region, but some caution still needs to be taken (see Information in the Bamako section later for more details).

The main annoyance for visitors are the young men who lurk outside hotels in Bamako, Mopti and other tourist towns, offering their services as guides (see the boxed text 'Guides in Mali' at the end of this chapter's Getting Around section).

BUSINESS HOURS

Government offices are open weekdays from 7 am to noon and 2 to 4.30 pm, except on Friday when they're closed (or as good as) after noon. Business and bank hours are from 8 am to noon and 3 to 6 pm (approximately)

on weekdays, and from 8 am to noon on Fridays. Shops and some businesses open on Saturday mornings.

PUBLIC HOLIDAYS & SPECIAL EVENTS

Public Holidays include the Muslim holidays plus 1 January (New Year's Day), 20 January, Easter Monday, 1 May, 25 May, 22 September (Independence Day) and 25 December. For a table of Islamic holiday dates, see the Public Holidays & Special Events section in the Regional Facts for the Visitor chapter.

Special events include the Biennal (September in even years), a national sport and cultural festival held in Bamako. Lots of regional bands enter the competitions, and it's

The Cattle Crossing at Diafarabé

In December every year, in a rite that goes back almost 200 years, the sleepy village of Diafarabé is transformed into a centre of activity as hundreds of thousands of cows (about one-third of Mali's total cattle population) are driven southwards across the River Niger to greener pastures. It's a happy time for the Fula herders, who have been in the fringes of the Sahara for many months. The crossing means reunion with their families and a time to celebrate. On the first day of the crossing, a festival of music and dance is held. This is unquestionably the most captivating event in Mali and one of the most interesting in West Africa.

Diafarabé is on the north bank of the River Niger about halfway between Ségou and Mopti. There's no regular public transport, but you can get there by boat from Mopti. The exact date of the crossing is not set until November because much depends on the water level, but it's usually during the first two weeks of December. If you can't make the crossing at Diafarabé, inquire about the dates of the others; they continue throughout December.

an excellent opportunity to hear live music. There are also annual Dogon ceremonies (usually held from March to May), which include masked dances.

ACTIVITIES

Trekking in Dogon Country is the most popular activity in Mali; see that section for details of routes and practicalities.

There's a world-class but little known rock-climbing area near Hombori, a village on the main road between Mopti and Gao. See the boxed text 'Rock Climbing' on p594.

ACCOMMODATION

Places to stay in large towns range from backstreet brothels to smart hotels. Between these two extremes are campements, where accommodation is simple but adequate, and sometimes good value; most towns have one. Some hotels add a tourist tax of CFA500 per person per night onto the cost of the room – wherever possible, this is included in the rates we quote. In Dogon Country, where many travellers go trekking, it's usual to sleep on the flat roof of a hut in a village, and a blanket or light sleeping bag may be required.

FOOD & DRINKS

Food in Mali is generally similar to that found in Senegal, with *poulet yassa* (chicken in an onion and lemon sauce) and *riz yollof* (rice with vegetables and/or meat) featuring on many menus. All along the River Niger, restaurants also serve *capitaine* (Nile perch), which is usually either grilled or deep fried, although more imaginative methods (such as baking or stewing) are occasionally employed.

Around markets and transport parks you find stalls selling tea and coffee, while small shops and stalls sell cold drinks. Mali is predominantly a Muslim country, so many locals do not drink alcohol, but most towns have at least one bar or hotel where you can buy beer. Castel is the most popular brand, while Flag is a more refined and expensive

brew. Local brews include millet beer – a thick brown liquid, which most travellers come across in Dogon Country. In the far southern parts of Mali, palm wine can occasionally be found.

Getting There & Away

AIR

Mali's main airport is on the outskirts of Bamako, and all international flights go to/from here. International airlines serving Mali include Air France and Sabena, while the main airline within West Africa is Air Afrique.

Airport tax is CFA7000 for flights to African countries, and CFA9000 for all other international flights.

Europe & the USA

European airlines serving Mali include Air France, Sabena and Aeroflot. Return flights are about US$600 to US$800, depending on the season and length of stay. There are also flights from Europe on Air Afrique and Royal Air Maroc. Many travellers go overland from Europe to Morocco and fly to Bamako from Casablanca on Royal Air Maroc; fares start at US$300. From the USA, you can take Air Afrique from New York, transferring to a regional flight in Dakar (Senegal) or Abidjan (Côte d'Ivoire). Otherwise you'll have to fly via Europe.

Africa

Air Afrique flies most days between Bamako and Dakar (CFA104,000 one way), and also serves Abidjan (CFA96,000). Air Mali goes twice-weekly to Dakar (CFA65,000) and Abidjan (CFA72,000). Air Dabia goes weekly to Banjul (Gambia) for CFA63,000 and also to Dakar. Air Burkina flies twice weekly to Ouagadougou (Burkina Faso). Other destinations include Niamey in Niger (Air Afrique or Ethiopian Airlines), Conakry in Guinea (Air Guinée and Air France) and Lagos (Nigeria Airways).

Border Crossings

Mali is a large country and shares borders with several neighbours. If you're heading for **Burkina Faso**, the main border crossing point is just south of Kouri, on the road between Koutiala or San and Bobo-Dioulasso. Many travellers use the quieter route, between Mopti and Ouagadougou, via Bankass, and Ouahigouya, crossing at the border village of Koro.

If you're heading for **Côte d'Ivoire**, the main crossing point is between Sikasso and Ferkessédougou, although many travellers going between Mali and Côte d'Ivoire go via Burkina Faso anyway.

If you're going to or from **Guinea**, the border is at Kourémalé, on the road to Siguiri and Kankan, but some of the traffic goes between Bougouni and Kankan, crossing the border at Badogo.

A much busier route on the west side of Mali is to/from **Senegal**, where by far the busiest border is between Kidira (Senegal) and Diboli (Mali), two small towns on either side of a river where both the main railway and the main road cross on bridges.

North of here, it's possible to cross the border between Mali and **Mauritania** to the north of Nioro, or to the west of Nara, to reach Ayoûn or Néma in Mauritania, but not many travellers go this way.

The border with Algeria is effectively closed to travellers, so your only other option is to the east, the route to/from **Niger**, where the main road between Gao and Niamey crosses the border at Labbe-ganza, between Ansongo and Ayorou.

Air Afrique and Ethiopian Airways have flights to Nairobi (Kenya) or Johannesburg (South Africa). Air Gabon goes to Libreville (twice weekly) with connections to Jo'burg.

LAND

Burkina Faso

Direct buses leave Bamako's Sogoniko gare routière daily for Ouagadougou (CFA12,500)

via Bobo-Dioulasso (CFA8000). Buses also go to Bobo-Dioulasso from Ségou, Sikasso and Mopti.

Côte d'Ivoire

Direct buses go daily from Bamako all the way to Abidjan for CFA15,000. The 1200km trip is supposed to take 1½ days but delays are common. One traveller called it 'the most broken-down, over-packed, sweaty, dirty, dusty, smelly, sweltering bus trip I have ever taken'. His bus took over four days! It's much more pleasant to do the trip in stages, breaking at Sikasso.

Guinea

Bush taxis run most days from Bamako's Djikoroni gare routière to the border at Kourémalé for CFA2500, or sometimes all the way to Siguiri, from where you can find transport to Kankan. There's a possibility that the road between Bougouni and Kankan could be improved. If this is true, more traffic will start using this route, leaving from the Sogoniko gare routière in Bamako.

Mauritania

The main route between Mali and Mauritania is via Nara and Néma, although public transport is especially light between the two towns and you'll probably have to resort to trucks. It's also possible to enter Mauritania from Nioro (see the Kayes section for details).

The Bamako to Nara road is in good condition. Between Nara and Néma it's sandy in the dry season and muddy in the wet (July and August), but from Néma the 'Trans-Mauritanienne' is tar all the way to Nouakchott.

Niger

Your only option is the bus between Gao and Niamey. See the Gao section for details.

Senegal

Bush Taxi Most travellers take the train between Bamako and Dakar, but roads linking Mali and Senegal have improved over the last few years, so travelling by bush taxi is quite straightforward. Bush taxis from Kayes to the Mali border town of Diboli cost CFA2500. Some vehicles continue to Kidira but if they don't, you can walk over the bridge to Kidira from where you can reach Tambacounda in a Peugeot 504 (CFA4000) or minibus (CFA2700). There are also trucks between Kayes and Tambacounda, carrying passengers for CFA6000.

Nearly all road traffic between Bamako and Kayes uses the northern road (via Nioro), but there isn't much as the road is terrible. The southern road (running next to the railway) is good between Bamako and Kita, but appalling thereafter – although it is due for upgrading all the way to Kayes in 1999 and 2000.

Train Express trains run between Bamako and Dakar twice per week in each direction, departing each city on Wednesday and Saturday mornings: from Bamako at 8 am and

---

Cars & Motorbikes on the Train

It's possible to put a car on the train between Bamako and Dakar, but the total cost can run into several hundred thousand CFA, once you've paid for space on a wagon, customs charges, loading fees, 'help' with loading and tying down – not to mention outright bribes just to get a space. Additional problems include the apparent lack of any proper loading ramp at Bamako. We heard from some drivers whose beloved 4WD was hoisted aboard by forklift truck. On top of these kinds of problems you might wait a week just to be loaded.

For motorbikes, it's a different matter. Two bikers from Scotland told us their trip on a freight train between Kayes and Bamako cost CFA6000 per bike, plus CFA4000 per passenger, plus another CFA7000 to cover 'incidentals' and loading (basically, a bunch of guys lifting), then CFA2000 to unload in Bamako.

---

from Dakar at 10 am. The whole journey takes at least 35 hours. For details of fares, see the getting There & Away section of the Senegal chapter. Some travellers take the slower, cheaper (by about 40%) 'local' train between Bamako and Kayes, then the express just to Tambacounda.

Car & Motorcycle See the notes on the condition of roads between Mali and Senegal in the Bush Taxi section earlier. At Diboli, a new road bridge takes you across to the Senegal border town of Kidira, from where a good dirt road (due to be tar by 1999) leads to Tambacounda.

We had a letter from intrepid overland driver Sarah Reilly, who entered Mali from Senegal and went from Kayes via Bafoula-bé to Mararitalis-Bingasi and the new dam at Manantali, from where Kita can be reached.

RIVER

A barge carrying passengers goes roughly once a week between Jukuroni (upstream from Bamako) and Kankan in Guinea from July to November, or when the river is high enough. The trip costs CFA5000 and takes four days. For details ask at the Compagnie Malienne de Navigation (CMN) office in Bamako (see Getting There & Away in that section).

Getting Around

AIR

Domestic flights are operated by Air Mali. Flights go to Kayes and Nioro twice per week, but the main route of interest is between Bamako and Timbuktu, via Mopti (the airport is at Sévaré) and Goundam, three times a week each way. Once a week the flight goes on to Gao. Flights usually depart Bamako at around 7 am, arriving in Mopti at 8.30 am and Gao at 11 am; they then depart Gao at noon, Mopti at around 2 pm and arrive in Bamako around 4 pm. The flight days vary, and delays are not uncommon, so you should inquire locally for more details. In Bamako and Mopti reservations are handled by most travel agents, and there are Air Mali offices or reps in the other touchdown towns.

Flights (with one-way fares) most often used by visitors are Bamako to Mopti (CFA40,000), Mopti to Timbuktu (CFA 44,000) and Mopti to Gao (CFA50,000). Fares are the same in either direction and returns are double. If you make your booking through an agency, their name might appear on the all-important passenger list instead of yours, so check this if your seat has apparently disappeared.

Airport departure tax is CFA2000 for flights within Mali.

BUS & BUSH TAXI
Several companies run safe and comfortable buses on long routes between the main towns. Fares are fixed so all companies charge the same, working out at around CFA10 per kilometre. For example, Bamako to Ségou CFA2000 (235km), Bamako to Mopti CFA6000 (640km) and Bamako to Gao CFA10,000 (1200km). You can normally buy tickets in advance, which reserves your seat.

Bush taxis and minibuses run on some long routes, and are generally slightly more expensive than the bus. On shorter routes bush taxis are usually the only option: either

Night Bus Arrivals

Many long-distance buses travel overnight, which saves on hotel bills but means you miss a lot of scenery. If the bus arrives before dawn, everyone just goes to sleep on the bus or in the nearby waiting room. The luggage isn't even unloaded until first light. There's no point going anywhere anyway, as all the cheap places to stay will be locked up and, especially in Bamako, you don't want to be wandering the streets with a rucksack in the dark.

Peugeot 504 seven-seaters, which carry nine people, or pick-ups (bâchés) with about 16 passengers. Bâchés are slower but about 25% cheaper than 504s.

TRAIN
The only rail journey within Mali is between Bamako and Kayes or Diboli, in the west of the country. Most people, on their way to/from Senegal, take this option, as road transport is very limited.

CAR
Self-drive car rental is rare, and not recommended because accident insurance for foreigners can be ineffective (even if you're not at fault). However, cars with drivers are easy to arrange through tour operators in Bamako and Mopti, with rates about CFA25,000 per day, plus CFA25 per kilometre. A 4WD will be around CFA70,000 per day, plus CFA75 per kilometre, although some companies offer daily flat rates irrespective of distance covered. On main routes petrol costs CFA400 per litre, diesel CFA260, although these prices rise in out of the way places.

BOAT
Passenger Boat
Large passenger boats, operated by the Compagnie Malienne de Navigation (CMN), ply the River Niger between Koulikoro (near Bamako) and Gao, stopping at Mopti, Korioumé (for Timbuktu) and several other riverside towns. They run usually from August to November, when the river is high. In December and January the service may run only between Mopti and Gao or be suspended altogether. In theory, one boat heads downstream from Koulikoro every Tuesday and arrives in Gao the following Monday, while another boat heads upstream from Gao every Thursday and arrives at Koulikoro a week later. The journey from Koulikoro to Mopti should take three days and from Mopti to Gao it should be four days, but schedules are very unreliable and each section can take twice as long.

Despite the vagaries of the timetable, the journey is fascinating as you get a close look at village life along the Niger. But it's not for everyone. There's a story about a couple from New York who imagined sipping piña coladas on a Caribbean-style cruise ship. What they found was a floating village, with sweltering cabins, loud music blasting away in the bar, dirty toilets and cargo spread everywhere with people on top. Another traveller's tale relates how the boat became stuck on a sandbank for two days, during which time the water pump broke and the restaurant started running out of food. But don't let this put you off – many travellers rate the river journey as one of the highlights of their trip.

There are three boats, although one always seems to be out of action: the *Kankan Moussa* is the best, the *Tombouctou* and *Général Soumaré* are more basic. It's not essential to do the whole trip: the two day section between Mopti and Korioumé (about 400km), for example, is a very popular way to reach Timbuktu. It's far less crowded between Mopti and Ségou, or Gao and Korioumé. Fares (in CFA) for sectors, in either direction, most used by travellers are listed in the following table:

route	luxe	1st	2nd	3rd	4th
Koulikoro to Mopti	60,000	35,000	27,000	15,000	5000
Ségou to Mopti	40,000	24,000	17,000	19,000	3000
Mopti to Korioumé	46,000	30,000	21,000	12,000	4000
Mopti to Gao	94,000	61,000	41,000	24,000	8000

The 'luxe' cabins have a bathroom and air-con, while 1st class cabins have two bunk beds, toilet and washbasin; 2nd class is a four berth cabin with a washbasin and shared toilets; 3rd class is an eight berth cabin. In 4th class all you get is space on the dirty and extremely crowded lower deck, although tourists are allowed into the bar-restaurant on the upper deck, as long as they

buy a few drinks. Try to get a cabin on the north side of the boat – it's cooler.

Except in 4th class, meals are included in the fare. Extra food can be bought from women cooking on the 4th class deck or at stops en route. Water is drawn from the river and 'purified' by the addition of bleach. This may not be reliable, but fortunately bottles of mineral water, soft drinks and beer are sold (although these sometimes run out).

In Bamako tickets often sell out, except for 4th class where space is seen as infinite. At offices in other towns they never sell out, so you can always get a ticket, although there may not be a berth when you get on the boat and you'll end up in 4th class anyway. However, during the trip you may be able to pay a supplementary fee for a bunk in 3rd class.

Pirogue & Pinasse

Pirogues are small canoes, either paddled by hand or fitted with a small outboard motor. They're usually the slowest form of river transport, but are OK for short journeys or if you're not in any kind of a rush. *Pinasses* are larger motorised boats, carrying cargo and anything from 10 to 100 passengers. Some are large enough to have an upper deck and a couple of basic cabins; smaller pinasses make do with a reed mat rigged up to keep off the sun. Pinasses can be faster than the CMN passenger boat (especially when it breaks down or runs aground – which is often), but they are equally unpredictable and can be extremely crowded. When loaded to the gunwales with cargo, the deck hovering just above the surface of the water, they look downright dangerous! The most popular pinasse route for travellers is Mopti to Korioumé (for Timbuktu).

ORGANISED TOURS

Tours around the whole country can be arranged in Bamako and Mopti, but these are tailor-made affairs of high cost and quality, usually based on the hire of a vehicle and driver plus fuel and all other items such as hotels, meals, guides and excursions. Some tour and travel agents offering this

Guides in Mali

In Bamako you may be approached by local guides offering tours around the country, for which you pay a daily fee (from CFA5000 plus expenses, or up to CFA70,000 including bus fares, hotels etc). They'll tell you horror tales of thieves and complex travel arrangements, which make their services seem attractive. But it's all hot air. If you're new to travel in Africa, or nervous about the great unknown, such a guide might be worth considering, although in reality they act more as escort or fixer. Otherwise, decline their offers. These guys are by no means required.

Note, however, that in places such as Djenné or Timbuktu, a knowledgeable and informative guide, hired on the spot for a few hours, can enhance your visit – although they're still not obligatory. The only place where guides are highly recommended is Dogon Country.

service are listed in the Bamako and Mopti sections.

For specialist adventure tours through the desert in Mali and Mauritania, you can arrange things in advance with Nomade Voyage (☎/fax 22 75 13; email nomade .voyage@djata.malinet.ml) in Bamako, run by the friendly and multilingual Juan Dobler. He also runs Dogon Country treks and pinasse tours, and can sometimes fit in individuals with groups already booked. Some other companies arranging tours are listed under information in the Bamako section.

Shorter local tours can also be arranged (for example from Mopti, Bandiagara or Bankass to Dogon Country, or from Timbuktu into the desert) and these are detailed in the relevant sections.

Bamako

Mali is such a poor country that many visitors expect the pace of life in Bamako to be pretty slow. Nothing could be further from the truth. The city centre is like one big market, with stalls on every pavement, metalworkers bashing out pots and pans, music blasting away in shop doorways and traders selling everything under the sun. The streets are full of people, cars and buzzing flocks of *mobylettes*. After the semi-European feel of Dakar or Abidjan, Bamako is quintessentially African. It can be hot and tiring, but if you're in the right mood the city provides hours of entertainment, even if you don't like shopping. In short, Bamako has buzz!

Orientation

Bamako's city centre is on the north bank of the River Niger, focused on the triangle formed by Ave Kassa Keita, Blvd du Peuple and the railway. From the northern end of Blvd du Peuple, two major roads extend eastward: Route de Koulikoro leads past the Hippodrome (horse racing track), while Route de Sotuba heads out to the smart suburb of Niaréla.

South of Ave Kassa Keita is Square Lumumba and, just beyond, the Pont des Martyrs which leads to Route de Ségou (also called Ave de l'Unité Africaine), the main road out of town. The area over the river is called Badalabougou. The Sogoniko gare routière is about 6km south of the city centre, the airport 15km. The Pont du Roi (west of Pont des Martyrs) carries a new highway which runs parallel to Route de Ségou direct to the airport.

Street Name Changes

Some of Bamako's main streets have been renamed. Ave de Fleuve is now Ave Modibo Keita. Route de Koulikoro has been officially retitled Ave Al Qoods, but *nobody* uses this new name, especially because this is the main route to – you've guessed it – Koulikoro. Streets without names have numbers – these have also changed recently, but are well signed.

MALI

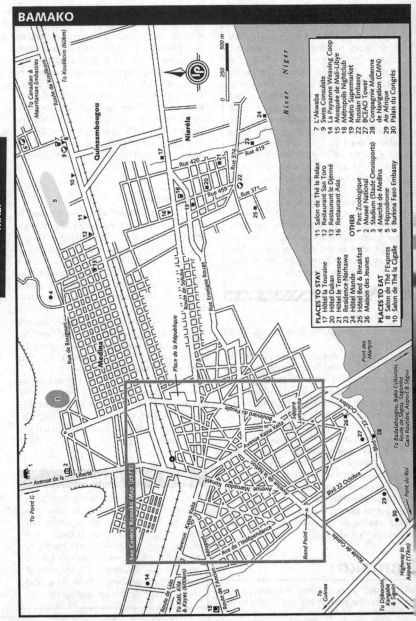

BAMAKO

500 m
250

River Niger

To Canadian &
Mauritanian Embassies

To Koulikoro (60km)

Route de Koulikoro

Quinzambougou

Niaréla

Rue 420
Rue 419
Rue 376
Rue 459
Rue 371

Rue de Bougouni

Medina

Route de Sotuba

Place de la République

Rue Enseigne Rouge

Pont des
Martyrs

See Central Bamako Map (p573)

Boulevard du Peuple

Square
Lumumba

To Badalabougou, Bako Djikoroni,
Route de Ségou, Sogoniko,
Gare Routière, Airport & Ségou

Octobre

Blvd

Avenue Kassa Keïta

Avenue Mamadou Konaté

Avenue de la Nation

Ave de l'Indépendance

Avenue de la   Liberté

To Point G

Pont du Roi

Blvd 22 Octobre

Rond Point

Route de Guinée

Highway to
Airport (17km)

To Djikoroni,
Kangaba
& Siguiri

To
Guinea

Route de l'Ancien

Route de Ségou (600km)

To Kéla, Kéla
& Kayes

Route de l'Ancien

Route de Uéo

To Kéla, Kéla
& Kayes

PLACES TO STAY
17 Hôtel la Touraine
20 Hôtel Dakan
21 Hôtel le Tennessee
23 Residence Narhawa
24 Hôtel Mande
25 Hôtel Bed & Breakfast
26 Maison des Jeunes

PLACES TO EAT
8   Salon de Thé l'Express
10 Salon de Thé la Cigalle
11 Salon de Thé le Relax
12 Restaurant San Toro
13 Restaurant le Djenné
16 Restaurant Asia

OTHER
1   Parc Zoologique
2   Musée National
3   Stadium (Stade Omnisports)
4   Marché de Medina
5   Hippodrome
6   Burkina Faso Embassy
7   L'Akwaba
9   Swiss Consulate
14 La Paysanne Weaving Coop
15 Mosquée de Mali-Libye
18 Métropolis Nightclub
19 Metro Supermarket
22 Russian Embassy
27 BCEAO Tower
28 Compagnie Malienne
    de Navigation (CMN)
29 Air Afrique
30 Palais du Congrès

Information

Tourist Information The Office Malien du Tourisme et de l'Hotellerie (OMATHO) is near the southern end of Rue Mohammed V. The office is not set up for independent tourists, but the staff are friendly and helpful where possible, and have a few historical booklets for sale.

A listings magazine called *Djembé*, available at tour agents, carries advertisements for local events, nightclubs and restaurants, and also has details of flights in and out of Bamako.

Money Banks for changing money include BIM on Ave de la Nation, and BDM and BMCD on Ave Kassa Keita. BMCD gives cash on Visa cards, charge-free: go in the morning with your card and passport, set the ball rolling and then come back in the afternoon to get your money. Moneychangers deal openly outside the banks; their rates are the same, although there's no commission and the process is quick. Wherever you change your money, note that a lot of unsavoury characters also lurk around this part of town so it's no place to be with wads of cash in your hand.

Post & Communications The main post office is on Rue Karamoko Diaby, and the main public telephone office is two blocks east on the same street. The poste restante is fine for letters (CFA300 to collect) but unreliable for packages.

As this book was going to press, we heard that an Internet and email bureau had opened, called Mali-Net, near the Restaurant Central.

Travel Agencies & Tour Operators There are several agencies dealing in international and regional flights. Two of the best are ATS Voyages (☎ 22 44 35) on Ave Kassa Keita, where the staff are helpful and speak English, and TAM (☎ 23 92 00, fax 22 05 47, email tvoyage@sotelma.net) on Square Lumumba, open till midnight Monday to Saturday, and on Sunday mornings. Both also organise car hire and tours around the

country. Other agencies arranging tours include: Tam Tam Tours (☎/fax 23 66 71), not to be confused with TAM; West Air Services (☎ 22 88 80 or 77 14 22, fax 23 27 65, email maya@westair.malinet.ml), run by the efficient and dynamic Mariama Mohamed, who speaks several languages including English; and Bani Voyages (☎ 23 83 83), with offices at the Grand Hôtel and other top end hotels around the country.

Bookshops The bookshops at the Amitié and Grand hotels sell *Time* and a few other English-language newspapers and books, but otherwise the choice is limited. For second-hand books you could try browsing among the stalls on Rue de Rochester or outside the main post office.

Cultural Centres The US Information Centre, near the train station, has magazines and books in its air-con library. The Centre Culturel Français on Ave de l'Indépendance also has a library, and often shows films.

Medical Services The Hôpital Gabriel Touré (☎ 22 27 12) is better for emergencies; otherwise, go to the Hôpital du Point G (☎ 22 50 02). Dr Traoré at Clinique Acacia (☎ 22 41 03) in the suburb of Quinzambougou has been recommended. The Hôtel de l'Amitié has a good pharmacy, and there are several others around the city centre. Imported tampons are available at the Azar supermarket on Route de Koulikoro.

Dangers & Annoyances Crime in Bamako is on the increase. We've heard from several travellers who were mugged in the area around the train station, even during the day. If you arrive on the train at night, either stay in the station building until dawn or take a taxi to your hotel. Another potential hot spot for muggings is in the streets just north of the Maison des Jeunes; to avoid this, it's best to approach it from the Square Lumumba side. Walking the streets off Rue de Rochester is dangerous at night. Bamako also has its share of pickpockets and bag

MALI

Bamako Scams

A common scam operated in the Grand Marché area involves hustlers who begin talking to you, meeting any resistance with a loud and obscene argument and an apparent potential for violence. It seems to be a ruse to get you off-guard. Don't rise to it. If necessary, go into a shop or restaurant and ask for help. Your 'assailant' will soon be chased off.

We've also had letters from several travellers who were all stung by the same con-men who hang around at the Ali Baba Snack Bar and other places frequented by tourists. The story goes like this. He knows somebody living in Bamako from Sydney/Washington/Manchester/Berlin (or wherever you're from) who's having a party tonight and would just love to meet some compatriots. There'll be music, beer and good times. In the evening you go to a house in the suburbs. Some other local guests have already arrived, and you're assured the Aussie/American/Brit/German you've come to meet will be here soon. In the meantime how about smoking some grass? You decline, but some of the other guests light up. Next minute, enter the police. The whole thing is a set-up. You get arrested, even if you never touched the joint, and of course only a very large fine will get you off the hook.

snatchers, and normal security precautions are definitely advisable.

Things to See & Do

Bamako's main attractions are the lively **markets**, described in more detail under Shopping, but well worth a walk around even if you don't want to buy anything. You almost certainly won't want anything from the **fetish stalls** on Blvd du Peuple near the Maison des Artisans – unless of course you're in desperate need of bones, skins, dried lizards and rotting monkey heads.

Photos are an absolute no-no here. Few tourists reach the **Marché de Medina** north of the Hippodrome – this large bustling place is where the locals do their shopping – so despite the throng there's rarely any hassle.

For a calmer atmosphere, the **Musée National** has one of the finest ethnographic displays in West Africa. The tapestry section is particularly good, featuring some extraordinary Fula wedding blankets. There are also masks, funeral objects and weapons. The museum is open from 9 am to 6 pm daily except Monday. Entrance is great value at CFA500, and French and English-speaking guides can be hired.

Places to Stay – Budget

In the city centre, the cheapest place is the *Maison des Jeunes*, near Square Lumumba, charging CFA1000 for a dormitory bed or CFA2000/3000 for single/double rooms. The place is a bit run-down and suffers from theft, although new management has started major renovations and promises improved security.

A much better option is the *Mission Catholique* (or Centre d'Accueil des Soeurs Blanches), just west of the centre, where a bed in a dorm (which sleeps six) costs CFA3000 and doubles are CFA8000. Missionaries have priority, and the French nuns in charge take no nonsense from travellers; you can only come and go from 7 am to 1 pm and from 4 to 10 pm. A friendlier alternative is the nearby *Chez Fanta*, where a bed costs CFA3000 to CFA4000 per night. There's no sign, but locals will point out the house.

Also worth considering is the *Mission Libanaise*, an old mission now run as a small hotel, off Ave Kassa Keita. Doubles with nets, fans and hot showers cost CFA6000. You can also camp or sleep in the yard for CFA2000, although this seems plagued by swarms of mosquitoes. If rooms are full, avoid at all costs the owner's 'other place' – a very unpleasant brothel.

World music or railway devotees may favour the *Hôtel-Buffet de la Gare* overlooking the tracks at the train station. It's noisy and none too clean, and poor value at

MALI

PLACES TO STAY
2 Grand Hôtel
4 Hôtel-Buffet de la Gare
30 Mission Catholique
31 Chez Fanta
36 Hôtel Lac Debo
46 Mission Libanaise
51 Hôtel de l'Amitié
58 Hôtel-Restaurant du Fleuve

PLACES TO EAT
7 Ali Baba Snack Bar
8 La Pizzeria
29 Café Mohammed à la Casa
32 Restaurant de la Paix
34 Bakery
35 Restaurant Central

40 Salon de Thé la Phoenicia
41 Restaurant le Gourmet
50 Le Bol de Jade Restaurant

OTHER
1 Hôpital Gabriel Touré
3 Train Station
5 US Information Centre
6 US Embassy
9 Bar Kaissa
10 Le Grand Muraille
11 Place de la République
12 Maison des Artisans
13 Grande Mosquée
14 Sotelma Public Telephone Office
15 Colis Postal (Parcel Office)
16 Post Office (PTT)

17 Place de la Liberté
18 Mairie
19 Sabena
20 Cinéma Babemba
21 Tennis Club
22 Petit Marché
23 Dabanani Intersection
24 Taxi Rank
25 Grand Marché
26 Place du Souvenir
27 Cathedral
28 Cinéma Vox
33 BMCD Bank
37 Sûreté (Immigration)
38 Taxi Rank
39 Aeroflot Office
42 L'Evasion Nightclub
43 Azar Supermarket
44 Disco Colombo

45 Jewellers
47 ATS Voyages
48 Tourist Office (OMATHO)
49 BDM Bank
52 Square Lumumba
53 Minibuses to Sogoniko Gare Routière; Petrol Station
54 TAM (Travel Agency)
55 French Embassy
56 Air France; Ethiopian Airlines; Air Mali
57 Senegal Embassy
59 Guinea Embassy
60 Rond Point
61 Centre Culturel Français
62 BIM Bank

To Musée National & Point G Plateau
Route de Koulikoro
Avenue van Vollenhoven
To Route de Lido
Avenue de la Liberté
Avenue Kassa Keita
To Niaréla
Rue Baba Diarra
Rue de Rochester
Rue Archinard
Rue Karamoko Diaby
Route de Sotuba
Blvd de la Paix
Route de l'Ancien Aéroport
Rue de la Fosse (R328)
Avenue de la République
Avenue de l'Indépendance
Rue 361
Rue 355
Rue Mamadou Konaté
Rue Bagayoko
Rue Diarra
Rue 221
Rue Mohammed V
Rue Gouraud
Boulevard du Peuple
Rue Fabolo Coulibaly
Ave de l'Artois
Rue Laperrive
Rue 358
Rue 324
Rue 319
Rue 222
Rue Enseigne Froger
Avenue de la Nation
Rue 136
Rue Poincaré
Avenue Moussa Travélé
Avenue Modibo Keita
Avenue Pasteur
Avenue de la Marne
Rue 311
Rue 329
Ave de Verdun
Avenue Ruault (R310)
Rue 317
Avenue de l'Yser
Rue 313
R306
Blvd 22 Octobre
To Pont des Martyrs, Airport & Gare Routière

0   125   250 m

CFA10,000/15,000, although this includes breakfast and dinner – but dessert is extra!

Places to Stay – Mid-Range

Highly recommended in this range is the safe and friendly *Hôtel Lac Debo* (☎ 22 96 35) on Ave Kassa Keita. Rooms with air-con and bathroom cost CFA15,000/18,000. Rooms with fans are cheaper. Breakfast, meals, beers and coffees are served in the street-front restaurant.

The *Hôtel-Restaurant du Fleuve* (☎ 22 65 03), just south of Ave de l'Yser, has double rooms with air-con and bathroom from CFA15,000 to CFA25,000 depending on size and other extras, such as TV and telephone. The hotel's restaurant gets lively, especially at weekends.

Further from the centre is the friendly *Hôtel Maxim* (☎ 23 98 56), in a back street off Route de Koulikoro near the Canadian embassy. Double rooms are CFA15,000.

There are several places in the suburb of Niaréla. The old-style, French-run *Hôtel la Touraine* (☎ 22 52 98), better known as Le Rabelais – the name of its restaurant – is on Route de Sotuba, with rooms from CFA 32,000 and breakfast at CFA3500. South a few blocks, the *Hôtel Dakan* (☎ 22 91 96) has a garden, very pleasant African ambience and decent rooms with air-con and bathroom for CFA15,000/19,000 with breakfast. The restaurant serves meals for CFA2000 to CFA3000. Nearby is the smarter *Hôtel le Tennessee* (☎ 22 36 77) with rooms at CFA30,000/33,000. In the same area, the friendly *Hôtel Bed & Breakfast* (☎ 22 01 04) has some small singles for CFA15,000 and larger doubles from CFA28,000 with bathroom, mosquito net, TV and even a bedside radio. Breakfast is included and other meals are CFA4000. Nearby is *Residence Narhawa* (☎/fax 22 40 29), small and welcoming, with simple rooms at CFA10,000/15,000 and larger rooms with bathroom and air-con at CFA28,000/33,000.

South of the centre, just off Route de Ségou and about 3km from the Pont des Martyrs, is the relaxed and popular *Hôtel les Colibris* (☎ 22 66 37) with rooms at CFA 12,500/15,000 with air-con and bathroom. They also have safe parking and allow camping for CFA2500. For getting to/from town, minibuses run regularly nearby. Also south of the river, about 5km west of the bridge in the suburb of Bako Djikoroni, is the *Hôtel des Arbres* (☎ 23 66 43). This is a great place, with clean double rooms for CFA 14,000 (CFA17,000 with air-con), or a mattress and net outside for CFA4000 and camping for CFA3000. There's a pool, bar, fair-priced meals and safe parking. It's ideal for travellers with wheels. Otherwise, you can get a green minibus from Square Lumumba.

Places to Stay – Top End

The *Hôtel Mande* (☎ 23 19 93, fax 23 19 96) has by far the best setting in the city, on the banks of the river south-east of Niaréla, excellent value with rooms at CFA29,000/32,000 and a breezy restaurant-bar with great views. A taxi to/from the centre is CFA2000.

The colonial-era *Grand Hôtel* (☎ 22 38 73, fax 22 26 01) is central but a major renovation has destroyed much of its charm. Rooms are CFA43,500/46,000, plus CFA 4500 for breakfast. Nonguests can use the pool for CFA2000.

The *Hôtel de l'Amitié* (☎ 22 43 21, fax 22 36 37), just off Square Lumumba, is the city's best, with rooms at CFA48,000 plus breakfast for CFA5000. It has most amenities of a typical four-star hotel, including a cinema, casino, mini-golf course and tennis courts. The swimming pool charges nonguests CFA7000.

Places to Eat

Cheap Eats At the taxi rank near the Cinéma Vox there are a couple of *food shacks* serving rice and sauce at rock-bottom prices. For a better atmosphere, try *Café Mohammed* opposite the Mission Catholique, with local dishes (including some vegetarian options) from CFA500 to CFA750. Nearby, on Rue Bagayoko, the friendly *Restaurant de la Paix* serves meals in the same price range; it also has a few basic double rooms for CFA6000. *Restaurant le Gourmet*, off Rue Mohammed V, is small and clean, with rice and sauce for CFA500 and poulet yassa for CFA1000.

Up a few grades but still relatively cheap is the *Ali Baba Snack Bar*, near the US embassy, serving chawarmas and local dishes from CFA800, and other meals up to CFA2000, plus pizzas, sandwiches, cakes and ice cream. The busy *Salon de Thé la Phoenicia* on Rue Mohammed V serves hot croissants for CFA150, chawarmas and snacks in the CFA750 to CFA1000 range, Lebanese food for around CFA1500 and other meals up to CFA2500. Big beers are CFA1000. Calmer and slightly more expensive is the nearby *Restaurant Central*.

African The best upmarket African restaurants are *Le Djenné* (☎ 22 30 82) and *San Toro*, on Route de Koulikoro, with the same management and excellent main courses around CFA3500; they also serve European food. San Toro has a garden and terrace, *kora* musicians in the evening and a gallery selling fine art and craftwork.

Asian The long-standing *Bol de Jade* (☎ 22 63 03) on Ave Ruault serves authentic Vietnamese cuisine, with main dishes from CFA3000 to CFA4000, a daily *menu* for CFA3500 and small beers for CFA500. On Route de Sotuba, *Restaurant Asia* is reputedly even better (but with higher prices).

European The *Hôtel-Restaurant du Fleuve* (see Places to Stay earlier) has steaks, fried fish, pizzas, lasagne and spaghetti from CFA2000 to CFA3000, with side orders for CFA500. For more Italian flavours try *La Pizzeria* on Rue Mohammed V, where pizzas and pastas cost CFA3000 to CFA5000, and small beers CFA700.

There are three popular *salons de thé* on and around Route de Koulikoro: the *Relax*, the *Cigalle* and the *Express*. All have similar fare and prices: chawarmas for CFA750, meals like steak and chips from CFA2000 to CFA3000, pizzas around CFA2500, plus ice cream, cakes and pastries.

The best restaurants in town are at the *Amitié* and *Grand* hotels, the former with main courses around CFA5000 and a *menu du jour* at CFA8000, the latter slightly less. For a complete blow-out, the Grand has a very good buffet for CFA7500. The *Hôtel Mande* charges CFA7000 for a vast buffet at Sunday lunch time.

Self-Catering For imported food, try *Azar Libre Service* just off Ave Kassa Keita. There's a much larger *Azar* supermarket on Route de Koulikoro, near the Hippodrome, and *Le Metro* in Niaréla is also good.

Entertainment

Bars & Live Music For a serious drinking den try *Bar Kaissa*, off Rue de Rochester. Very lively, although not for the faint-hearted, is the nearby *Grand Muraille* – a bar-restaurant (serving cheap beer and Chinese food) and unashamed brothel with rooms out the back rented by the hour (or less, in many cases). The *Carrefour des Jeunes* near Place de la Liberté is friendly, inexpensive and sometimes has live music; it also may have cheap rooms. Bands play some weekend evenings at the *Hôtel-Buffet de la Gare*, but don't expect the legendary Rail Band. If visiting any of these places, note that the station car park and the streets off Rue de Rochester are dangerous at night – get a taxi.

For more pleasant surroundings, the *Centre Culturel Français* occasionally has music events. Otherwise, most places are in the suburbs. Try the open-air *Bar Baron* in the back streets south of Route de Koulikoro, although you'll have to get here by taxi as it's impossible to find in the dark. The salons de thé Relax, Cigalle and Express along Route de Koulikoro also serve beer and sometimes have live music at weekends, although the atmosphere is often rather sedate. Behind the Express is the much livelier *L'Akwaba* (☎ 22 06 45), a very good restaurant-bar (meals around CFA2000, big beers CFA1500) and open-air nightclub with live bands a few times each week. Further along Route de Koulikoro is *L'Inta*, which is also recommended.

MALI

Nightclubs Most discos are in the centre and don't get going before 11 pm. Thursdays to Sundays are the lively nights. Cover charges are mostly around CFA2500 and usually include a drink, but after that they're expensive. Your choices include: *Colombo* on Ave de la Nation, with CFA2500 entry, beers at CFA2000 and a mix of African and disco music; *Golden Club*, diagonally opposite the US embassy, which is similar, but plays more rap and techno; and *L'Evasion*, just off Ave Kassa Keita, frequented by Bamako's bright young things, where entry is CFA5000 at weekends and all drinks are CFA2500. The *Métropolis* in Niaréla is another glitzy joint. More preferable is the low-key *Jazz Club*, behind L'Evasion, where entry and beers are CFA1000 and, despite the title, all sort of music is played.

Cinemas The cinema at the *Hôtel de l'Amitié* has air-con and daily showings at 9 pm. For karate flicks and Indian movies try the *Vox* on Rue Bagayoko, the *Babemba* on Ave Kassa Keita, and the *Rex* near the station.

Shopping

Sadly, the Grand Marché burnt down in 1993. It has since been rebuilt in local style using pink cement (so it now goes by the name of Marché Rose), but the merchants who moved their stalls onto the surrounding streets seem reluctant to move back indoors. As a result, the market area as a whole is very busy. You can find fabrics, tie-dyed and indigo cloth, traditional blankets and rugs, brass, incense, spices and local medicines.

There are several stalls selling cassettes behind the post office, and along Blvd du Peuple.

Leather goods and woodcarvings are made and sold at the Maison des Artisans, on Blvd du Peuple. This is also a good place for gold and silver, but note that both metals are sold by weight and bargaining is usually not possible. There are also several jewellers' shops along Ave de la Nation.

La Paysanne women's cooperative, west of the centre off Ave Kassa Keita, is friend-ly and sells some lovely fabrics, designed and printed by women from the surrounding area, including tie-dyes, bogolan mud cloth and ready-made clothes. They also make designs to order. Prices are slightly higher than at the market, and the clothes are more adapted to western tastes. It's open from 9 am to 4 pm; to noon on Saturday and closed on Sunday.

Getting There & Away

Air For flight details, see the main Getting There & Away and Getting Around sections earlier in this chapter. Airlines with offices in Bamako include: Air Burkina (☎ 22 01 78), Air Guinée (☎ 22 31 50), Royal Air Maroc (☎ 22 61 05) and Air Ivoire (☎ 22 48 70), all at the Hôtel de l'Amitié; and Air France (☎ 22 22 12), Air Mali (☎ 22 84 39) and Ethiopian Airlines (☎ 22 60 36), all on Square Lumumba. Sabena (☎ 22 71 01) is on Ave Kassa Keita and Air Dabia (☎ 22 13 02) is at Maxi-Voyages on Ave Kassa Keita, next to Hôtel Lac Debo. Air Afrique (☎ 22 58 02 or 22 56 05) is on Blvd 22 Octobre, near the river, and also has an office at the Grand Hôtel.

Bus Most long-distance buses go from the gare routière at Sogoniko, 6km south of the city centre along Route de Ségou. Several bus companies (mostly those for Sikasso, Bobo-Dioulasso and Abidjan) have their ticket offices inside the gare routière. Companies running to Ségou, Mopti and Gao have yards and ticket offices outside the gare routière, with Bani Transport and N'Ga just to the south, and Bamabus and Binke Transport slightly nearer town. SOMATRA-Balazan has a yard across the main road.

It's advisable (but not essential) to visit the gare routière the day before you travel to check departure times and buy your ticket (which reserves your seat). This also helps avoid the enthusiastic touts. (If you come by taxi, get dropped off just before the gare routière to escape their notice.)

Most bus prices are fixed, so your choice is likely to be determined by departure time and quality of bus. Sample fares include

THE MOSQUE AT DJENNÉ

Djenné's elegant mosque is a classic example of Sahel-style (or Sudanese) mud architecture – in fact, it's the largest mud-brick building in the world. The current mosque was built in 1905, but the design was based on the previous mosque, dating from the 11th century, which was famous even in Europe during medieval times.

The wooden spars which jut out from the walls, giving the mosque its 'spiky' appearance, are part of the wooden frame which helps support the mud bricks, but are also to support ladders and planks when the smooth mud-rendering which covers the bricks has to be renewed at the end of every rainy season. At this time the whole town is involved in the repair work – with up to 4000 people doing the job in less than a month.

Inside, a forest of wooden columns supporting the roof takes up almost half of the floor surface. A lattice of small holes in the roof allow beams of light to penetrate between the columns, and in the rainy season they're covered with ceramic pot lids.

Non-Muslim visitors cannot go inside (apparently after a European advertising company filmed scantily clad women here) but it's worth walking right around the mosque to see it from all sides. An excellent view of the mosque, with the market in the foreground, can be had from the roof of the Petit Marché.

Top: Passing the steps to the mosque.

Bottom: The stunning façade of Djenné mosque, with the market in the foreground.

A toguna – a shelter for men's meetings – in the Dogon region, Mali.

Boats on River Niger near Mopti, Mali.

Young boy copying verses of the Quran, Mali.

Camels and sand dunes on the desert fringe near Timbuktu, Mali.

Sikasso CFA3500, Mopti CFA6000 and Gao CFA10,000. Most buses leave between 4 and 8 pm (arriving at Mopti the next morning, and Gao the following afternoon), although a few depart at around 10 am.

SOMATRA buses go hourly to Ségou for CFA2000 (some go on to Mopti); you can only buy tickets on the same day.

Vehicles to Nara and Nioro (for Kayes and Mauritania) go from near the Marché de Medina, north of the Hippodrome. (For Burkina Faso and Côte d'Ivoire buses see the main Getting There & Away section earlier in this chapter.)

Train The train station is in the city centre. The ticket office is officially open daily from 6.30 to 11 am and 3 to 6 pm, but the clerk doesn't know this so you have to go along and hope for the best. The service most used by travellers is the twice weekly express to Tambacounda and Dakar. You can buy tickets in advance, but the queues are sometimes very long. You can also buy tickets from touts, but they charge a hefty premium and you never quite know what you might be buying.

The local service to Kayes leaves Bamako most mornings, and Friday evening, with fares about 40% less than the express.

Boat For details on the River Niger boat service see the main Getting Around section earlier in this chapter. To make bookings in Bamako go to the CMN office (☎ 22 38 02), a small building on the river bank 300m west of the Pont des Martyrs. It's open weekdays to 2.30 pm and Saturdays to noon.

Getting Around

To/From the Airport Bamako's airport is 15km south of the centre. A bus meets most international flights and goes into town for CFA1500, whereas taxis charge CFA5000 to CFA7500. Going from the centre to the airport is CFA4000 in a shared taxi, CFA6000 in a private taxi.

Minibus Battered green minibuses called *dournis* (from the Bambara word for 25, the

original fare – or the number of people they pack inside?) run from the centre to the outer suburbs, for a flat fare of CFA100. Those going along Route de Ségou leave from Square Lumumba. In addition, smart blue and white 'Taba' minibuses run on some routes. Taba bus stops are clearly marked, and all fares are CFA125.

Taxi All taxis in Bamako are yellow: those with a 'taxi' sign on the roof are shared – the driver may pick up other passengers going your way, but the fare is cheaper. Those without signs are for private hire (*déplacement*) only. The minimum charge for tourists across the city centre is CFA700. For longer trips across town or out to Sogoniko it's CFA1000 to CFA1500.

AROUND BAMAKO

The River Niger passenger boats start their journey in **Koulikoro**, 50km east of Bamako. Koulikoro was an important place in colonial days (when the train from Dakar terminated here), but despite the activity around the harbour and its beautiful situation, the town itself is uninspiring and not worth a visit unless you're catching the boat. If you do overnight in Koulikoro, the pleasant *Motel le Saloon* has air-con doubles for CFA12,500. We heard from some Dutch travellers who stayed here and did some rewarding hiking in the surrounding area, which is very peaceful with rocky hills, scattered villages and great views over the river. Bush taxis from Bamako leave from near the western end of Route de Koulikoro.

If you go upstream from Bamako for 90km, towards Siguiri, the riverside town of **Kangaba** is reported to be scenic. The *Hôtel Manding* has rooms and can arrange local guides. Bush taxis from the Djikoroni gare routière in Bamako cost CFA1600.

The River Niger Route

The classic journey through Mali follows the River Niger, either by road or by boat, as it carves a huge arc through the Sahel. The towns and cities along this route are listed here in order of distance from Bamako.

SÉGOU

Ségou is a large town about 230km east of Bamako. Often overlooked by visitors as they rush east to Mopti and Djenné, it's an interesting place to stop for a night or two, noticeably lacking the hassle which sometimes spoils the touristy towns. Ségou was an important centre in colonial days, and the headquarters of the vast Office du Niger irrigation scheme. The imposing, elaborate buildings and wide avenues give an idea of how French West African colonial towns looked.

Things to See & Do

The Grand Marché is open all week, but is especially good on Mondays. You can find Bambara pottery and Ségou strip cloth and blankets at very good prices. Tapestries and carpets are made and sold at the Nieleni Rug Cooperative, near the Marché de Medina, about 1.5km south of the main road. It's closed on Sunday.

Pirogue Trips & Tours

From the waterfront, piroguers can take you on excursions to a number of nearby sites on the river, such as **Kalabougou**, where pottery is made, **Farako**, a centre for mudcloth making, or the old city of **Ségou Koro**. The trips cost around CFA15,000 to CFA 20,000 per boat. You may be able to arrange something all the way to Mopti. Similarly priced trips are available at the Hôtel Esplanade, or at Balazan Tours, where the enthusiastic staff can also arrange guides and car hire.

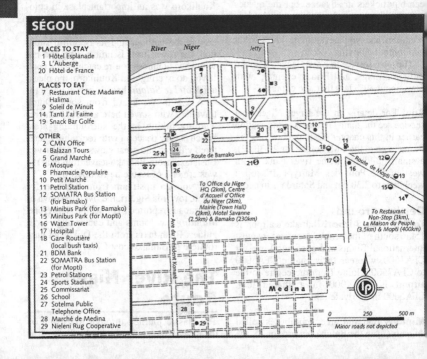

SÉGOU

PLACES TO STAY
1 Hôtel Esplanade
3 L'Auberge
20 Hôtel de France

PLACES TO EAT
7 Restaurant Chez Madame Halima
9 Soleil de Minuit
14 Tanti J'ai Faime
19 Snack Bar Golfe

OTHER
2 CMN Office
4 Balazan Tours
5 Grand Marché
6 Mosque
8 Pharmacie Populaire
10 Petit Marché
11 Petrol Station
12 SOMATRA Bus Station (for Bamako)
13 Minibus Park (for Bamako)
15 Minibus Park (for Mopti)
16 Water Tower
17 Hospital
18 Gare Routière (local bush taxis)
21 BDM Bank
22 SOMATRA Bus Station (for Mopti)
23 Petrol Stations
24 Sports Stadium
25 Commissariat
26 School
27 Sotelma Public Telephone Office
28 Marché de Medina
29 Nieleni Rug Cooperative

River Niger

Jetty

Route de Bamako

Route de Mopti

Ave du Président Konaré

To Office du Niger HQ (2km), Centre d'Accueil d'Office du Niger (2km), Mairie (Town Hall) (2km), Motel Savanne (2.5km) & Bamako (230km)

To Restaurant Non-Stop (3km), La Maison du Peuple (3.5km) & Mopti (400km)

Medina

0   250   500 m

Minor roads not depicted

Places to Stay

The *Centre d'Accueil*, 2km west of the centre, near the Office du Niger headquarters, has rooms at CFA6500. Nearby, the much friendlier *Motel Savanne* has rooms at the same price and meals for around CFA 1500. Your other cheap option is the *Maison du Peuple* about 3.5km east of the centre on the north side of the main road opposite a small mosque and near a large water tower. Rooms with fans cost CFA3000.

The *Hôtel de France* ('Chez Grand Griot') has rooms with bathroom for CFA 7500, set around a shady courtyard which becomes a lively bar-restaurant at night. Some rooms have seen better days, as has the Grand Griot himself.

L'Auberge (☎ 32 01 45) is popular with tour groups, and has singles/doubles from CFA9000/11,000 to CFA24,000/26,000, all with bathroom and some with air-con. The restaurant is good, with main dishes from around CFA2000, a *menu du jour* for CFA 4000 and large beers at CFA800. The friendly manager can help with information and offers a discount to all readers of this guidebook. But the biggest plus is the spotlessly clean swimming pool in the gardens behind the hotel – one of the few and certainly the best outside Bamako.

Overlooking the river, the plush *Hôtel Esplanade* is good value, charging CFA7500/11,000 for simple rooms and up to CFA 15,000/20,000 if you want air-con, bathroom and TV. The riverside bar is an excellent place to watch the sunset.

Places to Eat

There's a choice of cheap eating houses on the road just east of the centre, at the place where minibuses leave for Bamako and Mopti, including *Tanti J'ai Faime*, with local dishes from CFA250. *Chez Madame Halima*, in the centre, serves meals at similar prices – plus cheap beers.

The long-established *Snack Bar Golfe* is easy to find, with tables on the terrace or inside and excellent meals, such as chicken or fish with chips or vegetables, in the CFA1500 to CFA2000 range, plus coffee, snacks, cold drinks and beers. West of here, the friendly *Soleil de Minuit* serves similar fare at similar prices, and also has a very nice room to rent for a bargain CFA5000 – you really feel like you're part of the family.

Another favourite is *Restaurant Non-Stop*, 3km east of the centre on the Mopti road, renowned for its pizzas which cost around CFA2000. The garden bar serves cheap beers, and there's pleasant background music (and sometimes a griot or local blues guitarist playing).

Getting There & Away

Bus & Minibus SOMATRA buses leave for Mopti (CFA4000) from its yard, while its buses to Bamako (CFA2000) go hourly from the gare routière east of the centre. Minibuses to Bamako and Mopti go from the main road nearby, leaving when full, for the same fare. Generally, the big buses are a much better option. You can also get a daily bus to Sikasso (CFA3500) and Bobo-Dioulasso (CFA6000).

SAN

San is a junction town where you stop for a meal on the bus between Ségou and Mopti or change transport if you're heading to/from Burkina Faso. It's a pleasant place, with friendly people and a traditional ambience that the larger towns seem to have lost. The **mosque** and many **old houses** in the centre are mud brick, and San was described by one traveller as 'like Timbuktu without the legend'. The main market day is Monday.

Places to stay include the *Hôtel Relax* on the southern outskirts of town, with rooms for CFA3000; the bar gets fairly lively at night. The *Campement-Restaurant Teriya*, on the new bypass road, has similarly priced rooms and meals from CFA750 to CFA1500.

DJENNÉ

Djenné sits on an island in the River Bani about 130km south-west of Mopti and 30km off the main road. It is unquestionably one of the most interesting and picturesque towns in West Africa, and one of the oldest. Little has

MALI

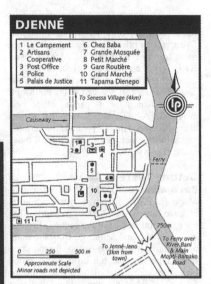

DJENNÉ

1 Le Campement
2 Artisans
  Cooperative
3 Post Office
4 Police
5 Palais de Justice
6 Chez Baba
7 Grande Mosquée
8 Petit Marché
9 Gare Routière
10 Grand Marché
11 Tapama Dienepo

To Senessa Village (4km)

Causeway

Ferry

750m

To Ferry over
River Bani
& Main
Mopti-Bamako
Road

To Jenné-Jeno
(3km from
town)

0   250   500 m
Approximate Scale
Minor roads not depicted

changed since its heyday during the 14th and 15th centuries when it profited, like Timbuktu, from the trans-Saharan trade. But while Timbuktu declined, Djenné remained wealthy. When the French explorer René Caillié visited here in the early 19th century, he reported that the inhabitants enjoyed a good standard of living and had plenty to eat, most could read, no one went barefoot and everyone seemed to be usefully employed.

Today, most of the houses and the world-famous mosque are still skilfully built with mud bricks and rendered in traditional Sahel style. Djenné's Monday market is incredibly large and lively, so come on this day if you can, but stay on for a day or two to enjoy the winding streets and sleepy atmosphere virtually undisturbed.

Things to See & Do

Top of the list is the **Grande Mosquée** (see the colour feature between pages 576 and 577), and in front of here is a wide open area for the **Grand Marché**. Most of the time it's quiet, but on market day (Monday) the place is packed with thousands of traders

and customers who come from many miles around. (Watch out for pickpockets in the crowd.) The sheer range of goods is amazing, but there's little in the way of souvenirs for tourists. This is very much a local's place, and the sights, sounds and smells, complete with the awesome mosque as a backdrop, make this one of the highlights of any visit to Mali, and even West Africa. Nearby is the **Petit Marché** which is busy every day.

As you go through the narrow streets and alleyways, you'll pass between the walls of **mud-brick houses**. Many are over a storey high; traditionally, the top part was for the masters, the middle floor for the slaves and the bottom floor for storage and selling. The porches of the houses are lined with wooden columns, while the wooden window shutters and doors are decorated with paint and metal objects. In one part of town, the houses are decorated in a Moorish style, dating from the period when Moroccan traders lived here and dominated the trade. Several inhabitants of Djenné claim Moroccan descent.

You will also pass a few **madrassa** schools where young children learn the Quran. There are more madrassas in Djenné than in any other town in Mali. With the help of a guide, you can also see the **old well** and the **house of the traditional chief**, whose role today is mainly as an adjudicator in local disputes (eg when Fula cattle eat Bambara crops).

Your guide may also want to show you **Tapama Dienepo**, the tomb of a young girl sacrificed here in the 9th century after a local religious leader decided the town was corrupt; there's nothing to see today, but this stroll to the edge of town is interesting.

Guides are not essential in Djenné but you'll be pestered all day by local youths offering their services, so hiring one will keep the others at bay. You'll also see a lot more than you would on your own. Your guide will be able to take you onto the roof of a private house to get a view of the town, ask permission from the locals to take photos, and show you where the various artisans (such as goldsmiths, woodcarvers and mud-cloth artists) work. Some guides speak English and, as

MALI

Fula Earrings

In Djenné, Mopti and other towns along the Niger, you will often see well-to-do Fula women dressed very elaborately, with large bracelets of silver and necklaces of glass beads. Most spectacular, however, are the huge 14-carat gold earrings called *kwotenai kanye*, worn by the wealthiest women. They are so heavy that the top of each earring is bound with red wool or silk to protect the ear, and sometimes supported with a strap over the top of the woman's head. Earrings are given as wedding gifts from the woman's husband, who will have had to sell off several cows to afford them, but Fula women remain financially independent of their husbands and so gold and jewellery is often passed down from mothers to daughters.

with anywhere else, it's worth getting a recommendation from another traveller before hiring anybody. Fees are negotiable; some guides start by asking for CFA2500 per person per hour, but you can soon get down to half that for a whole morning, and even less if there's four or five of you in a group.

Places to Stay & Eat

Most travellers favour *Chez Baba*, originally a basic eating house where you could crash on the floor, now a large restaurant and two-storey block of simple rooms for CFA2000 per person. The food is good – large meals of chicken or fish with chips or *brochettes* and rice cost CFA2000 – and Baba himself is still as friendly as ever. Breakfast includes a whole loaf of bread and honey.

Your other choice is *Le Campement*, which promises 'cuisine qualité et un accueil incomparable', but the group of sullen youths running the place are not very welcoming and the food is nothing special either. However, simple double rooms for CFA5000 are adequate, although four showers and toilets for up to 60 people is a bit tight. Rooms with bathroom cost CFA10,000, or you can sleep on the roof for a negotiable CFA2000. Breakfast is CFA1000, meals around CFA2500, small beers CFA500 and soft drinks CFA300.

Shopping

Djenné is famous for bogolan (or mud cloth, as described in the colour feature 'Textiles' between page 128 and 129), and some of the women artists in Djenné are very skilled. Most famous is Pama Sinatoa, whose workshop is near the small bridge where the road enters the town. There are several other workshops in the same area. It's also worth checking in the women artisans' cooperative next to the campement, where the quality is good and you can browse unhassled.

Getting There & Away

Bus & Bush Taxi Direct buses go from Bamako to Djenné a few days each week (mainly on Saturday and Sunday). Alternatively, you can catch something to Mopti and be dropped at the junction where the road to Djenné branches off from the main road, but you may have a long wait. If it's not market day (Monday), consider going to Mopti and finding transport back to Djenné from there.

In Mopti, bush taxis for Djenné leave most days, and always on Monday mornings. Bâchés cost CFA1500 but take at least three hours. Faster 504s cost CFA1750. Consider getting a group together to charter a 504 – it

MALI

Jenné-Jeno

About 3km from Djenné are the ruins of Jenné-Jeno, an ancient settlement which dates back to about 250 BC. Implements and jewellery have been discovered that suggest it may have been one of the first places in Africa where iron was used. In the 8th century Jenné-Jeno was a fortified city with walls 3m thick, but around 1400 it was abandoned. Today, there is nothing much to see – some mounds and millions of tiny pieces of broken pottery – so a visit is likely to be of interest only to archaeologists.

might be a bit more expensive but it saves lots of time. Between the main road and Djenné, cars have to cross the river by a ferry, which breaks down frequently and is occasionally rumoured to have sunk, but against all odds still seems to be running.

Boat There's no regular river transport between Djenné and Mopti, as nearly everything goes by road. However, we have heard from travellers who found rides on merchants' pinasses. It seems much easier to do this coming from Djenné rather than the other way. Local guides will help you out, and the fare should be around CFA3000.

MOPTI

Mopti lies at the junction of the Niger and Bani rivers, and the surrounding region is one of the most interesting parts of West Africa. In medieval times Mopti was largely overshadowed by Djenné and Timbuktu, but River Niger commerce increased during the colonial period, and Mopti's position between Bamako and Gao gave it a distinct advantage.

Today, with over 40,000 inhabitants, Mopti is thriving, with a large market, a beautiful mosque and the most vibrant port on the river. Boats come and go all day, loading and unloading passengers, piles of dried fish, bundles of firewood and baskets of spices and vegetables. Some of the merchandise is bought and sold by eager traders even before it gets to the market.

Mopti is surrounded by water, swamp and rice fields, inundated every rainy season, and is linked by a 12km causeway to the mainland proper at Sévaré on the main road.

Within a day's journey is the ancient city of Djenné and the fascinating Dogon Country. Mopti is also a good starting point for a trip to Timbuktu, and an ideal spot to meet locals and other travellers, with a good choice of bars and restaurants. Whatever you do, there's enough to keep you fully occupied for quite a few days.

Information

Money Service at the banks is slow, commissions are high and staff often refuse to accept any currency other than French francs. Some large hotels and tour companies in Mopti will change cash and travellers cheques (UK£, US$ and DM) into CFA with far less fuss, and some traders in the market will also change French francs.

Post & Communications The post office is in the centre, with the Sotelma telephone office next door. When Sotelma is closed you can make calls at the post office.

Travel Agencies & Tour Operators Frontrunners seem to be Ashraf Voyages (☎/fax 43 02 79, fax 43 00 66) and Bambara Tours (☎ 43 00 80), both in the town centre. They can assist with travel reservations on planes or boats to Timbuktu, and also run a range of tours in the surrounding area. Ashraf also offers half-day boat trips on the river and mountain bike hire.

Dangers & Annoyances Mopti is the centre of Mali's tourist industry, and your visit can be ruined by local youths continually offering their services as guides, or simply trying to sell you postcards and souvenirs. If you don't need their services, just ignore them completely or tell them you've already

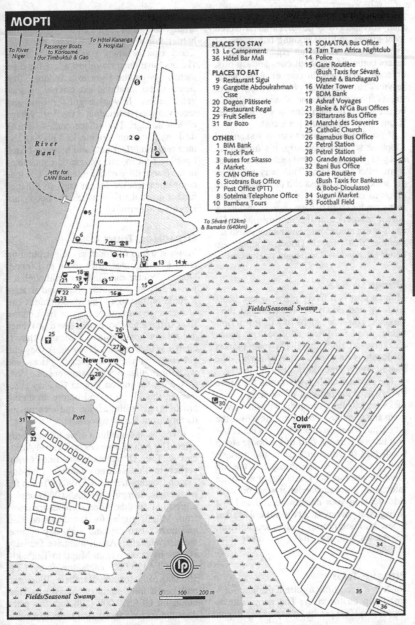

MOPTI

To River Niger

To Hôtel Kananga & Hospital

Passenger Boats to Korioumé (for Timbuktu) & Gao

River Bani

Jetty for CMN Boats

To Sévaré (12km) & Bamako (640km)

Fields/Seasonal Swamp

New Town

Port

Old Town

Fields/Seasonal Swamp

MALI

PLACES TO STAY
13 Le Campement
36 Hôtel Bar Mali

PLACES TO EAT
9 Restaurant Sigui
19 Gargotte Abdoulrahman Cisse
20 Dogon Pâtisserie
22 Restaurant Regal
29 Fruit Sellers
31 Bar Bozo

OTHER
1 BIM Bank
2 Truck Park
3 Buses for Sikasso
4 Market
5 CMN Office
6 Sicotrans Bus Office
7 Post Office (PTT)
8 Sotelma Telephone Office
10 Bambara Tours

11 SOMATRA Bus Office
12 Tam Tam Africa Nightclub
14 Police
15 Gare Routière (Bush Taxis for Sévaré, Djenné & Bandiagara)
16 Water Tower
17 BDM Bank
18 Ashraf Voyages
21 Binke & N'Ga Bus Offices
23 Bittartrans Bus Office
24 Marché des Souvenirs
25 Catholic Church
26 Bamabus Bus Office
27 Petrol Station
28 Petrol Station
30 Grande Mosquée
32 Bani Bus Office
33 Gare Routière (Bush Taxis for Bankass & Bobo-Dioulasso)
34 Suguni Market
35 Football Field

0   100   200 m

MALI

got something booked. We've heard from many travellers over the years who have used local guides and had nothing but praise for them. But we've had an equal number of letters complaining about cons and rip-offs, or about receiving torrents of abuse when services are declined. We've even heard stories about staged 'attacks' which will only be sorted out by the police if you pay a fee (from which the youths get a cut).

If you do want a guide to show you around Mopti or set up a boat trip, it's imperative that you get some personal recommendations from other travellers. That way the good guides keep in business and the bad ones are elbowed out. Don't rely on names alone: many guides seem to have several (including 'street' names) and the renting out of ID cards is not an uncommon practice. Also remember that trips to Dogon Country are better arranged in Bandiagara or Bankass.

Things to See

Mopti's **port** is a lively place, where boats from up and down the river unload their cargoes. You'll see slabs of salt from Timbuktu, dried fish, firewood, pottery, goats, chickens and much more. The main **market** for locals is on the east side of town – the busiest day is Thursday.

The classic Sahel-style **Grande Mosquée** towers over the old part of town. If you're lucky (or Muslim), the guardian will let you go in and climb the stairs for a view over the city. Otherwise, the man who lives next door will let you onto the roof of his house (for a small fee) so you can look at the mosque from there. East of the mosque is the old town, where tourists rarely venture. It's an interesting place to wander around, but consider leaving your camera behind and just *seeing* with your eyes. At the **Suguni Market** a new building houses traders selling fruit, vegetables, salt, fish, meat and other commodities.

Pirogue Trips

Dusk is a good time to hire a pirogue for a small trip on the river. The going rate is about CFA1000 per hour, especially if you

go straight to the boat owner rather than arrange things through a guide (although the harder you bargain, the shorter the trip). Check exactly where you're going – some visitors have been taken just a few hundred metres across the river to a 'village' that seems to be inhabited exclusively by souvenir sellers. If you've got the time and money, a good destination is the Bozo village of Kakalodaga. The village comes alive at dusk, with women cooking, kids playing and men repairing their nets and building boats. Spotting pelican, ibis and heron contributes to the tranquillity of the ride back. The tour companies arrange longer trips to villages further down the river, where the people are less used to tourists.

Organised Tours

Mopti is a hub for tours in the surrounding area. Local guides offer tours to Djenné, Dogon Country and Timbuktu, although it's just as easy to go to these places and arrange a guide on the spot. The Mopti guides can also arrange pirogue or pinasse trips on the river (from a few hours to a few days). Fees are totally negotiable – basically, they'll charge you as much as they think they can get away with. For an idea of prices, see what the regular tour operators are charging, or see the section on Dogon Country costs later in this chapter. And before arranging anything, get some advice and recommendations from fellow travellers.

If you want something more formal, tours offered by Ashraf Voyages (see Travel Agencies & Tour Operators under Information earlier in this section) include four-day Dogon Country treks at CFA90,000 each for two people, dropping to CFA50,000 each for a group of six (the price includes transport from Mopti, guide, food, accommodation and taxes); two-day and eight-day options are also available. An all-inclusive four-day voyage by pinasse from Mopti to Timbuktu costs CFA125,000 each for four, CFA 100,000 each for six. Bambara Tours can rent you a fully equipped pinasse to Timbuktu for CFA550,000 (although this price does not include food), and tours to Dogon

Country and elsewhere in the region range from CFA15,000 to CFA22,000 per person per day depending on destination and number in group. Dogon Country treks and excursions by boat or car can also be arranged with Askia Tours (☎ 43 00 32, fax 34 00 08), based at the Campement; for example, one day to Djenné costs CFA 28,000 for four to six people. Pinasse tours can also be arranged through Bar Bozo (see Places to Eat later in this section).

Places to Stay

The *Hôtel Bar Mali*, in the old town, has been the shoestringers only choice for many years. It's a dirty brothel with a kind of sleazy charm and singles/doubles/triples with fans for CFA4000/4500/7000. Upstairs is a corridor with a balcony at one end, and travellers generally get put in rooms along here. The bar serves cheap beer, and food is available if you order long in advance.

Mopti's single mid-range hotel is *Le Campement*, the hub of most tourist activity. Double rooms in the main building are reasonable and cost CFA16,000 with bathroom and air-con, while those in bungalows are more basic (although a renovation is planned) with dirty shared bathrooms and are overpriced at CFA10,000.

The other mid-range hotels are in Sévaré (12km from Mopti). Cheapest and relatively good value is the *Hôtel Oasis* a few blocks off the main road, near the local bush taxi park, with clean singles/doubles at CFA6000/7500. Breakfast costs CFA750, other meals are around CFA1500, and there's a useful map of the surrounding area (including Dogon Country) on the wall. Camping costs CFA2500.

On the main road, the *Motel de Sévaré* (☎ 42 00 82) has plain but acceptable rooms at CFA9000/13,000 with bathroom and breakfast. Air-con is an extra CFA3000. The bar is dingy and disreputable, but the garden courtyard is pleasant. Further out of town, near the airport turn-off, the smaller *Hôtel Débo* (☎ 42 01 24) charges CFA15,500/19,000 for good air-con rooms, with meals around CFA3000.

Back in Mopti, but 1km north of the centre, the top end *Hôtel Kananga* (☎ 43 05 00) has rooms at CFA23,500/28,500, plus CFA2250 for breakfast.

Places to Eat

The best place for *street food stalls* and basic *eating houses* is around the gare routière near the port and at the gare routière near the Campement. *Fruit sellers* congregate on the bridge to the old town.

The *Dogon Pâtisserie*, in the centre, is a bit more expensive but has excellent coffee (CFA250) and pastries (CFA150 to CFA 450). Round the corner is the simpler *Gargotte Abdoulrahman Cisse*, a bench in the street where coffee is CFA125, and omelettes and bread CFA300. Also good value is the nearby *Restaurant Regal*, with very friendly staff selling rice and sauce for CFA500, fish and chips for CFA1250 or half a chicken for CFA1000. There's another cheap place opposite the Sotelma telephone office.

Restaurant Sigui has a pleasant garden and an elaborate menu with meals from CFA3000, including Asian dishes such as *riz chinoise*. Small beers and soft drinks are CFA500. *Bar Bozo* on the harbour has good food at slightly lower prices, a great view and a few more mosquitoes.

In Sévaré a popular restaurant is *Mankan Té*, with inside or garden seating, excellent meals from CFA3000, small beers for CFA 500 and music or dancing at weekends.

Shopping

Mopti is famous for blankets. With hard bargaining, you can get all-wool blankets (made by combining six or seven long thin bands) from around CFA5000, wool-cotton mix for CFA7500, all-cotton ones with simple coloured squares for CFA10,000 and all-cotton ones with complex designs for CFA12,500. The much more ornate Fula wedding blankets can cost CFA50,000 or more, depending on the material. You'll find sellers at the Marché des Souvenirs and outside the better restaurants.

At the Marché des Souvenirs you can also buy printed and mud-cloth fabrics, Tuareg

MALI

swords and jewellery, old glass beads, leatherwork, and woodcarvings from many parts of West Africa. Look out for the igloo-shaped *sans-bois* huts surrounding the market – a new design to help reduce wood required for building.

A local trader called Oumar Cisse (widely known as 'Peace Corps Baba', because many volunteers buy his stuff) is highly rated. He sells carvings (old and antique), jewellery, blankets and many other items – mostly from Mali and all very good quality. Most items are at Baba's house, which is difficult to find in the depths of the old town – you'll probably need to ask a local guide to show you, but once inside there is absolutely no pressure to buy.

Getting There & Away

Air The airport is 15km from Mopti, 3km south of Sévaré. For details of Air Mali flights to/from Bamako, Timbuktu and Gao see the Getting Around section at the beginning of this chapter. The Air Mali office is at the Campement. Booking a flight here is unreliable, so it's worth paying a little extra to get a travel agency to make a reservation for you. A private taxi from Mopti to the airport costs CFA4000. Strangely, taxis do not always meet incoming flights.

Bus Several companies serve Mopti: the N'Ga, Binke, Bittartrans and Sicotrans ticket offices are on the waterfront; Bani is in the port area; Bamabus is near the centre; and SOMATRA is near the post office. All have services to Bamako, Ségou and Gao, usually at around 9 am and again at 4 pm. Note that some Gao buses go from Sévaré.

Buses to Sikasso (companies include Badegna and Zanga) go daily from near the main market. Some Sikasso buses go on to Bobo-Dioulasso (Burkina Faso), but departure days vary so you need to ask (and buy your ticket) in advance. Otherwise get a Sikasso bus to Koutiala and then go to Bobo by bush taxi.

All bus fares are fixed, and buying a ticket in advance reserves your seat. To Ségou it's CFA4000, Bamako CFA6000, Gao CFA6000, Sikasso CFA4500 and Koutiala CFA3250.

Bush Taxi Bâchés cover the 12km between Mopti and Sévaré throughout the day for CFA175, departing Mopti from the gare routière near the Campement. Transport also goes from here to Djenné (CFA1750 in a 504, CFA1500 in a bâché) and Bandiagara (CFA1500 by 504).

Bush taxis to most other destinations go from near the port. Bankass is CFA2500 by 504 and CFA2000 by bâché. You can also get 504s to Bobo-Dioulasso (CFA6500) from here, via San, overnighting at Kouri on the border.

Another option is the route direct to Ouagadougou. A bâché goes most mornings from Mopti to Koro, via Bankass, for CFA2500. It can take several hours to fill, but on Saturday (Koro's market day) it leaves early. From Koro a comfortable STMB bus to Ouagadougou departs on Saturday and Thursday afternoons. It waits on the Mali side, then crosses the border. The fare is CFA4000. Other days, you might have to overnight in Koro – but there's a good cheap campement. Bush taxis from Koro to Ouahigouya are CFA2500.

Car The tour companies in Mopti all have cars with drivers for hire. For example, Bambara Tours charges CFA35,000 per day plus petrol. Ashraf charges CFA20,000 to Bandiagara, CFA40,000 to Sanga or Bankass, and CFA65,000 for a one day return trip to Djenné.

Boat From Mopti, many travellers head for Korioumé (Timbuktu's port) by boat. For the large CMN passenger boats, the office is on the waterfront (see this chapter's main Getting Around section for timetables). Tickets can be hard to come by, as this is by far the busiest sector on the boat's itinerary (for locals because roads are bad, and for tourists because sailing to Timbuktu is a pretty cool thing to do). Sometimes clerks won't sell cabin tickets without payment of an extra 'booking fee', and occasionally tourists have bought tickets, only to find the cabin already full. You might consider using the services of a local guide or tour operator to get you a ticket, which will of course cost extra. Or, if it's just the boat trip you want to experience, consider going from Mopti to Ségou instead.

Alternatively, you can take a large *pinasse transporteur* (cargo pinasse) between Mopti and Korioumé. Some travellers go all the way, or take a pinasse just to Diré or Niafounké and continue from there to Timbuktu by land. Look out for the 80m-long *Baba Tigamba*, known as *Petit Baba*, going once per week in each direction, and taking only two days. It has proper seats, a roof and even a small upper deck which the owner calls the *cabine luxe*. Fares start at a ridiculous CFA 25,000, but after negotiation you should get a ride for about CFA10,000 or even less. On less fancy pinasses the fare for a space on the deck is around CFA3000 to Diré and CFA5000 to Korioumé. Smaller pinasses take about three days, but with breakdowns and stops to take on cargo they can take up to six.

Your third option is to get a group together and charter your own pinasse through a tour operator or local guide. In the last few years this has become an increasingly popular option for travellers, and is a very relaxing and fascinating way to see the River Niger. From Mopti to Korioumé usually takes four days, with stops at villages on the way and sleeping each night on the boat or the river bank. For an idea of prices see Organised Tours, earlier in this section.

TIMBUKTU (TOMBOUCTOU)

Strategically located on the southern edge of the Sahara Desert and at the top of the River Niger's 'great bend', Timbuktu is the

MALI

Timbuktu – Some Snippets of History

Timbuktu dates back to around 1100 AD when a group of Tuareg nomads settled around a small oasis here. An old woman was put in charge of the settlement while the men tended the animals. Her name was Bouctou, meaning 'large navel', possibly indicating a physical disorder. Tim simply means 'well', and the town became known as Timbouctou, later called Tombouctou, and anglicised to Timbuktu or Timbuctoo.

In 1494, Leo Africanus, a well travelled Spanish Moor, recorded in his *History and Description of Africa* that Timbuktu had 'a great store of doctors, judges, priests and other learned men, that are bountifully maintained at the king's expense'.

When the first European explorers arrived in the early 19th century, Timbuktu had declined, following repeated invasions and the loss of its trade monopoly. Early drawings show that it looked pretty much as it does today. A Scot called Gordon Laing is usually credited with being the first to arrive, but he was killed on his way home. The Frenchman René Caillié reached Timbuktu in 1828 after many years travelling through the desert disguised as a Moor, living to tell the tale. The third European explorer to arrive here was a German called Heinrich Barth, who came disguised as an Arab. His incredible five-year journey began in Tripoli and took him first to Agadez, then through Nigeria and finally, in September 1853, to Timbuktu. He stayed here gathering information for the better part of a year before narrowly escaping with his life and eventually reaching Europe to write an account of his travels.

During the 1990s Timbuktu was badly hit by fighting between Tuareg rebels, the Bambara-dominated army and Songhaï militias. There was no actual fighting here, but in the military crackdown Tuareg civilians and suspected sympathisers from other ethnic groups were arrested and imprisoned. Many people were reportedly executed in the sand dunes outside the town.

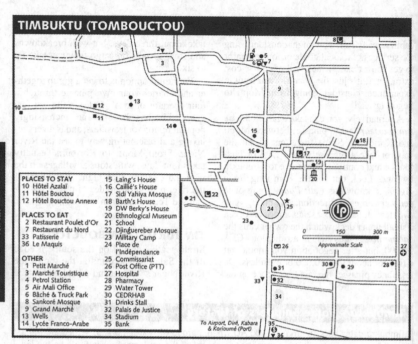

TIMBUKTU (TOMBOUCTOU)

PLACES TO STAY
10 Hôtel Azalaï
11 Hôtel Bouctou
12 Hôtel Bouctou Annexe

PLACES TO EAT
2 Restaurant Poulet d'Or
7 Restaurant du Nord
33 Patisserie
36 Le Maquis

OTHER
1 Petit Marché
3 Marché Touristique
4 Petrol Station
5 Air Mali Office
6 Bâché & Truck Park
8 Sankoré Mosque
9 Grand Marché
13 Wells
14 Lycée Franco-Arabe

15 Laing's House
16 Caillié's House
17 Sidi Yahiya Mosque
18 Barth's House
19 DW Berky's House
20 Ethnological Museum
21 School
22 Djinguereber Mosque
23 Military Camp
24 Place de l'Indépendance
25 Commissariat
26 Post Office (PTT)
27 Hospital
28 Pharmacy
29 Water Tower
30 CEDRHAB
31 Drinks Stall
32 Palais de Justice
34 Stadium
35 Bank

To Airport, Diré, Kabara & Korioumé (Port)

0   150   300 m
Approximate Scale

terminus of a camel caravan route across the desert that has linked West Africa and the Mediterranean since ancient times. Gold, ivory and slaves were transported north, eventually making their way to Europe and the Middle East. In return, West Africans wanted salt which came from former lakes deep in the desert. Timbuktu grew wealthy on the trade, by the 15th century becoming a powerful city-state and influential centre of Islamic learning.

Today, camel caravans still arrive with salt from the desert, and the town is a regional centre for trade, administration and relief work. But Timbuktu is a shadow of its former self – the population of 15,000 down from 100,000 in its heyday, the place a sprawl of low, flat-roofed buildings with sandy streets and alleyways winding between the houses. All you can see in any direction is sand dunes, and the city itself seems to be filling up with sand blown in from the desert, so that you now have to step *down* from street level into many of the houses.

For centuries, Timbuktu has been a by-word for an inaccessible place and is the favoured destination for travellers. Almost inevitably, some are disappointed when they arrive. Like the early European explorers, maybe they expect the streets to be paved with gold. One of the problems is that many visitors fly in and out, often spending only a day here. To get the most out of Timbuktu you really need to stay a bit longer, and give yourself time to understand the significance of this town – its isolation, its history and its continuing importance as a trading post on the salt trade route. It can be a fascinating place to visit, with an appeal and atmosphere quite unlike any other town along the River Niger.

Orientation & Information

The focus of Timbuktu is Place de l'Indépendance, a dusty traffic circle. South from here the road leads out towards the airport and the port at Korioumé (18km away). In the older part of town north of Place de l'Indépendance is the Grand Marché, the museum, three mosques and Timbuktu's two hotels.

Money The BDM and Banque National de Développement Agricole are on the main road south of the centre. The latter changes cash and some travellers cheques, including US$, and also has an excellent map of the surrounding area on the wall.

Post & Communications The post office sells postcards and stamps for that all-important postmark. It's open normal hours Monday to Friday and, 'for the best satisfaction of the clientele', on Saturday morning, too. These people understand service!

The Sotelma telephone office is next door. There's also a public phone which takes cards – sold by a guy who hangs around the Hôtel Bouctou.

Police The commissariat is on Place de l'Indépendance. You can register here or extend your visa if necessary.

MALI

The Timbuktu Salt Trade

Throughout the cool season, from October to March, a camel caravan arrives in Timbuktu every two or three days. Led by Tuareg and Arab traders, they come from the salt mines of Taoudenni, deep in the Sahara almost 900km north of Timbuktu. Some of the last genuine working caravans in Africa, they are continuing a trade that has gone unchanged for centuries.

Each caravan consists of 60 to 300 camels, and every camel carries four to six slabs of salt weighing about 45kg. The journey takes about 15 days, although because of the intense heat the caravans travel at night, with camels unloaded and rested during the day. On arrival in Timbuktu the salt is sold to merchants who then transport it downriver to Mopti, where it is sold again and dispersed all over West Africa, as far away as the coast. Salt is a valuable commodity that used to be traded weight for weight with gold. Nowadays, a good quality slab will fetch up to CFA5000 in Timbuktu, with its value increasing as it heads south.

The feudal relationships between the different tribes of the desert has also gone unchanged for centuries: Tuareg and the Arabs are the masters; the Bella and the Haratin, respectively, are their virtual slaves. Often the same Bella family has served the same Tuareg family for many generations. It's the Bella and the Haratin who look after the camels and actually mine the salt.

The salt comes from the beds of ancient lakes, which dried out many millennia ago, and the mining techniques are not noted for their attention to safety. The salt starts about 1m below the surface and is reached by a system of trenches and tunnels up to 6m deep and up to 200m long, using salt slabs as makeshift props. The salt is dug out in large blocks to be split into slabs on the surface.

Work in the mines is appallingly paid as well as hard and dangerous: each man earns about CFA30,000 for six months work, and is allowed to keep one in every four bars mined. But they don't bring many back. The nearest oasis to the mines is a three day camel journey away, and the masters provide water to their workers in exchange for salt. One *guerba* of water (about 30L) costs two slabs.

The salt caravans unload on the northern side of Timbuktu, where the Bella live in temporary camps, but the Tuareg and Arab traders do not welcome visitors. If you really want to see more, go with a reputable guide who knows the traders.

Tour Operators Local guides offer tours of the town and can help set you up with camel trips, trucks to Gao or boats to Mopti – if required. Their services are not essential, but they can make your walk around town more interesting and enjoyable.

Many tour operators in Bamako and Mopti bring groups here, but there are also a couple of local outfits who can arrange cars, long-distance camel trips, skilled guides etc. Sahel Expedition (☎/fax 92 10 48) is a joint German-Mali operation, headed by Ayouba Ag Moha. (In Germany contact New Adventure, ☎ 06221-809151, email nadventure@aol.com.)

A new company is due to be formed by respected senior guides Dramane Alpha and Oumar Dicko (☎ 92 10 12), who both speak excellent English and offer boat trips on the River Niger. Dramane's biggest job so far was organising a 50 day trip with 200 camels for a *National Geographic* film crew – but he caters for all visitors with a genuine interest.

Mosques

Timbuktu has three of the oldest mosques in West Africa. They're not large, architecturally impressive or in good repair – just old. You may be allowed in on payment of a CFA1000 fee, but sometimes this is only allowed if you are with a guide. **Djinguereber Mosque**, west of Place de l'Indépendance, is the oldest, dating from the early 14th century when Emperor Kankan Moussa, having taken control of the city from the Tuaregs, ordered its construction. From the top of the minaret you get a great view over the city. **Sidi Yahiya Mosque** is north of Place de l'Indépendance. Named after one of the city's saints, it was constructed in 1400. **Sankoré Mosque**, northeast of the Grand Marché, was built a century later. It also functioned as a university, which by the 16th century was one of the largest schools of Arabic learning in the Muslim world, with some 2500 students.

Museums

The **Ethnological Museum** is near Sidi Yahiya Mosque, with the well of Bouctou, which gave the city its name, in the grounds.

There's a good variety of exhibits, including furniture, jewellery and games, but they're not well labelled and at one point it's hard to differentiate between artefacts on display and items for sale. There are also some interesting photos from colonial times – including an incongruous display of bunting to welcome a governor. Admission is CFA500.

If you're keen on old manuscripts, responsible guides may be able to arrange a visit to the **Centre de Recherches Historiques Ahmed Baba** (CEDRHAB) – a collection of ancient books on religion and science from all over the Muslim world and the histories of local clans and families going back many centuries. Pride of place goes to the brash bumper-sized Quran presented to the centre by Libya's Colonel Gaddafi.

Explorer's Houses

The house where **René Caillié** stayed is south of the Grand Marché and west of Sidi Yahiya Mosque. It is unoccupied and in tumbledown condition, but a plaque remains on the wall. **Gordon Laing** stayed in a house a little west of Caillié's on the same winding street. It's very small, and you can't go inside as the floors are about to collapse. The house **Heinrich Barth** stayed in is in better repair; it's east of the Sidi Yahiya Mosque. Don't miss the house of **DW Berky** – leader of the first American Trans-Saharan Expedition of 1912 – almost opposite the museum.

Markets

The **Grand Marché** is the large covered building in the centre of town. It's not particularly grand: there are a few merchants selling cloth and other goods, some tailors and a man mending pots and pans. When we passed through, a new **Petit Marché** and **Marché Touristique** for local artisans to sell their wares were under construction on the west side of town. The Tuareg specialise in knives and swords with engraved blades and inlaid handles, and make bracelets, rings and talismans out of silver and brass. You can also buy various leatherwork items.

Desert Wells

Near the Hôtel Bouctou are some large, funnel-shaped wells, about 50m across at the top, with a line of steps leading down to a small pool at the bottom. They have to be this shape because of the sandy soil; a conventional well would soon collapse. Each well is surrounded by a small ring of vegetable plots, the tiny patches of vivid green quite a shock in this grey city of sand.

Camel Rides

Many visitors enjoy a short camel ride out into the surrounding desert to the west of the town. This is easily organised with the Tuaregs who tout for business at the Hôtel Bouctou, and the going rate for a three hour outing is CFA5000 per person, although opening prices can be 10 times this! You can choose to go to the dunes (the so-called 'Port de la Sahara' – Gateway to the Desert) or to one of the outlying Tuareg camps. Trips overnighting in a camp are a great way to see the desert by moonlight. These should cost CFA15,000 to CFA20,000 including a traditional meal.

On either trip you'll be given strong sweet Arab tea, and undoubtedly offered knives or leatherwork to buy. Some travellers have reported being taken for just a 30 minute ride, not even reaching the dunes, while others have been taken to tents that were set up as a tourist trap where they were submitted to hours of hard-sell. The only way to avoid this is to make it clear right from the start what you want and pay for the trip on your return, or to go with someone who's been recommended by other travellers.

If you're short of cash, it's easy to walk north-west from the town out into the dunes. The evening is the best time. You can't get lost, as the lights of Timbuktu show the way back.

For something more authentic, reputable guides can set you up with longer camel rides. A three day trip covering around 100km and visiting several genuine Tuareg camps costs about CFA50,000 per person. Other destinations include Lac Faguibine (three to four days each way by camel, for about CFA100,000 per person) or Araouane (see Around Timbuktu later in this chapter).

Places to Stay

The *Hôtel Bouctou* has a stranglehold on accommodation in this town, and basic single/double rooms are not worth the CFA 12,500/16,500 charged. Rooms with bathroom cost CFA14,500/19,000 plus an extra CFA2000 for air-con. Breakfast is CFA 1250 and other meals are made to order for about CFA3500, while big beers are CFA 1000 and soft drinks CFA500. The hotel annexe is older and quieter, with more character (and great views from the roof). Upstairs rooms with a mattress on the floor cost CFA5000 with dogged persistence.

Nearby is the *Hôtel Azalaï* (☎ 92 11 63), where soulless but clean rooms with air-con and bathroom cost CFA24,000/28,000. Breakfast is CFA2500 and meals CFA5000. If you're taking the better rooms at the Bouctou, you'll get more luxury at the Azalaï for only a little extra cost.

Places to Eat

Street food is hard to find, but the *Restaurant du Nord* near the Grand Marché serves coffee, bread and cheap meals for around CFA500. Near the Petit Marché is the friendly and good value *Restaurant Poulet d'Or*,

---

Private Lodgings in Timbuktu

It used to be illegal to stay in somebody's house in Timbuktu. It isn't any more, but it's still tricky and needs to be arranged through a local guide with some discretion. The hotels don't like to lose business, the police see it as undermining their 'control' of the town, and your hosts can get into trouble. We've even heard reports of visitors arranging overnight camel trips having a hotel night included in their fee, so that hotel managers can be placated, and the Tuareg permitted to tout for customers nearby.

where you need to order in advance and establish the total cost, as otherwise the menu arrives *after* the meal! Meat sauce with rice is CFA750, and larger meals like brochettes, fish and grilled chicken with chips cost around CFA2000, but try the tasty and filling *toucassou* – a local speciality made with meat and something like dumplings. Cheap rooms are also planned to open here.

On the south side of town, the *patisserie* sells coffee, beers and good cakes, plus meals for around CFA1500 in the evening. The friendly manager sometimes offers a couple of basic rooms for a low price. The adjacent *drinks stall* and shop has a tempting 'Glace' sign but not an ice cream in sight! Nearby, *Le Maquis* – a long way from Abidjan – serves evening meals for around CFA2000, but you need to order in the morning.

Getting There & Away

Air Timbuktu is served by Air Mali flights. The airport is about 5km from the town. A bus meets all flights, and takes you to the hotels for CFA1500 per person.

Land Battered old Land Rovers run from Mopti to Timbuktu a few times per week. The best but longest route from Mopti is east to Gossi and north to Gourma-Rharous where there's a ferry (which breaks down quite often), then west to Timbuktu. Another route goes via Douentza to Bambara-Maounde then to another ferry directly south of Timbuktu. In the dry season some vehicles go north to Korientze and Saraféré, on to Niafounké, then via Goundam to Timbuktu. Whichever way you go, the fare is around CFA12,500. The dry-season route usually takes about 1½ days, but can take much longer as breakdowns are common and you may still have to wade across a few rivers. You stop to sleep on the way, but your backpack stays firmly tied to the roof under tons of other baggage. Passengers are packed in tightly in the back of the vehicle, and the rough road makes this incredibly uncomfortable. Many travellers have written to highly recommend paying a few thousand CFA extra to get a seat at the front. Trucks also run

> ## Lightning Tours of Timbuktu
>
> The CMN passenger boat stops for four to 12 hours at Korioumé, so if you're travelling between Gao and Mopti, it's possible to make a mad dash to Timbuktu. The going rate for a round trip tour in a chartered taxi is CFA10,000 to CFA15,000 – there's no time to take a shared one.

irregularly between Mopti and Timbuktu. They'll take passengers for about the same price as the Land Rovers, but can take longer.

Leaving Timbuktu for Mopti, the same routes and prices apply. If you're heading east, trucks also run a couple of times each week between Timbuktu and Gao along the north side of the river. Ask around at the Grand Marché and prepare yourself for a tough two day trip.

Boat Between late July and late November, the large CMN passenger boats stop at Korioumé, Timbuktu's port. Alternatively, you can reach Timbuktu by pinasse. Most people come from Mopti – see Getting There & Away in that section for details. Once you've arrived at Korioumé, a place in a bâché to Timbuktu costs CFA350 to CFA500. A private taxi costs CFA5000.

If you want to leave Timbuktu on the CMN boat, the ticket office is in Kabala (the old port). Getting here is CFA200 by bâché, CFA5000 for the round trip by taxi or CFA2000 for someone with a mobylette to drive you there and back. If you're waiting for the boat, Korioumé has some food stalls, basic eateries and a small *case de passage*.

Public pinasses go to Diré a few times a week, especially Mondays (for Diré's Tuesday market), for about CFA2000. There you can find another pinasse to Mopti for around CFA3000.

There's very little transport to/from Gao, but every Monday a pinasse goes to Gourma-Rharous (to tie in with the Wednesday market). Here you might find another pinasse going to Gao or (more likely) a place in a truck for CFA12,500. Road transport also goes to Mopti from Gourma-Rharous.

Your final option by boat from Timbuktu to Mopti is one of the chartered pinasses which bring groups of tourists. This can be arranged in Mopti in advance (if you're coming from that direction); otherwise, ask the guides who hang around the Hôtel Bouctou. For an idea of prices, see the Mopti section, but be prepared for some heavy negotiation – and beware of guides charging you high prices for a chartered pinasse and then putting you on a public one. It's happened more than once!

AROUND TIMBUKTU

Diré

This small town on the River Niger is rarely visited by outsiders, but might be on your

route if you're travelling between Timbuktu and Mopti. You may have to change boats here, or switch to road transport for part of the journey, going via Goundam. Market day is Tuesday, and transport options are better on Mondays and Wednesdays. The old campement has closed, and the new one was still under construction when we were there, but the owner of the *quincaillerie* (hardware shop) on the main square has a **room** to rent for CFA10,000. Otherwise, ask around at the cheap eateries near the market. Pinasse prices are given in the Mopti and Timbuktu Getting There & Away sections. By sandy road, a truck from Diré to Timbuktu (CFA5000) takes around five hours.

Lac Faguibine

Lac Faguibine is about 50km to the north of Goundam. In years of normal rainfall it's

MALI

The Elephants of Timbuktu

It comes as a surprise to most visitors to learn that Mali is home to large elephant herds, especially as the Sahel seems unable to produce enough food even for people and their livestock. Despite their catchy handle, Mali's elephant herds don't actually live near Timbuktu, but inhabit the Gourma region between the River Niger and the border with Burkina Faso. During the rainy season they feed in the relatively lush southern area, and around November to January, as the vegetation withers, they move north to a chain of reliable water holes. The easiest place to see them is near Gossi, where they drink at a large lake, west of the main road between Mopti and Gao. They move south again in June, a welcome sign for local people of coming rain, often passing near the town of Boni. This annual 1000km circuit is the longest elephant migration in Africa.

The Mali elephants have adapted to the desert conditions by fattening themselves in the rainy season, and living on relatively little during the dry; they also have longer legs and shorter tusks than their East African cousins. They share the water holes with cows and other domestic animals, and have lived alongside local people (who do not hunt them for meat or ivory) for many centuries; herders are pleased when high branches on trees are pulled down by an elephant to be scavenged by goats.

But conditions in the Sahel have become very hard for farmers in recent years, and nomads turning to cultivation put increasing pressure on the land. There's not enough trees or bushes to keep even hardy elephants happy, so the crops are an inevitable temptation, and the ditches and fires which used to keep them out of the fields no longer work. Following the unrest which erupted in the early 1990s, guns are everywhere, and when hungry people are confronted by a raiding elephant, a desperate clash is inevitable. The easy coexistence looks set to end, and is yet another example of how the fate of Africa's wildlife and people are irrevocably intertwined.

MALI

the largest natural lake in West Africa, not counting Lake Chad (some 2000km east). Should you want to visit, guides in Timbuktu can set you up with a camel or 4WD, but the lake has been dry since the end of the 1980s (due either to changing world climate and lower rainfalls, or because so much water is taken out of the River Niger for irrigation) so you may want to check the latest situation before arranging anything.

Araouane

Araouane is a small oasis village deep in the desert, over 250km north of Timbuktu. It's completely surrounded by sand dunes, and is a major staging post on the camel caravan route from the salt mines of Taoudenni. The local people have started a project called Arbres pour Araouane (Trees for Araouane), with help from a guy called Ernest Aebi and a solar-powered water pump. They have built vegetable gardens and – astoundingly – a small hotel. This was destroyed during the Tuareg rebellion, but is being rebuilt and the price to stay here depends on the state of completion. Until it's finished you can lodge with local people for around CFA7500 per person, and all profits go towards funding the project.

For more information, contact the project's representatives in Timbuktu, Dramane Alpha (☎ 92 10 12) or Malik Alkady c/o Magasinier du PAM (World Food Program). Alternatively, in advance contact Trees for Araouane, 460 West Broadway, New York NY 10012, USA (☎/fax 212-473 8114).

Getting There & Away From Timbuktu to Araouane, a 4WD vehicle (seating up to six people) costs from CFA250,000 for the return trip. But it's far better to go by camel, which takes about a week, riding (or walking) for seven to eight hours each day, and costs around CFA10,000 per day (which includes food – typical Tuareg fare of rice and meat). The best time to go is between October and February. You need a sleeping bag, something to keep off the sun (a Tuareg turban, not surprisingly, does the job well), a large bottle and something to purify water.

It takes a bit of preparation, and is not something to enter into lightly, as the trip can be hard, but everyone who's done it rates it an absolutely fantastic experience.

HOMBORI

Hombori is a village on the main road between Mopti and Gao. What stands out about this place, quite literally, is a huge rock formation called **Hombori Tondo**, rising straight up from the plains to 1155m – the highest point in Mali. This is one of many huge sandstone buttresses or 'mesas' that punctuate the semidesert landscape in this area.

There are two small *hotels* in the village: the first is on the main road, with simple but clean rooms for CFA1500 per person, bucket showers and good food; the second is in the village, which is a quieter setting, with similar prices. For somewhere to eat, there

Rock Climbing

About 30km south-west of Hombori is a huge rock formation with needle-like towers called La Main de Fatma – the Hand of Fatma – rising some 600m above the plain. This is the single best place in West Africa for technical rock climbing and since the early 1990s it has attracted an increasing number of climbers from Europe. Several routes have been established, most of very high and demanding standard (British grades around E4, French grades around 7a). Some routes have been bolted and there's plenty of scope for new routes here and on surrounding towers. Anyone wanting to climb here should contact a Spanish climber called Salvador Campillo, who is married to a local woman and lives in a village nearby. He can arrange guides, negotiate access with local villagers and provide information. Before arrival in Mopti, messages should be sent c/o Pare Claret, 175 Etic, 08041 Barcelona, Spain. British climbers can get details from the March 1998 issue of *High* magazine.

are several **cheap eateries** and **street food stalls** on the main road. These cater mostly for passing traffic, and service can be sluggish if there's no bus due for a while.

This is a great area for hiking, although a few hours in the early morning is enough for most people as it gets very hot here. Start off by aiming for the two hills about 1½ hours walk away – one has a village on the top and provides great views; the manager at the hotel on the main road will explain the route. For anything further, you should take a guide. The area is still a bit tense after the Tuareg rebellion, and many local men carry guns.

To reach Hombori, get off any bus between Gao and Mopti – you'll probably have to pay full fare. Alternatively, the rare local bush taxi from Gao to Hombori costs CFA3000. A ride on a truck from Hombori to Mopti is CFA3500.

GAO

Gao is the easternmost town of any size in Mali. It's on the north bank of the Niger, while the long tar road from Bamako terminates on the southern side of the river; a ferry makes the crossing about 15km east of Gao. Since the early 1990s, when the trans-Saharan route from Algeria closed to foreigners, Gao has seen few visitors – just a few hardy overlanders on their way to or from Niamey and other points east. During the day it's a quiet town, the people stultified by the heat, but in the evenings a couple of lively outdoor bars and restaurants crank into gear.

The **market** and waterfront are interesting, and Gao also has a small ethnological **museum**. The only other thing coming close to a 'sight' is the **Tomb of the Askia** (a 16th century ruler), now used as a mosque and notable because the exposed beams typical of Sahel mud-brick buildings stick out even further than usual. Entry costs CFA500, and there are good views of the town. The river is picturesque here: you can rent a pirogue around dusk and watch the dunes turn orange as you drift along, or go further to the big **sand dunes** at Quema and Hondo – a

three hour trip which should cost around CFA3000 per person.

Information

All visitors are supposed to report to the police here, and they're more insistent about this in Gao than in any other part of Mali. Although a few travellers have failed to report and had no problems, others have been sent back to Gao from the ferry to the Bamako road, and even from the Niger border.

Gao's only bank, the BDM, is open in the morning, Monday to Friday. The staff are extremely slow and don't accept travellers cheques of any kind.

Places to Stay

Gao has three campements. The French-run **Camping Bangu** is about 2km north of the market on the route towards Tanezrouft, with

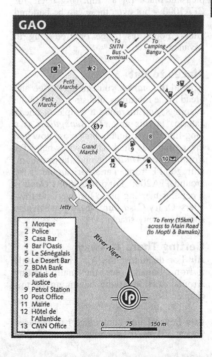

GAO

1 Mosque
2 Police
3 Casa Bar
4 Bar l'Oasis
5 Le Sénégalais
6 Le Desert Bar
7 BDM Bank
8 Palais de Justice
9 Petrol Station
10 Post Office
11 Mairie
12 Hôtel de l'Atlantide
13 CMN Office

To SNTN Bus Terminal
To Camping Bangu
Petit Marché
Petit Marché
Grand Marché
Jetty
River Niger
To Ferry (15km) across to Main Road (to Mopti & Bamako)

0   75   150 m

MALI

a friendly, laid-back atmosphere. Thatched bungalows cost CFA2500 per person, or you can rent a mattress on the terrace or pitch your own tent for CFA1500. The restaurant serves good food and is frequented by aid workers from the surrounding area. *Village Tizi-Mizi* is 4km along the airport road to the north-east of town, with camping or a mattress on the roof for CFA1500 and some rooms for around CFA6000. *Camping Yurga* is an older, more basic place outside Gao along the road towards the ferry, with similar but negotiable prices.

The old *Hôtel de l'Atlantide*, near the Grand Marché, has become very run-down but prices haven't dropped accordingly, with singles from CFA12,000 and up to CFA 29,000 for a double with bathroom, which is appalling value as there is frequently no water or electricity. However, all rates are negotiable, and you can sleep on the roof for CFA2500. Even if you don't stay here, it's a pleasant place for a drink (big beers for CFA1000 – but even these can be bartered for!) and a good place to meet other travellers. Food has to be ordered long in advance.

Places to Eat

Around the *market* you can get coffee and bread in the mornings, and street food in the evenings, and there are a couple of cheap eateries in this area. *Le Sénégalais* is a long-time favourite, but may close now that the patron has died. Otherwise, head for *Restaurant l'Amitié* behind the museum, with good European and African meals for around CFA2000. For drinks, *Bar l'Oasis* is a popular meeting place for overland travellers. Or try *Casa Bar*, where you can also sometimes buy snacks.

Getting There & Away

Air For details of the Air Mali schedule to/from Bamako see the main Getting Around section at the beginning of this chapter.

Bus Several bus companies run between Gao and Bamako, via Sévaré (near Mopti);

Boré

Travellers on the road between Mopti and Gao might like to stop over at the village of Boré, about 55km west of Douentza and 5km from the northern end of the Falaise de Bandiagara, the huge escarpment which runs through the heart of Dogon Country. The main attraction of Boré is the ancient Sahel-style mud-brick mosque. Unlike the more famous mosques in Mopti and Djenné, visitors are allowed inside (CFA 1000 fee) and up onto the roof for panoramic views. Tour groups stop here for a quick look, but very few tourists stay longer to appreciate this quiet desert village. Saturday is the main market day, and the local traders have established an artisan's shop (open every day) selling bogolan mud cloth, indigo dyed cloth, Tuareg jewellery etc. There's no hotel, but near the commandant's office is a hut where visiting government workers or tourists can stay. Buses between Mopti and Gao all stop here, and there are local bush taxis to Mopti and Douentza, especially on market days.

see the Bamako and Mopti Getting There & Away sections for details. Most vehicles leave from the ferry ramp on the south side of the river. After crossing the river by ferry, catch a local shared taxi to town.

Between Gao and Niamey the SNTN bus runs once a week in each direction, departing from Gao's SNTN office on the north-eastern side of town. In either direction, buses leave in the morning, stop overnight at the border and arrive the following day around sunset. The fare is CFA11,000.

Boat For details on the large passenger boat from Mopti, see this chapter's Getting Around section. Heading downstream, pinasses go most Wednesdays to Ansongo (market day on Thursday), and from there to Ayorou (in Niger).

THE DOGON

The Dogon people migrated to the Falaise de Bandiagara (Bandiagara Escarpment) from the surrounding plains in around 1300 AD, taking refuge from various other groups who were expanding into the area and introducing Islam. Today most Dogon follow their traditional religion, although about 35% are Muslim and a smaller minority are Christian (often two beliefs run side by side). It's not unusual for people in the same village to follow different religions, intermarriage between faiths being quite common. Tolerance is just one of the Dogon's many admirable characteristics.

Before the Dogon reached the escarpment, it was inhabited by the Tellem people. The origins of the Tellem are unclear – Dogon tradition describe them as small and red skinned – and none remain today, but their houses and cave dwellings built high on the escarpment can still be seen. The vertical cliff is several hundred metres high (overhanging in some places), yet the Tellem managed to build houses in the most inaccessible places. Most cannot be reached today, and the Dogon believe the Tellem could fly, or maybe used long ropes to lower themselves from the top of the escarpment. Another theory suggests that the wetter climate of the previous millennium allowed vines and creepers to cover the cliff, providing natural ladders for the early inhabitants. The Tellem also used the caves to bury their dead, and many are still full of ancient human bones.

The Dogon were first brought to the attention of the outside world through the work of the French anthropologist Marcel Griaule, whose influential book *Dieu d'Eau: Entretiens avec Ogotemmêli* (published in 1948) was the result of many years living and studying near the village of Sanga. During this time he was accepted into the local community, and built a dam outside the village to improve the water supply. Griaule died in France in 1956, and a plaque near the dam marks the spot where the Dogon believe his spirit resides. Griaule's book was published in English under the title *Conversations with Ogotemmêli* in 1965, and reprints are still available from specialist bookshops.

Dogon religion and culture (the two are inextricable) are incredibly complex and very hard for outsiders to appreciate. This section is therefore a very simplified introduction. For more details read *African Art of the Dogon* by Jean Laude.

Religion & Cosmology

The Dogon believe that the earth, moon and sun were created by a divine male being called Amma. The earth was formed in the shape of a woman, and by her Amma fathered twin snake-like creatures called the Nommo, which Dogon believe are present in streams and pools. Later, Amma made two humans – man and woman – who were circumcised by the Nommo and then gave birth to eight children, regarded as the ancestors of all Dogon. Eight is a significant number throughout Dogon culture, and the ancestors are represented by the snake, tortoise, scorpion, crocodile, frog, lizard, rabbit and hyena.

Today, circumcision is still very important in Dogon culture. For boys the removal of the foreskin is a sign of the first step into manhood. A large ceremony takes place every three years at Songo near Bandiagara, where up to 200 boys between 10 and 12 years old are initiated together. Female circumcision (which involves removal of the clitoris, and is sometimes more accurately called female genital mutilation) has officially been banned by the government, but is still quite widespread – especially in remote areas.

Amma is also credited with creating the stars, and a major feature of Dogon cosmology is the star known in the west as Sirius or the Dog Star, which was also held to be auspicious by the ancient Egyptians. The Dogon are able to predict Sirius' periodic appearance at a certain point above the skyline, and have long regarded it as three separate stars – two close together and a third invisible. The movements of these stars dictate the timing of the major Sigui festival which takes place about every 60 years. Although modern astronomers knew Sirius to be two stars, it was only in 1995 that powerful radio telescopes detected a third body of super-dense matter in the same area.

Aspects of Dogon religion more readily seen by visitors are the 'fetishes' or sacred objects dotted around most villages, often a simple dome of hard-packed mud, sometimes daubed with intricate red and black markings. Although these may have religious significance, they are not always held in silent awe. You might join a group of local men having a drink while lounging on or around a fetish and frequently dosing it with helpings of thick millet beer.

The focal point of any Dogon village is the *togu-na*, where the older men meet to discuss village matters or to just relax.

Masks & Ceremonies

Masks are very important in Dogon culture, and play an important role in religious ceremonies. The most famous ceremony is the Sigui, performed every 60 years (most recently during the 1960s), which features a large mask and headdress called the *iminana* in the form of a prostrate serpent, sometimes almost 10m high. During the Sigui, the Dogon perform dances recounting the story of their origin. After the ceremony, the iminana is stored in one of the caves high on the cliffs.

The iminana is also used during a major 'funeral' ceremony which takes place once every five or so years. According to Dogon tradition, when a person dies their spirit wanders about looking for a new residence. Fearful that the spirit might rest in another mortal, the Dogon bring out the iminana and take it to the deceased's house to entice the spirit to reside in the mask. The accompanying ceremony can last up to a week and celebrates the life of the dead person and the part they played in the village.

When important village members die, they are interred in a cave high on the cliffs (sometimes appropriating a Tellem cave), usually on the same day or the day after they die. The body is wrapped in colourful cloth and run head-high through the village, then lifted with ropes up to the cave. A smaller funeral ceremony takes place about five days later.

Most Dogon ceremonies, where you may see masks, take place from March to May, when the harvest is finished. These include Agguet, around May, in honour of the ancestors, and Ondonfile in the period leading up to the first rains.

Architecture

When the Dogon first moved into this area, for protection they built their houses on the high cliffs of the escarpment. These houses were made of mud on a wooden frame with a flat roof supported by wooden beams, while the smaller granaries had conical roofs. These were assembled on the ground and then hoisted into position.

In recent times, many of the cliff dwellings have been abandoned, and the people have moved onto the plains at the foot of the escarpment, although usually only a short distance from their former village.

The design of Dogon houses is unique. Each house, collectively built and made of rock and mud brick, consists of a number of separate rooms with flat roofs, surrounding a small yard and interlinked with stone walls. The granaries, with their conical straw roofs, stand on stone legs to protect the maize or other crops from vermin. The most notable features are the elaborately carved doors and shutters that art collectors are forever seeking.

The focal point of any village is the *togu-na*, a shelter and meeting place for the older men, where they discuss the affairs of the village or simply lounge, smoke, tell jokes and take naps. The togu-nas are built with a low roof, so that the men must remain seated (and thus prevent discussions from turning into arguments or fights), topped with eight thick layers of dried millet stalks. The wooden posts supporting the roof of the togu-na are often carved with figures of the eight Dogon ancestors.

Women are banned from the togu-na. Their closest equivalent are special houses on the outskirts of the village where they stay during menstruation, as this is considered an unclean time. Interestingly, all women (whether Muslim, Christian or traditional) use the same house.

Ancestor figures are carved onto granary doors to protect the food inside.

Agriculture

The Dogon are traditionally farmers and both men and women are very industrious, as work is a central feature of Dogon society. Lazy people lose respect in their village and find it hard to get a marriage partner. Dogon men are often employed to work on farms in other parts of the country, and Dogon women find work as housemaids in the cities. Dogon people are proud that there are no thieves in their villages – they say everybody's too busy.

Crops such as millet are planted in the fields below the escarpment. The tops of the escarpment are just bare rock, but in many areas plots have been created, using stones to build low circular walls which are filled with soil brought up from the plains. Water is carried up from a nearby stream in large pots to irrigate the crops. Some plots are only a few square metres in size, balanced on a ledge or even a flat-topped boulder out of reach from goats. In other areas, larger dams and plots have been established. Onions are the most popular crop, of high quality and distributed all over the country. Apparently, European agricultural experts were brought in not long ago to offer advice on onion production, but found the system impossible to improve.

Weekdays & Markets

The traditional Dogon week has only five days, and in most villages along the escarpment every fifth day is market day, which is always a lively and interesting event. Villages which are predominantly Muslim, or on the edge of Dogon Country where they've traded with outsiders, keep to a seven day week. If you're planning a visit, note that Dogon markets usually don't get going until around noon.

A successful market always ends with lots of drinking. Millet beer (*kojo* or *chakalow*), still fermenting, is usually poured into a large earthenware pot and then served in the shade to the men. Some markets are more important as social gatherings than as places for trading. At Djiguibombo, for example, there's plenty of beer and meat every Wednesday, but not much to buy.

Dogon villages form clusters, with market day held on a different day in each village in the cluster. The day of the week is named after the village where the market is held. Thus the same day may have different names, according to where you are. In the area most visited by tourists, the key markets are at Sanga and Dourou. If you know when these markets are held, you can calculate when other markets will be held in the surrounding area. Good guides in Bandiagara and elsewhere keep a record of Sanga's and Dourou's market days and mark them on a conventional calendar; this way they can calculate the next market day in that village, and by extension surrounding villages.

The following tables show which days are market days, according to the Dogon five day system and the conventional seven day system, and may help you plan your trek to coincide with a market.

Five Day Week	Dourou cluster	Sanga cluster	Others
1	Dourou	Tireli	Ibi
2	Nombori	Banani	
3	Idjeli	Amani	Yendouma
4	Komokani	Sanga	
5	Jingorou (near Begnimato)	Ireli	

Seven Day Week	Village
Monday (big) and Friday (small)	Bandiagara
Tuesday	Bankass
Sunday	Douentza, Endé
Thursday	Kani-Kombolé

Dogon Country

On everybody's list of the top 10 places in West Africa, the homeland of the Dogon people is the huge Falaise de Bandiagara (Bandiagara Escarpment) that extends some 150km through the Sahel to the east of Mopti. The landscape is stunning, and the Dogon people are noted for their complex and elaborate culture, their art forms, their unique houses and granaries – some clinging to the bare rock face of the escarpment – and their unique vegetable plots perched on ledges in the cliffs.

The best way to see Dogon Country (Pays Dogon) is to trek along the escarpment for anything between two and 10 days, walking slowly from village to village, giving yourself plenty of time to see and appreciate the people and the landscape. Distances are short, and it's usual to walk during the morning, rest during the heat of the afternoon, then explore a village and its nearby cliff dwellings in the early

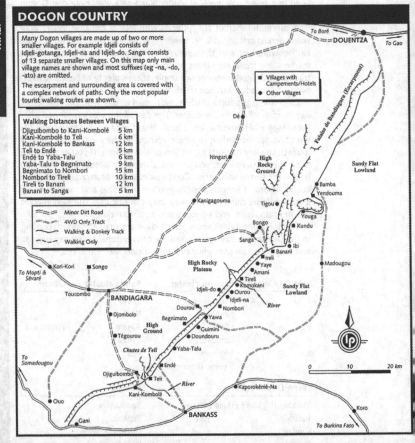

DOGON COUNTRY

Many Dogon villages are made up of two or more smaller villages. For example Idjeli consists of Idjeli-gotanga, Idjeli-na and Idjeli-do. Sanga consists of 13 separate smaller villages. On this map only main village names are shown and most suffixes (eg -na, -do, -ato) are omitted.

The escarpment and surrounding area is covered with a complex network of paths. Only the most popular tourist walking routes are shown.

Walking Distances Between Villages	
Djiguibombo to Kani-Kombolé	5 km
Kani-Kombolé to Teli	6 km
Kani-Kombolé to Bankass	12 km
Teli to Endé	5 km
Endé to Yaba-Talu	6 km
Yaba-Talu to Begnimato	9 km
Begnimato to Nombori	15 km
Nombori to Tireli	10 km
Tireli to Banani	12 km
Banani to Sanga	5 km

- ■ Villages with Campements/Hotels
- ● Other Villages

Minor Dirt Road
4WD Only Track
Walking & Donkey Track
Walking Only

To Boré · DOUENTZA · To Gao

Falaise de Bandiagara (Escarpment)

To Mopti & Sévaré

Kori-Kori · Songo

Toucombo · BANDIAGARA

Djombolo

Tégourou

Chutes de Teli

Djiguibombo · Teli · River

Kani-Kombolé · BANKASS

Ouo

Gani

De

Ningari

High Rocky Ground

Sandy Flat Lowland

Bamba · Yendouma

Kanigagouma · Tigou · Youga · Kundu

Bongo · Sanga · Banani · Ireli · Yaye · Amani

High Rocky Plateau · Tireli · Komokani · Ouroul · Idjeli-do · Idjeli-na

Dourou · Nombori · River

Begnimato · Yawa · Guimini · Doundouru

High Ground · Yaba-Talu

Endé

Madougou

Sandy Flat Lowland

Kaporokémié-Na

Koro

To Somadougou

To Burkina Faso

0   10   20 km

evening. You can find food and lodging in the villages, and guides are recommended and easy to find.

TREKKING PRACTICALITIES
When to Go
The hottest part of the year is March to May, with temperatures touching 40°C – too hot for hiking for most of the day, but the first few hours of the morning are OK and there are very few other visitors. The rainy season from June to September is not usually popular, although the rains don't affect hikers too much as downpours only last an hour or two. The air is clear and the waterfalls over the escarpment are spectacular at this time. By November to February it's cooler and the most popular period to visit, although daytime temperatures are still well over 30°C (but it's chilly enough for a blanket at night). This climate pattern and the nature of holidays in Europe mean December and January are the busiest times.

Starting Points
The three main starting points for treks in Dogon Country are the small towns of Sanga (also spelt Sangha), Bandiagara and Bankass. Sanga is right on the escarpment and usually where organised tour groups go, as it's hard to reach by public transport. Most independent travellers start at Bandiagara or Bankass, although local transport is used to reach the escarpment itself.

Guides
Guides in Dogon Country are not obligatory – you could follow the more straightforward routes alone – but without one you'll undoubtedly miss many points of interest. As well as showing you the way (essential if you want to follow more interesting routes), guides will make arrangements with villagers and take you to abandoned cliff dwellings. They will also explain something of the history and culture of the Dogon as you go along. All guides speak French (few local Dogon do) and some also speak English or other European languages.

It is usual (and much easier) to hire your guide at Bandiagara, Bankass or Sanga; many guides from these places go to Mopti to look for work, but making arrangements is more hassle there (but not necessarily more expensive). Guides hired in Mopti pay their own transport costs to the start of the trek, and all other trekking costs are more or less fixed.

When choosing your guide, write down all the expenses, as this aids memory on both sides, and ask lots of questions about market days, history, festivals etc, to see if they know their stuff. It's essential that your guide should be a Dogon, as other guides will have to subcontract a genuine local (who you pay for). It's worth spending an extra day or two asking around for recommendations from other travellers, rather than rushing off with the first guide you meet.

Note that in Bankass the guides operate a rota system, so you'll have to push to get a guide *you* want, such as one who speaks English or one who has been recommended.

Accommodation & Food
Several villages have *campements* for tourists, where you can sleep and eat. In smaller villages you might stay with a family. It's usual to unroll your sleeping bag on the flat roof of a house and sleep under the stars. This is a wonderful experience, particularly in the early morning as the sunlight hits the top of the giant cliffs and you listen to the sounds of the village stirring around you.

Evening meals are usually rice with a sauce of vegetables, meat or chicken. In the morning, you'll be given tea, bread and possibly millet porridge. You should bring other food with you. Biscuits, crackers, fruit, cheese and tins of sardines or meat can be bought in Bandiagara and Bankass. In some villages along the escarpment enterprising locals sell cold drinks.

An increasingly popular option is for guides to provide food for the entire trip. When arranging things make sure it's clear who will be paying for the guide's meals and lodging. It is usual for these to be covered by the fee you pay them.

Equipment

The general rule is to travel as light as possible as paths are steep or sandy in places. Footwear should be sturdy, but boots are not essential. It is vital to have a sunhat and a water bottle, as otherwise heatstroke and serious dehydration are real possibilities. You should carry at least a litre of water while walking. Plastic bottles can be bought in Mopti market, and you can get water from village pumps (always preferable to a well) along the way – although it needs to be purified. Tents are not required as all visitors are expected to stay in the villages. Nights are warm, although a light sleeping bag or blanket will keep off the pre-dawn chill from November to February. Dogon villages are dark at night, so a torch (flashlight) is useful. Wearing shorts for trekking is OK, as they do not offend Dogon culture, although women will feel more comfortable with a wrap-around skirt or long trousers when staying in a village, especially in remote areas.

Costs

Visitors to Dogon Country must pay for the privilege. Fees are reasonable, and provide the local people with a much needed source of income. It costs CFA500 to CFA1000 per person to enter a village; this allows you to take photos of houses and other buildings (but *not* people – unless you get their permission), and to visit nearby cliff dwellings. If possible, pay this fee direct to the village headman, not to your guide. If you're simply walking through on your way to the next place, you do not have to pay this fee. To sleep at a campement or private house costs around CFA1000 per night. Food is CFA500 for breakfast and between CFA750 and CFA1500 for dinner.

Fees for guides are usually from CFA3000 to CFA5000 per person per day, although this depends on the size of the group, the length of the trip and the quality of the guide. Negotiation is essential.

Your only other cost is reaching the escarpment. From Bandiagara, a local taxi to take you to the start of your trek (eg Djigui-bombo or Dourou, about 20km) is about CFA10,000. If you're alone it might be cheaper for you and the guide to hire a couple of mobylettes.

From Bankass to the escarpment at Endé or Kani-Kombolé (12km) by horse and cart is CFA3000. (The track is too sandy for mobylettes.) Of course, you can save money by walking this section, but you need to allow for the extra time it requires.

Many guides offer all-inclusive 'packages' (including transport, food, accommodation, fees etc), which can be worth considering if you want to make life easy, as it sometimes costs only a little more than doing it yourself. Prices range from CFA6000 to CFA12,500 per person per day, depending on the size of your group, the length of trek and quality of guide. All you pay extra is for drinks.

Note that for a four day trek guides often include four nights' accommodation in their calculations, even though you're only out for three, or they might charge the full rate for the first and last days of your trek, even if it's only a few hours, so check carefully just when your final day is expected to finish.

Your last cost is to cover payments to take photos (with permission of course) or

Dogon Souvenirs

The number of people visiting the Dogon region has the potential to destroy this unique culture, so travellers need to be particularly sensitive to local customs and do as little as possible to intrude into the locals' lives. You should also think hard about what you buy, as everything (carvings, masks, fetishes, even the doors off houses) is for sale. You can't blame the Dogon – especially when buyers offer an amount worth several years salary. But to stop the Dogon culture disappearing completely, you might consider only buying new doors and other objects specially made for tourists. In this way, you still get your souvenir, the culture stands a chance of remaining intact for a bit longer and the locals still make a bit of cash.

to visit a village's *hogon* (spiritual leader). It's usual to give him a small gift of around CFA500. Another good gift is kola nuts, which can be bought in Mopti or Bandiagara – but not always in Bankass or Sanga.

Hiking & Trekking Routes

The walking route you choose depends on the time and money you have available. It also depends on your energy. You may decide to walk between two villages on easy paths along the foot of the escarpment, or you might want to take a more interesting route up and down the cliff itself, winding through cɔves, scrambling on all fours, leaping from boulder to boulder or using ladders carved from logs to cover the steepest sections. People with no head for heights may feel a bit shaky, and routes of this nature usually involve walking all day, but the spectacular views you get along the way make it all worthwhile. The best information is always from other travellers, so ask around before finalising anything.

One Day If you are very short of time there are three circular walks from Sanga, aimed at tour groups on tight schedules who arrive by car. (With public transport it can easily take two or three days just getting to/from Sanga.) The Petit Tour goes to Gogoli (7km), the Moyen Tour goes to Gogoli and Banani (10km), and the Grand Tour goes to Gogoli, Banani and Ireli (15km).

Two Days Spending a night in a Dogon village gives you a much better impression of life on the escarpment than you can ever get on a one day trip. From Bandiagara, with a lift to Djiguibombo, you can walk down to the plain, spend the night in either Kani-Kombolé, Teli or Endé and return by the same route. You could also do a circular route from Dourou to Nombori. From Bankass, a short but rewarding circuit takes you to Kani-Kombolé, through Teli to Endé (spending the night at either) and then back.

Three to Five Days A good three day trek from Bandiagara starts with a lift to Djigui-

bombo. You descend to Teli for the first night and trek northwards to Begnimato (second night). On the third day continue to Yawa, then up the escarpment to Dourou, where you can either stay and walk back to Bandiagara on day four or arrange for a lift. You can add an extra day by diverting northward to Nombori. An easier trip from Bandiagara would be Djiguibombo, Teli and Endé, returning by the same route.

From Bankass, you can get to Teli or Endé and then walk northwards to Begnimato, Yawa or Nombori, before retracing your route.

Another option to avoid backtracking is to start from Bandiagara, go to Dourou, trek south to Endé or Teli and then continue southwards to Bankass, from where you can get transport back to Mopti or on towards Burkina Faso. Alternatively, you could start this route in Bankass and end at Bandiagara – the views are better this way.

From Sanga, a good four day route descends first to Banani then heads north to Kundu (first night), Youga (second night) and Yendouma (third night). On the fourth day you go up the cliffs to Tiogou and return over the plateau to Sanga. The escarpment is less well defined north of Banani, but unlike areas further south, it's rarely visited.

Six Days or More If you have plenty of time, any of the routes described above can be extended. From Sanga and Banani you can head southwards via Tireli and Yawa to reach Dourou (after three days) or Djiguibombo (after another two or three days), and then end your trek at Bandiagara or Bankass. This trek can also be done in reverse: to Djiguibombo, first night in Teli, second night in Begnimato, third night in Nombori, fourth night in Tireli and fifth night in Banani before going up the escarpment to Sanga.

Things to See & Do

If you are still trying to decide which route to take, the following information may be helpful. Working roughly south to north, **Kani-Kombolé** has an interesting mosque, while **Teli** and **Endé** are very picturesque

MALI

and have waterfalls nearby. Endé is also a good place to visit the village hogon. **Begnimato** and **Dourou** offer spectacular views of the plains, and picturesque Tireli is known for its pottery. At **Daga-Tireli**, on top of the escarpment, a large area of vegetable plots surrounds a dam. **Amani** has a sacred crocodile pool, and **Ireli** is a classic Dogon village with cylindrical granary towers at the foot of the cliffs, topped by a mass of ancient Tellem houses. **Banani** is within a few hours walk of Sanga and full of souvenir sellers, so worth avoiding. **Bongo** has spectacular views of the plains and is a good place to watch artisans at work and to purchase Dogon art.

BANDIAGARA

Bandiagara is a small, dusty town some 70km east of Mopti and about 20km from the top of the escarpment. In the heart of town is the market – the main day is Monday, and Friday is also busy. For trekking food, Alimentation Niang Ibrahim on the main street sells essentials like sardines, pasta, chocolate spread and toilet paper. The

bush taxi park is on the western side of town, just off the Mopti road, and there are several shops selling Dogon artefacts nearby. For a stroll in the evening, head out on the Sanga road past the Traditional Medicine Centre – an excellent example of the sans-bois style of architecture.

Places to Stay & Eat

A long-time favourite is *Auberge Kansaye* off the southern end of the main street, run by the friendly and helpful Boubacar Kansaye, son of 'Papa' Kansaye who ran this place for many years. The rooms are spartan but the beds have clean sheets and the price is reasonable at CFA2500 per person. The bar is busy with local guides and the restaurant is decorated with fabulous artwork, but most people eat and drink in the shady garden. To leave baggage costs CFA1000, and a shower (if you're not staying) is CFA500.

Near the bush taxi park is the small and quiet *Camping Satimbe*, with rooms for CFA2500 per person including breakfast. You can sleep on the roof terrace and relax in the garden. Slightly further out of town is

BANDIAGARA

To Sanga

To Hôtel Toguna (4km), Songo (10km) & Mopti (70km)

To Djiguibombo (20km)

1 Restaurant le Bon Coin
2 Mosque
3 Ruined Fula Palace
4 Hôtel Village
5 Police
6 Gare Routière
7 Camping Satimbe
8 Market
9 Bar Point Raid
10 Auberge Kansaye

0   125   250 m

the *Hôtel Village*, with singles/doubles at CFA2500/4000 and breakfast for CFA500. This is also a bar-restaurant, with music some evenings. The large yard is used by visiting overland trucks. To pitch a tent costs CFA 1000 per person.

About 4km outside town on the Mopti road, the simple *Hôtel Toguna* has rooms at CFA2500 per person, with open-air toilets, Dogon statues in the garden and good grilled chicken in the restaurant.

More upmarket is the French-run *Restaurant Cheval Blanc*, under construction when we passed through, but promising à la carte meals from CFA1500 to CFA2500 and comfortable doubles with bathroom from CFA12,000 to CFA18,000. Some rooms will have air-con and TV.

All the places to stay do meals, and there's street food around the market in the evening. The best seems to be *Le Bon Coin*, serving breakfast and good value meals like steak and chips or spaghetti bolognaise for CFA1500, big beers for CFA600 and soft drinks for CFA300. The *Bar Point Raid*, just off the main street, serves drinks at the same price and has a great upstairs terrace overlooking the town. It also does food to order.

About 5km outside Bandiagara on the Mopti road, a small dirt track leads for another 5km to the tranquil Dogon village of

New Road to Dogon Country

The road from Sévaré to Bandiagara is due for upgrading, and will be extended to Djiguibombo and rorced down the cliff to Kani-Kombolé and out to Bankass. It is apparently part of a long-term plan, funded by the World Bank, to improve links between this part of Mali and Burkina Faso. The project is welcomed by most local people as it will be easier to get to Mopti (where they have to go to buy or sell most things). But it will make access to the escarpment easier for tourists also, and will probably have a dramatic effect on the nature of trekking in this area.

Songo, which has a small *campement* and some interesting rock paintings in the surrounding area.

Getting There & Away
Bush taxis to Bandiagara go every day from the gare routière by the port in Mopti or from the main crossroads in Sévaré. The trip takes about two hours and costs CFA1500 by 504.

SANGA
Sanga (also spelt Sangha) is 120km from Mopti and about 40km to the north-east of Bandiagara. It's very close to the top of the escarpment and one of the largest Dogon villages in the region. Sanga is where most upmarket tour groups come, as the escarpment is within easy reach. For independent travellers it's not an ideal place, although some people end their trek here and get transport back to Bandiagara.

Places to Stay & Eat
The rustic *Hôtel Femme Dogon* has simple double rooms for CFA6000, or you can have a mattress on the roof for CFA2000. The shared shower has running water and the toilet flushes by bucket. Breakfast is CFA600 and good meals are available – although they're a bit steep at CFA1500 (but where else can you go?). The hotel has its own guides who can be hired for CFA3000 per day; all-inclusive treks are CFA7500 per person per day. To hire the hotel car to Bandiagara costs CFA15,000.

Tour groups stay at the *Campement-Hôtel Guinna*, where clean and spacious rooms with shower cost CFA10,000. With a fan and bathroom, doubles at CFA15,000 are good value. Breakfast is CFA1000 and a meal CFA3000. Electricity means the beer is cold, but expensive.

Getting There & Away
You first need to get to Bandiagara, from where you may find a truck or pick-up going to Sanga, especially on the morning of Sanga's market day or on the evening of Bandiagara's market day. There's no regular public transport. Chartering a bush taxi costs

MALI

CFA15,000 or getting a mobylette to drop you off costs CFA7500 (including petrol).

BANKASS

Bankass (also spelt Bankas) is about 120km from Mopti, and about 10km from the southern end of the escarpment. Because it's easy to reach and near the cliffs, this is one of the best starting points for a trek in Dogon Country. The guides are less pushy than in Bandiagara (but this may change as more visitors come here). Market day is Tuesday.

Places to Stay & Eat

The most popular place for travellers is *Camping Hogon*, on the edge of town as you come in from Mopti, with rooms in traditional-style huts for CFA5000 (single or double). Camping or sleeping on the roof is CFA1500. This place is run by the friendly Guindo brothers, sons of a Dogon elder, who hold some sway over guides in Bankass. Issa speaks French and English (and Russian!), and Malick speaks a bit of English too. Cheap local dishes are available to order. The brothers also run *Campement Hogon* in town, where prices are the same.

A smarter place to stay is *Hôtel les Abres*, where simple doubles cost CFA5000 (CFA 7500/16,000 with bathroom). Camping is CFA1500 per person, or you can sleep outside with a mattress and mosquito net for CFA3500. Meals are available, mostly with an Italian flavour, for around CFA2500, and there's also a shop on site selling useful items like mineral water and toilet paper.

Getting There & Away

Bush taxis leave Mopti from the gare routière by the port. It costs CFA2500 to Bankass in a 504 and CFA2000 in a bâché. If you're heading on to Burkina Faso, a bush taxi from Bankass to Koro is CFA2000.

The West

KAYES

Kayes (pronounced *khay*, to rhyme with 'eye') is near the border with Senegal and Mauritania. All that most travellers see of this town is the train station, as they pass through on the express between Bamako and Dakar. Kayes might be worth a stopover, however, although it's a hot and dusty place, and any charm it might have is not immediately apparent. There's plenty of activity, especially in the evening, and none of the hassle tourism has created in some of Mali's other towns. There's a thriving market, an interesting waterfront, and several colonial buildings from the time when Kayes was a major port on the River Senegal.

Places to Stay & Eat

Near the station, the *Centre d'Accueil de Jeunesse* (known as the Campement) has basic rooms for CFA4000/6000, and will let you sleep on the roof for a nominal fee. In town, the *Hôtel Amical* (known as Le Caisse Rond) has gloomy rooms for CFA3000. The street from the station to the town centre passes several cheap eateries (*Restaurant Wassu* seems one of the best), and *La Teranga* by the ferry is also worth a try.

Opposite the train station is a row of street food stalls. Just behind is the *Hôtel du Rail*, old and run-down but still the best place in town, although rooms with air-con and bathroom are a bit steep at CFA13,700/20,700. The garden bar is nice for a drink, even if you're not staying, and a good place to wait for trains.

Getting There & Away

Bush Taxi & Truck The only useable road between Kayes and Bamako is via Nioro, but it's long, bad and indirect which is why most people use the train. However, there are trucks and bush taxis every day to Nioro (CFA7500 to CFA9000) from where you can reach Mauritania. Some transport may go from Kayes Ndi on the north side of the river. From Kayes you can also reach Senegal.

Train The express train between Bamako and Dakar stops at Kayes – for more details see the main Getting There & Away section earlier in this chapter. A slower and cheaper

DOGON

The Dogon people live in the area around the Bandiagara Escarpment south of Mopti. Their villages are perched on cliffs and in between craggy rocks, with houses and granaries decorated with delicate relief patterns sculpted in mud. Wooden doors are intricately carved with images from myths and iron door fastenings are wrought in the shape of symbolic creatures and objects designed to protect the inhabitants.

Masks are an important part of Dogon culture. There are various types of mask, including the famous *iminana*, which can be up to 10m high, the bird-like *kanaga*, which protects against vengeance (of a killed animal), and the house-like *sirige*, which represents the house of the *hogon*, who is responsible for passing on Dogon traditions to younger generations.

Top: Bronze ceremonial container, Dogon. Photograph by Dennis Visken/Sidewalk Gallery.

Middle: Wooden granary doors like this one are greatly sought after by art collectors, and usually feature protective symbolism. Photograph by Dennis Visken/Sidewalk Gallery.

Bottom: Dogon people are famed for their masks used to evoke female and male ancestors.

JASON LAURÉ

BAMBARA

The Bambara (also known as Bamana) are the largest ethnic group in Mali. Although Muslim, many have retained traditional beliefs and customs.

The Bambara have an occupational caste system that includes farmers, leather workers, poets, and most important of all blacksmiths. Not only does the smith make hoes for producing food, but door locks that protect women and children, and guns that arm the village. All of these are furnished with spiritual power as well as utility. Door locks often have a water-lizard symbol to protect the house from thieves, or a long-eared creature like a bat that 'hears every sound' and protects women and children.

Blacksmiths are also carvers, Only those born into the blacksmith caste inherit the capacity to tap into the spiritual power Nyama that enables them to transform wood and iron into religious objects, such as the masks used in dances to invoke the aid of the spirit world. Because Nyama is inherited, blacksmiths must marry within their own occupational group. Each occupational group or caste has its own initiation rituals for which particular masks are required. Perhaps the best known image of the Bambara is the chiwara headdress, a stylised antelope with long arched neck and horns, Legend has it that the Creator sent an antelope to teach the Bambara how to cultivate grain.

Katie Abu, David Else

VICTOR ENGLEBERT

Top: Bronze chiwara, the characteristic antelope symbol of the Bambara. Photograph by Dennis Wisken/Sidewalk Galler

Middle: Bambara stool stools are often carved out of a single piece of wood, with a handle for transport. Photograph b Dennis Wisken/Sidewall Gallery.

Bottom: Bambara men i traditional dress, passing the time of day in Timbuktu, Mali.

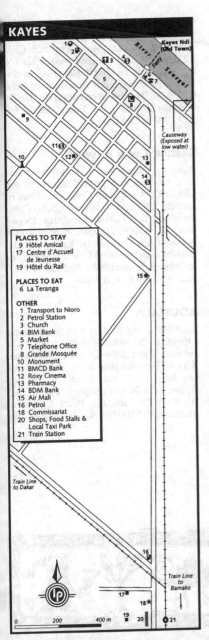

KAYES

Kayes Ndi (Old Town)

River Senegal

Ferry

Causeway (Exposed at low water)

Train Line to Dakar

Train Line to Bamako

PLACES TO STAY
9 Hôtel Amical
17 Centre d'Accueil de Jeunesse
19 Hôtel du Rail

PLACES TO EAT
6 La Teranga

OTHER
1 Transport to Nioro
2 Petrol Station
3 Church
4 BIM Bank
5 Market
7 Telephone Office
8 Grande Mosquée
10 Monument
11 BMCD Bank
12 Roxy Cinema
13 Pharmacy
14 BDM Bank
15 Air Mali
16 Petrol
18 Commissariat
20 Shops, Food Stalls & Local Taxi Park
21 Train Station

0   200   400 m

local train runs daily each way between Bamako and Kayes, leaving around 7 am and arriving in the late afternoon. The fare is about 40% less than the express. There are extra services at weekends but these are crowded.

Boat Intrepid travellers may want to inquire about motorised pirogues which take goods and passengers down the River Senegal to Bakel – for more details, see the Bakel entry in the River Senegal Route section of the Senegal chapter.

AROUND KAYES
The **Chutes de Felou** are a set of rapids and waterfalls on the River Senegal about 15km upstream from Kayes, although they're only really impressive when the river is high. To get there, you may be able to find a bâché heading for Diamou. Otherwise you can get a taxi there and back for CFA9000. On the way you pass **Fort de Medine** – one of the chain of defence posts built along the River Senegal in French colonial times – where you can see a ruined arsenal and officers' mess, a war memorial surrounded by wheel-less canons, an octagonal watchtower still in good condition, and an old station from when the place was linked to Kayes by railway. There's also a cemetery – one of the gravestones still legible reads 'M Sale, Canonnier, 12 Mars 1877, 23 ans'.

KITA
Kita is on the railway between Kayes and Bamako. Once a backwater, it's become a boom town since a large multinational company established a massive cotton enterprise here in the mid-1990s. Local farmers have stopped producing food crops and now grow cotton instead, which pays more money, so the market (main days Wednesday and Sunday) is very lively. It's a friendly town which rarely sees tourists, and an excellent place to slow down for a while. It's also a good base for walks in the surrounding hills.

Places to stay include the cheap and sleazy *Hôtel Lo-Lo* near the station, the

MALI

Relais Touristique, frequented by local expats and with doubles at CFA7500, and the similarly priced *Chat Rouge*. For meals and beers, *Chez Issa* has been recommended with steak and chips for CFA1000 and local meals for less.

Kita is linked to Bamako by a good new road, and there are plans to extend this road to Kayes by the year 2000. There's also a local train service, but the train to/from Kayes which stops here is much quicker.

The South

SIKASSO

Sikasso is in the far south of Mali, 373km from Bamako. Most travellers come here on the way to Ferkessédougou (Côte d'Ivoire) or Bobo-Dioulasso (Burkina Faso), but the town might be worth a visit for its own sake – possibly on the way between Bamako and Mopti. The market is lively, with no hassle, and the surrounding area is green and relatively lush – in contrast to the semidesert landscape most often associated with Mali. The only notable 'sight' is the Palais du Dernier Roi on the western side of town; guided tours are available.

Places to Stay & Eat
The cheapest place to stay is the *Hôtel Solo-Khan*, with basic rooms for CFA2500 and filthy shared bathrooms, although water in the bucket is hot. Up a grade is the *Hôtel Tata*, on the outskirts, with rooms from CFA 4000 to CFA7000 and good food. Sikasso's top address is the *Hôtel Mamelon*, in the town centre, which has air-con rooms from CFA6000. Nearby, *Restaurant le Vieille Marmite* serves good filling meals for CFA1000 to CFA1500.

Getting There & Away
Buses run daily between Sikasso and Bamako. You can also go to/from Mopti for CFA4500, or Ségou for CFA3500. If you're heading for Burkina, buses to Bobo-Dioulasso cost CFA3500 and to Ouagadougou they're CFA7500. The road on the Mali side is rough and very dusty, but tar on the Burkina side. South into Côte d'Ivoire, buses to Ferkessédougou are CFA5000 or CFA 8500 all the way to Abidjan.

KOUTIALA

Koutiala is the country's cotton-growing capital, at the junction of the main roads between Ségou, Bobo-Dioulasso, Mopti and Sikasso. Few travellers do more than change bus here, but if you decide to stay, the *Auberge Poulet Vert* has good value doubles for CFA6750 and the *Hôtel Cotonnier* charges CFA30,000 for doubles with air-con.

Mauritania

You'll definitely enjoy Mauritania if you like venturing through towns half blanketed in sand, riding camels in rolling sand dunes, sipping tea for hours with nomads in their colourful tents, crossing lunar-like landscapes characterised by rocky plateaus and deep gorges and looking at prehistoric rock drawings and ancient Saharan architecture. Mauritania is also one of the best bird-watching areas in the world. The 200km-long Banc d'Arguin is the mating place for hundreds of thousands of sea birds. Although it's the desert and often incredibly hot, the climate is comfortably dry, and from November to February the weather is actually quite pleasant.

Facts about Mauritania

HISTORY
It is hard to imagine that thousands of years ago Mauritania had large lakes, rivers and enough vegetation to support an abundance of elephant, rhino and hippopotamus. There is also evidence of early human habitation; you can find prehistoric rock drawings and arrowheads all over Mauritania. This came to an end when the Sahara started spreading about 10,000 years ago (for more details, see the History section of the Facts about the Region chapter).

Around the 3rd century AD the camel was introduced to the Berbers in Morocco. Now able to cover long distances, the Berbers established trading routes all over the western Sahara, including Mauritania. Salt, the primary commodity traded, was often valued on a par with gold. By the 9th and 10th centuries the gold trade, as well as slavery, had given rise to the first great empire in West Africa, the Soninké Empire of Ghana (the capital of which is believed to have been at Koumbi Saleh in south-eastern Mauritania). Under the Soninké, the Berbers in Mauri-

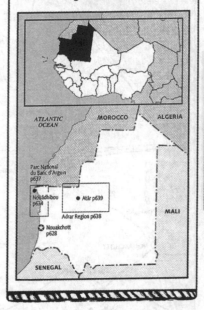

MAURITANIA AT A GLANCE

Capital: Nouakchott
Population: 2.4 million
Area: 1,030,700 sq km
Head of state: President Colonel Maaouya Sid'Ahmed Ould Taya
Official language: Arabic
Main local languages: Hassaniya, Fula, Wolof, Soninké
Currency: Ouguiya
Exchange rate: US$1 = UM200
Time: GMT/UTC
Country telephone code: ☎ 222
Best time to go: November to February

tania were reduced to vassals. (For more details on the Empire of Ghana and other early empires, see the History section of the Facts about the Region chapter.)

Islamic Beginnings

About this time, Islam began spreading throughout the area. One Muslim group stood out – the Almoravids. They gained control over the Berbers and established their capital in Marrakesh (Morocco), from where they ruled the whole of north-west Africa as well as southern Spain. In 1076 they pushed south and, with the assistance of Mauritanian Berber leaders, destroyed the Empire of Ghana. That victory led to the spread of Islam throughout Mauritania and the western Sahara – the Almoravids' most important legacy.

By this time, the Almoravid empire was in effect two: one in Morocco and a southern one ruled by the Berbers of Mauritania. In turn, the southern empire was subjugated by Arabs in 1674, after which virtually all Berbers adopted Hassaniya, the language of their conquerors.

In the late 15th century, Europe was busily draining the African continent of its people and its gold. Mauritania, however, remained

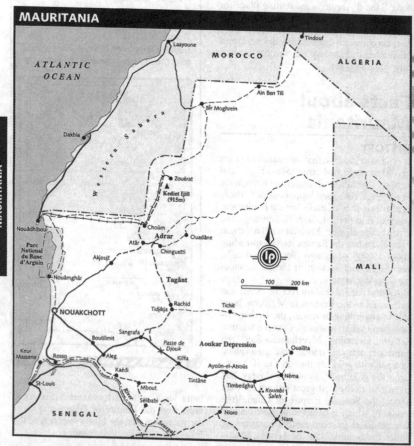

relatively unscathed. While gum arabic and slaves were sold to the Portuguese at the mouth of the River Senegal, no depopulation from slavery occurred elsewhere, there was no reorientation of the economy to cash crops and there was no exploitation of minerals. For France, Mauritania was seen as a buffer zone – troops were stationed here to protect the rest of French West Africa from raids by neighbours and ambitious European powers. The French also used the region as a place of exile for political prisoners.

In 1814 the Treaty of Paris gave France the right to explore and control the Mauritanian coast. French headquarters were installed in Senegal at St-Louis on the River Senegal, but in 1820 the slave trade ended, leaving only gum arabic as a revenue producer. The British, another contender for the gum arabic trade, withdrew from the region in 1857 in exchange for control of the River Gambia, and in 1904, having played one Moorish faction off against another, the French finally managed to make Mauritania a colonial territory. However, it took the French another 30 years to subjugate the Moors in the north and, thus diverted, only discovered Mauritania's huge iron-ore deposits on the eve of the country's independence.

Independence

Compared with the rest of West Africa, Mauritania was a political backwater in the lead-up to independence. While nationalist demands were being made all across French West Africa in the 40s and early 50s, Mauritania's representative to the French national assembly, Sidi el Mokhtar, continued to side with Charles de Gaulle. What broke the ice was Moroccan independence in 1956, after which King Hassan V began claiming much of Mauritania as part of a 'greater Morocco'. Partly in reaction to this, Mauritania's first political party, the Union Progressiste Mauritanienne, was formed and in 1957 won most of the seats in the territorial assembly elections. Mokhtar Ould Daddah, a lawyer with French backing, was elected vice president of the region's first governing council.

Independence came quickly. On 28 November 1958, Mauritania became an autonomous republic within the French community. Ould Daddah's party, the Parti du Regroupement Mauritanien, won every seat in the new national assembly and Ould Daddah became prime minister. When full independence came in 1960, Ould Daddah became the new president. The Moors declared Mauritania an Islamic republic and hastily set about building a new capital at Nouakchott. At the same time a 675km railway to the coast and a mining port at Nouâdhibou were built to take advantage of the sizeable iron-ore deposits in Zouérat. Production began in 1963.

The mines were operated by a foreign-owned consortium that paid its expatriate workers handsomely – their salaries accounted for two-thirds of the country's entire wages bill. When poorly paid Mauritanian miners went out on a two-month strike in the late 60s, the army intervened and eight miners were killed. Left-wing opposition to the government mounted and some miners formed a clandestine Marxist trade union in 1973. President Ould Daddah, who had by then eliminated all opposing political parties, survived the challenge from left-wing opponents by nationalising the company in 1974, withdrawing from the franc zone and substituting the ouguiya for the CFA.

Some years before, during the late 60s, Ould Daddah had alienated the southerners, who are mainly black Africans (the north is dominated by Moors), by making both Hassaniya and French the country's official languages and by compelling all school children to study in Arabic (lessening their opportunities for university education in French-speaking countries). Consequent rioting by southerners in Nouakchott was quickly suppressed by the army.

However, it was the issue of Western Sahara that finally toppled the government. In 1975 the Moroccans walked into the former Spanish colony. Mauritania entered into an agreement with Morocco and Spain to divide the former colony: Mauritania was to take an empty slab of desert in the south and Morocco was to get the mineral-rich northern two-thirds, with Spain relinquishing all claims. The inhabitants of what became known as the Western Sahara were understandably unhappy with this arrangement. Aided by Algeria, Libya and Cuba, militants in the region formed the Polisario Front and launched a guerrilla war to oust both Morocco and Mauritania from the area.

Mauritania was very vulnerable: the railway linking the iron-ore mines and the port at Nouâdhibou runs close to the border with the Western Sahara and the Polisario sabotaged it continually. In 1978 iron-ore exports were down 36% from their pre-war level.

The war was seemingly unwinnable. The inevitable, a (bloodless) coup took place in Mauritania in 1978, bringing in a new military government who renounced all territorial claims to the Western Sahara. Morocco wasted no time in moving its troops into the vacated territory. (For more details on the Western Sahara problem, see the boxed text 'Crossing the Sahara' in the main Getting There & Away chapter.)

Ould Taya in the 1980s

Despite promises to get the economy back on track, the new government, ruled by a committee of high-ranking military officers, was unable to do so. In 1984, there was another genteel palace coup, deposing Kohamed Khouna Haidalla, the last and longest serving of three presidents during this period. The coup brought the present ruler Colonel Maaouya Sid'Ahmed Ould Taya to power.

With World Bank support, Ould Taya immediately set about restructuring the economy, emphasising agricultural development in the south and fishing over traditional infrastructure projects. Topping his agenda, however, was the persecution of black Africans, who predominate in the south. In 1987, he jailed various prominent southerners thought to be connected with the distribution of a manifesto, published in Senegal, attacking the country's long suppression of black Africans. Subsequent rioting of southerners in Nouakchott and Nouâdhibou was partly quelled through the

The 1989 Race Riots

In 1989, in Mauritania and Senegal, bloody race riots broke out between Moors and black Africans. The riots were ignited by a familiar dispute: Moor-owned camels were grazing on the land of Soninké farmers and eating their crops. Moor border guards fired at Soninké onlookers, killing two farmers. Enraged, the Senegalese across the river rioted. The violence there spread like wildfire; hundreds of innocent Mauritanian shop owners had their shops vandalised by mobs. In Mauritania, the Moors retaliated with lynch mobs, brutal maiming, Gestapo-like raiding of homes, confiscation of property and forced deportation.

Bewildered deportees were 'returned home' to Senegal, a country most had never known. In all, some 70,000 black Africans were expelled – far more than the number of Moors deported from Senegal. Neither government did much to quell the violence but the Mauritanian government, through its anti-black actions leading up to the incident and the scale of the atrocities that it allowed on the Mauritanian side, deserved most of the blame.

introduction of strict Islamic law. Later that year, the government dismissed some 500 Tukulor soldiers from the army and soon after, the jailed author of the antiracist manifesto died in prison. The government's true colours were now all too obvious.

In 1989, race riots broke out in Mauritania and Senegal, resulting in massive deportations of southerners from Mauritania and in turn deportations of Mauritanians from Senegal. It was an ugly moment in both countries' histories and led to Taya's government becoming even more ethnocentric and xenophobic.

Mauritania in the 1990s

By 1990 Taya had sacked most southerners in government positions while black Mauritanians were deported to allow traditionally nomadic Moors to obtain land. Eliminating Tukulors was particularly important as they were the most outspoken group on the issue of civil and land rights. In November 1990, following trumped-up charges of an attempted coup spearheaded by Senegal, Mauritanian police rounded up and arrested some 300 southerners who were never heard of again. Many international aid organisations left, while aid poured in from Islamic border nations. By now Senegal and Mauritania had closed their joint border.

Taya, now regarded as an Islamic extremist, had alienated moderate Muslims, particularly the Algerians. His closest ally became Iraq (which he supported during the 1991 Gulf War), greatly diminishing Mauritania's chances of attracting loans from the west. During the last few months of 1990, 50 prominent Mauritanians signed an open letter denouncing the extent of the repression against black African civilians and soldiers.

As a result of criticism, Taya attempted to moderate his approach, pushing through a new constitution permitting opposition political parties. In early 1992, in the country's first open presidential elections, Taya was pitted against Ahmed Ould Daddah, half-brother of the country's first president, and was re-elected with 63% of the vote. However, electoral fraud was massive and the hotly contested election results won him little international respect. Opposition parties consequently voted to boycott the general elections later in the year.

With the country's economy crippled and with development focused primarily on the agricultural sector, the question of land ownership became increasingly important, further straining race relations. Bread riots in 1995, stemming from a new tax on bread, led to the arrest of Taya's principal political opponents, Ould Daddah and Hamdi Ould Mouknass – another sign that the crossover to a civilian government had not yet materialised.

In the presidential elections of December 1997, Taya's government had another chance to demonstrate its commitment to democratic reform. On the positive side, the government allowed opposition groups to appear on television and criticise the government. However, fearing massive vote rigging, the four main opposition groups boycotted the elections, while the remaining four candidates had no serious backing. The reported scale of Taya's victory was questioned by foreign observers.

Today, the question of repatriation still haunts the country. Although direct attacks have ceased, black Mauritanians continue to have difficulty recovering their land and obtaining jobs, identity cards and bank loans. They live in fear and are denied their civil rights. Meanwhile, the Taya regime refuses to acknowledge the problem. In 1993, many high-ranking government officials linked to past crimes were granted amnesty by the government.

Clearly, Mauritania's future rests on its ability to end racism and focus on a solid socioeconomic plan.

GEOGRAPHY

Mauritania is approximately twice the size of France. About three-quarters of the country, including Nouakchott, is desert, with huge expanses of flat plains broken by occasional ridges and rocky outcrops. Moreover, the desert is expanding southward, leading to a major exodus of nomads into the two largest cities, Nouakchott and Nouâdhibou.

The south is flat scrubland but as you move northward into the Sahara, there are more sand dunes and the scrub begins to disappear. The rocky plateaus of this desert region are some of the most spectacular sights in Mauritania. Most of them have been eroded so that only isolated peaks remain. One of the highest plateau areas (over 500m) is the Adrar, 450km north-east of Nouakchott, with its towns of Chinguetti and Ouadâne. These plateaus are often rich in iron ore, and there are especially large deposits at Zouérat about 200km north of Chinguetti. The highest peak is Kediet Ijill (915m) near Zouérat. Mauritania has some 700km of shoreline, which includes the Banc d'Arguin.

MAURITANIA

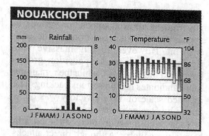

NOUAKCHOTT

CLIMATE

In the Sahara region, annual rainfall is usually less than 100mm or absent. Southward, in the Sahel zone, rainfall increases to about 600mm per year. There is a short rainy season in the south from July to September, which enables the narrow 400km strip of arable land to support cultivation.

It is extremely hot from April to October, especially from June to August when hot winds (*rifi*) from the north send temperatures soaring to 45°C and above. However, along the coast, the trade winds (*alizé*) blow from the ocean, causing average highs to be 5°C lower. The best weather is from December to March, when the highs and lows in Nouakchott are typically 29°C and 13°C, respectively. In cooler Nouâdhibou, you may need a light sweater at night.

ECOLOGY & ENVIRONMENT

Desertification looms as the greatest environmental problem. Nearly 75% of Mauritania's land surface is desert or near-desert and this is increasing. Augmented livestock herds, as a result of additional wells and human population growth, contribute to overgrazing. Deforestation results as villages grow and people seek more firewood. This latter trend may be in decline – wood has become so scarce that most cooking is now done on kerosene stoves.

FLORA & FAUNA

The uninhabited eastern desert is home to the addax antelope, an endangered species. Giraffes and lions have long gone – victims of desertification and the bullet. The last troop of elephants meanders in the hilly terrain between Kaédi and Ayoûn-el-Atroûs. One endangered species that you might see are monk seals off Cap Blanc near Nouâdhibou. Between there and Nouakchott is Parc National du Banc d'Arguin, where hundreds of thousands of birds migrate from Europe in the winter. It is one of the world's major bird breeding grounds and is on UNESCO's list of World Heritage natural sites. The new Parc National du Diawling along the River Senegal is helping to attract additional birds, including some endangered species.

GOVERNMENT & POLITICS

Mauritania is in the process of what it calls 'controlled democratisation'. In 1992, Mauritania became the first member of the Arab League to elect a head of state by universal suffrage. However, President Taya's election that year and his re-election in late 1997 were marred by what appeared to be heavy poll rigging.

The 1991 constitution declared Arabic the sole official language, introduced sharia (Islamic law), and legalised political parties but prohibited them from being organised on racial or regional lines or to be opposed to Islam, fuelling racial tensions. Some 16 political parties, including the president's party, the Parti Républicain Démocratique et Social (PRDS), are now registered. The two major opposition parties, which boycotted the 1997 elections, are the Union des Forces Démocratiques (UFD) and the Union pour la Démocratie et le Progrès (UDP) led, respectively, by Taya's old foes, Ould Daddah and Ould Mouknass.

Parliament consists of a 79 member chamber of deputies and a 56 member senate elected every five and six years, respectively. The presidential term is six years. Over 30 newspapers and periodicals are published on a regular basis. However, despite an attempt to appear democratic, the government continues to rely heavily on military support.

Sometimes labelled as one of the world's most racist countries, the regime nevertheless hopes to attract foreign aid. Taya's trump card is his opposition to Islamic fundamentalism; he says he will have difficulty halting its spread unless he can overcome the country's economic problems – and for this he needs assistance from the west.

ECONOMY

Mauritania's economy has stagnated. Over the past three decades, drought, resulting in the decimation of livestock and further desertification, have resulted in a mass exodus of traditionally nomadic Moors from the desert to Nouakchott. Today, only about 10% of the population is officially nomadic, compared with 83% in the late 1960s. The economic situation is exacerbated by debt (much of which has been incurred in the financing of dubious projects) and the high population growth rate (2.5%).

GNP per capita is just over US$500, relatively high for West Africa. However, life expectancy is 47 years (below the West African average) and doctors are scarce. Thus, the quality of life is very low. Agriculture along the River Senegal contributes to one-third of GNP, making this land a focal point for development. While irrigation there is increasing, the government encourages cattle-raising and rain-fed farming methods, traditionally Moorish activities, which is to the detriment of black Mauritanians.

Fishing and the iron-ore industry account for over 90% of export earnings. The waters off Mauritania are among the world's richest but over-fishing has devastated stocks. Mauritania has one of the world's largest reserves of iron ore, mainly around Zouérat, but falling world prices have affected exports. On a brighter note, gold-extracting operations began in 1992 in Akjoujt. Texaco and Amoco are also conducting oil exploration, and trade with the USA is increasing.

Mauritania's major problem is its external debt, among the highest in West Africa (as a percentage of GNP). As part of the IMF structural adjustment program the government periodically devalues the ouguiya and is slowly privatising state enterprises. The slow opening of the economy to foreign imports is increasing the food supply and lowering prices.

POPULATION & PEOPLE

Of Mauritania's 2.3 million inhabitants, most are Moors (or Maurs) of Arab and Berber descent. However, a long tradition of inter-ethnic marriage has blurred ethnic boundaries. The actual figure for Moors of Arab descent, called 'Bidan', is closer to 40%. As with most African ethnic groups, there's a strict class system among Bidan Moors.

The other major ethnic group are black Africans, ethnically split into two groups. The Haratin, or black Moors, the descendants of people enslaved by the Moors, have assimilated the Moorish culture and speak Hassaniya, an Arabic dialect. The longer a Haratin family has been associated with a Bidan family and the more it has intermarried with Bidans, the higher its status. Culturally, they have little affinity with the Mauritanians living in the south along the River Senegal, the 'Soudaniens'. The Soudaniens constitute 40% of the total population and are mostly Fula (sedentary or nomadic, also known as Peul) or the closely related Tukulor. These groups speak Fula (Pulaar) and are known jointly in Mauritania as Hal-Pulaar. There are also Soninké and Wolof minorities.

EDUCATION

While formal education is not compulsory, some 51% of school-age children attend primary school and about 15% go on to secondary school. The adult literacy rate is still only 34%, well below the sub-Saharan average of 51%.

ARTS

Although there is plenty of art and craftwork in Mauritania, as well as lots of opportunities to hear traditional Mauritanian music, there is essentially no literature or theatre. You may see one of the traditional Mauritanian sand games.

Art & Craftwork

Mauritania has a strong tradition of art and craftwork, especially silverwork. Most prized are wooden chests with silver inlay, but there are also silver daggers and silver and amber jewellery. There are also earth-tone rugs of camel and goat hair from Boutilimit, hand-painted Kiffa beads and other trade beads, hand-dyed leatherwork including colourful leather cushions and leather pipe pouches, camel saddles and sandals. Kaédi is famous for its colourful batik cloth. Other textiles include rugs made of white, beige or chest-nut-coloured wool with geometric designs, available in Nouakchott.

Music

The traditional music of Mauritania is mostly Arabic in origin, although along its southern border there are influences from the Wolof, Tukulor and Bambara. If Arabic music is your preferred style, you'll enjoy the power of Mauritanian singers. Mauritanian instruments include the *ardin* (harp) and the *tidnit*, a four-stringed plucked lute, similar to the *xalam* of the Wolof over the border in Senegal. Several singers with a more modern African inspiration have hit the international scene including a woman, Malouma, and a group headed by Khalifa Ould Eide and Dimi Mint Abba. But finding their recordings is difficult and hearing them sing in Mauritania is next to impossible.

SOCIETY & CONDUCT

The majority Moors were traditionally no-mads, living from raising cattle and sheep and from commerce, particularly transport with camel caravans. For some, this came to an end during the severe droughts of the 1970s and early 80s when most of their animals died and they had no choice but to come to Nouakchott and live in shanty towns. Today, most Moors live in cities and towns. Many gave up their nomadic exis-tence long ago, becoming city-based traders, and Moorish merchants are a common sight all over West Africa. The men characteristic-ally have Arab facial features and wear long light-blue African robes. Many have the

The Haratin & the Bidan

The Moors have one of the most stratified caste systems in Africa. The system is based on lineage, occupation and access to power. This division hampers any attempt to unify the people. However, colour has become a popular but inaccurate measure to determine status. At the top are the upper classes, the typically light-skinned Bidan Moors descended from war-riors and men of letters. Below them are commoners, mostly of Berber-Negroid stock. The lowest castes traditionally consisted of four groups: the Haratin Moors, artisans, *griots* and slaves with no rights of any kind.

The Haratin do all the house and field work, and tend to be as lean and sinewy as the palm trees they tend. Bidan women, on the other hand, tend to be plump because fat for them is beautiful. They even feed their daughters a special diet of milk and peanuts so that they will grow up desirably colossal.

In 1980, there were an estimated 100,000 Haratin slaves in Mauritania. It wasn't until then that Mauritania declared slavery illegal. But it's one thing to declare slavery illegal; it's another for it to happen. In fact slavery had been declared illegal three times before this. In the Adrar region, people are reportedly still being bought and sold. For one thing, freeing the slaves was conditional on the owners being compensated. Also, most slaves have been attached all their lives to Bidan families and have agreeable relationships. Once they walk out the door, they lose all their financial security. So it's not surprising that most continue living and working for their Bidan families while at the same time being part of, and cared for by, the extended family.

name Ould (son of) eg Ahmed Ould Mohamed. For women it's Mint (daughter of). Women are in a very disadvantaged position. Only a third as many women as men are literate and few are involved in commercial activities other than selling food and crafts. Culturally, however, they have more freedoms than women in many Arabic countries. For example, while women cover their heads, they are not obliged to cover their faces.

As in most of West Africa, elaborate greetings are traditional in Moorish society. Social activities revolve around tea, which is invariably strong and sweet. The first two glasses are almost obligatory but declining the third glass is not impolite.

RELIGION

Over 99% of the people are Sunni Muslims; religion provides a superficial unity between Moors and other peoples. Islamic fundamentalists are growing in number but remain a minority.

LANGUAGE

Arabic is the official language, but French is still spoken in all government sectors and is widely used in business. The everyday language of the Moor majority is a Berber-Arabic dialect called Hassaniya. In the south, other languages are spoken, including Fula (Pulaar), Wolof and Soninké. See the Language chapter for a list of useful phrases in French, Hassaniya, Fula and Wolof.

Facts for the Visitor

SUGGESTED ITINERARIES

If you have only a week to visit Mauritania, you should plan on spending your time in Nouakchott (two days) and the Adrar region. You could take a bush taxi or fly to Atâr and there arrange transport to Chinguetti. Plan at least a day and a half in Chinguetti so that you can enjoy a day's camel ride out into the desert.

If you have two weeks, you could then try arranging local transport to nearby

Highlights

Natural Beauty & National Parks

Parc National du Banc d'Arguin
(The Coast)
A birder's paradise, with hundreds of thousands of birds migrating from Europe.

Tagânt Plateau *(The East & South)*
Great views from the plateau, plus prehistoric rock paintings and old forts, mosques and traditional houses.

Adrar Plateau *(The North)*
Striking landscape, with prehistoric rock paintings, ancient towns and a huge crater, the Guelb er Richat.

People & Culture

Port de Pêche *(Nouakchott)*
Every afternoon the fishing boats return to shore, igniting a flurry of activity. A great spectacle, with a lively atmosphere.

Central Market *(Nouakchott)*
The main market in the capital is a great place to wander round, and offers a huge variety of goods.

Nouâdhibou to Zouérat Train *(The North)*
Riding this train – the longest in the world – makes a memorable trip and is a great way of meeting Mauritanians.

Activities

Beaches *(The Coast)*
Mauritania's entire coast is virtually one long strip of sand and mostly deserted except for Nouakchott.

Fishing *(The Coast)*
Surf casting is great all along the coast, and in Nouâdhibou deep-sea fishing is available.

Camel Rides *(The North)*
Chinguetti is ideal for riding camels as there are spectacular sand dunes just outside the city.

MAURITANIA

Ouadâne, another desert village of historical interest. Alternatively you could try the three day overland route from Atâr to Tidjikja along the panoramic Tagânt plateau. Very few travellers take this route, and the trip must be conducted by a tour agency because of the danger of getting lost.

If you have a third week, the place to head for would be the Parc National du Banc d'Arguin, which is remotely located along the Atlantic coast – you will need to arrange a guide and your own transport for this. A fourth week could be spent exploring southern Mauritania.

VISAS & DOCUMENTS
Visas
Visas are required for all except nationals of Arab League countries, some African countries, France and Italy. Visa prices vary from country to country, and multiple-entry visas are generally not available. The standard visa is valid for three months and good for a stay of one to three months from the date of entry. The embassy in Washington requires US$10, an itinerary and a photocopy of your latest bank statement. Applications take several days to process.

In Europe, visas are easy to get. While embassies here usually issue visas only to those arriving by air, they do not insist upon seeing your airline ticket. You can get a visa in the Canary Islands, but the process takes weeks. In Australia, the French consulate in Melbourne issues visas to Mauritania but the requirements are onerous – A$50, a recent bank statement, itinerary, flight details and a letter from your employer. Make sure they use the title 'Islamic Republic of Mauritania' as some travellers have had problems at borders when 'Islamic' was left out.

Getting a visa in Morocco is problematic. The embassy in Rabat requires a letter of introduction from your embassy (Australians can use the Canadian embassy) and a return airline ticket. Some embassies in Rabat, such as the Netherlands embassy, refuse to write letters of introduction for Mauritanian visas, and others, such as the Belgian embassy, are reluctant to do so. Without the letter and

ticket, you will not get a visa. If you bring both, they'll issue the visa on the spot. It is common practice for an overland traveller to buy an airline ticket in Rabat for the purpose of obtaining a visa and to sell the ticket once the visa is issued. The visa will indicate that it's valid for entry at Nouakchott airport but border officials ignore this.

In West Africa, getting visas is easy and sometimes cheap. In most countries, you can get visas on the spot or within 24 hours but often you need a letter of introduction from your embassy. If your government has no embassy, they'll probably waive the requirement. In countries without a Mauritanian embassy, the French embassy usually issues them and requires no *note verbale*, but the cost is higher, typically CFA20,000.

Visa Extensions Visa extensions can be obtained from the *commissariat central* on Ave Abdel Nasser in Nouakchott.

Other Documents
You may need proof of vaccination against cholera or yellow fever (if you're coming from an infected area). Those driving need a *carnet de passage en douane* and will have to get insurance, usually at the nearest customs office. An International Driving Permit (IDP) is not required; your own licence will suffice.

EMBASSIES & CONSULATES
Mauritanian Embassies & Consulates
In West Africa, Mauritania has embassies in Côte d'Ivoire, Gambia, Mali, Nigeria and Senegal, and a consulate in Niger. For more details, see the Facts for the Visitor section of the relevant country chapter.

Elsewhere, Mauritania has embassies and consulates in the following countries:

Belgium
  (☎ 02-672 47 47)
  6 rue de Colombie, Brussels 1050
France
  (☎ 01 45 48 23 88)
  89 rue du Cherche-Midi, 75006 Paris

Germany
(☎ 0228-36 40 24, fax 361 7888)
Bonnerstrasse 48, 53173 Bonn

Morocco
(☎ 07-75 68 28)
1 Rue de Normandie, Souissi, Rabat

Spain
(☎ 91-563 1090, fax 435 9531)
Velasquez 90, 28006

USA
(☎ 202-232 700, fax 319 2623)
2129 Leroy Place, NW, Washington, DC 20008

Mauritania also has embassies in Canada, and consulates in Austria, the Canary Islands, Germany and Switzerland. There's no Mauritanian representation in the UK.

Embassies & Consulates in Mauritania

The following countries are represented in Nouakchott:

France
(☎ 52337)
Rue Ahmed Ould Mohamed, just before the Monotel

Germany
(☎ 51729)
Rue Abdallaye

Mali
(☎ 54081, 54078)
Rue Mamadou Konaté, opposite the German embassy

Morocco
(☎ 51411, telex 550)
Ave du Général de Gaulle, near Hôtel Halima

Visas for Onward Travel

The French consulate issues three-month visas to Burkina Faso, Côte d'Ivoire and Togo in 24 hours. Bring two photos and UM5200 (less for five-day visas).

The Mali embassy takes 24 hours to issue visas, and requires UM1475, two photos and a photocopy of the information pages of your passport.

You can also get visas here for Morocco (embassy open until 3 pm; visas issued the same day) and Senegal.

Senegal
(☎ 57290)
Ave de l'Ambassade du Sénégal

USA
(☎ 52660, fax 51592)
Rue Abdallaye (consulate open Monday and Wednesday from 10 to 11.30 am)

Egypt, Spain and Tunisia also have embassies in Nouakchott.

CUSTOMS

It is illegal to bring any alcohol into the country. There are no longer currency declaration forms and there is no restriction on the amount of foreign currency you can bring in, but if you bring in a lot, you should declare it. Local currency cannot be imported or exported.

MONEY

The unit of currency is the ouguiya, UM, which equals five khoums.

Euro €1	=	UM245
1FF	=	UM37
UK£1	=	UM350
US$1	=	UM200

The currency is fairly stable and the exchange rate is increasing slowly. Banks are very slow in their operations. The street rate is about 25 to 33% higher than the official rate. Virtually everyone changes money on the street, and the market is usually the best place. Police do not control this. Shop around for the best rate. The larger towns have bureaus de change. Their rates are inferior but are usually better than those offered by banks, plus they're more efficient. The preferred currencies are US$ and French francs. The CFA is not convertible, even on the street, except with money dealers at the Senegal border.

At Nouakchott airport, you can exchange money at airport shops, which give a better rate than the bank (often closed). Hotels usually won't accept travellers cheques, but if it's your last resort, the top end ones will

MAURITANIA

usually take them. Upcountry, you can always find people willing to change ouguiya for US$ or French francs.

The Banque Mauritanienne pour le Commerce International (BMCI) and the Banque Nationale de Mauritanie (BNM) change travellers cheques but only their branches in Nouakchott and Nouâdhibou do this. Travellers sometimes experience difficulty cashing American Express travellers cheques. No banks give cash advances on credit cards. Credit cards are accepted only at top hotels and some travel agencies.

POST & COMMUNICATIONS

Post offices are open from 8 am to noon and 3 to 6 pm and are usually closed on Friday and Saturday. However, the one in Nouakchott is open seven days a week. Letters from here to Europe take about a week, sometimes more. The poste restante (in Nouakchott) is generally efficient.

The telephone system is connected to satellite. You can make international calls and send faxes at many post and telephone centres, but you can do the same more conveniently and for about the same price at one of the many privately run phone shops in the major cities and towns. Most are open late. The cost is about UM450/US$3 a minute to the USA or Europe and 25% less for calls within West Africa. Telephone area codes within Mauritania are as follows:

Nouakchott   ☎ 2
Rosso   ☎ 5
Nouâdhibou, Atâr & Zouérat   ☎ 7

BOOKS

Catherine Belvaude's La Mauritanie (in French) gives the best description of the country's culture, government and its people. The only bookshop worth a look is Librairie Vents du Sud in Nouakchott.

NEWSPAPERS & MAGAZINES

Since 1992, the local press has blossomed. Newspapers available locally in French include L'Opinion, Calame, La Tribune and Info Nouakchott; most others are in Arabic. Some can be quite critical of the government. Copies of Le Monde, Newsweek and the Herald Tribune are also available.

RADIO & TV

ORTM, state-run, operates the sole radio and TV stations. They broadcast news, sports and cultural programs.

PHOTOGRAPHY & VIDEO

Photo permits are not required. However, a police officer could cause problems if he sees you photographing something other than a tourist site. Taking photographs of government buildings including post offices, airports, ports, radio antennas and military installations is strictly forbidden. Some Mauritanians are delighted to have their photos taken, others are not, so it's best to always ask first. For more information and advice, see the Photography & Video section in the Regional Facts for the Visitor chapter. The only city where you can buy film is Nouakchott.

HEALTH

A yellow fever vaccination certificate is required unless you have come from a non-infected area and are staying less than two weeks. Malaria is a risk year-round except in the north around Nouâdhibou and Tiris. In Adrar and Inchiri malaria risk exists only during the rainy season. If you're travelling in the south, you should take appropriate precautions. See the Health section in the Regional Facts for the Visitor chapter for more information on these and other health matters.

The water in rural areas is generally safe as it comes from deep bore holes, but treating water is still recommended. In urban areas, the water can become contaminated by leaks in the pipes. In general, it's the unsanitary handling of the food that causes most stomach problems.

In an emergency, the hospital in Nouakchott (☎ 52135) has French doctors. There are also hospitals in Nouâdhibou, Atâr and Rosso. Pharmacies are quite well stocked, and many medicines are available over the counter which would require a prescription elsewhere.

WOMEN TRAVELLERS

Women can be subjected to sexual harassment, especially when alone or with other women. There have been attacks in Nouakchott. It's a good idea for women to dress conservatively, as miniskirts, shorts and swimsuits are offensive to many Mauritanians, especially outside Nouakchott. For more general information and advice, see the Women Travellers section in the Regional Facts for the Visitor chapter.

DANGERS & ANNOYANCES

Despite a rise in crime, particularly petty thefts, Nouakchott remains one of the safest capital cities in Africa – see Information in the Nouakchott section for more details.

The border with the Western Sahara is still unstable. There are thousands of land mines buried along the Mauritanian side. People have been killed here, so avoid it, including the area just west of Nouâdhibou on the peninsula. For those travelling overland to Mali: since the early 90s, the area north of Néma has on occasion been affected by the Tuareg insurgency. There have also been disturbances, some violent, in that area, involving cattle rustling and the weapons trade. Ask beforehand about conditions along the border and keep a watchful eye.

BUSINESS HOURS

Business hours are Sunday to Thursday from 8 am to noon and 3 to 6 pm; closed Friday and Saturday. Some businesses are open on Saturday mornings, and many shops are open every day. Government offices are open Saturday to Wednesday from 8 am to 3 pm; Thursday 8 am to 1 pm. Banking hours are Sunday to Thursday from 7 am to 12.30 pm (for changing money).

PUBLIC HOLIDAYS & SPECIAL EVENTS

Mauritania celebrates the usual Islamic holidays – see Public Holidays & Special Events in the Regional Facts for the Visitor chapter for a table of estimated dates of these holidays. In addition to these, Mauritania has holidays on 1 January (New Year's Day), 26 February (National Reunification Day), 1 May (Workers' Day), 25 May (African Liberation Day), 10 July (Army day), 28 November (Independence) and 12 December (anniversary of the 1984 coup).

ACCOMMODATION

Finding inexpensive accommodation (in the US$5 to US$10 range) is easy in cities and major towns. There are also air-con hotels meeting international standards in Nouakchott and Nouâdhibou and satisfactory air-con hotels in Atâr, Kiffa and Zouérat. In minor towns, accommodation is bad to nonexistent. Nevertheless, Mauritania is one of the easiest countries to find a place to sleep. Everywhere people will offer you a bed, and most restaurants will allow you to sleep on the floor if you buy a meal. In addition, there are camp sites in Nouakchott and Nouâdhibou. Camping elsewhere in open spaces is legal. A tent is often unnecessary but you'll need one on a windy day or during a sandstorm.

FOOD & DRINKS

The desert cuisine of the Moors wins no culinary awards. Dishes are generally bland and limited to rice, mutton, goat, camel or dried fish. Unsweetened, curdled goat or camel milk often accompanies meals served in private homes. However, Mauritanian couscous, similar to the Moroccan variety, is delicious. A real treat is to attend a *méchui*, a traditional nomad's feast where an entire lamb is roasted over a fire and stuffed with cooked rice. Guests tear off bits of meat with their hands.

The cuisine of southern Mauritania, essentially Senegalese, is excellent, with much more variety, spices and vegetables. Most cheap African restaurants, even in the north, are operated by Tukulors and Fulas from the south. Two of the most popular dishes are rice with fish and Senegalese *mafé* (a peanut-based stew), typically UM100 to UM150.

MAURITANIA

Soft drinks are available everywhere, and alcohol is available at some hotels and restaurants in Nouakchott and Nouâdhibou.

Getting There & Away

AIR

Airports & Airlines

Nouakchott and Nouâdhibou both have international airports. It's a good idea to reconfirm flights, especially during Ramadan. Flights are sometimes delayed due to sandstorms, especially in the winter. There is no airport departure tax.

Europe & the USA

Air France has twice-weekly flights to/from Paris (with connecting flights to/from London) as does Air Afrique. From Nouakchott, regular fares (UM75,520 or US$580 one way, economy class) are over 50% cheaper than the same class ticket purchased in France. Prices go down by as much as 10% during the low season (October to March), except around Christmas. You can also fly via Casablanca – Air Mauritanie, Air Algérie and Royal Air Maroc all offer one flight a week there. A one way fare is about US$350.

Air Mauritanie also flies a Nouakchott to Las Palmas (Canary Islands) round trip (UM45,000 one way, UM58,000 return), stopping in Nouâdhibou. The twice-weekly flights are often full for weeks, but if you try flying stand-by your chances of getting on are not bad.

Africa

You can fly between Nouakchott and Dakar (Senegal) five days a week on Air Mauritanie (UM20,250/CFA69,500), Air Afrique and Air France. There are flights twice weekly to/from Bamako (Mali) on Air Afrique and Air Mauritanie, to/from Banjul on Air Gambia and Air Mauritanie and to/from Abidjan (Côte d'Ivoire) on Air France and Air Afrique. There are once weekly flights

Border Crossings

The main border crossings are Rosso into Senegal, at Néma for Mali and north of Nouâdhibou for Morocco.

Crossing into **Mali**, on the Mauritanian side, have your passport stamped by police at the first town. You must also clear customs, which can be done only in Néma or Kiffa.

Crossing into **Senegal** at Rosso, note that immigration is only open on the Mauritanian side from 8 am to noon and 3 to 6 pm. The border crossing at Rosso, while easy for most travellers, is often a nightmare for vehicle owners. Police, customs officials and men hanging about collaborate on scams. They may take your health card hostage. Customs officials on both sides routinely demand vehicle owners pay bribes of as much as CFA10,000. One motorcycle owner recently reported that police on the Mauritanian side demanded UM3000 to stamp his passport; they settled for UM2500.

Going to **Morocco**, the trail is still a one way route – for more details, see the boxed text 'Crossing the Sahara' in the main Getting There & Away chapter at the beginning of this book. Mauritania considers the border dangerous because of land mines and does not permit crossings northward without special permission. Some dare-devils ignore the regulations and skirt the usual border crossing route, entering Morocco a few kilometres to the east. It's the first stopping point on the train (about an hour from Nouâdhibou). They use a guide, obtainable in Nouâdhibou for around UM25,000, to avoid the land mines and to find the Moroccan border post where they wait for the Moroccan army officer accompanying the convoy southward from Dakhla (Tuesday and Friday) to take them to Dakhla. Apparently those making it to Morocco are usually held by police there for questioning for several days. If you try it and are caught on the Mauritanian side you'll have lots of explaining to do.

to/from Algiers on Air Algérie and to/from Tunis on Tunis Air. One-way fares on Air Mauritanie are over 10% cheaper than those of most other airlines. Excursion and youth fares are available.

LAND
Mali
The main crossings are, east to west: at Néma, Timbedgha (both connecting with Nara in Mali), Ayoûn-el-Atroûs, Tîntâne and Kiffa (all connecting with Nioro in Mali). Petrol is usually available in Nioro, Nara, Néma, Ayoûn and Kiffa. The route via Tintâne is popular as it avoids the worst of the dunes. There are two routes between Nioro and Ayoûn; the westward route is better. Halfway between Nioro and Ayoûn there's a fork to the left (north-west) leading to Tintâne. Take it as it avoids the worst of the dunes. If you cross via Timbedgha, check out the excavations at Koumbi Saleh on the way.

Take everything you'll need, as petrol and supplies are not available en route. The trip, by whichever route, is roughly 230km and usually takes 1½ days (one day if you really push it). It's easy to lose the track, so take a compass. The Route de l'Espoir is sealed all the way from Nouakchott to Néma and is in good condition except for the 250km stretch between the Passe de Djouk and Aleg, which is appalling.

Morocco
For details on crossing between Morocco and Mauritania, see the boxed text 'Crossing the Sahara' in the main Getting There & Away chapter earlier in this book.

Senegal
Bush Taxi From Dakar to Nouakchott usually takes from 11 to 13 hours depending on the wait at Rosso. Most minibuses and bush taxis leave Dakar before 10 am to be sure of arriving in Rosso well before the border closing time (6 pm). At Rosso, most travellers without vehicles cross by pirogue (five minutes; UM100/CFA350) as the ferry crosses only four times daily.

Car & Motorcycle The Dakar to Nouakchott route involves crossing the River Senegal at Rosso, which takes only 10 minutes by ferry (*bac*). The ferry departs from the Mauritanian side at 9 am, 11 am, 3 pm and 5 pm, and from the Senegalese side some 45 minutes later. It costs UM2000 (CFA6500) for street cars, UM2200 (CFA 7150) for a Land Rover, and more for trucks. Procedures for getting car insurance (required by both countries) and passing through police and customs are efficient on the Senegalese side, less so on the Mauritanian side. Officials on both sides routinely demand large bribes in return for customs clearance.

There is also a river crossing west of Rosso; it's several hours longer as the track is very sandy. For more details, see the Getting There & Away section in the Senegal chapter.

Getting Around

AIR
Air Mauritanie, one of the better airlines in West Africa, flies twice daily from Nouakchott to Nouâdhibou and less frequently to Atâr, Néma, Zouérat, Tidjikja, Kaédi, Kiffa and Ayoûn-el-Atroûs. Prices are reasonable, for example UM9080 to Nouâdhibou. Departures are usually punctual, weather permitting. Make advance reservations as flights are often fully booked.

BUSH TAXI & TRUCK
Peugeot 504s, Land Rovers, minibuses and pick-ups (*bâchés*), in descending order of cost, are the four types of public transport. Overcharging is rare except with the baggage fee, which requires bargaining. Taxis go to all the major towns daily, but finding a taxi for small villages is challenging. You can also take large trucks, which are about a third cheaper but slower. Peugeot 504s are uncomfortable because you're crammed in four to a row, so consider paying for two seats to avoid the misery. The front two seats are less

cramped but they're also more expensive – and more dangerous.

Expect a long, hot and dusty trip with few or no toilet stops but frequent stops for prayer and tea, and occasional breakdowns. Take along plenty of water and something to munch on. If you choose a bâché, bring a *houli* (man's headwrap) to cover your head, nose and mouth.

TRAIN

The Nouâdhibou-Zouérat train, the world's longest train, is a great adventure. It's an iron-ore train with no passenger terminals, but for people travelling between these two towns it has become a passenger train for lack of alternatives. The trip takes 16 to 18 hours, but most travellers get off at Choûm, 12 hours from Nouâdhibou. You can put your car on board if you make prior arrangements with SNIM, the organisation that operates both the train and the iron-ore mines.

The dilapidated passenger carriage at the rear has no lights or porters, and the seats consist of long benches on either side. There

The Iron Ore Train

The Zouérat to Nouâdhibou train is the longest in the world – typically 2.3km long. When it arrives at the 'station' in Nouâdhibou, an unmarked place in the open desert, a seemingly endless number of ore wagons pass before the passenger carriage at the rear appears. Then the stampede to get on board begins. The lucky ones find a place on one of the two long benches; the rest stand or sit on the floor. There's little to see as the windows are small and many are shut. The train stops in the middle of nowhere every hour or so to let people off. The atmosphere can be quite jovial, with people playing cards on the floor. In the late afternoon, many men find space on the floor to pray and at dusk when the cabin becomes totally dark, chanting begins.

are compartments at either end with fold-down bunks, which cost extra, but getting one is difficult. The carriage is usually very crowded, but as the journey progresses and people get off, space opens up. If you're going only to Choûm and the train isn't too crowded, the journey will be much easier. In that case, if you don't get a seat, there will be space for sitting on the floor. You can ride on top, but you'll find it very cold. Riding free in one of the open-air ore wagons is also allowed on the return trip to Zouérat when the cars are empty. Be prepared for a very gruelling trip. Take a houli to keep sand and soot out of your eyes and enough clothes to keep warm as it gets very cold at night.

CAR & MOTORCYCLE

Petrol costs UM112 per litre. There's a new Japanese-financed road to Atâr, so driving there from Nouakchott is now a snap – six hours nonstop. The road from Atâr to Choûm and Chinguetti (both three hours) is reasonably good and doesn't require 4WD. Petrol is usually available in both towns but can be pricey if there's a shortage. You can also make it to Ouadâne without 4WD if you travel along the northern plateau road but not if you travel from Chinguetti onward via the more interesting but sandy southern route. You'll also need 4WD for Tidjikja.

The overland trip from Nouakchott to Nouâdhibou (525km) takes two to three days and requires 4WD. This route is far worse than any other section of the trans-Saharan route through Morocco and Mauritania. The first 155km from Nouakchott north to Cap Timiris is along the beach and passable only during low tide. This means a breakdown is potentially disastrous, so study the tide schedule beforehand. Thereafter you enter the worst section, full of dunes for almost 300km. For safety reasons go with at least one other vehicle and a guide (typically UM25,000) as you're almost guaranteed to get lost without one.

ORGANISED TOURS

There are numerous travel agencies in Nouakchott that offer tours around the country (see Information in that section for more details). Travel is usually by 4WD. The most popular destinations are the Adrar region, Tagânt plateau, and the Banc d'Arguin. Most trips are about one or two weeks. If there are at least four travellers, prices should average around UM15,000 per day.

Nouakchott

Nouakchott, meaning 'place of the winds' in Hassaniya, was hastily constructed in 1960 at independence. St-Louis, the administrative centre of the French territory Senegal-Mauritania, ended up on the Senegalese side, leaving Mauritania without a major city. The site of the new capital was originally a long way from the Sahara, but over the years the Sahara has moved in, and now the town is surrounded by rolling sand dunes.

Designed for 200,000 inhabitants, the city was planned with wide streets and space around public buildings and houses – quite unlike a typical African city. Today, surrounded by shanty towns, it has over triple that number. In 1990, in order to free land for middle-class Moors, the government moved the poor to new settlements far from town. You can see them along the road to Atâr and west of the Route de l'Espoir (to Néma), but from the highway you can't appreciate their vastness.

The main streets are Ave Abdel Nasser running east to west and Ave Kennedy running north to south. The nicest district is to the north while to the south, near where Abdel Nasser and Kennedy cross, is the Grand Marché and, 2km further south, the Cinquième quarter, a major shanty town with a busy market. The ocean is 5km west along Abdel Nasser, while the old Ksar district and airport are 3km north-east of the centre.

Information

Money Moneychangers hang out around the Grand Marché and at the gare routière. One of the numerous bureau de change is on Ave Abdel Nasser next to the BNM bank; another is half a block east on Ave du Général de Gaulle. Banks include the BNM and the BMCI (☎ 52826, fax 52045) on Ave Abdel Nasser.

Post & Communications The post office is on Ave Abdel Nasser. You can make phone calls there, but phone shops are quicker. There's one on Rue Mamadou Konaté in the centre of town, and another on Ave du Général de Gaulle just south of Ave Abdel Nasser. For information on telephone numbers or codes, call ☎ 12.

Travel Agencies & Tour Operators Soprage (☎ 53851, fax 51353) on Rue Alioune specialises in air travel. It accepts credit cards and represents American Express but does not sell travellers cheques. Others nearby include ATV (☎ 54749), Soreci Voyages (☎ 51207) and Golden Tours (☎ 53109).

Numerous agencies offer tours; quoted prices require a minimum of four people, sometimes more. VSTC (☎ 56953, fax 56955) on Ave Abdel Nasser charges US$755 per person (minimum four people) for an eight day all-inclusive trip to Chinguetti, Ouadâne, Guelb er Richat crater and Terjît, an eight day excursion to the Tagânt plateau (Tidjikja, Rachid and El Barka) or a six day excursion to the Banc d'Arguin.

Others agencies include Inchiri-Voyage (☎ 54796, fax 54905), AVR (☎ 57379) and Général Services (☎ 57356, fax 53855) on Ave Abdel Nasser and, possibly better, Randoneé Tours (☎ 59535, fax 59539) and Savana Tours (☎ 59443, fax 52073) on Ave du Général de Gaulle.

Bookshops The best bookshop is Librairie Vents du Sud (☎ 52684) on Ave Kennedy. It has postcards, foreign newspapers, magazines and books. Also check the top hotels.

Dangers & Annoyances Nouakchott is a relatively safe city, especially compared with other capital cities in the region. It's a late-night city, with many people walking around even at 11 pm. Even at those hours

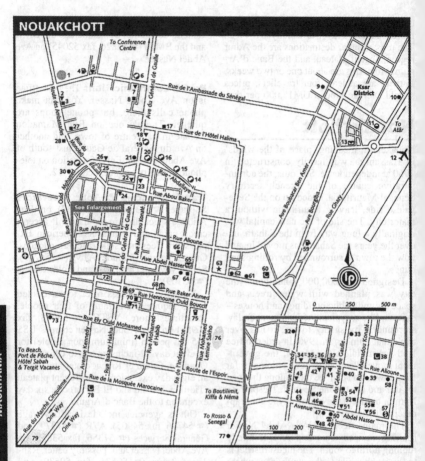

NOUAKCHOTT

walking is generally safe for men. The worst area is along the beach near the city as muggings and rapes have occurred there. No one, especially women, even in a group, should walk along the beach at night. Thefts there are common. Foreigners of African descent are sometimes subjected to harassment by the police and Moors.

Musée National

This museum, south-west of Hôtel Marhaba, is worth visiting, although it focuses on the culture of the Moors, excluding that of the black southerners. On the first level is a prehistoric gallery displaying bits of pottery and various ancient artefacts. The second level has a good display of beauty aids used by nomadic women, a model house from Oulâta, local games, camel saddles, leather cushions, boxes and bags, a floor covering for tents, carpets, old photographs, bowls, baskets, weaving and musical instruments. It's open from Saturday to Thursday from 9.30 am to 3 pm (Thursday to 12.30 pm).

NOUAKCHOTT

PLACES TO STAY		
3	Hôtel du Petit Paris	
8	Hôtel-Restaurant	
	Casablanca	
17	Hôtel Halima	
27	Auberge du Désert	
28	Monotel Dar-el-Barka	
45	Park Hôtel	
46	Hôtel El Amane	
52	Hôtel Chinguetti	
53	Hôtel Oasis	
55	Auberge de	
	Jeunesse l'Amitié	
64	Hôtel Marhaba	
70	Hôtel Adrar	

PLACES TO EAT		
2	Pizza Lina; Naf	
5	Oiseau de Paradis	
7	Welcome Burger	
18	Restaurant Guervoum	
22	X'Presso Café	
23	Le Bambou	
24	Restaurant la Dune	
26	Taska Karaoke; Mac Drive	
34	Le Prince; Royal Snack;	
	Fruit Stands	
35	Snack Irak; Restaurant-	
	Pâtisserie Rally	
36	Restaurant le Palmier	
41	Snack Al Moulouk	
42	Ali Baba	

43	La Nouvelle Boucherie	
48	Restaurant-Pâtisserie	
	Andalouss	
51	Restaurant El Kemal	
54	Restaurant Phenicia	
56	Restaurant Rimal	
71	Restaurant Taiba	
74	Restaurant Zoubeida	

OTHER		
1	Stade Olympique	
4	Petrol Station	
6	Senegal Embassy	
9	Market	
10	Centre National du Tapis	
11	Gare Routière	
12	Airport	
13	Post Office	
14	US Embassy	
15	Spanish Embassy	
16	German Embassy	
19	Moroccan Embassy	
20	Mali Embassy	
21	Arguin Tours	
25	St Joseph Cathedral	
29	French Embassy	
30	Alliance Française	
31	Hospital	
32	Tunis Air; Librairie	
	Vents du Sud	
33	Randonées Tours;	
	Savana Tours	

37	Petrol Station	
38	Mosquée Saudique	
	(Grande Mosquée)	
39	Golden Tours	
40	ATV; Soreci Voyages	
44	BNM Bank; Exchange	
	Bureau; VSTC Voyages,	
	Inchiri Voyage	
47	Air Algérie	
49	Phone Shop	
50	La Gazelle du Désert;	
	Général Services	
57	BMCI Bank	
58	Soprage (Amex)	
59	Petrol Station	
60	Friday Mosque	
61	Air France; Royal Air Maroc	
62	Air Mauritanie	
63	Commissariat Central	
65	Post Office	
66	Air Afrique	
67	GCAL Voyages (Europcar)	
68	Musée National	
69	L'Artisanal Féminin	
72	Grand Marché	
73	Stade de la Luttes	
	(Wrestling Arena)	
75	Racing Club	
76	Stade de la Capitale	
77	Centre Artisanal	
78	Moroccan Mosque	
79	Cinquième Marché	

MAURITANIA

Admission is officially UM300 but you may be charged UM500.

Mosques

The Grande Mosquée (better known as the Mosquée Saudique) in the centre on Rue Mamadou Konaté was donated by Saudi Arabia. The two other principal mosques are the Friday mosque on Ave Abdel Nasser and the new Moroccan mosque near the Cinquième district.

Port de Pêche

It's definitely worth checking out the small wharf and fish market, Port de Pêche; the best time is afternoons between 4 and 6 pm when the fishing boats return. You'll see teams of strong men dragging in heavy hand-knotted fishing nets. Small boys hurry back and forth with trays of fish which they sort, gut, fillet and lay out on large trestles to dry. The fishers, mostly Wolof and Fula, are friendly and will explain techniques, the different types of fish they catch and the going prices.

The cheapest way to get here is by shared taxi. Take one from the centre to the southwest edge of town (UM30) and another from there to the wharf (UM30). A 'course' taxi (one to yourself) from the centre of town to the fish market costs about UM300.

Le Ksar

This Moorish settlement is the oldest part of town but it lost much of its interest and old buildings when it was destroyed by a flood in 1950. However, if you're driving over the desert and need spare parts, the Ksar is the place to look. The two streets leading west from the gare routière are full of spare-part shops, each with a sign indicating the make of vehicle it covers.

Swimming

Pools The Monotel and Hôtel Marhaba have pools. The Monotel's is open only to guests but the Marhaba's, which should re-open soon, used to be free if you were eating there too.

Beaches The nearest beach to Nouakchott is 5km west of the centre. There's no shade, so bring sunscreen. To lessen the likelihood of theft, come on weekday mornings when the beaches are relatively deserted. If you have a 4WD, head for the unmarked, secluded **Tanit beach**, 61km to the north where there's a good camping spot.

Places to Stay – Budget

Most overlanders stay at *Tergit Vacanes* (☎ 56673) on the beach just north of Hôtel Sabah. Camping costs UM1000 a person. There are large huts with numerous bare mattresses (UM1200 a person) and smaller three-person huts (UM3500). Showers and parking are extra (UM300) as is laundry. Meals are available but relatively expensive. Kids walk about, so lock your valuables!

Auberge de Jeunesse l'Amitié (☎ 54419), just north of Ave Abdel Nasser, is a youth hostel. It's a spotless, friendly place with four beds to a room (UM1000 per person) and hot water showers.

Hôtel Adrar (☎ 52955), south-east of the Grand Marché, is friendly and decent. Single/double rooms with hot water showers cost UM2000/2500 (UM3000 with two beds) and have secure locks. *Auberge du Désert* (☎ 58701) is on the next road to the right beyond the Monotel and the third building in on your left – an unmarked two-storey house. Singles/doubles with shared bathroom cost UM1500/2600. Meals are expensive. *Hôtel du Petit Paris* nearby (see Places to Stay – Mid-Range, following) has a common room with mattresses and a shower (UM1500 per person). *Restaurant la*

Dune (☎ 56274), run by an ex-guide who is a good source of information, offers clean rooms and parking. Meals are good, but if you don't want food, say so on registering. It's on Rue Abou Baker and poorly marked; look for a gate with 'Saïd' next to the buzzer.

Places to Stay – Mid-Range

The pleasant French-run *Hôtel du Petit Paris* (☎/fax 56621) beyond the Monotel has reasonably priced singles/doubles for UM3500/4000 (UM5000/6000 with air-con). There's an outdoor patio for drinks, a good restaurant and a lively lounge. The sterile *Hôtel Oasis* (☎ 52011) on Ave du Général de Gaulle charges UM4000/5000 for renovated singles/doubles (UM1000 more with air-con) and may offer a reduction. *Hôtel Chinguetti* (☎ 53537) nearby is similar. Forget *Hôtel du Complexe Olympique* and *Hôtel Sabah*; they're virtually deserted and overpriced.

The somewhat remote *Hôtel-Restaurant Casablanca* (☎ 55965) has only six singles/doubles (UM6000/8000 with air-con) and a popular restaurant. Advance reservations are advisable. For years the most popular mid-range establishment has been *Hôtel El Amane* (☎ 52178, fax 57043) on Ave Abdel Nasser. It has singles/doubles with air-con for UM8000/10,000. The pleasant open-air terrace is a popular meeting place. The refurbished *Park Hôtel* (☎ 51444) nearby features a popular snack bar and has large air-con singles/doubles for UM7980/8550.

Places to Stay – Top End

All three hotels listed in this section accept credit cards and have satellite TVs. *Monotel Dar-el-Barka* (☎ 53526, fax 51831) on the road to the Stade Olympique and ex-Novotel remains the city's top hotel. Singles/doubles are UM13,900/16,700. Also with a pool, the *Hôtel Marhaba* (☎ 51686, fax 57854) was being renovated at the time of writing. The well-run *Hôtel Halima* (☎ 57920, fax 57922) has a classy restaurant and does good business despite having small rooms and no pool. Singles/doubles cost UM13,000/15,000.

Places to Eat

Cheap Eats There are many fast-food establishments on a stretch of Rue Alioune between Ave Kennedy and Ave du Général de Gaulle known as 'Avenue des Restaurants'. Open until 11 pm or later, most have a Lebanese bent. *Le Prince* and *Ali Baba* offer chawarma sandwiches, hamburgers, pizza and chicken sandwiches for UM300. *Restaurant-Pâtisserie Rally*, *Snack Irak*, *Snack Al Moulouk* and *Royal Snack* are similar. Others to the north include *Mac Drive* on Rue Abdallaye, *Welcome Burger* opposite the Senegalese embassy and *Nœf* near the Monotel. For a good continental breakfast (UM500), pastries and espresso coffee, treat yourself at the modern *X'Presso Café* on Ave de Gaulle. Open every day, it also serves cheap Lebanese fare.

Restaurant Taiba near Hôtel Adrar serves couscous for UM200 and rice with fish or meat for UM200. *Restaurant-Pâtisserie Andalouss* near the Grand Marché has similar fare. Both are open late. For something different, try *Restaurant Zoubeida* (☎ 52184) on Rue Ely Ould Mohamed. There's a carpeted room at the back where clients, usually all men, lounge on worn cushions. Open every day, it features Moroccan couscous (UM250) and Senegalese rice with fish sauce (UM200).

African The attractive, upmarket *Restaurant Guervoum* on Ave de Gaulle specialises in Cameroonian dishes, including *sauce feuille* and *sauce gombo* (UM700) and *n'dole viande* (UM1000). You can eat inside with air-con or on the veranda.

Asian *Oiseau de Paradis* near the Stade Olympique offers superb but expensive Chinese fare; it's open daily except Monday and Wednesday. The attractive *Le Bambou* on Ave du Général de Gaulle, open daily, serves good, less expensive Chinese and Vietnamese food. Most dishes cost UM650 to UM800.

European The air-con *Pizza Lina* (☎ 58662) near the Monotel is extremely popu-

lar and serves alcohol. The food is excellent and a wide variety of pizzas (UM700 to UM900) are available. *Hôtel El Amane* continues to get rave reviews for its fine French food, which comes in huge servings. For outside dining, try *Restaurant le Palmier* (closed Thursday) on 'Avenue des Restaurants', which serves decent French food and has a relaxing ambience. Less interesting, *Taska Karaoke* on Ave Abdallaye features French and Continental cuisine. *Hôtel du Petit Paris* has an air-con dining room, a small patio and a more limited menu but it's much better value: for example spaghetti or roast chicken and chips for UM550.

The *Restaurant El Kamal* (☎ 52382) on Ave Abdel Nasser features a terrace from which you can sip a Coke and take in the view, and has reasonable food, including pepper steak.

Lebanese The most popular Lebanese restaurants are *Rimal* (☎ 54832) on Ave Abdel Nasser and *Phenicia* (☎ 52575) nearby. Spacious and plain, they are open every day and close late. Most dishes at Rimal cost around UM600 including grilled chicken. The lively Phenicia is similar with some cheaper selections including chawarma sandwiches and yoghurt. The air-con *Hôtel-Restaurant Casablanca* several blocks south of the Senegalese embassy serves alcohol and specialises in good but expensive Lebanese and French cuisine.

Self-Catering The French-run *La Nouvelle Boucherie* on Ave Kennedy has imported cheeses, bread, pastries, meats and tinned goods. Nearby on Ave Kennedy are shops with tinned goods and drinks and stalls stacked with fresh fruit. Vendors are open until around 11 pm and prices are reasonable.

Entertainment

Bars & Nightclubs The top end hotels, as well as the hotels Casablanca, Park and Oasis and Pizza Lina, serve alcohol. A beer costs UM500.

Taska Karaoke (or Karaoke Club) near the French embassy and open from 7 pm, has lively music and enthusiastic singers. Admission is UM1500. *Le Palace*, open Tuesday and Thursday from 10 pm, features a dance floor and video screen. It's at Ceinture Verte (admission UM2000) and you'll need a taxi to get there. When you pass the *palais du congrès* coming from the TV station heading west, turn left; the house-like disco is at the end. For alcohol, head for the private *Racing Club* at the Stade de la Capitale; it accepts non-members but charges them 50% more. The bar is open daily from 5 to 10 pm, and the restaurant opens at 7 pm.

Cinema The *French Cultural Centre* on Rue Ahmed Ould Mohammed shows classic French films; its program is posted outside.

Wrestling Occasionally on Saturday afternoons there are wrestling matches at the Stade de la Luttes (wrestling arena) at the western end of Rue Ely Ould Mohamed.

Shopping

The womens' cooperative, L'Artisanal Féminin, near the Grand Marché, sells tablecloths, clothes, purses, pillows, camelhair rugs, colourfully painted leather cushions, nomad tents and fine straw mats at fixed prices. It's open daily except Friday from 8 to 11 am and 4 to 6 pm.

The Grand Marché (also called Marché Capital) offers a bit of everything. Potential souvenirs include brass tea pots, silver jewellery, traditional wooden boxes with silver inlay, pipes, leather bags, sandals, cushions, beads and *grisgris* (charms) such as dried frogs and bird claws. You'll find new and used jeans, as well as dress material and the inexpensive, crinkly *malafa* that Moor women use as veils.

The Cinquième Marché is good for browsing through and people watching, and has good vegetables, household wares and tailors. To get there look for a green minivan along Ave Kennedy and ask for 'le Cinquième'; the cost is about UM30.

At Hôtel El Amane, you can buy colourful Soninké tie-dyed material and Senegalese batiks. For wooden boxes with silver inlay,

daggers and jewellery, check outside Hôtel El Amane; prices are high and hard bargaining is required. At the Grand Marché you may find better bargains and possibly a wider variety. Also check the Centre Artisanal (or 'silver market'). Obscure and sometimes moribund, it's unmarked and not easy to find. Head south on the highway to Rosso – it's beyond the roundabout intersection for Boutilimit and on your right.

For rugs, try the unmarked Centre National du Tapis in the Ksar district on the road to Atâr. It's open Saturday to Thursday from 8 am to 3 pm. They're bulky to take home and expensive, but watching the weaving is fun.

Getting There & Away

Air For details of international and domestic flights to/from Nouakchott, see the Getting There & Away and Getting Around sections earlier in this chapter. For booking tickets or reconfirming flights, the following airlines have offices in Nouakchott: Royal Air Maroc (☎ 53564), Air France (☎ 51808), Air Mauritanie (☎ 52212 or 52216), Air Afrique (☎ 52545, fax 54944) and Air Algérie, all on or just off Ave Abdel Nasser; Tunis Air (☎ 52684) is on Ave Kennedy.

Bush Taxi The main gare routière is in the Ksar quarter. Vehicles to most destinations leave in the morning from around 9 am, but for Rosso (3½ hours by bush taxi) you may be able to find earlier ones. If you're headed for Senegal, remember that immigration on the Mauritanian side is closed from noon to 3 pm and time your departure accordingly. Most vehicles for Atâr leave around 5.30 pm or slightly later. Vehicles for Nouâdhibou usually leave in the morning before 11 am or in the late afternoon. Alternatively, catch a bush taxi to Atâr and the next day another to Choûm to connect with the afternoon train; you should arrive in Nouâdhibou around 6 am.

Getting Around

To/From the Airport The airport is in the Ksar district. There is no airport bus service but there are taxis and they accept US$ and French francs. The standard fare to the centre is between UM600 and UM700, but at night drivers demand more so consider sharing or hailing a taxi from the highway nearby; from here the fare to the centre (3km) shouldn't exceed UM250. Alternatively, wait for a public minibus.

Bus Transport Urbaines' yellow and green minibuses run throughout the city. Fares range from UM25 to UM35. In the centre, the best place to catch one is on Ave Kennedy next to the Grand Marché. They are best for long distances, eg to the Ksar quarter or the Cinquième market.

Taxi Taxis come in all colours and spotting them is fairly easy. They are most plentiful along Ave Abdel Nasser and Ave Kennedy, especially in the market area. On Ave Kennedy near the market you'll find numerous parked taxis. They leave when full, typically within several minutes (except at night).

You need to specify clearly whether you want a *course* or a *route* taxi. Route taxis operate like buses, with a specified route. Most routes start at the market stand. A 'course' is when you have the taxi to yourself, and you can then specify the exact destination.

Fares are UM25 to UM35 for a seat in a shared route taxi, UM250 for a short trip (*course*) anywhere around town, including the airport, and UM500 to UM600 by the hour (negotiable). Taxis do not have meters but drivers are fairly honest about fares.

Car All the agencies listed earlier in this section under Travel Agencies & Tour Operators also rent cars with drivers. In addition, one of the best agencies is the Europcar representative, GCAL Voyages (☎ 51163, fax 52285), on Ave Abdel Nasser. It accepts credit cards and has a variety of vehicles. Prices vary according to the destination and vehicle, for example UM14,000 including driver for a five-person vehicle to Adrar and UM6000 for a vehicle in town. Other tour operators include Arguin Tours (☎ 58560, fax 58607) on Ave du Général de Gaulle and La Gazelle du Désert (☎ 50669, fax 58162). You'll find many more agencies along the northern side of Ave Abdel Nasser, west of the intersection with de Gaulle.

The Coast

NOUÂDHIBOU

Called Port-Étienne during colonial days, Nouâdhibou (population 45,000) is on the Baie du Lévrier. It's in the middle of a narrow 35km-long peninsula. The eastern half of the peninsula is Mauritania and the western half, the Atlantic Ocean side, is Morocco. Be warned – there are many land mines planted in the sands on the western side, and this area is strictly off limits.

The sea on both sides is chilled by the Canary current, and it has one of the world's highest densities of fish. As a result, Nouâdhibou is famous for its fishing and ships come here from all over the world.

The city's main street, running north-south, is Blvd Médian. The northern side of town is Numerowat while the older fishing quarter, east of the stadium, is Tcherka. The latter was once a settlement of people from the Canary Islands. Today, it's a shanty town crammed with fishers. At the southern edge of town is the Port de Pêche Moderne (the container port) and 8km further south is Cansado. The latter used to be an enclave for expatriates, but most left when the iron-ore company was nationalised. Port Minéralier, 3km further, is where the train line ends and ore is loaded onto ships, while 4km beyond is Cap Blanc, the southern tip of the peninsula. (For a map of the area around Nouâdhibou, see p637.)

The BNM bank (☎ 45045) on Blvd Médian changes money, but most people do it on the parallel market, usually around the market. Overland travellers must get their passports stamped at the *sûreté* (☎ 45072) near the BNM, which closes at 2.30 pm. Those with vehicles must buy insurance. The entire process usually takes four to six hours.

MAURITANIA

NOUÂDHIBOU

PLACES TO STAY
2 Sabah Hôtel
3 Hôtel du Maghreb
13 Hôtel Niabina
22 Auberge de Jeunesse;
   National Park Office
25 Camping Baie du Lévrier;
   Claire de Lune
38 Camping Abba;
   Fast Food Basna

PLACES TO EAT
6 Restaurant El Ahram
7 Restaurant Amitié
10 Restaurant Beyrouth
14 Restaurant Continental
23 Restaurant Babylone;
   BNM Bank
33 Restaurant Sôl

OTHER
1 Airport
4 Mosque
5 Friday Mosque
8 Moroccan Consulate
9 Pharmacie Sahwa
11 Grand Marché
12 Garage Nouakchott
15 Galérie Mahfoud
16 AVL Tours
17 Soprage
18 May Tours
19 Post Office;
   Restaurant le Pêcherie
20 Air Mauritanie
21 Spanish Consulate
24 Sûreté
26 Air France; Petrol
27 Petrol
28 Government Offices
29 Catholic Church
30 Hospital
31 Fish Market
32 Stadium
34 Police
35 Hanna Tours
36 New Fish Market
37 BMCI Bank
39 Toyota Dealer
40 Naftec Station
41 Elf Station
42 Cité SNIM

Things to Do

For **fishing**, head for the Centre de Pêche Air Afrique or, more convenient, the fishing centre at the Oasian Hôtel. Count on paying about UM1400 for a surf casting pole and UM8400 a day for deep-sea fishing, including equipment.

The best beach is at **Cap Blanc**, a 20 minute taxi ride to the south. Arrange for a driver to pick you up. The monk seals (*phoque moine*) near the lighthouse are a major attraction. Resembling elephant seals, these grey-skinned animals have been hunted since the 15th century for their valuable skins and oil. The protected colony here of roughly 120 seals is reportedly the last one on earth; you may be lucky enough to see them at play.

Cansado beach is also nice and half the distance. People sometimes cross the unprotected Moroccan border illegally and bathe in the bay behind Faux Cap Blanc, but it's not worth the risk of getting caught.

Places to Stay

Auberge Abba (☎ 46044, fax 46056), also called Camping Abba, and *Camping Baie du Lévrier* are both on Blvd Médian. The friendly Abba has an inviting communal room and charges UM1000 a person for a spotlessly clean room with hot shower. The more central Lévrier (UM700 per person and UM1300 per vehicle) is sometimes full as it's the top choice of overland trucks from Europe (they reserve in advance). Both places have protected areas for vehicles.

If they're full, try the unmarked *Auberge de Jeunesse* near the Lévrier or the *camp site* some 6km north of the airport near the beach. The auberge is clean with secure parking and charges UM2000 for a double with bathroom. Some travellers have bargained the price down to UM1400. *Hôtel Niabina* (☎ 45983), two blocks south of the market, is tranquil and clean but overpriced at UM 2500/4000 for singles/doubles (no fan) with shared bathroom.

In the more expensive category, *Hôtel du Maghreb* (☎ 45544) and *Sabah Hôtel* (☎ 45317, fax 45419) are on the road to the airport. The old Maghreb charges UM4000/5000 for small singles/doubles without fan; the bar here is a good place for getting information. The well-maintained Sabah has singles/doubles for UM8000/11,000 plus 14% tax; rooms come with air-con, hot-water bathroom and satellite TV. The restaurant offers good service but disappointing food.

The *Oasian Hôtel* (☎ 49029, fax 49053) in Cansado has excellent air-con singles/doubles for UM7980/10,830. It accepts credit cards and has a deep-sea fishing centre and a beach nearby. The *Centre de Pêche Air Afrique* (☎ 45571) is 14km north of town on the Baie du Lévrier. Singles/doubles cost UM3800/4900 and fixed meals are UM2800. Air Afrique in Nouakchott offers an all-inclusive weekend special from Nouakchott for UM25,000.

Places to Eat

In the centre, you'll find a number of very cheap restaurants along Rue de la Galérie Mahfoud including *Restaurant Amitié*. Six short blocks south on the same street is *Restaurant Continental*, which is more spacious and good for the price (fish and rice UM100, couscous UM150).

Restaurant Beyrouth (☎ 45266) is a block east of the market, and *Restaurant El Ahram* (☎ 45018) is nearby. They are both Lebanese and inviting, with most dishes in the UM300 to UM500 range, including couscous for UM300. A third, *Restaurant Babylone*, on Blvd Médian, is more expensive, with full meals for UM700 to UM1000, but with chawarma sandwiches for UM300.

Restaurant le Pêchérie next to the post office is highly recommended. Servings are copious – a filling shrimp dinner costs UM350. *Fast Food Basna* next to Camping Abba features good croissants in the morning, as well as sandwiches, but they're not cheap. Further up Blvd Médian in the heart of town is the popular *Claire de Lune*. The menu includes espresso coffee, snacks, ice cream and fantastic apple turnovers.

Restaurant Sôl (☎ 45980) is the best restaurant in Nouâdhibou, and perhaps in Mauritania. The chef is Korean, the cuisine is Korean and French, and his cooking is fabulous. Main courses are in the UM1200 to UM1400 range. Alcohol (not on the menu) is available.

Getting There & Away

Air For details of international flights, see the main Getting There & Away section earlier in this chapter. Air Mauritanie (☎ 45011) has two flights on most days to/from Nouakchott (UM9080), and flights on Saturday to Atâr (UM7100) and on Tuesday to Zouérat (UM8200). For reservations, see Soprage (☎ 45574) on Blvd Médian. It represents American Express and accepts credit cards.

Boat With great luck, catching a boat to Las Palmas in the Canary Islands is possible. Two Spanish freighters, the *Cap Blanc* and the *Caribbean Trailer*, ply bi-weekly between Nouâdhibou and Las Palmas. The trip takes 1½ days. These vessels no longer take passengers, but the captain might agree. Expect to pay UM3500. Otherwise hang around the port and look for a fishing vessel headed that way. You may have to wait several weeks, however.

Train The train station is about 5km south of town, 3km before Cansado. There's no building, just a spot in the desert near the tracks. You can buy tickets, bottled water (UM160) and long-life milk here. On board, a man sells tea and cheap snacks. There are several trains but the one with a passenger car leaves daily around 2.30 pm, arriving in Choûm (UM600) around 2 am (where pick-up trucks for Atâr will be waiting) and Zouérat (UM850) around 7 am.

When the train arrives from the port, there's a mad scramble to get on board the passenger car at the rear. You could easily get robbed then, so carry nothing in your pockets and lock everything. If you're travelling with others, have one person join the scramble and grab seats for the others. For more details, see the boxed text 'The Iron Ore Train' in the main Getting Around section earlier in this chapter.

Car There are two routes to Nouakchott – via Choûm and Atâr (usually involving shipping your car on the train) or directly south along the beach. Driving this latter route by car is extremely difficult. At times there's not even a hint of a trail, and sand dunes are often impossible to skirt. The 525km trip typically takes two or three days. The first 70km north-eastward alongside the railway tracks is flat and easy, then you head south through the dunes where the driving becomes extremely difficult. There are poles every 5km to Nouâmghâr, the fishing village at Cap Timiris, but they will not keep you from getting lost if you have no guide. The last third is along the beach; you may have to wait several hours for the tide to recede. Avoid the soft sand at all cost! From Nouakchott, do this by departing as the tide recedes.

Travelling alone is perilous, as once the route leaves the beach, it's easy to get lost and getting stuck is almost guaranteed. Taking a guide is essential even if you're travelling in a convoy. It's easy to find guides in Nouâdhibou. Travelling in convoy makes the cost of a guide (typically UM 25,000) more affordable.

Alternatively, ship your vehicle by train to Choûm, and drive from there to Nouakchott, a day's drive. You must make arrangements at least a day in advance with SNIM (☎ 45174, fax 45396). It costs UM6500 to UM10,500, depending on vehicle size.

Bush Taxi Bush taxis ply daily between Nouâdhibou and Nouakchott (although they often get stuck). The route is partially along the beach and when the tide is high, vehicles must wait for it to recede. The trip usually takes 15 to 20 hours depending in part on the tides. Vehicles (pick-ups and Land Rovers) leave Nouâdhibou from Garage Nouakchott (behind the market) between 8 am and 11 am and again around 5 pm. The fare is UM5000 (UM3000 in the back of a pick-up).

Getting Around

Taxi Shared taxis are plentiful. Fares are fixed: UM25 within the centre and up to Numerowat, UM30 to the container port and UM50 to the train station and Cansado. Chartered black-and-yellow taxis charge UM500 from the airport to the centre (less if you share) and at least UM600 by the hour.

Car Rental AVL Tours (☎ 45334) opposite Galérie Mahfoud rents cars for travel around town (UM7500). For the Parc National du Banc d'Arguin, Hanna (☎ 46242, fax 46165) on Blvd Maritime charges UM50,000 for a standard two day tour. However, to tour the park properly you need at least three days because the trip there takes seven hours. Three-day trips are negotiable. Hanna asks UM80,000 (which includes petrol, driver, guide and tents) as does May Tours (☎ 45584) on Blvd Médian.

PARC NATIONAL DU BANC D'ARGUIN

The Banc d'Arguin is an important stopover for multitudes of birds migrating between Europe and southern Africa. Over two million broad-billed sandpipers (*limicoles*) have been recorded in the winter. Other species include pink flamingo (*flamant rose*), white pelican (*pélican blanc*), grey pelican, royal tern (*sternes royales*), gull-billed tern (*spatule blanche*), black tern (*sterne bridée*), white-breasted cormorant, spoonbill and several species of herons, egrets and waders.

The park extends 200km north from Cap Timiris (155km north of Nouakchott) and provides an ideal breeding environment for many species. The sea is clear and shallow, so fish are easy to find. Most birds are found on sand islands in the shallow ocean.

Park permits cost UM800 per person per day and are issued in Nouâdhibou at the park headquarters, which organises trips for large groups. In Nouakchott, contact the Ministre de la Pêche et de l'Économie Maritime (☎ 52476). Travel agencies in Nouakchott can arrange trips.

The best viewing time is December and January, which is also the mating season. During this period, you can't get too close to

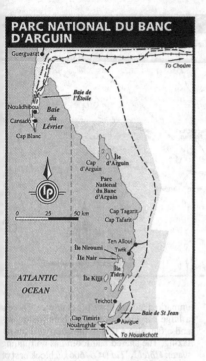

PARC NATIONAL DU BANC D'ARGUIN

Guerguarat

To Choûm

Baie de l'Étoile

Nouâdhibou
Cansado
Cap Blanc

Baie du Lévrier

Île d'Arguin

Cap d'Arguin

Parc National du Banc d'Arguin

Cap Tagarit
Cap Tafarit

Ten Alloul
Île Niroumi   Twik
Île Naïr
Île Tidra

ATLANTIC OCEAN

Île Kijji

Teichot

Baie de St Jean

Cap Timiris
Nouâmghâr   Awgue

To Nouakchott

0   25   50 km

the birds because the slightest disturbance can cause them to fly away and abandon their eggs. The only way to see them is by small boat. The main island, 30km long, is Tidra, and just to the west of the northern tip are two tiny islands, Niroumi and Naïr. There are other sandbanks but these three are the most accessible. The principal launching point is **Twik**, a fishing village on the mainland 6km north-east of Tidra. You can find boats here; they cost UM10,000 whether you stay out all day or only a few hours.

After, you could head to **Cap Tagarit**, 40km north of Tidra. You can fish, snorkel and *camp* here without government permission or a guide. The view from the cape is magnificent and the water is crystal clear, perfect for viewing fish. A catch of trout, sea bass and sea bream is almost guaranteed; just don't let the eerie wailing of jackals, or their presence near camp, bother you.

Getting There & Away

To get to Twik, head for the fishing village of Ten Alloul, which is roughly halfway between Nouâdhibou and Nouakchott. You can rent a vehicle in either city or, cheaper, take a bush taxi; most of those plying the Nouakchott to Nouâdhibou route stop here. You must pay the full fare (UM5000). From Ten Alloul it's 14km south-west along the coast and down a small peninsula to Twik.

If you're driving from Nouâdhibou, see the Getting There & Away section in that entry. Coming from Nouakchott, it's another 70km from Cap Timiris on a good sand track to where it divides; take the left track towards the sea for roughly 25km more to Twik. If you're headed for Cap Tagarit, continue northwards along the track. At 106km north of Cap Timiris, you'll reach two low rocky hills bisecting the track; head directly west by compass over sand dunes for 25km to Cap Tafarit The smaller Cap Tagarit is 5km to the north and better for camping.

The North

If you have time to visit only one area outside Nouakchott, head for the Adrar region. You'll see oases, nomads in their tents, striking rocky plateaus with deep gorges and ancient rock paintings, historical sites, a huge crater (Guelb er Richat), endless sand dunes and towns seemingly about to be buried under the desert. This is also a great area for riding camels. Outside Chinguetti, all you can see are rolling dunes – a good place for a camel ride.

ATÂR

Atâr (population 18,000) is the major northern commercial centre. It's also the starting point for several interesting side trips.

A large roundabout marks the centre of Atâr and the market is just north of it. Here, you'll find Moorish crafts but prices are no better than in Nouakchott and the selection is inferior. The area around the market is best for changing money (US$ and French

MAURITANIA

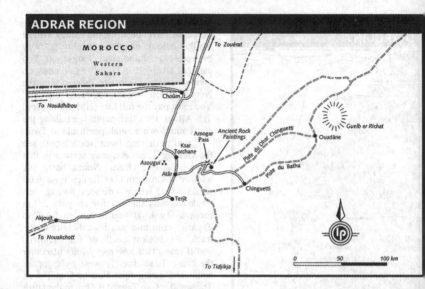

ADRAR REGION

MOROCCO
Western
Sahara

To Zouérat
To Nouâdhibou
Choûm
Guelb er Richat
Amogar Pass
Ancient Rock Paintings
Ksar Torchane
Piste du Dhar Chinguetti
Ouadâne
Azougui
Atâr
Piste du Batha
Chinguetti
Terjît
Akjoujt
To Nouakchott
To Tidjikja

0   50   100 km

francs), but the rates are not good. To see artisans at work, look to the east and north of the market. The small maze-like Ksar district, west of the market, is a good place to explore. It's the old residential quarter, with narrow winding streets, brick walls and carved doorways.

A good side trip from Atâr is to the ruins of **Azougui**, 10km or so north-west. It was from here in the 11th century that the Berber Almoravids to the north launched their attacks on the capital of the Empire of Ghana, Koumbi Saleh (in the south, near the Malian border), leading to the spread of Islam throughout West Africa. The ruins consist of a fort and the mausoleum of the warrior hero Imam Hadrami. If you walk here from Atâr (three or four hours), start early to avoid the heat. Otherwise, take a taxi. Either way you'll need a guide.

Places to Stay

Restaurant-Auberge Azouqui (☎ 64371), at UM500 per person, is good value. The woman owner of the restaurant, three blocks east of the roundabout, will lead you to her unmarked auberge five blocks away. There's a large carpeted room with bare mattresses and a fan, also a tent in the courtyard for relaxing. The shared bathroom has no running water. *Hôtel N'Tid* (☎ 64606), a block east of the roundabout, has small singles/doubles with fan for UM500/1000 and similar bathrooms. Ali, the manager, is reportedly very helpful. At both, if you take meals, settle the price first! The friendly, tranquil *Hôtel Dar Salam*, on the eastern outskirts of town or the Chinguetti road, is much better but a 25-minute walk from the centre. It charges UM1200 for a small room and UM3500 for a larger room with bathroom. You can get decent meals too. The moribund *Hôtel des Almouravides* (☎ 64383) is overpriced at UM6000/8000 for its air-con singles/doubles. On the south-western outskirts of town behind the army barracks, this old colonial establishment attracts little business and the restaurant is closed.

Places to Eat

From the roundabout head east on the Chinguetti road for a block, then turn left

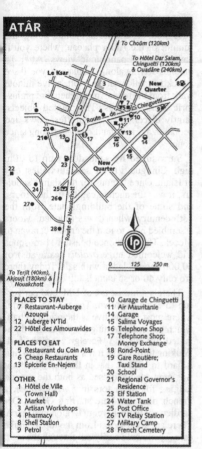

ATÂR

To Choûm (120km)

To Hôtel Dar Salam,
Chinguetti (120km)
& Ouadâne (240km)

Le Ksar

New
Quarter

Route de Chinguetti

New
Quarter

Route de Nouakchott

To Terjît (40km),
Akjoujt (180km) &
Nouakchott

0   125   250 m

PLACES TO STAY		10	Garage de Chinguetti
7	Restaurant-Auberge	11	Air Mauritanie
	Azouqui	14	Garage
12	Auberge N'Tid	15	Salima Voyages
22	Hôtel des Almouravides	16	Telephone Shop
		17	Telephone Shop;
PLACES TO EAT			Money Exchange
5	Restaurant du Coin Atâr	18	Rond-Point
6	Cheap Restaurants	19	Gare Routière;
13	Épicerie En-Nejem		Taxi Stand
		20	School
OTHER		21	Regional Governor's
1	Hôtel de Ville		Residence
	(Town Hall)	23	Elf Station
2	Market	24	Water Tank
3	Artisan Workshops	25	Post Office
4	Pharmacy	26	TV Relay Station
8	Shell Station	27	Military Camp
9	Petrol	28	French Cemetery

Most restaurants are along this road, and three have the same name – *Restaurant Moderne;* the best one is *Restaurant du Coin Atâr*. They are all run by Wolof and Fula and serve basically the same fare, including spaghetti, rice, fish and Senegalese *mafé* (peanut sauce) for UM100. The *Azouqui* and *N'Tid* auberges also serve food. There are many grocery stores near the roundabout on the Chinguetti road, but *Épicerie En-Nejem* with a friendly Moroccan owner near the N'Tid stands out. The

best *brochettes* are sold in the evening outside Garage de Chinguetti, two blocks east of the roundabout.

Getting There & Away

Air Air Mauritanie has flights from Nouâdhibou and Nouakchott.

Bush Taxi & Truck The main gare routière is opposite the roundabout, where you can get vehicles, mostly pick-ups, for Choûm and Nouakchott. Most vehicles headed for Nouakchott depart between 5.30 pm and 7 pm. Occasionally, one may depart midmorning. The fare is UM3000 (UM2000 in the back of a pick-up). Even though the straight driving time on the newly sealed road is only six hours, you may not arrive before the early morning as the vehicles stop en route at Akjoujt (180km). There are no hotels in Akjoujt but travellers eating at Restaurant Terjît (rice, meat and tea for UM170) at the gare routière may be able to sleep on its carpeted front terrace.

Battered Land Rovers and pick-up trucks headed for Chinguetti and Ouadâne leave from the tiny Garage de Chinguetti east of the roundabout. Departure can be at any time, usually mid-morning to late afternoon. The drivers go around looking for passengers, so you may not see any vehicle waiting.

Car Rental To rent a vehicle to Chinguetti, count on paying at least UM25,000 (plus food and lodging for driver and guide) and returning the next day (UM18,000 if you return the same day). You'll have to bargain hard.

Salima Voyages (☎/fax 64347), a couple of blocks south of Chinguetti road, is very professional. It charges UM18,000 a day to Chinguetti or Ouadâne, which includes petrol, driver, guide and their food and lodging. Independent guides (inquire around Restaurant Azouqui) are sometimes cheaper but they can ruin trips by constantly trying to get you to add side trips or by not delivering on promises.

MAURITANIA

The Guedra

In the Adrar region, a real treat is to see a performance of the Guedra, a ritual dance of love performed by women. Sometimes the dancer stands, but more often she squats, covered in a black veil. The dance is a ballet of complex movements of the hands and feet on which the women paint intricate designs with henna to draw attention to them. The dancers' hair is sumptuously decorated; every plait is embellished with pendants, talismans, carved shell discs and green and red glass beads.

CHINGUETTI

Getting to Chinguetti (population 4000), 120km east of Atâr, is half the fun. The road passes through the lunar-like Adrar plateau.

One barren gorge leads up to the **Amogar Pass** and, at about the 70km point, the summit of the Adrar plateau, where you'll have amazing panoramic views. After 15 minutes driving along the plateau, you'll see a rock formation on your left, a five minute walk from the road. Among them are prehistoric rock paintings. The painted objects, faintly discernible, are giraffes, cows and people in a grassy landscape – all long since gone.

Surrounded by sand dunes up to 20m high, Chinguetti is the seventh holiest city of Islam. Once famous for its Islamic scholars, it was the ancient capital of the Moors, and some of the buildings date from the 13th century, when it was founded. Moors assembled here to join the annual caravan to Mecca. The town once boasted 11 mosques and welcomed huge *azalais* (caravans) of 30,000 camels laden with salt. Today there are only 40 or so camels left in Chinguetti.

There's a tourist tax of UM1000 per person to enter the town. The modern quarter where most people live is the northern half, which you enter coming from Atâr. It's dominated by an old **Foreign Legion fort**. Walking through the fort's debris, you'll find it hard to believe that in the early 1980s it was renovated and used as both the set and lodging for the actors in *Fort Saganne*, a French film shot here starring Gérard Dépardieu about the Foreign Legion in Algeria. There are good views from the top, but take care – you could easily fall through the roof.

In the centre there's a flat wadi (dry riverbed) where palm trees grow, cutting this oasis town neatly in two. The town's old quarter, **Le Ksar**, is just beyond. More than half the structures, mostly of stone, are in ruins and unoccupied. The principal attraction is the 16th-century stone **mosque** (no entry to non-Muslims). Nearby is a **Quranic library**. It houses some 1300 ancient manuscripts. The most prized ones are not viewable except with a large gift. Check out the small market near the water tank; it's remarkable for how little produce is available.

Don't fail to go for a camel ride. The sand dunes are perfect and prices are reasonable –

UM1500 for a camel for the day. Each trip must be accompanied by a guide (UM2500). Plan on a full day's ride as you'll see little of the dunes in half a day. You'll probably have tea at a nomad camp. For a longer trip, head for Zarga, 20km south-west, a hilly area with rocks and sand dunes. There's an auberge here.

Places to Stay & Eat

The tranquil *Auberge de Bien Être de Chinguetti* in the centre charges UM1000 per person for a room with a mattress on the floor. It features a lovely courtyard and a nomad's tent for relaxing. Full board costs UM1000 a day. *Auberge des Oasis* in the old quarter charges the same but is inferior. Many travellers stay at the larger, cleaner *Auberge des Caravanes* (☎/fax Nouakchott 59759) at the entrance to town – UM1000 per person plus UM700 a day for food. This pleasant place has a bar and tents to relax in, as well as walled space for parking.

Getting There & Away

There is at least one vehicle a day to/from Atâr. The fare is UM1200 (UM1000 in the back of a pick-up), and the trip takes four hours (three hours by private vehicle), sometimes twice that.

OUADÂNE

Ouadâne was founded in 1147 by Berbers, and sits on the edge of the Adrar plateau 120km north-east of Chinguetti. For 400 years, it was a prosperous caravan centre and a transit point for dates, salt and gold – the last stopover for caravans heading to Oualâta in the south-eastern corner of the country. The decline began in the late 16th century when the powerful Moroccan prince Ahmed el Mansour gained control of this trans-Saharan route and diminished Ouadâne's commercial role.

The most interesting section is the old quarter, **Le Ksar el Kiali**. It's a steep rocky cliff covered in stone houses, mostly deserted, with a contrasting lush oasis below. From a distance, these crumbling structures and

the stones of the escarpment blend together, forming what seems to be a massive stone wall. Check out the crumbling mosque, also the small quranic library. You can get a good view from the old resthouse that was shelled by Polisario some years ago and is now in ruins. There's a tourist tax of UM1000 per person.

You can ride camels here but the terrain – sand mixed with rocks – is less interesting than around Chinguetti. The **Guelb er Richat** crater is 40km to the north-east. En route, stop at **Tin Labbé** (7km), a unique settlement where the large boulders prevalent in this area have been incorporated into the villagers' homes.

Places to Stay & Eat

Many travellers stay at the new well-marked *Auberge Guelb er Richât (Nouakchott ☎ 56285)* at the entrance to town. It has six rooms with bathrooms and protected vehicle parking. The owner has another establishment in town, *Auberge Agweidir*, consisting of some huts and tents. Both places charge UM1500 per person and serve meals. There is reportedly a cheaper *auberge* without parking in the centre of town. If you want to camp for free, try the wadi. Be prepared, however, for an onslaught of ragged children with packets of arrowheads for sale.

Getting There & Away

Finding transport to Ouadâne is not easy. Atâr is a much better place to look than Chinguetti as vehicles go between Atâr and Ouadâne on a fairly regular basis (but not every day). The trip (UM1600) normally takes about seven hours (five hours in private car).

Getting from Chinguetti to Ouadâne is a problem. There is no public transport and finding someone headed here is difficult; so you'll probably have to backtrack to Atâr. Those driving have two routes to choose from: the southerly Piste du Batha, which passes through sand dunes and definitely requires a guide, and the northerly Piste du Dhar Chinguetti along the plateau, which is in good condition but is less interesting and requires a local guide because of land mines. The latter route splits off from the Atâr-Chinguetti road 12km before Chinguetti.

TERJÎT

Some 40km south of Atâr as the crow flies is Terjît (also spelt Tergit), an unusually verdant oasis. What's special here is a natural pool in which you can swim. This lush place is wonderful – you'll think you're in the tropics.

The only place to stay is the *Auberge des Caravances*, which is very reasonable – UM1000 per person and UM700 per day for food. There's also a protected area for parking.

To get here by private car, drive 40km south of Atâr on the road to Nouakchott, then turn left and follow a good sand track eastward for 13km. The trip takes 1½ hours. For a tour, see Salima Voyages in Atâr.

ZOUÉRAT

Zouérat is an important iron-ore centre but has little to offer the visitor except a fascinating tour of the huge mining operations. These can be arranged at the mining company's *Hôtel Oasian* (☎ 49042, fax 49043). Singles/doubles with air-con here cost UM7980/10,830, which includes breakfast. There's a good restaurant as well. For cheaper accommodation, you'll have to rely on local hospitality. The train departs at 12.30 pm, arriving in Choûm around 5.30 pm and Nouâdhibou (UM850) in the morning. Air Mauritanie flies from Nouakchott (UM9900) on Tuesday and Thursday (via Atâr).

The East & South

Like the Adrar region, the Tagânt area east of Nouakchott offers impressive views from the plateau, prehistoric rock paintings, historical sites including old forts and fortresses, decaying towns such as Tidjikja and Tichit (with mountains of sand about to consume them), as well as the opportunity to look for Neolithic items in the sand. Getting here is difficult.

TIDJIKJA

Tidjikja (population 6000) is the capital of the Tagânt region. People here don't see many visitors, so register with the police to avoid suspicion. Children will follow you everywhere. Founded in 1680 and now surrounded by sand dunes, the town supports one of the country's more important palm groves (which dates from the 18th century), a busy market, numerous shops and Fort Coppolani (an old French military fort used in subduing the Moors).

The town is split in the middle by a spacious sandy wadi. You'll arrive at the 'modern' south-western section with wide streets and administrative buildings, including the police. The old quarter to the northeast is where you'll find the ancient palm grove, an old mosque and traditional houses (some are vacant and easily visited). Notice the decorative niches with geometric designs, the flat roofs with gargoyle-decorated drains for rainwater and double-panelled doors in place of windows.

A good side trip can be made to **Rachid**, 35km north on the track to Atâr. High up a cliff, it's one of the most beautiful spots in Mauritania and was once used as a site for launching attacks on caravans passing by. You can rent a 4WD vehicle in Tidjikja. Expect to pay about UM10,000.

Places to Stay & Eat

The *Centre d' Accueil de Tidjikja* (☎ 96-187) was still under construction when we visited. You may have to rely on people's hospitality for a place to sleep and eat. For food, there are some small shops and the *market*.

Getting There & Away

Air Mauritanie has flights from Nouakchott on Tuesday (UM6940).

By public transport, it's easy to get as far as Sangrafa (20km beyond Magta-Lahjar on the main road east from Nouakchott bu from there you'll have to hitchhike, an traffic is very light. You're better off holding out in Aleg until you find a vehicle. I you're driving, be prepared to get stuck i the sand on the final 205km leg. There's petrol in Tidjikja but it can never be guaranteed, so carry plenty.

It's possible to drive from Tidjikja to Atâr (470km). Travel agencies in Nouakchott can arrange this trip, as can Salima Voyages in Atâr. It takes 3½ days. A guide is essential and attempting it with only one vehicle inadvisable. Foreigners without guides have died on this route.

TICHIT

If you're adventurous and want to see a ghost town in the making, head for the isolated ancient town of Tichit, 255km east of Tidjikja. Driving here, you'll pass through barren landscape – the trees are bare, the scrub is twisted, and the ground is littered with the bleached bones of camels and goats. It's a bit like the Arctic, except sand rather than snow blankets everything. You should report to the police when you arrive.

The town once furnished water and precious supplies to desert caravans and boasted over 6000 people and 1500 houses. Today, fewer than 300 houses remain and only about half are inhabited. The main mosque is impressive, as are the old houses, which are made of local stone of different hues. They have decorative motifs on the exterior and solid, ornate doors with wooden latches, like those of the Dogon people in Mali.

The 1980 decree outlawing slavery has changed little here (for more details, see the boxed text 'The Haratin & the Bidan' in the Facts about Mauritania section). For most slaves (the Abid, who have their own section of town), there were only two choices – migrate to the city slums or continue working for their masters in return for food and lodging. Most chose the latter.

Getting There & Away

You'll need your own transport to get here. The tracks frequently disappear and there are few landmarks along the way, so you'll need a guide and enough petrol for a round trip. Also bring food as there's little here.

ROSSO

Rosso (population 28,000) is a busy little town with a Senegalese flavour but not much to see. Most travellers cross the border here and head on. For those without vehicles, the crossing is usually straightforward. If someone asks you to pay an 'exit tax', politely refuse. For those with vehicles, it can be a headache as bribery is endemic on both sides. For more details, see the boxed text 'Border Crossings' in the main Getting There & Away section earlier in this chapter.

Places to Stay & Eat

Restaurant du Fleuve near the ferry wharf has rooms (UM1500) with bare mattresses on the floor and shared bathrooms. Or ask around – there's reportedly at least one other basic hotel. The best place is the *Hôtel Union* (☎ 69029), 150m north of the gare routière. It has singles/doubles for UM3500/4500 with air-con and bathroom. For cheap food, try *Restaurant Marie*.

Getting There & Away

Peugeot 504 bush taxis from Nouakchott cost UM1100 (UM1000 by minibus). The trip takes at least 3½ hours, more by minibus. There are now only several police stops along the way and baggage checks are no longer frequent. The onward trip to Dakar costs CFA3000 by minibus and CFA4500 by Peugeot 504.

KAÉDI

South-east of Nouakchott on the River Senegal, Kaédi is the country's fourth largest city, with a mostly Tukulor population. It has become a site for development projects, including SNIM's extraction of high-grade ore from a nearby reserve. The market is good for Tukulor crafts and authentic Senegalese batik cloth. Prices here are lower than in Nouakchott and most cities in Senegal.

For a room, try the rustic *Sonader Case de Passage* near the centre or the *UNDP Guesthouse*. The latter has air-con rooms (UM5000), a dining room and a pool, and it's definitely worth the price. Travellers are welcome if there's room.

Diabandé – the Art of Home Decoration

If you make it to Sélibabi, south of Mbout (on the road between Kaédi and Kiffa), try to visit Tachott Botokholo, 30km to the south. It and other Soninké villages in the area are famous for their colourfully painted houses. Several decades ago, the women, given free rein over their homes as their husbands looked for work in Senegal, began painting the inside of their houses, a practice called *diabandé*. The designs have evolved over the years: in the 1970s the fad was for simple, bold checks painted in white, ochre and black, and covering entire walls. Today, some rooms may be painted in bold, wide strips, others in geometric shapes with abstract drawings. The white is made from limestone, the ochre from soil and the black from red clay mixed with cow dung. The grinding and mixing can take days and when it comes time to paint, five or six women may work together for a week on a single room. The overall effect is truly splendid.

Air Mauritanie no longer has regular flights here but minibuses (UM2000) and pick-ups go daily to/from Nouakchott (437km).

KIFFA

This town is the capital of the southern Assabe region and an important regional trading centre and crossroads. Much of the activity of this vibrant place (which doesn't have electricity) centres on the active market. The city is famous for its glass beads, check them out in the market, where they're made.

Hôtel de l'Amitié et du Tourism in the centre has basic singles/doubles with mattresses on the floor, fans and shared showers for UM2000/3000 (negotiable). The friendly Ghanaian woman here will cook you a meal if you ask. The best place to stay in southern Mauritania is the brand new *hotel* on the outskirts of town; it has air-con rooms and a restaurant. In town, a good place to eat is *Brahims*. It's run by an elderly man who specialises in couscous and mutton.

Getting here from Nouakchott costs UM2600 by minibus (10 hours) and UM 1600 by truck (15 hours). Alternatively, you can fly from Nouakchott (UM7000) on Air Mauritanie on Wednesday.

AYOÛN-EL-ATROÛS

For lodging in Ayoûn (population 30,000), try *Hôtel Ayoûn* (☎ 90079), which is in the centre and surprisingly nice. Rooms have balconies overlooking the city, and cost UM2000/3000 for singles/doubles with fan and bathroom. It also has air-con rooms but there's electricity only until midnight. For cheap food, try the restaurant across the street. It serves basic food, including omelettes and steaks.

A minibus costs UM3300 from Nouakchott. There's petrol here. You can also fly here for UM9300: Air Mauritanie's Sunday flight to Néma stops here if there is sufficient demand.

Koumbi Saleh

The legendary capital of the Empire of Ghana, West Africa's first medieval empire, Koumbi Saleh is one of the best known archaeological sites in West Africa. Traces of the town were uncovered in 1913, and although several digging campaigns have been carried out since then these have only scratched the surface. Large stone houses and a huge imposing mosque have been partially excavated, attesting to the large number of people, estimated in the tens of thousands, who once lived here. From Timbedgha (106km west of Néma), head south on the route to Nara in Mali for 65km, then head a few kilometres east.

NÉMA

In Néma, you'll find a market, petrol pump and bank. If you're headed to/from Mali, get your passport stamped by the police and, if you're driving, pass through customs here. There's no hotel but the police may be helpful in finding you a mat to sleep on. Minibuses from Nouakchott cost UM4300; the trip takes at least two days. Air Mauritanie has flights every Sunday morning from Nouakchott; the fare is UM11,100.

OUALÂTA

Dating from 1224, Oualâta, about 100km north of Néma, used to be the last resting point for caravans heading for Timbuktu. Ransacked on several occasions, the town has suffered considerably and its mosque is in a lamentable shape. Most interesting, however, is the decorative painting on the exterior and interior of the houses. If you're lucky, you may get invited inside one of them. The women paint geometric designs with dyes, typically red or indigo.

There's a *hotel-restaurant* owned by the mayor of the town; rooms cost about UM700. Pick-up trucks and Land Rovers ply between Néma and Oualâta but not every day. The best day for finding them in Néma is Sunday morning when the plane from Nouakchott arrives.

MAURITANIA

Niger

Warning

! Travel in northern Niger has been dangerous since the early 90s because of attacks by bandits. In the Agadez region, for example, lorries and tankers have been attacked and set on fire, and many 4WDs belonging to aid workers or visitors have been hijacked and stolen. The US embassy recommends avoiding travel beyond Tillabéri, Tahoua and Zinder.

If you travel beyond Tahoua to Agadez and Arlit, or beyond Agadez to Zinder, you can go with the *convoi militaire* (military convoy). It goes twice weekly from Tahoua and once a week (Monday) from Agadez to Zinder. Be warned that as recently as 1998, European 'go-it-aloners' have been killed for their vehicles beyond Agadez.

The Algerian side of the border is strictly no-go, with the fundamentalist Groupe Islamique Armée (GIA) in full control. Many foreigners and thousands of Algerians have died in the conflict which has been raging since 1993. Attempts to cross the border would be suicidal.

NIGER AT A GLANCE

Capital: Niamey
Population: 9.4 million
Area: 1,267,000 sq km
Head of state: President Ibrahim Baré Maïnassara
Official language: French
Main local languages: Hausa, Djerma, Fula, Tamashek
Currency: West African CFA franc
Exchange rate: US$1 = CFA600
Time: GMT/UTC +1
Country telephone code: ☎ 227
Best time to go: December to February

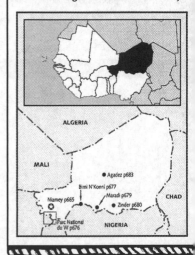

Niger is a fascinating destination. The capital, Niamey, has a distinctive character, with camels walking down the wide boulevards and interesting modern buildings that seem out of place in the Sahel. Outside Niamey, you'll find plenty more of interest. To the south is one of the best places for seeing wildlife in West Africa – Parc National du W (pronounced *dou-blay-vay*). To the north-east is the crumbling city of Agadez, teetering on the edge of the Sahara. North-east of Agadez lie the incomparable Aïr Massif and Ténéré Desert, not to be missed when travel in the region is safe. Any trip to Niger is tempered by the incredible poverty you encounter. In the back streets

and busy markets the struggle for life goes on as it has for centuries.

Facts about Niger

HISTORY

About 6000 years ago, rivers ran through grassy plateaus in parts of northern Niger that are now desert, and the region was populated by hunters and herders. As the Sahara became drier, these people migrated southwards. Towards the end of the 1st millennium BC, they had learnt the skills of metalwork and developed elaborate social organisations and complex forms of trade.

Empires were founded, with wealth and power based on the control of the trans-Saharan trade in gold, salt and slaves. The first was the Kanem-Borno Empire, which flourished between the 10th and 13th centuries AD, remaining a significant force until the 19th century in the eastern part of present-day Niger, around Lake Chad. During the same period, the large Hausa population expanded into southern Niger from the north of present-day Nigeria. They were followed, in the 17th century, by groups of Djerma people, descendants of the great Songhaï Empire.

Although the slave trade had been abolished in most other parts of West Africa, it was still going strong in Niger and Chad a hundred years ago. The sultans and chiefs were determined to keep it alive, and with an army of 12,000 soldiers the sultan of Zinder had little trouble attacking villages in his own kingdom, to capture the inhabitants and sell them into slavery whenever debts mounted.

The slave trade was the only way the sultan could support his 300 wives and numerous children, especially as the trans-Saharan trade in gold had diminished as the Portuguese started trading on the West African coast, breaking the monopoly of the Sahel empires. Agadez, once a great gold-trading centre, was also hit; its population shrank from 30,000 in 1450 to less than 3000 by the early 20th century.

As trade in gold declined, the value of salt rose. Mined at remote oases in the desert,

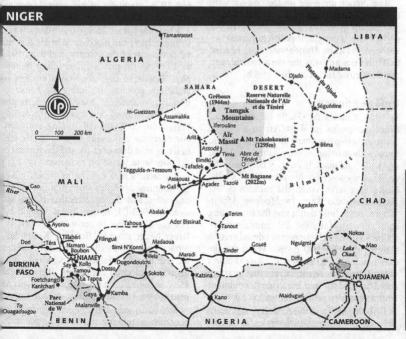

salt deposits were the prerogative of the Tuareg nomads; it was so rare in the Sahel that markets often traded it ounce for ounce for gold. It was salt that kept alive the huge trans-Saharan camel caravans, and as recently as 1906 a 20,000-camel caravan left Agadez to collect salt at Bilma, an oasis some 610km to the east.

Islam came via the trans-Saharan trade, but the rural people remained loyal to their traditional religions until the 19th century. Today, about 85% of the people are Muslim. Europe's first intruder was a Scot, the celebrated Mungo Park, who disappeared on the River Niger in 1806 (for more details, see the boxed text 'Mungo Park' on page 24). Although the French didn't arrive until 1890, their conquest was rapid and savage with bloody massacres in 1898 and 1899. Niger was made a military territory and by 1901 the slave trade was over. Tuaregs in the north kept resisting until the 1920s when Niger became a French colony.

The French did little for the colony, with the exception perhaps of the introduction of groundnuts (peanuts) in the 1930s. In the early 1950s a couple of political parties developed. Sawaba (Independence), headed by Djibo Bakari, was the most radical, and opposed close ties with the French.

Independence

In 1958, Charles de Gaulle offered the 12 French colonies in West Africa a choice between self-government in a French union or immediate independence. Guinea shocked de Gaulle and made history by becoming the only colony to reject his plan. Unofficially, Niger may have voted the same way. As Basil Davidson says in *Modern Africa*, 'There seems little doubt that the true voting returns were falsified by administrative action'. The French-supported administration claimed that 370,000 people voted for the union and 100,000 against – 750,000 didn't vote! It was clear, however, that nothing could stop Niger and the other 10 colonies from eventually gaining full independence.

Djibo Bakari and the Sawaba party campaigned for complete independence, and the infuriated government banned the party and sent Bakari into exile. This left Hamani Diori, leader of the Parti Progressiste Nigérien (PPN), in complete control and the only candidate for president when full independence arrived in 1960.

Diori maintained unusually close ties with the French and, despite several unsuccessful coups, survived until the great Sahel drought of 1973-74. Niger was probably the worst hit country of all: over 60% of the livestock was lost. Stocks of food were discovered in the homes of several of Diori's ministers, and soon after, Lt Col Seyni Kountché overthrew Diori in a bloody coup and set up a military council to rule the country, with himself as president.

Kountché & Saïbou

The new military government took a hard line on morality and in his early years, Kountché was known for his sensationalistic methods of governing. Twice, in 1975 and 1976, members of his government attempted unsuccessful coups.

Kountché was lucky in other ways. Uranium had been discovered in 1968 in the far north-east of the country, and from 1974 to 1979, world prices for uranium quintupled. Kountché embarked on a number of ambitious projects, including the construction of a 'uranium highway' to Agadez and Arlit, the centre of operations of the mainly French-owned SOMAIR mining company. Not everyone was smiling, however; the cost of living rose dramatically and the poorest of the poor were worse off than ever.

Kountché's luck ran out in the early 80s. Government revenues from uranium took a nose dive and the construction boom was over. In 1983-84, another great drought hit. For the first time in recorded history, the River Niger stopped flowing. Kountché's reputation for honesty helped him weather the resulting dissatisfaction, including a third unsuccessful coup attempt in 1983. But in 1987 he died after a long illness and was replaced by his chosen successor, Ali Saïbou.

Saïbou immediately began a process of constitution-making. In 1989, he formed a new political organisation called the Mouvement National pour une Société de Développement (MNSD), but at the same time he upheld the ban on political parties which Kountché had introduced after the 1974 coup. He then stood for presidential election, but with himself as the sole candidate in the interests of national unity.

Keenly aware of the profound political changes sweeping across West Africa, the Niger people weren't satisfied with Saïbou's cosmetic alterations. Political, industrial and ethnic unrest was flaring up everywhere. The government, and the whole country, was beginning to fall apart. The promise of political reform, seriously needed, failed to pacify the people. In February 1990, there were mass student demonstrations and strikes by workers.

Outside the capital, things were also far from peaceful. In May 1990, a band of armed Tuaregs launched a violent attack on the police post at Tchin Tabaraden, in northeastern Niger. This was precipitated by the lack of assistance given to Tuaregs recently returned from Algeria and the misappropriation of funds promised to them following Saïbou's accession to power. The raid also brought the country international attention, and was the final straw that led to Saïbou's downfall.

In 1991, a new constitution was drafted facilitating political pluralism. Saïbou was stripped of power and a transitional government was set up with a remittance to run the country until multiparty elections could be held. The new prime minister was Amadou Cheffou.

Ousmane Era

Multiparty elections were held in 1992, with delegates from several groups gaining seats in the new National Assembly. Nine of these parties formed a coalition called the Alliance des Forces de Changement (AFC), which had a majority in the national assembly and therefore became the government. Presidential elections followed in March 1993, which Mahamane Ousmane, a former government adviser, won with the backing of the AFC.

Tuareg Rebellion

The Tuareg form minorities in many Saharan countries, including Niger, Mali, Mauritania, Algeria, Senegal, Chad, Libya, Burkina Faso and Tunisia. Being a minority has put them at a disadvantage with the majority groups in any state when it comes to getting their fair share of the national budget, and they have been marginalised politically and economically. Another contributing factor for Tuareg dissatisfaction has been suffering as a result of droughts in the 1970s and 1980s, which decimated livestock and altered the way of life of these traditionally nomadic herders. In addition, increasing desertification and population growth have resulted in competition for scarce resources with other pastoral groups such as the Arabs and Fula, leading Tuareg frustrations to the point of rebellion.

In Niger the Tuareg are demanding a federal country, with a Tuareg autonomous region in the north. (In Mali, the Tuareg are demanding an independent state.) Since their armed struggle began in 1990, more than a hundred people, including rebels, police and civilians, have been killed in Niger. In 1992, as a result of the violent attacks on civilians, the Niger government banned travel in the north, and closed its main border with Algeria. It remained closed for over a year, halting the tourist flow across one of the Sahara's oldest routes and stifling Niger's tourist industry.

In early 1994, the Tuareg Front de Libération de l'Aïr et l'Azouack (FLAA) and Front de Libération Tamouist (FLT) agreed to an uneasy truce. A peace accord was signed in 1995 after the government and the Organisation de la Resistance Armée (ORA), representing the Tuareg groups, met in Ouagadougou. Tuareg refugees are now returning to Niger. The aftermath of the rebellion has been outbreaks of sporadic violence and banditry in the north and far east of the country, much of which remains off limits to the traveller.

NIGER

Although peace returned to the capital, unrest continued in the Tuareg areas, despite attempts by the new government to reach a settlement by peaceful means. Several Tuareg groups regarded the new government as untrustworthy, saw no benefit in negotiation and wanted to continue fighting for their freedom.

The problem was further complicated by armed bandits (possibly Tuareg or Arab, the Tuaregs' traditional enemy, or from other groups) taking advantage of the general breakdown in control. However, by June 1993, a truce was agreed with prominent Tuareg rebel groups. As a result, the government reopened negotiations and dropped the state of emergency which had prevented foreigners from travelling in the region.

Ousmane also had problems in Niamey. Parliament's smooth run was disrupted in 1994, when key members of the AFC defected to the MNSD, removing the AFC's majority and forcing another election in January 1995. Surprisingly, the MNSD won a majority in the national assembly. A truce was signed in May 1995 between the new government and the Organisation de la Résistance Armée (ORA) which represents six of the main Tuareg groups. But in spite of this success, the divided, weak and ineffectual government was short-lived.

Niger Today

In January 1996, a military junta headed by Colonel Ibrahim Baré Mainassara staged a coup and ousted Ousmane on the basis that the weak government threatened economic reforms. The constitution was suspended, parliament was dissolved and political parties were banned.

Mainassara reinstituted the constitution and another presidential election was held in July. The National Election Commission reported a couple of days later that Mainassara had polled over 50% of the vote (Ousmane had polled 20%). Elections were held for the 83 seat national assembly in November 1996 and January 1997. The authoritarian National Independents' Union for Democratic Renewal (UNIRD) managed to get

about 70% of the seats (56 of the 83); the nearest rival got eight seats. Mainassara's photograph now appears in most restaurants in Niger – a sure sign that he, like many other authoritarian African leaders, is here for the long haul.

Although disarmament (of Tuaregs and Arabs) was part of the peace deal, it is unlikely that weaponry will be quickly removed from the volatile northern areas, where skirmishes and banditry have been a way of life for centuries. Although the new peace accord has more chance of holding than any of the previous cease-fires, nothing is certain. Banditry is still rife and you have to join a military convoy to travel beyond Tahoua to Agadez and Arlit, or from Agadez to Zinder.

GEOGRAPHY

Niger is West Africa's second-largest country, over twice the size of France. It is landlocked, over 650km from the sea. The River Niger flows for about 300km in the south-western corner of the country.

Niger's most remarkable area is the Aïr Massif in the north-east, which you can see from the highest buildings in Agadez. Rising over 2000m and comprising dark volcanic formations culminating in the Bagzane peaks, the mountains are breathtakingly beautiful. Beyond the massif to the east is the Ténéré Desert, which has some of the most spectacular sand dunes in the Sahara.

CLIMATE

The hottest part of the year is March to June, the worst month being April when daytime temperatures reach 45°C (113°F) or more, with the heat becoming so intense that rain evaporates before reaching the ground. December to February is the coolest period, when temperatures in the desert can drop to freezing at night. This is probably the best time to visit Niger. The harmattan winds, however, usually come before the rains and blow a fine dusty fog that envelops everything. Visibility is cut to less than 1km. In late May, the rains come to the southern parts

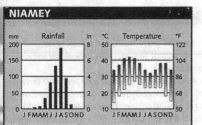

of the country, averaging around 50mm in that month. The annual total in the south is usually 550mm. In contrast, the northern parts receive less than 150mm of rainfall annually, even in the best of years. In the worst years it may not rain at all.

Do not underestimate the desert heat, especially during the hot seasons. Desert travel can be extremely harsh, with air temperatures way over 50°C (making sand and rocks hot enough to burn skin).

ECOLOGY & ENVIRONMENT
Today, two-thirds of Niger is desert and the rest is Sahel (the semidesert zone south of the Sahara). Over half of the country is uninhabitable – even by nomads.

Desertification is Niger's greatest environmental problem and is mostly due to deforestation as people cut wood to use as fuel for cooking. Fortunately, there have been some successful reafforestation schemes, particularly the community forestry project at Guesselbodi, outside Niamey, which has encouraged villagers to build windbreaks and establish nurseries.

Overgrazing is the other major cause of desertification. Animal health and well-digging programs have resulted in increases in herd sizes beyond the land's carrying capacity, although herds were severely depleted by the droughts in the early 1990s. To help rebuild stocks and generate income, one aid scheme 'loans' young goats to farmers who then tend the animals until they mature and reproduce. The animal offspring are then 'repaid' to the aid scheme.

FLORA & FAUNA
In spite of Niger's poverty there has been a concerted attempt to preserve the remaining wildlife of the south-west, especially in Parc National du W. The last giraffes of the Sahel are found in the south-west (especially around Tillabéri) and foreign agencies are attempting to establish a viable conservation project.

GOVERNMENT & POLITICS
Niger's remarkably smooth transition to a multiparty democracy was interrupted in 1996 by the Mainassara coup. Mainassara won the first election after reinstating the constitution, however, and Niger has supposedly returned to democratic rule.

The constitution provides that the president is elected by universal suffrage and serves for a five year term. Elections are next scheduled for 1998. The president appoints the prime minister, who heads the national assembly. This has 83 members elected by popular vote for five-year terms.

ECONOMY
Niger's economy is doing very badly. It has recorded negative GDP growth ever since 1990 and was one of the countries worst hit by the devaluation of the CFA franc in early 1994. The country would be economically lost without uranium. It owns about a fifth of the world's total uranium deposits and, despite the devastating collapse in world prices during the 1980s, uranium still accounts for about three-quarters of export earnings.

While only 3% of the land is arable and rainfall is unpredictable, subsistence farming and stock rearing contribute around half of GDP and nearly three-quarters of the labour force is employed in this sector. Exports include cotton, cowpeas (black-eyed peas) and groundnuts (peanuts). Principal subsistence crops, with the aid of irrigation projects, are millet, sorghum, cassava and rice, all of which help to make the country self-sufficient during the non-drought years.

The country struggles to repay its foreign debt, with the result that essential medical

Suffer the Children ...

Niamey, at first glance looks like a relatively prosperous city – truth is, it's the capital of one of the poorest countries on earth. And the major victims of the impoverishment are the children who live amid the worst health conditions imaginable.

The statistics are horrifying for children under five: a mortality rate of 320 per 1000 (infant mortality overall of 191 per 1000); 32% stunted; 16% wasted; 36% underweight; and only 20% immunised against measles. Studies in villages around Niamey have revealed that micronutrient deficiencies in pregnant women and school children are rife – 60% are anaemic (iron deficient) and iodine deficient, and vitamin A deficiency, the cause of xerophthalmia (night blindness) is widespread.

The problems have been compounded by the drought which currently ravages this part of the Sahel, especially the Tillabéri region. Families have been forced to migrate to Niamey and Agadez (already cluttered with Tuareg refugees), or to desperately fossick for and consume wild food. Women are reduced to sifting precious spilt grain from sand or to scratch for grain among ant hills.

The hungry period or *soudure*, which usually lasts from May to June, has lengthened in recent years. As a result cereal prices are 150% more than in 1997 and farmers, not self-sufficient even in good years, are forced to sell their grain early to pay taxes and then repurchase it during soudure at higher prices. It is believed that the current crisis affects 3,000,000 of the population.

One of the frightening consequences of the malnutrition has been the re-emergence of the 'Grazer' or noma, severe gangrene of the tissues of the mouth and face – often described as the 'African disease' and most prevalent in children. A minor case of gingivitis (gum infection), for example, caused by commonplace bacteria can develop into gangrene, when the flesh of the face is literally eaten away.

The noma could easily be prevented with adequate nutrition and antibacterials (mouthwash, ointments or antibiotics). The parents of the children, however, are ofter starving themselves, and have no money buy these. Once the disease has ravaged a victim's face even plastic surgery can't hide the hideous disfigurement – and such surgery is an impossibility in this country. Survivors are hidden away where no one can see their faces.

In spite of limited international aid, much of which has focused on the repatriation and feeding of refugees, the problem seems insurmountable. After a debilitating war, which sapped the government coffers and burdened the country with foreign debt, there are no funds left to put in place preventative health programs or provide basic medicines. Failure to take preventative measures against diseases such as measles, meningitis and malaria claims the majority of children.

Further facts point to the desperation of the situation – maternal mortality is 1 in 20 compared with 1 in 1000 in developed countries; each woman has on average seven children; only 15% of the births are aided by trained health workers (and only in Niamey); and in rural areas there is little or no pre or postnatal care; some 40% of women have given birth by the age of 17; and only 4% use some form of contraception. And it seems that the country is again plunging back into a state of internal turmoil with recent riots in several towns.

Only a massive international effort will avert further disaster. If you want to help, information about volunteering with the international medical aid organisation Médecins Sans Frontières (MSF) can be found on their Web site at www.msf.org.

services are neglected and much of the population faces hunger. One horrifying result is that one-third of Niger's children die before they reach the age of five. Another war would have even more disastrous results.

POPULATION & PEOPLE

An area of 1,267,000 sq km and 9.4 million people gives Niger one of the lowest population densities in West Africa: about seven people per square kilometre. (In contrast, Nigeria is three-quarters the size of Niger and has 14 times more people.) However, 90% of the population lives in the south of the country. Drought and heat have made it increasingly difficult for people to thrive in the northern regions.

The population is growing at 3.2% annually. This is combined with a very high infant mortality rate. Life expectancy is an estimated 43 years.

The population is extremely diverse, with numerous ethnic groups. The main group is the Hausa, who make up over 50% of the population. The second-largest group (22%) is the Songhaï-Djerma along the River Niger and in Niamey, followed by the Tuareg in the north (less than 10%) and the Fula (also called Peul; 9%). Other groups include the Kanouri in the eastern part of Niger between Zinder and Chad, and the Toubou in the north. Niger also has a minority of Arabs in parts of the country's north-east, related to groups in Libya and Chad. For more information on the Tuareg peoples, see the colour feature between page 672 and page 673.

The Songhaï were once known as traditional administrators and warriors. About 400 years ago, they migrated south and settled along the River Niger. Today, they constitute over half the population of Niamey. The Djerma (or Zarma) have common origins and speak the same language as the Songhaï. They are found in Dosso and south of Niamey.

The Fula are the second-largest nomadic group in Niger (after the Tuareg). The best known are the Bororo Fula, or Wodaabé,

Tuareg Culture

The Tuareg are Muslim, but although they celebrate most Muslim holidays, they ignore the annual Ramadan fast. The Tuareg are also one of the few groups in Africa who traditionally eat with utensils – a large wooden spoon – rather than their hands.

Tuareg women traditionally do no livestock keeping or domestic work. The Tuareg are effectively monogamous and women enjoy a degree of independence, owning their own livestock and spending the income on themselves, while men have to provide for the home. Chieftancy is passed to men through the female line. The young have choice in whom they marry and courtship is an established art involving instrumental music, songs and poetry. Most social activity takes place round family campfires at night.

from the Dakoro-Tanout region west of Agadez. They take great pride in being beautiful and, during festivals, wear lots of jewellery and have intricate hairstyles. Their annual Cure Salée festival in September, known as the Gerewol, is famous throughout Africa. For more details, see the boxed text 'La Cure Salée' in the Facts for the Visitor section following.

In Ayorou on market day you are likely to see representatives of all the major ethnic groups in their traditional dress, including Moorish (Mauritanian) merchants and the local Bella people.

EDUCATION

For a host of reasons, including the country's sparse widespread population, Niger ranks at the bottom of the world in terms of schooling for children. Education is available in most major towns and is compulsory and free of charge, but only 17% of school-age children attend school, one of the lowest rates in the world. University-level education is faring no better. The University of

NIGER

Niamey went bankrupt in 1993. Today, the average length of schooling for adults is less than two months – the lowest in the world along with Burkina Faso. About 10% of government expenditure is spent on education, but the results are hard to see.

ARTS

Niger is a crossroads for West Africa. Here you can see many forms of art and craftwork from the diverse groups who make up the population. Best known, perhaps, is the art and craftwork of the Tuareg, especially their silverwork, including jewellery (see the colour feature between pages 672 and 673) and intricately decorated dagger handles, and leatherwork, including sandals, cushions and magnificent camel saddles.

Also look out for *les couvertures Djerma*, large, bright strips of cotton sewn together into a large cloth, which are truly spectacular and unique to Niger.

RELIGION

Islam is a dominant force in the daily lives of the people of Niger, practised from birth until death. Nearly 85% of the population is Muslim and only a small percentage of urban dwellers are Christian. A few rural communities continue to practise the traditional animist religions.

LANGUAGE

French is the official language. The principal African languages are Hausa, spoken mainly in the south, and Djerma (also spelt Zarma), spoken mostly in the west, including around Niamey. Other languages include Fula and Tamashek (also spelt Tamachek and Tamasheq), the language of the Tuareg. See the Language chapter for useful phrases in French, Hausa, Fula and Tamashek.

Facts for the Visitor

SUGGESTED ITINERARIES

Niamey is an interesting town to explore, with a good market and museum, so you should allow a week here. Possible one-day

Highlights

Natural Beauty & National Parks

Ténéré Desert *(The North)*
The spectacular beauty of the Aïr Massif and endless rolling dunes of the Ténéré Desert are not to be missed.

Parc National du W *(The South)*
On the banks of the mighty River Niger, this national park is possibly the best place to see wildlife in West Africa; although the park straddles three countries, the Niger part is the easiest to reach.

People & Culture

Grand Marché *(Niamey)*
You'll find an amazing selection of art & craftwork from around the country here, and it's a good place to look for the colourful and distinctive *couvertures Djerma* and silver jewellery.

Zinder *(The South)*
The market here is one of the liveliest in the country; said to be home to the best leatherworkers in Niger.

Agadez Markets *(The North)*
The people dressed in traditional garb make the Grand Marché and the Tuareg market a kaleidoscope of colour; come in February when the salt caravans arrive, and there are hundreds of camels at the Tuareg market.

La Cure Salée *(The North)*
One of the most famous celebrations in Africa, held annually in the area around In-Gall.

Architecture

Agadez *(The North)*
Lose yourself in the labyrinthine back streets of the Vieux Quartier and marvel at the construction of the seven-storey mud mosque – like Timbuktu, but more extensive and interesting.

excursions include those to Boubon, Namaro, or the Sunday markets at Ayorou and Filingué. Allow another week for visiting Parc National du W in the south.

If you plan on going to Agadez, allow another week, and up to five weeks in total if you visit the fascinating Aïr Massif and Ténéré Desert. On the way to Agadez you could take in Zinder, with a possible stop at Birni N'Konni or Maradi. Count on spending at least a few days in Agadez as it's a fascinating town, possibly taking a camel ride into the surrounding areas for a day or more.

PLANNING

December to February is the best time to be here even though the harmattan can ruin photos. From March to June it is just too hot to travel in the desert (especially if the aircon packs it in).

It is hard to get good maps of Niger; your best bet is the Michelin map of West Africa, although it does have some errors.

TOURIST OFFICES

The Office National du Tourisme (ONT) has outlets in Niamey and Agadez, which have a limited amount of information – for more details see Information in the relevant sections later. There are no Niger tourist offices abroad.

VISAS & DOCUMENTS
Visas

Visas are required by almost everyone. Requirements change all the time, however, so check with the nearest Niger embassy. French visitors do not need visas except for stays of more than three months.

Getting a visa in Europe or North America is fairly straightforward if you're arriving by air, but not by land. In the USA, for example, the Niger embassy in Washington DC requires US$35, three photos, proof of yellow fever vaccination and a copy of your airline ticket proving onward travel. Other embassies outside Africa have similar requirements and charge up to US$40 for visas. In France, the Niger embassy in Paris,

open weekdays from 9.30 am to 12.30 pm, charges the same for multiple-entry visas as for single-entry ones and usually gives 24-hour service.

If you're travelling overland, note that Niger has only a few embassies in West Africa, and none in Central Africa, so getting a visa requires careful planning. In West Africa, most embassies do not impose an onward ticket requirement on overland travellers. Visas are easy to obtain in Benin (CFA22,500 for one month), and in Nigeria from the embassy in Lagos and the consulate in Kano (N3000 for one month). Both countries issue visas within 24 hours.

Niger visas are also available from embassies in Ghana and Côte d'Ivoire. You cannot get Niger visas in neighbouring Mali, Burkina Faso or Chad. You can, however, get visas in Liberia and Tunisia from the Côte d'Ivoire embassy. French embassies do not have authority to issue visas to Niger.

Visa Extensions For a visa extension, go to the *sûreté* in Niamey; it costs CFA7500 and takes 24 hours to issue.

Registration

It is necessary to register with the police in some towns and cities in Niger. If you pass through Diffa, Arlit or Agadez, register with the police (and get the *vu au passage* stamp in your passport) whether or not it's officially required. This will save you a lot of hassle at police checks further along the road (especially if you are heading from Tahoua to Agadez, Arlit or Zinder with the military convoy).

Wherever you register, you will be hassled endlessly for a bribe (perhaps up to CFA 5000); if you relent you may be spared waiting all day for your passport.

Other Documents

To enter Niger, you need a yellow fever vaccination certificate, which you must show at the airport if you fly in. Entering overland, a check usually depends on the mood of border officials.

EMBASSIES & CONSULATES
Niger Embassies

In West Africa, Niger has embassies in Benin, Côte d'Ivoire, Ghana and Nigeria. For more details see the Facts for the Visitor section of the relevant country chapter. Embassies elsewhere include the following:

Belgium
(☎ 02-648 61 40)
78 ave Franklin-Roosevelt, Brussels 1050
France
(☎ 01 45 04 80 60)
154 rue de Longchamp, 75016 Paris
USA
(☎ 227-483 4224)
2204 R St NW, Washington DC 20008

There are also embassies in Canada and Egypt. Niger does not have diplomatic representation in the UK.

Embassies & Consulates in Niger

All embassies and consulates are in Niamey.

Benin
(☎ 72 28 60)
On Rue des Dallois, 2km north-west of the centre, near Route de Tillabéri, BP 11544
France
(☎ 72 27 22 or 72 27 23)
On the corner of Ave Mitterrand and Blvd de la République, BP 10660; the consulate is open Monday to Saturday from 7.30 am to 12 pm
Germany
(☎ 72 25 34)
Ave du Général de Gaulle
Mali
(☎ 75 24 10)
On Ave Mali, 4km north of the city centre, BP 811
Nigeria
(☎ 73 24 10 or 73 27 95)
On Blvd de la République, 1km past the US embassy (after which the road becomes dirt), BP 617
USA
(☎ 72 26 61 or 64, fax 73 31 67, email usemb@intent.ne)
On Rue des Ambassades, 4km north-west of the centre, BP 11201

Other countries with diplomatic representation in Niamey include Canada and Chad.

Visas for Onward Travel

In Niger, you can get visas for the following neighbouring West African countries. For each visa you need between one and four photos.

Benin

The embassy is open weekdays from 8 to 10 am and issues visas in 48 hours. A one month visa costs CFA12,500 (CFA18,000 for multiple entry). You may also be able to get a temporary visa (CFA4000) at the border in Malanville but it's good only for 48 hours (though you can renew it in Cotonou).

Burkina Faso, Côte d'Ivoire & Togo

The French consulate issues visas to these countries (CFA10,000 for 14 days). It usually gives a no-hassle 24-hour service. Visas valid for up to 90 days cost CFA20,000.

Mali

The consulate is open weekdays from 9 am to 12 pm and 4 to 6 pm. Visas valid for up to 30 days cost CFA12,500 and are usually available the same day.

Nigeria

The embassy is open Monday to Thursday 10 am to 1 pm but will *not* issue visas to anyone who is not a resident of Niger. On occasion, travellers have been successful in getting around this requirement but you shouldn't come here counting on it.

CUSTOMS

Searches by customs officials vary greatly, but extensive searches are becoming increasingly rare except in the north where, due to the problems with bandits, you'll be stopped constantly.

There is no limit on the import of foreign currencies. If you plan to export large amounts of foreign currency, declare it upon arrival.

NIGER

If you fly into Niamey, there's a security check between the health check and customs. It's usually hassle-free, but ignore demands for 'special taxes' to cover cameras etc.

MONEY

The unit of currency is the CFA franc.

Euro €1	=	CFA660
1FF	=	CFA100
UK£1	=	CFA950
US$1	=	CFA600

Banks that change money include the Banque Internationale pour l'Afrique – Niger (BIA-Niger), the Bank of Africa Niger (BAN) and the Banque de Développement de la République du Niger (BDRN).

In Niamey, it's quicker and easier to change cash. At all banks, staff find French francs easiest to deal with, although US dollars are generally no problem. UK pounds and some other hard currencies are also accepted in the BIA-Niger, but not at the BAN. Usually, no commission is charged when you change cash. Banks in Niamey will also change travellers cheques, but commissions can be high and rates are often extremely variable.

Outside Niamey, finding a bank, especially one that accepts travellers cheques, is sometimes difficult. Banks are more likely to give bad rates and levy ridiculously high commissions (typically a flat rate of around CFA4000 but sometimes a percentage). If you're coming in from another country, bring enough cash, preferably French francs, to cover your trip from the border to Niamey.

POST & COMMUNICATIONS

Postal services outside the capital are slow and unreliable, so you should send everything from Niamey. As an example of rates, a 10g letter to Europe costs CFA450.

Currently it is almost impossible to send email from Niger by public means (unless you become a monthly subscriber and pay hefty fees), but this may change.

NEWSPAPERS & MAGAZINES

If you wish to read newspapers or magazines in English, go to the library at the American Cultural Center in Niamey. In the bigger hotels and some of the bookshops, you can get French newspapers and magazines.

PHOTOGRAPHY & VIDEO

A photo or video permit is not required. The usual restrictions on photographing or videoing people and places apply – for more details see the Photography & Video section in the Regional Facts for the Visitor chapter. Note that in Niger, you shouldn't take photos of Kennedy Bridge in Niamey or of people bathing in the river.

HEALTH

A yellow fever vaccination certificate is required for entry into Niger, and, although not officially enforceable, proof of cholera vaccination may also be asked for. Discuss with your doctor, but it may be advisable to get a meningococcal meningitis vaccination. Malaria is a risk year-round in the whole country, so you should take appropriate precautions. Dehydration and heat-stroke are real risks here, especially in the hot season, so make sure you drink plenty of treated or bottled water. Bring your own water purification tablets, as they are generally unavailable here.

For more general information on these and other health matters, see the Health section in the Regional Facts for the Visitor chapter.

WOMEN TRAVELLERS

Generally women have little trouble travelling in Niger. There have been incidents, however, of foreign women being abused or attacked for wearing what was seen as improper clothing. It is important to be aware that this is a Muslim country, where dress is taken very seriously. Shorts or singlets for either women or men show a lack of sensitivity and are not advised. Contraception is not widely available, so come prepared. For more general information and advice, see

NIGER

the Women Travellers section in the Regional Facts for the Visitor chapter.

BUSINESS HOURS

Business hours are from 8 am to 12.30 pm and 3 to 6.30 pm Monday to Friday, and from 8 am to 12.30 pm on Saturday. Government offices are open from 7.30 am to 12.30 pm and 3.30 to 6.30 pm Monday to Friday, and are closed Saturday and Sunday. Banking hours are generally from 8 to 11.30 am and 3.45 to 5 pm Monday to Friday.

La Cure Salée

One of the most famous annual celebrations in West Africa is the Cure Salée (Salt Cure), held by herders in Niger. The Cure Salée is held in the vicinity of In-Gall, where the land and water are especially salty, particularly around Tegguidda-n-Tessoum.

Each group of herders has its own Cure Salée, but that of the Wodaabé people is famous Africa-wide. Indeed, such is its importance on Niger's calendar that the government selects the festival site and it is the only Cure Salée that the country's top officials will attend. The festival lasts a week, usually during the first half of September, and the main event happens over two days.

The Wodaabé are a unique sect of nomadic Fula herders. When the Fula migrated to West Africa centuries ago, possibly from the Upper Nile, many converted to Islam; some even left

herding to become sedentary farmers. For the Fula who remained nomads, cattle retained their pre-eminent position. Valuing their freedom, the nomadic Fula despised their settled neighbours and resisted outside influences. Many called themselves 'Wodaabé' meaning 'people of the taboo' – those who adhere to the traditional code of Fula, particularly modesty. The sedentary Fula called them 'Bororo', a name derived from their cattle and insinuating something like 'those who live in the bush and do not wash'.

The Wodaabé men have long, elegant, feminine features, and they believe they have been blessed with great beauty. To a married couple, it is of upmost importance to have beautiful children. Men who are not good-looking have, on occasion, shared their wives with more handsome men to gain more attractive children. Wodaabé women have the same fine, elegant features and enjoy great sexual freedom before marriage, sleeping with unmarried men whenever they choose.

During the year, the nomadic Wodaabé are dispersed, tending to their animals. As the animals need the salt to remain healthy, when the grass can support large herds at the height of the rainy season, the nomads bring their

PUBLIC HOLIDAYS & SPECIAL EVENTS

The usual Islamic holidays are observed – for a table of estimated dates of these holidays see the Public Holidays & Special Events section in the Regional Facts for the Visitor chapter. Other public holidays include 1 January (New Year's Day), Easter Monday, 1 May (Labour Day), 3 August (Independence Day), 5 September (Settlers' Day), 18 December (Republic Day) and 25 December (Christmas Day).

La Cure Salée

animals to graze in the area around In-Gall, known for its high salt content. During the Cure Salée, you'll see men on camels trying to keep their herds in order, and camel racing. The event serves above all as a social gathering: a time for wooing the opposite sex, marriage and seeing old friends. Afterwards, some of the cattle are driven to Nigeria for sale. Believing that all work other than tending animals is demeaning, the Wodaabé use the money to buy rather than make items such as jewellery and leather goods.

For the Wodaabé, the Cure Salée is the time for their Gerewol festival. To win the attention of eligible women, single men participate in a 'beauty contest'. The main event is the Yaake, a late afternoon performance in which the men dance, displaying their beauty, charisma and charm. In preparation they will spend long hours decorating themselves in front of small hand

mirrors. They then form a long line and are dressed to the hilt with blackened lips to make the teeth seem whiter, lightened faces, white streaks down their foreheads and noses, star-like figures painted on their faces, braided hair, elaborate hats, anklets, all kinds of jewellery, beads and shiny objects. Tall, lean bodies, long slender noses, white even teeth and white eyes are what the women are looking for.

After taking special stimulating drinks, the men dance for long hours. Their charm is revealed in their dancing. Eventually, the women, dressed less elaborately, timidly make their choices. If a marriage proposal results, the man takes a calabash full of milk to the woman's parents. If they accept, he then brings them the bride price, three cattle, which are slaughtered for the festivities that follow.

Rivalry between suitors can be fierce, and to show their virility the young men take part in the Soro, an event where they stand smiling while others try to knock them over with huge sticks. At the end of the festival, the men remove their jewellery, except for a simple talisman. All of this is magnificently recorded in *Nomads of Niger* by Carol Beckwith and Marion Van Offelen.

The major event of the year in Niger, is the Cure Salée in September (see the boxed text on the previous page). We tried to reach the celebration of the arrival of the Tuareg salt caravan at Bilma, in the desert about 250km from Zinder – best of luck to those who make it!

ACTIVITIES

In Niamey it's possible to play tennis (a challenge in the heat) or to swim at one of the big hotels (a much better option). There aren't really any hiking options in Niger, although you can go for trips in the desert by 4WD or camel.

Alternatively, you can hire a pirogue along the River Niger, perhaps combining it with a walk through some of the riverside villages.

ACCOMMODATION

Budget places are relatively expensive in Niger, with the cheapest single rooms costing around CFA3000, and the quality is often very low. However, camping (which normally costs about CFA1500 per person) is possible in Niamey, Tahoua, Maradi and Birni N'Konni, Tillabéri and Parc National du W.

Mid-range hotels in Niger are more expensive than in neighbouring Nigeria, Benin and Togo, although on a par with Mali, with prices ranging from CFA6000 to CFA9000 for a double room with fan, and another CFA4000 to CFA5000 if you want air-con. There are decent mid-range hotels in Niamey, Zinder, Maradi, Tahoua, Ayorou and Parc National du W, but nowhere else.

Niamey, and a few other towns, have upmarket hotels, where rooms are CFA13,500 to CFA30,000 or more, but the country's only deluxe hotel of international standard is the Hôtel Gaweye Sofitel in Niamey.

FOOD & DRINKS

The traditional food of Niger is nothing to write home about. In the north, dates, yoghurt, rice and mutton are standard fare among the nomadic Tuaregs. In the south, rice and sauce is the most common dish. Couscous and ragout are also popular. Nevertheless, you're likely to enjoy meal times because in most instances you'll probably be eating in some open-air place, with your feet in the sand and, at night, with the starlit heavens above you. Standard fare at restaurants is usually grilled fish or chicken with chips, or beef *brochettes* and rice. You may be able to get vegetarian dishes at one of the Chinese restaurants in Niamey.

For drinks, you have a choice of tea or a Flag beer. Bottled water and soft drinks are also available.

Getting There & Away

AIR

There is only one international airport in Niger – Niamey. Airport tax is CFA2500 for flights within West Africa (CFA9000 for international flights). Some long-haul flights have the tax included, although this depends on the airline.

Europe & the USA

A couple of European airlines serve Niger. Air France (all flights via Paris) has a twice-weekly service. Economy return fares from Paris start at 7200FF (about US$1200), or a little more from other European capitals, and vary according to season and length of stay. There is a special return fare of US$614. From Niamey, a return fare to Paris is about CFA660,000. British Airways from London is UK£961 one way, but it offers occasional return specials for UK£785.

Ethiopian Airlines offers one-way/return fares between London and Niamey for UK£824/961.

The other option is Air Afrique, which has flights from London, Paris and some French cities to Niamey via Dakar (Senegal) or Abidjan (Côte d'Ivoire). Prices are the same as for Air France.

From the USA, you could take Air Afrique to Dakar or Abidjan and catch a connecting flight to Niamey, or fly to Paris and transfer there.

Africa

Within West Africa, most flights to/from Niamey are on Air Afrique, including: Abidjan (CFA138,600/152,250 one way/return) and Ouagadougou (Burkina Faso; CFA36,300/56,550), four times a week; Cotonou (Benin) for CFA95,700/105,050, Bamako (Mali) for CFA149,600 return and Ndjamena (Chad) for CFA198,000 return, all twice a week; and Dakar (CFA223,850/246,400), once a week.

You can also fly on Ethiopian Airlines once a week from Niamey to Bamako (CFA135,850 one way) and Dakar (CFA 235,400 one way).

The only flights to/from East Africa are on Ethiopian Airlines, which has two flights a week to/from Addis Ababa. From Addis you can fly to Nairobi and several other East African capitals, and from there to destinations in southern Africa.

Border Crossings

One of the great border crossings is no longer – that from Assamakka (Niger) into Algeria. This is because of Algeria's ongoing civil war and massacres. The border with Chad is similarly off limits because of rebel activity.

The four main entry points into Nigeria – east of Gaya, south of Zinder, Birni N'Konni and Maradi – all tax the patience of even the most hardened of travellers. Very few foreigners enter Nigeria this way and the Nigerian authorities have a field day, with about five standard checks (customs, immigration, luggage, drugs and bribe check).

The crossing into Benin (between Gaya and Malanville) is relatively painless, except that you have to do the trip in a couple of motorcycle-taxi rides between bus parks.

Not many travellers cross into Mali from Niger. The Burkina Faso border is a breeze but note that there is a time change.

Royal Air Maroc flies weekly between Niamey and Casablanca for CFA448,250 one way. An economy return fare to Paris via Casablanca is CFA276,650.

LAND

Benin

The road from Niamey to Cotonou is tar all the way, and the border between Niger and Benin closes at 7.30 pm. There are SNTN and private buses from Niamey to the border town of Gaya, but none cross the border. Across the border, bush taxis take you to points further south in Benin.

A Peugeot 504 bush taxi from the Wadata *autogare* in Niamey to Gaya costs CFA4500 and takes four to six hours. By minibus the same trip costs CFA3500, and between Dosso and Gaya costs CFA1750. You'll be let off at a junction 10km before Gaya, where motorcycle-taxis will take you to the Benin border town of Malanville. From there to Parakou it's six hours and CFA3500 by 504 (CFA2500 by minibus, but several hours longer). With good connections, you can make it from Niamey to Parakou in one long day.

Burkina Faso

Bus Only large buses (or minibuses operated by the big bus companies) can cross the border, making direct connections between Niamey and Ouagadougou. SNTN and SOTRAO have a service a week each between Niamey and Ouagadougou (CFA 7500). The buses are reasonably comfortable and fairly punctual, departing at 7 am and arriving 12 to 14 hours later, with over two hours at the border for checks. Tickets must be purchased a day or more in advance.

Buses also go between Niamey and the Burkina Faso border at Foetchango (CFA 3000). The waiting time at the border for a bus or bush taxi on the other side can be short or long depending on your luck.

On the Burkina side, Sans Frontière has a daily service from Ouagadougou to Kantchari (CFA4500) from where there is intermittent transport to the border.

Bush Taxi Despite what drivers may tell you, bush taxis do not cross the border and you must always change here. By bush taxi, Niamey to the border at Foetchango is about CFA2000. You can travel from Niamey to Ouagadougou by bush taxi in a long day, if you leave early and make fairly quick connections at the border.

Coming from Ouagadougou, it's also possible to make the entire trip to Niamey in one long day if connections at the border are good, but 1½ days is more typical, as departures seem to be later and you lose an hour en route because of the time change. Most bush taxis from Ouagadougou do not reach the border by the time it closes at 6.30 pm (Niger time), so most travellers end up sleeping at the border.

Bush taxis to Burkina leave from the gare routière which is on the right side of the River Niger (across the Kennedy Bridge). Follow the road to Burkina Faso – the gare routière is about 1km before the Rive Droite customs.

Car & Motorcycle The main road from Niamey to Ouagadougou is tar, and the trip usually takes about 10 hours. For an alternative, try the route starting west from Farié (62km north-west of Niamey) over the river by ferry towards Dori and Ouagadougou; the road is in good condition all the way. Bear in mind that the Niger-Burkina border closes at 6.30 pm Niger time (Niger is one hour ahead of Burkina Faso).

Chad

There is no public transport across the border and it is unlikely you would use it now if there was. This is a very dangerous area where banditry is rife. Information is provided here in the hope that the situation improves.

On the Niger side of the border, the farthest you can get is Nguigmi, about 100km from the border. Nguigmi is linked to Zinder most days by bush taxi (CFA8500; 16 hours). The trip between Diffa (between Zinder and Nguigmi) and Zinder costs CFA6000 and takes about 12 hours.

On the Chad side there's no public transport, although trucks and pick-ups trundle between Nguigmi and Nokou once every few days and take passengers for about CFA10,500. After more waiting you can find something between Nokou and Mao for about CFA3500, and from there you might be able to find something on to Ndjamena, probably after another few days of waiting.

One last thing: whichever way you go, don't forget to get your passport stamped in Diffa.

Mali

SNTN has a bus (actually a truck with a cabin on the back) that goes between Niamey and Gao once a week. The fare is CFA11,000. On a typical trip the bus leaves at noon, gets to the border around 9 pm and crosses over the next morning, arriving in Gao or Niamey around 6 pm. The road from Niamey to Tillabéri is tar and is fairly decent to Ayorou; from there it's sandy all the way to Gao. It's a hellish trip but even more so from July to September when the route is quite muddy.

There are no bush taxis ploughing the entire distance between Niamey and Gao. If you're headed for Gao and can't get a seat on the SNTN bus, try the gare routière in Niamey near the Rond-Point Yantala and Camping Touristique. Trucks for Gao leave from there on an irregular basis.

Nigeria

The cheapest way to get from Niamey to Nigeria is via Gaya (for details on getting to Gaya, see under Benin earlier in this section). At the junction 10km before Gaya, motorcycle-taxis (moto-taxis) will be waiting to whisk you across the border to Kamba for about CFA1000. From Kamba, you can catch a bush taxi (which are much cheaper than in Niger) almost immediately for Sokoto, which will take three to five hours. Minibuses to Niamey from Kamba take four to six hours (CFA3500).

You can also cross over into Nigeria from Birni N'Konni, Maradi and Zinder. From

Konni, you can take a motorcycle taxi to the border, while from Maradi and Zinder you have to take a bush taxi (which continues all the way to Katsina or Kano).

Getting Around

AIR
For getting around the country by air, there is no scheduled public service. Nigeravia (☎ 73 30 64) may have spare seats on their charter flights, so it might be worth stopping by at the Nigeravia office on the roundabout near the Grand Hôtel in Niamey to see if there's anything going.

BUS
The government's large SNTN buses are the best way to travel around Niger because they cover all the major routes, are comfortable, relatively fast and punctual. However, they are the most expensive form of public transport. For example, Niamey to Birni N'Konni (440km) costs CFA7950, and Niamey to Zinder (950km) costs CFA14,500. Seats must be reserved in advance, and the buses usually fill up fast, starting from the moment the previous one leaves. In each town, SNTN has its own bus station.

You can save about 20% by taking a private bus. They tend to have more frequent departures from the gares routière (also called autogares in Niger), although later departure times. The driving time is typically 50% longer.

BUSH TAXI
Because buses in Niger are fast and comfortable, many travellers prefer them to bush taxis, which tend to be neither. But bush taxis are cheaper and leave more frequently than the buses, although they are often very crowded. There are two types of bush taxi: Peugeot 504 seven-seater station wagons (504s), which normally carry about 12 people; and minibuses, which carry 30 people or more.

Bush taxis head in all directions: along the big roads between Niamey, Agadez and Zinder, and to the borders of Nigeria, Benin and Burkina Faso, as well as to many smaller places off the main routes. In rural areas you can also find converted trucks and pick-ups, called *fula-fulas*. These are cheap, but slow and terribly uncomfortable.

Note that baggage is always charged extra, usually about 5 to 10% of the passenger fare.

CAR & MOTORCYCLE
Main roads in Niger are excellent. From Niamey to Agadez and Arlit, to Zinder and Nguigmi, and to the Burkina Faso border, the roads are all tar.

The road between Zinder and Agadez is a nightmare, having been engulfed by the desert in the central section – it's 4WD only, as the promised repairs have never been carried out. Private vehicles (and public transport) have to join military convoys on the main road between Tahoua and Arlit via Agadez, and convoys still operate between Agadez and Zinder (see the Warning box at the beginning of this chapter). The distance from both Niamey to Agadez and Niamey to Zinder is about 950km. From Niamey to Agadez is currently a two day trip, with a compulsory overnight stop at Tahoua to await the military convoy which leaves early in the morning.

Private cars must pay a toll (*péage*) to use the main routes. You buy a ticket before travelling from a checkpoint on the edge of each town, either for a whole trip (eg Niamey to Agadez CFA1000) or in sections (eg Niamey to Tahoua CFA500, then Tahoua to Agadez CFA500). If you don't have a ticket when it's asked for at a checkpoint, you're fined on the spot by police.

ORGANISED TOURS
Your only choice in order to visit Parc National du W or the desert areas around Agadez may be with an organised tour. For more details see Information in the Niamey and Agadez sections later in this chapter.

NIGER

Niamey

Since becoming the capital, Niamey has experienced fantastic growth – from around 2000 people in the 1930s to over 600,000 today. However, the city is fairly spread out and uncongested, which means that getting around requires a little more walking than in other Sahel capitals.

If you've arrived from Ouagadougou or Bamako, you may be struck by the number of smart new government buildings in the centre, although their exteriors blend in with the environment far better than most modern structures. They are a reminder of the time when uranium prices were sky-high.

Yet despite the modern buildings, tar roads and street lights, Niamey still has a traditional African ambience that gives the city its charm. It is most noticeable on the eastern bank of the River Niger, spanned by the Kennedy Bridge. Dusk is the time to have a drink nearby and watch the activity. If you wait long enough, you are bound to see a camel or two crossing over it. (But beware – there are frequent muggings in this area.) At night, finding a place to eat, drink and chat outside under the stars is easy; and, as with anywhere in the desert, that's when you'll most appreciate being here.

Orientation

Like many African cities, street names in Niamey are virtually useless as nobody knows them, even though most streets have signs. The street pattern, however, is easier to understand than it looks. The two principal arteries intersect at the Grand Marché: Rue de Coulibaly Kalleye, running from the north-east to the south-west (towards the River Niger) and Blvd de la Liberté.

Rue de Coulibaly Kalleye is the main commercial drag, stretching south-west from the Grand Marché to the Kennedy Bridge, becoming Rue du Gaweye along the way. The city's top hotel, the Hôtel Gaweye Sofitel, is just before the bridge, overlooking the River Niger.

The other major axis, Blvd de la Liberté, runs alongside the market, heading south-east towards the airport and out of town (to Agadez, Zinder and Benin) and north-west towards the equally wide Route de Tillabéri. The latter route, also called Blvd de l'Indépendance, leads out though the smart Plateau *quartier* (suburb) to the Rond-Point Yantala on the north-western edge of town and, eventually, to Tillabéri and the border with Mali.

Information

Tourist Information The ONT (☎ 73 24 47, fax 72 33 47) is in the centre on Ave Luebké. It can arrange trips to Parc National du W, the riverside villages north of Niamey and to the Aïr Massif (from Agadez).

Air Afrique's free *Niger: Guide Touristique* provides a good account of the country and services. *Le Sahel* is a newspaper that publicises events such as films and shows at the cultural centres.

Money At the BIA-Niger (☎ 73 31 01) they charge between 1 and 2% to change travellers cheques, plus a handling charge per cheque. They give quick service and also handle Visa cash advances (but not always, so don't rely on it) and cash transfers by Western Union Money Transfer.

Post & Communications There are two main post offices, in the centre of town (Grande Poste) and in Plateau. The post office in Plateau has a poste restante service which is quick and reliable; letters are kept for up to four months. If you need to send something urgently, the courier service DHL has an office at the Hôtel Gaweye Sofitel.

Cheap telephone calls (and telexes) can be made from either of the post offices. Three minutes (the minimum charge) to Europe costs about CFA5000, plus CFA1600 per subsequent minute. To send a fax, the first page costs CFA3000, and subsequent pages CFA1500. The central post office also operates a 'fax restante' service; you can have faxes sent to you (fax 73 44 70) and pick them up free of charge.

NIAMEY

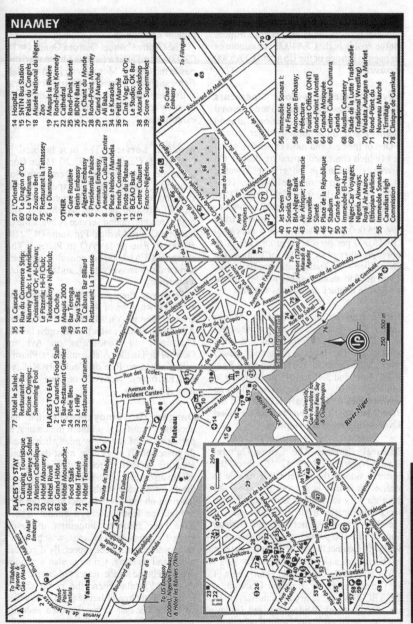

PLACES TO STAY
1 Camping Touristique
20 Hôtel Gaweye Sofitel
23 Mission Catholique
30 Hôtel Maourey
52 Hôtel Rivoli
63 Grand Hôtel
66 Hôtel Moustache;
   Food Stalls
73 Hôtel Ténéré
74 Hôtel Terminus
77 Hôtel le Sahel;
   Restaurant-Bar
   Piscine Olympic
   Swimming Pool

PLACES TO EAT
2 Les Canaries; Food Stalls
16 Bar-Restaurant Grenier
24 Poêle Bleu
32 Le Hilly
33 Restaurant Caramel
35 La Cascade
44 Rue du Commerce Strip;
   Niamey Club; Le Meridien;
   Croissant d'Or; Al-Diwan;
   Le Pizzeria; Hi-Fi Club;
   Takoubakoye Nightclub;
   La Cloche
48 Maquis 2000
49 Bar Terenga
51 Suya Stalls
53 La Cabana Bar Billiard
   Restaurant; La Terrasse

57 L'Oriental
60 Le Dragon d'Or
62 Le Vietnam
67 Zouzou Bert
75 Restaurant la Tattassey
76 Le Diamangou

OTHER
3 Gare Routière
4 Benin Embassy
5 Algerian Embassy
6 Presidential Palace
7 German Embassy
8 American Cultural Center
9 Place Nelson Mandela
10 French Consulate
11 Poste du Plateau
12 BCEO Bank
13 Centre Culturel
   Franco-Nigérien

14 Hospital
15 SNTN Bus Station
17 Palais du Congrès
18 Musée National du Niger;
   Zoo
19 Maquis la Rivière
21 Rond-Point Kennedy
22 Cathedral
25 Rond-Point Liberté
26 BDRN Bank
27 Le Chant du Monde
28 Rond-Point Maourey
29 Ali Baba
   Ali Bni Marché
31 Le Kaoke
34 Le Kaoke
36 Petit Marché
37 Ciné Vog; Epi d'Or;
   Le Studio OK Bar
38 Ascani Bookshop
39 Score Supermarket

40 Jet Seven
41 Sonida Garage
42 BIA-Niger Bank
43 Air Afrique; Pharmacie
   Nouvelle
45 Sûreté
46 Place de la République
47 Stadium
50 Grande Poste (PTT)
54 Niger-Car Voyages;
   Nigeria Airways;
   Royal Air Maroc;
   Ethiopian Airlines
55 Immeuble Sonara II:
   Canadian High
   Commission

56 Immeuble Sonara I:
   Air France
58 Moroccan Embassy;
   Préfecture
59 Tourist Office (ONT)
61 Rond-Point Monteil
64 Grande Mosquée
65 Centre Culturel Oumara
   Ganda
68 Muslim Cemetery
69 Stade de la Lutte Traditionelle
   (Traditional Wrestling)
70 Wadata Autogare & Market
71 Rond-Point du
   Nouveau Marché
72 L'Ermitage
78 Clinique de Gamkalé

The easiest place for international phone calls and faxes is the Hôtel Gaweye Sofitel, but the cost is high: CFA4000 per minute or per page to Europe or the USA and CFA6500 to Australia.

Travel Agencies & Tour Operators Most companies run tours to Parc National du W (and other destinations around Niamey), and to the north of Niger.

One of the best and most expensive agencies (which continued operating despite the Tuareg situation) is Niger-Car Voyages (☎ 73 23 31) in Immeuble El-Nasr. Their prices for a two day (one night) trip to Parc National du W, including simple accommodation, lunch and breakfast, range from CFA125,000 per person for two people to CFA55,000 per person for groups of six or more. Another place to try for tours is the ONT office – see Tourist Information earlier. If you need to make changes to your flights, it's best to contact the airlines directly.

Bookshops Indrap on Rue de Martin Luther King and Ascani on a side street behind the Score supermarket are good bookshops. The latter is better for newspapers and magazines and is open from 8 am to 12.15 pm and 3.45 to 6.45 pm Monday to Saturday. Also try Papeterie Burama between Rue de Coulibaly Kalleye and the Hôtel Maourey. The *tabac* behind the Hôtel Rivoli sells *Time* and *Newsweek*.

Cultural Centres The Centre Culturel Franco-Nigérien (☎ 73 42 40) faces the northern side of the museum off Ave de la Mairie. Its library is open to everyone and there's a busy schedule of lectures, exhibits, dance and theatre. It also regularly screens excellent French, American and African films at CFA500 per person (commencing at 8.30 pm). Contact the centre for more details.

The American Cultural Center (☎ 73 28 61) is on Ave du Général de Gaulle east of the German embassy. It shows CNN daily, the ABC news summary on Saturday at 10 am, movies every Wednesday and Friday, and has a large variety of cultural programs.

There's also an impressive library and regular exhibitions.

The Centre Culturel Oumara Ganda (☎ 74 09 03) named after a famous film maker, opposite the Grande Mosquée on Blvd de Mali Bero, sponsors a variety of African cultural activities, including wrestling, dancing, films by local film makers, concerts and art exhibitions.

Medical Services The best hospital is Clinique de Gamkallé (☎ 73 20 33) on Corniche de Gamkallé about 2km south of Kennedy Bridge. But it's expensive: the standard fee is CFA20,000 per consultation and CFA10,000 per test. A cheaper and highly recommended service is available at the new Centre Médical Pro Santé (☎ 72 26 50) at 10 Rue de la FAO in Plateau. The charge is CFA10,000 per consultation. Staff and facilities are very good, and there's also a pharmacy.

Otherwise, there are plenty of pharmacies around town. One of the best is Pharmacie Grand Marché on Blvd de la Liberté. Another good one, which stays open late, is Pharmacie du Rond-Point on Ave du Général de Gaulle. Also central are Pharmacie Kaocen on Rue de Coulibaly Kalleye and Pharmacie Nouvelle on Ave Luebké near Air Afrique.

Dangers & Annoyances Crime has become a significant problem in Niamey, in part because of attacks by newly urbanised, dispossessed Tuaregs. The most dangerous areas are the Petit Marché (where pickpockets are also a problem), Kennedy Bridge and the two Corniche roads running parallel to the river on the city side, including the area around the Hôtel Gaweye Sofitel. There have been frequent muggings and even knife-slashings in these areas, which should be avoided after sunset, especially if you are alone and walking. Crime is also a serious problem in the northern areas of Niamey, including Yantala where the camp site is located. The Grand Marché is relatively free of crime because it has its own security guards.

Markets

The **Grand Marché** on the Blvd de la Liberté is one of the best in West Africa, with a big selection of artisan goods from all over the country. It is quite impressive, with its modern architecture and fountains. Good times to visit are in the early morning and at the end of the noon siesta when activity is calmer. You can buy anything from vegetables and fabric to bicycle parts and toys.

The **Petit Marché** on Ave de la Mairie is closer to the river and mainly a food market, but it too merits a visit (make sure you watch your valuables).

Grande Mosquée

This impressive mosque, financed by Libya, is 1.5km north-east of the Grand Marché on Ave de la Grande Mosquée. Open to both male and female visitors, it has workers and guards who, if shown a little politeness, are often glad to give a short tour. A tip will be expected.

Musée National du Niger

Built in 1959, this museum, between Ave de la Mairie and Rue du Gaweye, is well worth a visit. You'll find life-sized models of traditional dwellings of the Tuareg, Hausa, Djerma, Fula and Toubou peoples, along with life-sized models in typical dress – a quick way to train the eye for detecting the differences in ethnic groups as you travel around the country. In addition, there is a series of pavilions, each with a different thematic display such as handicrafts, weapons and costumes. One pavilion contains an intact 100,000,000-year-old dinosaur skeleton (an iguanadon), found by uranium prospectors near Agadez, and other palaeontological treasures.

The most interesting area is the artisans' centre, where you can see how the various crafts are made. You can also get custommade sterling silver rings, bracelets, earrings, Tuareg crosses (such as the *croix d'Agadez*) and toe rings, which make great souvenirs.

The **zoo** is part of the museum and is depressing because of the small cages in which the animals are kept.

The museum and zoo are open from 8 am to 12 pm and 4 to 6.30 pm daily, except Monday. Admission is CFA100 (and a photography permit is CFA100).

Swimming

The cheapest place to swim is at the public Olympic-sized pool (CFA500; closed Friday) next to Hôtel le Sahel on Corniche de Gamkalé. During the week it's virtually empty, whereas at weekends it's packed. The top hotels have pools, with fees ranging from CFA500 to CFA2000 at the Hôtel Gaweye Sofitel. At the Hôtel Ténéré on Blvd de la Liberté, you can use the pool for free if you buy a drink and look presentable. The pool at the Grand Hôtel usually lacks water to swim in; when filled it costs CFA1000.

Pirogue Trips

Niger-Car Voyages and ONT can arrange pirogue rides along the river to see Niamey at sunset. Rates start at about CFA5000 per person for an hour-long trip, or you can arrange your own trip by going direct to the piroguers at the waterfront near the SNTN bus station. These boats only take four people in safety (around CFA5000 per hour for a boat would be reasonable).

Places to Stay – Budget

Camping The popular *Camping Touristique*, also called Camping Yantala (☎ 73 42 06), is 200m beyond Rond-Point Yantala on the road to Tillabéri, north-west of the centre. It costs CFA2500 a person plus the same for a vehicle (less for motorcycles). It's dusty and fairly unattractive with few trees, but it has reasonably clean showers and toilets. The restaurant becomes a noisy bar at night. There are plenty of stalls outside where the food is better. The price of a shared taxi into town is CFA300. Note, however, that many travellers have been robbed here.

Hotels Open to all, and highly rated, is the safe and peaceful *Mission Catholique* (☎ 73 32 03), north of the cathedral, on the north-western side of the city centre. Clean rooms cost CFA3200 per person and there's a kitchen for guests. In many parts of West Africa, Catholic missions have stopped accepting travellers because their hospitality has been abused, so make sure it doesn't happen here.

There are a handful of cheap hotels in town, but they are noisy and dirty. An exception is *Hôtel Moustache* (☎ 73 42 82), north of the centre at the intersection of Ave de l'Islam and Ave Soni Ali Ber. It has some good air-conditioned double rooms with bathroom for CFA7000 (and a few more *chambres de passage* which are much cheaper).

Places to Stay – Mid-Range

For years, the ageing, dirty and noisy *Hôtel Rivoli* (☎ 73 38 49) in the centre on Rue Nasser was a favourite with travellers, but no longer it seems. It is central, but you pay for the location: CFA8100/10,100 for singles/doubles with air-con. It has decent beds but its toilet facilities are badly in need of repair.

Much better value is the *Hôtel Maourey* (☎ 73 28 50), in the heart of town at Rond-Point Maourey, which charges CFA13,750/15,750 for air-con single/double rooms. The staff are friendly, and it's the only mid-range hotel that has a predominantly African clientele and ambience. The restaurant is good for breakfast but not so good for main meals.

If the Maourey is full, another option is *Hôtel le Sahel* (☎ 73 24 31 or 73 24 32) on Rue du Sahel. Singles/doubles are good value at CFA14,000/17,000 and comfortable suites are CFA25,000. The restaurant is decent and specialises in pizza. One problem is that it's a 15 to 20 minute walk from the centre, in an area noted for robberies, and there are few taxis.

The *Hôtel Terminus* (☎ 73 26 92 or 73 26 93), also on Rue du Sahel, has comfy bungalows for CFA22,500/26,500 including tax. There is a pool, tennis courts, a jazz club on Thursday, satellite TV, and the restaurant is outstanding. It is very popular with tour groups and is often fully booked.

Also in the mid-range is *Hôtel les Rôniers* (☎ 72 31 38), some 7km west of town on Rue Tondibia. It has top-quality bungalows for CFA18,500/21,000, an excellent restaurant, a pool and tennis courts.

Places to Stay – Top End

There are three top-end hotels, and all accept most credit cards except MasterCard. The long-standing *Grand Hôtel* (☎ 73 26 41) sandwiched between the river and Place de la Fraternité is looking a little frayed around the edges these days. It's comfortable, and has a pool and pleasant terrace overlooking the river; it's also only a 10 minute walk from the centre. The restaurant is popular but has unimpressive meals (with the exception of the sumptuous lunch buffet for CFA6000). Bungalows and doubles are CFA 27,000, superior rooms CFA34,500 and the best suites CFA41,500.

The *Hôtel Ténéré* (☎ 73 39 20) is near the centre on Blvd de la Liberté. It's 1km south-east of the market in the direction of the airport, and getting a taxi is easy. Part of the PLM chain found in many parts of West Africa, it has rooms on a par with the Grand's and a clean pool. Single/double rooms are about CFA20,500/24,700.

Built during the uranium boom, *Hôtel Gaweye Sofitel* (☎ 72 34 00, fax 72 33 47), adjacent to the Palais de Congrès, is Niamey's finest and most impressive hotel. Rooms cost from CFA66,000 to CFA71,000 with TV and video (suites are CFA90,000). It has a pool (CFA2000 for nonguests), tennis courts (CFA2000 for an hour with rackets and balls), travel agency, car hire, nightclub, casino, DHL service and business centre.

Places to Eat

Cheap Eats The best place for really cheap food is around the Grand Marché on Ave de la Mairie. *Street stalls* and basic *eating houses* serve *riz sauce* (rice with sauce of meat or chicken) for around CFA600, plus Nescafé, bread and fried-egg sandwiches in the morning until around 9.30 am and again in the evening from around 6.30 pm.

There are similar *stalls* outside the front of the Hôtel Moustache on Ave Soni Ali Ber near the mosque. The friendly *Zouzou Beri* bar on Rue du Cameroon has excellent chicken curry (CFA2000). If you are out partying along the disco strip of Rue du Commerce in the centre of town, there are some great *suya stalls* (*suya* is Hausa for brochette) opposite the nightclubs; CFA500 will see you well fed. Across the road from these is an excellent little bakery, *Croissant d'Or*, with bread, pastries and snacks. Fast food of all sorts is available from *Le Meridien*, not far north of the Croissant d'Or, where chawarma sandwiches are CFA700, hamburgers CFA750 (or CFA1100 for the 'kingburger') and there is a selection of Senegalese dishes. There are also several *cheap places* in the Petit Marché area.

From the Grand Marché, south-west along Rue de Coulibaly Kalleye towards the bridge, there are a number of popular cheap places to eat on or just off the street. On Rue de la Copro, between Rue de Coulibaly Kalleye and the Hôtel Maourey, is the animated *Le Hilly*, with bare tables and loud music. It serves food until around 10 pm and drinks until midnight or later. On the same street is *Restaurant Caramel* (☎ 73 40 40). It has great pastries, a basic menu with omelette and chips for CFA450, riz sauce for CFA600, steak for CFA650 and a strictly enforced no smoking policy.

The *Niamey Club* is on Rue du Gaweye diagonally across from the Hôtel Rivoli. It's a rustic open-air place with shady trees that's good for drinks and food. It's also a bar and nightclub, and can get lively after dark.

The excellent *Poêle Bleu* on Rond-Point Liberté has fast, friendly service and an enormous range of inexpensive meals, such as steak for CFA1200 and hamburgers for CFA600, plus chawarma, chips and other snacks. It's open after 6 pm.

Highly recommended is the *Restaurant-Bar Piscine Olympic*, very near (you guessed it) the swimming pool, behind Hôtel le Sahel. It serves brochettes for CFA300 and cheap meals for between CFA600 and CFA1200. Beers are cheap too, and this is a

wonderful place to watch the sun set over the River Niger.

On Rue du Gaweye, opposite the Sonara buildings, are the pleasant and very popular *La Cabana Bar Billiard Restaurant* and *La Terrasse*. Both of these restaurants are packed to the gunwales with locals at night, enjoying both the setting and inexpensive food. Mixed salads are CFA900, steaks are CFA2000 and burgers or chawarmas CFA1000.

For good but inexpensive African food, it's hard to beat *Les Canaries* (☎ 75 25 63) on the western side of town near the camp site at Rond-Point Yantala. The menu includes grilled fish, couscous, *sauce de mouton* (mutton) and other African specialities, as well as grilled chicken and pepper steak.

Just north of Rue du Maroc are some more good places. *Bar Terenga* is open from around noon to 11 pm, with a pleasant outdoor eating area under some shady trees, and rock-bottom prices eg CFA300 for couscous (CFA550 with meat).

African *Maquis 2000* (☎ 73 56 56) is a pleasant Ivoirian-style open-air restaurant, with dishes such as *poisson braisé* (braised fish), *crevette grillé* (grilled prawns) and *couscous d'igname* (couscous made from pounded yam) for around CFA2500.

Also recommended is *Restaurant la Tattassey*, a few blocks south-east of the Hôtel Terminus. It has an attractive garden setting and a good menu. Most dishes are in the CFA2300 to CFA2800 range.

Asian *Le Dragon d'Or*, serving a mix of Vietnamese and Chinese food, is opposite the Grand Hôtel and north of the Place de la Fraternité, with a pleasant garden setting and lots of Chinese lanterns (also inside air-con dining) and over 100 menu selections. The speciality here is the filling, delicious *pho* (a noodle soup with coriander, bean sprouts and beef) for CFA1300. The spring rolls (CFA1400), served with lettuce, mint and fish sauce are as good as you'll get anywhere. Another worthy Asian restaurant is the more expensive *Le Vietnam* on Rue du Terminus.

French Three of the top French restaurants are at hotels. *La Croix du Sud* (closed Sunday) at the Hôtel Gaweye Sofitel, the *Toukounia* (closed Monday) at the Hôtel Terminus and the restaurant in *Hôtel les Rôniers* are about as good as you'll find anywhere. The restaurant at Les Rôniers is slightly less expensive and is the only one open at lunch time.

For something less formal try *Bar-Restaurant Grenier* (☎ 73 32 62) between the bridge and the SNTN station; or *Le Diamangou*, also known as Le Bateau (☎ 73 51 43), on the Corniche de Gamkalé about 1.5km south of Kennedy Bridge. It has its own boat moored alongside, where guests can dine. Both restaurants are open evenings only and are fairly expensive. Their main attraction is the pleasant setting overlooking the river, although the food, mainly European, is good.

Another possibility is *La Cascade* in the heart of town a block north of the Score supermarket. The food is good and the owners are friendly but prices are on the high side. For example, fish soup is CFA 3600, large salads are from CFA3700, fish platters from CFA4000, soufflé CFA3800 (with prawns CFA4800) and beers CFA800.

Italian Hôtel Gaweye Sofitel is hardly cheap, but if you have a craving for pizza, at night head for *La Potinière*, the hotel's informal pool-side restaurant. It's the least expensive of this hotel's restaurants and the pizza is the best in town.

The pizzas at *Le Pizzeria* on Rue du Commerce are also excellent but expensive. In this expat hang-out the rarest thing is a smile from either staff or customers – perhaps they should arrange the ingredients on top of the pizza in one of those 'happy face' patterns. *La Cascade* also has good pizza and other Italian dishes.

For a wider choice, readers have recommended *Le Koudou*, a predominantly Italian place on Rue du Grand Hôtel.

Lebanese *L'Oriental* (☎ 72 20 15), to the east of Rond-Point Kennedy, has moderately priced daily specials for around CFA1500 to CFA2500, plus an expensive à la carte menu with fairly small portions and prices from CFA3000 to CFA4000. It's open every evening except Wednesday. Expats swear by *La Cloche*, south of Air Afrique on Rue du Combat, exhorting that it serves the best chawarma, humous and tabouleh in town; it's OK but we feel it doesn't deserve the rave. The food, however, is welcome after a disco blast in Takoubakoye next door. *Al-Diwan* around the corner on Rue du Commerce is also recommended.

Entertainment
Bars The most happening place in town for local company, football, food and cheap drinks is the *Ali Baba* on Rue du Festival south of Rond-Point Maourey. You can ask for a chair and be seated outside to watch the passing parade (and great Sahel nights). The friendly owner ensures all travellers have a good time. Just a few doors away is another African club, *Le Karaoke*, which attracts a rougher crowd.

The lively *Niamey Club* opposite the Hôtel Rivoli on Rue Nasser, popular with locals, has cheap drinks and tasty meals, and occasionally has live music at night. The nearby *La Cabana* and *La Terrasse* are also good places to meet locals and to share a beer.

A little rougher are the three bars near the Ciné Vog. The *Epi d'Or*, *Le Studio* and the *OK Bar* all look a bit dilapidated inside but the clientele is friendly. For an open-air bar with a rustic African feel, try the lively *Le Hilly*, between Rue de Coulibaly Kalleye and the Hôtel Maourey.

The poolside terrace at the *Grand Hôtel* provides the best views over the river; it has inexpensive brochettes and other snacks, as well as beers.

Another place for a beer at sundown on the river's edge is the *Maquis la Rivière* behind the palais du congrès – a great place to meet friends for a drink and a light lunch (chicken couscous is CFA2500).

Nightclubs Nightlife in Niamey is centred on the Rue du Commerce, a section of street squeezed between Rue du Gaweye and Rue le Coulibaly Kalleye. Here you will find the perennial *Hi-Fi Club*, one of those glitterball fantasias. Another long-time favourite is the rustic and breezy *Niamey Club*, and just around the corner is *Takoubakoye*, which drags in a healthy haul of expats and locals after dark. Another good place is *L'Ermiage*, on Blvd de la Liberté two blocks south-east of Hôtel Ténéré. The clientele is almost entirely African and the dancing, which starts around 10 pm and continues to about 3 am, is accompanied by a live band (except on Sunday); admission is CFA500.

The disco of Niamey discos is *Jet Seven*, across from the Score supermarket near the Petit Marché; admission is an expensive CFA3000. All the top end hotels have discos trying hard to imitate the latest in western trends – usually a couple of years behind.

Cinemas The air-con *Le Studio* cinema, in the centre on the street behind the Score supermarket, is the best in town. *Ciné Vog* is a block away and worth checking too. Films are also shown at the *Centre Culturel Franco-Nigérien*, at the *Palais du Congrès* and at the *American Cultural Center*.

Spectator Sports

Wrestling On some Sundays, you may have the opportunity to see African-style wrestling matches at the Stade de la Lutte Traditionelle, a block north-west of the Wadata autogare on the same street and 3km east of the Grand Marché. The crowds are very enthusiastic and the matches, held in an arena surrounded by a covered viewing stand, are definitely worth seeing.

Horse Racing Races are held almost every Sunday from 3 to 5 pm at the Hippodrome out near the airport – follow Ave de l'Amitié from the centre of town. You will probably be approached to assist in race lotteries, which are usually based on French racecourses.

Shopping
Supermarkets The largest supermarket is Score, in the heart of town facing the Petit Marché. Closed on Sunday, it's large and loaded with groceries from France. There are smaller Lebanese-owned stores in the city centre area that carry many products from the Arab world.

For fresh produce, the best place is the Petit Marché. Bottled water is now sold all over town.

Art & Craftwork At the Grand Marché there's an amazingly wide selection of goods, including Tuareg and Hausa leatherwork, silver jewellery, batiks, tie-dyed cloth and Djerma blankets.

Other markets include Marché Wadata, near the autogare, although this has a less extensive selection, or the nearby (and well signposted) Cooperative Village Artisanal, which has a wide range of high-quality merchandise. For jewellery, visit the Attaya Sahara Boutique near the mosque.

Music Cassettes of local and western music (originals and bootlegs) can be bought from several of the stalls in the Grand Marché. Other places to try include Le Chant du Monde at Rond-Point Maourey. It has an extensive selection and is open daily from 8.30 am to 1 pm and from 4 to 9 pm.

Getting There & Away
Air For details of international flights to/from Niamey, see the main Getting There & Away section earlier in this chapter. Airlines with offices in Niamey include:

Air Afrique
   (☎ 73 30 11 or 73 33 75 at the airport)
   3 Ave Luebké
Air Algérie
   (☎ 73 31 56)
   At Hôtel Rivoli
Air France
   (☎ 73 33 89)
   In Immeuble Sonara I on Rue du Gaweye
Ethiopian Airlines
   (☎ 73 50 52)
   In Immeuble El-Nasr

Nigeria Airways
In Immeuble El-Nasr
Royal Air Maroc
(☎ 73 28 85)
In Immeuble El-Nasr

Bus The SNTN bus station (☎ 72 30 20) is on Corniche de Yantala, north of Kennedy Bridge. The ticket office is open weekdays from 7.30 am to 12.30 pm and 3.30 to 6.30 pm, Saturday from 8 to 9 am and Sunday from 8 am to 12 noon. From Niamey, SNTN has buses to the following destinations (one-way fares in CFA):

destination	fare
Arlit	22,000
Agadez	17,500
Tahoua	10,750
Zinder	14,500
Maradi	10,850
Birni N'Konni	7950

Large private buses leave from the Wadata autogare on Blvd de Mali Bero east of the city centre. If you ask for directions, note that it's called autogare, not gare routière – its full name is ECO-Autogare Wadata. Private buses are about 20% cheaper than the SNTN buses.

Bush Taxi There are bush taxis to all the major towns. Most of them leave from the Wadata autogare on the eastern side of the city centre. Generally speaking they are slower than buses.

Bush taxis to Gaya (four to six hours) are frequent because there are few large buses on this route. The Peugeot 504s charge about CFA4500, and minibuses charge CFA3500. If you do this trip in stages, Niamey to Dosso costs CFA1750, and Dosso to Gaya is CFA2500.

To Birni N'Konni, 504s charge CFA5000 and minibuses CFA4000 (although by minibus this trip can easily take up to nine hours). To Tahoua, minibuses cost CFA7750 and can take up to 14 hours.

Bush taxis are also popular on the route between Niamey and the Burkina Faso border. The 130km trip takes roughly two hours and costs about CFA2000 (or CFA 2500 between Niamey and Kantchari). Bush taxis on this route leave Niamey from a small gare routière on the right bank of the Niger (see Burkina Faso in the Land section of the main Getting There & Away section earlier in this chapter for more details).

Getting Around
To/From the Airport A taxi from the airport to Niamey city centre (12km) costs about CFA5000 but this depends on your bargaining powers and the time of day. Luggage is extra. No buses serve the airport, but shared taxis (CFA5000 to the centre) run along the highway nearby.

Taxi Taxis around town don't have meters and are mostly shared, following set routes. Fares for shared taxis are around CFA150 per 'stage' (about 2.5km), and this rate doubles at night.

A taxi to yourself *(déplacement)* will cost about CFA1000 to CFA1500 for a short ride across town, say from the centre to the Wadata autogare, or about CFA2500 per hour and CFA20,000 by the day. You can find them at the Grand Marché, the Petit Marché and at the big hotels (although they charge higher rates). From around 10 pm taxis are as scarce as hen's teeth.

Car Rental The major car rental agency is Niger-Car Voyages (☎ 73 23 31), which has offices in Immeuble El-Nasr and at the airport. For the smallest car, a Toyota Starlet without air-con, it charges CFA13,500 a day plus CFA2000 per day for insurance, CFA130 per kilometre and tax (about 20%). It can only be used around town.

For travel outside Niamey, the cheapest car is a Toyota Corolla, which costs CFA15,000 per day, plus CFA2000 insurance, plus CFA130 per kilometre, plus obligatory chauffeur (at CFA6000 a day plus tax. This comes to almost CFA50,000 a day if you average around 200km, not including petrol.

TUAREG

These nomadic camel-owning Berber speakers used to roam across the Sahel from Mauritania to the western Sudan, although they have had to abandon their traditional way of life recently, mainly because of droughts, and have moved further south, to settle near cities.

Tuareg people still operate a rigid status system. The veils or *tagelmoust* that extend from a Tuareg man's turban are both a source of protection in the desert and a social requirement, for a Tuareg man does not show his face to one of higher status. You are unlikely to see a Tuareg man remove his shawl to expose the lower half of his face in company. When the men drink tea, they are supposed to pass the glass under their taguelmoust so as not to reveal the mouth.

The taguelmoust is the symbol of a Tuareg's identity, and the way it is wrapped changes from tribe to tribe. Typically 5m long and made of blue or black cotton, it helps keep out the desert winds and sand. You may be required to wear a taguelmoust when meeting a Tuareg chief or elders.

Top: Tuareg girl

Middle: The tagelmoust is a symbol of identity, as well as a vital protection against the harsh desert climate.

Bottom: Traditionally nomadic herders, Tuareg re seen throughout the Sahel countries.

ALL PHOTOS BY VICTOR ENGLEBERT

The Tuareg are sometimes known as 'blue people' because the indigo of their clothing rubs off on their skin, an effect that they admire. The women weave artificial strands into their plaits and attach cowrie shells. They wear large pieces of silver jewellery, preferring it to gold.

VICTOR ENGLEBERT

The *croix d'Agadez* is one of the best known of Tuareg artefacts, together with the intricately decorated dagger handles. The crosses are in silver filigree. The Tuareg believe they are powerful talismans to protect against 'the evil eye'. Those with phallus designs are fertility symbols for both sexes, while others are for good luck and protection. Inspect them closely – each desert town (Tahoua, Zinder, Bilma etc) has a slightly different design. The In-gall necklace is altogether different with a silver and amber pendant. The Tuareg men use the crosses as a form of currency to buy cattle, and between trades the crosses are worn by their wives as a sign of wealth.

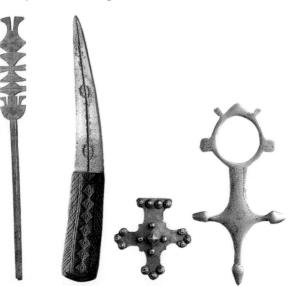

PHOTOS BY DENNIS WISKEN/SIDEWALK GALLERY

Top: Camels play an important role in Tuareg life; see for yourself at the Tuareg camel market at Agadez.

Bottom, from left to right: Protective symbolism on a Tuareg bed post; intricate silverwork on a Tuareg dagger handle; protective amulets, like this one, are often worn, and may contain a verse from the Quran; the croix d'Agadez, perhaps the best known Tuareg symbol.

AROUND NIAMEY

All three places listed in this section are easily reached by bush taxi from the Wadata autogare in Niamey.

Boubon

Boubon is 25km north-west of Niamey on the tar road to Tillabéri. The best time to come here is on Wednesday, when there's a marvellous market. But even better is simply being so close to the River Niger. You can hire a pirogue for a trip along the river. Most visitors, however, come just for a meal at the outdoor restaurant on the small island 200m from the village (you'll find someone with a pirogue to take you over).

Le Campement Touristique Boubon (☎ 73 24 27) is on the island and open year-round. It has a restaurant, a clean pool and thatched-roof cabins for about CFA3500.

Namaro

About 30km north of Boubon on the Tillabéri road, you come to Namaro and a sign pointing to the *Complexe Touristique de Namaro* (☎ 73 21 13), a popular weekend spot for expats. Simple cabins with double beds, air-con and filthy toilets are about CFA7500 to CFA9000 (CFA12,000 to CFA16,000 for rooms with four beds).

Kollo

Kollo is about 40km south-east of Niamey, on the east bank of the River Niger, linked to the capital by a good tar road. The day to come here is Friday, which is market day. The market isn't large but it is lively and colourful.

North of Niamey

From Niamey, one main road leads north-west along the River Niger, towards the Mali border. Beyond the villages of Boubon and Namaro are the larger settlements of Tillabéri and Ayorou, which see very few visitors except those hurrying to and from Gao, over the border in Mali. Even less frequently visited is Téra, some 100km west of the river, on the 'back road' to Burkina Faso.

TILLABÉRI

On the way to Ayorou, Tillabéri (also spelt Tillabéry) is one of Niger's biggest rice growing areas. If you're driving to Mali, get your passport stamped here. The most interesting day to visit is market day on Sunday, and you might also inquire about the local giraffe herd which, during the dry season, usually hangs out along the river bank, several kilometres south of Tillabéri. These are said to be the last giraffes living wild in West Africa.

The *Relais Touristique* is near the river on the northern side of town. It has a restaurant and charges CFA1500 per person for camping and about CFA7500/10,000 for singles/doubles with fan (CFA1000 more with air-con).

AYOROU

If you have a car, or can rent one for the day, Ayorou is an interesting one-day excursion from Niamey and highly recommended during the dry season. The major attraction of the town, particularly from November to April when it's most lively, is the livestock **market** (for cattle, camels, sheep and goats) held here every Sunday. It's the people who make this an unforgettable place: you'll see Tuareg, Fula, Bella and Moors, all in traditional dress. The market doesn't really warm up until around noon, so if you're there in the morning, go to the river to watch the cattle swimming across. It is not a bad idea to hire a guide (CFA3500 per day) as they will arrange photo permissions.

Make sure you leave time afterwards to take a trip on the river. You can rent pirogues in Ayorou or, more cheaply, in **Firgoun**, a small, rarely visited fishing village 11km to the north. A fee of CFA4000 for the boat is a fair price. You may see hippos – the piroguers know where they are.

Places to Stay & Eat

The *Campement* has some dirt-cheap huts where you can sleep on the floor, or you may find lodging with a local. For an inexpensive meal try *Restaurant à la Pirogue*, run by a local Tuareg. Otherwise bring some food with you, as there's little in town. At the other end of the scale is *Hôtel Amenokal* on the river bank. This good hotel has a pool, bar, restaurant and air-con rooms for CFA12,000/ 14,000 on weekdays (50% more on weekends). It's open only from November to April. You can reserve accommodation through Niger-Car Voyages (☎ 73 23 31) in Niamey.

Getting There & Away

Ayorou is served by the SNTN bus running between Niamey and Gao, and by bush taxis from Niamey (CFA3500 one way).

TÉRA

Some 175km north-west of Niamey, Téra receives few visitors. Those who do come here are usually travelling the alternative route to Ouagadougou via Dori (across the Burkina Faso border).

The only place to stay is *Campement de Téra*, which charges about CFA1250 per person for a big room. It has no running water or electricity, only kerosene lanterns and buckets of water. For cold drinks and better food, try the *bar-restaurant* on the other side of town.

If you're heading on to Burkina, the road from Téra to Dori has been improved and may now be possible to travel on in the rainy season. The distance to Dori is only 90km, but the trip can easily take several days as vehicles are so scarce.

Private buses to Téra from Niamey charge about CFA3000; the trip takes eight hours, depending on the delay when crossing the River Niger by ferry at Farié. You can also take an SNTN bus every Wednesday and Saturday; the fare is about 50% more. There are also daily bush taxis from Wadata autogare in Niamey.

FILINGUÉ

Filingué is 185km north-east of Niamey on a tar road, and another interesting place for

a day excursion (if you have your own transport). The market on Sunday, used primarily by the Fula and Songhaï-Djerma, is surprisingly active for such a small town and there are some good examples of traditional architecture in the town. It's at the base of a hill, which you can climb to get an excellent view of the town and the Dallol Bosso, a valley with a dry riverbed.

If you come on a Sunday, don't fail to stop in **Baleyara** (meaning 'where the Bella meet'), roughly halfway to Filingué. On Sunday, it has a very picturesque market under a canopy of shady trees – the animal bartering, which takes place on the town side of the market, is particularly worth seeing.

In Filingué, the rudimentary *Campement* is on your right as you enter town from Niamey, next to the fort. Singles cost about CFA3000 and the beds are big enough for two people. There's also a shower but no fans.

Bush taxis (CFA2500) for Filingué leave daily from the Wadata autogare in Niamey first thing in the morning.

The South

Niger's main arterial road leads from Niamey eastward along the southern edge of the country towards Chad, running roughly parallel to the Nigerian border. The strip of territory along this road, including several major towns, has been loosely termed 'the South'.

DOSSO

Some 140km south-east of Niamey, Dosso is the first major settlement reached on the main southern road. The name comes from 'Do-So', a Djerma spirit. Dosso was once an important Islamic centre and the home of the Djermakoye, the most important Djerma religious leader. Today Dosso is a crossroads south to Benin and west to Nigeria.

Places to Stay & Eat

The renovated and good value *Auberge du Carrefour* (☎ 65 00 17) is on the right a you enter town from Niamey, not far from the autogare, and has doubles for CFA4200 (CFA6200 with air-con) and a nice courtyard restaurant.

Even better is the *Hôtel Djerma* (☎ 65 02 06), on the main drag in the centre of town behind the Mobil station. Air-con singles/doubles with bathroom cost CFA9000/10,000. The rooms at the back, away from the lively bar, are quieter. The hotel has a decent restaurant, serving couscous, spaghetti (CFA1500) and steak with chips, plus a beer garden where the drinks are nearly always cold. The pool is due to be filled one day.

Cheaper good *street food* can be found along the main road, particularly at the autogare, and by SNTN. If you're self-catering, the *Mini-Bazaar* grocery store on the main east-west drag has a variety of goods. Near the Grand Marché is *Chez Rita* where the meals are good and cheap but the star attraction is Rita herself. There's also *Sous les Palmiers* which offers cheap meals and a place to stay.

Getting There & Away

Dosso sits at the junction of the main roads between Niamey and Zinder and south to Gaya (for Benin and Nigeria), so there are always plenty of bush taxis. Minibuses to/from Gaya cost CFA2500 and to/from Niamey CFA1750.

GAYA

Gaya is the only border town for Benin and one of four ones for Nigeria. The only place to stay is *Hôtel Dendi*, very near the market. Single/double rooms are CFA3000/4000 with electricity, fan and bucket shower. For cheap food, try the *Restaurant la Joie d'Été* next to the market. For a beer, try the rustic *Bar Station* across from the bus park.

Minibuses from Niamey to Gaya (four to six hours) cost about CFA3500; 504s cost CFA4500. The gare routière in Gaya is south of town, on the road to the port (and border crossing). The cheapest way to get to the Nigerian or Benin border is by motorcycle-taxi (CFA500).

PARC NATIONAL DU W

This excellent national park is on the western bank of the River Niger in an area of dry savanna woodland, a transition zone between the Sahel and moister savannas to the south. The W in the name comes from the double bend in the River Niger at the park's northern border. The park actually straddles the territory of three countries – Niger, Benin and Burkina Faso – although most people visit the Niger section as it's the easiest to reach.

Although there's a wide variety of wildlife, their total numbers, with the exception of antelope, are very small. Elephant number around 100 or less. Carnivores include lion, leopard, cheetah, hyena and jackal. Migratory birds arrive between February and May.

The best wildlife viewing time is towards the end of the dry season (March to May) when the animals are desperate for water and congregate around water holes. This is also the time of year when the park is most barren-looking. In the dry season, one of the favoured elephant haunts is the river near the park lodge.

The park is open from 1 December to late May, and the entrance is at La Tapoa, 145km south of Niamey. Admission is CFA4000 and a map is available. A guide costs from CFA3500 to CFA6000 a day. Guidebooks can be purchased at the park (CFA5000).

Organised Tours

Several travel agencies in Niamey offer guided tours to Parc National du W – for more details see Information in the Niamey section earlier.

Places to Stay & Eat

Camping inside the park or in one of the adjoining protected reserves is prohibited. The *camp site* just before the River Tapoa may be open (CFA2500 per person).

The only alternatives are finding someone in La Tapoa village to put you up for the night, or staying at the 35 room lodge called *Relais de la Tapoa* next to the camp site and the river. The lodge is open for the same

NIGER

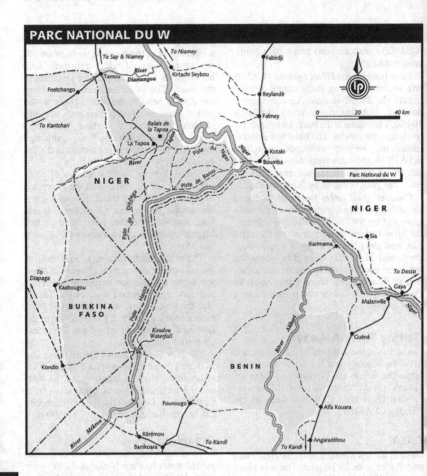

PARC NATIONAL DU W

period as the park. The cost of single/double bungalows with half board (bed, breakfast and dinner or lunch) is CFA17,500/27,000 (CFA20,000/31,500 with air-con). You can make a reservation at the ONT office (☎ 73 24 47) or at Niger-Car Voyages (☎ 73 23 31) in Niamey.

Getting There & Away

Access by public transport is very difficult. From Niamey take a bush taxi or minibus to Say from the small gare routière on the western side of Kennedy Bridge, then another on to Tamou. From Say or from Tamou you may find transport headed for La Tapoa, but don't count on it as the road is very lightly travelled. Remember that the only way in is by car, and walking around the park is not permitted because of lions.

If you're going by car, from Niamey take the conversation-stopping washboard road south to Say (50km) and on to Tamou (55km) at the Burkina Faso border, then 40km further south to La Tapoa.

DOGONDOUTCHI

'Doutchi' is a small town on the main road, about halfway between Dosso and Birni 'Konni. The nearby area is picturesque and the town is pleasant. Just outside the town is a small hill, which you can walk up, and about 15km away is an impressive escarpment *(falaise)* which, although not quite up to the standard of the Falaise de Bandiagara in Dogon Country in Mali, still offers good views.

The only place to stay (unless you find someone in the village to put you up) is the *Hôtel Magama* (☎ 282), well signposted near the centre of town. Rooms in pleasant bungalows cost CFA3500 and an air-con double is CFA8000. The shady restaurant serves meals for between CFA700 and CFA1500, and there's secure parking. If you dare, dine on the offal or carcasses (tails and all) provided in front of the SNTN bus station.

BIRNI N'KONNI

About 420km east of Niamey, Birni 'Konni (or simply 'Konni') is one of the four major border crossings with Nigeria. The two principal streets form a T, with the east-west highway between Niamey and Zinder about 500m north of the town centre, and the main road to Sokoto in Nigeria, extending south from it. The bank has closed, but moneychangers are everywhere.

Places to Stay & Eat

There's a friendly *Relais-Camping Touristique* (☎ 338) on the western outskirts of town on the road to Niamey, about 2km from the centre. The sign is much easier to see when you're coming out of Konni. Double rooms with fan cost about CFA6000 and camping is CFA1500 per person plus CFA1000 per vehicle.

In the centre of town on the main north-south drag is the *Hôtel Wadata* with basic rooms for CFA1800.

About 100m further north is the *Campement*, behind the Maquis 2001 nightclub sign. It has depressing double rooms for CFA3600, with fan and shower.

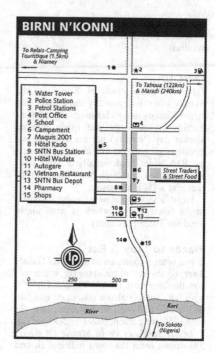

BIRNI N'KONNI

To Relais-Camping
Touristique (1.5km)
& Niamey

To Tahoua (122km)
& Maradi (240km)

Street Traders
& Street Food

1 Water Tower
2 Police Station
3 Petrol Stations
4 Post Office
5 School
6 Campement
7 Maquis 2001
8 Hôtel Kado
9 SNTN Bus Station
10 Hôtel Wadata
11 Autogare
12 Vietnam Restaurant
13 SNTN Bus Depot
14 Pharmacy
15 Shops

0   250   500 m

River   Kori

To Sokoto
(Nigeria)

The *Hôtel Kado* (☎ 296), across the street at the same intersection, is the best hotel and has friendly, helpful staff. It's an attractive place with air-con singles/doubles with bathroom for CFA8800/9800, and singles with fan and bathroom for CFA5800. The shady restaurant is one of the best in town.

Other places to eat include the *Vietnam Restaurant* just around the corner to the north of the SNTN depot, the buvette *Maquis 2001* and a number of *street stalls*, along the main north-south road.

Getting There & Away

The SNTN bus from Niamey to Zinder departs twice weekly and charges CFA7950 from Niamey to Konni. Between Zinder and Konni it costs CFA8500. There are also large private buses from Niamey to Konni every day; they charge about CFA6000 but are slower. Cheaper still, but even slower (up to

NIGER

nine hours), are 504 bush taxis from Niamey to Konni for CFA5500 (CFA4500 for a minibus).

TAHOUA

Tahoua, 122km north of Konni, is the country's fourth-largest city and a major stop on the Niamey to Agadez road. The main attraction is the large and lively market. Market day (Sunday) attracts a big crowd from outlying areas. For changing money, the BIA-Niger bank usually accepts travellers cheques (although don't count on it), charging a 2% commission.

Worth a visit is the new Centre Artisanal in the town centre, which is particularly good for Tuareg jewellery.

Places to Stay & Eat

If you want a room, go to the *Hôtel Galabi Ader*, north-west of the autogare, where air-con doubles cost CFA7500, or CFA5000 with fan. There's also a restaurant and bar, and a safe and well-shaded camp site for CFA1250 per person, plus CFA500 per car.

Les Bungalows de la Mairie (☎ 61 05 53) across from the town hall has air-con bungalow rooms (infested with mosquitoes) for around CFA8000 and a restaurant which serves good-value European food; there's a shady *bar* in the gardens (*jardin publique*) nearby.

Also worth checking out is the clean and well run *Hôtel l'Amitié* (☎ 61 01 53), also known by the name of its nightclub, Les Galaxies, on the main highway, 200m past the SNTN bus station on the road out of town towards the Niamey to Agadez fork – you won't miss it because of the giraffes outside. It charges around CFA10,000 for air-con rooms, and there's a friendly bar and restaurant with meals from CFA2000.

For traditional African food, head for the popular *Chez Fatima* at the roundabout just east of the BIA-Niger bank. There are several *café men* near the SNTN depot and lots of *food stalls* along the main Niamey to Agadez drag. There's also the upmarket and expensive European *Restaurant les Delices* across from Les Bungalows.

Getting There & Away

The SNTN buses between Niamey and Agadez stop here on Wednesday and Sunday); you join the convoi militaire the next day if you continue to Agadez. The fare between Tahoua and Niamey is CFA10,750. Bush taxis to/from Niamey charge CFA790 and if you choose a decrepit one, the trip can easily take 14 hours.

MARADI

With a population of about 60,000, Maradi is the country's third-largest city. It was destroyed by floods in 1945 but was rebuilt on higher ground. Outside Niamey it remains the administrative capital and commercial centre for agriculture.

To change money, try the BIA-Niger bank on Rue de la Sûreté or Sonibank on Route de Niamey across the road from the market; as everywhere in Niger, commissions on travellers cheques are outrageously high. For black market naira (for Nigeria), try the gare routière 200m north of Sonibank.

Don't miss the **market** in the heart of town on the main north-south drag. Also worth seeing is the **Maison des Chefs** at Place Dan Kasswa on the western side of town, which with its traditional geometric designs, is a fine example of Hausa architecture.

Places to Stay

The cheapest place is the *Campement* in green shady area 2km from the market on the south-western outskirts of town. Old and decaying, it has basic singles with shower for about CFA2200 and doubles for CFA4000. Camping is also possible; the charge is CFA1200 a person.

The *Hôtel Liberté* is on the western side of town at a major intersection, about 200m west of the catholic church near the centre of town. It charges CFA3300/6000 for rooms with shower and fan and CFA850 for better rooms with air-con and bathroom.

Hôtel Arewa, which is much better, is on the northern side of town behind the CNSS building, about 1km from the gare routière and well marked on the main highway.

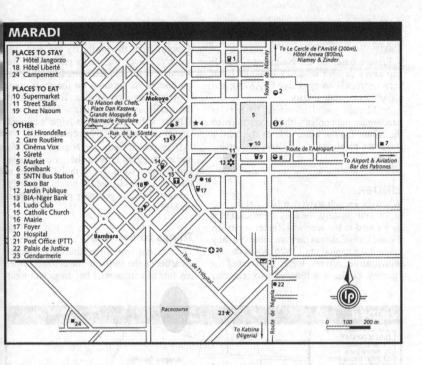

MARADI

PLACES TO STAY
7 Hôtel Jangorzo
18 Hôtel Liberté
24 Campement

PLACES TO EAT
10 Supermarket
11 Street Stalls
19 Chez Naoum

OTHER
1 Les Hirondelles
2 Gare Routière
3 Cinéma Vox
4 Sûreté
5 Market
6 Sonibank
8 SNTN Bus Station
9 Saxo Bar
12 Jardin Publique
13 BIA-Niger Bank
14 Ludo Club
15 Catholic Church
16 Mairie
17 Foyer
20 Hospital
21 Post Office (PTT)
22 Palais de Justice
23 Gendarmerie

To Maison des Chefs, Place Dan Kasswa, Grande Mosquée & Pharmacie Populaire

Mokoyo

Route de Niamey

To Le Cercle de l'Amitié (200m), Hôtel Arewa (800m), Niamey & Zinder

Rue de la Sûreté

Route de l'Aéroport

To Airport & Aviation Bar des Patrones

Bambara

Rue de l'Hôpital

Route de Nigeria

Racecourse

To Katsina (Nigeria)

0   100   200 m

has large clean singles/doubles with shower for CFA7300/9200 (extra for air-con).

The sprawling *Hôtel Jangorzo* (☎ 41 01 40), 500m to the east of the centre on the Route de l'Aéroport, is the nicest hotel but its standards are slipping. Air-con doubles cost CFA13,000 (smaller rooms cost CFA5500) but the plumbing is not the best. On the plus side, the atmosphere is pleasant, and the hotel's Pacific Bar is the hottest place in town at weekends.

Places to Eat

At night you'll find delicious grilled chicken and other snacks on the streets around the jardin publique across from the south-western corner of the market. Another place where the chicken is excellent is the Lebanese-run *Chez Naoum*, about 1km south-west of the centre; meals are around CFA1500.

In the centre, try the tranquil *Le Cercle de l'Amitié* on the main drag, 200m north of the gare routière. Another possibility is *Les Hirondelles* (☎ 41 00 85) facing Ciné Dan Kasswa on the northern side of town, though it's mainly a place for drinking.

Entertainment

For drinks, music and dancing, try the lively *Ludo Club* a couple of blocks north-east of the Hôtel Liberté, the *Foyer* around the corner from the mairie, and the *Saxo Bar* on Route de l'Aéroport across the road from the market. Unusually for West Africa, the airport has a booming restaurant (with good pizzas) and a friendly, relaxed bar, the *Aviation Bar des Patrones*.

Getting There & Away

There are SNTN buses between Niamey and Zinder, via Maradi, twice weekly in

NIGER

each direction. Niamey to Maradi is CFA10,850, and Maradi to Zinder is CFA 4500.

Private buses do the Niamey to Maradi trip every day for around CFA9000. Bush taxis to/from Niamey charge CFA8750, and CFA6500 to/from Dosso.

In Maradi you'll also find bush taxis heading for the border with Nigeria 50km to the south. On the other side of the border there are plenty of cheap 504s to Katsina and Kano.

ZINDER

When the French arrived in Niger at the end of the 19th century, the only significant city they found in the area was Zinder, a city on the old trans-Saharan caravan route. So they made it the capital until 1926, when the administrative offices were transferred to Niamey. Zinder was founded two centuries earlier by Hausa people emigrating from the Kano area. They were soon joined by the Kanouri from the north. By the mid-19th century, Zinder was in its prime. The importance of this old Hausa trading town was because of its location on the trade route between Kano and Agadez. Today, most of the traffic uses the uranium highway via Tahoua, although Zinder is Niger's second-largest city with 85,000 people.

If you want naira for Nigeria, look for moneychangers around the gare routière; you'll need some for a taxi to Kano or Katsina. Don't change too much, as moneychangers in Kano generally give better rates for US$.

Things to See & Do

The city has two old sections: the **Zengou Quartier** on the northern side of town, which has lots of commercial buildings and mud-

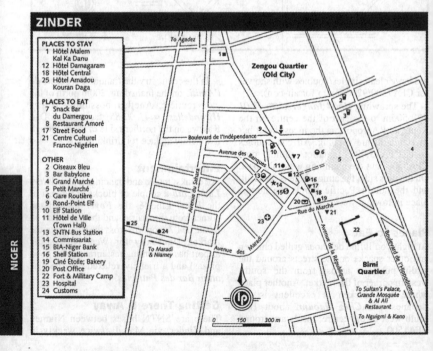

ZINDER

PLACES TO STAY
1 Hôtel Malem
   Kal Ka Danu
12 Hôtel Damagaram
18 Hôtel Central
25 Hôtel Amadou
   Kouran Daga

PLACES TO EAT
7 Snack Bar
   du Damergou
8 Restaurant Amoré
17 Street Food
21 Centre Culturel
   Franco-Nigérien

OTHER
2 Oiseaux Bleu
3 Bar Babylone
4 Grand Marché
5 Petit Marché
6 Gare Routière
9 Rond-Point Elf
10 Elf Station
11 Hôtel de Ville
   (Town Hall)
13 SNTN Bus Station
14 Commissariat
15 BIA-Niger Bank
16 Shell Station
19 Ciné Étoile; Bakery
20 Post Office
22 Fort & Military Camp
23 Hospital
24 Customs

To Agadez

Zengou Quartier
(Old City)

Boulevard de l'Indépendance

Avenue des Banques

Avenue du Sahara

Avenue des Marché

Rue du Marché

Avenue de la République

To Maradi
& Niamey

Birni
Quartier

To Sultan's Palace,
Grande Mosquée
& Al Ali
Restaurant

To Nguigmi & Kano

0   150   300 m

brick houses; and the picturesque **Birni Quartier** to the south-east. They are separated by the modern area with its wide streets, hotels, banks, markets and the gare routière.

A stroll through the narrow streets of the Birni Quartier is highly recommended. You'll find small gardens, friendly people, an old French fort on a hill overlooking the area and, best of all, some fine examples of traditional **Hausa architecture**. Even in Nigeria you won't see such a well preserved area of traditional Hausa buildings. The old *banco* (mud brick) houses are everywhere, easily identified by the geometrical designs in relief, usually colourfully painted. A good place to start is the **Grande Mosquée**, as there are some fine examples nearby. Behind it is the **Sultan's Palace**, built in the mid-19th century. Also worth checking out are the **markets**, which are some of the liveliest in Niger – the big day is Thursday. Look for leather goods as the best *artisans de cuir* in Niger are here. Be careful, though; Zinder seems to have more than its fair share of aggressive touts and rip-offs galore.

Places to Stay

One of the cheapest places is the homely *Hôtel Malem Kal Ka Danu* (☎ 51 05 68) on the main drag, 700m north of the town centre. The friendly owner charges CFA 3000/4000 for clean singles/doubles with fan and shared bucket shower (CFA6000 with bathroom). Cheap meals are available. You could inquire about other cheap places around the autogare.

The lively *Hôtel Central* (☎ 51 20 47) diagonally across the road from the post office, and once the favourite of British overland trucks, has recently taken a downward slide. Large doubles with fan/air-con go for about CFA8500/9500, although the air-con doesn't always work. The pleasant outdoor terrace is the city's most popular rendezvous in the evenings for expats, prostitutes and locals, and the food isn't bad either (chicken couscous is CFA2500). It is infested with touts, however, with the tenacity of leeches.

Zinder has two good quality hotels. *Hôtel Damagaram* (☎ 51 03 03) in the heart of

town on the main north-south drag has decent air-con doubles for about CFA10,000. It has a restaurant, a shaded patio and a modern nightclub at weekends with a CFA 1000 cover charge and drinks for CFA500.

Zinder's most prestigious hotel, and almost identically priced, is the newer, more tranquil *Amadou Kouran Daga* (☎ 51 07 42) on the road to Niamey on the western outskirts of town. It has attractive rooms with air-con (CFA10,500), a good restaurant and a pleasant terrace bar. As at the Damagaram, the water is often cut off during the day.

Places to Eat

Some of the best *street food* can be found in the square in front of Hôtel Central and on Blvd de l'Indépendance by the gare routière. There is a good *bakery* next door to the Ciné Etoile on the Rue du Marché, or try the *Snack Bar du Damergou* almost opposite the Hôtel Le Damagaram. All of the African favourites can be tasted underneath the *paillotes* at *Al Ali Restaurant*, on the road to the Sultan's Palace, and prices are reasonable.

For good food, including brochettes, *pâte* and chicken, head for the outdoor *Restaurant Amoré*; it's on Rond-Point Elf. Better still is the food at the *Centre Culturel Franco-Nigérien*, also on Rue du Marché; riz sauce is CFA1000, spaghetti CFA700 and big beers CFA420.

Entertainment

Near the Grand Marché are two popular bars, *Oiseaux Bleu* and *Bar Babylone*. For a better time, go with locals, as they are more likely to get you home along the labyrinthine streets with a degree of safety.

The *Centre Culturel Franco-Nigérien* screens movies at 8.30 pm on Monday and Friday and admission is CFA1000 for foreigners and CFA300 for locals. Occasionally, good movies are screened at *Ciné Etoile* on Rue du Marché.

Getting There & Away

SNTN buses (CFA14,500, 14 hours) run twice weekly in each direction between Niamey and Zinder. In Zinder, the SNTN

NIGER

bus station is on Ave des Banques, a couple of blocks north-west of Hôtel Central. Bush taxis run daily between Zinder and Niamey for CFA11,000; they leave from the gare routière near the Petit Marché.

SNTN buses between Zinder and Agadez only go once a week in each direction for CFA6800 (luggage is about CFA500) – you have to go with the convoi militaire. Bush taxis run between Zinder and Diffa, on the road to Chad, for CFA6000. Some go on to Nguigmi and charge CFA8500 for the whole trip.

If you're heading to Kano in Nigeria, you'll have no problem finding a bush taxi in the morning. The Zinder to Kano price is CFA3500. You can save money by going just to the border, from where Nigerian bush taxis will take you to Kano for the equivalent of about CFA800.

NGUIGMI

Nguigmi is a small town in the far east of Niger, at the end of the tar road, and the last settlement of any size before you reach Chad. The town has no hotels. There is a lively market area to the south of town where you can buy brochettes.

There are a few bush taxis between Zinder and Nguigmi, charging CFA8500. For transport to/from Chad, see the main Getting There & Away section earlier in this chapter. Realise that entry into Chad at this point is fraught with danger.

The North

AGADEZ

With its sandy streets, fine Sahel-style mud architecture, and Tuareg nomads, Agadez is a fascinating place. Like Timbuktu, it was a great city in medieval times due to its strategic position on the trans-Saharan trade routes.

Today, camels no longer carry gold and slaves across the desert but, unlike Timbuktu which seems to be dying, Agadez continues to thrive because of its important

Warning

When we visited Agadez in 1998 – with the military convoy from Niamey – it was reasonably safe to travel. Banditry is still rife and it is not a good idea (and probably illegal) to travel between towns in the north alone – eg Agadez to Zinder or Arlit. Check on the current situation before proceeding. Travellers have been killed for their vehicles.

Whichever way you're travelling, don't forget to get your passport stamped at the commissariat. If you fail to do this and continue on to Arlit, Niamey or Zinder, you may be constantly hassled by police along the way.

location on the uranium highway, and as a supply stop for trucks crossing the Sahara.

In the 1990s Agadez hit a slump but the city has seen the good times come and go before. In the 16th century, with a population of 30,000 people, it thrived off the gold caravans plying between Gao and Tripoli. As the gold trade waned, so did the city's population: down to about 3000 by 1900. Now, it's back up to 30,000, with uranium, the Trans-Saharan highway and Tuareg refugees all contributing.

Unfortunately, the success of this trade has also given rise to tribes of hustlers bent on making money from travellers one way or another. Most locals scorn the hustlers as well. You'll just have to learn to recognise them, then avoid them (but sometimes it is impossible to avoid them).

Information

Tourist Office The ONT (☎ 44 00 80) is on the city's main drag, south of the turn-off for Arlit. It's open from 7.30 am to 12.30 pm and 3 to 6 pm Monday to Friday and on Saturday morning. You can get a free map of the city here and approval of your itinerary for travelling in the Aïr Massif (if travel is possible). This is obligatory, as is a guide. We no longer recommend individual guides

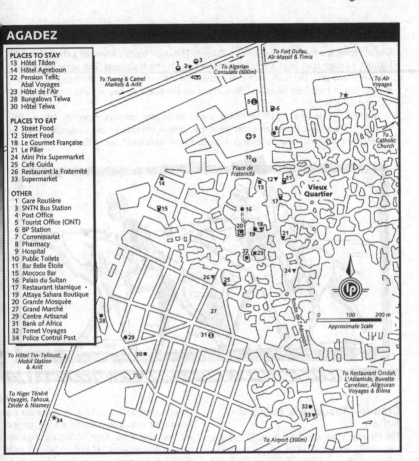

AGADEZ

PLACES TO STAY
13 Hôtel Tilden
14 Hôtel Agreboun
22 Pension Tellit;
   Abal Voyages
23 Hôtel de l'Aïr
28 Bungalows Telwa
30 Hôtel Telwa

PLACES TO EAT
2 Street Food
12 Street Food
18 Le Gourmet Française
21 Le Pilier
24 Mini Prix Supermarket
25 Café Guida
26 Restaurant la Fraternité
33 Supermarket

OTHER
1 Gare Routière
3 SNTN Bus Station
4 Post Office
5 Tourist Office (ONT)
6 BP Station
7 Commissariat
8 Pharmacy
9 Hospital
10 Public Toilets
11 Bar Belle Étoile
15 Mococo Bar
16 Palais du Sultan
17 Restaurant Islamique
19 Attaya Sahara Boutique
20 Grande Mosquée
27 Grand Marché
29 Centre Artisanal
31 Bank of Africa
32 Temet Voyages
34 Police Control Post

To Fort Dufau,
Aïr Massif & Timia

To Algerian
Consulate (600m)

To Tuareg & Camel
Markets & Arlit

To Aïr
Voyages

To
Catholic
Church

Place de
Fraternité

Vieux
Quartier

Route de l'Aéroport

Approximate Scale
0   100   200 m

To Hôtel Tin-Telioust,
Mobil Station
& Arlit

To Niger Ténéré
Voyages, Tahoua,
Zinder & Niamey

To Restaurant Oridah,
L'Atlantide, Buvette
Carrefour, Aligouran
Voyages & Bilma

To Airport (300m)

---

by name – get personal recommendations from other travellers if you can.

Money Most travellers change money with shopkeepers, as rates for cash are better than at the bank, although travellers cheques come in for a hefty commission.

Travel Agencies & Tour Operators
Aligouran Voyages (☎ 44 00 94), east of the centre on the road towards Bilma, is still in operation. Other possibilities are the ONT,

Aïr Voyages (☎ 44 01 25), Abal Voyages (☎ 44 01 25), Bagzane Voyages (☎ 44 08 76), Niger Ténéré Voyages, also known as the Société de Voyage Saharien (SVS; ☎ 44 02 74; BP 10734 Niamey) and Temet Voyages (☎ 44 00 51) on the road to the airport, 400m south-east of the Grand Marché.

Tours range from short camel rides on the Agadez outskirts through to trips to the Aïr Massif (starting at CFA50,000 per person per day for groups of four), and major expeditions into the Ténéré Desert or beyond.

Camel Racing

Camel racing is a favourite sport of the Tuareg. The usual routine involves a champion rider taking an indigo scarf from a woman and heading off into the desert. The other riders try to catch him and grab the scarf. Whoever succeeds is the winner. During the race, the women, decked out in their best silver jewellery, cheer on the riders by singing and clapping to the sound of drums.

The best time to be in Agadez is during one of the Muslim holidays, especially Tabaski. Following the feast, you can see one of the great spectacles of the desert – the 'cavalcade', a furious camel race through the narrow crowded streets to the square in front of the Palais du Sultan.

Grande Mosquée & Palais du Sultan

The Grande Mosquée dates from 1515 but it was totally rebuilt in 1844. Its pyramid-like minaret with wooden scaffolding is a classic of Sahel-style architecture and affords a view of the Aïr Massif. If you're not sporting lots of camera equipment, a CFA1000 *cadeau* is often sufficient to persuade the guardian to let you climb 27m to the top for photographs.

The three storey building just north of the mosque is the Palais du Sultan, the residence of the city's traditional ruler.

Markets

The **Grand Marché** near the mosque is the most animated place in town. The variety of people here, many dressed in traditional desert costumes, is at least as interesting as what's for sale. You can find a wide range of art and craftwork here including rugs and Tuareg leatherwork. If you're buying gold, silver or bronze, you're less likely to be cheated if you deal directly with the artisans.

There is also a **Tuareg market** on the north-western outskirts of town where the Tuaregs will trade just about anything with you. The best time to see it is in February when the salt caravans arrive with hundreds of camels. Sitting down for endless cups of tea is a highlight, but don't pay more than CFA1500 for a kilo of desert 'Tuareg tea' (in spite of what the touts and others tell you). If you wish to take photographs request permission from the chief of the market and expect to pay (perhaps CFA2500).

The marvellous **camel market**, part of the Tuareg market, is another must-see. It has wonderful colours – and not so wonderful smells emanating from the camels, goats and other animals for sale. You must get here early as the activity is over by 10.30 am.

Vieux Quartier

For a slightly more tranquil experience, head for the Vieux Quartier, the old section of town which surrounds the market, particularly the district facing the mosque. With its small crooked streets, tiny shops and interesting old Sahel-style houses with Hausa-inspired designs, it's the best place to go roaming around. Just ask for the houses with '*les belles façades*' (meaning 'beautiful façades'). You'll also find all kinds of artisan shops, including silversmiths making the famous croix d'Agadez (for more details see the colour feature between pages 672 and 673), leatherworkers producing Tuareg *samaras* (sandals), *coussins* (cushions) and magnificent *selles de chameau* (camel saddles), and bronzesmiths making a variety of objects, including jewellery.

The bargaining is intense but not disagreeable. You can usually take photographs of the artisans at work.

Camel Rides

For a bit of adventure, you can take a camel ride into the surrounding area for several days. Any number of Tuareg guides will do this. The price is often quoted for the camel and the guide, and starts at CFA15,000 per day (although there seems to be no distance limit). Just make sure your arrangements are absolutely clear before you start because unexpected extra charges always creep in. It is best that one of the travel agencies make all the arrangements for you. Permission from the *commissariat* is also required before you leave.

Places to Stay – Budget

Camping is no longer recommended. With the dearth of travellers in Agadez at this time, every crook in town flocks to your person and gear ready to rip off whatever is not tied down.

When the Paris-Dakar Motor Rally comes through Agadez (usually in January) hotel prices jump to three or four times the normal.

It's hard to beat the friendly *Hôtel Agreboun* (☎ 44 03 07), on the western edge of town, several blocks from the mosque. Run by a friendly Tuareg man, it has nine clean singles/doubles with fan and shower for CFA3000/4000 (more with air-con), a restaurant and a sandy courtyard where you can have cheap beers, park your car and, to be a bit cooler, drag your mattress out for sleeping.

If the Agreboun is full, try the equally friendly *Hôtel Tilden*, in the centre of town in Place de la Fraternité, which has doubles with fan/air-con for CFA10,000/12,000 and a bar and restaurant. Out near the Mobil station on the Niamey to Arlit road is the *Hôtel Tin-Telloust*, a newer, comfortable place with rooms for the same price as the Tilden; it also has a bar and restaurant.

Places to Stay – Mid-Range

If you're into history and atmosphere, the best place to stay is the famous and once-elegant *Hôtel de l'Aïr* (☎ 44 01 47), in the centre of town with a perfect view of the Grande Mosquée. Architecturally fascinating, with 1m-thick walls, the Aïr was formerly a Sultan's residence. Today, its rooms are not so grand, costing CFA13,500 for one or two people with fan and shared bathroom or CFA15,000 for a self-contained air-con double. Older rooms, actually in the palace itself, are a bit cheaper. There's no hot water but near the Sahara, who needs it? The restaurant has little to recommend it other than its architectural splendour, but a drink on the roof-top terrace, with great views of the city, is a real treat. The food is expensive – steak with beans is CFA3000 and spaghetti CFA2500.

If you're into comfort, and money is not a big problem, head for the friendly *Pension Tellit* (☎ 44 02 31), opposite the Aïr, which has excellent staff and a friendly Italian manager. The four rooms each have air-con,

NIGER

fan, small refrigerator and bathroom with hot water. Rooms for one to four people range from CFA12,250 (a single) to CFA26,000 (a suite).

Another possibility is the *Hôtel Telwa* (☎ 41 01 64) two blocks south-west of the Grand Marché. It lacks the Aïr's charm, but it's a decent government-run hotel with more comfortable rooms, costing from CFA10,000 to CFA15,000; the more expensive ones have air-con. About 200m to the north are the smart and secure *Bungalows Telwa* (☎ 44 02 64), connected to the hotel of the same name, where singles/doubles with TV and fridge cost CFA12,500/15,000 and an extra bed is CFA2000.

Places to Eat

For *street food*, check out the main northern road near the gare routière, on the eastern side of Place de la Fraternité or around the market. The *Café Guida* and *Restaurant la Fraternité*, across the road from the Grand Marché, are cheap alternatives with a good selection of Tuareg specialities. Self-caterers could try the *Mini Prix supermarket* on the road to the airport.

Probably the best of the traditional Sahel restaurants is *L'Atlantide* just off the road to Bilma in the Sabon Gari area, to the east of the Vieux Quartier. Here salads are CFA500, kebabs CFA700, *viande Tuareg* CFA800 and couscous CFA1300. Nearby is the equally pleasant *Restaurant Oridah*, where main meals are in the CFA700 to CFA1350 bracket.

European alternatives are *Le Gourmet Française*, to the east of the mosque, which in spite of its name also has a number of local dishes; and the very expensive *Le Pilier* (☎ 44 03 31), on Route de l'Aéroport, which has expensive Italian dishes (in the CFA5000 to CFA7000 range).

Entertainment

There are a number of good bars in town. Local hang-outs include the *Mococo Bar*, a block south of the Hôtel Agreboun, which often has musicians; *Restaurant Islamique* a block south of Place de Fraternité in the centre opposite the Mobil station; and the *Bar Belle Étoile* in the Vieux Quartier, not far from the Islamique. Best of all, however, is the open-air *Buvette Carrefour*, just along the street from the Restaurant Oridah on the road to Bilma. Meals and drinks here are cheap, the garden with its paillotes is pleasant and the staff are friendly.

Shopping

For buying jewellery and seeing silversmiths at work check out the Centre Artisanal on the south-western edge of town, or the Attaya Sahara Boutique near the mosque. At both places, some bargaining is required.

Getting There & Away

At the time of writing, two buses a week were leaving Niamey on Sunday and Wednesday for Agadez. The overnight stop is in Tahoua and the buses continue on to Agadez the next day and to Arlit the day after with the military convoy. There is a bus in the other direction which leaves Arlit on Sunday and Wednesday. The fare between Niamey and Agadez is about CFA17,600. The fare from Niamey to Arlit is CFA22,000. The SNTN bus station is next to the gare routière north of the town centre on the road to Arlit. The bus fare from Agadez to Arlit is CFA5000.

For details on the route between Agadez and Zinder, see the Zinder Getting There & Away section earlier in this chapter.

AÏR MASSIF & TÉNÉRÉ DESERT

Agadez is the main jumping-off point for expeditions into some of the most spectacular desert and mountain scenery in Africa. There are three principal zones: the Aïr Massif immediately to the north and north-east of Agadez, the Ténéré Desert further east and, to the north-east, the Plateau du Djado, about 1000km from Agadez via Bilma.

The Aïr Massif is close enough for travellers with wheels (or the money for a tour) and a few free days to visit. The other two destinations are extremely remote and require a lot more time and effort. A guide (or driver) and government authorisation are required for all trips; check at the ONT in Agadez before setting off.

Aïr Massif

The Aïr Massif is one of the most spectacular sights in West Africa. Covering an area the size of Switzerland, these mountains are of dark volcanic rock capped with unusually shaped peaks, the highest being Mt Bagzane (2022m), 145km from Agadez. They aren't as bare as the Hoggar Mountains in Algeria, and many different trees, plants and animals can be seen, including goats, camels, antelopes and birds.

The main route is rough but compacted and fairly well marked on the Michelin map. From Agadez the road goes north-east 45km to a fork in the road, called Téloua. The left fork takes you to the hot thermal springs at **Tafadek**; the right fork takes an anticlockwise route that rejoins the main road just before Elméki. On taking the left fork, after about 15km the road forks again; the left one goes to Tafadek and the right goes to Elméki, 65km to the north-east.

The next stop past Elméki is Kreb-Kreb, then the lovely green oasis of **Timia**, some 110km from Elméki. Timia is the second major destination on many tours and the waterfalls near town are a 'don't miss' attraction. The next oasis further north is Assodé, then **Iferouâne**, 180km north of Timia and 160km east of Arlit. This is a good place to stop as the oasis is beautiful and there are some interesting prehistoric sites in the area. You could then backtrack or head west to Arlit.

Ténéré Desert

The Ténéré Desert, some 500km as the crow flies north-east of Agadez, is an area of sand dunes and monotonous flat areas of hard sand. The desert is reputed to have some of the most extraordinarily beautiful sand dune areas in the entire Sahara. You'll need several days to reach them, so at a minimum it's a one week trip, preferably more. At least two vehicles are required for safety reasons. There are two main routes, both notoriously

difficult: east towards Bilma and then north, or north to Iferouâne and Tadéra, then east.

Heading east from Agadez towards Bilma, you'll come to Tazolé after 100km. To the south is a **dinosaur cemetery**, one of the world's most important ones. The fossils are spread over a belt 150km long. Continually covered and uncovered by the sand, they are silent witness to the fact that the whole Sahara Desert was once green and fertile. You may see a number of species, maybe even fossilised crocodiles.

After another 179km, you'll pass the famous **Arbre du Ténéré**, the only tree in Africa marked on the Michelin map – except it no longer exists. This sole tree in the middle of the desert, over 400km from the next nearest tree – the last acacia of the once great Saharan forests – was hit in 1973 by a Libyan truck driver. Incredible. All you'll see is a metal replica; the remnants of the real thing are in the museum in Niamey.

Some 171km further east is the salt-producing oasis of Fachi and, 610km from Agadez, **Bilma**, which is truly the end of the earth. This town satisfies every thought you ever had of an exotic oasis in the middle of a forbidding desert. It is fortified and surrounded by palm trees and irrigated gardens – everywhere are piles of salt destined for the market towns of southern Niger and northern Nigeria.

Years ago, there were caravans (*azalai*), 20,000 camels long, that did the trip from Agadez to pick up the salt. Today, they still come but not nearly as frequently and are only a fraction of the size. You'll see how salt is purified and poured into moulds made from large palm trunks, giving the salt its loaf-like form (in contrast, for example, to the door-like slabs from Mali).

If you continue on to the **Plateau du Djado** (a 10 to 14 day round trip from Agadez), you'll see some of the prehistoric cave paintings of antelope, giraffe and rhino for which the area is noted.

Getting There & Away

Note that there is no public transport to this area (for foreigners at least). You can only

NIGER

come here with a tour (see earlier) or in a private vehicle with a guide.

The ONT (☎ 44 00 80) in Agadez can help to arrange tours. For details of other tour operators in Agadez, see Information in the Agadez section earlier.

The price per person can be very high if you take an all-inclusive tour with tents, food, guide etc. For example, a seven day excursion that includes most of the Aïr Massif and the dunes at Temet, or a 12 day excursion that includes much of the Aïr Massif and the Ténéré Desert all the way to the Plateau du Djado, could start at CFA 60,000 per person per day.

Renting a vehicle is a lot cheaper than an all-inclusive tour – ask at the travel agencies mentioned earlier or the tourist office. You should also get the latest safety information from them before setting off. If you bargain well, a five passenger Land Rover and driver plus a guide (compulsory) and all food and petrol will cost about CFA100,000 a day.

If you leave one day at 4 pm and return the next at 3 pm you'll be charged for two full days. Discuss the itinerary in detail and, best of all, put something in writing or draw a map so the driver can't claim a misunderstanding. And keep hold of your documents.

ARLIT

Uranium was discovered here in 1965. Six years later, SOMAIR, the uranium mining company, created Arlit, Niger's most northern major town. Since then, this dusty

mining settlement has grown considerably. If you are here it is likely that you are on business. Very few travellers would bother passing through Arlit unless the trans-Saharan route from Tamanrasset (Algeria) to Assamakka was reopened.

The *Hôtel l'Auberge la Caravane* (☎ 45 22 78), in the centre west of the main street, has closed most of its rooms with the demise of the trans-Saharan trade. It has doubles with fan for around CFA7000 (CFA10,000 with air-con). Around the corner is the *Hôtel Tamesna* (☎ 45 23 30 or 45 23 32) which functions now as a bar and nightclub.

Behind the Tamesna you'll find the *Café des Arts* doing excellent meals for around CFA1200. Two other recommended bar-restaurants are *Au Bon Coin* and *Le Refuge*, both of which serve inexpensive European and African dishes. The bar-dancing *Sahel 2* is also a good place to enjoy a desert evening.

See Getting There & Away in the Agadez section of this chapter for details of buses between Niamey, Agadez and Arlit.

ASSAMAKKA

Assamakka, 200km north-west of Arlit, is a border checkpoint. At this time it is too dangerous to travel the trans-Saharan route north to Tamanrasset in Algeria; many people, travellers included, have been murdered near this border. It is almost certain that for a long time to come you will not be allowed to travel across the Algerian border north of Arlit.

WEST AFRICAN FIGURATIVE SCULPTURE

African tribal sculpture is considered one of the most dynamic and influential artforms. Once relegated to curio cabinets and dusty museum store rooms, and labelled as crude, barbaric and primitive, African carving was 'discovered' in the early 20th century by Picasso, Matisse, and other artists who found inspiration in its radical approach to the human form. The strange and uncompromising forms found in West African sculpture are not the unique creations of an inspired artist. The sculptures are made to fulfil specific functions required in tribal society.

Top: Dual spirits – Yoruba *ibeji* twins. Among the Yoruba, who have a particularly high rate of twin births, twins are welcomed as bringing good fortune to their parents, and are believed to be powerful spirits.

Bottom: Senoufo rhythm pounder (left) – these figures are used in dances in initiation ceremonies to mark the rhythm; they are lifted by their arms and the heavy bases are thumped on the ground. Stick figures – Senoufo pair (middle) and Lobi (right).

In West Africa, sculpture is mostly used in connection with ancestor or spirit worship. Many tribal groups believe that the spirit of the dead can have major effects, both positive and negative, on a person's life. Ancestor figures are carved and placed in shrines and altars where they receive libations and sacrificial blood. Some tribes carve figures which are cared for by women to ensure fertility and in the hope that the child will inherit the fine looks represented in the sculpture. The famous *akuaba* 'doll' of the Ashanti is the best known example of this. Prestige objects are also carved, such as figurative staffs of office, commemorative statues and other regalia which are used by kings, chiefs, traditional healers and diviners as emblems of power.

West African sculpture is usually created by a professional artist, usually male, who has learnt his craft via an apprenticeship. Mostly a family or caste-based occupation, the specific forms and skills required are passed down from generation to generation resulting in highly refined styles. Some tribes have no professional carvers, and the work is carved by any member of the group.

Top: Fanti fertility dolls (left) and Mossi fertility figure (right)

Bottom: Perfect pairs – Yoruba figures in traditional dress (left) and colonial-style dress (middle); seated Dogon pair (right).

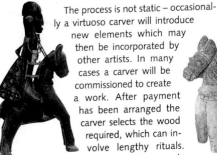

The process is not static – occasionally a virtuoso carver will introduce new elements which may then be incorporated by other artists. In many cases a carver will be commissioned to create a work. After payment has been arranged the carver selects the wood required, which can involve lengthy rituals. The carver blocks out the form using an adze, completing the finer details with a knife and, traditionally, sanding the carving with a species of rough leaf.

Of the many different tribal styles produced in West Africa, some common characteristics can be identified. Usually symmetrical, the figure faces forward, the features impassive and the arms held to the side with the legs slightly bent at the knees. Certain features may be exaggerated, and the head is almost always large in proportion to the body. The

Top: Equestrian figures – Bambara (left) and old terracotta figure from Djenné in Mali (right).

Bottom, from left to right: Baoulé, Lobi and Bambara figures

ALL PHOTOS BY DENNIS WISKEN/SIDEWALK GALLERY

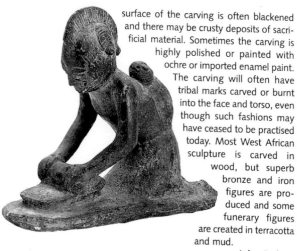

surface of the carving is often blackened and there may be crusty deposits of sacrificial material. Sometimes the carving is highly polished or painted with ochre or imported enamel paint. The carving will often have tribal marks carved or burnt into the face and torso, even though such fashions may have ceased to be practised today. Most West African sculpture is carved in wood, but superb bronze and iron figures are produced and some funerary figures are created in terracotta and mud.

John Graham

Top: Woman grinding grain (terracotta, Lobi). She carries a baby in typical West African fashion on her back.

Bottom, from left to right: Baoulé carving showing the exaggeratedly large head and trunk that is characteristic of the sculpture of many West African peoples, and seated Dogon man.

Nigeria

Nigeria is the veritable giant of West Africa. Recognised as the region's most influential country economically and militarily, it has more than half the area's population and one of its most highly educated workforces.

It is also off most travellers lists as a place to visit – its sights only accessible to the spartan ascetic or the truly masochistic voyager. And yet, if you don't visit, you can hardly say you've been to West Africa. Remember also, before you rush to pack your bags, that Nigeria was rated the world's most corrupt country (out of 52) in a Corruption Perception Index compiled by a Berlin company.

No visit to Nigeria is complete without some time in Lagos – West Africa's largest city and, by many criteria, Africa's worst, with one of the highest crime rates. The current harsh penalties meted out to armed robbers (death by firing squad with the scantiest of trials) and the accompanying 'Operation Sweep' have made conditions a little safer for travellers and locals. The biggest problem throughout the country is lack of fuel, giving rise to riots, lack of transport between cities and economic depression.

Places such as Kano, Katsina, Zaria, Jos, Sokoto, Calabar, Abraka, Maiduguri, villages in the delta states of Bayelsa and Rivers and the mountains in the far east along the Cameroon border are respites for those who don't appreciate the overwhelming bustle of Lagos and Ibadan. However, these places also have periodic flares of violence, lawlessness, curfews and frequent rough military intervention.

Facts about Nigeria

HISTORY

Northern and southern Nigeria are essentially two different countries, and their histories reflect this disparity. The first recorded empire to flourish in this part of West Africa was Kanem-Borno in the north around Lake

NIGERIA AT A GLANCE

Capital: Abuja
Population: 100 million
Area: 924,000 sq km
Head of state: General Abdulsalam Abubakar
Official language: English
Main local languages: Hausa, Igbo, Yoruba
Currency: Naira
Exchange rate: US$1 = N80
Time: GMT/UTC +1
Country telephone code: ☎ 234
Best time to go: Year-round

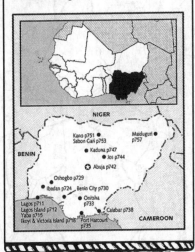

Chad. Its wealth was based on control of the important trans-Saharan trade routes from West Africa to the Mediterranean and the Middle East. Islam became the state religion quite early in Kanem-Borno's history. A number of Islamic Hausa kingdoms also flourished between the 11th and 14th centuries, based around the cities of Kano, Zaria and Nupe.

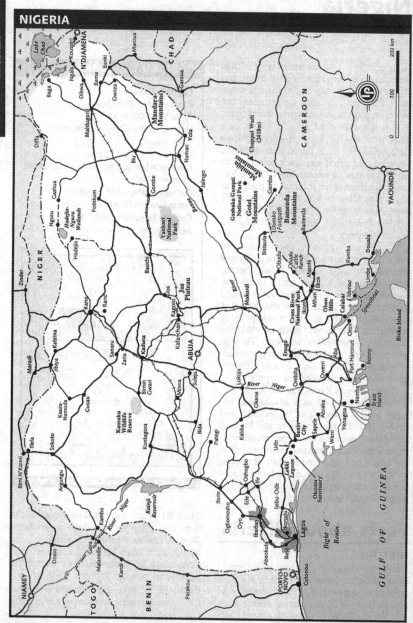

In the south-west a number of Yoruba kingdoms sprang up between the 14th and 15th centuries, centred in Ife, Oyo and Benin City, which became important centres of trade. The most famous was the Kingdom of Benin, which produced some of the finest bronze artwork in Africa. The political systems of these states rested largely on a sacred monarchy with a strong court bureaucracy, each retaining its traditional religion. Islam made very little headway here until the late 18th century. The obas (kings) of these traditional states retain considerable influence today. In the south-east, the Igbo and other peoples never developed any centralised empires but instead formed loose confederations. People here depended on agriculture, and a strong military was not needed.

The Colonial Period

The first contact between the Yoruba empires and Europeans was made in the 15th century by the Portuguese, who began trading in pepper, later supplanted by the more lucrative trade in slaves. In contrast, the northern Islamic states continued to trade principally across the Sahara and remained untouched by Europeans until well into the 19th century.

The Portuguese were gradually replaced by the northern European maritime nations throughout the 16th and 17th centuries, during which time the slave trade expanded dramatically (for more information on the slave trade, see the boxed text on p23).

In the north, important changes occurred towards the end of the slave-trade era. There was a revolutionary upheaval in the Hausa kingdoms by Fulani religious zealots (previously subjugated by the Hausa), leading to the replacement of the Hausa kings with Fulani rulers. They set up a caliphate based in Sokoto, and set about revitalising Islamic values.

During the so-called 'Scramble for Africa' in the late 19th century, Britain sent armies to Nigeria, storming Kano in 1902. Once military conquest was completed, the British ruled indirectly through local kings and chiefs, thereby guaranteeing a stable envir-

onment from which economic surplus could be extracted without disruption. The policy worked well in the north, but much less so in the south-west where none of the traditional Yoruba rulers had ever extracted taxes. In the south-east, where there had never been any centralised authority, the policy was even less successful.

Independence

As the demand for independence gathered force after WWII, the British attempted to put together a constitution taking into account the interests of the three main areas of the colony: the Hausa-dominated north, the Igbo-dominated south-east and the Yoruba-dominated south-west. It proved a difficult task. The northerners feared that the southerners had an educational advantage which would allow them to dominate politics and commerce. There was likewise considerable mistrust among southerners – a result of fierce competition for jobs in the civil service and for business contracts. The British solution was to divide the country into three regions, along ethnic lines. Each region was given its own civil service, judiciary and marketing boards (the main earners of foreign exchange).

Tensions arose over who was to dominate the federal parliament in Lagos. In the hard-fought elections of 1959, the Northern Peoples Congress party came out ahead but failed to win a majority. Its leader, Sir Abubakar Tafawa Balewa, a moderate northerner, was asked by the British to form a government.

The coalition government of the First Republic was a disaster. National politics degenerated into a vicious power game, corruption became rampant and the elite accumulated wealth by any means possible. The elections of 1965 were so outrageously rigged that protesting groups went on a rampage.

In early 1966, a group of young army officers, most of whom were Igbo, staged a coup. The prime minister, the premiers of the north and west and most of the senior army officers were assassinated. The head of the army, General Ironsi, an Igbo, took over as head of state.

Ironsi's accession to power was welcomed by many sections of the Nigerian public but it didn't last long. A few months later he was killed in a coup staged by a group of northern army officers after anti-Igbo riots had broken out in the north. A new regime was set up under the leadership of Lt Colonel Yakabu Gowon, a Christian from a minority group in the north.

The coup was viewed with horror in the east and the military commander of the area, Lt Colonel Ojukwu refused to recognise Gowon as the new head of state. His antipathy to the new regime was sealed when large-scale massacres of Igbo again took place in the north, triggering a return to the east of thousands of Igbo from all over the country. In May 1967, Ojukwu announced the secession of the east and the creation of the independent state of Biafra. Civil war began.

Seeing an opportunity to secure drilling rights in oil-rich Biafra, France and other countries threw their support behind the republic. Washington supported the federal government, but the press was pro-Biafra, showing scenes of mass starvation. Biafra was recognised by only a handful of African countries. The civil war dragged on for three years as the Igbo forces fought tooth and claw for every inch of territory that the federal forces took back. By early 1970, as a result of the blockade imposed by the federal government, Biafra faced famine and its forces were forced to capitulate. Somewhere between 500,000 and two million Biafran civilians had died, mainly from starvation.

Oil Boom

Reconciliation was swift and peaceful, and the horrors of the war were eclipsed in part by the oil boom. Oil production increased sevenfold between 1965 and 1973, and world prices rocketed. By 1975, Nigeria found itself with a US$5 billion surplus. The military government under Gowon went on a spending spree. Foreign contractors rushed to Lagos. Corruption was rife, and crime

was rampant – the chaos became unbearable. In July 1975, Gowon was overthrown in a bloodless coup led by General Murtala Mohammed.

The new government launched a clean-up of the civil service, the judiciary and the universities. However, despite his widespread popularity, Mohammed was assassinated in a coup attempt in early 1976. Other members of the regime survived and continued to implement his policies. In 1979, the military leaders declared they would adopt a US-style constitution and handed power back to a civilian government following elections in 1979. A northerner, Shehu Shagari was sworn in as president.

Within four years, the Second Republic had fallen. With Nigeria at the height of its political influence, Shagari squandered the country's wealth on grandiose and ill-considered projects until the next crisis loomed in the early 1980s when the price of oil plummeted and the supply of easy money dried up.

Unpaid contractors packed up and left. In an attempt to shore up the crumbling edifice, Shagari turned to bartering oil for essential commodities such as foodstuffs and transport. Next he turned on the millions of West Africans who had flocked to Nigeria in search of work during the oil boom. Some three million of them were suddenly expelled, causing massive disruption, unemployment and food shortages in neighbouring countries. Nigeria's action almost destroyed ECOWAS. On New Year's Eve 1983 Shagari was overthrown in a military coup, headed by General Mohammed Bahari.

Bahari clamped down heavily on corruption and made bold moves to get the country back on track economically. Many of Shagari's grandiose projects were postponed or cancelled. However, during Bahari's rule there were widespread abuses of civil liberties: torture, arbitrary arrests and incarceration without trial became common. In 1985, he was overthrown in another coup – the sixth since independence

– led by the army's chief of staff, General Ibrahim Babangida.

The Babangida Years

Babangida, the new head of state, gained instant popularity by releasing political prisoners, and by lifting press controls. Babangida also started something of an economic revolution. Going further than the IMF dared recommend, he devalued the naira fourfold, dismantled many of the major marketing boards, and privatised unprofitable public enterprises.

But devaluation and the other economic measures bore little fruit. Oil revenues dropped again and the country's debt rose to US$20 billion. Crime increased, with the police and soldiers often being the worst culprits. The country was broke.

A year after taking office, Babangida announced he would hand over power to a civilian government in 1990. In 1989, in the Abuja Declaration, he lifted the ban on political parties, declaring that there could be two parties. The Social Democratic Party (SDP) and the National Republican Convention (NRC) were formed as a result.

Return to civilian rule was postponed twice. Support for Babangida dwindled amid continuing economic difficulties and fuel shortages that caused heavy riots throughout the country.

The much delayed presidential elections finally went ahead in June 1993. The SDP candidate, Moshood Abiola, a wealthy Yoruba Muslim from the south, claimed victory. Two weeks later, Babangida annulled the results, resulting in widespread rioting, and announced that another election would be held.

Had the election results been allowed, Abiola would have become the first Yoruba to beat a Hausa candidate and become president. For the first time in Nigeria's history, people voted across ethnic and religious lines – a momentous break from past elections. The military, on the other hand, continued to be dominated by the Hausa, and their resistance to Abiola was viewed by many Yoruba as indicative of Hausa reluctance to share power.

Nigeria Today

Pressured by fellow army officers to hand over power, Babangida stepped down in August and appointed Ernest Shonekan as head of an interim civilian government, the Transitional Council (TC). Shonekan's first priority, he claimed, was to hold 'democratic' elections. He and newly appointed Vice President General Sani Abacha urged Nigerians to be patient, but violent rioting broke out around the country. Abiola, who by this time had fled the country, denounced the puppet government.

Shonekan lasted three months. Preempting an uprising by junior ranks, General Sani Abacha seized control in a bloodless coup in November, forcing Shonekan to announce his governments resignation and reinstating military rule. Abacha abolished all 'democratic' institutions including the two political parties, the national and state assemblies and local governments. Establishing a Provisional Ruling Council and appointing himself chairman, Abacha created a tightly constructed power base from which he could rule. In a surprise move, he chose a mainly civilian cabinet that included Abiola's running mate. Abiola, who had returned to Nigeria to claim the presidency, was arrested and charged with treason.

Under Abacha's rule corruption flourished once again. In Abacha's attempt to maintain a grip on power, many leading Nigerian politicians, intellectuals, labour leaders, politicians, prodemocracy leaders and retired military leaders were arrested. Crackdowns on the opposition also resulted in dozens of newspapers being shut down.

Among the victims was one of Nigeria's most prized authors and the first African to win the Nobel Prize, Wole Soyinka. He had to flee Nigeria in November 1994 to avoid arrest. Not so fortunate was Ken Saro-Wiwa, who was executed in November 1995 for allegedly plotting to overthrow the government. There was worldwide condemnation of this action, leading to the

NIGERIA

expulsion of Nigeria from the Commonwealth.

Abacha dissolved his cabinet in November 1997, later allowing the formation of five political parties (rejecting another 10 others because they were likely to oppose him). However, no one will ever know if Abacha really intended a return to civilian rule. In June 1998, he unexpectedly died of a heart attack, aged 54 (and estimated to be worth US$10 billion). His defence chief, Abdulsalam Abubakar, was sworn in as successor. There were immediate calls for a return to 'genuine democratic process'. Abubakar released some political prisoners, and promised reforms, saying 'It is clear that

Ken Saro-Wiwa

Ken Saro-Wiwa, the distinguished Nigerian novelist, playwright, and political activist, was hanged in November 1995, along with eight other Ogoni people, on the order of the military head of state General Sani Abacha. A hand-picked military tribunal found Saro-Wiwa guilty of complicity in the murder of four pro-government Ogoni chiefs. The trial was marked by numerous irregularities, the intimidation of witnesses and the refusal of the prosecution to present vital evidence.

Saro-Wiwa's conflict with the Nigerian government began in 1993 with the formation of a peaceful resistance organisation, the Movement for the Survival of the Ogoni People (MOSOP), which he led. The Ogoni, a minority tribal group of 500,000 people, inhabit a region of Rivers State which for decades has born the brunt of oil drilling operations by Anglo-Dutch company Shell, which extracts 300,000 barrels per day from more than 100 wells.

The environmental damage to the Ogoni territory has been severe and has rendered much of the land unusable. Between 1976 and 1991, there were almost 3000 oil spills, averaging 700 barrels each. Clean-up operations, when they have taken place at all, have been inordinately slow. In addition, gas flares, burning 24 hours a day (some of them for the past 30 years), are often near Ogoni villages, resulting in acid rain, massive deposits of soot and respiratory diseases in the surrounding community.

It was against this background that MOSOP was formed. Saro-Wiwa campaigned vigorously. Every protest mounted by the Ogoni (several of which involved hundreds of thousands of people) was met with violence from the armed forces. Hundreds of Ogoni have been killed, many more maimed and tens of thousands have been rendered homeless by vandalism.

Saro-Wiwa's execution caused international outrage, particularly after numerous appeals for clemency had been expressed by many world leaders, including Nelson Mandela. It led to Nigeria being expelled from the Commonwealth and to sanctions being applied by the USA and several European countries.

Nigerians want a country where fairness, justice and equity are not mere slogans'. It seemed probable that he also intended to release Abiola, still in prison. However, Abiola died unexpectedly on 7 July 1998, shortly after a visit by UN representatives.

So far Abubakar has been steering Nigeria down the road to democracy. He has promised to end military rule by 29 May 1999 which has been set as the inauguration date of the new government following the elections. Meanwhile, thousands of voter registration centres have been set up all over the country in preparation for local elections to be held on 5 December 1998 and the presidential elections set for 27 February 1999.

However, the elections are threatened by the ever-present conflict between the Hausa majority and the various southern groups headed by the Yoruba and Igbo. The northerners have dominated Nigerian politics far too long and the southern groups want not only to share power but are also demanding a true federal system. In particular, the southern groups demand to divide Nigeria into six federal regions, decentralise the armed forces so far dominated by the northerners, a fairer share of the oil revenue and a rotational system of the presidency between the major ethnic groups. Furthermore, many southerners are expecting the next president to be from their ranks and if he is not, more strife can be expected.

GEOGRAPHY

More than three times the size of the UK, Nigeria occupies 15% of West Africa (but has 56% of its people). Nigeria's only mountains are in the far east along the Cameroon border. They're spectacular but are too far off the beaten path for most people. In the centre around Jos is a plateau area (1500m), with the most pleasant climate in the country. With short grass and open scenery, this central savanna area offers some impressive sights. The north borders the Sahel and is largely savanna, with a drier climate. Cutting north-west to south is the River Niger, Africa's third-longest river. It forms a huge delta in the region around Port Harcourt. The

Benue flows west from Cameroon, emptying into the Niger near Lokoja.

The coastal oil-producing region is almost a different country, with lagoons, mangrove swamps, sandy beaches, innumerable streams and, as you move inland, thick forests.

CLIMATE

Nigeria's weather pattern differs substantially between the north and the south. In the north, the climate is like that of the Sahel – hot and dry, with one long rainy season from late May to the end of September. Between March and May temperatures reach around 40°C. Along the coast, temperatures average 5 to 10°C less, but the humidity can be unbearable. In the coastal regions, it rains most heavily between April and July, peaking in June; September to October is a second, shorter, rainy season.

ECOLOGY & ENVIRONMENT

Nigeria has extraordinary biological diversity. Most of it, however, is on a swift path to destruction. Nigeria's major environmental problems stem in large part from its

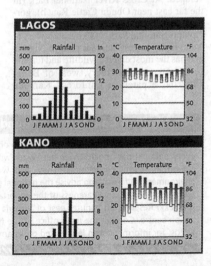

NIGERIA

rapidly increasing population. One consequence of this is deforestation. Between 1983 and 1993, Nigeria's forest cover decreased by 20%, second only to Côte d'Ivoire in West Africa. Overall, Nigeria has logged 95% of its original forests. Moreover, very little land in Nigeria is protected – less than one-third of the all-Africa average, which isn't very high. The failure to protect forests has allowed the destruction of animal habitats by human activity to go unabated.

A further problem is pollution in the oil-producing regions of the Delta. The economies of whole groups of villages have been wiped out, especially by pollution of rivers and estuaries, and little has been given in the way of compensation.

For more information on the fight to stop the pollution, see the boxed text 'Ken Saro-Wiwa' on p694.

FLORA & FAUNA

While Nigeria doesn't have a huge population of large mammals, you can still see a wide variety of wildlife (mostly ungulates) and the birdwatching is excellent. Yankari National Park, north-east of Abuja, is the best known Nigerian parks and the most developed. At Cross River National Park (in the far east near Obudu Cattle Ranch), gorillas have been spotted recently. Gashaka Gumpti National Park, 200km south-west of Yola, is the largest national park in Nigeria and has the most diverse wildlife and terrain.

The Okomu Sanctuary, west of Benin City, has a patch of rainforest. Kamuku Wildlife Reserve, west of Kaduna, is a great place for birdwatchers, as are the Hadejia-Nguru Wetlands near Nguru, about 200km north-east of Kano.

Apart from the Nigerian Conservation Foundation (see the boxed text in this section), another group involved in national parks and environmental matters is the British Voluntary Service Overseas (VSO). Its main office is in Kano and, although the staff are quite busy, they can provide travellers with information on current programs.

GOVERNMENT & POLITICS

Nigeria is a military dictatorship with the armed forces controlling the country. There are over 30 states, including the Federal Capital Territory based on Abuja. The governors of the states are all high-ranking military officials. If the return to civilian rule ever happens then Nigeria will have a bicameral legislature like the USA, with an elected president, senators and members of the House of Representatives. For a picture of the Nigerian political climate, see Nigeria Today in the History section.

ECONOMY

With such a turbulent political climate, Nigeria's economy has suffered. The country is frighteningly dependent on oil. As the world's sixth-largest producer, oil accounts for 90% of Nigeria's foreign exports and 80% of foreign earnings. Contrast this with the fact that in 1960 food accounted for 70% of Nigeria's exports and it was the largest

The Nigerian Conservation Foundation

The NCF is the most important conservation organisation in Nigeria and has one member on every national park board. Members work with teachers, and environmental studies is included in school curriculums. They also work to raise public awareness of Nigeria's environment and assist and advise the national parks. They have spearheaded efforts to create parks and to increase awareness of the importance of biological diversity. A good example is the Lekki Reserve, 20 minutes east of Victoria Island (Lagos), where the NCF has a conservation centre. Contact the main office of the NCF (☎ 01-268 6163) at 5 Moseley Rd, Ikoyi, Lagos, for information on less-visited parks and how the NCF's work is progressing.

producer of palm kernels and palm oil. Nigeria now imports cooking oil and food imports cost billions of dollars.

By mid-1994 Nigeria's foreign debt had grown from US$20 billion to a shocking US$34 billion, while the price of oil had dropped by more than one-third. With fraud and mismanagement running rampant in the oil industry and frequent oil strikes, there is little hope that the country can soon shrug off its debts. The government, trying to stimulate industry, reintroduced foreign exchange controls, but for companies needing foreign-sourced components the shortage of foreign currency has made matters worse. Thousands of barrels of local petrol are smuggled out of the country every day with the collusion of government officials and the army.

In sum, the situation is spiralling virtually out of control. Inflation is rampant; real incomes are at least one-third less than in 1974, and per capita GNP has dropped from US$860 in 1982 to US$280 in 1996. By some estimates, this is lower than it was in 1965, before Nigeria's oil began flowing. Most Nigerians face a very grim economic future.

POPULATION & PEOPLE

Nigeria has a population of roughly 100 million and this is a 'guesstimate', as there is a lack of census information. Almost one in two West and Central Africans is a Nigerian. Most importantly, the population is increasing by 3.3% annually (the fifth-highest growth rate in Africa) and doubling every 19 years. By 2025, with an estimated 285 million people, Nigeria will be the third most densely populated place, behind India and China but just ahead of the USA.

It is a scenario that does not bode well for the country's future. Efforts to curb population growth aren't working. During the late 1980s, the US government poured more money into population-control programs in Nigeria than into any other country in the world. Unlike similar programs in Asia and Latin America, the effort has had minimal impact. The number of couples using contraception is less than 10%.

Nigeria has more than 250 ethnic groups, most with their own language, but three (65% in total) stand out – the Hausa in the north, the Igbo (or Ibo) in the south-east and the Yoruba in the south-west around Lagos and Ibadan – see the colour feature between page 704 and 705 for more details about these three major people groups.

Countless smaller linguistic groups (Ido, Nupe, Efik, Idoma, Nembe etc) make up the rest of the population. In some ways, these minorities help unify Nigeria as a nation. Since none could be politically viable independently, they tend to forge alliances as it suits their interests, thereby blurring the tribal-political divisions.

There have always been these three major divisions, and ethnic rivalries are fiercer now than ever. In large part this is due to the scramble for national resources. The country's vast petroleum wealth is pooled at the centre and redistributed among the more than 30 states. The states compete for the federal government's favour, thus reinforcing the respective groups' strong community and ethnic identities. And political patronage – the bedrock of Nigerian politics – has in turn fed off these regional rivalries, further undermining national solidarity.

ARTS
Music

Some of Africa's best known singers come from Nigeria. Foremost among them are the late Fela Anikulapo Kuti (see the boxed text on p710), Femi Kuti (Fela's son) and Sunny Ade, followed by Sonny Okosun, Ebenezer Obey and the group Ghetto Blaster. Another well known Nigerian singer is Chief Stephen Osita Osadebe. Sunny Ade is king of the extremely popular *juju* music, a style unique to Nigeria (for more details see the illustrated section 'Music of West Africa' in the Facts about the Region chapter). His recordings with Onyeneka Onwenu, *Choices* and *Wait For Me*, encourage family planning, and royalties from the sales go to the Planned Parenthood Federation. Sonny Okosun plays a funk/highlife/Afro-pop synthesis called Afro-Soul.

Nigerian Art

Nigeria's vast and rich art heritage is unequalled anywhere in West Africa. The oldest sub-Saharan sculpture discovered so far are the 2000-year-old terracottas found near the village of Nok. Other ancient cultures renowned for sculpture include those of the Igbo-Ukwe, Ife, Owo and Benin, examples of which can be seen at the National Museum in Lagos.

Many tribal groups still produce fine sculptures and masks. The best known are the Yoruba, whose small twin figures, *ibeji*, are world famous. The Yoruba also carve figures for many deities and cults which make up their religion. A figure with a carved double axe balanced on its head represents Shango, the god of thunder. A kneeling couple portray Eshu, the representative of Olurin, the supreme or sky god. For the cults of *epa* and *gelede*, masks are carved with elaborate superstructures incorporating human and animal groups. The Yoruba are also known for their bronze casting and iron herbalist staffs which depict a large bird surrounded by many smaller birds.

The Igbo carve personal shrine figures called *ikeng*, which feature a horned man holding a sword in one hand and a severed head in the other. The Igbo also carve masks with open-work crests which represent a beautiful maiden. The Ekoi (or Ejagham), who live near the Igbo, use similar masks covered in skin, which are unique to West Africa. In the north-east, the Mumuye are renowned for their cubist approach to the human form, expressed in their ancestor figure carvings.

The soapstone figures from the Esie in Iloun, the pottery, metalwork and glass-making of the Nupe, and the applique banners and phenomenal beadwork of the Yoruba are just a few of the great reflections of precolonial Nigeria.

The latest sensation is tenor saxophonist Lagbaja (in Yoruba, 'someone of importance'), who hides his identity with a mask. Some know him incidentally from his Friday jazz program Ray Power 100FM and the highly successful single *Coolu Temper*, the 1994 debut album *Bad Leadership* – heavily infused with Yoruba music – and the 10-track album *C'est un African Thing*, influenced by John Coltrane and Cannonball Adderley. In a similar style to Afro-Soul is *fuji* music, of which Chief Sikiru Ayinde Barrister and King Wasiu Ayinde Marshal II are the main exponents. Fuji incorporates elements from juju and blends them with a diverse range of musical styles and instruments. Fuji music is gaining popularity in Nigeria over other musical forms.

Literature

Nigeria seems to have as many writers as the rest of black Africa combined. Chinua Achebe is probably Nigeria's most famous author, although he faces strong competition from Wole Soyinka, Ben Okri, Amos Tutuola, Cyprian Ekwensi and Ken Saro-Wiwa. These authors and their works are discussed in more detail in the Arts section of the Facts about the Region chapter.

Another notable writer is Flora Nwapa, an Igbo teacher and administrator, who was the first Nigerian woman to have a novel published. Most of her stories focus on the problems women face in marriage and with children. Critics have praised her skill in presenting her women characters sensitively as individuals and dealing with their special burdens.

Her first book, *Efuru* (1966), deals with the role of women in Igbo society. *Idu* (1970) concerns the importance of children in the African family. She has since formed her own publishing company, Flora Nwapa & Co, and published 12 books, seven of which she wrote. Her latest, *Once Is Enough*, is about a childless woman caught in a bad marriage. Buchi Emecheta has followed in Nwapa's footsteps, publishing seven novels and attaining some recognition as well.

SOCIETY & CONDUCT

In the Muslim north, strict dress standards apply (for more details, see the Society & Conduct section in the Regional Facts for the Visitor chapter). However, in the south, dress standards are much more relaxed and Lagos is *the* place to dress up – or down.

If someone is late for an appointment, they are probably delayed in the 'go slow' or are operating on 'African time' – it's nothing to get upset about.

RELIGION

Three primary religions are practised in Nigeria: Christianity, Islam and animism. In addition, there are countless cults and syncretic religions that combine, for example,

Christianity with local spirits and guardians. The tremendous number of cults, groups and religions is not surprising in a country with over 250 different languages.

Christians dominate the south, while Muslims predominate in the north. The Yoruba (and some Igbo groups) in the south practise animism.

Islam expanded into Nigeria via the trans-Sahara trading caravans and various holy wars. Today, evidence of its influence is seen in every aspect of life in the north. Christianity arrived much later, with the colonial powers.

LANGUAGE

English is the official language. The three principal African languages are Hausa in the north, Igbo in the south-east and Yoruba in the south-west around Lagos. See the Language chapter for a list of useful phrases in these languages.

Nigerian Speak

The following list of colloquial Nigerian English phrases and terms may be useful:

area boys	local gang members, petty thieves and criminals
buka	shanty restaurant
don	past tense, eg 'I don chop'
el hadjis	businessmen, rich people (literally a visitor to Mecca)
go	future tense, eg 'I go chop'
go slow	traffic jam in Lagos
hear	speak/know, eg 'I hear Igbo'
kiss	bump another car
moto	car
NEPA	Nigerian Electric Power Company, eg NEPA is 'offed' (which it is several times daily, or 'Never Electric Power Anytime')
night fighters	women who stay up all night with customers
NITEL	national telephone company which seldom works
o-ibo	white person
oga	boss, eg 'Oga, how work now?' (to ask a policeman how things are)
quench, squelch	to break down
sabi	know, eg 'I sabi am' (I know it)
shucking	drinking
tay	to stay
419	commercial fraud (the number of the relevant Act)

Facts for the Visitor

SUGGESTED ITINERARIES

Most people would advise getting out of Lagos as soon as possible and bypassing Ibadan on your way out. However, the brave should allow a week for Lagos, in part because one of the major highlights of any trip to Nigeria is an evening at one of the great nightclubs featuring live music.

Although Benin City has an interesting museum and the nearby Okomu Reserve, and Abraka has whitewater rafting and diving, cities in the southern half of the country have little to offer travellers. However, if you head to the far eastern section, you'll find some interesting parks and the country's best hiking area, especially along the eastern border. You could easily spend a week or more in this area, which in-

Highlights

Architectural & Historical

Hausa Cities   *(The Centre, The North)*
The Hausa cities of the north – Zaria, Katsina, Sokoto, Kaduna and Kano – are replete with sights, and with their imposing mosques, remnant city walls and seething markets are one of the best reasons to visit Nigeria.

Jos Museum   *(The Centre)*
The ethnological collection here is superb and the best of its kind in the country. The added bonus of a visit to Jos, one of the most English and most peaceful parts of Nigeria, is its cool climate, a welcome respite from the heat of the north and south.

National Parks & Activities

Yankari National Park   *(The Centre)*
The best of Nigeria's national parks for bird-watching, and a great place to escape the hustle and bustle of Nigeria's overcrowded cities.

Cross River National Park   *(The South)*
One of several parks run by the Nigerian Conservation Foundation, it's set in lush rainforest, and is a good place for hiking; there are gorillas in nearby Mbe Mountain National Park.

Gashaka Gumpti National Park *(The South)*
Nigeria's largest park, with the country's highest mountain; less developed than some of the other parks, but with diverse ecology and great birdwatching.

Trekking & Climbing
                                      (The South,
                                       The Centre)
Nigeria has some excellent hiking possibilities, especially in the south-east near the eastern border with Cameroon (at present off limits) and on the Jos plateau.

Relaxation

The Niger Delta
Palm-fringed creeks and waterways, mangrove swamps and traditional fishing villages; enjoy fresh fish, palm wine and the relaxed atmosphere of the islands in the delta – it's well worth the hassles you'll undoubtedly encounter along the way.

Food
The exotic smells of the street stalls, chop shops and market places will have you salivating in no time; you can eat cheaply on street food and it's a great way to interact with locals.

Music   *(Lagos)*
For the brave, a clubbing night out in Lagos, Nigeria, will be one of your most enduring experiences. You may even see King Sunny Ade, the masked Lagbaja or Shina Peters.

Survival

Sounds funny to include this here but those few independent travellers who make it to Nigeria, one of the world's most dangerous destinations, will relish the fact that they survived.

cludes Cross River National Park, Obudu Cattle Ranch and Gashaka Gumpti National Park. Towns in the Delta region are real delights – Brass and Bonny for instance. You have to be keen to make the effort to get there, but the adventurous will enjoy the palm-fringed islands and the speedboat trips through the labyrinthine mangroves.

Heading north, you could stop for a day or two at Kaduna, the northern capital; Jos, which has a fabulous sprawling ethnographical museum; Yankari National Park; and Zaria, with its interesting old quarter. Nigeria's main attraction, however, is Kano. Allow at least three days to explore this fascinating city.

PLANNING

Nigeria can be visited at any time when the political situation is stable. In the current state of political turmoil, chances are that one major region will be off limits. When summers (between March and May) are very hot and muggy along the coast, you can escape to the plateau and Jos.

WAPB Street Maps Lagos 1992 is the latest street guide to Lagos. The *Spectrum Road Map Nigeria* (1994) has contour colouring; the scale is 1:1,500,000.

VISAS & DOCUMENTS
Visas

Everyone needs a visa. Most embassies (including the high commissions in the UK and Australia and the embassies in Benin and Togo) issue visas only to residents and nationals of the country in which the embassy is located (although New Zealanders can get visas from the consulate in Canberra). The Nigerian embassy in Washington, as well as the consulates in New York and San Francisco, issue single-entry visas (valid for a month's stay) free of charge and process applications in two days. Nigerian embassies generally require forms in triplicate, evidence of a round-trip airline ticket, and a letter of invitation from a person/company in Nigeria detailing the reason for your visit. All applications require photos – bring plenty.

The cost of a visa depends on your nationality. For most it's about US$30 (or the equivalent) but it's a huge US$200 for UK citizens (a *quid pro quo* for visa restrictions placed on Nigerians by the British). For Australians it's A$36 and for New Zealanders a mere A$8. Processing takes from one to two weeks.

Visas usually allow for a stay of up to one month and remain valid for three months from the date of issue, not the date of arrival. Plan accordingly.

Visa Extensions These can be obtained in all the state capitals from the immigration department of the Federal Secretariat (in Lagos this is in Obalende). Extensions cost N800 and you will need a letter from a local citizen or resident vouching for you; in Kano you can get this from the manager of the Kano State Tourist Camp. A dash will speed up the process considerably.

Other Documents

You need proof of vaccination against yellow fever, if you are coming from an infected area.

EMBASSIES & CONSULATES
Nigerian Embassies & Consulates

In West Africa, Nigeria has embassies in all countries except Cape Verde. For more details, see the Facts for the Visitor section of the relevant country chapter.

Elsewhere, there are embassies in most European Union member states, as well as the following:

Australia
    (☎ 02-6286 1222)
    7 Terrigal Crescent, O'Malley, ACT 2606
Belgium
    (☎ 02-735 40 71)
    3B ave de Tervueren, Brussels 1040
France
    (☎ 01 47 04 68 65)
    173 ave Victor Hugo, 75016 Paris
Germany
    (☎ 0288-32 20 71 or 32 20 72)
    Goldbergweg 13, 53177 Bonn

UK
  (☎ 0171-353 3776 or 0891-600 199; from 22
  April 2000 ☎ 020-7353 3776)
  76 Fleet St, London EC4Y
USA
  (☎ 202-822 1500)
  2201 M St NW, Washington, DC 20037; also
  in New York (☎ 212-370 0856)

Embassies & Consulates in Nigeria

The majority of foreign embassies are in
Lagos (telephone code ☎ 01) on Ikoyi or
Victoria Island (VI).

Australia
  (☎ 261 8440, fax 261 8703)
  2 Ozumba Mbadiwe Ave, VI
Benin
  (☎ 261 4411)
  4 Abudu Smith St, VI
Burkina Faso
  (☎ 268 1001)
  15 Norman Williams St, Ikoyi
Cameroon
  (☎ 261 2226)
  5 Elsie Femi Pearse St, VI
Côte d'Ivoire
  (☎ 261 0963)
  5 Abudu Smith St, VI
France
  (☎ 260 3300)
  1 Oyinkan Abayomi Drive (formerly Queens),
  Ikoyi
Germany
  (☎ 261 1011)
  15 Louis Farrakhan Crescent, VI
Ghana
  (☎ 263 0015)
  23 King George V St, Lagos Island
Niger
  (☎ 261 2300)
  15 Adeola Odeku St, VI
Togo
  (☎ 261 1762)
  Plot 976 Oju Olobun Close, VI
UK
  (☎ 261 1551)
  11 Louis Farrakhan Crescent
USA
  (☎ 261 0050)
  2 Louis Farrakhan Crescent

Chad, Italy and Kenya also have embassies
in Lagos.

Visas for Onward Travel

In Nigeria, you can get the following visas
for neighbouring countries. Note that you
usually need at least two photos for each
application.

Benin

The embassy is open weekdays from 9 to
11 am and gives same-day service (collection at 2 pm). Visas (N600) are valid for 15
days but are easily renewable in Cotonou.

Cameroon

The embassy is open weekdays from 8 am
to 12.30 pm and issues 90-day multiple-
entry visas (N5000) in 24 hours. You'll
need an onward airline ticket. You can also
get visas with much less hassle in Calabar
in 24 hours; the consulate, at 21 Ndidan
Usang Iso Rd (formerly Marian Rd), is open
9 am to 2.30 pm weekdays; you may not
be asked for an onward ticket.

Niger

The embassy is open weekdays from 9 am
to 2.30 pm and issues visas (N3000 for visas
valid for one month) in 24 hours. You can
also get visas to Niger in Kano (same cost);
the consulate (☎ 645274) is at 12 Aliyu Ave
(just off Murtala Mohammed Way) on the
north-western side of town near Airport
Roundabout.

Although Abuja is the official capital few
countries have relocated their offices there.
The European Community House (☎ 523
3144), 63 Usuma St, Abuja, serves the diplomatic needs of citizens of many European
countries. The British High Commission
(☎ 523 2010) on North Shehu Shagari Way
attends to the needs of Commonwealth citizens, and the US embassy (☎ 523 0916) is at
9 Mambilla Way in Maitama.

CUSTOMS

It is illegal to import or export any more
than N50. Nigeria strictly enforces its laws

against exporting Nigerian antiquities; anything that looks old is likely to be confiscated by customs unless you have a certificate from the National Museum in Lagos.

MONEY

The unit of currency is the naira (N).

CFA1000	=	N130
Euro €1	=	N100
UK£1	=	N130
US$1	=	N80

The official rate is now almost on a par with the black market rate. At the time of the above rates, the black market rates were US$1 = N84, UK£1 = N135 and CFA1000 = N135. For the average traveller it is hardly an advantage to go to the black market any more. The plus is convenience, but there is a risk of being short changed.

Many travellers regret bringing travellers cheques instead of cash. Many bureaus de change won't accept cheques, and some banks won't either. If you're very lucky, you might get an exchange rate about 5 to 7% less than that for cash; you may waste an entire morning at the bank. Among the banks, try the First Bank of Nigeria (FBN); it gives better rates and its commissions are low.

Credit cards are virtually useless except at major hotels in Lagos and Abuja. Elsewhere, hotels don't accept them. Money transfers from overseas are confined to Western Union with FBN in Lagos (☎ 01-266 8176).

Changing money on the black market is a widespread practice in just about every town of any size. In Lagos, for example, you can drive by the Bristol or Federal Palace hotels in a taxi and do your transaction in the taxi quickly, but discretion is the key. US$ are the hot favourites, particularly US$100 bills, but UK, German and French currencies and CFA are all readily accepted in Lagos; outside Lagos US$ are best.

The major banks for changing money are the FBN, the International Bank for West Africa (IBWA), the Société Générale Banque Nigeria (SGBN), the Union Bank of Nigeria (UBN) and the United Bank for Africa (UBA).

POST & COMMUNICATIONS

Post

Postal rates are low – N40 a letter and N30 for an aerogram – but the service is questionable. Alternatively, try the EMS or DHL services; the documents are insured and are almost guaranteed to arrive at their intended destination. The cost to Europe is N1000 per 100g for these services.

Telephone

Telephone services tend to be erratic. Lagos is in the process of digitising its system, but many areas have not been covered. International telephone, fax and telex facilities are generally quite good and efficient; they are

Area Telephone Codes

The major city (and state) telephone codes are as follows:

Abeokuta	☎ 039
Abuja	☎ 09
Bauchi	☎ 077
Benin City	☎ 052
Calabar	☎ 087
Enugu	☎ 042
Ibadan	☎ 022
Ife	☎ 036
Ilorin	☎ 031
Jos	☎ 073
Kaduna	☎ 062
Kano	☎ 064
Katsina	☎ 065
Lagos	☎ 01
Maiduguri	☎ 076
Makurdi	☎ 044
Minna	☎ 066
Onitsha	☎ 046
Oshogbo	☎ 035
Port Harcourt	☎ 084
Sokoto	☎ 060
Zaria	☎ 068

NIGERIA

available at Nigeria Telecom's (NITEL) principal office in Lagos (14 Marina St) and at NITEL's offices throughout the country. The charges are reasonable: for example, N350 for a three minute call to North America.

BOOKS

The hefty tome, *Yoruba: Nine Centuries of African Art & Thought* (by Henry John Drewal, John Pemberton III and Rowland Abiodun), is a must for the art enthusiast. It covers the art of the Yoruba in detail, and has excellent photos. Other specialist art books include *Royal Benin Art* (Brian Freyer, 1987) and *The Art of Benin* (Paula Girshick and Ben Amos, 1995).

Nigeria: Giant of Africa (Peter Holmes, 1985) is an excellent coffee-table book.

Enjoy Nigeria (Ian Nason, 1993) is good for information on less-travelled roads and little-known towns, natural wonders and celebrations; it's available in Lagos.

PHOTOGRAPHY & VIDEO

No permit is required, but use great caution; you may find lots of people will be offended by being photographed. The usual restrictions on photographing military locations etc apply – see the Photography & Video section in the Regional Facts for the Visitor chapter for more general information. Be careful – the police are often looking for ways to extort bribes.

HEALTH

A yellow fever vaccination certificate is required of travellers coming from infected areas. Malaria risk exists year-round throughout the whole country, so you should take appropriate precautions. For more general information on these and other health matters, see the Health section in the Regional Facts for the Visitor chapter.

WOMEN TRAVELLERS

In the Muslim north, you should cover your arms and legs. Apart from the usual security concerns for a person of any gender travelling in Nigeria, women should enjoy

Safety in Nigeria

Lagos is one of the most dangerous cities in West Africa (Abidjan and Dakar are others). For travellers, armed thieves rather than burglars are the major problem. Taxi drivers seem to be involved in most of the thefts involving foreigners, so be careful when choosing a driver at the airport, particularly if you are arriving at night (to be avoided if at all possible). Drivers who are well known at the airport are safer; ask the luggage handlers or dispatchers. Be conspicuous about writing down the number of the taxi's licence plate. Also, avoid taxis where there is a second person riding along for some inexplicable reason. Carry your passport at all times – police stops are frequent – but keep it well hidden.

Bribery is everywhere. If the police stop you on the road and ask you to 'settle' the problem, they want money (a dash), not an explanation. In Nigeria, there's one law for the rich and another for the poor. Money can 'settle' anything.

Ife has recently been the scene of widespread sectarian violence and should be avoided at present. For further details see the Warning box in that section.

travelling in the south. This is a nation where women have made more gains (but not enough yet) than in most African countries.

You will find local women initially curious as to why you're here. After breaking the ice, they are usually very friendly. Life is tough for *all* in Nigeria – and for women, it's even tougher.

For more general information and advice, see the boxed text 'Tips for Travellers in Islamic Countries' in the Religion section of the Facts about the Region chapter, and the Women Travellers section in the Regional Facts for the Visitor chapter.

BUSINESS HOURS

Business hours are weekdays from 8.30 am to 5 pm. Government offices are open

YORUBA

Yorubaland extends from south-west Nigeria to neighbouring Benin. The Yoruba have always preferred to live in towns, migrating seasonally to the more distant farmlands. Their urban culture facilitated the development of trade and elaborate arts including the famous Benin bronzes. The old quarters of Yoruba cities contain huge household compounds of extended families. Every town has its crowned chief or Oba. The traditional head of all Yorubas is the Alafin who lives at Oyo, in Nigeria, while the chief priest is the Oni, who lives at Ife.

Formality, ceremony and hierarchy govern Yoruba social relations which are a minefield to the stranger. Great ostentation in dress and jewellery is a social requirement for women at traditional functions.

JASON LAURÉ

IGBO

Igbo (Ibo) occupy a large, densely settled farming area in south-east Nigeria. The third-largest ethnic group in Nigeria, they are predominantly Christian and have a reputation for hard work, ambition and a love of education.

Traditionally minded Igbo will not eat the new season's yam until Ikeji, the annual new yam festival, when thanks are given to the gods for a productive year. The most important Ikeji festival takes place in September at Arochukwu. Judges select the best village presentation of dance, parade and music.

An Igbo receives his destiny (Chi) directly from Chukwu, the benign god of creation. At death a person returns his Chi and joins the world of ancestors and spirits, there to watch over his living descendants and

Top: The famous Benin bronzes, like this one, were cast using the lost wax method. Photograph by Dennis Wisken/ Sidewalk Gallery.

Middle: A wedding unites Igbo and Yoruba.

maybe to return again one day with a different Chi. A traditionalist's daily preoccupation is the pleasing and appeasement of the Alusa, the lesser spirits who can blight a person's life if offended and bestow rewards if pleased. Those who died a bad death, for instance in childbirth or through suicide, used to be denied proper burial or entry into the realm of the ancestors and were thrown into the forest where they became harmful wandering ghosts.

HAUSA

Hausaland extends over much of northern Nigeria and into Niger. It is a culture deeply embedded in the Muslim religion. Quranic script intertwines with symbols of modern technology like bicycles and aeroplanes in the mud relief patterns on the walls of houses in the old quarters of Kano and Zaria. Women rarely step from behind the walls of those great compounds and many trade their home processed foods, crafts or petty goods from home, while children run the errands between compounds.

The emirs of the Hausa states live and travel in great state. Their bodyguards wear chain mail carry spears and ride gorgeously caparisoned horses whilst attendants on foot wear red turbans, and brilliant red and green robes. Often these days the Emir rides slowly in a big American car, with the horn sounding. The rural Hausa farm grains, cotton and above all groundnuts. Sacks of groundnuts stacked in pyramids are one of the distinctive sights of Kano market.

Hausaland is one of the few places in the world where cloth is dyed with natural indigo. The sight of the drying cloths, cleverly patterned in shades of blue on blue against a mud-red urban landscape, more than compensates for the smell of indigo.

Katie Abu

Top: Hausa women traditionally remain within their compounds sending children out to do their errands.

Bottom: Hausa herald at one of the Muslim feasts.

weekdays from 7.30 am to 3.30 pm, and Saturday until 1 pm. Banking hours are Monday to Thursday from 8 am to 3 pm, and Friday until 1 pm.

Sanitation day (when people are theoretically required to clean up) is the last Saturday of each month. You are not officially allowed onto the street between 7 am and 10 am.

PUBLIC HOLIDAYS & SPECIAL EVENTS

Islamic holidays are observed, even in the south – for a table of estimated dates of these holidays, see the Public Holidays & Special Events section of the Regional Facts for the Visitor chapter. Other public holidays include 1 January (New Year's Day), Good Friday, Easter Monday, 1 May, 1 October (National Day) and 25 to 26 December (Christmas).

Of all the festivals in West Africa, the most elaborate are the celebrations in northern Nigeria, in particular Kano, Zaria and Katsina, for the two most important Islamic holidays – the end of Ramadan and Tabaski, 69 days later. The principal event is the durbar, a cavalry procession which features ornately dressed men mounted on colourfully bedecked horses. The horsemen wear breastplates and coats of flexible armour and, on their scarlet turbans, copper helmets topped with plumes. The emir, draped in white and protected by a heavy brocade parasol embroidered with silver, rides in the middle of the cavalry, which is dressed in blue. He may be followed by traditional wrestlers flexing huge biceps, and lute players with feathered headdresses decorated with cowrie shells.

In mid to late February the three-day Argungu Fishing & Cultural Festival takes place on the banks of the River Sokoto in Argungu, 100km south-west of Sokoto. The fishers' customs and traditions are closely tied to Islamic religious practices. Several months before the festival, the River Sokoto is dammed. When the festival begins, hundreds of fishermen jump into the river with their nets and gourds. Some come out with fish weighing more than 50kg. It's quite a sight.

Around August, don't miss Nigeria's most photographed festival – the Pategi Regatta. Pategi is on the River Niger, halfway between Ibadan and Kaduna. There's swimming, traditional dancing, acrobatic displays, fishing and a rowing competition.

On the last Friday in August, the Oshun Festival takes place in Oshogbo, 86km north-east of Ibadan. It has music, dancing and sacrifices, and is well worth seeing.

ACCOMMODATION

Hotel room bills are subject to a hefty 15% tax; prices quoted in this chapter include it. The top end hotels and many mid-range hotels require a deposit, often twice the room rate.

Hotels in Nigeria are reasonably priced just about everywhere except Lagos and Abuja. Even in Lagos, however, if you're willing to stay in one of the suburbs, you can sleep cheaply. Elsewhere, Nigeria's large cities have hotels to suit all budgets, and you should be able to get a room for under US$5 or N450. In some cities, such as Jos, Sokoto, Ibadan and Kano, there are mission guesthouses with rooms at bargain prices. Few cities have camping facilities.

FOOD

Soup is a common lunch time food in Nigeria. It's usually eaten by scooping it up with a closed hand in the form of a spoon. As in most of Africa, you only eat with your right hand.

In the south, two favourites of the Yoruba are *egusi* soup and palm nut soup. The former is a fiery-hot yellow stew made with meat, red chillis, ground dried prawns and bits of green leaves. The latter is a thicker stew made with meat, chillis, tomatoes, onions and palm nut oil.

Other favourites include fish pepper soup, bitter leaf soup (made with greens and various meats and usually eaten with pounded yams), groundnut soup, *ikokore* (a main course made with ground yams and various fish, popular in the west of the

Hiking & Rock Climbing in Nigeria

HIKING

Nigeria offers great hiking possibilities, especially on its border with Cameroon. However, at present, the border between Nigeria and Cameroon is sensitive because of an ongoing dispute between the two countries over the Bakassi Peninsula. We can only suggest the alternatives.

Gashaka Gumpti National Park

Near the village of Gashaka, in the national park, are several good hikes, including a five hour walk to the Bat Forest. The terrain is rough, so bring sturdy shoes or boots. You can also go on extended walks, so bring all your camping equipment; guides can be hired in Serti.

Cross River National Park

This diverse park has several divisions within its boundaries, including the Obudu Cattle Ranch and the Oban Rainforest Reserve, and offers hikes from one to five days length. Hiking through the forests is a marvellous experience, but having an open schedule and an ability to rough it are definitely helpful.

The Obudu Cattle Ranch has a number of walks in an agreeable climate. At 1890m on the Oshie Ridge you may think you are in Scotland. Its 13km Gorilla Camp walk is rewarding.

The Oban Hills in the Oban Rainforest Reserve offer several hiking possibilities. Along the road from Oban to Ekang the World Wide Fund for Nature (WWF) has established a system of village liaison officers. They can organise hikes into the forest; inquire at Mfaninyen and Akor. The WWF is also active in the Mbe Mountain region. The WWF liaison officers in the towns of Kayang and Buanchor on the Ikom to Obudu road can organise hikes into the cloud forest (but don't count on seeing the gorillas). The camping along the trails is primitive, but the scenery is stupendous.

Gembu

Hikers should check out Gembu on the Cameroon border, sandwiched between the Gotel and Mambila mountains. It's in a hilly area of tea estates and cattle ranches way off the beaten track. The hikes are up to your imagination as there are few marked paths. If you head for the hospital at Waar Wa, you'll walk above, through and under the clouds. Gembu is a two hour bush taxi ride from Serti (N350); non-4WD vehicles can make the trip only with great difficulty.

Mandara Mountains

Gwoza, 115km south-east of Maiduguri, in the western foothills of the scenic Mandara Mountains is a good place for hiking. The scenery in this area is some of the most interesting in West Africa, but most hikers see it only from the Cameroon side, particularly the area around Mokolo. Head off in the early morning and return in the late afternoon to avoid the heat of

---

country). Then there's *ukwaka* (a steamed pudding based on corn and ripe plantains), various okra-based stews (which are usually very spicy and tasty), brown beans, paella-like *jollof* rice, and *moin-moin* (a steamed cake of ground dried beans with fish or boiled eggs eaten with *gari* – dried manioc flour – or yams). You'll also find lots of

snack food, including fried yam chips, fried plantains, boiled groundnuts, meat pastries, *akara* (a puffy deep-fried cake made with black-eyed peas and sometimes eaten with chilli dip), *kulikuli* (small deep-dried ball made of peanut paste), *suya* (a hot spicy kebab), and a few sweets such as *chinchin* (fried pastries in strips).

Hiking & Rock Climbing in Nigeria

the day. Keep a look out for unusual butterflies and monkeys. From Gwoza you can hike for four hours on a footpath east to Ngoshe.

To the south of the Mandara Mountains are even more hiking possibilities. You could explore the Muri Mountains near Kaltungo (eg the Tangale volcanic plug, a three hour climb), the Alantika Mountains east of Yola; and the Shebsi Mountains with isolated Vogel Peak (2042m) – Nigeria's highest point outside the Cameroon border region.

Bissaula to Dumbo
Chances are this route (about 40km) across a sensitive border will be off-limits for a while, but it rates as one of Africa's great footpaths. At the end of Nigeria's A4-3 road is Bissaula – from here you can walk for two tough days to Dumbo on the Bamenda Highlands Ring Rd in Cameroon. Navigation is difficult and a porter/guide would be a blessing; have all your papers in order and be prepared to dash.

Jos Plateau
The plateau surrounding Jos is the most significant hilly area after the Cameroon border ranges. The area around Bukuru, 24km south of Jos, is good for hiking, especially around Kurra Falls. To get there, take a minibus from Bukuru to Barakin Ladi. As you go out of Barakin Ladi, turn right towards Bokkos, and right again after about 10km towards Kurra village. At the village take the left fork (marked) towards the lake and falls.

Another area to visit, for those with time and transport, is the Assop Waterfalls, some 65km south of Jos, just before the town of Gimi. Go during the rainy season for the best views. No facilities are provided, but you could come prepared for a day hike or for longer (camping may be possible) in the Ganawuri Mountains.

ROCK CLIMBING
Climbing routes abound, especially on the 'sticky' granite inselbergs (outcrops) in the north. At Kagoro, at the junction of the Jos and Kaduna roads north of Kafanchan, is a large inselberg, separate from the main Jos plateau. It boasts the West Wall (300m, UIAA grade VI+/US grade 5.10a) and Cleavage Climb (230m, VI-/5.8; easy abseil descents). Rano, an hour's drive from Kano, has the Shike Pinnacle (60m, most routes IV/5.3) and the desperate Highway to Eternity (VII/5.10b/c) – it was once used as a lookout point. Near the village of Dal is a 120m rock (around V/5.5) and many inselbergs are found near Bauchi. Zomma Hill near Suleja in the Federal Capital Territory (Abuja) is a 300m granite plug ripe for the picking.

Between Gombe and Numan in the north-east, near Kaltungo, is basaltic Tangale, Nigeria's Matterhorn (with its rotten sandstone base). The north-west and south ridges have routes of 450m (VI/5.9 in places); you descend by the north-east ridge (II).

Getting There & Away

AIR
There are two international airports: one at Lagos and one at Kano. Getting in and out of Murtala Mohammed airport in Lagos will probably be one of your hardest travel experiences ever. It's worth considering flying to Kano instead, so that you can overcome the 'Nigeria shock' before setting out on your travels.

The departure tax of US$35 for international flights from Lagos and Kano is included in your ticket price. Check, and on no account pay departure tax to anyone at the airport – you will be asked!

Europe & the USA

There are flights to Lagos from Amsterdam, Brussels, Frankfurt, Geneva, London, Madrid, Moscow, Paris, Rome and Zürich.

Nigeria Airways stopped flying from London to Nigeria after the British protested about safety standards and unpaid insurance. In return, British Airways suspended its flights to Kano and Lagos. Recently, British-registered aircraft were again permitted to land in Nigeria. At the time of going to press, British Airways had daily flights between Gatwick and Lagos. British Airways also flies from London Gatwick to Accra in Ghana, from where you can get a Ghana Airways flight to Lagos (UK£470 one way; a return special is UK£499).

Air France flies from Paris to Lagos five times a week; the standard fare is US$1563 one way. If you're in Lagos looking for a one way ticket back to Europe, Balkan Airlines has special deals via Sofia (Bulgaria). Sabena via Brussels in Belgium can also be a cheap alternative. EgyptAir has special deals via Cairo (US$1240/1340 one way/return from Cairo).

There are no longer any direct Nigeria Airways flights to/from the USA. Travellers must pass through Europe, another West African country or through Addis Ababa (Ethiopia), Cairo, Harare (Zimbabwe) or Nairobi (Kenya).

Africa

There are daily flights between Lagos and Abidjan (Côte d'Ivoire), Accra, Cotonou (Benin), Lomé (Togo), Niamey (Niger), Yaoundé and Douala (both in Cameroon), and four flights to/from Dakar (Senegal) weekly. Most of these flights are on Nigeria Airways or Ghana Airways. As a guide, Lagos to Niamey is US$200/280 one way/return, to Cotonou US$35/45 and Yaoundé US$190/200.

Flights also operate to Nairobi with Ethiopian Airlines, Kenya Airways and Bellview

Border Crossings

No border crossing into Nigeria is going to be easy. Those in the north (Benin and Niger) seldom see western travellers, and after the initial shock a series of searches is carried out designed to get bribes. Your passport stamp can be delayed for up to half a day if you don't bribe, and luggage searches add to the hassle.

The crossing on the Cotonou to Lagos road in the south-east is probably the least difficult, because they are more used to seeing western travellers.

(all cost US$459). Foreigners must pay in hard currency and not naira. South African Airways now has a twice weekly service between Johannesburg and Lagos.

LAND
Benin

You can catch direct bush taxis from Cotonou to Lagos Island. You can also board a ferry on Lagos Island to Mile-2 (west of Apapa in Lagos), and catch Benin-bound vehicles from the motor park (bus and bush taxi park) there. Bush taxis charge N300 to Cotonou and the trip takes three hours in Peugeot 504s, and up to six hours in cheaper minibuses, which tend to be stopped frequently by police. The coastal border with Benin is open 24 hours.

Cameroon

You get a bush taxi in Ikom for the 25km trip to the border (Mfum-Ekok) or in Ekok for other points in Cameroon.

Niger

There are four major entry points into Niger. From east to west they are Kano to Zinder, Katsina to Maradi, Sokoto to Birni N'Konni and Kamba to Gaya. The last route is usually the least expensive way to Niamey as you travel more in cheap Nigeria and less in expensive Niger. If you are in a bush taxi, feel for your fellow passengers who may have to wait as the customs, immigration, police and army stop the vehicle every time they see a tourist.

SEA

When the current territorial dispute over the Bakassi Peninsula is over, you may be able to travel to Cameroon by boat from Oron, a short ferry ride from Calabar. For more details on this option, see Getting There & Away in the Calabar section later in this chapter.

Getting Around

AIR

In Lagos, flights for the interior do not go from Murtala Mohammed international airport but from an older domestic airport 10km away.

For air travel within Nigeria, the service on Nigeria Airways is sometimes good. You may find that you cannot book a ticket in advance – buy your ticket at the airport, and anticipate wasting lots of time as the flight departure schedules are a joke. Any number of expediters will offer to get your ticket, but beware – many are crooks. Flights are usually full because services have been cut back.

Don't overlook the private airlines, which are superior and generally more punctual than Nigeria Airways. They include ADC, Kabo Airlines (to Kaduna, Kano and Jos), Okada Air (to Port Harcourt, Benin City and Enugu), Gas Air (to Kano and Maiduguri), Express Airways (to Kaduna), Harco, Bellview and Concord Airlines. They all have their offices at Terminal 2 at the domestic airport (see Getting There & Away in the Lagos section later for telephone numbers).

Flights are cheap, and fares are roughly the same on all airlines. One-way fares for some popular routes include N5400 for Lagos to Port Harcourt, N7700 for Lagos to Calabar and N6000 for Lagos to Jos/Kano/Abuja; add 60% for return cost.

A N50 airport tax applies for all domestic flights.

BUS & BUSH TAXI

Travel by bus is safer, more comfortable (depending upon the condition of the bus) and cheaper than bush taxis on long-haul routes. Buses connect all the main cities. Each bus company has its own offices, but they're often not at the motor park so finding them isn't always easy. However, most companies tend to have their offices in the same general area.

The main advantage of bush taxis is that they leave at all hours. Nigeria's bush taxi system is unquestionably the fastest and most comfortable in West Africa – but it's dangerous. Two types of Peugeot bush taxis are used – the Peugeot 504 saloons that take five passengers (more expensive) and the 504 station wagons that take up to nine.

Minibuses are slower and generally at least 25% cheaper than Peugeot 504s. Bush taxis are cheaper in Nigeria than in any other country in West Africa – for example, N600 from Lagos to Kano (1028km).

TRAIN

More often than not trains are not running; don't let the schedules fool you as trains *never* arrive on time. Contact the now almost defunct Nigerian Railway Corporation (☎ 283 4302) to learn more.

There are three railway lines: one connects Lagos with Ibadan, Kaduna and Kano; another connects Port Harcourt with Maiduguri, passing through Enugu, Jos and Bauchi; and the third links Kaduna and Kafanchan.

CAR & MOTORCYCLE

The road system is excellent. However, driving is dangerous, especially on the expressway between Lagos and Ibadan, where it's like playing bumper cars at the carnival. Drive only during the day and be aware of frequent police roadblocks – often consisting of a nail-studded board across the road. Should you need help with car towing or a repair (and you are a member), contact the Automobile Club of Nigeria (☎ 296 0514) at 24 Mercy Eneli St, Surulere, Lagos – but don't hold your breath.

NIGERIA

HITCHING

Hitchhiking in Nigeria is very dangerous, and cannot be recommended. If you do resort to it, be careful. There is little you can do when the driver produces a gun – cheerily hand over everything and you may live to tell your story. See also the section on Truck & Hitching in the Getting Around the Region chapter earlier, for more on the dangers of hitching.

Lagos

Most travellers detest Lagos. The city's reputation for crime is known worldwide. Its number of inhabitants – perhaps 13,000,000 – doesn't help. In the last 30 years, the population has grown 20-fold, a world record for cities of more than one million people. About half of its inhabitants are under the age of 16. By 2025, Lagos is predicted to become one of the world's five largest cities.

Wide expressways connect the airport with the city centre and encircle Lagos Island (the heart) and nearby Ikoyi and Victoria Island, where you'll find top end hotels and posh residences. Underneath the freeways you'll find another city inhabited by people living in dilapidated cardboard shacks.

The city's main attraction is the music – Sunny Ade, Lagbaja, Shina Peters and Femi Kuti (son of the late great Fela Kuti) all have their nightclubs here. This hardly makes up for its other faults – hassles with the taxi drivers and police, high prices and violent crime. If you hear of people liking Lagos, chances are they made Nigerian friends. This seems to be the only way to enjoy it.

Orientation

The heart of Lagos is Lagos Island, where the major banks, department stores and large commercial establishments are found. The major road is Broad St, which passes Tinubu Square, a major intersection near the centre of the island, and ends at Tafawa Balewa Square, a large commercial complex. You'll find most of Lagos' airline offices and travel agencies on the southern side of the square and shops and restaurants on the northern side. The national museum is just south-east of the square, in Onikan.

Running roughly parallel with Broad St is Marina St, which overlooks the harbour and has numerous large commercial establishments. Within several blocks of the corner of Martins and Broad Sts are most banks, airline offices and black marketeers. The

Fela Kuti – the Legend Lives On

Fela Kuti, born in 1938 in Abeokuta, 100km north of Lagos, is one of Africa's most famous musicians. Immensely popular in Nigeria, he was also the most vocal politically, and various Nigerian governments took revenge. When he travelled to Los Angeles in 1964 he met Malcolm X who stirred black consciousness in him. On the musical front, James Brown influenced Fela greatly. On his return to Nigeria he mixed Brown's soul music with the many cultural intricacies of Nigerian music to create Afro-beat.

During the 1970s, he formed the Kalakuta Republic, a commune for playing music. The government burned it down in 1977, resulting in Fela's mother's death two days later. Exiled in Ghana from 1978 to 1980, he returned to Nigeria and continued playing music with lyrics critical of the regime. In 1985 he was jailed on currency smuggling charges, then released a year later when the judge admitted Fela had been framed. Fela was also accused in 1993 of killing a man whose body was found near his compound; Fela and his brother, a key figure in the group Campaign for Democracy, rebutted the charge as being politically motivated.

Confusion Breaks Bones is one of Fela's last albums (he died in 1997), in which he blasts the military; he has also targeted international organisations such as the IMF.

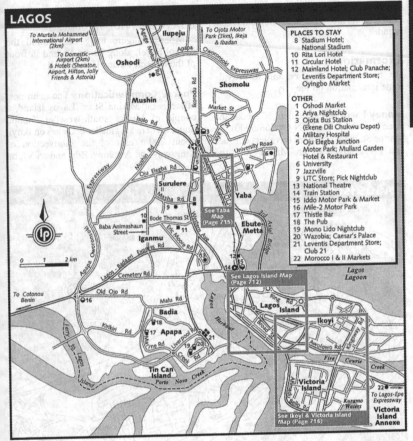

LAGOS

PLACES TO STAY
8 Stadium Hotel;
  National Stadium
10 Rita Lori Hotel
11 Circular Hotel
12 Mainland Hotel; Club Panache;
  Leventis Department Store;
  Oyingbo Market

OTHER
1 Oshodi Market
2 Ariya Nightclub
3 Ojota Bus Station
  (Ekene Dili Chukwu Depot)
4 Military Hospital
5 Oju Elegba Junction
  Motor Park; Mullard Garden
  Hotel & Restaurant
6 University
7 Jazzville
9 UTC Store; Pick Nightclub
13 National Theatre
14 Train Station
15 Iddo Motor Park & Market
16 Mile-2 Motor Park
17 Thistle Bar
18 The Pub
19 Mono Lido Nightclub
20 Wazobia; Caesar's Palace
21 Leventis Department Store;
  Club 21
22 Morocco I & II Markets

---

entire island is encircled by Ring Rd, a major expressway. Most of the embassies and big houses are on Victoria Island (universally referred to as VI) and Ikoyi, both just to the south-east of lagos Island. At either end of VI are the two leading central hotels – the Eko and the Federal Palace. On Ikoyi, the wide Kingsway Rd leads up to the Ikoyi Hotel. The liveliest street is Awolowo Rd, where there are many restaurants.

Most of the city's living quarters are to the north, in the direction of the airport, and are connected to Lagos Island by three bridges. From east to west they are 3rd Axial Bridge, Carter Bridge and Eko Bridge. Yaba, about 5km north of Lagos Island, and Surulere, north-west of it, are major nightclub areas with lots of inexpensive hotels and several markets. Two major expressways, Agege Motor Rd (leading to the airports) and Ikorodu Rd, along which you'll find Sunny Ade's nightclub and Ojota motor park, intersect in Yaba. Ikorodu Rd eventually intersects with the Lagos-Ibadan

Expressway, which leads to all points north. Both airports are in Ikeja, 22km from Lagos Island.

Information

The major hotels may be able to provide some information on the city.

Money Lagos has more than 50 banks; the three largest are the FBN (☎ 266 5900), 35 Marina St, which changes travellers cheques and gives advances on MasterCard; the

UBN (☎ 266 5439), 40 Marina St; and the UBA (☎ 266 7410), 97 Broad St.

Moneychangers hang out around the Bristol Hotel, along Broad St, and in front of the Federal Palace Hotel on VI.

Post & Communications The main post office is on Marina St on Lagos Island, a couple of blocks south-west of Tinubu Square. There are smaller branches on Ikoyi, about 200m east of the intersection of Kingsway and Awolowo Rds, and on VI, on

LAGOS ISLAND

Adeola Odeku St. They all close on weekends. The major hotels can organise air freight; DHL (☎ 268 1106) is at 1 Sumbo Jibowu St on Ikoyi.

For phone calls, your best bet is to dial through your hotel (most of which usually have direct dialling facilities).

After searching for ages we finally found a reliable public Internet service. InfoWeb (☎ 262 3475) is on the 1st Floor, NCWS House, PC14 Ahmed Onibudo St (off Adeola Hopewell St), VI. Connect time is N10 per minute and receiving email is N25 (four pages).

Travel Agencies There are many travel agencies in the Race Course Rd complex on the southern side of Tafawa Balewa Square on Lagos Island; pleasant touts will lead you to the offices. Most of the airline offices are in this area too. L'Aristocrate Travels & Tours (☎ 266 7322) at the corner of Davies and Broad Sts, is the agent for Thomas Cook. Mandilas Travel (☎ 266 3339) on Broad St, two blocks south-east of Martins St, is the agent for American Express and Hertz. On Ikoyi, Bitts Travel & Tours (☎ 268 4550) is at the Falomo Shopping Centre.

Bookshops One of the best in town is Glendora at the Falomo Shopping Centre on Ikoyi. It sells lots of imported books, including the Lonely Planet series. The Bestseller Bookshop next door carries mostly Nigerian publications. The bookshop at the Eko Hotel is small but has a few good books.

The largest bookshop is CSS Bookshop on Lagos Island, on the corner of Broad and Odunlami Sts; it carries primarily Nigerian publications, including maps of Nigeria.

Cultural Centres The British Council (☎ 269 2188 or 269 2192), 11 Kingsway on Ikoyi, carries various newspapers and magazines in its reading room; it's open from 10 am to 6 pm. The Centre Culturel Français (☎ 261 5592), just off Idowu Taylor Rd, VI, screens films every Thursday at 7 pm. The Goethe Institut (☎ 261 0717) is on Maroko Rd, VI.

Medical Services For emergencies, the best hospitals in Lagos are St Nicholas Hospital (☎ 263 1739), 57 Campbell St, on Lagos Island, and the clean, modern Medical Consultants Group, Flat 4, Eko Court Annexe, Kofo Abayomi Rd on VI.

Dr CO Da Silva (☎ 263 6997) is a general practitioner who accepts emergency cases without appointment. Drs M & D Seeman (☎ 268 4125) and Dr BR Bahl (☎ 268 3127) are also recommended. If you have a medical

LAGOS ISLAND

PLACE TO STAY	3	Isale Eko Market	22 Leventis Department Store
16 Bristol Hotel	4	Ebute Ero Market	23 KLM, Mandilas Travel (Amex)
30 Hotel Wayfarers;	5	Ebute Ero Motor Park	25 UBN Bank
Josanna Restaurant	6	Hospital	26 Main Post Office
36 YWCA	7	Jankara Market	27 NITEL Office
37 Ritz Hotel	8	Central Mosque	28 CMS Motor Park;
	9	Balogun Market	CMS Bookshop
PLACES TO EAT	11	UTB Bank	29 Ministry of External Affairs
10 Bagatelle Restaurant	12	L'Aristocrate Travel & Tours	32 NAL Towers;
19 Mr Bigg's		(Thomas Cook)	First Bank of Nigeria (FBN)
21 Chicken George	13	SGBN	33 Ferry Station
24 Cathay Restaurant	14	Market	34 Nigeria Airways
31 Mr Bigg's	15	Lufthansa	35 Aeroflot
	17	Kingsway Department Store	38 Police Headquarters
OTHER	18	UK High Commission	39 Ghanaian High Commission
1 Oba's Palace		(Consular Section)	40 National Museum
2 Udumata Bus Stop	20	UBA Bank	41 Onikan Stadium

problem, it might be worth contacting your diplomatic representatives for a list of reputable medical practitioners. The expat community is another good source of information of this kind.

Dangers & Annoyances Lagos is infamous for its violent crime. In some areas of the city home-owners take turns guarding their neighbourhoods. Walking alone at night anywhere in Lagos is extremely risky and should be avoided, particularly around hotels and other areas frequented by foreigners. For a more general discussion of safety issues in Nigeria, see the boxed text 'Safety in Nigeria' in the Facts for the Visitor section earlier in this chapter.

National Museum
This museum is definitely worth seeing. The star attractions are the Benin bronzes and ivory carvings. Equally memorable is the bullet-riddled car in which Murtala Mohammed, a former head of state, was assassinated. Architectural buffs will enjoy the numerous wooden doorways and house posts, and those interested in crafts should check out the craft shop here for a demonstration of *adire* cloth making (see the colour feature on textiles between page 128 and 129 for more details on adire cloth).

The museum is on Awolowo Rd, Lagos Island, 150m south-east of Tafawa Balewa Square, and is open daily from 9 am to 5 pm; entry is N10.

Markets
In Africa's largest city the many markets are by far the best attractions. A definite favourite is the labyrinthine Balogun Market north-west of the Bristol Hotel; you can really get lost in this busy maze that's reminiscent of Cairo's markets. Other Lagos Island delights are Isale Eko, Jankara and Ebute Ero. Thanks to the 'go slow', most market offerings are available as you wait in the embroilment of choked traffic.

At the south of VI, along Bar Beach, is Bar Beach Market. East of VI, on the way to Lekki Peninsula, are Morocco I and II, huge

lively evening markets which have to be seen to be believed.

The Ekpe Fish Market, east of the city, is vast, but the smell will blast away the most hardened traveller.

Other Things to See
Tafawa Balewa Square is a huge arena adorned by gargantuan horses. In the square is Remembrance Arcade, featuring memorials to Nigeria's WWI, WWII and civil war victims. The guard changes on the hour. Across the road, on Campbell St, is the 26 storey **Independence House**, built in 1963 to commemorate Nigeria's independence.

The residence of the traditional king of Lagos, the **Oba's Palace**, is extremely modest; it's near the northern tip of Lagos Island, four blocks east of Carter Bridge.

The **Brazilian Quarter** is a collection of distinctive houses built by former slaves and descendants who returned from Brazil; have a look along Kakawa and Odunfa Sts.

The **National Theatre** (☎ 283 0200) is the huge round building you can't miss on the drive in from the airport. It has galleries of modern Nigerian art, Nigerian crafts and

---

Joobeam

If you're hunting for miracle remedies, West Africa is the place to go. Ask around the markets for this one, proudly announced by the Idowya Royal Clinic:

Joobeam, for 'Libido, Impotence, failing Manhood, Loss and Weak erection, sexual fatigue, Impaired Male Fertility Protency (sic) are treated under 2 weeks (15 days) with Joobeam Super Power for Stimulant, Health, Strenght (sic) and more Vitality, It acts like Magic'.

And if you believe that 'Diabetes, Ulcer, Asthma, Yellow & Typhoid Fever, Hypertension, Heart-Beats, Hernia etc (without operations)' have recently plagued you, have we got a product for you!

other African arts. The best time to visit is Tuesday to Saturday between 10 am and 3 pm, when all three galleries are open.

Beaches

The once popular Bar Beach on the southern end of VI has been largely washed away by a flood. Some weekend favourite alternatives are Palasides Beach, Lekki Beach, Tarkwa Beach (no undertow) and, nearby, Lighthouse Beach (strong undertow).

The beaches are a delightful half-hour trip by water taxi through the port, across the lagoon and past fishing villages. Launches are available most readily on weekends and holidays. You'll find them on VI along Louis Farrakhan Crescent. The price is negotiable, with N200 per person (return) the maximum. Make arrangements to be picked up in the afternoon and don't pay beforehand. Ilekki Beach, 50km east of Lagos off the Ilekki-Epe Expressway, is also popular.

Places to Stay – Budget

Ikoyi & Lagos Island The *YMCA (77 Awolowo Rd)* on Ikoyi was once good value, but forget it in its present state. The *YWCA*, for women only, is on Lagos Island on the corner of Moloney and George V Sts, a block east of Tafawa Balewa Square. The N200 price of a dormitory bed includes breakfast. Unlike the YMCA, it is still good value.

Close by is the very nice *Ritz Hotel* (☎ *252 3148, 41 George V St)*, where aircon singles/doubles with clean bathrooms cost N650/800. It has a bar that has been described as 'cool and sleazy' – we agree.

Another option is *Hotel Wayfarers* (☎ *226 3011, 52 Campbell St)*, roughly in the centre of Lagos Island, at the intersection with Joseph St. It's overpriced at N1200 for air-con singles with reasonably comfortable beds and bathroom (bucket showers).

Mainland Yaba, 5km north of Lagos Island and easily reached by shared taxis, is livelier and much cheaper than the centre.

The old *Majestic Hotel (14 Popo St)*, two blocks north of Tejuosho (Yaba) Market, charges N350 for a decent single with fan

YABA

To Ikeja — *University Rd* — *To Lagos University*

0   100   200 m

1 Yaba Motor Park
2 Majestic Hotel
3 Granada Hotel
4 Mr Bigg's
5 Tejuosho (Yaba) Market
6 Niger Palace Hotel
7 Street Food
8 Tambest Bar-Restaurant
9 Onikirp Hotel

(N700 with air-con). The beds are wide enough for two people. The building is dilapidated, but the people are friendly. The nearby *Granada Hotel* (☎ *284 7980, 29 Jacob St)*, two blocks north-west of Tejuosho Market, has excellent air-con singles/doubles at N750/1050 for rooms with bathroom.

Just east of Western Ave is the *Mullard Garden Hotel & Restaurant* (☎ *283 7974, 89 Oju Elegba Rd)*; clean rooms with fan in this 'short-time' joint for couples cost N500/650.

Places to Stay – Mid-Range & Top End

Lagos Island Most of the pricier hotels require deposits, which are sometimes double the room cost. The Nigeria Hotels Ltd (NHL) *Bristol Hotel* (☎ *266 1204)*, near the corner of Martins and Broad Sts, was once the most famous hotel in Lagos.

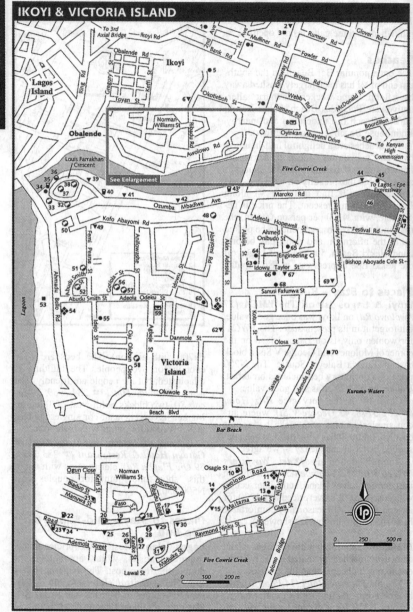

IKOYI & VICTORIA ISLAND

Ikoyi

To 3rd Axial Bridge — Ikoyi Rd
Obalende Rd
Gregory's St
Kefti St
Toyan St
Obalende Rd
Okotieboh St
Norman Williams St
Ribadu Rd
Awolowo Rd
Louis Farrakhan Crescent
See Enlargement
Lagos Island
Obalende
2nd Ave
Bank St
1st Ave
Mulliner Rd
Rumsey Rd
Glover Rd
Kingsway Rd
Fowler Rd
Brown Rd
Webb Rd
Rumens Rd
McDonald Rd
Bourdillon Rd
Oyinkan Abayomi Drive
To Kenyan High Commission
Fire Cowrie Creek
Maroko Rd
To Lagos - Epe Expressway
Ozumba Mbadiwe Ave
Kofo Abayomi Rd
Femi Pearse
Adeola Hopewell
Adetokunbo Ademola Street
Festival Rd
Samuel Manuwa St
Ahmed Onibudo St
Alukia St
Bishop Aboyade Cole St
Akin Adesola St
Abayomi Rd
Idowu St
Engineering C
Idowu Taylor St
Ahmadu Bello Rd
Abudu Smith St
Gerrard St
Adeola Odeku St
Arebele St
Danmole St
Idejo St
Oju Olobun Close
Oluwole St
Sanusi Fafunwa St
Kotun St
Olosa St
Savage Rd
Ademola Street
Kuramo Waters
Lagoon
Victoria Island
Beach Blvd
Bar Beach
Five Cowrie Creek
Falomo Bridge

Enlargement

Ogun Close
Kefti St
Norman Williams St
Biadu St
Manuwa St
Baso
Ribadu Rd
Datumola St
Osagie St
Awolowo Road
Maitama Sule St
Njoku St
Giwa St
Road
Ademola Street
Kanpe St
Maruke St
Lawal St
Raymond Njoku St
Abjo Rd
Five Cowrie Creek

0   250   500 m

0   100   200 m

0   250   500 m

IKOYI & VICTORIA ISLAND

PLACES TO STAY
3 Ikoyi Hotel
16 YMCA; Koreana Restaurant;
    Bhojosons Supermarket
47 B-Jay's Hotel;
    Cowrie Restaurant
53 Federal Palace Hotel;
    Mirage Restaurant
70 Eko Hotel; Shangri-La;
    Kuramo Lodge

PLACES TO EAT
2 Golden Gate Chinese
    Restaurant
6 La Verdure Restaurant
15 Les Amis Restaurant
19 Bacchus Restaurant;
    Water Gardens Chinese
    Restaurant
21 Josephine's
24 44 Restaurant
25 Burgy's Restaurant
29 Sherlaton Indian Restaurant
30 Al-Basha Restaurant
31 New Yorker's
39 After Hours Restaurant
41 Lagoon Restaurant
42 Mr Bigg's
44 Peninsula Waterfront &
    Calabash Restaurant
49 The Flamingo Restaurant

62 Frenchies
67 Tower Restaurant &
    Nightclub
69 La Brasserie Restaurant

OTHER
1 Federal Secretariat
    (Immigration Extensions)
4 Ikoyi Club
5 State House
7 British Council
9 French Embassy
10 AP Station
11 Falomo Shopping Centre
12 Batik Sellers
13 Batik Sellers
14 Ace Supermarket & Fast
    Food; Kebab Corner
17 Mobil Station
18 Burkina Faso Embassy
20 Total Station
22 Agip Station
23 Jazz 38; Chop Houses
26 Bureau de Change
27 Bureau de Change
28 Bureau de Change
32 British High Commission
33 German Embassy
34 Napex Supermarket;
    Captain Jack's Bar

35 Outside Inn Bar
36 Boats for Tarwa Bay
    & Lighthouse Beach
37 US Embassy
38 Italian Embassy
40 Koko's Bar
43 Fiki's Bar
45 Goethe Institut
46 1004 Apartments
    Housing Complex
48 Netherlands Embassy
50 Australian High
    Commission
51 Cameroon Embassy
52 Benin & Côte d'Ivôire
    Embassies
54 Payless 3 Shopping
    Complex
55 Air France
56 Chad Embassy
57 Niger Embassy
58 Togo Embassy
59 Post Office
60 Pack 'n' Carry
61 Payless
    Shopping Complex
63 Ethiopian Airlines
64 Sabena; Swissair
65 InfoWeb Internet Services
66 Air Afrique
68 British Airways

Singles/doubles cost N2300/3000 plus a deposit of N4000 (at least there is no non-resident rate). It's fallen on bad times; the lift is slow or not working, the restaurant is a shocker, but the terrace bar is atmospheric (as it overlooks the heart of town).

Mainland As with the cheap hotels, you'll get better value here. The *Niger Palace Hotel* (☎ 280 0010, 1 Thurburn Ave), at the intersection with Commercial Ave, 500m south-east of Yaba Market, is a bit pricey. It charges N2050 plus N3000 deposit for a double with carpet, TV and bathroom.

The well known *Stadium Hotel* (☎ 283 3593, 27 Iyun St), just north of the national stadium in Surulere, charges N1600 per twin room with air-con and TV; it is often full. The Stadium has one of Lagos' best highlife

venues and a nightclub which features a great floor show.

Other mainland choices include the friendly *Circular Hotel* (136 Bode Thomas St) in Surulere, with good double air-con rooms with TV for N1350; the Nigerian-run *Onikirp Hotel* (328 Borno Way), near the junction of Hughes Ave in Yaba, with clean, quiet air-con singles/doubles for N1100/1350.

You could also try the austere but comfortable and clean *Mainland Hotel* (☎ 280 0300, 2 Murtala Mohammed Way) , just to the north of Iddo motor park (and convenient if you arrive late), with doubles for N2500, and the *Rita Lori Hotel*, a little isolated on Baba Animashaun St in Ignamu (west of Ebute-Metta), has expensive singles/doubles for N1500/1650.

Ikoyi & Victoria Island Prices in this section are given in US$ because this is what tourists usually have to pay. Only the top end places take credit cards; ring them to find out which cards are in favour.

The NHL *Ikoyi Hotel* (☎ 269 1522 or 269 1531), on Kingsway Rd, Ikoyi, is poor value for its ordinary singles/doubles for US$110/115. The sad news for us poor travellers is that the resident rate is N2700/4300 – share a room with a Nigerian and get them to register! There is a filthy pool, casino, magazine stand, poor hotel restaurant and an overpriced Chinese restaurant (meals start at N600) on the premises.

The huge *Federal Palace Hotel* (☎ 262 3116 or 262 3125), at the intersection of Ahmadu Bello Rd and Abudu Smith St on VI, looks like a bomb hit it (and in this part of the world you don't joke about such things). The desk staff are unhelpful and the dreadful lobby bar and its lack of ambience makes you wish you were somewhere else – even though it overlooks the sea. The deluxe/business suites are US$160/300 (compared with N6000/8000 for deluxe singles/doubles for Nigerians). Even the pool costs N750 for a swim for nonguests.

Better is the expensive *Eko Hotel* (☎ 261 5339, fax 261 5205) and adjoining *Kuramo Lodge* on Adetokumbo Ademola St, also on VI. Rooms at the Kuramo are top quality, but cost 35% less than the Eko and yet include access to all facilities; make reservations to ensure a lower price. It costs big bucks (US$150 and over) to stay here; it's the haunt of the company credit card set.

The best value choice in Lagos (and an indication of the big gulf between privately owned and state-run (eg NHL) places) is the ultra-friendly *B-Jay's* (☎ 261 2391), a small boutique hotel opposite the 1001 Apartments at 24 Samuel Manuwa St on VI. This friendly place represents the best value accommodation in the country. Standard/ executive doubles with cable TV, shower (with little extras like shampoo and environmentally friendly soap) and refrigerator (with complimentary mineral water) cost US$80/85 (residents N6000/6500).

Airport Area For those in transit, staying in the airport area (Ikeja), 22km from the centre, makes sense. The huge old *Airport Hotel* (☎ 490 1001), on Obafemi Awolowo Rd, 3km north-east of the domestic terminal, has air-con rooms with TV for N4600/7200 for a double/business suite. It has a pool, tennis court, bookshop, car rental and a nightclub. You should be able to get a taxi from there to the airport for N200.

The *Sheraton* (☎ 490 0930 or 497 0321, 30 Mobolaji Bank, Anthony Way), 3km due east of the domestic terminal, exists for those too timid to go into town. The rooms are ridiculously expensive (more than US$150), considering that you are far removed from the excitement of Ikoyi, VI or Apapa; it has The Goodies, a kitsch English-style pub. For less than half the price you can stay at the much smaller *Hilton* (☎ 496 0601, 2 Ajayi St), 3.5km north-east of the domestic terminal. It isn't part of the Hilton chain, so the price of US$90 for doubles isn't surprising.

Places to Eat

Ikoyi The area with the highest concentration of good restaurants in Lagos is a 1km stretch along Awolowo Rd on Ikoyi. It has restaurants in all price ranges, although the street numbering system is confusing.

Among the cheapest of the Awolowo Rd food places is *Ace Supermarket & Fast Food* (99 Awolowo Rd), 100m east of the YMCA. Across the street at No 160 (the numbering system is confusing) is the popular *Les Amis Restaurant* with many Lebanese specialities, including felafel and kofta sandwiches for N160 and hamburgers for N240. The *Kebab Corner* at No 97 is pricey but has delectable Indian and Chinese takeaways, and *Al-Basha* at No 126 has pizzas from N350 and felafels from N160. You could also try *Josephine's* (10 Keffi St); she serves basic fare such as rice and soup.

The inexpensively priced *Sherlaton* at No 108 has been around for years; it's the city's best Indian restaurant by reputation.

The *Koreana Restaurant* (81 Awolowo Rd) serves the best Korean and Japanese fare in town; expect to pay from N600. Further west is the good *Water Gardens Chinese Restaurant*, which charges from N500 a plate. Two hundred metres east of it, the popular *Bacchus Restaurant* (closed Sunday), at No 57, is a dressy affair on Saturdays with a stiff N500 cover charge; the dancing is the attraction.

New Yorker's (59 Raymond Njoku St) is one of those imitation American diners; it's said to have the best hamburgers (N400) in Lagos. *La Verdure Restaurant* at the northern end of Ribadu Rd is a fancy large place with a predominantly French menu; the bar is popular with expats.

Big Treat, a pastry shop that doesn't live up to its name, is just west of Jazz 38 on Awolowo Rd.

The popular *44 Restaurant*, referred to as 'double 4', at 44 Awolowo Rd is an attractive upmarket cafe with pizza (N500) and Lebanese selections among other things.

Victoria Island For a fast food fix, there's a *Mr Bigg's* outlet on Ozumba Mbadiwe Ave. *Frenchies (29A Akin Adesola St)* is a popular pastry shop with éclairs (N100) and other cakes, bread, pizza (N450) and sandwiches (N200).

The *Calabash Restaurant (8 Maroko Rd)* serves a mean fish pepper soup for N200 and has an all-you-can-eat buffet for N650 on weekdays from 12 pm to 3 pm. The excellent *Cowrie Restaurant* at B-Jay's Hotel has the best African food in town, but it is expensive – chef's salad is N350, minestrone soup N200 and *fufu* with snail and stockfish N550. The Cowrie has bands on Friday and Saturday nights.

At the *Peninsula Waterfront Restaurant*, next to the Calabash, a meal with drinks costs between N850 and N1000. The *Mirage* at the Federal Palace is, unlike the hotel, maintaining its high standards; the Chinese restaurant *Shangri-La*, on the 14th floor of the Eko Hotel, has good food, atmosphere and views (from N1200 to N2000); and the *Golden Gate Restaurant*, on Kingsway Rd, 200m north of Mulliner Road, is well worth a splurge if you have bulging pockets. Two places that combine Chinese and Indian food are the casual *La Brasserie (52 Adetokumbo Ademola St)* and *The Flamingo (10 Kofo Abayomi Rd)*, which is more dressy, and serves dishes in the N700 range.

Two of the island's top restaurants are on the northern side of VI along Five Cowrie Creek. Both have patios overlooking the creek. The more easterly is the newer *Lagoon Restaurant* on Ozumba Mbadiwe Ave. It has European food and a cheaper section for takeaway pizza and banana splits. For a splurge try the other restaurant, *After Hours* on Louis Farrakhan Crescent; expect to pay N1000 per person – pizzas cost from N550 to N800, sandwiches from N250 to N600 and red wine is N200 by the glass.

Lagos Island On Lagos Island (and indeed all over Lagos) you will find *suya stalls* under nearly every flyover, and on the fringe of markets and motor parks. Favourites are the Cameroonian places scattered around the corner of Martins and Broad Sts near the Bristol Hotel and other stalls near Balogun Market.

For fast food there are the *Mr Bigg's* outlets at the junction of Broad and Joseph Sts (look for the red and yellow sign) and on Marina St; for some fowl, try *Chicken George* on Abibu Oki St. The snack bars at the large stores serve snacks and Nigerian fare, and include *UTC* on Broad St, *Leventis (42 Marina St)* and *Kingsway* at the southern end of Martins St.

You can try Nigerian specialities at the *Museum Kitchen* at the National Museum in Onikan, including *gwaten doya* (yam soup), *ikokore*, pepper soup and groundnut soup. Expect to pay N300 for *edikang ikong* (bitter leaf soup with beef); add another N300 for a piece of stockfish or some large snails.

The *Cathay Restaurant (68 Broad St)* serves good Chinese food (N500 to N750), although the atmosphere can sometimes be dead; it's closed on Sunday.

The *Bagatelle (☎ 266 2410, 208 Broad St)* on the 4th floor has been a Lagos institution for over 35 years and has excellent harbour views. It's an elegant place and men need to wear ties; it's closed on Sunday.

Yaba & Airport Area In Yaba, there is a *Mr Bigg's* restaurant across from Tejuosho Market, and many chop shops along Oju Elegba Rd and Commercial Ave. On the 1st floor of No 34 Oju Elegba Rd is *Mac Eating Home* – but you won't see Ronald; further west is *Pico Chicken Restaurant* with its 'Eat as You Earn' sign. Only 100m from the Onikirp Hotel, on Hughes Ave, is the *Tambest Bar-Restaurant*, which has cheap Nigerian food.

Readers recommend the *Club Panache* Chinese restaurant (closed on Sunday) in the Mainland Hotel near Iddo motor park for value meals.

For those staying at or near the Sheraton there is the *Taj Mahal Indian Restaurant* on Mobolaji Bank, Anthony Way. The *Sheraton* has four restaurants, including the excellent *Pili Pili Restaurant* and a good Italian restaurant (from N400 to N1000 for a meal).

Entertainment

Victoria Island & Ikoyi A fun watering hole at the water's edge is *Fiki's Bar*, a few blocks west of the Falomo Bridge on VI; this place has just relocated and is slowly building up its old reputation. (Fiki himself will ensure it succeeds.) Further west is *Kokos*, a 'respectable brothel bar' where a beer will set you back N120; a live band plays here on Friday and Saturday night.

Down the road on Louis Farrakhan Crescent, the bar at the *After Hours* restaurant is decidedly more upmarket and has a live band at the weekend.

Further west is the *Outside Inn* (☎ 261 4216), undoubtedly the best of the town's 'pick-up' joints, with an air-con 'inside' bar and an 'outside' bar; it has a good selection of ice cold beers. Nearby is *Captain Jack's*, where those temporarily barred from the Outside Inn seem to congregate. *Tower Restaurant & Nightclub* (18 Idowu Taylor St) is popular with the young expat set; the music tends to be loud rap and the cover charge is N350.

In Ikoyi, there's the open-air *Jazz 38* (☎ 268 4984, 38 Awolowo Rd). The star at-

traction is the Kuyobe Jazz Quintet. The cover charge is N300, and if you are a musician with an instrument, you can play with the band.

Mainland Three famous clubs are known by every taxi driver. The star nightclub is Fela's former *Shrine* in Ikeja. It's 500m east of Agege Motor Rd Expressway at the point where it intersects with the road from the domestic airport. It lacks Fela (who died in 1997) but the mantle has been assumed by his son Femi Kuti. Unfortunately, due to a re-zoning dispute it may close in the future; currently the cover is just N100.

The second club, where juju music reigns, is King Sunny Ade's *Ariya Nightclub* in Yaba. It's at 15 Ikorodu Rd (the major expressway towards the airport), a 15 minute ride north from Lagos Island. It's open every evening except Monday until dawn and the cover charge is N200; don't arrive before 11 pm unless you're coming to dance. KSA may play here Wednesday and Saturday.

Shina Peters, the Afro-juju master, performs periodically at the third club, at the *Stadium Hotel* (☎ 283 3593, 27 Iyun St) in Yaba. He usually sings on Thursday nights but you can call to check. For blues try *Jazzville* (☎ 286 7597, 21 Majaro St) in Onike. Jazz is also played here; there's a N100 cover charge.

On Opebi Rd near the airport you'll find *Nightshift*, a disco that's good for dancing. The crowd here is mostly young and rich; the cover charge is N200. Lagbaja's club *Motherland* is also on Opebi Rd. The *Pick Nightclub*, Adeniran Ogunsanya St in Surulere (near the UTC store), is one of those places where you have to dress up – drinks are priced accordingly.

The entertainment capital of the 'mainland' is Apapa, the port city; most places have a small entry fee if there is live music. One of the best venues to meet locals is *Wazobia* near the UTC store in central Apapa; it buzzes with live music on Friday and Saturday. Not far away is the famous *Mono Lido Nightclub*, which is known to every sailor who visits Lagos, and the

Lebanese-run *Caesar's Palace* near the Calcutta Rd Roundabout. By the Leventis store on Wharf Rd is the equally infamous *Club 21*. Near Marine Rd there are two good bars – the best is the *Thistle Bar* (aka Avondelle) at No 36 because of its live music. Equally popular, especially with expats, is the aptly named *The Pub*.

Shopping

Supermarkets & Shopping Centres On Lagos Island there is the Leventis Department Store (42 Marina St) and Kingsway.

On Ikoyi, head for Awolowo Rd, particularly the Falomo Shopping Centre on the corner of Njoku St, and the small Ace Supermarket & Fast Food 350m further west at 99 Awolowo Rd. Bhojosons Supermarket (77 Awolowo Rd) is well stocked.

On VI the Napex Supermarket is opposite the US embassy on Louis Farrakhan Crescent, Payless 3 is across from the Federal Palace Hotel on Ahmadu Bello Rd, and another Payless 3 shopping complex is on Adeola Odeku St. There is also a Pack 'n' Carry in Ikoyi, west of Payless 3 on Adeola Odeku St.

Art & Craftwork The best place for batiks is Njoku St, on the western side of the Falomo Shopping Centre in Ikoyi. They're sold along the street and the selection is extensive.

The National Museum has a non-profit-making crafts centre with batik, calabashes, woodcarvings and textiles at fixed prices.

Jankara Market, on Adeniji Adele Rd, 500m north of Tinubu Square, is the largest market in Lagos. You'll find traditional tie-dyed and indigo cloth, trade beads, jewellery and pottery, plus a fetishers market where they sell various medicines.

At the eastern end of Bar Beach on VI is a market where traders sell batik, baskets and calabashes.

Getting There & Away

Air International flights leave from Murtala Mohammed international airport and domestic flights leave from the older airport,

3km north-east by road. Airline offices on Lagos Island include the following:

Aeroflot
   (☎ 263 7223) Tafawa Balewa Square
Alitalia
   (☎ 266 2468) 2 Martins St
Cameroon Airlines
   (☎ 263 0909) Tafawa Balewa Square
EgyptAir
   (☎ 266 1102) 39 Martins St
Iberia
   (☎ 263 6950) Tafawa Balewa Square
KLM-Royal Dutch Airlines
   (☎ 266 0032) 96 Broad St
Lufthansa
   (☎ 266 4430) 150 Broad St
Nigeria Airways
   (☎ 263 1002) 15/19 Tafawa Balewa Square

Airline offices on VI and Ikoyi include:

Air Afrique
   (☎ 261 6467) 24 Amodu Tijani St, VI
Air France
   (☎ 262 1456) 4th floor ICON Building on Idejo St, VI
British Airways
   (☎ 261 3004) Near the corner of Sanusi Fafunwa and Oloshore Sts, VI
Ethiopian Airlines
   (☎ 263 7655) Idowu Taylor St, VI
Ghana Airways
   (☎ 266 1808) 130 Awolowo Rd, Ikoyi
Sabena and Swissair
   (☎ 261 1655) Plot PC10, Engineering Close, VI

Nigeria's major private airlines all have their offices at Terminal 2 at the domestic airport, including ADC (☎ 496 1942), Harco (☎ 493 3911), Okada Air (☎ 496 3881), Triax (☎ 493 7549), Gas Air (☎ 493 1199), Kabo Airlines (☎ 493 4404) and Bellview.

Bus Various bus companies connect Lagos with major cities in the country, and each has its own station. A major company serving the south (Benin City, Onitsha and Enugu) is Ekene Dili Chukwu, which has its station in Ojota on Ikorodu Rd. Many others, including those to Kano, are near Iddo motor park on the mainland, just north of Lagos Island. Young Shall Grow, serving the south-east (Calabar and Port Harcourt) leave from Oju Elegba motor park.

Bush Taxi From north to south, the main motor parks are: Ojota motor park (Ibadan, Oshogbo, Ife) on Ikorodu Rd in Ojota, roughly 10km north of Lagos Island; Oju Elegba Junction motor park in Surulere (Benin City, Onitsha, Enugu, Port Harcourt, Calabar) on Western Ave, at the intersection with Oju Elegba Rd; Iddo motor park (Kano, Kaduna, Jos, Sokoto, Zaria) on Murtala Mohammed Way on the mainland; and Ebute Ero motor park (Cotonou and Lomé) on the northern tip of Lagos Island between Carter and Eko bridges.

Typical fares are N100 to Ibadan, N300 to Benin City, N700 to Calabar, N800 to Kano and N700 to Jos.

Train The train station (☎ 283 4302) is on the mainland just north of Lagos Island, near Iddo motor park. See Train in the Getting Around section earlier in this chapter.

Getting Around

To/From the Airport Murtala Mohammed international airport has a restaurant and a Hertz agency, but no bureau de change, so you'll probably have to negotiate a taxi fare in dollars.

At the airport, taxis licensed to carry passengers will show you their identity cards; they are likely to be more reliable and safer. Haggle over the fare. A taxi from the international airport should cost less than N1000. However, you'll probably end up paying US$15 to US$20 (N1500) to Lagos Island (22km) or nearby VI and Ikoyi, N100 to the domestic airport and N200 to the Sheraton. A minibus from Agege Motor Rd to Lagos Island is N10.

Taxi & Minibus Minibuses provide the cheapest transport around Lagos; most go on fixed routes. They can cost as little as N5. The CMS bus park is on Ring Rd in Lagos Island. There are no longer any shared taxis in Lagos so you must charter the cab and haggle like crazy. A taxi costs N50 to go

anywhere on Lagos Island and N100 to VI and Ikoyi.

Car Self-drive rental cars are virtually unavailable in Lagos. By the hour, expect to pay about N800 with a driver. (Taxis by the hour are less than half this.) Hertz, Budget and Europcar have offices at the international airport. Hertz is also handled by Mandilas, Broad St, Lagos Island; and Avis by Nigerian Rent-a-Car (☎ 284 6336), 225 Apapa Rd, Inganmu.

Ferry Ferries provide the cheapest and quickest transport from Lagos Island to Apapa and to Mile-2, on the western side of town. The ferry fare is N10. The ferry terminal is the south side of Lagos Island, just south of Ring Rd.

AROUND LAGOS
Lekki Reserve

A mere 20 minute drive east from Lagos on the Lagos-Epe Expressway, opposite the Chevron Plant, is the Lekki Reserve. Run by the NCF (see the boxed text 'The Nigerian Conservation Foundation' in the Facts about Nigeria section earlier) it has 78 hectares of wetlands which have been set aside for viewing wildlife. Raised walkways enable you to see monkeys, crocodile and various birds; early morning is the best time. A conservation/visitors centre and a library are open daily; admission is free.

The easiest way to get there is to flag down a bus on VI along Maroko Rd; the cost is around N75.

Abeokuta

Abeokuta, 70km north of Lagos, translates as 'under the rock'; it's famous not only for being the birthplace of the late singer Fela Kuti and the writer Wole Soyinka (now in exile), but also for the Olumo rock. This chunk of granite is considered sacred and is used in various celebrations and rituals. Guides will take you to the top of the rock for commanding views of Lagos and the surrounding country. There are also caves and a shrine in the area. At the market you can buy adire cloth and plenty of juju material (charms, grisgris etc).

Bush taxis leave from Ojota motor park (N350, two hours).

The South

IBADAN

Roughly half the size of Lagos, Ibadan, with a population of 8,000,000, is an ugly, congested and sprawling Yoruba city. The capital of Oyo State, area-wise it's thought to be the largest city in Africa, and it's the second most populous city in West Africa after Lagos. It was the most populous from the late 1800s to the 1960s, which makes it all the more surprising that there's so little of interest to travellers.

The major sights are the huge, sprawling Dugbe Market, the University of Ibadan (UI) and the International Institute of Tropical Agriculture (IITA). Two interesting markets that are notably less hectic than Dugbe are Oje and Bode. Bode is the most fascinating because of its fabulous juju section.

Orientation

The commercial heart of town is the block-size triangle formed by Dugbe Market, the train station and Cocoa House. UI is on the northern outskirts of town and is connected to the centre (5.5km away) by Oyo Rd, which leads south-west to eventually become Fajuyi Rd and, near the market, Dugbe Rd and, further south-west beyond the train station, Yaganku and Abeokuta Rds. Bodija Rd leads directly south from UI, becoming Ogunmola St and eventually Lagos Rd.

Three major connecting roads running roughly east-west, are (from north to south): Queen Elizabeth II Rd, which connects the southern end of Oyo Rd with Bodija Rd; Lagos Bypass Rd, which connects the central triangle with Lagos Rd; and Ring Rd, which connects the southern end of Yaganku Rd with Lagos Rd. Further south on Lagos Rd is New Garage, which is the motor park for Lagos and points east (including Benin City and Port Harcourt).

The Cocoa House is the only high rise in Ibadan and is a good downtown reference point.

Information

There is no tourist information office. The map in this book is as good as you will find. Otherwise, rely on a taxi driver to negotiate a way through the labyrinth.

Money The National Bank of Nigeria, UBA, UBN and a bureau de change are all on Lebanon Rd next to Dugbe Market, while FBN is one block to the south, on New Court Rd, and the New Nigeria Bank is two blocks to the south, on Commercial St. The reliable Safe Bureau de Change is across from UI.

Post & Communications The post office is chaotic; it's on Abeokuta Rd, and it's open from 8 am to noon and 2 to 4 pm weekdays.

Cultural Centres The American Cultural Center is on Bodija Rd near the PI Hostel, while the Alliance Française is in the centre of town at 7 Lebanon Rd. There is also a branch of Alliance Française near the junction of Oshontokun Ave and Bodija Rd. The British Council library is on Magazine/Jericho Rd, 500m north-west of the train station.

Medical Services If you need medical help contact the IITA (☎ 241 2626) for a list of recommended doctors and clinics.

International Institute of Tropical Agriculture

This is the oasis of Nigeria, if you are lucky enough to be invited to stay. It has squash courts, a clean swimming pool, tennis courts, hiking trails, a lake for fishing, a superb restaurant, an outdoor bar, a golf course and comfortable accommodation in International House. It exists to study the main agricultural staples of the West African diet (cassava, yam etc) and scientists from just about every continent are represented on the staff. Part of the fenced grounds contain a remnant tract of indigenous forest, which

NIGERIA

IBADAN

PLACES TO STAY
5 JK Intercontinental Hotel
9 PI Hostel; American Cultural Center
11 Alma Guesthouse
18 Premier Hotel; Dragon d'Or Restaurant
23 Onireke Resthouse; Fortune Restaurant
33 D'Rovan Hotel
35 Kakanfo Inn; Indian Restaurant
44 Central Hotel

PLACES TO EAT
4 Express Fisheries Fast Food Restaurant
16 Chicken Out Restaurant
24 King's Dominion Restaurant
25 Mama Wale Food Centre
29 The Cabin Lebanese Restaurant
54 Chicken George
56 Koko Dome Restaurant; African Queen Bar; Legends Nightclub

OTHER
1 Safe Bureau de Change
2 Agbowo Shopping Complex
3 University of Ibadan (UI)
6 Town Taxis
7 Sango Motor Park
8 Transwonderland Amusement Park
10 Alliance Française
12 The Cotton Club
13 Platinum Nightclub
14 Secretariat of Oyo State
15 Leventis Department Store
17 Overnight Coaches to South-East Nigeria
19 University College Hospital
20 AP Station
21 Cinema
22 Adamasingba Sports Complex
26 Agip Motor Park
27 British Council Library

28 Hospital
30 Oje Market
31 The Cave Nightclub
32 Police Station
34 Mobil Station
36 Oke-Ado Market
37 Weavers
38 Bode Market
39 Texaco Station
40 Molete Motor Park
41 Challenge Motor Park
42 Texaco Station
43 Lufthansa; German Honorary Consul
45 Taxi-Bus Park
46 Dugbe Market
47 National Bank of Nigeria; Money Exchange Bureau
48 Train Station
49 Post Office
50 UBN Bank
51 UBA Bank
52 Standard Travel; Bureau de Change
53 Alliance Française
55 First Bank of Nigeria (FBN)
56 Cocoa House
57 AP Station
58 New Nigeria Bank; British Airways; Alitalia
60 Dutum Station

To Oyo Motor Park, International Institute of Tropical Agriculture (IITA) & the North

Old Airport

Ogbomosho Rd

Bodija

Ogbontokun Ave

Awolowo Ave

Mokola

Oyo Road

Parliament Road

Bodija Road

Magazine/Jericho Road

Links

GRA

Racecourse Road

Kudeti Rd

Queen Elizabeth II Road

Nalende

Adeoyo

To Ife

Total Roundabout

Bower Tower

Onireke Road

Egunjenmi Street

Hospital Street

Ogunmola Road

See Enlargement

Olubadan Stadium

Agbeni

Lebanon Rd

Oke-Foko

Mapo Hall

Bere Square

To Lafia Hotel & Abeokuta

Abeokuta Road

Yaganku Road

New Gra

Commercial Road

Adelabu Road

New Gra

Oke-Ado

Olaniyan Fagbemi Road

Liberty Stadium Road

Oluyole

Liberty Stadium

Lagos Bypass Road

Ijebi Rd

Molete

Lagos Road

0   250 m

Onireke Rd

Dugbe Road

Commercial Road (Lagos Bypass Rd)

Dugbe

Alawo Road

Egunjenmi Street

Lebanon Road

New Court Road

To New Garage Motor Park, Lagos & Benin City

0   0.5   1 km

is easy to explore and a rarity in this part of the world.

Other Things to See & Do
The University of Ibadan (UI) has a good **museum** in the Institute of African Studies building as well as good shopping for textiles and crafts.

Locals like to spend weekends wandering through the now largely defunct **Transwonderland Amusement Park**; consider the general state of all machinery with working parts in Nigeria before you hop on a ride.

Places to Stay – Budget
One kilometre to the south of UI on Bodija Rd is *PI (Pastoral Institute) Hostel* (☎ 2413928); look for the sign. It's a great place with clean rooms, mosquito nets and showers for about N500 a person, including breakfast. In the heart of town, try the *Central Hotel (30 Dugbe Alawo Rd)*, about 100m north of Dugbe Market. It charges N300 for a barely decent room with fan and shared bathroom.

Foreigners with wheels often prefer the more upmarket *Lafia Hotel (☎ 2316555)*, on the south-western outskirts of town in Apata Ganga, about 5km from Dugbe Market on Abeokuta Rd. It has singles/doubles for N2000/2750, which includes tax, plus a N600/900 refundable deposit. The air-con rooms have carpets, cable TV and bathroom, and the doubles also have refrigerators.

The *University Guest House (☎ 2413143)* on campus charges N2100 for a double plus a refundable deposit of N3500. Close by, on Bodija Rd, is the *JK Intercontinental* (☎ 2412221), where decent doubles with TV cost N2000, including tax, plus a refundable N1000 deposit. It has a car park, casino, decent restaurant and a nearby Lebanese supermarket (with luxuries like pesto sauce and ice cream Mars Bars). The small and quiet *Alma Guesthouse (☎ 2715657)*, about 1km further south on Bodija Rd (look for the sign pointing east of the road), has rooms for slightly less.

North of the city centre in a quiet area is the *Onireke Resthouse (☎ 2414607, 13 Kudeti Ave)*, 1km north of Dugbe Market. Singles/doubles with air-con, TV and shower cost N1300/1650.

Places to Stay – Mid-Range & Top End
The old, run-down *Premier Hotel* (☎ 2400340), a six storey structure off Oyo Rd on a hill with a commanding view of the city, has rooms for N2650 plus a N3000 deposit. The water supply is dependable and it has a casino and Olympic-size pool which nonguests can use for N150.

The posh *Kakanfo Inn (☎ 2311471, 1 Nihinlola St)* off Adebiyi St charges N2500 for air-con suites with large double beds (N2750 with two large beds) and cable TV. Breakfast costs N180; dinner in the hotel's Indian restaurant is around N450 (N200 per dish). It's in New Gra, 2km south-west of Dugbe Market and two blocks north-east of the Mobil Station Roundabout on Ring Rd.

The *D'Rovan Hotel (☎ 2312907)*, on Ring Rd, charges about N2500 for a tiny room with all the trimmings (they may be operating the resident/nonresident travesty of charging – if so expect to pay around US$80). The casino and nightclub can get quite lively (and there is often live music); they also feature snooker and darts.

The best accommodation is the *International House (☎ 2412626, email iita@cgnet .com)* in the IITA on Oyo Rd on the northern outskirts; you have to arrange a room in advance. Really tidy, spotless air-con double rooms with bathroom are N7000 and a full English breakfast is included.

Places to Eat
Cheap Eats A good central place for cheap Nigerian food is the rustic *Mama Wale Food Centre* at the northern intersection of Dugbe and Dugbe Alawo Rds. It's 30m down a dirt path; look for the sign. This is also a good area for *street food*, as is the area to the south around Dugbe Market.

Opposite Mama Wale is *King's Dominion Restaurant*, an inexpensive fast food restaurant with fried chicken, chips and the like. *Chicken George*, on Lebanon Rd, a block east of Dugbe Market, has similar food and prices (a quarter fried chicken, chips and Coke for N150) and is a little fancier.

In the UI area, try the UI *cafeteria*, the fancier *Staff Club*, or *Express Fisheries*, a fast food restaurant 100m south of the Agbowo shopping complex on Bodija Rd. There's also *Chicken Out* (we did!) on Oyo Rd, a fast food place down the hill from the Premier Hotel.

Asian One of Ibadan's best restaurants serves Chinese food. *Fortune Restaurant (27 Kudeti Ave)*, 150m beyond the Onireke Guesthouse has meals for around N500; it's open every day except Saturday for lunch and dinner; it's only open for dinner on Saturday. The other is the *Dragon d'Or* at the Premier Hotel; it's also quite good and has similar prices.

European The best food in town is found at the IITA's *restaurant*. For about N1000 you can get a three course meal – roasts, vegetables, soup and desserts. Every now and then they have live entertainment or theme nights eg French, when they provide cheese, wine and regional delicacies.

Lebanese Near Cocoa House is the *Koko Dome Restaurant*, which is pleasant and moderately priced, and has Middle Eastern and European selections for N400 per plate (the African dishes are a little more expensive). It also has a snack bar by the pool; if you order food you can use the pool for free (otherwise it's N100, or N150 on weekends). Another good Lebanese place is *The Cabin* on the street north of Egunjenmi St; it is known for its excellent mezzes.

Entertainment

Ibadan is a quiet place. *The Cave* on Ogunmola St features live music every night, usually a highlife or juju outfit. Watch for curious additions to your bill; beers are otherwise cheap. The *Cotton Club*, east of Oyo Rd, on Awolowo Rd, is a good bar with pool tables, TV and western-style food.

At the intersection of Awolowo and Bodija Rds is the *Platinum Nightclub*, which is a real squeeze on any night when there are promotions. The Koko Dome has the *African Queen Bar* downstairs and the *Legends Nightclub* upstairs; both are haunts of Lebanese businesspeople.

Getting There & Away

Bush Taxi Bush taxis and minibuses for Lagos and points east leave from New Garage motor park on the southern outskirts of town off Lagos Rd and from Challenge motor park near the junction of Lagos and Ring Rds.

Vehicles leave every few minutes for Lagos (N80 to N100), which is just over an hour away. Vehicles travelling east to Benin City (N300), Onitsha and other points east take longer to fill. Ojoo motor park , which also serves Lagos and is on the northern outskirts of town, has greater variety of vehicles, including Peugeot 504s (N110).

Vehicles headed for Kaduna, Kano and other points north leave from Sango motor park on Oyo Rd. Peugeot 504s to Kano (N1100, 11 hours) and Abuja (N900, eight hours) usually leave by 7 am. Bush taxis for Ife (N80) and Oshogbo (N80) leave from Egbede motor park on the south-east side of town at the junction of Ife and Lagos Rds.

To get here from Lagos, catch bush taxis (N100) at Iddo motor park.

Train This form of transport is so unreliable you would have to be studying the inefficiencies of rail transport in Nigeria to want to use it. Ask for details of services at the train station, a block west of Dugbe Market.

Getting Around

You'll find lots of inner-city minibuses and taxis on Dugbe Rd across from the market; get a share taxi there (N10 to N20).

OYO

This former capital of the Yoruba domain is now a small town (population 250,000) that stands in quiet contrast to Ibadan, the present-day capital of Oyo State. Here you can wander around the various stalls of the Akasen Market, which extends from the Town Hall to the Alafin of Oyo's Palace. Munch on a *moin-moin* (steamed bean cake) and keep your eyes open for carved and blue-dyed *igba* (gourds), pots, baskets and talking drums.

Halfway between Oyo and Ilorin is the industrial city of Ogbomosho (population 1 million), to be passed through as quickly as possible.

Places to Stay & Eat
The *Merrytime Hotel* (☎ 230344) is conveniently located by the Agip station, which is where you will be dropped off by a bush taxi. A basic single with fan and bucket bath costs N600 (N300 more with air-con); it has a friendly bar and provides cheap, hearty meals.

Those with a car can try the *Labamiba Hotel* (☎ 230443) on Ibadan Rd. A double with air-con, TV and shower costs about N2200.

Getting There & Away
Bush taxis for Ibadan and Lagos leave from Owode motor park, south of the Agip station.

ILORIN
Ilorin is an economic and cultural gateway between the north and south. Here, in the capital of Kwara State, you can feel and see a strong Muslim influence, which is quite different from other cities in Yorubaland. A huge blue-domed mosque and four towering minarets dominate the skyline of this busy trading centre. The Kwara Hotel on Ahmadu Bello Ave is a good place to change money.

Places to Stay & Eat
The *White House Hotel* (☎ 220770, 183 Lagos Rd) has singles/doubles with TV, bucket bath and fan or air-con for N1000/ 1500.

Doubles with TV, shower and phone at the *Kwara Hotel* (☎ 221490), on Ahmadu Bello Ave, cost nonresidents/residents N3000/2200 plus a hefty deposit of double

the room price. Its *Prince Garden Chinese Restaurant* is OK but, like the rest of the hotel, it's overpriced (about N500 per dish).

Getting There & Away
The Marara motor park for Kaduna, Kano and Zaria is on Murtala Mohammed Rd on the northern outskirts of town. Bush taxis to Lagos and Ibadan leave from Lagos motor park, 500m north of the White House Hotel on Lagos Rd.

IFE
Ife (officially known as Ile-Ife), in Osun State, is the legendary home of the founder of the Yoruba. It has three major attractions besides its numerous colonial-era houses: the Oni's Palace and nearby Ife Museum at the eastern end of town, and, 5km away on the north-western outskirts, the sprawling Obafemi Awolowo University campus.

Places to Stay & Eat
The university's *Conference Centre Guest House* (☎ 230705), just east of the campus, is excellent and you don't have to be connected with the university to stay here. Clean doubles (no singles) cost N1350. The rooms have hot showers, TV, air-con and balconies; the food and service are excellent. There are two bars, and the *Olokun Restaurant* serves Nigerian and European dishes for around N400 (breakfast N250). The nearby *Leventis supermarket* is the best place for groceries.

Warning

Ife has recently been the scene of widespread sectarian violence, with a virtual state of war existing between Ife and neighbouring Modakeke since March 1997. This dispute is caused by disagreement over the location of local governments. Nearly 300 people have been killed or injured, many are missing and thousands have fled their homes. It should be avoided at present. Note that a bomb exploded here on 23 April 1998, killing 20 people.

NIGERIA

Yoruba Mythology

According to the Yoruba creation myth, the world began at Ife and spread outwards from there. The sky god Olurun gave a chain, a piece of earth and a five-toed chicken to Orishala, the god of whiteness, and told him to drop the earth on the water below and climb down the chain with the chicken. But Orishala became drunk at a party of the gods and it was his brother Odua who climbed down the chain and placed the chicken on the piece of earth. The chicken scratched at it, spreading it ever wider across the primeval water. Odua built his home there at Ife but when Orishala woke up he claimed that the earth was his. They fought until Olurun declared that Odua should rule the earth, and Orishala should create human beings.

So Odua became the first king of Ife and all Yoruba are believed to be descended from him, the royal families tracing their descent from his 16 sons.

Katie Abu

Most hotels are on the western side of town not far from the university's long entrance. On Ibadan Rd is *Hotel Diganga* (☎ 233200), the best top end option. Singles/doubles with air-con, TV and shower cost N1500/2000.

Getting There & Away

From Lagere motor park in the centre, frequent bush taxis go to Oshogbo, Ibadan and Lagos (N220). Transport to Benin City (N220) leaves from the motor park, near the Ibadan and Ondo Rds junction.

OSHOGBO

This quiet but unattractive town (population 500,000), the capital of Osun State, was once one of the most creative and artistic places in Africa. Unfortunately, the art attractions and related centres are looking decidedly tired these days. On the last Friday in August, the town hosts the colourful Oshun Festival.

Sacred Forest

Oshogbo is also famous for its Sacred Forest on the outskirts of town, a half-hour walk from the Oba's Palace. Some of this collection of sacred shrines to various Yoruba gods appear to be reverting to the forest as their cement and laterite mix crumbles and vines encroach into the inner sanctums. However, much work is being done to maintain the shrines: see the boxed text 'The Sacred Forest' in this section for more information. For a tour, ask the caretakers (priestesses) – who now seem to require donations at every shrine.

The Sacred Forest

Since the 1950s Austrian sculptor Suzanne Wenger has been working in the Sacred Forest outside Oshogbo to bring the Yoruba shrines back to life through her imaginative 'restorations'.

Called Aduni Olosa, the Adored One, by the local inhabitants, she is now so highly regarded that the local women have made her the priestess of two cults.

With the help of local artisans she has worked on restoring the old shrines while adding her own touches. The result is a forest of spectacular, monumental and truly unique shrines. While they are totally different in style from that traditionally associated with African art, the inspiration is still Yoruba.

The principal shrine is that of the river goddess Oshuno, in a grove enclosed by an imaginatively designed wall. By the sacred river, near the Lya Mapa grove where huge new sculptures soar skywards, you can see a monumental and complex cement sculpture to Ifa, the divine Yoruba oracle. Another impressive sculpture, approximately 5m high, is the shrine to Onkoro, the mother goddess.

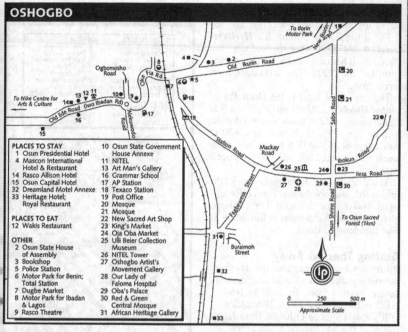

OSHOGBO

To Ilorin
Motor Park

To Nike Centre for
Arts & Culture

Ogbomosho
Road

Old Ikurin Road

Old Ede Road (Iwo Ibadan Rd)

Station Road

Mackay
Road

Ibokun Road

Ilesa Road

Fagbewesa Street

To Osun Sacred
Forest (1km)

Buraimoh
Street

Osun Shrine Road

Sabo Road

New Ikurin Rd

Approximate Scale
0   250   500 m

PLACES TO STAY
1 Osun Presidential Hotel
4 Mascon International
   Hotel & Restaurant
14 Rasco Allison Hotel
15 Osun Capital Hotel
32 Dreamland Motel Annexe
33 Heritage Hotel;
   Royal Restaurant

PLACES TO EAT
12 Wakis Restaurant

OTHER
2 Osun State House
   of Assembly
3 Bookshop
5 Police Station
6 Motor Park for Benin;
   Total Station
7 Dugbe Market
8 Motor Park for Ibadan
   & Lagos
9 Rasco Theatre

10 Osun State Government
   House Annexe
11 NITEL
13 Art Man's Gallery
16 Grammar School
17 AP Station
18 Texaco Station
19 Post Office
20 Mosque
21 Mosque
22 New Sacred Art Shop
23 King's Market
24 Oja Oba Market
25 Ulli Beier Collection
   Museum
26 NITEL Tower
27 Oshogbo Artist's
   Movement Gallery
28 Our Lady of
   Faloma Hospital
29 Oba's Palace
30 Red & Green
   Central Mosque
31 African Heritage Gallery

Art Galleries

In its heyday, Oshogbo was the flourishing centre of the Oshogbo School of Art, a movement which was started in the 1960s by a European couple, Ulli and Georgina Beier. Their students experimented with beads, wool, plastic strips and wood. To see some of the artists' works, you'll have to visit their individual studios, as there is no central outlet for the sale of Oshogbo art other than the Nike Centre for Arts & Culture, 1km out of town.

Two galleries stand out: the Art Man's Gallery on Old Ede Rd and Jimoh Buraimoh's African Heritage Gallery at 1 Buraimoh St. There is also a small museum on Station Rd that houses the Ulli Beier collection. The New Sacred Art Shop, 41a Ibokun Rd, sells copies of Austrian sculptor Suzanne Wenger's *Sacred Groves of Oshogbo* as well as pieces of art.

Other Things to See

Be sure to see the Oja Oba Market across from the Oba's Palace. The market is packed with stalls selling juju material and a number of shrines to various gods. The richly painted building decorated with intricate carvings and facing the present palace is reputed to be the first Oba's palace in Oshogbo.

Places to Stay & Eat

On Iwo Ibadan Rd, there are two relatively cheap hotels that charge N350 for a single room with fan and shared bathroom. The *Osun Capital Hotel* (☎ 230396) is friendly and clean and the *Rasco Allison Hotel* (☎ 233046) has an open bar, but the rooms are grimy.

Singles/doubles at the *Mascon International Hotel & Restaurant*, just off Old Ikurin Rd cost N300/480 for fans and bathroom with bucket bath; the nightclub here is busy on weekends but the upstairs restaurant serves abysmal food and offers little choice.

The artist Jimoh Buraimoh's **Heritage Hotel** (☎ 234285) is 1km south of town on Okefia St. It has comfortable air-con singles with TV for N900. The restaurant here serves suya.

The city's best hotel is the **Osun Presidential Hotel** (☎ 232399), on Olk Ikurin Rd, on the eastern side of town, where a double with air-con, TV and shower costs N3000 plus a deposit of N4000. It has a cinema (on weekends) a nightclub, and an overpriced restaurant.

You'll find many restaurants along Iwo Ibadan Rd; just look for the 'Food is Ready' signs. **Wakis** is on this strip. For a splurge go to the **Royal Restaurant** in Buraimoh St near the Heritage Hotel.

Getting There & Away
Bush taxis leave throughout the day from the motor park on Oke Fia Rd near the town centre; typical fares are N80 to Ibadan, N175 to Lagos and N350 to Benin City.

It's easy to get to Oshogbo from Lagos (Iddo) or Ibadan (Egbede motor park).

Getting Around
For getting around town, expect to pay about N30 for a taxi trip across town.

BENIN CITY
Until the British sacked it, Benin City was one of the great cities of West Africa, dating back to the 10th century AD. Human sacrifice was a part of Bini culture and was thought to appease the gods. When a British contingent arrived in 1897, a ceremony was held in an attempt to ward off the invaders. On entering the walled city, the conquering troops encountered a shocking, seemingly savage sight – countless decapitated corpses. However, this didn't stop the British carting back to Europe 2000 bronze statutes from the Oba's Palace. The western world was astounded by their quality and museums pounced on the work. The bronzes of Benin became one of the first styles of African art to win worldwide recognition.

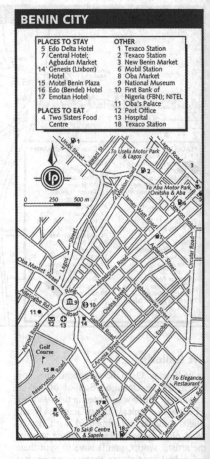

BENIN CITY

PLACES TO STAY	OTHER
5 Edo Delta Hotel	1 Texaco Station
7 Central Hotel; Agbadan Market	2 Texaco Station
14 Genesis (Lixborr) Hotel	3 New Benin Market
15 Motel Benin Plaza	6 Mobil Station
16 Edo (Bendel) Hotel	8 Oba Market
17 Emotan Hotel	9 National Museum
	10 First Bank of Nigeria (FBN); NITEL
PLACES TO EAT	11 Oba's Palace
4 Two Sisters Food Centre	12 Post Office
	13 Hospital
	18 Texaco Station

Today Benin City (population 400,000), capital of Edo State, is a sprawling, undistinguished place. However, it has several interesting sights that locals will proudly show you, including the Okada's House opposite the Edo Hotel. It is opulent, and has many interesting statues outside.

Orientation
Fortunately you can find your way through the sprawl to most of the sights and services, as they are near the Ring Rd. This circles

King's Square, which has the National Museum at its centre. Akpakpava Rd runs north-east, and Sapele and Sapoba Rds south-east, from Ring Rd. You will find plenty of places to stay, restaurants, shops and local transport along these routes.

Information
The official guides at the National Museum are great sources of information, and make up for the lack of an information office (a small tip is appreciated). The post office is on Airport Rd next to the hospital and the FBN bank is on Ring Rd. A good time to visit Benin City is December, when the seven-day Igue/Ewere Festival and the nine-day New Yams Festival take place around Edo State.

National Museum
The museum, built in 1973, is the city's major landmark, and is in the centre of town, circled by Ring Rd. It's open daily from 9 am to 6 pm; admission is N10. The star attraction is the famous bronzework, produced mainly for the king's court. The pieces on display are good but not spectacular: more notable pieces of Benin art are on show in London. Photographs make up a sizeable part of the collection. Upstairs is an excellent Okokaybe dancer's costume and headdress as well as masks, stools, doorways, terracotta, pottery and ivory carvings.

Oba's Palace
The mud-walled Oba's Palace, a block south-west of the museum, is quite spectacular. The palace contains sculptures, brass relics and other art depicting historical events during Benin's heyday. It also has an impressive array of traditional crafts, historic bronzes, ivory and other works of art. You need the secretary's permission to visit, but he's a busy man. Moreover, you're supposed to request permission a week or so in advance, so few travellers see it.

Places to Stay
The *Central Hotel* (☎ 200780, 76 Akpakpava Rd), is looking a bit rough around the edges, but it is friendly and has reasonable singles/doubles with fan at N350/480 and doubles with air-con for N550. The rooms all have their own bathrooms (with buckets, of course) and the hotel has a restaurant and a bar (with live music). The quiet and pleasant *Edo Delta Hotel* (128 Akpakpava Rd) has singles/doubles with fan and shared bathroom for N550/600 (air-con suites with bathroom are N850).

For convenience, you can't beat the friendly *Genesis Hotel* (☎ 240066, 4 Sapoba Rd), formerly Lixborr, just off the King's Square. Rooms with air-con and bathroom are good value at N800/1100. It has a vibrant bar but the restaurant is a bit pricey.

The best value is the old *Edo Hotel* (☎ 200120), formerly the Bendel Hotel, 1km south-west of the museum on 1st Ave. Singles/doubles are N850/1050 with fan and doubles with air-con are N1350. It is set in extensive manicured grounds and has a lot of old colonial character.

The well maintained *Emotan Hotel* (☎ 200130, 1 Central Rd) just off Sapele Rd is the best buy in the 'slightly upmarket' category. Spacious rooms with colour TV and bathroom cost N2300, and there is a restaurant. The nearby *Motel Benin Plaza* (☎ 201430, 1 Reservation Rd) charges N2500/ 2800 plus a deposit of N4000 for air-con singles/doubles with TV.

Places to Eat
There are many *street stalls* along Akpakpava Rd, especially in the Agbadan Market next to the Central Hotel, around the Oba Market, and many stalls (including suya places) around the New Benin Market on Lagos Rd. A great cheap place is the clean and friendly *Two Sisters Food Centre* opposite the Edo Delta Hotel, which serves generous meals for around N150. Another excellent choice for cheap Nigerian dishes is the *Elegance Restaurant* on the corner of Sapoba Rd and Murtala Mohammed Way. The Motel Benin Plaza's restaurant has African meals for around N600.

For European food, the best places are the *Emotan Hotel* (with meals for N450) and the *Saidi Centre* on Sapele Rd; the latter also serves Chinese food.

For groceries, try *Leventis supermarket* on Sapoba Rd near the Genesis Hotel.

Getting There & Away

The motor park for Onitsha, Enugu and other points east is Aba motor park on Akpakpava Rd, several kilometres north-east of the museum. For Lagos (N300) and Ibadan (N250), the Uselu motor park is on Lagos Rd on the north-western outskirts of town. Large buses also serve all of these cities and are slightly cheaper than bush taxis. Ekene Dili Chukwu, one of the main companies, has offices at Mile-2 bus stop along Urubi St.

Getting Around

Around town, shared taxis are N30, and a motorcycle N10 to N20 depending upon distance.

OKOMU SANCTUARY

Nature lovers wanting to see one of the few remaining areas of rainforest in Nigeria should head for this sanctuary near Udo, 40 minutes by car north-west of Benin City. The NCF (see the boxed text 'The Nigerian Conservation Foundation' in the Facts about Nigeria section earlier) is the major force behind this important sanctuary, home to the endangered white-throated monkey and elusive forest elephant, to say nothing of birds and butterflies. You can birdwatch from a treehouse, a dizzying 65m above the ground, overlooking the lake. The reserve also has an educational centre.

The NCF has a *dormitory* at the educational centre with simple/plush rooms for N750/2200. There's better lodging at the African Timber & Plywood *guesthouse*.

For permission to enter the sanctuary and to book accommodation, contact the NCF (☎ 01-268 6163), 5 Moseley Rd, Ikoyi, Lagos. To get here, you'll need your own transport or to take a taxi.

ABRAKA

This small town on the River Benin, 110km south-east of Benin City, is a real escape from the hectic cities to the north. It was a pivotal town in the slave trade and has a long and interesting history. Ask at the Delta State University for information.

The *Abraka Hotel* is the most popular (and best value) place to stay, although not many foreigners visit here. It costs about N4000 for private, clean doubles and good meals are available. It is very close to the river where there is good scuba diving for old Portuguese gin bottles (once used as currency for slave trading) and excellent white-water tubing through rapids.

ONITSHA

Onitsha, in Anambra State, is a veritable wasteland in the heart of the most densely populated area in Africa after the Nile valley. Before the Biafran War, traders from as far away as Cameroon converged on its large market, but the fighting destroyed much of the city, including the market.

Today, this city on the banks of the River Niger has regained some of its vitality. As author Chinua Achebe explains, it has always attracted the 'exceptional, the colourful and the bizarre'. It is famous for its 'market writers', who produced short and often moralistic paperback novels (really just thin pamphlets). The writers, including Cyprian Ekwensi, started producing these cheap and easy to read works in the late 1940s; by 1960 there were more than 200 titles.

Places to Stay & Eat

The friendly *Eleganza Hotel* (☎ 212256, 4 O'Connor St) near DMJ's Roundabout, charges N550 for a single with fan and shared bathroom or N900 for a room with TV, air-con and bathroom. The hotel has a bar and restaurant.

The best of the cheapies is the *People's Club Guesthouse* (☎ 212717). Air-con singles/doubles with TV, fridge and bathroom cost N800/1250. It's frequently fully booked, and has a comfortable bar and a decent restaurant. To get there, cross the overpass from the main motor park on the Lagos-Enugu Expressway and continue

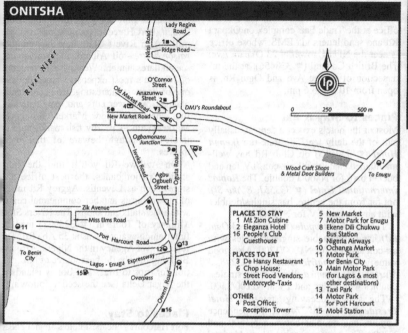

ONITSHA

PLACES TO STAY
1 Mt Zion Cuisine
2 Eleganza Hotel
16 People's Club Guesthouse

PLACES TO EAT
3 De Hansy Restaurant
6 Chop House; Street Food Vendors; Motorcycle-Taxis

OTHER
4 Post Office; Reception Tower
5 New Market
7 Motor Park for Enugu
8 Ekene Dili Chukwu Bus Station
9 Nigeria Airways
10 Ochanga Market
11 Motor Park for Benin City
12 Main Motor Park (for Lagos & most other destinations)
13 Taxi Park
14 Motor Park for Port Harcourt
15 Mobil Station

about 500m south on Owerri Rd; you'll come to the unmarked left turn-off for the hotel.

The best hotel is the small *Mt Zion Cuisine (3 Lady Regina Rd)* just off Ridge Rd. Comfy air-con singles/doubles with colour TV and hot showers cost N1500/1850 plus a deposit of N1500; it has a good Chinese restaurant.

A great cheap place to eat is *De Hansy* not far from Ogbomonanu Junction; a plate of rice or gari with fish or meat costs N100. Another good cheap place is the *Apple Rock Restaurant* on O'Connor St. A *supermarket*, inexpensive *restaurants* and *street food* can be found at the junction of Old and New Market Rds.

Getting There & Away

The bus company, Ekene Dili Chukwu, is on Oguta Rd, 250m south of DMJ's Round-

about. Bush taxis and minibuses for most cities (Lagos, Abuja etc) leave from the motor park just north of the overpass on the expressway, while the motor park for Enugu is on the eastern side of town. The motor park for Benin City is west of town, on the Lagos-Enugu Expressway just before it crosses the river.

ENUGU

Enugu, the centre of Nigeria's coal-mining region, is the capital of Enugu State. It is a typical sprawling Igboland city of nearly 500,000 inhabitants, and is of limited interest to travellers. It was the headquarters for the Igbo (Biafran) army in the tragic civil war and was fortunate to survive pretty much intact.

The city's main street, running roughly north-east to south-west, is Okpara Ave, along which you'll find many businesses, banks and, nearby, the post office. You can make international calls from the NITEL office at the Trade Fair complex on Okpara Rd and send letters via EMS, whose office is near the NITEL tower at 23 Okpara Ave. The British Council (☎ 338456), at the intersection of Chime Ave and Ogui Rd, is open from 10 am to 6 pm.

Places to Stay & Eat

Most of the hotels expect a deposit, usually half of the daily fee. The state-run *Ikenga Hotel* (☎ 334055) on Club Rd has well-maintained chalets with air-con, TV, fan and bucket bath for N800 a double. The *Romas International Hotel* (☎ 333551, 8 Aku St), not far from the centre, has singles/doubles with air-con and TV for N950/1450.

The *Hotel Metropole* (☎ 255411, 13 Ogui Rd) has comfortable singles/doubles with air-con and TV for N1000/1200. Also good value is the *Panafric Hotel* (☎ 335248, 6 Murtala Mohammed Way), with singles/doubles with fridge and TV at N2200/2500.

The slowly decaying state-run *Hotel Presidential* (☎ 337274), at Independence Layout, has doubles between N1500 and N3000. The more expensive, glitzy *Modotel Enugu* (☎ 338870, 2 Club Rd), has air-con singles/doubles with TV and showers for N3000/4000; it has a bar and restaurant.

For quick and cheap chop, try *Ideal Cuisine* (15 Edinburgh Rd); *Den's French Bakery* on Kingsway Rd, east of the roundabout; and *Danny Boy Fast Food* near the Hotel Metropole. *Genesis Restaurant* (36 Zik Ave) serves good Chinese dishes for around N350.

Getting There & Away

Nigeria Airways has several flights each week to Calabar and Lagos. Private airlines service northern centres.

Bush taxis for Onitsha leave from the New Market motor park; vehicles for Port Harcourt and the south leave from Ogbete motor park near the Holy Ghost Cathedral; and vehicles for Abuja, Jos and the north leave from Ogbete, but on the western side of the market.

PORT HARCOURT

Built as a port for exporting coal from Enugu, Port Harcourt (population over one million) in Rivers State now has another *raison d'être* – oil. All around town you can see oil flares at night. Wealth has made it one of Nigeria's most expensive cities but not one of its most interesting. It is continually plagued by power cuts and, enigmatically fuel shortages. New Market, Bonny St Market (with its nearby fish market) are of interest, although beware of the many thieves.

On Azikwe Rd you'll find the train station, major banks, the post office and stores such as Leventis. Aggrey Rd in the old township is another commercial centre with food stalls and shops. The Rivers State Ministry of Tourism (☎ 334901) may be functioning again; it was at 35 Aba Rd. The Ideal Travel Agency in the Nigeria Airways Building may be the best source of information for trips to Brass and Bonny islands in the Niger Delta (see the section following).

Places to Stay

Port Harcourt's cheapest hotels are not cheap compared with hotels elsewhere in Nigeria, Lagos excepted. At the *Alhaja Titilope (2 Rumuadaolu Rd)*, a single with fan and shared bathroom costs N500, while an air-con double goes for N750. The best value is the *Anneta Guest House* (4 Kalagbar St) where air-con singles with shared bathroom cost N450. The staff here are super friendly.

A good choice is the *Delta Hotel* (☎ 300190, 1-3 Harley St), but it's a little removed from the interesting part of town. Well-maintained singles/doubles with air-con, TV and telephone cost N1200/1600. It has a decent bar and restaurant. The *Seane International* (☎ 332141, 2 Okorodo St) has small dark rooms and charges N1250 for singles with fans and N1400 for doubles with air-con.

The *Cedar Palace Hotel* (☎ 300180), on Harbour Rd in the central port area, charges N1500/2200 for a single/double with TV, fridge and shower. The restaurant serves basic meals and the popular bar attracts

PORT HARCOURT

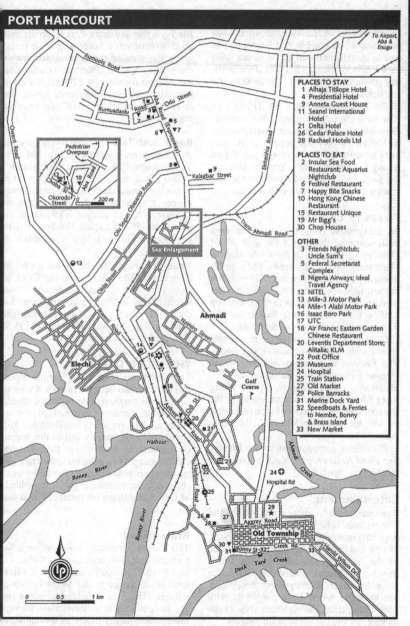

To Airport,
Aba &
Enugu

Rumuola Road

Rumuadaolu

Aba Road – Odu Street

Owerri Road

Pedestrian
Overpass

Choba

Okorodol
Street

Aba Road

200 m

Kalagbar Street

Ekfeoshia Road

Olu Segun Obasanjo Road

Trans-Ahmadi Road

See Enlargement

Okija Street

Iwerri Road

Elechi

Namini Street

Ahmadi

Forces Avenue

Golf
Course

Aptive St

Old St

Harbour Road

Harbour

Bonny River

Bonny River

Hospital Rd

Ahmadi Creek

Old Township

Aggrey Road

Bonny St

Creek Rd

Harold Wilson Dr

Dock Yard Creek

0   0.5   1 km

PLACES TO STAY
1   Alhaja Titilope Hotel
4   Presidential Hotel
9   Anneta Guest House
11 Seanel International
    Hotel
21 Delta Hotel
26 Cedar Palace Hotel
28 Rachael Hotels Ltd

PLACES TO EAT
2   Insular Sea Food
    Restaurant; Aquarius
    Nightclub
6   Festival Restaurant
7   Happy Bite Snacks
10 Hong Kong Chinese
    Restaurant
15 Restaurant Unique
19 Mr Bigg's
30 Chop Houses

OTHER
3   Friends Nightclub;
    Uncle Sam's
5   Federal Secretariat
    Complex
8   Nigeria Airways; Ideal
    Travel Agency
12 NITEL
13 Mile-3 Motor Park
14 Mile-1 Alabi Motor Park
16 Isaac Boro Park
17 UTC
18 Air France; Eastern Garden
    Chinese Restaurant
20 Leventis Department Store;
    Alitalia; KLM
22 Post Office
23 Museum
24 Hospital
25 Train Station
27 Old Market
29 Police Barracks
31 Marine Dock Yard
32 Speedboats & Ferries
    to Nembe, Bonny
    & Brass Island
33 New Market

sailors. Close by is the new *Rachael Hotels Ltd* (☎ *334191, 4 Harbour Rd*), which was twice voted best hotel in Port Harcourt. The air-con doubles with all facilities are good for the N3450 price tag but only if the auxiliary power is on (otherwise the air-con, lifts and lights don't work).

The *Presidential Hotel* (☎ *310400*) on Aba Rd is the city's top hotel. For nonresidents it has rooms which seem overpriced at N6500 plus a N10,000 deposit. ADC Airlines have their office here and you'll find it easy to change money. You can also use the pool for N100, visit the town's best cinema or dine in the 4-5-6 Restaurant.

Places to Eat

For inexpensive chop, try any of the *suya stalls* scattered throughout the grid of old township or the stalls at Bonny St Market. These stalls are all lit by lamps, and with the frequent power cuts in the port it is probably the best light you'll get. For predictable fast food, try *Mr Bigg's* just north of Leventis on Azikwe Rd or *Happy Bite Snacks* on Aba Rd just south of the Federal Secretariat.

On Aba Rd are some better restaurants with a wider range of cuisines and prices. The *Festival Restaurant* and *Restaurant Unique* serve delicious European fare. For reasonable Chinese meals, try the *Hong Kong Chinese Restaurant* on Aba Rd or the *Eastern Garden Chinese* a block to the east of Aba Rd, south of Mile-1 Alabi motor park.

For elegant surroundings, try the *Insular Sea Food Restaurant*, a block off Aba Rd; lobster is its speciality.

Entertainment

Aquarius, not far from the corner of Aba and Rumuadaolu Rds, is one of the city's most popular nightclubs (N100 entry). *Friends*, nearby and known to all taxi drivers, is one of the hottest places (N100), but *Uncle Sam's*, entered from Friends, is even hotter (an additional N200 entry). Both these places are basically white male hang-outs with prostitutes galore. The nightclub at the *Presidential* is more comfortable for women.

Getting There & Away

Air Flying to and from Port Harcourt is a good alternative to buses and bush taxis, given the state of roads to nearby major cities. The airport is 20km north on the Aba Rd. Nigeria Airways (☎ 229931) has daily flights to Lagos and a number of private airlines (Kabo, Okada and ADC) fly to other regional centres.

Bus & Bush Taxi The main motor park for all destinations is on Owerri Rd at Mile-3. You'll probably arrive here. The smaller Mile-1 Abali motor park on Azikwe Rd is better for certain destinations. From there, expect to pay N100 to Aba, N350 to Calabar, N200 to Enugu, N350 to Benin City and N650 to Lagos. The best way to get here from Lagos is by overnight bus.

Boat Speedboats to the Delta towns of Nembe and Brass leave from the Creek at Bonny St Wharf (see the Brass Island Getting There & Away section following for details). The huge public ferries are cheaper but dangerous; one went down in April 1998 with the loss of at least 200 lives.

THE NIGER DELTA

This is Nigeria's most fascinating region and anyone who perseveres with a visit to Nigeria, the toughest of destinations, should not miss it. It makes the hardships of travelling in Nigeria seem worthwhile. You could easily get happily lost in this region of convoluted waterways, palm-fringed creeks, mangroves, palm oil distilleries and traditional fishing villages. The best way to see it is to set yourself a goal – the island of Bonny and Brass for instance – and just go.

Brass Island

This Nembe community is a paradise: it has a vehicle-free town centre, loads of places to buy fresh fish, comfy bars, and it offers tourists the chance to stay in the houses of villagers. However, it is hard to get to and you have to want to go there. Have all your immigration papers handy as the immigration officials will do anything to get a dash – don't give in!

Brass Island got its name from a misunderstanding. When the British arrived, eager to map this relatively unknown part of the world, they sought information from a lone woman on Brass beach. One officer gripped the woman by the shoulder and demanded 'Where are we?' She retaliated with 'Barasi' ('Leave me alone' in Nembe). The map makers gleefully jotted the location down as 'Brass'! The British traditions live on and you will see the village elders dressed in top hats and buttoned-up turn-of-the-century striped shirts and sporting walking sticks or ornamental umbrellas.

Once you get to Brass you have really arrived in remote Africa. It's reminiscent of Lamu in Kenya. Wander the streets, enjoy the food (periwinkles, scampi and lady fish), talk with the locals, watch future football champions battle it out barefoot on the dusty oval, sample good palm wine and enjoy the peaceful surroundings and 24 hour electricity.

Places to Stay & Eat There are two nice *hotels* in Brass, one known locally as Uncle Erasmus – both are in the southern part of town near the creek. A bed in either will cost about N1200: the rooms have fans and windows with mosquito screens. Both have bars and restaurants.

You can also stay with locals, as we did. Ask at the wharf for *Nana Begold* – a stay at her home will be a highlight. The amenities are basic, but the food and hospitality are superb (N1500 would be fair for meals and bed).

There is a great *bar* near the creek. It has a rickety pool table, sumptuous African meals and cheap, cold beers.

Getting There & Away Brass can be reached from Port Harcourt, or from Yenagoa, the capital of the newly created Bayelsa State (the former western section of Rivers). A speedboat from Yenagoa takes just over two hours to get to Brass (N250 to N500) and from Port Harcourt four hours (N500 to N600); local ferries cost N150 and N200 respectively. To get to Yenagoa from Port Harcourt take a bus from Mile-1 Alabi motor park (N100, two hours) and enjoy the travelling salesman's hilarious sales pitch along the way.

A Conversation between Two Kids on Brass Island

Two locals (aged six and seven) followed me, an *o-ibo* (white person), as I left the jetty on Brass to go to my lodgings in the village. They spoke in Nembe, but a bystander interpreted for me. Much laughter followed.

1st Kid: Why are you wasting your time following that o-ibo? He is not going to give you money.

2nd Kid: You think I am following him because I want money from him. You think that I have not seen money before? I have seen lots of money before. I have even eaten N200 before. (This is an incredible sum for a kid who earns N5 for carrying bags from the jetty – and to consume it all in one day!)

1st Kid: You are a liar. You have not eaten that much before. If you have, then you stole it from your mother.

After that, the two intrepid entrepreneurs gave up and returned to the beach to play.

Jeff Williams

NIGERIA

CALABAR

In the far south-east, with twice as much rainfall as Lagos, old colonial Calabar is popular with travellers passing through Nigeria, especially those headed for Cameroon, 25km away. High on a hill, Calabar commands a fine view of the River Calabar, the city on its eastern banks and the frenetic fish market at Hawkins Beach (busy on Thursday, Friday, Sunday and Monday).

Calabar is small by Nigerian standards, which makes it liveable and likeable. If you don't care to walk, motorcycle-taxis are everywhere and are dirt cheap.

The beautiful old governor's residency on the hill overlooking the river has been converted into the city's museum. Open daily from 9 am to 6 pm, entry is only N5. It's well worth a visit. This fascinating and impressive collection covers the precolonial days, the slave era, the palm-oil trade, the British invasion in the late 19th century and independence. It also has a great view of the river.

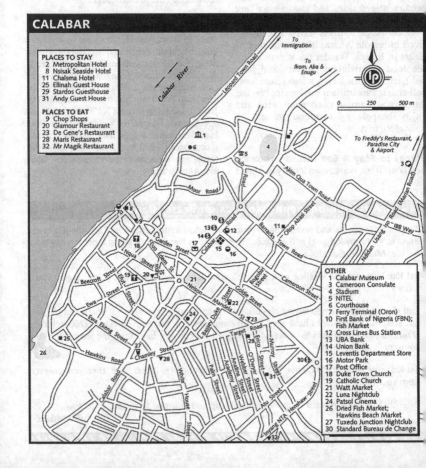

CALABAR

PLACES TO STAY
2 Metropolitan Hotel
8 Nsisak Seaside Hotel
11 Chalsma Hotel
25 Ellinah Guest House
29 Stardos Guesthouse
31 Andy Guest House

PLACES TO EAT
9 Chop Shops
20 Glamour Restaurant
23 De Gene's Restaurant
28 Maris Restaurant
32 Mr Magik Restaurant

OTHER
1 Calabar Museum
3 Cameroon Consulate
4 Stadium
5 NITEL
6 Courthouse
7 Ferry Terminal (Oron)
10 First Bank of Nigeria (FBN); Fish Market
12 Cross Lines Bus Station
13 UBA Bank
14 Union Bank
15 Leventis Department Store
16 Motor Park
17 Post Office
18 Duke Town Church
19 Catholic Church
21 Watt Market
22 Luna Nightclub
24 Patsol Cinema
26 Dried Fish Market; Hawkins Beach Market
27 Tuxedo Junction Nightclub
30 Standard Bureau de Change

NIGERIA

Places to Stay

The most inviting place to stay for cheap accommodation is the family-run *Stardos Guesthouse (7a O'Dwyer St)*. A furnished room with fan and bathroom with bucket shower costs N350 (N500 with air-con). *Andy Guest House* on Erico St has air-con singles/doubles with bathroom for N450/600. The *Chalsma Hotel* (☎ 221942, 7 Otop Abasi St), is also a good choice in the budget range – singles/doubles with air-con and bathroom cost from N900/1500 and smaller rooms with fan only are a couple of hundred naira less. A place with excellent value meals, great river and fish market (and sunset) views is the *Ellinah Guest House* (☎ 223151, 20 Hawkins Rd). Clean singles/doubles with TV and fridge are very reasonably priced at N400/600. Enjoy a pot of tea on their small terrace.

For N800/1000 a single/double, the *Nsisak Seaside Hotel (45 Edem St)* has panoramic views from its 3rd floor glassed-in bar, perfect for watching sunsets.

The city's finest hotel, the *Metropolitan Hotel* (☎ 220913) on Calabar Rd, is decidedly utilitarian. Doubles with TV, air-con and bathroom cost about N3200 (plus N2500 deposit).

Places to Eat

At *Mr Magik Restaurant*, just off Inyang NTA Henshaw St, Mr and Mrs Magik will make you anything, but check the price before ordering. The Calabar soup with periwinkles and the local delicacy, *ekpang nkukwo ikpong* (cocoyam wrapped in cocoyam leaves), N150, are delicious. Oh, and the scampi with sauce tartare is a steal at N45. They also offer pounded yam (N30) and pork kebabs (N120) – yum. Give them time to prepare the food.

Other places to eat include the *chop shops* on Edem St; *Glamour Restaurant (77 Egerton St)*, where gari costs N100; the *Maris Restaurant* on Chamley St for bush meat and plantain; the spotlessly clean *De Gene's (36 Nelson Mandela St)*; and *Freddy's Restaurant* (☎ 222821, 90 Atekong

Drive) for humous (N375), fish pepper soup (N300) and ice cream (N175).

Entertainment

The *Luna Nightclub (18 Nelson Mandela St)* has live music and also serves food. *Tuxedo Junction (147 Calabar Rd)*, at the intersection with Chamley St, is also popular for music. *Paradise City* is the most popular of the discos.

Getting There & Away

Air Nigeria Airways and ADC have flights between Calabar and Lagos.

Bush Taxi & Minibus Bush taxis and minibuses leave from the motor park next to Leventis on Mary Slessor Ave (Cameroon Rd). Cross Lines bus station is across the street and charges N700 to Lagos, N600 for the 12 hour bus to Abuja and N750 for the marathon ride to Kaduna; the condition of the buses is variable.

One way into Cameroon is north via Ikom and Mfum. Bush taxis to Mfum cost N50; from there you can walk into Cameroon. The other way is to go from Ekang (at the end of the Oban Forest Rd) to Otu; inquire in Calabar for details.

Boat Note that, at the time of going to press, it was not possible for travellers to go to Oron, because of the ongoing dispute over the Bakassi Peninsula. The following details are given in case this route opens up again – you should check in Calabar on the current situation before setting out.

From Cross Lines on the wharf you can catch a ferry or 'flying boat' (speedboat) to Creek Town. To Oron there's a ferry (N60) twice a day, leaving Calabar at 8.30 am and 1.30 pm, arriving two hours later and returning at 11 am and 4 pm. There is also a more expensive speedboat.

Sea travel is not possible from Oron or Ikang at the moment, which means travellers cannot use this route to travel to/from Cameroon. If the dispute is resolved then there should be two options. You could take the flying boat that leaves Oron around 10 am for Idenao (eight passengers; three to four hours, N600 per person). Otherwise, find five other people and go direct to Limbe (six passengers; five hours, N800). Land crossings may still be possible (see the beginning of this section for more details).

AROUND CALABAR

A good day trip is to the tranquil village of **Creek Town**, a short, relaxing trip up the river. You meet locals going about their business as you wander along the dusty roads. Look out for the incongruous colonial church.

In **Oron**, reached by ferry, there is an excellent museum opposite the ferry wharf. It's open daily from 9 am to 5.30 pm, and has a wonderful collection of woodcarvings. However, with the present Bakassi Peninsula conflict, travellers cannot go to Oron. It is the usual sea departure point for Cameroon.

CROSS RIVER NATIONAL PARK

This large park is north of Calabar and set in a lush rainforest which contains waterfalls, birds and gorillas. You can hike in the park: see the boxed text 'Hiking in Nigeria' in the Facts for the Visitor section of this chapter for details. The park has an office in Calabar at 3 Ebuta Crescent, Ette Agbor Layout. Ask there for information and an introductory letter; they also have information on nearby Mbe Mountain National Park.

Cross River National Park is managed jointly by the World Wide Fund for Nature (WWF) and the NCF, which have a centre near Kanyang 1, north of Ikom on the road to Obudu. You can arrange for a guide there as well as get information on the **Mbe Mountain Conservation Project**, where the gorillas live.

The WWF has advised that the Ikrigon Forest Reserve, part of the park, is under threat from logging. The state government, in spite of the recommendations of an Environmental Impact Assessment has approved a massive 54,143 hectare concession to a logging company.

If you're caught in Ikom for the night, the **Lisbon** on Calabar Rd is a really cheap place (N450) which allows vehicle parking in its secure grounds.

Getting There & Away

From Calabar take a bush taxi north to Ikom (N150), then get an onward taxi towards Obudu. After 45 minutes you'll come to Kanyang 1, the closest village to the NCF/WWF centre. You can walk from the village to the nearby centre.

OBUDU CATTLE RANCH

This unlikely but well known resort is on the Cameroon border, at the base of the Sonkwala Mountains on the Oshie Ridge, 110km east of Ogoja. On the way you'll pass through tall, dense forests where the branches form a canopy that shuts out the sun entirely. As you drive up the plateau, you'll see rolling mountain ranges.

Built during the 1950s by Scottish ranchers, this was at one time a well-functioning ranch-resort. These days it's run-down but it is slowly being renovated (with VSO help). The *Obudu Ranch Hotel* has chalets, tennis courts and horses. The rooms are not cheap (around N2750); for reservations write to: Obudu Cattle Ranch, PO Box 40, Obudu, Cross River State. (See also the boxed text 'Hiking in Nigeria' in the Facts for the Visitor section of this chapter.)

Getting There & Away

By vehicle the 110km drive east from Ogoja to the ranch via Obudu is straightforward and is tar road part of the way. Take a motorcycle or bush taxi from Obudu, which is 44km west of the ranch.

GASHAKA GUMPTI NATIONAL PARK

Gashaka Gumpti is Nigeria's largest national park and has the country's highest mountain, **Chappal Wadi** (2418m). Within its large area is a plethora of rivers and the most diverse ecology of any Nigerian park, including guinea savanna, grasslands and pockets of mountain (or gallery) forest. Elephant, hippopotamus, waterbuck, buffalo, monkeys and big cats are all found here, and birdwatchers will be in their element. You have to be adventurous to want to see it, as it is less developed than the better known Yankari National Park.

The national park headquarters is on the edge of **Serti**, about 1km from the motor park (N20 by taxi). From here you can hire a vehicle (the price is negotiable) from the national park authorities to get to the heart of the park at **Gashaka**, 40km away on a rough 4WD road. The park entrance fee is N60 per person.

Places to Stay

There is basic *accommodation* in Serti at the park headquarters (N300). You'll need to bring all your food, but there is electricity and plenty of water. In Gashaka you can probably stay in the NCF's *lodge* (N200 per person) which has a wood-burning stove, lamps, plenty of water (fetched from the river) and a great veranda to sit on and appreciate 'sundowners' – tip the caretaker.

The only place to stay in Gembu (140km south of Serti) is the *Daula Hotel*, which has single/doubles with shared bucket showers for N100/150 (N200 to N350 for larger rooms with private bathrooms).

Getting There & Away

Unless you have your own transport, you will have to juggle several bush taxis. To get to Serti (N400), start on the A4 in Jalingo or Wukari. To get to the park from Gembu, take a bush taxi on the road to Serti (N300).

The Centre

ABUJA

During the oil-boom days of the 1970s, the Nigerian government decided to construct a new capital in an undeveloped central area. Construction began in the early 1980s, which was the worst time possible, as oil revenues were then beginning to slide. As a result, construction has proceeded at a snail's pace. The mosque (brilliantly lit at night), the law courts and the presidential guesthouse are finished, but the wide boulevards have rela-

tively few vehicles and many lots are still vacant. During the monthly three hour clean-up the town is as quiet as a morgue.

Abuja is only slowly becoming Nigeria's actual capital; ex-president Abacha moved his government here to a veritable fortress (he needed it!) on Aso Rock. While many official functions are now held in Abuja, the Federal Capital Territory (FCT), many ministries are still in Lagos.

One of Nigeria's more famous landmarks is **Zuma Rock**, only 55km from Abuja. This huge granite outcrop is approximately 300m high and 1km long. It's not exactly a spine-tingling sight, but it is somewhat impressive. To get there from Wuse market take a minivan to Suleja (about N75).

Information

The Sheraton and Nicon Noga Hilton hotels have information desks. For phoning, the NITEL office is on Faskari St in the Garki district. There's a post office and EMS parcel service are in the Wuse Shopping Centre. Nigeria Airways has an office at the UTC shopping complex, while the private airlines have desks at the Sheraton (ADC, Bellview and Okada).

Places to Stay – Budget

There are not many 'cheap' hotels in Abuja. The cheapest appears to be the *Eddie-Vic Hotel*, which is off Mohammed Buhari Way and quite isolated. It charges N700 for a single room with a wretched shared bathroom. If you pay a little more, you'll get better value.

The *Sonny Guest Inn (41 Areal St)* off Benue Crescent behind the old Garki motor park is slightly better, but the location is less than desirable. It's pleasant and clean and charges N750 for a single with fan (N1000 with air-con).

The *Sharon International Hotel (220 Fortlammy St)* off Bissau St and the *Tamara Guest Inn (2059 Abidjan St)* have singles for about N1250 plus a deposit of N600 and doubles for N1500 plus a deposit of N750.

The best hotel for the money is the *Savannah Suites* in the Garki district off JS

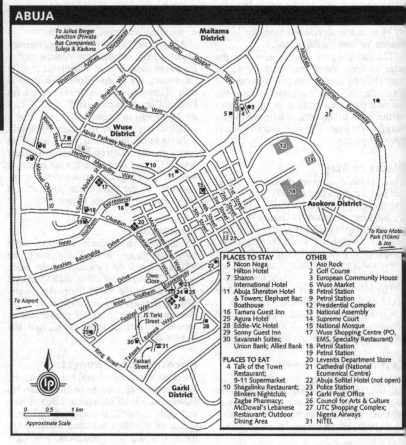

ABUJA

To Julius Berger
Junction (Private
Bus Companies),
Suleja & Kaduna

Maitama
District

Wuse
District

Asokoro District

To Karu Moto
Park (10km)
& Jos

To Airport

Garki
District

0   0.5   1 km

Approximate Scale

PLACES TO STAY
5   Nicon Noga
    Hilton Hotel
7   Sharon
    International Hotel
11 Abuja Sheraton Hotel
    & Towers; Elephant Bar;
    Boathouse
16 Tamara Guest Inn
25 Agura Hotel
28 Eddie-Vic Hotel
29 Sonny Guest Inn
30 Savannah Suites;
    Union Bank; Allied Bank

PLACES TO EAT
4   Talk of the Town
    Restaurant;
    9-11 Supermarket
10 Shagalinku Restaurant;
    Blinkers Nightclub;
    Zagbe Pharmacy;
    McDowal's Lebanese
    Restaurant; Outdoor
    Dining Area

OTHER
1   Aso Rock
2   Golf Course
3   European Community House
6   Wuse Market
8   Petrol Station
9   Petrol Station
12 Presidential Complex
13 National Assembly
14 Supreme Court
15 National Mosque
17 Wuse Shopping Centre (PO,
    EMS, Speciality Restaurant)
18 Petrol Station
19 Petrol Station
20 Leventis Department Store
21 Cathedral (National
    Ecumenical Centre)
22 Abuja Sofitel Hotel (not open)
23 Police Station
24 Garki Post Office
26 Council for Arts & Culture
27 UTC Shopping Complex;
    Nigeria Airways
31 NITEL

Tarki St, between the Union and Allied banks. Comfortable, clean rooms cost N2000 plus a deposit of N1000.

Places to Stay – Mid-Range & Top End

The top class hotels in town all have swimming pools, tennis courts, free airport shuttle service and so on. Of these, the best value is the *Abuja Sheraton Hotel & Towers* (☎ 5230225 or 5230244) at Ladi Kwali Way, where standard doubles cost US$140 plus a

deposit of US$210. It has a huge atrium and is close to cheap restaurants (you won't wan to dine in the hotel too often unless you ar extremely wealthy).

The *Nicon Noga Hilton* (☎ 5234811 o 5234840), Africa's largest hotel, charge US$160 plus for doubles plus a heft deposit. Both the Hilton and Sheraton have resident rate which is considerably lowe (the Sheraton's is N9200 for the cheapes double room); get a Nigerian to make you booking so you can pay in naira.

The *Agura Hotel* (☎ *5231753*) in Festival Way offers the comforts of the bigger hotels for much less. It has a pool, tennis courts and shops and the comfortable rooms are about N8000 for doubles. The *Abuja Sofitel* on Festival Way is closed.

Places to Eat

For *cheap chop* try one of the little stands around Wuse market or those outside the bus stations near the Julius Berger junction in the north-west of the city. If you crave a few western delights go to the *9-11 Supermarket* just off Shehu Shagari Way North, near the European Community House.

The biggest collection of restaurants is about 300m west of the Sheraton in Addis Ababa Crescent, just off Herbert Macauley Way. There are a couple of cheap places, including an unnamed *outdoor dining area* and bar protected by a wall of sackcloth – the harmattan can be pretty fierce here. The other places are relatively expensive. *McDowal's* is a great Lebanese place that has shish kebab for N160, tabouleh for N170 and hearty salads for about N250. *Shagalinku* is a Muslim place just around the corner (there is no alcohol and smoking is forbidden) with very good food: their excellent jollof rice is N170.

The town's most expensive restaurant, outside of the hotels, is *Talk of the Town*, just off Shehu Shagari Way North. It serves Indian specialities.

Entertainment

The city's best attractions are probably the classy bars and nightclubs, catering to construction workers and visitors. You will find the *Elephant Bar* and *Boathouse* at the Sheraton much better than the bars at the Hilton. If you want to listen to a band and meet locals then *Blinkers* near Addis Ababa Crescent is your best choice.

Getting There & Away

Nigeria Airways, ADC, Okada Airlines and Bellview Airlines have daily flights to Lagos; it is about N5950/10,000 one way/ return to Lagos (payable in US$ only). The airport is 40km west of town.

Bush taxis leave from the new Karu motor park, 10km west of town on the Jos road. The major routes are to Kano (N350, five hours), Kaduna (N200, two hours), Jos (N350, three hours), Makurdi (N250, three hours), Onitsha (N500, four hours) and Lagos (N800, twelve hours).

The private buses are much better. Chisco and CN Okoli, both near Julius Berger junction, charge about N1200 for an overnight trip ('night flight') to Lagos. The buses depart at 7 pm and reach Lagos at about 5 or 6 am the following morning.

JOS

Jos (an abbreviation of 'Jesus Our Saviour'), with a population between one and two million, is one of the more popular destinations in Nigeria. The two major attractions are the cooler climate and the unique Jos museum complex. At 1200m above sea level, the Jos plateau is noticeably cooler than most other areas of the country. The stone-covered rolling hills also make it more scenic. Ask a Nigerian – they'll lift their arms in the air and utter sweetly 'Jos!'

Orientation & Information

The city has two main north-south drags. One is Bauchi Rd, along which you'll find the large, covered market, the train station and some commercial establishments; it transforms into Murtala Mohammed Way in the south. Roughly 1km to the west is Zaria Rd, which becomes Gomwalk Rd further south. Beach Rd ('The Beach') runs parallel to the now defunct railway line.

The post office (which has an email service via Lagos) is on Ahmadu Bello Way in the city centre, while the pitiful NITEL office is on the outskirts of town on Yakubu Gowon Way, out near the old airport junction. Abbas Bureau de Change opposite the post office will change travellers cheques at a reasonable rate. The Rayfield Travel Agency on Ahmadu Bello Way can make all travel bookings. Ross Clayton Internet on Ahmadu Bello Way could be your best

NIGERIA

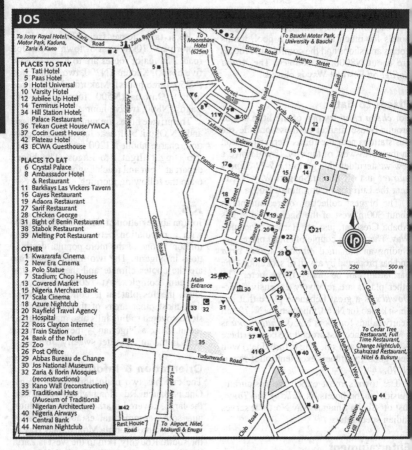

JOS

To Jossy Royal Hotel, Motor Park, Kaduna, Zaria & Kano

PLACES TO STAY
4 Tati Hotel
5 Paas Hotel
9 Hotel Universal
10 Varsity Hotel
12 Jubilee Up Hotel
14 Terminus Hotel
34 Hill Station Hotel; Palace Restaurant
36 Tekan Guest House/YMCA
37 Cocin Guest House
42 Plateau Hotel
43 ECWA Guesthouse

PLACES TO EAT
6 Crystal Palace
8 Ambassador Hotel & Restaurant
11 Barkliays Las Vickers Tavern
16 Gayes Restaurant
19 Adaora Restaurant
27 Sarif Restaurant
28 Chicken George
31 Bight of Benin Restaurant
38 Stabok Restaurant
39 Melting Pot Restaurant

OTHER
1 Kwararafa Cinema
2 New Era Cinema
3 Polo Statue
7 Stadium; Chop Houses
13 Covered Market
15 Nigeria Merchant Bank
17 Scala Cinema
18 Azure Nightclub
20 Rayfield Travel Agency
21 Hospital
22 Ross Clayton Internet
23 Train Station
24 Bank of the North
25 Zoo
26 Post Office
29 Abbas Bureau de Change
30 Jos National Museum
32 Zaria & Ilorin Mosques (reconstructions)
33 Kano Wall (reconstruction)
35 Traditional Huts (Museum of Traditional Nigerian Architecture)
40 Nigeria Airways
41 Central Bank
44 Neman Nightclub

To Bauchi Motor Park, University & Bauchi

To Moonshine Hotel (625m)

To Cedar Tree Restaurant, Full Time Restaurant, Change Nightclub, Shahrazad Restaurant, Nitel & Bukuru

To Airport, Nitel, Makurdi & Enugu

0   250   500 m

chance to get an email message home in months.

Jos Museum Complex

The highly recommended museum complex is really four separate museums and a zoo. The Railroad Museum, Tin Mining Museum and zoo are not very exciting. However, the pottery and much older terracotta collections (including Nok pottery from 500 BC) at the Jos National Museum are superb. The Museum of Traditional Nigerian Architec-

ture is more unusual. Spread out over 20 hectares are full-scale reproductions of buildings from each of Nigeria's major regions. You can see a reconstruction of the Kano wall (and go for a frightening walk along it), the old Zaria mosque with a Muslim museum inside, the Ilorin mosque and examples of the major styles of village architecture, such as the circular *katanga* buildings of the Nupe people, with beautifully carved posts supporting a thatched roof.

The museum complex is open daily from 8.30 am to 5.30 pm and has an entrance fee of N10 (check out the bat-infested Australian eucalypts at the entrance). Ask for one of the knowledgeable guides; they will open up a world of understanding and are well worth a tip of N150 for a two hour excursion.

Jos Wildlife Park

This park is 14km south-west of town on the Bukuru Rd. It's better than the town's sad zoo offering and is open from 10 am until sunset.

Places to Stay – Budget

One of the best places, the cheery *Cocin Guest House* on Noad Ave, charges N170 per bed in a two-bed room with bathroom. Opposite, the *Tekan Guest House/YMCA* (☎ 453036), a Christian missionary centre, has dormitory rooms with beds for N160 a person. Good cheap European or African meals are available here. The tranquil *ECWA Guesthouse* (☎ 454482), another Protestant missionary centre just off Kano Rd, is similar. For a dorm room with shared bathroom (cold water only) it charges N130 a person or N280 for a room with bathroom and hot water.

The *Hotel Universal* (*11 Pankshin Rd*) has doubles with fans, shared bathrooms and towels for N250 (N300 with bathroom) and they bring steaming buckets of hot water to your door in the morning! One block behind (south-east of) the Universal, at 1 Nnamdi Azikiwe Ave (Zik Ave), is the slightly more expensive *Varsity Hotel*. Immaculate singles/doubles with bathroom cost N300/400; the hotel has a restaurant and sedate bar.

Several hotels have the name Jubilee, but only one gives cause for celebration. The *Jubilee Up* (☎ 455457, *32 Adebayo St*) has clean singles with shared bathroom for N300/420; doubles with bathroom, TV and fan cost N600, or N780 with air-con. The *Jubilee Down* on Zaria Bypass should be avoided. On Enugu Agidi St is the good-value *Moonshine Hotel* (☎ 455645), where rooms with shared bathroom go for N300 (N550 with TV and bathroom). The *Moon-shine Annexe* across the street has air-con singles/doubles for N500/650.

Places to Stay – Mid-Range & Top End

The popular, modern *Tati Hotel* (☎ 455897 *or 452554*) at the intersection of Zaria Rd and Zaria Bypass has good air-con rooms for N800 with bathroom, and N1250 for a suite, plus a deposit of N1000. The breakfasts in the restaurant are disappointing, but the staff are very friendly. The *Paas Hotel* (☎ 453851, *42 Ndagi Farouk Close*), is the best mid-range hotel. Rooms with balconies, air-con, TV, telephone, bathroom and one/two beds cost N750/900.

If you prefer to be in the heart of town, the run-down *Terminus Hotel* (☎ 454831), on Tafawa Balewa Rd, a few blocks west of the covered market, charges N900 for a room with two single beds, fan, telephone, and bathroom. The water supply is not always reliable and the street can be noisy. We only learnt about the *Jossy Royal Hotel* on Zaria Rd after we had left town. Reports are that it is good value at N800/1800 for singles/ doubles and N3000 for suites.

The *Hill Station Hotel* (☎ 455398), on Tudun Wada Rd, is nicely perched on a hill on the western side of town. Singles/doubles cost N2000/2300 plus a deposit of N4000 ('plateau' rooms are N7150). Even if you don't stay here, it's a good place to come for a drink or to swim in the freezing pool for N100. The *Plateau Hotel* (☎ 455741) on Rest House Rd, half a kilometre south of the Hill Station, is much better value with air-con doubles at N1600 plus a deposit of N1250.

Places to Eat

There are plenty of cheap *chop houses* near the stadium, some with the ubiquitous goat's head soup. Within walking distance, on or close to Zik Ave, are the *Ambassador*, *Crystal Palace* (with burgers and coffee), *Barkliays Las Vickers Tavern* and the more expensive *Gayes Restaurant*. Try local dishes here such as *koko da kosat*, a custard-style corn mash (N60), super tasty *fura da nano*, cow's milk with millet, or *tuwan shinkafa* with egusi and chicken (N120).

Other good Nigerian restaurants are *Adaora* on Rwang Pam St and *Sarif* on Beach Rd; meals range from N50 to N150. The *Stabok Restaurant (8 Bank Rd)* has toasted sandwiches, and African and European dishes from N110. For fast food addicts there is *Chicken George* on Bauchi Rd.

A wonderful place for lunch is the *Bight of Benin* restaurant at the Jos Museum complex. It offers an interesting variety of reasonably priced Nigerian dishes, and you get to eat in a replica of a chief's house. Also good for lunch is the *Melting Pot* on Ahmadu Bello Way, although it is a little more expensive.

One of the best restaurants is the Lebanese *Cedar Tree Restaurant* (☎ 454890), 5km south of the market on Bauchi/Bukuru Rd, opposite Tilley Gyado House; humous is N200, felafel sandwiches N150, kofta N180, a mixed grill N300 and a large Guinness N100. The *Shahrazad* on Yakubu Gowon Way also serves excellent Lebanese food in the same price range. The pick of the town's Lebanese restaurants, with considerably lower prices, is *Full Time* (closed Monday), not far south of the Cedar Tree. Humous is N150 and felafel sandwiches N120.

Entertainment

The best watering hole in the centre is *Azure Nightclub* on Langtang St. It is a gathering place for the town's drug dealers, prostitutes and criminals, but they leave their professions behind when they are socialising.

For live music, try the ever-popular *Shahrazad* (see Places to Eat), one of the best nightclubs in town which often features local bands. *Change Nightclub*, 500m closer to the town centre on the same road, also frequently has live music (N100 entry), as does the popular *Neman Disco* on Bauchi Rd (also called Murtala Mohammed Way).

Two cinemas, *Kwararafa* and *New Era*, both on the Zaria Bypass, have the usual kung-fu and Indian offerings. There's also the *Scala Cinema* on Ndagi Farouk Close.

Getting There & Away

Air Nigeria Airways (☎ 452298) has numerous flights to Lagos (N5000) but virtually none to other cities. Its office is on Bank Rd. Okada Airlines have daily flights to Lagos; their office is in the Hill Station Hotel. The airport is 40km south of town and the taxi trip costs N500.

Bus On long-distance routes, you can save a small amount by taking a large bus instead of a Peugeot 504 bush taxi. Buses to Lagos cost N700 to N800 and take 12 or so hours. Plateau Express and Assisted Mass Transit leave from the sports complex (on Tafawa Balewa Rd). Companies with buses east to Bauchi and Maiduguri, such as Yankari Express, and south to Calabar, such as Cross Lines, operate next to the Bauchi motor park on Bauchi Rd, north of town.

Bush Taxi & Minibus Bush taxis and minibuses all depart from the Bauchi motor park. Minibuses charge N250 to Abuja and Kano; the trip to either one can take up to four hours. Bush taxis go to Abuja (N350, three hours), to Kaduna (N300, 3½ hours; N250 by minibus), to Kano (N400, six hours because of the road), to Enugu (N800, six hours) and to Calabar (N1000, nine hours).

Getting Around

For trips around town, expect to pay from N30 on a motorcycle-taxi and double that for a regular taxi.

KADUNA

Although intended by the British in the early 20th century to be the seat of power in the north, Kaduna has few points of historical interest.

The main street running north-south through the centre of town is the wide Ahmadu Bello Way, which becomes Junction Rd further south towards the stadium.

The tourist information centre on Wurne Rd, off Ali Akilu Rd, may be open. The British Council (☎ 236033) is on Yakubu Gowon Rd, near the post office and banks. The NITEL office on the corner of Lafia

KADUNA

PLACES TO STAY
5 Durbar Hotel;
   Street Food Vendors
17 Safari Club
18 Durncan Hotel
19 Kaduna Guest Inn
21 Central Guest Inn
23 Zodiac Hotel Annexe
24 Fina White House
   Hotel
25 Fina White House
   Hotel
26 Fina White House
   Hotel

PLACES TO EAT
2 Chicken George
7 Arewa Chinese
   Restaurant
8 Sherlaton Restaurant
9 Mayfair Restaurant

13 Nanet Restaurant
20 Chop House
22 Golden Fried Chicken
30 La Cabana

OTHER
1 Post Office
3 Racecourse
4 Maharajah Disco
6 German Consulate
10 Leventis Department
   Store
11 British Council
12 Post Office; Union
   Bank
14 Main Motor Park
15 Central Market
16 Union Bank
27 Stadium
28 Total Station
29 Train Station

and Kukawa Rds is open 24 hours. The British deputy high commission (☎ 233380) is at 2 Lamido Rd and the German consulate (☎ 223696) is on Ahmadu Bello Way.

The museum, at the northern end of the city on the road to Kano (Ali Akilu Rd) and across from the Emir's palace, has a little bit of everything – masks, pottery, musical instruments, brasswork, door posts, woodcarvings and leather displays; the entrance fee is N10. It is open daily from 9 am to 6 pm, but closes if NEPA's offed.

Places to Stay

The cheapest place in town is the *Kaduna Guest Inn (15 Ibadan St)*, which charges N250 for a room with fan and shared bathroom and is often full. The noisy *Central Guest Inn (182 Benue Rd)* charges N250 for a double with a clean shared bathroom. Another cheap, lively place is the *Safari Club (☎ 211838, 10 Argungu Rd)*. It has singles with fans for N300, clean bathrooms with bucket showers and a huge, active bar.

The three *Fina White House Hotels (☎ 211852)*, the main one at 23 Constitution Rd – look for the large four-storey building with the 'Motor Oil' sign on top – has cramped doubles for N500 with noisy aircon and bathroom. The management will farm you out to one of the better buildings if you ask – rooms with TV, air-con and bathroom cost from N1200.

For a clean room, good food and peaceful surroundings, the *Zodiac Hotel Annexe (☎ 234863)* on Yauri St is a good choice; large singles/doubles with large bed, air-con and fans are N550/750. On Katsina Rd the *Durncan Hotel* has comfy doubles with fan for N800 (N1100 with air-con and TV).

The excellent *Durbar Hotel (☎ 201108)* is near the centre, on the corner of Waff Rd and Independence Way. Its rooms with TV and fridge cost N4800 plus a deposit of N6000. It has a bookshop, pharmacy, bank, 50m pool (N200 for nonguests), four restaurants, a nightclub and bars. It is easy to change cash and travellers cheques here. The *Hamdala Hotel (☎ 211005)*, a block to the east, is very clean, and has comfortable

NIGERIA

doubles with TV and video for N4000 plus a deposit of N3000.

Places to Eat

For non-African fare, a popular place on Ahmadu Bello Way is *Chicken George*, a fast food chain. For more fast food, check out *Golden Fried Chicken* on Yoruba Rd. For grilled chicken and beef, try the vendors opposite the Durbar Hotel. For cheap African food, the no-name *chop house* at the intersection of Ahmadu Bello Way and Argungu Rd is unbeatable. The food is cooked in big, steamy pots and dished up by huge, sweaty women. It is very popular, open from lunch time until 9 pm and a plate is about N100.

On Ahmadu Bello Way is *Nanet Restaurant* which serves good Nigerian food in a middle-class setting (uniformed waiters and tablecloths); it's open from 6.30 am to 10 pm and a sound three course meal can be had for N450 to N600. The *Mayfair Restaurant*, 100m north and on the other side of the road, is a good choice for a hearty English breakfast.

The *Jakaranda Farm & Pottery*, 20km south of town on Kachia Rd, is a popular weekend jaunt known for its excellent buffets (a selection of African and European dishes) and pottery sales.

For an excellent meal in the N200 to N300 range you can't beat the *Arewa Chinese Restaurant* (☎ 212380) on Ahmadu Bello Way. It's open every day and has an all-you-can-eat buffet every Sunday (N1000). The *Unicorn Chinese Restaurant* at the Hamdala Hotel is quite good and has more than 120 choices for around N500 each; it's open daily.

For superb Indian food don't miss *Sherlaton* on Ahmadu Bello Way, where generally you won't spend more than N850 for a feast.

For Lebanese and French food, head for the fancy *La Cabana*, on Junction Rd 2km south of the central market. It's open every evening.

Entertainment

The *Central Guest Inn* has a lively bar. The weekend nightclub at *La Cabana* is for those looking for an upmarket place with dancing and drinking. The disco at the Durbar Hotel and the nightclub next door to the Hamdala Hotel are others. The buzz place at the moment is the *Maharajah Disco* on the corner of Independence Way and Kashim Ibrahim Rd; entry is N50.

Getting There & Away

Air Nigeria Airways (☎ 210174, 26 Ahmadu Bello Way), has two flights a day to Lagos, on average, and several flights a week to Port Harcourt. Kabo Air (☎ 242248) on Ahmadu Bello Way, 2km north of the central market, has flights to Lagos and other centres.

Bus & Bush Taxi The town's main motor park on Gombe Rd is across from the central market. For Lagos go to the Mando motor park in the north on Ali Akilu Rd. The cheapest way to get to Lagos is on one of the overnight buses.

Bush taxis cost N250 for the 3½ hour trip to Jos and leave from the New Kawo motor park. Bush taxis to Zaria cost N50 and take one hour. To reach either Mando or Kawo, catch a minibus from the main motor park; the fare is N10.

ZARIA

An old city and once one of the seven Hausa states, Zaria retains its traditional character. A 14km mud wall, now largely disintegrated, surrounds part of the old section of the city. Look for it on the southern side, towards Kaduna, south of the River Kubani and behind an old gate. The old market and the Friday mosque are both inside; while the mosque is modern, it has the magnificent original interior vaulting.

The streets of the old town contain fine examples of traditional **Hausa homes** with patterned mud walls. The most notable is the Emir's palace, complete with colourfully garbed guards and the occasional blast on the ram's horn to announce the arrival of someone of importance at the Babang Kofa, the festively decorated main gate.

At the **market**, look for dye pits, blacksmiths and other artisans at work; other artisans spin thread for the traditional *kaptani*, the knee length embroidered shirt for men. The **Nigerian Army Museum** on RWAFF Rd is open from 8 am to 2.30 pm weekdays; it has an interesting exhibit on the Biafran War.

Many of Zaria's houses show intricate mud decorations on the external walls. Spot the bicycle – prestige items like this are often worked into the pattern.

Places to Stay

Most hotels are in Sabon Gari, the new section north of the River Kubani. The first you'll come to is the friendly *Royal Guest House (8 Park Rd)*; it charges N450 for a good air-con single with bathroom and hot water. The *Zaria Central Hotel (26 Park Rd)*, 100m further north is similar in style and price.

The old *Kuta Hotel (☎ 33268, 8 Aliyu Rd)* 200m south of the bridge off Hospital Rd has a central courtyard and is decent for the price (N500 a double).

The city's two nicest hotels are the *Zaria Hotel (☎ 32875)*, on Sokoto Rd on the northern edge of town, 500m north of the main post office, and the *Kongo Conference Hotel (☎ 32872)*, in the centre of Sabon Gari, on Old Jos Rd. The Kongo charges N4500 for a double, while the Zaria is a bit cheaper. Both have air-con rooms and while the Kongo has a pool, the Zaria offers 'scintillating makossa music from 9 pm to dawn' in its nightclub on weekends.

Places to Eat

For Nigerian food, the *Ify Groove Restaurant (16 Park Rd)* serves inexpensive dishes such as moin-moin and gari; the *Efficient Restaurant (F3 Kaduna Rd)* has good salads for N120; and the *Unique Restaurant* on RWAFF Rd is as typical as you got. At the superb *Shakalinku* on Kongo Rd in Tudan Wada, you can eat local dishes (N150) in a traditional setting – sitting on the floor with your shoes off.

The *restaurant* at the Zaria Central Hotel serves typical Nigerian dishes for N100.

Getting There & Away

The motor park is in Sabon Gari. To Kano it costs N150 by minibus (two hours) and N200 by bush taxi. Bush taxis to Jos cost N300, while minibuses cost N200 (three hours).

BAUCHI

This city, capital of Bauchi State and a convenient stop on your way to or from Yankari National Park, is unpretentious and not very exciting. Students of politics may enjoy Tafawa Balewa's Mausoleum, open daily from 7 am to 6 pm; free admission.

Places to Stay & Eat
The *De Kerker Lodge*, behind the stadium, is cheap, friendly and has ultra-basic rooms with fans for N250. The communal toilet is dirty and water comes from the courtyard well. The impersonal *Sogiji Hotel* on Maiduguri Rd offers a large bed with either a fan/air-con for N800/950.

The *Zaranda Hotel* (☎ 435902) is several kilometres west of town on the Jos Rd. It charges N2000 (plus a deposit of N1000) for very comfortable rooms, and has a booking office for Yankari National Park. In town, the *Horizontal Bar*, opposite Chicken George on Jos Rd, has comfortable motel-style rooms for N1600.

Terry's Chinese Restaurant on the Maiduguri Bypass Rd serves a good meal with cold beer for around N400. *Vital Inn*, two blocks from the De Kerker Lodge, is the best watering hole in this mostly 'dry' town.

Getting There & Away
Bush taxis leave from Maiduguri motor park on Ningi Rd for Kano, while those for Jos depart from Jos motor park, Jos Rd. Transport to Yankari leaves from Minivan motor park.

YANKARI NATIONAL PARK
Open for wildlife viewing all year round, Yankari is 225km east of Jos, and covers an area of 2244 sq km. It's a good, cheap place to visit. Around 600 elephants live here, by far the largest number in any West African wildlife park. Bushbuck and waterbuck are the most common animals and are too numerous to count. The park is also home to buffalo, hippopotamus, lion, monkeys, warthog, waterbuck, crocodile and plenty of baboons.

Another great attraction of Yankari is the lake formed by the Wikki Warm Springs, near the park lodge. About 200m long and 10m wide, the springs are wonderful and scenic. Their crystal-clear mineral water is

a constant 31°C and, most importantly, is free of bilharzia. Baboons, and occasionally elephants, come down to the springs.

The best time to see animals is from late February to late April, before the rains, when the thirsty animals congregate at the River Gaji. Driving is permitted in the park, but most people take advantage of the park's two-hour tours at 7.30 am and 3.30 pm in specially converted trucks and buses. The tours are excellent value at N100 per person. The park entrance fee is N100, and N100 for a camera permit.

Places to Stay & Eat
Wikki Warm Springs Hotel (☎ 077-41174) in the park is often full at weekends, so reservations are advisable. It has circular bungalows that are ageing rapidly. They cost a quite reasonable N500 per room and have air-con and bathrooms. The restaurant, too, is reasonably priced at N250 for good three-course meals. You can camp for N150 per person and get water from the lodge.

Getting There & Away
Minibuses leave from Gombe motor park in Bauchi and charge N80. From the main gate wait for transport going into the park and cross your fingers; there is more traffic on the weekends (expect to pay N100 to get to the hotel). Also, Yankari has a VW bus for charter; arrangements can be made at the Zaranda Hotel.

The North

KANO
Dating back more than 1000 years, Kano is the oldest city in West Africa. For centuries it was one of the most active commercial centres in the region – a very important centre at the crossroads of the trans-Saharan trading routes. Today, it is Nigeria's third-largest city (with a population of two million plus), the centre for the north and number one on most travellers' lists of places to see in Nigeria. At the end of Ramadan (Sallah) and 69 days later (Tabaski), Kano comes

KANO

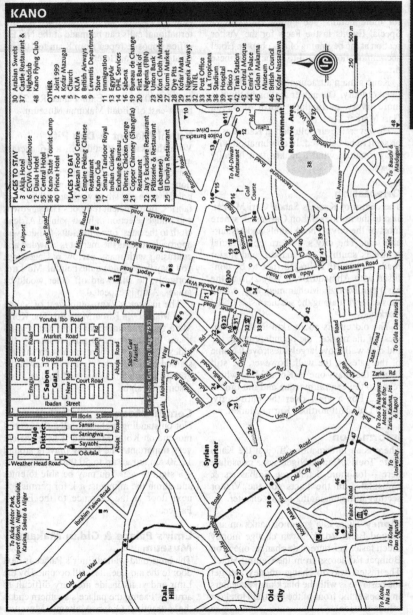

PLACES TO STAY
3 Akija Hotel
6 ECWA Guesthouse
12 Daula Hotel
35 Central Hotel
36 Kano State Tourist Camp
40 Prince Hotel

PLACES TO EAT
1 Akesan Food Centre
10 Empire Peking Chinese
   Restaurant
15 Kano Club
17 Smarts Tandoor Royal
   Indian Cuisine;
   Exchange Bureau
18 Diners; Chicken George
21 Copper Chimney (Shangrila)
   Restaurant
22 Jay's Exclusive Restaurant
24 Pâtisserie & Restaurant
   (Lebanese)
25 El Duniya Restaurant

30 Arabian Sweets
37 Castle Restaurant &
   Nightclub
48 Kano Flying Club

OTHER
2 Joint 999
4 Kofar Mazugai
5 Church
7 KLM
8 British Airways
9 Leventis Department
   Store
11 Immigration
13 EgyptAir
14 DHL Services
16 Sabena
19 Bureau de Change
20 First Bank of
   Nigeria (FBN)
23 Union Bank
26 Kon Cloth Market
27 Kurmi Market
28 Dye Pits
29 Kofar Mata
31 NITEL
32 Post Office
34 La Tropicana
38 Stadium
39 Hospital
41 Disco J
42 Train Station
43 Central Mosque
44 Emir's Palace
45 Gidan Makama
   Museum
46 British Council
47 Kofar Nassarawa

alive with a huge durbar (cavalry parade) – for more details, see Public Holidays & Special Events in the Facts for the Visitor section at the beginning of this chapter. Hotel accommodation is hard to come by at these times.

Kano's main attraction is the much over-rated old city. The newer section of town is more lively, particularly north of Sabon Gari Market.

However, the air pollution in Kano has to be seen to be believed. In combination with the harmattan wind it makes you literally choke.

Orientation

The centre of Kano is Sabon Gari Market. Just to the north is Sabon Gari itself, where most of the city's cheap hotels and restaurants are. The city's modern commercial centre is south of the market, and major roads include E Bello Rd (not to be confused with Ahmadu Bello Way 2km to the east) and Murtala Mohammed Way, which runs east-west along the southern side of the market.

The old city is about 1km to the south-west of the market, the boundary being the old city wall, now largely destroyed. Some of the gates in the wall, however, are still intact; the main one is Kofar Mata which leads to the central mosque and the Emir's palace. For a view over the entire city, climb Dala Hill north of Kurmi Market.

Information

There is an information office at the Kano State Tourist Camp. Niger has a consulate here – for more details see Embassies & Consulates in the Facts for the Visitor section at the beginning of this chapter.

Money There is a group of banks on and around Bank Rd. You can change money much faster at a bureau de change; one is on Bompai Rd across from the Central Hotel. The fastest way to change money and get the best rate is with the black market dealers in shops at the front of the Central Hotel (or others outside).

Post & Communications The post office is at the eastern end of Post Office Rd. International calls can be made at the NITEL office opposite (open from 8 am to 10 pm) or at the Central Hotel.

Cultural Centres The British Council (☎ 626500) is at 10 Emir Palace Rd, 200m north-east of Gidan Makama Museum.

Kurmi Market & Dye Pits

With thousands of stalls in a 16 hectare area, Kurmi Market is one of the largest markets in Africa and the city's main attraction. It's a centre for African crafts, including gold, bronze and silver work and all types of fabrics, from ancient religious Hausa gowns and a huge selection of hand-painted African cloth to the latest imported suits. Guides will approach you. As the market is crowded and confusing with many narrow passageways, you may find a guide quite helpful. Most importantly, he will ward off other would-be guides. A tip is expected.

The market is 2km south-west of Sabon Gari Market via Kofar Mata Rd. The Kofar Mata gate is unimpressive, but just beyond it are the famous dye pits, reputedly the oldest in Africa, where men with indigo-stained hands dip the cloth into pots in the ground filled with natural indigo dye. It's a fascinating sight.

Central Mosque

Not outstanding architecturally, the central mosque on Kofar Mata Rd is nevertheless very important. The Friday prayers around 12.30 pm attract up to 50,000 worshippers – a sight to see. You may be able to enter and climb the minarets; ask for permission next door at the entrance to the Emir's Palace.

Emir's Palace & Gidan Makama Museum

The huge mud-walled Emir's Palace is next door to the mosque. It is still occupied by the Emir and visits inside are very difficult to arrange. Facing the palace's southern end is the attractive Gidan Makama Museum.

Built in the 15th century for the 20th Emir of Kano, it is now completely restored and very interesting architecturally. On display are photographs of Kano architecture, a fascinating photographic history of Kano (including the taking of Kano in 1902 by the British) and various crafts, including leather, baskets and fabrics. Open daily from 10 am to 4 pm, entry is a nominal N10; it's well worth an extended visit.

Gida Dan Hausa

An outstanding example of Kano's architecture, blending Hausa and Arab styles, is the Gida Dan Hausa. It's the remarkable centuries-old home of the first British administrator and is on the southern side of town 200m south of State Rd, near the Ministry of Works, which is on Bello Kano Rd.

Places to Stay – Budget

The *Kano State Tourist Camp* (☎ 646309, 11a Bompai Rd) is still the haunt of the few overland trucks which pass these days. It charges N160 for a bed in a dorm, and N400/600 for singles/doubles with fans and shared bathrooms. You can also pitch a tent for N120 a person and use the communal bathrooms. The friendly managers will organise laundry and will change money (cash and travellers cheques). Group meals can be ordered in advance from the Indonesian Dewi Restaurant in the tourist camp.

The quiet *ECWA Guesthouse* charges N100 for dorm beds with shared bathrooms and N350/700 for decent singles/doubles with fans and shared bathrooms; meals are available. It's also strictly nonsmoking. It's east of the market on Tafawa Balewa Rd.

Sabon Gari has many squelched flea pits and 'short time' places, many of which suffer whenever NEPA's offed. However, a clean and good value one is the *Universal Guest Inn (86 Church Rd)*, which charges N300 for rooms with fans, showers and African-style toilets. On Ibadan St is the *Criss Cross Hotel* (☎ 620972); singles/doubles with fans are N350/450, and more with air-con. The nice courtyard and friendly staff make this place quite popular.

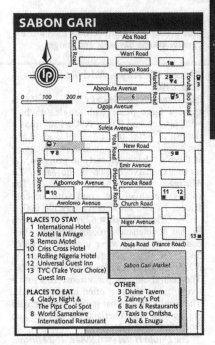

SABON GARI

PLACES TO STAY
1 International Hotel
2 Motel la Mirage
9 Remco Motel
10 Criss Cross Hotel
11 Rolling Nigeria Hotel
12 Universal Guest Inn
13 TYC (Take Your Choice) Guest Inn

PLACES TO EAT
4 Gladys Night & The Pips Cool Spot
8 World Samankwe International Restaurant

OTHER
3 Divine Tavern
5 Zainey's Pot
6 Bars & Restaurants
7 Taxis to Onitsha, Aba & Enugu

The grubby *TYC (Take Your Choice) Guest Inn* (☎ 647491) is on the corner of Abuja and Yoruba Ibo Rds. It asks N800 for its air-con rooms with TV and refrigerator (neither of which usually work) and waterless bathroom. The management's signs, posted everywhere, will keep you laughing for ages; note the bar rules in the Ultra Modern Bar and those around the treeless 'roof-top garden' – perhaps TYC means 'Take Your Chances'? A better choice is the *Rolling Nigeria Hotel (82 Church Rd)*. It charges N750 for a clean single with fan and bathroom.

The well-maintained *Remco Motel* (☎ 628600, 61 New Rd) has very tidy doubles with air-con, TV (which works), fridge and bathroom with bucket showers for N800. The restaurant serves good meals for about N160.

The popular *Akija Hotel* (☎ 645327) on Ibrahim Taiwo Rd, 1km west of Sabon Gari

Market, has singles/doubles from N600/850 plus a hefty deposit of N1000; the more expensive rooms have TV and fridge.

Places to Stay – Mid-Range & Top End

The *International Hotel (30 Enugu Rd)* is quite a large place with singles/doubles with air-con and TV at N900/1200 plus a deposit of N300; the restaurant is good and the hotel has a big bar (which can get noisy if there's a bachelor party in progress). A more expensive choice is the *Motel La Mirage* just across the road at No 27. The rooms are small but good with air-con, fridge, TV and showers for N1250/1600.

The *Central Hotel (☎ 625141)* on Bompai Rd has double/studio rooms with noisy air-con and an erratic water supply for N4350/5800 for nonresidents (resident rate is N2250/3000) plus a deposit of N5000/6000. The central outdoor patio transforms into a lively bar at night; it often has live music. The nearby air-con bar is very popular with expats, and with overlanders who drift up from the tourist camp.

The *Daula Hotel (☎ 628842, 152 Murtala Mohammed Way)* has better rooms (with telephone, fridge and cable TV) for the same price as the Central; it also has a pool. The *Prince Hotel (☎ 639402)* on Tamandu Close charges N5500 plus a deposit of N3000 for a nice room with fridge, TV and phone; it has an almost elegant restaurant with Euro-Afro cuisine for around N650.

Places to Eat

Diners, on Bompai Rd opposite the Central Hotel, is just one place in an enclave of fast food outlets; it sells Nigerian and continental dishes for about N160. Nearby are *Smarts Tandoor Royal Indian Cuisine*, which also has takeaway, and a *Chicken George* with its limited menu.

Throughout Sabon Gari, especially at the southern end of New Rd, there are plenty of cheap *chop houses* which serve great pepper soup, chicken pepper soup, goat's head soup (eyeballs and all) and gari. One good place is *World Samankwe International Restaur-*

ant, where for N80 you can stuff yourself. The 'best name' award for a chop house goes to the *Gladys Night & the Pips Cool Spot* on Abeokuta Ave; the food isn't bad either.

Elsewhere in the city, the *Akesan Food Centre (37 Weather Head Rd)*, is a rustic chop house open from noon to 5 pm. *El Duniya Restaurant (63 Ibrahim Taiwo Rd)*, is similar. Many of the cheap African restaurants close by 6 or 7 pm; hotel restaurants stay open later.

The long-established *Castle Restaurant* on Ahmadu Bello Way, just east of the stadium, is expensive and the food nothing special. For excellent Lebanese in the N400 to N600 range, you can't beat *Al-Diwan (41D Hadejia Rd)*; it has a great Sunday brunch for N750.

The *Empire Peking Chinese Restaurant (2 Bompai Rd)* is one of the best expensive restaurants; a meal can easily cost N1000 or more. For good, reasonably priced Indian food, the *Copper Chimney (Shangrila) Restaurant (15 Beirut St)* has soups, samosas and tandoori for reasonable prices.

The *Kano Flying Club (24 Magajin Rumfa Rd)* serves the cheapest European fare in town; you'll need to take out a temporary membership for N100. Similarly, the *Kano Club* on Bompai Rd has superb, cheap meals, but you have to be introduced by a member. For pizza go to *Jay's Exclusive Restaurant (2b Niger St)*.

Pastry & Ice Cream Shops For pastries and the best ice cream in town (N100), head for *Arabian Sweets* on Beirut Rd. At 7 E Bello Rd is the *Pâtisserie & Restaurant*, a similar Lebanese pastry shop with good takeaway meals.

Entertainment

Bars Sabon Gari has heaps. The roof-top garden of the *TYC Guest Inn* has good views over the city, but that's about all. The Ultra Modern Bar downstairs will make you laugh – check out the bar rules written up on the walls. A couple of Sabon Gari favourites are *Zainey's Pot* on Abeokuta Ave and the *Divine Tavern* on Ibo Rd. The bars at the

Central Hotel are busy until about 11.30 pm (when people move to the nightclubs).

Nightclubs There are two nightclubs on Sani Abacha Way (formerly Airport Rd) – *Mingles* and *Le Circle* both get going around midnight. *La Tropicana* on Niger Rd is yet another of the glitterball palaces, as is the very popular *Disco J* on Tamandu Cl, near the Prince Hotel; the latter starts moving about 1 am and has a hefty N300 cover charge. Lovers of fine music will appreciate *Joint 999*, a Cameroonian nightclub on Odutala Rd in Waje district, west of Sabon Gari.

Getting There & Away

Air International flights to/from Kano include the EgyptAir service to London via Cairo, KLM to Amsterdam and Sabena to Brussels. EgyptAir (☎ 630759) is on Murtala Mohammed Way, KLM (☎ 632632) is on Airport Rd just north of Murtala Mohammed Way and Sabena is on Bompai Rd (in the grounds of the Central Hotel).

Nigeria Airways (☎ 623891), 3 Bank Rd, has daily flights to Lagos, as does Kabo Air, Harco Air Services and Okada. Okada has two flights a week to Yola. Harco flies to Sokoto once a week and to Maiduguri three times weekly.

Bush Taxi & Minibus Kuka motor park, on the road to the airport on the western side of town, is the motor park for Sokoto and Katsina and, in Niger, Zinder and Maradi. Naibowa motor park, which serves points south (Zaria, Jos, Kaduna, Lagos etc), is on Zaria Rd on the southern outskirts of town. You can get minibuses and shared taxis for both from Sabon Gari Market. A third motor park on Murtala Mohammed Way, east of Sabon Gari Market, serves points east, including Maiduguri.

Bush taxis to Sokoto (five hours) cost N500 and N250 to Katsina. To Zaria, expect a two hour ride for N200. The three to five hour ride to Maradi, Niger, costs N550. The trip from Zinder takes from six to eight hours by minibus (CFA3000).

From the Naibowa motor park Lagos is a 15 hour ride by bush taxi and costs N800. Bush taxis go to Benin City (N500, eight hours), Zaria (N150, 1½ hours), Jos (N400, six hours), Maiduguri (N550, eight hours) and Kaduna (N200, 2½ hours).

Getting Around

The Kano international airport is 8km northwest of Sabon Gari Market. An airport tax of N200 applies to all domestic flights. A motorcycle-taxi ride to the airport from town will cost N40; a taxi is N60.

In town, taxis and motorcycle-taxis are everywhere and cost from N50 depending upon the length of your trip.

AROUND KANO

About 35km east of the town of Nguru is the **Hadejia-Nguru Wetlands Conservation Project**. This area is a great place for the avid birdwatcher, as it is an important resting point for birds migrating to or from Europe and is home to many indigenous water birds. The intrepid ornithologist interested in visiting this area should stop at the VSO office in Kano for further details. At the time of research, this office was in the process of moving – ask at the British Council in Kano for its new address.

KATSINA

This old Hausa city, 174km north-west of Kano, has lost some of its old structures, but parts of the old city wall and gates, the Emir's Palace, the Gobir Minaret (which can be climbed) and some old Hausa burial mounds outside town remain. Katsina's claim to fame is the spectacular **Durbar festival,** celebrated at the end of Ramadan (see Public Holidays & Special Events in the Facts for the Visitor section earlier in this chapter for more details).

Places to Stay & Eat

Just off Kano Rd and Ring Rd junction is *Liberty Camp*, where rough rooms with fan and bathroom are N300; it has a lively bar. The *Makurdi Hotel Annexe (3 Kano Rd)*, closer to town, has basic doubles for N500

(N650 with bathroom). Also on Kano Rd is the *Abuja Guest Inn* (☎ *30319*), where a basic single with shared bathroom costs N300. The *Liyata Palace Hotel* (☎ *31165*), outside town, is the only top end hotel. It has tennis courts, pool, and beautifully clean rooms and charges N2800 (plus a deposit of N1600).

The restaurant at the Markurdi Hotel Annexe serves large portions of great food; otherwise try *Katsina City Restaurant* on IBB Way for tasty chicken pepper soup and other Nigerian favourites.

SOKOTO

In the far north-western corner of Nigeria, Sokoto is known for the Sultan's Palace and its market. The town became important in the early 19th century as the seat of the caliphate established after Usman dan Fodio's Islamic jihad in 1807, which brought together the various Hausa city states. The present sultan, Dasuki, effectively remains the head of Nigeria's Muslims today.

If you go to the Sultan's Palace on a Thursday between 9 and 11 pm, you can hear Hausa musicians outside playing to welcome in the Holy Day, Friday (see the boxed text 'Hausa Bands' in this section). The Shehu Mosque is nearby. At the end of Ramadan, long processions of musicians and elaborately dressed men on horseback make their way from the prayer ground to the Sultan's palace.

The market, well known for its handmade leather goods, is held every day except Sunday; it's best on Friday.

Sokoto can be used as a base to visit the spectacular **Fishing & Cultural Festival** held every February in Argungu, 100km to the south-west. (For more details, see Public Holidays & Special Events in the Facts for the Visitor section of this chapter.)

Places to Stay & Eat

On the southern side of town, 200m from the post office, the old government-run *Catering Rest House* (☎ *232505*) is run-down and fairly dirty and has rooms for N600. The *Shukura Hotel* (☎ *200019*) on Gusau Rd, south of the centre, charges N2400 for an air-

---

Hausa Bands

A typical Hausa band consists of three *kakaki*, three *alghaita* and some drums. The kakaki is a remarkably long (about 3m) tin trumpet with an impressive, shattering timbre. It produces barely two notes but its majestic tone augments the orchestral ensemble. The conical alghaita is an African oboe with a metal tube through it that widens out into a bell at the end. What's remarkable about it, apart from its piercing tone, is the way it's played. The musician inhales a large amount of air, puffs his cheeks and remains that way, using the reed in a manner that allows him to play without interruption, for hours on end.

---

con double. For less expensive (N1100) but decent accommodation, try the *Ibro International Hotel* (☎ *232510*) on Abdullahi Fodio Rd, near the intersection of the bypass road.

The *Shalom Restaurant*, close to the Ibro, on Abdullahi Fodio Rd, has a wide range of cheap meals from N100.

Getting There & Away

Nigeria Airways (☎ *232252*) has flights three times weekly to Lagos; make sure your booking is secure.

Lots of bush taxis in Sokoto head for Kano, Zaria and Kaduna, Lagos and Illela/Birni N'Konni (the Niger border). They leave from the motor park facing the market on the northern side of town.

MAIDUGURI

Maiduguri is the booming capital of Borno State in the far north-eastern corner of Nigeria. From March to May temperatures often reach 48°C. Very few travellers come here – usually just those on their way to or from northern Cameroon, if border crossings are possible.

Gomboru Market, or Monday Market, is in the heart of town just north of the NEPA

NIGERIA

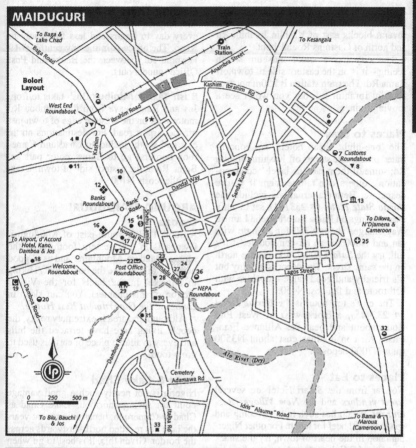

MAIDUGURI

To Baga &
Lake Chad

Baga Road

To Kesangala

Train
Station

Anamora Street

West End
Roundabout

Kashim Ibrahim Rd

Ibrahim Road

Bolori
Layout

Kashim

Kashim Ibrahim Rd

Dandal Way

Senda Kura Road

Customs
Roundabout

Banks
Roundabout

Bank
Road

Shehu Lamisu

To Dikwa,
N'Djamena &
Cameroon

To Airport, d'Accord
Hotel, Kano,
Damboa & Jos

Hospital Rd

Welcome
Roundabout

Post Office
Roundabout

Ahmadu Bello

Lagos Street

Damboa Road

NEPA
Roundabout

Damboa Road

Italba Rd

Cemetery
Adamawa Rd

Alo River (Dry)

To Bama &
Maroua
(Cameroon)

0   250   500 m

Idris Alauma Road

To Biu, Bauchi
& Jos

To Bama

PLACES TO STAY		
4	Deribe Hotel	
30	Safari Hotel	
33	Borno State Hotel	

PLACES TO EAT		
3	Chinese Restaurant	
8	Fish Restaurants	
21	Bosco Café	
23	Lalle Restaurant	
28	New Villager Restaurant;	
	Street Food Vendors	

OTHER		
1	Lively Bar Area; Cheap Hotels	

2 Motor Park for Geidam,
   Gashua & Baga
5 Police Station
6 Kamuri Market (New
   Market)
7 Motor Park for Mafa &
   Cameroon Border
9 Shehu's Palace
10 Stadium
11 Alliance Française
12 Leventis
   Department Store
13 Museum
14 Banks
15 Nigeria Airways

16 UTC Department Store
17 Supermarket
18 Ramat Polytechnic
19 Mosque
20 Motor Park for Biu, Gombe,
   Bauchi, Jos & Kano
22 Post Office; NITEL
24 Gomboru Market
   (Monday Market)
25 University Hospital
26 Molai Motor Park
27 Mosque
29 Zoo
31 Open-Air Theatre
32 Motor Park for Bama

Roundabout, while Kamuri Market, or New Market, is on the eastern side of town, several blocks east of Kashim Ibrahim Rd and north of Customs Roundabout.

The city has a small museum worth seeing – it is on the eastern side of town off Bama Rd. The train station is 250m north of Kashim Ibrahim Rd, but you won't see a moving train.

Places to Stay

The 'one-night cheap hotels' are concentrated on the side streets off Kashim Ibrahim Rd; some of them rate the label 'accommodation', others don't. Use them if you're desperate. Better alternatives include the *Borno State Hotel* (☎ 233191), set in leafy surroundings on Italba Rd off Shehu Lamisu Way charges about N350 for a single with fan and N600 for an air-con double. If it's full, try the *Safari Hotel*, a kilometre north on the same street. The decor is gloomy but it's friendly and good value – doubles with bathroom and fan cost N450.

The city's top hotel is the *Deribe Hotel* (☎ 232445), a block west of West End Roundabout and near the Alliance Française. Air-con doubles cost about N3500 (plus N7000 deposit).

Places to Eat

Not far from the Safari Hotel are several *street vendors* and the *New Villager Restaurant*, which has suya in the evening and spaghetti and beef for lunch. For other Nigerian chop in the heart of town, try the snack bar at the *UTC department store* on Kashim Ibrahim Rd, the *Bosco Café* between UTC and the post office, or *Lalle Restaurant* on Post Office Roundabout. For fresh fish go to the collection of *restaurants* near Customs Roundabout.

The excellent *Chinese Restaurant* is between the train line and West End Roundabout; it has reasonable prices and is also a good place to come for a drink.

Entertainment

For cheap bars and dancing, head for the 'hotel' area north of Kashim Ibrahim Rd.

Getting There & Away

Air Nigeria Airways has flights almost every day to Lagos and less frequently to Kano. The office is in the city centre, at 19 Hospital Rd, between the Banks and Post Office roundabouts.

Bush Taxi & Minibus Bush taxis to/from Jos and Kano leave from the Damboa Rd motor park on the western edge of town just off the airport road. For destinations north, east and south (including Chad and Cameroon borders) go to Bama motor park on Bama Rd at the eastern side of town; a taxi to either costs N100.

AROUND MAIDUGURI
Gwoza

Around 115km south-east of Maiduguri, Gwoza is in the western foothills of the scenic Mandara Mountains and is a good place for hiking (see the boxed text 'Hiking in Nigeria' in the Facts for the Visitor section of this chapter). You can sleep in Gwoza at the *Government Rest House*.

Although the area is extremely rocky, the people living here have terraced the hills and every available piece of earth is used to grow food.

Baga & Lake Chad

Nigeria is not nearly such a good vantage point for seeing enormous Lake Chad as Chad or Cameroon, because in recent years the lake has receded north-eastwards across the border. Given this, it is best to go when the water is at its highest, between December and February; Baga, 170km north-east of Maiduguri (and north of Dikwa), is the place to go. Be prepared, as immigration police are sure to hassle the hell out of you (because of incursions by Chadian rebels).

A 13km canal goes out to the Nigerian part of Lake Chad and the birdwatching is excellent; check with the Chad Basin Development Authority in Baga for permission to visit. Minibuses and bush taxis leave from Baga motor park in Maiduguri. You can stay at the *Baga State Hotel* or in rough huts in nearby Doro.

Senegal

More visitors come to Senegal than to any other country in West Africa. One reason for this might be the capital, Dakar, a lively city with a breezy climate and cosmopolitan mix of Afro-French characteristics. Nearby is the historically and culturally fascinating Île de Gorée, and to the south stretch the long sandy beaches of the Petite Côte. Another attraction is the verdant Casamance region, the part of Senegal south of Gambia, where local communities have built a network of good-value *campements*. There's a lot for wildlife enthusiasts too, including Parc National du Niokolo-Koba, one of West Africa's major national parks, as well as Parc National aux Oiseaux du Djoudj and Parc National de la Langue de Barbarie, which are among the most important bird sanctuaries in the world.

Facts about Senegal

HISTORY

Remains of organised societies from early in the 1st millennium AD have been discovered in several parts of Senegal, and the area was part of the great Islamic Sahel empires of Ghana (which flourished between the 8th and 11th centuries), Mali (13th to 15th centuries) and Songhaï (16th century). Smaller empires or kingdoms were also established during this period: along the River Senegal, the Tuklur Empire was established by the Tuklur people in the 9th to 10th centuries; and as Mali's power began to wane, the Wolof people established the Empire of Jolof in the central region of today's Senegal, although at this time they resisted Islamic influence. For more general details on the pre-European period, refer to the History section in the Facts about the Region chapter.

European Arrival

The year 1443 marks medieval Europe's first direct contact with West Africa, when Portuguese explorers reached the mouth of

SENEGAL AT A GLANCE

Capital: Dakar
Population: 8.7 million
Area: 196,192 sq km
Head of state: President Abdou Diouf
Official language: French
Main local languages: Wolof, Mandinka, Fula, Sérèr, Diola
Currency: West African CFA franc
Exchange rate: US$1 = CFA600
Time: GMT/UTC
Country telephone code: ☎ 221
Best time to go: November to February

the River Senegal. The following year they landed at Cap Vert, near present-day Dakar, and later settled on Île de Gorée – a vital base for ships trading along the coast.

Around 1600, the Dutch and the English entered the scene. The islands of Gorée and St-Louis changed hands several times before they were finally secured by the French in the late 17th century. For the next hundred years or so, all along the West African coast the European nations traded with powerful local chiefs for gold, ivory and, most importantly, slaves.

During the 18th century, St-Louis grew in size and importance, but after the slave trade was banned in 1815, the French were forced to look for new sources of wealth. Louis Faidherbe was appointed governor in 1845 and forced the local people around the River Senegal to grow groundnuts (peanuts) as a cash crop. With similar ruthlessness, over the next few decades French forces systematically moved inland, and Senegal became the gateway to the new territory of Afrique Occidentale Française (French West Africa).

Meanwhile, a marabout or Islamic leader called Omar Tall had established a vast empire based around the town of Ségou in today's Mali. His soldiers spread west into Senegal where they clashed with the French forces moving inland. To protect the new colony from the north and east, Faidherbe established a chain of forts along the River Senegal (including Bakel, Matam and Po-

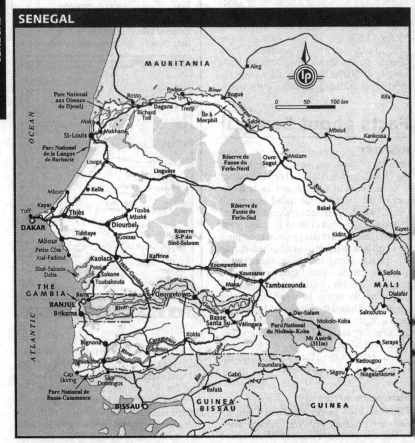

SENEGAL

dor) which can still be seen today. Faidherbe also established a settlement on the peninsula opposite Île de Gorée, which became Dakar.

The Marabouts

Omar Tall's forces were finally defeated by the French in 1864, but his missionary zeal inspired followers to continue the 'Marabout Wars', as they were called, for another three decades. By this time, the Wolof had embraced Islam and now fought fiercely against French expansionism. Soldiers of the Wolof king Lat Dior repeatedly hindered French attempts to build a railway line between Dakar and St-Louis, neatly symbolising the conflict between the new and old orders. Another thorn in the French side was a marabout called Amadou Bamba – for more details, see the boxed text 'Bamba' in the Diourbel section later in this chapter. The last significant Wolof battle was in 1889 at Yang-Yang in northern Senegal (near present-day Linguere) where the army of Alboury Ndiaye was defeated by the French. Eventually, superior European firepower and a divided marabout-led army allowed the French to gain control of the whole region.

The Colonial Period

At the Berlin Conference of 1884-85, following the 'Scramble for Africa', the continent was divided between powerful European states. While Britain (with Germany and Portugal) got most of East and southern Africa, the greater part of West Africa was allocated to France. At the end of the 19th century, French West Africa stretched from the Atlantic to present-day Niger.

In 1887, Africans living in the four largest towns in Senegal (Dakar, Gorée, St-Louis and Rufisque) were granted limited French citizenship but, compared with the British, the French did little to educate their colonial subjects. Only those needed to work for the French administration received secondary education in Dakar, which by this time had become the capital of French West Africa. (St-Louis remained the capital of Senegal-Mauritania.)

But in the early 20th century, things began to change. In 1914, Senegal elected its first African delegate, Blaise Diagne, to the French national assembly in Paris. After WWI, it became fashionable for politically conscious Senegalese to join French parties – particularly the increasingly powerful Socialists and Communists – and several Senegalese intellectuals went to France to study. One was Leopold Senghor, who became the first African secondary-school teacher in France. He began writing poetry and after WWII he helped found *Présence Africaine*, a magazine promoting the values of African culture.

Senghor was an astute politician, and shrewdly began building a personal power base which resulted in his election as Senegal's representative to the French national assembly. Meanwhile, the marabouts had become increasingly involved in politics, and through the 1950s Senghor made secret deals with leading figures, allowing them a certain amount of autonomy and control of the lucrative groundnut economy in return for their public support (ensuring safe votes from their followers in rural areas).

During the same period, the impending demise of France's African colonies became a major issue. Senghor promoted independence and a strong federal union of all French territories in Africa to prevent them from being divided and still dependent on their former ruler. His rival was Côte d'Ivoire's leader Houphouët-Boigny, who feared that within a union the richer territories would have to subsidise the poorer ones.

Independence

In the late 1950s, Senghor gained support from French Soudan (now Mali), Upper Volta (Burkina Faso) and Dahomey (Benin) to form the Mali Federation, but the latter two withdrew under pressure from France and Côte d'Ivoire. On 20 June 1960, Senegal and Mali became independent, while remaining within the French union, and Senghor became the first president. But two months later, the Senegal-Mali union broke up. Houphouët-Boigny had won the day, and

French West Africa became nine separate republics.

Senegal's early independent years did not always run smoothly. In 1968, in the wake of protests in France and amid mounting economic difficulties at home, students rioted at the University of Dakar. Senghor sent in the military, but the national trade union supported the students and called for a general strike. The situation was not resolved until workers and students were promised reforms.

The 1970s were less turbulent: Senghor held on to his position and remained a popular figure. In 1980, after 20 years as president, he did what no other African head of state had done before – he voluntarily stepped down. His hand-picked successor Abdou Diouf took over.

The First Diouf Decade

One of Diouf's first major moves was to help the president of Gambia, Dawda Jawara, who had been ousted in a coup. With help from Senegalese troops Jawara was restored, and this cooperation was formalised in the establishment of the Senegambia Confederation later in the same year.

In 1983, eight parties contested parliamentary elections, which Diouf's Parti Socialiste (PS) won with over 83% of the vote. His major opponent, Abdoulaye Wade, spearheaded an effort to unite the opposition parties but in 1985 a rattled Diouf banned the organisation on the grounds that it violated election law.

In 1988, Wade contested the presidency, but during the campaign violence erupted. Diouf's response was to ban all political meetings, station tanks throughout Dakar and arrest Wade, charging him with intent to subvert the government. Official results showed Diouf with 73% of the vote and Wade with 26%, but rumours of rigging were rampant. Wade received a one year suspended sentence and left for France.

By this time the Senegambia Confederation was in trouble, and in 1989 it was completely dissolved. But while Diouf was contending with this break-up and calls for political reform, he had two other major

The Mauritanian Crisis

There is a long history of resentment between the Senegalese and the Mauritanian Moors. The problem is complex and stems from the time when the Moors raided the villages of black Africans in Senegal for slaves.

In 1989, two Senegalese peasants were killed by Mauritanian border guards in a clash over grazing rights. In Senegal, people reacted by looting Mauritanian-owned shops in Dakar, and killing several people. Mauritania retaliated by deporting thousands of Senegalese, hundreds of whom were killed in the process. The Senegalese retaliated by deporting Mauritanians. Horrendous atrocities were committed on both sides.

Following the outbreaks of violence, the borders between Senegal and Mauritania were closed, and diplomatic relations were broken off for two years, resuming in April 1992. Today all borders are open and you can once again travel overland between these two countries.

problems to deal with: a dispute with Mauritania and a campaign against separatists in the southern region of Casamance (for more details on the Casamance conflict, see the Casamance section later in this chapter).

The 1990s

Abdoulaye Wade returned from political exile in 1990, which brought huge crowds out onto the streets chanting *sopi* (Wolof for 'change') and calling for Diouf's resignation. In an attempt at appeasement, some opposition parties were allowed a role in government and Wade was made Minister of State, but with little real effect.

Wade stood against Diouf in the presidential election of 1993, which Diouf won with 58% of the vote (against Wade's 32%) and was thus elected for a third term. In the parliamentary elections, Wade's party, the

Parti Démocratique Sénégalais (PDS) improved its performance, but the PS still obtained over two-thirds of the seats in the national assembly. Emboldened by its success, in August the same year the government introduced a number of austerity measures, which led to strikes and considerable unrest around the country. A major devaluation of the CFA franc in early 1994 did nothing to improve the situation.

Despite the protests, Diouf and the PS held onto power, although the situation took another turn for the worse in 1997 when serious fighting once again broke out in Casamance. Tired of government intransigence, a leading PS figure, Djibo Ka, broke away to form the Renouveau Démocratique party. In the parliamentary elections of 24 May 1998 they won 11 seats, disturbing the traditional split between the PS and PDS, who won 93 and 23 seats, respectively. Following the election, unsurprisingly, the PDS and other opposition parties accused the PS of rigging the results.

New election laws allow the president a seven year term, so Diouf remains in power until at least May 2000, when Wade and Ka will probably stand against him. In the meantime, most observers believe that Diouf will keep his opponents in check by offering limited power in a coalition government, and the country will trundle along as usual. But such predictions can never be certain, and more dramatic events may yet come to Senegal.

GEOGRAPHY

Senegal has an area of just under 200,000 sq km, and is largely flat, with low-lying hills in the south-east. To the west, the country is fringed by the Atlantic Ocean coastline, some 600km in length, running roughly north-south and divided by the Cap Vert peninsula on which Dakar was built. Senegal's three major rivers flow east-west across the country into the Atlantic. In the north, the River Senegal forms the border with Mauritania. In south-eastern Senegal, the River Gambia flows through Parc National du Niokolo-Koba before crossing into

Gambia itself. South of Gambia is the River Casamance, which gives its name to the surrounding Casamance area.

CLIMATE

In northern and central Senegal the rainy season is July to September, while in Casamance it's June to early October. Rainfall ranges from an annual average of 300mm in the north to almost six times that amount in the south, with about 600mm in Dakar. The rainy season is also the hottest time of year, with temperatures around 30°C. November to March is dry and relatively cool, with temperatures around 24°C, but from December the skies are clouded by the dust of the harmattan.

ECOLOGY & ENVIRONMENT

In common with many West African countries, pressing environmental issues in Senegal include deforestation and soil erosion. These are linked to the ever-increasing demand for land for cultivation, both small-scale plots for subsistence farmers and larger commercial plantations. See the boxed text 'Groundnuts' over the page for a wider discussion of these issues.

Meanwhile, off the coast of Senegal, overfishing to supply a growing local population and lucrative export market means fish stocks are declining. The problem is exacerbated by unsustainable fishing methods such as the use of dynamite to stun shoals, although this way only about a quarter of the fish killed can be 'caught' – the rest sink out of reach. In the area around Dakar, local fishermen were persuaded to stop using this

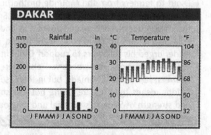

DAKAR

Groundnuts

Groundnuts (peanuts) grow like beans on low bushes, and can survive in relatively dry areas. Senegal's annual groundnut production is around 600,000 tonnes; the harvested nuts are crushed to make oil, which is exported to Europe for use in food manufacture. Groundnut plantations cover about one million hectares (around 40% of the country's arable land) and the industry employs a million people. The main groundnut growing region is around the towns of Diourbel, Touba and Kaolack which, not uncoincidentally, are centres of the powerful Muslim brotherhoods whose marabouts (leaders) dominate much of Senegal's political and economic life. Many marabouts derive their wealth and power from the groundnut plantations on their land. This is particularly the case among the followers of the Mouride brotherhood, for whom work (on behalf of their marabout) is considered a great virtue.

The nuts are harvested after the rains, mainly from October to January, but also up until June, and then transported to the crushing mills. As you travel around, you'll often see huge yellow trucks, perilously overloaded with sacks of groundnuts, trundling along the roads.

Although groundnuts may contribute to the economy, the plantations prevent local farmers growing their own food and have a devastating effect on the environment. The crop absorbs nutrients and at harvesting the whole plant – roots and all – is picked, leaving loose, dry soil exposed. The soil is soon exhausted or simply blown away, and new plantations have to be established, meaning grassland, bush or other natural vegetation has to be cleared. This reduces wildlife habitats and is a major issue in central Senegal as groundnut farmers expand into grazing reserves (réserves sylvo-pastorale) supposedly set aside for seminomadic people such as the Fula.

A specific incident occurred at a reserve called Mbegué, part of which was 'given' by President Abdou Diouf to farmers from the Mouride brotherhood in 1991. Writing in the New Internationalist magazine, environmental scientist Karen Schoonmaker-Freudenburger reported that over five million trees were chopped down, the land ploughed and groundnuts planted, while 6000 Fula people and 100,000 cows were forced off the land. The following year, the Mouride leader urged his followers to support Diouf in the national elections.

Similar invasions have occurred elsewhere in Senegal. It's a classic example of conflict between farmers and nomads, but in this case the continuing quest for new groundnut plantations means the Fula are facing not just small-scale cultivators, but the combined power and strength of Senegal's political and religious establishment.

method when a French scuba diver showed them video films of the sea bed covered in dead fish.

Of even more cause for concern are the factory ships from Europe and East Asia which use vast nets and highly efficient methods to land huge catches. Most have negotiated fishing rights with the Senegalese government and provide a vital source of income for the country (although there are frequent reports of extra ships fishing illegally and of legal ships exceeding quotas) but for the local fishermen in their traditional boats, making a living from the sea becomes increasingly precarious.

FLORA & FAUNA

Senegal lies in the Sahel zone, with a natural vegetation of well-dispersed trees and low scrub. In the north, along the border with Mauritania, the landscape comes close to being desert, while the wetter Casamance region in the south is a fertile zone of forest and farmland.

Most of the birds occurring in Gambia can also be seen in Senegal (in fact the latter has about 80 more species recorded) but the more widely dispersed nature of good birdwatching sites means Senegal has yet to become a major destination for ornithologists, and there is no comparable set-up with guides and local tours.

The coast and large estuaries of the rivers Senegal, Saloum and Casamance are notable staging points for waders, shore birds and vast flocks of European migrants, while avid birdwatchers can use the Cap Vert peninsula as a base from which to observe sea birds. Inland, the dry Sahel landscape supports several arid-savanna species which are hard to see elsewhere in Africa. Highly recommended is *A Field Guide to Birds of The Gambia & Senegal* by Clive Barlow and Tim Wacher. (For more information on birds, see the special section 'Birds of West Africa' earlier in this book.)

Easily recognised mammal species in forested areas include baboon and three types of monkey (vervet, patas and red colobus), while Parc National du Niokolo-Koba contains chimpanzee populations, their most northern outpost in West Africa. This park also has drier grassland areas where antelope species include cob, roan, waterbuck and Derby eland, and there's a chance of seeing hyena and buffalo, plus a few lonely hippopotamus. The park has populations of lion, leopard and elephant (although it's thought that less than 20 elephants remain in all Senegal). In wooded areas around the country you may also see oribi, duiker, warthog and bush pig.

National Parks

Senegal has six national parks: Parc National du Niokolo-Koba in south-east Senegal, the largest, with a wide range of habitat types and associated wildlife; Parc National de Basse-Casamance, an area of woodland and mangrove in the Casamance region; Parc National du Delta du Saloum, just north of Gambia, with mainly coastal lagoons, mangroves, sandy islands and a section of dry woodland; the Îles de la Madeleine, near Dakar; and, in northern Senegal, Parc National aux Oiseaux du Djoudj and Parc National de la Langue de Barbarie, both noted for their birdlife. Other protected areas include the Ferlo wildlife reserves in the north-central part of Senegal, the Réserve de Bandia near the Petite Côte, and the Biosphere Reserve at Sambadia (also written Samba Dia) on the northern fringe of the Siné-Saloum Delta.

GOVERNMENT & POLITICS

Senegal is a republic, with the president and 140 members of the national assembly elected every seven years and five years, respectively. The political system is a multiparty democracy dominated by the Parti Socialiste (PS) which despite – or because of – several changes of name and ideology over the years has never been defeated in elections. There are several opposition parties; the main ones being the Parti Démocratique Sénégalais (PDS) and Renouveau Démocratique.

Although the country's human rights record is by no means unblemished, it is still

SENEGAL

SENEGAL

one of the least politically repressive countries in West Africa, although the unofficial but essential links between the ruling PS and the Islamic brotherhoods remain a major feature of the political scene.

ECONOMY

Senegal's economy is based on agriculture, with groundnuts providing about 20% of export earnings. Some diversification, notably into cotton and rice, has been achieved, but production of subsistence crops such as millet is declining and Senegal now imports 35% of its food requirements. Fishing is a major activity on the coast, and in the 1980s, the value of fish exports outstripped that of groundnuts, although not without cost (see the boxed text 'Groundnuts' earlier in this section).

As with many other developing countries, foreign debt remains a huge problem. Senegal owes around US$4 billion to commercial banks and international bodies such

as the World Bank. This absorbs a major portion of the country's export earnings, but while trade figures remain negative, the loans cannot be cleared, and the interest keeps having to be paid.

POPULATION & PEOPLE

The population of Senegal was estimated a 8.7 million in mid-1997. The dominant ethnic group is the Wolof (about 35% of the total), found mostly in the central area, north and east of Dakar, and along the coast. The Sérèr (17%) are also found in the central regions, while the Fula (12%), also called Fulani, Fulbe and Peul, are found throughout northern and eastern Senegal, although they look on the Futa Toro region as their homeland. Other groups include: the Tukulo (also spelt Toucouleur), inhabiting the north the Mandinka, in the areas bordering Gambia; the Malinké in the north-east; and the Diola (also called Jola) found almost exclusively in the Casamance. Minor group

Bukut: A Diola Masking Tradition

The Bukut is an initiation ceremony that takes place every 20 to 25 years and involves the gaining of knowledge and social status by young Diola men. Preparations for the Bukut start months in advance as the celebrations require huge feasts involving the sacrifice of many cattle. It is during these preparations that mothers compose songs that are sung by the initiated during a ritual involving the passing of cloth called Buyeet. Each youth has his own song

which will not be sung again publicly until his death.

Distinctive woven cane masks called Ejumbi, which have tubular eyes and are surmounted by a pair of massive cattle horns, are worn by the initiates when they return from the sacred forest. Not all initiates wear these masks, but those who do are considered to possess special powers of clairvoyance. The masks are created by the initiates with the assistance of tribal elders.

The Bukut represents Diola identity and is still considered a very important event. It has survived and adapted to Christianity and Islam.

John Graham

include the Bassari and Bédik, found in the remote south-eastern part of Senegal, and the Lebu, who are found almost exclusively in the town of Yoff outside Dakar.

Most Senegalese speak Wolof and about 85% are Muslim. Further homogeneity derives from the *cousinage*, or 'joking cousins', relationship that exists between different ethnic groups or clans, which allows very jocular and personal conversations even among strangers, and symbolises a deeper level of support against outsiders.

ARTS

Art & Craftwork

While Senegal is not noted for its traditions of carving wooden masks and sculpture (unlike other countries in the region), arts and crafts from many other parts of West Africa are available in Senegal, especially in the market in Dakar.

Fabrics of various styles and designs also feature largely in Senegalese life, and travellers will find a wide range of clothes, wraps and wall-hangings available in markets. The tapestries of Thiès (see the boxed text in the Thiès section for more details) are world-famous and worth seeing, although they sell for thousands of dollars and are way beyond the budget of most travellers!

Literature

Senegal's most influential writer is Leopold Senghor, the country's first president. He coined the term *negritude*, which emphasised indigenous ideas and culture, and his combined position as leading politician and leading literary figure made him unique in Africa.

Of the few Senegalese writers translated into English, probably the most famous is Sembéne Ousmane. His classic *God's Bits of Wood* (1970) describes the struggles of striking railway workers in the late 1940s and the emergence of grassroots political consciousness in pre-independence Africa. His other

Pop Music in Senegal

The father of modern Senegalese music is Ibra Kassé, who formed the Star Band de Dakar to play at his nightclub, The Miami, in the early 1960s. Through the 1970s, the music scene in Senegal, Mali and Guinea was dominated by large bands or 'orchestras'. The most famous of these, Orchestra Baobab, has recently reformed, with three CDs available internationally, plus numerous local cassettes. Other great ensembles included Canari de Kaolack, the Royal Band and Étoile de Dakar – whose *mbalax* mix of Wolof drum rhythms and western rock shot Youssou N'Dour to stardom. He still plays on occasion with his band Le Super Étoile at his Thiosanne nightclub in Dakar.

Touré Kunda (meaning Touré family – the band was founded by four brothers) is another very popular group, as is the vocalist Thione Seck, formerly with Orchestra Baobab. The Latin influence is very strong in Senegal, and is realised best through the music of Africando. In contrast, Baaba Maal, a northern Fula, has stayed close to his musical roots.

Some other names to look out for include Lamine Konté, who blends the lighter Casamance style of *kora* playing with Cuban rhythms and folk music; Ismael Lô – sometimes called the Senegalese Bob Dylan – and his band Ilopro; and Idrissa Diop, who sings in Wolof and has performed before huge international audiences with his group Les Gaiendes (their music features percussion instruments of various kinds). The group Xalam developed a unique style combining African music, jazz and rhythm and blues, and was one of the first West African bands to gain recognition in Europe. They no longer play live, but Xalam albums are still widely available. Others worth trying are Le Super Cayor, Mansour Seck, Super Diamono, and Étoile 2000.

SENEGAL

Baaba Maal

Baaba Maal hails from the Fouto Toro region of Senegal, which borders Mauritania and Mali. Sources of inspiration for his music are the traditional Fula songs of this area, especially the kora music, and his popularisation of them has led to a greater interest in Fula music in general – no mean feat in a country where the mbalax and salsa styles dominate. His music incorporates elements from reggae and jazz, and is characterised by tight, interlocking drum rhythms. Traditional instruments, such as the balafon, are used on all of his recordings and are backed up by electric guitar. Although not a griot by birth, Maal sees himself as a commentator on all facets of life in Senegal. His lyrics frequently address the difficulties and aspirations of youth, as well as political issues. He sees music as a way of building greater understanding between people and as having an educative role. His first recording, Djam Leeli (made with his 'mentor' the griot Mansour Seck), is recommended, as is his superb Firin' in Fouta.

Graeme Counsel

books include *Black Docker*, based on his experiences in the port of Marseilles in the 1950s, and *Xala*, an attack on the privileged elites of Dakar.

A more recent Senegalese writer is Mariama Bâ, whose short but incisive novel *So Long a Letter* was first published in 1980 and won international acclaim. The common theme of ungainly transition between traditional and modern society is explored by a woman narrator whose much-loved husband takes a second wife.

Another woman writer is Aminata Sow-Fall; her 1986 novel *The Beggars Strike* is an ironic story which highlights the differences between rich and poor and questions the power of the political elite – a consistently popular theme in modern Senegalese literature.

SOCIETY & CONDUCT

Among the Wolof, weddings are very important and enjoyed with great enthusiasm. Legal and religious ceremonies are performed early so that the rest of the day can be spent celebrating.

In a traditional wedding, the grandmother and great aunts take the bride to the marriage chamber, lecture her and summon the husband to consummate the marriage. When this is done the older women exhibit the bloodstained sheet to the guests, after

which the bride is smothered with gifts. (If you want to make a gift at any ceremony, a small amount of money is perfectly acceptable.)

Christian ceremonies are observed in Senegal, particularly in the cities, where a larger proportion of the population (although still a minority) is non-Muslim.

At Christmas in St-Louis and Île de Gorée crowds of people carry around large lanterns called *fanals* which are made in the shape of boats or houses, and are brightly painted with intricate decorations. This fascinating tradition originated during French colonial times, although it may have been introduced by Portuguese settlers, when wealthy inhabitants going to midnight mass would be led by slaves carrying lamps. Today, the people sing and chant as they parade their fanals around the streets, while onlookers donate a few coins as a sign of appreciation.

RELIGION

In Senegal over 80% of the population is Muslim, mainly the Wolof, Tukulor, Lebu, Fula and Mandinka people, while the Diola and Sérèr favour Christianity, although many people also follow traditional beliefs.

An all-pervading aspect of Islam in Senegal is the power of the marabouts and Islamic brotherhoods.

FULA

The Fula (also called Fulani, or Peul in French-speaking countries) were originally nomadic cattle herders, tall, lightly-built people, who have been settling across savanna West Africa for centuries. The Tukulor (Toucouleur) and the Wolof of Senegal and the Fulbe Jeeri of Mauritania are all of Fula origin.

Many Fula are now settled farmers, while others continue to follow their herds seasonally in search of pasture, living in beehive like grass huts. Those with no cattle of their own work as herdsmen in many parts of West Africa looking after other people's cattle.

The nomadic Fula, the Wodaabé, put boys through a public initiation ceremony into manhood in which they are lashed with long rods to the accelerating rhythm of drums. Everyone, including potential brides is watching, and they must show no fear, though their ordeal leaves them scarred. At the annual Gerewol festival, where the young meet prospective marriage

Top: Fula woman by the River Niger.

Middle: Married Fula women may wear huge gold earrings like this one, made of a single strip of gold, beaten into curves. Photograph by Dennis Wisken/ Sidewalk Gallery.

Bottom: This goatherder on his way to the water hole wears a characteristic Fula hat.

VICTOR ENGLEBERT

VICTOR ENGLEBERT

partners, men pay great attention to their appearance, adorning themselves with bold shining jewellery, feathers, sunglasses and elaborate make-up, anything to create an impression, and to look their best for the women!

WOLOF

The Wolof heartland is Senegal where they comprise about 36% of the population. They are active in the Muslim brotherhoods of which the Mourides are one of the most powerful.

As with many West African people, Wolof society is hierarchical, with hereditary castes determining traditional occupations and status. Tradiional family status is now only important for marriage and traditional occupations, such as blacksmiths and praise singers (griots).

Although Islam has been an influence in the Wolof area since the 11th century many traditional beliefs persist. The main street of a Wolof village is always crooked, for a straight one would invite bad spirits, and there is a belief in a snake monster so terrible that to look upon it causes death. Against witches and other forms of evil people wear leather-bound amulets that often contain written verses of the Quran.

The Wolof tend to be tall, and look magnificent in their traditional flowing robes of white, dark blue or black. The women wear a series of loose layered gowns, each a little shorter than the one underneath. Men wear long gowns over loose white pantaloons that overhang the knee.

Katie Abu, David Else

JASON LAURÉ

Bottom: Wolof woma carrying her child in t traditional way.

Marabouts & Brotherhoods

An understanding of Senegal's marabouts and the power of the Islamic brotherhoods (con-fréries) is fundamental to an understanding of Senegal itself. The subject involves religion, politics, economy, God and the State, and is remarkably complex, but this short section will hopefully provide an insight.

Whereas orthodox Islam holds that every believer is directly in touch with Allah, the trad-itionally hierarchical societies of North and West Africa found it more natural to have religious leaders ascribed with divine power providing a link between God and the common populace. These intermediaries became known as marabouts, and many are venerated by their disci-ples (talibés) as saints. The concept of brotherhoods – groups who followed the teachings of a particular marabout – was imported from Morocco. The leader of a brotherhood was known as a cheik, or khalif, and these terms are still used today.

The earliest brotherhood established south of the Sahara (in the 16th century) was the Qadiriya, which encouraged charity and humility and attracted followers throughout the northern Sahel. It spread through Senegal in the 19th and 20th centuries. Today, most Qadiriya followers are Mandinka from the south of Senegal and in Gambia.

The Moroccan-based Tijaniya brotherhood was introduced to Senegal by Omar Tall in the mid-19th century, and remains powerful today, with large and important mosques in the towns of Tivaouane and Kaolack. Later in the 19th century, a smaller brotherhood called the Layen broke away from the Qadiriya under a marabout called Saidi Limamou Laye, who is believed to be a reincarnation of the Prophet Mohammed. Most Layen are Lebu people, who inhabit the town of Yoff outside Dakar.

The Mouridiya was founded by a marabout called Amadou Bamba in the late 19th century (for more details see the boxed text 'Bamba' in the Touba section) and is now the largest brotherhood, with over two million followers. One of Bamba's followers was Ibra Fall, who took readily to hard work but found prayer and study difficult. With Bamba's blessing he founded the Baye Fall sect for whom labour became religious observance. His followers called him Lamp Fall, and Bamba excused them from prayer and fasting during Ramadan so long as they worked hard – yet another Senegalese spin on conventional Islam.

Today, you'll see images of Lamp Fall and Bamba painted on walls and buses all over Senegal, and the Baye Fall disciples, with their dreadlocks, patchwork robes and begging bowls, are a constant reminder that Mouridism continues to thrive. Bamba's return to Senegal in 1907 after being exiled by the French is celebrated by the annual Magal pilgrimage to Touba, and it's significant that this is the major Mouride event, rather than any other Islamic holiday.

The alliance between the brotherhoods and the government is still a major feature of modern Senegalese life. The Parti Socialiste (PS) relies on marabout backing – especially from the khalif of the Mourides, who has about a quarter of the population hanging onto his every word – particularly at election time. To keep the brotherhoods sweet, the government pub-licly reinforces the marabouts' power and behind the scenes allows them a free hand in the all-important groundnut harvest (and, increasingly, other areas of the economy). If things look uncertain, the PS is allegedly not beyond the odd spot of outright largesse – see the boxed text 'Groundnuts' earlier in this chapter.

Both sides recognise the irony of a supposedly democratic left-wing party in cahoots with a rigidly hierarchical and conservative religious institution. But they need each other to main-tain the status quo from which they both benefit, and so the ministers and the marabouts remain faithful, if mistrustful, bedfellows.

LANGUAGE

French is the official language and Wolof the principal African language. Other languages include Mandinka (and the closely related Malinké), Fula, Sérèr and Diola (not to be confused with Dioula, spoken in Côte d'Ivoire). English is spoken a little, in some tourist areas only. See the Language chapter for a list of useful expressions in French, Wolof, Mandinka/Malinké and Fula.

Facts for the Visitor

SUGGESTED ITINERARIES

Starting in Dakar, you could spend a day or two visiting the frenetic markets and peace-ful Île de Gorée, before heading north to St-Louis, from where you can visit the spectacular wildlife reserves of Parc National aux Oiseaux du Djoudj and Parc National de la Langue de Barbarie (allow one day each). Alternatively, you could head south to the beaches of the Petite Côte and the Siné-Saloum Delta.

With three weeks the options expand further. Starting in Dakar, you could do a circular tour, heading south to the Petite Côte, Siné-Saloum Delta and Kaolack before going east to Tambacounda, perhaps returning to Dakar through Gambia. Another option would be to do the eastward leg through Gambia and the westward leg through the beautiful Casamance region, to

Highlights

Natural Beauty & National Parks

The Siné-Saloum Delta
A vast maze of mangrove creeks and forest-ed islands best appreciated by boat or on foot. Discover ancient shell mounds, spot birds, practise your fishing or just relax.

Parc National du Niokolo-Koba *(Eastern Senegal)*
The best place in the region to see large mammals in the wild; plus excellent birdwatching. You may be lucky and see chimpanzee, lion and elephant.

Casamance
Lush inland delta – the beautiful coastline and inexpensive traditional accommodation combine to make this a magnet for all travellers in Senegal.

River Senegal *(Northern Senegal)*
Parc National aux Oiseaux du Djoudj and Parc National de la Langue de Barbarie are bird sanctuaries of global significance around the creeks, flood plains, estuaries, shores and islands of the River Senegal.

People

Traditional Wrestling *(Dakar, Casamance)*
Join locals in watching one of their favourite traditional sports. Matches are held in the evening most weekends in the dry season in many towns, but are easiest to find in Dakar and Ziguinchor.

Fish Markets *(Central & Northern Senegal, Petite Côte)*
In many coastal villages and towns, including St-Louis and Mboro, a huge variety of fish, sharks, eels, and shellfish are sold by women on the beach after the boats come in from the ocean (usually in the late afternoon).

Marché Sandaga *(Dakar)*
You can buy anything in this vast, busy labyrinth of shops and stalls; take a deep breath and plunge in ...

History & Architecture

Île de Gorée *(Around Dakar)*
Beautiful island with a strong Mediterranean feel, thriving community, castles, colonial houses, good museums and dark reminders

Ziguinchor and the beaches at Cap Skiring before returning north for your flight home. To do all this might be a rush in three weeks, but four should be enough.

With five or six weeks, or even two months, you could do the above route in a much more relaxed manner, including detours off the circuit to the mosque at Touba, the Parc National du Niokolo-Koba and the little-visited wilds of Bassari Country in the far south-east.

PLANNING
When to Go
The best time is November to February when conditions are dry and relatively cool.

From December to February is also the local 'trading season', when the harvest is completed and the markets are busier. From March to May, the weather is dry but hotter. June to October is the rainy season, usually considered not so good for travelling – although some visitors prefer this time; just before and after the rains conditions are humid with no storms to clear the air.

Maps
The locally available *Carte du Senegal* (at a scale of 1:912,000) is good, and includes an excellent street map of Dakar. Also good is the IGN *Senegal Carte Routière* (at a scale of 1:1,000,000).

SENEGAL

Highlights

of the slave trade – a perfect escape from the hassles of Dakar.

St-Louis *(Central & Northern Senegal)*
The old capital dates from the 17th century, and many imposing colonial buildings remain in the city centre. Its unique coastal island setting and relaxed atmosphere make it a great place to hang out for a few days.

Touba, Diourbel and Kaolack *(Central & Northern Senegal)*
Huge, elaborate mosques in the heartland of the powerful Muslim brotherhoods.

Casamance
Discover the elaborate traditional architecture of this beautiful region, such as houses with roofs designed to trap water and two-storey mud buildings.

Activities
Birdwatching
Endless possibilities for spotting both endemic and migrant species, especially along the coast and estuaries, and plenty for those with only a passing interest.

Music & Dance *(Around Dakar, Casamance)*
Several hotels and campements offer opportunities for learning to play djembe drums and other traditional instruments, or study local dance.

Cycling *(Casamance, Eastern Senegal)*
One of the best ways to explore the Casamance and Kafountine areas of Senegal is by bicycle. Mountain biking is also becoming increasingly popular in the hills around Kedougou. In some places you can hire bicycles, but the quality varies considerably – consider bringing your own.

Beaches *(Eastern & Central Senegal, Petite Côte, Casamance)*
The Senegalese coast is one long beach, but south of Dakar conditions are better and places to stay easy to find, from large lively resorts to secluded hideaways.

Fishing *(Dakar, Casamance)*
Numerous opportunities for relaxed days with rod and line on the rivers and mangrove creeks, or for serious deep-sea sport fishing out in the Atlantic.

VISAS

Visas are not needed by citizens of Belgium, Britain, Denmark, France, Germany, Italy, Ireland, Luxembourg, the Netherlands and the USA. Tourist visas for one to three months cost US$20.

EMBASSIES & CONSULATES
Senegal Embassies & Consulates

In West Africa, Senegal has embassies in Burkina Faso, Cape Verde, Côte d'Ivoire, Gambia, Guinea, Guinea-Bissau, and Mali. For more details, see the Facts for the Visitor section of the relevant chapter. Elsewhere, embassies and consulates include the following:

Belgium
(☎ 02-673 00 97)
196 ave Franklin-Roosevelt, Brussels 1050
France
(☎ 01 44 05 38 48)
22 rue Hamelin, 75016 Paris
Germany
(☎ 0228-21 80 08)
Argelanderstrasse 3, 53115 Bonn
UK
(☎ 0171-938 4048; from 22 April 2000 ☎ 020 7938 4048)
39 Marloes Rd, London W8 6LA
USA
(☎ 202-234 0540)
2112 Wyoming Ave, NW, Washington, DC 20008

Embassies & Consulates in Senegal

Most embassies are in or near central Dakar, but some are in the Point E and Mermoz areas, about 5km north-west of the centre.

Belgium
(☎ 821 40 27)
Route de la Corniche-Est
Cape Verde
(☎ 821 39 36)
3 Blvd el Haji Djily Mbaye
Côte d'Ivoire
(☎ 821 34 73)
2 Ave Albert Sarraut
France
(☎ 839 51 00)
1 Rue Assane Ndoye, near the Novotel

The Gambia
(☎ 821 72 30 or 821 44 76)
11 Rue de Thiong
Germany
(☎ 823 25 19)
20 Ave Pasteur

Visas for Onward Travel

In Senegal, you can get visas for the following neighbouring West African countries. All embassies are open weekday mornings; for visas it's best to go first thing in the morning. You usually need to provide two photos.

Burkina Faso & Togo

The French embassy issues visas to these countries. The visa section is open weekdays from 8 am to 10.30 am, the fee is CFA3500 and visas are ready for collection at 5 pm the same day.

Cape Verde

Visas cost CFA6600 and take 24 hours. Open weekdays from 8.30 am to 12.30 pm, and 3 to 6 pm, Saturdays from 8.30 am to 12.30 pm.

Gambia

Visas cost CFA15,000 and are issued within 24 hours.

Guinea

Visas cost CFA20,000 and are issued in 24 hours.

Guinea-Bissau

Visas cost CFA10,000 for one month and are issued in 24 hours. There is also a consulate in Ziguinchor.

Mali

Visas cost CFA7500 and take 48 hours.

Mauritania

Visas cost CFA6000 to CFA9000, depending on nationality, and are issued on the spot by the consulate. Visas are not issued at the embassy in Mermoz.

Guinea
(☎ 824 86 06)
Rue 7, Point E
Guinea-Bissau
(☎ 824 59 22)
Rue 6, Point E
Mali
(☎ 823 48 93)
46 Blvd de la République
Mauritania (consulate)
Rue 37, Kolobane
Morocco
(☎ 824 69 27)
Ave Cheikh Anta Diop, Mermoz
The Netherlands
(☎ 823 94 83)
37 Rue Kléber
UK
(☎ 823 73 92)
20 Rue du Dr Guillet
USA
(☎ 823 34 96 or 823 34 24)
Ave Jean XXIII

Canada also has an embassy in Dakar.

CUSTOMS

There are no limits on the amount of foreign currency tourists are allowed to bring into Senegal, although CFA200,000 is the maximum amount of local currency foreigners can export.

MONEY

The unit of currency is the CFA franc.

Euro €1	=	CFA660
1FF	=	CFA100
UK£1	=	CFA950
US$1	=	CFA600

Banks include Citibank, CBAO (Compagnie Bancaire de l'Afrique Occidentale), BICIS (Banque Internationale pour le Commerce et l'Industrie Sénégalaise) and BCS (Banque Commerciale du Sénégal). There are branches in all main towns and at Dakar airport. If the airport branch is closed, you can change money at the airport bookshop, where commissions are lower.

Cashing travellers cheques in any major currency is easy in Dakar, but difficult else-

Bank Security

Some banks ask to see your proof of purchase receipt when changing travellers cheques. Travellers using cards to draw cash over the counter have also been asked for their PIN number. You may have no choice if you need some money, but keep a good record of the date and time, and if possible the name of the clerk serving you.

where if cheques are not in French francs. In Dakar, St-Louis, Ziguinchor and Kaolack, banks will give cash on Visa cards – usually on the spot. The Western Union Money Transfer agent is CBAO.

POST & COMMUNICATIONS
Post

Senegal's postal service is good, and items sent to or from the country generally arrive. A 10g letter to France/Europe/North America and Australasia is CFA300/320/460. The country's main poste restante is in Dakar.

Telephone & Fax

Senegal's phone service is good. Calls or faxes from public SONATEL offices cost about CFA1100 per minute to Europe (not

New Telephone Numbers

There are no city codes in Senegal, but most telephone numbers changed from six-digit to seven-digit numbers in 1997. Numbers beginning with 2 or 3 are now preceded by 8, except for mobile phone numbers (ie those starting with 28 and 38), which are preceded by 6. Note that 628 and 638 numbers are more expensive to call. All numbers starting with 4, 5, 6, 7, 8 and 9 are preceded by 9. There is no change to numbers beginning with 1 or any other number with less than six digits.

774 Facts for the Visitor

including France, which is less) and about CFA1400 to the USA and Australia. Rates are reduced by about 20% between 10 pm and 6 am Monday to Friday and all day at weekends.

In addition, you'll find privately owned *télécentres* (some are smart offices, others just a tiny booth in the corner of a shop or bar) with a *compteur* (meter) showing the number of units used. Most télécentres are open until late evening, although their rates are more than SONATEL's (eg around CFA1500 to CFA2000 per minute to the UK).

Email & Internet Access

There are Internet bureaus in Dakar and Ziguinchor. For more details see Information in the relevant town entries later.

BOOKS

Senegalese literature is discussed under Arts in the Facts about Senegal section earlier in this chapter, and some general books that include coverage of Senegal are listed in the Books section of the Regional Facts for the Visitor chapter. Locally produced guidebooks include *On Dakar Time* (CFA5000), covering the city and surrounding area, and *Gorée – The Island and the Historical Museum*.

NEWSPAPERS & MAGAZINES

Most newspapers and magazines are published in French, with a few in Wolof and other local languages. Senegal's main daily paper is *Le Soleil*, nominally independent but with close links to the ruling Parti Socialiste.

RADIO & TV

The government radio stations broadcast in French, Wolof and other local languages. Government TV is all in French. Independent radio stations, also French-language, include Dakar FM and the lively Sud-FM. Independent TV is dominated by Canal + Horizons and French satellite stations, although most large hotels have sets tuned into CNN or BBC World.

PHOTOGRAPHY & VIDEO

You can photograph most things (providing the usual rules of politeness are observed) – even the Presidential Palace – although snapping military installations, airports and government buildings could still get you into trouble. For more general information and advice, see the Photography & Video section in the Regional Facts for the Visitor chapter earlier.

HEALTH

Proof of yellow fever vaccination is mandatory if you are coming from an endemic area. Malaria exists year-round throughout the country, so you should take appropriate precautions. For more general information on these and other health matters, see the Health section in the Regional Facts for the Visitor chapter earlier in this book.

In Dakar you'll find the country's main hospitals as well as many private clinics and doctors. Around the country, most large towns have hospitals, doctors and clinics; if you need to find any of these, ask at a good hotel in the town.

WOMEN TRAVELLERS

Senegal does not pose any specific problems for women travellers. For more general information and advice, see the Women Travellers section in the Regional Facts for the Visitor chapter.

DANGERS & ANNOYANCES

There are two main dangers you may encounter: the possibility of civil unrest in Casamance (see the Warning box in the Casamance section of this chapter later) and the possibility of being robbed in Dakar (see Information in the Dakar section of this chapter).

BUSINESS HOURS

Businesses are open from 8 am to noon and 2.30 to 6 pm on Monday to Friday, and on Saturday from 8 am to noon. Government offices keep the same hours. Most banks are open Monday to Friday, typically from 8.30

to 11.30 am or noon, and 2.30 to 4.30 pm. Some banks open on Saturday until 11 am.

PUBLIC HOLIDAYS & SPECIAL EVENTS

The main public holidays are 1 January (New Year's Day), 4 April (Independence Day), Easter Monday, 1 May (Labour Day), 15 August, 1 November and 25 December (Christmas Day). Islamic holidays are also celebrated – see the Public Holidays & Special Events section in the Regional Facts for the Visitor chapter for a table of dates. The major holidays are Independence Day, the end of Ramadan and Tabaski.

Other festivals include the Grand Magal pilgrimage in Touba, 48 days after the Islamic new year; the International Music Festival of Dakar in December and the St-Louis International Jazz Festival, held every May. There's also the Paris-Dakar Rally (for more details see the boxed text on p 120), which ends in Dakar around the second week of January.

ACTIVITIES

Most major hotels have swimming pools that nonguests can use for a fee. Otherwise, Senegal's coast has many good beaches, although large waves, steep shelves and a heavy undertow can make some dangerous.

At hotels on the coast, you can hire sailboards, or arrange water-skiing and several other motor-assisted sports. Dakar is also a base for diving and kayaking.

Deep-sea sport fishing can be arranged in Dakar and other coastal centres. Depending on the season, ocean catches include barracuda, tuna, sailfish and blue marlin.

Alternatively, you could learn drumming – places in Yoff and Malika, near Dakar, and in and around Kafountine run drumming courses.

ACCOMMODATION

Senegal offers everything from top class hotels and coastal resorts to dirty dosshouses in Dakar. There is a good choice of campements and simple hotels in the smaller towns

and rural areas. All hotels charge a tourist tax of CFA600 per person. Sometimes this is included in the price, and sometimes it isn't – you have to ask.

Some hotels charge by the room, so it makes no difference to the price (apart from the tourist tax) if you are alone or sharing. In others, couples may be allowed to share a single. Breakfast is usually extra.

The high season for hotel rates is usually from October to May. Other times may be cheaper, but some hotels close outside the high season. The notable exception is Casamance, which successfully promotes itself as a year-round destination, with tour groups from Europe coming as often in July and August as they do in December and January.

FOOD

Senegal has some of the finest cuisine in West Africa – a very enjoyable feature of travel here. Common dishes include *mafé*, a groundnut-based stew, and *domodah*, the same stew with meat or vegetables added to it. Sometimes deep-orange palm oil is also added. *Tiéboudienne* (pronounced *chey-boujen* and also spelt 'thieboudjienne', and numerous other ways) is Senegal's national dish and consists of rice baked in a thick sauce of fish and vegetables. *Thieb khonkhe* (pronounced *cheb-honk*) is a similar dish which comes with a tomato paste. Also popular is *poulet yassa* – grilled chicken in onion and lemon sauce. Variations on the theme are *poisson yassa* (fish) and *viande yassa* (meat), or sometimes simply *yassa* – a bit of a lucky dip. Another equally variable favourite is *riz yollof*, also called *thieb yape*, which consists of vegetables and/or meat cooked in oil and tomatoes, served with rice.

DRINKS

Tea comes in two sorts: western-style tea made with a tea bag, and local tea made with green leaves and served with loads of sugar in small glasses. Coffee is almost exclusively instant Nescafé. Soft drinks are widely available.

Senegalese beer is good. Gazelle comes in 500mL bottles and costs between CFA500 and CFA900. Flag is a stronger, more up-market brew. A 330mL bottle costs CFA500 in a cheap bar and CFA1200 or more in posh hotels (where they wouldn't dream of offering Gazelle). Flag is also available in larger bottles and on draught.

Getting There & Away

AIR
Senegal's main international airport is Dakar. Major airlines servicing Dakar include Air Afrique, Air France and Swissair. Airport tax is charged when you leave, but is usually included in your ticket price. If it is not included, the tax (levied at the airport) is US$20 or CFA10,000.

Europe & the USA
Airlines from Europe serving Senegal include Air Afrique, Air France, Swissair, Alitalia, TAP Air Portugal and Aeroflot. Fares on scheduled flights from London to Dakar range from about UK£400 (US$600) to UK£500 (US$750), rising by another UK£100 (US$150) in the high season (October to May). Return fares from Paris to Dakar range from 2750FF to 3000FF, and up to 4000FF in the high season. Brussels to Dakar costs up to Bf30,000 (return) in the high season, although charter flights to Senegal with French and Belgian package tour companies are cheaper.

In Senegal, the best agency for charter flights is Nouvelles Frontières in Dakar (for contact details see the Information entry in the Dakar section later), with singles to Paris for around 2000FF (US$350).

From the USA, Air Afrique has flights twice a week between New York and Dakar (with APEX return fares around US$1200), but most other flights go via Europe.

Africa
Dakar is linked to all other capital cities in West Africa, with a wide choice of regional airlines. Air Afrique flies to Abidjan (Côte d'Ivoire) daily, Bamako (Mali) five times per week (CFA104,000 one way), Ouagadougou (Burkina Faso) three times weekly, and Conakry (Guinea) five times per week. Air Dabia serves Banjul (Gambia) and Conakry, and Ethiopian Airlines serves many West African regional capitals. Air Mali flies twice weekly to Bamako for CFA69,100 one way. Air Bissau flies twice a week to Bissau for CFA98,000 return.

Air Afrique and Ethiopian Airlines offer flights to Nairobi (Kenya) or Johannesburg (South Africa), and many travellers fly from Dakar to Casablanca (Morocco) to avoid the difficult overland section through Mauritania and Western Sahara. The usual one-way fare on Royal Air Maroc is US$530, and youth tickets are US$350.

LAND
Gambia
From Dakar there are buses (CFA2500 to CFA3500) and bush taxis (CFA3600) south to Barra in Gambia, from where you get the ferry across the River Gambia to Banjul.

Border Crossings

Senegal completely surrounds Gambia. There are three main border points of interest for travellers: at Karang, north of Barra on the main road to/from Kaolack and Dakar in central Senegal; Seleti, south of Brikama, on the main road to Ziguinchor in southern Senegal; and Sabi, east of Basse on the road to Vélingara. Other border crossing points include just south of Soma, and just north of Farafenni where the Trans-Gambia Highway between north and south Senegal cuts through Gambia.

From Senegal to Guinea, the main crossing point is between Tambacounda and Labé. For Guinea-Bissau, the main crossing point is at São Domingos. Most travellers heading for Mali take the train, but the main road crossing point is at Kidira, between Tambacounda and Kayes. The main border point between Senegal and Mauritania is at Rosso.

From southern Senegal, bush taxis run regularly between Ziguinchor and Serekunda (CFA2500), and between Kafountine and Brikama (CFA1200). It's also possible to travel between Tambacounda in eastern Senegal and Basse Santa Su in Gambia via Vélingara.

Guinea
Most traffic goes between Tambacounda and Labé in Guinea, usually via Koundara, and less often via Kedougou. For more details, see the Tambacounda and Kedougou sections later in this chapter.

Guinea-Bissau
Bush taxis and minibuses run several times daily between Ziguinchor and Bissau via São Domingos (the border) and Ingore, for CFA2500. The road is in good condition, but the ferries on the stretch between Ingore and Bissau can make the trip take anything from four to eight hours. Other options are to go from Tanaf to Farim or from Tambacounda via Vélingara to Gabú.

Mali
Bush Taxi Most travellers go by train but improved roads mean a bush-taxi option is available. From Tambacounda to the border

at Kidira a Peugeot 504 costs CFA4000, and a minibus CFA2700. In Kidira, you cross the new road bridge to Diboli, from where bush taxis go to Kayes for CFA2500.

Train Trains run between Dakar and Bamako twice a week in each direction. The trip is scheduled to take 35 hours but 40 hours or longer is more typical. You can get on or off at Tambacounda (eastern Senegal) or Kayes (western Mali), although between Kayes and Bamako the train is your only real option.

Seats are numbered, although in 2nd class you should get to the train in good time. The 1st class seats are large and comfortable, while 2nd class seating is more crowded. Sleepers (couchettes) are basic but adequate. The train has a restaurant car and you can get cheap food at stations along the way.

If there are no seats available, look out for touts on the platform selling unused tickets. Another option is go to Tambacounda by road and buy your train ticket there, although usually only 1st class tickets are available.

At each border post you take a short hike to the immigration office. Your passport may be taken by an officer on the train, but you still have to collect it yourself.

Theft is a problem; if you leave your seat, especially at night, ask a fellow passenger to watch your gear.

Trains between Senegal & Mali

The *Mistral International* (Senegalese) train departs Dakar on Wednesday at 10 am. Tickets are sold on Mondays and Tuesdays from 8 am to noon and 1.30 to 6 pm. The *Express International* (Malian) train departs Dakar on Saturdays at 10 am. Tickets are sold on Fridays from 8 am to noon and 1 to 6 pm. Times and fares (in CFA) for the *Mistral International* are as follows:

destination	arrival time	1st	2nd	sleeper
Thiès	11.30	8600	6900	n/a
Tambacounda	19.00	14,000	10,800	26,900
Kidira	23.30	18,500	14,100	31,300
Kayes	03.30	21,000	16,000	34,000
Bamako	15.30	34,700	26,400	51,000

Times for the *Express International* are the same and fares are about 10% less.

Car & Motorcycle The route from Tambacounda to Kayes is straightforward, but beyond here the direct route beside the railway is in very bad condition as far as Kita (although it's due to be upgraded). In the past, overlanders have loaded vehicles onto the train, but this is a very time-consuming and expensive process, so most go via Nioro, although this road is also in terrible condition.

Mauritania

Bush Taxi The main border point is at Rosso, where a ferry crosses the River Senegal. You can go direct to Rosso from Dakar, but most travellers stop off at St-Louis, from where a Peugeot 504 to Rosso is CFA1450. You cross the river on the large ferry, which is free for passengers, or by pirogue (CFA200). From the Mauritanian immigration point it's 500m to the gare routière, from where bush taxis go to Nouakchott.

There are plenty of moneychangers, but don't change on the Senegal side as it's illegal to bring ouguiya into Mauritania.

Car & Motorcycle To avoid the notorious hassle at Rosso, drivers can cross the River Senegal at several ferries east of here, and at the Maka Diama barrage, north of St-Louis, although the *piste* between the barrage and the main road on the Mauritanian side of the border is very soft sand.

SEA

Pirogues go between the Siné-Saloum Delta and Banjul. For more details see Getting There & Away in the Palmarin & Djifer section later in this chapter.

Getting Around

AIR

Air Senegal has daily flights from Dakar to Ziguinchor for CFA35,000 one way (which continue to Cap Skiring four times per week). This service is not very reliable but is due for privatisation, so things may change.

BUS, BUSH TAXI & MINIBUS

Long-distance routes between large towns are served by buses (*grand cars*), which usually carry about 35 people. Most are white Mercedes buses, sometimes called N'Diaga N'Diaye (pronounced *njagga-njaye*), and generally in quite good condition, leaving when full and only stopping occasionally. Everybody gets a seat. There are also a few bigger buses (50 to 60 seats) on some long-distance routes and it's likely that more will appear, as they are cheaper than other buses and just as good.

Minibuses (*petit cars*) carrying 15 to 20 people also run on many routes. These tend to be slower and have less regard for passenger limits. On many routes you also find misleadingly named *cars rapides* – minibuses, usually painted orange and blue, which are battered, slow, crowded and worth avoiding. Your other option for long-distance journeys are comfortable seven-seater Peugeot 504 bush taxis (*taxis brousse*).

All public transport fares are fixed by the government. To give an idea: a 504 from Dakar to Kaolack is CFA2000, from Dakar to St-Louis is CFA2800, and from Dakar to Ziguinchor is CFA6000. Minibuses are typically about 20 to 25% cheaper than 504s, and buses about 30 to 35% cheaper.

TRAIN

Many visitors take the express train that runs between Dakar and Bamako (Mali), but few use this line to travel by train around Senegal itself, although you could use it between, say, Dakar and Tambacounda. For more details, see the entry under Mali in the Getting There & Away section earlier in this chapter.

CAR

Most car hire companies are based in Dakar – for more details see the Dakar Getting Around section. Petrol costs around CFA 450 per litre. Diesel is CFA300 to CFA350.

BOAT

The MS *Joola* runs between Dakar and Ziguinchor via Île de Carabane, and is a very

Boat Fares

from	to	economy	2nd	1st (cabin 4 bunks)	1st (cabin 2 bunks)
Dakar	Ziguinchor	3500	6000	15,000	18,000
Dakar	Carabane	3000	6000	12,000	15,000
Ziguinchor	Carabane	1000	–	–	–

pleasant way of travelling. The trip takes about 20 hours. The boat usually leaves Dakar on Tuesday evening, stops at Île de Carabane early Wednesday morning and arrives in Ziguinchor around midday. Going the other way, the boat leaves Ziguinchor at noon on Thursday, stops at Carabane a few hours later, then arrives in Dakar on Friday morning. The boat also leaves Dakar on Friday and departs Ziguinchor on Sunday.

One-way fares (in CFA) for the different classes on the MS *Joola* are listed in the table.

There are seats in economy class but no guaranteed places, while 2nd class has reservable reclining seats. The restaurant-bar offers reasonable meals and, on some voyages, live music. One reader wrote to tell us of a trip where the band played, and most of the passengers danced, all through the night.

ORGANISED TOURS

If you're short of time you could get around the country on an organised tour. Most organised tours require a minimum of six to eight passengers, although there are some options for two or four. A small selection based in Dakar is included here. For tours in northern Senegal, see also the St-Louis section, and for trips to Parc National du Niokolo-Koba see the Tambacounda section.

Inter Tourisme
(☎ 822 45 29) 3 Allées Delmas. Friendly and relatively cheap; offers one-day trips to Lac Rose for CFA20,000 per person, two-day trips to Siné-Saloum for CFA85,000 each for two people and five-day trips to Parc National du Niokolo-Koba and Bassari Country for CFA200,000 per person (a minimum of six).

Nouvelles Frontières
(☎ 823 34 43, fax 822 28 17) 3 Blvd de la République. Local office of French international tour operator. Offers a wide range of excursions, and helps with hotel reservations.
Safari-Evasion
(☎ 822 47 38) 12 Ave Albert Sarraut. Mainly arranges flights, but a few tours to popular destinations are also available.
Senegalair Voyages
(☎ 825 80 11) Ave Leopold Senghor. Offers two-day trips to Siné-Saloum at CFA85,000 each for two people, or CFA70,000 each for four. Three-day trips to Parc National du Niokolo-Koba are CFA185,000 each for two people, or CFA130,000 for four.

For more specialised, active tours, contact Bruno at the Orisha souvenir shop (☎ 822 56 09) on Rue Mohamed V in Dakar. He's connected to the Kayak Club, which offers island, coast and river trips, plus treks in Bassari Country.

Dakar

Dakar is arguably one of the finest cities in West Africa, with a cosmopolitan atmosphere, temperate climate, wide range of restaurants, bars and nightclubs, and many interesting things to see and do. The central area is easy to walk around, and city buses run frequently to the suburbs. Also within reach are several good beaches, traditional fishing communities and some fascinating islands of historical and ecological interest.

Despite these attractions, some people just can't stand Dakar. The noise, fumes and crowds can be bad sometimes, but the main problem when strolling around town is the unwanted attention you'll get from pestering traders and the danger of theft. For advice on

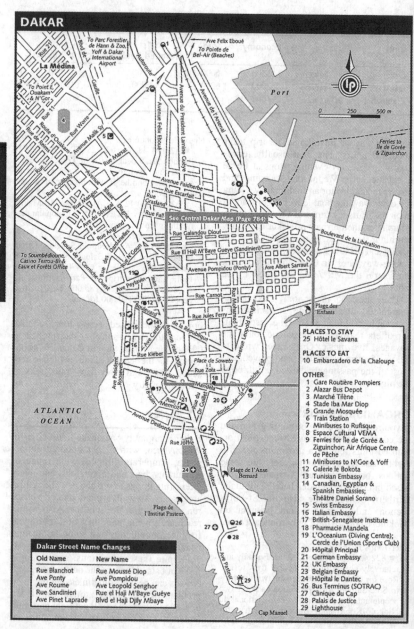

DAKAR

To Parc Forestier
de Hann & Zoo,
Yoff & Dakar
International Airport

La Médina

Ave Felix Eboué

To Pointe de
Bel-Air (Beaches)

Port

Rue 27

Blvd de...

Autoroute

Avenue du Président Lamine Guèye

Avenue de l'Arsenal

Ave Felix Eboué

To Point E,
Ouakam
& N'Gor

Rue 11

Route d'Ouakam

Rue Wiorte

Avenue Malik Sy

Rue Marsat

Route de Reims

Rue Coly

Avenue Blaise Diagne

Rue Mangin

Ave du Senegal

Rue Angrand

Rue N'Goun

Rue des Dadselles

Route de la Corniche Ouest

Rue Galandou Diouf

Rue El Haji M'Baye Gueye (Sandinieri)

Avenue Pompidou (Ponty)

Ave Albert Sarraut

Rue Carnot

Rue Jules Ferry

Rue Mohamed V

Avenue Léopold Senghor

Boulevard de la Libération

Ferries to
Île de Gorée
& Ziguinchor

See Central Dakar Map (Page 784)

Avenue Faidherbe

Rue Escarfait

Rue Grasland

Rue Fall

Plage des
Enfants

To Soumbédioune,
Casino Terrou-Bi &
Eaux et Forêts Office

Avenue de la République

Ave Peyravin

Ave Jean Jaures

Boulevard

Ave Cerlio

Avenue Jean XXIII

Place de Soweto

Rue Zola

Route de la Corniche Est

ATLANTIC
OCEAN

Avenue Nelson-Mandela

Rue Kléber

Ave Président Roosevelt

Ave Ponty

Rue 18 Juin

Rue Mermoz

Avenue Desbordes

Rue Joffre

Rue du Dr Guillet

Avenue Pasteur

Plage de l'Anse
Bernard

Plage de
l'Institut Pasteur

Cap Manuel

PLACES TO STAY
25 Hôtel le Savana

PLACES TO EAT
10 Embarcadero de la Chaloupe

OTHER
1 Gare Routière Pompiers
2 Alazar Bus Depot
3 Marché Tilène
4 Stade Iba Mar Diop
5 Grande Mosquée
6 Train Station
7 Minibuses to Rufisque
8 Espace Cultural VEMA
9 Ferries for Île de Gorée &
  Ziguinchor; Air Afrique Centre
  de Pêche
11 Minibuses to N'Gor & Yoff
12 Galerie le Bokota
13 Tunisian Embassy
14 Canadian, Egyptian &
  Spanish Embassies;
  Théâtre Daniel Sorano
15 Swiss Embassy
16 Italian Embassy
17 British-Senegalese Institute
18 Pharmacie Mandela
19 L'Oceanium (Diving Centre);
  Cercle de l'Union (Sports Club)
20 Hôpital Principal
21 German Embassy
22 UK Embassy
23 Belgian Embassy
24 Hôpital le Dantec
26 Bus Terminus (SOTRAC)
27 Clinique du Cap
28 Palais de Justice
29 Lighthouse

Dakar Street Name Changes	
Old Name	**New Name**
Rue Blanchot	Rue Moussé Diop
Ave Ponty	Ave Pompidou
Ave Roume	Ave Leopold Senghor
Rue Sandinieri	Rue el Haji M'Baye Guèye
Ave Pinet Laprade	Blvd el Haji Djily Mbaye

SENEGAL

Dangers in Dakar

Dakar is notorious for thefts and muggings against visitors, frequently in broad daylight. The worst areas for muggings are the beaches around Dakar and the Corniche roads near the coast, the areas around the markets, Ave Pompidou and Place de l'Indépendance (especially outside the banks). Pickpockets operate wherever wealthy tourists can be surrounded by crowds, such as at the railway station and on the Île de Gorée ferry.

Thieves may work in groups. One guy will touch your back, causing you to stop. A second tries to grab your wallet, while a third acts as a decoy. Watch out for 'traders' with only one item to sell. Beware too of people offering small gifts 'for friendship'; it's just another way to slow you down.

Genuine street traders, of course, are not thieves, but many are desperate for a sale and if you show the slightest bit of interest you'll be hassled mercilessly until you crack. Some, however, may work with thieves to slow down potential targets. Unless you genuinely want something ignore them, or try a firm but civil 'non merci' (no thank you). Don't forget that these aggressive guys are not typical. Most Senegalese are genuinely hospitable and wouldn't dream of hassling guests in their country.

coping with these notorious hustlers and muggers, see the boxed text. If your courage fails, it's easy enough to spend time in parts of the city that tourists, and consequently the bad guys, don't frequent.

Orientation

The hub of Dakar is the Place de l'Indépendance from which Ave Leopold Senghor leads south in the direction of the Palais Présidentiel, Ave Pompidou leads west to Marché Sandaga and Ave Albert Sarraut leads east towards Marché Kermel. A good selection of shops, hotels, restaurants, cafes, bars and nightclubs are in this central area.

From the Palais Présidentiel, Blvd de la République extends west, past the cathedral. South of here is Place de Soweto, the IFAN Museum, the national theatre and several embassies.

From Marché Sandaga, Ave Émile Badiane turns into Ave Blaise Diagne and heads north-west to become Route d'Ouakam, passing through the suburbs of Point E, Mermoz and Ouakam, to finally reach Pointe des Almadies and N'Gor.

Information

Tourist Information A free listings magazine called *Le Dakarois* is available in large hotels and travel agencies, and includes telephone numbers for restaurants, travel agents, embassies and hospitals.

Money On the west side of Place de l'Indépendance are BICIS, CBAO and Citibank, which all change money. CBAO has the quickest service, and BICIS is the next best. There's an exchange bureau inside the nearby Hôtel de l'Indépendance.

Post & Telephone The main post office is on Blvd el Haji Djily Mbaye, near Marché Kermel. The poste restante is at a smaller post office at the eastern end of Ave Pompidou, but is unreliable, holds letters for only 30 days and charges CFA250 per letter. It's open only in the evening.

For phone calls, SONATEL has offices on Rue Wagane Diouf and on Blvd de la République (both open from 7 am to 11 pm), and there are also many private télécentres, although their rates may be higher.

Email & Internet Access Metissacana (☎ 822 20 43, email metissacana@metissacana.com) on Rue de Thiong charges CFA2000 per hour for terminal use. Cyber-Business Centre (☎ 823 32 23, fax 826 96 14) on Ave Leopold Senghor, open daily from 8 am to midnight, has helpful English-speaking staff and a much more business-like atmosphere. One hour on a terminal is CFA 1600. Other services include public telephones and fax. Although sending

SENEGAL

email is no problem, neither place allows you to receive one-off messages.

Travel Agencies & Tour Operators For flights to Europe or other parts of Africa, agencies include Senegal Tours (☎ 823 31 81, fax 823 26 44) at 5 Place de l'Indépendance (American Express agent), SDV Voyages (☎ 839 00 81) at 51 Ave Albert Sarraut (Diners Club agent) and M'boup Voyages (☎ 821 18 63) on Place de l'Indépendance, where some staff speak English. For details of Dakar-based tour companies, see Organised Tours in the main Getting Around section of this chapter.

Bookshops Librairie Clairafrique near Place de l'Indépendance, and Librairie aux Quatres Vents on Rue Félix Faure, have a wide range of books and magazines (although very little in English) and also sell maps. Best for English titles is the bookshop at Auberge Keur Beer on Île de Gorée (see the Around Dakar section) and the second-hand bookstalls in the streets around Marché Sandaga, where traders will part exchange.

Cultural Centres The American Cultural Centre on Rue Carnot, off Place de l'Indépendance, has a big library of books in English. The British Council on Blvd de la République and the British-Senegalese Institute on Rue 18 Juin, near Place de Soweto, also have libraries. The lively Centre Cultur-el Français (also called the Alliance Franco-Sénégalaise) is on Rue Gomis. All have films and performances, usually advertised on their notice boards, which are good places to find out about other Dakar cultural events.

Medical Services For major accidents, the Hôpital Principal (☎ 823 27 41) is at the far southern end of Ave Senghor, and Hôpital le Dantec (☎ 822 24 20) is on Ave Pasteur. Otherwise you could try Clinique du Cap (☎ 821 36 27) just south of Hôpital le Dantec, Clinique Pasteur (☎ 821 25 48) west of Place de l'Indépendance or Clinique Internationale (☎ 824 44 21) at 33 Blvd Dial

Diop, which has some English-speaking staff.

Dakar has many pharmacies. Those with 24-hour service include Pharmacy Mandela (☎ 821 21 72) on Ave Nelson Mandela near the Hôpital Principal.

Things to See

The IFAN Museum (Institut Fondamental d'Afrique Noir) is one of the best museums in West Africa. Lively, imaginative displays show masks and traditional dress from the whole region (including Mali, Guinea-Bissau, Benin and Nigeria) and provide an excellent overview of styles, without bombarding you with so much that you can't take it all in. You can also see beautiful fabrics and carvings, drums, musical instruments and agricultural tools. The museum's open daily from 8 am to 12.30 pm and 2 to 6.30 pm; admission is CFA200.

The handsome white **Palais Présidentiel** is surrounded by sumptuous gardens and guards in colonial-style uniforms. Other interesting buildings from the same era include the **Gouvernance** and the **Chambre de Commerce** on Place de l'Indépendance, the fine old **Hôtel de Ville** (Town Hall) on Allées Delmas, and the church-like **train station**, a short distance further north.

Out of the city centre is the **Grande Mosquée**, built in 1964, with its landmark minaret, which is floodlit at night. The surrounding area, called **La Médina**, while not picturesque, is a lively, bustling place contrasting sharply with the sophisticated city centre. Another reason to visit is that few tourists come here, so there's little hassle.

West of the centre, a visit to the fishing beach and market of **Soumbédioune** is good in the late afternoon when the fishing boats return. This is also a major centre of pirogue building, and behind the fish market you'll see carpenters turning planks and tree trunks into large ocean-going canoes.

Markets

Marché Sandaga is very much aimed at locals, and you can buy just about anything here, although don't expect too many sou-

Soumbédioune Boat Race

In the manner of all great boating people, the Lebu of Soumbédioune have an annual regatta, the main event being a pirogue race. Each fishing village along the coast sends one team of about 25 crew in a specially built racing pirogue. It is a great spectacle, especially as the teams are fanatically competitive. So competitive that in 1996 and 1997 the race was cancelled following all-out warfare at sea between the crews before they even reached Dakar. If this obstacle can be overcome in subsequent years, the race apparently takes place on Independence Day, and would be well worth watching.

venirs. The sheer choice of fabric stalls is a real attraction. Colourful cotton trousers and shirts are popular, but you can buy any cloth you fancy and have it made up into something by the local tailors according to your own design for around CFA2000.

The stalls in and around **Marché Kermel** east of Place de l'Indépendance on Rue le Dantec have more for tourists, with carvings, baskets, leatherwork and other souvenirs, as well as flowers and fruit. Unfortunately, both Marché Sandaga and Marché Kermel are plagued by hustlers, offering to be your 'guide'. If you can't ignore them, complain to a stall holder that it's putting you off buying. Alternatively, hire one to minimise the hassle from others.

Well worth a visit is **Marché de Tilène**, at the heart of La Médina, crowded with the sights and sounds of a traditional African market and relatively free of tourists (and thieves). You may need a guide as the original market hall is hard to find among the sprawl of tin-roofed shops and houses.

Activities

Swimming Bel-Air, 3km north-east of the city centre, has two private beaches where personal safety is not a problem. Both have

CFA500 entry fees. Plage Monaco is the locals' favourite, while the smarter Plage Voile d'Or seems to be favoured more by Europeans, although the clientele at both is mixed. N'Gor and Yoff also have beaches – see the Around Dakar section following.

Most top end hotels have pools which are open to nonguests. The Hôtel Teranga has a pool overlooking the ocean and charges CFA4500 (free if you eat at the Assiette Grill). The Hôtel de l'Indépendance charges CFA2000 for its roof-top pool with a great view of Dakar (free if you have a drink).

Diving The French-run L'Oceanium (☎ 822 24 41, fax 821 02 24, email oceanium@dkar .acrhimedia.fr) on the Corniche-Est hires out equipment (from CFA3500) and arranges a wide range of trips and courses including a complete beginners' introductory dive for CFA10,000.

Kayaking You can rent kayaks at the L'Oceanium. Kayaking trips are also arranged by a local organisation contactable through the Orisha souvenir shop – see Organised Tours in the main Getting Around section of this chapter for more details.

Fishing You can arrange deep-sea sport fishing at the Air Afrique Centre de Pêche, next to the Île de Gorée ferry port. During the fishing high season (May to October), a day out costs a mere CFA280,000.

Places to Stay

It can sometimes be difficult to find a room in Dakar, especially in the lower price bracket, but wandering around with a rucksack on is not recommended. If you find a room anywhere within your price range, take it for one night and look for something cheaper the next day. Several other budget places are listed in the Around Dakar section later in this chapter.

Prices for budget hotels include tourist tax. At mid-range and top end hotels, prices do not include tax, but all have rooms with private bathrooms, restaurants serving breakfast and other meals.

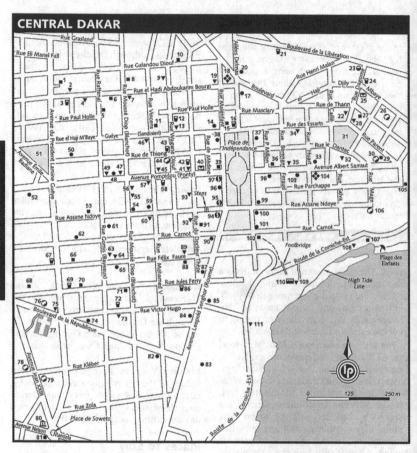

CENTRAL DAKAR

Places to Stay – Budget

Hôtel Mon Logis just off Ave du President Lamine Guéye charges CFA5000 for grubby rooms, trickling showers and dirty toilets. It's down an alley, upstairs and unmarked. Even worse is *Hôtel du Prince (49 Rue Raffenal)*, behind a grey steel gate, with double rooms for CFA4800. With more to recommend it is *Hôtel du Marché (3 Rue Parent)*, near Marché Kermel, charging CFA7800 per double. Nearby, north of the main post office, is the *Bar Masalia* which has a few doubles out the back for CFA10,000.

The *Hôtel l'Auberge Rouge* on Rue Moussé Diop gets mixed reviews. Some travellers describe it as peaceful; others complain of noisy comings and goings at night. Either way, double rooms are CFA8000.

A very popular place is the *Hôtel Provençal (☎ 822 10 69, 19 Rue Malenfant)* near Place de l'Indépendance, with singles/doubles/triples with fan from CFA8600/11,200/13,800. As with all cheapies, this place is also a brothel, but it's fairly low-key. Rooms upstairs are quiet and airy and reserved for tourists. The bathrooms are

CENTRAL DAKAR

PLACES TO STAY
1 Hôtel Mon Logis
5 Hôtel du Prince
6 Hôtel Al Baraka
8 Hôtel Continental Annex
10 Hôtel Continental
11 Hôtel-Restaurant Farid
15 Hôtel Provençal
27 Hôtel Oceanic
29 Hôtel du Marché
36 Hôtel Croix du Sud
39 Hôtel de l'Indépendance
53 Hôtel Ganalé; Restaurant '?' 1
66 Hôtel St-Louis Sun
68 Hôtel du Plateau
70 Hôtel Al Afifa
71 Hôtel l'Auberge Rouge
88 Hôtel le Miramar
91 Hôtel Nina
102 Hôtel Teranga (Sofitel)
105 Novotel
107 Hôtel Lagon II

PLACES TO EAT
2 Restaurant One-Way
4 La Pizzeria
7 Chez Bove Snacks
9 Touba Restaurant
13 Restaurant au Centre
19 Patio de Thierry
22 Restaurant Angkor
28 Le Dagorne
32 Restaurant le Sarraut
34 Restaurant Darou Salam
35 Gentina
41 La Palmeraie
45 Café de Paris
46 Keur N'Deye
47 Chawarma Donald;
   Salon du Thé le Capitol
49 Restaurant la Plaza
55 Chez Loutcha

56 Chez Georges
57 Ali Baba Snack Bar
60 Restaurant '?' 2
63 Touba Restaurant
64 Gargotte Diarama
73 Le Bambou
75 Patisserie Laeticia
89 Jaipur Restaurant
92 Restaurant Lunch
93 Restaurant Chez Nanette
108 Restaurant-Bar Lagon I
109 Assiette Grill
111 Restaurant Niani

OTHER
3 Night Club Jet Set
12 Le Tringa Hotel des Artes
14 Librairie Clairafrique
   (Bookshop)
16 Bar L'Imperial
17 Inter Tourisme (Tours)
18 Le Supermarché
20 Hôtel de Ville (Town Hall)
21 Bar Gorée
23 Place Leclerc (SOTRAC Bus
   Terminal)
24 Bar Marsalia
25 Main Post Office (PTT);
   Poste Restante
26 Cape Verde Embassy
30 Côte d'Ivoire Embassy
31 Marché Kermel
33 Safari-Evasion (Tours)
37 Gouvernance
38 Chambre de Commerce
40 Small Post Office (PTT)
42 Sene Keur (Bar/Nightclub)
43 Chez Claudette (Bar/Nightclub)
44 The Gambia High Commission
48 Cinéma le Plaza
50 Internet Café Metissicana
51 Marché Sandaga

52 Air Guinée
54 Air Bissau; TACV
   (Cabo Verde Airlines)
58 Bar Ponty
59 Orisha Art Shop
61 French Cultural Centre
62 Senecartours
65 Librairie aux Quatres Vents
   (Bookshop)
67 Bar Colisée 9
69 Le Play-Club (Nightclub)
72 King's Club (Nightclub)
74 British Council
76 Mali Embassy
77 Cathedral
78 US Embassy
79 Netherlands Embassy
80 IFAN Museum
81 Assemblée Nationale
82 Nouvelles Frontières
   (Travel & Tours)
83 Palais Présidentiel
84 Cyber-Business Centre
85 Senegalair Tours
86 Keur Samba Jazz Nightclub;
   Restaurant la Petite Côte;
   Restaurant Galerie Guygi
87 Ethiopian Airlines
90 American Cultural Centre
94 BICIS Bank
95 Citibank
96 Sabena; M'boup Voyages;
   Air Mauritanie
97 CBAO Bank
98 Air France; SDV Voyages
99 Senegal Tours
100 Air Afrique
101 Cinéma le Paris
103 Air Senegal
104 Score Supermarket
106 French Embassy
110 Hôtel Teranga Swimming Pool

SENEGAL

cleaned daily and the manager is a friendly guy called Hassan, who can assist with local information.

The decent and well organised **Hôtel Continental** (☎ 822 10 83, 10 Rue Galandou Diouf) has a wide choice of rooms from CFA10,500/11,500 up to CFA11,500/13,000 with air-con and bathroom. Rooms at their annexe two blocks west at 57 Rue Moussé Diop are about CFA1000 cheaper.

Places to Stay – Mid-Range

The **Hôtel Oceanic** (☎ 822 20 44, fax 821 52 28, 9 Rue de Thann) north of Marché Kermel is very good value, with spotless air-con single/doubles at CFA14,000/ 17,000. North-west of the centre, the **Hôtel-Restaurant Farid** (☎ 821 61 27, 51 Rue Vincens) has air-con rooms with shower for CFA16,500/19,000. The nearby **Hôtel Al Baraka** (☎ 822 55 32, fax 821 75 41, 35 Rue el Hadj Abdoukarim Bourgi) has doubles for CFA21,000.

South-west of the centre, *Hôtel du Plateau* (☎ 823 44 20, fax 822 50 24, 62 Rue Jules Ferry) is good value with doubles for CFA18,000. A block to the east is the smarter *Hôtel Al Afifa* with rooms for CFA28,000/33,000. The older *Hôtel St-Louis Sun* (☎ 822 25 70) on Rue Félix Faure has pleasant air-con singles/doubles/triples at CFA15,000/19,000/23,000 and arranges safe parking for cars.

The busy *Hôtel le Miramar* (☎ 823 55 98, fax 823 35 05, 25 Rue Félix Faure) has rooms with air-con, shower and TV for CFA17,000/22,000 including breakfast. The nearby *Hôtel Nina* (☎ 821 22 30, fax 821 41 81, 43 Rue du Docteur Thèze) is calmer, with small air-con rooms for CFA18,000/24,000 including breakfast. Best value in this price range is the swish *Hôtel Ganalé* (☎ 821 55 70, fax 822 34 30, 38 Rue Assane Ndoye), charging CFA18,000/21,000.

Also good is the old-style *Hôtel Croix du Sud* (☎ 823 29 47, fax 823 26 55, 20 Ave Albert Sarraut), which has a pleasant French ambience and single/double rooms for CFA 25,000/29,000.

Places to Stay – Top End

Hôtel de l'Indépendance (☎ 823 10 19, fax 822 11 17, Place de l'Indépendance) is the most central of the top end hotels, although it's rather dreary and pricey at CFA45,500/51,000. Nearby, also on Place de l'Indépendance, is Sofitel's giant *Hôtel Teranga* (☎ 823 10 44, fax 823 50 51), a tour group favourite, with rooms for CFA52,000.

The *Novotel* (☎ 823 88 49, fax 823 89 29) just off the southern end of Ave Albert Sarraut is uninspiring, with rooms at CFA50,000/ 56,000. Nearby is the smaller and more interesting *Hôtel Lagon II* (☎ 823 58 31) on Route de la Corniche-Est, perched on stilts at the edge of the ocean, with excellent rooms at CFA50,00/55,000. Top of the lot is *Hôtel le Savana* (☎ 823 60 23, fax 823 73 06, email savana@telecomplus.sn), on Route de la Corniche-Est, where rooms start at CFA60,000.

Places to Eat

In this section, restaurants are arranged according to the cuisine, but there's a lot of overlap, and you might easily find African, French, Lebanese and Vietnamese food on the same menu. For some self-catering ideas, see the Shopping section later.

Cheap Eats All over Dakar are sandwich booths and coffee stalls. For something more substantial, along Rue Assane Ndoye you'll find women serving *rice and sauce* for around CFA300, although most close by mid-afternoon. Chawarmas are sold throughout the city for around CFA650. A favourite with many travellers is *Chawarma Donald* on Ave Pompidou. *Ali Baba Snack Bar* one block east across the street is also good, but you pay a bit extra for the classy surroundings. *Chez Bove* on Rue el Hadj Abdoukarim Bourgi is quieter.

Gargotte Diarama on Rue Félix Faure serves simple meals in the CFA500 to CFA 750 range. Just around the corner on Rue Gomis is the similar *Touba Restaurant* and several other cheapies. There's another, slightly smarter, *Touba Restaurant* on Rue Wagane Diouf which has meals in the CFA600 to CFA1000 range. Nearby, on the corner of Rue el Haji M'Baye Guéye and Rue Wagane Diouf is *Restaurant du Centre* with dishes for CFA1000 to CFA1500. Similarly priced options include *Restaurant Lunch* (despite the name, it's also open in the evening) on Rue du Docteur Théze and *Restaurant la Petite Côte* on Rue Jules Ferry.

On the other side of the centre, *Restaurant Darou Salam* on Rue des Essarts serves filling African meals for around CFA800 to CFA1000. It's very popular at lunch time and closed in the evening.

Best value in this range are two places called *Restaurant '?'* (ask for 'Restaurant Point d'Interrogation') on Rue Assane Ndoye – both are clean and friendly, open in the evening as well as all day, with filling African dishes from CFA900 to CFA1500.

African Cheapest among the mid-range restaurants, and highly recommended, is

Keur N'Deye (68 Rue Vincens), with well prepared Senegalese specialities from CFA 2000. The friendly and popular *Chez Loutcha* (☎ 821 03 02, 101 Rue Moussé Diop), closed Sunday, offers Cape Verdean and 'Euro-Africaine' cuisine for around CFA 2500 to CFA3500 – specials from its 30-page menu include flights to Praia! To the north, *Chez Georges* is similar. Dakar's fanciest African restaurant is *Keur Samba* (☎ 821 60 45) on Rue Jules Ferry (what's special is the jazz played here), and almost next door is *Restaurant Galerie Guygi*, with a peaceful open-air courtyard and meals in the CFA3000 to CFA5000 range.

Asian & Indian The most colourful is the Chinese *Restaurant Angkor* (☎ 822 12 60) near Marché Kermel, open every day except Sunday, with dishes from CFA2500 to CFA4000. Next door is the similarly priced *Restaurant la Grande Muraille*.

The excellent *Jaipur* (☎ 823 36 46) on Rue Félix Faure offers curries and baltis (including vegetarian) from CFA2500 to CFA4500.

European One of the best French restaurants is *Le Dagorne* (☎ 822 20 80) north of Marché Kermel, with many tempting choices for CFA5000 to CFA10,000. Also good is *Restaurant le Sarraut* (☎ 822 55 23) on Ave Albert Sarraut, with a CFA7500 three course *menu du jour*, and *Restaurant la Plaza* (☎ 822 27 68) on Ave Pompidou, with dishes from CFA4000 to CFA6000. If money is no concern, *Le Bambou* (☎ 822 06 45, 19 Rue Victor Hugo) gets top marks for food and service.

You get a good Portuguese three-course meal from CFA2500 at *Restaurant Chez Nanette* on Rue du Docteur Thèze, while *La Pizzeria* (☎ 821 09 26, 47 Rue el Hadj Abdoukarim Bourgi) has excellent pizzas for CFA2500 to CFA3900 and pastas for up to CFA4000.

Seafood *Restaurant One-Way* (☎ 822 98 38) on the Rue el Hadj Abdoukarim Bourgi does a good range of seafood dishes from

around CFA5000. *Restaurant-Bar Lagon I* on the Route de la Corniche-Est, done out like an old-style cruise liner, complete with sails, rails and lifeboats, is more expensive.

Cafes & Patisseries Dakar has some excellent French-style patisseries and *salons de thé*, also selling ice cream, *crêpes* (pancakes), sandwiches and snacks. Busy places along Ave Pompidou include *La Palmeraie* opposite Alitalia, *Café de Paris* opposite Bar Ponty, and *La Gondole* near the Cinéma le Plaza. *Patisserie Laeticia* opposite the cathedral on Blvd de la République is much calmer. Most patisseries open for breakfast and close around 7.30 pm, although some on Ave Pompidou sell beer and stay open until late.

Entertainment

Bars The best known watering hole is *Bar Ponty* on Ave Pompidou, which manages to be smart and slightly disreputable at the same time. If you can afford a drink (small beers are CFA900), it's worth sampling. Other bars off Ave Pompidou include *Chez Claudette* on Rue Wagane Diouf, *Bar Alexandria* next door, and *Sene Keur* on Rue du Docteur Thèze. All are open evenings only and are often quite busy, more like small nightclubs in the later evening.

Much calmer are *Bar l'Imperial* on the northern side of Place de l'Indépendance and *Bar Colisée 9* on Ave du President Lamine Guéye – both smart with small draught beers for around CFA700.

Down near the Île de Gorée ferry terminal, *Bar Gorée* on Blvd de la Libération has cheap beer, snacks and food, music and dancing most evenings and a bit of a rough edge.

Music Venues, Nightclubs & Discos Dakar is one of the best cities in West Africa for live music and has several nightclubs where Senegalese bands perform at weekends – especially Saturday night – while discos are usually held on Thursday, Friday and Sunday. Most places have an entry fee of about CFA1000 to CFA2000 (although women often get in free) and up to CFA4000 if a band is playing. Sometimes the entry fee includes your first 'free' drink; otherwise beers are about CFA700 to CFA1500, depending on how smart the place is. Check the papers and listings magazines to see what's on. And don't expect the music to start before midnight – most places don't even start to fill up until about 11 pm.

World music fans should head for the hot and crowded *Club Thiossane* roughly 4km north of Marché Sandaga in Rue Coulibaly. It's owned by the legendary Youssou N'Dour, and the man himself sometimes performs here. Similarly popular is *Le Sahel* about 3km north-west of Marché Sandaga. The more sedate *Casino Terrou-Bi* on Route de la Corniche-Ouest has a nightclub, restaurant and bars, and often has live bands playing.

Other clubs and discos include the flashy *Club Kilimanjaro* by the Village Artisanal at Soumbédioune; the smart *Play-Club* on Rue Jules Ferry; the equally fancy *King's Club* on Rue Victor Hugo; and *Sene Keur* on Rue du Docteur Thèze, with cheap entry and cheap beers.

Chez Georges (see Places to Eat earlier) is also a jazz club, with music at weekends and some other nights; there's no entry fee if you eat. Other restaurants with music include *Keur Samba* (entry CFA2000) and *Restaurant Galerie Guygi* nearby. *Le Tringa Hotel des Artes* on Rue Wagane Diouf has bands playing jazz, traditional African music and pop.

Cinemas *Le Plaza* on Ave Pompidou and *Le Paris* opposite the Hôtel Teranga on Rue Carnot both show major releases and charge about CFA1000. Films in English are dubbed into French. *Le Tringa Hotel des Artes* on Rue Wagane Diouf occasionally shows films by local film-makers, while the *British-Senegalese Institute* and *American Cultural Centre* show films in English.

Shopping
Supermarkets For imported items and food, try the Score supermarket on Ave

Albert Sarraut or Le Supermarché three blocks north of Place de l'Indépendance, where stock is more limited. Fruit and vegetable vendors sell their produce outside Le Supermarché. Other supermarkets include Leader Price near Marché Kermel, or the smaller Bon Prix on Ave Pompidou next to Café de Paris. Most other supermarkets are out in the suburbs.

Art & Craftwork The Village Artisanal at Soumbédioune is the most popular place for souvenirs. You'll find a tremendous display of woodcarvings, metalwork, gold and silver jewellery, ivory, tablecloths, blankets, leather goods and clothing, but a lot of the stuff is churned out very quickly and you have to search hard for good quality pieces.

For better quality African art, head for Rue Mohamed V off Ave Pompidou where several small shops have masks, carvings and other objects from all over West Africa. On the same street, shops sell Moroccan or Algerian-style carpets, leatherwork and pottery.

For gold and silver, the best place is La Cour des Mours in a small alley at 69 Ave Blaise Diagne, north of Marché Sandaga. Even if you're not interested in jewellery, a trip to this fascinating old district is highly recommended. Silver is often sold by weight, so it's worth checking current prices with a local before you buy.

If you want music cassettes, youths with boxes full of tapes stroll the sidewalks. Prices depend on the playing time, the popularity of the musician and the quality of the tape, but most go for around CFA1500. For a wider choice, there are also stalls in and around Marché Sandaga on Rue des Essarts. Another option is Disco Star at 59 Ave Pompidou, which sells local cassettes from CFA3000 and imported CDs for CFA 130,000 to CFA190,000.

Getting There & Away
Air Details of international flights to/from Dakar are given in the Getting There & Away section earlier in this chapter. Within Senegal, there is just Air Senegal's service between Dakar, Ziguinchor and Cap Skiring

– see the individual entries later for more details.

For international flight inquiries, reconfirmations and reservations, airline offices in Dakar include the following:

Aeroflot
(☎ 822 48 15) Blvd de la République
Air Afrique
(☎ 839 42 00 or 839 42 03) Place de l'Indépendance
Air Bissau & TACV Cabo Verde Airlines
(☎ 820 00 83 or 821 39 68) Rue Assane Ndoye
Air France
(☎ 823 49 49 or 823 23 44) Ave Albert Sarraut
Air Guinée
(☎ 821 44 42) Ave Pompidou
Air Mali
(☎ 823 24 61) Rue el Haji M'Baye Gueye, near Rue Vincens
Air Mauritanie
(☎ 822 81 88) Place de l'Indépendance
Air Senegal
(☎ 823 49 70) 45-47 Ave Albert Sarraut
Alitalia
(☎ 823 31 29 or 823 38 74) 5 Ave Pompidou
Ethiopian Airlines
(☎ 821 32 98) 16 Ave Leopold Senghor
Ghana Airways
(☎ 822 28 20) Rue des Essarts, just off the Place de l'Indépendance
Iberia
(☎ 823 34 77) Place de l'Indépendance
Royal Air Maroc
(☎ 822 32 67) Place de l'Indépendance
Sabena
(☎ 823 49 71) Place de l'Indépendance
Swissair
(☎ 823 48 48) Immeuble Faycal behind Air France, just off Place de l'Indépendance
TAP Air Portugal
(☎ 821 01 13) Immeuble Faycal behind Air France, just off Place de l'Indépendance
Tunis Air
(☎ 823 14 35) 24 Ave Leopold Senghor

Bus, Bush Taxi & Minibus Buses and Peugeot 504 bush taxis for long-distance destinations leave from Gare Routière Pompiers, 3km north of Place de l'Indépendance. To get there from Marché Sandaga, take a SOTRAC city bus No 5, 6 or 18. A taxi from Marché Sandaga or the Place de l'Indépendance should cost about CFA500.

Some incoming transport may terminate at Gare Routière Kolobane, about 5km north of the centre on the other side of the autoroute. Some sample fares (in CFA) from Dakar are listed in the table.

destination	504	minibus	big bus
Barra (Gambia)	3600	3000	2500
Kaolack	2100	1500	1250
Mbour	950	750	650
Richard Toll	4600	3600	3200
Rosso	4600	3600	3200
St-Louis	2800	2300	2000
Tambacounda	6300	5100	4400
Thiès	900	700	600
Ziguinchor	7000	5300	4500

To give you an idea of journey times, from Dakar to St-Louis by 504 takes about three hours, to Tambacounda about six hours and to Ziguinchor from eight to 10 hours. Buses take about half as long again, while the journey time in a minibus can be double. If you want to take a 504, walk past the minibus stands (and the touts who will try to tell you they've all gone and push you onto a minibus) to where the 504s are lined up with signs indicating destinations.

For Tambacounda, Kaolack, Touba or St-Louis, the Transport Alazar buses (known as 'Le Car Mouride') are fast, reliable and comfortable if you get a proper seat rather than a stool in the aisle. Fares are about 70% of 504 prices eg to Tambacounda is CFA4000. Buses leave from a petrol station at an intersection on Ave Malik Sy, near the autoroute; go the day before you travel to reserve a seat and check departure times.

Train The train from Dakar goes to Bamako in Mali via several towns, including Thiès, Diourbel and Tambacounda. However, most people go by road to these destinations because it's quicker and cheaper. Passenger trains from Dakar to Kaolack no longer run, and they only go to St-Louis at holiday times.

Boat The MS *Joola* goes from Dakar to Ziguinchor via the Île de Carabane at the

SENEGAL

mouth of the River Casamance on Tuesday and Friday at 8.30 pm. Departure times can vary, however, so you should check details at the port (☎ 821 58 52). For more information on this service, see the main Getting Around section earlier in this chapter.

There's also a regular ferry service to Île de Gorée (CFA3000).

Getting Around

To/From the Airport The official taxi rate from the airport to central Dakar is CFA3000 (CFA4760 from midnight to 6 am). The drivers will swear to Allah that the posted rates no longer apply, so bargaining is required.

A taxi from the airport to Yoff should be CFA1500, but the drivers still charge CFA3000 (because after the short ride they must go to the back of the queue at the airport). From the city centre to the airport, the fare should be around CFA2000. You can also get bus No 7 or No 8.

Bus Large, clean and efficient SOTRAC buses serve the city centre and places around Dakar. They cost CFA140 for short rides and up to CFA200 for the longest rides. You get on at the back door and buy your ticket from the conductor's booth. Major lines include the following:

Warning

Arriving at Dakar airport, be prepared for touts and hustlers offering their services. A common trick is for the tout to 'find' you a taxi (there's always loads at the rank just outside the terminal building) and then come with you into town. On the way he'll tell you whatever hotel you're heading for is full, and you're welcome to stay at his place for a small fee. This may be a genuine earner or it may be a con. We've also heard of isolated incidents where touts and taxi drivers have colluded to rob passengers. The best way to deal with either case is to find your own taxi.

No 4 Train station to Marché de Tilène in La Médina.

No 5 Place Lat Dior, Marché Sandaga, Gare Routière Pompiers, then north along the autoroute.

No 6 Place Lat Dior, Place de l'Indépendance, train station, Gare Routière Pompiers, port, Plage Bel-Air, then along the main road between Yoff and Castors.

No 7 Palais de Justice, Ave Pompidou, Marché Sandaga, Ave Blaise Diagne, Point E, Mermoz, Ouakam. Alternate buses continue to Pointe des Almadies, N'Gor, the airport and Yoff.

No 8 Palais de Justice, Hôpital Principal, Blvd de la République, Marché Sandaga, La Médina, autoroute, Yoff and the airport.

No 10 Palais de Justice, Route de la Corniche-Ouest, Soumbédioune, Fann, university, then north through the suburbs to Castors.

No 12 Palais de Justice, Hôpital Principal, Marché Sandaga, Ave Blaise Diagne, Route d'Ouakam, Point E and Mermoz.

No 13 Palais de Justice, Hôpital Principal, Place de l'Indépendance, Ave Pompidou, Grande Mosquée, then along Ave Mbaké (also called Rue 13) to Castors.

No 15 Palais de Justice, Hôpital Principal, Place de l'Indépendance, industrial area, then east around the bay to Rufisque and Bargny.

No 18 Marché Sandaga, Gare Routière Pompiers, then north-east out to Castors.

No 21 Palais de Justice, Hôpital Principal, Blvd République, Ave du President Lamine Guèye and eventually north-east out of town to Tiaroye-Mer and Malika. Alternate buses continue to Keur Massar.

Following the SOTRAC bus routes are privately owned buses, usually white 30-seater Mercedes N'Diaga N'Diaye buses, with fares at about 30% of SOTRAC prices. Destinations and routes are not marked, so you'll have to ask.

There are two main bus terminals. For directions north of the city centre including N'Gor and Yoff, N'Diaga N'Diaye buses go from near Ave Peytavin. For places east of Dakar, such as Rufisque, the main terminus is on Blvd de la Libération.

Minibus Dilapidated blue-and-yellow minibuses (known as *cars rapides*), stuffed with people, cost about 25% less than other buses but their destinations aren't marked, so you'll have to listen carefully to the destinations the young assistants yell out.

Taxi Taxis around Dakar are plentiful, but taxi drivers prefer to quote flat rates for fares rather than use the meter. For a short ride across the city centre, the fare should be around CFA250 to CFA400. From the Place de l'Indépendance to the Gare Routière Pompiers you'll probably pay CFA750. At night all rates are double.

Car The major self-drive car hire agencies in Dakar are:

Avis (☎ 823 33 00 or 823 32 30, fax 821 21 83)
34 Ave du President Lamine Guéye, near the end of the autoroute
Budget (☎ 822 25 13, fax 822 25 06)
At the junction of Ave du President Lamine Guéye and Ave Faidherbe
Europcar (☎ 822 06 91, fax 822 34 77)
Junction of Blvd de la Libération and Allées Delmas
Hertz (☎ 821 56 23 or 822 20 16, fax 821 17 21)
With branches at the airport and Hôtel Teranga

All the major agencies have similar rates. For the smallest models, they charge between CFA13,000 and CFA15,000 per day, as well as CFA130 to CFA150 per kilometre, around CFA4000 per day, for insurance and 20% tax.

Of the independent car hire companies, Senecartours (☎ 822 42 86 or 822 94 54, fax 821 83 06) at 64 Rue Carnot is reliable, with good vehicles and lower prices than the internationals. It also does special weekend and *prix forfeiture* (lump sum) deals; for example, a small car for one week including all tax, insurance and 1500km is CFA 210,000. Auto Service Bayeux (☎ 821 42 08), a repair yard opposite the Centre Culturel Français, sometimes has cheap cars for hire from CFA 30,000 per day, with 100km per day free.

AROUND DAKAR
Île de Gorée
Île de Gorée, about 3km east of Dakar, is a wonderfully peaceful place, with colonial-style houses, narrow streets, trailing bougainvillea and a strong Mediterranean feel. The island is a popular bolt hole from Dakar, and the small beach is often busy at weekends. Guides can add considerably to the enjoyment of your visit, but are not obligatory. Official guides at the *syndicat d'initiative* (tourist office) charge CFA2500 per person for a half-day tour, while freelancers wait at the ferry jetty and charge whatever they can get away with!

The excellent **IFAN Historical Museum** at Fort d'Estrées on the northern end of the

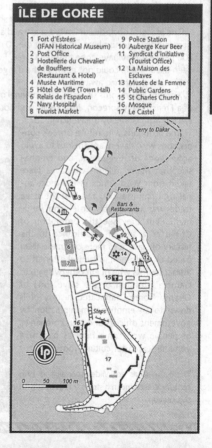

ÎLE DE GORÉE

1 Fort d'Estrées (IFAN Historical Museum)
2 Post Office
3 Hostellerie du Chevalier de Boufflers (Restaurant & Hotel)
4 Musée Maritime
5 Hôtel de Ville (Town Hall)
6 Relais de l'Espadon
7 Navy Hospital
8 Tourist Market
9 Police Station
10 Auberge Keur Beer
11 Syndicat d'Initiative (Tourist Office)
12 La Maison des Esclaves
13 Musée de la Femme
14 Public Gardens
15 St Charles Church
16 Mosque
17 Le Castel

Ferry to Dakar

Ferry Jetty

Bars & Restaurants

Steps

0   50   100 m

SENEGAL

SENEGAL

La Maison des Esclaves

Île de Gorée was a busy trading centre during the 18th and 19th centuries, and many merchants built houses where they lived or worked in the upper storey and stored their cargoes on the ground floor. The Maison des Esclaves (Slave House) is one of the last remaining 18th-century buildings of this type on Gorée. It was built in 1786 and renovated in 1990, with French assistance. With its famous doorway opening directly from the storeroom onto the sea, this building has enormous spiritual significance for some visitors, particularly African-Americans whose ancestors were slaves.

Walking around the dimly lit dungeons, particularly after a visit to the IFAN Historical Museum, you begin to imagine the horrors of incarceration. The curator will provide further gruesome details. In reality, however, despite the name, it's unlikely that the Maison des Esclaves was used to hold many captive slaves, apart from those who 'belonged' to the merchant and maybe a few for trading. In fact, some historians have pointed out that although the island was a vital trading centre and strategic port, and an important slave culture existed here, Gorée itself was never a major shipment point for slaves.

The practical obstacles of limited space and a lack of drinking water alone would have made transferring large numbers difficult. Of the 20 million slaves who were taken from Africa, only 300 per year may have gone through Gorée. Even then, the famous doorway would not have been used: a ship could not get near the dangerous rocks and the town had a perfectly good jetty a short distance away.

Additionally, records show that the original owners of the house were the mixed-race family of a French Navy surgeon, Jean Pepin, and not (as it is claimed) Dutch merchants – they were ejected from Gorée by the French in 1677.

The historians who refute Gorée's connections with slavery are anxious to avoid accusations of revisionism, and emphasise that many millions of slaves *were* taken from West Africa in the most appalling circumstances, and that the slave trade was undeniably cruel and inhumane. But they see the promotion of Gorée as a site of significance to the history of slavery as mere commercialism based on distortion, a cynical attempt to attract tourists who might otherwise go to Gambia's Jufureh or the slave forts of Ghana. Gorée's fabricated history boils down to an emotional manipulation by government officials and tour companies of people who come here as part of a genuine search for cultural roots.

Thanks to Chris de Wilde (specialist in 19th century West African history) for his help with this section.

DAVID ELSE

island has superb exhibits and the **Musée de la Femme** has imaginative displays on the role of Senegalese women in traditional and modern societies. There is also the **Musée Maritime** and the **Maison des Esclaves** – for more information see the boxed text. The museums are open daily, except Monday, and charge CFA200 to CFA500.

Le Castel is a rocky plateau giving good views of the island and across to Dakar. It's covered with fortifications dating from different periods including two massive WWII guns, and is now inhabited by a group of Baye Fall disciples (for more information on these, see the boxed text 'Marabouts & Brotherhoods' in the Facts about Senegal section).

Just behind the row of restaurants facing the jetty there's a little **tourist market** with crafts and materials, and where the bargaining is far more relaxed than in Dakar.

Places to Stay & Eat The *syndicat d'initiative* across the road from the public gardens provides good rooms from CFA 10,000. Just up the road, the stylish *Auberge Keur Beer* (☎/fax 821 38 01) has friendly management and double rooms from CFA 15,000. To find a room in a *private home*, ask in the restaurants near the ferry jetty. Rates start at CFA7500.

The old *Hostellerie du Chevalier de Boufflers* (☎ 822 53 64) is best known as a restaurant. It has main courses for around CFA5000, but you pay as much for the location and the shady terrace overlooking the harbour as for the food.

Most other places to eat are in a rectangle facing the ferry jetty, with meals from around CFA2000; prices are chalked up on boards outside. For cheaper fare, hunt out *Chez Madame Siga*, a private house near Le Castel, serving plates of rice and fish for CFA750.

Getting There & Away A ferry runs roughly every one to two hours between 6 am and 11 pm from the port in Dakar to Île

de Gorée. The trip across takes 20 minutes and costs CFA3000 return for foreigners.

Îles de la Madeleine

The Îles de la Madeleine are a national park about 4km off the mainland west of Dakar, consisting of a main island called Sarpan and two other islets. The islands are home to some interesting dwarf baobab trees, and the park is particularly noted as a good place to spot sea birds. A visit, combined maybe with some swimming or snorkelling, makes for a great day out.

To get there, you will first need to pay CFA1000 at the office of the Eaux et Forêts department on the Route de la Corniche-Ouest near the Casino Terrou-Bi. Then go to Soumbédioune and negotiate for a boat. The usual fee is CFA2000 per person, with a minimum charge of around CFA8000. Always pay on the way back.

Sometimes the hassle of hiring a boat spoils the trip to the island, so you might be better off taking a tour. L'Oceanium (listed under Activities in the main Dakar section) regularly runs visits for CFA5000 per person, or you can charter a small boat for CFA 30,000 for half a day. You can arrange this through the supermarket at the suburb of Virage – phone ☎ 820 30 99 or 820 57 74 for details.

Pointe des Almadies & N'Gor

The **Pointe des Almadies**, Africa's westernmost point, is only 13km from central Dakar. You just scramble over some black rocks sticking out between the waves, and that's it. There's no novelty signpost pointing across the sea to New York. Just a rubbish-strewn car park and a line of ugly restaurants. In mitigation, these serve good food and are popular at night – *L'Armatan* has dishes from CFA3000 and gets good reviews.

East of the point, the sheltered beach at **N'Gor** is good for swimming, and has a much better atmosphere, with a collection of shack-like restaurants, where you can enjoy cheap seafood and a cold beer. *Le Grand Bleu* has friendly staff, excellent shrimp sandwiches for CFA1000 and grilled prawns

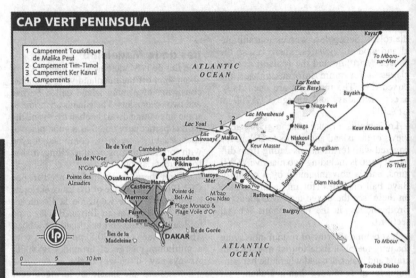

CAP VERT PENINSULA

1 Campement Touristique
  de Malika Peul
2 Campement Tim-Timol
3 Campement Ker Kanni
4 Campements

ATLANTIC OCEAN

Kayar

To Mboro-sur-Mer

Lac Retba
(Lac Rose)

Bayakh

Niaga-Peul

Lac Mbeubeusé

Niaga

Keur Moussa

Lac Youi

Lac Chirouayé   Malika

Île de Yoff   Cambérène

Keur Massar

Niakoul Rap

Sangalkam

To Thiès

Île de N'Gor

Yoff

Dagoudane Pikine

N'Gor

Route de Rufisque

Pointe des Almadies

Ouakam   Hann

Tiaroye-Mer

M'bao Niaye

Route de Bayakh

Diam Niadia

Castors

Mermoz

Pointe de Bel-Air

M'bao Gou Ndao

Rufisque

Bargny

To Mbour

Fann

Plage Monaco & Plage Voile d'Or

Soumbédioune

Îles de la Madeleine

Île de Gorée

DAKAR

ATLANTIC OCEAN

Toubab Dialao

0   5   10 km

for CFA3000. Much smarter is *La Brazzerade* with a *menu du jour* for CFA4900 and pleasant double rooms from CFA17,000.

Other accommodation options include the dirty brown *Hotel N'Gor Diarama*, which charges CFA40,000 per room, and *Club le Calao* (☎ 820 05 40) where double thatched bungalows cost CFA25,000. With luck you'll avoid the *Club Med*, which caters almost exclusively for groups (rates start at about CFA45,000 per person), but it's hard to miss the huge *Hôtel Meridien President* (☎ 820 15 15, fax 820 30 30), which has every facility (including golf course and heliport) for CFA75,000 per room.

To reach N'Gor, take a No 7 bus from central Dakar. Some only go to Ouakem, but alternate buses continue on to Pointe des Almadies and N'Gor.

Île de N'Gor is a short boat ride (CFA500 return) north of N'Gor village. It has the best beach of all, two restaurants, with meals from CFA2500, plus a couple of huts selling drinks and cheaper food. You can also hire simple sun shelters and water sports equipment. Along from the main beach, *Chez*

Carla (☎ 820 15 86) serves seafood dishes for around CFA3000 and has a few rooms from CFA15,000.

Yoff

A short distance east of N'Gor, but sharply contrasting in feel, is the town of Yoff. It may look like just another suburb but there's a vital sense of community here which marks it out from other places around Dakar. The town is self-administering, with no government officials, no police force 'from Senegal' and no crime. The people are almost exclusively Lebu, a fiercely independent group, and nearly all are members of the Layen, smallest of the four Islamic brotherhoods. Their founder's mausoleum, topped with a green dome, is at the eastern end of town.

The main fishing beach is about 1km west, where large pirogues are launched into the rollers and women sell recent catches, still glistening, on the sand. Even if the waves weren't dangerously large, and even if the beach wasn't covered in the town's detritus, Yoff is no place for basking: skimpy clothing is most inappropriate in this staunchly Mus-

Yoff Healers

One of the most interesting aspects of life in Yoff is the traditional *ndeup* ceremonies where people with a mental illness are treated and healed. People come to be cured from all over Senegal and Gambia and even from other neighbouring countries like Mali and Guinea-Bissau. Despite the town's Islamic heritage, the ceremonies are totally animistic, and based on a belief that psychological sickness is the result of possession by spirits. The leaders of the Leyen brotherhood turn a blind eye to the 'pagan' ceremonies and the two beliefs comfortably coexist.

The healing ceremonies usually last one day, but can be longer for serious illnesses, and usually take place about twice a month. The traditional healers sacrifice animals (a chicken or cow depending on the serious-ness of the illness) to invoke intervention from guardian spirits, and place the sick people into a trance-like state which allows malevolent spirits to be drawn out. Some observers have noted that the process is similar to voodoo ceremonies which take place in other parts of West Africa. The healers' services are not cheap; families of people who need treatment reportedly pay large sums (the equivalent of many years' salary), and often several sufferers are treated at the same time.

The ceremonies take place in the centre of Yoff and can attract large crowds of local people. Tourists are tolerated, but even watching can be a disturbing experience for spectators and not at all suitable for the faint-hearted. It's best to go with a local and keep to the sidelines. Waving a zoom lens around would be the height of insensitivity.

lim community. Forget about 'entertainment' too: there are no clubs or bars in Yoff, and drunkenness, even in private, is definitely frowned upon. This is a place to wander around slowly and respectfully, properly dressed and without a camera.

Places to Stay & Eat The long-standing *Campement le Poulagou* (☎ 820 23 47) charges CFA6000 per person including breakfast, and has a fine balcony overlooking the beach from where the fishing boats are launched. If you phone in advance the owner will pick you up from the airport.

The nearest Dakar has to a travellers lodge is *Via Via* (☎/fax 820 54 75, email viavia@ metissacana.com) on Route des Cimetières, east of Yoff. The rooms are clean and bright-ly decorated, the food is good and the atmosphere is friendly and relaxed. Rooms with shared bathroom are CFA7000/12,000. Rooms for four people are CFA5500 per person. All rates include breakfast, while snacks and meals in the bar-restaurant are CFA1000 to CFA4000. Guests can send and receive email for a nominal fee and an airport transfer is CFA1500 per person. The multilingual management can provide plenty of information about Senegal and arrange language or drumming courses.

Getting There & Away Yoff is near the airport, and easily reached from there by taxi – the fare is CFA1500. From Dakar centre, a taxi to Yoff should cost around CFA2000. By public transport, take a SOTRAC bus No 7 or 8 (but check it goes all the way to Yoff). Buses loop through Yoff centre, but to reach Campement le Poulagou or Via Via you have to get off on the main road and walk down a small street towards the beach. Both places are signposted.

Malika

About 20km from Dakar centre, and beyond the vast urban sprawl of Dagoudane-Pikine (now larger than Dakar itself), is the village of Malika – a great place to escape from the city and enjoy the beaches on the north side of the Cap Vert peninsula. *Campement Touristique de Malika Peul* has basic huts for CFA4000 and camping for CFA2000 per tent. There's a small bar-restaurant, and local musicians sometimes perform or hold work-shops. If you want to learn how to drum or play the *kora*, a teacher can be arranged for around CFA1500 to CFA2500 per three-hour session. About 1km east along the beach, *Campement Tim-Timol* has enthusiastic management and also offers dance, drum and music lessons. Huts cost CFA2800, half board is CFA7000 per person and camping is negotiable. There's a bar and restaurant, and you can just come for the day to lounge under their parasols.

Unfortunately there have been isolated reports of travellers being hassled while walking to the campements, or disturbed in their tents at night by prowlers. Taking taxis and staying in huts rather than camping might be worth the investment.

Getting There & Away From Dakar, take bus No 21 to Malika, and opposite the terminus follow a sandy track towards the ocean. After about a 15 minute walk, you pass a football field with a wall around it; take the left fork to the Campement Touristique or the right to Tim-Timol. Either way, it's another 15 minutes. Alternatively, a taxi from Dakar is CFA4000.

If you're driving, continue 6km beyond Tiaroye-Mer to a left turn signposted 'Sedima'. After 3km you reach a crossroads. The road straight ahead goes to Keur Massar and the road to the left goes to Malika.

Lac Retba

Lac Retba (also called Lac Rose) is about 10 times saltier than the ocean and famous for its pink hue when the sun is high – particularly in the dry season. If pink water and effortless floating aren't enough to entice you, the small-scale salt-collecting industry on the south side of the lake may be of more interest. Locals scrape salt from the shallow lake bed and load it into boats, before piling it onto the shore for sale. The lunch-time coachloads of tourists from Dakar can be disturbing, but morning and evening at Retba can be very peaceful. You can also walk over the dunes to the ocean.

Places to Stay & Eat About 3.5km southwest of the lake, *Campement Ker Kanni* has pleasant bungalows for CFA13,000 per person including breakfast and evening

meal. In Niaga village *Restaurant Madame Diara* serves a huge plate of tiéboudienne for CFA1000.

At the lake most places cater for tour groups. *Campement Intertourism* is the most pleasant option, with rustic cabins at CFA6000 for one to three people.

Getting There & Away Take bus No 21 to Keur Massar (not to be confused with Keur Moussa, further to the east), then a local minibus to Niaga (CFA300), but the last 5km walk from Niaga to the lake can be a real sweat. A round trip by taxi from Dakar will cost about CFA15,000.

Rufisque

Drivers will find *Camping WAS* (☎ 638 53 35) an ideal place to meet other overlanders, arrange spares, change sump oil etc. It's on the main road on the western edge of Rufisque. Camping is CFA2500, although those with no truck will feel distinctly left out, and not too comfortable on the gravel either.

Rufisque is on the main road out of Dakar and there's plenty of transport, including SOTRAC bus No 15 (the fare is CFA175), plus frequent N'Diaga N'Diaye buses and *cars rapides*.

The road is notoriously congested and slow, so you might consider taking the local commuter train – there are several services each day.

Keur Moussa Monastery

The Benedictine monastery at Keur Moussa, about 50km from Dakar between Rufisque and Kayar, has a beautiful Sunday mass at 10 am with music combining African instruments and Gregorian chants. Afterwards, the monks sell CDs and cassettes of their music, prayer books, beautifully made *koras*, homemade jam and goat's cheese.

From Rufisque catch a minibus heading to Bayakh or Kayar. Ask the driver to drop you off at a junction 2km after the minibus turns off the main road, from where a dirt track leads east for 1.5km to the monastery – it's signposted and all the drivers know it. Getting a lift back to Dakar shouldn't be difficult as many people will be going that way after the mass.

Central & Northern Senegal

This section covers a vast area, from the edge of the busy Cap Vert peninsula just a short distance from Dakar, to the remote outer edges of northern Senegal on the border with Mauritania. It includes the Grande Côte and the inland rural heartland of Senegal. Places in this section are described roughly from the south to the north and east.

THIÈS

Just 70km east of Dakar, Thiès is officially Senegal's second-largest city and a gateway to the central region. Nevertheless, it feels quite small and relaxed, with a pleasant at-mosphere, lots of shady trees and several good restaurants. Thiès also has one major attraction – a world-famous tapestry factory.

Places to Stay

The best choice is the central *Hôtel-Bar Rex*, with small, clean doubles with bath-room for CFA5400. The staff are friendly and there's safe parking. The nearby *Hôtel Man-Gan de Thiès* on Rue Amadou Sow has a nice garden courtyard and musty doubles with air-con and bathroom for CFA13,800. For a taste of the past, the old *Hôtel du Rail* east of the town centre has large, tranquil air-con singles/doubles with bathroom for CFA8900/9300.

Places to Eat

All the hotels do food. Otherwise, a stroll down Ave Léopold Senghor will reveal the cheapie *Restaurant International*, the clean

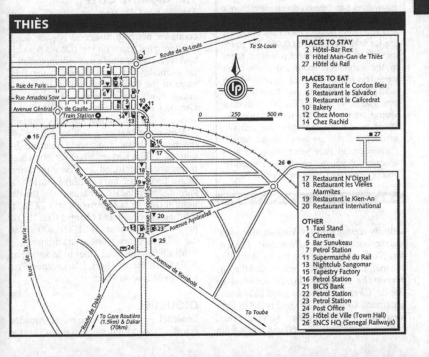

The Tapestries of Thiès

The factory of the Manufactures Séné-galaises des Arts Décoratifs (☎/fax 951 11 31) was one of the many artistic endeav-ours inspired by President Senghor during the 1960s. Today, the factory is run as a cooperative, with designs for the tapestries chosen from paintings submitted by Sene-galese artists.

Sizes of the tapestries vary but most are around 3m high by 2m wide. Preparing the design is a fascinating and elaborate process, taking many weeks. A large sketch of the painting is produced for the weavers to use as a pattern, but is a reverse of the original because tapestries are made on the loom upside down.

All the weaving is done on manual looms, and two weavers complete about 1 sq m per month. Only eight tapestries are made from each design. Most find their way around the world as gifts from the government to foreign dignitaries; there's a huge tapestry hanging in Atlanta airport and another in Buckingham Palace. Others are for sale, but at CFA500,000 per sq m, most of us will be content to admire them in the exhibition room, which is open weekdays from 8 am to 12.30 pm and 3 to 6.30 pm, and Saturday from 8 am to 12.30 pm. The entry fee is CFA500. Individual visitors are not normally shown the work-shops where the tapestries are actually made, but if you are genuinely interested, the exhibition supervisor might be able arrange for you to be shown around. If you phone ahead, your chances are better.

and tidy *Restaurant les Vieilles Marmites*, and the more expensive *Restaurant le Kien-An*. North of the railway tracks is another cheapie, *Chez Momo*, a *bakery* and the *Su-permarché du Rail*. On Ave Général de Gaulle, *Chez Rachid* does good chawarmas for around CFA650. Opposite is the smarter *Restaurant le Cailcedrat*, serving beers, coffees, snacks for CFA750 and meals from CFA2500 to CFA4000. Nearby on Rue de Paris is a cluster of good-value restaurants including *Le Salvador* and *Le Cordon Bleu*, with local food for around CFA500 and western dishes from CFA750.

Entertainment

For a cheap drink, try *Bar Sunukeau* next to the cinema. For something more lively, the *Nightclub Sangomar* on Ave Général de Gaulle opens at weekends, with an entry charge of CFA1000 for men.

Getting There & Away

Bush taxis and minibuses leave from the gare routière on the southern outskirts. A private taxi between the town centre and the gare routière costs CFA325. Typical fares for 504s are CFA900 to Dakar, CFA1600 to Kaolack and CFA2150 to St-Louis.

THE GRANDE CÔTE

The Grande Côte starts where the Cap Vert peninsula merges with the mainland and continues north to St-Louis. It's one long, uninterrupted beach (at low tide it's possible to drive a car the whole way – demonstrated, most notably, by competitors in the final stage of the Paris-Dakar Rally), but strong ocean winds and dangerous seas mean the Grande Côte has not been settled in a big way, nor has it been developed for tourism.

Mboro-sur-Mer is a fishing village off the beaten track and rarely reached by tourists, unlike Kayar (30km south), which is regularly included in tour itineraries. Some travellers have arranged informal *lodgings* with locals. Alternatively, the de-lightful *Gîte de la Licorne* (☎ 955 77 88) is right on the beach and charges CFA10,000 per person. Half board is CFA18,400 or you can self-cater (reservations are advised).

Minibuses run from Thiès to Mboro town (CFA600), from where it's another 5km walk to Mboro-sur-Mer.

DIOURBEL

Diourbel is the former home of Amadou Bamba, the founding marabout of the

Mouride Islamic brotherhood. The main mosque is smaller, neater and, it has to be said, more aesthetically pleasing than the vast and more famous structure at Touba.

The *Hotel le Baobab* has rooms from CFA14,000/16,000 with expensive drinks and an empty swimming pool.

By Peugeot 504, the fare to/from Dakar is CFA1600, Thiès CFA800 and Touba CFA500.

TOUBA

Touba, 50km north of Diourbel, is the sacred focus of the Mouride Islamic brotherhood, and Amadou Bamba is buried in the giant mosque which dominates the town. For more background information, see the boxed text 'Marabouts & Brotherhoods' in

Bamba

Amadou Bamba was born around 1850 and is still Senegal's most famous and influential marabout. He was a charismatic Islamic evangelist and, as a relation of the Wolof leader Lat Dior and member of the wealthy land-owning Mbacke clan, was accorded very high status. By 1887 he had gained a large following and founded the Mouride brotherhood which emphasised the importance of physical labour (ideally working in Bamba's own plantations) as a path to spiritual salvation. This initially fitted neatly with the French administration's attempts to improve their territory's economic output, but Bamba's anticolonial stance and local power base led eventually to him being exiled. Bamba returned to Senegal in 1907 and, despite his continued anticolonial rhetoric, became a secret ally of the French; they both had much to gain from keeping peasants working in the groundnut fields. Even today, Bamba remains an iconic figure, and the convenient alliance between the brotherhoods and the government is still a major feature of modern Senegalese politics.

the Facts about Senegal section. Touba's high point is the Grand Magal pilgrimage, held 48 days after the Islamic new year, which celebrates Bamba's return from exile. At this time, about half a million Mourides flock into town, and every bus seat and hotel bed within a day's journey is occupied. At all times of the year, Friday is also busy.

Outside prayer times, guides are available to show you around the mosque and mausoleums, and it is inappropriate to enter without one. Some speak English. Fees should be agreed beforehand; about CFA 1000 for an hour's tour is fair. The complex is still expanding to cater for the ever-growing crowds of followers, and the various stages of construction – from solid concrete columns to delicate hand-painted plaster reliefs – are interesting to observe.

No alcohol or cigarettes are allowed anywhere in Touba, and even hotels are seen as dens of iniquity. The nearest place to stay is at **Mbaké**, 10km to the south, which makes a good base for a day trip. *Campement Touristique le Baol* here has spartan singles/doubles (perhaps to get pilgrims in an ascetic mood) for CFA9900/12,300 and the friendly English-speaking staff can arrange guides.

To reach Touba from Dakar costs CFA 2000 in a Peugeot 504, and CFA1200 by minibus.

ST-LOUIS

The city of St-Louis – the first French settlement in Africa – was founded in 1659 on a strategic island near the mouth of the River Senegal. By the 1790s it was a busy port and trade centre with a population of 10,000 including Africans, Europeans and many of mixed race. Most notable among the residents of St-Louis at this time were the *signares* – women of mixed race who temporarily 'married' European merchants based in the city, and thereby gained great wealth and privilege. They initiated the festival of decorated lanterns (fanals) which still occurs in St-Louis in the weeks around Christmas.

In the early 19th century, St-Louis became the capital of France's new African colonies. Dakar became the capital of French West

ST-LOUIS

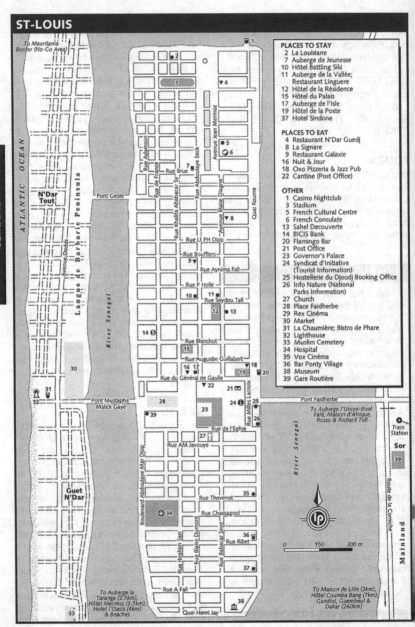

PLACES TO STAY
2 La Louisiane
7 Auberge de Jeunesse
10 Hôtel Battling Siki
11 Auberge de la Vallée;
   Restaurant Linguere
12 Hôtel de la Résidence
15 Hôtel du Palais
17 Auberge de l'Isle
19 Hôtel de la Poste
37 Hotel Sindone

PLACES TO EAT
4 Restaurant N'Dar Guedj
8 La Signare
9 Restaurant Galaxie
16 Nuit & Jour
18 Oxo Pizzeria & Jazz Pub
22 Cantine (Post Office)

OTHER
1 Casino Nightclub
3 Stadium
5 French Cultural Centre
6 French Consulate
13 Sahel Decouverte
14 BICIS Bank
20 Flamingo Bar
21 Post Office
23 Governor's Palace
24 Syndicat d'Initiative
   (Tourist Information)
25 Hostellerie du Djoudj Booking Office
26 Info Nature (National
   Parks Information)
27 Church
28 Place Faidherbe
29 Rex Cinéma
30 Market
31 La Chaumière; Bistro de Phare
32 Lighthouse
33 Muslim Cemetery
34 Hospital
35 Vox Cinéma
36 Bar Ponty Village
38 Museum
39 Gare Routière

Camels in Nouâdhibou, Mauritania: an important means of transport in the desert regions.

Adding beauty to functionality: colourful decoration on a Hausa dwelling in Nigeria.

The port and city centre of Dakar, Senegal.

Celebrating the New Year, West African-style, in Kabala, Sierra Leone.

Urban life in Kabala, Sierra Leone.

Bicycle repair men, Vogan, Togo.

Ewé fishermen pulling in a net, Togo.

Africa in 1904, but St-Louis remained the capital of Senegal (and Mauritania) until 1958, when everything was moved to Dakar.

Today St-Louis covers the island plus parts of the mainland (called Sor) and the Langue de Barbarie peninsula. With its unique setting and relaxed atmosphere, most visitors find St-Louis one of the most congenial towns in Senegal. On the island, which was once the European quarter, you can see many grand old houses, a few still with gracious wrought-iron balconies and verandas which give the town its air of faded elegance and have earned it a deserved UNESCO World Heritage site award.

Information

The syndicat d'initiative near the bridge on the island has helpful staff, a notice board with news of local events, and leaflets, including *St-Louis de Senegal – Ville d'Art et d'Histoire*, which has a city map and suggested walking tours to various historical features. Nearby on the quay at the far eastern end of Rue de l'Eglise is the national parks information office (called Info Nature) for Djoudj, Langue de Barbarie and Guembeul.

BICIS on Rue de France changes money, and the Centre Culturel Français on Ave Jean Mermoz has books, films, concerts and exhibitions. In various parts of town, you'll find local hustlers and unofficial guides offering tours and souvenirs, although most will accept refusal if you don't need their services.

Things to See

Originally built to cross the Danube and transferred here in 1897, the **Pont Faidherbe** bridge linking the mainland and island is a grand piece of 19th-century engineering. The middle section used to rotate to allow ships to steam up the River Senegal. Taxis run across the bridge, but it's worth walking for the view.

Immediately after crossing the bridge onto the island, to the right you'll see the old **Hôtel de la Poste**. Opposite is the post office, where, for a small fee, local guides will take you onto the roof which offers

good views of the bridge and surrounding city. Behind the post office is the former **governor's palace**, which was a fort during the 18th century and is now a government building; across the road is a **church** which dates from 1828 – the oldest in Senegal.

North and south of Place Faidherbe, with a statue of its namesake, the famous French colonial governor, are some of the island's **19th-century houses**. There are several good examples on Quai Henri Jay. At the southern tip of the island is a **museum** containing some fascinating old photos of St-Louis and other exhibits relating to the northern region. It's open 9 am to noon and 3 to 6 pm; admission is CFA500. Don't miss the 'totem poles' outside, carved from palm-tree stumps.

From Place Faidherbe **Pont Mustapha Malick Gaye** (formerly Pont Servatius) links the island to the Langue de Barbarie peninsula and the fishing settlement of **Guet N'Dar** to the south. After crossing the bridge, go straight ahead to reach the lighthouse and **beach**. Forget sunbathing though: every morning, some 200 pirogues are launched from here into the sea. They return in the late afternoon, surfing in spectacularly on the waves, to unload their fish on the sand. A line of trucks waits to take the catch to Dakar, from where some of it is shipped to Europe.

At the southern end of the village, on the river side, pirogues are lined up on the beach and fish dry on racks by the side of the road. Women boil up fish in vast drums, and the steam mixes odiously with the early morning sea mist. Further south is the Muslim **cemetery**, where each fisherman's grave is covered with a fishing net.

Further down the Langue de Barbarie peninsula you'll find several hotels and campements and can also begin looking for good beach spots. This area is called l'Hydrobase, and was a vital refuelling point for flying boats travelling between Europe and South America in the 1930s. A **monument** to early aviator Jean Mermoz stands next to the road.

You may be stopped by police if you go north from Guet N'Dar, as the border with

Mauritania is only 3km away, marked by a line of trees visible from the north end of the island.

Places to Stay

Mainland (Sor) Cheapest is the *Maison de Lille*, a community hostel, 2km south of the bridge on the mainland, with singles/doubles for CFA4000/4600 including breakfast. Another shoestringers' favourite is *Auberge l'Union-Bool Falé* (☎ 961 38 52) on the north side of Sor, where simple rooms with fan cost CFA4000 per person or CFA7500/11,000 with bathroom. A mattress on the roof is CFA1000. In the same area as the auberge is the small and clean *Maison d'Afrique* (☎ 961 45 00), charging CFA9400/11,000 with breakfast. About 7km south of the bridge, the large upmarket *Hôtel Coumba Bang* (☎ 961 18 50) has rooms at CFA 19,600/22,000, plus CFA2500 for breakfast.

Island The ancient *Hôtel Battling Siki* on Rue Abdoulaye Seck has grubby rooms for CFA5000/6000. Much better are *Auberge de la Vallée* on Ave Blaise Diagne and *Auberge de Jeunesse* on Rue Abdoulaye Seck, both clean and friendly. They charge CFA4500 to CFA5000 per person which is good value if you're in a double, but a bit steep for the eight bed dorm. Another option is the spartan *Auberge de l'Isle*, charging CFA4400 per person.

At the northern end of the island, *La Louisiane* (☎ 961 42 21) is a small, peaceful guesthouse where rooms with bathroom cost CFA10,600/15,200 (CFA2500 less if you have your own towel and sheet sleeping bag). The *Hôtel du Palais* on Rue Blanchot charges CFA12,600/14,700 but is dreary, with sluggish staff. Much better is the *Hôtel de la Résidence* (☎ 961 12 59) on Rue Blaise Diagne where air-con rooms with bathroom cost CFA15,600/18,200 plus CFA2500 for a sumptuous buffet breakfast. The hotel bar is the centre of well-to-do St-Louis nightlife, and the friendly French owners can help with local information.

At the charming *Hôtel de la Poste* on Rue du Général de Gaulle (☎ 961 11 18) rooms are CFA18,000/21,500 plus breakfast for CFA2500. For colonial flashbacks, visit the hotel's Safari Bar, complete with balding animal heads on the wall. On the quay nearby is the hotel's swimming pool. Top of the range is the stylish *Hôtel Sindone* (☎ 961 42 45) on Quai Henri Jay, with rooms from CFA19,600/22,200.

Langue de Barbarie Places to stay within 4km of the centre are listed here. Some other accommodation options on the Langue de Barbarie peninsula are listed in the Around St-Louis section following.

About 2.5km south of town, *Auberge la Teranga* is aimed squarely at backpackers, charging CFA4400 per person. The roof-top restaurant offers three-course *menus* in the CFA2000 to CFA4000 range. Next along is the relaxed *Camping l'Ocean* (☎ 961 31 18), ideal for travellers with vehicles and/or tents, charging CFA2500 per person. You can hire a tent for an extra CFA1000. They also have rooms from CFA7000/10,000.

About 1km further south is the *Hôtel Mermoz* (☎ 961 36 68), with comfortable bungalows from CFA7600/11,200 to CFA 10,600/13,200. Many travellers recommend the *Hôtel l'Oasis* (☎/fax 961 42 32, email nicooasissl@ns.arc.sn), about 4km south of the centre. Simple, good quality huts are CFA8600/13,200 (up to CFA27,000 for five people); high standard bungalows with bathroom are CFA12,600/18,200 – all with breakfast. Meals start at CFA2500 and cost up to CFA4500 for a three course *menu*. Snacks are also available – the prawn baguettes will sustain you all day. The friendly multilingual management also offers an email service for a nominal charge. Almost next door is the smarter *Hotel Cap St-Louis* (☎ 961 39 39), with simple rooms for CFA10,600/15,200 and air-con bungalows for CFA20,600/27,200. Facilities include a swimming pool, strictly for guests, and a tennis court.

Places to Eat

All the hotels do food. Otherwise, in the city centre on Rue du Général de Gaulle there are a couple of *chawarma joints* and the smarter *Nuit & Jour*, offering fast food and grills. In the post office yard is a workers' *cantine* serving cheap lunches (could this be the Poste Restaurante?). North of here, *Restaurant Galaxie* on Rue Abdoulaye Seck, *Restaurant Linguere* on the ground floor under Auberge de la Vallée and *Restaurant N'Dar Guedj* on Ave Jean Mermoz all do good Senegalese food for around CFA1500 to CFA2000. Up a grade is the *Oxo Pizzeria* near Hôtel de la Poste on Quai Roume, and the smartest place is *La Signare* on Ave Blaise Diagne, with a top-notch *menu du jour* for CFA7000.

Entertainment

The bar at *Hôtel Battling Siki* has cheap drinks but is frequented by hustlers and other lowlifes. At *Bar Ponty Village* the drinks are only slightly more expensive and the surroundings much better. They also do food and there's often live music. Next door is a *nightclub*, open at weekends. At the other end of the island, the *Casino Nightclub* is lively on Friday and Saturday, and also has a good restaurant.

In Guet N'Dar, *La Chaumière* bar and nightclub is popular with both locals and tourists. The place hops at weekends, al-

---

St-Louis Jazz

Jazz is a big thing here, and it's not just the shared name with Saint Louis in Mississippi, USA, where blues and jazz originated. Way back in the 1940s, jazz bands from St-Louis (Senegal) were playing in Paris and Europe. Worldwide interest was revived in the early 1990s with the introduction of the annual St-Louis International Jazz Festival, held every May, attracting performers and audiences from all over the world. Come if you're a jazz fan, but be prepared for full hotels and inflated rates. More information is available from the Centre Culturel Français (☎ 961 15 78, fax 961 22 23, email ccfsl@syfed.refer.sn).

---

though it seems to have a bit of a rough edge. Entry is CFA1000 for men. Next door, the *Bistrot du Phare* serves drinks until late.

Getting There & Away

The gare routière is on the mainland 250m south of Pont Faidherbe (a taxi from here to the city centre on the island costs CFA250). The fare to/from Dakar is CFA2000 by bus, CFA2300 by minibus and CFA2800 by Peugeot 504. To or from Richard Toll by 504 costs CFA1400. A 504 to Gandiol, from where boats to the Parc National de la Langue de Barbarie leave, costs CFA250.

Getting Around

Car & Motorcycle Cars can be hired from Senecartours (☎ 961 38 12) on Rue Blaise Diagne or Sahel Decouverte (see the Organised Tours section, following). Rates at Senecartours are the same as those offered by their Dakar office.

Siloc Location de Moto (near Auberge la Teranga and contactable through Hôtel l'Oasis) hires 125cc motorcycles for CFA 20,000 and 600cc motorcycles for CFA 30,000 per day.

Bicycle To get around St-Louis and the surrounding area, several hotels and auberges hire out steel roadsters for about CFA2500 and mountain bikes (VTTs in French) for CFA5000 per day.

Organised Tours You can also hire cars from tour operator Sahel Decouverte.

Tour Operators Some hotels arrange tours but the leading operator is Sahel Decouverte (☎ 961 42 63, fax 962 42 64, email residence@sonatel.senet.net) on Rue Blaise Diagne. They have excursions to Parc National de la Langue de Barbarie for CFA 21,000 per person, Parc National aux Oiseaux du Djoudj for CFA23,000 or a fascinating day trip into Mauritania for CFA 33,000. Longer tours, including a desert tour, cost about CFA50,000 per day. All prices are based on a minimum of four people, but individuals can usually join groups.

SENEGAL

Local Guides You can organise a tour to Djoudj or Langue de Barbarie national park with a local guide. Some are members of a professional organisation and peg their rates to Sahel Decouverte's (although guides offer tours with a minimum of one client). Independent guides charge CFA4000 per person per day. On top of this you pay for transport (usually a taxi – for sample prices see the Taxi Tours section following), plus CFA 2000 park entry fee (for either park) and the cost of the boat ride (CFA3000 for Djoudj or CFA2500 for Langue de Barbarie).

Taxi Tours To get to Djoudj or Langue de Barbarie under your own steam you could just hire a taxi and not take a guide at all. Daily rates are around CFA15,000 to Djoudj and CFA7500 to Langue de Barbarie. However, entry to Djoudj costs another CFA 5000 for the car (official guides have a permit which waives this charge). It's very important to hire a taxi in good mechanical condition, with a driver who knows the way (especially for Djoudj). Also, make it clear beforehand what time you plan to return and never pay the whole fare in advance.

AROUND ST-LOUIS
Guembeul & Gandiol

About 12km south of St-Louis, **Réserve de Faune de Guembeul** is small, easy to reach and a good place to explore on foot. It protects endangered Sahel animals including dama gazelle, patas monkey and sulcata tortoise. Also, 190 bird species have been spotted here. The park is open daily from 7.30 am to 6.30 pm; admission is CFA1000.

The park is easy to reach by any bush taxi going between St Louis and Gandiol, or by private taxi or rented bike.

Gandiol is a small village on the mainland about 18km south of St-Louis. From the lighthouse north of the village, ferries cross the estuary to the campements on the southern end of the Langue de Barbarie, and this is also the starting point for organised boat tours of the national park.

About 2km south of Gandiol is **Mouit** and the **national park office**. Nearby, on the

edge of the river, the excellent *Zebrabar* offers camping for CFA2000 and huts for CFA6000/9000, and can set you up for boat rides or visits to the park.

A bush taxi runs a few times each day from St-Louis to Gandiol (CFA250), Sometimes this taxi continues to Mouit, otherwise you'll have to walk the last 2km from Gandiol to Mouit and 2.5km to Zebrabar. A private taxi all the way from St-Louis to Zebrabar is CFA2500.

Parc National de la Langue de Barbarie

This national park includes the far southern tip of the peninsula, some small islands, the estuary and a section of the mainland, and is home to numerous water birds – notably flamingo, pelican, cormorant, heron and egret. From November to April, these numbers are swelled by the arrival of migrants from Europe.

The usual (and best) way to experience the park is by boat, which will cruise slowly past the mud flats and islands where the birds feed and roost.

Places to Stay In a wonderful position at the southern end of the peninsula, about 20km from St-Louis centre, are the smart *Campement Langue de Barbarie*, run by Hôtel de la Poste (CFA12,600/16,000 in cottages), and the more relaxed and good-value *Campement Ocean et Savane*, run by Hôtel de la Résidence, with accommodation in large Mauritanian-style tents (CFA4400). Both places provide meals, boat transfers and opportunities for fishing and sailboarding. Reservations are essential.

Although sometimes approachable from St-Louis, they are usually reached from Gandiol village on the mainland.

Getting There & Away The usual approach is by boat from the mainland, normally from Gandiol or Mouit. Another option is to join an organised tour from St-Louis – see the St-Louis Getting Around section earlier for more details.

Parc National aux Oiseaux du Djoudj

This national park is 60km north of St-Louis, and incorporates a stretch of the River Senegal, with numerous channels, creeks, lakes, ponds, marshes, reedbeds and mud flats, plus surrounding areas of dry woodland. This range of habitats (and being one of the first places with permanent water south of the Sahara) means the park attracts numerous species, making it a sanctuary of global significance with UNESCO World Heritage and Ramsar status.

The park is most famous for its vast flocks of pelican and flamingo. Even if you have no interest in ornithology, observing these comical birds at such close quarters is fascinating. Other easily recognisable species include spur-winged goose, purple heron, egret, spoonbill, jacana, cormorant and harrier. From November to April, various migrants from Europe, especially waders, arrive. Keen birdwatchers will recognise many of the European species, but the sheer numbers which assemble here are very impressive. Around three million individual birds pass through the park annually, and almost 400 separate species have been recorded.

There are a few mammals and reptiles in the park, most notably populations of warthog and mongoose and a famously large python that lurks by the edge of the lake. Other mammals include jackal, hyena, monkey and gazelle.

The park is open daily year-round, from 7 am to dusk. Entry costs CFA2000 per person, plus CFA5000 per car. To see the pelican colony you need to take a boat ride; this costs CFA 3000 per person for a standard two hour trip.

Places to Stay At the park headquarters and main entrance is the low-key *Campement du Djoudj* mainly for research groups, but open to the public, with clean rooms for CFA5000 per person. Camping is allowed. Also at the park entrance is the large *Hostellerie du Djoudj* (☎ 963 87 00, fax 963 87 01) with comfortable rooms at

Tours

The tour companies, hotels and guides in St-Louis offer tours which all follow the same pattern, leaving at around 7 am to reach the park by 8.30 am. First they drive to the jetty for a two hour boat ride through the creeks, the highlight of which is the enormous pelican colony. (The boats are owned by the hotel and the first trip goes at about 9 am.) After lunch at the hotel, you drive to see flamingo flocks on the lake's edge.

Trying to do something 'unusual' will cause all sort of confusion and, notwithstanding Djoudj's global status, there is no real set-up for ornithologists. Keen birdwatchers hoping to see a good range of species on an organised day trip from St-Louis are likely to find the visit quite frustrating. A better option might be to forget the local guides and hire your own taxi, or spend several days exploring the national park alone.

CFA15,600/20,000. You can charter a boat or 4WD for around CFA10,000 per hour, or hire mountain bikes.

Getting There & Away Most visitors reach the park on an organised tour or with a local guide (for more details see Getting Around in the St-Louis section earlier). If you're driving from St-Louis, take the paved highway towards Rosso for about 25km. Near Ross-Bethio you'll see a sign pointing to the park, which is about 25km further along dirt tracks.

Travellers have also reported that it's possible to join a tour from St-Louis but rather than return with the group, you can stay in the park for a few days and then hitch a ride out with some other tourists.

THE RIVER SENEGAL ROUTE

The River Senegal marks the country's northern and eastern border. In the 19th century, French colonial forces built a chain of forts – Dagana, Podor, Matam, Bakel and Kayes (in present-day Mali) – which later developed into major settlements and were linked by boats from St-Louis. Today, most of the traffic is on the main road which runs parallel to the river (but rarely close enough to see it). The road provides a rarely travelled route between St-Louis and Tambacounda, and between the national parks of Djoudj and Niokolo-Koba. Overland drivers linking Mauritania and Mali also find this route straightforward and enjoyable.

North of the river, the deserts of Mauritania mark the edge of the Sahara, and a journey along this road is as near to the desert as you can get in Senegal. The landscape is dry and the vegetation sparse. Sand drifts across the road, and the traditional *banco* (mud-brick) houses would blend almost completely into the background were it not for the Tukulor custom of decorating the outer walls in bold stripes of red, brown and yellow. To the south, the great Ferlo Plains stretch deep into central Senegal, with some parts set aside as wildlife reserves, although these dry areas are very hard to reach and have no tourist facilities.

Rosso & Richard Toll

The flyblown frontier town of Rosso-Senegal is some 100km north-east of St-Louis on the River Senegal. From here a ferry crosses to Rosso-Mauritanie. The main street is full of hustlers, smugglers, moneychangers and minibus touts, and worth escaping quickly. If you get stuck, the depressing *Auberge du Walo*, 2km from the ferry, has rooms for CFA6000. To St-Louis is CFA1400 by Peugeot 504 and CFA900 by bus. A local bush taxi to Richard Toll is CFA300.

Richard Toll was once a colonial town and is now the centre of Senegal's sugar industry. If you overnight here, an evening stroll to the tumbledown Chateau de Baron Roger at the eastern end of town whiles away an hour or two. The attached overgrown ornamental park was laid out by one Claude Richard, hence the name Richard Toll, which means Richard's Garden. Cheap places to stay seem

nonexistent. The *Hotel la Taouey* on the river, north of the main street, has adequate but bare rooms for CFA13,600/17,200 and the smarter *Gîte d'Étape* charges CFA 16,000/19,000. On the main street are several eateries; *Restaurant le Teddungal* has tablecloths, cold drinks and big meals (CFA750 to CFA1000).

Podor & Île à Morphil

Podor has a large fort and several old colonial buildings – but only history fans will get excited. The *Gîte de Douwaya*, charges CFA6000/8000 for rooms with bathroom, including breakfast. To get here, buses stop at Treji (also spelt Tredji or Taredji) on the main road and local bush taxis shuttle passengers to Podor 20km away.

Podor is at the western end of Île à Morphil, which stretches for 100km between the main River Senegal and a parallel channel. A road runs along the island all the way to Saldé at its eastern end, where a ferry crosses over to Ngoui, near Pete. Travellers with wheels and plenty of time have reported that this is an interesting route and that the traditional villages of Guede and Alwar are particularly scenic.

Between Podor and St-Louis is CFA2700 by Peugeot 504. If you're heading east, to Ouro Sogui is CFA2000 in a minibus or CFA2500 in a 504.

Matam & Ouro Sogui

Matam is 230km south-east of Podor, and is reached via a turn-off from Ouro Sogui. Over the years Matam has declined, while Ouro Sogui has grown into a lively trading centre and transport hub.

In Ouro Sogui, the *Auberge Sogui* has reasonable rooms for CFA4500/6000 and there are several cheap eateries on the same street including *Restaurant Teddoungal* where beef and spaghetti costs CFA750.

A Peugeot 504 to Dakar is CFA8500. From Ouro Sogui to Bakel costs CFA3600 in a 504 and CFA2000 in a bus. The road east of Ouro Sogui was in terrible condition when we passed through, but is due to be tarred all the way to the Mali border at Kidira by 1999.

Bakel

Bakel is an interesting and picturesque place, set among rocky hills overlooking the river. The abandoned Pavillon René Caillié on a hill next to two large water tanks gives great views. The old fort is still in good condition, but closed to the public. The large octagonal lookout tower at the southern edge of town and the nearby military cemetery are easily reached.

The *Hôtel Islam* has simple rooms for CFA4000/6000 and the nearby streets have several restaurants and food stalls. *Bar-Resto Mbodick*, on the waterfront, has beers and meals to order for CFA1500. The friendly patron, Mamadou Loum, is building a cheap *campement* and also knows the schedules and prices of boats going up and down the river.

From Bakel to the border town of Kidira is CFA900 by minibus, and vehicles go a few times a week to Tambacounda (a 504 costs CFA5000). For the adventurous, motorised pirogues go between Matam, Bakel and Kayes, leaving Bakel from the 'port' next to the Bar-Resto Mbodick. There is no set schedule – you just have to ask around.

The Petite Côte

The Petite Côte is south of Dakar, stretching for about 70km between Rufisque and Joal-Fadiout. The south-western aspect, reliable weather conditions and clean sands make this Senegal's second-best beach area after Cap Skiring, and by far its most popular in terms of visitor numbers.

Beyond Rufisque, smaller roads turn off the main artery and lead down to coastal villages such as **Popenguine** and **Somone**, which have beaches and a couple of low-key accommodation options.

TOUBAB DIALAO

The fishing village of Toubab Dialao is about 10km from Bargny, and many travellers rave about *Sobo-Bade*, built on a small cliff, surrounded by beautiful gardens and overlooking the beach and ocean, with double bungalows from CFA12,000 and

rooms with four beds for CFA3700 per person. Meals are from CFA2500, with vegetarian choices and a *menu* for CFA5500. Run by a Frenchman named Gerard, this place offers artistic workshops in dance, percussion and sculpture.

To get here from Dakar, take anything for Mbour and get off at the big junction where the roads to Thiès and Kaolack divide; local minibuses run from here to Toubab Dialao. Alternatively, in Bargny, you may find something direct.

SALY

Saly-Portugal consists of a cluster of about 10 big ocean-front hotels, 3km off the main road, grouped together in a *domaine touristique* (tourist zone) with restaurants, banks, shops and casino, and is packed with European tourists during winter. If you fancy some luxury, and money is of little concern, a small selection of hotels is listed here, although most cater for groups and do not even have rates for individuals. If you phone before arrival, discounts may be available, but this is more easily done through a tour agency in Dakar; many offer special rates.

Less fancy than most hotels in Saly, *Les Cocotiers* (☎ 957 14 91) has single/double bungalows at CFA27,500/37,500 per night, or CFA190,000/257,000 per week. *Hôtel Village Club des Filao* (☎ 957 11 80) has bed and breakfast at CFA21,000 per person and half board for CFA29,000. *Savana Saly* (☎ 957 11 12, fax 957 10 45, email savana@ elecomplus.sn) is a top end place with singles/doubles at CFA45,000/55,000 for half board.

The area between Saly and Mbour seems to be called, quite reasonably, **Saly-Mbour**. The village of **Saly-Niakhniakhale** is just south of the big hotels, where the small and highly rated *Auberge Khady* (☎ 957 25 18), with Belgian-Senegalese management, is set in lovely gardens near the sea. Simple but comfortable rooms with bathroom and breakfast costs CFA10,000/14,000 and half board is CFA13,000/20,000.

Further south towards Mbour is the slightly ramshackle *Ferme de Saly*, established as

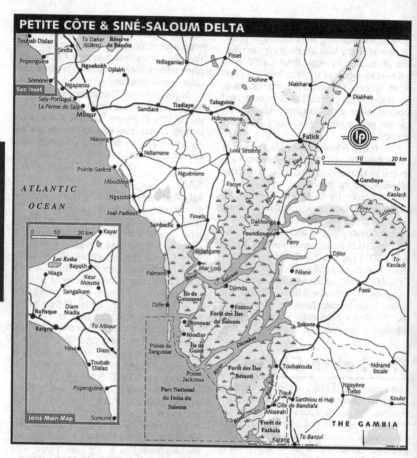

PETITE CÔTE & SINÉ-SALOUM DELTA

a *gîte rural* but rapidly becoming surrounded by new buildings. It's in an excellent position under trees on the beach. Huts cost CFA 15,000 per person for half board. In the low season (June to November) this drops to CFA8000 for bed and breakfast. It's a 3km walk off the main road along a maze of tracks.

Both the Auberge Khady and the Ferme de Saly arrange excursions and fishing trips, and the flashy places at Saly-Portugal offer water sports for nonguests. A taxi from Mbour is CFA1000.

MBOUR

Mbour is about 80km south of Dakar, a lively trading centre and good jumping-off point for places along the coast. The fishing market on the beach is a favourite spot for tour groups from Saly, attracting a motley crew of hustlers. The best way to avoid them is to go some way south along the beach.

Places to Stay

The friendly *Centre d'Accueil* near the main market has singles/doubles with breakfast for

CFA7000/10,500 and a wonderful garden. South from here, along the sandy street that runs nearest to the ocean, are several places where local people have opened rooms to travellers including **Chez Zeyna**, **Chez Charley** and **Chez Marie**, all charging a negotiable CFA5000 per person. Up a few grades is the affordably comfortable **Centre Touristique Coco Beach** (☎ 957 10 04) where doubles with bathroom and air-con cost CFA14,000.

Places to Eat

Just off the main street about 500m south of the centre **Restaurant le Djembe** has meals from CFA500. **Restaurant Luxembourg** near the market has dishes from CFA1700. Round the corner is a **snack bar** with chawarmas at CFA700.

Getting There & Away

Between Mbour and Dakar costs CFA950 in a Peugeot 504 and CFA670 in a bus. Minibuses south to Joal-Fadiout are CFA400.

NIANING

Nianing is 10km south of Mbour and boasts another line of hotels, although many of these are smaller and more pleasant than the Saly strip, and the village itself is quieter than Mbour. **Les Bourgain Villees** is close to the beach, with rooms from CFA7000; **Hôtel Le Ben'Tenier** has bungalows in a quiet garden for CFA10,600/17,000; and the similarly priced **Auberge des Coquillages** has a small pool and private beach.

JOAL-FADIOUT

The twin villages of Joal and Fadiout are interesting – and an easy day trip for tour groups from Dakar or Saly, so it can sometimes be crowded around midday. Joal is on the mainland, while Fadiout covers a small island reached by long wooden bridge. The island is composed entirely of clam shells that have accumulated over the centuries, and everything in the village seems made of shells too: they cover the maze of narrow streets, and are embedded in the walls of the houses. Parts of Fadiout, particularly the

rubbish tips near the water's edge, feel fairly squalid but the centre has a definite charm.

Contributing to Fadiout's unique atmosphere is the strong Christian influence – several shrines to the Virgin Mary are dotted around town, and there's a large church. The Christian cemetery is built on a separate shell island, also reached by a bridge. Nearby is a group of curious basket-like granaries on stilts over the water. The idea is that even if the village burns down, at least the food for the rest of the year will be safe. Joal-Fadiout also has a Muslim community, and the two groups seem to get along fine. When we visited a funeral was in progress – Muslims and Christians streamed across the bridge to the cemetery together.

Places to Stay & Eat

The best cheap place to stay in Joal is the **Relais 114**, run by the friendly Mamadou Baldé, who is very proud of his performing pelicans. Basic clean rooms cost CFA7000 (for one to three people), which includes one breakfast. An extra breakfast is CFA1500. Simple meals start from CFA2000. More upmarket, but lacking the Relais's soul, is the **Hôtel le Finio** with prices ranging from CFA5000 per person for simple huts to aircon singles/doubles at CFA9000/19,000. On Fadiout island **Campement les Paletuviers** has bed and breakfast in simple rooms for CFA4000 per person.

Getting There & Away

A minibus to/from Mbour is CFA400. If you're heading on down the coast, from Joal to Palmarin is CFA400. A Peugeot 504 goes direct to Dakar most mornings (without changing at Mbour) for CFA1300.

PALMARIN & DJIFER

The village of Palmarin (actually four villages in a group) is 20km south of Joal-Fadiout, where the beaches of the Petite Côte merge with the labyrinthine creeks of the Siné-Saloum Delta. The road here takes you through a shimmering flat-lands dotted with

SENEGAL

palm groves, traditional villages, shallow lagoons, mud flats and patches of salt marsh which attract huge flocks of wading birds.

The fishing village of Djifer is another 15km further south on the sandy Pointe de Sangomar peninsula jutting between the Atlantic Ocean and the mouth of the River Saloum. At the far end of village is a huge fish market and port where many colourful fishing boats are drawn up on the beach.

Places to Stay & Eat

In Palmarin, the superb Casamance-style *Campement de Palmarin* is on a sandy beach under the palms where half board in thatched bungalows costs an unbeatable CFA7000. This place is run by a friendly manager on behalf of the villagers. Behind the campement is a large lagoon – an excellent area to see wading birds.

Djifer has two campements, both charging CFA6000 per person with breakfast: the smarter *Campement Pointe de Sangomar* is popular with tour groups; the quieter *Campement la Mangrove* is 2km north of Djifer, close to a nice beach, and allows camping.

The campements all provide food; otherwise, there are several basic *gargottes* in Djifer; *Restaurant Lat Dior* and *Chez Khalid* both do good, big fisherman-sized helpings for CFA350.

Getting There & Away

Bush taxis go from Mbour or Joal-Fadiout to Palmarin and Djifer via Sambadia (also written Samba Dia). From Joal to Sambadia costs CFA400 and from Sambadia to Djifer is CFA700.

Another option is by pirogue to or from Ndangane or Foundiougne (see the Siné-Saloum Delta section following). If you're heading to Gambia, cramped, uncomfortable and notoriously unsafe pirogues go from Djifer to Banjul a few times per week for around CFA2500 per person. The trip takes about five hours, but may involve an overnight stop on a midway island. You have been warned! On arrival in Banjul go to the immigration office at the port and not the one in the city centre.

AROUND DJIFER

Places to visit near Djifer include the islands of **Guior** and **Guissanor**, on the other side of the River Saloum from the Pointe de Sangomar. This comes close to the heart of the Siné-Saloum Delta – beautiful, tranquil and almost completely devoid of tourist facilities. On Guior are the small fishing villages of **Niodior** and **Dionouar** and an upmarket lodge for anglers. The campements in Djifer run excursions to the islands from about CFA15,000 per boat for a half-day trip, or you can charter a pirogue yourself at the fishing beach for lower rates. A cheaper option is the public boat which runs between Djifer and Dionouar for CFA250 per person, but it only goes once a day in each direction, usually in the afternoon.

The Siné-Saloum Delta

South of the Petite Côte, between Kaolack and the Gambian border, the vast Siné-Saloum Delta is one of the most beautiful parts of Senegal. Formed where the Siné and Saloum rivers meet the tidal waters of the Atlantic Ocean, it's an area of channels, lagoons, open forests, dunes and sand islands, and vast tracts of mangroves.

Part of the area is included in the Parc National du Delta du Saloum, which abounds with monkeys, and the range of habitats makes it particularly good for birding. Highly recommended is a trip by pirogue to see birds, including pelican, flamingo, as well as traditional island fishing villages, or just to admire the fascinating scenery.

KAOLACK

Kaolack is a regional capital, the centre of Senegal's groundnut industry, and a handy gateway to the Siné-Saloum Delta. Although often regarded by travellers as little more than a junction town, it's a lively place and well worth visiting for a day or two.

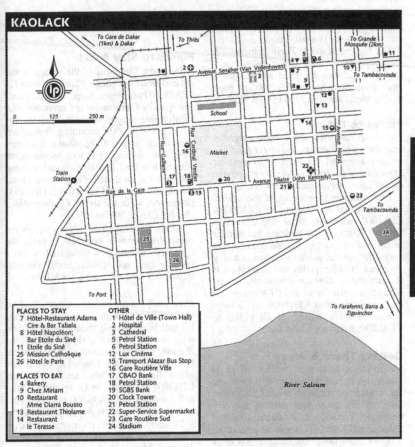

KAOLACK

To Gare de Dakar (1km) & Dakar
To Thiès
To Grande Mosquée (2km)
To Tambacounda

Avenue Senghor (Van Vollenhoven)

School

Market

Rue Cardinal Verdier
Rue Gallène

Train Station

Rue de la Gare

Avenue Filiatre (John Kennedy)

Avenue Noirat

To Tambacounda

River Saloum

To Port

To Farafenni, Barra & Ziguinchor

PLACES TO STAY
7 Hôtel-Restaurant Adama
  Cire & Bar Tabala
8 Hôtel Napoléon;
  Bar Etoile du Siné
11 Etoile du Siné
25 Mission Catholique
26 Hôtel le Paris

PLACES TO EAT
4 Bakery
9 Chez Miriam
10 Restaurant
  Mme Diarra Bousso
13 Restaurant Thiolame
14 Restaurant
  le Terasse

OTHER
1 Hôtel de Ville (Town Hall)
2 Hospital
3 Cathedral
5 Petrol Station
6 Petrol Station
12 Lux Cinéma
15 Transport Alazar Bus Stop
16 Gare Routière Ville
17 CBAO Bank
18 Petrol Station
19 SGBS Bank
20 Clock Tower
21 Petrol Station
22 Super-Service Supermarket
23 Gare Routière Sud
24 Stadium

SENEGAL

Things to see include the large Moroccan-style **Grande Mosquée** north of the town centre – the pride of the Tidjaniya brotherhood – and reputed to be the second-largest covered **market** in Africa (after Marrakesh in Morocco). Despite these attractions few tourists come here, so there's very little hassle. It's a great place just to wander around and soak up the atmosphere.

Banks include CBAO and SGBS, and you can change money at the Super-Service supermarket on Ave Filiatre.

Places to Stay

Cheapest in town is the *Hôtel Napoléon*, but it's grotty and grossly overpriced at CFA 4000 per double. Nearby is the *Hôtel-Restaurant Adama Cire*, a smarter brothel but clean and friendly enough, with doubles for CFA7000. The *Mission Catholique* might be worth a try, with single rooms for CFA4000 or a dormitory bed for CFA2000, but it's often full.

The best value is the friendly *Etoile du Siné* on the main road to Tambacounda.

Spotless doubles cost CFA9500 with breakfast; other meals can be prepared to order, and safe parking is available.

The top end *Hôtel le Paris* charges CFA 16,500/20,300 for singles/doubles with aircon. The facilities are good and include a small pool. Breakfast is CFA2500 and good quality meals are CFA3000 to CFA5000.

Places to Eat

For cheap eats there are several *gargottes* near the gares routière, and *street food* can be found around the market. *Restaurant Mme Diarra Bousso*, on Ave Senghor to the east of town, serves meals for CFA350.

Chez Miriam, north-east of the centre, has chawarmas and burgers for CFA500 to CFA1000 and meals for around CFA2500. Nearby, *Restaurant Thiolame* has similar prices, but on quiet nights the management may offer special deals to anyone perusing the menu. Best for quality and atmosphere is *Restaurant le Terasse* around the corner with chawarmas for around CFA600, pizzas and omelettes from CFA1000 and a huge choice of main meals for CFA1500 to CFA2500. Beers are CFA450.

Getting There & Away

The town has three gare routières: Gare de Dakar, on the north-western side of town, for western or northern destinations; Gare Sud, on the south-east side of the city centre, for Ziguinchor, Gambia and Tambacounda; and Gare Ville for local bush taxis.

To or from Dakar by Peugeot 504 costs CFA2100, minibus CFA1500 and bus CFA1250. A 504 to the Gambian town of Barra is CFA2100; to Thiès is CFA1600.

NDANGANE & MAR LODJ

Ndangane (pronounced *dan-gahn*) is on the northern side of the delta. Once a sleepy backwater, it has grown considerably over the last few years into a thriving tourist centre. From here you can get boats across the river to the village of Mar Lodj (also spelt Mar Lothie), a peaceful haven cut off by a branch of the River Saloum from the rest of the country. Several good campements make this a great place to slow down for a while.

Places to Stay & Eat

Ndangane The focus of the village is the top end *Hôtel le Pelican* where half board is CFA29,000 per person. Opposite is the small and friendly *Campement le Cormoran* with comfortable single/double bungalows for CFA13,000/20,000 including breakfast. Next to the jetty is *Chez Mbake*, a solitary bungalow sleeping up to four people which you can hire for CFA10,000. Another cheap choice is the local-style *Campement Fouta Torro*, where bed and breakfast is CFA6500 per person, while the stylish *Cordons Bleus* charges CFA22,500/39,000.

All the hotels do food. Otherwise, try the cheap *Restaurant le Bon Coin*, opposite the Cormoran. Nearby is a street stall, where a friendly lady sells coffee, bread and omelettes (her husband runs Chez Mbake).

Mar Lodj All the budget campements here charge CFA6000 with breakfast or CFA9000 for half board. These include *Mbine Diam* with double huts in a shady garden; *Le Bazouk*, small and relaxed, with pirogues for hire; and the larger *Limboko*, which also offers fishing and boat excursions from CFA2000 per person, and a day trip to Djifer and Dionouar at CFA36,000 per boat. Several more places are under construction.

Further along the river, the upmarket *Campement Mar Setal* and *Campement Hakuna Matata* deal mainly with groups, and advance reservations are essential.

Getting There & Away

Take any bus between Kaolack and Mbour, and get off at Ndiosomone, from where bush taxis shuttle back and forth to Ndangane. You can go direct from Dakar to Ndangane for CFA1200. From Mbour you can take bush taxis via Sambadia and Fimla.

To reach Mar Lodj from Ndangane there's an occasional public boat charging CFA250 one way. Otherwise, you have to charter. This should cost CFA4000 for the boat, but if there are more than four tourists the fare is CFA1000 each.

You can charter a pirogue between Ndangane and Djifer for about CFA15,000. To or from Foundiougne is about CFA25,000.

FOUNDIOUGNE

At the north-western edge of the delta, the relaxed village of Foundiougne is easy to reach and a good place to arrange pirogue trips around the delta. For a place to stay, a long-time favourite, and still one of the best, is *Campement le Baobab* where clean single/double rooms with spotless shared bathroom are CFA5500/10,000 including breakfast. For a private bathroom you pay CFA3000 more. Very good three-course meals cost CFA2500. Other options include *Campement Indiana* where simple rooms with shared bathroom cost CFA11,800 per person with breakfast, and *Auberge les Bolongs* which is slightly cheaper and has a nice bar on the beach. The upmarket *Hôtel les Piroguiers* has a beautiful setting on the river and comfortable air-con bungalows for CFA24,400/38,800/40,200.

All places to stay in Foundiougne arrange excursions from around CFA15,000 per half-day and CFA25,000 per day for the boat (depending on petrol and the length of time required). Alternatively, ask around at the ferry jetty, where cheaper deals can be negotiated.

Getting There & Away

A minibus from Kaolack to Foundiougne is CFA600. Alternatively, get anything between Kaolack and Karang on the Gambian border, and get off at Passi. From Passi to Foundiougne is CFA325.

From Dakar or Mbour, take anything heading for Kaolack, and get off at Fatick, then take a bush taxi to Dakhonga and catch a ferry across to Foundiougne. Leaving Foundiougne, the first ferry at 7.30 am connects with a minibus at Dakhonga, which goes all the way to Dakar for CFA1300.

To reach other parts of the delta by boat, you can charter a pirogue to Djifer or Ndangane for around CFA25,000. To Toubakouta

is CFA30,000 and Missirah CFA35,000. Alternatively, ask around for the public pirogue service which goes most days from Foundiougne to Djifer via villages along the River Saloum.

SOKONE

In Sokone, on the main road south of Kaolack, *Campement le Caïman* (☎ 948 31 40) could be a good place to arrange trips into the delta. Comfortable single/double bungalows with bathroom are CFA13,500/19,000 with breakfast, and all day excursions are CFA60,000 for the boat

TOUBAKOUTA

South of Sokone, and about 70km from Kaolack, Toubakouta is a good base for exploring the southern side of the delta. Birding is good in this area, but even if you're not a big fan of feathered friends, you'll enjoy watching pelican, flamingo, fish eagle, heron and egret, especially when they roost at night at the *reposoir des oiseaux* a short boat-ride away.

Hôtel les Palétuviers (☎ 948 77 76, fax 948 77 77) is one of the best quality places on the whole delta, with around 50 double cottages in large grounds. All have air-con and private bathrooms and are furnished to a high standard. Singles/doubles cost CFA33,000/36,000 with breakfast and half board is CFA41,000/52,000. There's a wide choice of excursions, and tours by pirogue range from CFA8000 per person for an evening trip to CFA17,500 for an all-day tour to the mouth of the Saloum where dolphins are sometimes seen. You can also arrange fishing.

Nearby, the *Hôtel Keur Saloum* (☎/fax 948 77 16) has rustic bungalows for CFA 24,900/40,400 half board, and a very nice bar overlooking the small beach beside the river. This place is dedicated to huntin', shootin' and fishin' (as the photos in the bar indicate), and boats are available for hire.

Bush taxis from Kaolack to Barra via Karang (CFA2100) will drop you off at Toubakouta, but you won't get any discount for getting off early. It's cheaper to go by

Mangroves

The mangrove is a tropical evergreen plant that grows on tidal mud flats and inlets all along the coast of West Africa. It plays a vital role for the local populations, as well as for the wildlife, and has a fascinating reproduction system, perfectly adapted to its watery environment. It is one of very few plants which thrive in salt water, and this allows rapid colonisation of areas where no other plant would have a chance. In Senegal, the best place to see mangroves is the Siné-Saloum Delta, although they also grow in other river estuaries, and a long way upstream in the River Gambia.

Two types of mangrove can be seen and easily identified. The **red mangrove** (of which there are three species – although to the untrained eye they all look the same) is most prominent. It's easy to recognise by its leathery leaves and dense tangle of stilt-like buttress roots. The seeds germinate in the fruit while still hanging on the tree, growing a long stem called a 'radical'. When the fruit drops, the radical lodges in the mud and becomes a ready-made root for the new seedling. If the tide happens to be in when the seed drops off, it will float around with the radical pointing downwards, ready to start growing as soon as it's washed ashore.

The **white mangrove** is less common and is found mainly on ground that is only covered by particularly high tides. It does not have stilt roots. Its most recognisable characteristic is the breathing roots, with circular pores, that grow out of the mud from the base of the tree.

Mangrove trees catch silt, vegetation and other floating debris in their root systems. The mangrove's own falling leaves are added to the pile. As this mire becomes waterlogged and consolidated, it forms an ideal breeding ground for young mangroves. In this way, the mangrove actually creates new land. As the stands expand on the seaward side, the older growth on the landward side gradually gets further from the water. Eventually they die, leaving behind a rich soil which is good for cultivation.

The mangrove has many other uses. Oysters and shellfish cling to the roots as the tide comes in. When it retreats, they are left exposed and easily captured by local people who cruise the creeks in pirogues or wade through the mud and water. Mangroves are also used for fishing as fish like the darkness between the roots.

---

minibus. The fare to/from Kaolack is around CFA1000.

MISSIRAH

This small village south of Toubakouta is one of the nearest points to the **Parc National du Delta du Saloum**. The vegetation includes tidal mud flats, mangrove swamps and the dry open woodland of the Forêt de Fathala, so there's a good range of birds and animals, including the plentiful but shy red colobus monkey. The park headquarters is 6km south of Missirah village, and admission is CFA2000.

Near Missirah, the *Gîte de Bandiala* (☎ 948 77 35 or 941 23 41) is peaceful, low-key and good value, making it a great base for exploring this part of the delta. Half board in simple bungalows is a bargain CFA9700 and full board is CFA14,500 (plus tax). The friendly management can make suggestions for forest walks, and in the bar-restaurant are some useful bird charts with names in French and English. The gîte also has a water hole, where monkeys, warthog and other animals come to drink. Tours by pirogue on the nearby creeks and lagoons cost CFA3500 per person for a half day, with a minimum of two people. Fishing can also be arranged.

From Kaolack take any vehicle going along the main road towards Karang, get off at Santhiou el Haji (about 80km from Kaolack) and walk 6km west on a pleasant sandy track through the forest. Another option is to get a private taxi from Kaolack for a negotiable CFA15,000.

Casamance

Casamance is the part of Senegal south of Gambia, a beautiful region which, for a variety of reasons, differs culturally and geographically from the rest of the country – the majority of people here are non-Muslim Diola (Jola), while the River Casamance is a verdant labyrinth of creeks and lagoons dotted by small islands, palm groves, forest and mangroves – perfect for touring on foot, by bike or by pirogue. The area has an excellent system of village-run Campements Rurals Integrés (CRIs) which enable you to get a feel for traditional rural life. Casamance also includes Cap Skiring, quite simply the finest beach in the country.

The region divides into three main areas: Basse Casamance (Lower Casamance) is west of Ziguinchor and south of the river; Casamance Nord is north of the river; and Haute Casamance (Upper Casamance) is east of Ziguinchor.

History

In the 19th and early 20th centuries, the French colonial authorities controlled their territory through local chiefs. In Casamance, however, the Diola people do not have a hierarchical society and thus had no recog-

Warning

The differences between Casamance and the rest of Senegal are quickly appreciated by tourists and felt strongly by local people too. A separatist movement has existed here since the 1950s, sometimes almost forgotten, but at other times armed and active.

When we were researching this book, a cease-fire was in place, and most public transport was running normally, but troops were maintaining a highly visible presence. Several areas remained off limits, either because they were sites of possible rebel incursions or because land mines had reportedly been planted.

Before venturing into rural Casamance, it is essential to check on the latest security situation. In Ziguinchor, ask at your hotel or the CRI office. If you're coming from Gambia, you can contact your embassy for information, while a more grass roots picture can be gleaned by talking to Senegalese bush-taxi drivers in Serekunda.

Due to the unrest, some campements have closed or fallen into disrepair, but others remain impressively spick and span. More places are likely to open up as tourism picks up and you will probably find many other changes by the time you visit.

nised leaders. The French installed Mandinka chiefs to administer the Diola, but they were resented as much as the Europeans, and Diola resistance against foreign interference remained strong well into the 1930s.

In 1943, the last Diola rebellion against the French was led by a traditional priestess called Aline Sitoe Diatta, from Kabrousse. The rebellion was put down and Aline Sitoe was imprisoned at the remote outpost of Timbuktu in neighbouring Mali, where she eventually died. She has been called the Casamance Joan of Arc, and for many years the Diola people of Kabrousse believed she would return and lead them to freedom.

The most recent conflict originates from a pro-independence demonstration held in

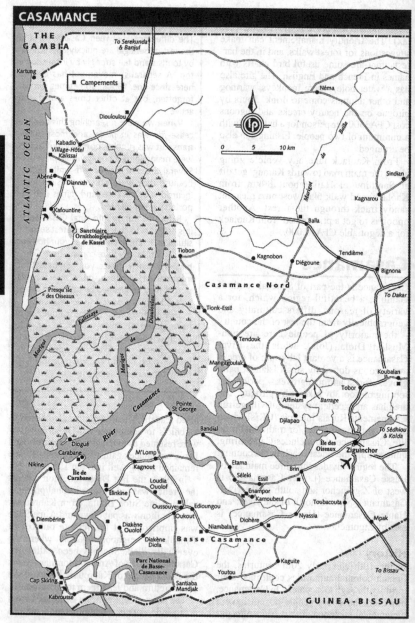

CASAMANCE

THE GAMBIA

To Serekunda & Banjul

Kartung

■ Campements

ATLANTIC OCEAN

SENEGAL

0   5   10 km

Diouloulou

Néma

Kabadio
Village-Hôtel
Kalissai

Abéné

Diannah

Kafountine

Sanctuaire
Ornithologique
de Kassel

Sindian

Kagnarou

Baïla

Presqu'île
des Oiseaux

Tioban

Kagnobon   Diégoune   Tendième

Casamance Nord

Bignona

To Dakar

Kalissaye

Diouloulou

Marigot de

Baïla

Tionk-Essil

Tendouk

Mangagoulak

Koubalan

Casamance River

Pointe
St George

Affiniam   Barrage

Tobor

Djilapao

Île des
Oiseaux

To Sédhiou
& Kolda

Ziguinchor

Dioguè

Carabane

Île de
Carabane

Nikine

M'Lomp

Bandial

Etama

Brin

Kagnout

Séléki   Essil

Diembéring

Elinkine

Loudia
Ouolof

Enampor
Kamoubeul

Toubacouta

Mpak

Oussouye

Diakène
Ouolof

Edioungou
Oukout

Diohère

Nyassia

Niambalang

Cap Skiring

Kabrousse

Diakène
Diola

Parc National
de Basse-
Casamance

Santiaba
Mandjak

Youtou

Kaguite

To Bissau

GUINEA-BISSAU

Ziguinchor in 1982, after which the leaders of the Mouvement des Forces Démocratique de la Casamance (MFDC) were arrested and jailed. Over the next few years the army clamped down with increasing severity, but this only galvanised the local people's anti-Dakar feelings and spurred the movement into taking more action.

In 1990, the MFDC went on the offensive and attacked some military posts. The army responded by attacking MFDC bases in southern Casamance and over the border in Guinea-Bissau. (The Bissau government gave covert support to the rebels, following a coastal territorial dispute with Senegal.) As always, it was local civilians who came off worse. Villages were hit by gunfire or bombs, and both the Senegalese army and the MFDC were accused of committing atrocities against any people thought to be sympathisers of the opposite side.

A cease-fire signed in May 1991 held for several months, but a major clash in September 1992 left another 60 people dead. After long negotiations between the government and the separatists, a cease-fire was declared in June 1993 and an uneasy peace returned to Casamance.

In 1995, four French people touring Casamance disappeared. The Senegalese government blamed the MFDC for their disappearance, while Father Diamacoune Senghor, the MFDC's leader, accused the army of trying to turn international opinion against the rebels. However, peace talks continued, this time with some optimism as President Diouf promised an Amnesty International delegation that his government would investigate and put an end to human rights violations.

But in mid-1997, Amnesty International announced that no such investigation had been held, later reporting that atrocities against civilians were being routinely committed by both Senegalese troops and MFDC soldiers. At the same time, a group of hard-liners broke away from the MFDC and resumed fighting, following the government's refusal to consider independence for Casamance. An audacious attack on an army post in Ziguinchor backfired when mortar shots instead hit a nearby village, killing and wounding some children.

Meanwhile, Father Diamacoune urged his supporters to continue the search for reconciliation with the government. A peace march in Ziguinchor, supported by local Diola, Mandinka and Wolof people, seemed to confirm his wishes, and in late 1997 a new cease-fire was agreed upon. Through the first half of 1998 the combination of a continued army presence, a divided rebel force, dwindling support from Guinea-Bissau and a genuine desire for peace among most of the civilian population means things have been relatively calm in Casamance. Only a genuine agreement accepted by all sides – one that addresses the issue of regional autonomy – can finally put an end to the struggle. Until that is achieved, the future of Casamance is far from certain.

ZIGUINCHOR

Ziguinchor (pronounced zig-an-shor) is the main access point for travel in the Casamance region. As you come into town, the quiet and dusty streets don't look too promising, but soon the attractions begin to reveal themselves. The central area is quite compact and can easily be covered on foot. There's a pleasant, laid-back atmosphere, very little hassle and the best choice of places to stay and eat for all budgets in the whole country.

Information

The nearest Ziguinchor has to a tourist office is the bureau of the Campements Rurals Integrés (☎ 991 13 75) at the Centre Artisanal. Manager Adama Goudiaby can provide details on the campements or help with general queries. The people who run Hôtel le Flamboyant on Rue de France are a mine of local information, and are happy to share their knowledge with anybody stopping by for a drink or meal.

The best bank for changing money is the CBAO on Rue de France, while tour operators include Diatta International Tours (☎ 991 27 81, fax 991 29 81) on Rue du

SENEGAL

Touring Casamance – Suggested Itineraries

Casamance can be toured by car, public transport, bicycle or on foot. The walking is not difficult, although occasionally you will encounter marshy areas or creeks where someone with a pirogue will take you across for a small fee.

For cycling, the smaller *pistes* (tracks) are often too sandy, even for fat-tyred mountain bikes, but there are several rideable dirt roads. The main tar roads are also OK on a bicycle, although what little traffic there is tends to go quite fast and with little room for error. If you get tired, you can always load your bike onto a bush taxi.

Through a combination of hiking and public transport, a full circuit of Basse Casamance can be done in seven to 12 days. Go from Ziguinchor by bush taxi to Brin, hike to Enampor, and then hike on to Diohère, Niambalang or Oussouye, or take a bush taxi back to Ziguinchor via Brin. From Oussouye, hike or catch a bush taxi to Elinkine, take the boat to the Île de Carabane, return to Elinkine, and either retrace your steps to Oussouye or go directly by pirogue to Diakène Ouolof. Get a boat or bush taxi from here to Cap Skiring and then return to Ziguinchor by bush taxi.

A tour by bicycle through Basse Casamance might take you from Ziguinchor to Brin, with a detour to Enampor, to Oussouye and then on to Elinkine via M'Lomp on the tar road. Go over to Carabane by boat (leaving the bike at Elinkine), return to Elinkine and then Oussouye on the old road via Loudia Ouolof, before continuing to Cap Skiring and/or Diembéring.

Casamance Nord is also ideal for cycling. The tracks are green and shady, although there are a few difficult patches of deep sand. From Ziguinchor you could catch the public ferry across to Affiniam, ride to Tionk-Essil (a good base for two days or more) and then on to Baïla, returning via Bignona to Koubalan.

Wherever you go, it's worth resting during the hot midday hours. At any time, take a hat and lots of water.

If you want to explore quieter areas by bike, pirogue or on foot, a local guide is recommended. As well as showing you the way (a maze of paths and tracks crosses the region), guides can also introduce you to aspects of Casamance life that you might otherwise miss. You'll feel less of a stranger and probably be greeted more easily by local people. Trips are often punctuated by informal visits to far-flung friends and relatives in distant villages.

To find a guide, ask around at your hotel or at places which hire bicycles. A personal recommendation from other travellers is always worth seeking as some 'guides' are less reliable than others. The Hôtel Relais Santhiaba and Hôtel le Flamboyant in Ziguinchor can recommend reliable, enthusiastic and knowledgeable guides for about CFA10,000 per day.

Général de Gaulle. There are post offices on Rue du Général de Gaulle and on Rue du Dr Olivier south of the Centre Artisanal, and several télécentres along Rue Javelier. You can send and receive email for CFA500 at Le Cybercafé (☎ 991 29 24, email sudinfo@telecomplus.sn) on Rue de France.

The Guinea-Bissau consulate (☎ 991 10 46) is opposite the Hôtel le Flamboyant and is open weekdays from 8.30 am to noon.

With CFA5000 and a photo, you can get a visa the same day. The Alliance Franco-Sénégalaise is on Ave Lycée Guignabo, with exhibitions, courses, cultural events and a pleasant garden restaurant.

Things to See & Do

The lively **Marché St-Maur** on Ave Lycée Guignabo 1km south of the centre caters mainly for locals, selling fresh food and other items, but is well worth a visit. Further south, vendors at the Centre Artisanal sell a wide variety of crafts from the area including woodcarvings and fabrics. This is also where the town's hustlers lurk.

Places to Stay – Budget

A good-value cheapie is *Auberge Kadiandou* south of the gare routière with small clean doubles for CFA3500. On the other side of town, *Restaurant Bambadinka* on Ave Cherif Bachir Aidara has filthy rooms for CFA2500 (up to three people), but this is only for the desperate. Nearby, and much better, *Hôtel le Bel Kady* just south of the market has been popular for years, with friendly management, good atmosphere and basic but decent rooms for CFA2500/3000, plus CFA1000 if you want a fan and mosquito net. Breakfast is CFA600, and meals cost from CFA800 to CFA1500.

About 3km west of the centre is *Centre Touristique de Colobane Fass*, with rooms and meals at CRI rates (for more details see

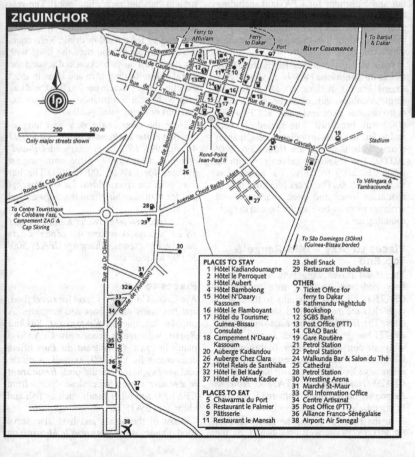

ZIGUINCHOR

SENEGAL

0   250   500 m
Only major streets shown

Ferry to Affiniam
Ferry to Dakar
Port
To Banjul & Dakar
River Casamance

Rue du Commerce
Rue du Général de Gaulle
Rue Javelier
Rue Fargues
Rue Lemoine
Rue Dialba
Rue de Truch
Rue du Dr
Rue de France
Rue de la Poste
Rue de Boucotte

Avenue Gavralho
Stadium

Rond-Point Jean-Paul II

Route de Cap Skiring
To Vélingara & Tambacounda

To Centre Touristique de Colobane Fass, Campement ZAG & Cap Skiring

Avenue Cherif Bachir Aidara

To São Domingos (30km) (Guinea-Bissau border)

Rue du Dr Oliver
Route de l'Aviation
Ave Lycée Guignabo

PLACES TO STAY
1 Hôtel Kadiandoumagne
2 Hôtel le Perroquet
3 Hôtel Aubert
4 Hôtel Bambolong
15 Hôtel N'Daary Kassoum
16 Hôtel le Flamboyant
17 Hôtel du Tourisme; Guinea-Bissau Consulate
18 Campement N'Daary Kassoum
20 Auberge Kadiandou
26 Auberge Chez Clara
27 Hôtel Relais de Santhiaba
32 Hôtel le Bel Kady
37 Hôtel de Néma Kadior

PLACES TO EAT
5 Chawarma du Port
6 Restaurant le Palmier
9 Pâtisserie
11 Restaurant le Mansah
23 Shell Snack
29 Restaurant Bambadinka

OTHER
7 Ticket Office for ferry to Dakar
8 Kathmandu Nightclub
10 Bookshop
12 SGBS Bank
13 Post Office (PTT)
14 CBAO Bank
19 Gare Routière
21 Petrol Station
22 Petrol Station
24 Walkunda Bar & Salon du Thé
25 Cathedral
28 Petrol Station
30 Wrestling Arena
31 Marché St-Maur
33 CRI Information Office
34 Centre Artisanal
35 Post Office (PTT)
36 Alliance Franco-Sénégalaise
38 Airport; Air Senegal

the boxed text 'Village Campements' at the end of the Ziguinchor section), plus CFA600 tourist tax. The ambience is slightly better at the nearby and identically priced *Campement ZAG* 100m further along the Cap Skiring road on your right. Both places also hire bicycles and arrange pirogue trips.

In the centre, the peaceful *Campement N'Daary Kassoum* has singles/doubles at CFA4000/5000 with shower, and CFA6000 for double with bathroom. A better deal is *Auberge Chez Clara*, just south of the town centre, with small rooms at CFA6000. Upstairs are some large clean airy rooms with fan and bathroom for CFA7000 including breakfast. This place has a family atmosphere, and Clara's husband plays in a jazz band, providing live music some evenings which can go on until late.

Also highly recommended is the *Hôtel Relais de Santhiaba* (☎ 991 11 99) off Ave Cherif Bachir Aidara. Small and basic singles/doubles with clean beds and mosquito nets are excellent value at CFA4000/6000 with breakfast. The shared showers and toilets are also very clean. Less spartan rooms with bathroom are from CFA7500/10,000. The restaurant serves good meals from CFA2200 to CFA2700, and pizzas from CFA1500. The hotel hires out decent mountain bikes and basic roadsters, and arranges tours by bike and/or boat in the surrounding area.

Places to Stay – Mid-Range & Top End

The *Hôtel Bambolong* between the ferry jetty and port has very nice rooms for CFA7500, but their proximity to the hotel's nightclub means disturbed sleep at weekends. The *Hôtel N'Daary Kassoum* (☎ 991 14 72) has good but rather austere rooms with air-con and modern bathroom for CFA11,000/13,000. The restaurant has an impressive looking menu with barracuda for CFA2900 and steaks for CFA3800. *Hôtel le Perroquet* on Rue du Commerce is similarly priced.

In the heart of town, the *Hôtel Aubert* (☎ 991 13 79) is well established, as the

beautiful gardens show, and good quality, with rooms for CFA12,500/15,000. Facilities include a small pool, car hire and an excellent restaurant, with meals for around CFA4000.

For many years the *Hôtel du Tourisme* on Rue de France has been popular with locals and visitors, and in 1997 the managers opened *Hôtel le Flamboyant* (☎ 991 22 23, fax 991 22 22, email flambzig@telecom plus.sn) opposite. Rooms with bathroom, air-con and TV are excellent value at CFA12,500/15,000. After a hot day on the road, it's tempting to leap off the balcony straight into the swimming pool! The restaurant offers pizzas from CFA1500 or main courses for around CFA3000. It's worth stopping by for a meal or drink; Veronique, the Frenchwoman who runs the hotel with her husband Philip, backpacked around the world before settling here and likes to meet travellers (and practise her English), and can help with local information, setting up excursions or hiring local guides.

Near the river is the new and tongue-twisting *Hôtel Kadiandoumagne* (☎ 991 11 46, fax 991 16 75), pronounced *kaj-and-oum-an*), a top quality place with singles/doubles for CFA15,600/19,200. The bar overlooks the river – ideal for sundowners and for watching birds and boats go up and down.

The fancy *Hôtel le Nema Kadior* (☎ 991 18 24) around 2km from the centre, caters mainly for groups, charging CFA27,500/33,000 for rooms.

Places to Eat

Ave Lycée Guignabo is good for *street food*, and has many cafes, bars and gargottes. A popular cheapie is *Restaurant Sokhna Busso*, with meals from only CFA350 a plate. In town, *Chawarma du Port* offers chawarmas for CFA700, as well as pizzas and sandwiches. Near the port, *Restaurant le Palmier* serves Senegalese dishes from CFA1000 and other meals such as fish and chips for CFA1500.

Most of the hotels and bars also serve food. Otherwise, *Restaurant le Mansah* on

Rue Javelier is recommended, with meals such as grilled chicken, *tiéboudienne* and prawn brochettes in *sauce piquant*, all with chips, for CFA1300.

Entertainment

Most hotels serve beers. The terrace bar at the *Hôtel le Flamboyant* is a good meeting place. For a more local feel, *Shell Snack* near Rond-Point Jean-Paul II does cold drinks and coffee, plus meals for CFA1000 to CFA1500. Also on the rond-point is the completely different *Walkunda Bar & Salon du Thé*, where beers are CFA900. The *Hôtel Bambolong* has a smart nightclub, while *Kathmandou* on Rue du Général de Gaulle is less flashy with cheaper drinks.

The jazz at *Auberge Chez Clara* (see Places to Stay earlier in this section) has been highly recommended.

Spectator Sports

Wrestling matches usually take place during the dry season on Sundays around 4 pm at the 'arena' (a dusty field) east of Ave Lycée Guignabo. For more information on this entertaining sport, see the boxed text 'Traditional Wrestling' in the Gambia chapter.

Getting There & Away

Air Air Senegal has an office (☎ 991 10 81) at the airport and flies daily to Dakar for CFA35,000. Some flights go via Banjul and some go to Cap Skiring.

Bus & Bush Taxi The gare routière is 1km east of the centre. Some sample fares (in CFA) are listed in the table.

Most transport to Dakar leaves between 7 am and noon, but there are also night buses that leave around midnight and reach Dakar at about noon. The fare is CFA3800 to CFA4500. You can get on the bus any time during the evening and sleep there until departure.

For details on routes to Serekunda (Gambia) and Bissau (Guinea-Bissau) see the main Getting There & Away section earlier in this chapter.

destination	504	minibus	bus
Bissau	2500	–	–
Cap Skiring	1250	900	–
Dakar	7000	4300	3800
Elinkine	1000	750	–
Kafountine	1500	750	–
Kaolack	5000	3000	2500
Kolda	2500	2000	–
Oussouye	1000	750	–
Serekunda (Gambia)	2500	–	–
Soma	2500	2000	–
Tambacounda	6000	4000	–

Boat The most interesting way to travel between Ziguinchor and Dakar is on the MS Joola which runs twice weekly in each direction via Île de Carabane. The boat departs Ziguinchor at noon on Thursday and Sunday. For more details of timetable and prices, see the main Getting Around section earlier in this chapter. Departure times may vary, so you should check details at the port (☎ 691 22 01).

Getting Around

Taxi The official rate for a taxi between Ziguinchor centre and the gare routière is CFA330. It's supposed to be the same for anywhere in town, but for longer rides you'll probably pay CFA500 to CFA750.

Car The set-up for hiring cars in Ziguinchor is quite informal, but Diatta International Tours (see Information earlier in this section) and most hotels will be able to help. Minor details such as insurance are sometimes a little hazy, but cars usually come with a driver which cuts the hassle with paperwork or deposits. Expect to pay around CFA 20,000 per day plus fuel. Another option is to hire a taxi; if you pay for fuel, the daily rate should be around CFA15,000.

Bicycle For getting around town, or for touring Casamance in relaxed style, you can't beat a bicycle. These can be hired from several hotels and campements (see Places to Stay earlier). Mountain bikes cost about CFA 5000 a day and old steel roadsters half this,

SENEGAL

although you can negotiate good deals if you hire one for a week or so.

AROUND ZIGUINCHOR

The **Ferme Animalière de Djibelor** is a small farm-cum-zoo-cum-nature-centre, 5km west of town on the road towards Cap Skiring. There's an interesting selection of tropical plants and animals, and you can stroll along pleasant paths through the forest. Admission is CFA1000.

Another popular day trip is a pirogue ride to the villages of **Affiniam** and **Djilapao** on the north bank of the River Casamance. For more information on Affiniam, see the separate entry in the Casamance Nord section later. At Djilapao you can visit some unusual two storey mud-brick buildings *(cases étages)* and the house of a local artist which is decorated with murals, some rather risqué. Most trips also go to the **Île des Oiseaux** where you can see pelican, flamingo, kingfisher, stork, sunbirds and many other species of birds.

You can arrange pirogue rides at some of the hotels or at Restaurant le Mansah on Rue Javelier where rates for day trips are around CFA15,000 per person including lunch. Local boatmen who loiter at the jetty near the Hotel Kadiandoumagne charge around CFA25,000 per boat, but this is negotiable, especially if you don't want lunch. Rates are also cheaper if you go for a shorter time, but this way you'll spend most of your trip crossing the river and miss the banks or mangrove creeks where the birds are more interesting. Once you've agreed on the trip duration, don't hand over the full payment until you get back.

A final option to consider is the public ferry – for more details see the Affiniam entry in the Casamance Nord section later.

BASSE CASAMANCE
Brin

Brin is on the road between Ziguinchor and Cap Skiring, where the track to Enampor branches off. *Campement le Filao* has bungalows in a lush garden, charging slightly lower than CRI prices. Brin is often over-

Village Campements

One of Casamance's major attractions are the places to stay called Campements Rurals Integrés (CRIs), often simply termed the 'village campement' (*campement du village*). They are built by villagers and run as cooperatives, with profits reinvested to build schools and health centres. Most CRI campements are built in a local style, with lighting by oil lamp, although most showers and toilets have running water. During the separatist fighting some campements became neglected and run-down. Assuming tourism picks up, the campements will swiftly be knocked back into shape.

Prices at all CRIs are standardised: bed (with mosquito net) CFA3000, breakfast CFA1800, three-course lunch or dinner CFA2500, full board CFA9800, beer CFA 750, soft drink CFA400 and mineral water CFA1000.

The CRI office is at the Centre Artisanal in Ziguinchor. Even if Casamance gets busier, their reservation system only works with at least a month's notice. As things stand, if you turn up on spec you'll almost certainly get a bed (although evening meals need a few hours warning, especially if you're vegetarian). If a campement is full, a room will be found for you at a private house in the village.

As well as the CRIs, there are now many privately owned campements with similar facilities and prices, although the profits go to the owner rather than to the village as a whole.

looked, but it's in a nice area. You can walk in the surrounding forest or fields, or take pirogue rides.

Enampor

The *village campement* charges standard CRI prices; it's a huge round mud house, called a *case à impluvium*, which is worth a visit even if you're not staying. Rainwater is funnelled into a large tank in the centre of the house through a hole in the roof (admitting a wonderful diffuse light). There are other such houses in Casamance, but this is a particularly good example. The grumpy manager will show you around for CFA250.

There's a daily minibus to Enampor from Ziguinchor in the afternoon (CFA400), returning in the morning.

Diohère

Diohère is a small village on the main road between Brin and Oussouye. Its *village campement* was closed in 1997; if it reopens, standard CRI prices will apply.

Niambalang

Niambalang is between Diohère and Oussouye The campement here is called *Chez Theodor Balouse* and visitors stay with the friendly Balouse family in very simple surroundings with rates lower than CRI prices, although several hours notice is required for meals.

Oussouye

Oussouye is between Ziguinchor and Cap Skiring, and the main town in Basse Casamance. It's a sleepy place, although the market gets lively on some mornings. For more activity, Casamance VTT (☎ 993 10 04) rents mountain bikes for CFA7000 per day and organises cycling, hiking and pirogue tours from CFA9500 per day. At Galerie Bahisen local artists make well-finished works in wood, terracotta and other traditional materials to contemporary designs.

Places to Stay & Eat The *village campement* is 1km north of town and is a beautiful example of local mud architecture, with two storeys, conical pillars and low doorways. Accommodation and meals are standard CRI prices. The *Auberge du Routard* near the village campement on the same road has nice bungalows and slightly higher rates. East of town, near the village of Edioungou (a centre for local pottery manufacture), the ambitiously large *Campement des Bolongs*

is in a tranquil setting overlooking the water, with singles/doubles for CFA5000/8000.

Restaurant 2000 on the main street in Oussouye has good cheap meals for around CFA700. Other places with similar prices are *Chez Rachel* in the market, *Restaurant Sud* on the main street, and *Khadim Rassoul* by the traffic circle. The nearby *Télécentre et Buvette du Rond-Point* is an ideal place for a quiet drink and any urgent phone calls you may need to make.

M'Lomp

On the tar road between Oussouye and Elinkine you'll pass through the village of M'Lomp, which has several two storey cases étages, and some other houses with brightly decorated walls and pillars, all unique to this part of West Africa. The old lady who lives in the largest *case étage* near the main road will give you a tour for a small fee. Tourists on day trips from Cap Skiring also visit M'Lomp, which explains the postcards of Rome and Mont Blanc proudly pinned to the wall, and the local youths outside offering cheap souvenirs.

In front of the largest *case étage* is an enormous fromager tree, at least 400 years old, and sacred in the village. Nearby, look for the museum of Diola culture, established by an enterprising young man who encourages local people to bring ancient implements and sacred objects so that traditional Diola customs can be preserved.

Pointe St George

Pointe St George lies to the north of M'Lomp on the River Casamance. The Hôtel Pointe St George remains closed, but a new *village campement* is almost finished, and local reports already have it billed as the best in the region.

Elinkine

Elinkine is a busy fishing village with a very pleasant atmosphere; from here you can get boats to Île de Carabane. The *village campement* charges standard CRI prices, with huts in a perfect setting among palm trees (complete with hammocks) on a sandy beach at the water's edge. *Campement le Fromager* is next to the road, with rates which are slightly lower, although it's a bit busier and noisier than the village campement.

Highly recommended is *Le Combassou*, a small and homely guesthouse run by a French-Casamançois couple. Bed and breakfast is CFA6000, with discounts for longer stays. The management is passionate about Casamance, and this place is ideal if you're looking for personal contacts and deeper insights.

Île de Carabane

Île de Carabane (sometimes spelt Karabane) is a beautifully peaceful island in the River Casamance. It was an important settlement and trading station in early colonial times, but it has now been almost totally reclaimed by bush. You can still see the ruined Breton-style church and the remains of a school. Along the beach is a cemetery with settlers' graves dating from the 1840s, many now half-covered in sand. The beach is good for swimming (you may see dolphins in the distance) and the island is also an excellent birdwatching site.

Places to Stay & Eat *Campement Barracuda* caters mainly for anglers – both locals and visitors – with a lively bar and half board at CFA6500. Fishing excursions cost CFA20,000 to CFA35,000 per boat. Shorter trips for birding or visiting local villages cost around CFA8000.

More tranquil and less macho is *Campement Badji Kunda* about 1km further along the beach, where prices are slightly higher, but a bed-only deal is just CFA4000. The owner is a sculptor and painter; his works (and those of other local artists) are on display or for sale here. If you're staying for a few days and you don't mind paying for materials, you can try your hand at local glass painting or pottery.

The delightful and well maintained *Hôtel Carabane* is set in a lush and shady tropical garden on the beach between the two campements. This was formerly a mission – the chapel is now the bar! – with rooms which

are very good value at CFA10,000/16,000 including breakfast and a three course *menu du jour* for CFA3500.

Getting There & Away Île de Carabane is reached by pirogue from Elinkine. There is no regular service, although there's usually a boat each evening which waits for the minibus to arrive from Ziguinchor. It comes back early next morning. Otherwise, you need to hang around on the waterfront until you see a boat leaving. The fare is CFA700 and the ride takes 30 minutes. Alternatively, you can charter a boat for about CFA5000 each way.

You can also get to Île de Carabane on the MS *Joola* which stops here on its trip between Dakar and Ziguinchor. For more information on times and fares, see the main Getting Around section earlier in this chapter.

Diakène Ouolof

The village of Diakène Ouolof is north of the road between Oussouye and Cap Skiring. *Campement Eguaye* is on an island near the village and is the most 'remote' campement in Basse Casamance. Rates are slightly higher than CRI prices, and birdwatching trips by pirogue can be arranged. A lift to Carabane costs CFA8000 for the boat. To reach the campement, get off at the junction 3km west of Diakène Diola. It's a 3km walk north along the sandy track to Diakène Ouolof, where you need to ask around for the owner, Abdou N'Diaye; he will paddle a canoe for you out to the campement.

CAP SKIRING

The beaches of Cap Skiring are some of the finest in West Africa. This is where you find several top end and mid-range hotels, plus several cheaper campements and a high concentration of foreigners. If you want a few easy days of sun and sand, this is the place. But if you're trying to see the 'real' Africa, pass on.

The village of Cap Skiring is 1km north of the junction where the main road from

Ziguinchor joins the north-south coast road. It has shops, restaurants, a market and gare routière. Just outside the village you can't miss the high walls of the Club Med complex, or the *prison touristique* as it's known locally. Most other hotels and campements are south of Cap Skiring, along the coast road towards Kabrousse, 5km away.

Places to Stay – Budget

There's a row of campements near the beach, close to the junction with the main Ziguinchor road. *Auberge de la Paix* is friendly but tatty, making the simple rooms a tad pricey at CFA3000 per person. The next door *Campement le Paradise* has more character and is better value. Spotless singles/doubles are CFA3000/5000 (or CFA8000/10,000 with bathroom) and meals in the attractively decorated bar are around CFA3000. *Campement M'Ballo* has a quiet and friendly feel and has rooms for CFA3000. Back from the beach, *Campement le Bakine* has half board from CFA5000, and traditional cultural evenings in the bar-restaurant, which are open to all.

Places to Stay – Mid-Range & Top End

Auberge le Palmier in Cap Skiring village has double rooms at CFA8000. The bar-restaurant serves meals from CFA5000 and seems particularly popular with visiting Frenchmen and local women. About 2km north, the plush *Hôtel Savana* has attractive bungalows from around CFA40,000 per person.

The *Hôtel la Paillote* (☎ 993 51 51, fax 993 51 17) has bungalows overlooking the ocean from CFA30,000 per person half board, and is renowned for its superb French food and refined ambience. It also has a private beach with water-sports equipment for hire.

South towards Kabrousse is the wonderful *Villa des Pêcheurs Aline Sitoe* (☎ 993 52 53, fax 993 51 80), a small, secluded place with just six rooms (all with bathroom) overlooking a tranquil stretch of beach. The managers have adopted the Casamance as their home and warmly welcome guests like friends

(they also speak some English). The atmosphere is convivial and the food is excellent. Fishing, boat trips and car hire can be arranged. For more information, including prices, contact the Hôtel le Flamboyant in Ziguinchor.

Near Kabrousse are the *Cap Casamance* and *Le Kabrousse* (☎ 993 51 19), two large and slightly pompous deluxe hotels, catering almost exclusively for groups. Half board in the high season is around CFA50,000/60,000. Further on is the infinitely preferable *Hôtel les Hibiscus* (☎ 993 14 36), a small and tasteful place in lush gardens on the beach, where cool bungalows decorated with stunning murals and local fabrics cost from CFA15,000 to CFA20,000 per person with breakfast.

Places to Eat

South of the row of campements, on the road towards Kabrousse, is the small and clean *Chez Max* bar-restaurant, with friendly atmosphere and good-value food such as sandwiches for CFA500 or chicken and chips for CFA1500.

Cap Skiring village has several cheap eateries with dishes in the CFA350 to CFA750 range. The smarter *Restaurant le Flamboyant* does meals between CFA1000 and CFA4000.

Up a grade is the *Restaurant la Pirogue*, near the Hôtel la Paillote, with a good three-course *menu* for CFA5000.

Getting There & Away

Bush taxis (CFA1250) and minibuses (CFA900) run regularly throughout the day between Ziguinchor and Cap Skiring, although there's more traffic in the morning.

Getting Around

Most hotels and campements have bicycles for hire and can arrange car hire or pirogue trips on the creeks inland from the coast. Day trips start at around CFA15,000 for the boat. Alternatively, you can arrange to be dropped off at Diakène Ouolof, Elinkine or Carabane. The repair shop in Cap Skiring also hires mobylettes.

SENEGAL

AROUND CAP SKIRING
Diembéring

To escape the hustle and bustle of Cap Skiring, head for Diembéring, 9km to the north, where its authentic African feel is in marked contrast to its touristy neighbour. The quiet and hassle-free beach is about 1km from the village. The spacious and peaceful *Campement Asseb* has rooms and meals at CRI rates. In the heart of the village, *Campement Aten-Elou* also has CRI-linked rates, but was hit harder than most by the drop in tourist numbers, although things may improve in future.

Diembéring can be reached by bicycle, although the road is sandy and hard work in the heat. A private taxi costs CFA5000 each way, or you can get the daily minibus from Ziguinchor, which passes through Cap Skiring around 5 pm and returns early next morning.

Parc National de Basse Casamance

This national park, east of Cap Skiring, contains tropical forest, open grassland, tidal mud flats and mangrove swamps, and animals include red colobus monkey and duiker, as well as a herd of forest buffalo and populations of bushbuck, porcupine, mongoose, crocodile and leopard. The park fee is CFA1000 per day, plus CFA5000 for a car. There's a good network of trails, plus *miradors* (hides) for viewing birds and animals.

Unfortunately, the park was closed at the time of research, as separatist rebels came through from their bases in neighbouring Guinea-Bissau (for more information, see the Warning box at the beginning of the Casamance section). The campement was also destroyed. If and when the park reopens, the best option is to stay in Oussouye and visit for the day by bike or taxi – but check the latest security situation first.

CASAMANCE NORD
Affiniam

Affiniam is a popular day trip destination from Ziguinchor (see the Around Ziguinchor section earlier). The main feature at Affini-am is the splendid *case à impluvium* (similar to the one at Enampor – see the Basse Casamance section earlier). It's worth staying longer than a day if you can to visit the surrounding area. The *village campement* charges standard CRI prices but the rooms are a little neglected, although bathrooms are clean and the manager is very friendly.

The public ferry from Ziguinchor runs several times a week. It stops at 'le port d'Affiniam' (about 1km from the campement) for one hour and then returns. The fare is CFA500. Alternatively, you can reach Affiniam by bike or car: turn off the main road from Ziguinchor about 8km south of Bignona and cross the barrage to the northeast of Affiniam. A short cut turns off the main road at Tobor, but this track is very sandy.

Tionk Essil

The village of Tionk Essil (also spelt Thionck-Essyl) is about 20km north-west of Affiniam, in the transition zone between the mangrove swamps and sandy forests, making its campement one of the most remote in Casamance. But getting here is well worth the effort; the surrounding area is peaceful and beautiful, and there's a remarkably good community spirit among the villagers. The *village campement* charges CRI prices, and the switched-on managers are very friendly and helpful. (When we passed through, the campement was occupied by the military so we were given lodgings in the mayor's house. That's how friendly they are here!)

Koubalan

Koubalan is about 2km east of the road between Ziguinchor and Bignona. The *village campement*, overlooking a quiet creek, charges standard CRI prices, and the welcoming manager keeps the place in good condition. Bush taxis run from Ziguinchor (CFA500) but, if the tide is right, you can come by pirogue almost to the door!

Bignona

Bignona is a crossroads town near the Trans-Gambia Highway junction. The basic *Hôtel le Kelumack* has singles/doubles at CFA3000/4000, but the old colonial-style *Hôtel le Palmier* is better, with rooms for CFA4000 (up to CFA7000 with bathroom) and breakfast for CFA700.

Baïla

Just off the main road between Bignona and Diouloulou, the *village campement* at Baïla is a quiet place with clean rooms and good food at standard CRI prices. It's run by a friendly manager who enjoys showing visitors around the village, which is off most tourist itineraries. It's also a very good place to see birds.

Diouloulou

This village is about 20km south of the Gambia border, where the road to Kafountine branches off the main route between Serekunda and Ziguinchor. The small *Campement Miriam* has simple bungalows for CFA1000 per person, or CFA3500 if you want a private bathroom (with bucket shower). Half board is CFA5000. We heard from two travellers who were promised music in the evening by the friendly manager. After sunset, the village electricity supply came on, and so did the radio!

KAFOUNTINE & ABÉNÉ

Kafountine and Abéné are on the coast, separated from the rest of Casamance Nord by a large branch of the River Casamance called Marigot Diouloulou (*marigot* means creek). Traditionally, this area looks more to the north than to the south: there's a relatively large proportion of Muslim Mandinka and Wolof mixed in with the Diola population, and people go to Brikama in Gambia for their shopping more often than they go to Ziguinchor.

The area has attracted artists from various parts of Senegal and Europe, and many of the campements arrange courses in drumming, dance and batik-making. This is a very good place to slow down for a few days and experience the local culture. Most weekends there's a performance somewhere; you just need to ask around.

Birdwatching

The creeks and lagoons around Kafountine are wonderful areas for watching birds, especially waders and shore birds. The most accessible place is the small pool near the Campement Sikoto. A bit further away are several *bolongs* (rivers) and *marigots* (creeks) which are also rewarding; the campements in Kafountine can arrange pirogue rides to reach these more easily.

The Sanctuaire Ornithologique de la Pointe de Kalissaye is a group of sandy islands at the mouth of the Marigot Kalissaye, but at the time of writing these were covered in water. Most birdwatchers now head for the highly rated Sanctuaire Ornithologique de Kassel, which is about 5km south-east of Kafountine.

Another place is the Presqu'ile des Oiseaux, a narrow spit of land between the ocean and a creek, noted for its huge populations of Caspian tern. It lies south of the Hotel Karone; the hotel's management can arrange trips by 4WD vehicle, and are happy to provide keen birdwatchers with more information.

Kafountine

Kafountine is a large, spread-out village about 2km from the ocean, at the end of the tar road from Diouloulou. On the coast is a large fish market and busy working beach. Fishing times depend on the tide, and it's fascinating to see the boats being launched or coming back after a long day at sea, surfing in on the rollers. Northwards, a huge empty beach leads up the coast past Abéné towards the Gambian border. This is a wonderful place for simply lounging in the sun, although the waves can make swimming dangerous.

Opinions vary about Kafountine itself; some travellers have found it tranquil, others call it 'pleasantly lively', while a few complain about local youths trying to sell souvenirs, touting boat rides or otherwise being a nuisance. A lot depends on your own attitude.

Places to Stay & Eat There are a few cheap eateries around the market, some with a couple of rooms, but most of the good places are beyond Kafountine village, just off the dirt road leading to the ocean, or along the beach. They all charge CFA2500 per person, although some have doubles for CFA3500, and offer meals from CFA1000 to CFA2500. These include the quiet, local-style *Campement Africa*, with good, clean huts in a sandy compound; the more basic *Campement le Kumpo*; and the large and well organised *Kunja Campement* with bungalows in a shady garden, shared bathroom and reliable running water.

At the end of the road, near the beach, *Campement le Filao* has bungalows with bathroom at CFA2500/3500/5000 for one/two/three people. It was run-down when we visited, but renovations are planned. About 100m from Le Filao is *A la Nature Resto-cases*, an elaborate two-storey venture with a hippyish feel, lush garden, hammocks, drummers and basic bungalows for CFA 2500 per person. Only the dirty bathrooms let this place down.

On the beach behind the Filao are a couple of cheap *gargottes* catering mainly for the local fishermen. Nearby are two more touristy places, offering meals from CFA1500 (advance notice required): *Le Senegalois* offers free tea while you flip through the menu, and *Soko Bantan* also has basic huts for CFA2000 per person.

On the beach about 700m north of the Filao the village-run *Campement Sitokoto* has rooms and meals at standard CRI prices. Rooms are basic but very clean and the shared bathrooms have running water.

North of here are several smarter places including *Fouta Djalon Campement-Hotel*, with bungalows in wonderful gardens. The French management offers half board for CFA13,300 plus bike hire, birding and fishing trips. Near the Fouta Djalon Campe-ment-Hotel is *Bateau Batik*, a cafe and fabric workshop where you can come for a drink, look at the batiks on exhibition, maybe buy one, or learn to make your own. Lessons cost CFA2500 per hour.

South from Kafountine, about 1km along the beach, is the clean, quiet and friendly *Campement-Hôtel Nandy* where simple rooms with bathroom cost CFA2500 per person, breakfast costs CFA1000 and other meals are around CFA2500. The only draw-back is its distance from the centre, but that's why it's so quiet. About 2km further south is the upmarket *Hôtel le Karone* (☎/fax 994 85 25) in extensive gardens right on the beach. Good quality thatched bunga-lows with air-con and hot shower cost CFA17,600 per person for half board.

Getting There & Away From Ziguinchor bush taxis run direct to Kafountine. Or take any vehicle heading for Serekunda and change at Diouloulou, from where local bush taxis run to Kafountine for CFA500.

You can also get bush taxis to Kafountine from Serekunda or Brikama (Gambia), al-though some traffic goes via the back road and the sleepy Darsalam border rather than the main crossing at Seleti. Brikama to Kafountine is CFA1200 (D30). Another option is to cross the border just south of Kartung.

All bush taxis stop in the centre of Kafountine, from where shared taxis travel down the dirt road to the fishing beach.

Getting Around Bicycles can be hired from a shop in the market, and from some of the campements. Rates are standardised at CFA2500 per day but the quality varies considerably, and rates may be negotiable.

Abéné

Abéné is north of Kafountine, with a selec-tion of places to stay in the village and on the beach. It's much quieter than Kafountine and harder to reach by local transport, so prepare for a few kilometres of hot walking.

In the heart of the village is the relaxed but well organised *Campement la Bell Danielle*, charging CFA2300 per person, or

CFA5400 for half board. Bikes and excursions are available.

From the village it's 2km along a sandy track to the beach, where **Restaurant Chez Vero** has meals for around CFA2000. Next door, the smart **Casamar** has cool white bungalows in an extensive garden, charging CFA4900 per person, and CFA10,000 for half board. Near the Casamar is the similarly priced German-managed **Maison Sunjata** and the village-run **Campement Samaba Diabang**, which charges standard CRI prices.

Along the beach is the more upmarket and very friendly French-run **Campement le Kossy**, where comfortable bungalows in a beautiful bougainvillea-laden garden cost CFA5000 per person. Next door is the relaxed **O'Dunbaye Land Ecole de Danse**, known as Chez Thomas, where high quality drum and dance lessons cost CFA8500 per session. Simple accommodation is also available, with half board for CFA6000 per person.

A few kilometres further north is the more expensive **Village-Hôtel Kalissai** (☎ 993 51 88, fax 993 51 17), which has air-con bungalows in a shady palm grove and manicured gardens very near the beach at CFA24,000 for half board.

All public transport between Diouloulou and Kafountine stops at the turn-off 2km from Abéné, near a village called **Diannah**. A traveller wrote to recommend Diannah's simple and relaxed **Campement Badala**, charging CFA3000 per person.

HAUTE CASAMANCE
Sédhiou & Kolda

East of Ziguinchor, Sédhiou and Kolda may be on your way to or from Tambacounda, or form part of a loop through this little visited part of Casamance. Sédhiou is on the north bank of the river, where **Hôtel la Palmeraie** caters mostly for hunting and fishing, with smart air-con single/double bungalows for CFA12,500/20,000. Local bush taxis go from Tanaf to Sandinièr, from where a ferry crosses to Sédhiou. There are also bush taxis which go between Sédhiou and Bounkiling on the Trans-Gambia Highway.

Kolda is a larger place, where very few travellers stop, but it has an easy atmosphere and friendly people – ideal for experiencing typical southern Senegalese life. The **Hôtel Hobbe** has rooms for CFA11,000/16,250; the **Hôtel Moya** is cheaper with doubles at CFA7800. There's good **street food** near the market, and bar-restaurants include **Restaurant Teddingal** and **Chez Bintu** serving evening meals from CFA1000 to CFA2500. The **Bamboo Bar** opposite the Moya is also good for a drink, while **Fuladou Dance Club** attracts Kolda's bright young things at weekends.

Eastern Senegal

Eastern Senegal is hot and flat, with a dry savanna landscape covered by bush and baobab trees. In the far south-east the plains give way to the rolling foothills of the Fouta Djalon in neighbouring Guinea. The region's main attraction is Parc National du Niokolo-Koba – one of the largest parks in West Africa – where visitors have a good chance of seeing large mammals. The town of Kedougou and surrounding Bassari Country also attracts adventurous travellers wanting to explore the green hills and picturesque villages that contrast strikingly with other parts of the country.

TAMBACOUNDA

Tambacounda is a major crossroads town and the gateway to Eastern Senegal. It has two main streets: Blvd Demba Diop, which runs east-west parallel to the train tracks, and Ave Leopold Senghor, which runs north-south. The latter has shops (including the well stocked Nouvelle Epicerie) and the SGBS bank which changes money and gives cash advances on a Visa card. The main gare routière (called *garage* here) is at the southern end of town, west of Ave Leopold Senghor). Taxis around town, eg from the train station to the main *garage*, are CFA250.

Places to Stay

The unmarked **Chez Dessert** on Ave Leopold Senghor has been a shoestringers favourite

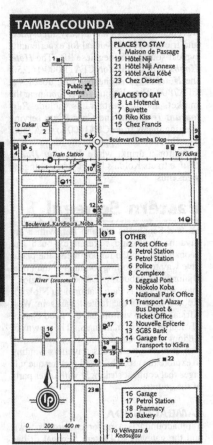

TAMBACOUNDA

PLACES TO STAY
1 Maison de Passage
19 Hôtel Niji
21 Hôtel Niji Annexe
22 Hôtel Asta Kébé
23 Chez Dessert

PLACES TO EAT
3 La Hotencia
7 Buvette
10 Riko Kiss
15 Chez Francis

OTHER
2 Post Office
4 Petrol Station
5 Petrol Station
6 Police
8 Complexe Leggaal Pont
9 Niokolo Koba National Park Office
11 Transport Alazar Bus Depot & Ticket Office
12 Nouvelle Epicerie
13 SGBS Bank
14 Garage for Transport to Kidira
16 Garage
17 Petrol Station
18 Pharmacy
20 Bakery

To Dakar
Public Garden
Train Station
Boulevard Demba Diop
To Kidira
Avenue Léopold Senghor
Boulevard Kandioura Noba
River (seasonal)
0   200   400 m
To Vélingara & Kedougou

Places to Eat

There's a wide choice of *gargottes* at the main *garage*, and another cluster of cheap eateries around the junction where the street to the main *garage* turns off Ave Leopold Senghor. The *buvette* near the junction of Blvd Diop and Ave Leopold Senghor has deck chairs, shade, cold drinks, snacks and sometimes other meals on offer.

The most popular spot in town is *Restaurant-Bar Chez Francis* on Ave Leopold Senghor, serving good meals for around CFA2000 and small beers for CFA500. Similarly priced are *Riko Kiss*, a quiet place with nice outdoor seating (but no beer); *La Hotencia*, near the station; and the outlandishly large *Complex Leggaal Pont*, also a nightclub.

Getting There & Away

Bus & Bush Taxi From the *garage* on the eastern side of town vehicles go to the Mali border at Kidira (CFA4000 by Peugeot 504, CFA2700 by minibus). Vehicles to most other destinations go from the larger *garage* on the southern side of town. (It swarms with touts, so watch your gear.) A minibus to Vélingara is CFA1000, from where you can cross into Gambia. To Dakar by 504 is CFA 6300, and by bus CFA4400. The safe and comfortable Transport Alazar bus, Le Car Mouride, leaves daily at 6 am for Dakar (CFA4000) and Kaolack (CFA2500), but buy a ticket from the Transport Alazar ticket office just south of the train station early the day before to get a good seat. If you're heading for Guinea, most days a battered bush taxi goes to Koundara via Medina Gounas and Sambaïlo (where you may have to change); this rough, slow trip costs around CFA8000.

Train The express train between Dakar and Bamako (Mali) comes through Tambacounda twice a week in each direction. For more details see the main Getting There & Away section of this chapter. Heading for Bamako it passes through Tambacounda on Wednesday and Saturday evening; the timetable says it departs at 18.59, but it's usually

for many years. Beds in simple rooms are CFA3000 per person. Breakfast is CFA1000, and there is a small kitchen where you can prepare your own food. To the north of Chez Dessert are the *Hôtel Niji*, which has good singles/doubles with bathroom for CFA 8200/10,700, and the top end *Hôtel Asta Kébé* (☎ 981 10 28, fax 981 17 44) with rooms at CFA18,600/23,200 and a swimming pool which nonguests can use for CFA2000. West of the centre, *Keur Khoudia* offers bungalows with air-con and bathroom for CFA12,300/17,000.

nearer 9 pm. Officially, a section of seating is reserved for passengers who board at Tambacounda. In reality, 2nd class is nearly always full, but 1st class tickets are usually available. Fares from Tambacounda are CFA5000/6900 (2nd/1st class) to Kayes and CFA14,200/19,400 to Bamako. Look out for touts selling unused tickets on the platform, but make sure your ticket relates to a real seat!

PARC NATIONAL DU NIOKOLO-KOBA

Niokolo-Koba is Senegal's major national park, a beautiful area of wilderness covering about 900,000 hectares, designated as a World Heritage site and International Biosphere Reserve. The landscape is relatively flat, with plains which become marshy after rain, interspersed with hills – the highest is **Mt Assirik** (311m) in the south-east. The

park is transected by the River Gambia and two tributaries – the Niokolo-Koba and the Koulountou. Vegetation includes dry savanna woodland and grassland, gallery forest, patches of bamboo and marshland.

Some 350 species of bird and about 80 species of mammal inhabit the park, including African classics such as lion and leopard, and the last few elephant in Senegal. These are very rarely seen (apart from the leopards in the enclosure near Simenti), but you have a good chance of spotting waterbuck, bushbuck, kob, baboon, monkeys (green and hussar), warthog, roan antelope, giant Derby eland, hartebeest and possibly buffalo. Chimpanzee troops are occasionally seen in the eastern part of the park. Hippo and three types of crocodile – Nile, slender-snouted and dwarf – live in the rivers.

The park was neglected until the early 1990s, and poaching became a problem, but

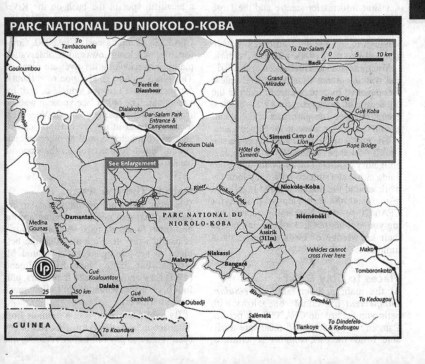

recent international funding for development as part of the Parc Transfrontalier Niokolo-Badiar trans-national ecosystem (which includes areas in neighbouring Guinea) is likely to improve the situation.

During the rains, and until late November, most park tracks are impassable. In December and January, conditions are pleasantly cool, but the best viewing time for wildlife is during the hot season in April and May, when the vegetation has withered and animals congregate at water holes.

A useful book is *Les Grands Mammiferes du Niokolo-Badiar,* available at the park entrance. It's mostly in French, but has useful pictures and animal names in English and German, as well as their scientific titles.

Information

The main access point for Parc National du Niokolo-Koba is **Simenti**, about an hour's drive from the park entrance at Dar-Salam. A visitor information centre and the large Hôtel de Simenti are here. Many animals are concentrated around the Simenti area, although to see a wider selection you have to travel into the eastern sector of the park.

You must be in a vehicle to enter the park, and walking is not usually allowed unless accompanied by a park ranger. Even in the dry season all tracks require 4WD vehicles, except between the park gate and Simenti and on some other tracks in the Simenti area.

The entrance fee is CFA2000 per person and CFA5000 per vehicle for 24 hours. It is obligatory to hire an official park-approved guide either at Tambacounda (they look for work around the popular tourist hotels and restaurants), the park gate or Simenti, for CFA6000 per day. They are good at showing you around, but lack of training means their knowledge of birds and animals is limited.

Places to Stay & Eat

At the main park entrance, *Dar-Salam Campement* has double bungalows with bathroom for around CFA3000 per person. Camping is possible, and meals are available. Inside the park *camping* is permitted,

although this is very unusual and there are no facilities at all.

Most people stay at *Hôtel de Simenti*, a large, ugly building, but in an excellent position overlooking the River Gambia. Plain rooms are CFA14,000/19,000 and simple thatched huts are CFA7000 for one or two people. Breakfast is CFA1200, and good and filling meals are served for CFA4200. The hotel organises half-day drives for CFA6000 per person (minimum of four people), and the nearby visitor centre offers boat rides for CFA3500 per person (with a minimum of two people and a maximum five) or walks in the bush with a ranger for CFA2500. You can also walk to a nearby hide overlooking a water hole/grazing area (depending on the season), where you'll almost certainly see as many animals as you would from the back of a vehicle.

Camp du Lion is a small campement 6km east of Simenti (reachable without 4WD) in a beautiful spot in the bush on the River Gambia. Very simple huts cost CFA6000 plus CFA600 per person, and meals are CFA3000. Camping costs CFA3000. Comfortable stone bungalows and an observation platform overlooking the river are planned. This place isn't so good if you're without car, as they don't have a vehicle or boat for excursions. The only place you can walk to from here is the nearby Pointe de Vue, overlooking a bend in the river. Hippo can be sighted from here, as well as other animals coming down to the river on the opposite bank to drink.

Getting There & Away

Whatever transport option you take, remember that morning and evening are the best times to see animals, so a one day trip is hardly worth it. Note also that the best place to see chimpanzees is around Mt Assirik, but getting here from Simenti (4WD is essential) can take four hours, plus four hours back, which doesn't allow much time for viewing.

By public transport, take a minibus from Tambacounda heading towards Kedougou (you'll have to pay full fare, CFA2000) and get off at the Dar-Salam entrance, where you can try hitching into the park. Or ask the Keur Khoudia hotel in Tambacounda (which has the same management as the Hôtel Simenti) if their staff vehicle has space for extra passengers.

Taxi Hire Most travellers hire a taxi (Peugeot 504) in Tambacounda to at least reach the Simenti area (although to see more of park, you need a 4WD). Rates are around CFA25,000 per day, with fuel. Those who haggle hard can get it down to CFA15,000. To this price add entrance fees (for you and the car), food and accommodation, plus the obligatory guide. Teaming up with other travellers obviously works out cheaper. The driver pays for his own food and accommodation, where necessary (the campement does not charge drivers).

If you don't want to launch headlong into haggling, ask the *chef du garage* (who has the respect of all the drivers) to help you find something suitable. Before clinching a deal, carefully check the taxi's condition, and if the rains have not long finished call at the main park headquarters in Tambacounda to ensure the track to Simenti is passable by 2WD.

We met some Dutch travellers who hired a taxi to take them to Simenti. They stayed at the hotel for three nights, going out for walks, car safaris and boat rides – all arranged on the spot. On the fourth day they hitched a ride onwards with some other tourists.

Car Rental Another option is to arrange car hire with official guides in Tambacounda. This costs around CFA40,000 per day including fuel, driver and an entrance charge for the car. To this, add your own costs (accommodation, entry etc) and the guide fee. An all-inclusive two day tour (car, fuel, driver, guide, entry for car and passengers, boat ride, food and accommodation at Camp du Lion) costs a total of CFA120,000 for four people.

Hôtel Niji and Hôtel Asta Kébé also have cars for hire, and arrange tours, starting at CFA60,000 per day for a car with fuel, or CFA50,000 per person per day all-inclusive.

BASSARI COUNTRY

The far south-east corner of Senegal is often called Bassari Country after the local Bassari people, who are particularly noted for their traditional way of life and picturesque villages. The Bassari often feature on tour itineraries, but they are in fact just one of many tribes who inhabit this area. Other groups include Wolof, Bambara, Malinké, Fula and Bedik.

The landscape is hilly – a northern extension of neighbouring Guinea's Fouta Djalon region – and well vegetated, making it a pleasant contrast to the hot and dusty plains elsewhere in Senegal, and an increasingly popular destination for hiking. Only a few years ago, you would have had a hard time explaining why you wanted to go walking in the bush to the tops of nearby hills. Now the guides find you.

Kedougou

Kedougou is the starting point for visits to Bassari Country. It has lost some of its remote feel now the new tar road from Tambacounda links it to the rest of Senegal, but it's still a relaxed town, with an interesting mix of people and a busy market. Other facilities include a petrol station and télécentre.

Places to Stay & Eat Your choice of places to stay includes the tranquil *Campement Diaw* with double huts for CFA5000, and the similarly priced but livelier *Campement Moïse* where the bar-restaurant is a popular meeting spot. Both arrange tours in the surrounding area, or to Parc National du Niokolo-Koba. The upmarket *Relais* is aimed mainly at hunters and has double huts for CFA8600 and an annexe called *Hippo Lodge Safari* about 4km out of town.

There's a good choice of *cheap eateries* around the market and garage. In the same area, *Restaurant Sirimana* has a nice dining room and breezy patio, with basic meals from CFA600 and more elaborate evening meals for around CFA1500.

SENEGAL

Getting There & Away Tambacounda to Kedougou is CFA2000 in a minibus and CFA3000 in a Peugeot 504. The main road goes straight through Parc National du Niokolo-Koba (a source of great controversy when it was widened and tarred), but park fees are not payable if you are just in transit. Minibuses occasionally go to the town of Mali (also called Mali-ville) in Guinea, from where a 504 to Labé is GF7000.

Around Kedougou

Kedougou makes an excellent base from which to explore the many traditional villages in the surrounding hills on foot, by bush taxi or a combination of the two. Bicycles can also be hired at some of the campements.

One of the nearest villages is **Bandafassi**, noted for its basket-makers. There's a shop selling cold drinks where you can refuel before hiking to the top of the nearby hill which gives wonderful views. **Ibel** is a mainly Fula village 7km west of Bandafassi, and from here it's another 2km uphill to the Bedik village of **Iwol**, dominated by a huge and sacred baobab tree.

Salémata, 75km west of Kedougou by good dirt road, is in the heart of Bassari Country. The surrounding hills – some more than 400m high – are beautiful, and chimpanzees can be seen here occasionally. The best day to arrive is Tuesday, when the *lumo* (weekly market) is held. Every year (usually in May) there's a major Bassari circumcision ceremony held here. Salémata has a small and friendly *campement*, where double huts are CFA7500 and meals are around CFA3500. Steep prices, but you pay for the remote location. A good day-walk from here is to **Etiolo**, a 15km round trip.

The village of **Dindefelo** is about 30km south of Kedougou. The lumo is on Sunday, when the village is lively and there's quite a lot of traffic. The Casamance-style *village campement* charges CFA2500 per person.

From the campement you can hike 2km to a spectacular waterfall with a deep green pool at the bottom, wonderful for cooling off in, but only in the dry season. We heard from some readers who swam here during the rainy season and were nearly swept away as 'the quiet creek was transformed into a dangerous torrent in a few minutes'. The campement will insist you take a guide to reach the waterfall, but it isn't really necessary. They also try to charge for looking at the waterfall, although the money is reportedly for the village fund.

Onwards from Kedougou

We had a very interesting report from Belgian traveller Arne van Dongen about his rather unusual route into Guinea.

Arne reached Dindefelo from Kedougou by bush taxi easily enough, and after visiting the waterfall, started to look around for something going further south. There was a minibus to Mali-ville, the first town in Guinea, but after waiting for a day it was still only half full and showed no signs of leaving. So Arne decided to walk. The campement manager introduced him to a Fula trader who had come from Mali-ville to sell at the *lumo* and was now returning home. They walked for three days through the bush, mostly uphill, covering about 70km along narrow paths which were too steep in places even for donkeys. There are very few villages, so Arne and his companion carried food, but stayed in remote huts each night where the locals are used to traders passing through on this route (but not European backpackers!).

In Mali-ville, Arne registered his arrival with the police, and shortly afterwards he saw the minibus from Kedougou finally arrive!

Sierra Leone

After more than eight months of junta rule, much of Sierra Leone is now calm. The watershed event of 1998 was the reinstatement of President Ahmed Tejan Kabbah in March, after which Sierra Leoneans could begin the long process of recovery from junta destruction, and from the civil war which ravaged much of the country from the early 1990s until late 1996. Despite these positive developments, Sierra Leone is still not a place for independent travellers. While the government controls major towns, rebel fighting continues in some areas in the east and north and the overall security situation remains tenuous.

Should the situation stabilise, Sierra Leone holds many attractions, including beautiful beaches, lush and varied tropical landscapes, a dynamic culture and friendly people.

Facts about Sierra Leone

HISTORY

The region now called Sierra Leone was on the southern edge of the great Empire of

SIERRA LEONE AT A GLANCE

Capital: Freetown
Population: 4.6 million
Area: 72,325 sq km
Head of state: President Ahmed Tejan Kabbah
Official language: English
Main local languages: Krio, Mende, Temne
Currency: Leone
Exchange rate: US$1 = Le1000
Time: GMT/UTC
Country telephone code: ☎ 232
Best time to go: Mid-November

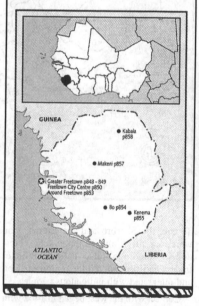

Mali, which flourished between the 13th and 15th centuries (for more details on this and other early empires, see the History section in the Facts about the Region chapter). Early inhabitants included the

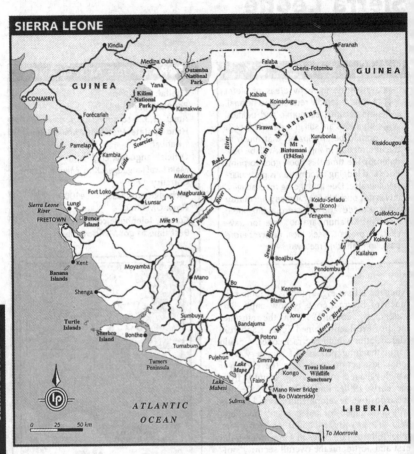

SIERRA LEONE

Temne, the Sherbro and the Limba, who were organised into independent chiefdoms. Mandingo (also called Malinké) traders had also entered the region early on and integrated with indigenous peoples.

Contact with the west began in 1462 with the arrival of Portuguese navigators who called the area Serra Lyoa (Lion Mountain), later modified to Sierra Leone. Around 120 years later, Sir Francis Drake stopped here during his voyage around the world. However, the British did not control the area until the 18th century when they began to dominate the slave trade along the West African coast.

The turmoil of the American War of Independence in the 1770s provided an opportunity for thousands of slaves to gain freedom by fighting for Britain. (Slavery was still legal in Britain, but a 1772 court ruling had determined that a freed slave was free for life.) When the war ended, over 15,000 ex-slaves made their way to London, where they suffered unemployment and poverty. In 1787, a group of philanthropists – inspired by John Wesley's religious revival to improve the conditions of the poor – purchased 52 sq km of land near Bunce Island in present-day Sierra Leone from a local chief for the purpose of founding a 'Province of Freedom' in Africa for the ex-slaves. This became Freetown. That same year, the first group of about 400 men and women (300 ex-slaves and 100 Europeans) arrived.

Within three years, all but 48 settlers had died of disease or in fights with the local inhabitants, or had deserted. But in 1792 the determined British philanthropists sent a second band of settlers, this time 1200 ex-slaves who had fled from the USA to Nova Scotia. Later, they sent 550 more from Jamaica. To the chagrin of the philanthropists, some settlers, both white and black, joined in the slave trade. In 1808, the British government took over the Freetown settlement and declared it a colony.

The Colonial Period

By the early 1800s, slavery had been abolished in Britain. Over the next 60 years, British warships plied the West African coast, trying to intercept slave ships destined for America. Freetown became the depot for thousands of 'recaptives' from all over West Africa as well as many migrants from the hinterland. By 1850, over 100 ethnic groups were represented in the colony. Yet they lived in relative harmony, each group in a different section of town.

Like the previous settlers, the recaptives became successful traders and intermarried, and all non-indigenous blacks became known collectively as Krios. Many were Christian, and received an education at Fourah Bay College outside Freetown. British administrators favoured the Krios and appointed many to senior posts in the civil service.

Towards the end of the 19th century, the tide started to turn against the Krios, who were outnumbered 50 to one by the indigenous people. Britain declared the hinterland a protectorate and imposed a hut tax, which led to a war between the two groups in which many Krios were killed. Lebanese merchants began migrating to the area, and by WWI had displaced the Krios as the leading traders with the tribes of the interior. In Freetown, British entrepreneurs favoured the more tractable indigenous people, thus squeezing Krio merchants out of business.

In 1924, the British administrators established a legislative council with elected representatives, to the advantage of the more numerous indigenous people. Many Krios, who continued to monopolise positions within the civil service, reacted by allying with the British. While other colonies clamoured for independence, they proclaimed loyalty to the Crown, and one group even petitioned against the granting of independence. They were far from enamoured of Wallace Johnson, a liberal Krio journalist, who led the independence movement in the 1930s.

Independence

When independence was achieved in 1961, it seemed that western-style democracy would work. There were two parties of roughly equal strength but they became divided along ethnic lines. The Sierra Leone People's Party (SLPP) was the party of the Mendes (the dominant ethnic group in southern Sierra Leone), and represented the tribal structure of the old colony. The All People's Congress (APC), formed by trade unionist Siaka Stevens, became identified with the Temnes of the north and voiced the dissatisfaction of the small, modernising elite. The Krio community threw its support behind the SLPP, whose leader, Milton Margai, became the first prime minister.

Following Margai's death in 1964, his brother Albert took over and set about replacing the Krios in the bureaucracy with Mendes. The Krios took revenge in the 1967 elections by supporting the APC, which won a one seat majority. A few hours after the results were announced, a Mende military officer led a coup, placing Siaka Stevens under house arrest. Two days later, fellow officers staged a second coup, vowing to end the corruption that was so widespread under the Margai brothers.

SIERRA LEONE

Stevens went into exile in Guinea and with a group of Sierra Leoneans began training in guerrilla warfare techniques for an invasion. This became unnecessary when a group of private soldiers mutinied and staged a third coup 13 months later – an African record for the number of coups in such a short period.

Siaka Stevens returned and formed a new government, but his first decade in office was turbulent. He declared a state of emergency, banned breakaway parties from the APC and tried a number of SLPP members for treason. Meanwhile, the economy continued to deteriorate. The iron-ore mine closed, diamond revenues dropped, living costs increased, students rioted, and Stevens again declared a state of emergency. The 1978 election campaign resembled a mini civil war between the major ethnic groups; the death toll topped 100. Stevens won, and Sierra Leone became a one party state. Politically, matters calmed down, but the economy continued to stagnate and the country sank deeper into debt.

Despite the one party system, the 1982 elections were the most violent ever. Stevens was forced to give Mendes and Temnes equal representation in the cabinet, although this did not stop deterioration of economic and social conditions. With virtually no support left, Stevens finally stepped down in 1985 at the age of 80, naming as his successor Major General Joseph Momoh, head of the army.

Under Momoh, the economy continued its downward spiral. By 1987 the inflation rate was one of the highest in Africa, budget deficits were astronomical, and smugglers – allegedly with close government connections – continued to rob Sierra Leone of up to 90% of its diamond revenue. Foreign exchange reserves dried up, and only with occasional loans from members of the powerful Lebanese business community was the government able to halt total economic collapse.

Things worsened in late 1989 when civil war broke out in neighbouring Liberia. By early 1990, thousands of Liberian refugees had fled into Sierra Leone. The following year, fighting spilled across the border and Sierra Leonean rebels opposed to Momoh took over much of the eastern part of the country.

Through 1990 and early 1991 there was growing clamour for reform and multiparty democracy, but the Momoh government used the war in the east as an excuse to postpone elections. Finally, in September 1991, a new constitution was adopted to allow for a multiparty system. But in April 1992, before an election date could be announced, a group of young military officers overthrew Momoh. The National Provisional Ruling Council (NPRC) was set up, and 27-year-old Captain Valentine Strasser was sworn in as head of state. Despite an attempted coup later that year and the execution of at least 25 suspects, Strasser was a popular leader. Elections and a return to civilian rule were promised for 1995. Economic reforms started to have effect and a campaign encouraging people to pay their income tax was successful.

Soon, however, the optimism began to fade. A major drain on resources was the continuing fighting in the east against the antigovernment rebels, now called the Revolutionary United Front (RUF). They were bolstered after the coup by supporters of the previous Momoh regime, and by escaping rebels from Liberia. It soon became apparent that none of these groups were fighting for a political objective, but rather to control the territory and its diamond and gold fields. By late 1994 northern and eastern parts of the country had descended into near anarchy with private armies led by local warlords, government soldiers, rebel soldiers and deserters from both sides (Sierra Leone and Liberia) roaming the area at will and terrorising local communities.

In January 1996, Strasser was overthrown in a coup by Brigadier General Julius Maada Bio. Despite NPRC efforts at postponement, previously scheduled elections went ahead, and in March, Ahmed Tejan Kabbah – leader of the SLPP – was elected president. Kabbah's government continued peace talks with the RUF that had been initiated by the previous military government. In November 1996, a peace agreement was finally signed, officially ending almost six years of civil war.

During the six month respite following the accord, over 500,000 internally displaced Sierra Leoneans returned to their communities. However, progress was short lived. On 25 May 1997, a group of junior military officers staged a coup in Freetown. President Kabbah fled to neighbouring Guinea, and a wave of looting, terror and brutality engulfed the capital. Guerrilla warfare spread throughout much of the country, perpetrated by a junta comprising disenchanted military and RUF rebels. By early 1998, there were few areas that had not been affected. Food and fuel supplies were scarce almost everywhere, and thousands of Sierra Leoneans had fled the country.

In February 1998, a Nigerian-led West African peacekeeping force (ECOMOG), succeeded in ousting the junta leaders and in taking control of Freetown and many upcountry areas – although not before fleeing rebels had looted and destroyed much in their path. President Kabbah was reinstated in March. The next presidential election is scheduled for 2000.

While daily life in many areas is returning to normal, Sierra Leone still has a long road ahead before the causes underlying the conflicts of the past decades can be addressed and a stable political situation created.

GEOGRAPHY

The coastal zone, consisting of mangrove swamps, beaches and islands, is flat except for the 40km-long Freetown peninsula – the only place in West Africa where mountains rise near the sea. Inland is an undulating, forested and extensively cultivated plateau. In the north-east are the Loma Mountains; south of these are the twin towns of Koidu and Sefadu in Kono, the country's major diamond area.

Only about 5% of Sierra Leone's original forest cover remains today, much of it destroyed by mining and detrimental agricultural practices.

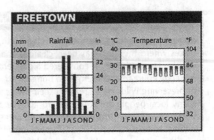

CLIMATE

Sierra Leone is one of the wettest countries in West Africa, with an average annual rainfall of over 3150mm. The rainy season stretches from mid-May to November, with July and August the wettest months. Humidity is particularly high in the coastal regions, although sea breezes afford some relief. The country's annual average temperature is 27°C; inland it gets much warmer. December and January are the coolest, driest months, but skies can be hazy from the harmattan (desert winds).

FLORA & FAUNA

Despite its small size, Sierra Leone is endowed with a broad range of vegetation zones, home to a variety of bird and animal species. The government has established several parks and reserves where this wildlife can be protected, although due to the security situation most are now off limits to tourists. These include the Gola Forest Reserve and Tiwai Island Wildlife Sanctuary near Kenema, and Mamunta-Mayoso Wildlife Sanctuary and Outamba-Kilimi National Park in the north of the country. For more details, see the individual entries later in this chapter, or contact the Conservation Society of Sierra Leone (☎ 229716) at 4 Sanders St, Freetown, which has a reference library and dated but interesting leaflets about the country's protected wildlife areas. Alternatively, you could contact the Forestry Division's Wildlife Conservation Branch (☎ 225352) in the Government Building at Tower Hill in Freetown.

SIERRA LEONE

Wildlife Conservation in Sierra Leone

Many Sierra Leoneans, particularly in the north, view farmland and settlements favourably as places where the bush has been cleared, and where the morals of their ancestors can be upheld. The bush itself is considered a dangerous place of threatening supernatural powers, requiring courage and strength to bring it within the farming cycle. Thus, the western notion of preserving wilderness areas for their own sake is not always shared by traditional people. Many local people are struggling to achieve a better standard of living or, in some cases, simply to survive. Most protected nature areas include lands of subsistence farmers, but it's difficult to be a conservationist if your family is hungry.

Although western attitudes towards the environment may seem incompatible with local concepts, it is still possible to protect natural ecosystems without local people having to give up their beliefs or ambitions. To do this, conservationists and government officials must create a situation where protecting natural areas and indigenous plant and animal life will offer significant practical advantages for local people.

Before the 1997 coup, several groups were working together with communities to identify areas of compatibility and to prevent further environmental degradation. The Conservation Society of Sierra Leone (CCSL) supports schemes where local people are involved in setting up protected areas and benefiting from them in a tangible manner. Another group, the Environmental Foundation for Africa (EFA, also known as ENFOSAL), focuses on increasing awareness and education while working via community-based projects to reclaim lands destroyed by mining or detrimental agricultural practices.

To support the work of CCSL, you can buy the booklet *Wildlife & Nature Reserves* (from which parts of this section were extracted) and other leaflets from their offices in Freetown (see the Flora & Fauna section in this chapter) or visit one of the reserves described in this chapter should the security situation stabilise. EFA has several short but informative videos highlighting the frightening degree of environmental damage that has already been inflicted on many areas of Sierra Leone and suggesting ways to counteract further degradation. They can be contacted in Freetown at ☎ 232347 or in the UK (☎ 0171-834 6120; from 22 April 2000 ☎ 020-7834 6120).

GOVERNMENT & POLITICS

Sierra Leone is divided into 150 chiefdoms, each governed by a paramount chief and a council of elders. Paramount chiefs wield considerable influence, both at the local and national levels. Twelve seats of Sierra Leone's 80-seat parliament are occupied by paramount chiefs, one from each of the country's national districts.

ECONOMY

Sierra Leone – already one of the poorest countries in the world prior to the 1997 coup – is now even worse off. During the months that the junta controlled the government, food and fuel supplies were almost exhausted. Prices of remaining goods skyrocketed, sustained by a vigorous black market which sprung up after the imposition of economic sanctions by ECOWAS. With the restoration of peace, goods are again coming freely into the country although supply to more remote areas is erratic. Living conditions remain difficult, with an estimated 80% of the population living below the poverty line. Foreign investment has been hampered by the ongoing political instability. Under almost any scenario, Sierra Leone will remain heavily dependent on international aid for the foreseeable future.

The country's economy is based on subsistence agriculture. Principal crops include cassava and rice. Civil strife has limited exploitation of large reserves of bauxite, diamonds and gold.

POPULATION & PEOPLE

Sierra Leone is one of the more densely populated countries in West Africa. There are over 15 indigenous ethnic groups. The two largest groups, the Temnes and Mendes, each comprise about one-third of the population. Other groups include the Limba and Koranko in the north, the Kissi in the east and the Sherbro in the south-west.

Krios, most of whom reside in Freetown, constitute less than 2% of the population and are predominantly Christian. Many of the country's intellectuals and professionals are Krios. There are significant numbers of Mandingo (also called Malinké) and Fula (also called Peul) concentrated in the north and east, and a sizeable Lebanese business community.

ARTS

Sierra Leone is known for its fabrics, especially country cloth and *gara*. Country cloth is a coarse material woven from wild cotton into narrow strips that are joined to make blankets and clothing, then coloured indigo, green or brown using natural dyes. Gara is a thin cotton material, tie-dyed or batik-printed either with synthetic colours or natural dyes.

The Mendes produce the best known masks. These are often used in initiation ceremonies of the women's Bundu societies

Temnes & Mendes

Although ethnic conflict is minimal between Sierra Leone's Temnes and Mendes when compared with some other West African countries, great differences and considerable competition exist between these groups.

The Temnes inhabit northern Sierra Leone, and share cultural traditions with the savanna-dwelling peoples of Guinea, southern Senegal and southern Mali. They follow Islam, and place considerable importance on the idea of hereditary kingship. Ceremonies that confirm the power of local kings or chiefs are important and often quite elaborate. However, the Temnes are not traditionally warlike, and have generally coexisted peacefully with neighbouring groups, such as the Loko in the west or the Koranko around Mt Bintumani.

The Mendes are primarily in the south and their culture is linked more to the forest-dwelling peoples of Liberia and Côte d'Ivoire. Traditionally, Mendes are animists, although many have embraced Christianity and a few are Muslim. Mendes traditionally see themselves as superior to neighbouring smaller groups, such as the Gola around Kenema and the Sherbro along the coast, who are gradually abandoning their own traditions and adopting Mende language and culture.

Both Mendes and Temnes maintain strong traditions. Village chiefs wield considerable power and it is they (rather than civil judges) who have primary jurisdiction over local disputes. The Mendes are known for their culture of 'secret societies', locally called Bundu (although this is actually a Krio word). These societies, including the Poro for men and the Sande for women, are very influential – their responsibilities include training children in matters of tribal law and crafts, thus helping with their education and keeping traditional culture alive. If you see young children with their faces painted white, you'll know that they're in the process of being initiated. Masks are an important feature in Bundu ceremonies and are highly prized.

SIERRA LEONE

(see the boxed text 'Temnes & Mendes' on the previous page).

The Temnes and Kissi use stone heads and figures as protectors and cult items. These bear a strong resemblance to the Afro-Portuguese ivories which were commissioned for export in the 15th century.

Another traditional craft is the distinctive Temne basketry, made in the north of Sierra Leone.

RELIGION

About 40% of the population is Muslim, concentrated in the north. The remainder are Christians or adherents of traditional religions, which are still strong and which exert significant influence on the practice of Christianity.

LANGUAGE

There are more than a dozen tribal languages, the most common of which are Mende and Temne. English is the official language and Krio the most widely spoken. See the Language chapter for a list of useful phrases in Krio.

Facts for the Visitor

SUGGESTED ITINERARIES

If things stabilise and Sierra Leone becomes safe for independent travel, a good itinerary would be to spend a few days in Freetown getting to know the city, including a visit to Lumley Beach and an excursion to River Number 2. Then, you could head out to Bo and Kenema, perhaps including a visit to Tiwai Island Wildlife Sanctuary, before either heading back to Freetown or north to Mt Bintumani and Outamba-Kilimi National Park.

PLANNING

The best time to visit is mid-November, after the rains and before dusty harmattan winds spoil the views.

The dated Shell map (1988) has the country on one side (1:396,000) and Freetown on the other. It's readily available on the street in Freetown (US$6). Country maps available outside Africa include one in the International Travel Map series (1997; 1:560,000) and one published by the Fachhochschule Karlsruhe (1994; 1:800,000).

VISAS & DOCUMENTS

All visitors need visas or entry permits; they're not available at the border. You'll also need an certificate of vaccination for yellow fever and cholera.

Visas, normally valid for 30 days, can be extended in Freetown at the Immigration Department offices (☎ 223034) at the corner of Siaka Stevens and Rawdon Sts.

Before leaving Sierra Leone you will need to get a 'police clearance' (no cost) at police headquarters on George St between Siaka Stevens and Lightfoot Boston Sts. Clearances are issued daily between 8 am and 6 pm, usually with a minimum of hassle, but will only be granted within 48 hours of your departure. You'll need to show your passport and provide your departure date. The clearances can be used before the departure date given, but not afterwards.

EMBASSIES & CONSULATES
Sierra Leone Embassies

Within West Africa, Sierra Leone has embassies where you can get visas and entry permits in Guinea and Liberia, and, if they have reopened, also in Côte d'Ivoire, Gambia, Senegal and Nigeria. For more details see the Facts for the Visitor section of the relevant country chapter. In countries with no Sierra Leone embassy, try the British high commission.

Elsewhere, Sierra Leone has the following embassies:

Belgium
  (☎ 02-771 0052)
  410 ave de Terveuern, Brussels 1150
Germany
  (☎ 0228-35 20 01)
  Rheinallee 20, 53173 Bonn
UK
  (☎ 0171-636 6483; from 22 April 2000 ☎ 020-7636 6483)
  33 Portland Place, London W1N 3AG

USA
(☎ 202-939 9261)
1701 19th St NW, Washington, DC 20009

Embassies & Consulates in Sierra Leone

Embassies and consulates in Freetown which have resumed operations or are likely to reopen soon include the following:

Germany
(☎ 222511)
Santanno House, 10 Howe St
Ghana
(☎ 223461)
16 Percival St
Guinea
(☎ 232584)
Wilkinson Rd, 500m west of Congo Cross roundabout. Visas are issued within 72 hours and cost approximately US$45.
Ireland
(☎ 222017)
8 Rawdon St
Mali
(☎ 231781)
40 Wilkinson Rd
Nigeria
(☎ 224202)
Nigeria House, Siaka Stevens St. Visas are not normally issued to nonresidents.
Spain
(☎ 223551)
10 Siaka Stevens St, at IPC Travel
UK
(☎ 223961)
6 Spur Rd
USA
(☎ 226481)
1 Walpole St

CUSTOMS

Importing or exporting more than US$5 in leones is illegal; you cannot convert excess leones back into foreign currency at the airport.

You can't take antiquities out of the country. Certificates of non-authenticity (for things that look old) were previously available from the national museum.

MONEY

The unit of currency is the leone (Le). A unit of 100 leones is often referred to as a 'block'.

Euro €1	=	Le1000
1FF	=	Le160
UK£1	=	Le1500
US$1	=	Le1000

Apart from the exaggerated inflation occasioned by the coup, prices have been fairly stable in real terms, and are expressed in US$ throughout this chapter. Top hotels require payment in hard currency.

There is no black market. However, rates and commissions vary among the various banks and foreign exchange (forex) shops. Cash gets good rates at forex shops, especially for large denomination bills. Some shop owners are often also willing to change cash for you. Be wary of con-artists offering good rates on the street.

POST & COMMUNICATIONS

The postal service in Sierra Leone is unreliable for sending and receiving letters.

The telephone network within Freetown and to some upcountry towns is fairly good. Phonecards for domestic and international calls are on sale in Freetown at the main post office. Regional area codes include the following:

Freetown	☎ 022
Bo	☎ 032
Makeni	☎ 052

If you want to send or receive email, you can get online in Freetown; one access number is ☎ 228850. Additional access numbers can be obtained by contacting SierraTel.

BOOKS

A wealth of English-language material exists on Sierra Leone. *Fighting for the Rain Forest* (Paul Richards) is an analysis of issues underlying the country's ongoing political instability. *The Gullah* (Joseph Opala) is a pamphlet published by the US Information Service with fascinating information about the links between Sierra Leone and the Gullah peoples of south-eastern USA. *Tales*

SIERRA LEONE

of the Forest (Thomas Decker) is a collection of local folktales.

In a different category altogether is *The Heart of the Matter* by Graham Greene, a novel of colonial times, where Freetown becomes a the setting for a tale of human weakness, waste and frustration.

FILMS
Amistad (1997, directed by Steven Spielberg) tells the story of Mende slaves, led by Sengbe Pieh, who in 1839 revolted to obtain their freedom while being shipped from one Cuban port to another. The Amistad case so fuelled anti-slavery feelings in the USA that it is considered one of the catalysts of the American Civil War. The case also gave rise to American missionary activity in Sierra Leone. Students from schools established by these early missions were later influential forces in Sierra Leone's drive for independence.

NEWSPAPERS & TV
The most respected paper for news about current events is *For Di People*. The Sierra Leone Broadcasting Corporation has the only television station in the country; the news is broadcast every evening at 8 pm.

PHOTOGRAPHY & VIDEO
Photo permits are not required, but use caution until the security situation stabilises; don't snap government buildings, military sites, airports or harbours. For more general information on photography restrictions, see the Photography & Video section in the Regional Facts for the Visitor chapter.

WEIGHTS & MEASURES
Distances on signposts are often in miles. A term sometimes heard in markets is 'pint' – the size of a standard beer bottle (330mL) – used to measure cooking oil and other fluids.

HEALTH
You'll need proof of yellow fever vaccination, and, although not an internationally agreed requirement, proof of vaccination against cholera. Malaria risk exists year-round throughout the whole country, so you should take appropriate precautions. See the Health section in the Regional Facts for the Visitor chapter for more details on this and other health matters.

The water is not safe to drink: it is best to boil, filter or otherwise purify the water, or drink mineral water. A good pharmacy in Freetown is Marz the Chemist, on Siaka Stevens St.

WOMEN TRAVELLERS
Sierra Leone does not present any specific problems for women travellers. For more general information and advice, see the Women Travellers section in the Regional Facts for the Visitor chapter.

DANGERS & ANNOYANCES
Although Freetown and some upcountry towns are now under the control of ECOMOG troops, many areas, particularly in the east, remain rebel territory. Banditry, skirmishes and worse continue; before venturing out, get an update in Freetown.

Some land mines were planted during the 1997 fighting near Hastings airfield and at some locations around the Freetown peninsula. Seek local advice if you're planning to hike, especially on the Freetown peninsula.

In most areas of the country there's a midnight to 6 am curfew (from 10 pm in some upcountry towns). Much of Freetown has electricity in the evenings although power cuts are common. Upcountry, electricity is generally sporadic or nonexistent.

There are ECOMOG checkpoints on many roads in Freetown. Checkpoints on upcountry roads slow travel significantly.

BUSINESS HOURS
Business hours are 8 am to 5 pm Monday to Saturday although many places close at 1 pm on Saturday. Government offices are open 8 am to noon and 12.30 to 3.45 pm weekdays, and alternate Saturday mornings. Banking hours are 8 am to 1.30 pm Monday to Thursday (2 pm on Friday).

PUBLIC HOLIDAYS & SPECIAL EVENTS

Public holidays and special events include 1 January, Easter Friday, Easter Monday, 27 April (Independence Day), 29 April (Revolution Day), 25 and 26 December, and Islamic holidays. For a table of estimated dates of Islamic holidays, see p119.

If you're in Freetown on Easter Monday, visit the beach for National Kite-Flying Day celebrations. In major towns, the last Saturday of every month is Cleaning Day; there's a virtual curfew until 10 am while everyone cleans their yard or section of road, and fines of up to US$125 are levied on those found out on the roads during this time.

ACTIVITIES

The ocean is calm and swimming is generally safe. Deep-sea fishing off the coast is considered to be among the best in the region. Once security stabilises there are many excellent hiking areas, especially on Freetown peninsula and in the mountains of the north-east, although for now caution should be exercised on the Freetown peninsula due to the danger of land mines. Ask knowledgeable locals before setting off.

ACCOMMODATION

As of mid-1998, many hotels in Freetown had not yet reopened. Lodging selection upcountry is limited.

FOOD

Sierra Leone is known for its cuisine and every town has at least one chop bar (basic eating house) serving tasty, filling food. Rice is the staple and *plasas* (chopped potato leaves and pounded or ground cassava leaves cooked with palm oil and fish or beef) is the most common sauce. Other typical dishes are okra sauce, palm-oil stew, groundnut stew, pepper soup and, for special occasions, jollof rice. Street food favourites include roasted groundnuts, roasted corn, beef sticks, steamed yams, fried plantains, fried dough balls and fried yams with fish sauce. *Benchi* (black bench peas with palm oil and fish) are often served with bread for breakfast.

DRINKS

Star, the local beer, is reasonable. Poyo (palm wine), is light and fruity, but getting used to the smell and the wildlife floating in your cup takes a while. The spicy ginger beer sold on the streets is a nonalcoholic alternative, but you can easily get sick from it as the water is rarely boiled.

Getting There & Away

AIR

Freetown has two airports. Lungi is the main airport and most regional flights depart from here, with the exception of West Coast and InterTropic flights. Hastings is a small airfield used for domestic flights and for regional flights on West Coast and InterTropic airlines. When buying your ticket, clarify which airport you will be using for departure. Airport departure tax for regional flights is US$20 (payable in US dollars).

Intercontinental flights into Sierra Leone have been cancelled, although some may restart in 1999. Airlines which previously offered flights into Freetown include KLM (via Amsterdam), Sabena (via Brussels), and Air Afrique from New York (via Dakar in Senegal or Abidjan in Côte d'Ivoire).

For flights within West Africa see the table on the following page.

LAND

Guinea

As of late 1998, the border crossings at Pamelap and Kabala were not safe due to sporadic local fighting; inquire locally before setting out. The Koindu to Nongoa crossing is off limits to travellers. A daily SLRTC bus goes to Pamelap (US$7), where you'll find taxis to Conakry (US$5). There may also be a direct bus service between Freetown and Conakry; inquire at the SLRTC station.

Bush taxis run between Freetown and Conakry (330km, 10 hours, US$15) direct or with a change of vehicle at Pamelap. It's

SIERRA LEONE

Flights from Freetown (within West Africa)

destination	flights per week	airline	one way/ return fare (US$)
Abidjan	four	Air Afrique, Ghana Airways, Weasua	272/389
Accra	four	Ghana Airways	278/412
Banjul	two	Bellview, Air Dabia, Air Afrique	177/247
Conakry	six	West Coast, InterTropic, Air Guinée	80/160
Lagos	one	Bellview, ADC	308/464
Monrovia	five	Weasua, Air Guinée, West Coast	143/275

also possible to cross at Medina Oula (Medina Dula) between Makeni and Kindia and between Kabala and Faranah, although there's little transport on this route; you'll probably have to hire a motorbike in Kabala to take you to the border or on to Faranah.

Liberia

The main route between Freetown and Monrovia is via Kenema, Zimmi and Bo (Waterside) on the border. The journey takes two days in the dry season (650km, US$28). There's a border post north of Bo (Waterside) at Kongo, although it's in poor condition and rarely crossed. The route via Koindu towards Voinjama is unsafe.

SEA

A ferry service is scheduled to resume between Freetown and Conakry. Inquire at Government Wharf in Freetown for details.

Border Crossings

There are border crossings between Sierra Leone and Guinea at Pamelap, Medina Oula (also called Medina Dula) and Gberia-Fotombu. To/from Liberia, there are border crossings at Bo (Waterside) and Kongo.

Before setting out for any of these borders, make inquiries locally: many have been shut at various times due to the security situation.

Getting Around

AIR

West Coast Airways and InterTropic have daily (except Sunday) flights between Freetown and Bo (US$50) and Kenema (US$70). Departures are from Hastings.

BUS

The SLRTC runs daily buses between Freetown and Pamelap (six hours, US$7), Makeni (four hours, US$3), Kambia (US$4), Bo (seven hours, US$4), Kenema (eight hours, US$5) and Kabala (eight hours, US$5).

BUSH TAXI & MINIBUS

Bush taxis and minibuses (poda-podas) run between Freetown and many upcountry towns including Bo, Kenema, Makeni, Pamelap, Kambia and Kabala, though it's usually safer and more reliable to take the bus. They also link upcountry towns with each other and with surrounding villages.

Freetown

Freetown's pep and optimism, while dampened by the events of 1997, have not been extinguished. The capital is once again bustling and energetic, although scars from the extensive looting during the coup will take more time to heal.

Beautiful nearby beaches and stunning views of sea and mountains compensate for the chaos of downtown and for the city's all-too-frequent traffic jams.

Orientation

Central Freetown is set out on a grid pattern with Siaka Stevens St the main thoroughfare, running north-east to south-west. Halfway along is the huge Cotton Tree. Within a few blocks of the tree are the post office, markets, banks and offices. Away from the central area, winding streets climb the surrounding hills. Mt Aureol and Leicester Peak overlook the city.

The main road to the east is Kissy Rd; some taxis and poda-podas alternatively go along Fourah Bay Rd through the dock area. Going west, the main road follows Sanders St, Brookfields Rd and Main Motor Rd towards Aberdeen and Lumley. Some westbound transport goes via Kroo Town Rd and Congo Town Rd.

At the north-western tip of Freetown peninsula, 10km from the centre, are Aberdeen village and Lumley Beach.

Information

Tourist Offices Neither the National Tourist Board (at the Cape Sierra hotel) nor the Ministry of Tourism and Culture (Government Wharf) have maps or leaflets. IPC Travel (☎ 223551) is a good source of information for travellers.

Money Barclays on the corner of Siaka Stevens and Charlotte Sts, and Union Trust Bank on Howe St changes travellers cheques in UK pounds or US dollars. Barclays also sells travellers cheques, and gives cash against Visa or MasterCard (US$20 plus 0.75% commission for an approved transaction, US$3 cable charges if it's denied). There are forex shops on and around Siaka Stevens St which give good rates for cash, lower for travellers cheques.

Post & Communications The main post office, on the corner of Siaka Stevens and Gloucester Sts, is open from 8 am to 4.45 pm weekdays (1 pm on Saturday). There's no poste restante.

International calls can be made at the post office (phonecard only), or at Sierra Leone External Telecommunications (SLET) behind the bus station, open 24 hours daily. For a three-minute (minimum) call to the USA/UK/Australia it costs about US$5/5/6.

You can also send and receive faxes at SLET (fax 224439). Incoming faxes are held indefinitely, although there's no registration system.

Travel Agencies & Tour Operators IPC Travel (☎ 223551), on the corner of Siaka Stevens and Rawdon Sts, is good for airline bookings and for group excursions (once security stabilises). Lion Travel (☎ 226618), 13 Howe St, is also helpful.

Medical Services Doctors in Freetown who have been recommended include Dr VR Willoughby (☎ 225804) and Dr Mansour (☎ 22875). For serious illness you'll need to go to Abidjan in Côte d'Ivoire.

Dangers & Annoyances Watch out for pickpockets and bag-snatchers, although violent robbery is unlikely during the day. At night, avoid the port area. The beaches in front of hotels and restaurants are generally safe during the day.

In the city centre, beware of con-artists pretending to be customs officials and asking whether you've arrived recently. Just ignore them.

Things to See & Do

The first order of the day should be a walk down Siaka Stevens St. Halfway along is the 500-year-old **Cotton Tree**, the heart of town and the city's principal landmark. Up the hill from the tree is the **State House** (closed to the public). To the west of the Cotton Tree is the **National Museum**, which suffered during the 1997 coup.

On the corner of Lightfoot Boston and Gloucester Sts is the dilapidated **City Hotel** from the 1920s, where Graham Greene wrote *The Heart of the Matter* while working here for the British Colonial Service during WWII.

GREATER FREETOWN

SIERRA LEONE

Some of the old wood-framed **Krio houses** scattered throughout Freetown are fascinating. Most date from the late 19th century; a few are even older.

The **Parliament** building is on Tower Hill, inland from the Paramount Hotel, although there's no access to it. On top of Mt Aureol is **Fourah Bay College**, founded in 1827 by the Church Missionary Society and one of the oldest English-language universities in sub-Saharan Africa. From the Paramount Hotel head up Parliament Rd (which turns into Berry St), then turn on Barham Rd to the college; it's about an hour on foot.

Places to Stay – Budget & Mid-Range

Maronda Guest House (☎ 225306, 7 Rush St), just off Circular Rd, has a kitchen and decent rooms with shared bathroom for US$8/12 single/double.

Opposite the petrol station at Aberdeen Junction, the pleasant *Jay's Guest House* (☎ 272470), has clean rooms with bathroom and fan/air-con for US$20/27. Staff are very friendly and will help with meal arrangements.

The *Cockle-Bay Guest House & Relaxation* (☎ 272789, 46a Cockle-Bay Rd), about 700m west of Aberdeen Junction, has basic, dirty singles/doubles for US$7/9 (US$12 with bathroom), and breakfast on request. Just across the bridge off Aberdeen Rd is the nicer *Lagoon Bleu Hotel & Restaurant* (☎ 272237) with comfortable air-con bungalows for US$40/45.

The *Sierra Light House* restaurant (☎ 272110 or 225221) – see Places to Eat later in this section – will soon be opening rooms overlooking the water (approximate-

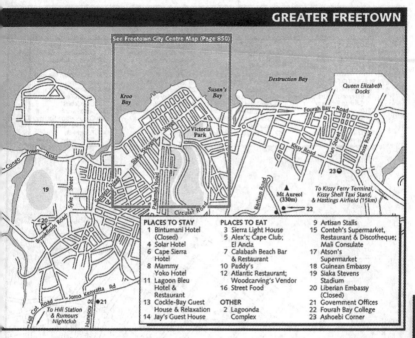

GREATER FREETOWN

PLACES TO STAY
1 Bintumani Hotel (Closed)
4 Solar Hotel
6 Cape Sierra Hotel
8 Mammy Yoko Hotel
11 Lagoon Bleu Hotel & Restaurant
13 Cockle-Bay Guest House & Relaxation
14 Jay's Guest House

PLACES TO EAT
3 Sierra Light House
5 Alex's; Cape Club; El Ancla
7 Calabash Beach Bar & Restaurant
10 Paddy's
12 Atlantic Restaurant; Woodcarving's Vendor
16 Street Food

OTHER
2 Lagoonda Complex
9 Artisan Stalls
15 Conteh's Supermarket, Restaurant & Discotheque; Mali Consulate
17 Atson's Supermarket
18 Guinean Embassy
19 Siaka Stevens Stadium
20 Liberian Embassy (Closed)
21 Government Offices
22 Fourah Bay College
23 Ashoebi Corner

SIERRA LEONE

ly US$30 for a double with bathroom). The setting is ideal; it would be well worth checking out the rooms once renovations are completed. The only drawback may be noise from the restaurant below.

For cheap lodging near the beach, your only option is the isolated *Dr Bendu's Guest House* (☎ 272522) at the southern end of Lumley Beach with grungy rooms for US$7. Staff will help with meals. Sleeping on Freetown's beaches is illegal and unsafe.

Places to Stay – Top End

The three hotels listed in this category are all in Aberdeen, at the western end of the peninsula. The only luxury hotel operating is the *Cape Sierra* (☎ 272272), at the northern end of Lumley Beach, overlooking an attractive stretch of the beach. It has a relaxing ambience, fairly comfortable single/double rooms for US$135/160 (cash only),

swimming pool and dilapidated tennis courts. Meals at the restaurant start at about US$11. The nearby *Solar Hotel* (☎ 272531) 200m off Cape Rd, and opposite the old Mammy Yoko Hotel, is a bit run-down but relatively comfortable, with blocks of studio apartments for US$40; US$80/120 for chalets (two people) or cottages (four people). All accommodation has air-con, kitchenettes and fridges. Meals at the restaurant start at about US$10. There is also a small swimming pool.

The *Mammy Yoko Hotel* (☎ 272444), on Cape Rd on Lumley Beach, was formerly Freetown's best but was badly damaged during the coup. It has not yet reopened.

Places to Eat

For inexpensive food in a lively atmosphere try *Ram Jam* on Garrison St opposite Victoria Park in the city centre. Meals start at

FREETOWN CITY CENTRE

PLACES TO STAY
13 City Hotel
38 Paramount Hotel
41 Maronda Guest House

PLACES TO EAT
8 Crown Bakery
15 Santanno House Cafeteria; German Embassy
22 Ram Jam
23 Street Food

OTHER
1 Government Wharf

2 Ministry of Tourism & Culture
3 SLET
4 SLRTC Bus Station
5 Intertropic Airways
6 Union Trust Bank
7 Air Guinée
9 Irish Consulate
10 Choitram's Supermarket
11 Basket Market (Big Market)
12 St George's Cathedral
14 Lion Travel

16 Sacred Heart Cathedral
17 Immigration; Ghana Airways; Haifa Supermarket
18 IPC Travel
19 East Street Market
20 Bush Taxis for Conakry (Guinea)
21 Victoria Park Market
24 West Coast Airways
25 Forex Shops
26 Barclays Bank
27 Post Office
28 Police Headquarters

29 King Jimmy Market
30 Connaught Hospital
31 Bellview Airlines
32 Ghanaian Embassy
33 US Embassy; Nigerian Embassy
34 National Museum
35 Cotton Tree
36 Law Courts
37 State House
39 Conservation Society of Sierra Leone
40 Tower Hill; Government Offices

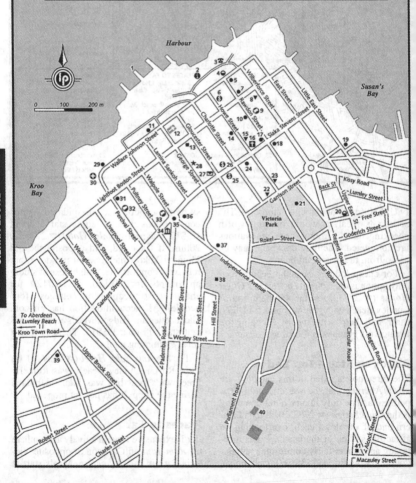

SIERRA LEONE

US$1. Howe St has good *street food*, as does Aberdeen Junction.

The friendly and quiet *Santanno House Cafeteria* on the 4th floor of Santanno House at 10 Howe St has very good meals from US$1. It's open weekdays between 12 and 3 pm.

Crown Bakery (☎ 222545, 6 Wilberforce St) near the corner with Lightfoot Boston St is very popular. Fried chicken starts at US$2; there are also sandwiches from US$2.50, and main dishes for US$10.

The popular *Paddy's*, on Aberdeen Rd about 2km beyond Aberdeen Junction, has pizzas and grills from US$5. It's open daily, evenings only.

Calabash Beach Bar & Restaurant (☎ 272002) on Lumley Beach just down from the Cape Sierra Hotel is open daily from noon onwards. Meals start at US$5 (US$2 for sandwiches).

Down the hill from the Mammy Yoko Hotel are *Alex's* and *Cape Club*, two popular and moderately priced bar-restaurants overlooking the bay. Both serve grills and seafood for US$3 to US$11, and are good places for a drink. They're open from 4 pm daily (noon on Sunday).

On the opposite side of the bay is the attractively situated *Sierra Light House* (☎ 272110), with good fish and grills from US$5. It's open from 7 pm daily.

To reach these last three places get a shared taxi to Aberdeen Junction, then another to the Aberdeen village roundabout (just past the Mammy Yoko Hotel) and walk the last few hundred metres. At night taxis are hard to find (you cannot phone for one), and walking isn't safe. You may be able to find a lift to town if you ask in the car parks.

The *Atlantic Restaurant* at the southern end of Lumley Beach has good fish dishes for about US$10 and a terrace which is great for drinks at sunset.

Entertainment

Most restaurants listed earlier are also bars. For a taste of the past, visit the *Rumours Nightclub* at Hill Station above the city, with views across the peninsula. This was Freetown's social centre in colonial times (Graham Greene was a member), though now the club is just a shadow of its former self. To get here take a taxi up Hill Cot Rd (walking isn't advised after sunset).

Attitude Disco at the Lagoonda Complex at the end of Lumley Beach in Aberdeen, opposite the Cape Sierra Hotel has reopened and has good dancing on weekends. There is a US$7 admission charge. *Conteh's* on Wilkinson Rd also has good dancing, and features a local band on Sunday evenings. There's a US$5 admission charge on weekends. *Calabash Beach Bar & Restaurant* (see Places to Eat earlier) has live bands on most weekend nights. It's US$5 admission, although you can listen on the beach for free.

Shopping

Supermarkets On Rawdon St, Choitram's Supermarket is well stocked but expensive. Haifa Supermarket, on the corner of Rawdon and Siaka Stevens Sts, is slightly cheaper. Two other good choices are Atson's and Conteh's, both on Wilkinson Rd.

Art & Craftwork Sierra Leone is a good place to buy fabrics including country cloth and gara. In Freetown, the market stalls at Victoria Park have the best selection of country cloth. Material is sold by the lapa (about two metres), and is often pre-cut into 'double-lapa' lengths.

First visit Victoria Park Market, then try the shops along Howe St leading down from the market. You could also try the street stalls along Lightfoot Boston St. For baskets, and just about anything else, head for the Big Market (usually called the Basket Market) at the foot of Lamina Sankoh St. For woodcarvings, try the small stall 500m from the end of Lumley Beach near the Atlantic Restaurant or the stalls just down from the Mammy Yoko Hotel.

Getting There & Away

Air Airlines with offices in Freetown include the following: Air Guinée (☎ 225534), 5 Rawdon St; Bellview Airlines (☎ 227311), 31 Lightfoot Boston St; Ghana Airways

(☎ 224871), 15 Siaka Stevens St; InterTropic (☎ 224944), 16 Wallace Johnson St; and West Coast Airways (☎ 227561), 18 Siaka Stevens St. Other airlines can be booked through IPC Travel. Sabena (☎ 226072) has recently reopened; the office is at 14 Wilberforce St.

Bus SLRTC buses leave in the mornings from the bus station (formerly the train station) at the corner of Rawdon and Wallace Johnson Sts. The buses are very crowded; you'll need to arrive at least an hour early to get a seat.

Bush Taxi & Minibus Bush taxis and poda-podas leave from various sites in Freetown (all in the centre or east of the centre), depending on their destination: the corner of Free and Upper East Sts for Conakry; Dan St for Bo and Kenema; Ashoebi Corner (2km east of centre on Kissy Rd) for Makeni and Kabala; and Kissy Shell station (5km east of centre on Kissy Rd) for these and other locations.

Getting Around
To/From Lungi Airport Lungi airport (for regional flights) is about 25km from central Freetown, on the other side of the bay. You can cross the bay in various ways.

Via Hovercraft A hovercraft service connects Tagrin ferry terminal near Lungi with Government Wharf (US$30, 15 minutes). Included in the price is a shuttle bus which runs between the airport and Tagrin dock. There's no set schedule, but the hovercraft coordinates with most regional flights. For information, inquire at the hovercraft office (Mammy Yoko Tours) at Government Wharf (☎ 226661 or 224218), or at Freetown travel agencies.

Via Ferry There's a dilapidated ferry sporadically connecting Tagrin with the Kissy ferry terminal (US$1.50/0.50, 1st/2nd class). From Lungi to Tagrin, it's around US$3 in a private taxi. Shared taxis cost US$0.30; walk 200m out of the airport to the main road and

flag down any taxi going towards the left, as you exit the airport gates. From the Kissy ferry terminal private taxis go to Freetown (US$5); alternatively, walk up to the main highway and get a shared taxi from there into the centre.

To/From Hastings Airfield Hastings airfield (for domestic flights) is about 20km east of central Freetown (US$15 in a taxi). Allow at least 45 minutes to get there from downtown.

Taxi Freetown taxis don't have meters. From Siaka Stevens St to the Lumley Beach area costs about US$2 if you bargain well. Longer hires in the city are about US$4 per hour. Shared taxis in Freetown cost US$0.15 per ride (US$0.10 for a poda-poda).

Car IPC Travel may be able to help with car rental. Expect to pay about US$150 per day with driver within Freetown, US$200 around the Freetown peninsula, and up to US$350 per day for 4WDs upcountry.

AROUND FREETOWN
Be warned: land mines were planted in some areas of the Freetown peninsula during the 1997 fighting. Make inquiries locally before venturing off main roads.

Beaches
Freetown lies at the northern end of a 40km-long mountainous peninsula with some of the best beaches in West Africa stretching along the western side of the peninsula. **Lumley Beach** is nearest Freetown and reached by hailing any taxi headed west on Siaka Stevens St. Ask for Aberdeen Junction, 5km from the centre, from where shared taxis go to the beach area. To reach the other beaches by shared taxi, stay in the taxi past Aberdeen Junction to Lumley village, 4km further south, from where bush taxis and poda-podas run down the coastal road. Some tracks to the beaches aren't clear, so you may have to ask for directions.

South of Lumley village, 4km after Goderich village junction, is the turn-off for

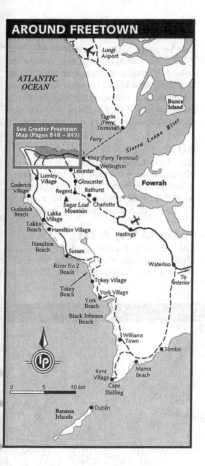

AROUND FREETOWN

ATLANTIC OCEAN

Lungi Airport

Bunce Island

Tagrin (Ferry Terminal)

See Greater Freetown Map (Pages 848 – 849)

Ferry

Sierra Leone River

Kissy (Ferry Terminal)
Wellington

Lumley Village
Leicester
Gloucester

Fowrah

Goderich Village
Regent
Bathurst

Sugar Loaf Mountain
Charlotte

Goderich Beach

Lakka Village
Lakka Beach
Hamilton Village

Hamilton Beach

Hastings

Sussex

River No 2 Beach

Tokey Village

Waterloo

To Interior

Tokey Beach

York Village

York Beach

Black Johnson Beach

Williams Town

Tombo

Kent Village

Mama Beach

Cape Shilling

0   5   10 km

Banana Islands

Dublin

---

town. You'll save time and money if you bring fuel for the excursion with you five to seven gallons. For a shorter trip, go up River No 2 to the waterfalls. The hills behind the beach, though overgrown, are good for hiking. South of River No 2 is the rockier but attractive **Tokey Beach**, although there's no infrastructure any more.

A few kilometres further south is York village with **York Beach** nearby and Black Johnson Beach across the bay (5km by road). Some 20km further at the end of the peninsula is Kent village, where you can also hire a boat to the **Banana Islands**.

Diving and snorkelling off the Banana Islands is superb. The fishing is said to be good too. In Dublin village, on the northern tip of the main island, there's a Portuguese church and the remains of a slave centre. Tours to the Banana Islands and River No 2 Beach are available from travel agencies in Freetown. From June until the end of the

---

Lakka Beach. Lakka village is 2km further south, after the now-closed Cotton Club, and then **Hamilton Beach**.

The choicest beach of all is **River No 2**, halfway down the peninsula. Basic *beach huts* can be hired for US$3 per day; there's also a more expensive stone hut with simple beds and mosquito nets. Otherwise, you can pitch a tent. Bring your own drinking water. Meals can be arranged with locals.

You can hire a boat here to the Banana Islands much more cheaply than from Free-

---

Bunce Island

Bunce (pronounced *bun-see*) Island is at the mouth of the Sierra Leone River, 18km from Freetown. Its major attraction is the ruined fortress. First built in 1663 by the British as a trading base, it was levelled to the ground in 1702 by French warships. The ruins are of a second fort built soon after.

After the original British and French occupations, the fort was held by the Dutch, the Portuguese and, again, the British. From 1750 to 1800, the island became notorious as one of the major collection points for slaves destined for Europe and the Americas. (The Gullah people of South Carolina are thought to have come from here.) Efforts are now being made to preserve its long-forgotten ruins.

Hiring a boat for yourself to Bunce is prohibitively expensive, so a tour may be the only feasible way to visit. Inquire at Freetown travel agencies to see whether excursions have resumed.

rainy season, the seas are much too rough for excursions.

Regent & Gloucester

These villages are in the hills overlooking the city, just a short ride (US$0.50) by bus or poda-poda via the village of Leicester. The villages have several interesting Krio-style houses, some dating from the early 19th century. From Regent you can walk though Krio villages to Charlotte Falls or climb **Sugar Loaf Mountain**, one of the highest points on the peninsula. It's a logging area and paths are often indistinct, but you can find guides in Regent. The top is a one to two hour climb, and offers sweeping panoramas of the bay. The Conservation Society of Sierra Leone (☎ 229716) can assist with planning hiking routes here and elsewhere on the peninsula, but caution should be exercised due to the danger of land mines.

The South & East

South-eastern Sierra Leone is humid, low-lying and forested. It also contains the country's major diamond mining areas, notably Tongo Fields between Kenema and Koidu-Sefadu which, along with Koindu in the far eastern corner of the country, are also diamond trading and smuggling centres.

BO

Bo, Sierra Leone's second city, is a lively, pleasant town in the heart of Mende country. Although it suffered during recent fighting, with almost all residents at least temporarily uprooted, it's now bustling again.

Places to Stay & Eat

The relaxing, family-run *MACEC Guest House* has comfortable rooms for US$7 (US$10 with bathroom). It's a 30 minute

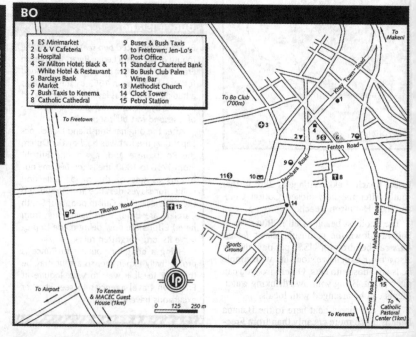

BO

1 ES Minimarket
2 L & V Cafeteria
3 Hospital
4 Sir Milton Hotel; Black & White Hotel & Restaurant
5 Barclays Bank
6 Market
7 Bush Taxis to Kenema
8 Catholic Cathedral
9 Buses & Bush Taxis to Freetown; Jen-Lo's
10 Post Office
11 Standard Chartered Bank
12 Bo Bush Club Palm Wine Bar
13 Methodist Church
14 Clock Tower
15 Petrol Station

To Makeni
Kissy Town Road
To Bo Club (700m)
To Freetown
Fenton Road
Dambara Road
Tikonko Road
Mahebollima Road
Sports Ground
To Airport
To Kenema & MACEC Guest House (1km)
Sewa Road
To Kenema
To Catholic Pastoral Center (1km)

0   125   250 m

SIERRA LEONE

walk from the centre. Meals are available on request.

Sir Milton Hotel in the centre has clean singles/doubles with bathroom for US$10/15 (US$23 with air-con). The restaurant and outdoor patio are being renovated and should be open soon. The *Black & White Hotel & Restaurant*, an old favourite, is up and running again. It has one large airy double for about US$15 and excellent groundnut stew and other local dishes for about US$5.

The *Catholic Pastoral Center*, 2km from the centre, should be reopening soon. Basic rooms were previously around US$3, with priority given to church workers.

For an inexpensive meal, try the *L & V Cafeteria* opposite the cinema. They're open daily from 7 am and serve a great groundnut soup for US$1. There are also numerous *chop bars* near the market.

Entertainment
At dusk in Bo, the town's many palm-wine bars fill up with men socialising. One popular spot is the *Bo Bush Club* on the corner of Tikonko Rd and the Kenema highway.

Table tennis and billiards fans may want to try the *Bo Club*, 700m beyond the hospital at the foot of Candy Mountain. It's owned by former Sierra Leonean tennis champion Charles Hubbard, who gives tennis lessons and has rackets and balls you can rent. The club also has a bar and a pleasant terrace.

The breezy upstairs bar at the *Black & White* (see Places to Stay & Eat earlier) is a good place to relax in the afternoon. The popular *Jen-Lo's* at the taxi stand on Dambara Rd is a good place for drinks in the evening.

Getting There & Away
Bush taxis go regularly to Freetown (US$6, from Dambara Rd) and Kenema (US$2, from Fenton Rd). There's a daily SLRTC bus to Freetown (6½ hours, US$4), departing about 7.30 am from the bus and bush taxi stand on Dambara Rd. The buses are always full; queues begin as early as 5 am. If you're driving, note that the main road

between Freetown and Kenema bypasses Bo, 2km south of town.

KENEMA
Kenema is Sierra Leone's timber capital. On the edge of town is the **Kambui Hills Forest Reserve**, a large, densely vegetated woodland area and a good place for a walk.

Places to Stay & Eat
Lodging options prior to the coup included the *Maryland Guest House*, with clean

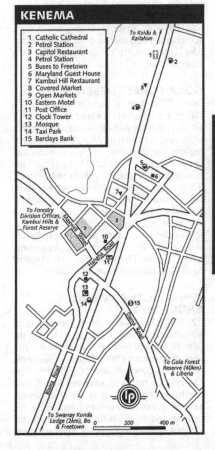

KENEMA

1 Catholic Cathedral
2 Petrol Station
3 Capitol Restaurant
4 Petrol Station
5 Buses to Freetown
6 Maryland Guest House
7 Kambui Hill Restaurant
8 Covered Market
9 Open Markets
10 Eastern Motel
11 Post Office
12 Clock Tower
13 Mosque
14 Taxi Park
15 Barclays Bank

To Koidu & Kailahun
To Forestry Division Offices, Kambui Hills & Forest Reserve
To Gola Forest Reserve (40km) & Liberia
To Swarray Kunda Lodge (2km), Bo & Freetown

0   200   400 m

SIERRA LEONE

rooms for US$6; the *Eastern Motel*, with rooms from US$11; and the *Swarray Kunda Lodge*, 3km from the centre on Blama Rd, with singles/doubles for US$3/8.

For cheap eats try the *Kambui Hill Restaurant*. *Capitol Restaurant* had good African and Lebanese meals.

Getting There & Away
SLRTC buses to Freetown (US$5) depart every morning from the bus station north of the centre. Bush taxis to Bo (US$2), Monrovia in Liberia (about US$20) and most other destinations depart from the taxi park near the clock tower. The hour-long ride to Bo is on a good tar road. However, the ride south towards Monrovia is long and bumpy. Kenema to Fairo and the Mano River bridge (the Liberian border) is an all-day trip in the rainy season.

GOLA FOREST RESERVE
Some 40km east of Kenema are the Gola Hills, a pocket of lowland tropical rain forest originally part of the larger forest that once covered much of West Africa's coastal region. Because this forest was separated from those in Central Africa, there are several unique species of birds and animals. To get here, head south-east on the Monrovia road to Joru, then 10km east to Lalehun. There are no facilities at present and as of mid-1998, this area was off limits to travellers; get a thorough briefing before setting out. The Conservation Department in the Forestry Division offices on Maxwell St in Kenema may have information.

TIWAI ISLAND WILDLIFE SANCTUARY
Tiwai is a beautiful reserve 50km south of Kenema on a small island (13 sq km) in the Moa River. The forest environment is virtually pristine with a high though increasingly threatened concentration of primates. You can hike on tracks all over the island; with careful stalking, you may see chimpanzee, several types of monkeys including the colobus and the beautiful diana monkey (the symbol of the park), pygmy hippopotamus,

crocodile, and more than 120 bird species, including hornbill, kingfisher and the rare white-breasted guinea fowl. Tiwai Island is also home to bats, bushbabies and hundreds of butterflies.

Unfortunately, it has been impossible to reach Tiwai since 1990 due to fighting in the area. For information on the current situation, contact the Conservation Society of Sierra Leone in Freetown (for contact details see Flora & Fauna in the Facts about Sierra Leone section) or the Conservation Department on Maxwell St in Kenema.

If security stabilises, the easiest way to reach Tiwai is via Potoru by bush taxi from Bo. (If you can't find anything to Potoru, take transport going towards Pujehun, get off at the Potoru junction and try to find onward transport from there.) From Potoru, head for Kambama village (16km) along the river's western bank; you may have to walk this bit. At Kambama, you can arrange overnight accommodation and hire a canoe to the island.

By car, take the major road east from Kenema to Joru (30km), then south towards Fairo for about 50km to the junction for Baoma village, then west to Baoma. Mapuma village is 2km beyond, on the river's eastern bank, where you can hire a canoe for the island.

KOIDU-SEFADU (KONO)
The twin towns of Koidu and Sefadu are usually called Kono, the name of the surrounding area. Kono is a major diamond trading centre. As of mid-1998, it was a centre of rebel activity and off limits to travellers.

The North

Northern Sierra Leone is the homeland of the Temne people. The landscape is higher and drier than in the south-east. Where they haven't been cultivated, the undulating hills are covered in light bush or savanna woodland, although ribbons of dense forest run along the major rivers. The hills become mountains in several places, with many peaks rising above 1500m. At the heart of the Loma

Mountains in the north-east is Mt Bintumani (1945m) which is the highest point in West Africa, as long as you put Mt Cameroon and several peaks along the Cameroon-Nigerian border in Central Africa!

MAKENI

Makeni, capital of the northern province, is a busy town with a beautiful mosque. The surrounding area has been traditionally renowned for two crafts: shukublais, distinctive Temne basketry, and gara cloth (for more details on gara cloth, see Arts in the Facts about Sierra Leone section earlier).

Many places in Makeni were badly looted following the coup. Previously, the *Thinka Motel*, south-west of the centre, had rooms from US$3.

Solokus Restaurant on Mapanda Rd had inexpensive chop. A Makeni institution was *Pa Kargbo's Bar* next to the Catholic Pastoral Center; check to see if it's reopened.

Bush taxis go daily to Freetown (US$5) and Kabala (US$3). The daily SLRTC bus to Freetown costs US$3. There's also transport to Kamakwie or to Kindia in Guinea.

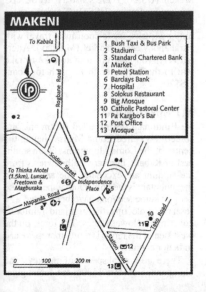

MAKENI

1 Bush Taxi & Bus Park
2 Stadium
3 Standard Chartered Bank
4 Market
5 Petrol Station
6 Barclays Bank
7 Hospital
8 Solokus Restaurant
9 Big Mosque
10 Catholic Pastoral Center
11 Pa Kargbo's Bar
12 Post Office
13 Mosque

To Kabala

Rogbane Road

Soldier Street

To Thinka Motel (1.5km), Lunsar, Freetown & Magburaka

Mapanda Road

Independence Place

Teko Road

Station Road

0   100   200 m

MAMUNTA-MAYOSO WILDLIFE SANCTUARY

This small reserve (20 sq km) protects a wetland area 30km south of Makeni, and provides a refuge for many species of birds and small mammals, and the rare short-nosed crocodile. All facilities were destroyed during the 1997 fighting, and the area remains off limits to travellers. You reach the reserve via Magburaka and the main road towards Mile 91. After 7km look for the MMWS signpost. Updated information on the sanctuary is available from the Conservation Society of Sierra Leone (for contact details, see Flora & Fauna in the Facts about Sierra Leone section).

OUTAMBA-KILIMI NATIONAL PARK

Outamba-Kilimi National Park (also called Kamakwie National Park or OKNP) near the Guinean border is a beautiful, peaceful place where you can experience some real West African wilderness. The park is easily reached by 4WD, or by public transport in the dry season. There are no roads inside the park, so visitors are encouraged to explore on foot or by canoe.

The park has two sections. The northern Outamba section consists of rolling hills, grasslands, flood plains and rainforests, intersected by several rivers, including the Little Scarcies. Before the coup, the park headquarters, visitors' centre and *camping ground* were in this section, on the riverbank. Several kilometres upstream is a waterfall. The Kilimi section to the southwest is flatter, less ecologically intact and not as interesting. Large animals in the park include elephant, leopard, buffalo, warthog, duiker, bushbuck, baboon, chimpanzee and several types of monkeys. In or near the rivers you may see otter, hippopotamus and crocodile. The various habitats support many bird species, including kingfisher, hornbill, heron, hawk, eagle, weaver, sunbird and the great blue turaco, one of the most spectacular birds in this region.

The park is presently off limits to travellers. If security stabilises, you may be able

SIERRA LEONE

to hire a canoe and arrange guides at park headquarters, though you'll need to bring a tent as those at the camp were looted. Water is available from the river, but must be treated; bring all your own food. For further information, inquire in Freetown at the Wildlife Conservation Branch or at the Conservation Society of Sierra Leone (for contact details see Flora & Fauna in the Facts about Sierra Leone section earlier).

Getting There & Away

From Makeni, take the main road north towards Kabala. After a few kilometres there's a junction where a dirt road leads west to Kamakwie (90km from Makeni). Beyond Kamakwie you have to cross the Little Scarcies River on a basic ferry. From there, continue towards Fintonia for 7km to the camp turn-off and park headquarters; it's 7km further east down a dirt track, about 25km from Kamakwie. In a 4WD, Makeni to park headquarters takes four hours, along a rough, hilly road. You can make it from Freetown in a day if the ferry is working.

With public transport, there's usually a bush taxi every morning from Makeni to Kamakwie (US$3). From Kamakwie, pick-ups go to Fintonia. Seven kilometres after the ferry crossing is the junction where the track leads east to the park. It's a 7km walk from there. Your other option is to hire a taxi in Kamakwie to the camp (US$15).

To get to the Kilimi section of the park, follow the directions above, then stay on the road until Sainya village. Villagers can point out the road leading into the park; the boundary is about 2km further.

KABALA

Kabala, the largest town in northern Sierra Leone, is at the end of the tar road and the last place of any size en route to Faranah across the border in Guinea. It's quiet and friendly and well worth a visit.

Prior to the coup, the *Gbawuria Guest House* (pronounced *bow-ree-ah*) on the west side of town, had clean rooms for US$3. There are *food stalls* on the main street north of the bus park. *Pa Willy's Bar*, north of the

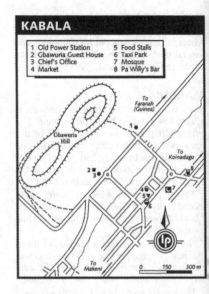

KABALA

1 Old Power Station
2 Gbawuria Guest House
3 Chief's Office
4 Market
5 Food Stalls
6 Taxi Park
7 Mosque
8 Pa Willy's Bar

To Faranah (Guinea)

Gbawuria Hill

To Koinadugu

To Makeni

0   150   300 m

centre, was a pleasant place; check to see if it's reopened.

Bush taxis go to Freetown (US$8) and Makeni (US$3). There's also a daily SLRTC bus to Freetown (US$5). To Faranah in Guinea, the road is bad and usually plied only by trucks; try to coordinate travel with Faranah's weekly market (Monday). Alternatively, you can hire a motorbike to take you to the border or to Faranah for about US$20.

MT BINTUMANI

Mt Bintumani (also spelled Bintimani, and sometimes called Loma Mansa) lies at the centre of the Loma Mountains, 60km southeast of Kabala. In clear weather, views from the summit are excellent. The area around the mountain is the homeland of the Koranko people; some sections have been listed as a reserve, protecting the highland rainforest covering the lower slopes. The forest on the west side of the range is more impressive and in better condition.

There are several species of monkeys, and chimpanzee. Above 1500m the forest gives way to grassland where you can spot baboon, warthog, duiker, porcupine and even buffalo. In the rivers you may see pygmy hippopotamus and dwarf crocodile, both very rare. The endangered rufous fishing-owl can also be seen in this area.

You can approach the mountain from Kabala via Koinadugu and Firawa, but it's more usual to approach from **Yifin** village (from where it's at least a four day walk to and from the summit), east of the dirt road between Kabala and Bumbuna, or from **Kurubonla**, north of Kono (three days).

Wherever you start, take a guide (many paths are overgrown) and possibly porters, as you need to be self-sufficient with camping gear and food for at least five days. Buy all your food in Makeni, Kabala (or Kono, if it has reopened to travellers). Before setting out, get a briefing on the security situation in Freetown or in Kabala.

Pay your respects to the chief in either Firawa, Yifin or Kurubonla (a gift of kola nuts or about US$1 is sufficient), and he'll help you find a guide and porters (about US$1 per day), and arrange accommodation with local people (also around US$1). Pay a small tip (US$0.50) or give some nuts to the chief of each village where you stay.

On the summit is a cairn and a bottle full of messages. The original bottle, which had been on the mountain since the turn of the century, was removed by the president in the 1960s when he reached the top by helicopter, but the messages from the last 30 years still make good reading.

Hiking Routes

From Yifin The route goes via the villages of Kondembaia and Sinikoro (four hours from Yifin). From there the path goes steeply uphill to reach 'Base Camp', a place for camping between the forest and the grassland, about five to seven hours from Sinikoro. From there to the summit is another four to five hours, but with an early start you can get back to Base Camp in a day. It's another one or two days back to Yifin.

From Kurubonla The route goes through the village of Sokurela (four to five hours from Kurubonla). From there the path goes steeply up to 'Camp Two', where you can pitch a tent, about five to seven hours from Sokurela. From there to the summit is only two hours, which means you can get back to Sokurela or even Kurubonla the same day.

SIERRA LEONE

Togo

Tiny Togo is one of the least known countries in modern Africa, even though it has suffered recent and violent coup attempts. It's only a thin strip of land but it's interesting enough to entice travellers.

Lomé, the capital city, and the nearby beaches are the main attractions. On the coast at Aného you can observe life in a traditional fishing village or you can cross nearby Lac Togo in a canoe and visit Togoville, a fetish centre.

Upcountry, you'll pass through some beautiful hills and plateaus on your way to the national parks in the north. The region around Kpalimé, near the Ghanaian border in the south-west, is particularly scenic and is known for its butterflies. The famous fortress-like mud-brick houses of the Tamberma people can be seen in the Kabyé region around Kara, a place that has withstood the onslaught of modernisation.

Facts about Togo

HISTORY

The region that is now Togo was once at the edge of several empires, including the Benin and Akan-Ashanti (see the History section in the Facts about the Region chapter for more details on these early empires), but never played a pivotal role in any. Various tribes moved into the country from all sides – the Ewé from Nigeria and Benin, and the Mina and Guin from Ghana. These tribes settled along the coast.

When the slave trade began in earnest in the 16th century, the Mina benefited the most. They became ruthless agents for the European slave-traders and would travel north to buy slaves from the Kabyé and other northern tribes. Europeans built forts along the coast in neighbouring Ghana and Benin (at Ouidah), but not in Togo, which had no natural harbours. Some of the slaves who were sent off to Brazil were eventually freed and, on their return, settled along the West

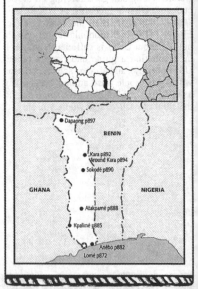

TOGO AT A GLANCE

Capital: Lomé
Population: 4.51 million
Area: 56,000 sq km
Head of state: President Gnassingbé Eyadéma
Official language: French
Main local languages: Ewé, Mina, Kabyé
Currency: West African CFA franc
Exchange rate: US$1 = CFA600
Time: GMT/UTC
Telephone country code: ☎228
Best time to go: Mid-July to mid-September

Dapaong p897

BENIN

Kara p892
Around Kara p894
Sokodé p890

GHANA   NIGERIA

Atakpamé p888

Kpalimé p885

Aného p882
Lomé p872

African coast between Accra (Ghana) and Lagos (Nigeria). They, in turn, became heavily involved in the slave trade. (For more details about the slave trade in West Africa, see the boxed text on p23.)

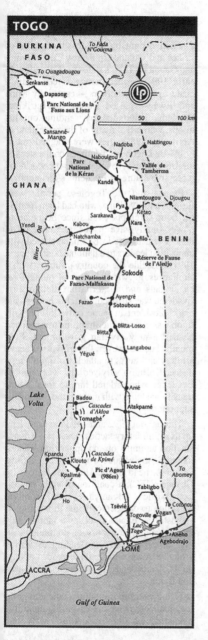

TOGO

BURKINA FASO

To Fada N'Gourma

To Ouagadougou

Senkanse

Dapaong

Parc National de la Fosse aux Lions

0   50   100 km

Sansanné-Mango

Nadoba   Natitingou

Naboulgou

Parc National de la Kéran

Vallée de Tamberma

Kandé

GHANA

Niamtougou   Djougou

Pya   Kétao

Sarakawa   Kara

Kabou

Yendi   Natchamba   Bafilo   BENIN

Bassar

Réserve de Faune de l'Aledjo

Sokodé

Parc National de Fazao-Malfakassa

Ayengré

Fazao   Sotouboua

Blitta-Losso

Blitta

Langabou

Yégué

Anié

Lake Volta   Badou

Cascades d'Akloa   Atakpamé

Tomagbé

Kpandu   Cascades de Kpimé

Klouto   Notsé

Pic d'Agou   To Abomey

Kpalimé   ▲ (986m)

Tabligbo

Ho

Tsévié   To Cotonou

Togoville   Vogan

Lac Togo   Aného

LOMÉ   Agebodrajo

ACCRA

Gulf of Guinea

River Oti

Colonial Period

When the slave trade started dying out in the mid-19th century, the Europeans turned their attention to trade in commodities – palm and coconut oil, cacao (the seeds from which cocoa and chocolate are made), coffee and cotton. The rivalry between Britain and France was fierce. Germany, which initially showed no interest in colonial expansion, surprised the British and French by sending a ship to the coast of 'Togoland', as they called this area, in 1884. They signed a treaty in Togoville with a local king, Mlapa, agreeing to 'protect' the local inhabitants in return for German sovereignty.

Under the Germans, Togoland, like the neighbouring Gold Coast (Ghana), underwent considerable economic development before WWI. Through the introduction and cultivation of cacao, coffee and cotton, Germany developed the colony's agricultural resources, which were soon paying for all its colonial expenses.

The Togolese, however, didn't appreciate the forced labour, direct taxes and 'pacification' campaigns of the Germans, in which thousands of local people were killed. As a result, large numbers of Togolese started migrating to the neighbouring Gold Coast. In 1914, with the outbreak of WWI, the Togolese welcomed British forces with open arms. Encircled by British and French colonies, the Germans surrendered – the Allies' first victory in WWI. After the war, Togoland was divided in two. According to the League of Nations mandate, France was to administer the eastern two-thirds of the country and Britain the remainder. The Ewé and several other tribal groups found themselves divided by an arbitrary border.

During the colonial period, the Mina, by virtue of their strategic position on the coast and long association with Europeans, came to dominate Togo's economic and political life to the exclusion of northern groups such as the Kabyé.

Independence

After WWII, political groups on both sides of divided 'Togo' agitated for reunification. In

TOGO

1956, hopes of reunification were dashed when British Togoland, in a plebiscite which was irregular and unilateral, voted to be incorporated into the Gold Coast, which was on the brink of independence.

In 1956, French Togoland to the east became an autonomous republic. Nicolas Grunitzky was appointed prime minister, and was succeeded two years later by Sylvanus Olympio. Olympio, an Ewé from the south, became Togo's first president in April 1960 when the country achieved full independence from the French.

In 1963, Togo became the first country on the continent to experience a military coup following independence. Olympio, as part of the southern elite, appeared to disregard the interests of northerners (whom he described as *petits nordiques*). When he refused to integrate into his small army some 600 soldiers returning from service for France in the Algerian War, these predominantly Kabyé northerners rebelled. Olympio was killed at the gates of the US embassy as he sought refuge. Thousands of exiles previously driven out of Togo by the repressive Olympio government returned, including Nicolas Grunitzky, who was put in charge. He lasted four years until deposed in a bloodless coup headed by Étienne Eyadéma, a Kabyé from the north.

Eyadéma set out to unify the country's disparate tribal groups, insisting on one trade union confederation and one political party, the Rassemblement du Peuple Togolais (RPT). He systematically established a cult of personality, surrounding himself with sycophantic staff and a chorus of cheering women in traditional dress. He championed 'authenticity' and dropped his French name, Étienne, in favour of the African Gnassingbé. On 24 January 1974, Eyadéma's private plane crashed near Sarakawa. Convinced that he had survived an assassination attempt, he became even more irrational and unpredictable.

Togo Today

In 1990, France began putting great pressure on Eyadéma to announce his support for a multiparty system. Eyadéma resisted and tried to portray African multiparty systems in a negative light by broadcasting scenes of strikes and violence in nearby Côte d'Ivoire and Gabon on Togo's state-run TV station. In early 1991, prodemocracy forces, mainly made up of southerners – especially Mina and Ewé – started rioting and striking. Eyadéma responded by sending out his troops, who killed many of the protesters. In April 1991, 28 bodies were dragged out of Lomé-Bé Lagoon and dumped on the steps of the US embassy, to indicate to the world the repressive nature of Eyadéma's dictatorship.

France and the Togolese people were furious, and Eyadéma, who had been fending off coup attempts ever since he came to power, finally gave in. Just as Kérékou had done a year before in Benin, he agreed with opposition leaders to a national conference in 1991 to decide the country's future, with a similar result. After 24 years of ruling Togo by slogans and authoritarian dictatorship, Eyadéma was stripped of all his powers and made president in name only. Joseph Koffigoh was elected interim prime minister and headed a new civilian government. Four months later, however, the army used heavy artillery and tanks to attack Koffigoh's residence. Koffigoh survived and was taken to Eyadéma, who ordered him to form a new transitional team with more of the president's supporters.

Throughout 1992 and 1993 the army kept up its intimidatory tactics. There were assassination attempts on the opposition leaders, including the serious wounding of Gilchrist Olympio, head of the Union of Forces for Change (UFC), a coalition of eight opposition parties. Meanwhile, the promised transition to democracy came to a complete standstill as Eyadéma became increasingly intransigent. The opposition continued calling for general strikes, leading to further violence by the army and the exodus of hundreds of thousands of southerners to Ghana and Benin.

Using every intimidating tactic and political manoeuvre at his disposal, including disqualifying one opposition party and causing another to refuse to participate, Eyadéma won the August 1993 presidential elections unopposed, although up to 90% of registered voters boycotted the elections. Repression immediately returned.

Eyadéma then proceeded with parliamentary elections in early 1994. The lead-up to the elections, however, was marred by widespread shooting almost every night in Lomé, frequent dusk-to-dawn curfews and at least one coup attempt. On election day, local observers were not permitted into the polling stations. Nevertheless, the main opposition grouping, the Committee for Renewed Action (CAR) headed by Yao Abgoyibo won 34 out of 78 seats, making it the best represented party in parliament. The Union Togolaise Démocratique (UTD), headed by Edem Kodjo, won six seats. Instead of becoming the ruling party, however, the CAR was effectively pushed aside when Eyadéma reached a deal with Kodjo, appointing him prime minister. Kodjo, looking more and more like a tool of the president, rewarded Eyadéma by giving some key ministerial posts to the president's supporters and none to the CAR.

Presidential elections were held on 21 June 1998, and the outcome was unsurprising. After 30 years as president, Eyadéma, claiming a majority of just over half the votes cast, started on a new five-year term. The leading opposition candidate, Gilchrist Olympio (who is now in exile in Ghana) of the UFC, received 34% of the vote, and the CAR candidate received 9.5%. The European Union and the USA both expressed their concern at the manner in which the elections were conducted. The National Election Commission president resigned, claiming she had been severely intimidated, and opposition supporters reacted by taking to the streets. Bullets and tear gas were fired at crowds on Lomé's streets and clashes were reported throughout the country. Another five years ...

GEOGRAPHY

Togo measures roughly 540km by 110km, with only 56km of coastline. Lagoons stretch intermittently along the sandy coastline, and further inland are rolling hills covered with forest. Around Kpalimé, in the south-west, the hills are excellent for growing coffee. In the north, the hills drop down to savanna plains.

Sokodé, about halfway between Lomé and the northern border, is the largest city in the interior, with about 70,000 inhabitants, followed by Kara, Kpalimé and Atakpamé.

CLIMATE

Rains fall from May to October. In the south there's a dry spell from mid-July to mid-September. In the north there is no such interlude, but on the whole the north is much drier than the south. The coast, including Lomé and up to 10km inland, is also fairly dry. From mid-February (after the harmattan wind lifts) to mid-April is the hottest period throughout the country.

ECOLOGY & ENVIRONMENT

Togo is one of the most densely populated countries in West Africa. Land pressure, combined with lack of government commitment, scarce financial resources and entrenched traditional pressures such as slash-and-burn agriculture, have taken a heavy toll on the environment. Only recently have attempts been made by forestry managers to involve local communities in the care of reafforested areas. In return for access to forests to retrieve fruits etc and some firewood, local farmers are asked to help in the prevention of forest fires – in the past they often deliberately lit fires to show

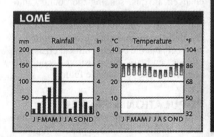

TOGO

their resentment at being denied access to protected areas.

The situation in Togo's national parks is particularly bad and very little wildlife remains. Poaching and deforestation go on unhindered. The coastline is also in a precarious state. Since the construction of a second pier at Lomé's port several beaches have disappeared. Pollution compounds the situation.

FLORA & FAUNA

The two main wildlife reserves – Parc National de la Kéran and Parc National de Fazao-Malfakassa – are disappointing as most of the large mammals have been killed off. The Swiss Fondation Franz Weber is desperately trying to resurrect the latter park.

GOVERNMENT & POLITICS

Togo is technically a republic with an elected president. However, you have to question how democratic a country is when the same president has been in power for more than 30 years. See the History section earlier in this chapter for more details.

ECONOMY

At the beginning of 1990, the economy was on a modest upturn even though the country's main export crop, cacao, continued to suffer from low world prices. Even though Togo was ranked badly in terms of its human suffering – taking into account such factors as literacy, clean water and nutrition – the country was virtually self-sufficient in food production in nondrought years. The political crisis, however, has changed all this, sending the country into severe recession. By 1994, government revenues were down by more than one-third. By 1996, economic growth was reported to be at 6%, but the current political crisis may put an end to any positive economic outcome in the foreseeable future.

POPULATION & PEOPLE

With about 40 ethnic groups and a population of nearly four million people, Togo has

Ewé Beliefs

According to the Ewé, once a person dies their reincarnated soul, or *djoto*, will come back in the next child born into the same lineage, while their death soul, or *luvo*, may linger with those still living, seeking attention and otherwise creating havoc. Funerals are one of the most important events in Ewé society and involve several nights of drumming and dancing, followed by a series of rituals to help free the soul of the deceased and influence its reincarnation.

one of the more heterogeneous populations in Africa. The two largest groups are the Ewé and the Kabyé. The Kabyé (related to the Tamberma), who count President Eyadéma among their number, are concentrated in the north around Kara and in the centre. They are known as hard-working people, skilled in terrace farming. Travelling north of Atakpamé, you can tell when you reach the Kabyé area by the design of the houses. The predominantly rectangular huts give way to round Kabyé houses with conical roofs, joined together by a low wall. The compound is known as a *soukala* and is designed for an extended family.

The Ewé-related people are concentrated in the south, particularly on the cacao and coffee plantations in the south-west (see the colour feature between pages 384 and 385 for more information about the Ewé). They include the Anlo, Adja, Pla-Peda, Mina and Guin people. Although they call themselves Ewé, some of these groups, such as the Mina and the Guin, are not ethnic Ewé. The Guin are Ga people from Accra, while the Mina are Fanti people from the coast of Ghana.

ARTS

The tribal groups of Togo produce no masks and few carved figures, the most notable being the small Ewé dolls carved for the Abiku cult. These function in a similar way to the Yoruba twin figures (see the Arts entry in the Nigeria chapter for more details) as receptacles for a dead child's spirit. The Ewé are also known for their *kente* cloth, which is usually less brilliantly coloured than the more famous Ashanti kente cloth.

Togo's best known author is Tété-Michel Kpomassie, who was raised in a traditional Togolese family. Kpomassie's most famous book is *An African in Greenland*, which is an autobiography containing his fascinating and unique perspective on Arctic life.

SOCIETY & CONDUCT

Female circumcision, or more specifically infibulation (removal of the labia and closing the vagina by sewing together the vulva), is practised by some groups in Togo. Over 20% of women have undergone infibulation, with most cases occurring in the north, especially in the Sokodé region. This spiritual and cultural ritual dates back to ancient Egyptian times, but only in recent years have the health problems associated with this grossly mutilating and often less than hygienically performed operation gained prominent attention. (For a more general discussion of this issue, see the boxed text 'Female Genital Mutilation' in the Facts about the Region chapter.)

This subject was covered in the poignant *Do They Hear You When You Cry?* (1998), a story of one woman, Fauziya Kasinga, who defied this tribal custom and fought for her freedom in the USA – after 16 months imprisonment and a number of court cases, she was finally granted asylum in the USA in 1996.

RELIGION

Approximately 20% of Togolese are Christians, 10% (concentrated around Sokodé) are Muslims and the remainder are animists. Most of the Christians, many of whom are Ewé, live in the south.

LANGUAGE

French is the official language. About half the people speak or understand Ewé. The second most widely spoken African language is Mina. Kabyé, the language of the current president, is widely spoken in the north. Refer to the Language chapter for useful phrases in French, Ewé, Mina and Kabyé.

Facts for the Visitor

SUGGESTED ITINERARIES

Allow one week for exploring Lomé and surrounds, two weeks if you include Kpalimé and the central towns, and three weeks if you venture to the far north to spend a few days in Tamberma country.

The Friday market in Vogan is particularly interesting; you can combine this trip with one to Aného, and spend a few days at Lac Togo. The area around Kpalimé, north-east of Lomé, is a great place to go hiking. From here, you could head for Atakpamé and the Akloa waterfalls outside Badou, then continue on to Kara, which is in a good area for cycling. The Tamberma Valley in the far north is home to the fascinating Tamberma people and well worth a visit. Also worth a short visit are Togo's two national parks: Fazao-Malfakassa in the central region and Kéran in the north.

PLANNING

The best time to visit is during the dry season (mid-July to mid-September in the south) when the roads are in good order. Unfortunately, this coincides with the harmattan wind and is a rotten time for photos.

TOURIST OFFICES

The only source of tourist information outside Lomé is the Togo Information Service (☎ 202-569 4330), 1625 K St NW, Washington, DC 20006, USA.

VISAS & DOCUMENTS
Visas

Nationals of ECOWAS countries do not need visas. All other nationals need visas. French embassies in Africa have authority to issue visas for Togo where there is no Togo embassy.

TOGO

Highlights

Natural Features

Kpalimé   *(The South)*
Beautiful hill country, on the border with Ghana, well known for its butterflies; great camping and hiking opportunities.

Markets

Fetish market   *(Lomé)*
This famous market in Akodessewa (Lomé) has an amazing collection of traditional medicines and fetishes on offer – fascinating to browse through, even if nothing tempts you to buy ...

Grand Marché   *(Lomé)*
Famed for its Mama Benz, the smart and wealthy women traders who seem to control all the goings on; you can get just about anything you want here – and have fun bargaining with the Mama Benz.

Architecture

Vallée de Tamberma   *(The North)*
Built without tools, the *tata* compounds are an extraordinary collection of towers with conical roofs – not to be missed.

Activities & Relaxation

Beaches   *(Around Lomé, The South)*
Robinson's Plage is a secluded beach away from the hustle of Lomé; the Aného beach is one of the main attractions of the south.

Water Sports   *(Around Lomé)*
You can windsurf or water-ski on the inland lagoon of Lac Togo, only 30km east of Lomé; combine it with a trip to Togoville by pirogue, or pay one of the local fishermen to take you out for the day.

Food

Togo has some of the best food in West Africa, much of it French-influenced, and each area has its culinary specialities – the variety of food on offer, especially in Lomé is astounding.

Visa Extensions The *sûreté* in Lomé on Rue du Maréchal Joffre issues visa extensions in 24 hours. They are usually good for 14 days, one month or three months, require photos, and cost about CFA10,000. The visa section is open from 7.30 to 11.30 am and 2.30 to 5.30 pm Monday to Friday, and from 8 am to noon on Saturday.

Other Documents

You need proof of yellow fever vaccination. If you're driving, you need an International Driving Permit.

EMBASSIES & CONSULATES

Togo Embassies & Consulates

In West Africa, Togo has embassies in Ghana and Nigeria. For more details, see the Facts for the Visitor section of the relevant country chapter.

Outside West Africa, embassies and consulates include the following:

Belgium
  (☎ 02-770 17 91 or 770 55 63)
  264 ave de Tervueren, Brussels 1150
France
  (☎ 01 43 80 12 13)
  8 rue Alfred Roll, 75017 Paris
Germany
  (☎ 228-35 50 91)
  Beethovenstrasse 13 D, 5300 Bonn 2
USA
  (☎ 202-234 4212)
  2208 Massachusetts Ave NW, Washington, DC 20008

Togo also has embassies in Congo-Zaïre, Gabon and Canada, and consulates in four cities in Germany (Berlin, Bonn, Hanover and Bremen), three in France (Bordeaux, Marseille and Nice), and in Switzerland and Austria.

Embassies & Consulates in Togo

The following countries have diplomatic representation, all in Lomé:

France
  Embassy:
  (☎ 21 25 71)
  51 Rue du Colonel de Roux, BP 337

Consulate:
(☎ 21 25 76)
Rue Bissaguet, BP 337

Germany
(☎ 21 23 38)
Blvd de la Marina (Route d'Aflao), BP 289

Ghana
(☎ 21 31 94)
Behind Gare de Kpalimé, Tokoin

Nigeria
(☎ 21 34 55)
311 Blvd du 13 Janvier

USA
(☎ 21 29 91 or 21 29 92, fax 21 79 52)
Corner of Rue Pelletier Caventou and Rue
Vauban

The Netherlands also has an embassy in
Lomé. Honorary consuls include those of

Visas for Onward Travel

In Togo, you can get visas for the following neighbouring West African countries.

Benin
There's no Benin embassy in Lomé but you
can get visas at the southern border on the
highway between Lomé and Cotonou. The
border is open 24 hours, but you can't
always get visas at night. The visas are
good for only two days, cost CFA4000,
and can be extended to one month at Immigration in Cotonou for CFA12,000
(takes three to five days).

Burkina Faso & Côte d'Ivoire
You can get visas (CFA20,000 for visas
valid for three months) at the French consulate. It's open weekdays from 8 to 11.30
am and issues visas within 48 hours if you
put your request in before 11 am.

Ghana
The embassy is open from 8 am to 2 pm
Monday to Friday, requires photos and
takes 48 hours to issue visas. They're good
for one-month stays and cost CFA12,000
(CFA10,000 for Commonwealth citizens).

Senegal (☎ 21 26 37), the UK (☎ 21 89 92)
and Denmark (☎ 21 34 45).

CUSTOMS
There is no restriction on the importation of
local currency. Declare any large sums of
foreign currency you bring in because the
export of foreign currency must not exceed
the amount declared on arrival. Theoretically, you're not supposed to export more
than CFA25,000.

Unlike many West African countries, exporting artwork requires no clearance from
a museum.

MONEY
The unit of currency is the CFA franc.

Euro €1	=	CFA660
1FF	=	CFA100
UK£1	=	CFA950
US$1	=	CFA600

If you want to change hard currency, ask at
your accommodation – they will usually
know of a reputable dealer or can change
money for you, which is much quicker than
changing at the banks.

Banks for changing cash or travellers
cheques include: BIA-Togo; UTB (Union
Togolaise de Banque) ☎ 21 64 11, the agent
for Western Union Money Transfer;
Ecobank and the BTCI (Banque Togolaise
pour le Commerce et l'Industrie).

POST & COMMUNICATIONS
The poste restante at the main post office in
Lomé is reliable. A postcard to Europe or the
USA costs CFA200, and small packages cost
about CFA2500 per kilogram by surface
mail, and considerably more by air mail.

The international telephone service is
good. It is possible to use International Direct Dialling (IDD) with phonecards in some
parts of Lomé, but the cards are gobbled up
quickly. Calls to the USA and Europe are
expensive (about CFA2000 a minute).

There are no area codes. Although you
may see them quoted, these relate to the first

TOGO

two digits of the actual telephone number. The telephone directory, *Annuaire Officiel des Abonnes au Telephone*, is surprisingly up to date for this part of the world.

There is an Internet service available in Lomé – see Information in the Lomé section later for more details.

BOOKS

The Village of Waiting (1988), by George Packer, is an interesting observation on life in Togo. One of the best books yet on the Peace Corps experience, it's about a volunteer's two years in Lavié and it's quite candid about the country's autocratic politics.

NEWSPAPERS & MAGAZINES

The *Togo Presse* (in French, with some articles in Kabyé and Ewé) tends to take the official presidential line. Occasionally you may see opposition magazines. The cultural centres and big hotels may have week-old international newspapers and even older magazines.

PHOTOGRAPHY & VIDEO

A photo permit is not required. Take care around the presidential palace, as travellers caught taking photos of this have been beaten by the police. See also the Photography & Video section in the Regional Facts for the Visitor chapter.

HEALTH

A yellow fever vaccination certificate is required of all travellers. Malaria risk exists year-round throughout the country, so you should take appropriate precautions. See the Health section in the Regional Facts for the Visitor chapter for more general information on these and other health matters.

WOMEN TRAVELLERS

In the predominantly Muslim northern towns of Sokodé, Bafilo and Kara long dresses and long sleeves are a must. For more information and advice, see the Women Travellers section in the Regional Facts for the Visitor chapter.

DANGERS & ANNOYANCES

The recent political strife in Lomé has made the city relatively dangerous – see Information in the Lomé section later for more details.

BUSINESS HOURS

Business hours are from 8 am to noon and 3 to 6 pm Monday to Friday, and from 7.30 am to 12.30 pm on Saturday. Government offices are open from 7 am to noon and 2.30 to 5.30 pm Monday to Friday. Banking hours are generally from 7.30 to 11 am and 2 to 3 pm Monday to Friday.

PUBLIC HOLIDAYS & SPECIAL EVENTS

Public holidays in Togo include 1 January (New Year's Day), 13 January (Meditation Day), 24 January, Eid al-Fitr (end of Ramadan), 27 April (National Day), 1 May (Labour Day), Ascension Day, Whit Monday, Tabaski, Day of the Martyrs (21 June), 15 August, 1 November and 25 December (Christmas Day). See p119 for a table of estimated dates for the Islamic holidays.

Special events include Evala, the wrestling festival in the Kabyé region around Kara, in July; the Dzawuwu-Za harvest festival in Klouto and the Ayiza harvest festival in Tsévié in August; and the Igname (yam) festival in Bassar in September. There are many others; see the *Calendar of Traditional Festivals*, free from the tourist office in Lomé (but realise it is a bit out of date).

ACTIVITIES

There are plenty of hiking opportunities in Togo, particularly in the Taberma region (see the boxed text 'Hiking in the Kpalimé Area' in the Kpalimé section of this chapter for more details) and around the national parks.

For swimming, there are some good beaches near Lomé, including Robinson's Plage and Le Ramatou, and there is a secluded beach at Aného. Several of the top hotels have swimming pools and tennis courts. Water sports can be arranged at Lac Togo, and there are a couple of places in Lomé where horse riding is possible.

ACCOMMODATION

Accommodation in Togo is among the least expensive in West Africa – finding a room for as little as CFA3000 per night is not difficult. For just a little more, you'll get a spacious hotel room with bathroom and fan. For CFA6000 to CFA10,000, your room will have air-con.

Top end hotels with swimming pools and other amenities can be found in Lomé, on Lac Togo (Agebodrafo) and in Kara. Prices quoted in the Places to Stay sections in this chapter are per room, not per person, unless otherwise indicated.

FOOD

The food in Togo is some of the best in West Africa and there are lots of places to try it, especially in Lomé. As in most of West Africa, meals are usually based on a starch staple accompanied by sauce. Sauces and starches come in many varieties – see the boxed text for a guide on these as well as a list of Togolese regional specialities. You'll find rice with groundnut (peanut) sauce *(riz sauce arachide)* most places.

Most towns have a Fan Milk outlet where you can get deliciously refreshing yoghurt and ice cream.

DRINKS

Togo also has its fair share of local brews. In the north, the preferred drink is *tchakpallo*, which is fermented millet with a frothy head, often found in the market areas. In the south, the most popular brews are palm wine and, to a lesser extent, *sodabe*, an unusually strong, clear-coloured alcohol distilled from palm wine which will knock your socks off.

Getting There & Away

AIR

The international airport is near Lomé, 7km north-east of the city centre.

Europe & the USA

From Europe, there are three direct flights a week from Paris (or daily via Abidjan in Côte d'Ivoire), two a week from Amsterdam and one a week from Brussels, Geneva and Frankfurt. The cheapest flights between Lomé and Europe are on Aeroflot, which has flights once a month via Paris (CFA 420,000 return). Corsair has one flight a week to Paris (around CFA200,000 one way). Sabena (US$795), Air France (US$ 606) and KLM (US$930) also periodically

---

Togolese Tucker

Sauces

aglan – crab
arachide – groundnut (peanut)
aubergine – eggplant
épinard – spinach
gboma – spinach and seafood
lamounou déssi or *sauce de poisson* – fish

Staples

ablo – a slightly sweet *pâte* made with corn and sugar
djenkoumé – a red-coloured *pâte* made with palm oil, tomatoes and corn
foufou – mashed yams

gari – a couscous-like grain made with manioc
monplé – a slightly sour *pâte* made with fermented corn
pâte or *akoumé* – a dough-like substance which can be made of millet, corn, plantains, manioc or yams

Togolese Specialities

abobo – snails cooked like a brochette
egbo pinon – smoked goat
koklo mémé – grilled chicken with chilli sauce
koliko – fried yams, a popular street food
millet couscous – especially popular in the north

TOGO

have good return deals, although normal fares are very expensive. It may be cheaper to fly to Cotonou (Benin) or Accra (Ghana) and take a bush taxi from there.

From the USA, you'll have to take Air Afrique or Ghana Airways from New York, transferring in Dakar (Senegal), Abidjan or Accra, or go via Europe.

Africa

Air Cameroon has flights to/from Ouagadougou for CFA108,900/119,900 one way/return. Nigeria Airways and Air Afrique have a number of flights between Lomé and various West African cities, including Abidjan, Bamako (Mali), Cotonou and Niamey (Niger). From other parts of the continent, Ethiopian Airlines flies between Nairobi and Lomé via Kinshasa and Aeroflot has a flight between Lomé and Johannesburg (South Africa).

LAND
Benin & Ghana

Bush taxi Peugeot 504s and minibuses from Lomé to Cotonou (155km) or Accra (200 km) cost CFA2500 and CFA2000, respectively. The Ghanaian border closes at 6 pm sharp, whereas the southern Benin border is open 24 hours. There are always lots of ve-

hicles headed in either direction, so you never have to wait long. You can reach Niamey in Niger via Benin (1217km). The roads are tar all the way. Alternatively you could go via northern Togo.

It's possible to get to Côte d'Ivoire from Lomé via the coastal route through Ghana. Air-conditioned STIF buses go from Lomé to Abidjan. The STIF depot is about 750m beyond Hôtel Palm Beach as you head towards Cotonou.

If you've got your own transport, an interesting but longer way to reach Accra is to go via Kpalimé, north-west of Lomé. From there, you go west to the Ghanaian border, then south-west along Lake Volta. This route is tar all the way.

Burkina Faso

Lomé to Ouagadougou usually takes about 36 hours, with the night spent at the border. A bush taxi or minibus direct to Ouagadougou costs CFA15,000; it's cheaper (about CFA5000 less) to go to Dapaong and get another bush taxi or minibus from there. Buses for Ouagadougou leave from the Gare de Kara in Agbalepedo.

You can reach Niamey in Niger via northern Togo and Burkina Faso (two long days from Lomé), although the roads via Benin are better.

Togo's northern border closes around 6 pm, but cars can usually get through after this by paying a dash.

Border Crossings

The border with Ghana slams shut as soon as there is any political instability in Lomé (as there was after the presidential elections in June 1998). Check before setting off whether the border is open or not. You can cross the border just west of Lomé, or, more interesting but longer, you can go via Kpalimé to Ho or Kpandu.

The Benin border at Hilla-Condji is relatively trouble-free, and it is possible to get a 48 hour visa here, which can be extended in Cotonou.

The border post north of Dapaong between Togo and Burkina Faso closes at 6 pm and crossings are generally hassle-free.

Getting Around

BUSH TAXI & MINIBUS

For travel upcountry, minibuses are the primary means of transport, and most are in fairly good condition. There are many police checkpoints, so travelling can be agonisingly slow. A supplementary charge is levied for luggage and you'll have to bargain furiously because they'll sometimes ask for as much as a third of the ticket price. To Kpalimé, for example, the fare is CFA 1000 and the typical luggage fee is CFA200; for Dapaong, it's CFA4500 and CFA500, respectively.

TOGO

TRAIN

For total submersion in African life, try the train. There is now only one line, from Lomé to Blitta. The train leaves from Lomé on Tuesday, Thursday and Saturday morning and returns the following day; it stops at Tsévié, Notsé and Atakpamé. The cost is CFA1160 one way. Take drinks with you as none are sold on the train.

CAR & MOTORCYCLE

Roads in Togo are in fairly good condition. The one major exception is the stretch between Atakpamé and the north, which is potholed.

Lomé

Before the country's political troubles in the 1990s, Lomé (population 600,000) was the pearl of West Africa, with tranquil beaches, exotic markets and friendly people. A few hotels are still doing good business, but the majority, especially the large ones, are almost deserted. Should the country's political disturbances subside, a fast recovery is likely as Lomé has more than its fair share of attractions. As well as the beaches, it has a lively nightlife, great restaurants and an intriguing fetish market.

Orientation

Orienting yourself is fairly easy in Lomé. Most places of interest to travellers are in or just outside the D-shaped central area defined by the coastal highway and the semicircular Blvd de 13 Janvier (often called Blvd Circulaire).

The heart of town is around the intersection of Rue de la Gare and Rue du Commerce, which becomes Rue du Lac Togo beyond the market area . The market is a few blocks to the east of the intersection and the landmark SGGG supermarket is about six blocks north along Rue de la Gare. A block north of the SGGG is Ave du 24 Janvier, which runs east-west. Ave Maman N'Danida (formerly Rue d'Amoutivé), which becomes Route d'Atakpamé, leads north from the centre out to the airport, university and, eventually, Atakpamé.

Maps For detailed maps of Lomé, try the Direction de la Cartographie Nationale on Ave Sarakawa.

Information

Tourist Information The tourist office (☎ 21 43 13) on Rue du Lac Togo, just west of Chez Marox, usually has maps of Togo and Lomé, but no other information. Air Afrique's free *Togo: Guide Touristique* has some additional information.

Money The major banks, including BIA-Togo, BTCI, UTB (agent for Crédit Lyonnais) and Ecobank, are all conveniently clustered in the centre at or near the corner of Rue de la Gare and Rue du Commerce. Ecobank's commissions are typical – 2% on travellers cheques and nothing for cash (they have a board displaying rates). Proof of purchase is required to change travellers cheques.

SDV Togo Voyages (☎ 21 26 11 or 21 69 16, fax 21 26 12) in the centre of town at 2 Rue du Commerce is the American Express representative.

Post & Communications The main post office is on Ave de la Libération, between Blvd du 13 Janvier and Ave du 24 Janvier. Poste restante here is reliable and efficient. There is a small fee for each item you collect (about CFA200) and the items are held for two months.

There are international telephone and telex facilities at the major hotels (expensive but reliable), but it's cheaper to use the telephones behind the main post office.

On the southern boundary of the Université du Benin at 1542 Blvd de la Kara there is an Internet service – Computer Services (☎ 22 42 20, fax 21 26 88, email cstogo@cafe.tg).

Travel Agencies & Tour Operators There's no lack of travel agencies. Many offer excursions to the interior, typically

TOGO

LOMÉ

Gulf of Guinea

To Marché des
Féticheurs (2km) &
Gare d'Agbodessewa

To Restaurant-
Pili Pili (14km)

Route d'Aného

To Foyer
des Marins, Hôtel
de la Paix Pullman, Bar
Belgica, Hôtel Sarakawa (3km),
Alt Munchen, Robinson Plage &
Le Ramatou (7km), Chez Alice (13km),
Lac Togo, Aného & Benin

To Airport (5km), Gare de
Kara & Atakpamé

To Ramco
Supermarché,
Tokoin & Université
du Bénin

Military
Camp

To Gare de Kpalimé,
Ghanaian Embassy
(1.5km) & Kpalimé

Lac Ouest (La Laguna)

Nyekonakopé

Leodjoviakopé

To Aflao (Ricardo's) & Ghanaian Border (400m)

Boulevard du 13 Janvier

Rue Lassey

Avenue de Gaulle

Avenue Sarraut

Avenue Duckboh

Boulevard de la Marina

Route d'Aflao

Avenue Georges Pompidou

Rue du Golfe

Rue de Kouromé

Rue de la Marina

Boulevard de la Marina

Boulevard de la Marina

Avenue Georges Pompidou

Rue du Commerce

Rue du Maréchal Foch

Avenue Maman N'Danida

Boulevard du 13 Janvier

Rue du Grand Marché

Rue de la Gare

Boulevard de la Marina

TOGO

300 m
150
0

500 m
250
0

LOMÉ

PLACES TO STAY
5 Hôtel du Boulevard
16 Hôtel Avenida
17 Hôtel Ahoefa
22 Secourina Hôtel
38 Hôtel Palm Beach;
    Le Privilège Discotheque;
    Ethiopian Airlines
44 Hôtel du Golfe
65 Hôtel Mawuli
75 Hôtel du 2 Février Sofitel
79 Hôtel Ahodikpé Éboma
82 Hôtel le Bénin
85 Hôtel le Galion
86 Hôtel le Maxime
88 Hôtel California
89 Hôtel Lily
91 Salam Motel

PLACES TO EAT
1 Le Kilimanjaro
3 Le Shanghai
6 Street Food
8 La Bodega
9 Restaurant Fouta Djalon
10 Ristorante Da-Claudio
11 Lebanese Restaurant
15 Restaurant Keur Rama
18 Ristorante Big Boss
19 Restaurant la Pirogue
20 Golden Crown
24 Chez Marox
35 Restaurant Sénégalais
    de la Paix
36 Le Square Taverne
41 Croissant Chaud
52 Restaurant (no name)

53 Restaurant de l'Amitié
58 Restaurant Mini-Brasserie
59 Le Gatto Bar
61 Papillon
63 Au Relais de la Poste
67 Café Brussels; Circus
    Nightclub
77 Okavango
78 Bar Fifty-Fifty (Free Time)
90 L'Auberge Provençale

OTHER
2 Maladise (Bookshop)
4 BTCI Bank
7 Le Robinet
12 Le Byblos
13 Bar Panini
14 Nigerian Embassy
21 Mobil Station
23 Tourist Office
25 Netherlands Embasssy
26 STIF Buses to Abidjan
27 Taxi Stand
28 US Embassy
29 American Cultural Center
30 Goethe Institut
31 Cathedral
32 Gare de Contonou
    (Aného & Contonou)
33 Ecobank
34 Couronne de Mai
    Supermarché
37 SDV Togo Voyages (Amex)
39 Immeuble Taba (Yildizzard
    Lebanese Restaurant;
    Air France; Ghana
    Airways; KLM; Sabena)

40 Goyi Score Supermarket
42 Church
43 Immeuble Vendôme
    (Nigeria Airways;
    Nouvelles Frontières Corsair)
45 Artisan Stalls
46 BTCI Bank
47 Togo Voyages
48 BIA-Togo Bank
49 Librairie Bon Pasteur
50 Grand Marché
51 UTB Bank;
    Air Afrique
54 Le Mandingue Jazz Club
55 Z Nightclub
56 Domino Snack Bar
57 L'Abreuvoir
60 Boston Pub
62 Centre Culturel Français
64 Post Office;
    Telecom
66 Village Artisanal
68 Train Station
69 Musée National;
    Palais du Congrès
70 Place des Martyrs
71 SGGG Supermarket
72 Sûreté (Immigration)
73 Direction de la
    Cartographie Nationale
74 Place de l'Indépendance
76 Stadium
80 French Consulate
81 Tennis Club
83 Presidential Palace
84 Bric à Brac
87 German Embassy

CFA80,000 for a three day trip to the north. One of the best is SDV Togo Voyages, the American Express representative (for contact details see Money earlier in this section). Another reliable agent is Togo Voyages (☎ 21 12 77) at 13 Rue du Grand Marché. The Nouvelles Frontières-Corsair (☎ 21 08 03) office is in the Immeuble Vendôme on Rue du Maréchal Foch.

Bookshops The two best bookshops are Librairie Bon Pasteur (☎ 21 36 28), a block west of the cathedral on Rue Aniko Palako; and Maladise, which is behind the *commis-sariat central*. They have street maps of Lomé (CFA3000) and occasionally have publications in English such as the *International Herald Tribune* and *Time* magazine.

Cultural Centres The US Cultural Center is opposite the US embassy on Rue du Maréchal Foch. The Centre Culturel Français near the corner of Ave de la Libération and Ave du 24 Janvier has a good selection of books and papers, including *Le Monde*.

Medical Services For medical treatment, a good place to try is Clinique de l'Union

TOGO

(☎ 21 77 13) near the École Française in Nyekonakopé. The Hôpital Tokoin (☎ 21 25 01) on the Route de Kpalimé, about 3km north of the centre of Lomé usually has a French physician.

Dangers & Annoyances Petty crime is a problem in Lomé. There are lots of pickpockets around the Grand Marché and along Rue du Commerce, and muggings are frequent, some at knife-point. The worst thing you could do is walk along the beach alone at night. Indeed, walking anywhere around the city at night is very dangerous – take a taxi. Even then, avoid the bars at the Ghanaian border (eg Ricardo's), which resemble the famous intergalactic bar scene in *Star Wars*. Also avoid the Blvd de la Marina at night – the police roadblocks there are an unofficial revenue collection exercise (and a foreigner was killed at one in 1996).

Place de l'Indépendance

The gilded bronze statue of President Eyadéma and the statue of his mother were taken down in 1991 during the civil disturbances. On the east side of the square is the Palais du Congrès, previously the headquarters of Eyadéma's RPT party.

Musée National

The entrance to the museum is at the back of the Palais du Congrès in Place de 'Indépendance. It houses historical artefacts, pottery, costumes, musical instruments, woodcarvings, traditional medicinal remedies and 'thunder stones' and cowrie shells, both formerly used as legal tender. It's open from 8 am to noon and 3 to 5.30 pm Monday to Friday, and admission is CFA300.

Marché des Féticheurs

The fetish market is in the Akodessawa area, 4km north-east of the centre. It has a remarkable supply of traditional medicines used by sorcerers, including skulls of monkeys and birds, porcupine skin, warthog teeth and all sizes of bones and skulls. It's also a great place to buy grisgris, charms

Fetishes can take many forms, such as this elaborately decorated fertility staff.

which are worn around the neck to ward off various evils.

From the Grand Marché, take a shared taxi (CFA250 or CFA600 for a taxi to yourself) along Blvd Notre Dame. This photogenic area has become quite touristy of late, and there are some very persistent touts.

Activities

The surf in Lomé is very dangerous because of a strong undertow, and drownings are common – be careful. Many of the beaches are also used as the local toilet. The best by default is in front of the Hôtel le Bénin. The beaches east of Lomé are better and more secluded – see the Around Lomé section following.

The pool at the Hôtel Sarakawa is Olympic size (CFA3000 for nonguests). Hôtel le

Bénin and the Foyer des Marins charge nonguests CFA2000 and CFA1000, respectively, to use their pools, which are clean but crowded at weekends.

Apart from swimming, there are tennis courts at the large hotels and there is a horse riding centre just beyond the airport. Horse riding is also possible along the beach near the Hôtel Sarakawa (Baguida Plage) and near Foyer des Marins.

Places to Stay

Listed here are accommodation options within 5km of the centre of town. Some other options (including camping) further from the centre are listed in the Around Lomé section following.

Places to Stay – Budget

The very cheap *Hôtel Atlantique* in a rough area on the western outskirts of town, 500m from the Ghanaian border, has clean rooms without fan for CFA3000.

Near the central area, the best by far is the *Hôtel Mawuli* (☎ 21 55 05, 21 Rue Maoussas). Secure doubles with fan and clean shared bathroom cost CFA5000. It's in the Zongo district a block or two south of Blvd du 13 Janvier and a block east of the mosque.

The *Salam Motel* on Blvd de la Marina has clean cramped rooms with twin beds, fan and grubby shared bathroom for CFA 4000. Recently it has attracted its share of drug dealers and lowlifes. A block east on the same road is *Hôtel Lily*, which has small rooms with fan and bathroom for CFA3800, most of them occupied by prostitutes.

Better value is the *Hôtel California* (☎ 21 78 75), which is a poorly signposted four-storey establishment two blocks west of the Hôtel le Maxime and just a block from the seafront. Single/double rooms with fan, balcony and hot shower cost CFA6500/9000. There's a good restaurant and a *paillote* bar outside.

If you don't mind paying a bit more, check out the excellent *Hôtel le Galion* (☎ 22 00 30, 12 Rue des Camomilles). There's a lounge upstairs with relaxing armchairs and shelves full of books, and a bar

downstairs, which is popular with locals and travellers. Ice cold beers are CFA300. Bright, attractive doubles with fan and clean bathroom cost CFA6500 (CFA9000 with air-con). They have a great CD collection and Emile, the owner, often jams on flute with a group of friends accompanying on guitar. You will probably be roped into a game of *pétanque*.

Hôtel Ahodikpé Éboma (☎ 21 47 80, 45 Blvd du 13 Janvier), also on the western side of town, is mentioned here as a place to avoid as it has recently suffered an influx of piratical permanents. Doubles with fan/air-con are CFA4000/6500; water and electricity are rare.

Two possibilities on the eastern side of town are the *Hôtel du Boulevard* (☎ 21 15 91, 204 Blvd du 13 Janvier), half a block west of the intersection with Route d'Atakpamé, and the *Hôtel Ahoefa* (☎ 21 42 48) further east, a block behind the Hôtel Avenida. They charge CFA5000 for a tidy room with fan and bathroom. The Boulevard is in a good location that's lively at night, while the Ahoefa is on a quiet side street and has a more African feel. It has a small shady area outside for drinks and polite service – the hotel's hallmark.

The *Bar-Carnaval New Look* (☎ 22 21 67) 3km north of the centre, behind the train station in Tokoin, is good value at CFA6500 for a large air-con room with bathroom.

Places to Stay – Mid-Range & Top End

A great place for the price is the *Foyer des Marins* (☎ 27 53 51) on the Route d'Aného 5km east of the centre, just before the Rond-Point du Port. It has singles/doubles with fan and shared bathroom for CFA5000/7000 (CFA7500/9500 for apartments with kitchens). Other features include a pool, snack bar and a bar. The only problem for travellers is that the owner must give first priority to sailors, so call in advance.

For a place closer to the centre, try *Hôtel le Maxime* (☎ 21 74 48), 1.5km west of the centre on the Route d'Aflao. This long-standing French-run place has rooms with

TOGO

bathroom and air-con for CFA12,000, and a pleasant patio.

Closer to the centre is the *Secourina Hôtel* (☎ 21 60 20) on Rue du Lac Togo, at the intersection with Route d'Aného. It has air-con singles with shower and telephone for CFA7500 to CFA9500, and doubles for CFA8500 to CFA10,500. The well maintained *Hôtel Avenida* (☎ 21 46 72), half a block east of Blvd du 13 Janvier near the Nigerian embassy, has a decent restaurant and singles/doubles for CFA9000/12,000.

The *Hôtel du Golfe* (☎ 21 51 41/2, 5 Rue du Commerce), isn't a bad place but it's a bit hit and miss as to the quality of the rooms you get. A good room is worth the CFA15,000 you will pay for it.

The best buy among the top end hotels is unquestionably the long-standing *Hôtel le Bénin* (☎ 21 24 85) on Blvd de la Marina, 500m west of the town centre. At this well maintained independence-era hotel, renovated rooms cost from CFA23,000.

A popular, new high-rise hotel is *Hôtel Palm Beach* (☎ 218511) at the corner of Rue de Kouromé and Blvd de la Marina, which has rooms from CFA45,000. Features include a pool, weight room and cable TV; the town's most upmarket disco, Privilège, is nearby.

The best beachfront hotel is the PLM *Hôtel Sarakawa* (☎ 21 65 90) 3km east of the town centre on the Benin road. Expect to pay CFA30,000 a room (CFA45,000 with ocean view). Features include a wonderful pool, horse riding, tennis court, a hairdresser, shops and a paucity of guests.

The only other ocean-view hotel is the fast declining *Hôtel de la Paix Pullman* (☎ 21 52 97), which has a beach opposite, a pool, casino and tennis court. Rooms cost from CFA23,000 to CFA35,000.

The top hotel is the somewhat beleaguered *Hôtel du 2 Février Sofitel* (☎ 21 00 03) just west of Place de l'Indépendance. It costs about the same as the Sarakawa but half of the rooms have been closed off and are only reopened when there is a political party meeting or conference – in which case visitors may well be asked to relocate.

Places to Eat

Cheap Eats One of the best places for *street food*, day and night is north of Blvd du 13 Janvier along the Route d'Atakpamé. On Blvd du 13 Janvier, at the junction with Rue de Bé, *Restaurant Fouta Djalon* is a great place which offers several African dishes (riz sauce arachide is CFA500).

In the heart of town, there is a terrific, cheap, *unmarked place* half a block north of the UTB bank on a north-south side street. It usually has four sauces to choose from (the sauce aubergine is great, as is the sauce de poisson); a CFA350 serving is filling.

Another area for inexpensive food is around the SGGG department store on Rue de la Gare.

African Lomé has a good selection of African restaurants. The *Restaurant de l'Amitié (17 Rue du Grand Marché)* is a popular place, offering mostly Senegalese dishes (CFA600 to CFA1200). *Restaurant Sénégalais de la Paix* is at the intersection of Rue du Commerce and Rue de la Gare. Most dishes are in the CFA850 to CFA1400 range. Both places are open until around 8 pm.

On the eastern side of town, on Blvd du 13 Janvier near the Nigerian embassy, is *Keur Rama* (closed Monday). The cuisine is Senegalese and Togolese and most dishes cost from CFA2000 to CFA2500. *Restaurant la Pirogue*, several blocks south at the junction of Blvd du 13 Janvier and Rue de la Paix, has similar prices, with French dishes as well as an African selection.

Also on Blvd du 13 Janvier, just east of Ave du Nouveau Marché, is *Le Kilimanjaro*, the city's only Ethiopian restaurant. A huge plate of vegetarian sauces and *injera* (Ethiopian bread), plenty for two people, costs CFA3000 per person, more with meat.

The *Jerusalem Bar* is a living monument to Bob Marley and reggae. It has good food (breakfast CFA1000, meals CFA3000) and on Wednesday evening they put on a dinner with traditional dishes and music.

Asian The best Chinese restaurants are all on Blvd du 13 Janvier. Starting at the eastern end, at the intersection with the ocean road, there's the long-standing **Golden Crown** which has good quality food at moderate prices. Halfway along Blvd du 13 Janvier near the commissariat central is **Le Shang-hai**. Closed on Wednesday, it's one of the best and most popular Chinese restaurants and has an extensive menu.

European At the **Ristorante Da-Claudio** (☎ 22 26 65) on Blvd du 13 Janvier just north of the intersection with Blvd Notre Dame you'll find pizzas for CFA2000 to CFA4000, pasta dishes for CFA2000 to CFA3500 and, best of all, a choice between air-con dining inside and a relaxing terrace outside. Highly recommended is **Le Gatto Bar** on Ave du 24 Janvier. The food is not cheap (most dishes are CFA3500 to CFA 5000) but the decor is pleasant.

Au Relais de la Poste on Ave de la Libération opposite the post office has a friendly atmosphere, and wandering minstrels sometimes play during the meal. An omelette and chips costs CFA1000. The **Restaurant Mini-Brasserie** has a convivial atmosphere and is a long-standing favourite. The food is good, with main dishes in the CFA3000 to CFA6000 range. It's one of the best places to meet other travellers and have an ice-cold beer (CFA500).

For a French meal in the CFA2300 to CFA3000 range, try **Hôtel le Galion**. One of their favourites is **cuisses de grenouille** (frogs' legs) for CFA1800. They provide snack food all day long. A block away, towards the beach, is the more expensive, but not as good, restaurant at **Hôtel le Maxime**. Salads are from CFA2000, lobster brochettes CFA6000, steak dishes about CFA4500 and profiteroles CFA2800.

One place described as 'very French' by an expat is **Okavango** on Blvd du 13 Janvier. It has an outdoor area with a garden and an air-con indoors section. Excellent meals are from CFA4000 to CFA5000.

The **Ristorante Big Boss** on the eastern side of town on Blvd du 13 Janvier, about 250m north of the ocean road, is an expensive place, with most main courses starting at CFA5000. Another upmarket French restaurant, which also features African dishes, is **Pili-Pili** on the eastern side of town on Rue de l'Entente behind Hôtel de la Paix (dishes start from CFA2500). Other upmarket French choices are **Le Square Taverne** between the Hôtel du Golfe and Blvd de la Marina, and **Le Maleson** on Ave du 24 Janvier near the Centre Culturel Français.

L'Auberge Provençale on the coastal road near the Ghanaian border has become a culinary institution. The cuisine is southern French and the seafood is superb. You can dine inside or outside; it's closed Tuesday.

At the eastern end of Rue du Lac Togo is **Chez Marox**, a popular open-air German beer garden and delicatessen. The food is not cheap (eg sausages with salad and chips costs CFA5000), however, and the service is slow. Somewhat better is the attractively decorated German-run **Alt München** (closed Tuesday) on the Route d'Aného, just east of the Hôtel Sarakawa. The seafood is particularly good here and the service is excellent.

For Spanish food there is only one choice. **La Bodega** on Blvd du 13 Janvier, near the intersection with Rue de la Marne, serves tapas, paella and other dishes for CFA3500.

Lebanese **Yildizzard** on the first floor of the Immeuble Taba, behind the Hôtel Palm Beach, is very popular with the Lebanese community; hearty dishes cost from CFA 3000. The former Le Pacha nightclub on Blvd Notre Dame is now a small nameless **Lebanese restaurant**. It has a good selection of mezzes and other inexpensive dishes.

Cafes & Patisseries Sadly, there are no cafes in Lomé where you can get a good cup of coffee. The city's best patisserie is **Croissant Chaud** on Rue de Kouromé, near the church. It also serves mediocre brewed coffee. For the yummiest fresh fruit juices (CFA300 to CFA1500) in town, try the air-con **Papillon** on Ave 24 du Janvier. The **Café Brussels** on the corner of Route de Kpalimé and Ave Nicolas Grunitsky is the best place to go for ice cream (CFA800 to

TOGO

CFA2000). Upstairs there is a Moroccan restaurant, which has meals from CFA3500 and serves Belgian beers.

Bar Fifty-Fifty (aka Free Time) on the western side of Blvd du 13 Janvier, just north of the Hôtel Ahodikpé, is very popular and lively. Food is served only in the evenings. You can also get good food at the *Boston Pub* opposite the Centre Culturel Français.

Entertainment

Bars Lomé is a great place for drinking because the beer in Togo is the cheapest in West Africa. Two of the most popular more upmarket places are *Chez Marox* and the air-con *Restaurant Mini-Brasserie* (see Places to Eat earlier for more details). Both cater primarily for foreigners.

For a bit of Wild West atmosphere you have two good choices. Perched on the Ghanaian border on the fringes of the city, *Ricardo's* is not for the faint-hearted. It's an outdoor place with a regular crowd of 'contrabandistas', drug dealers, car smugglers and prostitutes. In town, *Le Robinet (217 Blvd du 13 Janvier)* is another very popular outdoor place that fairly buzzes at night. It can get a bit rough here at times, but the local crowd will probably keep an eye on you.

Further east on Blvd du 13 Janvier is the cosy *Bar Panini*, a great place to enjoy a beer and a late-night snack. A couple of blocks west of the Hôtel Sarakawa on Route d'Aného, at the corner of Rue Garibonne, you'll find the friendly *Bar Belgica*. It's a good out-of-town option for a beer and a bite to eat.

The air-con *bar* at the airport is expensive (CFA800 for a small beer) – join airport workers at the *bar* across the road from the airport entrance where beer is only CFA375.

Nightclubs The European-oriented, disco-like nightclubs are expensive and have cover charges, typically CFA3000, which usually include a drink. The hottest and best known is *L'Abreuvoir* in the centre of town on Rue de la Gare. Small beers are CFA 2000, and there's a snack bar. Just across

the road is the popular bar and nightclub *Domino*, an infamous pick-up joint. (The locals know the area bounded by the Restaurant Mini-Brasserie, Domino and L'Abreuvoir as the Bermuda Triangle – once you get inside you lose all bearings!)

On Blvd du 13 Janvier, just north of the Nigerian embassy, is *Le Byblos* (open weekends only), which has a Caribbean theme and is frequented by rich young Togolese. North of Hôtel du 2 Février Sofitel is the *Circus (8 Ave de Nicolas Grunitsky)*, formerly Maquina Loca. It occasionally has live bands.

Other discos include *The Blue Night*, which is on the north side of the lagoon on Route de Kpalimé; the *Z Nightclub* on Rue de Colonel Maroix (a stiff CFA4000 cover charge); and the glitzy *Le Privilège* near the Hôtel Palm Beach (a barn-like place popular with teenagers and with a CFA3500 entry and expensive drinks).

Music Venues For live entertainment, head for *Chez Alice* about 12km from the heart of Lomé on the coastal highway to Aného. Every Wednesday night, the Togolese dance group Sakra performs here. It's great fun and is always packed till the early hours of the morning. The cost for nonresidents, with dinner, is about CFA4500.

Le Mandingue on Rue de la Gare is transformed from a bar-restaurant into a jazz club at the weekend. There is no cover charge but the price of the drinks is high (beers from CFA800 and cocktails from CFA2000).

Cinemas The best cinema, the air-conditioned *Concorde* (☎ 21 00 03), is at Hôtel du 2 Février, with shows at 6.30 and 9 pm. There's another cinema, *Opéra* (☎ 21 69 77), on Rue du Commerce.

Shopping

Supermarkets Goyi Score on Rue du Kouromé in the centre of town is the largest supermarket, followed by Supermarché Couronne de Mai on Ave de la Libération, just south of Rue du Commerce. Another option is the Indian-run Ramco Supermarché just south of the bridge on Ave de la Libération. It sells lots of American goods.

Art & Craftwork The Grand Marché has plenty of colourful cotton material, most of it wax cloth from Holland and cheaper African material. It's sold by the *pagne* (about 2m), the amount needed for a complete outfit. Don't be surprised if they sometimes refuse to sell less than this – it's not always easy to sell the remainder. The market is open every day except Sunday, and closes at 4 pm sharp.

For woodcarvings and brasswork, take a walk along Rue des Artisans, a short alley in the centre of town on the eastern side of Hôtel du Golfe, where there are many Senegalese and Malian traders. Their opening prices are usually ridiculously high, so expect lots of hard bargaining.

For high quality art, your best bet by far is Bric à Brac (☎ 210245) a block east of Hôtel le Maxime on Blvd de la Marina. Messie Catherine, the friendly owner, has a showroom of good-quality West African pieces from around West Africa and her fixed prices are very reasonable.

The Village Artisanal on Ave du Nouveau Marché, between Ave du 24 Janvier and Blvd du 13 Janvier, is an easygoing place to shop. You'll see Togolese artisans weaving cloth, carving statues, making baskets and lampshades of rattan, sewing leather shoes and constructing cane chairs and tables – all for sale at reasonable fixed prices.

Lomé is famous for leather sandals. They were originally all made at the Village Artisanal, but you can also buy them around the Grand Marché for about CFA3000.

Getting There & Away

Air Most of the major airlines are in the heart of Lomé and include Ghana Airways (☎ 21 56 91), Air France (☎ 21 69 10), KLM (☎ 21 63 60) and Sabena (☎ 21 75 55, 21 73 33) in Immeuble Taba; Air Afrique (☎ 21 20 42) at 12 Rue du Commerce; and Nigeria Airways (☎ 58 26 32) in Immeuble Vendôme on Rue du Maréchal Foch. Aeroflot (☎ 21 04 80) at 7 Ave du 24 Janvier has the

cheapest flights to Europe, while Swissair (☎ 21 31 57) is on the eastern side of town on Rue du Lac Togo near Chez Marox.

Bus, Bush Taxi & Minibus Taxis and minibuses travelling east to Aného and Cotonou leave from the Gare d'Akodessewa (5km east of the centre and 1km beyond Bé market) and, more conveniently, from the smaller gare routière (Gare de Cotonou) on Rue du Commerce just south of the market.

Buses for Accra leave from just across the Ghanaian border in Aflao; those for Kpalimé (CFA1000) leave from Gare de Kpalimé, 3km from the centre on the Route de Kpalimé; most of the rest, including those for Kara, Atakpamé and Dapaong leave from Gare Routière du Lycée, which is several kilometres north of the centre towards the airport. The Gare de Kara 10km north of the centre in Agbalepedo, off the road to Atakpamé, is not used much, although this is where buses to Ouagadougou go from.

A bush taxi from Gare d'Akodessewa to the Ghanaian border should cost no more than CFA250, but getting that price is difficult. Most minibuses are in excellent condition. Some destinations and fares from Lomé include: Atakpamé (CFA1500), Bassar (CFA3050), Cotonou in Benin (CFA 1500 to CFA2000), Dapaong (CFA4850), Kara (CFA3200), Kpalimé (CFA1000) and Sokodé (CFA2750). There's an extra charge for baggage (eg CFA400 to Kara) and CFA100 for Assistance Secours (a sort of insurance). Bush taxis to Ouagadougou cost CFA15,000 direct and CFA8225 if you go to Dapaong and get another from there.

Train The train station is in the centre of town at the intersection of Ave du Nouveau Marché and Ave du 24 Janvier. There is now only one train from Lomé to Blitta; see the main Getting Around section earlier in this chapter for more details.

Getting Around

To/From the Airport A taxi from the airport into Lomé (6km) costs at least

CFA3000, but it's only CFA1500 to CFA 2000 from town to the airport.

Taxi The city has no public buses, so your only choice is a *line* (fixed route) taxi or a private hire. Taxis are abundant, even at night, and have no meters. Fares are CFA200 for a shared taxi (CFA300 after 6 pm), more to the outlying areas, and CFA 750 for a *course* (short trip in a taxi to yourself). At the hotels you'll pay more, and rates double at midnight. A taxi by the hour should cost CFA2500 if you bargain well.

Motorcycle-taxis are also extremely popular (and dangerous). From the Ghanaian border to the centre of Lomé is CFA100 and from the border to the airport is CFA300.

Car Hertz (☎ 21 44 79, 22 04 69), Europcar (☎ 21 13 24) and Avis (☎ 21 10 33) all have booths at the airport. In town, Europcar is on the western end of Blvd du 13 Janvier, while Avis is at 252 Blvd du 13 Janvier, next door to Le Robinet and across the street from Hertz at 215 Blvd du 13 Janvier. A Toyota Starlet with air-con costs roughly CFA 30,000 per day plus petrol for travel not exceeding 150km.

AROUND LOMÉ
Beaches
East of Lomé, on or just off the highway to Lac Togo and Aného, are several popular beach resorts where you can camp or stay in bungalows. The first you come to, 9km from the centre, are Le Ramatou and Robinson's Plage. The well marked turn-off is 1km east of the large roundabout at the port. A taxi from the Grand Marché in the centre of town should cost no more than CFA700. A shared taxi to Lomé from the main road costs CFA150. At weekends, you could try hitching with expats.

Le Ramatou (☎ 21 43 53) has big plain bungalows with up to four single beds, mosquito nets and shared bathroom for CFA 2000 and CFA6000/10,000 for rooms with fan/air-con and bathroom. Lately, much of the picnic area seems to have fallen into the sea but swimming is still possible, although

much of the camping area (CFA1000 per person) was washed away.

Robinson's Plage next door has a slightly more formal atmosphere and superb restaurant. The spacious thatched-roof bungalows have twin beds and mosquito nets and cost CFA3500 (CFA5000 with bathroom). There are also rooms with air-con and bathroom for CFA8000/CFA9000. Food is also available, with menus from CFA3500 to CFA6000. Be warned – walking on the beach at night is very dangerous.

About 4km east of Robinson's Plage, just off the highway to Aného, is the tiny village of Avéposo. You can camp here at *Chez Alice* (☎/fax 27 91 72) for CFA1000, or you can stay in basic bungalows (CFA3500) with shared bathroom. There are also rooms (CFA6000) with fan and clean shared bathroom (CFA10,000 with bathroom and closer to the sea). There's live entertainment most nights – see Entertainment in the Lomé section for more details. A bush taxi from Lomé is CFA150.

About 13km east of Lomé is the *Camping Bar Boukts* (☎ 21 29 03), a relaxed place near the palm-fringed Baguida Plage, with camping (CFA1000 per person), guest rooms and a restaurant.

Lac Togo
The popular access point to the lake is Agebodrafo, 30km east of Lomé. The lake is part of the inland lagoon which stretches all the way from Lomé to Aného, and is good for windsurfing and water-skiing. You can eat lunch or stay overnight here or hire a pirogue across the lake to Togoville.

Places to Stay & Eat There are two hotels on the southern side of Lac Togo. From Lomé, the first one you come to is *L'Auberge du Lac* (☎ 27 09 10), which is about halfway to Aného. It's just outside the village of Kpéssi. The auberge is beautifully situated among palm trees on an elevated knoll overlooking the lake. It has a friendly manager, a restaurant and spacious comfortable bungalows with two beds and bathroom for CFA8000.

Several kilometres further east on the highway from Lomé to Cotonou is the top hotel on the lake, the French-run *Hôtel le Lac* (☎ *35 00 05)*, which is well signposted off the main highway. Facilities include a good restaurant, a saltwater pool (CFA1000 for nonguests) and water-skiing (CFA4500 per trip). Air-con singles/doubles cost CFA12,000/16,000. The *menu du jour* is CFA6000, and you can get snacks at the bar.

Getting There & Away The cheapest way to get to the lake from Lomé is to hop on a minibus (CFA500) to Aného and get off at the turn-off for whichever hotel you choose.

Togoville

On the northern banks of Lac Togo, Togoville is mainly interesting for its history. It was from here that voodoo practitioners were taken as slaves to Haiti, now a major centre for voodoo. And it was here in 1884 that chief Mlapa III signed a peace treaty with the German explorer Nachtigal which gave the Germans rights over all of Togo. Today, the only attractions are the chief's house, the church and the artisanal. The artisanal is between the village's main pier and the nearby church, and consists of several buildings. The church has some beautiful stained-glass windows.

About 100m west of the church is an interesting modern structure called the Maison Royal, the chief's house. The only reason to come here is to meet the chief, Mlapa V Moyennant, who will gladly show you a room (the 'museum') which houses his throne as well as some interesting old photos of his grandfather. A gift may be expected. The best time to visit is early on Saturday morning when he holds court (*fait la justice)* on the patio of his compound.

Alternatively, you could offer one of the local fishermen a small *cadeau* (gift) to take you with them on their daily fishing excursion, departing around 5.30 am and returning around noon.

Places to Stay & Eat The cheapest accommodation is at the dumpy *Auberge de l'Arbre à Palabre* two blocks east of the market. It has cell-like rooms without electricity for CFA6000 a month, so you should be able to get one for CFA1500 or so a night.

The best place to stay by far is the surprisingly nice *Hôtel Nachtigal* (☎ *21 64 82)* 100m west of the market. Clean, small rooms with fan and bathroom cost CFA6000 (or from CFA8000 with air-con). There is also a large paillote where you can get sandwiches from CFA1500 or a decent three-course meal for CFA5000. You can play table tennis here and then go have a drink at one of the nearby *bars*.

Getting There & Away Getting here from Lomé is a bit of a hassle. You can either go all the way to Aného, then around the lagoon to Togoville, or much quicker, go to Agebodrafo, which is about 10km before Aného, and take a canoe across the lagoon for about CFA1000 return. The canoe trip takes about 20 minutes and canoes leave periodically during the day. If you hire a canoe to yourself, with hard bargaining expect to pay about CFA2500 for the trip over and back. You can also get to Togoville by bush taxi from Aného, about 12km away (CFA250).

Vogan & Agoégan

The Friday market at Vogan is one of the largest and most colourful in Togo and should not be missed. It's a good place for practical items, although there isn't much art or craftwork. There's also a well stocked voodoo section. The activity starts about sunrise and lasts until mid-afternoon.

The *Hôtel Medius* (☎ *33 10 00)* not far from the market has clean rooms with fan for around CFA6000 (CFA8000 with air-con) and a bar-restaurant.

On Monday, there's also a market in Agoégan, which is on the intercoastal canal dividing Togo and Benin and is less than half an hour's taxi ride from Aného. It's one of the most picturesque markets in Togo, relatively untouched by outside influences.

The trip on the tar road from Lomé takes one hour and costs about CFA500 by bush taxi. If you're driving, go to Aného and take a left turn (north) to Vogan, circling around the lagoon. On Friday morning, finding a minibus in Lomé at Gare d'Akodessewa direct to Vogan should not be a problem; otherwise, change in Aného. From Togoville, bush taxis (CFA200) to Vogan leave only on Friday morning.

The South

ANÉHO

The colonial capital of Togo until 1920, Aného is about 40km east of Lomé and 2km west of the Benin border. The town is dissected by the river (formerly the lagoon); the newer section is south of the bridge. Aného looks like it's going with the wind, but it can be interesting to walk around and look at the old buildings that are still standing. You could also watch the fishermen as

they haul in their nets in the late afternoon. The major attraction is the beach. The lagoon and the ocean used to be separated by a thin strip of sand but now the lagoon flows directly into the sea. This means that the old lagoon is regularly flushed out and swimming is possible right in front of Hôtel de l'Oasis.

At night, Aného comes alive with a surprising amount of activity for such a tiny town. Along the streets you'll hear music playing and find vendors selling a variety of food.

Places to Stay

The best place to stay is **Hôtel de l'Oasis** (☎ 31 01 25) on the water's edge 40m northeast of the bridge. It has beautiful views and rooms with fan/air-con and bathroom cost CFA6500/8000, but they're usually fully booked at the weekend.

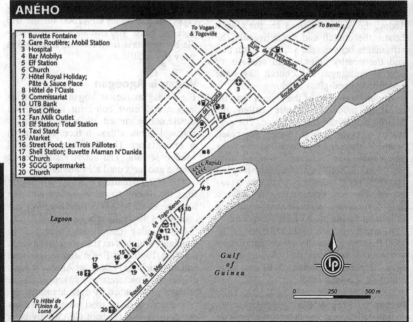

ANÉHO

1 Buvette Fontaine
2 Gare Routière; Mobil Station
3 Hospital
4 Bar Mobilys
5 Elf Station
6 Church
7 Hôtel Royal Holiday; Pâte & Sauce Place
8 Hôtel de l'Oasis
9 Commissariat
10 UTB Bank
11 Post Office
12 Fan Milk Outlet
13 Elf Station; Total Station
14 Taxi Stand
15 Market
16 Street Food; Les Trois Paillotes
17 Shell Station; Buvette Maman N'Danida
18 Church
19 SGGG Supermarket
20 Church

The ordinary *Hôtel Royal Holiday* (☎ 31 00 27) two blocks away on the noisy Rue de l'Hôpital asks CFA7500 for a large, clean room with bathroom (often no water) and fan (CFA8500 with air-con), but you can bargain the price down.

Well away from the water, *Hôtel de l'Union* (☎ 31 00 69) at the south-western entrance to town on the main highway is overpriced at CFA12,000 for a room with air-con and bathroom.

Places to Eat

On the north-eastern side of the bridge, there's a good *pâte and sauce place* hidden behind Hôtel Royal Holiday; you have to go to the end of an alley to find it. Opposite Buvette Fontaine, 200m east of the gare routière, there's a no-name *food hut* with cheap simple fare.

On the south-western side of the bridge, there are *street vendors* in the market area across from the SGGG supermarket. At night they sell omelettes, chicken, stews, brochettes, and pâte with sauce.

Entertainment

For a drink, head for the open-air *Buvette Jardin Maman N'Danida* 150m west of the market on the Route de Togo-Benin. Other bars include *Bar Mobilys* on Rue de l'Hôpital and *Les Trois Paillotes* near the market.

For dancing, try *Le Maquis* east of the bridge; entry is CFA300. To get there, catch a motorcycle-taxi (CFA100).

Getting There & Away

From Lomé, take a minibus from the Gare d'Akodessewa or from the smaller Gare de Cotonou in the centre near the market (CFA500). In Aného, bush taxis and minibuses for Lomé depart from the taxi stand opposite the market and from the gare routière near the hospital.

KPALIMÉ

Kpalimé, 120km north-west of Lomé, is in the centre of the mountainous cacao and coffee region, considered by many to be the prettiest area in Togo, and a good area for hiking. Kpalimé is noted for its mild climate, market and artisans cooperative, the Centre Artisanal (see Shopping later in this section). Nearby is Klouto, noted for its fantastic butterflies. Mt Agou, Togo's highest peak at 986m, is 20km away.

Kpalimé is spread out, so covering it on foot takes time. There are four major tar roads leading out of town – north-west towards Klouto, north-east to Atakpamé, south-west to Ho (Ghana) and south-east to Lomé. The heart of the commercial district is the Rond-Point Texaco. If you're looking for a guide, ask at the Hôtel-Restaurant Domino. A full day of guiding by motorcycle costs CFA7500.

The waterfalls, **Cascades de Kpimé**, about 12km north of Kpalimé, are usually a trickle but nonetheless a good spot for a swim in the middle of the day. Admission to the falls is CFA500.

Places to Stay – Budget

The cheap, dumpy *Chez Solo* has cell-like rooms with filthy shared toilets and a lone basic shower for CFA2050. Meals are CFA1500. The one plus is the reasonable garden. It's on the south-eastern side of town on the Route du Zongo, 1km from the centre. Almost as bad is *Hôtel le Boabab* about 1km from the centre along Rue de Kpadapé. Rooms are CFA3500 and dinner is about CFA1800.

The friendly *Auberge Amoto Zomanyi* (☎ 41 01 94) is on the south-western outskirts of town on Rue de Kpadapé (the road to Ho), about 2km from the centre. It has clean, spacious singles/doubles with fan and shared bathroom for CFA2500/3500. Two other good budget places are *Auberge Laurore* on Route d'Atakpamé (CFA4500 for a room with shower), which has a good restaurant; and *Le Palace*, just off Route de Nyivémé (CFA3500/5000 per room without/with shower).

In the centre, the long-standing *Hôtel-Restaurant Domino* (☎ 41 01 87), opposite the Rond-Point Texaco, has small rooms with fan and clean shared bathroom for

Hiking in the Kpalimé Area

The wooded Kpalimé area is great for hiking because of the thick vegetation, hilly terrain and noticeably cooler climate. But it's the butterflies that make it unique.

Take a taxi from Kpalimé up the hill to Campement de Klouto (670m), 12km to the north-west of Kpalimé. From the campement you can hike up **Mt Klouto** (741m) nearby and look over into Ghana.

The village of **Klouto**, some 600m from the campement, is the starting point for hikes to see the butterflies. Early morning is the best time to go. It's a good idea to take a guide – in the village you'll find any number of young men eager to guide you to the butterfly areas. With bargaining you should be able to get the rate down to CFA1000 per person in a group. Afterwards, you could hike alone and take some back routes down to Kpalimé.

A kilometre or so before you reach the campement you'll pass the paved turn-off for **Château Viale**. It's an astonishing medieval-style fortress of stone built by a Frenchman in 1944 as a retreat for his wife. She spent three days there, then split for France. On a clear day, there are views of Lake Volta (Ghana), but since the government purchased the chateau it has been off limits to the public. It's now a frequent weekend retreat for President Eyadéma.

Alternatively, you could climb the **Pic d'Agou** (986m), 20km south-east of Kpalimé. It is also possible to see Lake Volta from here, but during the harmattan season the views are disappointing. To get to the base of the climb at Agou Nyogbo, take a taxi from Lomé or Kpalimé and get off at the Hôpital Evangélique (in Agou Nyogbo). Finding a shared taxi (CFA500) headed to Agou can be difficult, except on market day every Friday, so you may have to charter one. In Agou, hire a boy to guide you for the first hour or so until the ascent is clear. After that just ask people along the way. The walk to the top takes three hours. The top itself is disappointing because of the antenna, fences and guards, but the walk up is peaceful and beautiful. Bring your passport because there's a sensitive TV station antenna on top and the police guards may ask to see your documents. Alternatively, you could take a taxi all the way to the top of the mountain (about CFA5000). From there you could hike back down to the main Kpalimé to Lomé highway.

Another option would be to go to the waterfalls, **Cascades de Kpimé**, north of Kpalimé. Take a taxi or a minibus north from Kpalimé in the direction of Atakpamé. After 9km you come to Kpimé-Séva, where the waterfalls are signposted. You can see them clearly in the distance. There's no need for a guide; just walk westward down the main track for 30 minutes until you reach a closed gate, then walk through a gap in it. The base of the waterfalls is 200m or so from the gate. The guardian will request CFA500.

The waterfalls are spectacular during the rainy season, but almost dry the rest of the year. From the base you can hike to the top of the falls, where there's a lake and a panoramic view, and then hike back to Kpalimé, perhaps taking a remote back route.

Yet another possibility would be to climb in the **Plateau de Danyi** area. To get there, continue north another 9km beyond Kpimé-Séva to Adéta and then turn left onto a tar road for the plateau. You'll find the seven room Motel Concordia in N'Digbé, which is on the plateau, and, a few kilometres further, the Benedictine Convent and Monastery.

CFA3000 (CFA3500 with bathroom and CFA6000 with air-con), although these are not particularly good value; prices for *chambres de passage* on request! The touts who continually pester you make this place one of Kpalimé's least attractive options.

KPALIMÉ

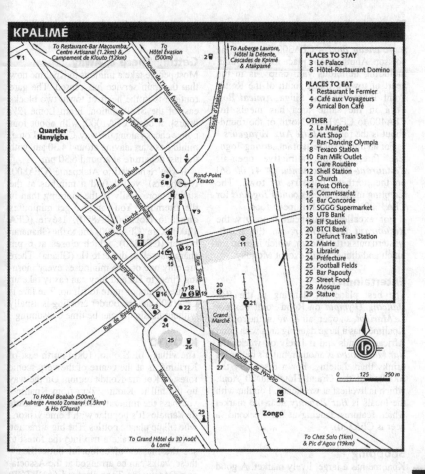

To Restaurant-Bar Macoumba,
Centre Artisanal (1.2km) &
Campement de Klouto (12km)

To
Hôtel Évasion
(500m)

To Auberge Laurore,
Hôtel la Détente,
Cascades de Kpimé
& Atakpamé

Quartier
Hanyigba

Route de l'Hôtel Évasion

Route d'Atakpamé

Rue de Nyaéme

Rue de Bakula

Rue de Missahohé

Rue de Marché

Rue de Hanyigba

Rue de Sinaé

Rue de Kpodapé

Rond-Point
Texaco

Grand
Marché

Route de Nyogbo

Route de Lomé

Zongo

To Hôtel Boabab (500m),
Auberge Amoto Zomanyi (1.5km)
& Ho (Ghana)

To Grand Hôtel du 30 Août
& Lomé

To Chez Solo (1km)
& Pic d'Agou (19km)

0   125   250 m

PLACES TO STAY
3 Le Palace
6 Hôtel-Restaurant Domino

PLACES TO EAT
1 Restaurant le Fermier
4 Café aux Voyageurs
9 Amical Bon Café

OTHER
2 Le Marigot
5 Art Shop
7 Bar-Dancing Olympia
8 Texaco Station
10 Fan Milk Outlet
11 Gare Routière
12 Shell Station
13 Church
14 Post Office
15 Commissariat
16 Bar Concorde
17 SGGG Supermarket
18 UTB Bank
19 Elf Station
20 BTCI Bank
21 Defunct Train Station
22 Mairie
23 Librairie
24 Préfecture
25 Football Fields
26 Bar Papouty
27 Street Food
28 Mosque
29 Statue

Places to Stay – Mid-Range & Top End

The *Hôtel la Détente*, is signposted 100m off the Route d'Atakpamé, about 1.5km from the town centre. Rooms with fan and shared bathroom cost CFA4500 (CFA7500 with air-con and bathroom). This is a quiet, pleasant place and food is available. It's similar in many respects to the tranquil but inconveniently located *Hôtel Évasion* (☎ 41 01 85) 1km due north of town on a dirt road, Route de l'Hôtel Évasion, between Rue Mis-

sahohé and the Route d'Atakpamé. Single/double rooms with fan cost CFA3600/5000 (CFA7000 with air-con), and you can get food here as well. The tranquil *Grand Hôtel du 30 Août* (☎ 41 00 95) 2km south of town on Route de Lomé has large air-con singles/doubles for CFA9000/12,500.

The nicest hotel in the area, *L'Auberge de Bethania* (☎ 21 35 51), has bungalows, a pool and tennis courts, but it's 30km south of Kpalimé in Avétonou on the road to Lomé.

Places to Eat

Several women opposite the Grand Marché serve *cheap food* – CFA300 for sauce de poisson. Another good place for *street food*, including delicious yam chips, is in the heart of town a block south of the Rond-Point Texaco on Rue Singa. *Amical Bon Café* in the same area has meals for CFA400 to CFA1500. North of the roundabout is the reliable *Café Aux Voyageurs*.

For an upmarket restaurant serving Togolese fare, try the attractive open-air *Restaurant-Bar Macoumba* (☎ 41 00 86) on the northern outskirts of town. The tempting menu includes *poulet Togolais* for CFA1600 as well as European food.

For excellent European food, try the *Restaurant le Fermier*, on the north-western outskirts of town, which is open for lunch and dinner daily except Monday.

Entertainment

The best place for dancing is the *Bar Dancing Olympia* on Rond-Point Texaco. *Le Marigot*, an open-air *boîte* on the road to Kpalimé, has a large dancing area with good African sounds and is lively on weekends. *Bar Macoumba* is another, but it's better for drinks than dancing. For a disco, try the *Akpéssé* at the Grand Hôtel du 30 Août, which is liveliest at weekends. Popular with the locals is *Bar Papouty* near the market which features dancing at the weekend (a beer is CFA350).

Shopping

Kpalimé has a large, lively market. A good selection of Ghanaian kente cloth is sold here, but prices are higher than in Kumasi. The long-standing Centre Artisanal is about 2km north of the centre on the road to Klouto. Here you'll find a vast array of woodcarvings, including chiefs' chairs and tables carved out of solid blocks of wood, as well as pottery, macramé and batiks. It's open from 7 am to noon and 2.30 to 5.30 pm Monday to Saturday, and from 8.30 am to 1 pm Sunday and public holidays. The Art Shop, a small box-like structure opposite Hôtel-Restaurant Domino, also has a good selection of art and craftwork (*djembe* drums, masks and statuettes).

Getting There & Away

Most people take a minibus to Kpalimé now that the train service has ceased. The gare routière is in the heart of town, two blocks east of the Shell station. From Lomé (2½ hours), it costs CFA1000, with about four police checks along the way. Going to Lomé, minibuses start leaving around 4.30 am, with the last departure at around 6.30 pm.

If you're headed to Atakpamé (CFA800, two hours), you'll find a minibus at the station more easily in the morning than in the afternoon. You can also get minibuses direct to Notsé (CFA800), Tsévié (CFA 1200), Kara (CFA3500) and to the Ghanaian border (CFA350), which closes at 6 pm sharp, as well as direct to Ho (Ghana). There are only one or two minibuses every morning direct to Ho and they can easily take up to three hours or more to fill up. The fare is CFA1000 and the border crossing is usually without hassle but can be time consuming.

KLOUTO

The village of Klouto, 10km north-east of Kpalimé, is at the centre of the very scenic forested Kouma-Konda region. On the way up the hill to Klouto, 7km from Kpalimé, you pass the mineral water spring Cascade de Kamalo. It's popular with Lomé visitors, who fill up plastic bottles. The big attraction in Klouto is to take a trip into the forest to see the masses of colourful butterflies – these walks can be arranged at the Association Découverte Togo Profond (ADETOP) and the Auberge des Papillons. See the boxed text 'Hiking in the Kpalimé Area' for more details.

Places to Stay & Eat

The friendly *Auberge des Papillons* is run by the inimitable M Prosper, the 'Butterfly Man'. It's fairly primitive but clean. Doubles cost CFA2000, and cheap meals are available (eg foufou with fish CFA2700).

Another good place in Klouto is the comfortable *ADETOP* (fax 41 02 28). A bed is

CFA2500, breakfast CFA400, and lunch or dinner CFA2000. The main reason to come here is to learn the secrets of the forest – a guided walk is CFA5000 and the evening entertainment (singing, drumming and lessons on traditional medicine etc) is CFA7000.

For solitude, stay at the 16 room *Campement de Klouto* (☎ 41 00 95), which was a German hospital before WWI. It's on top of a mountain, 12km north-west of Kpalimé, and a 30 minute walk from Klouto on the road to Ghana. It is quiet, shady, moist and cool, with a constant breeze. Fairly large singles/doubles/triples cost CFA5300/7600/11,900 with breakfast. Lunches and dinners are CFA4000, soft drinks CFA400 and beers CFA600.

Getting There & Away

To get from Kpalimé to Klouto, most people charter a taxi. The price should be about CFA4000 return. Taking a shared taxi is much cheaper, usually CFA300 from town to the police checkpoint. From there it's an easy walk to either the Campement de Klouto or Klouto village. To get a taxi back to Kpalimé, go to the checkpoint and wait for a shared taxi. The campement also has a telephone which you can use to call a taxi.

ATAKPAMÉ

Once the favourite residence of the German administrators, Atakpamé is in the heart of a mountainous area. It's also the centre of Togo's cotton-growing belt and has a textile mill. You may see tourist posters in Lomé of dancers on stilts, sometimes 5m high – this is where they come from. There's a good public pool (CFA500) near the gare routière, but it's frequently not functioning.

The southern entrance to town is marked by a T-junction, the eastern leg of which bypasses the centre and continues on to Kara. The north-south leg is the highway from Lomé which continues into the centre of town.

Places to Stay

The Peace Corps' *Maison de Passage* may still accept travellers. It costs CFA2000 per person, which includes a mattress with sheets and mosquito net. It's a centrally located yellow-and-blue house on a hill south of the Station de Kpalimé; everybody knows where it is.

The *Auberge le Retour* (☎ 40 05 40), on the highway opposite Station de Lomé, the main gare routière, has rooms with bucket shower for CFA2500, but no fan. On the main highway, just north of the gare routière, is the poorly marked *Foyer des Affaires Sociales*. This dormitory-like place has no restaurant, but its bare clean rooms with shared bathroom, fan and one or two beds are a good deal at CFA3000 (CFA4000 with air-con and bathroom).

A much better place, is the homely *Hôtel Miva* (☎ 40 04 37). Entering town from the south, it's on the left, about 100m north of the T-junction. It has small, spotless singles/doubles with fan and clean shared bathroom for CFA3500/4000.

The best place is the *Hôtel Roc* (☎ 40 02 37) just up the hill from Station de Lomé. It's on a plateau with a panoramic view of the city and surrounding hills. Air-con singles/doubles cost about CFA8000/10,000.

Hôtel le Kapokier (☎ 40 02 84) on the main drag 200m east of the market has spacious air-con rooms with bathroom for CFA6500.

Relais des Plateaux (☎ 40 02 32) on Rue de la Station de Lomé, just south of the commissariat, is more expensive and no better. Single/double rooms with fan and shower are CFA5600/7000 (CFA6500/7300 with air-con).

Places to Eat

A great place for African food is *Buvette à la Sueur* just behind the Mobil station near Hôtel le Kapokier. During the day you'll find several women here offering a choice of sauces, and if you order a drink you can eat inside; for western-style food, you'll have to pay more. *La Sagesse* is on Rue du Marché, 100m north of the market. This rustic place, open from 11 am to 2 pm and from 6 pm to midnight, serves surprisingly good food, with African dishes of your choice from

TOGO

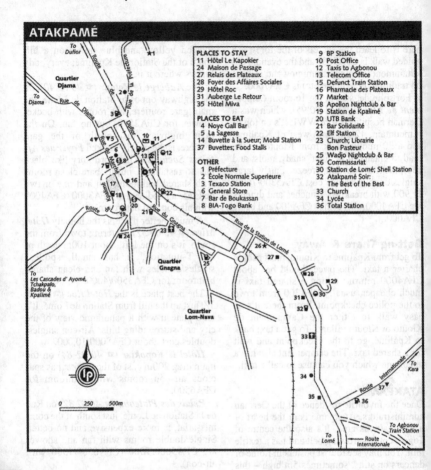

ATAKPAMÉ

PLACES TO STAY
11 Hôtel Le Kapokier
24 Maison de Passage
27 Relais des Plateaux
28 Foyer des Affaires Sociales
29 Hôtel Roc
31 Auberge Le Retour
35 Hôtel Miva

PLACES TO EAT
4 Noye Gall Bar
5 La Sagesse
14 Buvette à la Sueur; Mobil Station
37 Buvettes; Food Stalls

OTHER
1 Préfecture
2 École Normale Superieure
3 Texaco Station
6 General Store
7 Bar de Boukassan
8 BIA-Togo Bank
9 BP Station
10 Post Office
12 Taxis to Agbonou
13 Telecom Office
15 Defunct Train Station
16 Pharmacie des Plateaux
17 Market
18 Apollon Nightclub & Bar
19 Station de Kpalimé
20 UTB Bank
21 Bar Solidarité
22 Elf Station
23 Church; Librairie Bon Pasteur
25 Wadjo Nightclub & Bar
26 Commissariat
30 Station de Lomé; Shell Station
32 Atakpamé Soir: The Best of the Best
33 Church
34 Lycée
36 Total Station

CFA1500 and desserts and salads from CFA500. Across the road is the reasonable *Noye Gali Bar*.

There are a number of roadside *buvettes* at the southern end of town, about 200m east of the Total station, where you can get delicious Togolese dishes. For western-style food in this area, your best bet is the restaurant at the *Hôtel Miva*. Also, on the way into town you can stop at the *Fan Milk outlet* near Station de Lomé for ice cream or yoghurt.

Entertainment

Good places for beer include the *Bar de Boukoussan* opposite the market with draught beer for CFA150 a glass; *Apollon Nightclub & Bar* just south of the market and down the hill; and *Wadjo* 500m south of the market. The *Bar Solidarité* 200m south of the market is a rustic bar that's good for a large, cold beer (CFA280).

At night, one of the most popular places is *Atakpamé Soir: The Best of the Best*, a bar-dancing opposite the Station de Lomé.

Getting There & Away

Bush Taxi The main gare routière, Station de Lomé, is on the north-south highway leading into town, a kilometre north of the T-junction and 2km south-east of the centre. Minibuses and bush taxis go from here to Lomé (CFA1350) and Kara (CFA2000). Station de Kpalimé, which serves Kpalimé and Badou, is in the centre of town on Route de Kpalimé, 200m south of the market. Minibuses leave frequently throughout the day to Kpalimé (CFA800) and less frequently to Badou (CFA800). Roads are tar and in good condition to Lomé, Kpalimé and Badou.

Train The train from Lomé to Blitta stops at Agbonou station east of Atakpamé on Tuesday, Thursday and Saturday; it passes through Agbonou on its return the following day.

BADOU

Badou, in the heart of the cacao area, is 88km west of Atakpamé by a rough but tar road. The major attraction is **Les Cascades d'Akloa** (also spelt Akrowa) 11km south-east of town. Just before entering Badou, you'll see a large rock with a painting of the waterfalls on it. Access to the falls, however, is at **Tomagbé**, 9km to the south. There are minibuses from Badou to the waterfalls, but the walk from Badou to Tomagbé is pleasant. You have to pay CFA500 to the villagers at Tomagbé, which includes a guide if you want one.

The hike up the hill from Tomagbé to the waterfalls takes 40 minutes. It's a pleasant walk and not too strenuous, except in the rainy season. The trip is worth it as the waterfalls are beautiful and you can swim beneath them.

There is a UTB bank in town, a large Elf station and a pharmacy.

Apart from the 'by-the-hour' rooms at the *Carrefour 2000*, the only hotel is the *Hôtel Abuta* (☎ 43 00 16), which has doubles with fan from CFA5500. Camping is permitted in the grounds for CFA1200 per person.

In Atakpamé at Station de Kpalimé near the market you can get a minibus or old Toyota truck to Badou. The 1½ hour trip costs CFA800, and the road is rough with numerous police checkpoints. Minibuses (CFA300) go from Badou to the waterfalls all day.

PARC NATIONAL DE FAZAO-MALFAKASSA

This 200,000 hectare national park is in the beautiful Malfakassa Mountains of central Togo, an area of thickly wooded savanna with plenty of waterfalls, cliffs and rocky hills.

The park was badly managed for a long time, so the chances of seeing much wildlife other than birds and monkeys are slim. In recent years it has been taken over by the Fondation Franz Weber of Switzerland which has concentrated on animal rehabilitation, the construction of trails and the provision of 4WD excursions.

Adjoining Fazao is the Malfakassa Zone de Chasse. It's an excellent area for hiking, and affords some great views over the surrounding countryside. If you want to hike, ask at the Hôtel Parc Fazao for permission. Hikers should fill up with water at the River Mô in Malfakassa as other streams in the park can dry up; you will need to purify the water.

There are many good animal trails to follow in Malfakassa; the best run along the mountain tops and head south into the park. Orientation is easy even when you're hiking off trails because of the wide views from the mountain tops. In the rainy season, walking up the slopes through the tall grass takes considerable effort.

Places to Stay & Eat

Perched on a hill near Fazao village, and built like an African village, the *Hôtel Parc Fazao* (☎ 50 02 96) has air-con rooms and a restaurant. A single room is a stiff CFA 17,000, but includes breakfast, dinner, use of the pool and a guided tour of the village. There are no hotels in Malfakassa, but there are many good places to *camp* in the reserve.

Getting There & Away

The marked turn-off for the Fazao section of the national park is in the village of Ayengré 50km south of Sokodé on the main highway. You may have to wait a while for a ride to the Hôtel Parc Fazao at Fazao. To get to the Malfakassa Zone de Chasse, catch a minibus from Sokodé towards Bassar and get off at the semi-abandoned village of Malfakassa in a pass near the highest point of these small mountains. From the village, hike south from the highway into the park.

The North

SOKODÉ

There are no major sights in Sokodé, apart from the central market, which is particularly active on Monday. Nevertheless, Togo's second-largest city, with some 70,000 (mainly Muslim) inhabitants is a pleasant place to spend a day or two. The town is spread out with shade trees everywhere, especially colourful flamboyants and mango trees. The heart of town is the T-junction just south of the market.

Places to Stay

Le Campement (☎ 50 07 86) charges CFA2500/3000 for spacious singles/doubles with sheets, fan and bathroom. You can also get a set three-course meal here for CFA 2000. It's in a tranquil setting, up the hill from the *douane* (customs post) on the southern edge of town, a good walk from the centre. It's better than the filthy *Hôtel Tchaoudjo* in the centre of town on Route de Bassar, which is to be avoided at all costs (normally CFA2000). *Hôtel Kododji*, which is a block south, offers equally bad rooms with finicky fans for the same price.

Hôtel les Trois Fontaines (☎ 50 04 00) on Route de Lomé about 200m south of the T-junction is centrally located and is much better value. It charges CFA2750 for a large room with fan, fresh sheets and clean shared bathroom. Further south on the main highway the *Relais de la Cigale* (☎ 50 00

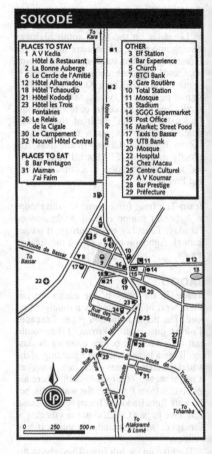

SOKODÉ

PLACES TO STAY	
1	A V Kedia Hôtel & Restaurant
2	La Bonne Auberge
6	Le Cercle de l'Amitié
12	Hôtel Alhamadou
18	Hôtel Tchaoudjo
21	Hôtel Kododji
23	Hôtel les Trois Fontaines
26	Le Relais de la Cigale
30	Le Campement
32	Nouvel Hôtel Central

PLACES TO EAT	
8	Bar Pentagon
31	Maman J'ai Faim

OTHER	
3	Elf Station
4	Bar Experience
5	Church
7	BTCI Bank
9	Gare Routière
10	Total Station
11	Mosque
13	Stadium
14	SGGG Supermarket
15	Post Office
16	Market; Street Food
17	Taxis to Bassar
19	UTB Bank
20	Mosque
22	Hospital
24	Chez Macau
25	Centre Culturel
27	A V Koumar
28	Bar Prestige
29	Préfecture

19) has neat spartan rooms with fan and clean shared bathroom for CFA4000.

If you're desperate, try *Hôtel Alhamdou* 500m east of the town centre near the stadium, or as a better alternative, *La Bonne Auberge* (☎ 50 02 35) 2km north of the centre on Route de Kara. The former has simple rooms with fan for CFA2200 (CFA3500 with air-con), while the latter has small clean rooms with bathroom and air-con for CFA6000.

Just north of Bonne Auberge is the recommended and very clean *A V Kedia Hôtel*

& *Restaurant*, with a hotel, bar and restaurant and tidy rooms from CFA3000. *Le Cercle de l'Amitié* on Route de Kara south of the Bonne Auberge is another bar-restaurant with rooms (CFA3000 a double).

The *Nouvel Hôtel Central* (☎ 50 01 23) is a large, quiet place on shady grounds at the southern end of town. It has clean, spacious rooms and tiled bathroom with hot water for CFA8500 (CFA11,000 for bungalows).

Places to Eat

The most attractive and relaxing hotel restaurant in town is at the *Relais de la Cigale*. Most dishes on the long menu are in the CFA1500 to CFA2500 range. For the best genuine Togolese food, head for *Maman J'ai Faim* on the southern side of town. Prices are low eg CFA350 for a filling meal of pâte or foufou with gboma sauce. For *street food*, try the area around the central market.

Entertainment

A good place for beer is *Bar Prestige* on the main drag south of the central area. It's a lively open-air place with loud African music and small draught beers for CFA150. If you're too hot to go dancing, head for *Bar Pentagon* on Route de Bassar, on the western side of town near the gare routière. In addition to loud music it has food, typically a *plat du jour* for CFA800. You would be surprised at the number of other bars in this Muslim town. Worth mentioning are *A V Koumar*, a bar-dancing behind Relais de la Cigale (CFA325 for a large beer); *Saint Ésprit*, a bar-dancing north of the Hôtel Kododji which also serves African food; the dependable *Chez Macau* near the Hôtel les Trois Fontaines; and *Bar Experience* north of the BTCI Bank on the Route de Kara, serving Togolese dishes from CFA300 to CFA1000.

Getting There & Away

The gare routière is on Route de Bassar, several blocks west of the central market. Bush taxis cost CFA550 to Bassar, CFA700 to Kara, CFA1500 to Atakpamé and CFA 2750 to Lomé.

BASSAR

Renowned for its traditional hunters, Bassar is 57km on tar road to the north-west of Sokodé. It is also the site of the annual Igname (yam*)* festival in September, which involves lots of dancing, including fire dances.

The cheapest place to stay is *Le Campement*, with modest, reasonably priced rooms. The best place is the state-run *Hôtel de Bassar* (☎ 63 00 40), which has bungalows from CFA6000; it also has a disco.

There are lots of *food stalls* in and around the market, and a number of bars, the best of which is *Le Palmier* about 100m from the market.

Bassar can be easily reached by bush taxi from Sokodé.

BAFILO

The predominantly Muslim town of Bafilo is in a very picturesque setting just north of the **Faille d'Aledjo**, where the road passes through a natural break in the cliff, and is surrounded by a magnificent tract of forest.

Bafilo is a good place to stop for at least a day just to see weavers in action and to buy pagnes of cloth at very reasonable prices. The *Masa Esso* on Route de Kara is about the only place to stay. It has a choice of rooms with fan or air-con (around CFA5000) and a restaurant.

KARA

Formerly called Lama-Kara, Kara is in Kabyé country. Because President Eyadéma comes from Pya, a Kabyé village about 20km to the north-east, he has pumped a lot of money into Kara, constructing a second brewery, a radio station and, most impressively, the party headquarters. As a result, the town has grown quickly to about 60,000 people.

Laid out by the Germans on a spacious scale, it's a pleasant town and a good base from which to visit the interesting area to the north.

The Mobil intersection on the Route Internationale is where the tar road east to Benin and west to Ghana begin. The gare routière,

TOGO

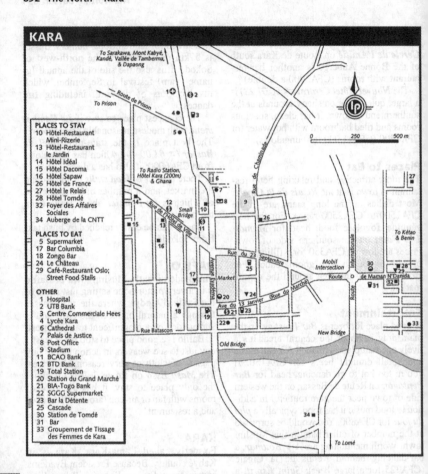

KARA

PLACES TO STAY
10 Hôtel-Restaurant Mini-Rizerie
13 Hôtel-Restaurant le Jardin
14 Hôtel Idéal
15 Hôtel Dacoma
16 Hôtel Sapaw
26 Hôtel de France
27 Hôtel le Relais
28 Hôtel Tomdé
32 Foyer des Affaires Sociales
34 Auberge de la CNTT

PLACES TO EAT
5 Supermarket
17 Bar Columbia
18 Zongo Bar
24 Le Château
29 Café-Restaurant Oslo; Street Food Stalls

OTHER
1 Hospital
2 UTB Bank
3 Centre Commerciale Hees
4 Lycée Kara
6 Cathedral
7 Palais de Justice
8 Post Office
9 Stadium
11 BCAO Bank
12 BTD Bank
19 Total Station
20 Station du Grand Marché
21 BIA-Togo Bank
22 SGGG Supermarket
23 Bar la Détente
25 Cascade
30 Station de Tomdé
31 Bar
33 Groupement de Tissage des Femmes de Kara

Station de Tomdé, is just east of the intersection and the centre of town is about 500m to the west. That's where you'll find the big Tuesday market. To change money, go to the UTB or the front desk of the Hôtel Kara.

Places to Stay

The cheapest place to stay is the *Foyer des Affaires Sociales* (☎ 60 61 18) 100m east of the gare routière on the highway to Benin. This large, well run centre with a bar-restaurant and TV charges CFA1500 to CFA 2000 per person for a dorm bed in a room with three bunk beds and fan. The shared bathrooms are clean. A room with fan costs CFA3000 (CFA4500 with air-con and bathroom). Another budget choice near the gare routière is the *Hôtel Tomdé* (☎ 60 07 12), with clean, spacious rooms and fan for CFA3500.

A notch up in price is the popular and well maintained *Auberge de la CNTT* (☎ 60 62 32) on the south side of town on the Route Internationale, about 1km south of the

TOGO

gare routière. It charges CFA3000/4000 for singles/doubles with fan (CFA5000/6000 with air-con).

West of the market towards the Hôtel Kara are several cheap hotels. **Hôtel Dacoma** charges CFA1100 for a room with bathroom but no fan. It's a block west of **Hôtel Sapaw** (☎ 60 14 44), which charges CFA3000 for doubles with fan and clean shared bathroom; you can get food here as well. A block north of the Dacoma is the rather dreary **Hôtel Idéal**, which charges CFA2500 for a large room with fan.

Another budget choice is **Hôtel de France** (☎ 60 03 42) in Rue de Chaminade, with large, attractive rooms with air-con and shower for CFA5000.

Rooms at **Hôtel-Restaurant Mini-Rizerie** (☎ 60 61 54) on Ave Eyadéma opposite the post office, cost CFA5600 with fan and CFA 7600 with air-con. It's close to the centre and there's a popular bar and restaurant.

The tranquil **Hôtel le Relais** (☎ 60 62 98) has dark rooms which cost CFA3500 with fan and CFA6000 with air-con. It's 500m down a dirt road leading north from the gare routière; follow the signs.

The **Hôtel Kara** (☎ 60 60 20 or 60 60 21) on Rue de l'Hôtel de Ville has a pool, volleyball and tennis courts, shops, a nightclub (La Féve) and three classes of rooms, from CFA20,500 to CFA27,000 for singles and CFA25,500 to CFA32,500 for doubles. **Hôtel-Restaurant le Jardin** (☎ 60 01 34) is off Rue de l'Hôtel de Ville, just west of the bridge. This attractive, popular place with a garden has four pleasant rooms with air-con (CFA7500), and Kara's top restaurant.

Places to Eat

Kara has a number of cheap places serving superb Togolese food. One of the most popular is the open-air **Bar Columbia**. The women pound away all morning on the corn and millet; by lunch time it's hard to find a seat. Their specialities are pâte and foufou. It's a block west of the market. **Zongo Bar** two blocks west of the market is run by the same family and is just as good, with a variety of sauces to choose from. Both

places are open until around 10.30 pm (closed Sunday). In the same area, 50m towards the market from the Columbia, is an **Ewé woman** who makes reputedly the best pâte in town. Also worth a look is **Café-Restaurant Oslo** near Station de Tomdé, with meals for CFA1200.

For reasonable prices and good quality, you can't beat **Le Château** (☎ 60 60 40), an attractive bar-restaurant (closed Monday) 50m east of the market on Ave du 13 Janvier. It has ice-cold beers for CFA200, sandwiches from CFA1000 and an extensive menu with both African and European dishes. It also serves expensive desserts, including *crêpes suzettes* and ice-cream sundaes for CFA900.

Another winner is the long-standing **Hôtel-Restaurant Mini-Rizerie**. Breakfast costs CFA900 and most dishes are in the CFA1500 to CFA2000 range (couscous with chicken is CFA1900). It serves three-course French meals and will also prepare Togolese food. Its large beers are a mere CFA375.

The city's best restaurant is at **Hôtel-Restaurant le Jardin**. The *crêpe chocolat* (chocolate pancake) here is particularly good and well worth the price.

Entertainment

The hottest African nightclub in town is the **Bar la Détente** on Ave du 13 Janvier near the market (large Bière Béninois are CFA250 and *pressions* are only CFA150 – perhaps the cheapest beer in Africa?).

The **Centre Commerciale Hees** on the Dapaong road has a good bar and restaurant and has lately been quite popular, as has the **Cascade** on Rue du 23 Septembre. There is a good nameless **bar** opposite the gare routière which is a good place to meet locals. The disco at the **Hôtel Kara**, open only at the weekend, has a cover charge of CFA800.

Shopping

For African fabrics, check out the Groupement de Tissage des Femmes de Kara on the eastern side of town. It sells high-quality material. From the Mobil station intersec-

TOGO

tion, take the tar road east for 200m and just beyond Affaires Sociales turn right, heading south on a dirt road, and follow the signs.

Getting There & Away

The main gare routière is Station de Tomdé at the intersection on the Route Internationale. Minibuses go to Sokodé (CFA700), Lomé (CFA3200), Dapaong (CFA1650) and Kétao (CFA300). The trip to Parakou in Benin (193km) takes a day, with taxi changes at the border and Djougou. The

chances of making it in one day to Tamale (256km) in Ghana are not as good. Both routes are tar only in Togo. Station du Grand Marché, in the centre next to the market, is better for catching vehicles at night to many destinations.

AROUND KARA
Sarakawa

Sarakawa, 23km to the north-west of Kara, is not worth a special visit, but if you are passing through, check out the huge monu-

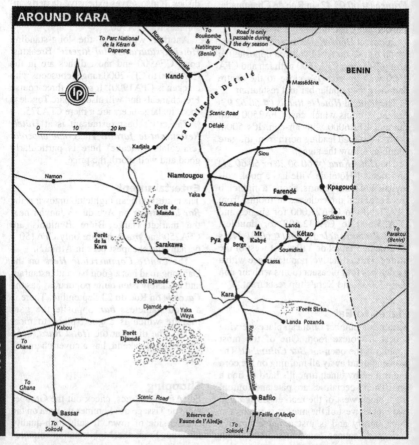

AROUND KARA

ment commemorating the site where Eyadéma's plane crashed in 1974. The statue has Eyadéma pointing to the ground and saying, 'They almost killed me here'. To get here, take the Route Internationale north for about 10km, then the tar road west for 13km.

Mt Kabyé & Around

Mt Kabyé is roughly 15km north-east of Kara (as the crow flies), in one of the most scenic areas in Togo. Heading from Kara, stop first in **Landa**, a village 15km north-east of Kara where women make a variety of goods. Some 4km further east, on the main highway, is **Kétao**. The huge Wednesday market here is fascinating and the second-largest in Togo.

From here, head north on a dirt road for about 20km or so to **Kpagouda**, where you may be able to hear traditional music (ask the chief). The main attractions, however, are the mountains, including Mt Kabyé. The *Hôtel de Kpagouda* is in a stunning location and has a bar-restaurant and tennis court. It charges CFA6000 for a spacious air-con chalet.

From Kpagouda you can head west into an area renowned for its *forgerons* (blacksmiths) and on to **Pya**, Eyadéma's birthplace,

on the Route Internationale, then south for about 14km back to Kara.

NIAMTOUGOU

Niamtougou is 34km north of Kara on the north-south Route Internationale and makes a good base for visits to the nearby Vallée de Tamberma. The traditional Sunday market here is one of Togo's most vibrant and fascinating, and there's a good selection of baskets and ceramic bowls. In addition, there's a great Centre Artisanal on the southern side of town, which has well made cloth and dresses (CFA5500).

The *Môtel de Niamtougou* is similarly equipped to the hotel in Kpagouda and has air-con rooms for about the same price. It also has a bar, restaurant and disco.

KANDÉ

Kandé (sometimes spelt Kanté) is on the Route Internationale, 28km north of Niamtougou; the stretch between these two towns is the most scenic on the entire highway. The valley of the Tamberma people, with their fascinating fortress-like houses, is accessible from Kandé. If you ask around, you should be able to find one of the dirt tracks leading east for about 27km to one of the Tamberma villages near the Benin border.

Tamberma Compounds

A typical Tamberma compound, called a *tata*, consists of a series of towers connected by a thick wall with only one doorway to the outside. In the past, the castle-like nature of these extraordinary structures helped ward off invasions by neighbouring tribes and, in the late 19th century, the Germans. Inside, there's a huge elevated terrace of clay-covered logs where the inhabitants cook, dry their millet and corn, and spend most of their leisure time.

Skilled builders, the Tamberma use no tools, and only use clay, wood and straw. The walls are *banco*, a mixture of unfired clay and straw, which is used as a binder. The towers, which are capped by picturesque conical roofs, are used for storing corn and millet. The other rooms are used for sleeping, bathing and, during the rainy season, cooking. The animals are kept under the terrace, protected from the rain.

Inside the compounds, there may be fetish animal skulls on the walls and ceilings and a tiny altar for sacrificing chickens. You may see a man and his son going off to hunt with bows and arrows. When the son gets old enough to start his own family, he shoots off an arrow and where it lands is where he'll construct his own tata.

TOGO

Kandé has the run-down *Campement de la Nouvelle Marché* with rooms for CFA2500 (CFA4000 with air-con) and food; it's on the main drag. In town you can find boys, or they'll find you, who will offer you huts to stay in for CFA800 per person.

Most travellers without their own transport end up walking the 27km from Kandé to the Tamberma villages. Not only is walking more interesting, but the people are much more likely to give you a warm welcome. You'll have to bring your own food and water. From Kandé, walk east for 20km to Warengo, then another 7km to Nadoba, the most important village. Alternatively, you might try your luck by looking for a shared taxi in Kandé; this is much easier on Tuesday, market day.

PARC NATIONAL DE LA KÉRAN

During the dry season, a visit to what is left of the Parc National de la Kéran is recommended, although in recent years much of it has been gobbled up by farmland. Heading north from Kandé towards Dapaong, look for a sign pointing to the park's entrance, which is 2km from the road. The turn-off for Naboulgou, inside the park, is 32km north of Kandé. This is the site of the well marked but now defunct Môtel de Naboulgou.

Unless you're very lucky, you won't see many animals. There are a number of good tracks throughout the park which are clearly marked on the map at the defunct motel. The main track heading south from the lodge is the one locals use to get to the villages beyond the southern boundary. It's the best track to follow during the rainy season because, unlike other paths, it remains dry for the most part.

Sansanné-Mango is a small village at the northern edge of the park. Stop here if you're interested in seeing hippo, which can be found in the River Oti nearby. There's also an SGGG supermarket in town where you can buy camping supplies.

Places to Stay & Eat

The *Hôtel-Bar l'Oti* (☎ 71 71 16) in Sansanné-Mango to the north of the village centre

has rooms for CFA2500. It's very clean and the friendly owner will arrange private lifts going south. At the restaurant you can get cheap drinks and a meal for CFA850.

DAPAONG

Only 30km from the border with Burkina Faso, Dapaong (population 25,000) is a pretty little town with a mild climate. It has an attractive setting overlooking the countryside, in a group of small hills which provide a welcome break in the otherwise flat landscape. The Route Internationale passes around to the east of the town, so it's possible to pass through this place without stopping. Dapaong is noted for its Saturday market.

Places to Stay

The cheapest place is the *Foyer des Affaires Sociales* (☎ 70 80 29) on the main road heading north out of town, the Route de Nasablé. A bare room with shared bathroom (with running water) costs CFA1800 (CFA2200 with fan and CFA3200 with air-con).

On the opposite side of town on the main street leading to the centre is *Hôtel Lafia*, which is similar in many respects. It has clean rooms with fan, shower and basin, and running water for CFA3000 (CFA4500 with air-con). Another possibility is *Hôtel le Rônier* a few blocks north-west of the centre. It has plain rooms with fan and shared bathroom for CFA2800 (CFA4500 with air-con and bathroom), but there's no running water. *Hôtel le Sahelien* (☎ 70 81 84) is in the heart of town and has large rooms with fan and shared bathroom for CFA3000 (CFA 4000 with bathroom and CFA6000 with air-con). The hotel's best feature is its paillote restaurant.

Hôtel le Campement (☎ 70 80 55) on the main road into town is a short walk up a hill from the centre. It's an attractive and relaxing place to stay. Rooms with fan and decent bathroom are CFA7500 (CFA9500 with air-con), and there's an active bar with the only draught beer in town (CFA400) and one of the best restaurants.

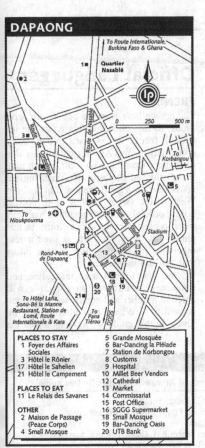

DAPAONG

To Route Internationale,
Burkina Faso & Ghana

Quartier
Nasablé

To
Korbangou

To
Nioukpourma

Stadium

Rond-Point
de Dapaong

To Hôtel Lafia,
Sonu-Bé la Manne
Restaurant, Station de
Lomé, Route
Internationale & Kara

To
Pana
Tiérou

PLACES TO STAY		5	Grande Mosquée
1	Foyer des Affaires Sociales	6	Bar-Dancing la Pléiade
		7	Station de Korbongou
3	Hôtel le Rônier	8	Customs
17	Hôtel le Sahelien	9	Hospital
21	Hôtel le Campement	10	Millet Beer Vendors
		12	Cathedral
PLACES TO EAT		13	Market
11	Le Relais des Savanes	14	Commissariat
		15	Post Office
OTHER		16	SGGG Supermarket
2	Maison de Passage (Peace Corps)	18	Small Mosque
		19	Bar-Dancing Oasis
4	Small Mosque	20	UTB Bank

The *Sonu-Bé la Manne Restaurant* near
Station de Lomé a couple of kilometres out
of the centre has four spotless rooms (about
CFA4500 each) with fan and bathroom.

Places to Eat

In addition to eating at the hotels, good
places to eat, drink and meet travellers
include the spacious open-air *Bar-Dancing
la Pléiade*, the *Bar-Dancing Oasis*, the
terrace of *La Flamboyante*, the *Hôtel
Chinois Vietnamien* on Place du Marché
and *Le Relais des Savanes* near the market.

Getting There & Away

Station de Korbongou is several blocks
north of the market and has vehicles leaving
for the Burkina Faso border and nearby villages. The main gare routière is Station de
Lomé on the Route Internationale, 2km
south of the centre. You can get minibuses
and bush taxis to the border (CFA500), to
Ouagadougou (CFA4000), Kara (CFA2000)
and Lomé (CFA4500, 12 to 16 hours).
Baggage is extra and typically costs about
CFA500 to Lomé. Most vehicles for Lomé
leave in the morning before 8 am and again
in the evening starting around 5 pm.

PARC NATIONAL DE LA FOSSE AUX LIONS

If you'd like to take a hike through some
typical savanna woodland, the Fosse aux
Lions might be of interest – but it's no longer
a 'pit of lions'! It's 12km south of Dapaong,
and the Route Internationale runs right
through it, making access easy (take any
bush taxi going on the highway). The entrance is signposted and there's no entrance
fee. The Fosse lies in a flat area of woodland
savanna at the base of a steep ridge. Hike up
the cliffs for an excellent view of the surrounding countryside. Several seasonal
streams flow through the savanna, but stock
up on food and water in Dapaong as the
water is not safe to drink.

TOGO

Language

Across West Africa, the region's myriad ethnic groups speak several hundred local languages, many subdivided into numerous distinct dialects. The people of Nigeria – West Africa's most populous country – speak at least 350 languages and dialects, while even tiny Guinea-Bissau (population just over one million) has around 20 languages.

Consequently, common languages are essential, and several are used. These may be the language of the largest group in a particular area or country. For example, Hausa has spread out from its northern Nigerian heartland to become widely understood as a trading language in the eastern parts of West Africa. Similarly, Dioula is a common tongue in markets over much of the western part of the region. Also widespread are the former colonial languages of French, English and Portuguese. In some areas, the common tongue is a creole – a combination of African and European languages.

Official Languages

FRENCH

Though we have used the polite verb form 'vous' in the following phrase list, the informal form 'tu' is used much more commonly in West Africa; you'll hear *s'il te plaît* more than *s'il vous plaît*, which may be considered impolite in France unless spoken between good friends. If in doubt in West Africa (when dealing with police, border officials or older people) it's always safer to use the polite 'vous' form. In this phrase list the polite form is used unless otherwise indicated – 'inf' for the informal, 'pol' for the polite.

Note that French uses masculine and feminine word forms; an adjective will agree in number and gender with the noun it modifies. Where two alternatives are given, in this guide we have indicated the

Don't Be Lost For Words in ...!

Country	Official Language	Principal African Languages (in this guide)
Benin	French	Fon, Hausa, Yoruba
Burkina Faso	French	Dioula, Fon, Hausa, Moré, Senoufo
Cape Verde	Portuguese	Crioulo
Côte d'Ivoire	French	Dan (Yacouba), Dioula, Hausa, Senoufo
Gambia	English	Diola (Jola), Mandinka, Wolof
Ghana	English	Ewé, Ga, Hausa, Twi
Guinea	French	Fula (Futa Djalon), Malinké, Susu
Guinea-Bissau	Portuguese	Crioulo
Liberia	English	Dan (Yacouba)
Mali	French	Bambara, Malinké, Sangha dialect, Senoufo, Tamashek
Mauritania	Arabic (French still in common use)	Dioula, Fula (Fulfulde), Hassaniya, Wolof
Niger	French	Djerma, Fon, Hausa, Tamashek
Nigeria	English	Hausa, Igbo, Yoruba
Senegal	French	Crioulo, Diola, Fula (Fulfulde), Malinké, Mandinka, Wolof
Sierra Leone	English	Krio
Togo	French	Ewé, Fon, Kabyé, Mina

masculine form with 'm', the feminine form with 'f'. Also note that where singular and plural forms of words are given, the singular is marked 'sg' and the plural, 'pl'.

Basics

I	*je*
you (sg)	*tu* (inf)/*vous* (pol)
he/she	*il/elle* (m/f)
we	*nous*
you (pl)	*vous*
they	*ils/elles* (m/f)

Hello/Good morning.	*Bonjour.*
Good evening.	*Bonsoir.*
Goodbye.	*Salut* or *A bientôt/ Au revoir.* (inf/pol)
Good night.	*Bonne nuit.*
How are you?	*Ça va/Comment allez-vous?* (inf/pol)
Fine, thanks.	*Bien, merci.*
Yes.	*Oui.*
No.	*Non.*
No, thank you.	*Non, merci.*
Please.	*S'il vous plaît.*
Thank you.	*Merci.*
You're welcome.	*De rien/ Je vous en prie.*
Excuse me.	*Excusez-moi/Pardon.*
What's your name?	*Comment vous appelez-vous?*
My name is ...	*Je m'appelle ...*

Language Difficulties

Do you speak English?	*Parlez-vous anglais?*
I understand.	*Je comprends.*
I don't understand.	*Je ne comprends pas.*

Getting Around

I want to go to ...	*Je veux aller à ...*
What's the fare to ...?	*Combien coûte le billet pour ...?*
When does (the) ... leave/arrive?	*À quelle heure part/ arrive ...?*
bus	*le bus*
train	*le train*
boat	*le bateau*

Signs

ENTRÉE	ENTRANCE
SORTIE	EXIT
CHAMBRES LIBRES	ROOMS AVAILABLE
COMPLET	NO VACANCIES
RENSEIGNEMENTS	INFORMATION
OUVERT/FERMÉ	OPEN/CLOSED
INTERDIT	PROHIBITED
(COMMISSARIAT DE) POLICE	POLICE STATION
TOILETTES, WC	TOILETS
HOMMES	MEN
FEMMES	WOMEN

Where is (the) ...?	*Où est ...?*
airport	*l'aéroport*
bus station/ bush taxi park	*la gare routière*
ferry terminal	*la gare maritime*
ticket office	*la billeterie*
train station	*la gare*

I'd like a ... ticket.	*Je voudrais un billet ...*
one-way	*aller simple*
return	*aller retour*
first class	*première classe*
second class	*deuxième classe*

Which bus goes to ...?	*Quel bus part pour ...?*
Does this bus go to ...?	*Ce bus-là va-t-il à ...?*
How many buses per day go to ...?	*Il y a combien de bus chaque jour pour ...?*
Stop here, please.	*Arrêtez ici, s'il vous plaît.*
Wait!	*Attendez!*
May I sit here?	*Puis-je m'asseoir ici?*

first	*premier*
next	*prochain*
last	*dernier*
the ticket	*le billet*
the timetable	*l'horaire*

crowded	*beaucoup de monde*
daily	*chaque jour*

early	tôt
late	tard
on time	à l'heure
quickly	vite
slowly	lentement

the address	l'adresse
the city	la ville
the number	le numéro
the street	la rue
village	le village

Where can I rent (a) ...?	Où est-ce que je peux louer ...?
bicycle	un vélo
car	une voiture

Directions

How far is ...?	À combien de kilomètres est ...?
Where (is ...)?	Où (est ...)?
Go straight ahead.	Continuez tout droit.
Turn left.	Tournez à gauche.
Turn right.	Tournez à droite.

near	proche
far	loin
here/there	ici/là
next to	à côté de
opposite	en face
behind	derrière
north	nord
south	sud
east	est
west	ouest

Around Town

For other common French terms which may prove useful as you move 'around town' see the Glossary following this chapter.

a bank	une banque
the beach	la plage
the ... embassy	l'ambassade de ...
the market	le marché
a pharmacy	une pharmacie
the post office	la poste
a public telephone	une cabine téléphonique
a restaurant	un restaurant

Emergencies

Help!	Au secours!
Call the police!	Appelez la police!
Call a doctor!	Appelez un médecin!
I've been robbed.	On m'a volé.
Go away!	Allez-vous-en!
I'm lost.	Je me suis égaré(e).

I want to change ...	Je voudrais changer ...
(cash) money	de l'argent
travellers cheques	des chèques de voyage

| What time does it open/close? | Quelle est l' heure de ouverture/ fermeture? |

Accommodation

Where is ...?	Où est ...?
the campground	le camping
the the hotel	l'hôtel

| Do you have any rooms available? | Avez-vous des chambres libres? |

I'd like a ... room.	Je cherche une chambre ...
single	à un lit
double	double

Can I see the room?	Puis-je voir la chambre?
How much is it per night?	Quel est le prix par nuit?
How much is it per person?	Quel est le prix par personne?
That's too much for me.	C'est trop cher pour moi.
Do you have a cheaper room?	Avez-vous une chambre moins chère?
This is fine.	Ça va bien.

air-conditioning	climatisation
a bed	un lit
a blanket	une couverture
full/no vacancies	complet
hot water	eau chaude

a key	*une clef/clé*
a sheet	*un drap*
a shower	*une douche*
the toilet	*les toilettes*

Shopping

I'm looking for the market?	*Je cherche le marché?*
Where can I buy ...?	*Où est-ce que je peux acheter ...?*
Do you have ...?	*Avez-vous ...?*
How much/many do you want?)	*(Vous en désirez combien?)*
That's enough.	*Ça suffit.*
I'd like (three).	*J'en voudrais (trois).*
How much is it?	*Ça coûte combien?*
How much for (two)?	*Combien ça fait pour (deux)?*

batteries	*des piles*
coffee	*du café*
gas cylinder	*une bonbonne de gas*
matches	*des alumettes*
newspaper	*un journal*
stamps	*des timbres*
toothpaste	*du dentifrice*
washing powder	*de la lessive*

big/small	*grand/petit*
more/less	*plus/moins*
open/closed	*ouvert/fermé*

Health

I need a doctor.	*J'ai besoin d'un médecin.*
Where is the hospital?	*Où est l'hôpital?*
I feel dizzy.	*J'ai des vertiges.*
I feel nauseaous.	*J'ai des nausées.*
I'm pregnant.	*Je suis enceinte.*

I'm ...	*Je suis ...*
diabetic	*diabétique*
epileptic	*épileptique*
asthmatic	*asthmatique*
allergic to antibiotics	*allergique aux antibiotiques*

aspirin	*l'aspirine*
condoms	*des préservatifs*

diarrhoea	*la diarrhée*
medicine	*le médicament*
sanitary napkins	*des serviettes hygiéniques*
tampons	*des tampons hygiéniques*

Time, Days & Numbers

What time is it?	*Quelle heure est-il?*
It's (two) o'clock.	*Il est (deux) heures.*
It's quarter past six.	*Il est six heures et quart.*
It's quarter to seven.	*Il est sept heures moins le quart.*
At what time?	*À quelle heure?*
When?	*Quand?*

now	*maintenant*
after	*après*
today	*aujourd'hui*
tomorrow	*demain*
yesterday	*hier*
(in the) morning	*(du) matin*
(in the) afternoon	*(de l') après-midi*
(in the) evening	*(du) soir*
day	*jour*
night	*nuit*
week/month/year	*semaine/mois/an*

Monday	*lundi*
Tuesday	*mardi*
Wednesday	*mercredi*
Thursday	*jeudi*
Friday	*vendredi*
Saturday	*samedi*
Sunday	*dimanche*

January	*janvier*
February	*février*
March	*mars*
April	*avril*
May	*mai*
June	*juin*
July	*juillet*
August	*août*
September	*septembre*
October	*octobre*
November	*novembre*
December	*décembre*

LANGUAGE

0	*zéro*
1	*un*
2	*deux*
3	*trois*
4	*quatre*
5	*cinq*
6	*six*
7	*sept*
8	*huit*
9	*neuf*
10	*dix*
11	*onze*
12	*douze*
13	*treize*
14	*quatorze*
15	*quinze*
16	*seize*
17	*dix-sept*
18	*dix-huit*
19	*dix-neuf*
20	*vingt*
21	*vingt-et-un*
22	*vingt-deux*
30	*trente*
40	*quarante*
50	*cinquante*
60	*soixante*
70	*soixante-dix*
80	*quatre-vingts*
90	*quatre-vingt-dix*
100	*cent*
101	*cent un*
125	*cent vingt-cinq*
200	*deux cents*
300	*trois cents*
400	*quatre cents*
1000	*mille*

one million   *un million*

PORTUGUESE

Like French, Portuguese is a Romance language (ie one closely derived from Latin). In West Africa it's the official language in Cape Verde and Guinea-Bissau.

Note that Portuguese uses masculine and feminine word endings, usually '-o' and '-a' respectively – to say 'thank you', a man will therefore say *obrigado*, a woman, *obrigada*.

Greetings & Civilities

Hello.	*Bom dia/Olá/Chao.*
Good morning.	*Bom dia.*
Good evening.	*Boa tarde.*
Goodbye.	*Adeus/Chao.*
See you later.	*Até logo.*
How are you?	*Como está?*
I'm fine, thanks.	*Bem, obrigado/a.* (m/f)
Yes/No.	*Sim/Não.*
Maybe.	*Talvez.*
Please.	*Se faz favor/por favor.*
Thank you.	*Obrigado/a.*
Excuse me.	*Desculpe/Com licença.*
Sorry/Forgive me.	*Desculpe.*
What's your name?	*Como se chama?*
My name is ...	*Chamo-me ...*

Language Difficulties

Do you speak English?	*Fala inglès?*
I understand.	*Percebo/Entendo.*
I don't understand.	*Não percebo/entendo.*

Getting Around

I want to go to ...	*Quero ir a ...*
How long does it take?	*Quanto tempo leva isso?*
What time does the ... leave/arrive?	*A que horas parte/ chega o ...?*
bus	*autocarro*
train	*combóio*
boat	*barco*
next	*próximo*
first	*primeiro*
last	*último*
timetable	*horário*
Where is the ...?	*Onde é a ...?*
airport	*aeroporto*
bus stop	*paragem de autocarro*
train station	*estação ferroviária*
I'd like a ...ticket.	*Queria um bilhete ...*
one way	*simples/de ida*
return	*de ida e volta*
1st class	*primeira classe*
2nd class	*segunda classe*

Signs

ENTRADA	ENTRANCE
SAÍDA	EXIT
ENTRADA GRÁTIS	FREE ADMISSION
INFORMAÇÕES	INFORMATION
ABERTO	OPEN
ENCERRADO	CLOSED
(OR *FECHADO*)	
O POSTO DA	POLICE STATION
POLÍCIA	
PROÍBIDO	PROHIBITED
EMPURRE/PUXE	PUSH/PULL
QUARTOS LIVRES	ROOMS
	AVAILABLE
LAVABOS/WC	TOILETS
h, HOMENS	MEN
s, SENHORAS	WOMEN

I'd like to hire ...	*Queria alugar ...*
a car	*um carro*
a bicycle	*uma bicicleta*

How do I get to ...?	*Como vou para ...?*
Is it near/far?	*É perto/longe?*
Go straight ahead.	*Siga sempre a direito.*
Turn left.	*Vire á esquerda.*
Turn right.	*Vire á direita.*

Accommodation

I'm looking for ...	*Procuro ...*
a guesthouse	*uma pensão*
a hotel	*uma hotel*
a youth hostel	*uma pousada de*
	juventude
a bed	*uma cama*
a cheap room	*um quarto barato*
a single room	*um quarto individual*
a double room	*um quarto de casal*
(with twin beds)	*(duplo)*

Do you have any	*Tem quartos livres?*
rooms available?	
How much is it per	*Quanto é por noite/*
night/per person?	*por pessoa?*
Is breakfast	*O pequeno almoço*
included?	*está incluído?*
Can I see the room?	*Posso ver o quarto?*
Where is the toilet?	*Onde ficam os lavabos*
	(as casas de banho)?

It is very dirty/	*É muito sujo/*
noisy/expensive.	*ruidoso/caro.*

Health

I need a doctor.	*Preciso um médico.*
Where is a hospital/	*Onde é um hospital/*
medical clinic?	*um centro de saúde?*

I'm ...	*Sou ...*
diabetic	*diabético/a*
epileptic	*epiléptico/a*
asthmatic	*asmático/a*
allergic to	*alérgico/a a*
antibiotics	*antibióticos*

aspirin	*aspirina*
condoms	*preservativo*
diarrhoea	*diarreia*
dizzy	*vertiginoso*
medicine	*remédio/medicamento*
nausea	*náusea*
sanitary napkins	*pensos higiénicos*
tampons	*tampões*

Time, Dates & Numbers

What time is it?	*Que horas são?*
When?	*Quando?*
today	*hoje*
tonight	*hoje á noite*
tomorrow	*amanhã*
yesterday	*ontem*
morning/afternoon	*manhã/tarde*

Monday	*segunda-feira*
Tuesday	*terça-feira*
Wednesday	*quarta-feira*
Thursday	*quinta-feira*
Friday	*sexta-feira*
Saturday	*sábado*
Sunday	*domingo*

Emergencies

Help!	*Socorro!*
Call the police!	*Chame a polícia!*
Call a doctor!	*Chame um médico!*
I've been robbed.	*Fui roubado/a.*
Go away!	*Deixe-me em paz!*
I'm lost.	*Estou perdido/a.*

1	*um/uma*
2	*dois/duas*
3	*três*
4	*quatro*
5	*cinco*
6	*seis*
7	*sete*
8	*oito*
9	*nove*
10	*dez*
100	*cem*
1000	*mil*

one million   *um milhão*

Indigenous Languages

BAMBARA/DIOULA

Differences between Bambara and Dioula (also known as Jula) are relatively minor and the two languages share much of their vocabulary, eg 'Goodbye' in Bambara is *kan-bay*, in Dioula it is *an-bay*.

Bambara (called *bamanakan* in Bambara) is the predominant indigenous language of Mali, while Dioula is widely spoken as a

What's Spoken Where?

COUNTRIES (WHERE SPOKEN):

INDIGENOUS LANGUAGE:	Benin	Burkina Faso	Cape Verde	Côte d'Ivoire	Gambia	Ghana	Guinea	Guinea-Bissau	Liberia	Mali	Mauritania	Niger	Nigeria	Senegal	Sierra Leone	Togo
Bambara/Dioula	–	■	–	■	–	–	–	–	–	■	■	–	–	–	–	–
Crioulo	–	–	■	–	–	–	–	–	–	–	–	–	–	■	–	–
Dan (Yacouba)	–	–	–	■	–	–	–	–	■	–	–	–	–	–	–	–
Diola (Jola)	–	–	–	–	■	–	–	–	–	–	–	–	–	■	–	–
Djerma (Zarma)	–	–	–	–	–	–	–	–	–	–	–	■	–	–	–	–
Ewé	–	–	–	–	–	■	–	–	–	–	–	–	–	–	–	■
Fon (Fongbe)	■	–	–	–	–	–	–	–	–	–	–	–	–	–	–	■
Fula (Pulaar)	–	–	–	–	–	–	■	–	–	–	–	–	■	■	–	–
Ga (Adangme)	–	–	–	–	–	■	–	–	–	–	–	–	–	–	–	–
Hassaniya	–	–	–	–	–	–	–	–	–	–	■	–	–	–	–	–
Hausa	■	■	–	–	–	■	–	–	–	–	–	■	■	–	–	–
Igbo	–	–	–	–	–	–	–	–	–	–	–	–	■	–	–	–
Kabyé	–	–	–	–	–	–	–	–	–	–	–	–	–	–	–	■
Krio	–	–	–	–	–	–	–	–	–	–	–	–	–	–	■	–
Malinké	–	–	–	–	–	–	■	–	–	–	–	–	–	■	–	–
Mandinka	–	–	–	–	■	–	–	–	–	–	–	–	–	■	–	–
Mina	–	–	–	–	–	–	–	–	–	–	–	–	–	–	–	■
Moré	–	■	–	–	–	–	–	–	–	–	–	–	–	–	–	–
Sangha dialect	–	–	–	–	–	–	–	–	–	■	–	–	–	–	–	–
Senoufo	–	■	–	–	–	–	–	–	–	■	–	–	–	–	–	–
Susu	–	–	–	–	–	–	■	–	–	–	–	–	–	–	–	–
Tamashek	–	–	–	–	–	–	–	–	–	■	–	■	–	–	–	–
Twi	–	–	–	–	–	■	–	–	–	–	–	–	–	–	–	–
Wolof	–	–	–	–	■	–	–	–	–	–	–	–	–	■	–	–
Yoruba	■	–	–	–	–	–	–	–	–	–	–	–	■	–	–	–

first language in Côte d'Ivoire and Burkina Faso. Dioula is one of West Africa's major lingua francas (a common language used for communication between groups with different mother tongues) so the words and phrases included below can be used not only in Burkina Faso, Côte d'Ivoire and Mali but also in south-eastern Mauritania (Néma and south), eastern Senegal, and parts of Gambia. In addition there are also distinct similarities between Bambara/Dioula and the Mandinka of northern Gambia and parts of southern Senegal, and most Senoufo speakers in southern Mali (Sikasso region), south-western Burkina Faso, and northern Côte d'Ivoire (Korhogo region) can speak Bambara/Dioula. It's not hard to see that some knowledge of it will prove very useful in this part of West Africa!

Bambara and Dioula are normally written using a phonetic alphabet; in this guide we've mostly used letters common to English. Some specific pronunciations you'll need to be aware of are:

a	as in 'far'
e	as in 'bet'; the combination **eh** is pronounced somewhere between 'ey' and the 'e' in 'bet'
i	as in 'marine'
o	as in 'hot'
u	between the 'u' in 'pull' and the 'oo' in 'boot'
g	always hard, as in 'get'
j	as in 'jet'
ñ	as in the 'ni' in 'onion'
ng	as the 'ng' in 'sing' – indicates that the preceding vowel is nasal
r	almost a 'd' sound

In the following phrase lists variation in vocabulary is indicated by (B) for Bambara and (D) for Dioula.

Greetings The response to any of the following greetings (beginning with *i-ni-* ...) is *n-ba* (for men) and *n-seh* (for women).

Hello.	*i-ni-cheh*
Hello. (to someone working)	*i-ni-baa-rah* (literally, to you and your work)

> **Note** In this guide bold letters indicate where the stress falls within a word.

Good morning.	*i-ni-soh-goh-mah* (sunrise to midday)
Good afternoon.	*i-ni-ti-leh* (12 noon to 3 pm)
Good evening.	*i-ni-wu-lah* (3 pm to sunset)
Good night.	*i-ni-suh* (sunset to sunrise)
Goodbye.	*kan-beng* (B) *an-beng* (D)
Please.	*S'il vous plaît.* (French)
Thank you.	*i-ni-cheh/ bah-si-tay* (lit: no problem)
Sorry/Pardon.	*ha-keh-toh*
Yes.	*ah-woh*
No.	*ah-yee* (B)/*uh-uh* (D)
How are you?	*i-kah-kéné*
I'm fine.	*tuh-roh-teh*
And you?	*eh-dung?*
Can you help me please?	*ha-keh-toh, i-bay-say-kah nn deh-meh wa?*
Do you speak English?	*i-beh-say-kah ahng-gih-lih-kahng meng wa?*
Do you speak French?	*i-beh-seh-kah tu-bah-bu-kan meng wa?*
I only speak English.	*nn-beh-seh-kah ahng-gih-lih-kahng meng doh-rohn*
I speak a little French.	*nn-beh-seh-kah tu-bah-bu-kan meng doh-nee*
I understand.	*nn-y'ah-fah-mu*
I don't understand.	*nn-m'ah-fah-mu*
What's your (first) name?	*i-toh-goh?*
My name is ...	*nn-toh-goh ...*
Where are you from?	*i-beh-boh-ming?*

I'm from ...	*nn-beh-boh* ...
Where is ...?	*... beh-ming?*
Is it far?	*ah-kah-jang-wah?*
straight ahead	*ah-beh-tih-leng*
left	*nu-man-boh-loh-feh*
	(lit: nose-picking hand)
right	*ki-ni-boh-loh-feh*
	(lit: rice-eating hand)
How much is this?	*ni-ñeh-joh-li-yeh?*
That's too much.	*ah-kah-geh-leng –*
	bah-ri-kah!
	(lit: lower the price)
Leave me alone!	*boh'i-sah!*

1	*keh-leng*
2	*fih-lah* (or *flah*)
3	*sahb-bah*
4	*nah-ni*
5	*du-ru*
6	*woh-roh*
7	*woh-lon-flah*
8	*shay-ging*
9	*koh-nohng-tahng*
10	*tahng*
11	*tahng-ni-kay-len*
12	*tahng-ni-flah*
13	*tahng-ni-sah-bah*
14	*tahng-ni-nah-ni*
15	*tahng-ni-doo-ru*
16	*tahng-ni-woh-roh*
17	*tahng-ni-woh-lon-flah*
18	*tahng-ni-shay-ging*
19	*tahng-ni koh-nohn-tahng*
20	*mu-gang*
30	*bi-sahb-bah*
31	*bi-sahb-bah-ni-keh-leng*
40	*bi-nah-ni*
50	*bi-du-ru*
60	*bi-woh-roh*
70	*bi-woh-lon-fla*
80	*bi-shay-ging*
90	*bie-koh-nohn-tahng*
100	*keh-meh*
1000	*wah*
5000	*wah-duru*

one million	*wah-wah* or *millar*

With thanks to Andy Rebold.

CRIOULO

Crioulo is a Portuguese-based creole spoken (with more or less mutual intelligibility) in the Cape Verde islands, Guinea-Bissau (where it's the lingua franca and 'market language') and parts of Senegal and Gambia. Nearly half the Crioulo speakers of Cape Verde are literate in Portuguese but since independence in 1975 Crioulo has become increasingly dominant; upwards of 70% of the country's population speak Crioulo. Even allowing for regional differences the phrases listed below should be understood in both Cape Verde and Guinea-Bissau.

Good morning.	*bom-dee-ah*
Good evening.	*bow-ah no-tay*
Goodbye.	*nah-buy*
How are you?	*ou-kor-poh*
	ees-tah-bon?
I'm fine.	*tah-bon*
Please.	*puhr-fah-bohr*
Thank you.	*ob-ree-gah-doh*
How much is it?	*kahl eh preh-suh*

1	*ahn*
2	*dohs*
3	*trehs*
4	*kwah-tuh*
5	*sin-kuh*
6	*say-ehs*
7	*seh-tee*
8	*oy-tuh*
9	*noh-vee*
10	*dehs*
11	*ohn-zee*
12	*doh-zee*
13	*treh-zee*
14	*kah-toh-zee*
15	*kihn-zee*
16	*dee-zah-say-ehs*
17	*dee-zah-seh-tee*
18	*dee-zoy-tuh*
19	*dee-zah-noh-vee*
20	*vin-tee*
30	*trin-tah*
100	*sehn*
1000	*meel*

DAN (YACOUBA)

Dan (also known as 'Yacouba') is one of the principal African languages spoken in Côte d'Ivoire (in and around Man). There are also a significant number of Dan speakers in Liberia (where it's referred to as 'Gio'). There are a couple of major dialects and more than 20 sub-dialects; as a result most communication between different language groups in the region is carried out in Dioula (see the Bambara/Dioula section in this guide for a comprehensive list of Dioula words and phrases).

Good morning.	*un-zhoo-bah-boh* (man)
Good morning.	*nah-bah-boh* (woman)
Good evening.	*un-zhoo-attoir* (man)
Good evening.	*nah-attoir* (woman)
How are you?	*bwee-ahr-way*
Thank you.	*bah-lee-kah*

DIOLA (JOLA)

The Diola people inhabit the Casamance region of Senegal, and also the south-western parts of Gambia, where their name is spelt Jola. Their language is Diola/Jola, which should not be confused with the Dioula/Jula spoken widely in other parts of West Africa. Diola society is segmented and very flexible, so several dialects have developed which may not be mutually intelligible between different groups even though the area inhabited by the Diola is relatively small.

Hello/Welcome.	*kah-sou-mai-kep*
Greetings. (reply)	*kah-sou-mai-kep*
Goodbye.	*ou-kah-to-rrah*

DIOULA (JULA)

Refer to the Bambara/Dioula section earlier in this language guide.

DJERMA (ZARMA)

After Hausa, Djerma (pronounced *jer-mah*) is Niger's most common African language (people with Djerma as their first language make up around a quarter of the country's population). It's spoken mostly in the western regions including around Niamey,

and it is one of the official national languages used for radio broadcasts.

Good morning.	*mah-teen-keh-nee*
Good evening.	*mah-teen-hee-ree*
How are you?	*bar-kah?*
Thank you.	*foh-foh*
Goodbye.	*kah-lah ton-ton*

EWÉ

Ewé (pronounced *ev-vay*) is the major indigenous language of southern Togo. It is also an official language of instruction in primary and secondary schools in Ghana where it's spoken mainly in the east of the country; you'll find that Twi (the language of the Ashanti and the Fanti) is the more universally spoken language of Ghana. There are also several closely related languages and dialects of Ewé spoken in Benin.

Good morning/ evening.	*nee-lye-nee-ah*
	mee-lay (response)
What's your name?	*n-koh-woh-day?*
My name is ...	*nk-nee-n-yay ...*
How are you?	*nee-foh-ah?*
I'm fine.	*mee-foh*
Thank you.	*mou-doh, ack-pay-now*
Goodbye.	*mee-ah doh-goh*

FON (FONGBE)

Fon (called Fongbe in the language itself) belongs to the Kwa group of the Gbe language family, *gbe* being the Fon word for 'language'. It is another of the major lingua francas of West Africa, spoken for the most part in Nigeria and Benin, but also used widely in Côte d'Ivoire, Burkina Faso, Niger and Togo. While Fon is subject to clear dialectal variation depending on region, you should find that the list of words and phrases below will be universally understood.

The Fon language is written using the IPA (International Phonetic Alphabet); for the sake of simplicity we've used a pronunciation system which uses letters common to English. Fon is a tone language (ie intended meaning is dependent upon changes in pitch within the normal range of a speaker's voice) with a standard system of five tones; in this guide we have simplified things by using only two written accents for tones (acute accent, eg **á**, for a high tone, grave accent, eg **à**, for a low tone) – an unmarked vowel has a mid-tone.

Pronounce letters as you would in English, keeping the following points in mind:

a	as in 'far'
e	as in 'met'
i	as in 'marine'
o	either as in 'hot' or as in 'for'
u	as in 'put'
g	as in 'go'
h	silent
hng	indicates that the preceding vowel is nasalised, eg the 'ing' sound in 'sing'
ñ	as the 'ni' in 'onion'

Hello.	*ò-kú*
Goodbye.	*é-dà-bòh*
Please.	*kèhng-kéhng-lèhng*
Thank you.	*àh-wàh-nu*
You're welcome.	*é-sù-kpéh-ah*
Sorry/Pardon.	*kèhng-kéhng-lèhng*
Yes.	*ehng*
No.	*éh-woh*
How are you?	*neh-àh-dèh-gbòhng?*
I'm fine.	*ùhn-dòh-gàhng-jí*
And you?	*hweh-loh?*
Can you help me please?	*kèhng-kéhng-lèhng-dá-lòh-mì?*
Do you speak ...?	*àh-sèh ... àh?*
English	*glèhng-síhng-gbè*
French	*flàng-sé-gbè*
I only speak English.	*glèhng-síhng-gbè kéh-déh-wèh-ùn-sèh*
I speak a little French.	*ùn-sèh flàng-sé-gbè kpèh-dèh*
I understand.	*ùn-mòh-nu-jéh-mèh*
I don't understand.	*ùn-mòh-nu-jéh-mèh-ah*
What's your name?	*neh-àh-nòh-ñí?*
My name is ...	*ùn-nòh-ñí ...*
Where are you from?	*tòh-téh-mèh-nùh-wéh-ñí-wèh?*
I'm from ...	*... nùh-wéh-ñí-mì*

Where is ...?	*fi-téh-wéh ...?*
Is it far?	*eh-lihng-wéh-ah?*
straight ahead	*treh-leh-leh*
left	*àh-myòh*
right	*àh-dì-sí*
How much is this?	*nà-bí-wèh-ñí-éh-lòh?*
That's too much.	*éh-vá-khìh-díhng*
Leave me alone!	*joh-mí-dóh!*

1	*òh-deh*
2	*òh-wèh*
3	*à-tòhng*
4	*eh-nèh*
5	*à-tóhng*
6	*à-yì-zéhng*
7	*teh-weh*
8	*ta-toh*
9	*téhng-nèh*
10	*woh*
11	*woh-dòh-kpóh*
12	*weh-wèh*
13	*wah-tòhng*
14	*weh-nèh*
15	*à-fòh-tòhn*
16	*à-fòh-tòhng-nù-kúhng-dòh-póh*
17	*à-fòh-tóhng-nu-kúhng-wèh*
18	*à-fòh-tóhng-nu-kúhng-à-tòhng*
19	*à-fòh-tóhng-nu-kúhng-èh-neh*
20	*kòh*
30	*gbàhng*
40	*kàhng-déh*
50	*kàhng-déh-woh*
60	*kàhng-déh-koh*
70	*kàhng-déh-gbàhng*
80	*kàhng-wèh*
90	*kàhng-wèh-woh*
100	*kàhng-wèh-kòh*
1000	*à-fàh-tóhng*

one million	*mì-yóhng-dòh-kpóh*

With thanks to Aimé Avolonto.

FULA (PULAAR)

Fula or Pulaar is one of the languages of the Fula people found across West Africa, from northern Senegal to Sudan in the east, and as far south as Ghana and Nigeria. The Fula are known as Peul in Senegal (they are also called Fulani and Fulbe).

There are two main languages in the Fulani group:

- Fulfulde, spoken mainly in northern and southern Senegal (includes the dialects known as Tukulor and Fulakunda).
- Futa Fula (also known as Futa Djalon), the main indigenous language of Guinea, also spoken in eastern Senegal.

It's worth noting that these far-flung languages have many regional dialects which aren't always mutually intelligible between different groups.

Fulfulde

The following words and phrases should be understood through most parts of Senegal. Note that **ng** should be pronounced as one sound (like the 'ng' in 'sing'); practise isolating this sound and using it at the beginning of a word. The letter **ñ** represents the 'ni' sound in 'onion'.

Hello.	*no ngoolu daa* (sg)
	no ngoolu dong (pl)
Goodbye.	*ñalleen e jamm*
	(lit. Have a good day)
	mbaaleen e jamm
	(lit. Have a good night)
Please.	*njaafodaa*
Thank you.	*a jaaraama* (sg)
	on jaaraama (pl)
You're welcome.	*enen ndendidum*
Sorry/Pardon.	*yaafo* or
	achanam hakke
Yes.	*eey*
No.	*alaa*
How are you?	*no mbaddaa?*
I'm fine.	*mbe de sellee*
... and you?	*... an nene?*
Can you help me please?	*ada waawi wallude mi, njaafodaa?*
Do you speak English/French?	*ada faama engale/faranse?*
I only speak English.	*ko engale tan kaala mi*
I speak a little French.	*mi nani faranse seeda*
I understand.	*mi faami*
I don't understand.	*mi faamaani*

What's your name?	*no mbiyeteedaa?*
My name is ...	*ko ... mbiyetee mi*
Where are you from?	*to njeyedaa?*
I'm from ...	*ko ... njeyaa mi*
Where is ...?	*hoto woni?*
Is it far?	*no woddi?*
straight ahead	*ko yeesu*
left	*nano bang-ge*
right	*nano ñaamo*
How much is this?	*dum no foti jarata?*
That's too much.	*e ne tiidi no feewu*
Leave me alone!	*accam!* or
	oppam mi deeja!

1	*go-o*
2	*didi*
3	*tati*
4	*nayi*
5	*joyi*
6	*jeego*
7	*jeedidi*
8	*jeetati*
9	*jeenayi*
10	*sappo*
11	*sappoygoo*
12	*sappoydidi*
13	*sappoytati*
20	*noogaas*
30	*chappantati*
100	*temedere*
1000	*wujenere*

one million	*miliyong goo*

With thanks to Fallou Ngom.

Futa Fula (Futa Djalon)

This variety of Fula known as Futa Djalon is predominant in the Futa Djalon region of Guinea. It is named after the people who speak it, and is distinct from the variety known as Fulfulde which is spoken in northern and southern Senegal.

Good morning/ Good evening.	*on-**jaa**-rah-mah*
How are you?	*ta-nah-alah-**ton**?*
Where is ...?	*koh-hon-toh woh-nee?*
Thank you.	***jaa**-rah-mah*
Goodbye.	*on-**ount**-tou-mah*

GA/ADANGME

Ga (and its very close relative Adangme) is one of the major indigenous languages spoken in Ghana, mostly around Accra.

Good morning/ Good evening.	*meeng-gah-bou*
How are you?	*toy-yah-tain?*
I'm fine.	*ee-oh-joh-bahn*
What's your name?	*toh-cho-boh-tain?*
My name is ...	*ah-cho-mee ...*
Thank you.	*oh-gee-wah-dong*
Goodbye.	*bye-bye*

HASSANIYA

Hassaniya is a Berber-Arabic dialect which is spoken by Moors of Mauritania. It's also the official language of Mauritania.

Good morning.	*sa-**la**-mah ah-**lay**-koum*
Good evening.	*mah-sah el-**hair***
How are you?	*ish-**tah**-ree?*
Thank you.	***shuh**-krahn*
Goodbye.	*mah-sa-**lahm***

HAUSA

Hausa is spoken and understood in a vast area of West Africa and beyond. Dialectal variation is not extreme in Hausa so the phrases included in this language guide will be universally understood, and will prove useful in Benin, Burkina Faso, Côte d'Ivoire, Niger, Nigeria and northern Ghana (where it is the principal language of trade).

Hausa is a tone language (where pitch variation in a speaker's voice is directly related to intended meaning) with three basic tones assigned to vowels: low, high and rising-falling. Standard written Hausa isn't marked for tones – our pronunciation guide for the words and phrases included below doesn't show them either. Your best bet is to learn with your ears by noting the inflection of African speakers.

The consonants **b**, **d** and **k** have 'glottalised' equivalents where air is exhaled forcefully from the larynx (the voice box); these glottal consonants are represented in this guide by **B**, **D** and **K** respectively.

The difference between short and long vowels is also overlooked in standard written Hausa; to help with pronunciation long vowels are represented in this guide by double vowels, eg *aa'aa* (no).

Hello. (greeting)	*sannu*
Hello. (response)	*yauwaa sannu*
Good morning.	*eenaa kwanaa*
Good morning. (response)	*lapeeyaloh*
Good evening.	*eenaa eenee*
Good evening. (response)	*lapeeyaloh*
Goodbye.	*sai wani lookachi*
Please.	*don allaah*
Thank you.	*naa goodee*
Don't mention it/ It's nothing.	*baa koomi*
Sorry, pardon.	*yi haKurii, ban ji ba*
Yes.	*ii*
No.	*aa'aa*
How are you?	*inaa gajiyaa?*
I'm fine.	*baa gajiyaa*
And you?	*kai fa?*
What's your name?	*yaayaa suunanka?*
My name is ...	*suunaanaa ...*
Where are you from?	*daga inaa ka fitoo?*
I'm from ...	*naa fitoo daga ...*
Can you help me please?	*don allaah, koo zaa ka taimakee ni?*
Do you speak English/French?	*kanaa jin ingiliishii/ faransancii?*
I speak only English.	*inaa jin ingiliishii kawai*
I speak a little French.	*inaa jin faransancii kaDan*
I understand.	*naa gaanee*
I don't understand.	*ban gaanee ba*
Where is ...?	*inaa ...?*
Is it far ...?	*da niisaa ...?*
straight ahead	*miiKee sambal*
left	*hagu*
right	*daama*
How much is this?	*nawa nee wannan?*
That's too much.	*akwai tsaadaa ga wannan*
Leave me alone!	*tafi can!*

1	*d'aya*
2	*biyu*
3	*uku*
4	*hud'u*
5	*biyar*
6	*shida*
7	*bakwai*
8	*takwas*
9	*tara*
10	*gooma*
11	*gooma shaa d'aya*
12	*gooma shaa biyu*
13	*gooma shaa uku*
14	*goma shaa hud'u*
15	*goma shaa biyar*
16	*gooma shaa shida*
17	*gooma shaa bakwai*
18	*gooma shaa takwas*
19	*gooma shaa tara*
20	*ashirin*
30	*talaatin*
40	*arba'in*
50	*hamsin*
60	*sittin*
70	*saba'in*
80	*tamaanin*
90	*casa'in*
100	*d'arii*
1000	*dubuu*

one million   *miliyan d'aya*

With thanks to Dr Malami Buba.

IGBO (IBO)

Igbo is the predominant indigenous language of Nigeria's south-east, where it is afforded the status of official language; it's used in the media and in government, and is the main lingua franca of the region. There are over 30 dialects of Igbo, each with varying degrees of mutual intelligibility.

Good morning.	*ee-**bow**-lah-chee*
Good evening.	*nah-**no**-nah*
How are you?	*ee-**may**-nah ahn-**ghan**?*
Thank you.	*ee-**may**-nah*
Goodbye.	*kay-**may**-see-ah*

KABYÉ

After Ewé, Kabyé is Togo's most common African language, predominant in the Kara region. One Kabyé word you'll always hear is *yovo* (white person).

Good morning	*un-lah-**wah**-lay.*
How are you?	*be-jah-un-sema*
I'm fine.	*ah-**lah**-fia*
Thank you.	*un-lah-**bah**-lay*
Goodbye.	*be-**lah**-bee-tasi*

KRIO

Krio is Sierra Leone's most common non-colonial language. Its major ingredient is English, but its sound system and grammar have been enriched by various West African languages. Because Krio was imported by different slave groups, there are strong differences between the Krio spoken in various regions, so strong in fact that some people find it easier to understand the Krio of Nigeria than the Krio spoken in other parts of Sierra Leone.

Hello.	***kou**-shay*
Hi mate.	*eh bo*
How are you?	*how-dee boh-dee?*
I'm fine.	***boh**-dee fine/no bad* (more common)
Thank God.	*ah tel god tenk-kee*
Thank you.	***tenk**-kee*
Please.	***dou**-yah (ah-beg)* (added for emphasis)
Goodbye.	*we go see back*
How much?	*ow mus?*
food	*chop*
Sierra Leone	*salone*

MALINKÉ

Malinké is spoken in the region around the borders between Senegal, Mali and Guinea. It's one of Senegal's six national languages. While it's very similar in some respects to the Mandinka spoken in Gambia and Senegal (they share much of their vocabulary), the two are classed as separate languages.

Good morning	*nee-soh-mah*
Good evening	*nee-woo-lah*

How are you?	tan-ahs-teh?
Thank you.	nee-kay
Goodbye.	m-bah-ra-wa

MANDINKA

Mandinka is the language of the Mandinka people found largely in central and northern Gambia, and in parts of southern Senegal. The people and their language are also called Mandingo and they're closely related to other Mande-speaking groups such as the Bambara of Mali, where they originate. Mandinka is classed as one of Senegal's national languages.

In this guide, **ng** should be pronounced as the 'ng' in 'sing' and **ñ** represents the 'ni' sound in 'onion'.

Hello.	i/al be ñaading (sg/pl)
Good bye.	fo tuma doo
Please.	dukare
Thank you.	i/al ning bara (sg/pl)
You're welcome.	mbee le dentaala/ wo teng fengti (lit: It's nothing)
Sorry/Pardon.	hakko tuñe
Yes.	haa
No.	hani
How are you?	i/al be kayrato? (sg/pl)
I'm fine.	tana tenna (lit: I'm out of trouble) kayra dorong (lit: peace only)
And you?	ite fanang?
What's your name?	i too dung?
My name is ...	ntoo mu ... leti
Where are you from?	i/al bota munto? (sg/pl)
I'm from ...	mbota ...
Can you help me please?	i/al seng maakoy noo, dukare? (sg/pl)
Do you speak English/French?	ye angkale/faranse kango moyle?
I speak only English.	nga angkale kango damma le moy
I speak a little French.	nga faranse kango domonding le moy
I understand.	ngaa kalamuta le/ ngaa fahaam le
I don't understand.	mmaa kalamuta/ mmaa fahaam

Arabic Islamic Greetings

Traditional Arabic Islamic greetings are very common in Muslim West Africa – they're easy to learn and will be much appreciated.

| Greetings. | salaam aleikum (peace be with you) |
| Greetings to you too. | aleikum asalaam (and peace be with you) |

Where is ...?	... be munto?
Is it far?	faa jamfata?
Go straight ahead.	sila tiling jan kilingo
left	maraa
right	bulu baa
How much is this?	ñing mu jelu leti?
That's too much.	a daa koleyaata baake
Leave me alone!	mbula!

1	kiling
2	fula
3	saba
4	naani
5	luulu
6	wooro
7	woorowula
8	sey
9	kononto
10	tang
11	tang ning kiling
12	tang ning fula
13	tang ning saba
20	muwaa
30	tang saba
100	keme
1000	wili kiling

| one million | milyong kiling |

With thanks to Fallou Ngom.

MINA

Mina (also known as Gengbe) is the language of trade in southern Togo, especially along the coast. It belongs to the Gbe ('gbe' meaning 'language') subgroup of the vast Kwa language family. Other Gbe languages of Togo include Ajagbe, Fongbe, Maxigbe and Wacigbe.

Good morning.	*soh-bay-doh*
(reply)	*dosso*
How are you?	*oh-foin?*
I'm fine.	*aaaa* ('a' as in 'bat')
Thank you.	*ack-pay*
Goodbye.	*soh-day-loh*

MORÉ

Moré (the language of the Mossi) is spoken by more than half the population of Burkina Faso – with over 4½ million speakers it's the country's principal indigenous language.

Good morning.	*yee-bay-roh*
Good evening.	*nay-zah-bree*
How are you?	*lah-fee-bay-may?*
I'm fine.	*lah-fee-bay-lah*
Thank you.	*un-pus-dah bar-kah*
Goodbye.	*when-ah-tah-say*

SANGHA DIALECT

Sangha is one of the main dialects (from around 48 others!) spoken by the Dogon people who inhabit the Bandiagara Escarpment in central Mali. Dialectal variation can be so marked that mutual intelligibility between the many Dogon groups is not always assured.

Good morning.	*ah-gah-poh*
Good evening.	*dee-gah-poh*
How are you?	*ou say-yoh?*
I'm fine.	*say-oh*
Thank you.	*bee-ray-poh*
Goodbye.	*ee-eyeh-ee way-dang*
Safe journey!	*day-gay-day-yah*

SENOUFO

The Senoufo words and phrases listed below should prove useful if you're travelling through southern Mali, south-western Burkina Faso and northern Côte d'Ivoire.

Senoufo pronunciation can be a very difficult prospect for foreigners, and with no official written form the task of matching the

Note In this guide bold letters indicate where the stress falls within a word.

sounds of the language with letters on a page presents quite a challenge. The pronunciation system used in this guide provides rough approximations only. Try to pick up the sounds and inflections of the language by listening to fluent Senoufo speakers.

a	as in 'far'
e	as in 'bet'; the combination **eh** is pronounced somewhere between 'ey' and the 'e' in 'bet'
é	as the 'ay' in 'bay'
i	as in 'marine'
o	as in 'hot'
u	between the 'u' in 'pull' and the 'oo' in 'boot'
g	always hard, as in 'get'
ñ	as in the 'ni' in 'onion'
ng	as the 'ng' in 'sing' – indicates that the preceding vowel is nasal

Hello.	*kéné*
Goodbye.	*wu-ñeh-té-reh*
Thank you.	*fah-nah*
Sorry/Pardon.	*yah-hé-yah*
Yes.	*huh* or *mi-loh-goh*
No.	*mé-tyeh*
How are you?	*mah-choh-loh-goh-lah?*
I'm fine.	*min-bé-gé-bah-mén*
And you?	*mohn-dohn?*
What's your name?	*mehn-mah-mi-ihn-yeh?*
My name is ...	*mehn-mihn-yeh* ...
Do you speak ...?	*mun-nah ... chi-yé-ré-lu-gu-lah?*
English	*ahn-gih-lih-kan*
French	*tu-bah-bu-kan*
I only speak English.	*min-nah ahn-gih-lih-kan chi-yé-reh-yeh-ké-né*
I speak a little French.	*min-nah tu-bah-bu-kan chi-yé-reh tyeh-rih-yeh*

Can you help me please?	nah-**pu**-gu?
I understand.	**mihn**-i-**tyeng** or mah-loh-**goh**
I don't understand.	**mihn**-nay-**chi**-mehn
Where are you from?	shi-moh-**nah** yih-rih-**ré**?
I'm from ...	**mihn**-na-**yih**-rih ...
Where is ...?	shi-**ohng**-yeh ...?
Is it far?	kah-lé-**li**-lah?
left	kah-**mohn**
right	**kin**-yih-kah-**nih**-gi-heh-**yeh**-ré
How much is this?	jur-gi-**nah**-**deh**-leh?
That's too much.	kah-lah-**rah**-wah-ah, deh!
Leave me alone!	**yi**-ri-wah! or meh-**yah**-bah!

Numbers

Numbers in Senoufo can be a very complicated affair. For example, the number 'one hundred' translates literally as 'two-times-five-times-two-times-four-plus-two-times-ten' – use the numbers in the Bambara/Dioula section earlier in this guide and you'll have no trouble being understood.

With thanks to Andy Rebold.

SUSU

Susu is Guinea's third most common indigenous language. It's spoken mainly in the south around Conakry.

Good morning.	tay-nah mah-ree
Good evening.	tay-nah mah-fay-yen
How are you?	oh-**ree** toh-nah-moh?
Thank you.	ee-noh-wah-lee
Goodbye.	une-**gay**-say-gay

TAMASHEK

Tamashek (spelt variously 'Tamasheq', 'Tamachek', 'Tamajeq' and more!) is the language of the Tuareg. There are two main dialects, Eastern (spoken in western Niger and eastern Mali) and Western (spoken in western Niger, the Gao region of Mali, and northern Nigeria).

How do you do?	met-al-ee-khah (pol) oh-yeek (inf)
I'm fine.	eel-kharass
How's the heat?	min-ee-twixeh (a traditional greeting)
Good/Fine.	ee-zott
How much?	min-ee-kit?
Thank you.	tan-oo-mert
Goodbye.	harr-sad

TWI

Twi (pronounced 'chwee'), the language of the Ashanti, is the most widely spoken African language in Ghana, where it is the official language of education and literature. Along with Fanti it belongs to the large Akan language family. Most of the dialects within this group are mutually intelligible.

Hello.	ah-**kwah**-bah
Hello. (in reply)	yaah
Good morning.	mah-**cheeng**
Good evening.	**mah**-joh
How are you?	ay-tah-sein?
I'm fine.	**ay**-yah
Please.	meh-**pah**-woh-cheh-oh
Thank you.	may-**dah**-say
Yes.	aahn
No.	dah-beh
Do you speak English?	woh-teh **broh**-foh ahn-nah
I don't understand.	uhm-**tah** seh
I'd like ...	meh-**pay** ...
Are you going to (Accra)?	yah-coh (accra)?
Let's go.	**yen**-coh
Safe journey.	nan-tee yee-yay
Goodbye.	mah-**krow**

1	bee-**ah**-koh
2	ah-bee-**ehng**
3	ah-bee-**eh**-sah
4	ah-**nahng**
5	ah-**nuhm**
6	ah-**see**-yah
7	ah-**sohng**
8	ah-**woh**-tweh
9	ah-**kruhng**
10	duh
11	duh-bee-**ah**-koh
20	**ah**-dwoh-nuh
100	oh-**hah**
1000	ah-**pehm**

WOLOF

Wolof (spelt Ouolof in French) is the language of the Wolof people, who are found in Senegal, particularly in the central area north and east of Dakar, along the coast, and in the western regions of Gambia. The Wolof spoken in Gambia is slightly different to the Wolof spoken in Senegal; the Gambian Wolof people living on the north bank of the River Gambia speak the Senegalese variety. Wolof is used as a common language in many parts of Senegal and Gambia, often instead of either French or English, and some smaller groups complain about the increasing 'Wolofisation' of their culture.

For some traditional Arabic Islamic greetings which are used in Muslim West Africa see the boxed text earlier in this guide.

Most consonants are pronounced as they are in English; when doubled they are pronounced with greater emphasis. Some vowels have accented variants.

a	as in 'at'
à	as in 'far'
e	as in 'bet'
é	as in 'whey'
ë	as the 'u' in 'but'
i	as in 'it'
o	as in 'hot'
ó	as in 'so'
u	as in 'put'
g	as in 'go'
ñ	as the 'ni' in 'onion'
ng	as in 'sing'; practise making this sound at the beginning of a word
r	always rolled
s	as in 'so', not as in 'as'
w	as in 'we'
x	as the 'ch' in Scottish *loch*

Hello.	*Na nga def.* (sg)
	Na ngeen def. (pl)
Good morning.	*Jàmm nga fanaane.*
Good afternoon.	*Jàmm nga yendoo.*
Goodnight.	*Fanaanal jàmm.*
Goodbye.	*Ba beneen.*
Please.	*Su la nexee.*

Thank you.	*Jërëjëf.*
You're welcome.	*Agsil/agsileen ak jàmm .* (sg/pl)
Sorry/Pardon.	*Baal ma.*
Yes.	*Waaw.*
No.	*Déedéet.*
How are you?	*Jàmm nga/ngeen am?* (sg/pl) (lit: Have you peace?)
I'm fine.	*Jàmm rekk.*
And you?	*Yow nag?*
How is your family?	*Naka waa kër ga?*
What's your first name?	*Naka nga/ngeen tudd?* (sg/pl)
What's your last name?	*Naka nga sant?*
My name is ...	*Maa ngi tudd ...*
Where do you live?	*Fan nga dëkk?*
Where are you from?	*Fan nga/ngeen jòge?* (sg/pl)
I'm from ...	*Maa ngi jòge ...*
Do you speak English/French?	*Dégg nga.Angale/ Faranse?* (sg/pl)
I speak only English.	*Angale rekk laa dégg.*
I speak a little French.	*Dégg naa tuuti Faranse.*
I don't speak Wolof/French.	*Màn dégguma Wolof/ Faranse.*
I understand.	*Dégg naa.*
I don't undestand.	*Dégguma.*
I'd like ...	*Dama bëggoon ...*
Where is ...?	*Fan la ...?*
Is it far?	*Sore na?*
straight ahead	*cha kanam*
left	*cammooñ*
right	*ndeyjoor*
Get in!	*Dugghal waay!*
How much is this?	*Lii ñaata?*
It's too much.	*Seer na torob.*
Leave me alone!	*May ma jàmm!*

Monday	*altine*
Tuesday	*talaata*
Wednesday	*àllarba*
Thursday	*alxames*
Friday	*àjjuma*
Saturday	*gaawu*
Sunday	*dibéer*

0	*tus*
1	*benn*
2	*ñaar*
3	*ñett*
4	*ñeent*
5	*juróom*
6	*juróom-benn*
7	*juróom- ñaar*
8	*juróom- ñett*
9	*juróom- ñeent*
10	*fukk*
11	*fukk-ak-benn*
12	*fukk-ak- ñaar*
13	*fukk-ak- ñett*
14	*fukk-ak-ñeent*
15	*fukk-ak-juróom*
16	*fukk-ak-juróom benn* (lit: ten-and-five one)
17	*fukk-ak-juróom ñaar*
18	*fukk-ak-juróom ñett*
19	*fukk-ak-juróom ñeent*
20	*ñaar-fukk* (lit: two-ten)
30	*fanweer*
40	*ñeent-fukk* (lit: four-ten)
50	*juróom-fukk* (lit: five-ten)
60	*juróom-benn-fukk* (lit: five-one-ten)
70	*juróom-ñaar-fukk* (lit: five two-ten)
80	*juróom-ñett-fukk*
90	*juróom-ñeent-fukk*
100	*téeméer*
1000	*junne*

one million *tamñareet*

With thanks to Mamadou Cissé.

YORUBA

Yoruba belongs to the Kwa group of the Ede language family (*ede* is the Yoruba word for 'language'). Along with Fon it is one of the main lingua francas in much of the eastern part of West Africa but it is principally spoken as a first language in Benin and Nigeria. As with the majority of indigenous West African languages, Yoruba is subject to a degree of dialectal variation, not surprising given the broad geographical area its speak-

ers are found in; fortunately, the majority of these variants are mutually intelligible.

Yoruba is normally written using the IPA (International Phonetic Alphabet). It is a tone language, ie changes in voice-pitch are important in giving words their intended meaning. To give a comprehensive description of the five-tone Yoruba vowel system would require more space than we have available here. For simplicity we have used an acute accent (eg á) to represent a high tone, a grave accent (eg à) to represent a low tone; unmarked vowels take a mid-tone.

The pronunciations we give for the words and phrases below are rough approximations only. Pronounce letters as you would in English, keeping the following points in mind:

a	as in 'far'
e	as in 'met'
i	as in 'marine'
o	as in 'hot'; as in 'or'
u	as in 'put'
g	as in 'go'
h	not pronounced
hng	indicates that the preceding vowel is nasalised, eg the 'ing' in 'sing'

Hello.	*báh-oh*
Goodbye.	*óh-dà-bòh*
Please.	*eh-dá-kuhn*
Thank you.	*eh-sheh-wuh*
You're welcome.	*eh-woh-lèh*
Sorry/Pardon.	*eh-dá-kuhn*
Yes.	*eh*
No.	*èh-ré-woh*
How are you?	*shéh-wà-dá-dah?*
I'm fine.	*àh-dúh-kpéh*
And you?	*èh-nyi-na-nkóh?*
What's your name?	*bá-woh-leh-má-jéh?*
My name is ...	*moh-máh-jéh ...*
Where are you from?	*à-ráh-iboh-loh-jéh?*
I'm from ...	*à-ráh ... ni mi*
Can you help me please?	*eh-dá-kuhn eh-ràhng-mí-lóh-wóh?*
Do you speak English?	*sheh-gbóh geh-sì?*
Do you speak French?	*sheh-gbóh frahng-séh?*

only speak English.	*geh-sì ni-kahng nì-moh-gbóh*	10	*eh-wah*
speak a little French.	*moh-gbóh frahng-séh dí-èh*	11	*móh-kàhng-lah*
understand.	*óh-yéh-mi-sí*	12	*mé-ji-lah*
don't understand.	*kòh-yéh-mi-sí*	13	*méh-tà-lah*
Where is ...?	*iboh nih ...?*	14	*méh-ri-lah*
Is it far?	*oh jin-ni*	15	*má-rùhng-lah*
straight ahead	*troh-loh-loh*	16	*méh-rihng-dóh-gúhng*
left	*òh-túhng*	17	*méh-tá-dóh-gúhng*
right	*òh-sìhng*	18	*méh-jì-dóh-gúhng*
How much is this?	*é-loh-lèh-yi?*	19	*òh-kahng-dóh-gúhng*
That's too much.	*ó-wáhng-jùh*	20	*òh-gúhng*
Leave me alone!	*fi-mí-nlèh!*	30	*méh-wah-lé-lóh-gbòhng*
		40	*òh-gbòhng*
		50	*méh-wàh-lé-lóh-gbòhng*
1	*eh-ní*	60	*òh-góhng-lé-lóh-gbòhng*
2	*èh-ji*	70	*òh-góhng-méh-wa-lé-lóh-gbòhng*
3	*eh-tah*	80	*òh-gbòhng-méh-jì*
4	*eh-rihng*	90	*méh-wah-lé-lóh-gbohng-mé-jì*
5	*à-rúng*	100	*òh-gúhng-lé-lóh-gbong-mé-jì*
6	*èh-fàh*		
7	*èh-jeh*	one million	*mi-lì-yohng kahng*
8	*èh-joh*		
9	*eh-sahng*	With thanks to Aimé Avolonto.

Glossary

The following is a list of words and acronyms used in this book and that you are likely to come across in West Africa. The glossary has been subdivided into the following broad categories:

For terms you're likely to see on the maps in this book and on the ground in the French-speaking towns, see the boxed text on p922. You might also want to refer to the Language chapter for more words and phrases.

Food & Drinks

afra – grilled meat, or grilled-meat stall
agouti – see *grasscutter*
akoumé – see *pâte*
aloco – fried bananas with onions and chilli
arachide – see *groundnut*
attiéké – grated *manioc*

benchi – black bench peas with palm oil and fish
bisap – purple drink made from water and hibiscus leaves
brochette – cubes of meat or fish grilled on a stick
buvette – small bar or drinks stall

caféman – man serving coffee (usually Nescafé), sometimes tea, and French bread with various fillings; found in Francophone countries mainly, usually only in the morning
cane rat – see *grasscutter*
capitaine – Nile perch (fish)
carte – menu
cassava – a common starch staple derived from the root of the cassava plant, usually ground to a powder and eaten as an accompaniment like rice or couscous; the leaves are eaten as green vegetable. Also called *gari* or *manioc*.

chakalow – millet beer
chawarma – a popular snack of grilled meat in bread, served with salad and sesame sauce; originally from Lebanon, it's now found in towns and cities all over West Africa
chop – meal, usually local style
chop shop – a basic local-style eating house or restaurant (English-speaking countries); also called a *rice bar*
cocoyam – starch-yielding food plant, also called taro
couscous – semolina or millet grains, served as an accompaniment to *sauce*

dibieterie – grilled-meat stall
domodah – groundnut-based stew with meat or vegetables

épinard – spinach

felafel – Lebanese-style deep-fried balls of ground chickpeas and herbs, often served with chickpea paste in sandwiches
feuille sauce – sauce made from greens (usually *manioc* leaves)
foufou – see *fufu*
foutou – sticky yam or plantain paste similar to *fufu*; a staple in Côte d'Ivoire
frites – hot potato chips or French fries
fufu – a staple along the southern coast of West Africa, made with fermented *cassava*, *yams*, *plantain* or *manioc* which is cooked and puréed; sometimes spelt 'foufou'

gargotte – simple basic eating house or stall in Senegal, parts of Mali and Gambia; also spelt 'gargote' or 'gargot'
gari – powdered *cassava*
gari jollof – *gari* with rice and tomatoes; see also *jollof rice*
gombo – okra or lady's fingers

grasscutter – a rodent of the porcupine family, known as *agouti* in Francophone countries. Sometimes called *cane rat*, it's popular in stews.

groundnut – peanut; 'arachide' in French

haricot verte – green bean

igname – see *yam*

laxatu – bitter flavouring

jollof rice – common dish throughout the region consisting of rice and vegetables with meat or fish; called *riz yollof* in Francophone countries

kedjenou – Côte d'Ivoire's national dish, slowly simmered chicken or fish with peppers and tomatoes

kinkiliba – leaf that is sometimes used in coffee, giving it a woody tang

kojo – millet beer

koutoukou – a clear, strong alcohol homemade in Côte d'Ivoire

mafé – *groundnut*-based stew; also spelt 'mafay'

Maggi – brand name for a ubiquitous flavouring used in soups, stews etc throughout the region

maquis – rustic open-air restaurant originating in Côte d'Ivoire, primarily serving braised fish and grilled chicken with *attiéké*, and traditionally open only at night

menu du jour – the meal of the day, usually at a special price; often shortened just to 'menu'

palaver sauce – there are regional variations, but this sauce is usually made from spinach or other leaves plus meat/fish; also spelt 'palava'

palm wine – a milky-white low-strength brew collected by tapping palm trees

patate – sweet potato

pâte – starch staple, often made from millet, corn ('pâte de maïs'), *plantains*, manioc or *yams*, eaten as an accompaniment to sauce; also called 'akoumé'

pito – local brew in northern Ghana

plantain – a large green banana, which has to be cooked before eating

plasas – pounded potato or *cassava* leaves cooked with palm oil and fish or beer

plat du jour – the dish of the day, usually offered at a special price

poisson – fish

pomme de terre – potato

poulet – chicken

poulet yassa – grilled chicken in onion and lemon sauce; a Senegalese dish that is found in many countries throughout the region; similarly you get 'poisson yassa' (fish), 'viande yassa' (meat) and just 'yassa' (whatever at hand)

pression – draught beer

rice bar – see *chop shop*

riz – rice

riz sauce – very common basic meal (rice with sauce)

riz yollof – see *jollof rice*

rôtisserie – food stall selling roast meat

salon de thé – literally 'tearoom'; café

sauce – basis of meals throughout the region; usually made from whatever is available and eaten with an accompanying starch staple like rice or *fufu*

snack – in Francophone Africa this means a place where you can get light meals and sandwiches, not the food itself. 'Bar–Snack' is where you can get a beer or coffee too.

sodabe – a spirit made in Togo

spot – simple bar

sucrerie – soft drink (literally 'sweet thing')

suya – *Hausa* word for *brochette*

tiéboudienne – Senegal's national dish, rice baked in thick sauce of fish and vegetables; also spelt 'thieboudjenne'

tô – millet or sorghum-based *pâte*

tomate – tomato

viande – meat

yam – edible starchy root; called 'igname' locally

yassa – see *poulet yassa*

yollof rice – see *jollof rice*

Getting Around

autogare – see *gare routière*
autoroute – major road or highway

bâché – covered pick-up ('ute') used as a basic bush taxi (from the French word for tarpaulin)
brake – see *Peugeot 504*
bush taxi – along with buses, this is the most common form of public transport in West Africa. There are three main types of bush taxi in West Africa: *Peugeot 504*, minibus and pick-up (*bâché*).

car – large bus, see also *petit car*
cinq-cent-quatre – see *Peugeot 504*
compteur – meter in taxi
couchette – sleeping berth on a train
car rapide – minibus, usually used in cities, often decrepit, may be fast or very slow
courrier postale – postal van; sometimes the only means of public transport between towns in rural areas

déplacement – a taxi or boat that you 'charter' for yourself
dournis – minibus

essence – petrol (gas) for car

fula-fula – converted truck or pick-up; rural public transport

garage – bush taxi and bus park
gare lagunaire – lagoon ferry terminal
gare maritime – ferry terminal
gare routière – bus and bush-taxi station (Francophone countries), also called 'gare voiture' or 'autogare'
gare voiture – see *gare routière*
gasoil – diesel fuel
goudron – tar (road)

IDP – International Driving Permit

line – fixed-route shared taxi
lorry park – see *motor park*

mobylette – moped

motor park – bus and bush taxi park; also called 'lorry park'

occasion – a lift or place in a car or bus (often shortened to 'occas')

péage – toll
petit car – minibus
pétrole – kerosene
Peugeot 504 – one of the main types of bush taxi; also called 'brake', 'cinq-cent-quatre', 'Peugeot-taxi' or *sept-place*
pinasse – large *pirogue*, usually used on rivers, for hauling people and cargo
pirogue – traditional canoe, either a small dugout or large narrow sea-going wooden fishing boat
piste – track or dirt road
poda-poda – minibus

quatre-quatre – 4WD or 4x4, a four wheel drive vehicle

sept-place – *Peugeot 504* seven-seater (usually carrying up to 12 people)

taxi brousse – bush taxi
taxi-course – shared taxi (in cities)
town trip – private hire (taxi)
tro-tro – a minibus or pick-up

woro-woro – minibus

zemi-john – motorcycle-taxi

Cape Verde & Guinea-Bissau

aluguer – for hire (sign in minibus)
arroz de marisco – seafood and rice

banco – bank
barco – large boat

cachupa – the Cape Verde national dish; a tasty stew of several kinds of beans plus corn and various kinds of meat, often sausage or bacon
cajeu – cashew nut

caldo – soup
caldo de peixe – fish soup
caña – home-brew rum
canoa – motor-canoe
casa de pasto – no-frills restaurant
cascata – waterfall
Ceris – bottled local brew
cidade – city
coladeiras – old-style music; romantic, typically sentimental upbeat love songs
correios – post office

estrada – street

fado – haunting melancholy blues-style Portuguese music
funaná – distinctive fast-paced music with a Latin rhythm, great for dancing; usually features accordion players and percussion

gelado – ice cream

horário – timetable

ilha – island

jardim – garden

kandonga – truck or pick-up

lagoa – lagoon
largo – small square
livraria – bookshop

macaco – monkey; a popular meat dish in upcountry Guinea-Bissau
mercado – market
mornas – old-style music; mournful and sad, similar to the Portuguese *fado* style from whence they may have originated
museu – museum

papelaria – newsagency
paragem – bus and bush taxi park
pastel com diablo dentro – literally 'pastry with the devil inside'; a mix of fresh tuna, onions and tomatoes, wrapped in a pastry made from boiled potatoes and corn flour, deep fried and served hot
pastelaria – pastry and cake shop

pensão – hotel or guesthouse
platô – plateau
pousada – guesthouse
pousada municipal – town guesthouse
praça – park or square
praia – beach

residencial – guesthouse
ribeiro – stream
rua – street

toca-toca – small minibus in Bissau

verde – green
vinhos verde – semi-sparkling Portuguese white wine

Miscellaneous

abusua – clan or organisation of the *Akan*
adinkra – hand-made printed cloth from Ghana worn primarily by the *Ashanti* on solemn occasions
Afrique Occidentale Française – see *French West Africa*
Afro-beat – a fusion of African music, jazz and soul originated and popularised by Fela Kuti of Nigeria; along with *juju* it's the most popular music in Nigeria
Akan – a major people group along the south coast of West Africa; includes the Ashanti and Fanti peoples
akuaba – *Ashanti* carved figure
animism – the base of virtually all traditional religions in Africa; the belief that there is a spirit in all natural things and the worship of those spirits, particularly human spirits (those of ancestors) which are thought to continue after death and have the power to bestow protection
Asantehene – the king or supreme ruler of the *Ashanti* people
Ashanti – the largest tribal group in Ghana, concentrated around Kumasi
aso adire – a broad term for dyed cloth, a common handicraft found in many markets in Nigeria
auberge – in France it's a hostel, but in West Africa it's used (occasionally) to mean any small hotel

French Towns & Maps

carrefour – crossroads
commissariat – police

douane – customs

église – church

falaise – escarpment

gendarmerie – police

hôtel de ville – town hall

immeuble – building

jardin – garden
jardin publique – public garden

librairie – bookshop

mairie – city hall
marché – market
mosquée – mosque

palais – palace
palais de justice – law courts
palais du congrès – house of congress
palais présidentiel – presidential palace
papeterie – stationer's shop
pâtisserie – pastry shop
place – square
pont – bridge
préfecture – police headquarters
(for documents etc)

quartier – literally quarter; district
of a town

rond-point – roundabout
rue – street

supermarché – supermarket
sûreté – security police

tabac – news stand/tobacconist

balafon – xylophone
Bambara – the major ethnic group of Mali
concentrated in the centre and south and

famous for their art, especially wooden
carvings
banco – clay or mud used for building
bar-dancing – term widely used through
out the region for a bar which also has
music (sometimes live) and dancing in the
evening
barrage – dam across river, or roadblock
bic – disposable ball-point pen ('Biro')
bidon – large bottle, container or jerry can
bidonville – shantytown
board – see *pension*
bogolan cloth – often simply called *mud
cloth*, this is cotton cloth with designs
painted on using various types of mud for
colour. It's made by the *Bambara* people of
Mali but is found throughout the region.
boîte – small nightclub (literally 'box')
bolong – literally 'river' in Mandinka, but
when used in English context it means
creek or small river
bombax tree – see *fromager tree*
boubou – the common name for the elaborate robe-like outfit worn by men and
women; also called 'grand boubou'
BP – boîte postale (PO Box)
Bundu – Krio word for 'secret society';
used in Liberia and in certain parts of Sierra
Leone and Côte d'Ivoire; includes the Poro
society for men and the Sande for women

cadeau – gift, tip, bribe or a handout
campement – could be loosely translated
as 'hostel', 'inn' or 'lodge', or even 'motel',
but it is not a camping ground (ie a place for
tents). Traditionally, campements offered
simple accommodation but many today are
on a par with mid-range hotels.
carnet – document required if you are
bringing a car into most of the countries of
the region
carrefour – literally 'crossroads', but also
used to mean meeting place
carrefour des jeunes – youth centre
case – hut
case de passage – very basic place to
sleep, often near bus stations; with a bed or
mat on the floor and little else, and nearly
always doubling as a brothel; also called
'chambre de passage' or 'maison de passage'

case étage – two-storey mud house

CFA – the principal currency of the region, used in Benin, Burkina Faso, Côte d'Ivoire, Guinea-Bissau, Mali, Niger, Senegal and Togo

chambre – room

chambre de passage – see *case de passage*

chambre ventilé – room with a fan

charms – see *fetish*

chassée submersible – see *pont submersible*

chèche – light cotton cloth, in white or indigo blue, that *Tuareg* men wear to cover their head and face

chiwara – a headpiece carved in the form of an antelope and used in ritualistic dances by the *Bambara*

climatisée – air-conditioned; often shortened to 'clim'

commissariat – police station

cotton tree – see *fromager tree*

CRI – Campements Rurals Integrés; system of village-run *campements* in the Casamance region of Senegal

croix d'Agadez – *Tuareg* talisman that protects its wearer from the 'evil eye'

Dahomey – the pre-independence name of Benin

dash – bribe or tip (noun); also used as a verb, 'You dash me something ...'

demi-pension – half board (dinner, bed and breakfast)

djembe – type of drum

Dogon – people found in Mali, east of Mopti; famous for their cliff dwellings, cosmology and art

durbar – ceremony or celebration, usually involving a cavalry parade eg in the Muslim northern Nigerian states

ECOMOG – *ECOWAS* Monitoring Group; a military force made up of soldiers from the member armies of *ECOWAS*

ECOWAS – Economic Community of West African States

Eid al-Fitr – feast to celebrate the end of *Ramadan*

Eid al-Kabir – see *Tabaski*

Empire of Ghana – no geographic connection with the present-day country of Ghana; one of the great *Sahel* empires that flourished in the 8th to 11th centuries AD and covered much of today's Mali and parts of Senegal

Empire of Mali – Islamic *Sahel* empire that was at its peak in the 14th century, covering the region between present-day Senegal and Niger; its capital was at Koumbi Saleh in southern Mauritania

en suite – a French term used in Britain to mean a hotel room with private bathroom attached. Also used in some English-speaking countries in West Africa (although not in French-speaking countries!).

fanals – large lanterns; also the processions during which the lanterns are carried through the streets

fanicos – laundry men

Fanti – part of the Akan group of people based along the coast in south-west Ghana and Côte d'Ivoire; traditionally fishing people and farmers

fast food – European or American style snacks (eg hot dogs, hamburgers) not necessarily served quickly

fête – festival

fêtes des masques – ceremony with masks

fetish – sacred objects in traditional religions, sometimes called 'charms'

fiche – form (to complete)

French West Africa – area of West and Central Africa acquired by France at the Berlin Conference in 1884-85 which divided Africa up between the European powers; 'Afrique Occidentale Française' in French

fromager tree – found throughout West Africa and also known as the 'bombax', 'kapok' or 'cotton tree', it is recognisable by its yellowish bark, large pod-like fruit and exposed roots

Fula – a people spread widely through West Africa, predominantly nomadic cattle herders; also known as 'Fulani' or 'Peul'

gara – thin cotton material

GDP – gross domestic product

gendarmerie – police station/post

girba – water bag

gîte – in France, this mean a small hotel or holiday cottage with self-catering facilities. In West Africa it is occasionally used interchangeably with *auberge* and *campement*.

GNP – gross national product

Gold Coast – pre-independence name for modern state of Ghana

Grain Coast – old name for Liberia

grand boubou – see *boubou*

griot – traditional musician or minstrel (praise singer) who also acts as historian for a village, clan or tribe or family going back for many centuries. The term is actually French in origin (it is pronounced 'gree-oh') and is probably a corruption of the *Wolof* 'gewel' or Tukulor 'gawlo'. The Mandinka word is 'jali'.

grisgris – a charm or amulet worn to ward off evil (pronounced 'gree-gree' also written 'grigri' or 'grisgri')

gué – ford or low causeway across river

harmattan – wind from the north which carries dust from the desert, causing skies to become hazy throughout West Africa from December to March

Hausa – people originally from northern Nigeria and southern Niger, mostly farmers and traders

highlife – a style of music, originating in Ghana, combining West African western influences

hôtel de ville – town hall

ibeji – *Yoruba* carved twin figures

Igbo – one of the three major people groups in Nigeria, concentrated in the south-east

IGN – Institute Géographique National. The French IGN produces maps of most West African countries. Several West African countries have their own IGN institution, although maps are not always available.

IMF – International Monetary Fund

immeuble – large building, such as an office block

impluvium – large round traditional house, with roof constructed to collect rain water in central tank or bowl

insha'allah – God willing, ie hopefully (Arabic, but used by Muslims in Africa)

jali – see *griot*

juju – see *voodoo*

juju music – the music style characterised by tight vocal harmonies and sophisticated guitar work, backed by traditional drums and percussion; it is very popular in southern Nigeria, most notably with the *Yoruba*

kandab – a large belt used to climb trees to collect palm wine

kapok tree – see *fromager tree*

kente cloth – probably the most expensive material in West Africa, made with finely woven cotton, and sometimes silk, by Ghana's *Ashanti* people

Kingdom of Benin – no relation to the present-day country, this was one of the great West African kingdoms (13th to 19th centuries), based in Nigeria around Benin City and famous for its bronzes

kola nuts – extremely bitter nuts sold everywhere on the streets and known for their mildly hallucinogenic and caffeine-like effects; they are offered as gifts at weddings and other ceremonies

kora – harp-like musical instrument with over 20 strings

Koran – see *Quran*

kwotenai kanye – earrings

Lobi – people based in south-west Burkina Faso and northern Côte d'Ivoire, famous for their figurative sculpture and compounds known as *soukala*

lumo – weekly market, usually in border areas

luttes – traditional wrestling matches

lycée – secondary school

mairie – town hall; mayor's office

maison de passage – see *case de passage*

malafa – crinkly voile material worn as a veil by women in Mauritania

Malinké – Guinea's major ethnic group, and also found in southern Mali, north-western Côte d'Ivoire and eastern Senegal;

closely related to the *Bambara* and famous for having one of the great empires of West Africa; also related to the *Mandinka* people

Mandinka – people group based in central and northern Gambia and Senegal; also the name of their language which is closely related to Malinké. Both Malinké and Mandinka are part of the wider Manding group.

marabout – Muslim holy man

marigot – creek

Maurs – see *Moors*

mestizos – people of mixed European and African decent

Moors – also called 'Maurs'; the predominant nomadic people of Mauritania, now also well known as merchants and found scattered over French-speaking West Africa

Moro-Naba – the king of the *Mossi* people

Mossi – the people who occupy the central area of Burkina Faso and comprise about half the population of Burkina Faso as well as the bulk of Côte d'Ivoire's migrant labour force

Mourides – the most powerful of the Islamic brotherhoods in Senegal

mud cloth – see *bogolan cloth*

nomalies – sandstone ancestor figures

OAU – Organisation of African Unity

oba – a *Yoruba* chief or ruler

orchestra – in West Africa, this means a group playing popular music

pagne – a length of colourful cloth worn around the waist as a skirt

paillote – thatched sun shelter (usually on beach or around open-air bar-restaurant)

palava – meeting place

paletuviers – mangroves

patron – owner, boss

peintures rupestres – rock paintings

pension – simple hotel or hostel, or 'board'; see also *demi-pension*

pension complet – full board (lunch, dinner, bed and breakfast)

pension simple – bed and breakfast

Peul – see *Fula*

pont submersible – a bridge or causeway across a river which is covered when the water is high

posuban – an ensemble of statues representing a proverb or notable event in Fanti culture

préfecture – police headquarters

PTT – post (and often telephone) office in Francophone countries

Quran – Islamic holy book, also written 'Koran'

Ramadan – Muslim month of fasting

Ramsar – an international convention primarily concerned with the conservation of wetland habitats and associated wildlife

Sahel – dry savanna area, south of Sahara Desert; most of Senegal, Gambia, Mali, Burkina Faso and Niger

Samory Touré – Guinean hero who led the fight against the French colonialists in the late 19th century

Scramble for Africa – term used for the land-grabbing frenzy in the 1880s by the European powers in which France, Britain and Germany laid claim to various parts of the continent

serviette – towel (in bathroom)

serviette de table – table napkin, serviette

serviette hygiénique – sanitary pad (feminine pad, feminine towel)

sharia – Muslim law

shukublai – distinctive baskets, traditionally made by Temne women in Sierra Leone

Songhaï – ethnic group located primarily in north-eastern Mali and western Niger along the Niger River

soukala – a castle-like housing compound of the Lobi tribe found in the Bouna area of southern Burkina Faso

spirale antimostique – mosquito coil

syndicat d'initiative – tourist information office

Tabaski – Eid al-Kabir; also known as the Great Feast, this is the most important celebration throughout West Africa

taguelmoust – shawl or scarf worn as headgear by *Tuareg* men

tama – hand-held drum

tampon – stamp (eg in passport)

tampon hygiénique – tampon; see also *serviette hygiénique*

tampon periodique – see *tampon hygiénique*

tata somba – a castle-like house of the Betamaribé tribe in north-western Benin

télécentre – privately run telecommunications centres

togu-na – traditional *Dogon* shelter where men sit and socialise

totem – used in traditional religions, similar to a fetish

toubab – white person; term used primarily in Gambia, Senegal, Mali and some other *Sahel* countries

Tuareg – nomadic descendants of the North African Berbers; found all over the Sahara, especially in Mali, Niger and southern Algeria

ventilé – see *chambre ventilé*

voodoo – the worship of spirits with supernatural powers widely practised in southern Benin and Togo; also called 'juju'

wassoulou – singing style made famous by Mali's Oumou Sangaré

WHO – World Health Organization

Wolof – Senegal's major ethnic group; also found in Gambia

Yoruba – a major ethnic group concentrated in south-western Nigeria

Acknowledgments

Many thanks to the travellers who used the last edition and wrote to us with helpful hints, useful advice and interesting anecdotes:

Nicole, Karin Aarsheim, Doug, Sylvanus Akakpo, James Allen, Tristan Allen, Victoria Alvarez, Janice Andersen, Renmans Antoon, John Archibald, Sarah Armstrong, Becky Arnold, John Asafo-Kudzo, Mohammad Ayanah, Hans Baars, Ailsa J Bain, David Barkshire, Chris Baumgartner, Michele Beasley, Richard Bedell, Esther Beneder, Tia Benn, Robert Bennett Lubic, Chris Berggren, Tim Bewer, Tiffany Bishop, Rudi Blacker, Robert Blewett, Prof A Blum, Arryn Blumberg, Axel Boes, Louis Bont, Kris Borring Prasada Rao, P C V Lynette Bouchie, Roland Brandenberg, Tobias Brandner, George Bringham, Bill Brodie, S Calder, E J Carpenter, Jennifer Cerasoli, Abbie Challenger, Jane Chesters, Greg Clarke, Rosemary Clossun, Geoffrey Coats, Barbie Campbell Cole, Alex Conder, A Couch, Graeme Counsel, Josh Crosslin, Florence Crovato, Mariano Cukar, Sarah Cummings, James Dalphonse, Simon Day, Liza Debevec, Walter T Decoene, Dale & Adrian DeKrester, Yann Delmas, Roberto Di Noto, Stefan Django, Kathy Duarte, Rossana Dudziak, Frank Dux, Robert Egg, Gista Ekmans, Jane Ellison, Sam R Emmanuel, J & I Epps, Matt Evans, Jennifer Fagan, Javier Falcon, Brian Farenell, Ferninand Fellinger, Suzanne Ferrie, Michael Fischer, D Flynn , Douglas Franks, Brian Fredrickson, Donatella Gatti, Michael Gildersleeve, Christelle Girard, Dr Valerie Godsalve, Les Goedbloed, Brooke Goode, Bart Goossens, Marcus Gould, Phil & Philippa Grant, Gunilla Green, Roby Greenwald, Amber Grove, Adam Guy, Bart Haex, Morten Hagen, Stephan Hagers, Beth Haise, Sue Hall, Hans-Peter Hauschild, Kevin Hedges, Ana Henriques, Matthew Henry, Alan & Michelle Hinde, Angie Hirata, Janneke Hogenboom, Gordon Humphreys, Michael & Gretchen Husted, Helen Jerry, Eric Johnson, Bianca Kamps, Cristiana Katsu, Roy Kellett, Findlay Kember, Torsten Kern, Christoph Kessel, K Linda Kiri, P Klompen, Mark Koepke, Kiros Kokkas, Carsten Kolle, Ruth Kondrup, Nadja Kos, Anja Koster, Raoul Kuiper, Britta Kunz, Greg Lane, Jutta Langlote, Paul Lascelles, Heinz Lauben, Kate Lee, Ruby S Lehman, David Leibson, Dieter Leonhard, Lucy Licence, Thomas Linhart, Manuel Lins, Krista Loynachan, Marcel Lucht, Andrea Tara Luff, Andrew Lyon, Joseph Machnica, Alan Macina, Kirk MacManus, Amy Manos, Saskia Marijnissen, Todd Markson, Amy Marsh, Chloe Marshall, Trixi Martin, Brent Maupin, Colin McCorquodale, Peter McFadden, Iain McIntyre, Sallyanne McKern, Andrew McNeil, Martin Meulenberg, Lydia Mickunas, Kathleen Miszuk, Susan Mobbs, Ram Mohan, Franco Del Monaco, P Murphy, George Musser, R N McLean, Stephanie Newell, Pam Newton, S Nies , Pavel Novotny, Ernest & Barbara Omoyuyi, Angelique Orr, Ian G Paskin, Henry Pearce, Ariana Pearlroth, Antoine Pecoud, John Peterkin, Anne-Marie Pogorelc, Marcel Pointet, Mark Pollock, Paul P Pometto, Maaike Poppinga, Cassandra Postema, Mark Quik, Petra Raddatz, Hafeezur Rahman, Laurie Rall, Norbert Reintjes, Terry Ann Repak, Joanna Revelo, Rodney Reviere, Alan & Margaret Reynolds, M Rijs, A Roberts, Louise Robertson, Marvin Rogers, D F Roy, Campbell Rule, Yasuharu Sano, Richard Santalla, Esther Sarda, Sara Satti, A Savelius, Bart Scheerlinck, Jill Schinas, Leen Schuyvinck, Joachim Schwab, Laura J Schwartz, Dominique Seurin, Lyn Shaw, P L Shinnie, Brian & Min Shu, Ingo Siedermann, Valerie Silensky, Delyla Saul Simon, Wilf Smedley, Harold Smits, Adrian Stabler, David Stanley, ME van der Steen, Kurt Steinbach, Laura Steinberger, Nick & Tim Stokes, Matthew Strahan, Christophe Streibl, J & M Swartwood, John Talbot, James Tartaglia, Ruud Teeuwen, Ulrich Thalheimer, Siffer Thomas, Paul Thompson, Corine Tiebosch, P Timmermans, Nicole Tod, Fiona & Jim Towers, Michael Turner, Jorge Tutor, Marianne Vetter, M J Vink, Jocelyn Vitale, Guy De Vos, Isabelle Waterschoot, Roger K Western, Monica Westin Addy, Laura White, Vincent Wiers, Chris de Wilde, James A Williams, Steve Windows, Roelof Wittnink, Sie Wixley, Bob Wong, Sandra Wood, Kim Wroblewski, Michael Zelba, Christian Zettler, Tilley Ziegler, Simonas V Zmuidzinas, Hendrik Jan Zonneveld.

LONELY PLANET

Guides by Region

Lonely Planet is known worldwide for publishing practical, reliable and no-nonsense travel information in our guides and on our Web site. The Lonely Planet list covers just about every accessible part of the world. Currently there are sixteen series: Travel guides, Shoestring guides, Condensed guides, Phrasebooks, Read This First, Healthy Travel, Walking guides, Cycling guides, Watching Wildlife guides, Pisces Diving & Snorkelling guides, City Maps, Road Atlases, Out to Eat, World Food, Journeys travel literature, Traveller's Advice titles and Illustrated pictorials.

AFRICA Africa on a shoestring • Cairo • Cairo Map • Cape Town • Cape Town Map • East Africa • Egypt • Egyptian Arabic phrasebook • Ethiopia, Eritrea & Djibouti • Ethiopian (Amharic) phrasebook • The Gambia & Senegal • Healthy Travel Africa • Kenya • Malawi • Morocco • Moroccan Arabic phrasebook • Mozambique • Read This First: Africa • South Africa, Lesotho & Swaziland • Southern Africa • Southern Africa Road Atlas • Swahili phrasebook • Tanzania, Zanzibar & Pemba • Trekking in East Africa • Tunisia • Watching Wildlife East Africa • Watching Wildlife Southern Africa • West Africa • World Food Morocco • Zimbabwe, Botswana & Namibia
Travel Literature: Mali Blues: Traveling to an African Beat • The Rainbird: A Central African Journey • Songs to an African Sunset: A Zimbabwean Story

AUSTRALIA & THE PACIFIC Aboriginal Australia & Torres Strait Islands • Auckland • Australia • Australian phrasebook • Australia Road Atlas • Bushwalking in Australia • Cycling Australia • Cycling New Zealand • Fiji • Fijian phrasebook • Healthy Travel Australia, NZ and the Pacific • Islands of Australia's Great Barrier Reef • Melbourne • Melbourne Map • Micronesia • New Caledonia • New South Wales & the ACT • New Zealand • Northern Territory • Outback Australia • Out to Eat – Melbourne • Out to Eat – Sydney • Papua New Guinea • Papua New Guinea Phrasebook • Pidgin phrasebook • Queensland • Rarotonga & the Cook Islands • Samoa • Solomon Islands • South Australia • South Pacific • South Pacific phrasebook • Sydney • Sydney Map • Sydney Condensed • Tahiti & French Polynesia • Tasmania • Tonga • Tramping in New Zealand • Vanuatu • Victoria • Walking in Australia • Watching Wildlife Australia • Western Australia
Travel Literature: Islands in the Clouds: Travels in the Highlands of New Guinea • Kiwi Tracks: A New Zealand Journey • Sean & David's Long Drive

CENTRAL AMERICA & THE CARIBBEAN Bahamas, Turks & Caicos • Baja California • Bermuda • Central America on a shoestring • Costa Rica • Costa Rica Spanish phrasebook • Cuba • Dominican Republic & Haiti • Eastern Caribbean • Guatemala • Guatemala, Belize & Yucatán: La Ruta Maya • Havana • Healthy Travel Central & South America • San Diego & Tijuana • Jamaica • Mexico • Mexico City • Panama • Puerto Rico • Read This First: Central & South America • World Food Mexico • World Food Caribbean • Yucatán
Travel Literature: Green Dreams: Travels in Central America

EUROPE Amsterdam • Amsterdam Map • Amsterdam Condensed • Andalucía • Austria • Baltic States phrasebook • Barcelona • Barcelona Map • Belgium & Luxembourg • Berlin • Berlin Map • Britain • British phrasebook • Brussels, Bruges & Antwerp • Brussels Map • Budapest • Budapest Map • Canary Islands • Central Europe • Central Europe phrasebook • Copenhagen • Corfu & the Ionians • Corsica • Crete • Crete Condensed • Croatia • Cycling Britain • Cycling France • Cyprus • Czech & Slovak Republics • Denmark • Dublin • Dublin Map • Eastern Europe • Eastern Europe phrasebook • Edinburgh • England • Estonia, Latvia & Lithuania • Europe on a shoestring • Europe Phrasebook • Finland • Florence • France • Frankfurt Condensed • French phrasebook • Georgia, Armenia & Azerbaijan • Germany • German phrasebook • Greece • Greek Islands • Greek phrasebook • Hungary • Iceland, Greenland & the Faroe Islands • Ireland • Istanbul • Italian phrasebook • Italy • Krakow • Lisbon • The Loire • London • London Map • London Condensed • Madrid • Malta • Mediterranean Europe • Milan, Turin & Genoa • Moscow • Mozambique • Munich • The Netherlands • Normandy • Norway • Out to Eat – London • Paris • Paris Map • Paris Condensed • Poland • Polish Phrasebook • Portugal • Portuguese phrasebook • Prague • Prague Map • Provence & the Côte d'Azur • Read This First: Europe • Rhodes & the Dodecanese • Romania & Moldova • Rome • Rome Condensed • Rome Map • Russia, Ukraine & Belarus • Russian phrasebook • Scandinavian & Baltic Europe • Scandinavian phrasebook • Scotland • Sicily • Slovenia • South-West France • Spain • Spanish phrasebook • St Petersburg • St Petersburg Map • Sweden • Switzerland • Trekking in Spain • Tuscany • Ukrainian phrasebook • Venice • Vienna • Walking in Britain • Walking in France • Walking in Ireland • Walking in Italy • Walking in Spain • Walking in Switzerland • Western Europe • World Food France • World Food Ireland • World Food Italy • World Food Spain
Travel Literature: A Small Place in Italy • After Yugoslavia • Love and War in the Apennines • On the Shores of the Mediterranean The Olive Grove: Travels in Greece • Round Ireland in Low Gear

LONELY PLANET

Mail Order

onely Planet products are distributed worldwide. They are also available by mail order from Lonely Planet, so if you have difficulty finding a title please write to us. North and South American residents should write to 150 Linden St, Oakland, CA 94607, USA; European and African residents should write to 10a Spring Place, London NW5 3BH, UK; and residents of other countries to Locked Bag 1, Footscray, Victoria 3011, Australia.

INDIAN SUBCONTINENT Bangladesh • Bengali phrasebook • Bhutan • Delhi • Goa • Healthy Travel Asia & India • Hindi & Urdu phrasebook • India • Indian Himalaya • Karakoram Highway • Kerala • Mumbai (Bombay) • Nepal • Nepali phrasebook • Pakistan • Rajasthan • Read This First: Asia & India • South India • Sri Lanka • Sri Lanka phrasebook • Tibet • Tibetan phrasebook • Trekking in the Indian Himalaya • Trekking in the Karakoram & Hindukush • Trekking in the Nepal Himalaya
Travel Literature: The Age of Kali: Indian Travels and Encounters • Hello Goodnight: A Life of Goa • In Rajasthan • A Season in Heaven: True Tales from the Road to Kathmandu • Shopping for Buddhas • A Short Walk in the Hindu Kush • Slowly Down the Ganges

ISLANDS OF THE INDIAN OCEAN Madagascar & Comoros • Maldives • Mauritius, Réunion & Seychelles
Travel Literature: Maverick in Madagascar

MIDDLE EAST & CENTRAL ASIA Bahrain, Kuwait & Qatar • Central Asia • Central Asia phrasebook • Dubai • Farsi (Persian) phrasebook • Hebrew phrasebook • Iran • Israel & the Palestinian Territories • Istanbul • Istanbul Map • Istanbul to Cairo on a shoestring • Istanbul to Kathmandu • Jerusalem • Jerusalem Map • Jordan • Lebanon • Middle East • Oman & the United Arab Emirates • Syria • Turkey • Turkish phrasebook • World Food Turkey • Yemen
Travel Literature: Black on Black: Iran Revisited • The Gates of Damascus • Kingdom of the Film Stars: Journey into Jordan

NORTH AMERICA Alaska • Boston • Boston Map • Boston Condensed • British Colombia • California & Nevada • California Condensed • Canada • Chicago • Chicago Map • Deep South • Florida • Great Lakes • Hawaii • Hiking in Alaska • Hiking in the USA • Honolulu • Las Vegas • Los Angeles • Los Angeles Map • Louisiana & The Deep South • Miami • Miami Map • Montreal • New England • New Orleans • New York City • New York City Map • New York City Condensed • New York, New Jersey & Pennsylvania • Oahu • Out to Eat – San Francisco • Pacific Northwest • Puerto Rico • Rocky Mountains • San Francisco • San Francisco Map • San Diego & Tijuana • Seattle • Southwest • Texas • Toronto • USA • USA phrasebook • Vancouver • Virginia & the Capital Region • Washington DC • Washington DC Map • World Food Deep South, USA • World Food New Orleans
Travel Literature: Caught Inside: A Surfer's Year on the California Coast • Drive Thru America

NORTH-EAST ASIA Beijing • Beijing Map • Cantonese phrasebook • China • Hiking in Japan • Hong Kong • Hong Kong Map • Hong Kong Condensed • Hong Kong, Macau & Guangzhou • Japan • Japanese phrasebook • Korea • Korean phrasebook • Kyoto • Mandarin phrasebook • Mongolia • Mongolian phrasebook • Seoul • Shanghai • South-West China • Taiwan • Tokyo • World Food – Hong Kong
Travel Literature: In Xanadu: A Quest • Lost Japan

SOUTH AMERICA Argentina, Uruguay & Paraguay • Bolivia • Brazil • Brazilian phrasebook • Buenos Aires • Chile & Easter Island • Colombia • Ecuador & the Galapagos Islands • Healthy Travel Central & South America • Latin American Spanish phrasebook • Peru • Quechua phrasebook • Read This First: Central & South America • Rio de Janeiro • Rio de Janeiro Map • Santiago • South America on a shoestring • Santiago • Trekking in the Patagonian Andes • Venezuela
Travel Literature: Full Circle: A South American Journey

SOUTH-EAST ASIA Bali & Lombok • Bangkok • Bangkok Map • Burmese phrasebook • Cambodia • East Timor Phrasebook • Hanoi • Healthy Travel Asia & India • Hill Tribes phrasebook • Ho Chi Minh City • Indonesia • Indonesian phrasebook • Indonesia's Eastern Islands • Jakarta • Java • Lao phrasebook • Laos • Malay phrasebook • Malaysia, Singapore & Brunei • Myanmar (Burma) • Philippines • Pilipino (Tagalog) phrasebook • Read This First: Asia & India • Singapore • Singapore Map • South-East Asia on a shoestring • South-East Asia phrasebook • Thailand • Thailand's Islands & Beaches • Thailand, Vietnam, Laos & Cambodia Road Atlas • Thai phrasebook • Vietnam • Vietnamese phrasebook • World Food Thailand • World Food Vietnam

ALSO AVAILABLE: Antarctica • The Arctic • The Blue Man: Tales of Travel, Love and Coffee • Brief Encounters: Stories of Love, Sex & Travel • Chasing Rickshaws • The Last Grain Race • Lonely Planet Unpacked • Not the Only Planet: Science Fiction Travel Stories • Lonely Planet On the Edge • Sacred India • Travel with Children • Travel Photography: A Guide to Taking Better Pictures

Lonely Planet Journeys

JOURNEYS is a unique collection of travel writing – published by the company that understands travel better than anyone else. It is a series for anyone who has ever experienced – or dreamed of – the magical moment when they encountered a strange culture or saw a place for the first time. They are tales to read while you're planning a trip, while you're on the road or while you're in an armchair in front of a fire.

These outstanding titles explore our planet through the eyes of a diverse group of international writers. JOURNEYS books catch the spirit of a place, illuminate a culture, recount a crazy adventure or introduce a fascinating way of life. They always entertain, and always enrich the experience of travel.

MALI BLUES
Traveling to an African Beat
Lieve Joris (translated by Sam Garrett)

Drought, rebel uprisings, ethnic conflict: these are the predominant images of West Africa. But as Lieve Joris travels in Senegal, Mauritania and Mali, she meets survivors, fascinating individuals charting new ways of living between tradition and modernity. With her remarkable gift for drawing out people's stories, Joris brilliantly captures the rhythms of a world that refuses to give in.

THE GATES OF DAMASCUS
Lieve Joris (translated by Sam Garrett)

This best-selling book is a beautifully drawn portrait of day-to-day life in modern Syria. Through her intimate contact with local people, Lieve Joris draws us into the fascinating world that lies behind the gates of Damascus. Hala's husband is a political prisoner, jailed for his opposition to the Assad regime; through the author's friendship with Hala we see how Syrian politics impacts on the lives of ordinary people.

SONGS TO AN AFRICAN SUNSET
A Zimbabwean Story
Sekai Nzenza-Shand

Songs to an African Sunset braids vividly personal stories into an intimate picture of contemporary Zimbabwe. Returning to her family's village after many years in the west, Sekai Nzenza-Shand discovers a world where ancestor worship, polygamy and witchcraft still govern the rhythms of daily life – and where drought, deforestation and AIDS have wrought devastating changes. With insight and affection, she explores a culture torn between respect for the old ways and the irresistible pull of the new.

THE RAINBIRD
A Central African Journey
Jan Brokken (translated by Sam Garrett)

Following in the footsteps of famous Europeans such as Albert Schweitzer and HM Stanley, Jan Brokken journeyed to Gabon in central Africa. *The Rainbird* brilliantly chronicles the encounter between Africa and Europe as it was acted out on a sidestreet of history in a kaleidoscope of adventures and anecdotes. A compelling, immensely readable account of the author's own travels in one of the most remote and mysterious regions of Africa.

Index

Abbreviations

Text

MAP LEGEND

BOUNDARIES

━━━━━	International
━━━━━	State
━ ━ ━	Disputed

HYDROGRAPHY

	Coastline
	River, Creek
	Lake
	Intermittent Lake
	Salt Lake
	Canal
⊙ ⟶	Spring, Rapids
⤚	Waterfalls
	Swamp

ROUTES & TRANSPORT

	Freeway
	Highway
	Major Road
	Minor Road
	Unsealed Road
	City Freeway
	City Highway
	City Road
	City Street, Lane

	Pedestrian Mall
⇉ ⇉	Tunnel
⊢⊢⊢●⊢⊢	Train Route & Station
	Walking Track
	Ferry Route

AREA FEATURES

	Building
✿	Park, Gardens
+ × ×	Cemetery

	Market
	Beach, Desert
	Urban Area

MAP SYMBOLS

○ CAPITAL	National Capital
● CITY	City
● Town	Town
● Village	Village
○	Point of Interest
■	Place to Stay
▲	Camping Ground
⌂	Hut or Chalet
▼	Place to Eat
🍺	Pub, Bar or Nightclub
✈	Airport
	Ancient or City Wall
∴	Archaeological Site

💲	Bank
🏊	Beach
🏰	Castle or Fort
⌒	Cave
⛪ 🏛	Church
	Cliff or Escarpment
	Dive Site
◎	Embassy
⊕	Hospital
☪	Mosque
▲	Mountain or Hill
🏛	Museum
☂	National Park

⟵	One Way Street
)(	Pass
⛽	Petrol
★	Police Station
✉	Post Office
❖	Shopping Centre
	Swimming Pool
☎	Telephone
	Temple
○	Toilet
❶	Tourist Information
☺	Transport
🐘	Zoo

Note: not all symbols displayed above appear in this book

LONELY PLANET OFFICES

Australia
Locked Bag 1, Footscray, Victoria 3011
☎ 03 8379 8000 fax 03 8379 8111
email: talk2us@lonelyplanet.com.au

USA
150 Linden St, Oakland, CA 94607
☎ 510 893 8555 TOLL FREE: 800 275 8555
fax 510 893 8572
email: info@lonelyplanet.com

UK
10a Spring Place, London NW5 3BH
☎ 020 7428 4800 fax 020 7428 4828
email: go@lonelyplanet.co.uk

France
1 rue du Dahomey, 75011 Paris
☎ 01 55 25 33 00 fax 01 55 25 33 01
email: bip@lonelyplanet.fr
www.lonelyplanet.fr

World Wide Web: www.lonelyplanet.com or AOL keyword: lp
Lonely Planet Images: lpi@lonelyplanet.com.au